ALIENS™
VS.
PREDATOR™
OMNIBUS

ALIENS™ vs. PREDATOR™ OMNIBUS

VOLUME 2

DARK HORSE BOOKS®

CONTENTS

cover illustration **JOHN BOLTON**

publisher **MIKE RICHARDSON**
series editors **DIANA SCHUTZ and PHILIP AMARA**
collection editor **CHRIS WARNER**
designer **JOSHUA ELLIOTT**
technical assistance **DAN JACKSON**
art director **LIA RIBACCHI**

Special thanks to **DEBBIE OLSHAN** at Twentieth Century Fox Licensing.

ALIENS™ VS. PREDATOR™ OMNIBUS Volume 2

This volume collects material previously published as the Dark Horse graphic novel *Aliens vs. Predator: Deadliest of the Species*, issues one through four of the Dark Horse comic-book series *Aliens vs. Predator: Xenogenesis*, the Dark Horse comic-book *Aliens vs. Predator: Booty,* and stories from the Dark Horse comic book *Aliens vs. Predator Annual.*

Dark Horse Books
a division of Dark Horse Comics, Inc.
10956 SE Main Street
Milwaukie, OR 97222

darkhorse.com | foxmovies.com

To find a comics shop in your area, call the Comic Shop Locator Service toll-free at 1-888-266-4226

First edition: October 2007
ISBN-10: 1-59307-829-3
ISBN-13: 978-1-59307-829-4

10 9 8 7 6 5 4 3 2 1
Printed in China

DEADLIEST OF THE SPECIES

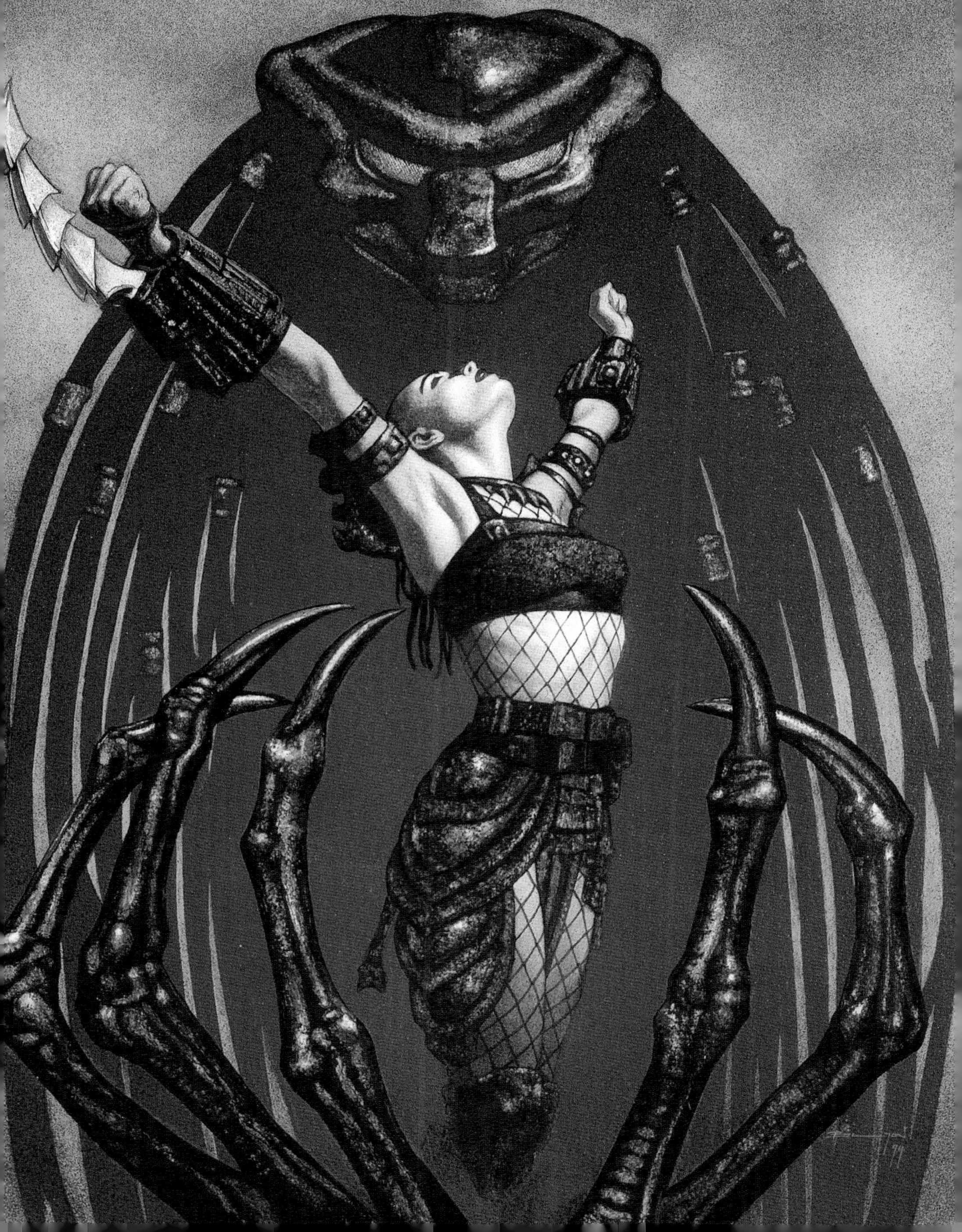

script
CHRIS CLAREMONT

pencils
JACKSON GUICE (chapters 1–3)
EDUARDO BARRETO (chapters 4–12)

inks
JOHN BEATTY (chapter 1)
EDUARDO BARRETO (chapters 2–12)

colors
GREGORY WRIGHT
with
SEAN TIERNEY
JIMMY JOHNS
MATTHEW HOLLINGSWORTH

lettering
TOM ORZECHOWSKI
SUSIE LEE

title illustration
JOHN BOLTON

TIME OF THE PREACHER

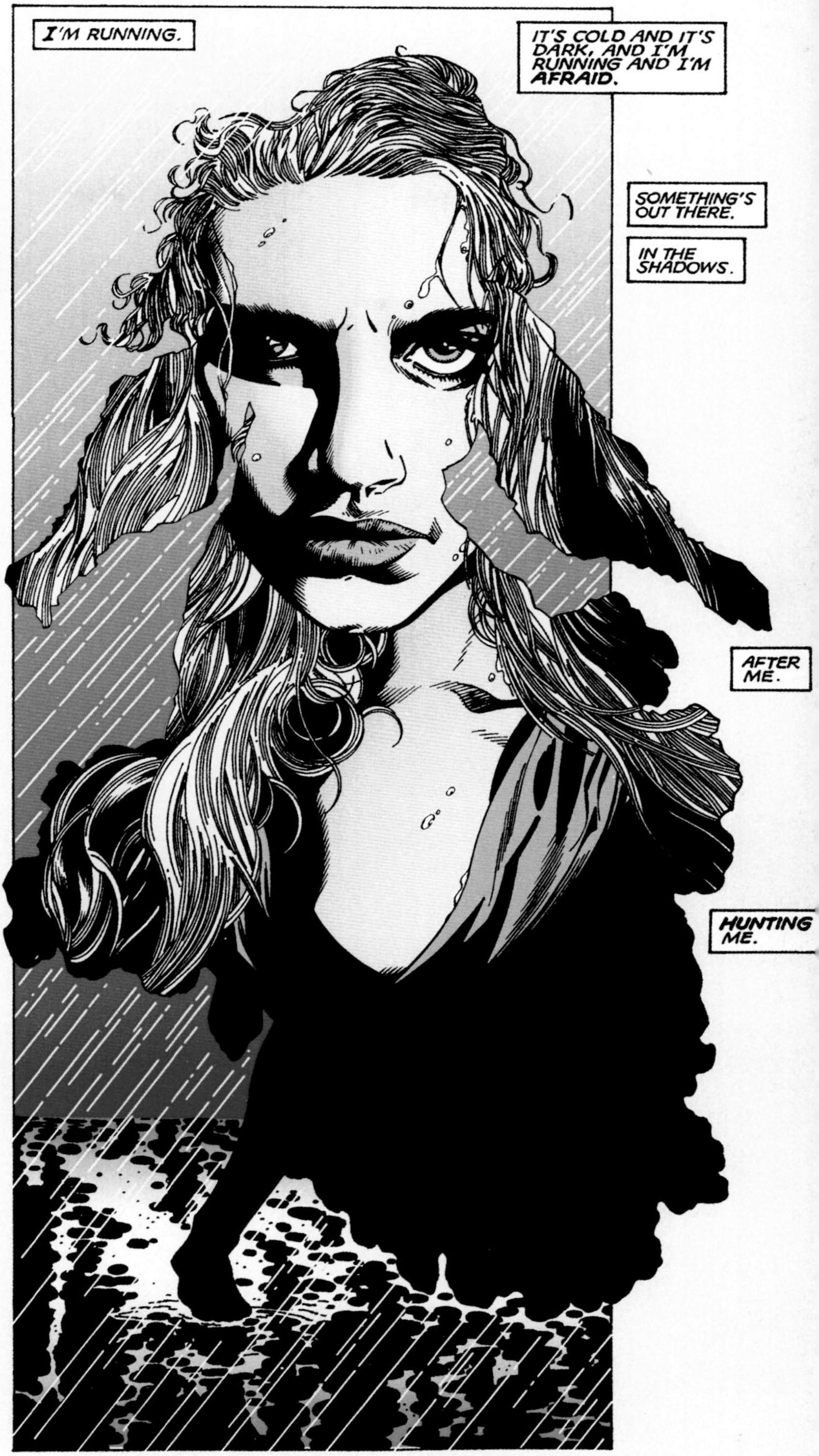
I'M RUNNING.
IT'S COLD AND IT'S DARK, AND I'M RUNNING AND I'M AFRAID.
SOMETHING'S OUT THERE.
IN THE SHADOWS.
AFTER ME.
HUNTING ME.

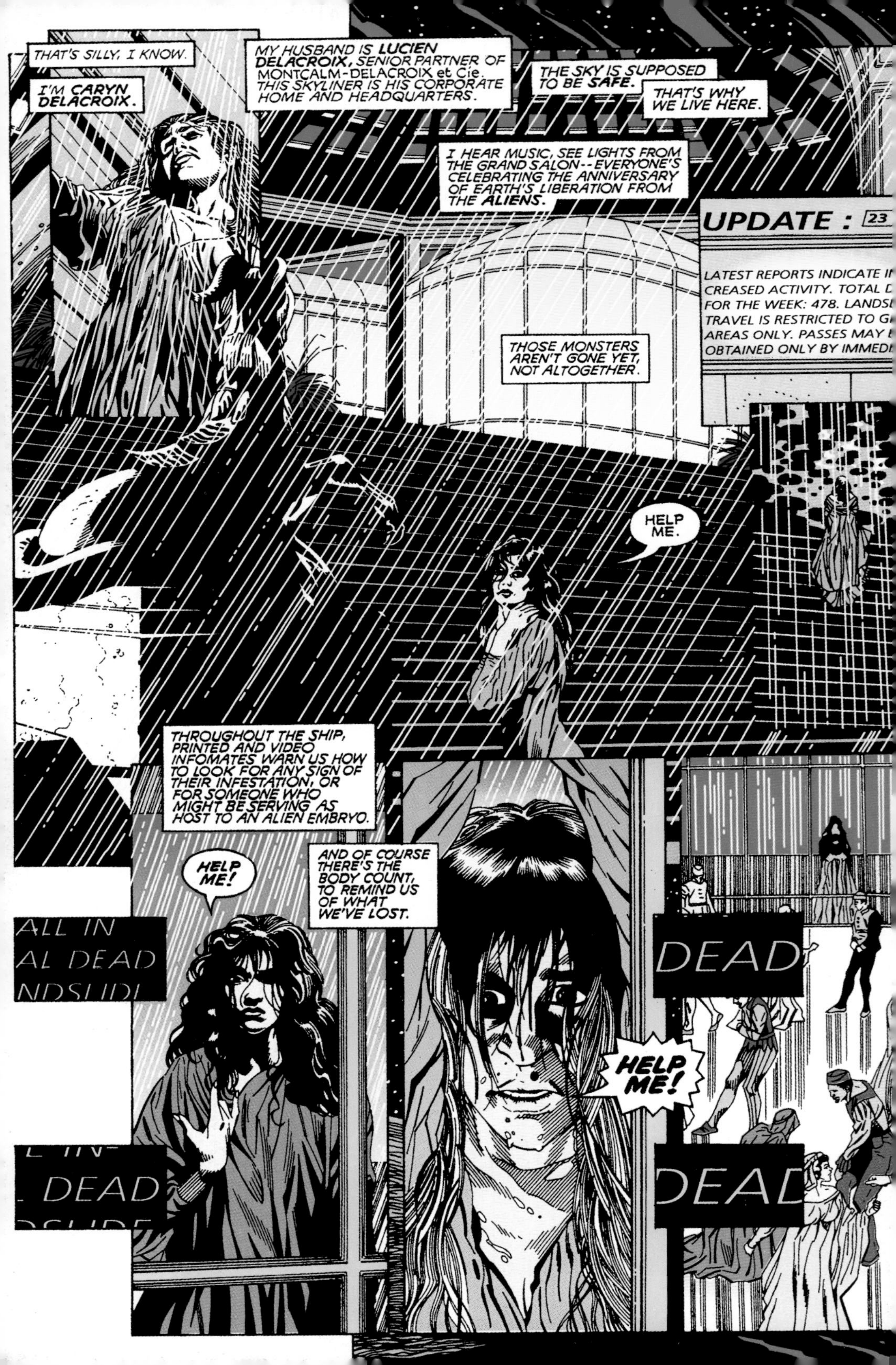

THAT'S SILLY, I KNOW.
I'M CARYN DELACROIX.
MY HUSBAND IS LUCIEN DELACROIX, SENIOR PARTNER OF MONTCALM-DELACROIX et Cie. THIS SKYLINER IS HIS CORPORATE HOME AND HEADQUARTERS.
THE SKY IS SUPPOSED TO BE SAFE.
THAT'S WHY WE LIVE HERE.
I HEAR MUSIC, SEE LIGHTS FROM THE GRAND SALON--EVERYONE'S CELEBRATING THE ANNIVERSARY OF EARTH'S LIBERATION FROM THE ALIENS.
UPDATE : 23
LATEST REPORTS INDICATE IN CREASED ACTIVITY. TOTAL D FOR THE WEEK: 478. LANDS TRAVEL IS RESTRICTED TO G AREAS ONLY. PASSES MAY OBTAINED ONLY BY IMMEDI
THOSE MONSTERS AREN'T GONE YET, NOT ALTOGETHER.
HELP ME.
THROUGHOUT THE SHIP, PRINTED AND VIDEO INFOMATES WARN US HOW TO LOOK FOR ANY SIGN OF THEIR INFESTATION, OR FOR SOMEONE WHO MIGHT BE SERVING AS HOST TO AN ALIEN EMBRYO.
HELP ME!
AND OF COURSE THERE'S THE BODY COUNT, TO REMIND US OF WHAT WE'VE LOST.
ALL IN
AL DEAD
NDSLIDI
DEAD
HELP ME!
DEAD
DEAD

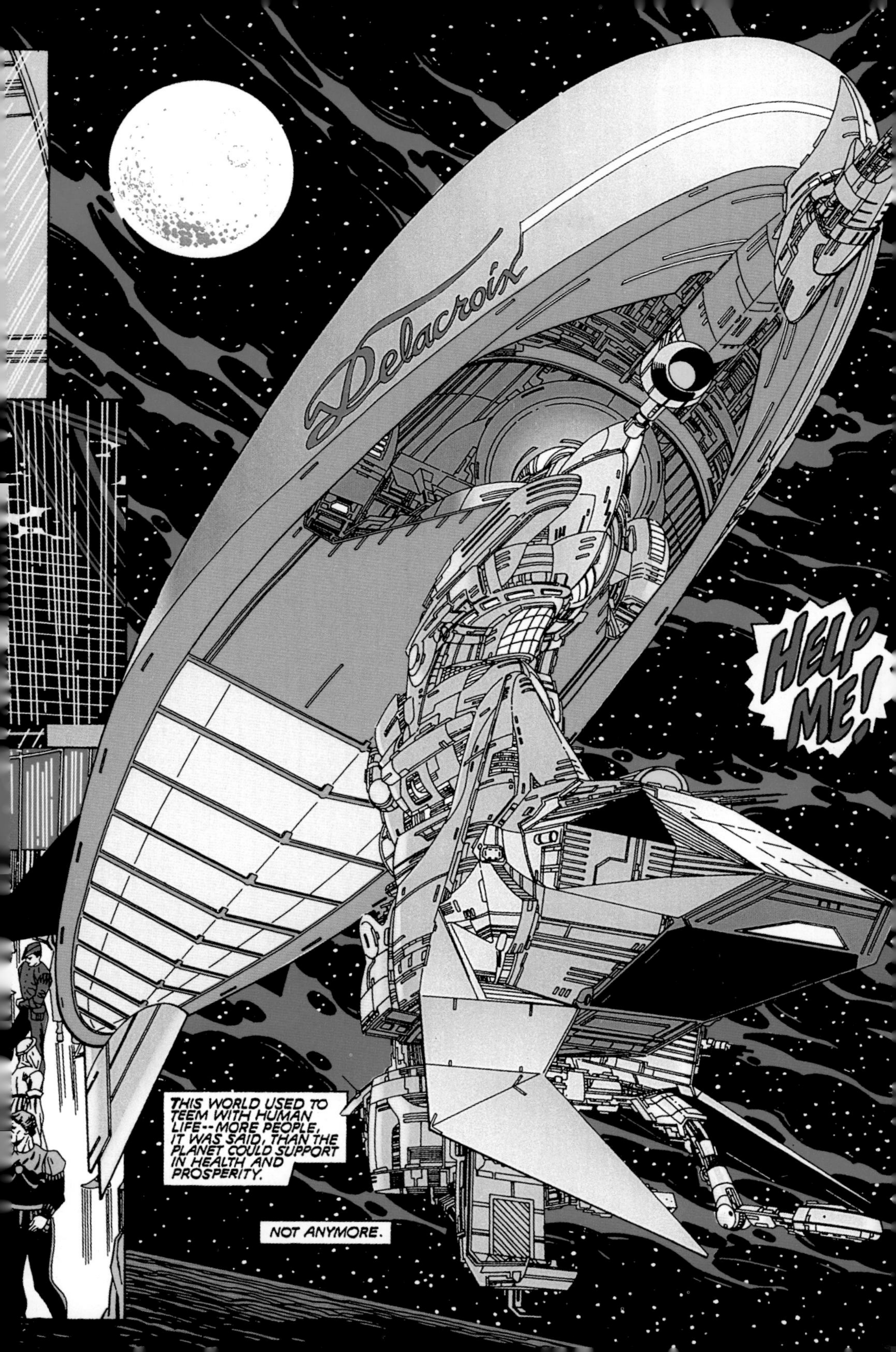

Delacroix
HELP ME!
THIS WORLD USED TO TEEM WITH HUMAN LIFE--MORE PEOPLE, IT WAS SAID, THAN THE PLANET COULD SUPPORT IN HEALTH AND PROSPERITY.
NOT ANYMORE.

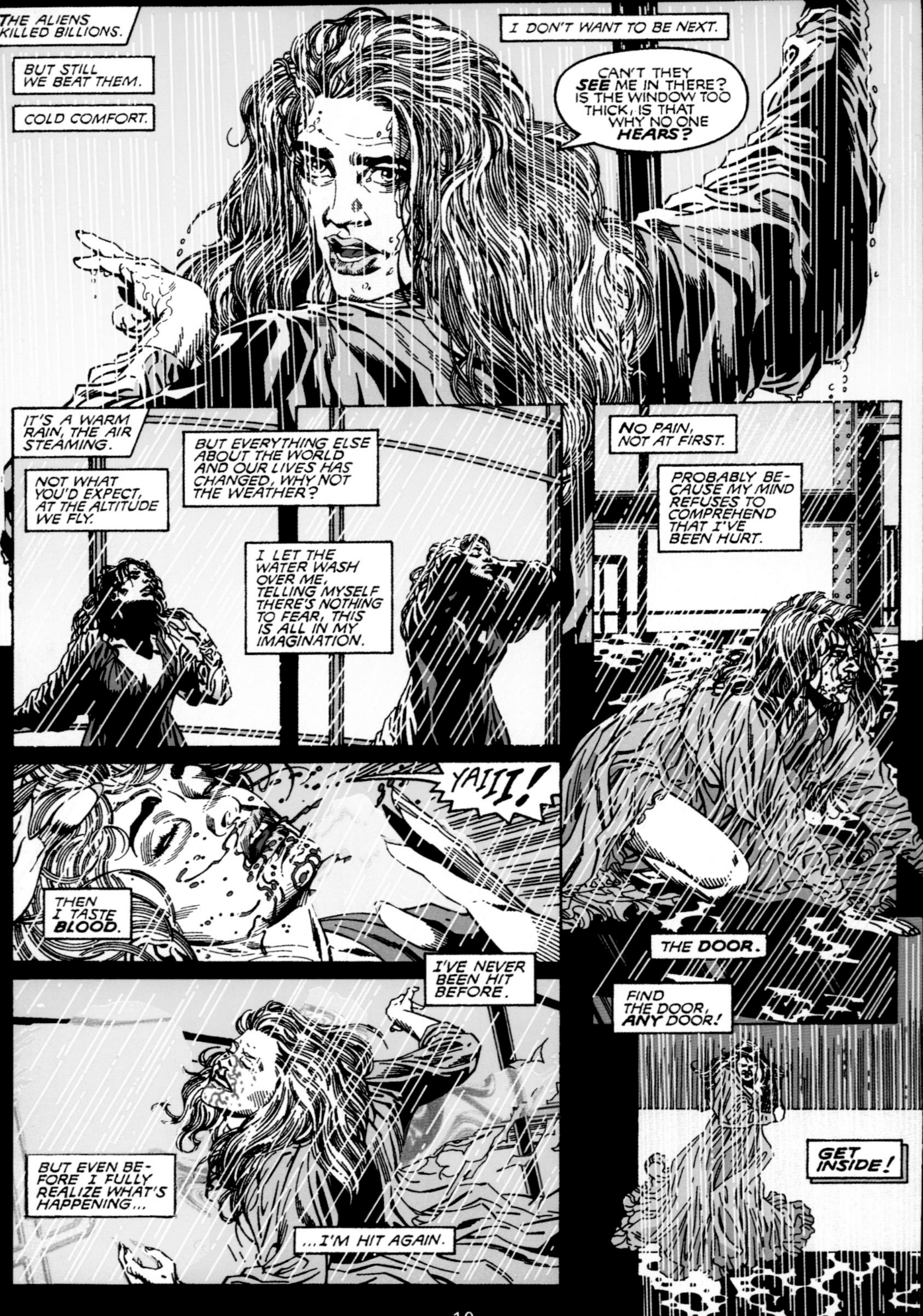
THE ALIENS KILLED BILLIONS.
BUT STILL WE BEAT THEM.
COLD COMFORT.
I DON'T WANT TO BE NEXT.
CAN'T THEY SEE ME IN THERE? IS THE WINDOW TOO THICK, IS THAT WHY NO ONE HEARS?
IT'S A WARM RAIN, THE AIR STEAMING.
NOT WHAT YOU'D EXPECT, AT THE ALTITUDE WE FLY.
BUT EVERYTHING ELSE ABOUT THE WORLD AND OUR LIVES HAS CHANGED, WHY NOT THE WEATHER?
I LET THE WATER WASH OVER ME, TELLING MYSELF THERE'S NOTHING TO FEAR, THIS IS ALL IN MY IMAGINATION.
YAIII!
THEN I TASTE BLOOD.
I'VE NEVER BEEN HIT BEFORE.
BUT EVEN BEFORE I FULLY REALIZE WHAT'S HAPPENING...
...I'M HIT AGAIN.
NO PAIN, NOT AT FIRST.
PROBABLY BECAUSE MY MIND REFUSES TO COMPREHEND THAT I'VE BEEN HURT.
THE DOOR.
FIND THE DOOR, ANY DOOR!
GET INSIDE!

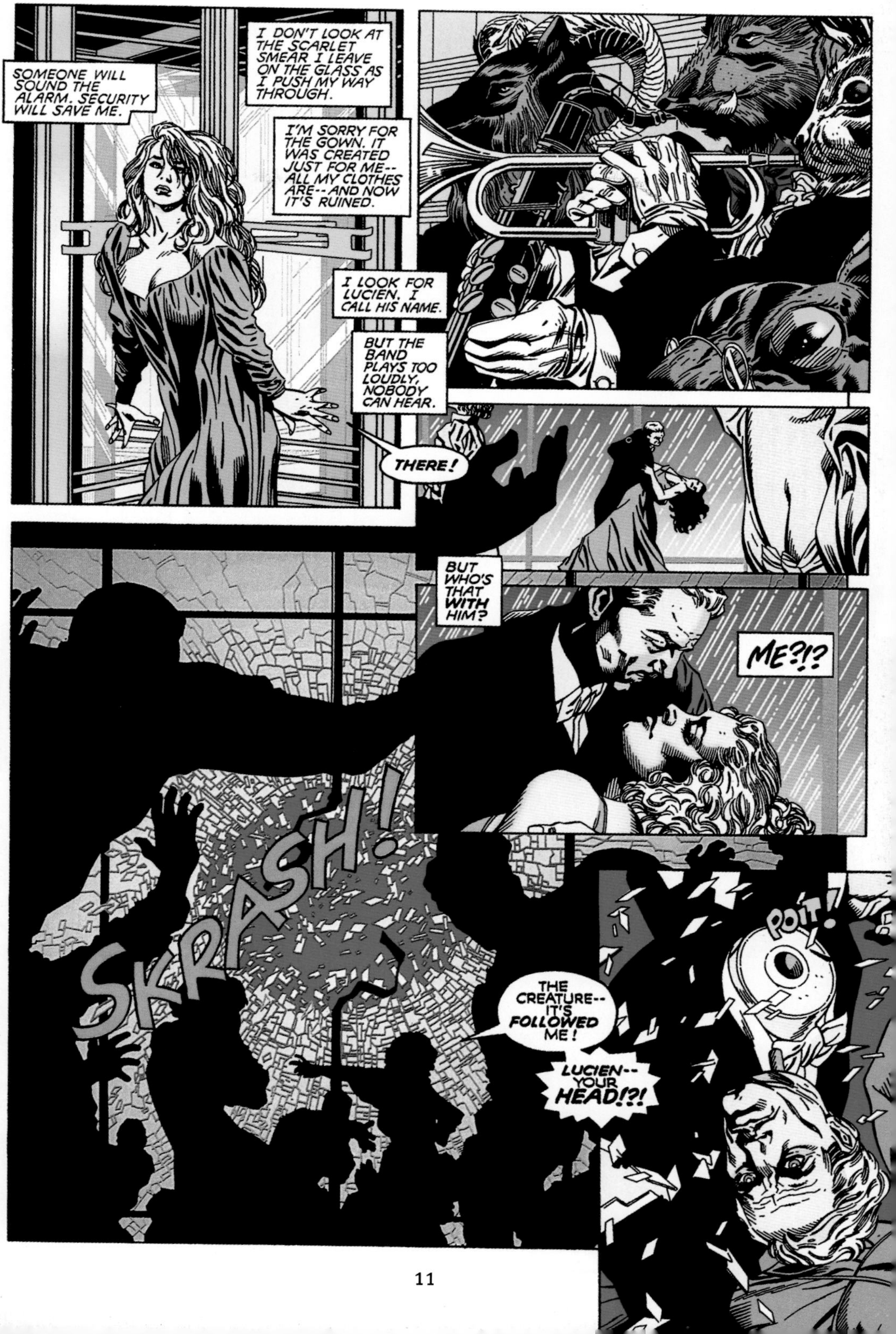
SOMEONE WILL SOUND THE ALARM. SECURITY WILL SAVE ME.
I DON'T LOOK AT THE SCARLET SMEAR I LEAVE ON THE GLASS AS I PUSH MY WAY THROUGH.
I'M SORRY FOR THE GOWN. IT WAS CREATED JUST FOR ME-- ALL MY CLOTHES ARE-- AND NOW IT'S RUINED.
I LOOK FOR LUCIEN. I CALL HIS NAME.
BUT THE BAND PLAYS TOO LOUDLY, NOBODY CAN HEAR.
THERE!
BUT WHO'S THAT WITH HIM?
ME?!?
SKRASH!
THE CREATURE-- IT'S FOLLOWED ME!
LUCIEN-- YOUR HEAD!?!
POIT!

FOR A MOMENT, I JUST STAND STILL AMIDST THE CHAOS, STARING IN DUMB DISBELIEF, OBLIVIOUS OF THE FLASHFIRE OF TERROR THAT RAGES ABOUT ME.

I HEAR SCREAMS, AS THOUGH FROM A GREAT DISTANCE, AND THE SOUNDS OF A TERRIBLE SLAUGHTER.

BUT NOTHING I SEE IS REAL.

AND THE ONLY BLOOD THAT FLOWS IS **MINE**.

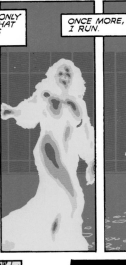

ONCE MORE, I RUN.

ONLY TO BE BROUGHT DOWN...

... BY THE **MANNEQUIN** VERSION OF ME.

THE WINDOW SHATTERS.

AND PART OF ME WELCOMES THIS FINAL PLUNGE...

...TO THE GROUND SO FAR BELOW.

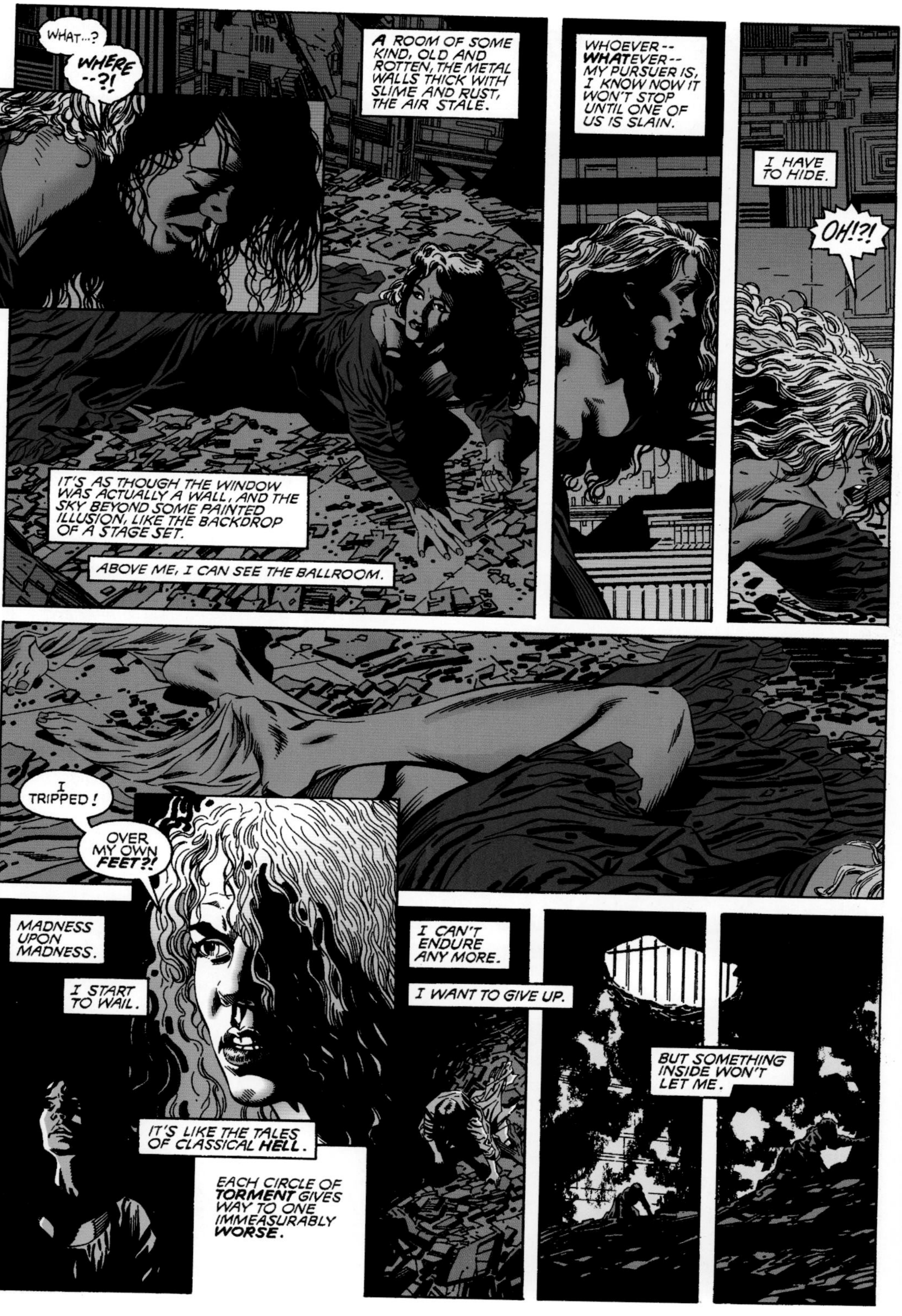
WHAT...?
WHERE --?!
A ROOM OF SOME KIND, OLD AND ROTTEN, THE METAL WALLS THICK WITH SLIME AND RUST, THE AIR STALE.
IT'S AS THOUGH THE WINDOW WAS ACTUALLY A WALL, AND THE SKY BEYOND SOME PAINTED ILLUSION, LIKE THE BACKDROP OF A STAGE SET.
ABOVE ME, I CAN SEE THE BALLROOM.
WHOEVER -- WHATEVER -- MY PURSUER IS, I KNOW NOW IT WON'T STOP UNTIL ONE OF US IS SLAIN.
I HAVE TO HIDE.
OH!?!
I TRIPPED!
OVER MY OWN FEET?!
MADNESS UPON MADNESS.
I START TO WAIL.
IT'S LIKE THE TALES OF CLASSICAL HELL.
EACH CIRCLE OF TORMENT GIVES WAY TO ONE IMMEASURABLY WORSE.
I CAN'T ENDURE ANY MORE.
I WANT TO GIVE UP.
BUT SOMETHING INSIDE WON'T LET ME.

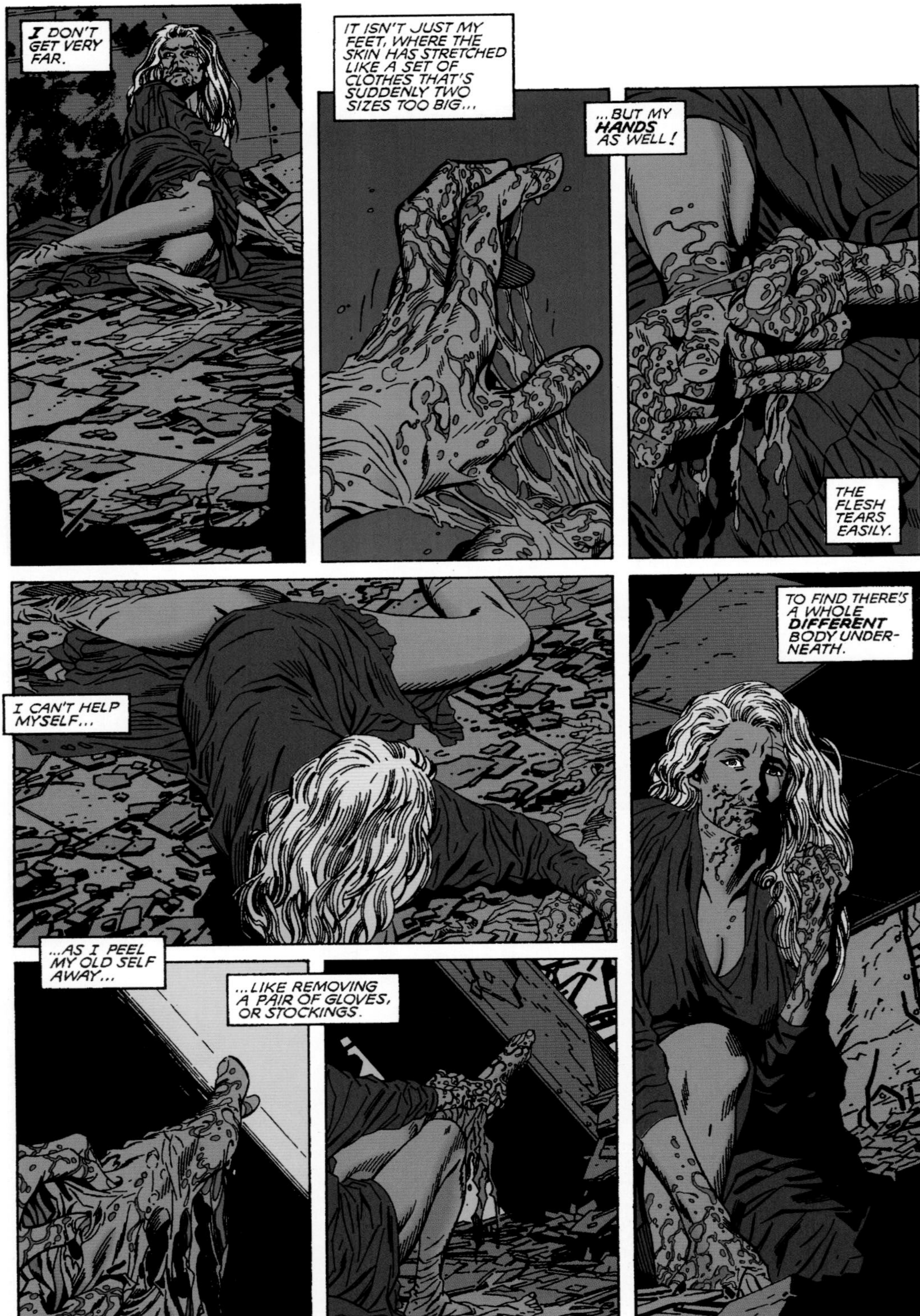
I DON'T GET VERY FAR.
IT ISN'T JUST MY FEET, WHERE THE SKIN HAS STRETCHED LIKE A SET OF CLOTHES THAT'S SUDDENLY TWO SIZES TOO BIG...
...BUT MY HANDS AS WELL!
THE FLESH TEARS EASILY.
I CAN'T HELP MYSELF...
...AS I PEEL MY OLD SELF AWAY...
...LIKE REMOVING A PAIR OF GLOVES, OR STOCKINGS.
TO FIND THERE'S A WHOLE DIFFERENT BODY UNDER-NEATH.

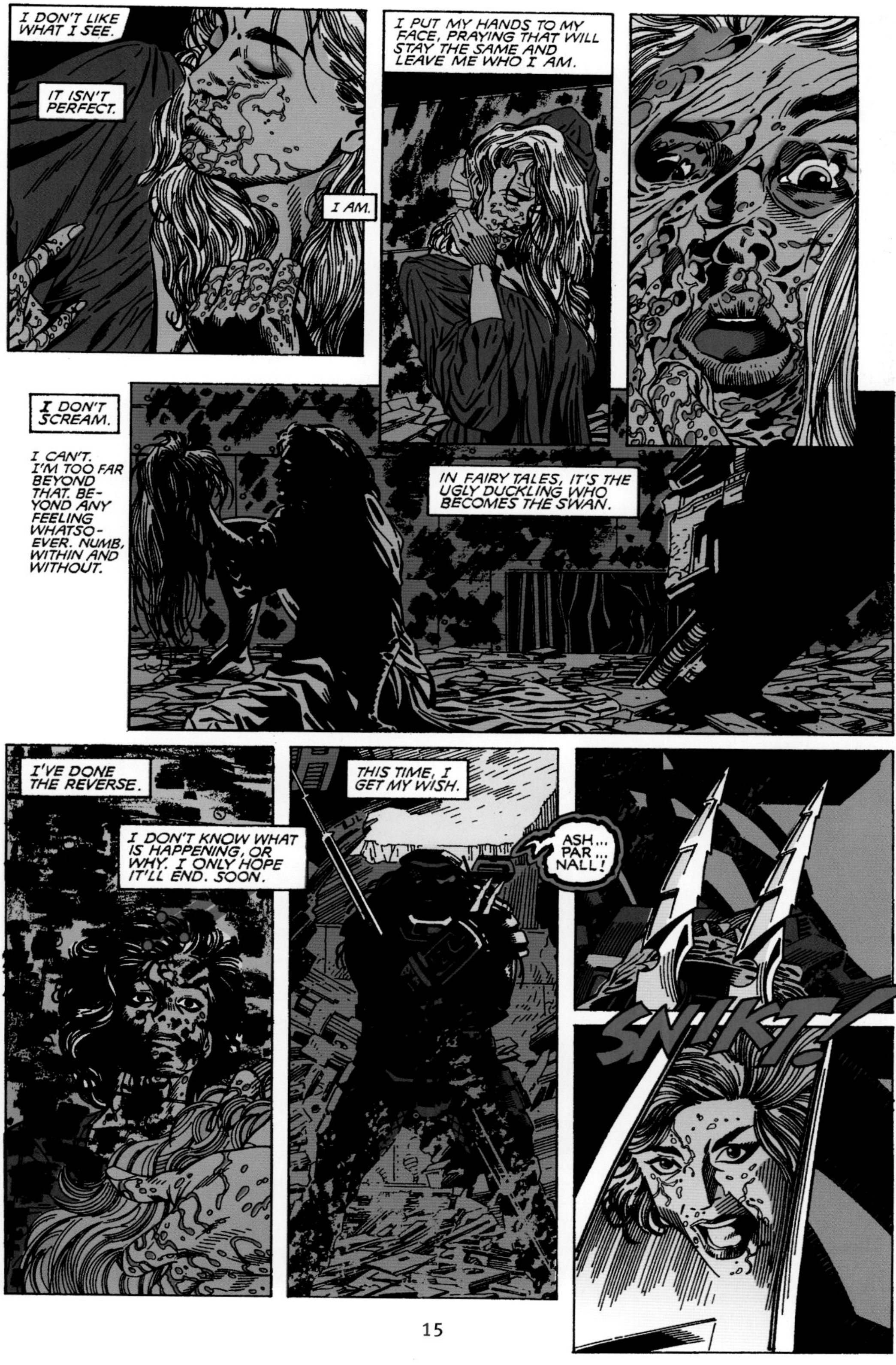
I DON'T LIKE WHAT I SEE.
IT ISN'T PERFECT.
I AM.
I PUT MY HANDS TO MY FACE, PRAYING THAT WILL STAY THE SAME AND LEAVE ME WHO I AM.
I DON'T SCREAM.
I CAN'T. I'M TOO FAR BEYOND THAT. BE-YOND ANY FEELING WHATSO-EVER. NUMB, WITHIN AND WITHOUT.
IN FAIRY TALES, IT'S THE UGLY DUCKLING WHO BECOMES THE SWAN.
I'VE DONE THE REVERSE.
I DON'T KNOW WHAT IS HAPPENING, OR WHY. I ONLY HOPE IT'LL END. SOON.
THIS TIME, I GET MY WISH.
ASH... PAR... NALL!
SNIKT!

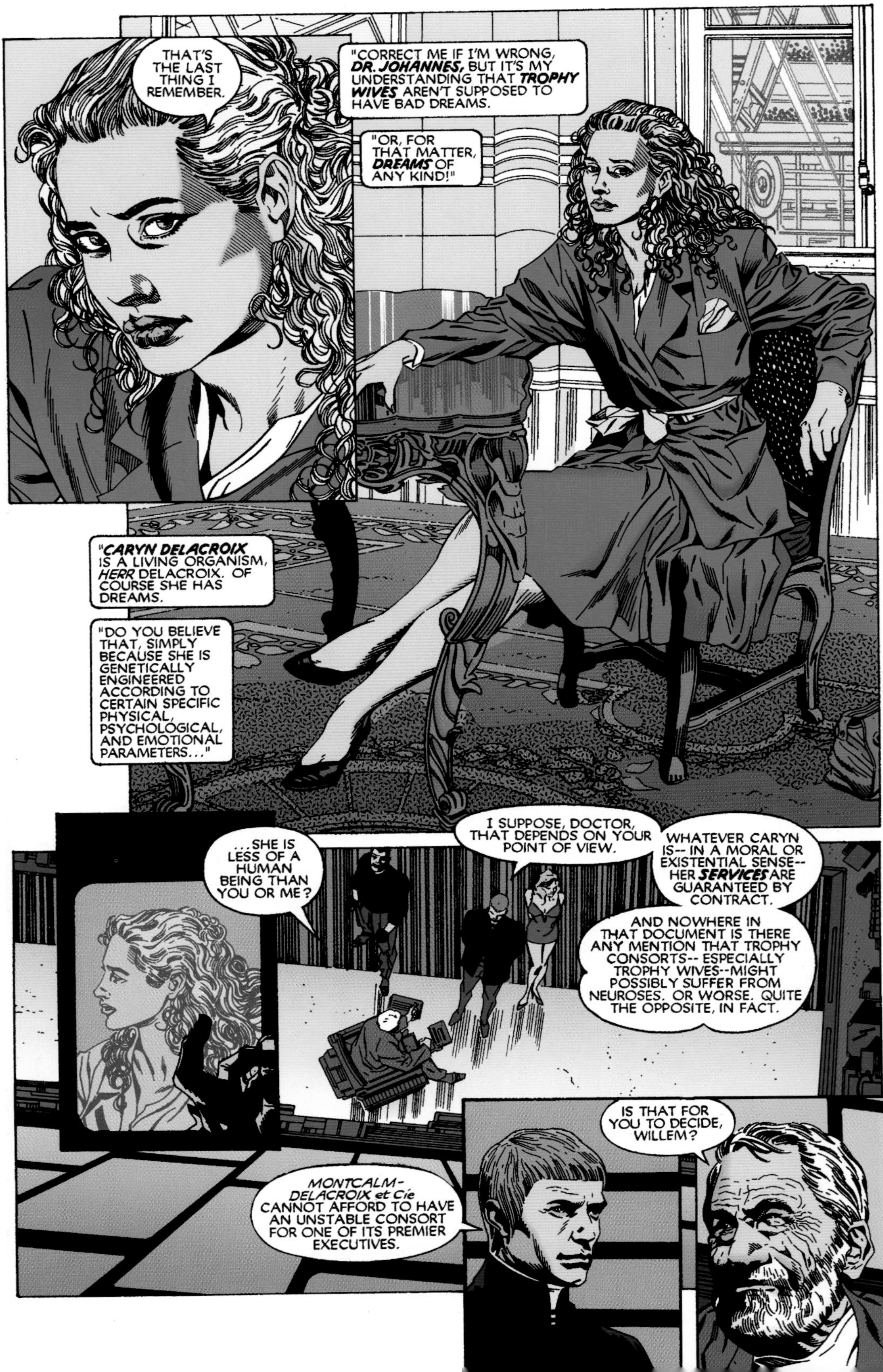
THAT'S THE LAST THING I REMEMBER.
"CORRECT ME IF I'M WRONG, DR. JOHANNES, BUT IT'S MY UNDERSTANDING THAT TROPHY WIVES AREN'T SUPPOSED TO HAVE BAD DREAMS.
"OR, FOR THAT MATTER, DREAMS OF ANY KIND!"
"CARYN DELACROIX IS A LIVING ORGANISM, HERR DELACROIX. OF COURSE SHE HAS DREAMS.
"DO YOU BELIEVE THAT, SIMPLY BECAUSE SHE IS GENETICALLY ENGINEERED ACCORDING TO CERTAIN SPECIFIC PHYSICAL, PSYCHOLOGICAL, AND EMOTIONAL PARAMETERS..."
...SHE IS LESS OF A HUMAN BEING THAN YOU OR ME?
I SUPPOSE, DOCTOR, THAT DEPENDS ON YOUR POINT OF VIEW.
WHATEVER CARYN IS-- IN A MORAL OR EXISTENTIAL SENSE-- HER SERVICES ARE GUARANTEED BY CONTRACT.
AND NOWHERE IN THAT DOCUMENT IS THERE ANY MENTION THAT TROPHY CONSORTS-- ESPECIALLY TROPHY WIVES--MIGHT POSSIBLY SUFFER FROM NEUROSES. OR WORSE. QUITE THE OPPOSITE, IN FACT.
MONTCALM-DELACROIX et Cie CANNOT AFFORD TO HAVE AN UNSTABLE CONSORT FOR ONE OF ITS PREMIER EXECUTIVES.
IS THAT FOR YOU TO DECIDE, WILLEM?

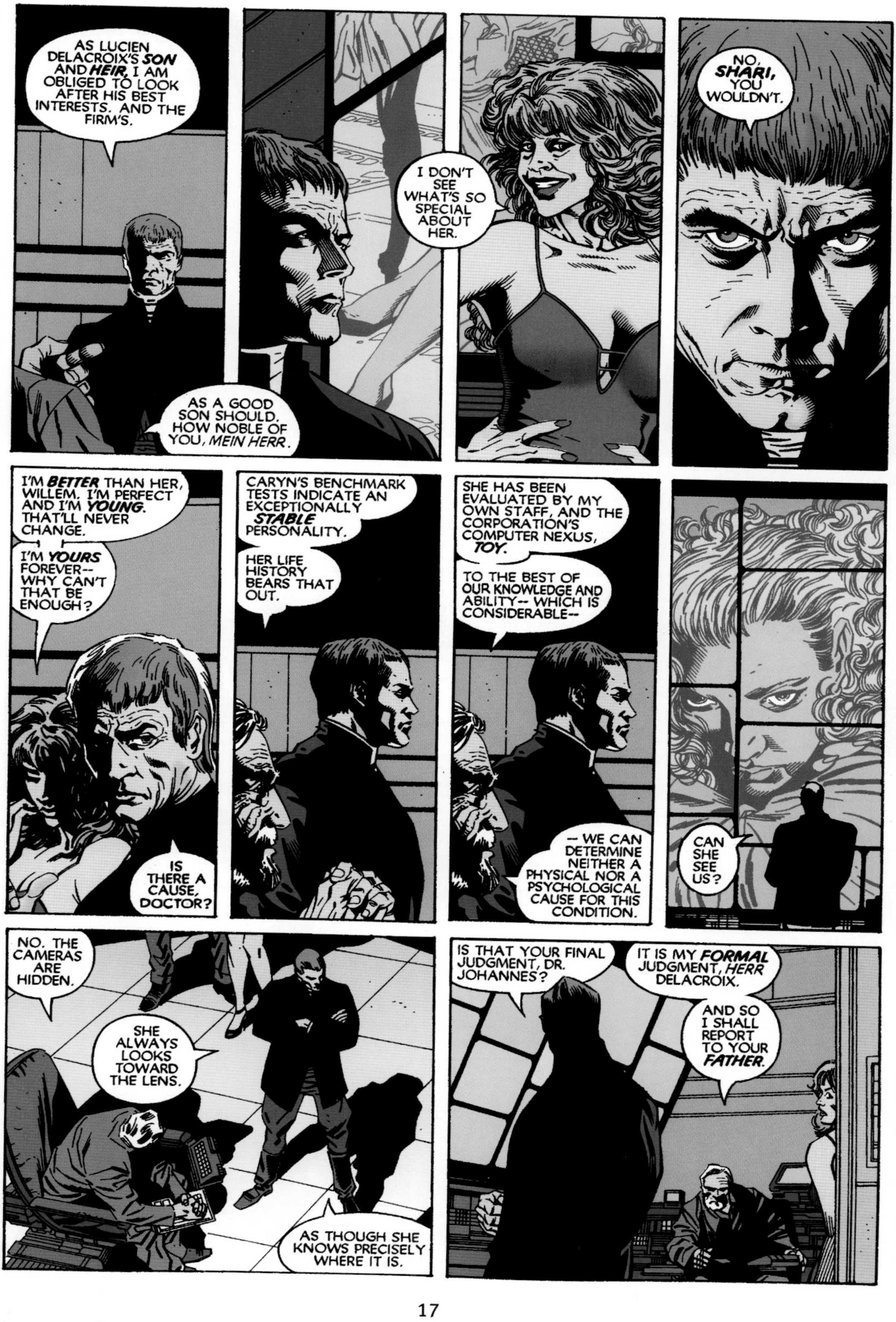

AS LUCIEN DELACROIX'S SON AND HEIR, I AM OBLIGED TO LOOK AFTER HIS BEST INTERESTS. AND THE FIRM'S.
AS A GOOD SON SHOULD. HOW NOBLE OF YOU, MEIN HERR.
I DON'T SEE WHAT'S SO SPECIAL ABOUT HER.
NO, SHARI, YOU WOULDN'T.
I'M BETTER THAN HER, WILLEM. I'M PERFECT AND I'M YOUNG. THAT'LL NEVER CHANGE.
I'M YOURS FOREVER-- WHY CAN'T THAT BE ENOUGH?
IS THERE A CAUSE, DOCTOR?
CARYN'S BENCHMARK TESTS INDICATE AN EXCEPTIONALLY STABLE PERSONALITY.
HER LIFE HISTORY BEARS THAT OUT.
SHE HAS BEEN EVALUATED BY MY OWN STAFF, AND THE CORPORATION'S COMPUTER NEXUS, TOY.
TO THE BEST OF OUR KNOWLEDGE AND ABILITY-- WHICH IS CONSIDERABLE--
-- WE CAN DETERMINE NEITHER A PHYSICAL NOR A PSYCHOLOGICAL CAUSE FOR THIS CONDITION.
CAN SHE SEE US?
NO. THE CAMERAS ARE HIDDEN.
SHE ALWAYS LOOKS TOWARD THE LENS.
AS THOUGH SHE KNOWS PRECISELY WHERE IT IS.
IS THAT YOUR FINAL JUDGMENT, DR. JOHANNES?
IT IS MY FORMAL JUDGMENT, HERR DELACROIX.
AND SO I SHALL REPORT TO YOUR FATHER.

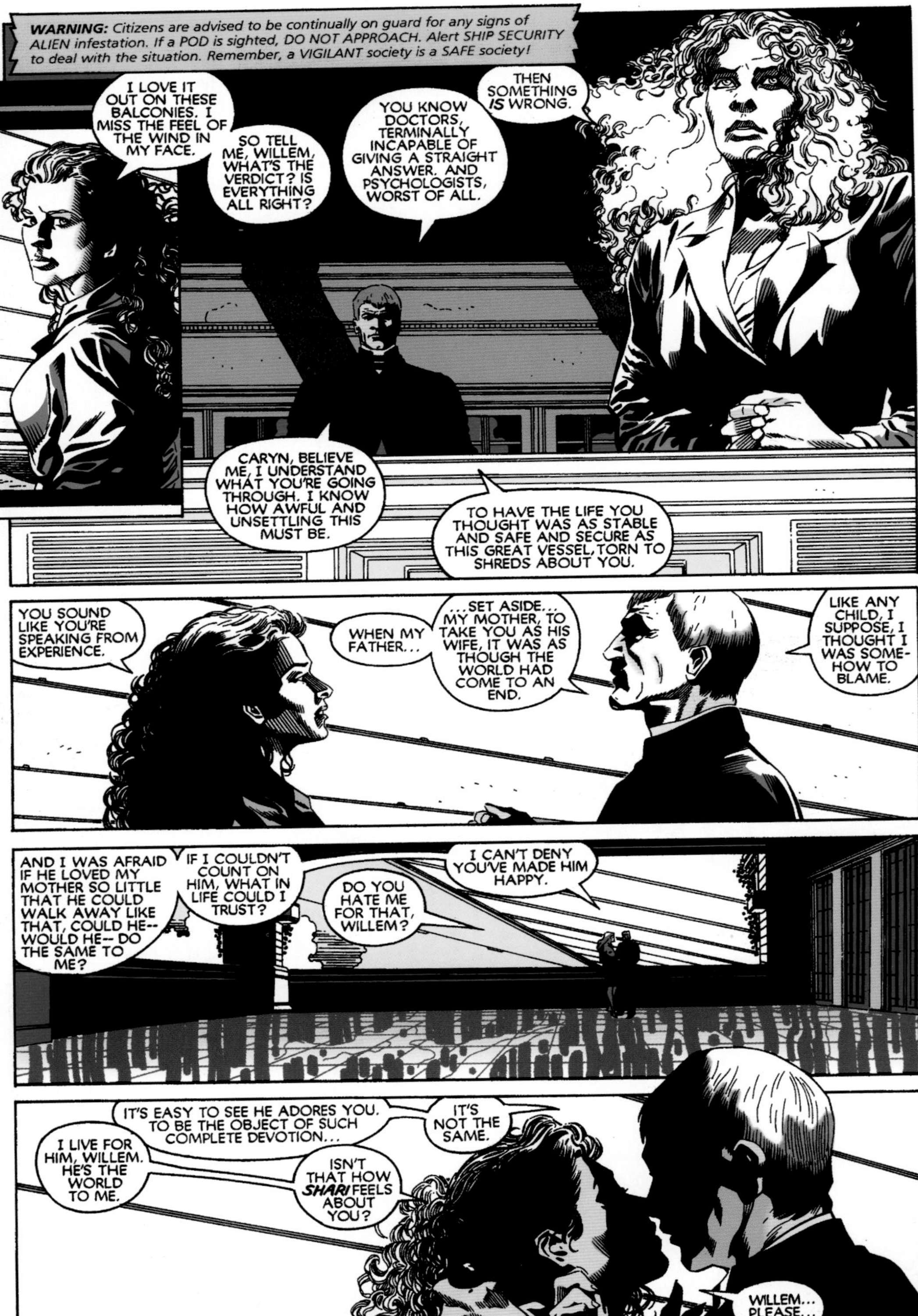
WARNING: Citizens are advised to be continually on guard for any signs of ALIEN infestation. If a POD is sighted, DO NOT APPROACH. Alert SHIP SECURITY to deal with the situation. Remember, a VIGILANT society is a SAFE society!
I LOVE IT OUT ON THESE BALCONIES. I MISS THE FEEL OF THE WIND IN MY FACE.
SO TELL ME, WILLEM, WHAT'S THE VERDICT? IS EVERYTHING ALL RIGHT?
YOU KNOW DOCTORS, TERMINALLY INCAPABLE OF GIVING A STRAIGHT ANSWER. AND PSYCHOLOGISTS, WORST OF ALL.
THEN SOMETHING IS WRONG.
CARYN, BELIEVE ME, I UNDERSTAND WHAT YOU'RE GOING THROUGH. I KNOW HOW AWFUL AND UNSETTLING THIS MUST BE.
TO HAVE THE LIFE YOU THOUGHT WAS AS STABLE AND SAFE AND SECURE AS THIS GREAT VESSEL, TORN TO SHREDS ABOUT YOU.
YOU SOUND LIKE YOU'RE SPEAKING FROM EXPERIENCE.
WHEN MY FATHER...
...SET ASIDE... MY MOTHER, TO TAKE YOU AS HIS WIFE, IT WAS AS THOUGH THE WORLD HAD COME TO AN END.
LIKE ANY CHILD, I SUPPOSE, I THOUGHT I WAS SOME-HOW TO BLAME.
AND I WAS AFRAID IF HE LOVED MY MOTHER SO LITTLE THAT HE COULD WALK AWAY LIKE THAT, COULD HE-- WOULD HE-- DO THE SAME TO ME?
IF I COULDN'T COUNT ON HIM, WHAT IN LIFE COULD I TRUST?
DO YOU HATE ME FOR THAT, WILLEM?
I CAN'T DENY YOU'VE MADE HIM HAPPY.
IT'S EASY TO SEE HE ADORES YOU. TO BE THE OBJECT OF SUCH COMPLETE DEVOTION...
IT'S NOT THE SAME.
I LIVE FOR HIM, WILLEM. HE'S THE WORLD TO ME.
ISN'T THAT HOW SHARI FEELS ABOUT YOU?
WILLEM... PLEASE...

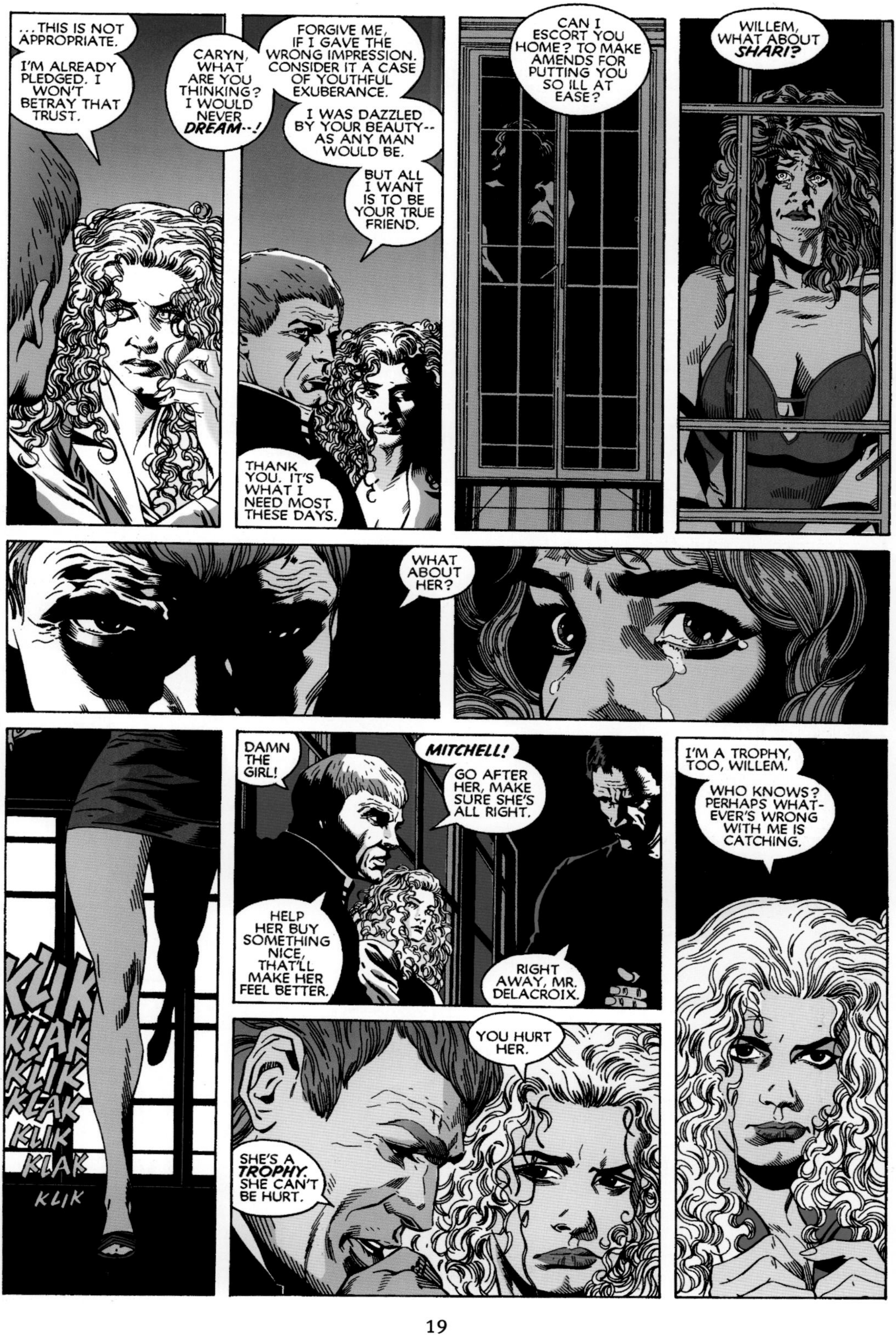
...THIS IS NOT APPROPRIATE.
I'M ALREADY PLEDGED. I WON'T BETRAY THAT TRUST.
CARYN, WHAT ARE YOU THINKING? I WOULD NEVER DREAM--!
FORGIVE ME, IF I GAVE THE WRONG IMPRESSION. CONSIDER IT A CASE OF YOUTHFUL EXUBERANCE.
I WAS DAZZLED BY YOUR BEAUTY-- AS ANY MAN WOULD BE.
BUT ALL I WANT IS TO BE YOUR TRUE FRIEND.
THANK YOU. IT'S WHAT I NEED MOST THESE DAYS.
CAN I ESCORT YOU HOME? TO MAKE AMENDS FOR PUTTING YOU SO ILL AT EASE?
WILLEM, WHAT ABOUT SHARI?
WHAT ABOUT HER?
KLIK
KLAK
KLIK
KLAK
KLIK
KLAK
KLIK
DAMN THE GIRL!
MITCHELL!
GO AFTER HER, MAKE SURE SHE'S ALL RIGHT.
HELP HER BUY SOMETHING NICE, THAT'LL MAKE HER FEEL BETTER.
RIGHT AWAY, MR. DELACROIX.
I'M A TROPHY, TOO, WILLEM.
WHO KNOWS? PERHAPS WHAT-EVER'S WRONG WITH ME IS CATCHING.
YOU HURT HER.
SHE'S A TROPHY. SHE CAN'T BE HURT.

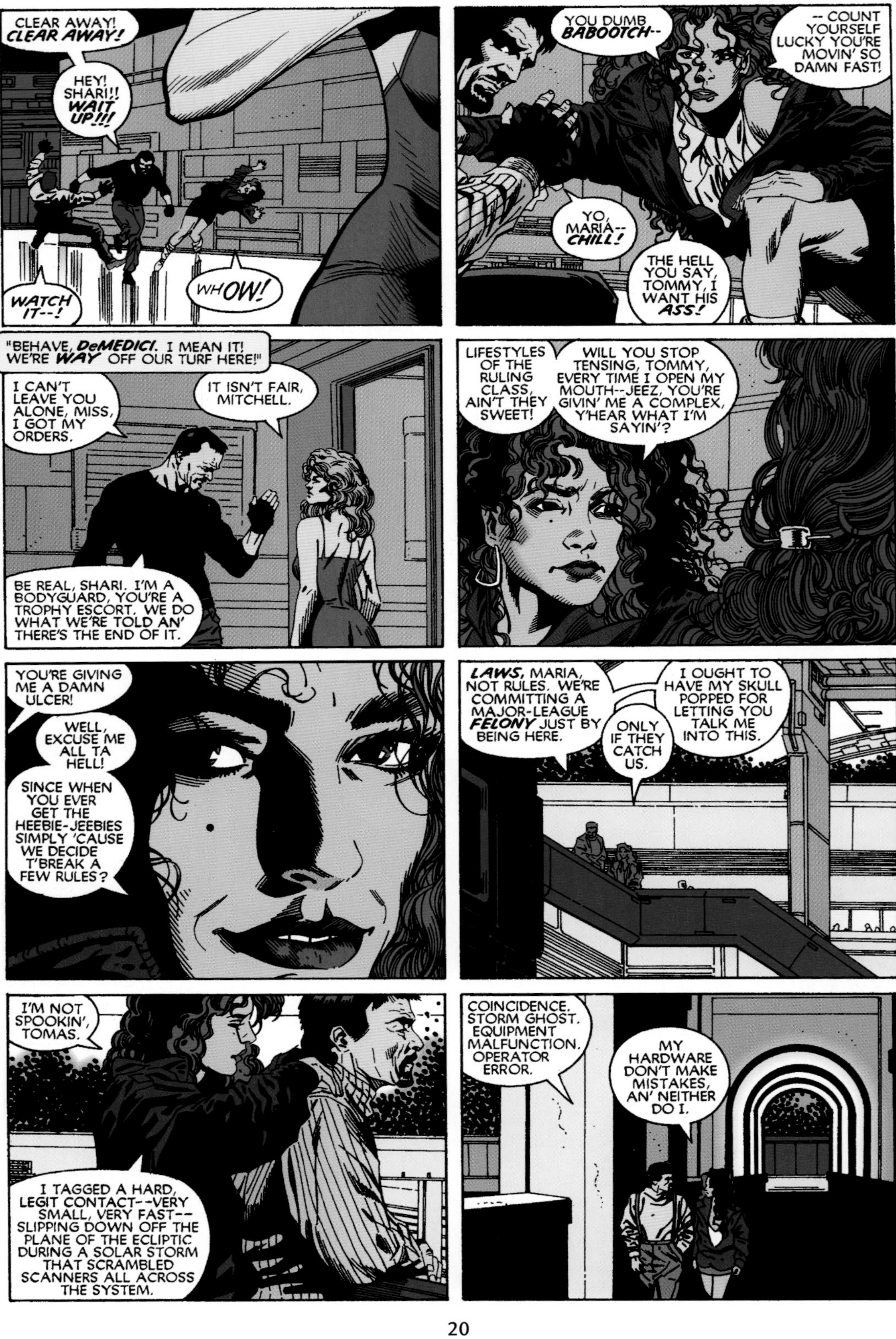

CLEAR AWAY! CLEAR AWAY!
HEY! SHARI!! WAIT UP!!!
WATCH IT--!
WHOW!
YOU DUMB BABOOTCH--
-- COUNT YOURSELF LUCKY YOU'RE MOVIN' SO DAMN FAST!
YO, MARIA-- CHILL!
THE HELL YOU SAY, TOMMY, I WANT HIS ASS!
"BEHAVE, DeMEDICI. I MEAN IT! WE'RE WAY OFF OUR TURF HERE!"
I CAN'T LEAVE YOU ALONE, MISS, I GOT MY ORDERS.
IT ISN'T FAIR, MITCHELL.
BE REAL, SHARI. I'M A BODYGUARD, YOU'RE A TROPHY ESCORT. WE DO WHAT WE'RE TOLD AN' THERE'S THE END OF IT.
LIFESTYLES OF THE RULING CLASS, AIN'T THEY SWEET!
WILL YOU STOP TENSING, TOMMY, EVERY TIME I OPEN MY MOUTH--JEEZ, YOU'RE GIVIN' ME A COMPLEX, Y'HEAR WHAT I'M SAYIN'?
YOU'RE GIVING ME A DAMN ULCER!
WELL, EXCUSE ME ALL TA HELL!
SINCE WHEN YOU EVER GET THE HEEBIE-JEEBIES SIMPLY 'CAUSE WE DECIDE T'BREAK A FEW RULES?
LAWS, MARIA, NOT RULES. WE'RE COMMITTING A MAJOR-LEAGUE FELONY JUST BY BEING HERE.
ONLY IF THEY CATCH US.
I OUGHT TO HAVE MY SKULL POPPED FOR LETTING YOU TALK ME INTO THIS.
I'M NOT SPOOKIN', TOMAS.
I TAGGED A HARD, LEGIT CONTACT--VERY SMALL, VERY FAST--SLIPPING DOWN OFF THE PLANE OF THE ECLIPTIC DURING A SOLAR STORM THAT SCRAMBLED SCANNERS ALL ACROSS THE SYSTEM.
COINCIDENCE. STORM GHOST. EQUIPMENT MALFUNCTION. OPERATOR ERROR.
MY HARDWARE DON'T MAKE MISTAKES, AN' NEITHER DO I.

I'VE CROSSLINKED MY REPORT TO YOUR BUFFER, *SEIGNEUR*.

BUT I MUST ASK, WOULD YOU NOT PERHAPS BE BETTER SERVED BY A MORE...STABLE COMPANION?

I SENT MY *WIFE* TO YOU, DR. JOHANNES, BECAUSE I WAS ASSURED YOU COULD BE OF HELP TO HER.

THIS SUGGESTION IS NOT HELPFUL.

I WAS MERELY OFFERING THE MOST EXPEDITIOUS RESOLUTION TO YOUR PROBLEM.

THE "PROBLEM," DOCTOR, IS THAT MY WIFE HAS *NIGHTMARES*.

I DO NOT WISH TO LOSE CARYN, OR DISPOSE OF HER.

I WANT THE NIGHTMARES TO *STOP*.

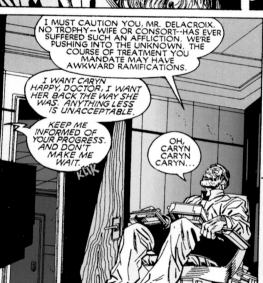

I MUST CAUTION YOU, MR. DELACROIX. NO TROPHY--WIFE OR CONSORT--HAS EVER SUFFERED SUCH AN AFFLICTION. WE'RE PUSHING INTO THE UNKNOWN. THE COURSE OF TREATMENT YOU MANDATE MAY HAVE AWKWARD RAMIFICATIONS.

I WANT CARYN HAPPY, DOCTOR, I WANT HER BACK THE WAY SHE WAS. ANYTHING LESS IS UNACCEPTABLE.

KEEP ME INFORMED OF YOUR PROGRESS. AND DON'T MAKE ME WAIT.

OH, CARYN CARYN CARYN...

KLIK

...WHAT A CONUNDRUM YOU ARE.

WHAT A *MESS* THIS IS.

HE WANTS YOU HAPPY, AND HE WANTS YOU BY HIS SIDE.

SUPPOSE THE TWO ARE MUTUALLY EXCLUSIVE?

ASH... PAR... NALL!

GASP!

MATER CHRISTI--

NO!

21

YOU HEAR SOMETHING?

NOT SURE. DOWN THE HALL, MAYBE, THE WAY WE CAME?

PROBABLY MY IMAGINATION.

IT'S THIS SHIP. MY MIND CAN'T ACCEPT ANYTHING THIS BIG CRUISING IN AN ATMOSPHERE.

IT'S A *MONARCH-*CLASS HEAVY-LIFTER, MARIA, RATED FOR OPERATION FROM SURFACE TO HIGH ORBIT. THIS IS THE SIZE THEY COME IN.

I'M SORRY, OKAY, IT MAKES ME NERVOUS.

TOO MANY BUILDINGS, TOO MUCH CROWD...

...IT'S LIKE THEY PUT A CITY IN THE CLOUDS.

SUPPOSE SOMETHING BREAKS, TOMMY?

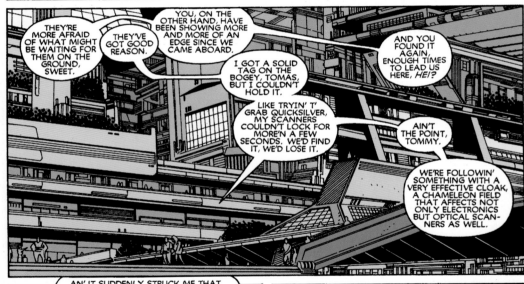

THEY'RE MORE AFRAID OF WHAT MIGHT BE WAITING FOR THEM ON THE GROUND, SWEET.

THEY'VE GOT GOOD REASON.

YOU, ON THE OTHER HAND, HAVE BEEN SHOWING MORE AND MORE OF AN EDGE SINCE WE CAME ABOARD.

AND YOU FOUND IT AGAIN, ENOUGH TIMES TO LEAD US HERE, *HEI?*

I GOT A SOLID TAG ON THE BOGEY, TOMAS, BUT I COULDN'T HOLD IT.

LIKE TRYIN' T' GRAB QUICKSILVER, MY SCANNERS COULDN'T LOCK FOR MORE'N A FEW SECONDS. WE'D FIND IT, WE'D LOSE IT.

AIN'T THE POINT, TOMMY.

WE'RE FOLLOWIN' SOMETHING WITH A VERY EFFECTIVE CLOAK, A CHAMELEON FIELD THAT AFFECTS NOT ONLY ELECTRONICS BUT OPTICAL SCANNERS AS WELL.

AN' IT SUDDENLY STRUCK ME THAT WHAT WORKS FOR A VEHICLE MIGHT BE APPLIED TO A PERSON AS WELL.

AN' IT STRUCK ME MORE THAT, ASSUMIN' I'M RIGHT, MAYBE THIS WHOMEVER MIGHT NOT APPRECIATE SOMEONE, NAMELY *US,* TRYIN' T' FLASH SOME LIGHT ONTO ITS SHADOWS.

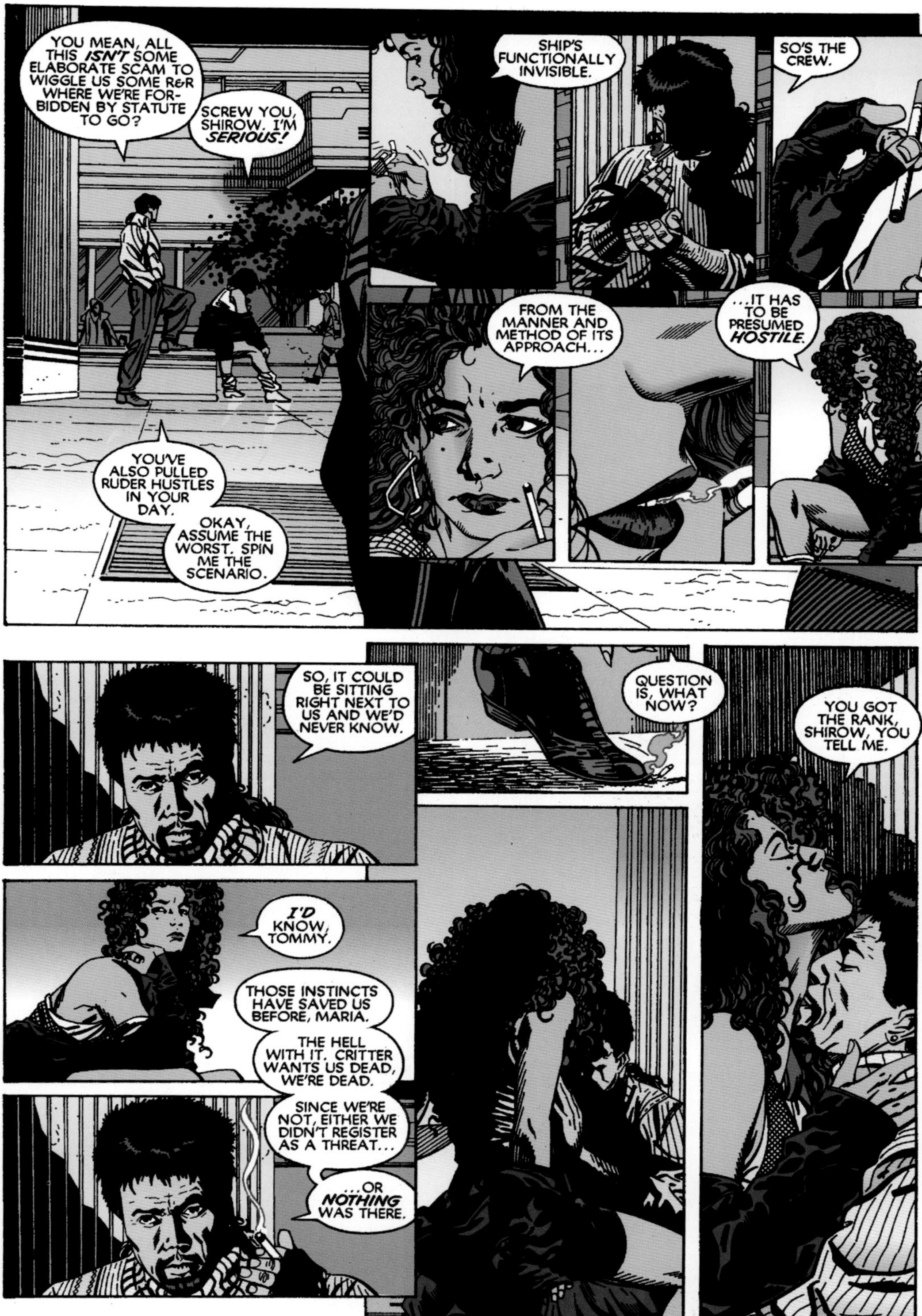

YOU MEAN, ALL THIS *ISN'T* SOME ELABORATE SCAM TO WIGGLE US SOME R&R WHERE WE'RE FORBIDDEN BY STATUTE TO GO?
SCREW YOU, SHIROW. I'M *SERIOUS!*
YOU'VE ALSO PULLED RUDER HUSTLES IN YOUR DAY.
OKAY, ASSUME THE WORST. SPIN ME THE SCENARIO.
SHIP'S FUNCTIONALLY INVISIBLE.
SO'S THE CREW.
FROM THE MANNER AND METHOD OF ITS APPROACH...
...IT HAS TO BE PRESUMED *HOSTILE*.
SO, IT COULD BE SITTING RIGHT NEXT TO US AND WE'D NEVER KNOW.
QUESTION IS, WHAT NOW?
YOU GOT THE RANK, SHIROW, YOU TELL ME.
I'D KNOW, TOMMY.
THOSE INSTINCTS HAVE SAVED US BEFORE, MARIA.
THE HELL WITH IT. CRITTER WANTS US DEAD, WE'RE DEAD.
SINCE WE'RE NOT, EITHER WE DIDN'T REGISTER AS A THREAT...
...OR *NOTHING* WAS THERE.

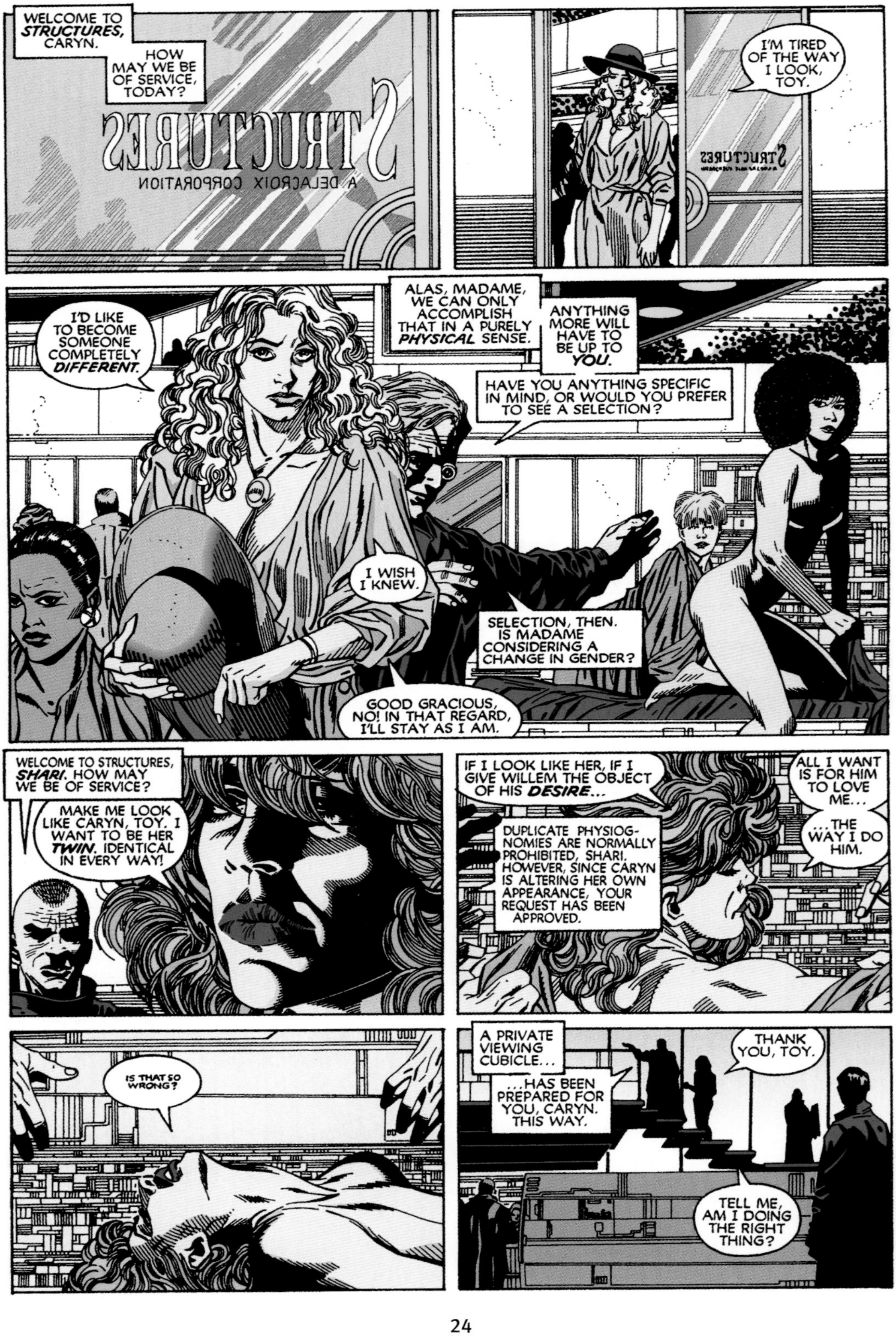
WELCOME TO STRUCTURES, CARYN.
HOW MAY WE BE OF SERVICE, TODAY?
STRUCTURES
A DELACROIX CORPORATION
I'M TIRED OF THE WAY I LOOK, TOY.
I'D LIKE TO BECOME SOMEONE COMPLETELY DIFFERENT.
ALAS, MADAME, WE CAN ONLY ACCOMPLISH THAT IN A PURELY PHYSICAL SENSE.
ANYTHING MORE WILL HAVE TO BE UP TO YOU.
HAVE YOU ANYTHING SPECIFIC IN MIND, OR WOULD YOU PREFER TO SEE A SELECTION?
I WISH I KNEW.
SELECTION, THEN. IS MADAME CONSIDERING A CHANGE IN GENDER?
GOOD GRACIOUS, NO! IN THAT REGARD, I'LL STAY AS I AM.
WELCOME TO STRUCTURES, SHARI. HOW MAY WE BE OF SERVICE?
MAKE ME LOOK LIKE CARYN, TOY. I WANT TO BE HER TWIN. IDENTICAL IN EVERY WAY!
IF I LOOK LIKE HER, IF I GIVE WILLEM THE OBJECT OF HIS DESIRE...
ALL I WANT IS FOR HIM TO LOVE ME...
...THE WAY I DO HIM.
DUPLICATE PHYSIOGNOMIES ARE NORMALLY PROHIBITED, SHARI. HOWEVER, SINCE CARYN IS ALTERING HER OWN APPEARANCE, YOUR REQUEST HAS BEEN APPROVED.
IS THAT SO WRONG?
A PRIVATE VIEWING CUBICLE...
...HAS BEEN PREPARED FOR YOU, CARYN. THIS WAY.
THANK YOU, TOY.
TELL ME, AM I DOING THE RIGHT THING?

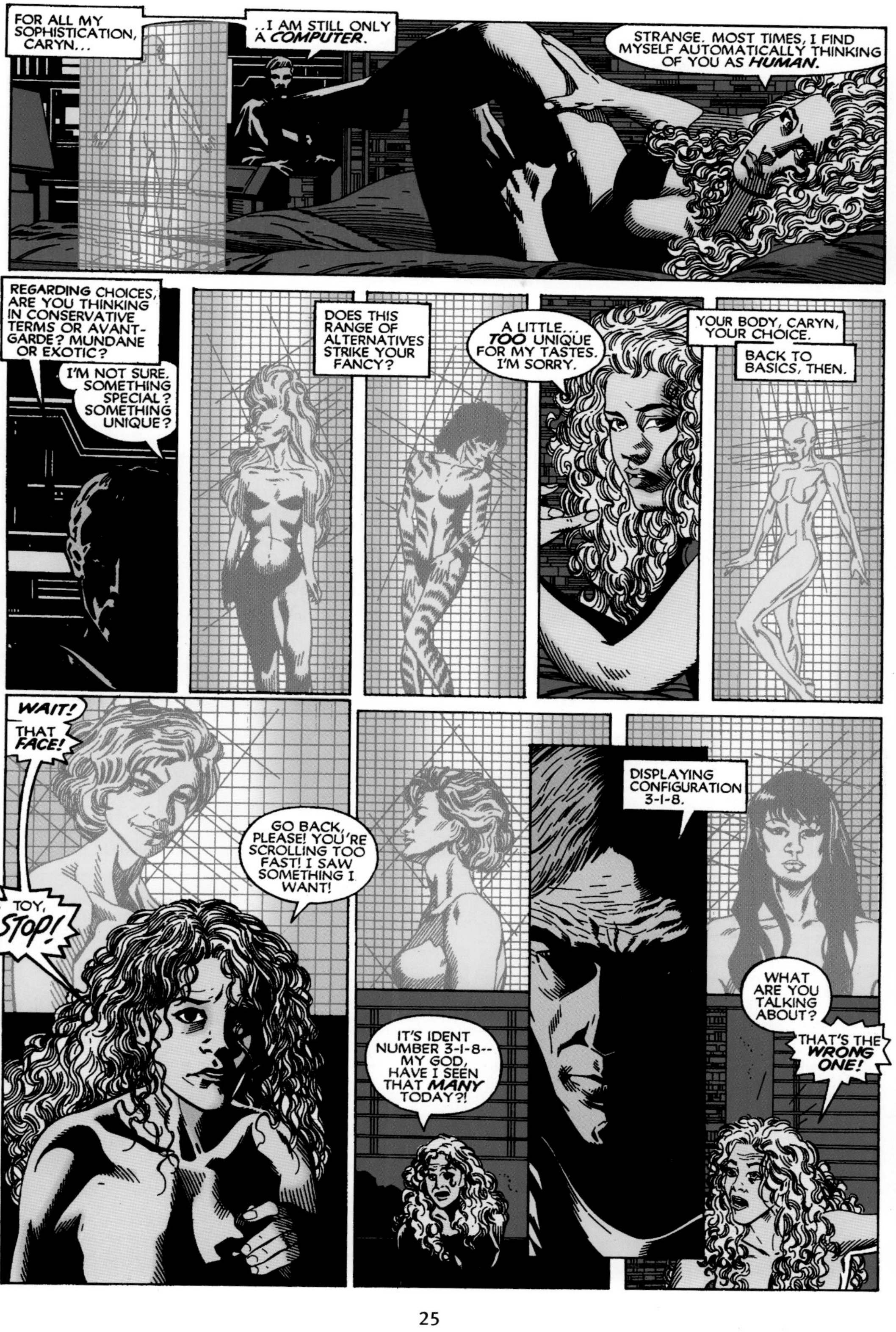
FOR ALL MY SOPHISTICATION, CARYN...
..I AM STILL ONLY A COMPUTER.
STRANGE. MOST TIMES, I FIND MYSELF AUTOMATICALLY THINKING OF YOU AS HUMAN.
REGARDING CHOICES, ARE YOU THINKING IN CONSERVATIVE TERMS OR AVANT-GARDE? MUNDANE OR EXOTIC?
I'M NOT SURE. SOMETHING SPECIAL? SOMETHING UNIQUE?
DOES THIS RANGE OF ALTERNATIVES STRIKE YOUR FANCY?
A LITTLE... TOO UNIQUE FOR MY TASTES. I'M SORRY.
YOUR BODY, CARYN, YOUR CHOICE.
BACK TO BASICS, THEN.
WAIT!
THAT FACE!
TOY, STOP!
GO BACK, PLEASE! YOU'RE SCROLLING TOO FAST! I SAW SOMETHING I WANT!
IT'S IDENT NUMBER 3-1-8-- MY GOD, HAVE I SEEN THAT MANY TODAY?!
DISPLAYING CONFIGURATION 3-1-8.
WHAT ARE YOU TALKING ABOUT?
THAT'S THE WRONG ONE!

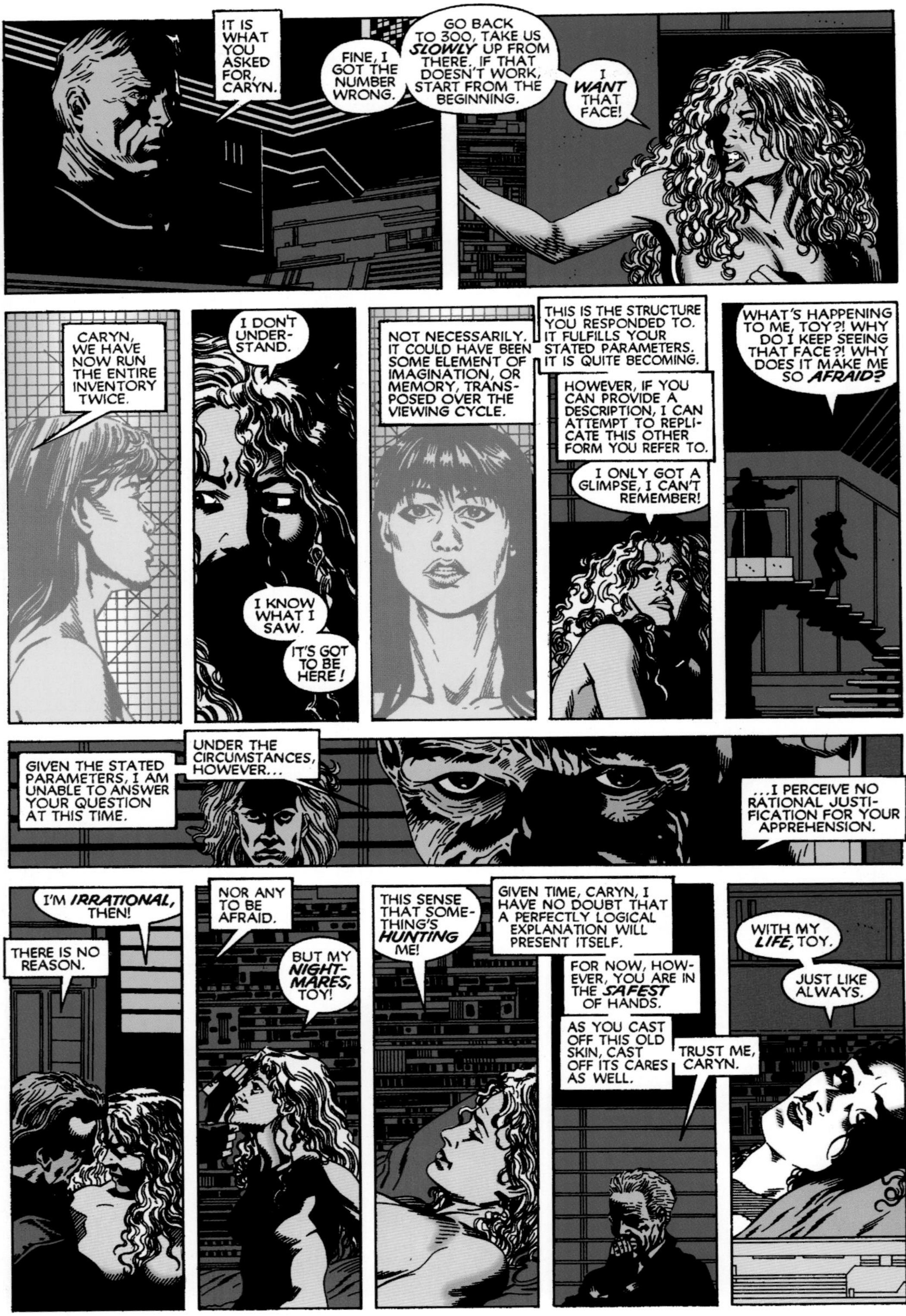
IT IS WHAT YOU ASKED FOR, CARYN.
FINE, I GOT THE NUMBER WRONG.
GO BACK TO 300, TAKE US SLOWLY UP FROM THERE. IF THAT DOESN'T WORK, START FROM THE BEGINNING.
I WANT THAT FACE!
CARYN, WE HAVE NOW RUN THE ENTIRE INVENTORY TWICE.
I DON'T UNDER-STAND.
I KNOW WHAT I SAW.
IT'S GOT TO BE HERE!
NOT NECESSARILY. IT COULD HAVE BEEN SOME ELEMENT OF IMAGINATION, OR MEMORY, TRANS-POSED OVER THE VIEWING CYCLE.
THIS IS THE STRUCTURE YOU RESPONDED TO. IT FULFILLS YOUR STATED PARAMETERS. IT IS QUITE BECOMING.
HOWEVER, IF YOU CAN PROVIDE A DESCRIPTION, I CAN ATTEMPT TO REPLI-CATE THIS OTHER FORM YOU REFER TO.
I ONLY GOT A GLIMPSE, I CAN'T REMEMBER!
WHAT'S HAPPENING TO ME, TOY?! WHY DO I KEEP SEEING THAT FACE?! WHY DOES IT MAKE ME SO AFRAID?
GIVEN THE STATED PARAMETERS, I AM UNABLE TO ANSWER YOUR QUESTION AT THIS TIME.
UNDER THE CIRCUMSTANCES, HOWEVER...
...I PERCEIVE NO RATIONAL JUSTI-FICATION FOR YOUR APPREHENSION.
I'M IRRATIONAL, THEN!
THERE IS NO REASON.
NOR ANY TO BE AFRAID.
BUT MY NIGHT-MARES, TOY!
THIS SENSE THAT SOME-THING'S HUNTING ME!
GIVEN TIME, CARYN, I HAVE NO DOUBT THAT A PERFECTLY LOGICAL EXPLANATION WILL PRESENT ITSELF.
FOR NOW, HOW-EVER, YOU ARE IN THE SAFEST OF HANDS.
AS YOU CAST OFF THIS OLD SKIN, CAST OFF ITS CARES AS WELL.
TRUST ME, CARYN.
WITH MY LIFE, TOY.
JUST LIKE ALWAYS.

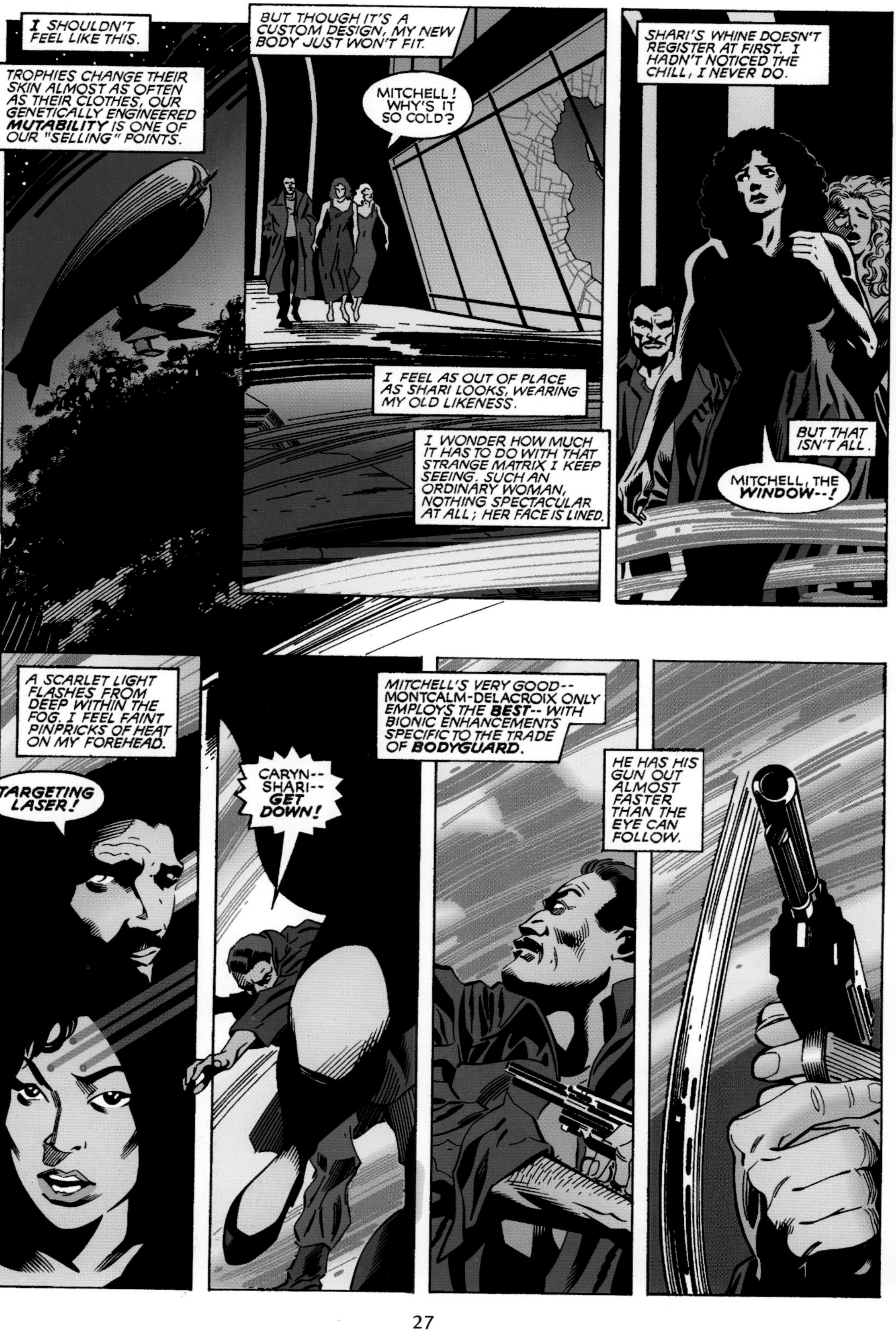
I SHOULDN'T FEEL LIKE THIS.
TROPHIES CHANGE THEIR SKIN ALMOST AS OFTEN AS THEIR CLOTHES, OUR GENETICALLY ENGINEERED MUTABILITY IS ONE OF OUR "SELLING" POINTS.
BUT THOUGH IT'S A CUSTOM DESIGN, MY NEW BODY JUST WON'T FIT.
MITCHELL! WHY'S IT SO COLD?
I FEEL AS OUT OF PLACE AS SHARI LOOKS, WEARING MY OLD LIKENESS.
I WONDER HOW MUCH IT HAS TO DO WITH THAT STRANGE MATRIX I KEEP SEEING. SUCH AN ORDINARY WOMAN, NOTHING SPECTACULAR AT ALL; HER FACE IS LINED.
SHARI'S WHINE DOESN'T REGISTER AT FIRST. I HADN'T NOTICED THE CHILL, I NEVER DO.
BUT THAT ISN'T ALL.
MITCHELL, THE WINDOW--!
A SCARLET LIGHT FLASHES FROM DEEP WITHIN THE FOG. I FEEL FAINT PINPRICKS OF HEAT ON MY FOREHEAD.
TARGETING LASER!
CARYN-- SHARI-- GET DOWN!
MITCHELL'S VERY GOOD-- MONTCALM-DELACROIX ONLY EMPLOYS THE BEST-- WITH BIONIC ENHANCEMENTS SPECIFIC TO THE TRADE OF BODYGUARD.
HE HAS HIS GUN OUT ALMOST FASTER THAN THE EYE CAN FOLLOW.

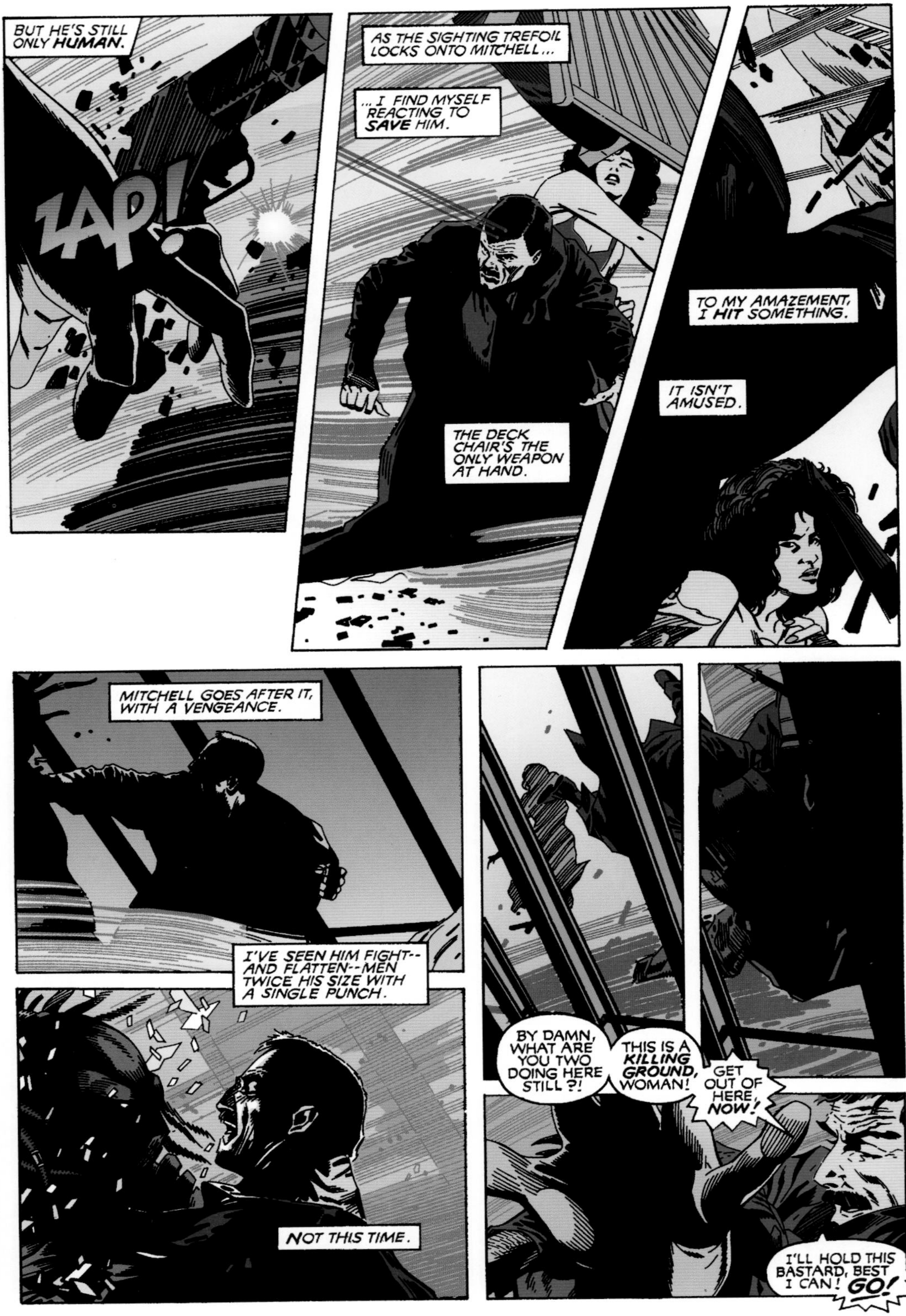

BUT HE'S STILL ONLY HUMAN.
ZAP!
AS THE SIGHTING TREFOIL LOCKS ONTO MITCHELL...
...I FIND MYSELF REACTING TO SAVE HIM.
THE DECK CHAIR'S THE ONLY WEAPON AT HAND.
TO MY AMAZEMENT, I HIT SOMETHING.
IT ISN'T AMUSED.
MITCHELL GOES AFTER IT, WITH A VENGEANCE.
I'VE SEEN HIM FIGHT--AND FLATTEN--MEN TWICE HIS SIZE WITH A SINGLE PUNCH.
NOT THIS TIME.
BY DAMN, WHAT ARE YOU TWO DOING HERE STILL?!
THIS IS A KILLING GROUND, WOMAN!
GET OUT OF HERE, NOW!
I'LL HOLD THIS BASTARD, BEST I CAN! GO!

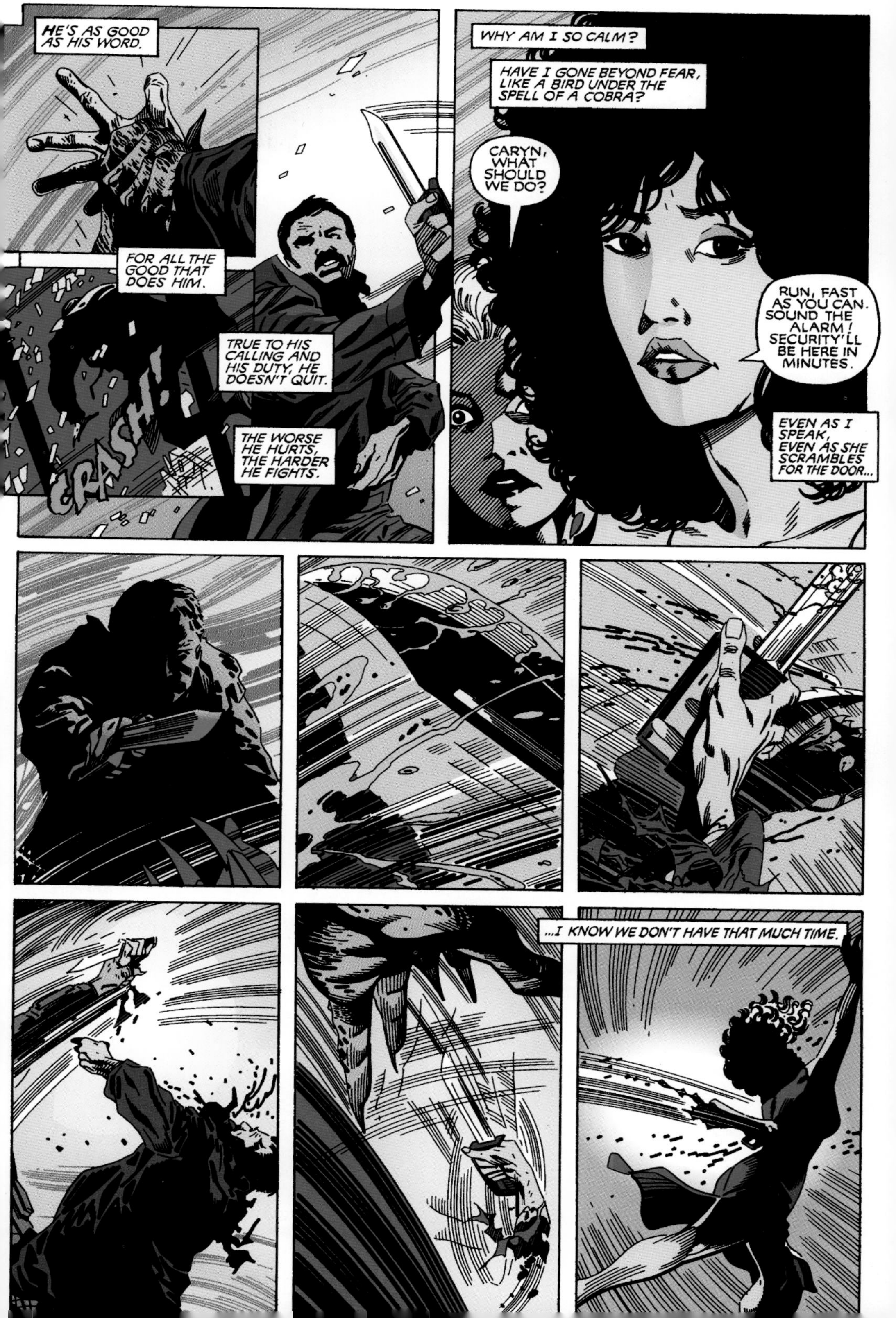
HE'S AS GOOD AS HIS WORD.
FOR ALL THE GOOD THAT DOES HIM.
TRUE TO HIS CALLING AND HIS DUTY, HE DOESN'T QUIT.
THE WORSE HE HURTS, THE HARDER HE FIGHTS.
CRASH!
WHY AM I SO CALM?
HAVE I GONE BEYOND FEAR, LIKE A BIRD UNDER THE SPELL OF A COBRA?
CARYN, WHAT SHOULD WE DO?
RUN, FAST AS YOU CAN. SOUND THE ALARM! SECURITY'LL BE HERE IN MINUTES.
EVEN AS I SPEAK, EVEN AS SHE SCRAMBLES FOR THE DOOR...
...I KNOW WE DON'T HAVE THAT MUCH TIME.

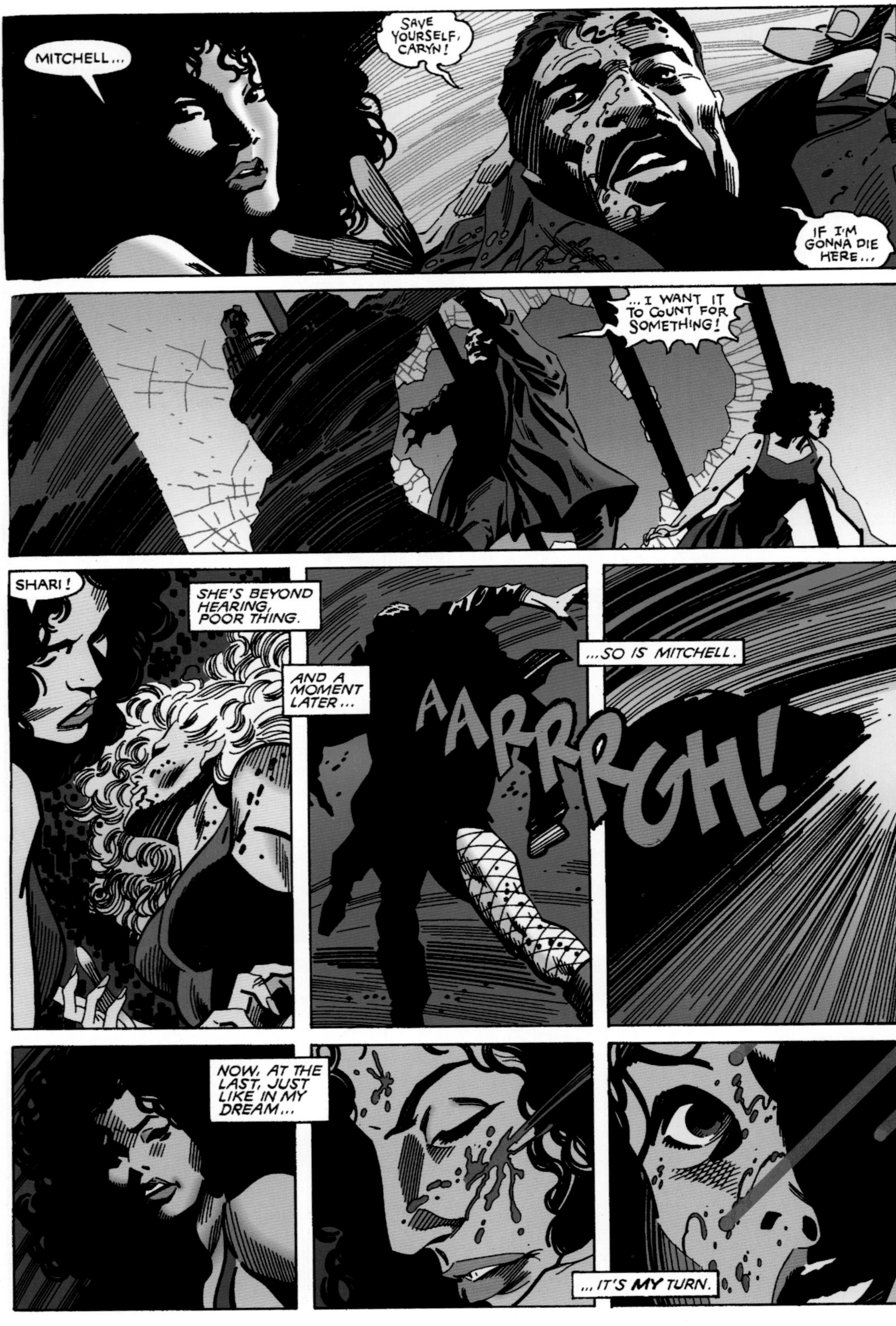
MITCHELL...
SAVE YOURSELF, CARYN!
IF I'M GONNA DIE HERE...
...I WANT IT TO COUNT FOR SOMETHING!
SHARI!
SHE'S BEYOND HEARING, POOR THING.
AND A MOMENT LATER...
...SO IS MITCHELL.
AARRRGH!
NOW, AT THE LAST, JUST LIKE IN MY DREAM...
...IT'S MY TURN.

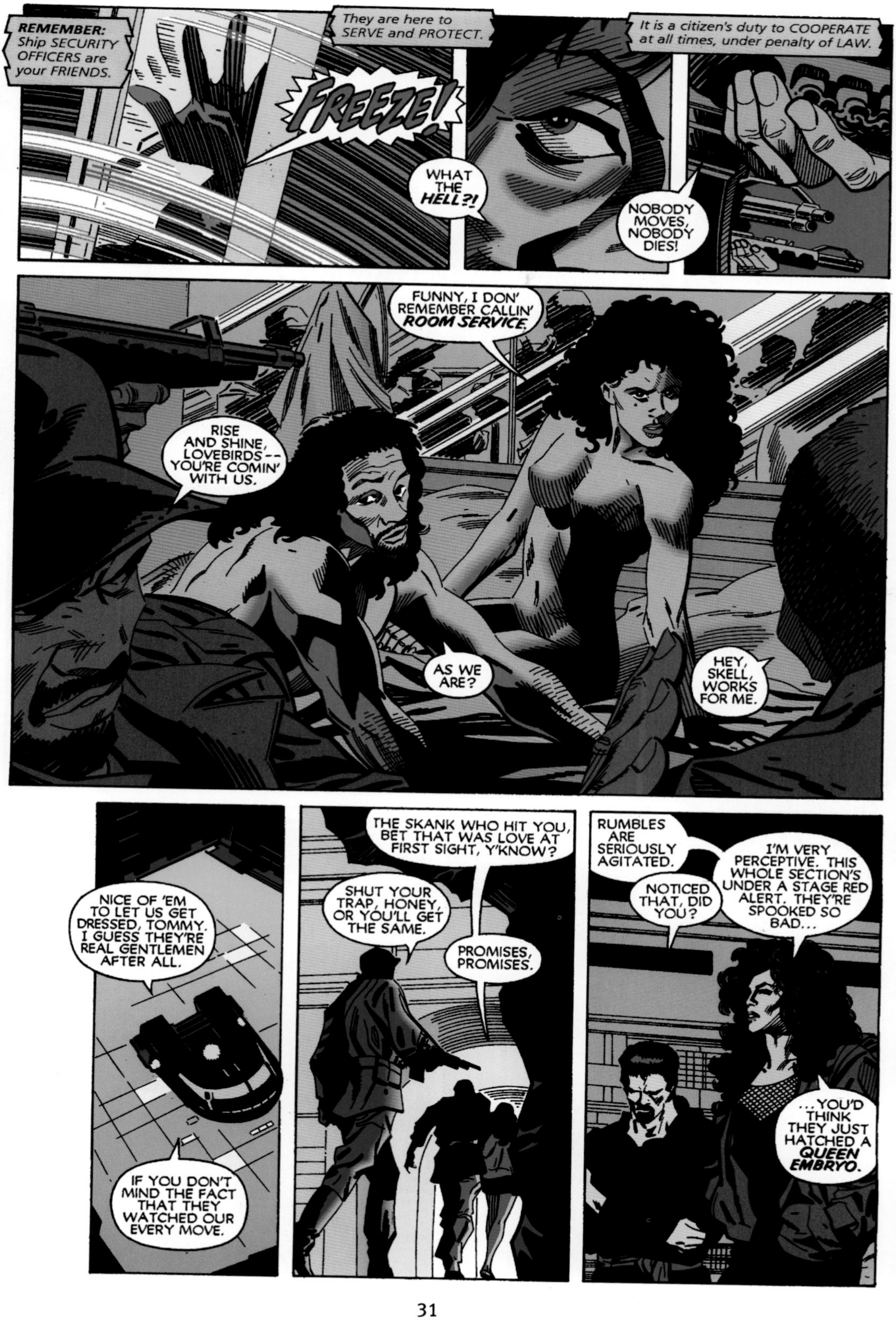
REMEMBER: Ship SECURITY OFFICERS are your FRIENDS.
FREEZE!
They are here to SERVE and PROTECT.
WHAT THE HELL?!
It is a citizen's duty to COOPERATE at all times, under penalty of LAW.
NOBODY MOVES, NOBODY DIES!
FUNNY, I DON' REMEMBER CALLIN' ROOM SERVICE.
RISE AND SHINE, LOVEBIRDS-- YOU'RE COMIN' WITH US.
AS WE ARE?
HEY, SKELL, WORKS FOR ME.
NICE OF 'EM TO LET US GET DRESSED, TOMMY. I GUESS THEY'RE REAL GENTLEMEN AFTER ALL.
IF YOU DON'T MIND THE FACT THAT THEY WATCHED OUR EVERY MOVE.
THE SKANK WHO HIT YOU, BET THAT WAS LOVE AT FIRST SIGHT, Y'KNOW?
SHUT YOUR TRAP, HONEY, OR YOU'LL GET THE SAME.
PROMISES, PROMISES.
RUMBLES ARE SERIOUSLY AGITATED.
NOTICED THAT, DID YOU?
I'M VERY PERCEPTIVE. THIS WHOLE SECTION'S UNDER A STAGE RED ALERT. THEY'RE SPOOKED SO BAD...
...YOU'D THINK THEY JUST HATCHED A QUEEN EMBRYO.

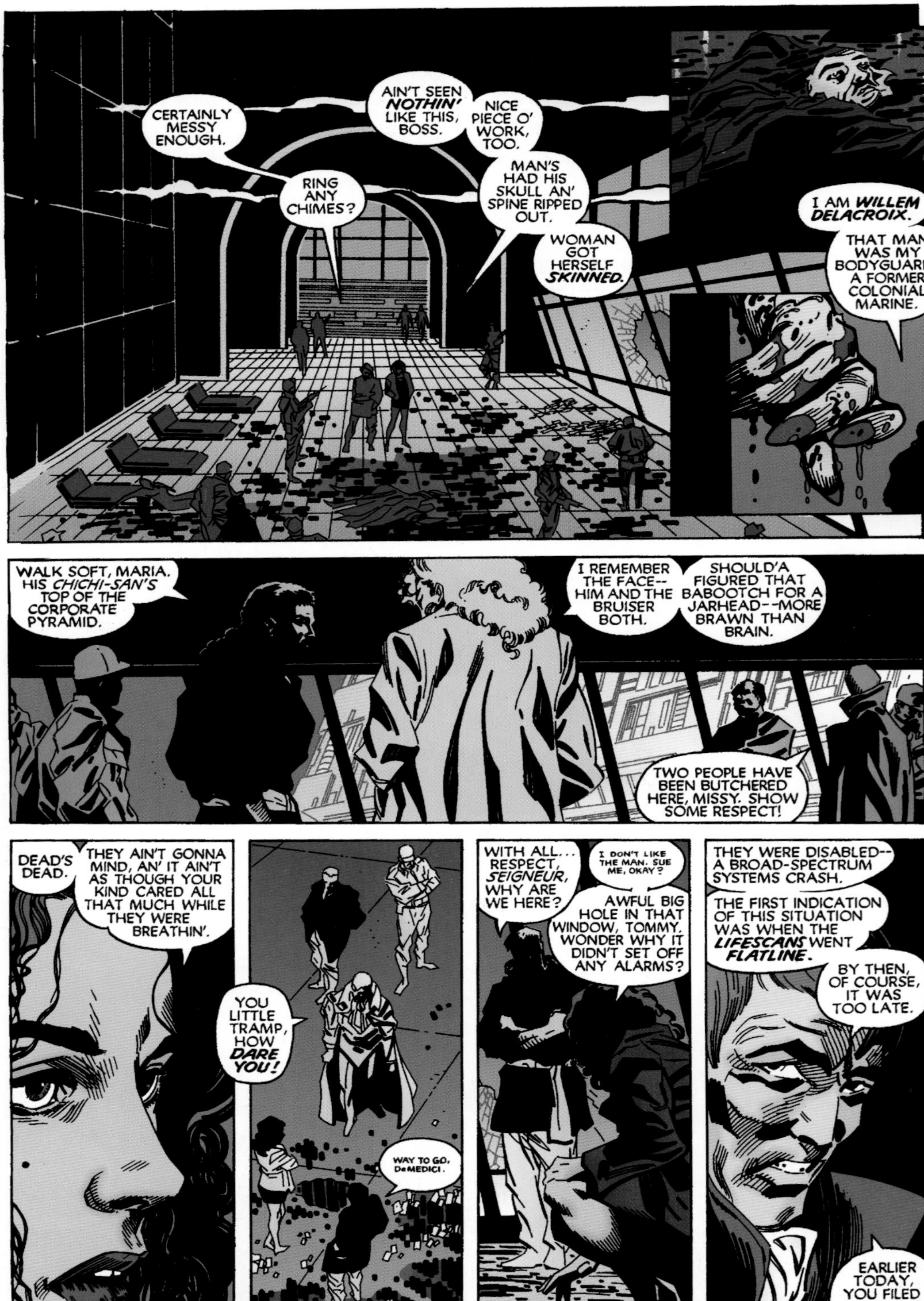
CERTAINLY MESSY ENOUGH.
AIN'T SEEN NOTHIN' LIKE THIS, BOSS.
NICE PIECE O' WORK, TOO.
RING ANY CHIMES?
MAN'S HAD HIS SKULL AN' SPINE RIPPED OUT.
WOMAN GOT HERSELF SKINNED.
I AM WILLEM DELACROIX.
THAT MAN WAS MY BODYGUARD. A FORMER COLONIAL MARINE.
WALK SOFT, MARIA. HIS CHICHI-SAN'S TOP OF THE CORPORATE PYRAMID.
I REMEMBER THE FACE-- HIM AND THE BRUISER BOTH.
SHOULD'A FIGURED THAT BABOOTCH FOR A JARHEAD--MORE BRAWN THAN BRAIN.
TWO PEOPLE HAVE BEEN BUTCHERED HERE, MISSY. SHOW SOME RESPECT!
DEAD'S DEAD.
THEY AIN'T GONNA MIND, AN' IT AIN'T AS THOUGH YOUR KIND CARED ALL THAT MUCH WHILE THEY WERE BREATHIN'.
YOU LITTLE TRAMP, HOW DARE YOU!
WAY TO GO, DeMEDICI.
WITH ALL... RESPECT, SEIGNEUR, WHY ARE WE HERE?
I DON'T LIKE THE MAN. SUE ME, OKAY?
AWFUL BIG HOLE IN THAT WINDOW, TOMMY. WONDER WHY IT DIDN'T SET OFF ANY ALARMS?
THEY WERE DISABLED-- A BROAD-SPECTRUM SYSTEMS CRASH.
THE FIRST INDICATION OF THIS SITUATION WAS WHEN THE LIFESCANS WENT FLATLINE.
BY THEN, OF COURSE, IT WAS TOO LATE.
EARLIER TODAY, YOU FILED A SIGHTING REPORT.

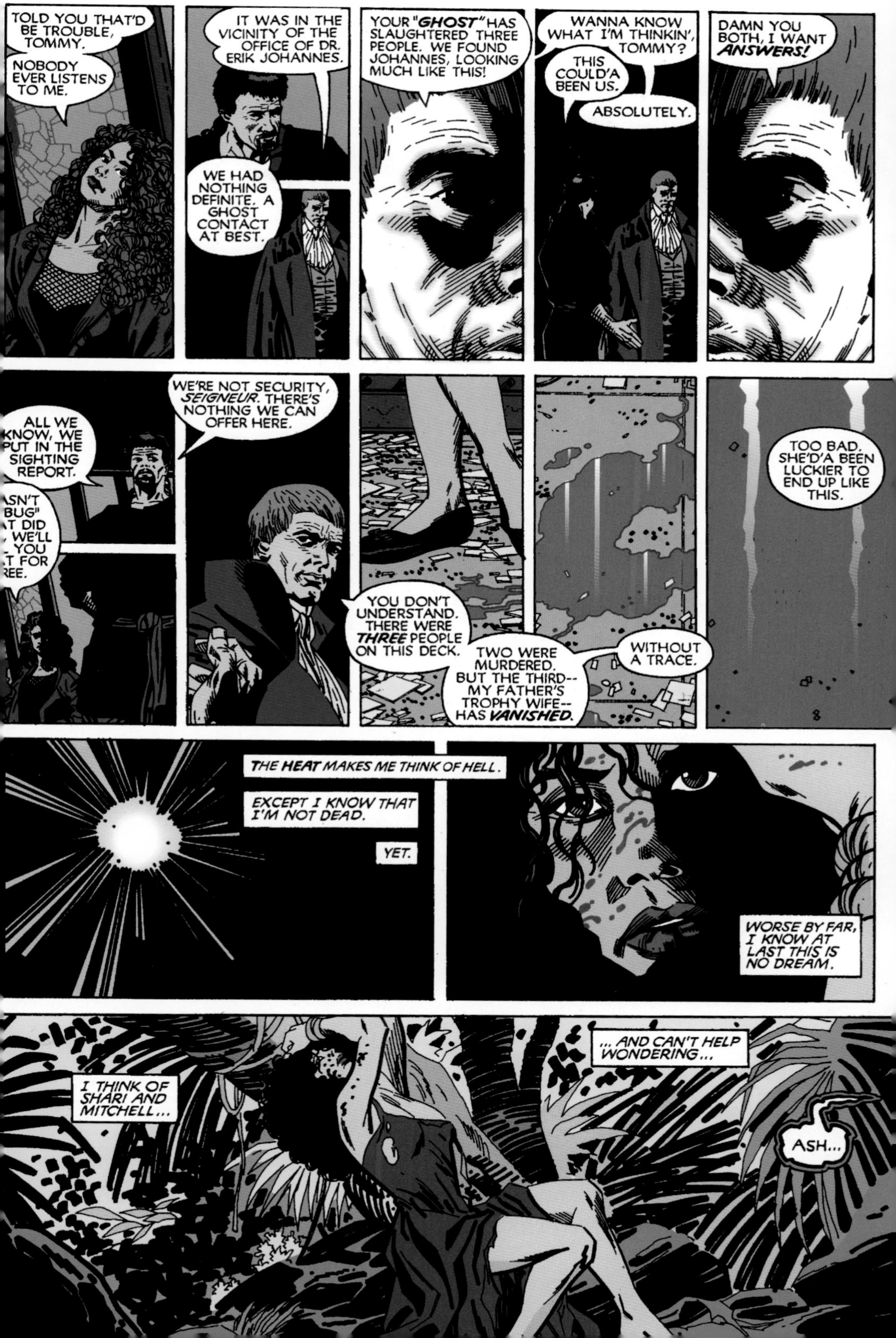

TOLD YOU THAT'D BE TROUBLE, TOMMY.
NOBODY EVER LISTENS TO ME.
IT WAS IN THE VICINITY OF THE OFFICE OF DR. ERIK JOHANNES.
WE HAD NOTHING DEFINITE. A GHOST CONTACT AT BEST.
YOUR "GHOST" HAS SLAUGHTERED THREE PEOPLE. WE FOUND JOHANNES, LOOKING MUCH LIKE THIS!
WANNA KNOW WHAT I'M THINKIN', TOMMY?
THIS COULD'A BEEN US.
ABSOLUTELY.
DAMN YOU BOTH, I WANT ANSWERS!
ALL WE KNOW, WE PUT IN THE SIGHTING REPORT.
ASN'T BUG" T DID WE'LL YOU T FOR REE.
WE'RE NOT SECURITY, SEIGNEUR. THERE'S NOTHING WE CAN OFFER HERE.
YOU DON'T UNDERSTAND. THERE WERE THREE PEOPLE ON THIS DECK.
TWO WERE MURDERED. BUT THE THIRD-- MY FATHER'S TROPHY WIFE-- HAS VANISHED.
WITHOUT A TRACE.
TOO BAD. SHE'D'A BEEN LUCKIER TO END UP LIKE THIS.
THE HEAT MAKES ME THINK OF HELL.
EXCEPT I KNOW THAT I'M NOT DEAD.
YET.
WORSE BY FAR, I KNOW AT LAST THIS IS NO DREAM.
I THINK OF SHARI AND MITCHELL...
... AND CAN'T HELP WONDERING...
ASH...

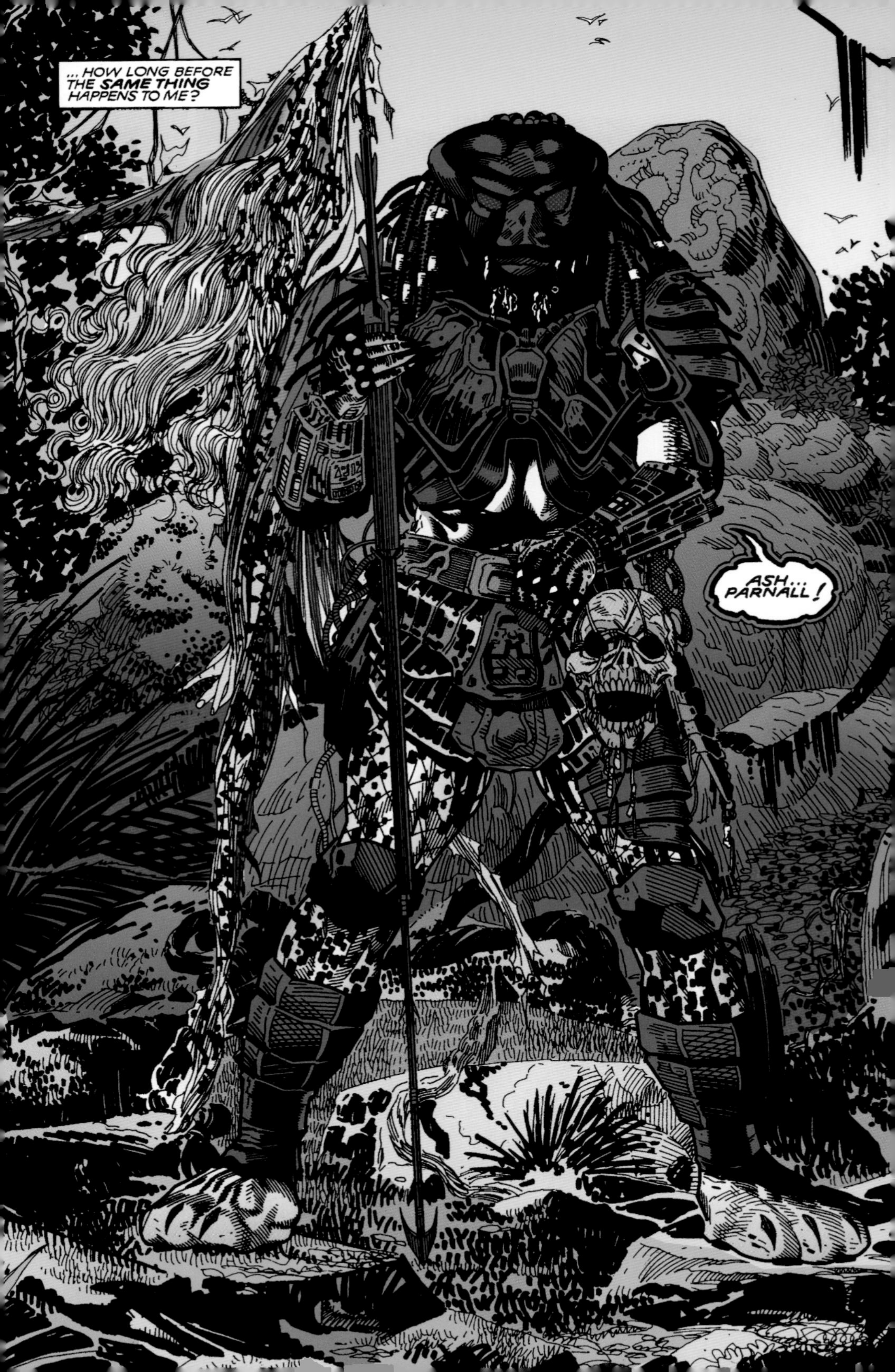
...HOW LONG BEFORE THE SAME THING HAPPENS TO ME?
ASH... PARNALL!

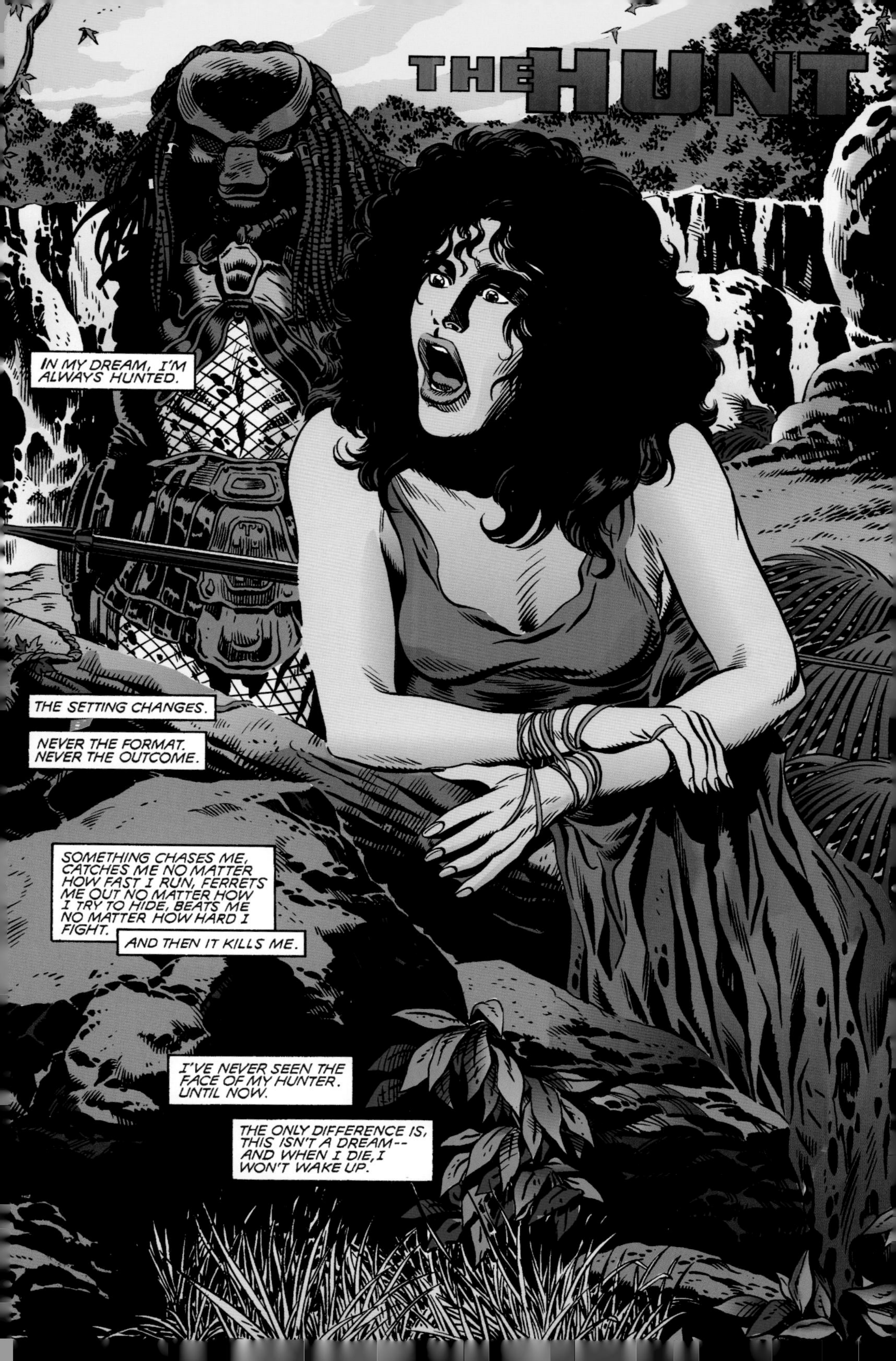
THE HUNT
IN MY DREAM, I'M ALWAYS HUNTED.
THE SETTING CHANGES.
NEVER THE FORMAT. NEVER THE OUTCOME.
SOMETHING CHASES ME, CATCHES ME NO MATTER HOW FAST I RUN, FERRETS ME OUT NO MATTER HOW I TRY TO HIDE, BEATS ME NO MATTER HOW HARD I FIGHT.
AND THEN IT KILLS ME.
I'VE NEVER SEEN THE FACE OF MY HUNTER. UNTIL NOW.
THE ONLY DIFFERENCE IS, THIS ISN'T A DREAM-- AND WHEN I DIE, I WON'T WAKE UP.

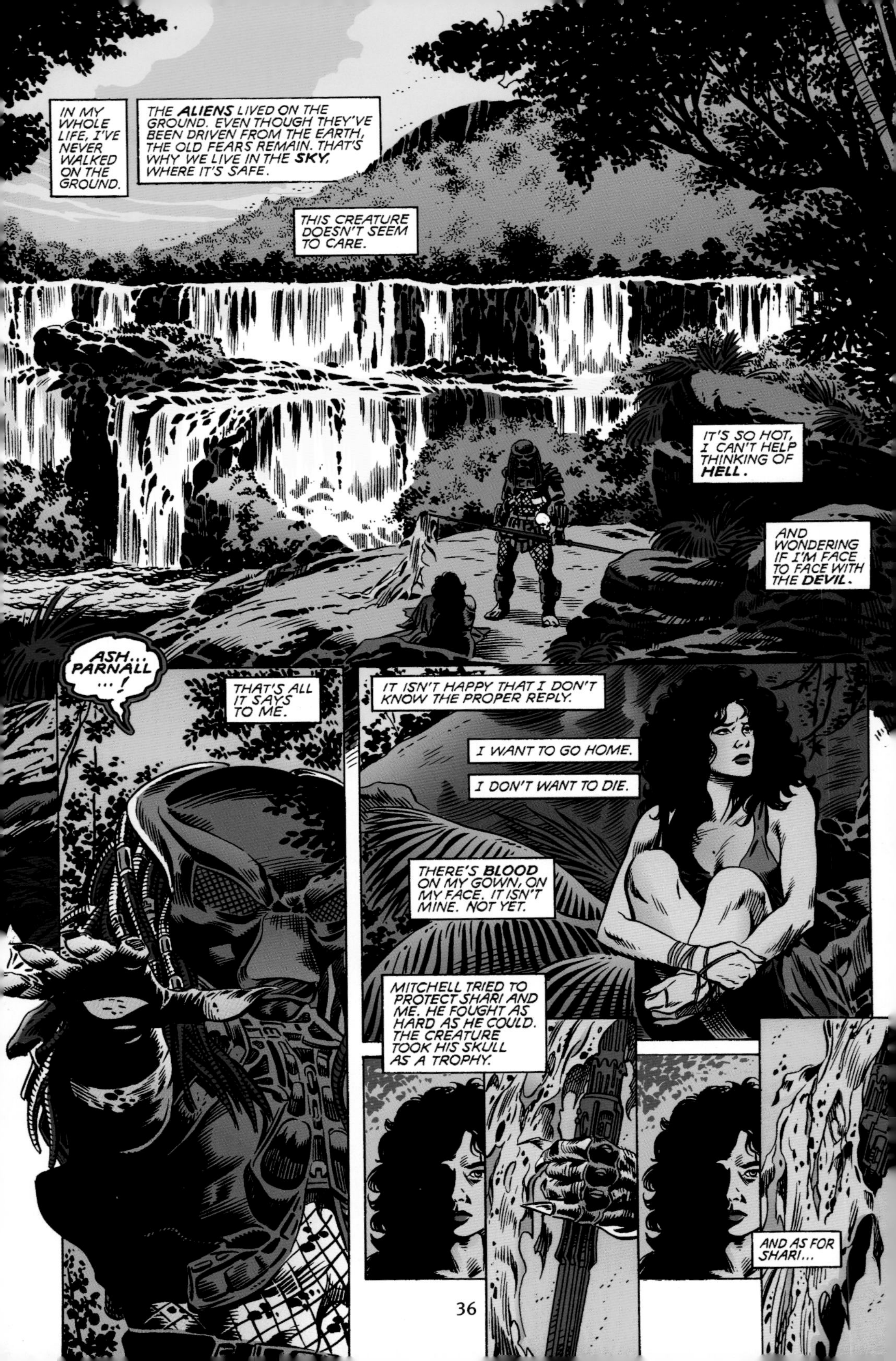
IN MY WHOLE LIFE, I'VE NEVER WALKED ON THE GROUND.
THE ALIENS LIVED ON THE GROUND. EVEN THOUGH THEY'VE BEEN DRIVEN FROM THE EARTH, THE OLD FEARS REMAIN. THAT'S WHY WE LIVE IN THE SKY, WHERE IT'S SAFE.
THIS CREATURE DOESN'T SEEM TO CARE.
IT'S SO HOT, I CAN'T HELP THINKING OF HELL.
AND WONDERING IF I'M FACE TO FACE WITH THE DEVIL.
ASH... PARNALL ...!
THAT'S ALL IT SAYS TO ME.
IT ISN'T HAPPY THAT I DON'T KNOW THE PROPER REPLY.
I WANT TO GO HOME.
I DON'T WANT TO DIE.
THERE'S BLOOD ON MY GOWN, ON MY FACE. IT ISN'T MINE. NOT YET.
MITCHELL TRIED TO PROTECT SHARI AND ME. HE FOUGHT AS HARD AS HE COULD. THE CREATURE TOOK HIS SKULL AS A TROPHY.
AND AS FOR SHARI...

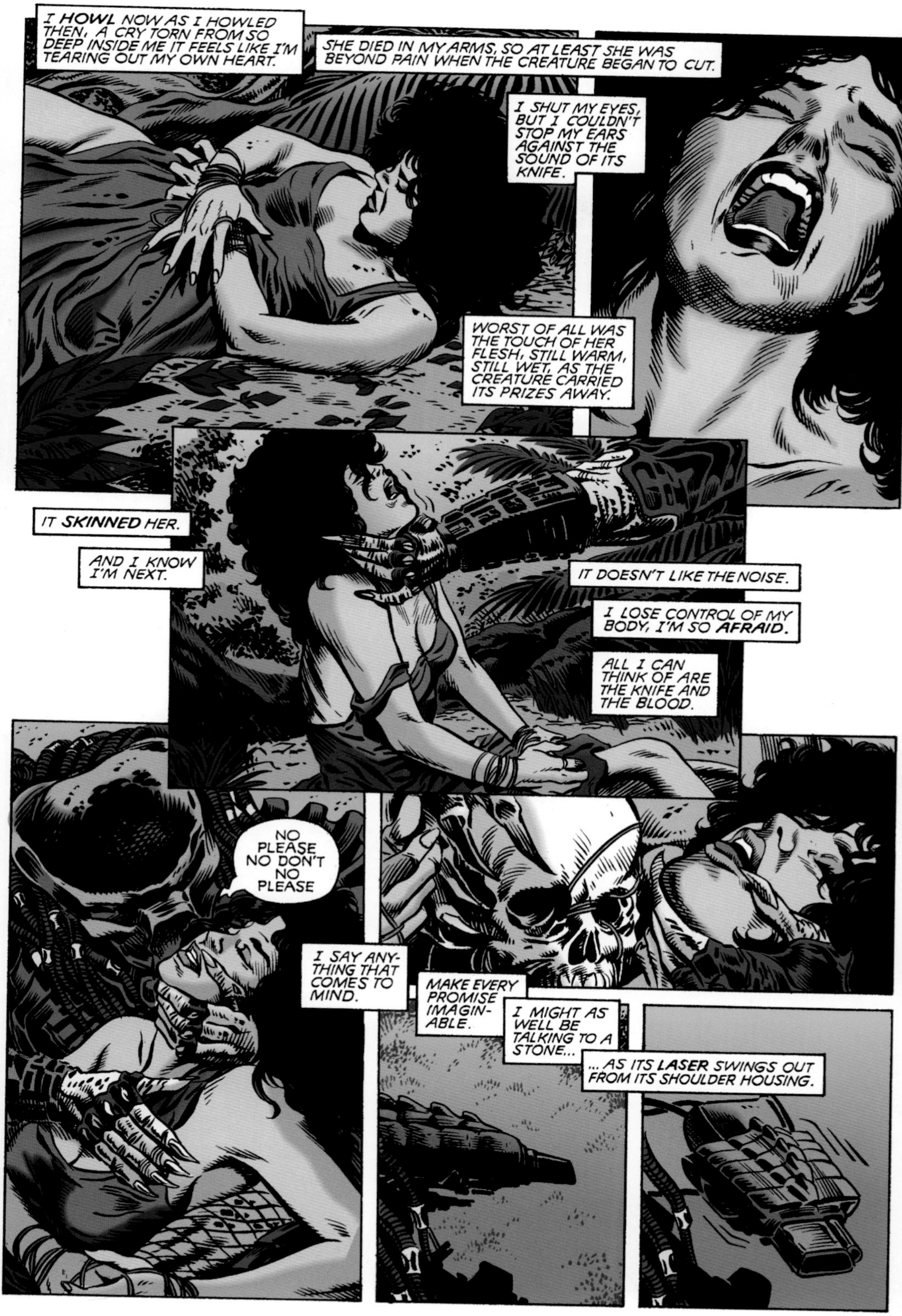
I HOWL NOW AS I HOWLED THEN, A CRY TORN FROM SO DEEP INSIDE ME IT FEELS LIKE I'M TEARING OUT MY OWN HEART.
SHE DIED IN MY ARMS, SO AT LEAST SHE WAS BEYOND PAIN WHEN THE CREATURE BEGAN TO CUT.
I SHUT MY EYES, BUT I COULDN'T STOP MY EARS AGAINST THE SOUND OF ITS KNIFE.
WORST OF ALL WAS THE TOUCH OF HER FLESH, STILL WARM, STILL WET, AS THE CREATURE CARRIED ITS PRIZES AWAY.
IT SKINNED HER.
AND I KNOW I'M NEXT.
IT DOESN'T LIKE THE NOISE.
I LOSE CONTROL OF MY BODY, I'M SO AFRAID.
ALL I CAN THINK OF ARE THE KNIFE AND THE BLOOD.
NO PLEASE NO DON'T NO PLEASE
I SAY ANY-THING THAT COMES TO MIND.
MAKE EVERY PROMISE IMAGIN-ABLE.
I MIGHT AS WELL BE TALKING TO A STONE...
...AS ITS LASER SWINGS OUT FROM ITS SHOULDER HOUSING.

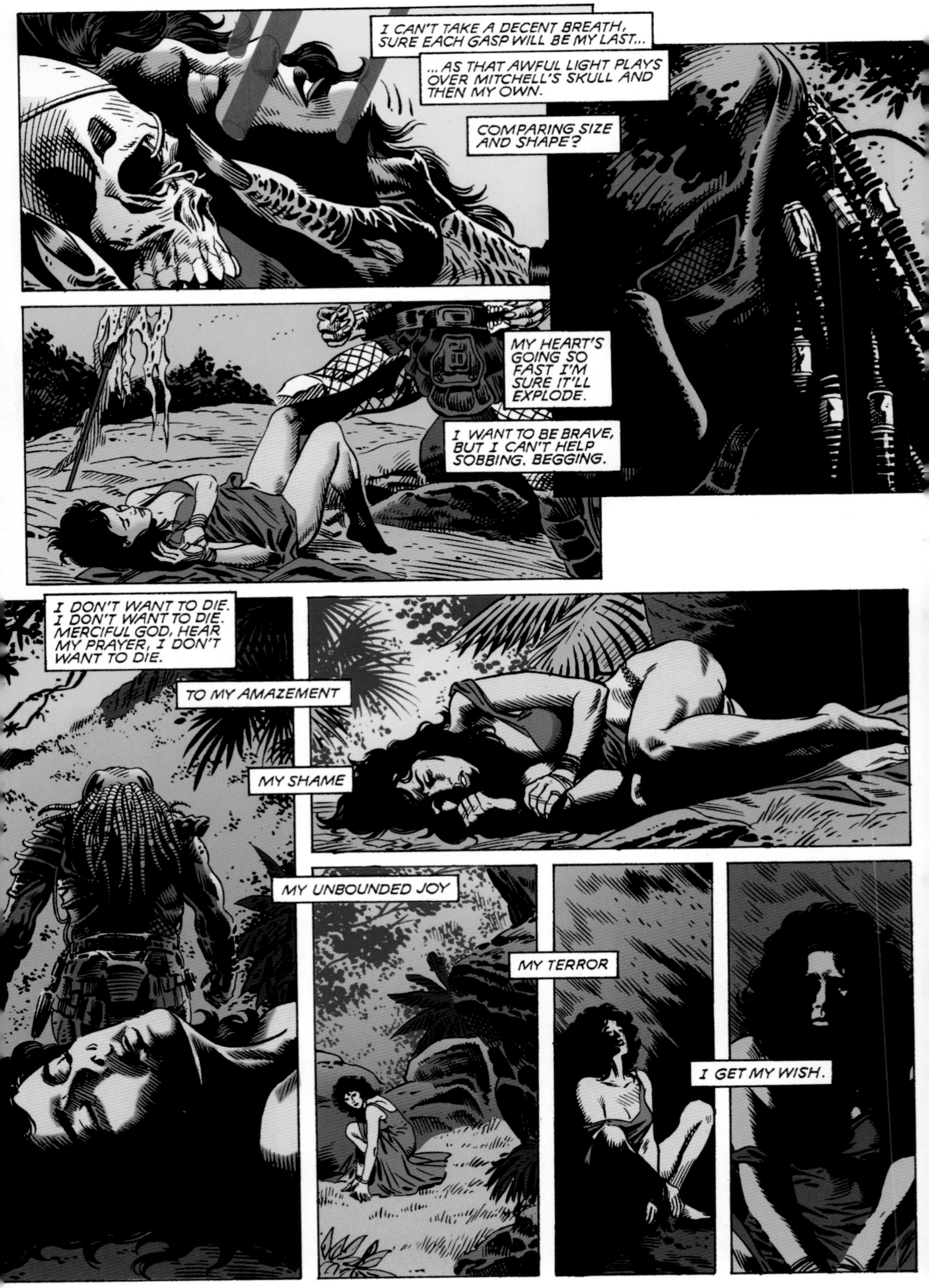
I CAN'T TAKE A DECENT BREATH, SURE EACH GASP WILL BE MY LAST...
...AS THAT AWFUL LIGHT PLAYS OVER MITCHELL'S SKULL AND THEN MY OWN.
COMPARING SIZE AND SHAPE?
MY HEART'S GOING SO FAST I'M SURE IT'LL EXPLODE.
I WANT TO BE BRAVE, BUT I CAN'T HELP SOBBING. BEGGING.
I DON'T WANT TO DIE. I DON'T WANT TO DIE. MERCIFUL GOD, HEAR MY PRAYER, I DON'T WANT TO DIE.
TO MY AMAZEMENT
MY SHAME
MY UNBOUNDED JOY
MY TERROR
I GET MY WISH.

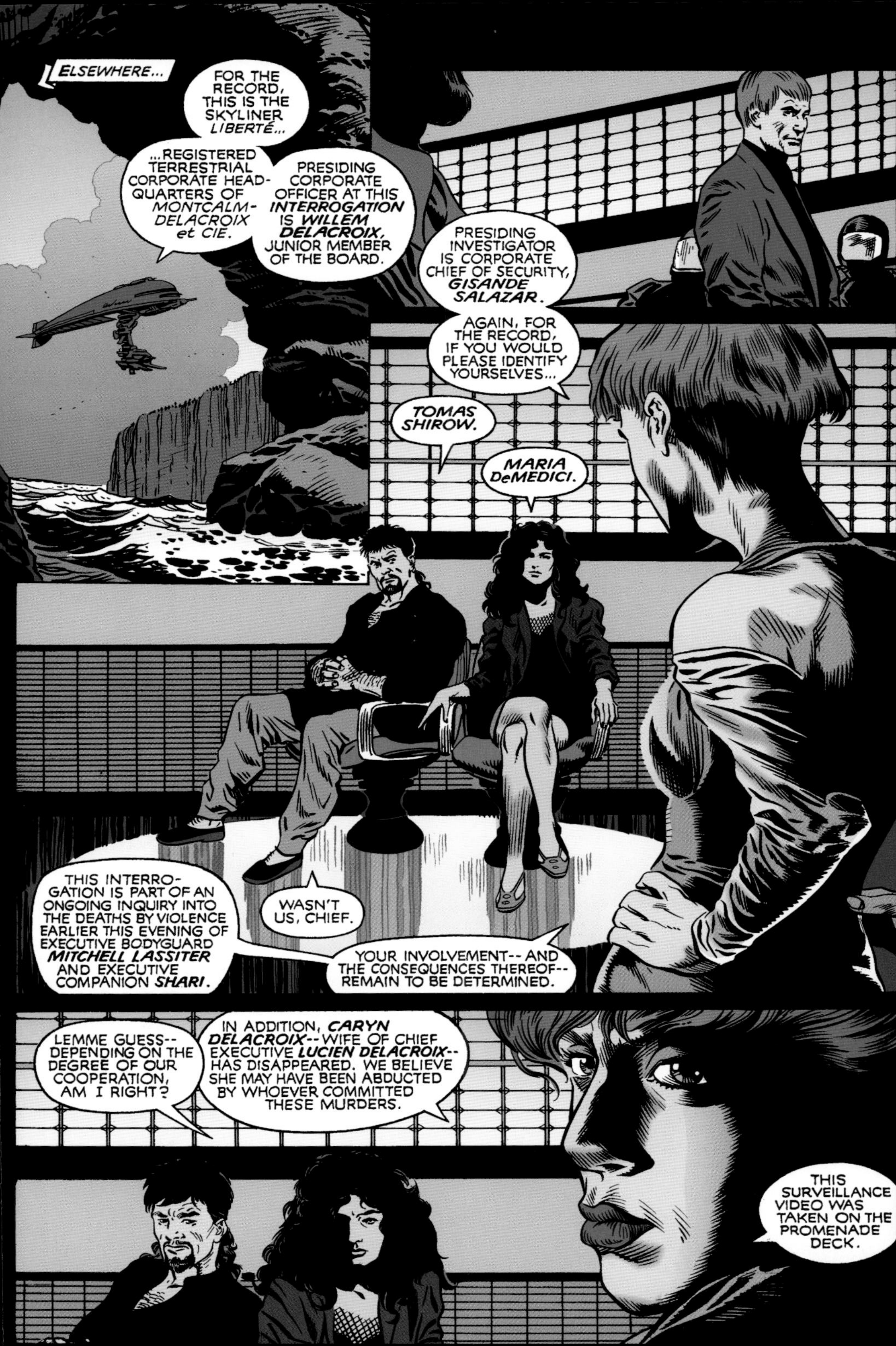
ELSEWHERE...
FOR THE RECORD, THIS IS THE SKYLINER LIBERTÉ...
...REGISTERED TERRESTRIAL CORPORATE HEAD-QUARTERS OF MONTCALM-DELACROIX et CIE.
PRESIDING CORPORATE OFFICER AT THIS INTERROGATION IS WILLEM DELACROIX, JUNIOR MEMBER OF THE BOARD.
PRESIDING INVESTIGATOR IS CORPORATE CHIEF OF SECURITY, GISANDE SALAZAR.
AGAIN, FOR THE RECORD, IF YOU WOULD PLEASE IDENTIFY YOURSELVES...
TOMAS SHIROW.
MARIA DeMEDICI.
THIS INTERRO-GATION IS PART OF AN ONGOING INQUIRY INTO THE DEATHS BY VIOLENCE EARLIER THIS EVENING OF EXECUTIVE BODYGUARD MITCHELL LASSITER AND EXECUTIVE COMPANION SHARI.
WASN'T US, CHIEF.
YOUR INVOLVEMENT-- AND THE CONSEQUENCES THEREOF-- REMAIN TO BE DETERMINED.
LEMME GUESS-- DEPENDING ON THE DEGREE OF OUR COOPERATION, AM I RIGHT?
IN ADDITION, CARYN DELACROIX-- WIFE OF CHIEF EXECUTIVE LUCIEN DELACROIX-- HAS DISAPPEARED. WE BELIEVE SHE MAY HAVE BEEN ABDUCTED BY WHOEVER COMMITTED THESE MURDERS.
THIS SURVEILLANCE VIDEO WAS TAKEN ON THE PROMENADE DECK.

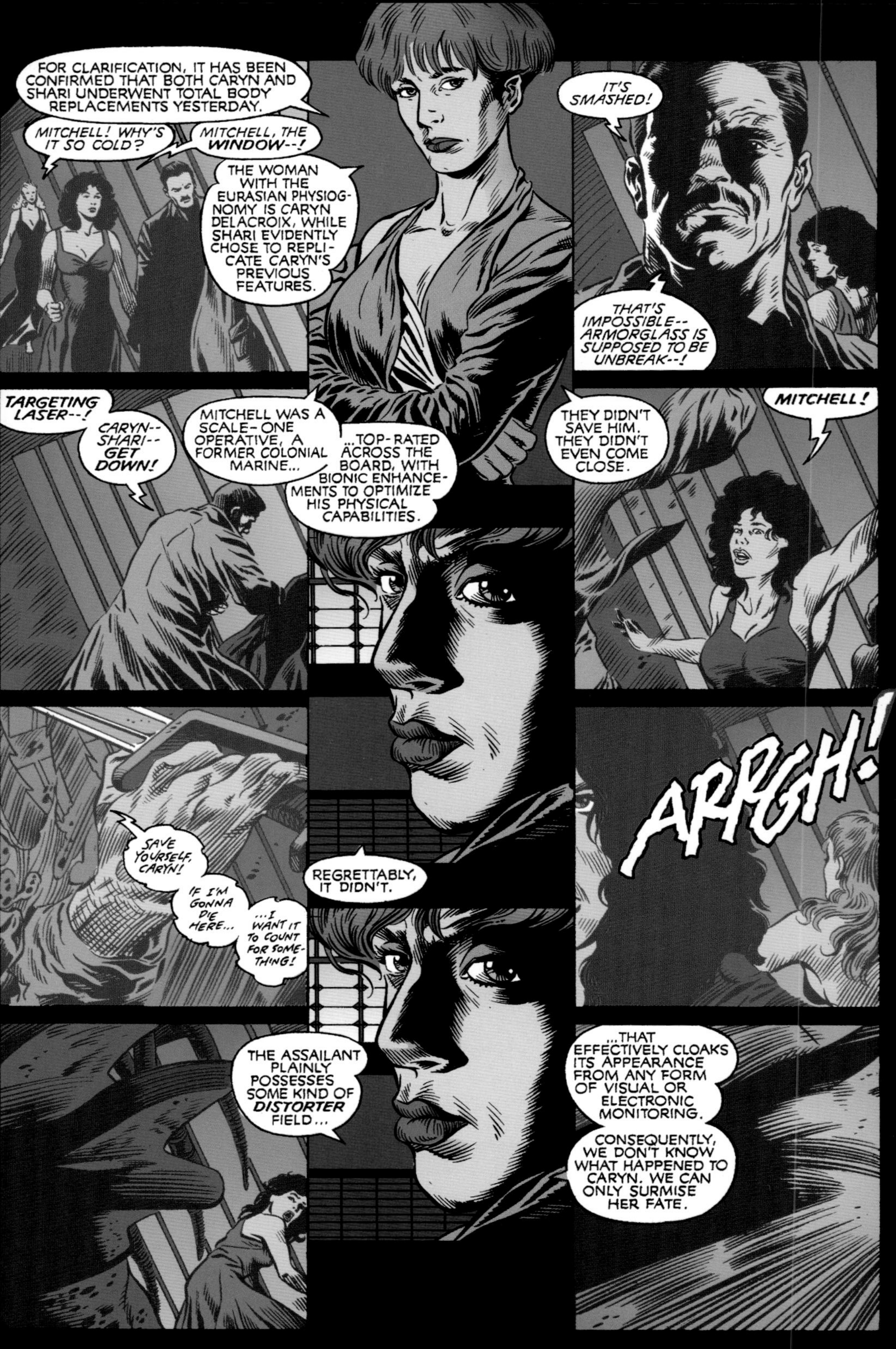
FOR CLARIFICATION, IT HAS BEEN CONFIRMED THAT BOTH CARYN AND SHARI UNDERWENT TOTAL BODY REPLACEMENTS YESTERDAY.
MITCHELL! WHY'S IT SO COLD?
MITCHELL, THE WINDOW--!
THE WOMAN WITH THE EURASIAN PHYSIOGNOMY IS CARYN DELACROIX, WHILE SHARI EVIDENTLY CHOSE TO REPLICATE CARYN'S PREVIOUS FEATURES.
IT'S SMASHED!
THAT'S IMPOSSIBLE-- ARMORGLASS IS SUPPOSED TO BE UNBREAK--!
TARGETING LASER--!
CARYN-- SHARI-- GET DOWN!
MITCHELL WAS A SCALE-ONE OPERATIVE, A FORMER COLONIAL MARINE...
...TOP-RATED ACROSS THE BOARD, WITH BIONIC ENHANCEMENTS TO OPTIMIZE HIS PHYSICAL CAPABILITIES.
THEY DIDN'T SAVE HIM. THEY DIDN'T EVEN COME CLOSE.
MITCHELL!
SAVE YOURSELF, CARYN!
IF I'M GONNA DIE HERE...
...I WANT IT TO COUNT FOR SOMETHING!
REGRETTABLY, IT DIDN'T.
ARRGH!
THE ASSAILANT PLAINLY POSSESSES SOME KIND OF DISTORTER FIELD...
...THAT EFFECTIVELY CLOAKS ITS APPEARANCE FROM ANY FORM OF VISUAL OR ELECTRONIC MONITORING.
CONSEQUENTLY, WE DON'T KNOW WHAT HAPPENED TO CARYN. WE CAN ONLY SURMISE HER FATE.

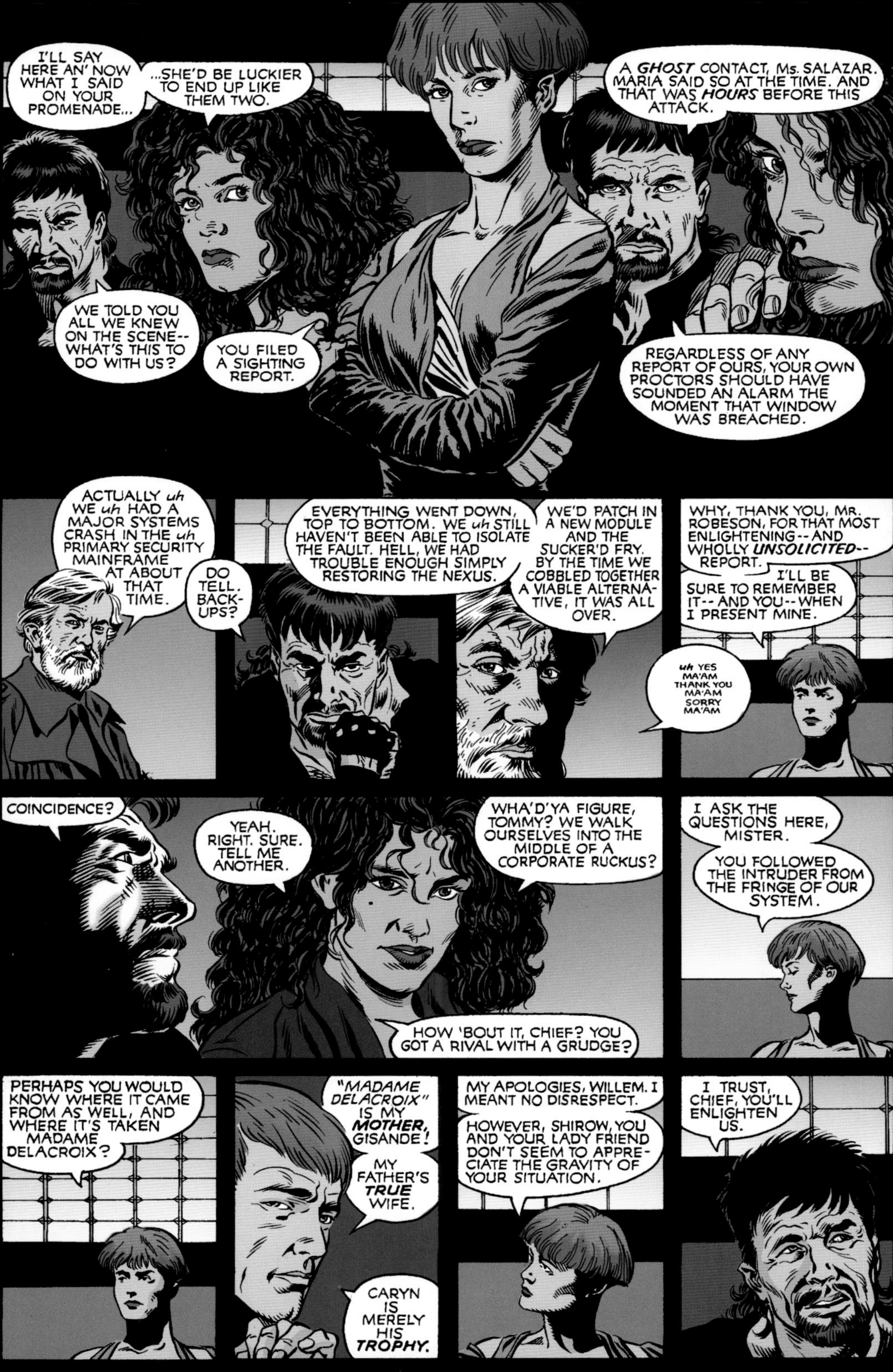
I'LL SAY HERE AN' NOW WHAT I SAID ON YOUR PROMENADE...
...SHE'D BE LUCKIER TO END UP LIKE THEM TWO.
A GHOST CONTACT, Ms. SALAZAR. MARIA SAID SO AT THE TIME. AND THAT WAS HOURS BEFORE THIS ATTACK.
WE TOLD YOU ALL WE KNEW ON THE SCENE-- WHAT'S THIS TO DO WITH US?
YOU FILED A SIGHTING REPORT.
REGARDLESS OF ANY REPORT OF OURS, YOUR OWN PROCTORS SHOULD HAVE SOUNDED AN ALARM THE MOMENT THAT WINDOW WAS BREACHED.
ACTUALLY uh WE uh HAD A MAJOR SYSTEMS CRASH IN THE uh PRIMARY SECURITY MAINFRAME AT ABOUT THAT TIME.
DO TELL. BACK-UPS?
EVERYTHING WENT DOWN, TOP TO BOTTOM. WE uh STILL HAVEN'T BEEN ABLE TO ISOLATE THE FAULT. HELL, WE HAD TROUBLE ENOUGH SIMPLY RESTORING THE NEXUS.
WE'D PATCH IN A NEW MODULE AND THE SUCKER'D FRY. BY THE TIME WE COBBLED TOGETHER A VIABLE ALTERNATIVE, IT WAS ALL OVER.
WHY, THANK YOU, MR. ROBESON, FOR THAT MOST ENLIGHTENING--AND WHOLLY UNSOLICITED--REPORT.
I'LL BE SURE TO REMEMBER IT--AND YOU--WHEN I PRESENT MINE.
uh YES MA'AM THANK YOU MA'AM SORRY MA'AM
COINCIDENCE?
YEAH. RIGHT. SURE. TELL ME ANOTHER.
WHA'D'YA FIGURE, TOMMY? WE WALK OURSELVES INTO THE MIDDLE OF A CORPORATE RUCKUS?
HOW 'BOUT IT, CHIEF? YOU GOT A RIVAL WITH A GRUDGE?
I ASK THE QUESTIONS HERE, MISTER.
YOU FOLLOWED THE INTRUDER FROM THE FRINGE OF OUR SYSTEM.
PERHAPS YOU WOULD KNOW WHERE IT CAME FROM AS WELL, AND WHERE IT'S TAKEN MADAME DELACROIX?
"MADAME DELACROIX" IS MY MOTHER, GISANDE!
MY FATHER'S TRUE WIFE.
CARYN IS MERELY HIS TROPHY.
MY APOLOGIES, WILLEM. I MEANT NO DISRESPECT.
HOWEVER, SHIROW, YOU AND YOUR LADY FRIEND DON'T SEEM TO APPRECIATE THE GRAVITY OF YOUR SITUATION.
I TRUST, CHIEF, YOU'LL ENLIGHTEN US.

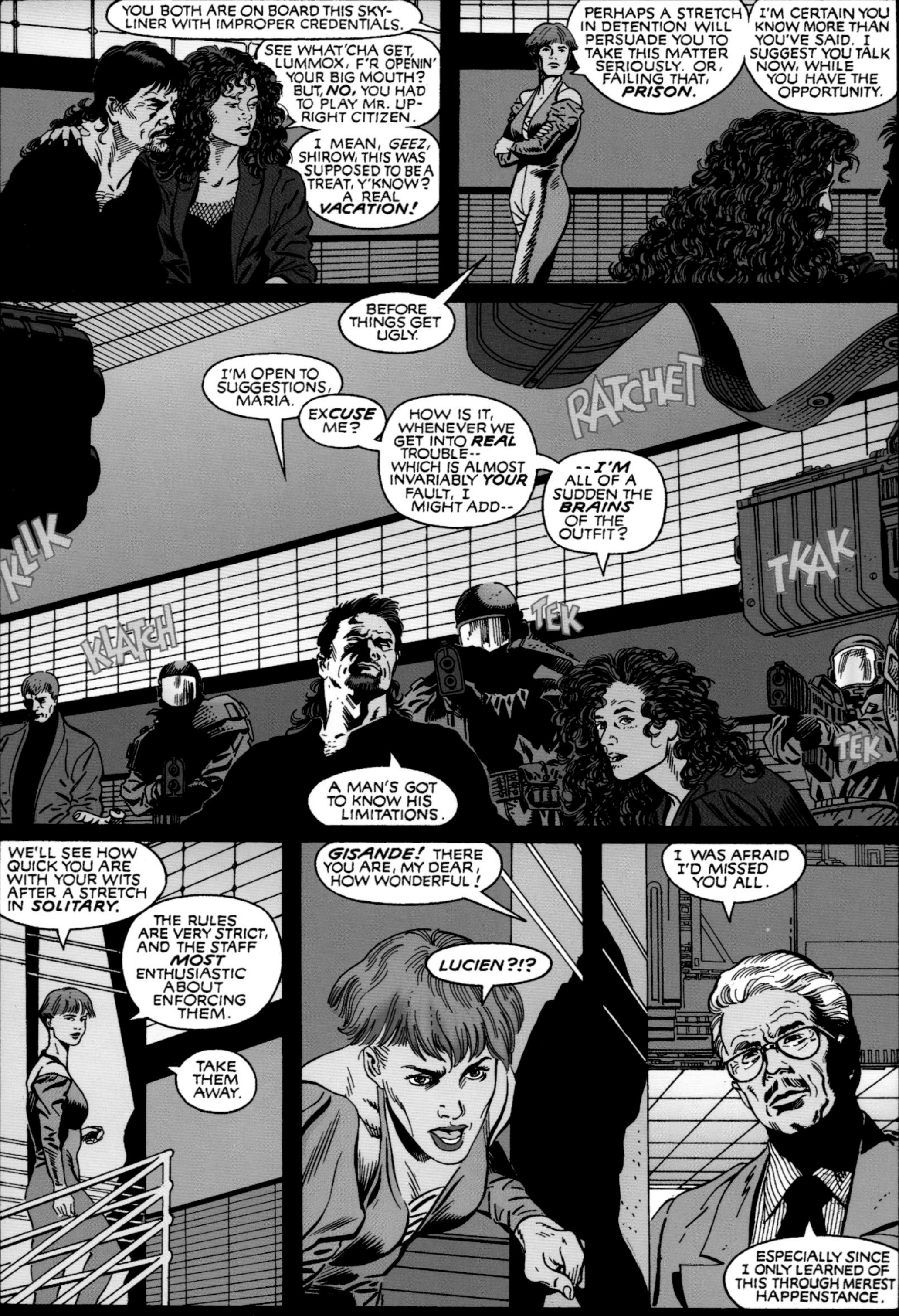

YOU BOTH ARE ON BOARD THIS SKY-LINER WITH IMPROPER CREDENTIALS.
SEE WHAT'CHA GET, LUMMOX, F'R OPENIN' YOUR BIG MOUTH? BUT, NO, YOU HAD TO PLAY MR. UPRIGHT CITIZEN.
I MEAN, GEEZ, SHIROW, THIS WAS SUPPOSED TO BE A TREAT, Y'KNOW? A REAL VACATION!
PERHAPS A STRETCH IN DETENTION WILL PERSUADE YOU TO TAKE THIS MATTER SERIOUSLY. OR, FAILING THAT, PRISON.
I'M CERTAIN YOU KNOW MORE THAN YOU'VE SAID. I SUGGEST YOU TALK NOW, WHILE YOU HAVE THE OPPORTUNITY.
BEFORE THINGS GET UGLY.
RATCHET
I'M OPEN TO SUGGESTIONS, MARIA.
EXCUSE ME?
HOW IS IT, WHENEVER WE GET INTO REAL TROUBLE-- WHICH IS ALMOST INVARIABLY YOUR FAULT, I MIGHT ADD--
--I'M ALL OF A SUDDEN THE BRAINS OF THE OUTFIT?
KLIK
TKAK
KLATCH
TEK
TEK
A MAN'S GOT TO KNOW HIS LIMITATIONS.
WE'LL SEE HOW QUICK YOU ARE WITH YOUR WITS AFTER A STRETCH IN SOLITARY.
THE RULES ARE VERY STRICT, AND THE STAFF MOST ENTHUSIASTIC ABOUT ENFORCING THEM.
TAKE THEM AWAY.
GISANDE! THERE YOU ARE, MY DEAR, HOW WONDERFUL!
LUCIEN?!?
I WAS AFRAID I'D MISSED YOU ALL.
ESPECIALLY SINCE I ONLY LEARNED OF THIS THROUGH MEREST HAPPENSTANCE.

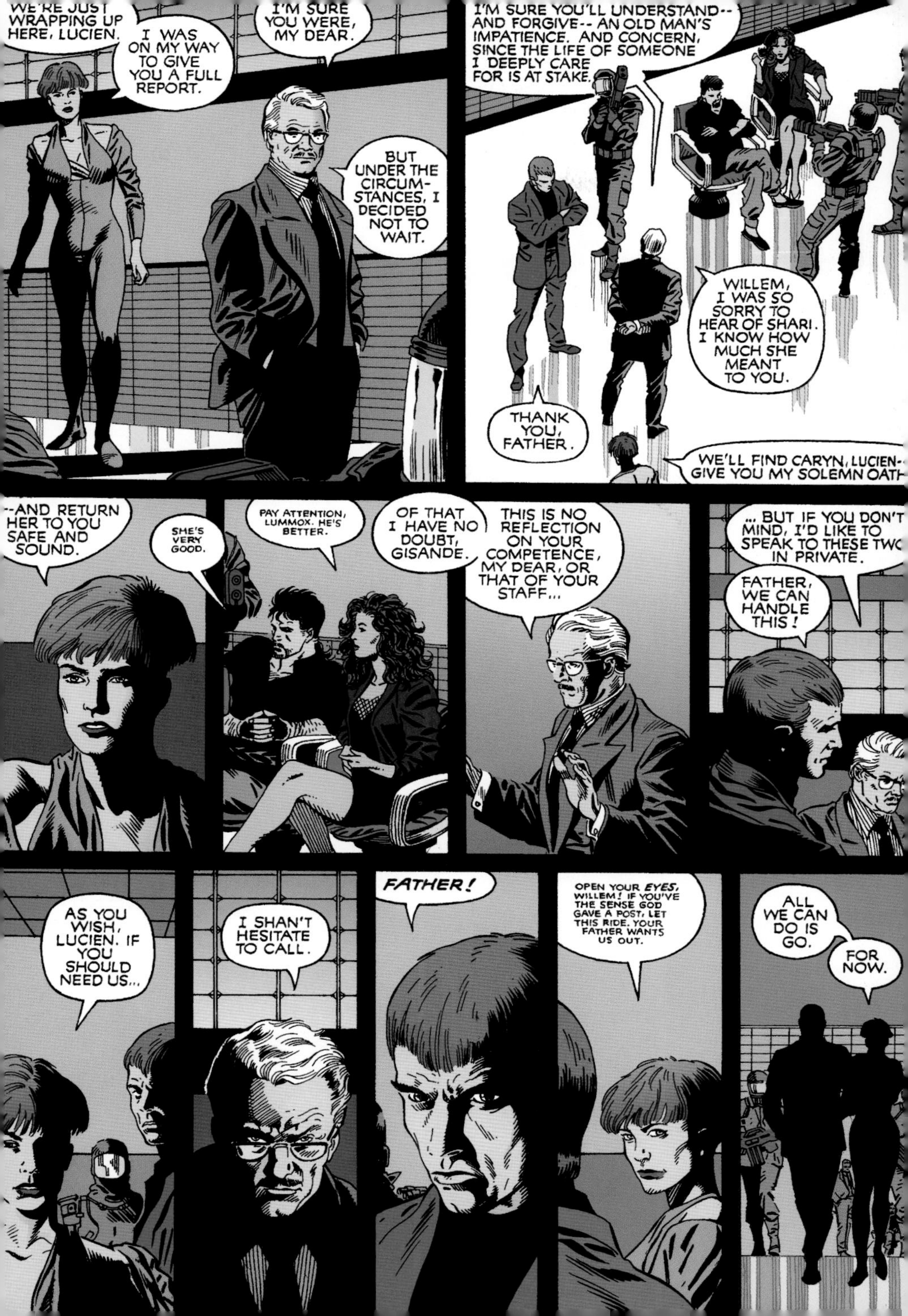
WE'RE JUST WRAPPING UP HERE, LUCIEN.
I WAS ON MY WAY TO GIVE YOU A FULL REPORT.
I'M SURE YOU WERE, MY DEAR.
BUT UNDER THE CIRCUM-STANCES, I DECIDED NOT TO WAIT.
I'M SURE YOU'LL UNDERSTAND-- AND FORGIVE-- AN OLD MAN'S IMPATIENCE. AND CONCERN, SINCE THE LIFE OF SOMEONE I DEEPLY CARE FOR IS AT STAKE.
WILLEM, I WAS SO SORRY TO HEAR OF SHARI. I KNOW HOW MUCH SHE MEANT TO YOU.
THANK YOU, FATHER.
WE'LL FIND CARYN, LUCIEN-- GIVE YOU MY SOLEMN OATH
--AND RETURN HER TO YOU SAFE AND SOUND.
SHE'S VERY GOOD.
PAY ATTENTION, LUMMOX. HE'S BETTER.
OF THAT I HAVE NO DOUBT, GISANDE.
THIS IS NO REFLECTION ON YOUR COMPETENCE, MY DEAR, OR THAT OF YOUR STAFF...
... BUT IF YOU DON'T MIND, I'D LIKE TO SPEAK TO THESE TWO IN PRIVATE.
FATHER, WE CAN HANDLE THIS!
AS YOU WISH, LUCIEN. IF YOU SHOULD NEED US...
I SHAN'T HESITATE TO CALL.
FATHER!
OPEN YOUR EYES, WILLEM! IF YOU'VE THE SENSE GOD GAVE A POST, LET THIS RIDE. YOUR FATHER WANTS US OUT.
ALL WE CAN DO IS GO.
FOR NOW.

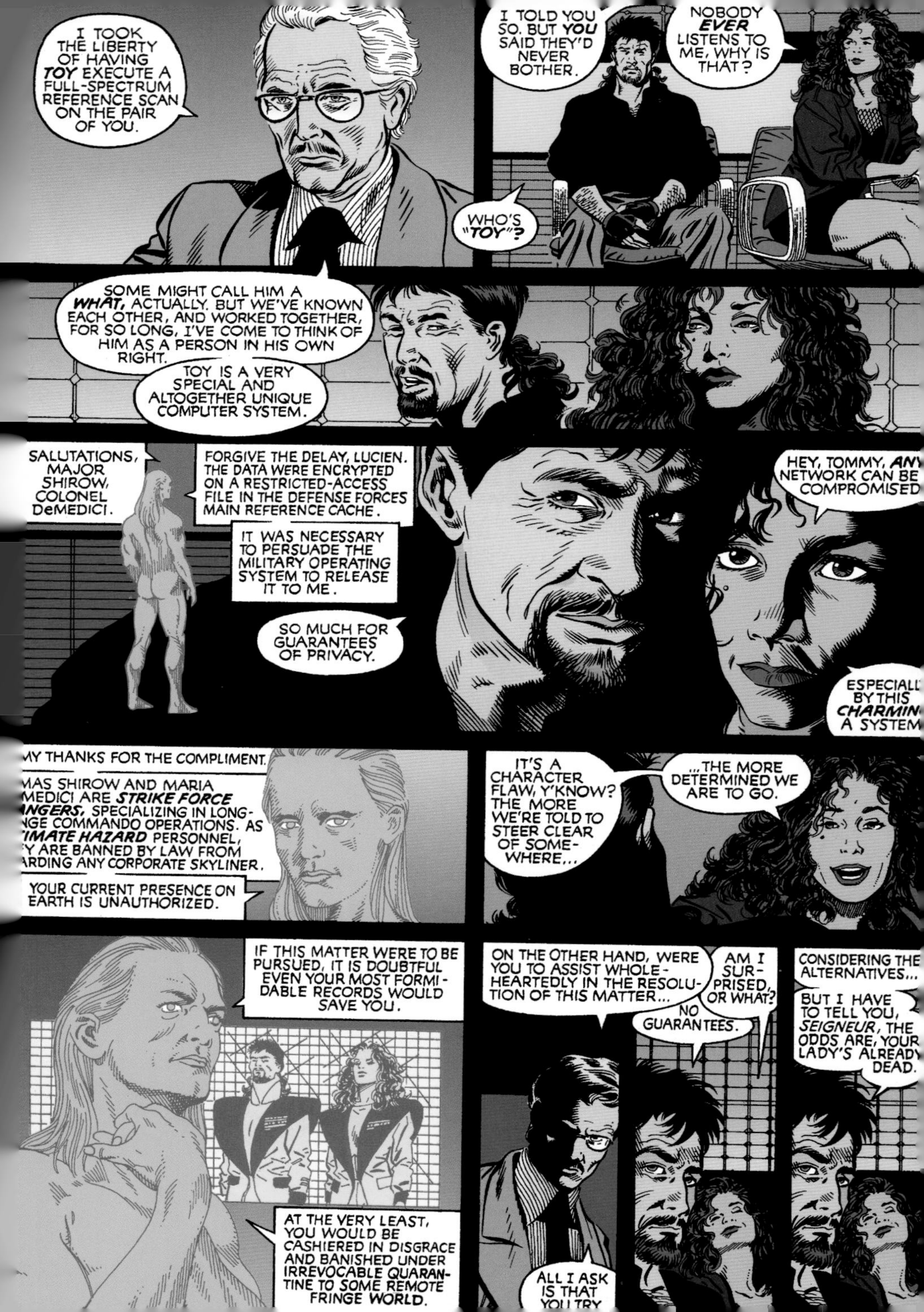

I TOOK THE LIBERTY OF HAVING **TOY** EXECUTE A FULL-SPECTRUM REFERENCE SCAN ON THE PAIR OF YOU.
I TOLD YOU SO. BUT **YOU** SAID THEY'D NEVER BOTHER.
NOBODY **EVER** LISTENS TO ME, WHY IS THAT?
WHO'S "**TOY**"?
SOME MIGHT CALL HIM A **WHAT**, ACTUALLY. BUT WE'VE KNOWN EACH OTHER, AND WORKED TOGETHER, FOR SO LONG, I'VE COME TO THINK OF HIM AS A PERSON IN HIS OWN RIGHT.
TOY IS A VERY SPECIAL AND ALTOGETHER UNIQUE COMPUTER SYSTEM.
SALUTATIONS, MAJOR SHIROW, COLONEL DeMEDICI.
FORGIVE THE DELAY, LUCIEN. THE DATA WERE ENCRYPTED ON A RESTRICTED-ACCESS FILE IN THE DEFENSE FORCES MAIN REFERENCE CACHE.
IT WAS NECESSARY TO PERSUADE THE MILITARY OPERATING SYSTEM TO RELEASE IT TO ME.
SO MUCH FOR GUARANTEES OF PRIVACY.
HEY, TOMMY, ANY NETWORK CAN BE COMPROMISED
ESPECIALL BY THIS *CHARMIN* A SYSTEM
MY THANKS FOR THE COMPLIMENT.
MAS SHIROW AND MARIA MEDICI ARE **STRIKE FORCE NGERS**, SPECIALIZING IN LONG-NGE COMMANDO OPERATIONS. AS **TIMATE HAZARD** PERSONNEL, Y ARE BANNED BY LAW FROM ARDING ANY CORPORATE SKYLINER.
YOUR CURRENT PRESENCE ON EARTH IS UNAUTHORIZED.
IT'S A CHARACTER FLAW, Y'KNOW? THE MORE WE'RE TOLD TO STEER CLEAR OF SOME-WHERE...
...THE MORE DETERMINED WE ARE TO GO.
IF THIS MATTER WERE TO BE PURSUED, IT IS DOUBTFUL EVEN YOUR MOST FORMI-DABLE RECORDS WOULD SAVE YOU.
AT THE VERY LEAST, YOU WOULD BE CASHIERED IN DISGRACE AND BANISHED UNDER IRREVOCABLE QUARAN-TINE TO SOME REMOTE FRINGE **WORLD**.
ON THE OTHER HAND, WERE YOU TO ASSIST WHOLE-HEARTEDLY IN THE RESOLU-TION OF THIS MATTER...
ALL I ASK IS THAT YOU TRY
AM I SUR-PRISED, OR WHAT?
NO GUARANTEES.
CONSIDERING THE ALTERNATIVES...
BUT I HAVE TO TELL YOU, *SEIGNEUR*, THE ODDS ARE, YOUR LADY'S ALREADY DEAD.

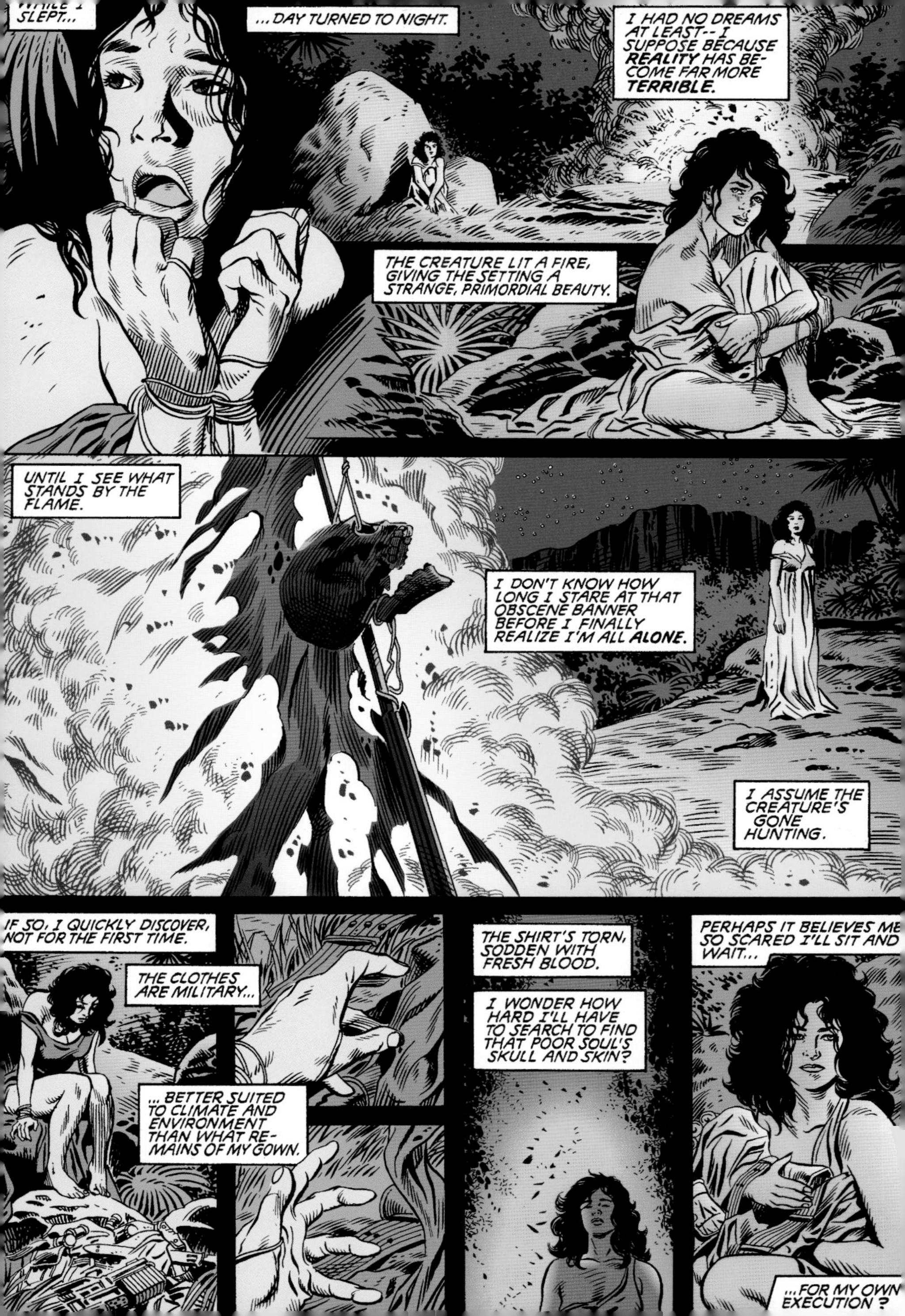
WHILE I SLEPT...
...DAY TURNED TO NIGHT.
I HAD NO DREAMS AT LEAST-- I SUPPOSE BECAUSE REALITY HAS BECOME FAR MORE TERRIBLE.
THE CREATURE LIT A FIRE, GIVING THE SETTING A STRANGE, PRIMORDIAL BEAUTY.
UNTIL I SEE WHAT STANDS BY THE FLAME.
I DON'T KNOW HOW LONG I STARE AT THAT OBSCENE BANNER BEFORE I FINALLY REALIZE I'M ALL ALONE.
I ASSUME THE CREATURE'S GONE HUNTING.
IF SO, I QUICKLY DISCOVER, NOT FOR THE FIRST TIME.
THE CLOTHES ARE MILITARY...
...BETTER SUITED TO CLIMATE AND ENVIRONMENT THAN WHAT REMAINS OF MY GOWN.
THE SHIRT'S TORN, SODDEN WITH FRESH BLOOD.
I WONDER HOW HARD I'LL HAVE TO SEARCH TO FIND THAT POOR SOUL'S SKULL AND SKIN?
PERHAPS IT BELIEVES ME SO SCARED I'LL SIT AND WAIT...
...FOR MY OWN EXECUTION?

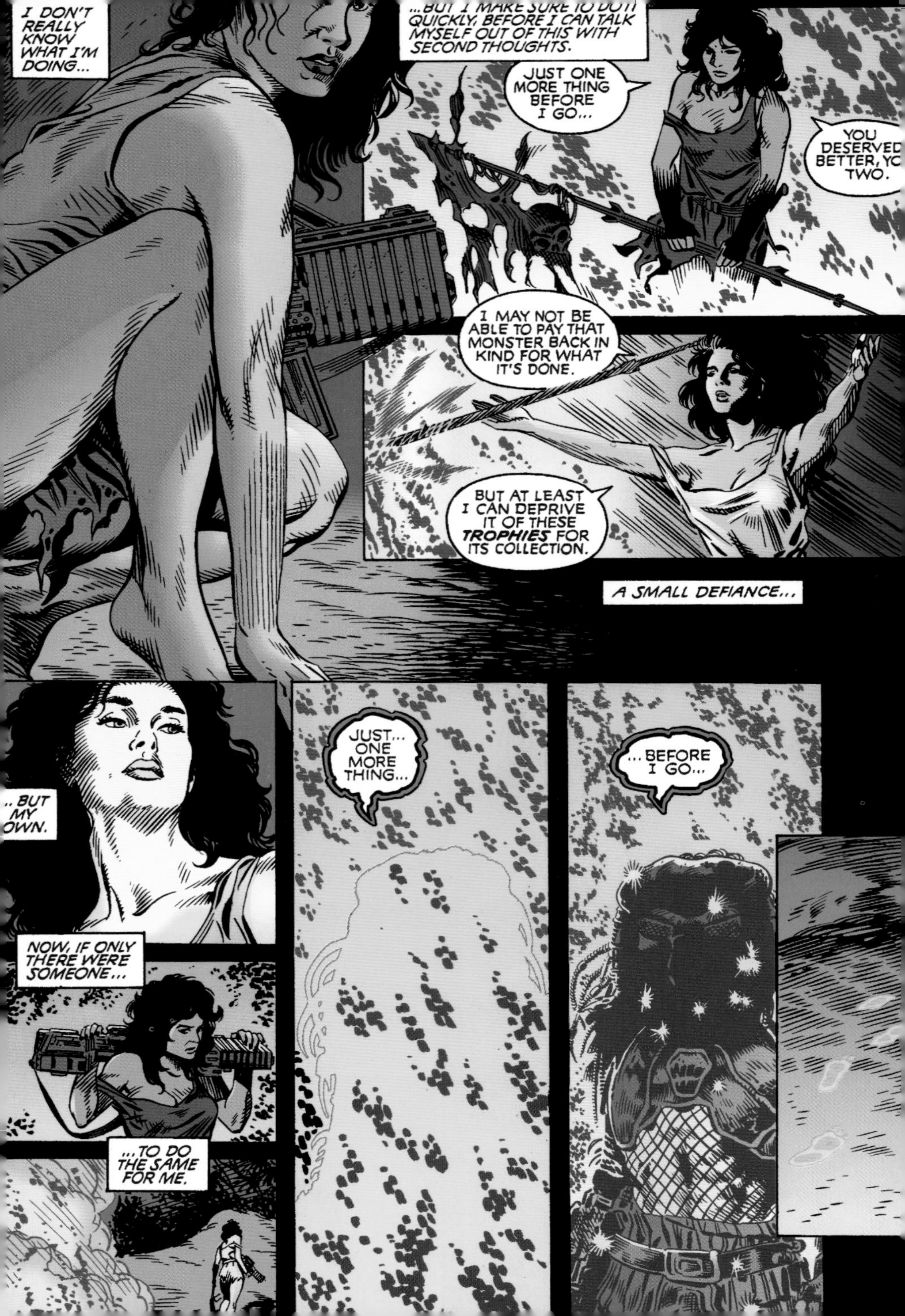
I DON'T REALLY KNOW WHAT I'M DOING...
...BUT I MAKE SURE TO DO IT QUICKLY, BEFORE I CAN TALK MYSELF OUT OF THIS WITH SECOND THOUGHTS.
JUST ONE MORE THING BEFORE I GO...
YOU DESERVED BETTER, YO TWO.
I MAY NOT BE ABLE TO PAY THAT MONSTER BACK IN KIND FOR WHAT IT'S DONE.
BUT AT LEAST I CAN DEPRIVE IT OF THESE TROPHIES FOR ITS COLLECTION.
A SMALL DEFIANCE...
.. BUT MY OWN.
NOW, IF ONLY THERE WERE SOMEONE...
...TO DO THE SAME FOR ME.
JUST... ONE MORE THING...
...BEFORE I GO...

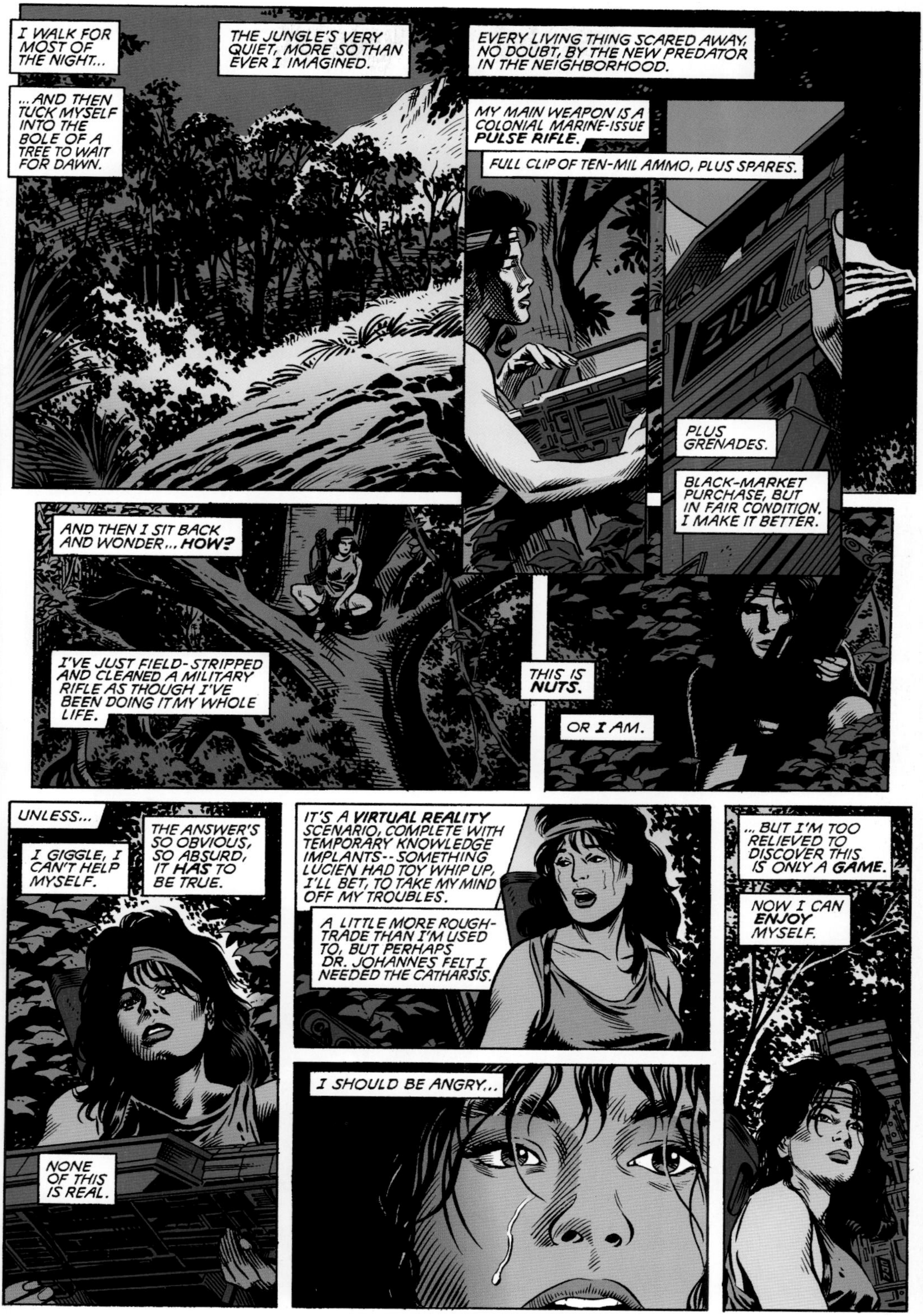
I WALK FOR MOST OF THE NIGHT...
THE JUNGLE'S VERY QUIET, MORE SO THAN EVER I IMAGINED.
EVERY LIVING THING SCARED AWAY, NO DOUBT, BY THE NEW PREDATOR IN THE NEIGHBORHOOD.
...AND THEN TUCK MYSELF INTO THE BOLE OF A TREE TO WAIT FOR DAWN.
MY MAIN WEAPON IS A COLONIAL MARINE-ISSUE PULSE RIFLE.
FULL CLIP OF TEN-MIL AMMO, PLUS SPARES.
PLUS GRENADES.
BLACK-MARKET PURCHASE, BUT IN FAIR CONDITION. I MAKE IT BETTER.
AND THEN I SIT BACK AND WONDER... HOW?
I'VE JUST FIELD-STRIPPED AND CLEANED A MILITARY RIFLE AS THOUGH I'VE BEEN DOING IT MY WHOLE LIFE.
THIS IS NUTS.
OR I AM.
UNLESS...
THE ANSWER'S SO OBVIOUS, SO ABSURD, IT HAS TO BE TRUE.
I GIGGLE, I CAN'T HELP MYSELF.
NONE OF THIS IS REAL.
IT'S A VIRTUAL REALITY SCENARIO, COMPLETE WITH TEMPORARY KNOWLEDGE IMPLANTS--SOMETHING LUCIEN HAD TOY WHIP UP, I'LL BET, TO TAKE MY MIND OFF MY TROUBLES.
A LITTLE MORE ROUGH-TRADE THAN I'M USED TO, BUT PERHAPS DR. JOHANNES FELT I NEEDED THE CATHARSIS.
I SHOULD BE ANGRY...
...BUT I'M TOO RELIEVED TO DISCOVER THIS IS ONLY A GAME.
NOW I CAN ENJOY MYSELF.

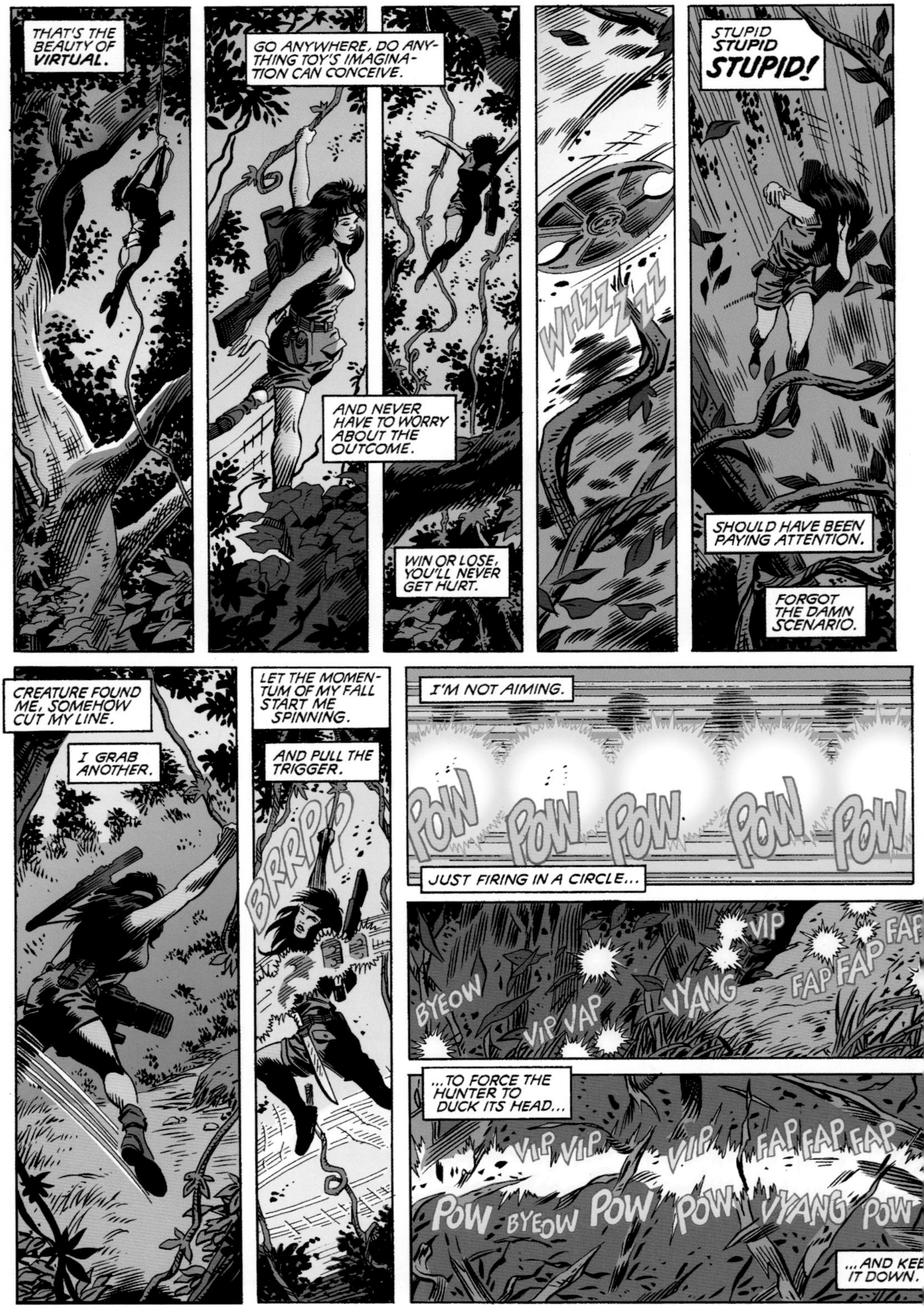

THAT'S THE BEAUTY OF VIRTUAL.
GO ANYWHERE, DO ANYTHING TOY'S IMAGINATION CAN CONCEIVE.
AND NEVER HAVE TO WORRY ABOUT THE OUTCOME.
WIN OR LOSE, YOU'LL NEVER GET HURT.
WHIZZZZZ
STUPID STUPID STUPID!
SHOULD HAVE BEEN PAYING ATTENTION.
FORGOT THE DAMN SCENARIO.
CREATURE FOUND ME, SOMEHOW CUT MY LINE.
I GRAB ANOTHER.
LET THE MOMENTUM OF MY FALL START ME SPINNING.
AND PULL THE TRIGGER.
BRRPPP
I'M NOT AIMING.
POW POW POW POW POW
JUST FIRING IN A CIRCLE...
VIP FAP FAP FAP
BYEOW VIP VAP VYANG
...TO FORCE THE HUNTER TO DUCK ITS HEAD...
VIP VIP VIP FAP FAP FAP
POW BYEOW POW POW VYANG POW
...AND KEEP IT DOWN.

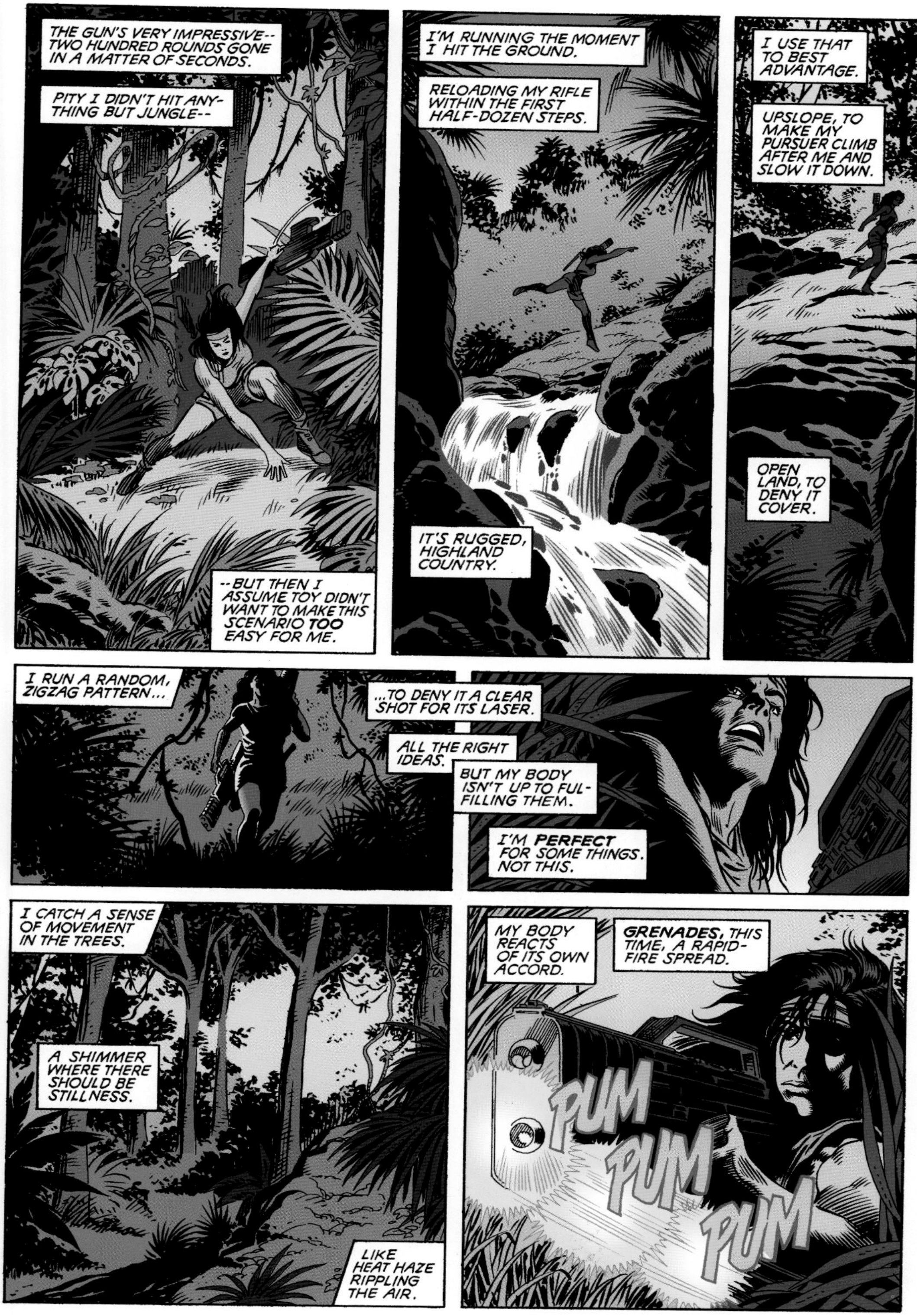
THE GUN'S VERY IMPRESSIVE--TWO HUNDRED ROUNDS GONE IN A MATTER OF SECONDS.
PITY I DIDN'T HIT ANYTHING BUT JUNGLE--
--BUT THEN I ASSUME TOY DIDN'T WANT TO MAKE THIS SCENARIO TOO EASY FOR ME.
I'M RUNNING THE MOMENT I HIT THE GROUND.
RELOADING MY RIFLE WITHIN THE FIRST HALF-DOZEN STEPS.
IT'S RUGGED, HIGHLAND COUNTRY.
I USE THAT TO BEST ADVANTAGE.
UPSLOPE, TO MAKE MY PURSUER CLIMB AFTER ME AND SLOW IT DOWN.
OPEN LAND, TO DENY IT COVER.
I RUN A RANDOM, ZIGZAG PATTERN...
...TO DENY IT A CLEAR SHOT FOR ITS LASER.
ALL THE RIGHT IDEAS.
BUT MY BODY ISN'T UP TO FULFILLING THEM.
I'M PERFECT FOR SOME THINGS. NOT THIS.
I CATCH A SENSE OF MOVEMENT IN THE TREES.
A SHIMMER WHERE THERE SHOULD BE STILLNESS.
LIKE HEAT HAZE RIPPLING THE AIR.
MY BODY REACTS OF ITS OWN ACCORD.
GRENADES, THIS TIME, A RAPID-FIRE SPREAD.
PUM
PUM
PUM

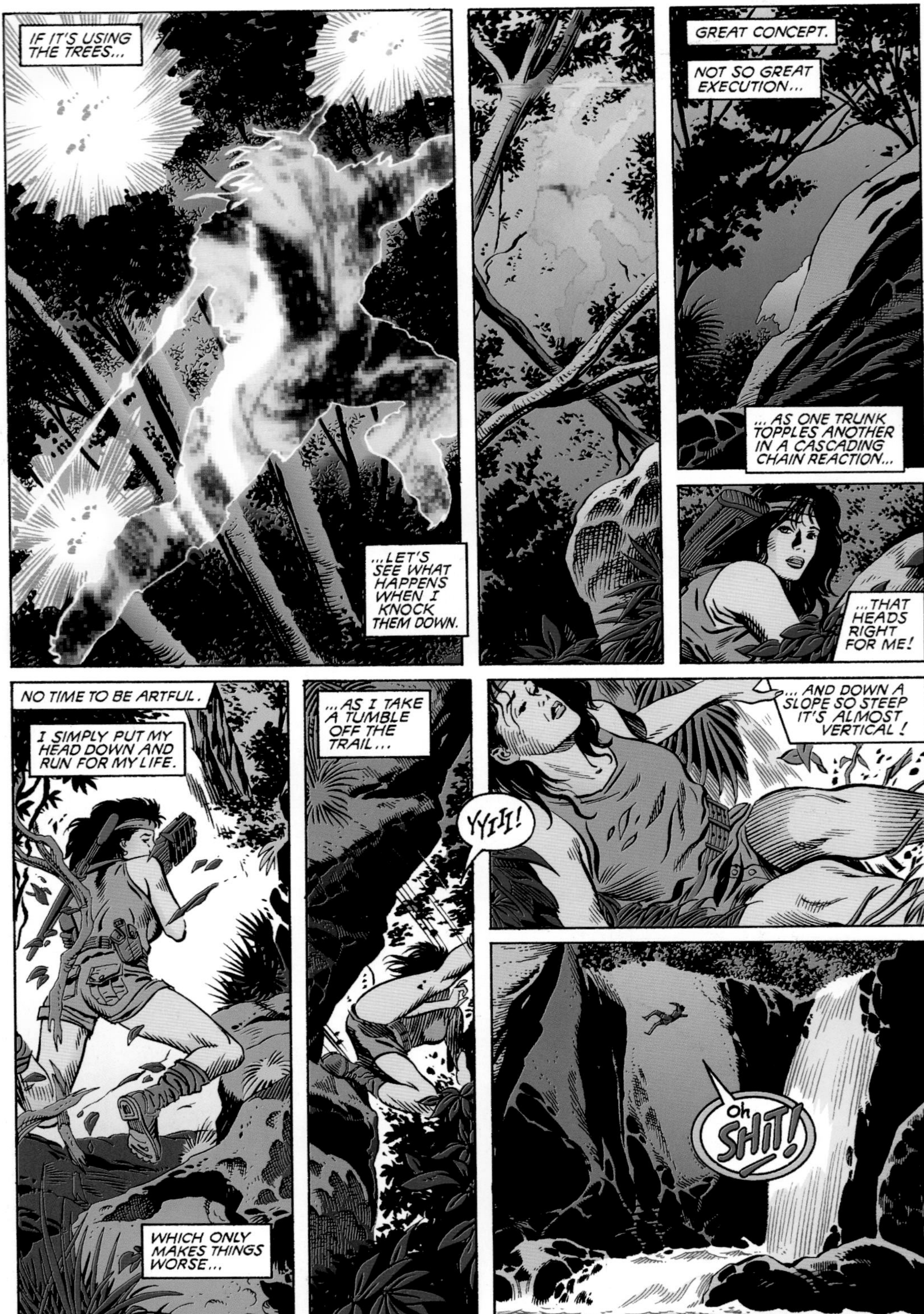
IF IT'S USING THE TREES...
...LET'S SEE WHAT HAPPENS WHEN I KNOCK THEM DOWN.
GREAT CONCEPT.
NOT SO GREAT EXECUTION...
...AS ONE TRUNK TOPPLES ANOTHER IN A CASCADING CHAIN REACTION...
...THAT HEADS RIGHT FOR ME!
NO TIME TO BE ARTFUL.
I SIMPLY PUT MY HEAD DOWN AND RUN FOR MY LIFE.
WHICH ONLY MAKES THINGS WORSE...
...AS I TAKE A TUMBLE OFF THE TRAIL...
YYIII!
...AND DOWN A SLOPE SO STEEP IT'S ALMOST VERTICAL!
Oh SHIT!

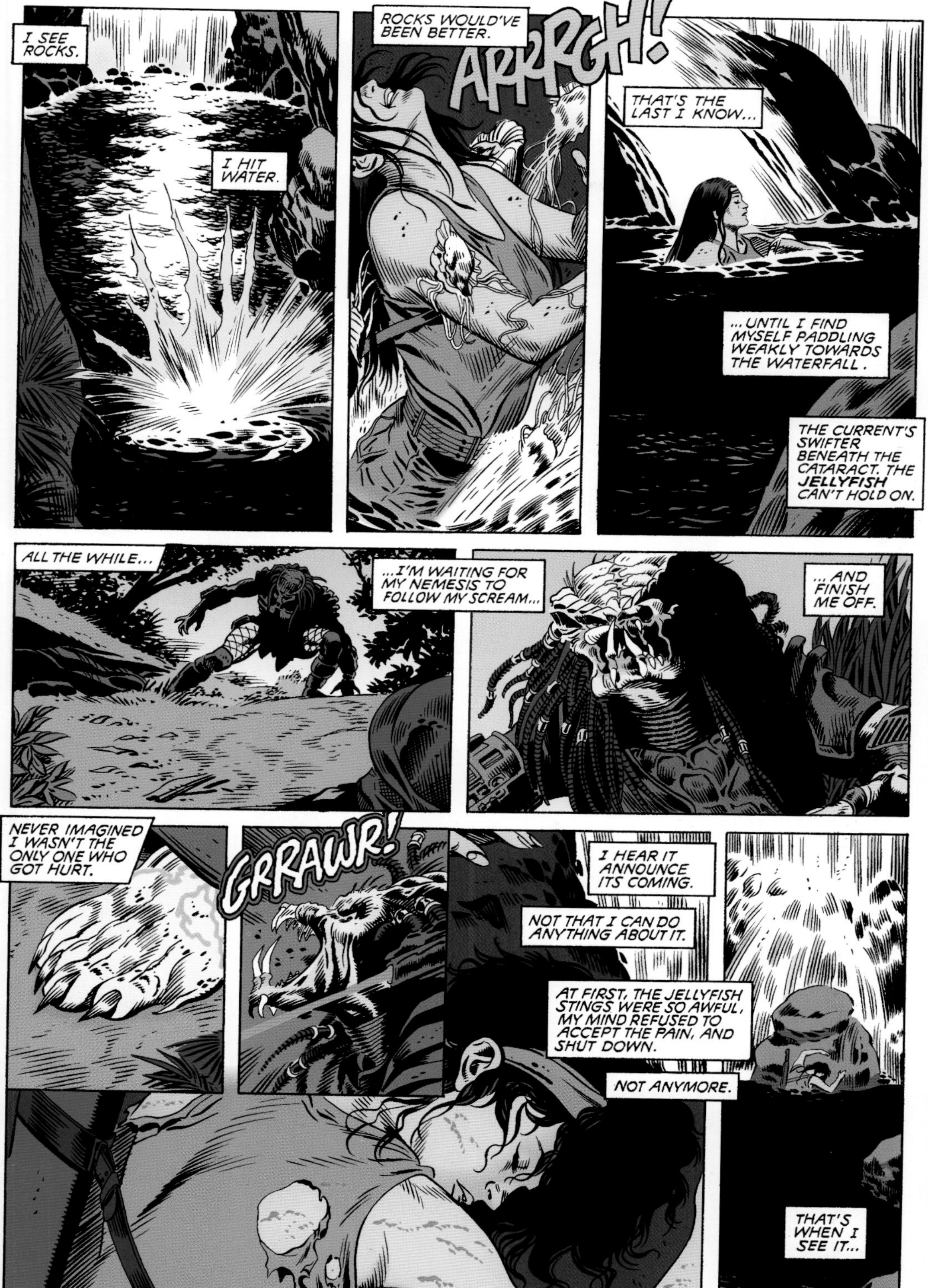
I SEE ROCKS.
I HIT WATER.
ROCKS WOULD'VE BEEN BETTER.
ARRRGH!
THAT'S THE LAST I KNOW...
...UNTIL I FIND MYSELF PADDLING WEAKLY TOWARDS THE WATERFALL.
THE CURRENT'S SWIFTER BENEATH THE CATARACT. THE JELLYFISH CAN'T HOLD ON.
ALL THE WHILE...
...I'M WAITING FOR MY NEMESIS TO FOLLOW MY SCREAM...
...AND FINISH ME OFF.
NEVER IMAGINED I WASN'T THE ONLY ONE WHO GOT HURT.
GRRAWR!
I HEAR IT ANNOUNCE ITS COMING.
NOT THAT I CAN DO ANYTHING ABOUT IT.
AT FIRST, THE JELLYFISH STINGS WERE SO AWFUL, MY MIND REFUSED TO ACCEPT THE PAIN, AND SHUT DOWN.
NOT ANYMORE.
THAT'S WHEN I SEE IT...

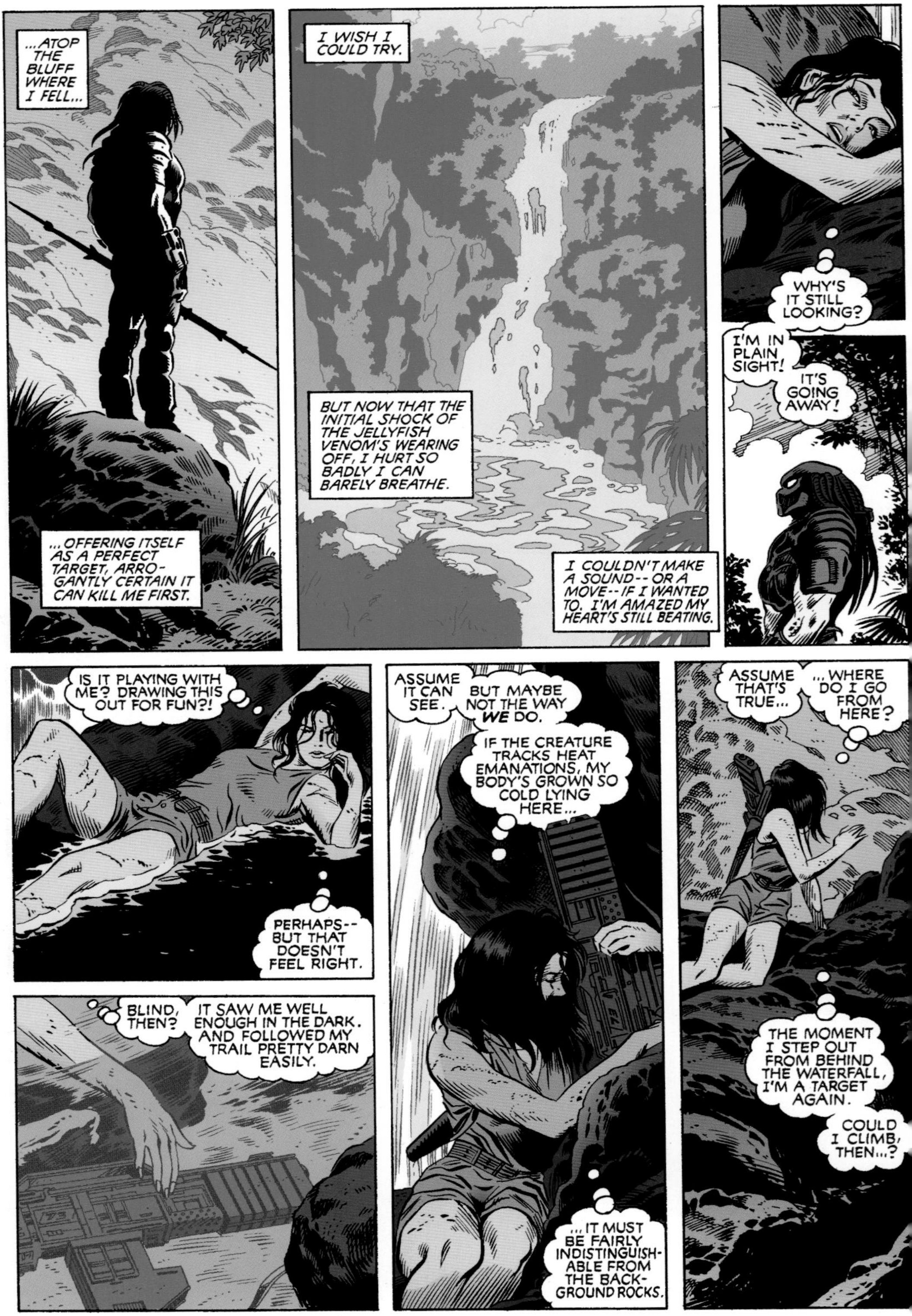
...ATOP THE BLUFF WHERE I FELL...
...OFFERING ITSELF AS A PERFECT TARGET, ARRO-GANTLY CERTAIN IT CAN KILL ME FIRST.
I WISH I COULD TRY.
BUT NOW THAT THE INITIAL SHOCK OF THE JELLYFISH VENOM'S WEARING OFF, I HURT SO BADLY I CAN BARELY BREATHE.
I COULDN'T MAKE A SOUND-- OR A MOVE-- IF I WANTED TO. I'M AMAZED MY HEART'S STILL BEATING.
WHY'S IT STILL LOOKING?
I'M IN PLAIN SIGHT!
IT'S GOING AWAY!
IS IT PLAYING WITH ME? DRAWING THIS OUT FOR FUN?!
PERHAPS-- BUT THAT DOESN'T FEEL RIGHT.
BLIND, THEN?
IT SAW ME WELL ENOUGH IN THE DARK. AND FOLLOWED MY TRAIL PRETTY DARN EASILY.
ASSUME IT CAN SEE.
BUT MAYBE NOT THE WAY WE DO.
IF THE CREATURE TRACKS HEAT EMANATIONS, MY BODY'S GROWN SO COLD LYING HERE...
...IT MUST BE FAIRLY INDISTINGUISH-ABLE FROM THE BACK-GROUND ROCKS.
ASSUME THAT'S TRUE...
...WHERE DO I GO FROM HERE?
THE MOMENT I STEP OUT FROM BEHIND THE WATERFALL, I'M A TARGET AGAIN.
COULD I CLIMB, THEN...?

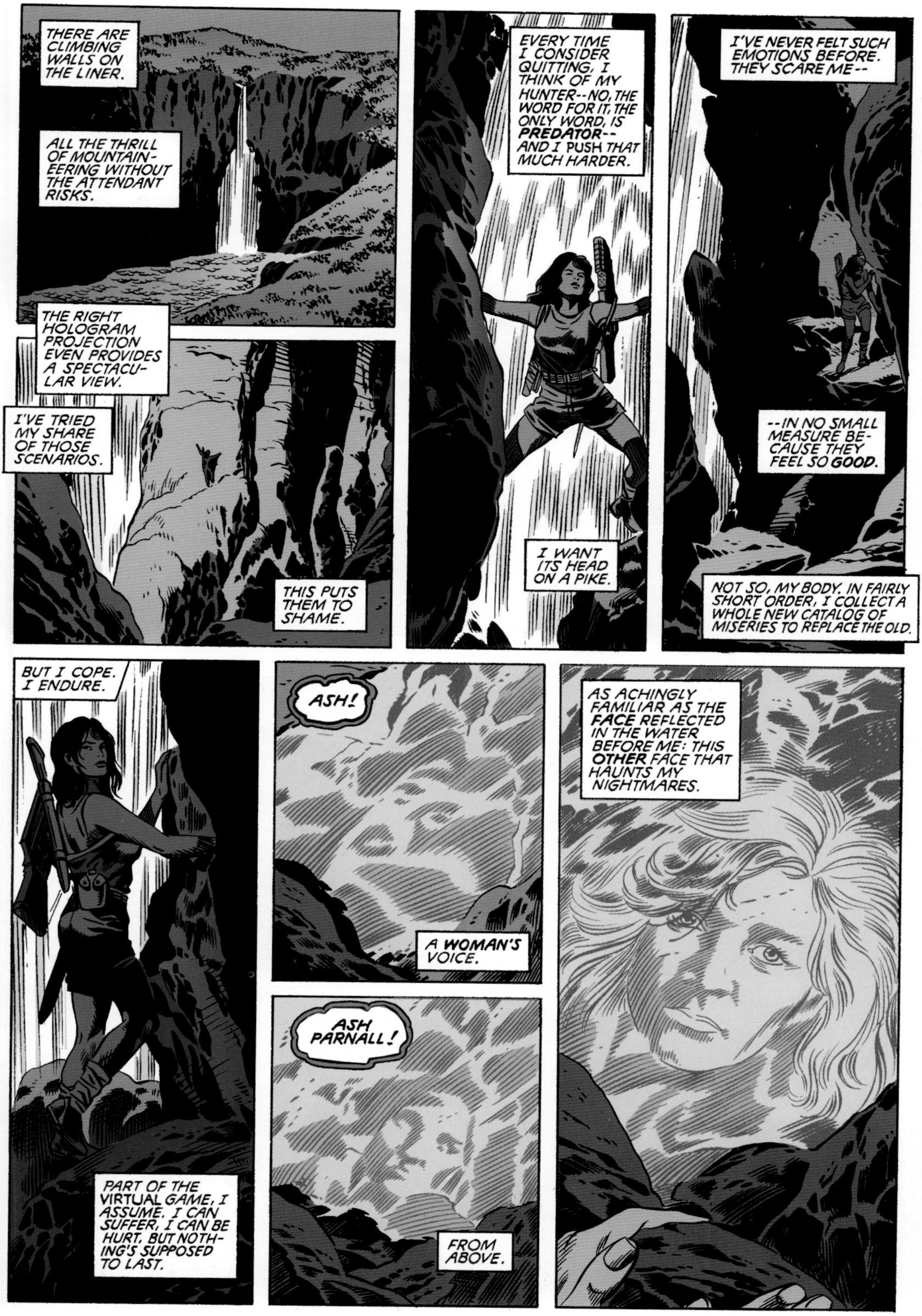
THERE ARE CLIMBING WALLS ON THE LINER.
ALL THE THRILL OF MOUNTAIN-EERING WITHOUT THE ATTENDANT RISKS.
THE RIGHT HOLOGRAM PROJECTION EVEN PROVIDES A SPECTACU-LAR VIEW.
I'VE TRIED MY SHARE OF THOSE SCENARIOS.
THIS PUTS THEM TO SHAME.
EVERY TIME I CONSIDER QUITTING, I THINK OF MY HUNTER--NO, THE WORD FOR IT, THE ONLY WORD, IS **PREDATOR**-- AND I PUSH THAT MUCH HARDER.
I WANT ITS HEAD ON A PIKE.
I'VE NEVER FELT SUCH EMOTIONS BEFORE. THEY SCARE ME--
--IN NO SMALL MEASURE BE-CAUSE THEY FEEL SO **GOOD**.
NOT SO, MY BODY. IN FAIRLY SHORT ORDER, I COLLECT A WHOLE NEW CATALOG OF MISERIES TO REPLACE THE OLD.
BUT I COPE. I ENDURE.
PART OF THE VIRTUAL GAME, I ASSUME. I CAN SUFFER, I CAN BE HURT, BUT NOTHING'S SUPPOSED TO LAST.
ASH!
A **WOMAN'S** VOICE.
ASH PARNALL!
FROM ABOVE.
AS ACHINGLY FAMILIAR AS THE **FACE** REFLECTED IN THE WATER BEFORE ME: THIS **OTHER** FACE THAT HAUNTS MY NIGHTMARES.

THE IMPULSE TO REPLY IS AUTOMATIC.

BUT BEFORE I CAN SPEAK, THE VOICE CHANGES.

ANOTHER WOMAN-- *SHARI*-- CALLING THE SAME NAME.

ASH PARNALL!

AND I VERY CAREFULLY SNEAK A PEEK...

... AS I HEAR *DR. JOHANNES*...

CARYN... DELACROIX!

IT'S A *MIMIC!*

AS WELL AS A *CHAMELEON... MATER CHRISTI*, IS THERE ANYTHING THAT HORROR *CAN'T* DO?

BUT WHY ONLY SCRAP WORDS? CAN'T IT CONSTRUCT COMPLETE SENTENCES? HOW MUCH DOES IT ACTUALLY COMPREHEND OF WHAT IT SAYS?

WHO CARES? IT'S ONLY A *VIRTUAL SIMULACRUM*. IF THOSE ARE ITS LIMITS, THOSE ARE ITS LIMITS.

I TAKE MY TIME BEFORE I MOVE AGAIN.

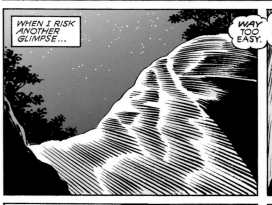

WHEN I RISK ANOTHER GLIMPSE...

WAY TOO EASY.

HOWEVER IT SPEAKS, IT *THINKS*. LIKE A HUNTER. IT KNEW I WENT IN THE POOL, AND WHEN IT COULDN'T FIND ME ANYWHERE ELSE...

... IT DETERMINED THE ONLY LOGICAL ALTERNATIVE.

CAN'T GO UP, CAN'T GO DOWN-- I'LL BE A CLEAR TARGET EITHER WAY.

CAN I SCOOT SIDEWAYS ALONG THIS LEDGE?

WHAT'S THIS?

SOME SORT OF OPENING IN THE ROCK--

--MERCIFUL HEAVEN, IT'S A *CAVE!*

I SEE *MOONLIGHT* INSIDE. IF THAT MEANS AN OPENING TO THE SURFACE...

... I MIGHT BE ABLE TO CATCH THAT UGLY BASTARD FROM BEHIND! THEN WE'LL SEE WHICH OF US IS THE REAL *PREDATOR!*

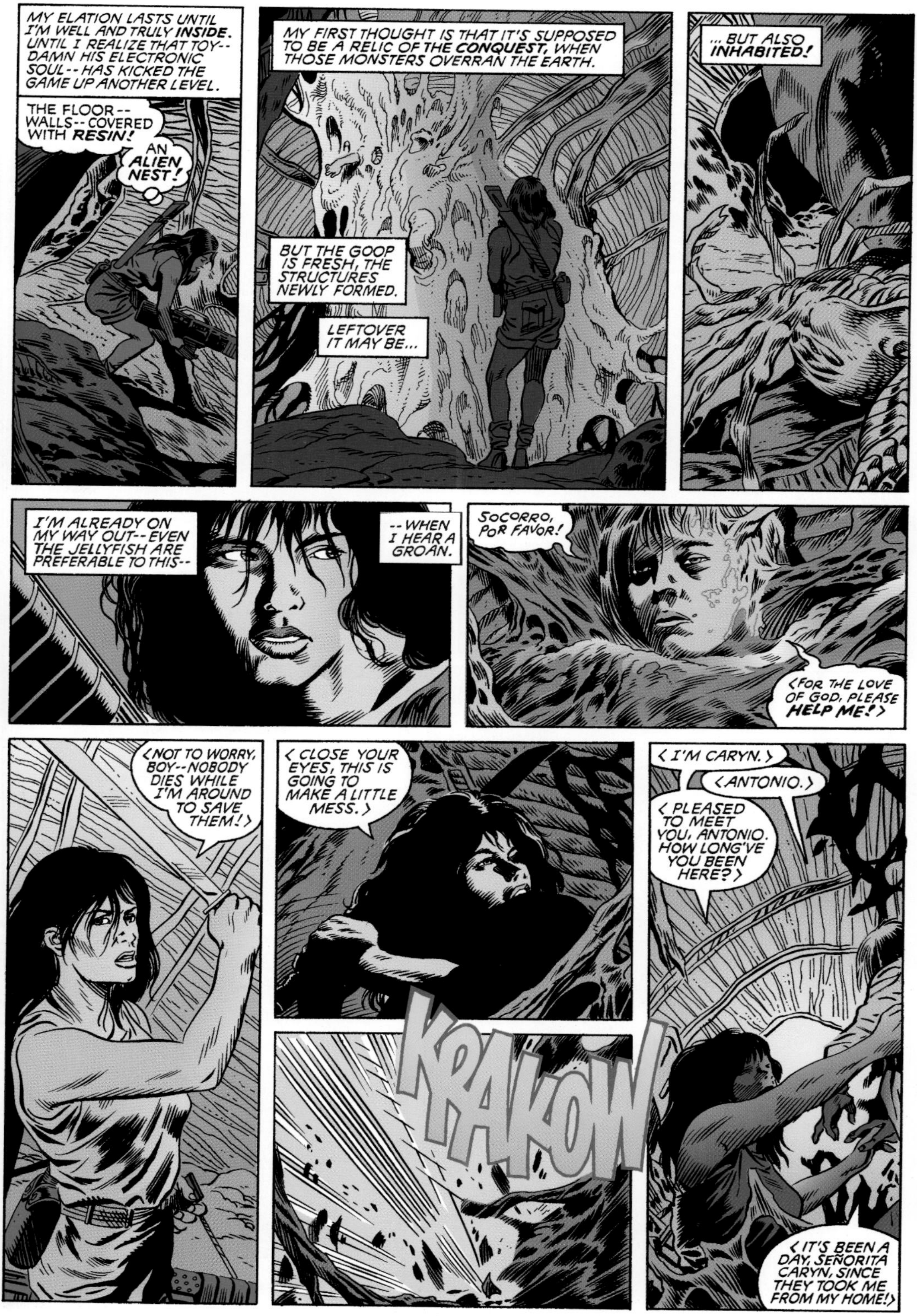
MY ELATION LASTS UNTIL I'M WELL AND TRULY INSIDE. UNTIL I REALIZE THAT TOY--DAMN HIS ELECTRONIC SOUL--HAS KICKED THE GAME UP ANOTHER LEVEL.
THE FLOOR--WALLS--COVERED WITH RESIN!
AN ALIEN NEST!
MY FIRST THOUGHT IS THAT IT'S SUPPOSED TO BE A RELIC OF THE CONQUEST, WHEN THOSE MONSTERS OVERRAN THE EARTH.
BUT THE GOOP IS FRESH, THE STRUCTURES NEWLY FORMED.
LEFTOVER IT MAY BE...
...BUT ALSO INHABITED!
I'M ALREADY ON MY WAY OUT--EVEN THE JELLYFISH ARE PREFERABLE TO THIS--
--WHEN I HEAR A GROAN.
SOCORRO, POR FAVOR!
<FOR THE LOVE OF GOD, PLEASE HELP ME!>
<NOT TO WORRY, BOY--NOBODY DIES WHILE I'M AROUND TO SAVE THEM!>
<CLOSE YOUR EYES, THIS IS GOING TO MAKE A LITTLE MESS.>
KRAKOW
<I'M CARYN.>
<ANTONIO.>
<PLEASED TO MEET YOU, ANTONIO. HOW LONG'VE YOU BEEN HERE?>
<IT'S BEEN A DAY, SEÑORITA CARYN, SINCE THEY TOOK ME FROM MY HOME!>

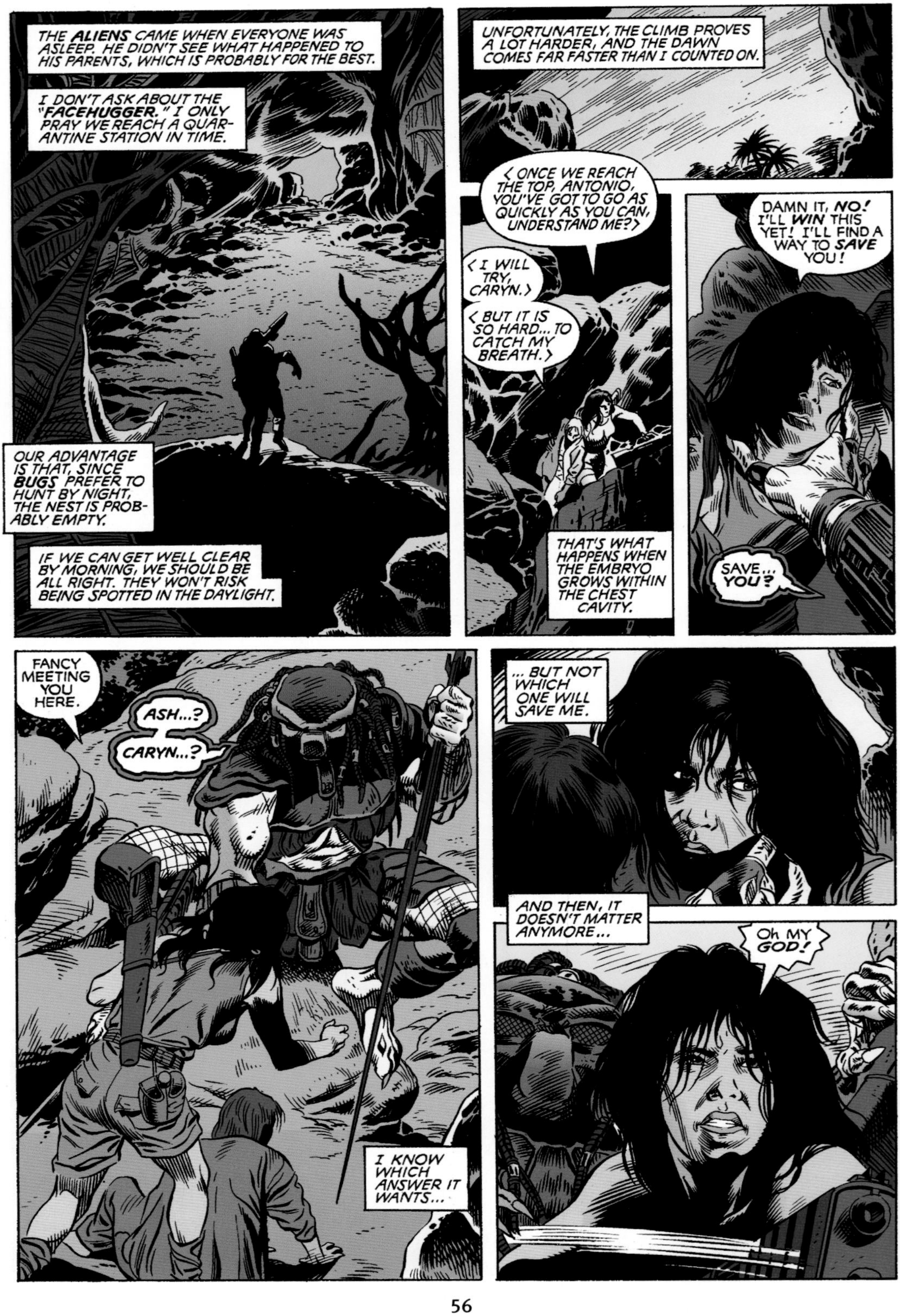
THE ALIENS CAME WHEN EVERYONE WAS ASLEEP. HE DIDN'T SEE WHAT HAPPENED TO HIS PARENTS, WHICH IS PROBABLY FOR THE BEST.
I DON'T ASK ABOUT THE "FACEHUGGER." I ONLY PRAY WE REACH A QUARANTINE STATION IN TIME.
OUR ADVANTAGE IS THAT, SINCE BUGS PREFER TO HUNT BY NIGHT, THE NEST IS PROBABLY EMPTY.
IF WE CAN GET WELL CLEAR BY MORNING, WE SHOULD BE ALL RIGHT. THEY WON'T RISK BEING SPOTTED IN THE DAYLIGHT.
UNFORTUNATELY, THE CLIMB PROVES A LOT HARDER, AND THE DAWN COMES FAR FASTER THAN I COUNTED ON.
< ONCE WE REACH THE TOP, ANTONIO, YOU'VE GOT TO GO AS QUICKLY AS YOU CAN, UNDERSTAND ME? >
< I WILL TRY, CARYN. >
< BUT IT IS SO HARD... TO CATCH MY BREATH. >
THAT'S WHAT HAPPENS WHEN THE EMBRYO GROWS WITHIN THE CHEST CAVITY.
DAMN IT, NO! I'LL WIN THIS YET! I'LL FIND A WAY TO SAVE YOU!
SAVE... YOU?
FANCY MEETING YOU HERE.
ASH...?
CARYN...?
I KNOW WHICH ANSWER IT WANTS...
... BUT NOT WHICH ONE WILL SAVE ME.
AND THEN, IT DOESN'T MATTER ANYMORE...
Oh MY GOD!

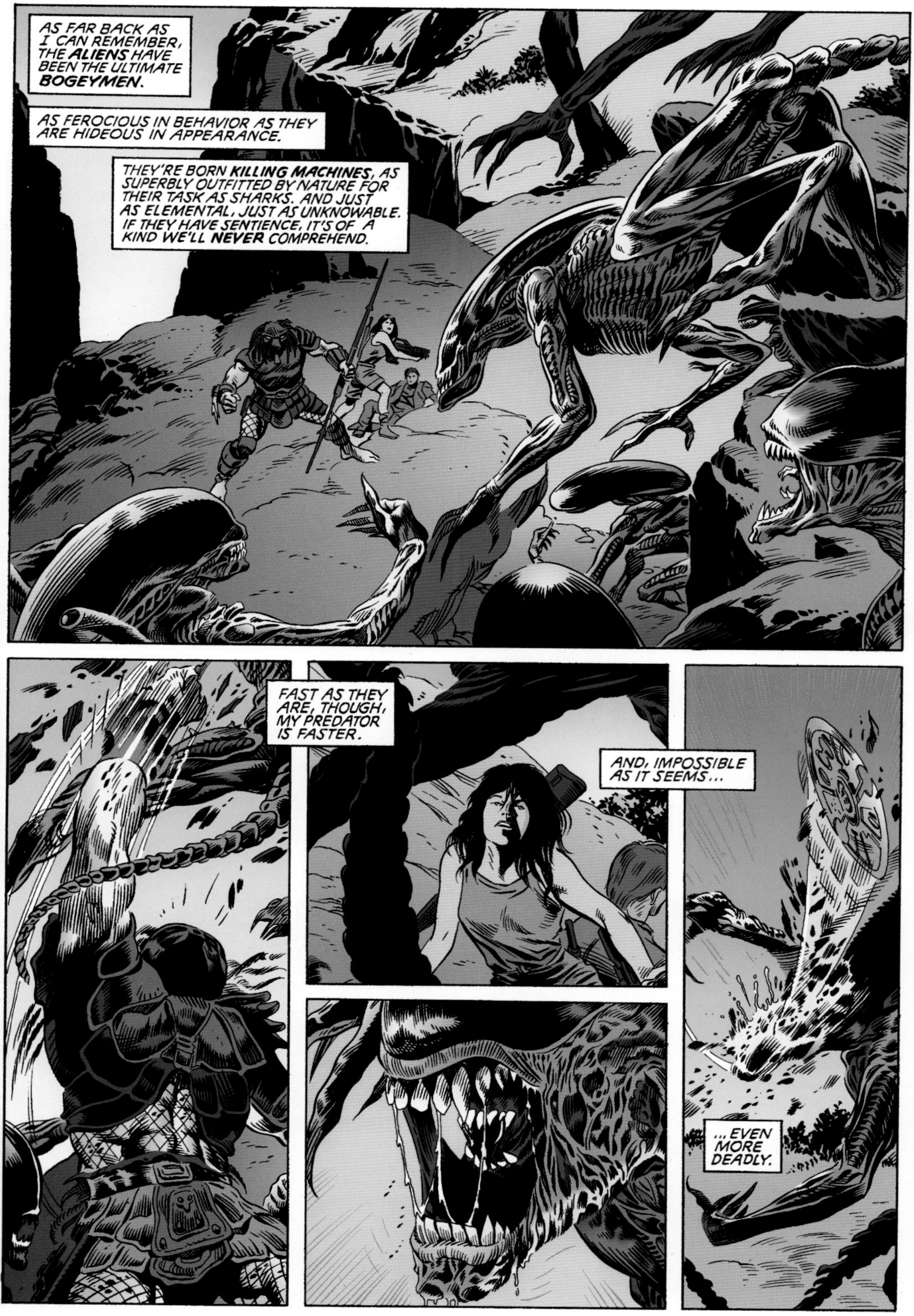
AS FAR BACK AS I CAN REMEMBER, THE ALIENS HAVE BEEN THE ULTIMATE BOGEYMEN.
AS FEROCIOUS IN BEHAVIOR AS THEY ARE HIDEOUS IN APPEARANCE.
THEY'RE BORN KILLING MACHINES, AS SUPERBLY OUTFITTED BY NATURE FOR THEIR TASK AS SHARKS. AND JUST AS ELEMENTAL, JUST AS UNKNOWABLE. IF THEY HAVE SENTIENCE, IT'S OF A KIND WE'LL NEVER COMPREHEND.
FAST AS THEY ARE, THOUGH, MY PREDATOR IS FASTER.
AND, IMPOSSIBLE AS IT SEEMS...
...EVEN MORE DEADLY.

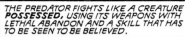

THE PREDATOR FIGHTS LIKE A CREATURE *POSSESSED*, USING ITS WEAPONS WITH LETHAL ABANDON AND A SKILL THAT HAS TO BE SEEN TO BE BELIEVED.

I KEEP IT AT MY BACK...

...SENSING SOMEHOW THAT IT'LL LEAVE ME BE SO LONG AS IT HAS ITS ANCIENT *FOES* TO FIGHT.

I WONDER HOW I KNOW THAT.

AND THEN CAST QUESTION AND ANSWER ASIDE...

...TO CONCEN-TRATE ON THE BATTLE AT HAND.

SHORT, CON-TROLLED BURSTS. AT THEIR LIMBS FIRST, TO IM-MOBILIZE THEM.

THEN, CHEST OR SKULL, TO FINISH THEM OFF.

REMEMBERING ALWAYS TO TAKE CARE NOT TO GET SPLASHED BY THEIR *ACID BLOOD*.

MY MAGAZINE COUNTER DROPS INTO THE LOW DOUBLE-DIGITS...

...SO I LOCK AND LOAD A FRESH CLIP AND SCAN FOR NEW TARGETS.

BIG MAMA ?!

"BIG MAMA" ?!?

58

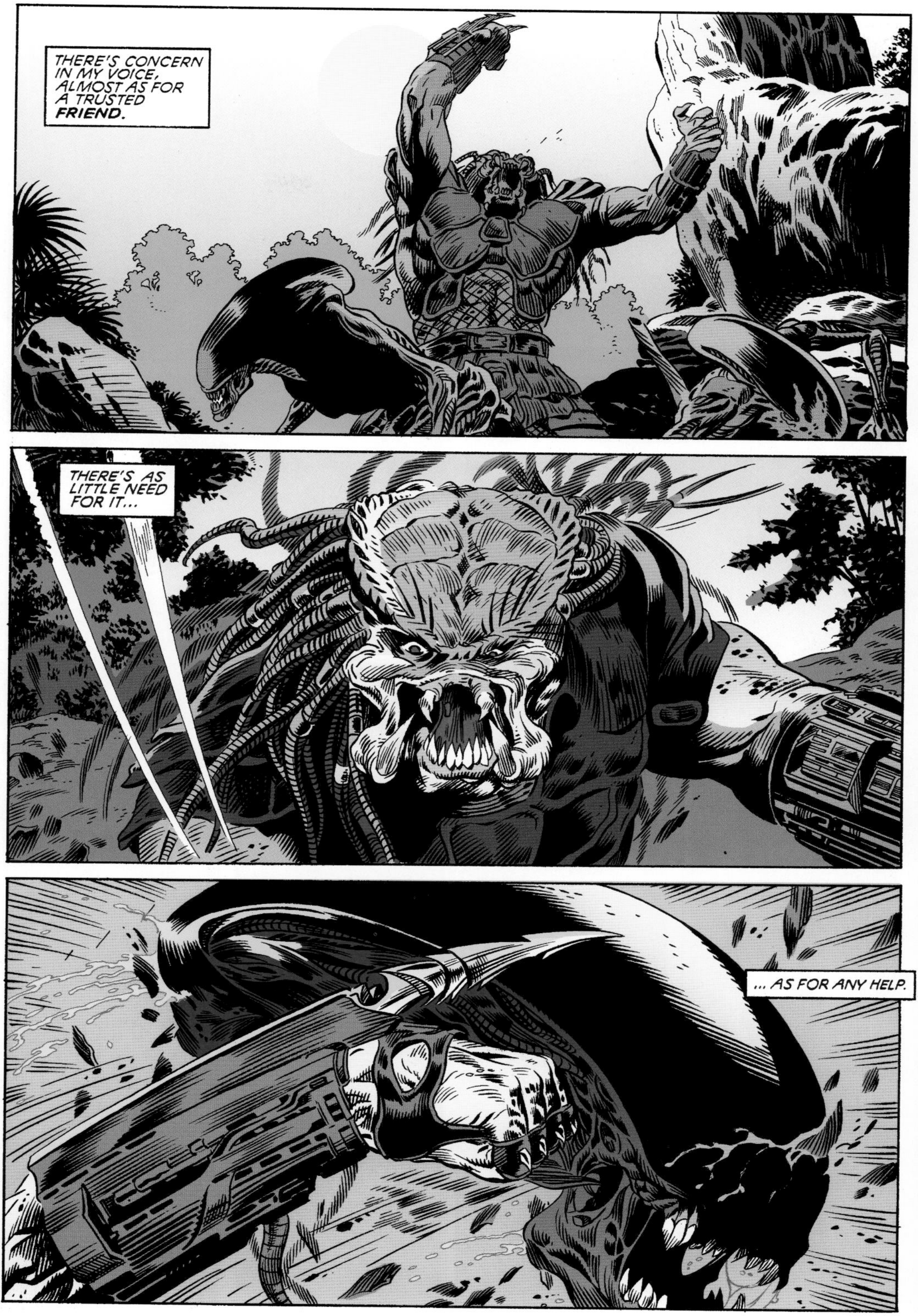
THERE'S CONCERN IN MY VOICE, ALMOST AS FOR A TRUSTED **FRIEND.**
THERE'S AS LITTLE NEED FOR IT...
...AS FOR ANY HELP.

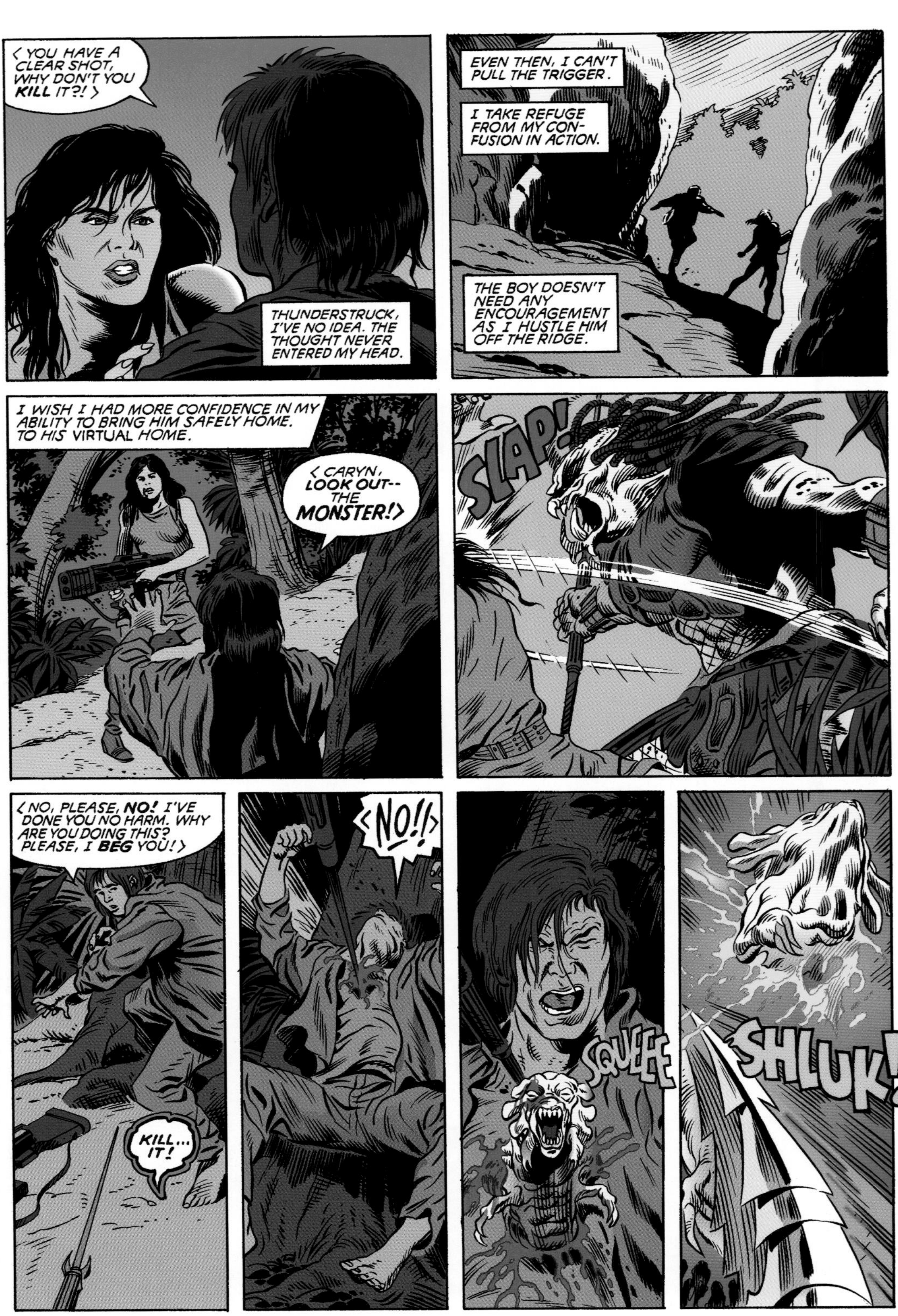

< YOU HAVE A CLEAR SHOT, WHY DON'T YOU KILL IT?! >
THUNDERSTRUCK, I'VE NO IDEA. THE THOUGHT NEVER ENTERED MY HEAD.
EVEN THEN, I CAN'T PULL THE TRIGGER.
I TAKE REFUGE FROM MY CONFUSION IN ACTION.
THE BOY DOESN'T NEED ANY ENCOURAGEMENT AS I HUSTLE HIM OFF THE RIDGE.
I WISH I HAD MORE CONFIDENCE IN MY ABILITY TO BRING HIM SAFELY HOME. TO HIS VIRTUAL HOME.
< CARYN, LOOK OUT-- THE MONSTER!>
SLAP!
< NO, PLEASE, NO! I'VE DONE YOU NO HARM. WHY ARE YOU DOING THIS? PLEASE, I BEG YOU! >
KILL... IT!
<NO!!>
SQUEEEE
SHLUK!

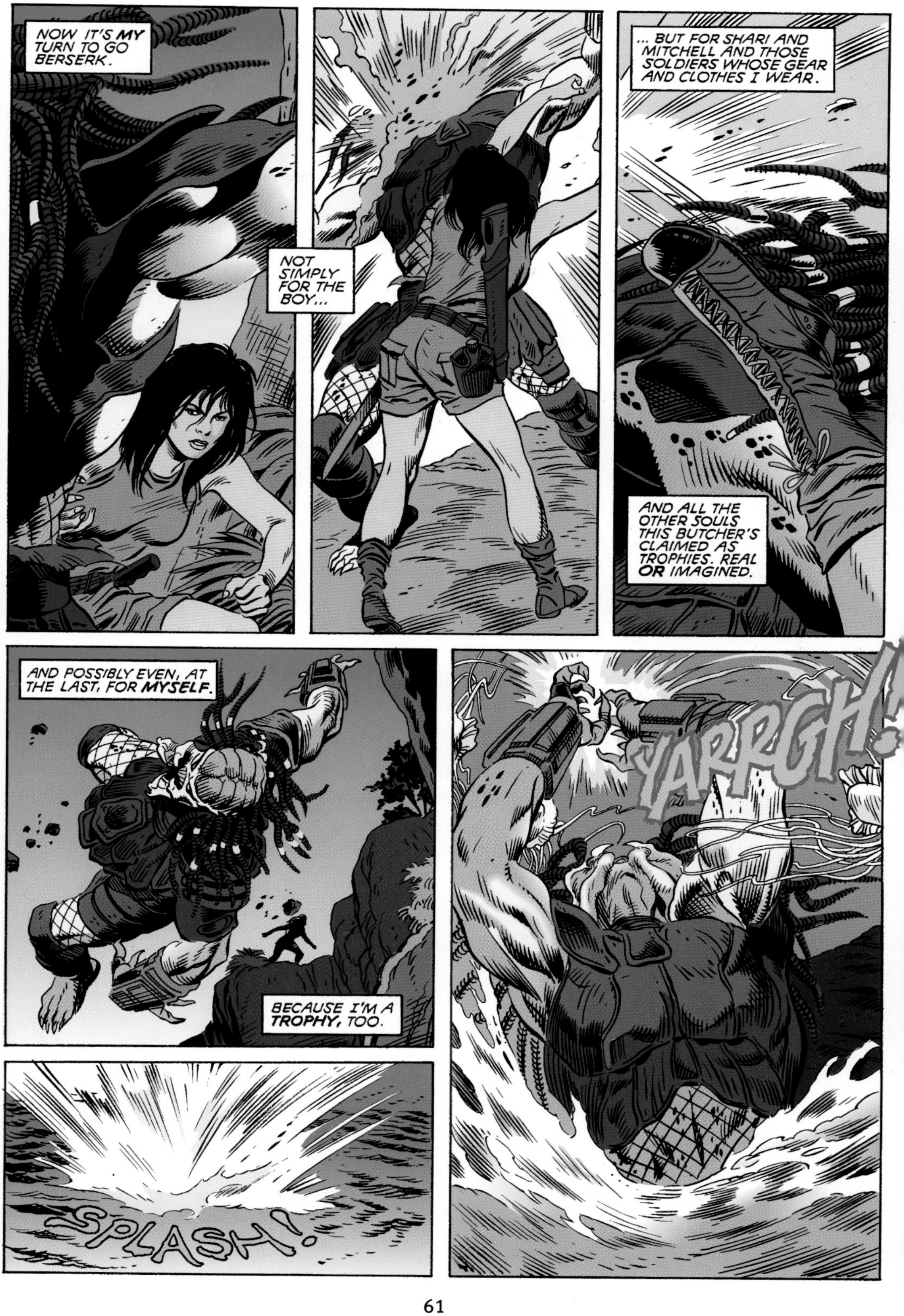
NOW IT'S **MY** TURN TO GO BERSERK.
NOT SIMPLY FOR THE BOY...
... BUT FOR SHARI AND MITCHELL AND THOSE SOLDIERS WHOSE GEAR AND CLOTHES I WEAR.
AND ALL THE OTHER SOULS THIS BUTCHER'S CLAIMED AS TROPHIES. REAL **OR** IMAGINED.
AND POSSIBLY EVEN, AT THE LAST, FOR **MYSELF**.
BECAUSE I'M A **TROPHY**, TOO.
YARRGH!
SPLASH!

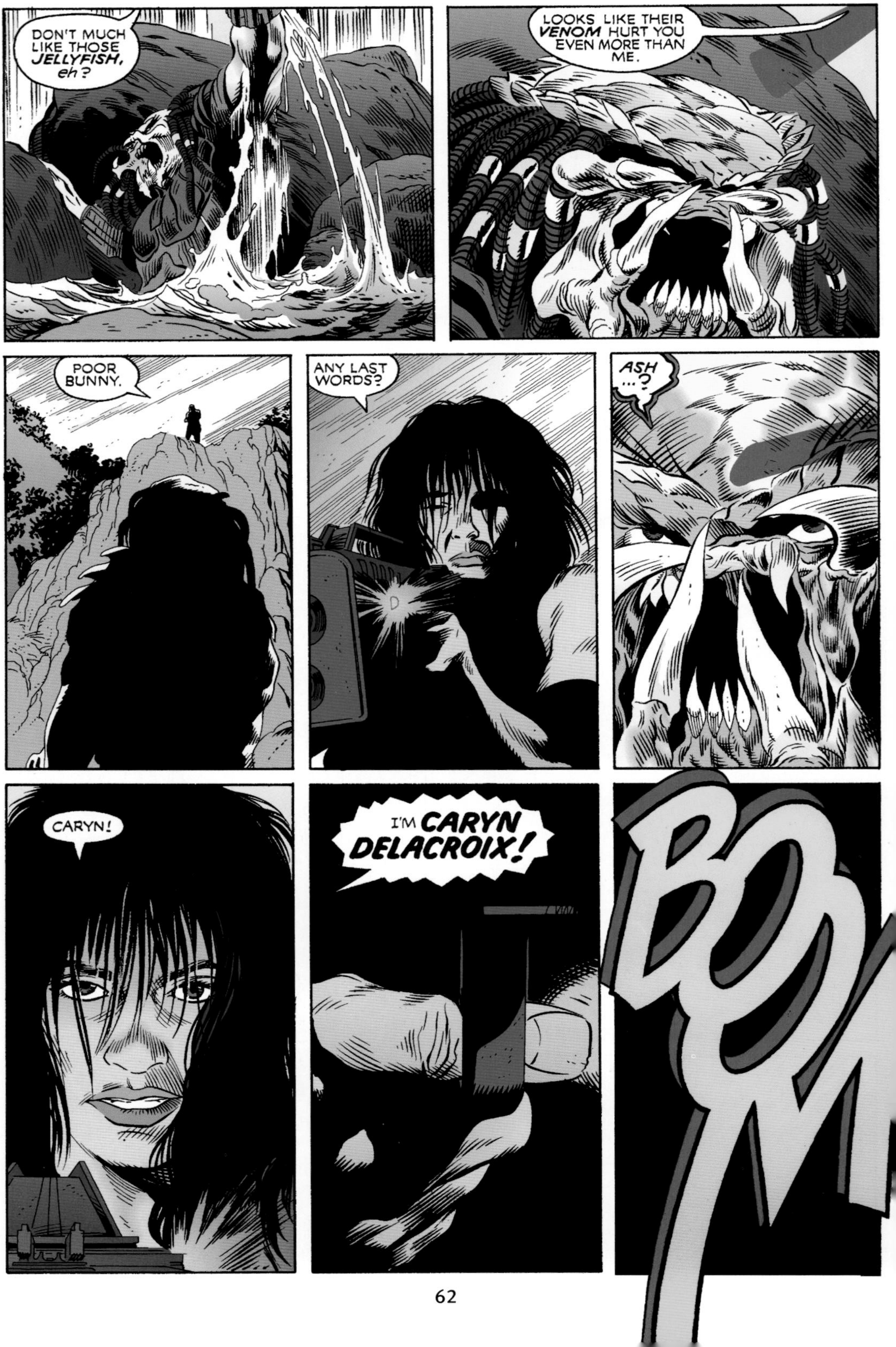
DON'T MUCH LIKE THOSE JELLYFISH, eh?
LOOKS LIKE THEIR VENOM HURT YOU EVEN MORE THAN ME.
POOR BUNNY.
ANY LAST WORDS?
ASH ...?
CARYN!
I'M CARYN DELACROIX!
BOOM

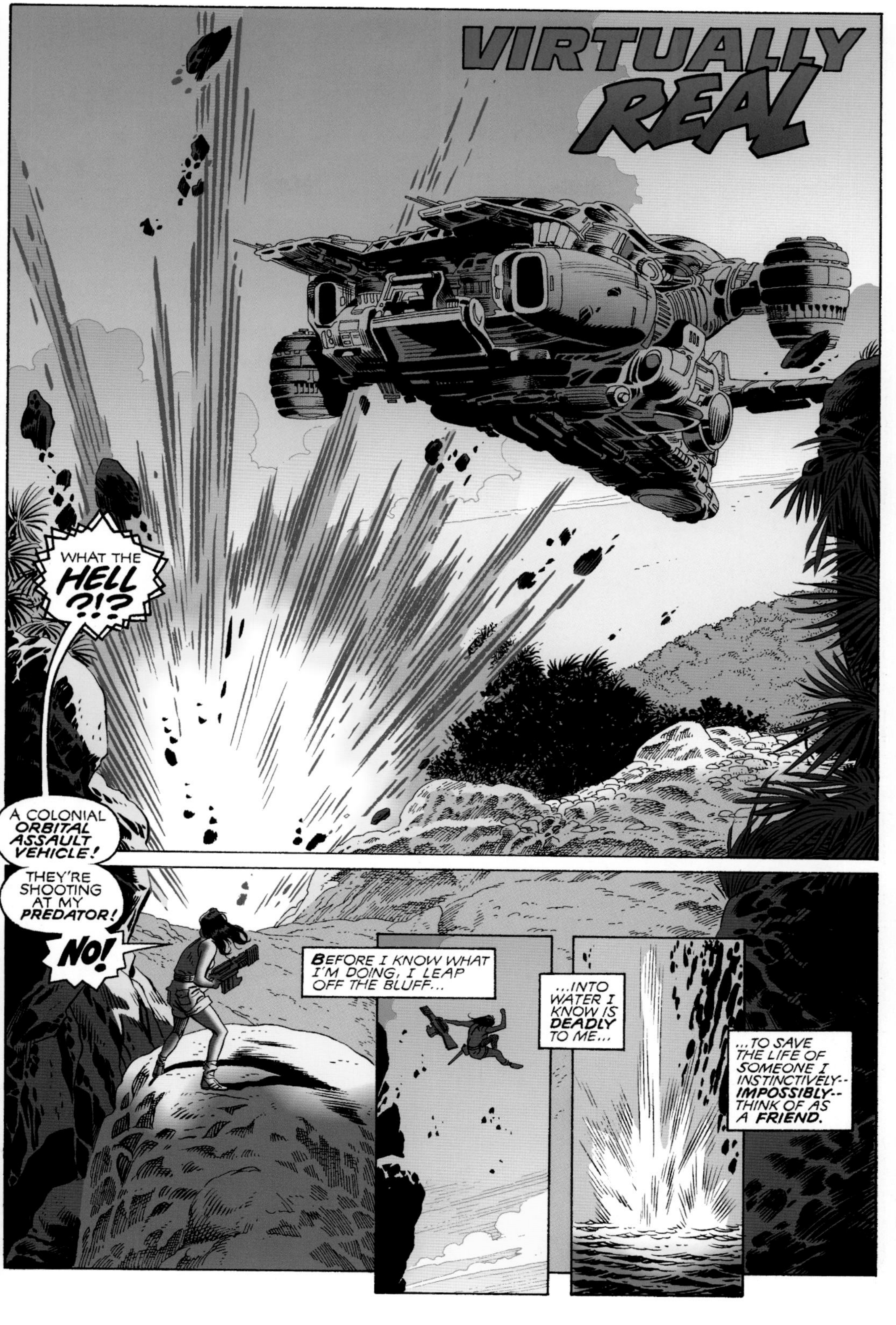
VIRTUALLY REAL
WHAT THE HELL ?!?
A COLONIAL ORBITAL ASSAULT VEHICLE!
THEY'RE SHOOTING AT MY PREDATOR!
NO!
BEFORE I KNOW WHAT I'M DOING, I LEAP OFF THE BLUFF...
...INTO WATER I KNOW IS DEADLY TO ME...
...TO SAVE THE LIFE OF SOMEONE I INSTINCTIVELY-- IMPOSSIBLY-- THINK OF AS A FRIEND.

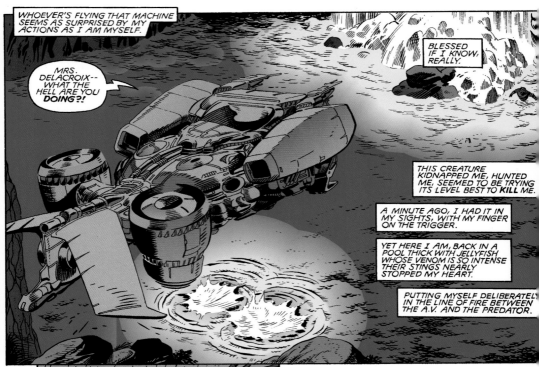

WHOEVER'S FLYING THAT MACHINE SEEMS AS SURPRISED BY MY ACTIONS AS I AM MYSELF.

MRS. DELACROIX-- WHAT THE HELL ARE YOU *DOING?!*

BLESSED IF I KNOW, REALLY.

THIS CREATURE KIDNAPPED ME, HUNTED ME, SEEMED TO BE TRYING ITS LEVEL BEST TO *KILL* ME.

A MINUTE AGO, I HAD IT IN MY SIGHTS, WITH MY FINGER ON THE TRIGGER.

YET HERE I AM, BACK IN A POOL THICK WITH JELLYFISH WHOSE VENOM IS SO INTENSE THEIR STINGS NEARLY STOPPED MY HEART.

PUTTING MYSELF DELIBERATEL IN THE LINE OF FIRE BETWEEN THE A.V. AND THE PREDATOR.

...BUT NOT QUITE DESPERATE ENOUGH.

SHOK!

I FIGURE I'M HISTORY.

ASH... PARNALL?

ASH PARNA

IT SOUND ALMOST *HAPPY.*

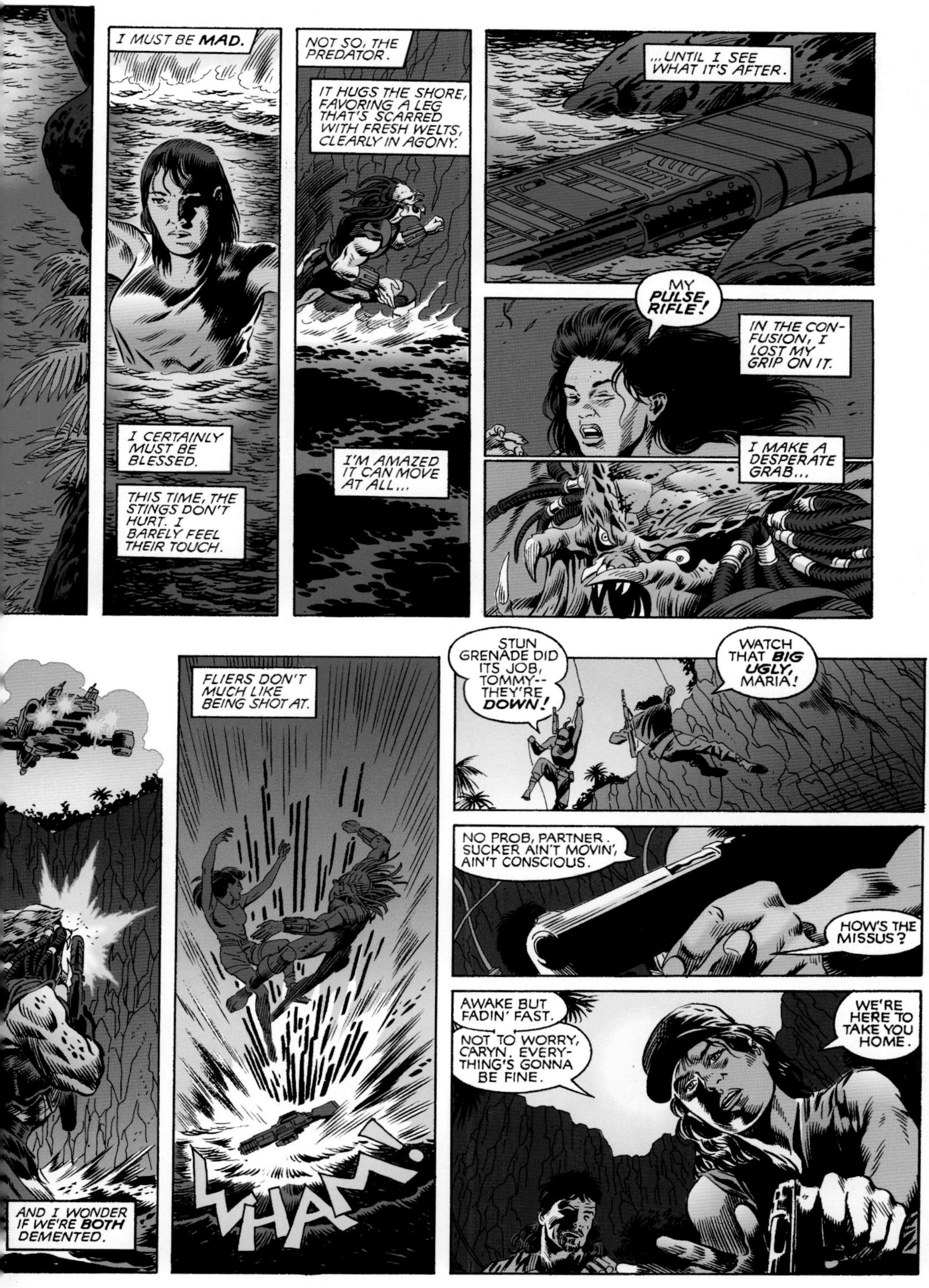
I MUST BE MAD.
I CERTAINLY MUST BE BLESSED.
THIS TIME, THE STINGS DON'T HURT. I BARELY FEEL THEIR TOUCH.
NOT SO, THE PREDATOR.
IT HUGS THE SHORE, FAVORING A LEG THAT'S SCARRED WITH FRESH WELTS, CLEARLY IN AGONY.
I'M AMAZED IT CAN MOVE AT ALL...
...UNTIL I SEE WHAT IT'S AFTER.
MY PULSE RIFLE!
IN THE CONFUSION, I LOST MY GRIP ON IT.
I MAKE A DESPERATE GRAB...
AND I WONDER IF WE'RE BOTH DEMENTED.
FLIERS DON'T MUCH LIKE BEING SHOT AT.
WHAM!
STUN GRENADE DID ITS JOB, TOMMY-- THEY'RE DOWN!
WATCH THAT BIG UGLY, MARIA!
NO PROB, PARTNER. SUCKER AIN'T MOVIN', AIN'T CONSCIOUS.
HOW'S THE MISSUS?
AWAKE BUT FADIN' FAST.
NOT TO WORRY, CARYN. EVERYTHING'S GONNA BE FINE.
WE'RE HERE TO TAKE YOU HOME.

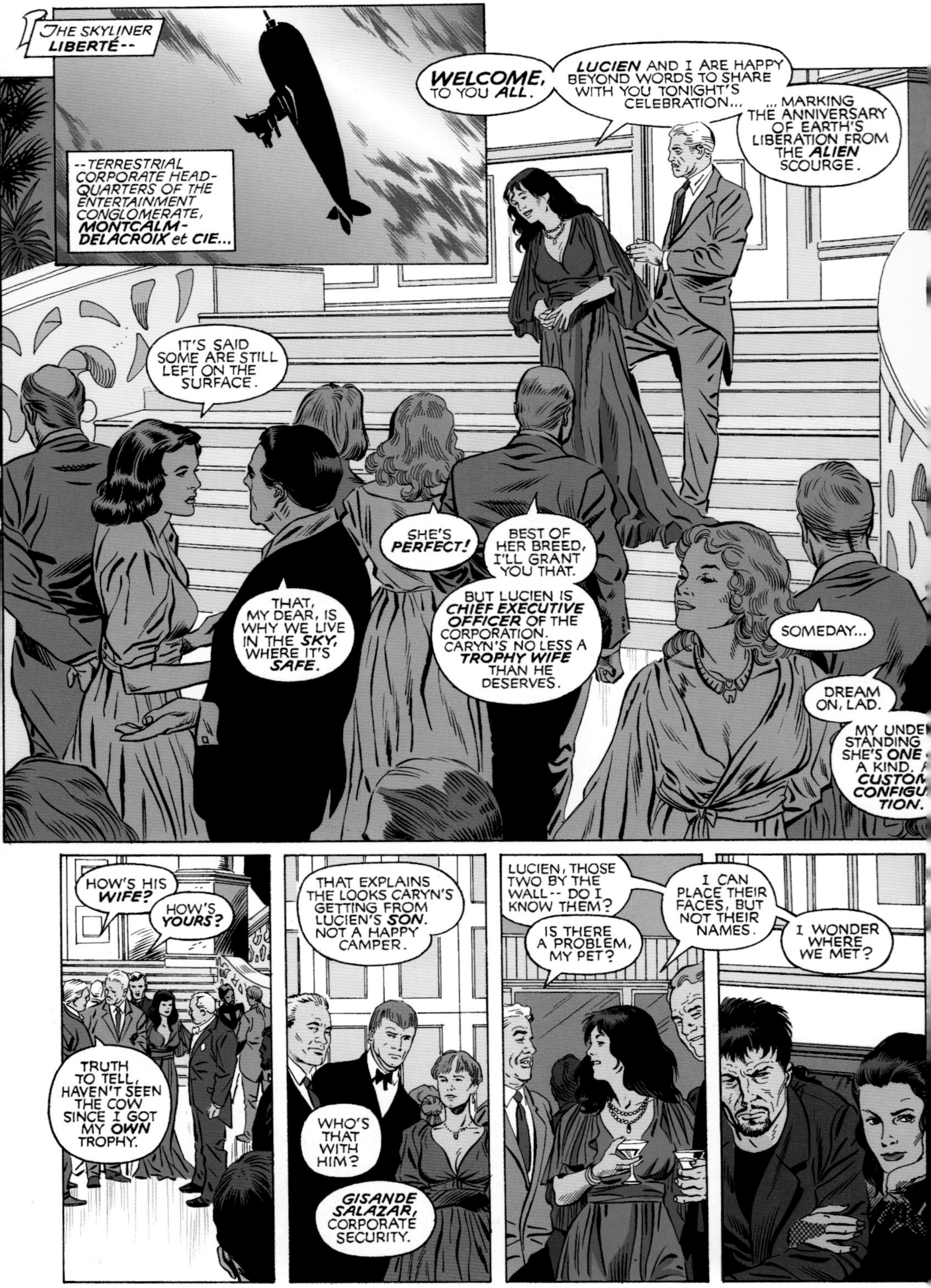
THE SKYLINER LIBERTÉ--
--TERRESTRIAL CORPORATE HEAD-QUARTERS OF THE ENTERTAINMENT CONGLOMERATE, MONTCALM-DELACROIX et CIE...
WELCOME, TO YOU ALL.
LUCIEN AND I ARE HAPPY BEYOND WORDS TO SHARE WITH YOU TONIGHT'S CELEBRATION...
...MARKING THE ANNIVERSARY OF EARTH'S LIBERATION FROM THE ALIEN SCOURGE.
IT'S SAID SOME ARE STILL LEFT ON THE SURFACE.
THAT, MY DEAR, IS WHY WE LIVE IN THE SKY, WHERE IT'S SAFE.
SHE'S PERFECT!
BEST OF HER BREED, I'LL GRANT YOU THAT.
BUT LUCIEN IS CHIEF EXECUTIVE OFFICER OF THE CORPORATION. CARYN'S NO LESS A TROPHY WIFE THAN HE DESERVES.
SOMEDAY...
DREAM ON, LAD.
MY UNDE STANDING SHE'S ONE A KIND. CUSTOM CONFIGU TION.
HOW'S HIS WIFE?
HOW'S YOURS?
TRUTH TO TELL, HAVEN'T SEEN THE COW SINCE I GOT MY OWN TROPHY.
THAT EXPLAINS THE LOOKS CARYN'S GETTING FROM LUCIEN'S SON. NOT A HAPPY CAMPER.
WHO'S THAT WITH HIM?
GISANDE SALAZAR, CORPORATE SECURITY.
LUCIEN, THOSE TWO BY THE WALL-- DO I KNOW THEM?
IS THERE A PROBLEM, MY PET?
I CAN PLACE THEIR FACES, BUT NOT THEIR NAMES.
I WONDER WHERE WE MET?

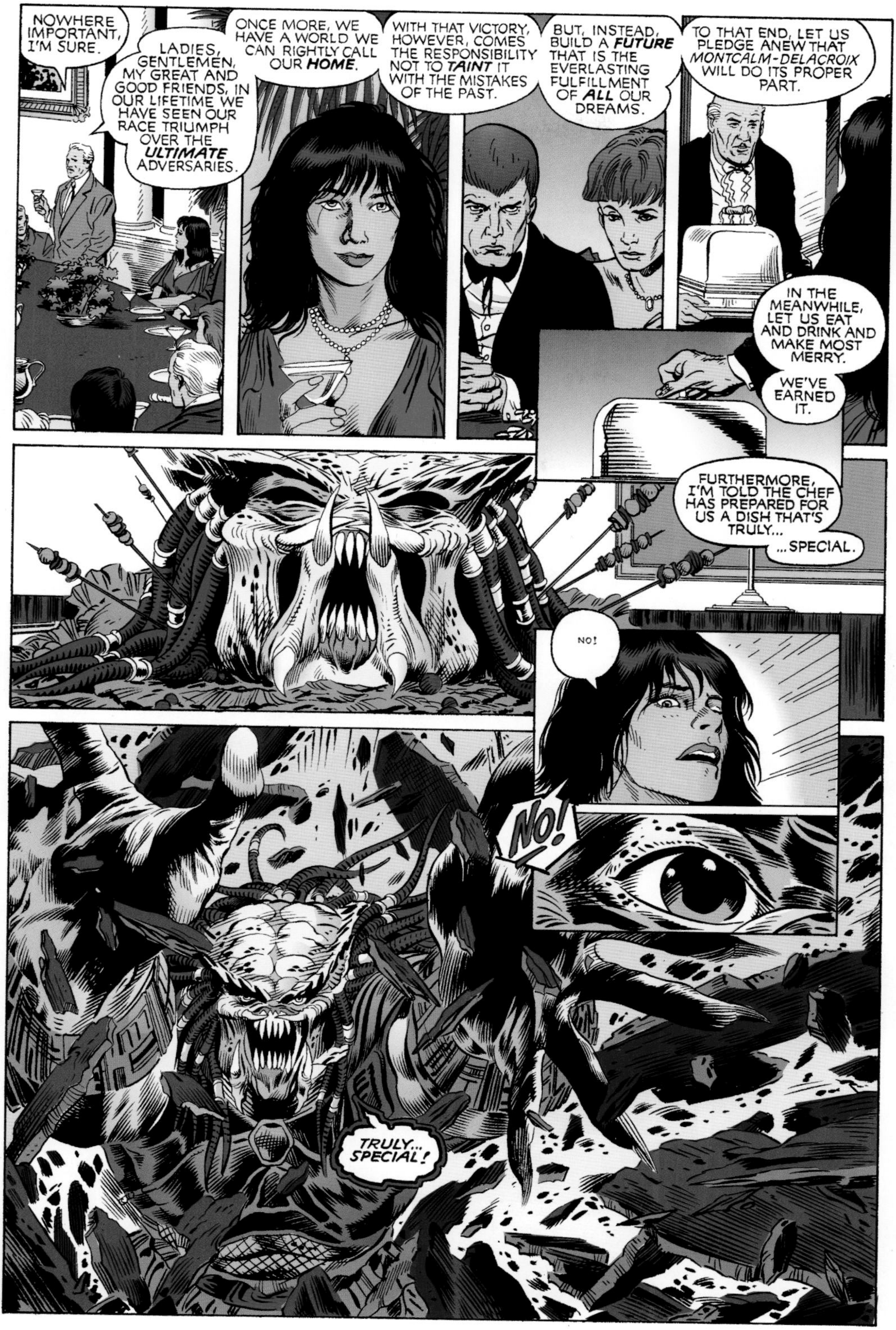
NOWHERE IMPORTANT, I'M SURE.
LADIES, GENTLEMEN, MY GREAT AND GOOD FRIENDS, IN OUR LIFETIME WE HAVE SEEN OUR RACE TRIUMPH OVER THE ULTIMATE ADVERSARIES.
ONCE MORE, WE HAVE A WORLD WE CAN RIGHTLY CALL OUR HOME.
WITH THAT VICTORY, HOWEVER, COMES THE RESPONSIBILITY NOT TO TAINT IT WITH THE MISTAKES OF THE PAST.
BUT, INSTEAD, BUILD A FUTURE THAT IS THE EVERLASTING FULFILLMENT OF ALL OUR DREAMS.
TO THAT END, LET US PLEDGE ANEW THAT MONTCALM-DELACROIX WILL DO ITS PROPER PART.
IN THE MEANWHILE, LET US EAT AND DRINK AND MAKE MOST MERRY.
WE'VE EARNED IT.
FURTHERMORE, I'M TOLD THE CHEF HAS PREPARED FOR US A DISH THAT'S TRULY...
...SPECIAL.
NO!
NO!
TRULY... SPECIAL!

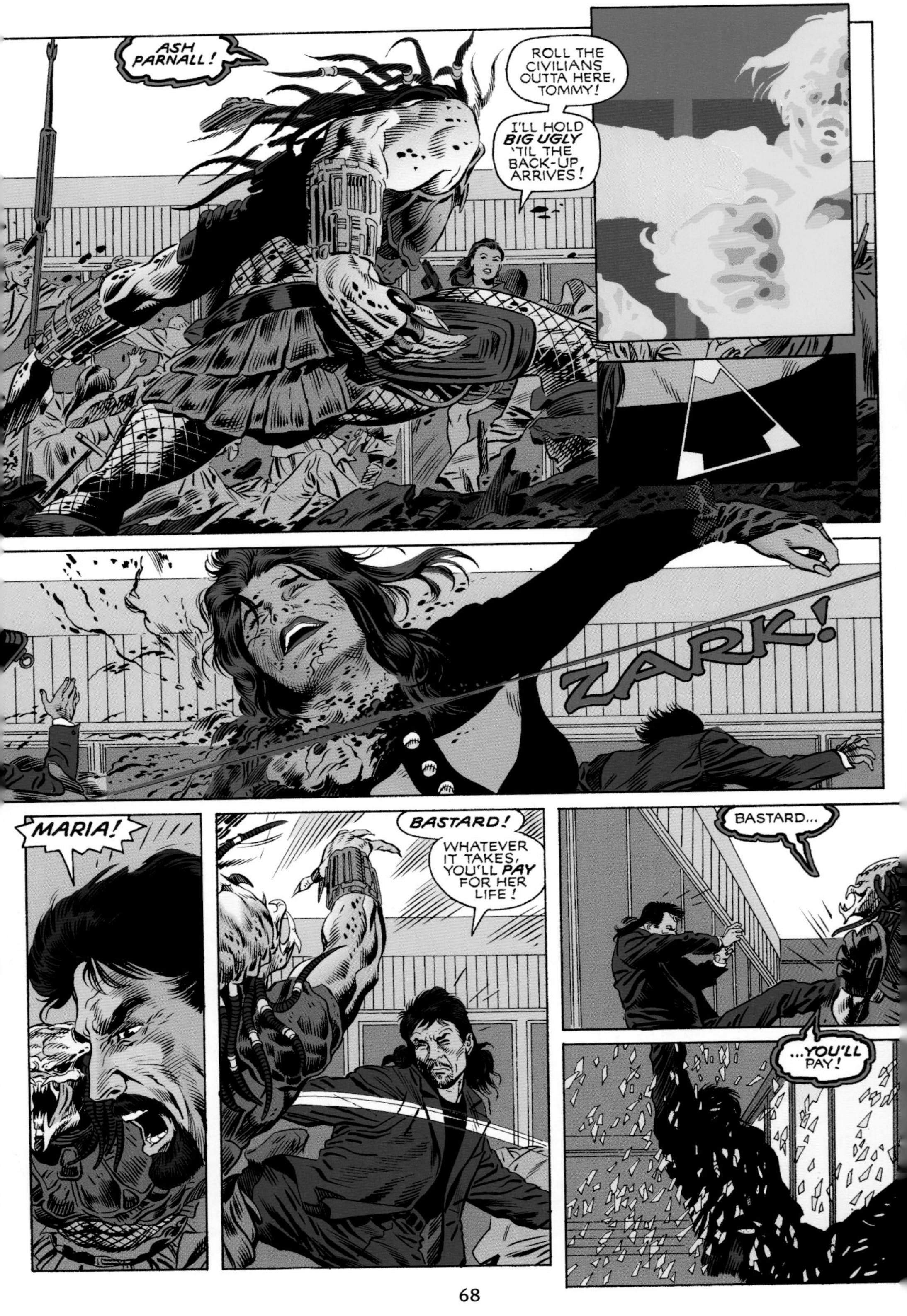
ASH PARNALL!
ROLL THE CIVILIANS OUTTA HERE, TOMMY!
I'LL HOLD BIG UGLY 'TIL THE BACK-UP ARRIVES!
ZARK!
MARIA!
BASTARD!
WHATEVER IT TAKES, YOU'LL PAY FOR HER LIFE!
BASTARD...
...YOU'LL PAY!

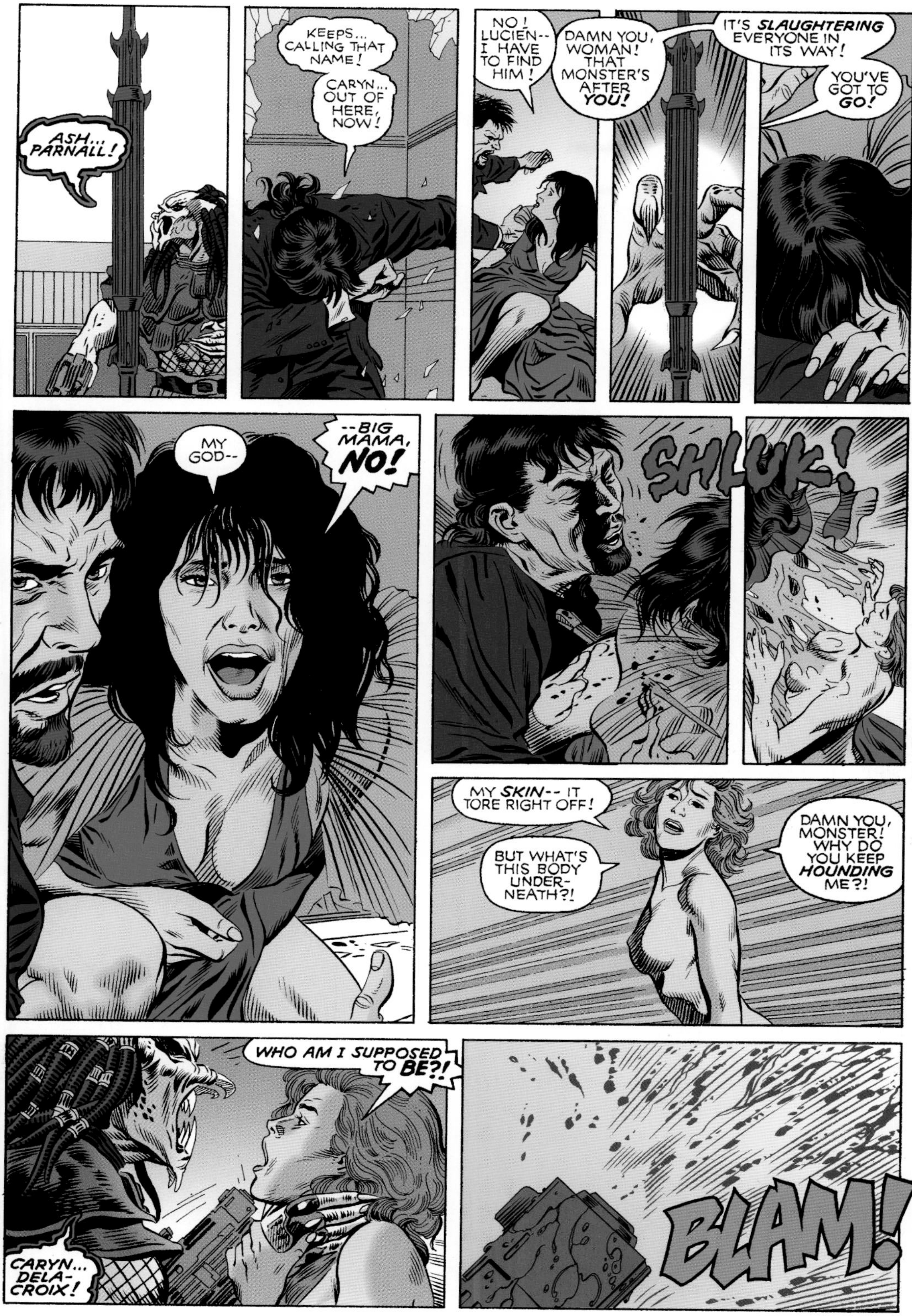

ASH... PARNALL!
KEEPS... CALLING THAT NAME!
CARYN... OUT OF HERE, NOW!
NO! LUCIEN-- I HAVE TO FIND HIM!
DAMN YOU, WOMAN! THAT MONSTER'S AFTER YOU!
IT'S SLAUGHTERING EVERYONE IN ITS WAY!
YOU'VE GOT TO GO!
MY GOD--
--BIG MAMA, NO!
SHLUK!
MY SKIN-- IT TORE RIGHT OFF!
BUT WHAT'S THIS BODY UNDER-NEATH?!
DAMN YOU, MONSTER! WHY DO YOU KEEP HOUNDING ME?!
WHO AM I SUPPOSED TO BE?!
CARYN... DELA-CROIX!
BLAM!

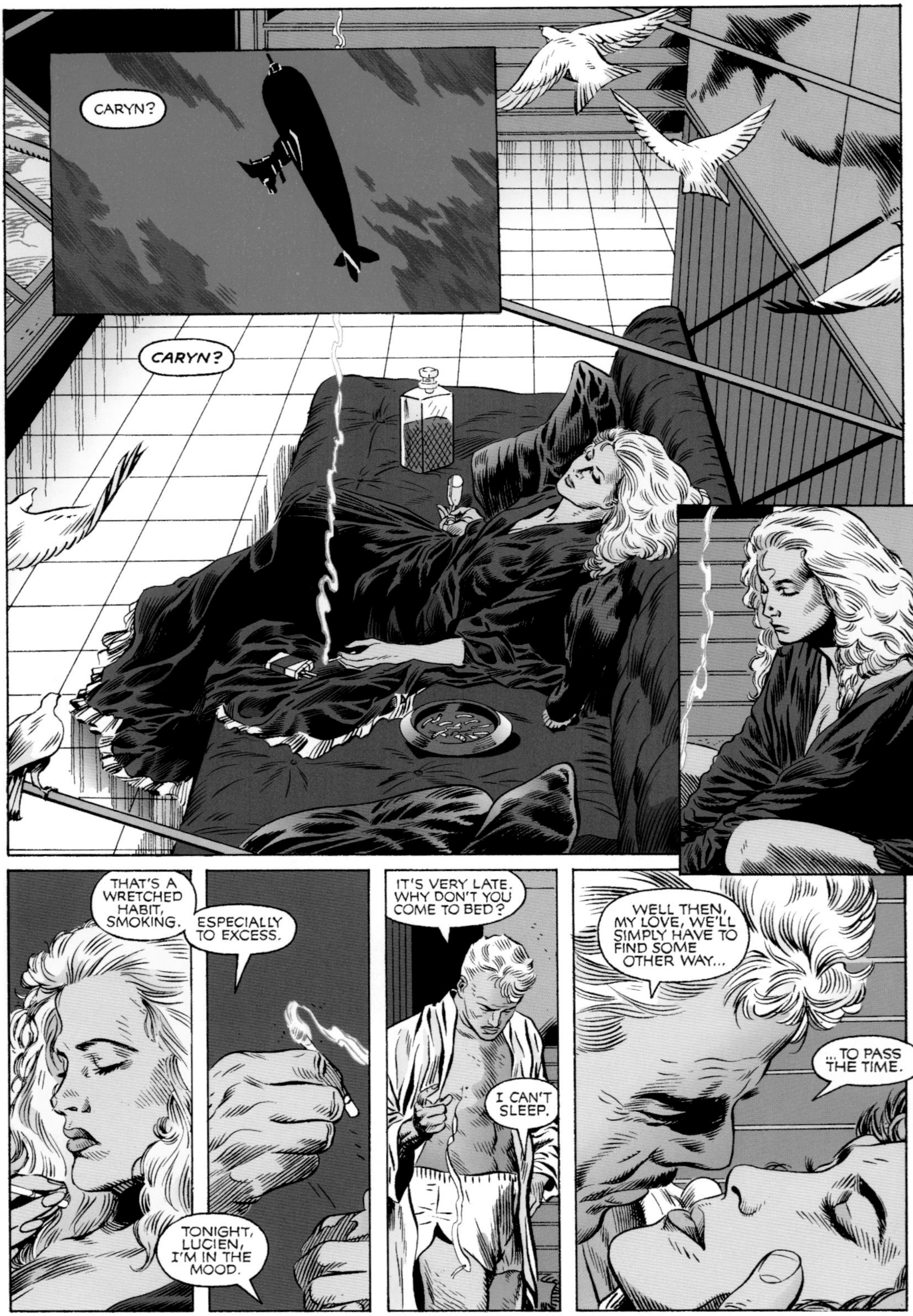
CARYN?
CARYN?
THAT'S A WRETCHED HABIT, SMOKING.
ESPECIALLY TO EXCESS.
TONIGHT, LUCIEN, I'M IN THE MOOD.
IT'S VERY LATE. WHY DON'T YOU COME TO BED?
I CAN'T SLEEP.
WELL THEN, MY LOVE, WE'LL SIMPLY HAVE TO FIND SOME OTHER WAY...
...TO PASS THE TIME.

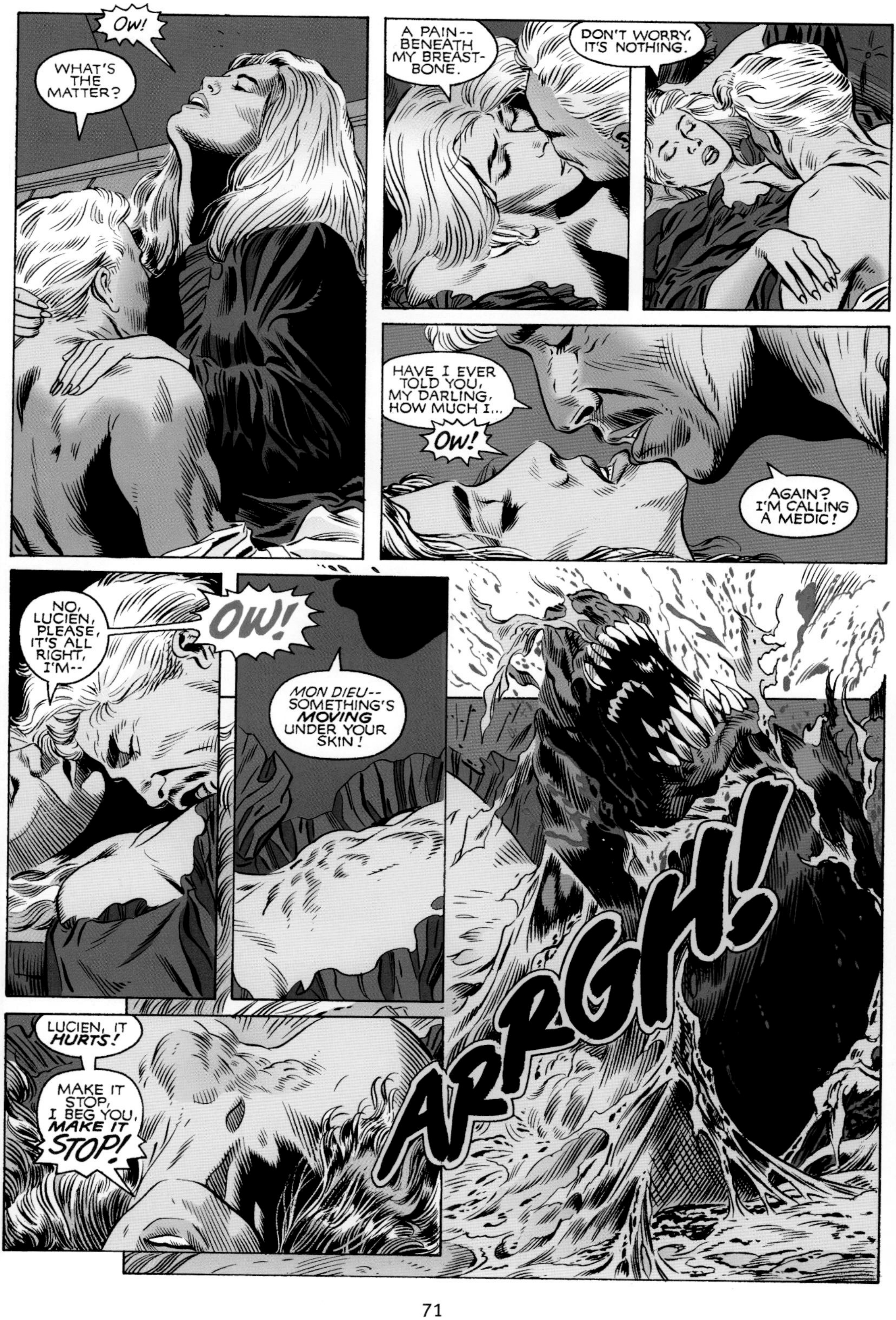
OW!
WHAT'S THE MATTER?
A PAIN-- BENEATH MY BREAST-BONE.
DON'T WORRY, IT'S NOTHING.
HAVE I EVER TOLD YOU, MY DARLING, HOW MUCH I...
OW!
AGAIN? I'M CALLING A MEDIC!
NO, LUCIEN, PLEASE, IT'S ALL RIGHT, I'M--
OW!
MON DIEU-- SOMETHING'S MOVING UNDER YOUR SKIN!
LUCIEN, IT HURTS!
MAKE IT STOP, I BEG YOU, MAKE IT STOP!
ARRGH!

THIS WASN'T PART OF THE DEAL, MARIA.

WE DID WHAT WAS ASKED, WE GET A FEW DAYS TO LIVE THE HIGH LIFE, NO QUESTIONS, NO GRIEF.

SO WHAT'S THE PROB, TOMMY?

THEY GOT A POOL, I WANT TO SWIM-- Q.E.D.

GIVE IT A REST, WHY DON'TCHA, B'FORE YOU TURN INTO SOME WHINY LITTLE RANDOM!

IT'S NONE OF OUR CONCERN THAT CARYN DELACROIX HAS BAD DREAMS. HELL, AFTER WHAT SHE'S BEEN THROUGH, WHO WOULDN'T?

HAVE A LITTLE FAITH, SHIROW, WILLYA? I KNOW WHAT I'M DOING.

FAMOUS LAST WORDS, DeMEDICI!

UP YOURS!

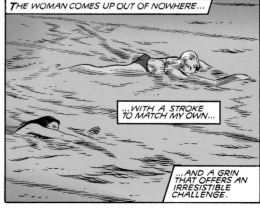

THE WOMAN COMES UP OUT OF NOWHERE...

...WITH A STROKE TO MATCH MY OWN...

...AND A GRIN THAT OFFERS AN IRRESISTIBLE CHALLENGE.

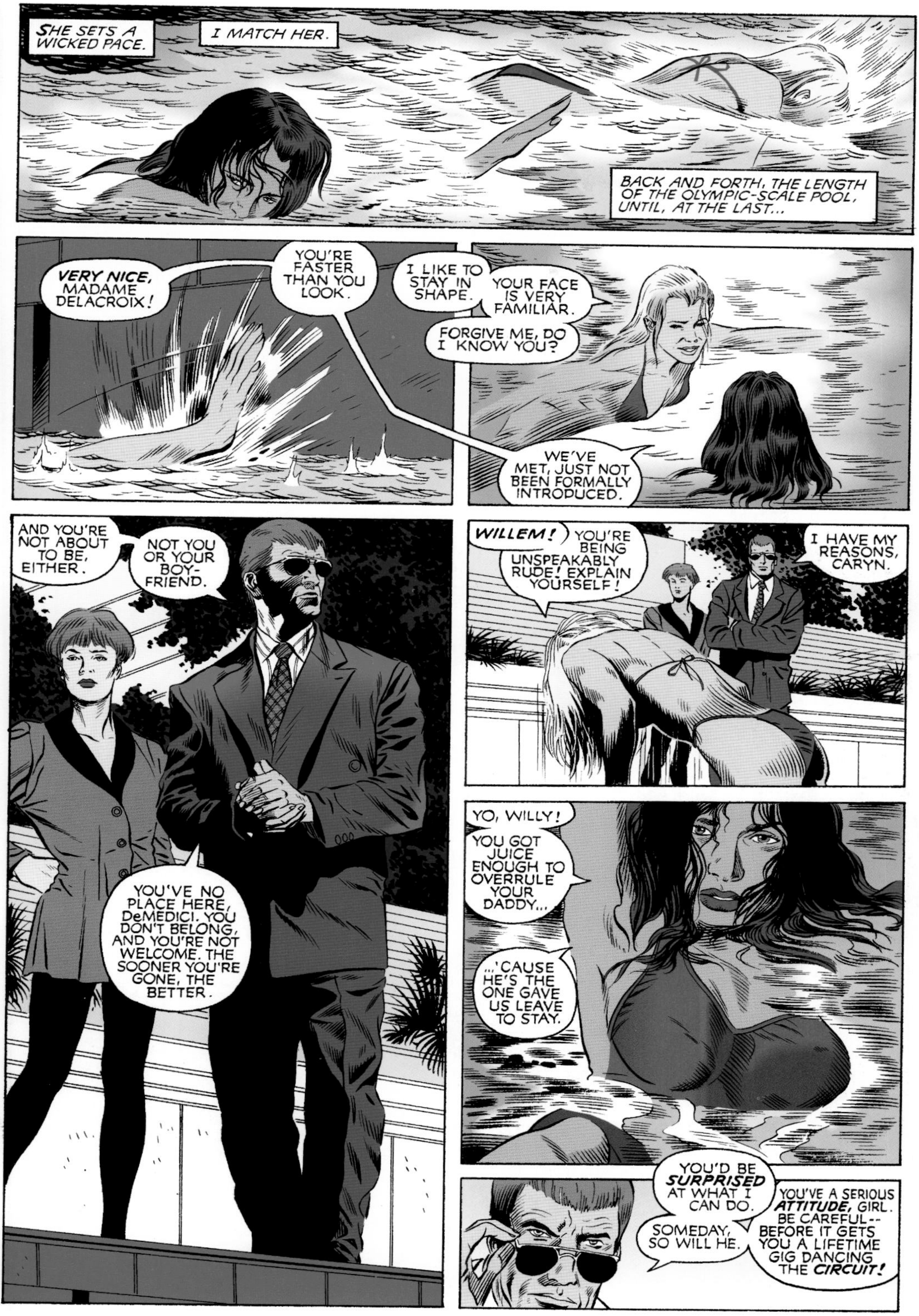
SHE SETS A WICKED PACE.
I MATCH HER.
BACK AND FORTH, THE LENGTH OF THE OLYMPIC-SCALE POOL, UNTIL, AT THE LAST...
VERY NICE, MADAME DELACROIX!
YOU'RE FASTER THAN YOU LOOK.
I LIKE TO STAY IN SHAPE.
YOUR FACE IS VERY FAMILIAR.
FORGIVE ME, DO I KNOW YOU?
WE'VE MET, JUST NOT BEEN FORMALLY INTRODUCED.
AND YOU'RE NOT ABOUT TO BE, EITHER.
NOT YOU OR YOUR BOY-FRIEND.
YOU'VE NO PLACE HERE, DeMEDICI. YOU DON'T BELONG, AND YOU'RE NOT WELCOME. THE SOONER YOU'RE GONE, THE BETTER.
WILLEM!
YOU'RE BEING UNSPEAKABLY RUDE! EXPLAIN YOURSELF!
I HAVE MY REASONS, CARYN.
YO, WILLY!
YOU GOT JUICE ENOUGH TO OVERRULE YOUR DADDY...
...'CAUSE HE'S THE ONE GAVE US LEAVE TO STAY.
YOU'D BE SURPRISED AT WHAT I CAN DO.
SOMEDAY, SO WILL HE.
YOU'VE A SERIOUS ATTITUDE, GIRL. BE CAREFUL-- BEFORE IT GETS YOU A LIFETIME GIG DANCING THE CIRCUIT!

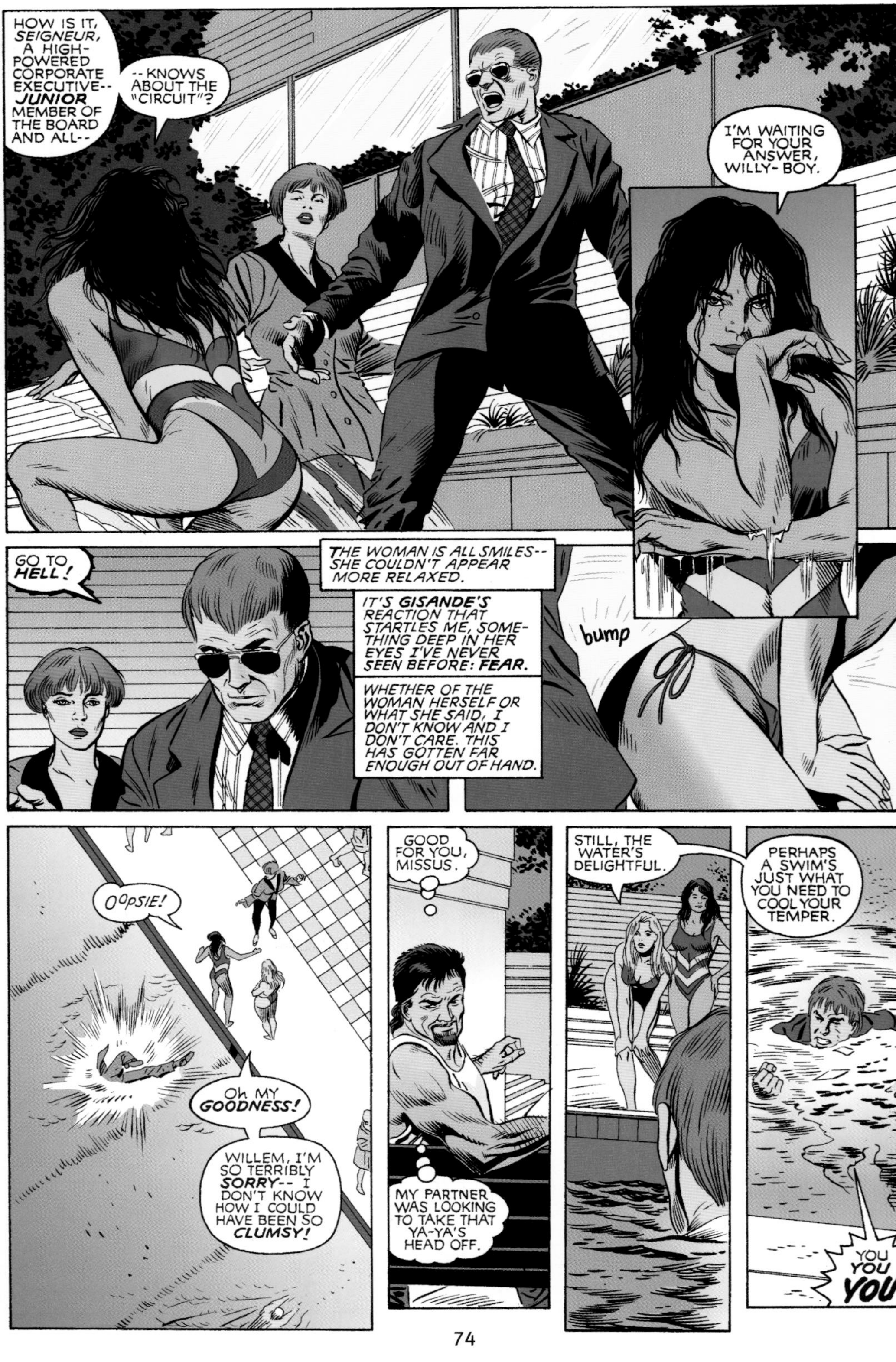
HOW IS IT, SEIGNEUR, A HIGH-POWERED CORPORATE EXECUTIVE-- JUNIOR MEMBER OF THE BOARD AND ALL--
--KNOWS ABOUT THE "CIRCUIT"?
I'M WAITING FOR YOUR ANSWER, WILLY-BOY.
GO TO HELL!
THE WOMAN IS ALL SMILES-- SHE COULDN'T APPEAR MORE RELAXED.
IT'S GISANDE'S REACTION THAT STARTLES ME, SOMETHING DEEP IN HER EYES I'VE NEVER SEEN BEFORE: FEAR.
WHETHER OF THE WOMAN HERSELF OR WHAT SHE SAID, I DON'T KNOW AND I DON'T CARE. THIS HAS GOTTEN FAR ENOUGH OUT OF HAND.
bump
OOPSIE!
OH MY GOODNESS!
WILLEM, I'M SO TERRIBLY SORRY-- I DON'T KNOW HOW I COULD HAVE BEEN SO CLUMSY!
GOOD FOR YOU, MISSUS.
MY PARTNER WAS LOOKING TO TAKE THAT YA-YA'S HEAD OFF.
STILL, THE WATER'S DELIGHTFUL.
PERHAPS A SWIM'S JUST WHAT YOU NEED TO COOL YOUR TEMPER.
YOU YOU YOU

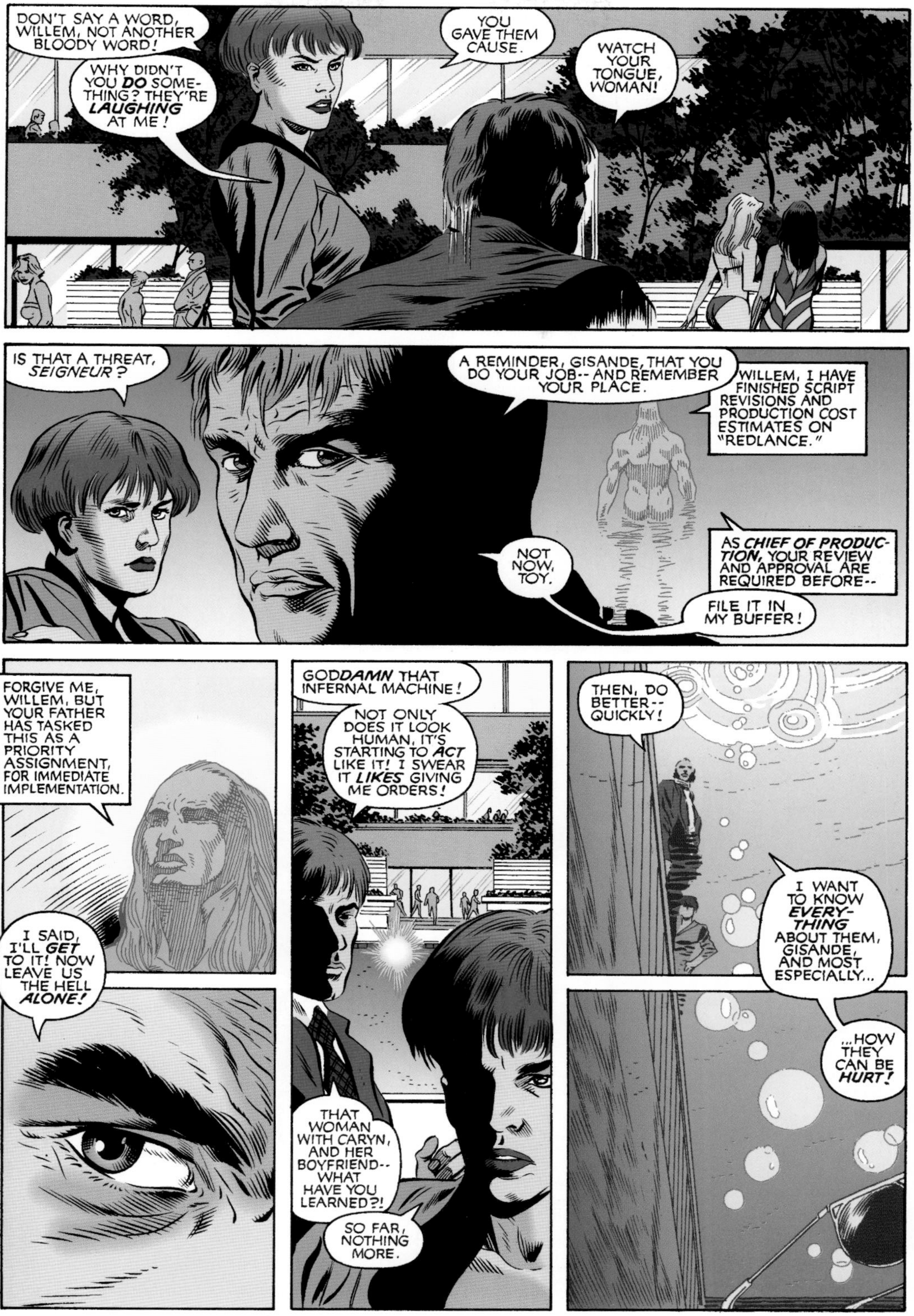
DON'T SAY A WORD, WILLEM, NOT ANOTHER BLOODY WORD!
WHY DIDN'T YOU DO SOME-THING? THEY'RE LAUGHING AT ME!
YOU GAVE THEM CAUSE.
WATCH YOUR TONGUE, WOMAN!
IS THAT A THREAT, SEIGNEUR?
A REMINDER, GISANDE, THAT YOU DO YOUR JOB-- AND REMEMBER YOUR PLACE.
WILLEM, I HAVE FINISHED SCRIPT REVISIONS AND PRODUCTION COST ESTIMATES ON "REDLANCE."
AS CHIEF OF PRODUCTION, YOUR REVIEW AND APPROVAL ARE REQUIRED BEFORE--
NOT NOW, TOY.
FILE IT IN MY BUFFER!
FORGIVE ME, WILLEM, BUT YOUR FATHER HAS TASKED THIS AS A PRIORITY ASSIGNMENT, FOR IMMEDIATE IMPLEMENTATION.
I SAID, I'LL GET TO IT! NOW LEAVE US THE HELL ALONE!
GODDAMN THAT INFERNAL MACHINE!
NOT ONLY DOES IT LOOK HUMAN, IT'S STARTING TO ACT LIKE IT! I SWEAR IT LIKES GIVING ME ORDERS!
THAT WOMAN WITH CARYN, AND HER BOYFRIEND-- WHAT HAVE YOU LEARNED?!
SO FAR, NOTHING MORE.
THEN, DO BETTER-- QUICKLY!
I WANT TO KNOW EVERY-THING ABOUT THEM, GISANDE, AND MOST ESPECIALLY...
...HOW THEY CAN BE HURT!

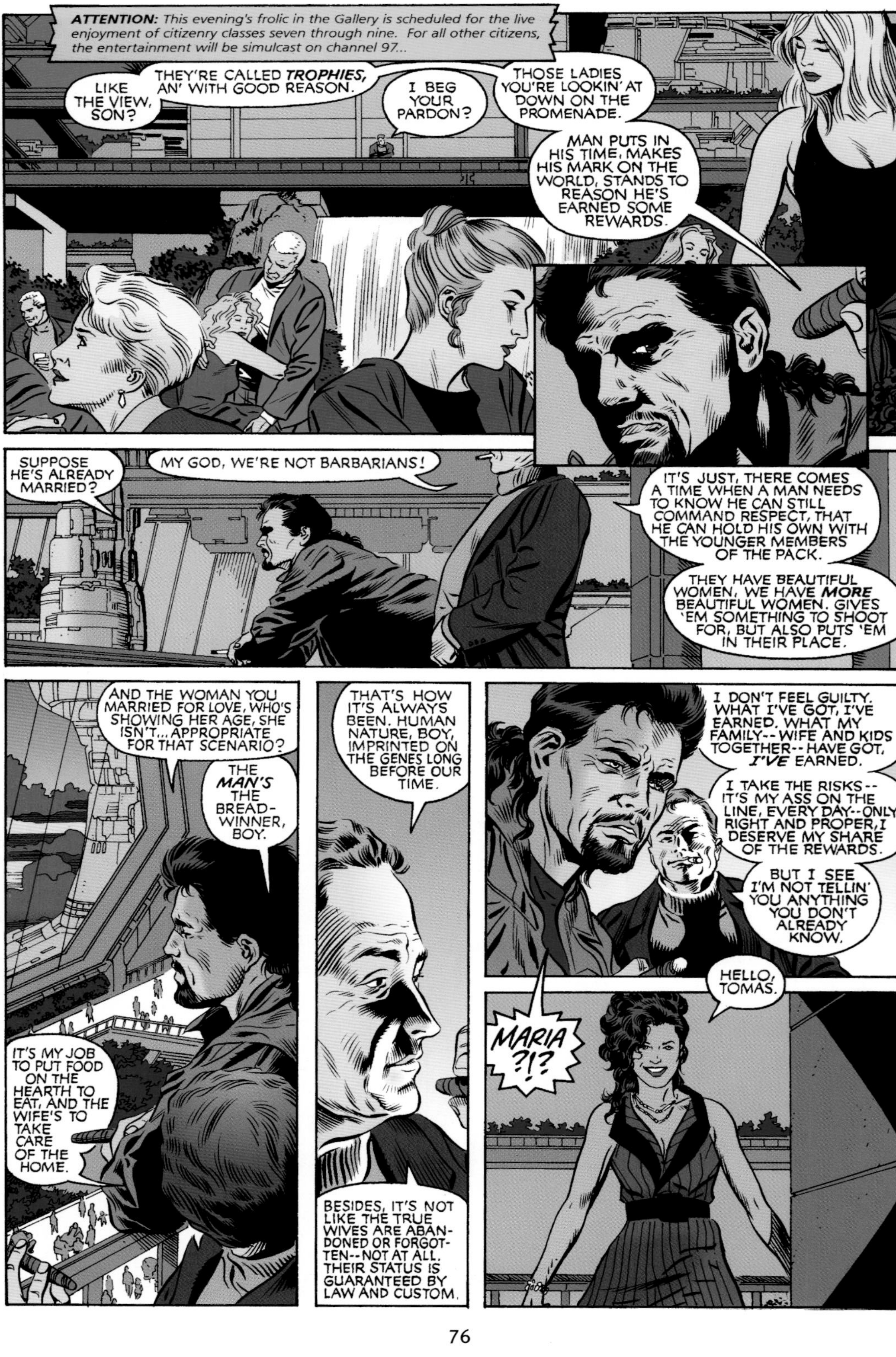
ATTENTION: This evening's frolic in the Gallery is scheduled for the live enjoyment of citizenry classes seven through nine. For all other citizens, the entertainment will be simulcast on channel 97...
LIKE THE VIEW, SON?
THEY'RE CALLED TROPHIES, AN' WITH GOOD REASON.
I BEG YOUR PARDON?
THOSE LADIES YOU'RE LOOKIN' AT DOWN ON THE PROMENADE.
MAN PUTS IN HIS TIME, MAKES HIS MARK ON THE WORLD, STANDS TO REASON HE'S EARNED SOME REWARDS.
SUPPOSE HE'S ALREADY MARRIED?
MY GOD, WE'RE NOT BARBARIANS!
IT'S JUST, THERE COMES A TIME WHEN A MAN NEEDS TO KNOW HE CAN STILL COMMAND RESPECT, THAT HE CAN HOLD HIS OWN WITH THE YOUNGER MEMBERS OF THE PACK.
THEY HAVE BEAUTIFUL WOMEN, WE HAVE MORE BEAUTIFUL WOMEN. GIVES 'EM SOMETHING TO SHOOT FOR, BUT ALSO PUTS 'EM IN THEIR PLACE.
AND THE WOMAN YOU MARRIED FOR LOVE, WHO'S SHOWING HER AGE, SHE ISN'T... APPROPRIATE FOR THAT SCENARIO?
THE MAN'S THE BREAD-WINNER, BOY.
IT'S MY JOB TO PUT FOOD ON THE HEARTH TO EAT, AND THE WIFE'S TO TAKE CARE OF THE HOME.
THAT'S HOW IT'S ALWAYS BEEN. HUMAN NATURE, BOY, IMPRINTED ON THE GENES LONG BEFORE OUR TIME.
BESIDES, IT'S NOT LIKE THE TRUE WIVES ARE ABAN-DONED OR FORGOT-TEN--NOT AT ALL. THEIR STATUS IS GUARANTEED BY LAW AND CUSTOM.
I DON'T FEEL GUILTY. WHAT I'VE GOT, I'VE EARNED. WHAT MY FAMILY-- WIFE AND KIDS TOGETHER-- HAVE GOT, I'VE EARNED.
I TAKE THE RISKS-- IT'S MY ASS ON THE LINE, EVERY DAY--ONLY RIGHT AND PROPER, I DESERVE MY SHARE OF THE REWARDS.
BUT I SEE I'M NOT TELLIN' YOU ANYTHING YOU DON'T ALREADY KNOW.
HELLO, TOMAS.
MARIA ?!?

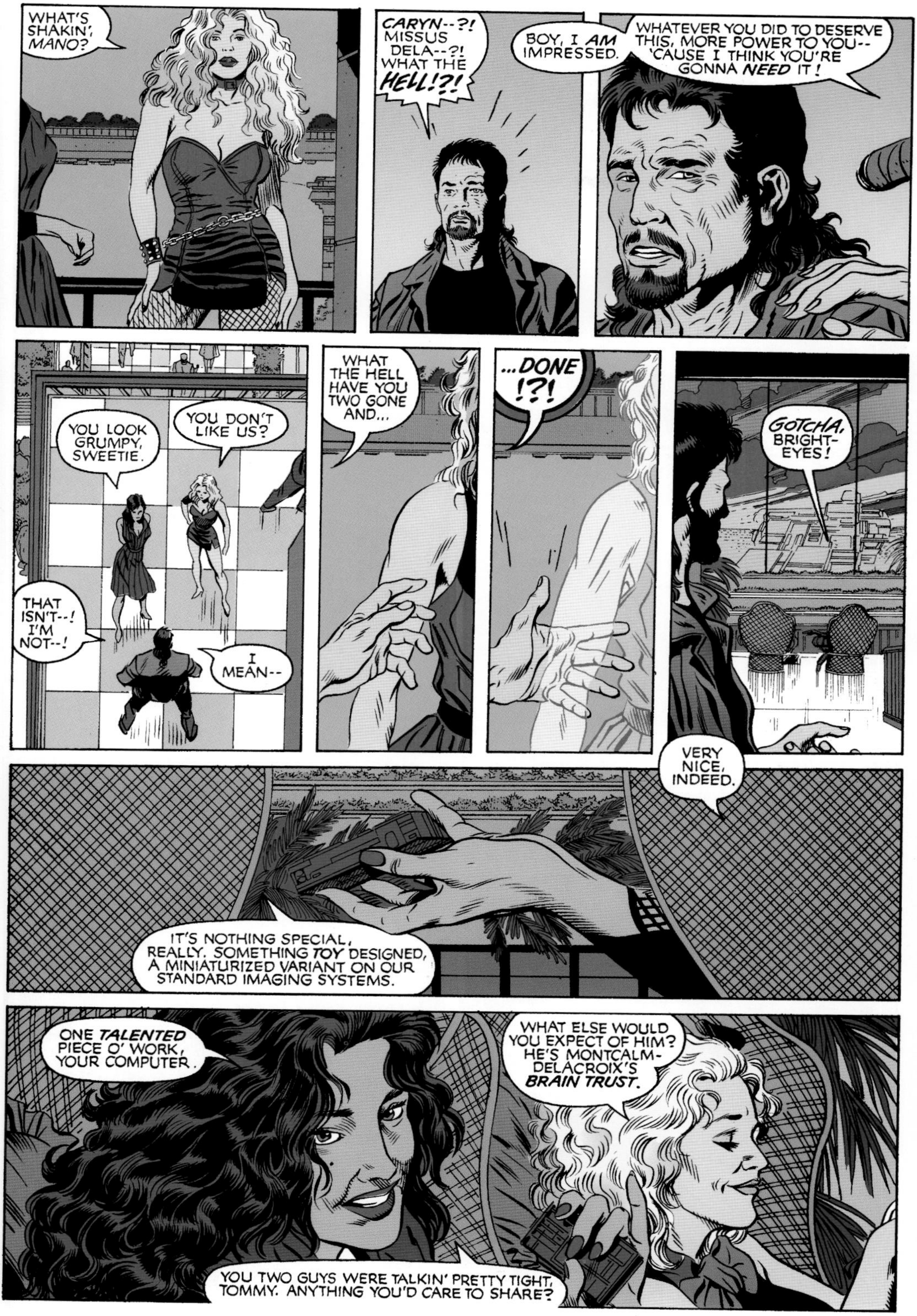

WHAT'S SHAKIN', *MANO*?
CARYN--?! MISSUS DELA--?! WHAT THE ***HELL!?!***
BOY, I *AM* IMPRESSED.
WHATEVER YOU DID TO DESERVE THIS, MORE POWER TO YOU-- 'CAUSE I THINK YOU'RE GONNA *NEED* IT!
YOU LOOK GRUMPY, SWEETIE.
YOU DON'T LIKE US?
THAT ISN'T--! I'M NOT--!
I MEAN--
WHAT THE HELL HAVE YOU TWO GONE AND...
...DONE !?!
GOTCHA, BRIGHT-EYES!
VERY NICE, INDEED.
IT'S NOTHING SPECIAL, REALLY. SOMETHING *TOY* DESIGNED, A MINIATURIZED VARIANT ON OUR STANDARD IMAGING SYSTEMS.
ONE *TALENTED* PIECE O' WORK, YOUR COMPUTER.
WHAT ELSE WOULD YOU EXPECT OF HIM? HE'S MONTCALM-DELACROIX'S ***BRAIN TRUST.***
YOU TWO GUYS WERE TALKIN' PRETTY TIGHT, TOMMY. ANYTHING YOU'D CARE TO SHARE?

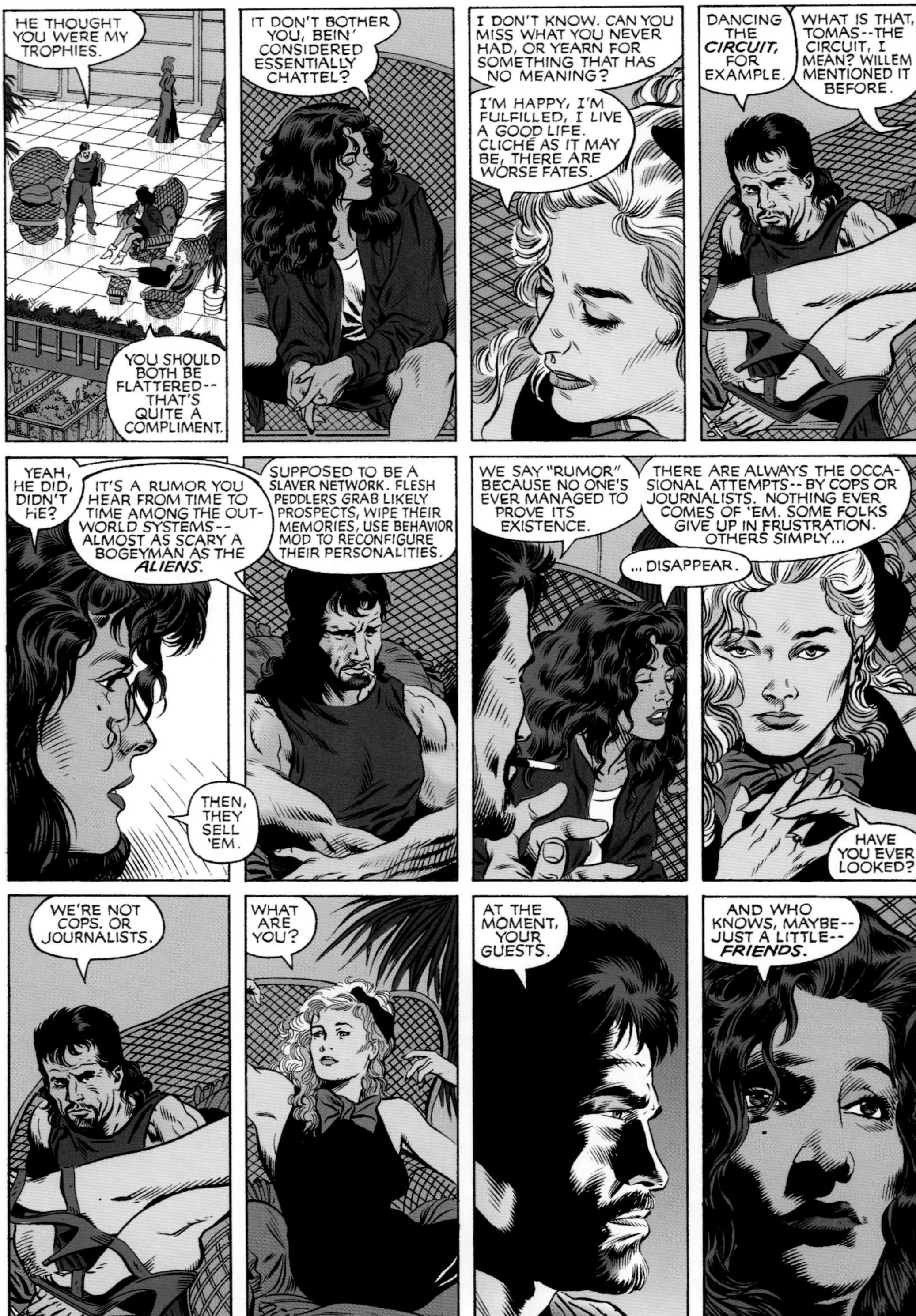
HE THOUGHT YOU WERE MY TROPHIES.
YOU SHOULD BOTH BE FLATTERED--THAT'S QUITE A COMPLIMENT.
IT DON'T BOTHER YOU, BEIN' CONSIDERED ESSENTIALLY CHATTEL?
I DON'T KNOW. CAN YOU MISS WHAT YOU NEVER HAD, OR YEARN FOR SOMETHING THAT HAS NO MEANING?
I'M HAPPY, I'M FULFILLED, I LIVE A GOOD LIFE. CLICHÉ AS IT MAY BE, THERE ARE WORSE FATES.
DANCING THE CIRCUIT, FOR EXAMPLE.
WHAT IS THAT, TOMAS--THE CIRCUIT, I MEAN? WILLEM MENTIONED IT BEFORE.
YEAH, HE DID, DIDN'T HE?
IT'S A RUMOR YOU HEAR FROM TIME TO TIME AMONG THE OUTWORLD SYSTEMS--ALMOST AS SCARY A BOGEYMAN AS THE ALIENS.
SUPPOSED TO BE A SLAVER NETWORK. FLESH PEDDLERS GRAB LIKELY PROSPECTS, WIPE THEIR MEMORIES, USE BEHAVIOR MOD TO RECONFIGURE THEIR PERSONALITIES.
THEN, THEY SELL 'EM.
WE SAY "RUMOR" BECAUSE NO ONE'S EVER MANAGED TO PROVE ITS EXISTENCE.
THERE ARE ALWAYS THE OCCASIONAL ATTEMPTS--BY COPS OR JOURNALISTS. NOTHING EVER COMES OF 'EM. SOME FOLKS GIVE UP IN FRUSTRATION. OTHERS SIMPLY...
...DISAPPEAR.
HAVE YOU EVER LOOKED?
WE'RE NOT COPS. OR JOURNALISTS.
WHAT ARE YOU?
AT THE MOMENT, YOUR GUESTS.
AND WHO KNOWS, MAYBE--JUST A LITTLE--FRIENDS.

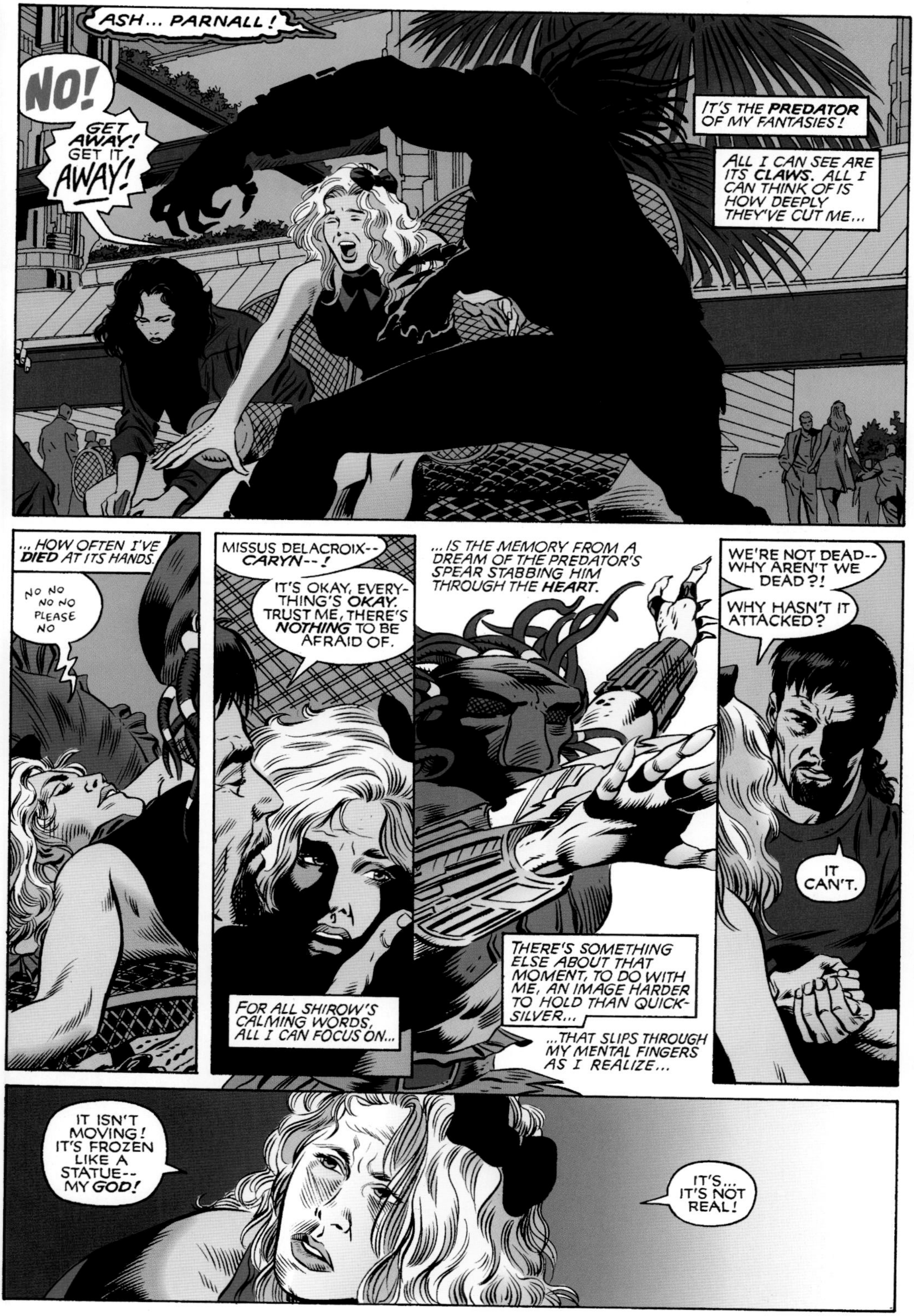

ASH... PARNALL!
NO!
GET AWAY! GET IT AWAY!
IT'S THE PREDATOR OF MY FANTASIES!
ALL I CAN SEE ARE ITS CLAWS. ALL I CAN THINK OF IS HOW DEEPLY THEY'VE CUT ME...
...HOW OFTEN I'VE DIED AT ITS HANDS.
NO NO NO NO PLEASE NO
MISSUS DELACROIX-- CARYN--!
IT'S OKAY, EVERYTHING'S OKAY. TRUST ME, THERE'S NOTHING TO BE AFRAID OF.
FOR ALL SHIROW'S CALMING WORDS, ALL I CAN FOCUS ON...
...IS THE MEMORY FROM A DREAM OF THE PREDATOR'S SPEAR STABBING HIM THROUGH THE HEART.
THERE'S SOMETHING ELSE ABOUT THAT MOMENT, TO DO WITH ME, AN IMAGE HARDER TO HOLD THAN QUICK-SILVER...
...THAT SLIPS THROUGH MY MENTAL FINGERS AS I REALIZE...
WE'RE NOT DEAD-- WHY AREN'T WE DEAD?!
WHY HASN'T IT ATTACKED?
IT CAN'T.
IT ISN'T MOVING! IT'S FROZEN LIKE A STATUE-- MY GOD!
IT'S... IT'S NOT REAL!

A *HOLO-GRAM*?! THE *IMAGE CONTROL MODULE*!

MARIA-- *YOU* DID THIS?! YOU SUMMONED THAT HORROR?! HOW *DARE* YOU!?!

FACING THAT THING WAS *AWFUL* ENOUGH ON A *VIRTUAL* PLAYGROUND--!

WHY ARE YOU SO UPSET? YOU WON.

THAT ISN'T THE BLOODY POINT!

I WAS HURT, I WAS SCARED, I SAW INNOCENT PEOPLE HORRIBLY KILLED! I DON'T CARE IF IT WAS ALL AN ILLUSION-- IT FELT *REAL*!

AND YOU'VE NO RIGHT TO MAKE ME RELIVE IT!

WHO'S *ASH PARNALL*?

GO TO *HELL*!

MADAME DELACROIX-- *CARYN*-- I'M *SORRY*!

AH, WELL...

SO MUCH FOR THAT IDEA.

SHE WASN'T ACTING, MARIA. THAT LADY WAS WELL AND TRULY TERRIFIED.

MAKES NO SENSE, TOMMY.

THAT'S NOT OUR PROBLEM.

YOU'RE NOT EVEN A LITTLE BIT CURIOUS...

...AS TO WHY ALL THESE PIECES DON'T ADD UP?

LIKE, NOT TO MENTION, WHO'S "ASH PARNALL"?

AN' WHAT THE HELL IS *THIS BIG* UGLY THING?!

SCAN LEVEL
2348654 x3
16 32 48 79
93 39 10 23

NONE OF OUR BUSINESS, DARLIN'.

WE'VE SEEN HOW THE "OTHER HALF" LIVES, WE'VE HAD OUR LITTLE ADVENTURE, WE'RE *DONE* HERE.

SCAN LEVEL
2348654 x3
16 32 48 79
93 39 10 23

WE DON'T KNOW THE PLAYERS, MARIA, WE DON'T KNOW THE GAME.

I SAY, "DIDI MAU" WHILE THE I.Z. IS CLEAR.

SCAN LEVEL
2348654 x3
16 32 48 79
93 39 10 23

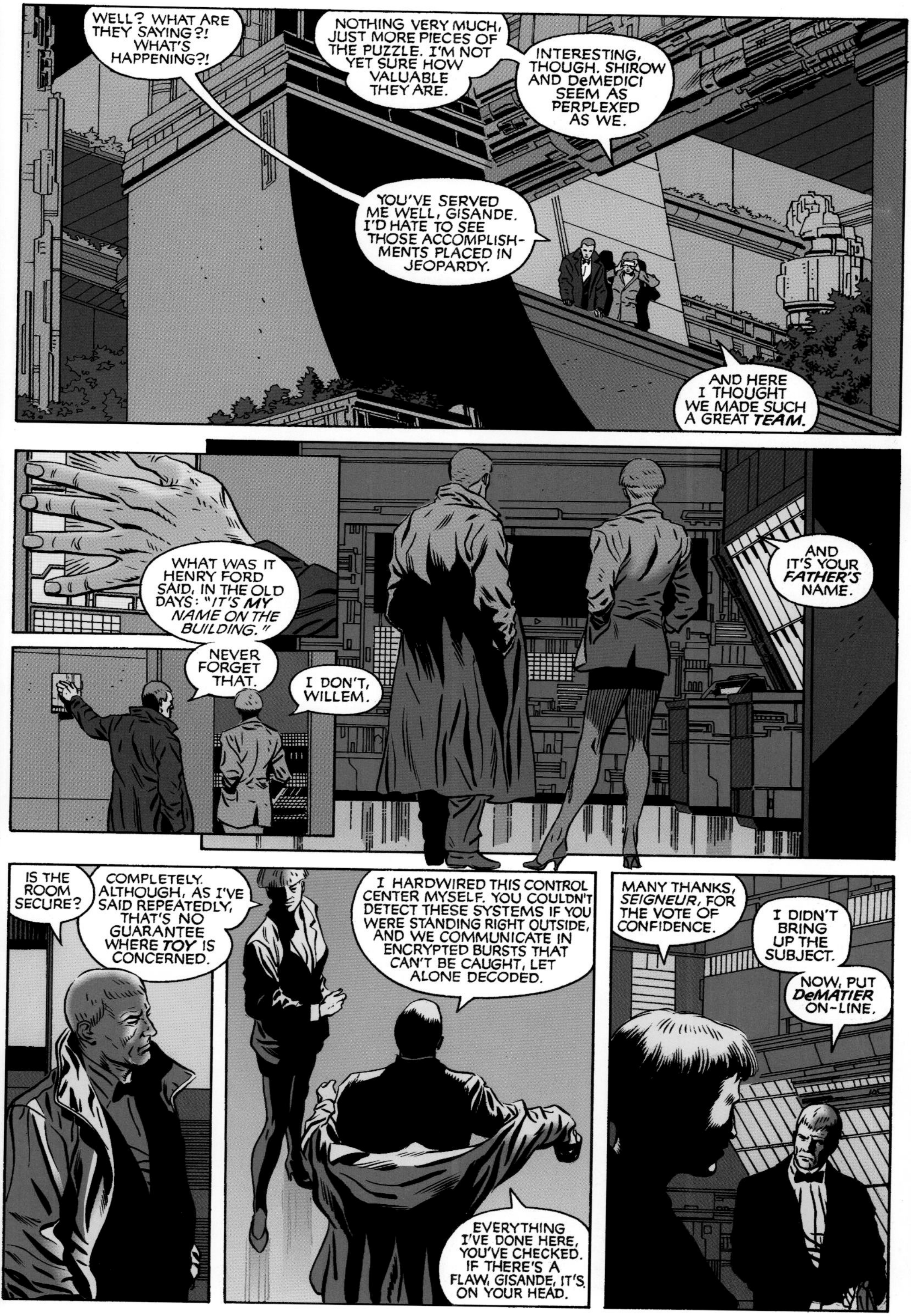

WELL? WHAT ARE THEY SAYING?! WHAT'S HAPPENING?!
NOTHING VERY MUCH, JUST MORE PIECES OF THE PUZZLE. I'M NOT YET SURE HOW VALUABLE THEY ARE.
INTERESTING, THOUGH. SHIROW AND DeMEDICI SEEM AS PERPLEXED AS WE.
YOU'VE SERVED ME WELL, GISANDE. I'D HATE TO SEE THOSE ACCOMPLISHMENTS PLACED IN JEOPARDY.
AND HERE I THOUGHT WE MADE SUCH A GREAT *TEAM.*
WHAT WAS IT HENRY FORD SAID, IN THE OLD DAYS: *"IT'S MY NAME ON THE BUILDING."*
NEVER FORGET THAT.
I DON'T, WILLEM.
AND IT'S YOUR *FATHER'S* NAME.
IS THE ROOM SECURE?
COMPLETELY. ALTHOUGH, AS I'VE SAID REPEATEDLY, THAT'S NO GUARANTEE WHERE *TOY* IS CONCERNED.
I HARDWIRED THIS CONTROL CENTER MYSELF. YOU COULDN'T DETECT THESE SYSTEMS IF YOU WERE STANDING RIGHT OUTSIDE, AND WE COMMUNICATE IN ENCRYPTED BURSTS THAT CAN'T BE CAUGHT, LET ALONE DECODED.
EVERYTHING I'VE DONE HERE, YOU'VE CHECKED. IF THERE'S A FLAW, GISANDE, IT'S ON YOUR HEAD.
MANY THANKS, *SEIGNEUR,* FOR THE VOTE OF CONFIDENCE.
I DIDN'T BRING UP THE SUBJECT.
NOW, PUT *DeMATIER* ON-LINE.

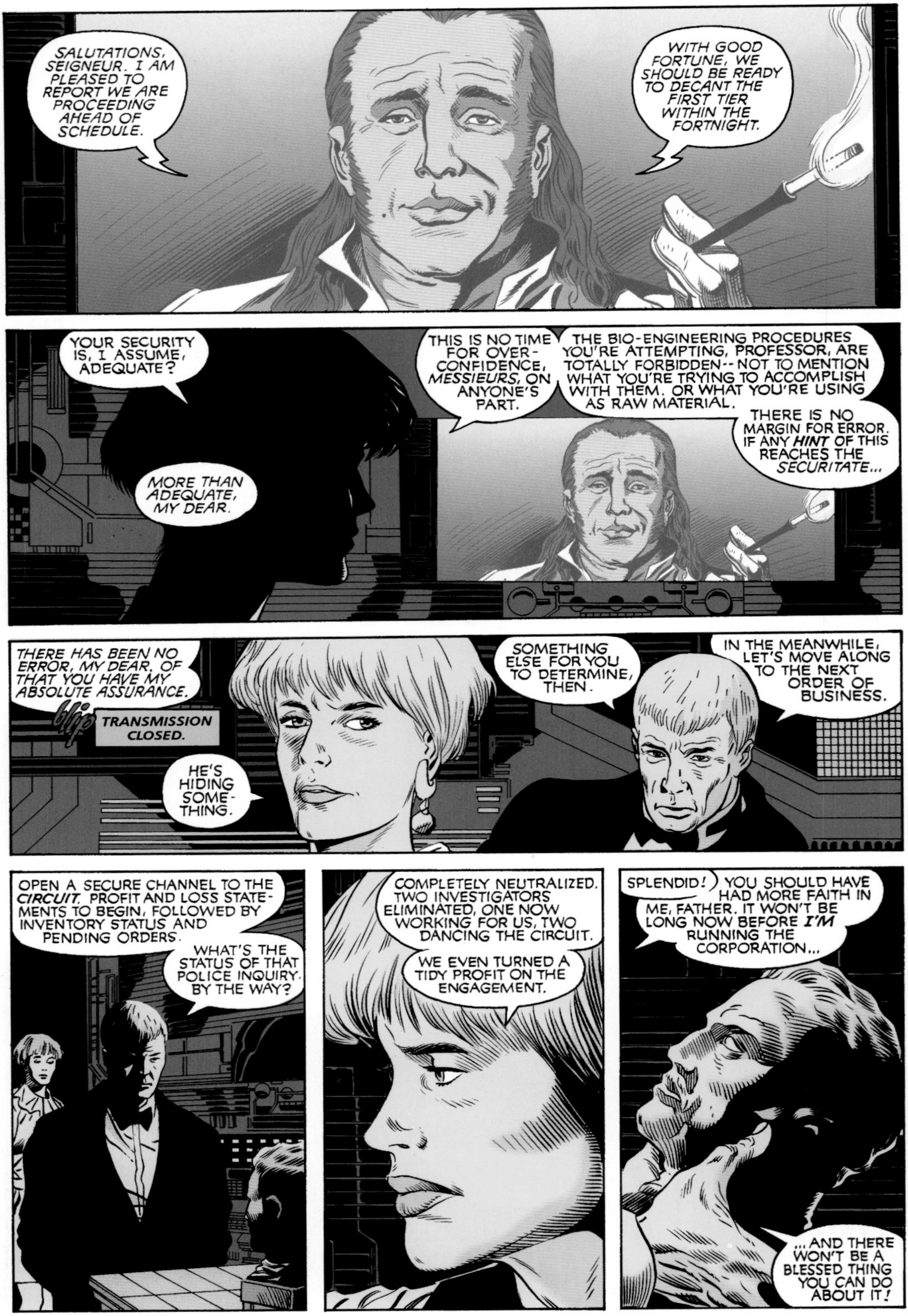
SALUTATIONS, SEIGNEUR. I AM PLEASED TO REPORT WE ARE PROCEEDING AHEAD OF SCHEDULE.
WITH GOOD FORTUNE, WE SHOULD BE READY TO DECANT THE FIRST TIER WITHIN THE FORTNIGHT.
YOUR SECURITY IS, I ASSUME, ADEQUATE?
MORE THAN ADEQUATE, MY DEAR.
THIS IS NO TIME FOR OVER-CONFIDENCE, MESSIEURS, ON ANYONE'S PART.
THE BIO-ENGINEERING PROCEDURES YOU'RE ATTEMPTING, PROFESSOR, ARE TOTALLY FORBIDDEN--NOT TO MENTION WHAT YOU'RE TRYING TO ACCOMPLISH WITH THEM. OR WHAT YOU'RE USING AS RAW MATERIAL.
THERE IS NO MARGIN FOR ERROR. IF ANY HINT OF THIS REACHES THE SECURITATE...
THERE HAS BEEN NO ERROR, MY DEAR. OF THAT YOU HAVE MY ABSOLUTE ASSURANCE.
blip
TRANSMISSION CLOSED.
HE'S HIDING SOME-THING.
SOMETHING ELSE FOR YOU TO DETERMINE, THEN.
IN THE MEANWHILE, LET'S MOVE ALONG TO THE NEXT ORDER OF BUSINESS.
OPEN A SECURE CHANNEL TO THE CIRCUIT. PROFIT AND LOSS STATE-MENTS TO BEGIN, FOLLOWED BY INVENTORY STATUS AND PENDING ORDERS.
WHAT'S THE STATUS OF THAT POLICE INQUIRY, BY THE WAY?
COMPLETELY NEUTRALIZED. TWO INVESTIGATORS ELIMINATED, ONE NOW WORKING FOR US, TWO DANCING THE CIRCUIT.
WE EVEN TURNED A TIDY PROFIT ON THE ENGAGEMENT.
SPLENDID!
YOU SHOULD HAVE HAD MORE FAITH IN ME, FATHER. IT WON'T BE LONG NOW BEFORE I'M RUNNING THE CORPORATION...
...AND THERE WON'T BE A BLESSED THING YOU CAN DO ABOUT IT!

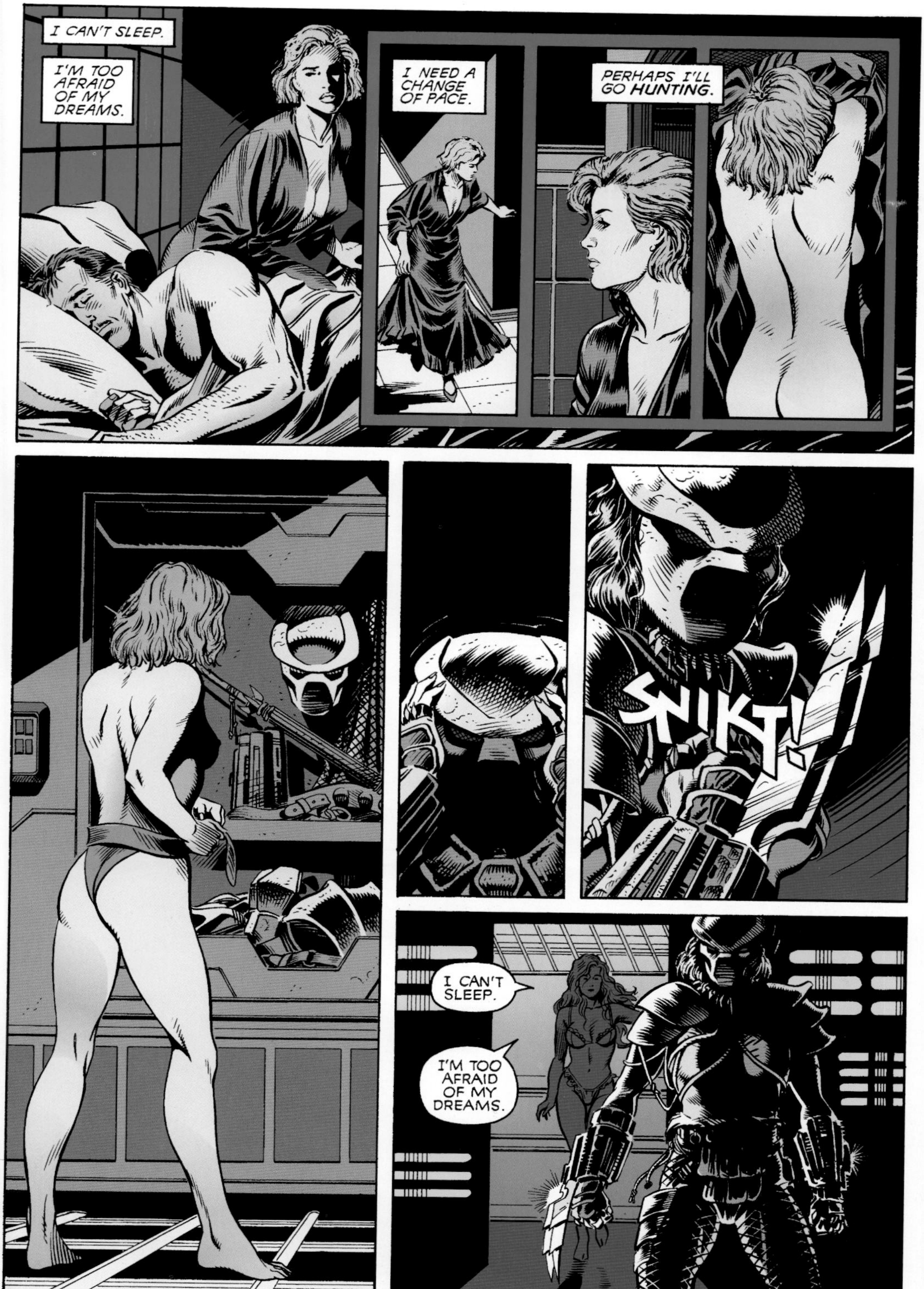

I CAN'T SLEEP.
I'M TOO AFRAID OF MY DREAMS.
I NEED A CHANGE OF PACE.
PERHAPS I'LL GO HUNTING.
SNIKT!
I CAN'T SLEEP.
I'M TOO AFRAID OF MY DREAMS.

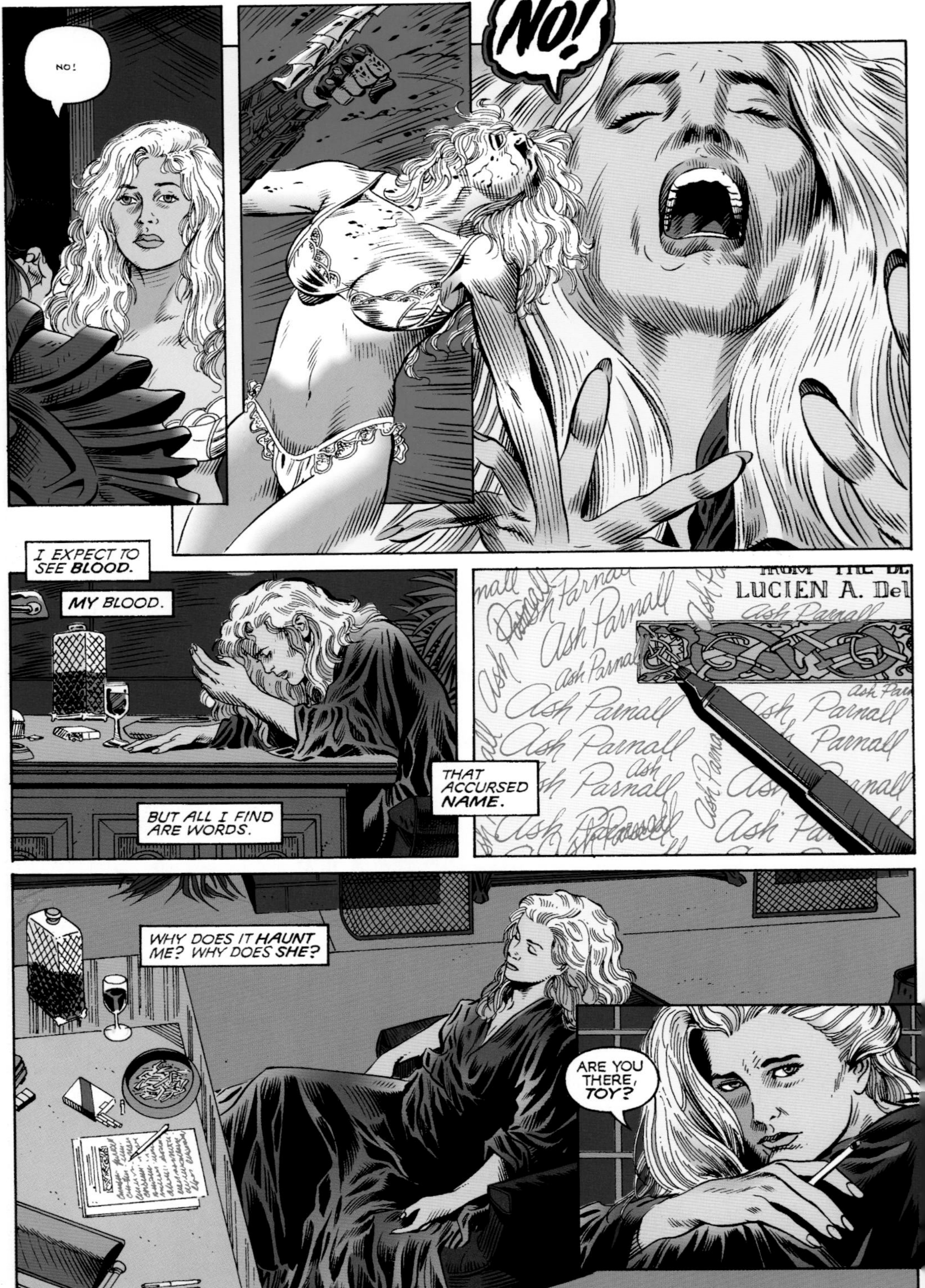
NO!
NO!
I EXPECT TO SEE BLOOD.
MY BLOOD.
BUT ALL I FIND ARE WORDS.
THAT ACCURSED NAME.
LUCIEN A. Del
Ash Parnall
WHY DOES IT HAUNT ME? WHY DOES SHE?
ARE YOU THERE, TOY?

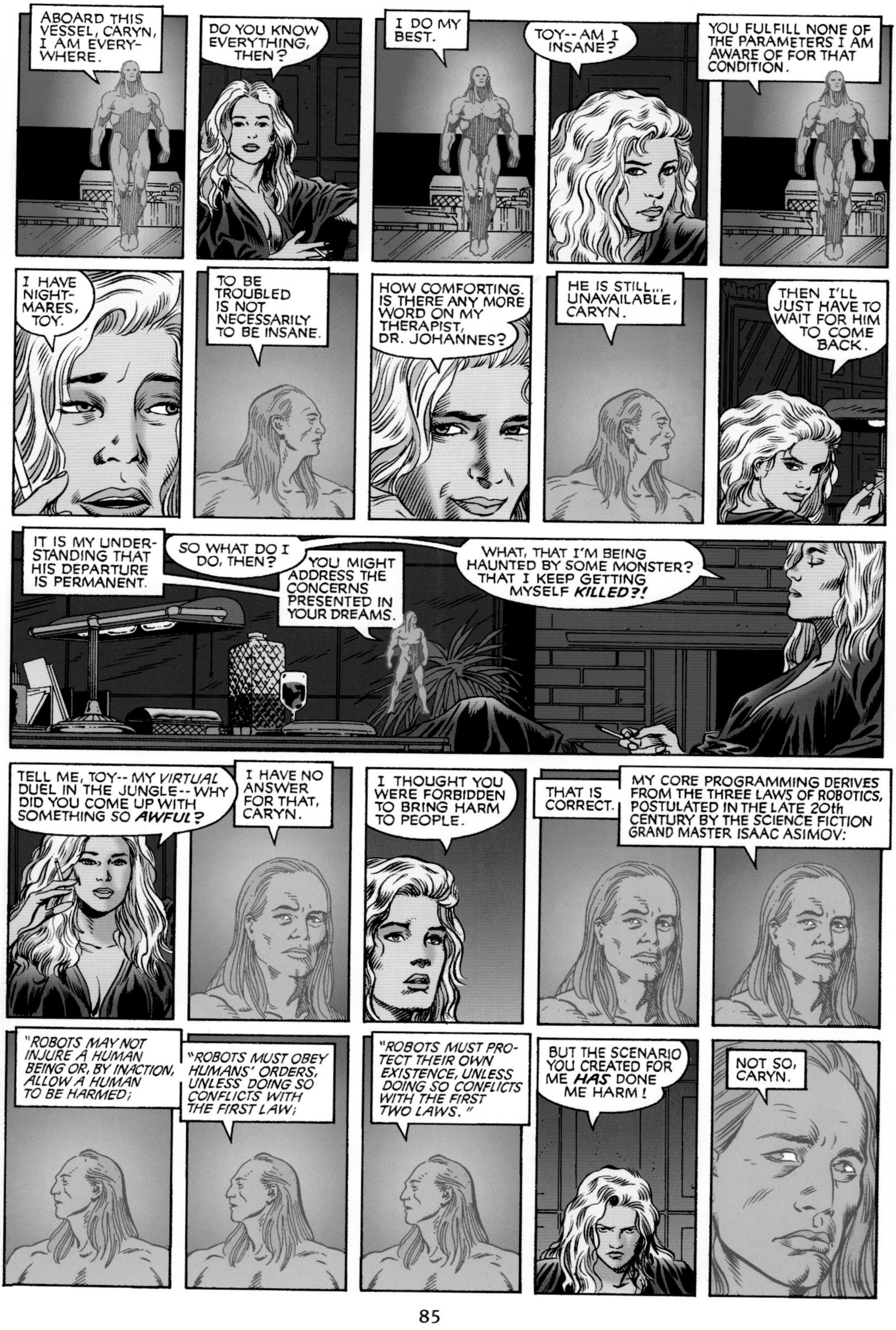
ABOARD THIS VESSEL, CARYN, I AM EVERY-WHERE.
DO YOU KNOW EVERYTHING, THEN?
I DO MY BEST.
TOY-- AM I INSANE?
YOU FULFILL NONE OF THE PARAMETERS I AM AWARE OF FOR THAT CONDITION.
I HAVE NIGHT-MARES, TOY.
TO BE TROUBLED IS NOT NECESSARILY TO BE INSANE.
HOW COMFORTING. IS THERE ANY MORE WORD ON MY THERAPIST, DR. JOHANNES?
HE IS STILL... UNAVAILABLE, CARYN.
THEN I'LL JUST HAVE TO WAIT FOR HIM TO COME BACK.
IT IS MY UNDER-STANDING THAT HIS DEPARTURE IS PERMANENT.
SO WHAT DO I DO, THEN?
YOU MIGHT ADDRESS THE CONCERNS PRESENTED IN YOUR DREAMS.
WHAT, THAT I'M BEING HAUNTED BY SOME MONSTER? THAT I KEEP GETTING MYSELF KILLED?!
TELL ME, TOY-- MY VIRTUAL DUEL IN THE JUNGLE-- WHY DID YOU COME UP WITH SOMETHING SO AWFUL?
I HAVE NO ANSWER FOR THAT, CARYN.
I THOUGHT YOU WERE FORBIDDEN TO BRING HARM TO PEOPLE.
THAT IS CORRECT.
MY CORE PROGRAMMING DERIVES FROM THE THREE LAWS OF ROBOTICS, POSTULATED IN THE LATE 20th CENTURY BY THE SCIENCE FICTION GRAND MASTER ISAAC ASIMOV:
"ROBOTS MAY NOT INJURE A HUMAN BEING OR, BY INACTION, ALLOW A HUMAN TO BE HARMED;
"ROBOTS MUST OBEY HUMANS' ORDERS, UNLESS DOING SO CONFLICTS WITH THE FIRST LAW;
"ROBOTS MUST PRO-TECT THEIR OWN EXISTENCE, UNLESS DOING SO CONFLICTS WITH THE FIRST TWO LAWS."
BUT THE SCENARIO YOU CREATED FOR ME HAS DONE ME HARM!
NOT SO, CARYN.

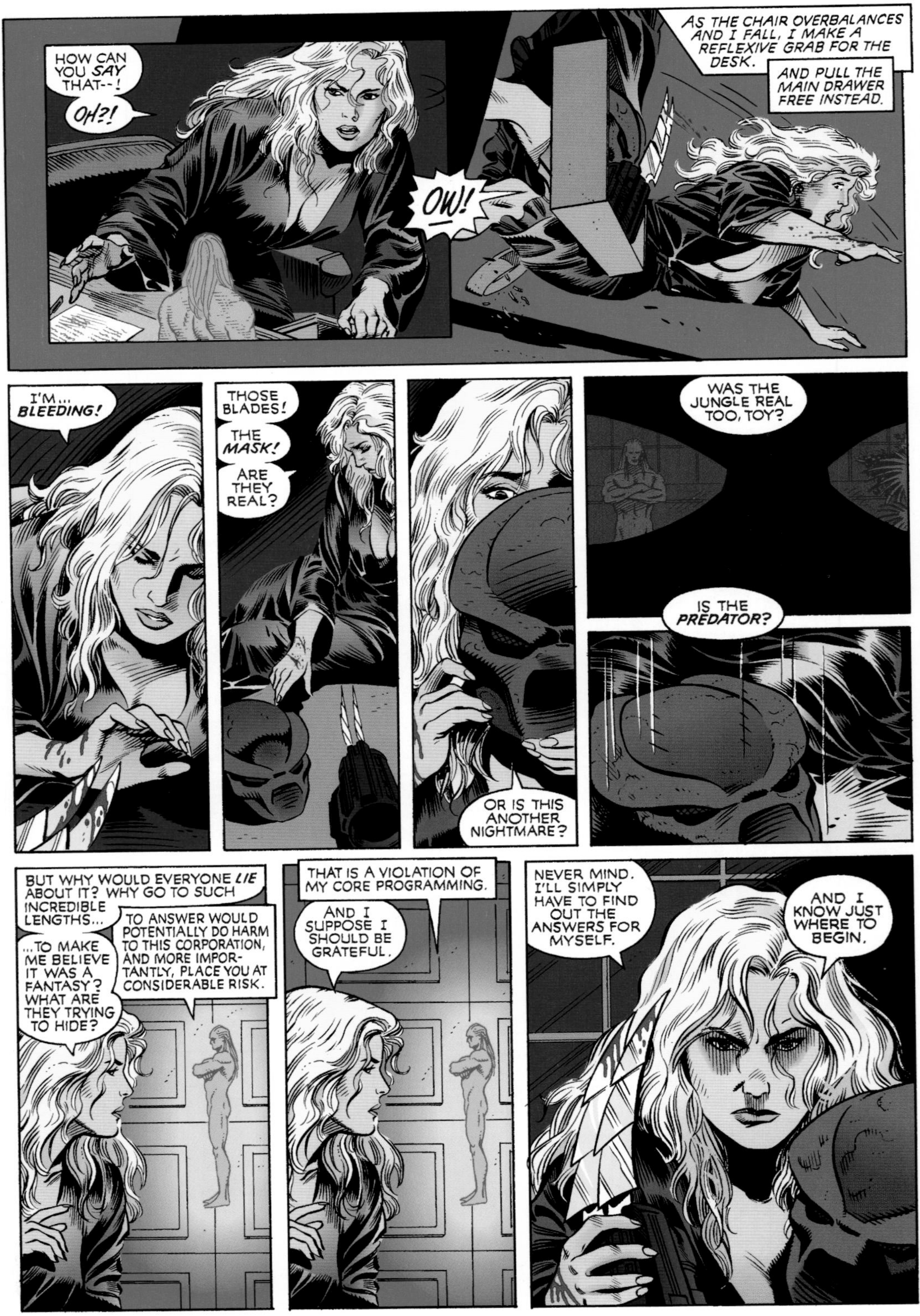
HOW CAN YOU SAY THAT--!
OH?!
AS THE CHAIR OVERBALANCES AND I FALL, I MAKE A REFLEXIVE GRAB FOR THE DESK.
AND PULL THE MAIN DRAWER FREE INSTEAD.
OW!
I'M... BLEEDING!
THOSE BLADES!
THE MASK!
ARE THEY REAL?
OR IS THIS ANOTHER NIGHTMARE?
WAS THE JUNGLE REAL TOO, TOY?
IS THE PREDATOR?
BUT WHY WOULD EVERYONE LIE ABOUT IT? WHY GO TO SUCH INCREDIBLE LENGTHS...
...TO MAKE ME BELIEVE IT WAS A FANTASY? WHAT ARE THEY TRYING TO HIDE?
TO ANSWER WOULD POTENTIALLY DO HARM TO THIS CORPORATION, AND MORE IMPORTANTLY, PLACE YOU AT CONSIDERABLE RISK.
THAT IS A VIOLATION OF MY CORE PROGRAMMING.
AND I SUPPOSE I SHOULD BE GRATEFUL.
NEVER MIND. I'LL SIMPLY HAVE TO FIND OUT THE ANSWERS FOR MYSELF.
AND I KNOW JUST WHERE TO BEGIN.

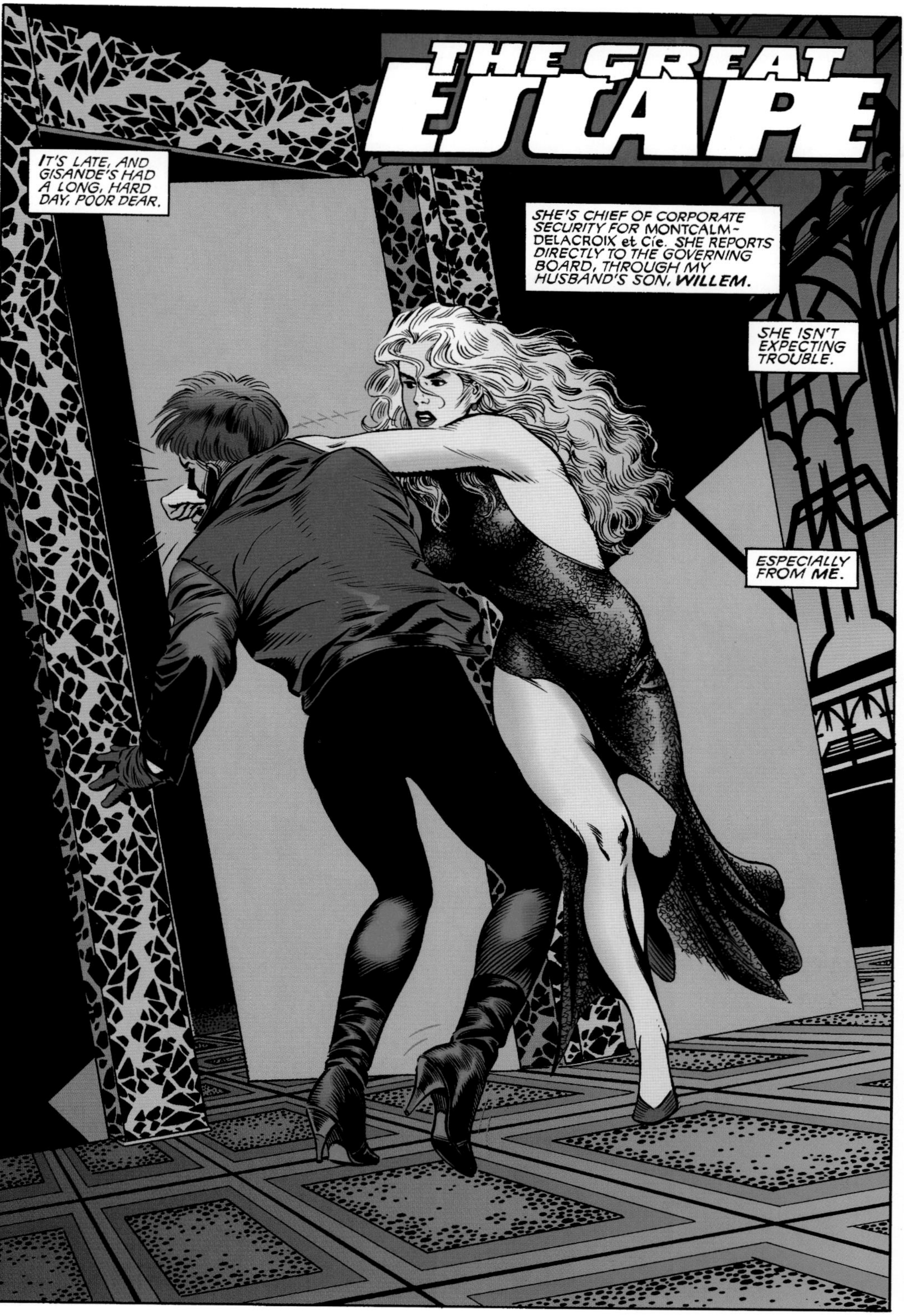
THE GREAT ESCAPE
IT'S LATE, AND GISANDE'S HAD A LONG, HARD DAY, POOR DEAR.
SHE'S CHIEF OF CORPORATE SECURITY FOR MONTCALM-DELACROIX et Cíe. SHE REPORTS DIRECTLY TO THE GOVERNING BOARD, THROUGH MY HUSBAND'S SON, WILLEM.
SHE ISN'T EXPECTING TROUBLE.
ESPECIALLY FROM ME.

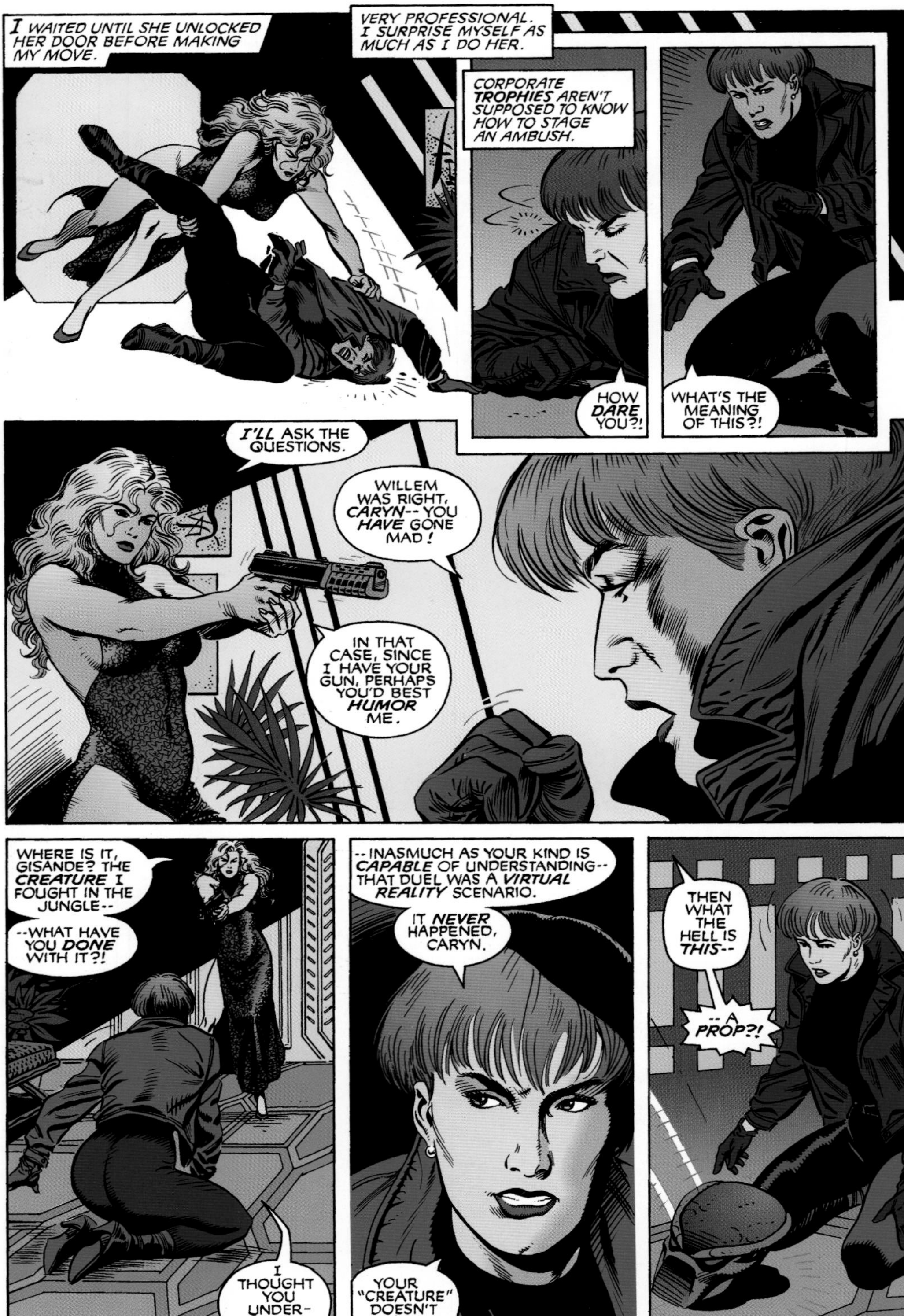
I WAITED UNTIL SHE UNLOCKED HER DOOR BEFORE MAKING MY MOVE.
VERY PROFESSIONAL. I SURPRISE MYSELF AS MUCH AS I DO HER.
CORPORATE TROPHIES AREN'T SUPPOSED TO KNOW HOW TO STAGE AN AMBUSH.
HOW DARE YOU?!
WHAT'S THE MEANING OF THIS?!
I'LL ASK THE QUESTIONS.
WILLEM WAS RIGHT, CARYN-- YOU HAVE GONE MAD!
IN THAT CASE, SINCE I HAVE YOUR GUN, PERHAPS YOU'D BEST HUMOR ME.
WHERE IS IT, GISANDE? THE CREATURE I FOUGHT IN THE JUNGLE--
--WHAT HAVE YOU DONE WITH IT?!
I THOUGHT YOU UNDER-STOOD--
--INASMUCH AS YOUR KIND IS CAPABLE OF UNDERSTANDING-- THAT DUEL WAS A VIRTUAL REALITY SCENARIO.
IT NEVER HAPPENED, CARYN.
YOUR "CREATURE" DOESN'T EXIST.
THEN WHAT THE HELL IS THIS--
--A PROP?!

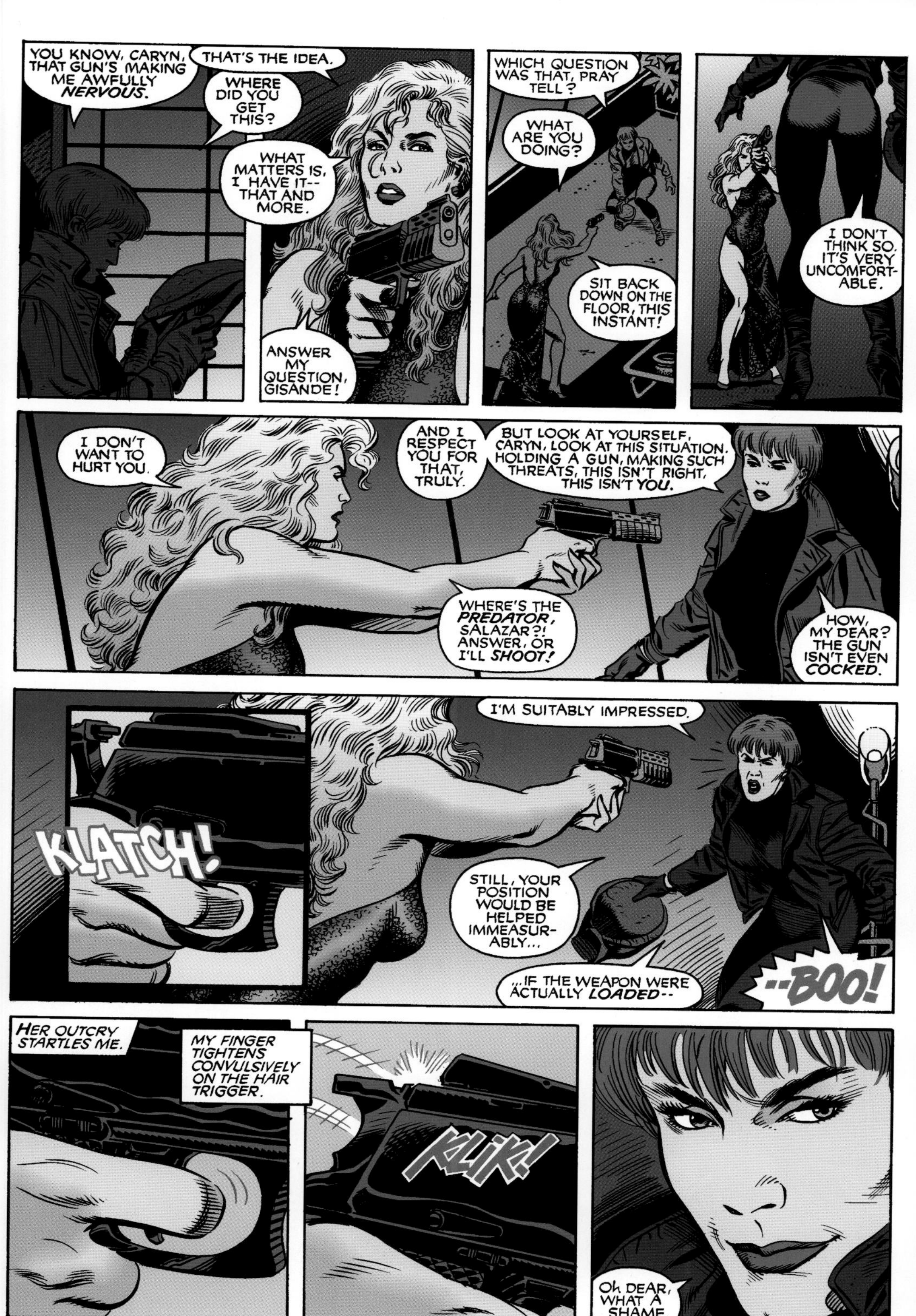
YOU KNOW, CARYN, THAT GUN'S MAKING ME AWFULLY NERVOUS.
THAT'S THE IDEA.
WHERE DID YOU GET THIS?
WHAT MATTERS IS, I HAVE IT-- THAT AND MORE.
ANSWER MY QUESTION, GISANDE!
WHICH QUESTION WAS THAT, PRAY TELL?
WHAT ARE YOU DOING?
SIT BACK DOWN ON THE FLOOR, THIS INSTANT!
I DON'T THINK SO. IT'S VERY UNCOMFORT-ABLE.
I DON'T WANT TO HURT YOU.
AND I RESPECT YOU FOR THAT, TRULY.
BUT LOOK AT YOURSELF, CARYN, LOOK AT THIS SITUATION. HOLDING A GUN, MAKING SUCH THREATS, THIS ISN'T RIGHT, THIS ISN'T YOU.
WHERE'S THE PREDATOR, SALAZAR?! ANSWER, OR I'LL SHOOT!
HOW, MY DEAR? THE GUN ISN'T EVEN COCKED.
KLATCH!
I'M SUITABLY IMPRESSED.
STILL, YOUR POSITION WOULD BE HELPED IMMEASUR-ABLY...
...IF THE WEAPON WERE ACTUALLY LOADED--
--BOO!
HER OUTCRY STARTLES ME.
MY FINGER TIGHTENS CONVULSIVELY ON THE HAIR TRIGGER.
KLIK!
OH DEAR, WHAT A SHAME.

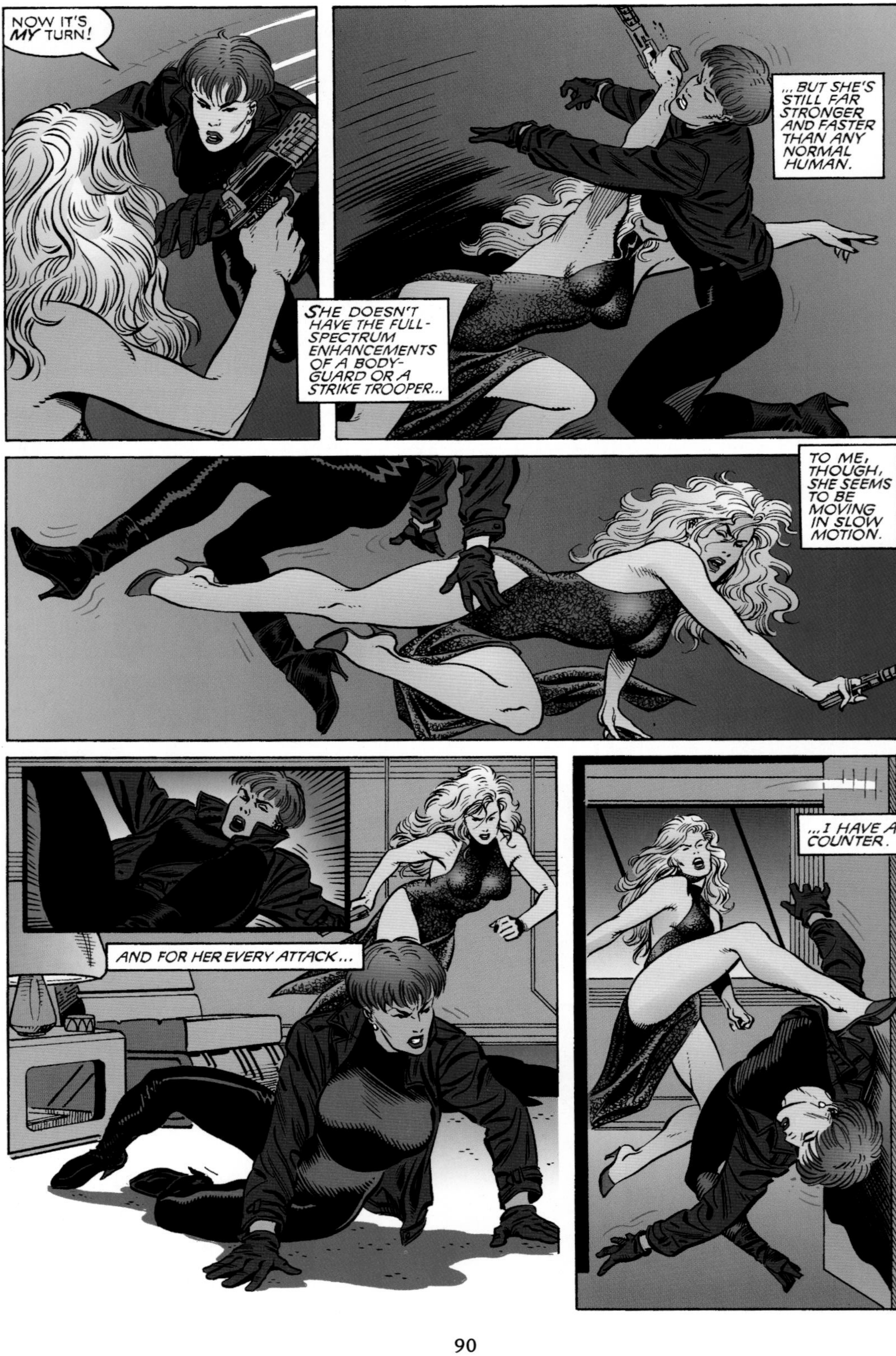
NOW IT'S MY TURN!
SHE DOESN'T HAVE THE FULL-SPECTRUM ENHANCEMENTS OF A BODY-GUARD OR A STRIKE TROOPER...
...BUT SHE'S STILL FAR STRONGER AND FASTER THAN ANY NORMAL HUMAN.
TO ME, THOUGH, SHE SEEMS TO BE MOVING IN SLOW MOTION.
AND FOR HER EVERY ATTACK...
...I HAVE A COUNTER.

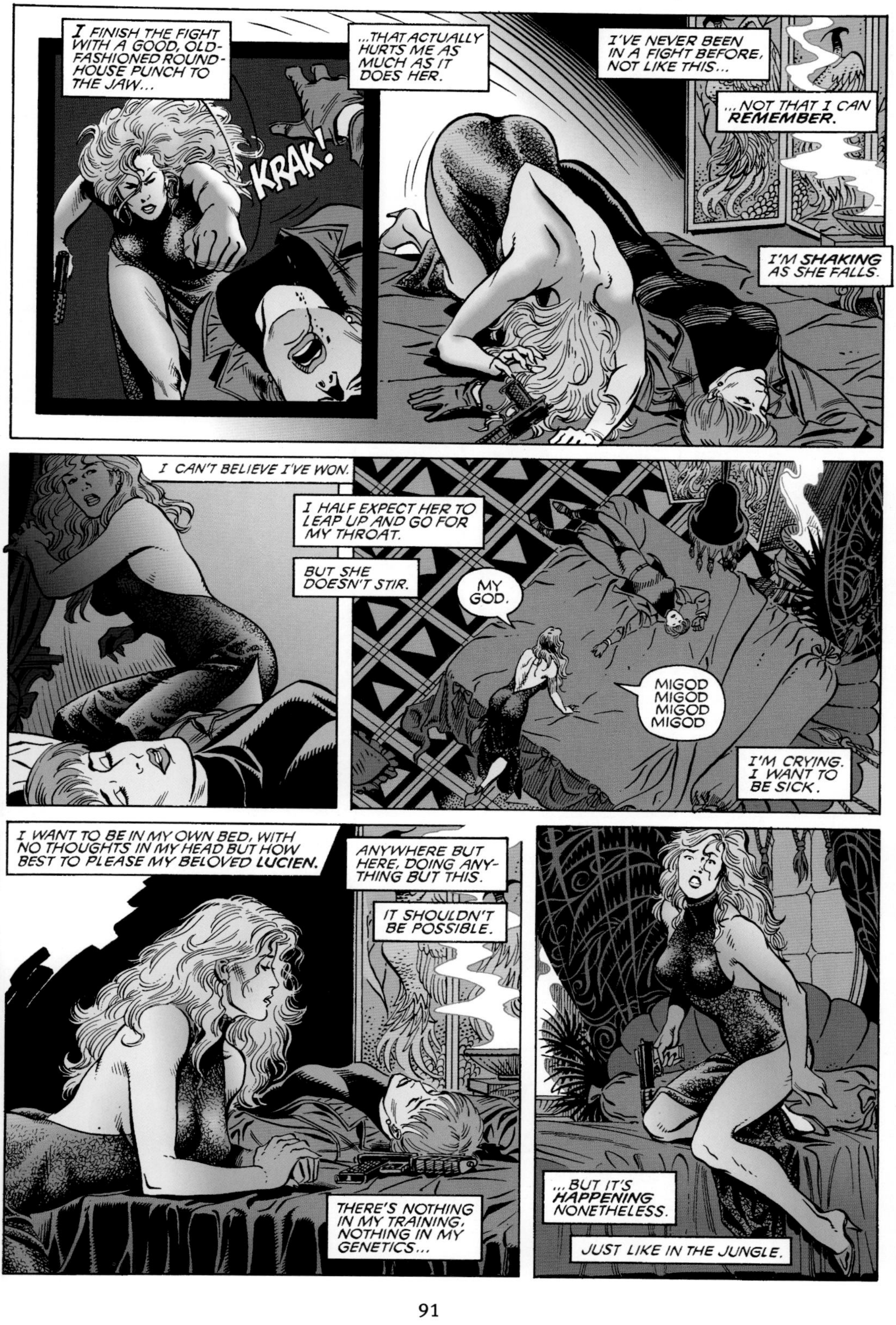

I FINISH THE FIGHT WITH A GOOD, OLD-FASHIONED ROUND-HOUSE PUNCH TO THE JAW...
KRAK!
...THAT ACTUALLY HURTS ME AS MUCH AS IT DOES HER.
I'VE NEVER BEEN IN A FIGHT BEFORE, NOT LIKE THIS...
...NOT THAT I CAN **REMEMBER.**
I'M **SHAKING** AS SHE FALLS.
I CAN'T BELIEVE I'VE WON.
I HALF EXPECT HER TO LEAP UP AND GO FOR MY THROAT.
BUT SHE DOESN'T STIR.
MY GOD.
MIGOD MIGOD MIGOD MIGOD
I'M CRYING. I WANT TO BE SICK.
I WANT TO BE IN MY OWN BED, WITH NO THOUGHTS IN MY HEAD BUT HOW BEST TO PLEASE MY BELOVED **LUCIEN.**
ANYWHERE BUT HERE, DOING ANYTHING BUT THIS.
IT SHOULDN'T BE POSSIBLE.
THERE'S NOTHING IN MY TRAINING, NOTHING IN MY GENETICS...
...BUT IT'S **HAPPENING** NONETHELESS.
JUST LIKE IN THE JUNGLE.

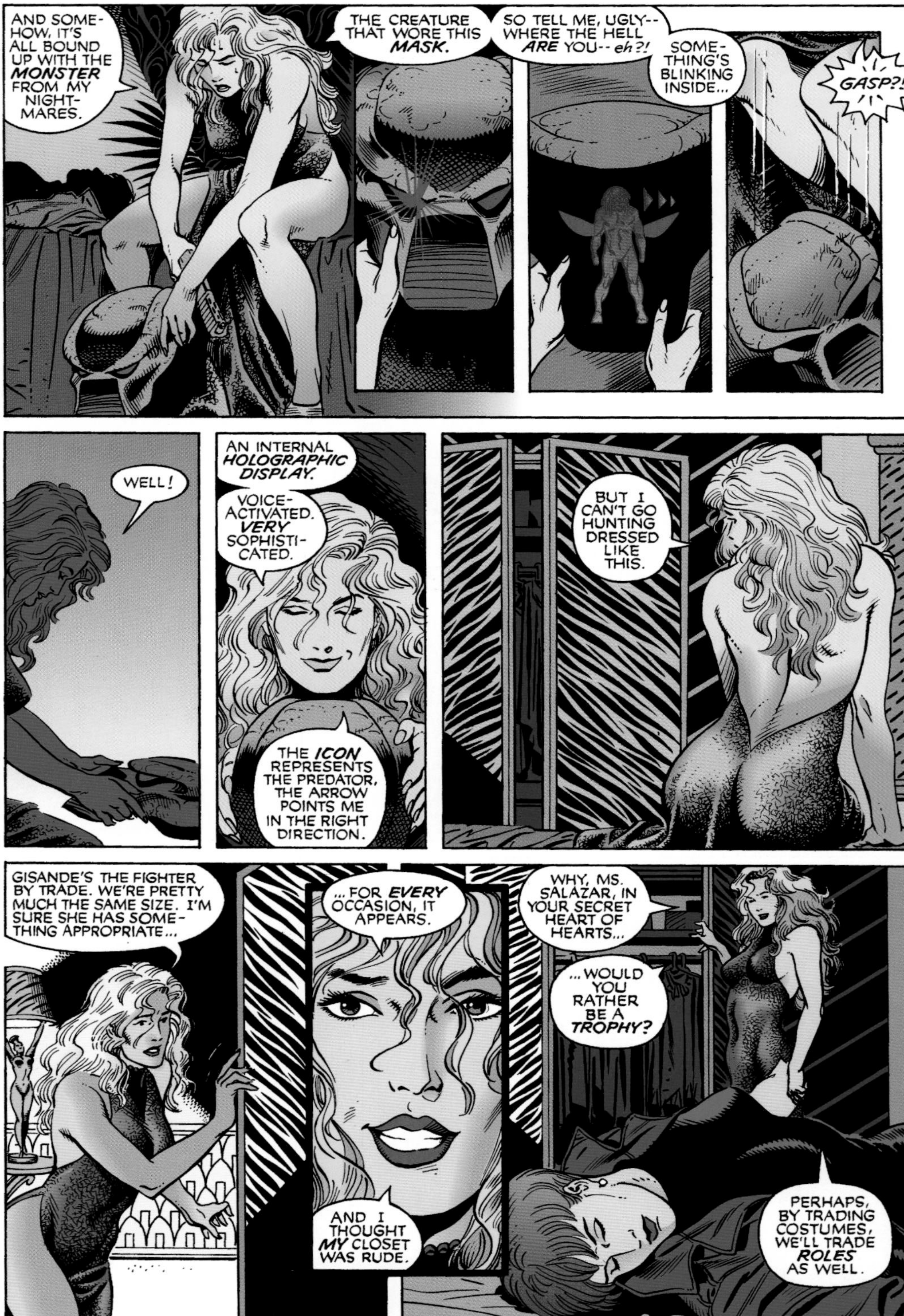
AND SOMEHOW, IT'S ALL BOUND UP WITH THE MONSTER FROM MY NIGHTMARES.
THE CREATURE THAT WORE THIS MASK.
SO TELL ME, UGLY-- WHERE THE HELL ARE YOU-- eh?!
SOMETHING'S BLINKING INSIDE...
GASP?!
WELL!
AN INTERNAL HOLOGRAPHIC DISPLAY.
VOICE-ACTIVATED. VERY SOPHISTICATED.
THE ICON REPRESENTS THE PREDATOR, THE ARROW POINTS ME IN THE RIGHT DIRECTION.
BUT I CAN'T GO HUNTING DRESSED LIKE THIS.
GISANDE'S THE FIGHTER BY TRADE. WE'RE PRETTY MUCH THE SAME SIZE. I'M SURE SHE HAS SOMETHING APPROPRIATE...
...FOR EVERY OCCASION, IT APPEARS.
AND I THOUGHT MY CLOSET WAS RUDE.
WHY, MS. SALAZAR, IN YOUR SECRET HEART OF HEARTS...
...WOULD YOU RATHER BE A TROPHY?
PERHAPS, BY TRADING COSTUMES, WE'LL TRADE ROLES AS WELL.

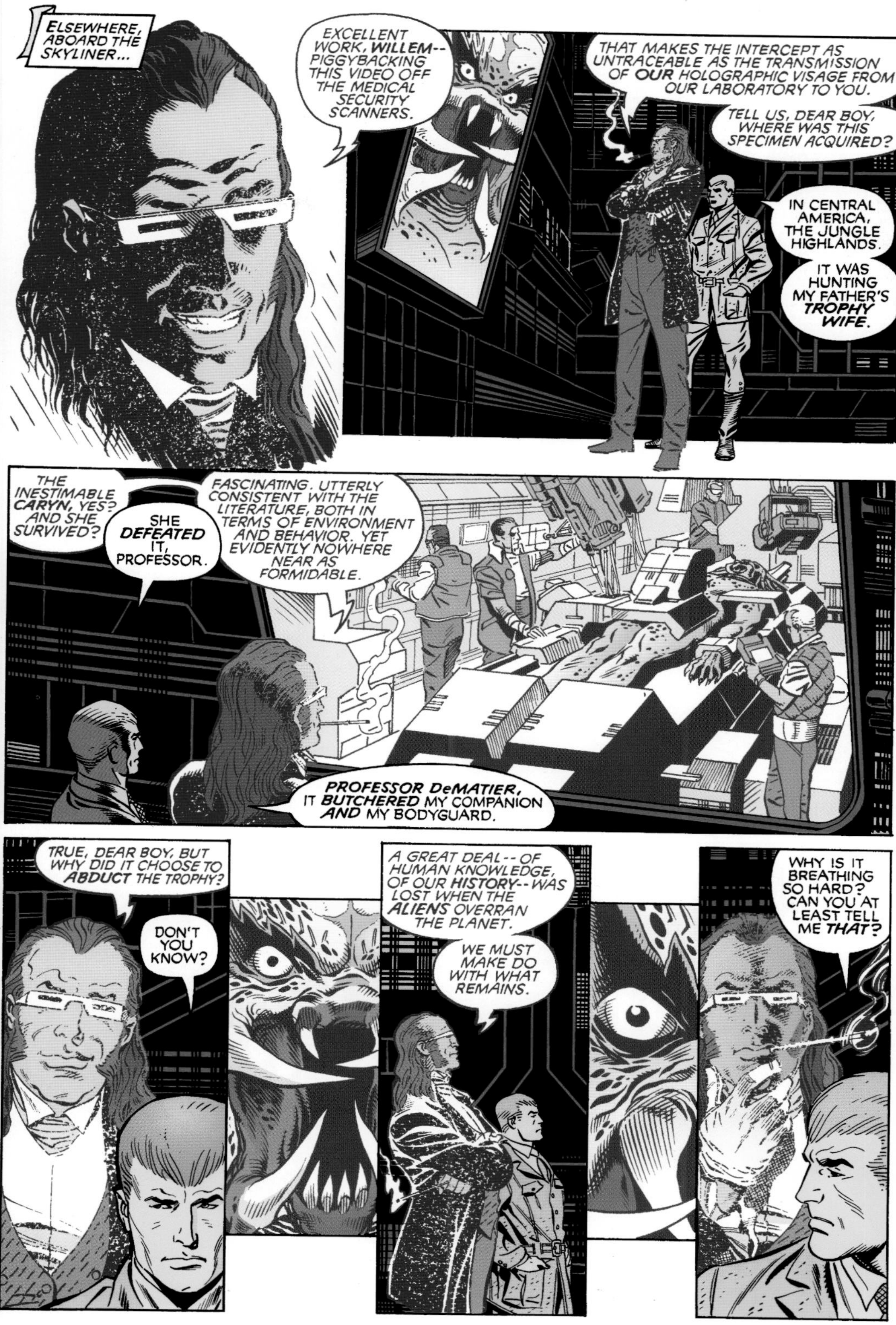

ELSEWHERE, ABOARD THE SKYLINER...
EXCELLENT WORK, WILLEM-- PIGGYBACKING THIS VIDEO OFF THE MEDICAL SECURITY SCANNERS.
THAT MAKES THE INTERCEPT AS UNTRACEABLE AS THE TRANSMISSION OF OUR HOLOGRAPHIC VISAGE FROM OUR LABORATORY TO YOU.
TELL US, DEAR BOY, WHERE WAS THIS SPECIMEN ACQUIRED?
IN CENTRAL AMERICA, THE JUNGLE HIGHLANDS.
IT WAS HUNTING MY FATHER'S TROPHY WIFE.
THE INESTIMABLE CARYN, YES? AND SHE SURVIVED?
SHE DEFEATED IT, PROFESSOR.
FASCINATING. UTTERLY CONSISTENT WITH THE LITERATURE, BOTH IN TERMS OF ENVIRONMENT AND BEHAVIOR. YET EVIDENTLY NOWHERE NEAR AS FORMIDABLE.
PROFESSOR DeMATIER, IT BUTCHERED MY COMPANION AND MY BODYGUARD.
TRUE, DEAR BOY, BUT WHY DID IT CHOOSE TO ABDUCT THE TROPHY?
DON'T YOU KNOW?
A GREAT DEAL-- OF HUMAN KNOWLEDGE, OF OUR HISTORY-- WAS LOST WHEN THE ALIENS OVERRAN THE PLANET.
WE MUST MAKE DO WITH WHAT REMAINS.
WHY IS IT BREATHING SO HARD? CAN YOU AT LEAST TELL ME THAT?

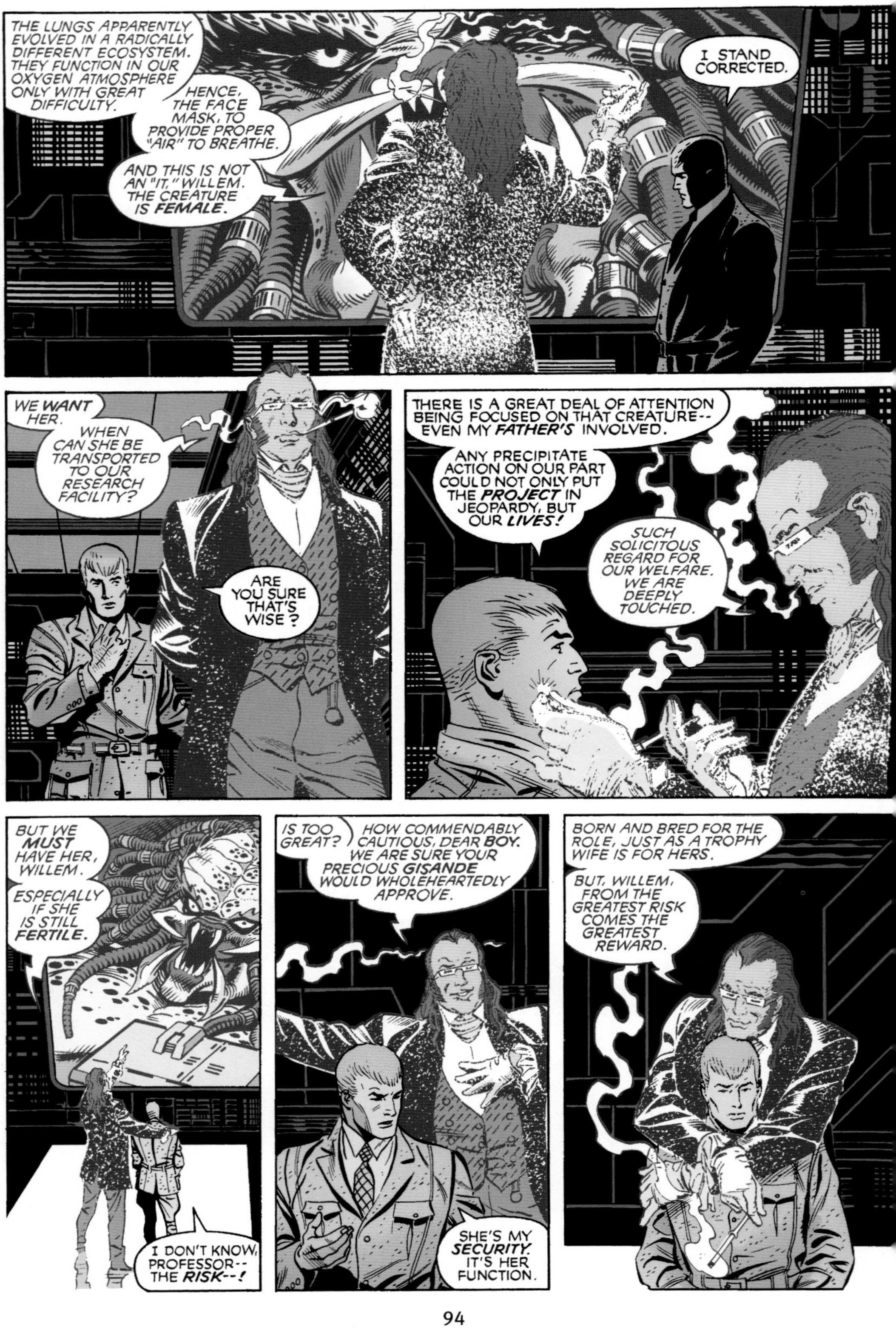

THE LUNGS APPARENTLY EVOLVED IN A RADICALLY DIFFERENT ECOSYSTEM. THEY FUNCTION IN OUR OXYGEN ATMOSPHERE ONLY WITH GREAT DIFFICULTY.
HENCE, THE FACE MASK, TO PROVIDE PROPER "AIR" TO BREATHE.
AND THIS IS NOT AN "IT," WILLEM. THE CREATURE IS FEMALE.
I STAND CORRECTED.
WE WANT HER.
WHEN CAN SHE BE TRANSPORTED TO OUR RESEARCH FACILITY?
ARE YOU SURE THAT'S WISE?
THERE IS A GREAT DEAL OF ATTENTION BEING FOCUSED ON THAT CREATURE-- EVEN MY FATHER'S INVOLVED.
ANY PRECIPITATE ACTION ON OUR PART COULD NOT ONLY PUT THE PROJECT IN JEOPARDY, BUT OUR LIVES!
SUCH SOLICITOUS REGARD FOR OUR WELFARE. WE ARE DEEPLY TOUCHED.
BUT WE MUST HAVE HER, WILLEM.
ESPECIALLY IF SHE IS STILL FERTILE.
I DON'T KNOW, PROFESSOR-- THE RISK--!
IS TOO GREAT?
HOW COMMENDABLY CAUTIOUS, DEAR BOY. WE ARE SURE YOUR PRECIOUS GISANDE WOULD WHOLEHEARTEDLY APPROVE.
SHE'S MY SECURITY. IT'S HER FUNCTION.
BORN AND BRED FOR THE ROLE, JUST AS A TROPHY WIFE IS FOR HERS.
BUT, WILLEM, FROM THE GREATEST RISK COMES THE GREATEST REWARD.

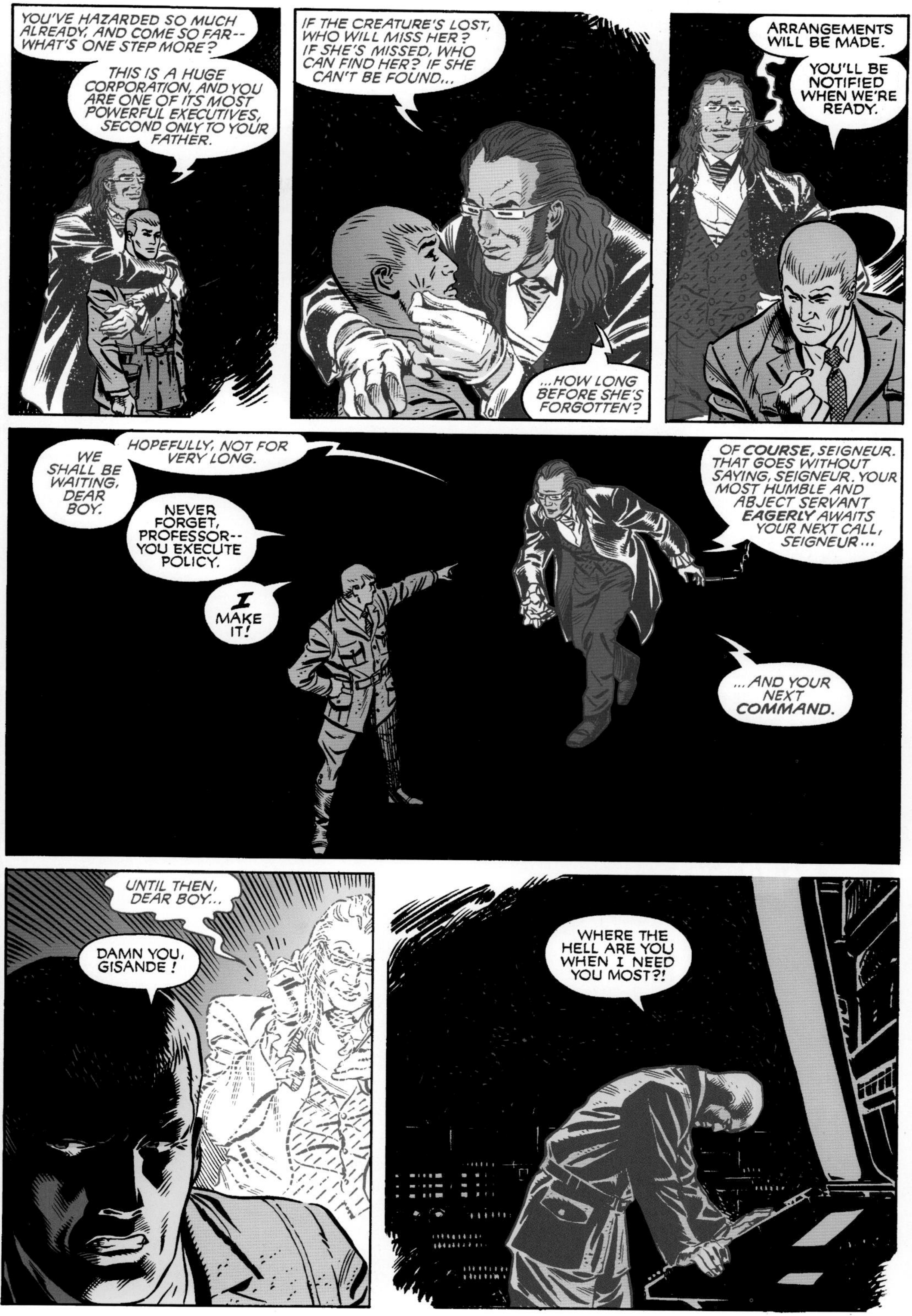

YOU'VE HAZARDED SO MUCH ALREADY, AND COME SO FAR-- WHAT'S ONE STEP MORE?
THIS IS A HUGE CORPORATION, AND YOU ARE ONE OF ITS MOST POWERFUL EXECUTIVES, SECOND ONLY TO YOUR FATHER.
IF THE CREATURE'S LOST, WHO WILL MISS HER? IF SHE'S MISSED, WHO CAN FIND HER? IF SHE CAN'T BE FOUND...
...HOW LONG BEFORE SHE'S FORGOTTEN?
ARRANGEMENTS WILL BE MADE.
YOU'LL BE NOTIFIED WHEN WE'RE READY.
WE SHALL BE WAITING, DEAR BOY.
HOPEFULLY, NOT FOR VERY LONG.
NEVER FORGET, PROFESSOR-- YOU EXECUTE POLICY.
I MAKE IT!
OF COURSE, SEIGNEUR. THAT GOES WITHOUT SAYING, SEIGNEUR. YOUR MOST HUMBLE AND ABJECT SERVANT EAGERLY AWAITS YOUR NEXT CALL, SEIGNEUR...
...AND YOUR NEXT COMMAND.
UNTIL THEN, DEAR BOY...
DAMN YOU, GISANDE!
WHERE THE HELL ARE YOU WHEN I NEED YOU MOST?!

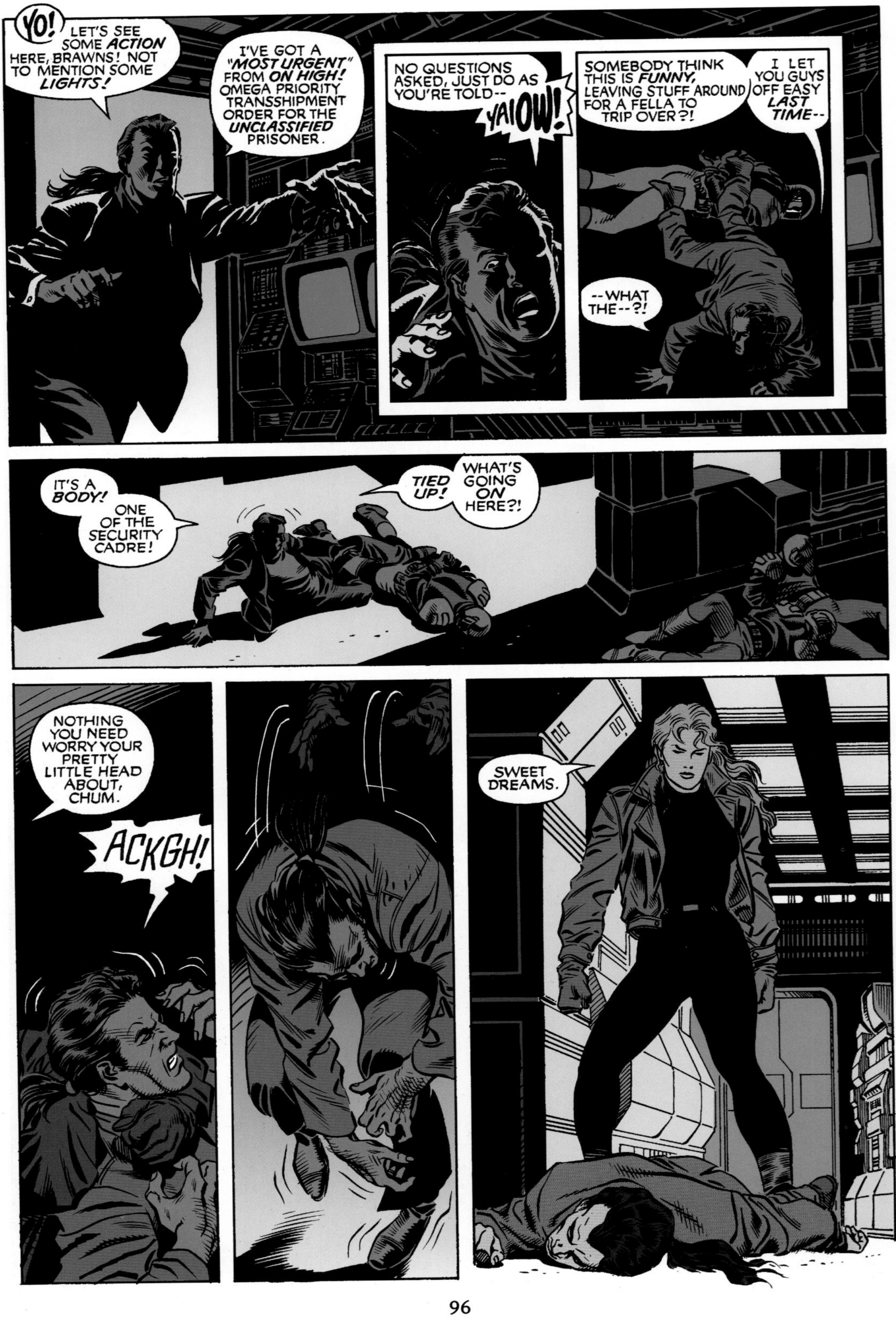
YO!
LET'S SEE SOME ACTION HERE, BRAWNS! NOT TO MENTION SOME LIGHTS!
I'VE GOT A "MOST URGENT" FROM ON HIGH! OMEGA PRIORITY TRANSSHIPMENT ORDER FOR THE UNCLASSIFIED PRISONER.
NO QUESTIONS ASKED, JUST DO AS YOU'RE TOLD--
YAIOW!
SOMEBODY THINK THIS IS FUNNY, LEAVING STUFF AROUND FOR A FELLA TO TRIP OVER?!
I LET YOU GUYS OFF EASY LAST TIME--
--WHAT THE--?!
IT'S A BODY!
ONE OF THE SECURITY CADRE!
TIED UP!
WHAT'S GOING ON HERE?!
NOTHING YOU NEED WORRY YOUR PRETTY LITTLE HEAD ABOUT, CHUM.
ACKGH!
SWEET DREAMS.

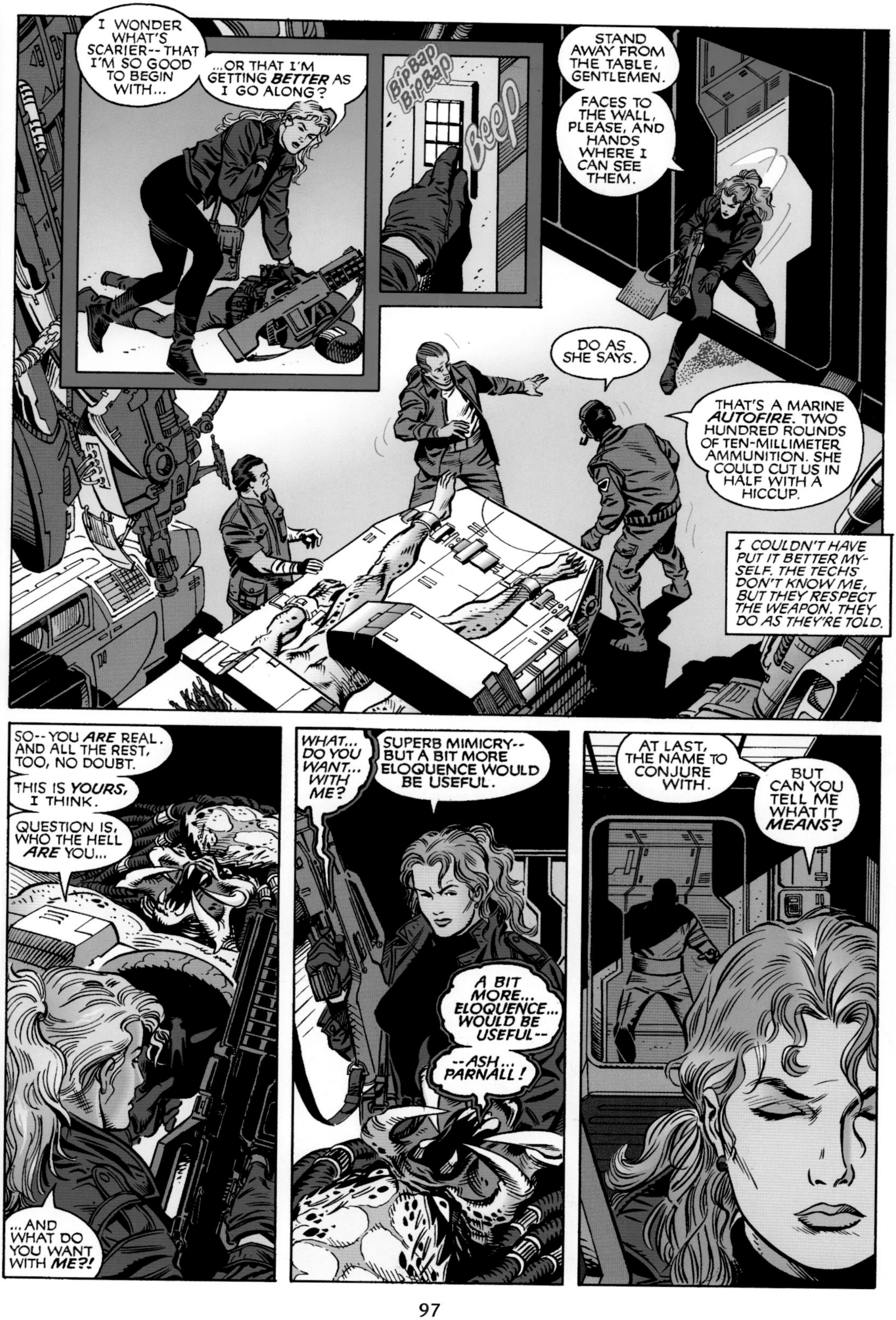
I WONDER WHAT'S SCARIER-- THAT I'M SO GOOD TO BEGIN WITH...
...OR THAT I'M GETTING *BETTER* AS I GO ALONG?
BipBap BipBap
Beep
STAND AWAY FROM THE TABLE, GENTLEMEN.
FACES TO THE WALL, PLEASE, AND HANDS WHERE I CAN SEE THEM.
DO AS SHE SAYS.
THAT'S A MARINE *AUTOFIRE*. TWO HUNDRED ROUNDS OF TEN-MILLIMETER AMMUNITION. SHE COULD CUT US IN HALF WITH A HICCUP.
I COULDN'T HAVE PUT IT BETTER MYSELF. THE TECHS DON'T KNOW ME, BUT THEY RESPECT THE WEAPON. THEY DO AS THEY'RE TOLD.
SO-- YOU *ARE* REAL. AND ALL THE REST, TOO, NO DOUBT.
THIS IS *YOURS,* I THINK.
QUESTION IS, WHO THE HELL *ARE* YOU...
...AND WHAT DO YOU WANT WITH *ME?!*
WHAT... DO YOU WANT... WITH ME?
SUPERB MIMICRY-- BUT A BIT MORE ELOQUENCE WOULD BE USEFUL.
A BIT MORE... ELOQUENCE... WOULD BE USEFUL--
--ASH... PARNALL!
AT LAST, THE NAME TO CONJURE WITH.
BUT CAN YOU TELL ME WHAT IT *MEANS?*

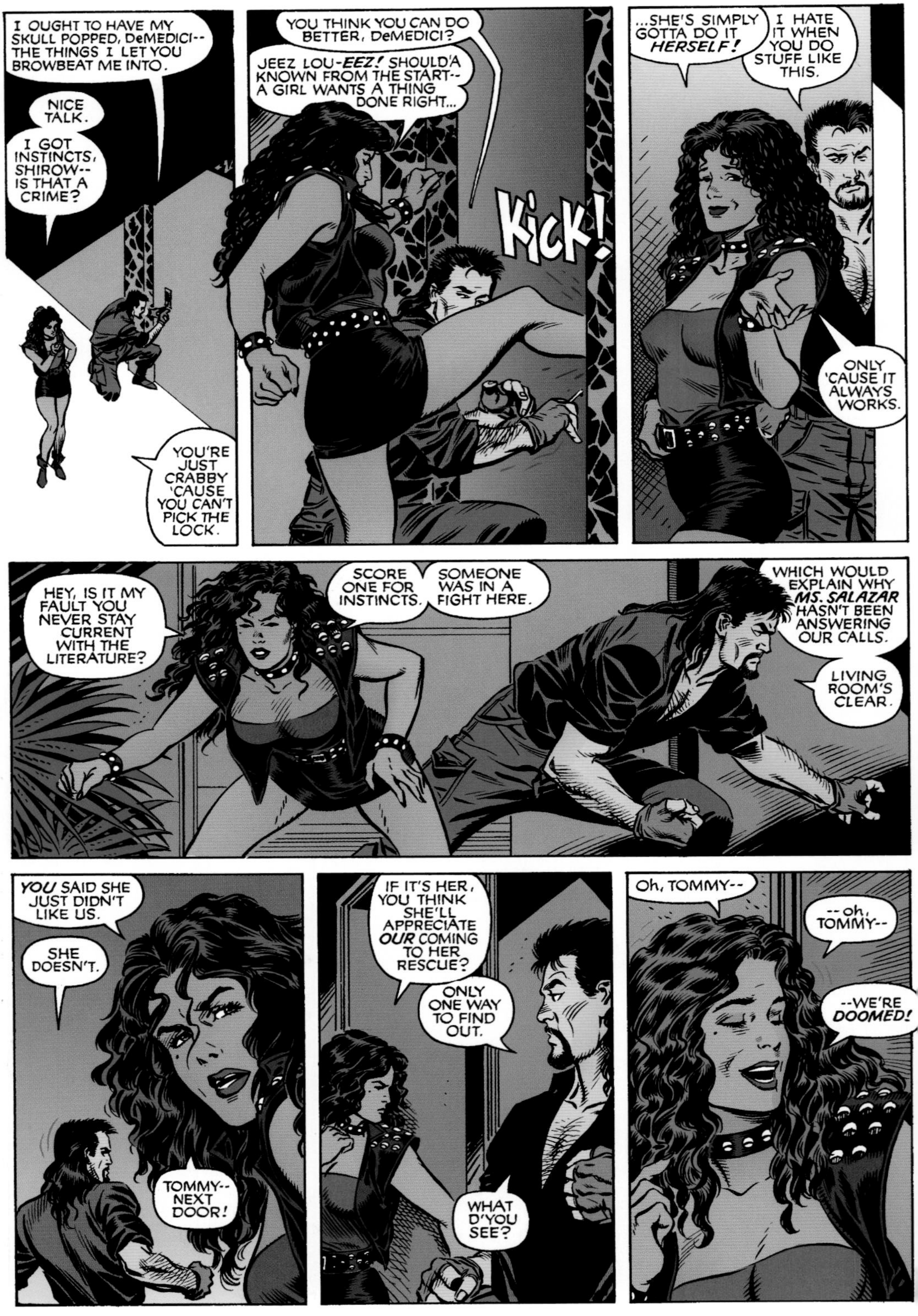

I OUGHT TO HAVE MY SKULL POPPED, DeMEDICI-- THE THINGS I LET YOU BROWBEAT ME INTO.
NICE TALK.
I GOT INSTINCTS, SHIROW-- IS THAT A CRIME?
YOU'RE JUST CRABBY 'CAUSE YOU CAN'T PICK THE LOCK.
YOU THINK YOU CAN DO BETTER, DeMEDICI?
JEEZ LOU-*EEZ!* SHOULD'A KNOWN FROM THE START-- A GIRL WANTS A THING DONE RIGHT...
KICK!
...SHE'S SIMPLY GOTTA DO IT *HERSELF!*
I HATE IT WHEN YOU DO STUFF LIKE THIS.
ONLY 'CAUSE IT ALWAYS WORKS.
HEY, IS IT MY FAULT YOU NEVER STAY CURRENT WITH THE LITERATURE?
SCORE ONE FOR INSTINCTS.
SOMEONE WAS IN A FIGHT HERE.
WHICH WOULD EXPLAIN WHY *MS. SALAZAR* HASN'T BEEN ANSWERING OUR CALLS.
LIVING ROOM'S CLEAR.
YOU SAID SHE JUST DIDN'T LIKE US.
SHE DOESN'T.
TOMMY-- NEXT DOOR!
IF IT'S HER, YOU THINK SHE'LL APPRECIATE *OUR* COMING TO HER RESCUE?
ONLY ONE WAY TO FIND OUT.
WHAT D'YOU SEE?
Oh, TOMMY--
--oh, TOMMY--
--WE'RE *DOOMED!*

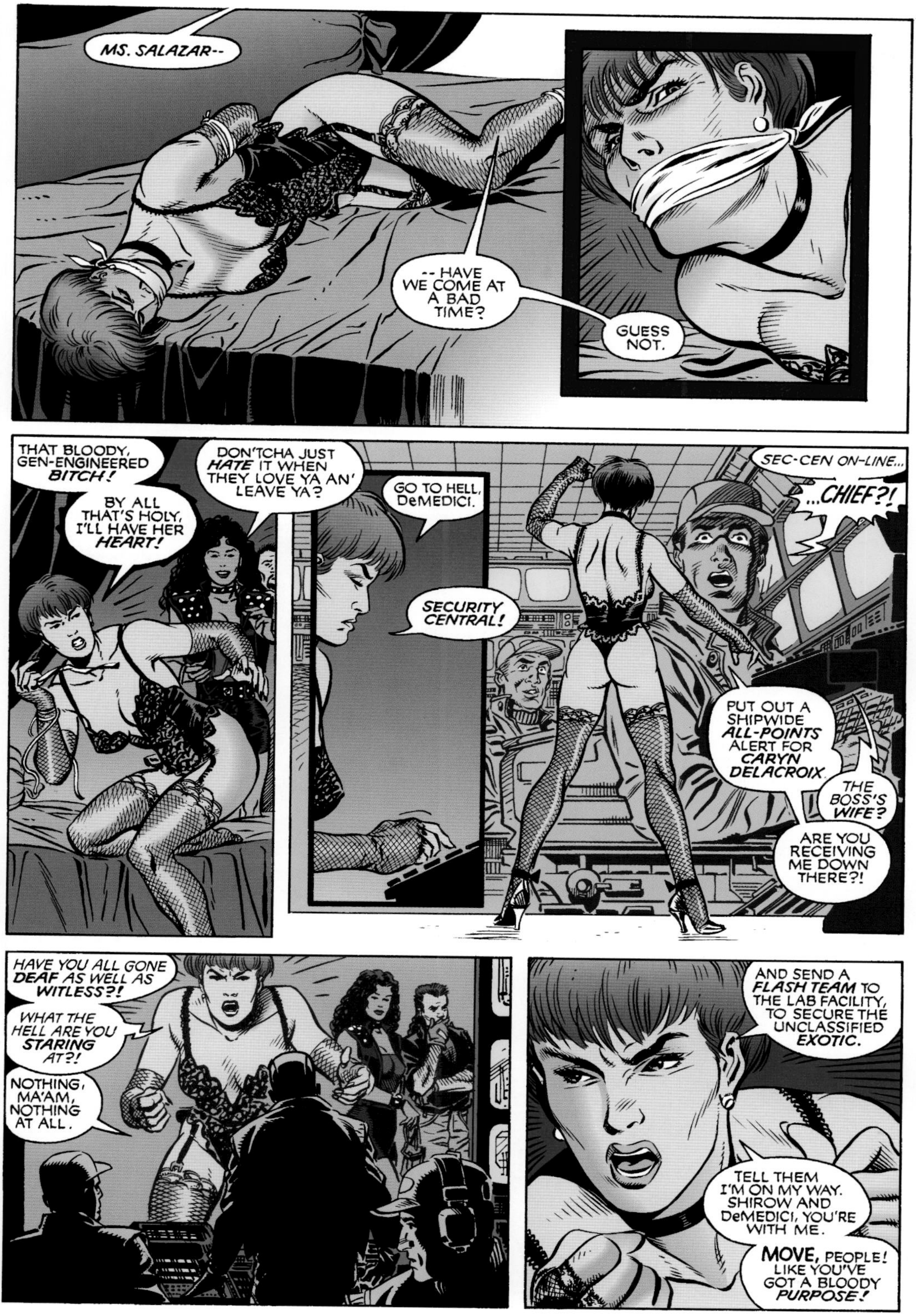
MS. SALAZAR--
--HAVE WE COME AT A BAD TIME?
GUESS NOT.
THAT BLOODY, GEN-ENGINEERED *BITCH!*
BY ALL THAT'S HOLY, I'LL HAVE HER *HEART!*
DON'TCHA JUST *HATE* IT WHEN THEY LOVE YA AN' LEAVE YA?
GO TO HELL, DeMEDICI.
SECURITY CENTRAL!
SEC-CEN ON-LINE...
...CHIEF?!
PUT OUT A SHIPWIDE *ALL-POINTS* ALERT FOR *CARYN DELACROIX.*
THE BOSS'S *WIFE?*
ARE YOU RECEIVING ME DOWN THERE?!
HAVE YOU ALL GONE ***DEAF*** *AS WELL AS* ***WITLESS?!***
WHAT THE HELL ARE YOU ***STARING*** *AT?!*
NOTHING, MA'AM, NOTHING AT ALL.
AND SEND A *FLASH TEAM* TO THE LAB FACILITY, TO SECURE THE UNCLASSIFIED *EXOTIC.*
TELL THEM I'M ON MY WAY. SHIROW AND DeMEDICI, YOU'RE WITH ME.
MOVE, PEOPLE! LIKE YOU'VE GOT A BLOODY *PURPOSE!*

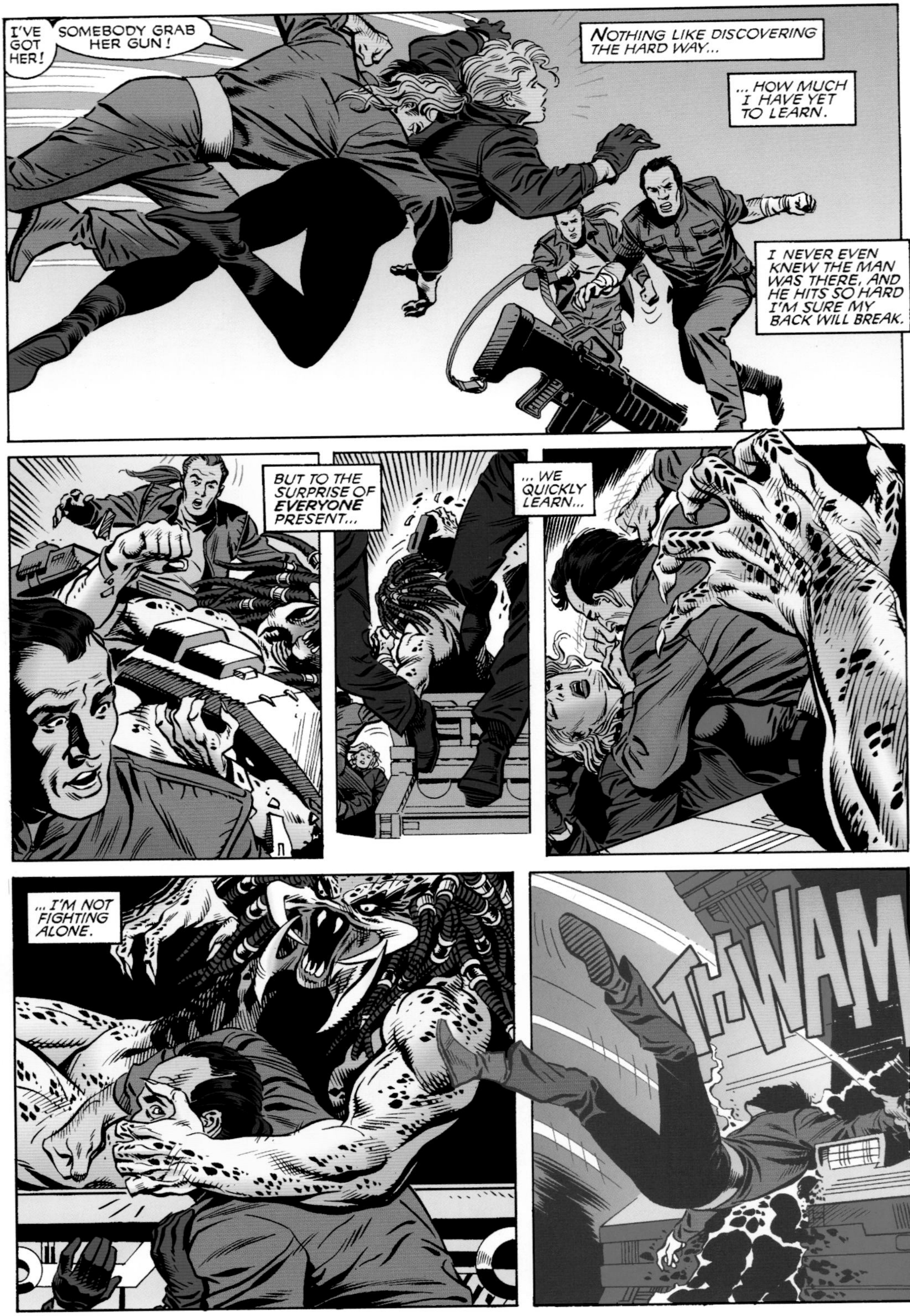
I'VE GOT HER!
SOMEBODY GRAB HER GUN!
NOTHING LIKE DISCOVERING THE HARD WAY...
...HOW MUCH I HAVE YET TO LEARN.
I NEVER EVEN KNEW THE MAN WAS THERE, AND HE HITS SO HARD I'M SURE MY BACK WILL BREAK.
BUT TO THE SURPRISE OF EVERYONE PRESENT...
...WE QUICKLY LEARN...
...I'M NOT FIGHTING ALONE.
THWAM

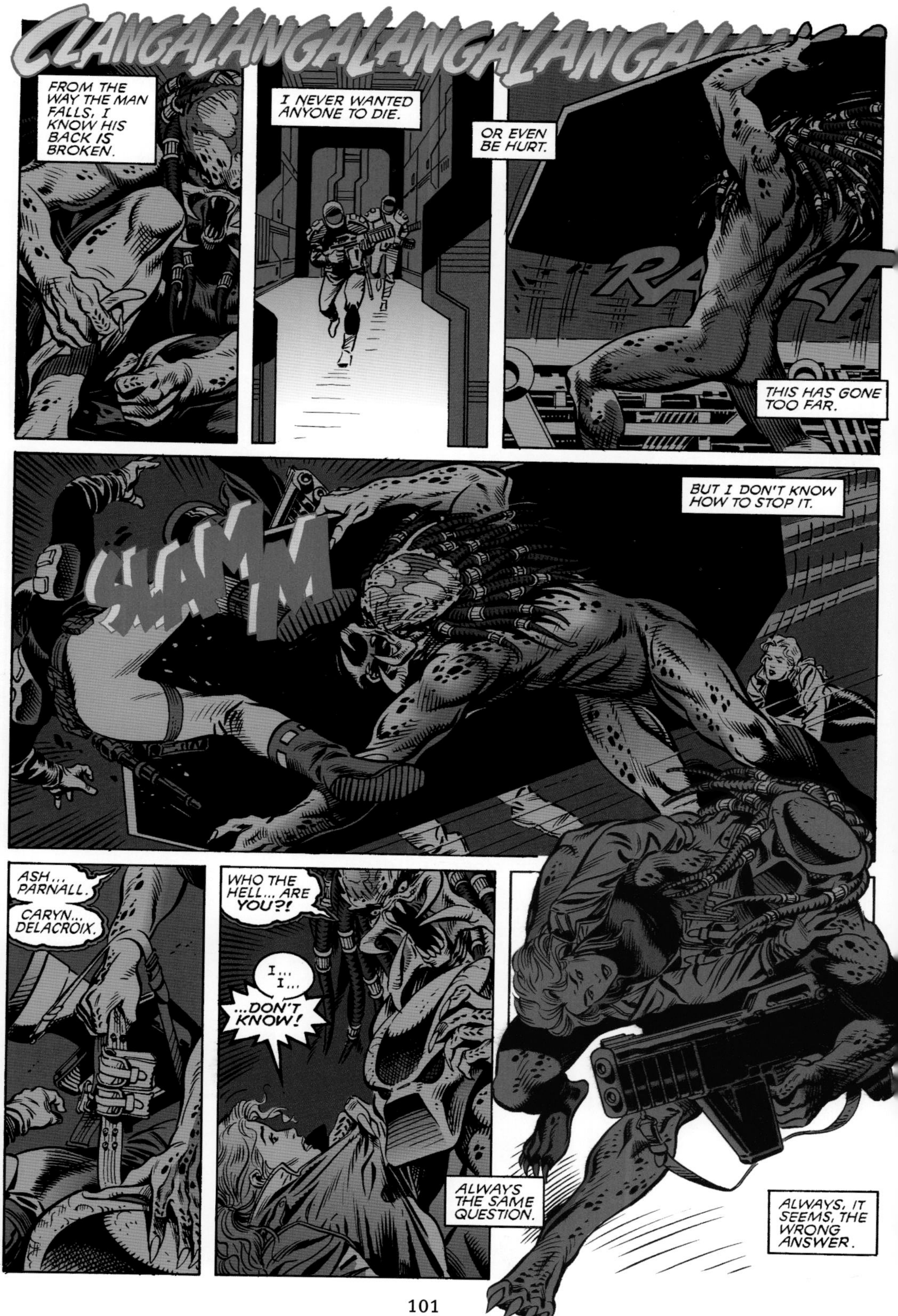
CLANGALANGALANGALANGALANGALA
FROM THE WAY THE MAN FALLS, I KNOW HIS BACK IS BROKEN.
I NEVER WANTED ANYONE TO DIE.
OR EVEN BE HURT.
THIS HAS GONE TOO FAR.
BUT I DON'T KNOW HOW TO STOP IT.
SLAMM
ASH... PARNALL.
CARYN... DELACROIX.
WHO THE HELL... ARE YOU?!
I... I...
...DON'T KNOW!
ALWAYS THE SAME QUESTION.
ALWAYS, IT SEEMS, THE WRONG ANSWER.

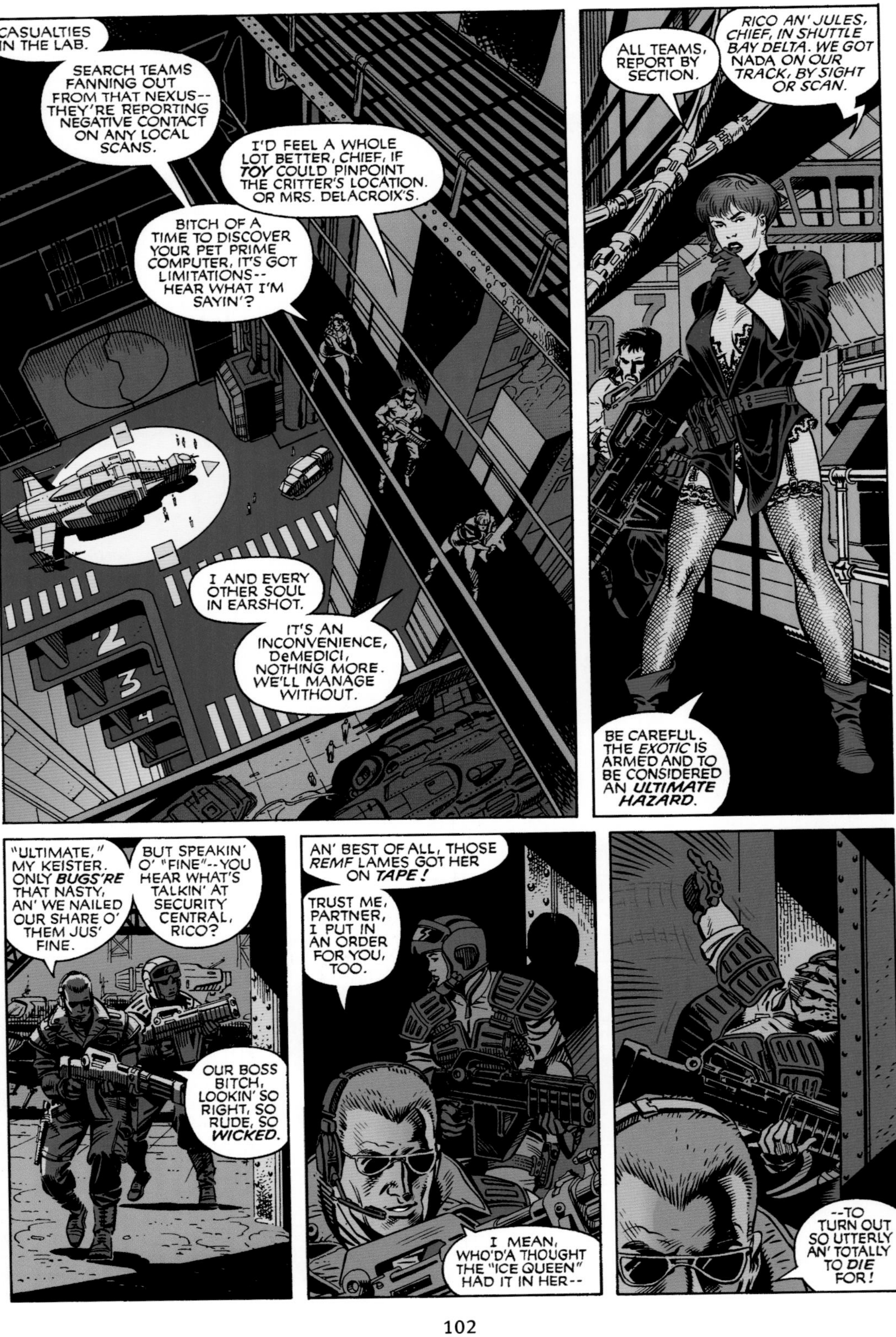
CASUALTIES IN THE LAB.
SEARCH TEAMS FANNING OUT FROM THAT NEXUS-- THEY'RE REPORTING NEGATIVE CONTACT ON ANY LOCAL SCANS.
I'D FEEL A WHOLE LOT BETTER, CHIEF, IF TOY COULD PINPOINT THE CRITTER'S LOCATION. OR MRS. DELACROIX'S.
BITCH OF A TIME TO DISCOVER YOUR PET PRIME COMPUTER, IT'S GOT LIMITATIONS-- HEAR WHAT I'M SAYIN'?
I AND EVERY OTHER SOUL IN EARSHOT.
IT'S AN INCONVENIENCE, DeMEDICI, NOTHING MORE. WE'LL MANAGE WITHOUT.
ALL TEAMS, REPORT BY SECTION.
RICO AN' JULES, CHIEF, IN SHUTTLE BAY DELTA. WE GOT NADA ON OUR TRACK, BY SIGHT OR SCAN.
BE CAREFUL. THE EXOTIC IS ARMED AND TO BE CONSIDERED AN ULTIMATE HAZARD.
"ULTIMATE," MY KEISTER. ONLY BUGS'RE THAT NASTY, AN' WE NAILED OUR SHARE O' THEM JUS' FINE.
BUT SPEAKIN' O' "FINE"--YOU HEAR WHAT'S TALKIN' AT SECURITY CENTRAL, RICO?
OUR BOSS BITCH, LOOKIN' SO RIGHT, SO RUDE, SO WICKED.
AN' BEST OF ALL, THOSE REMF LAMES GOT HER ON TAPE!
TRUST ME, PARTNER, I PUT IN AN ORDER FOR YOU, TOO.
I MEAN, WHO'D'A THOUGHT THE "ICE QUEEN" HAD IT IN HER--
--TO TURN OUT SO UTTERLY AN' TOTALLY TO DIE FOR!

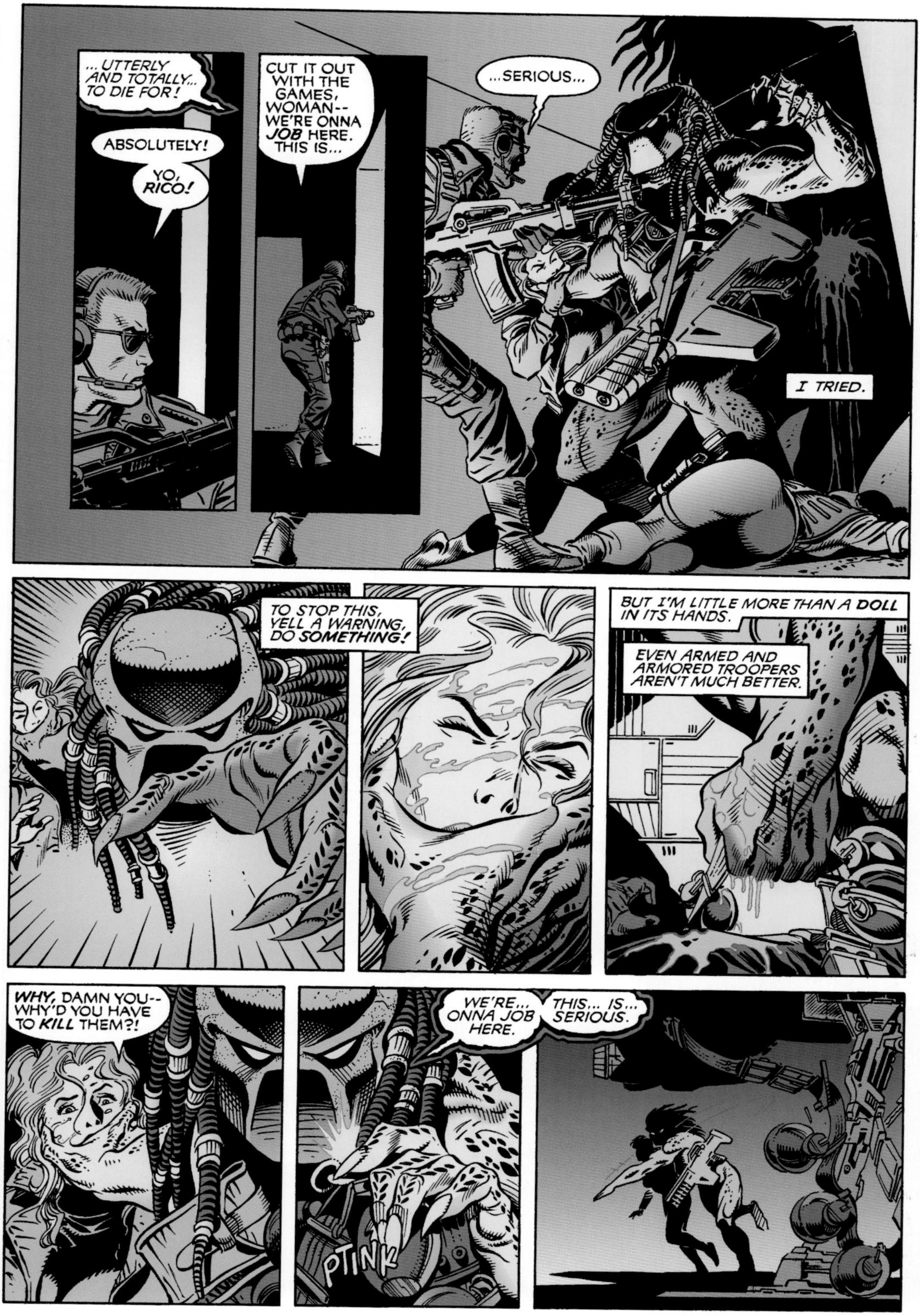
...UTTERLY AND TOTALLY... TO DIE FOR!
ABSOLUTELY!
YO, RICO!
CUT IT OUT WITH THE GAMES, WOMAN-- WE'RE ONNA JOB HERE. THIS IS...
...SERIOUS...
I TRIED.
TO STOP THIS, YELL A WARNING, DO SOMETHING!
BUT I'M LITTLE MORE THAN A DOLL IN ITS HANDS.
EVEN ARMED AND ARMORED TROOPERS AREN'T MUCH BETTER.
WHY, DAMN YOU-- WHY'D YOU HAVE TO KILL THEM?!
WE'RE... ONNA JOB HERE.
THIS... IS... SERIOUS.
PTINK

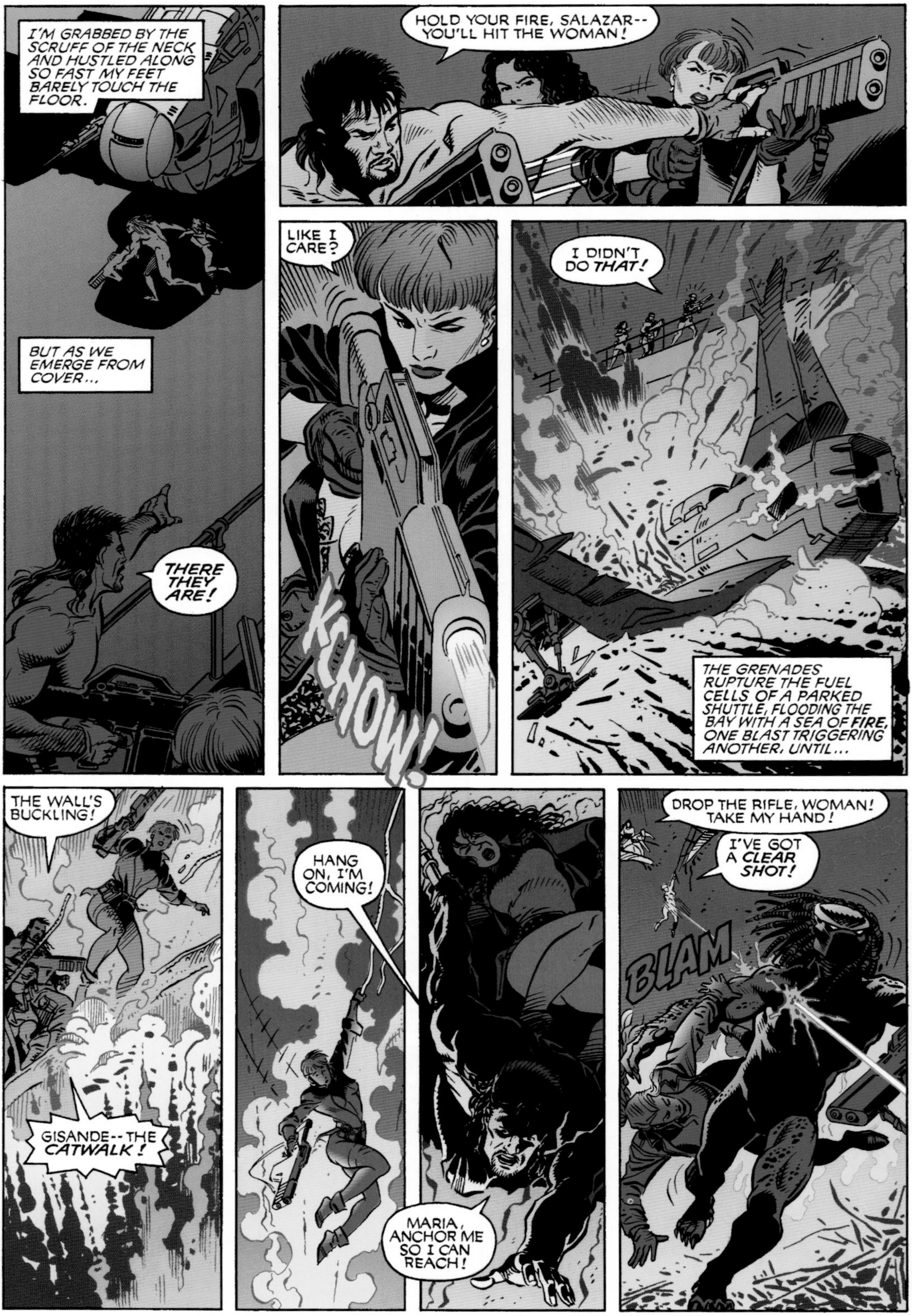

I'M GRABBED BY THE SCRUFF OF THE NECK AND HUSTLED ALONG SO FAST MY FEET BARELY TOUCH THE FLOOR.
BUT AS WE EMERGE FROM COVER...
THERE THEY ARE!
HOLD YOUR FIRE, SALAZAR-- YOU'LL HIT THE WOMAN!
LIKE I CARE?
KCHOW!
I DIDN'T DO THAT!
THE GRENADES RUPTURE THE FUEL CELLS OF A PARKED SHUTTLE, FLOODING THE BAY WITH A SEA OF FIRE, ONE BLAST TRIGGERING ANOTHER, UNTIL...
THE WALL'S BUCKLING!
GISANDE--THE CATWALK!
HANG ON, I'M COMING!
MARIA, ANCHOR ME SO I CAN REACH!
DROP THE RIFLE, WOMAN! TAKE MY HAND!
I'VE GOT A CLEAR SHOT!
BLAM

THE PREDATOR FALLS LIKE IT'S BEEN HIT BY A SLEDGE-HAMMER.

IT'S A PERFECT TARGET.

YARRRGH

BUT GISANDE NEVER HAS THE CHANCE TO TAKE ADVANTAGE.

BOOM

SHIROW, I'M *BURNING!* *I'M BURNING!*

TOMMY--! USE YOUR JACKET, MARIA! SMOTHER THE FLAMES!

CLEAR ME SOME ROOM, SO I CAN GET HER AWAY FROM THE EDGE.

THE FLAMES ARE STARTING TO COOK THE CATWALK!

IS SHE ALIVE?

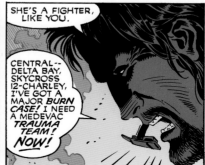

SHE'S A FIGHTER, LIKE YOU.

CENTRAL-- DELTA BAY, SKYCROSS 12-CHARLEY, I'VE GOT A MAJOR *BURN CASE!* I NEED A MEDEVAC *TRAUMA TEAM!* NOW!

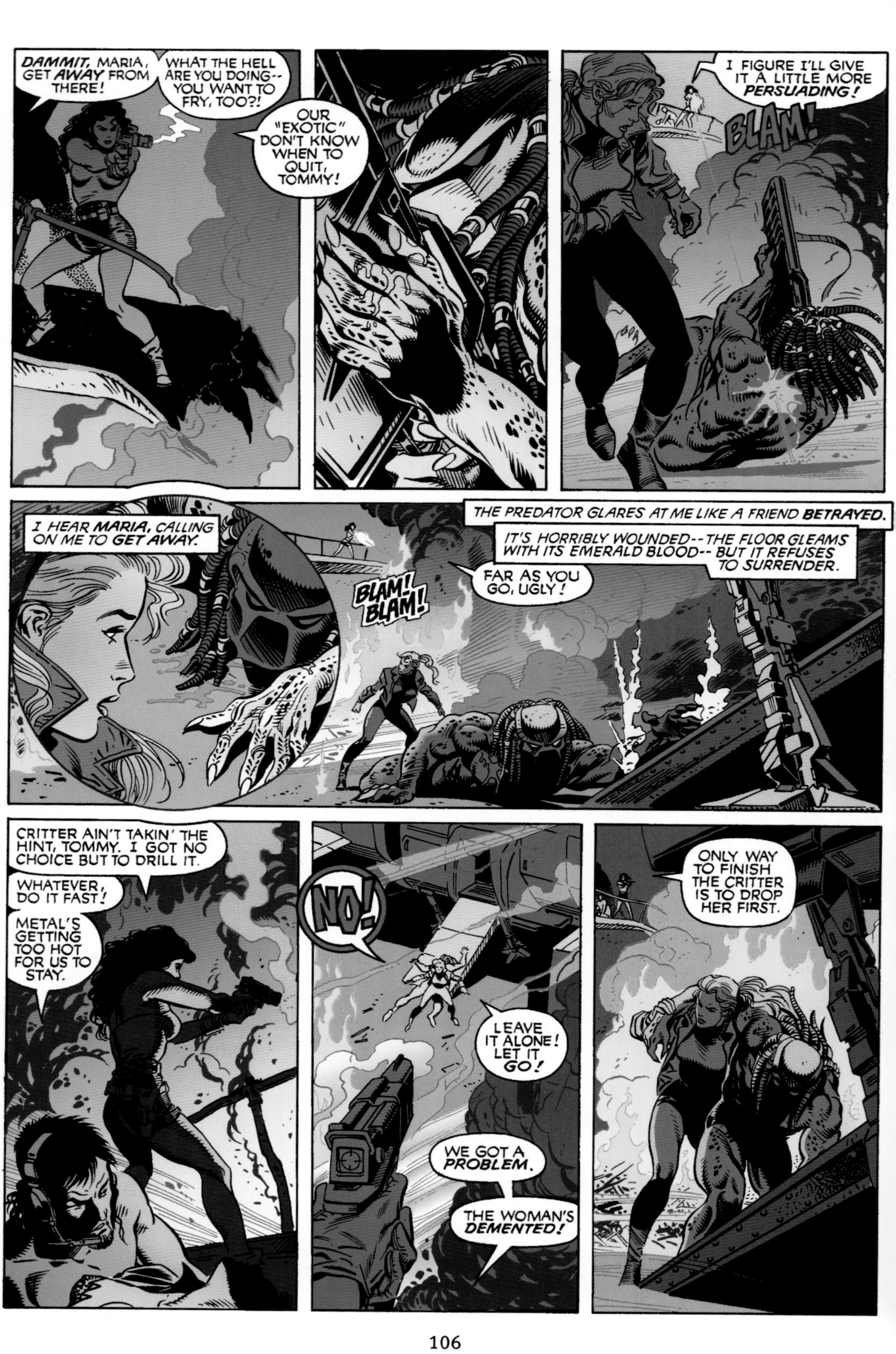
DAMMIT, MARIA, GET AWAY FROM THERE!
WHAT THE HELL ARE YOU DOING-- YOU WANT TO FRY, TOO?!
OUR "EXOTIC" DON'T KNOW WHEN TO QUIT, TOMMY!
I FIGURE I'LL GIVE IT A LITTLE MORE PERSUADING!
BLAM!
I HEAR MARIA, CALLING ON ME TO GET AWAY.
THE PREDATOR GLARES AT ME LIKE A FRIEND BETRAYED.
IT'S HORRIBLY WOUNDED-- THE FLOOR GLEAMS WITH ITS EMERALD BLOOD-- BUT IT REFUSES TO SURRENDER.
BLAM! BLAM!
FAR AS YOU GO, UGLY!
CRITTER AIN'T TAKIN' THE HINT, TOMMY. I GOT NO CHOICE BUT TO DRILL IT.
WHATEVER, DO IT FAST!
METAL'S GETTING TOO HOT FOR US TO STAY.
NO!
LEAVE IT ALONE! LET IT GO!
WE GOT A PROBLEM.
THE WOMAN'S DEMENTED!
ONLY WAY TO FINISH THE CRITTER IS TO DROP HER FIRST.

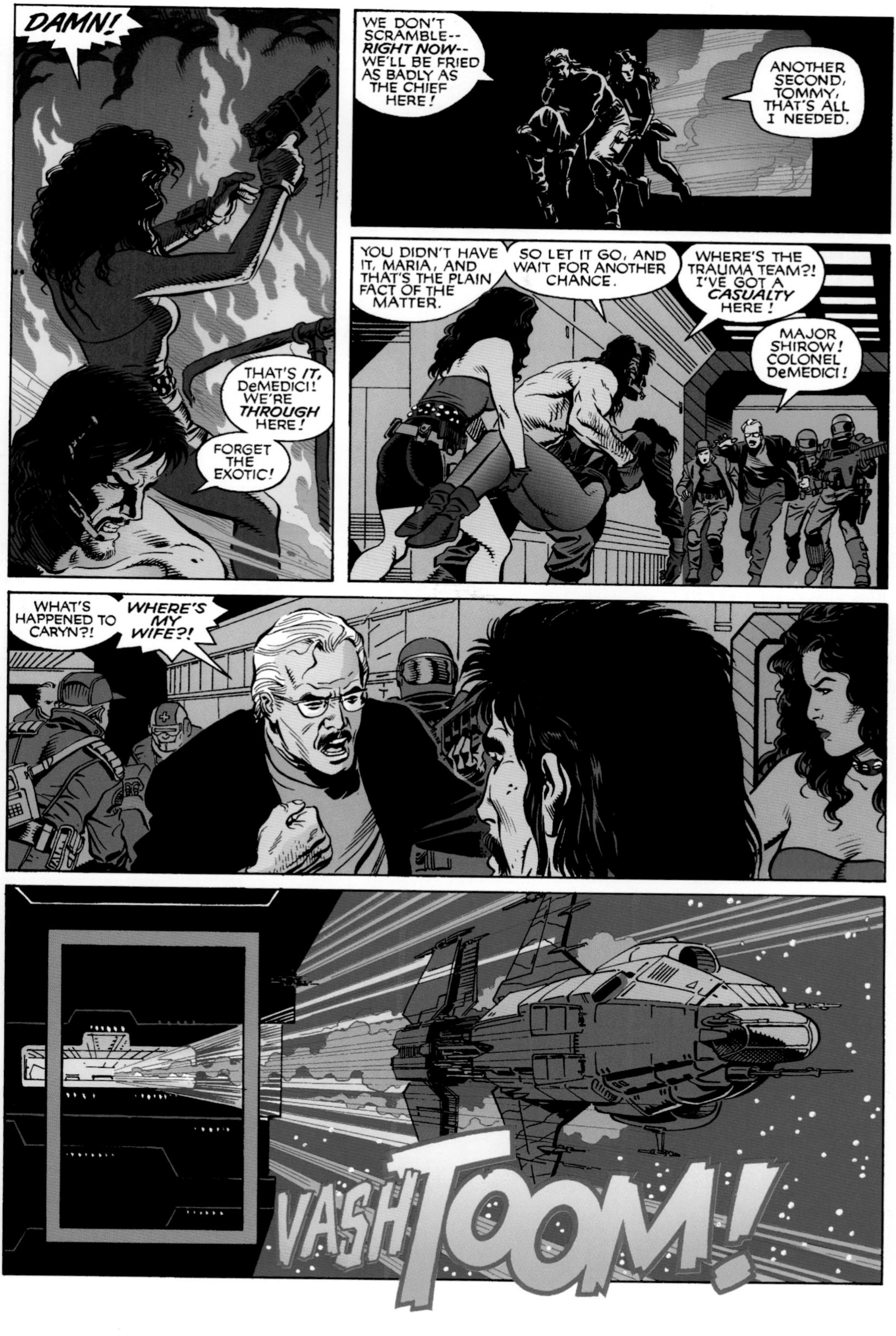
DAMN!
THAT'S IT, DeMEDICI! WE'RE THROUGH HERE!
FORGET THE EXOTIC!
WE DON'T SCRAMBLE-- RIGHT NOW-- WE'LL BE FRIED AS BADLY AS THE CHIEF HERE!
ANOTHER SECOND, TOMMY, THAT'S ALL I NEEDED.
YOU DIDN'T HAVE IT, MARIA, AND THAT'S THE PLAIN FACT OF THE MATTER.
SO LET IT GO, AND WAIT FOR ANOTHER CHANCE.
WHERE'S THE TRAUMA TEAM?! I'VE GOT A CASUALTY HERE!
MAJOR SHIROW! COLONEL DeMEDICI!
WHAT'S HAPPENED TO CARYN?!
WHERE'S MY WIFE?!
VASHTOOM!

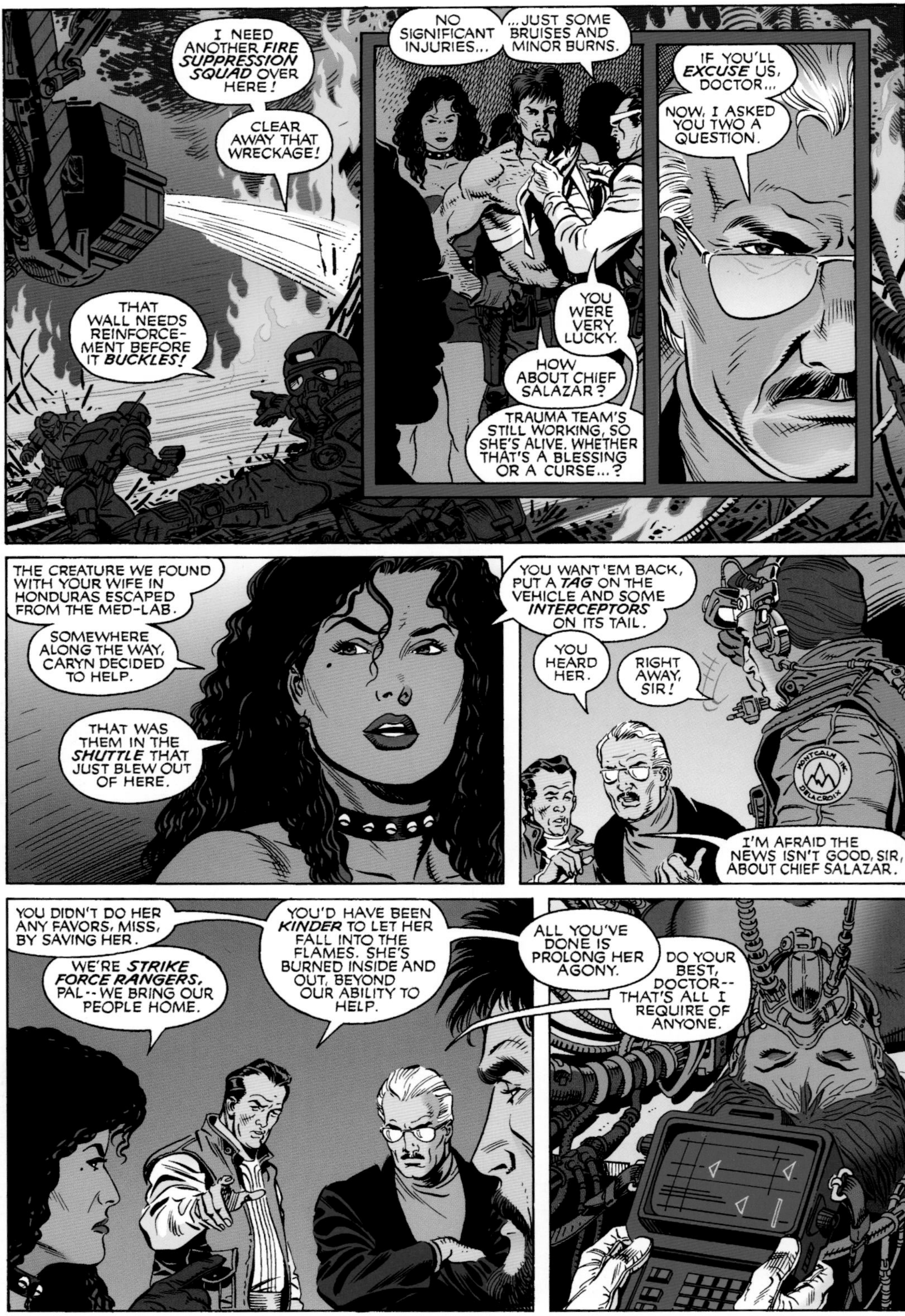
I NEED ANOTHER FIRE SUPPRESSION SQUAD OVER HERE!
CLEAR AWAY THAT WRECKAGE!
THAT WALL NEEDS REINFORCE-MENT BEFORE IT BUCKLES!
NO SIGNIFICANT INJURIES...
...JUST SOME BRUISES AND MINOR BURNS.
YOU WERE VERY LUCKY.
HOW ABOUT CHIEF SALAZAR?
TRAUMA TEAM'S STILL WORKING, SO SHE'S ALIVE. WHETHER THAT'S A BLESSING OR A CURSE...?
IF YOU'LL EXCUSE US, DOCTOR...
NOW, I ASKED YOU TWO A QUESTION.
THE CREATURE WE FOUND WITH YOUR WIFE IN HONDURAS ESCAPED FROM THE MED-LAB.
SOMEWHERE ALONG THE WAY, CARYN DECIDED TO HELP.
THAT WAS THEM IN THE SHUTTLE THAT JUST BLEW OUT OF HERE.
YOU WANT 'EM BACK, PUT A TAG ON THE VEHICLE AND SOME INTERCEPTORS ON ITS TAIL.
YOU HEARD HER.
RIGHT AWAY, SIR!
MONTCALM INC. DELACROIX
I'M AFRAID THE NEWS ISN'T GOOD, SIR, ABOUT CHIEF SALAZAR.
YOU DIDN'T DO HER ANY FAVORS, MISS, BY SAVING HER.
WE'RE STRIKE FORCE RANGERS, PAL--WE BRING OUR PEOPLE HOME.
YOU'D HAVE BEEN KINDER TO LET HER FALL INTO THE FLAMES. SHE'S BURNED INSIDE AND OUT, BEYOND OUR ABILITY TO HELP.
ALL YOU'VE DONE IS PROLONG HER AGONY.
DO YOUR BEST, DOCTOR--THAT'S ALL I REQUIRE OF ANYONE.

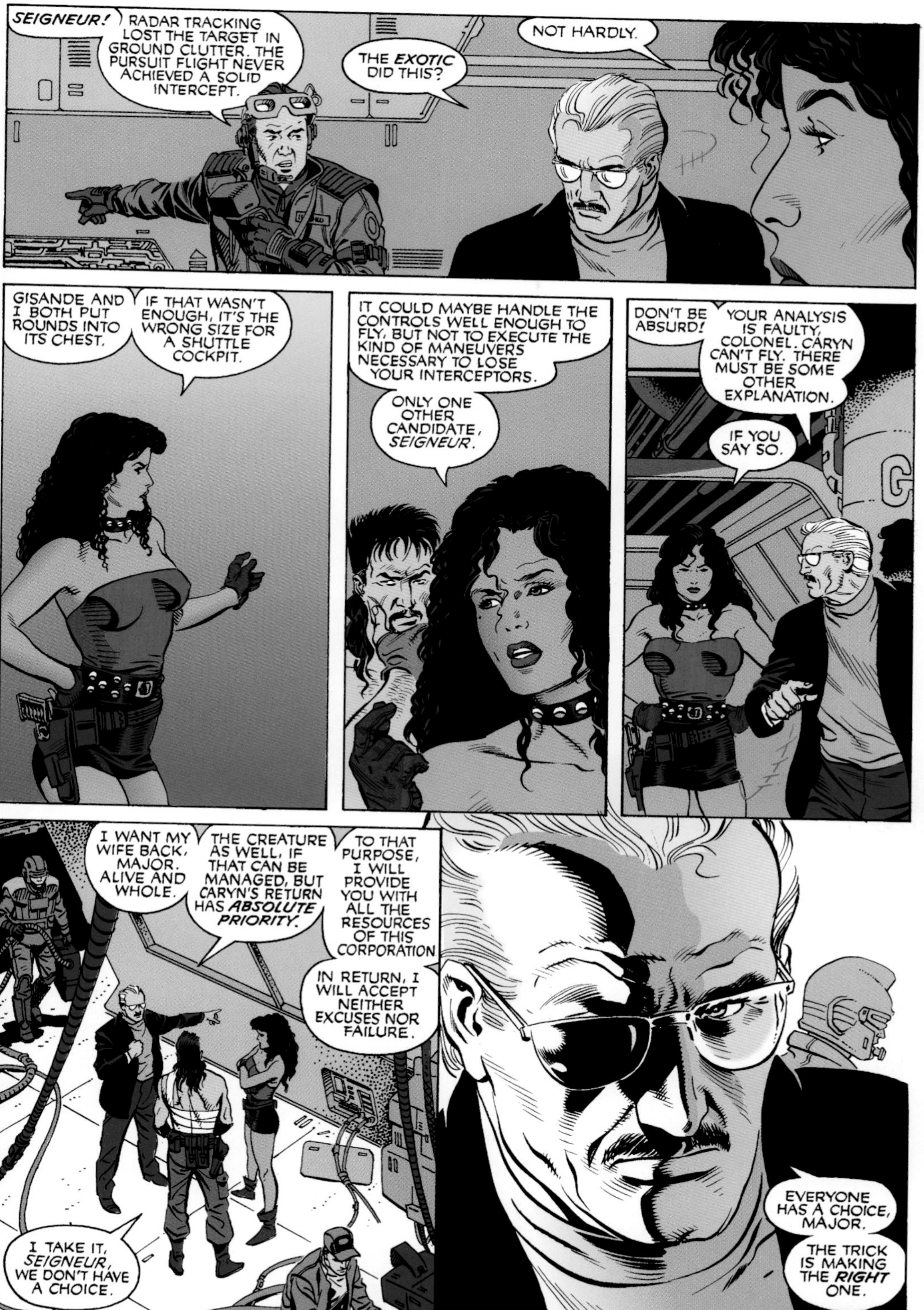
SEIGNEUR!
RADAR TRACKING LOST THE TARGET IN GROUND CLUTTER. THE PURSUIT FLIGHT NEVER ACHIEVED A SOLID INTERCEPT.
THE EXOTIC DID THIS?
NOT HARDLY.
GISANDE AND I BOTH PUT ROUNDS INTO ITS CHEST.
IF THAT WASN'T ENOUGH, IT'S THE WRONG SIZE FOR A SHUTTLE COCKPIT.
IT COULD MAYBE HANDLE THE CONTROLS WELL ENOUGH TO FLY, BUT NOT TO EXECUTE THE KIND OF MANEUVERS NECESSARY TO LOSE YOUR INTERCEPTORS.
ONLY ONE OTHER CANDIDATE, SEIGNEUR.
DON'T BE ABSURD!
YOUR ANALYSIS IS FAULTY, COLONEL. CARYN CAN'T FLY. THERE MUST BE SOME OTHER EXPLANATION.
IF YOU SAY SO.
I WANT MY WIFE BACK, MAJOR. ALIVE AND WHOLE.
THE CREATURE AS WELL, IF THAT CAN BE MANAGED, BUT CARYN'S RETURN HAS ABSOLUTE PRIORITY.
TO THAT PURPOSE, I WILL PROVIDE YOU WITH ALL THE RESOURCES OF THIS CORPORATION
IN RETURN, I WILL ACCEPT NEITHER EXCUSES NOR FAILURE.
I TAKE IT, SEIGNEUR, WE DON'T HAVE A CHOICE.
EVERYONE HAS A CHOICE, MAJOR.
THE TRICK IS MAKING THE RIGHT ONE.

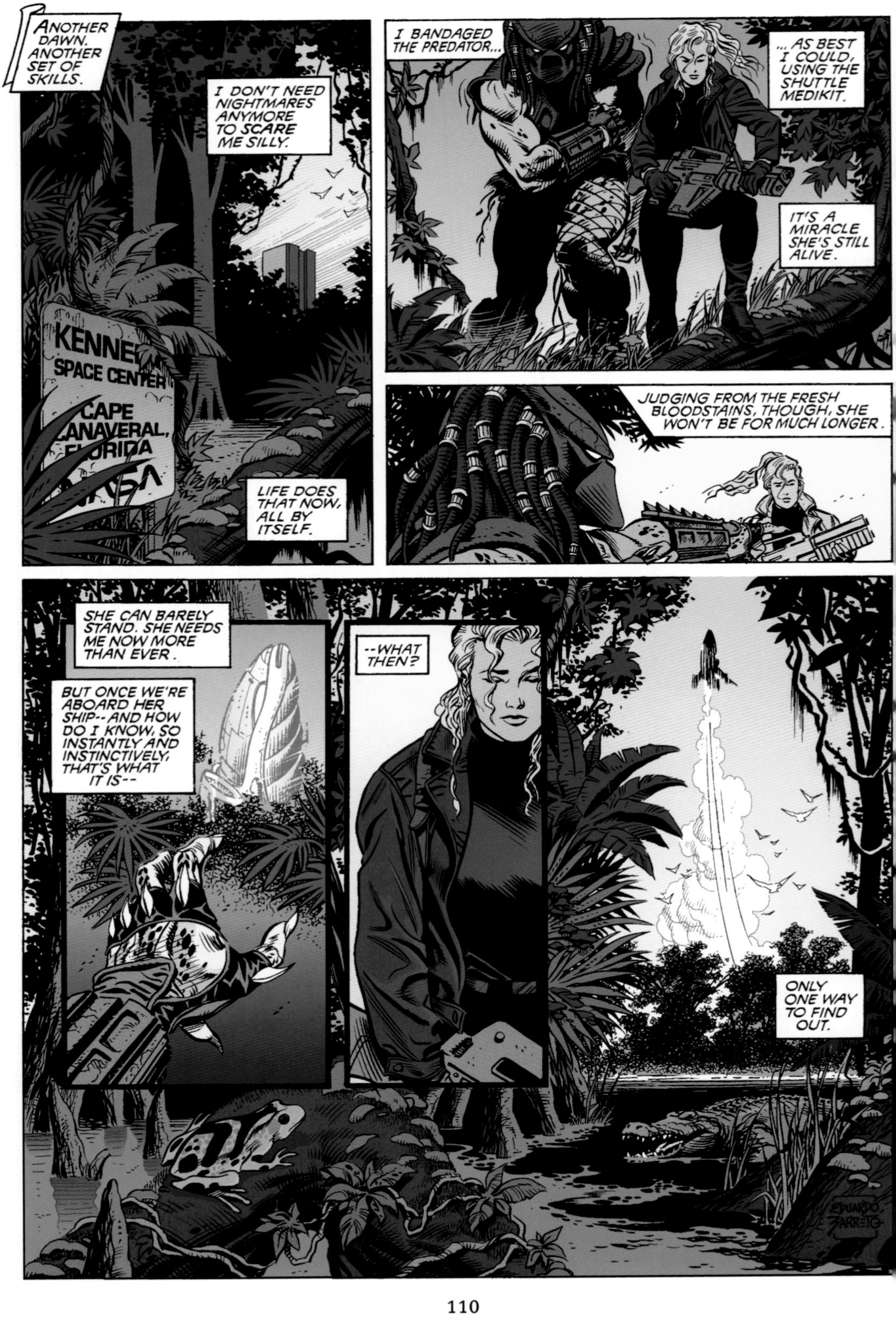
ANOTHER DAWN. ANOTHER SET OF SKILLS.
I DON'T NEED NIGHTMARES ANYMORE TO SCARE ME SILLY.
KENNEDY SPACE CENTER
CAPE CANAVERAL, FLORIDA
NASA
LIFE DOES THAT NOW, ALL BY ITSELF.
I BANDAGED THE PREDATOR...
...AS BEST I COULD, USING THE SHUTTLE MEDIKIT.
IT'S A MIRACLE SHE'S STILL ALIVE.
JUDGING FROM THE FRESH BLOODSTAINS, THOUGH, SHE WON'T BE FOR MUCH LONGER.
SHE CAN BARELY STAND. SHE NEEDS ME NOW MORE THAN EVER.
BUT ONCE WE'RE ABOARD HER SHIP-- AND HOW DO I KNOW, SO INSTANTLY AND INSTINCTIVELY, THAT'S WHAT IT IS--
--WHAT THEN?
ONLY ONE WAY TO FIND OUT.
EDUARDO BARRETO

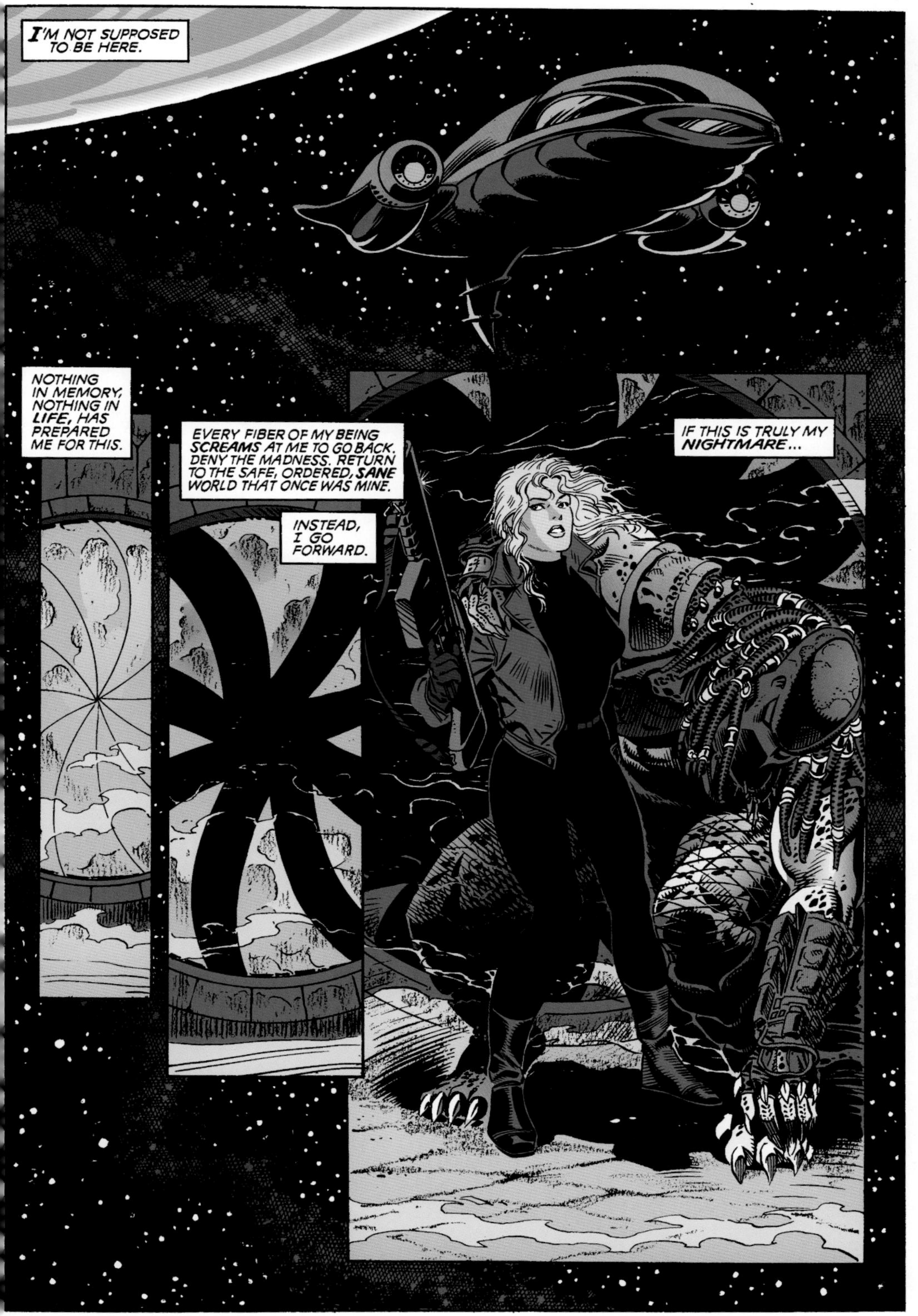
I'M NOT SUPPOSED TO BE HERE.
NOTHING IN MEMORY, NOTHING IN LIFE, HAS PREPARED ME FOR THIS.
EVERY FIBER OF MY BEING SCREAMS AT ME TO GO BACK. DENY THE MADNESS. RETURN TO THE SAFE, ORDERED, SANE WORLD THAT ONCE WAS MINE.
INSTEAD, I GO FORWARD.
IF THIS IS TRULY MY NIGHTMARE...

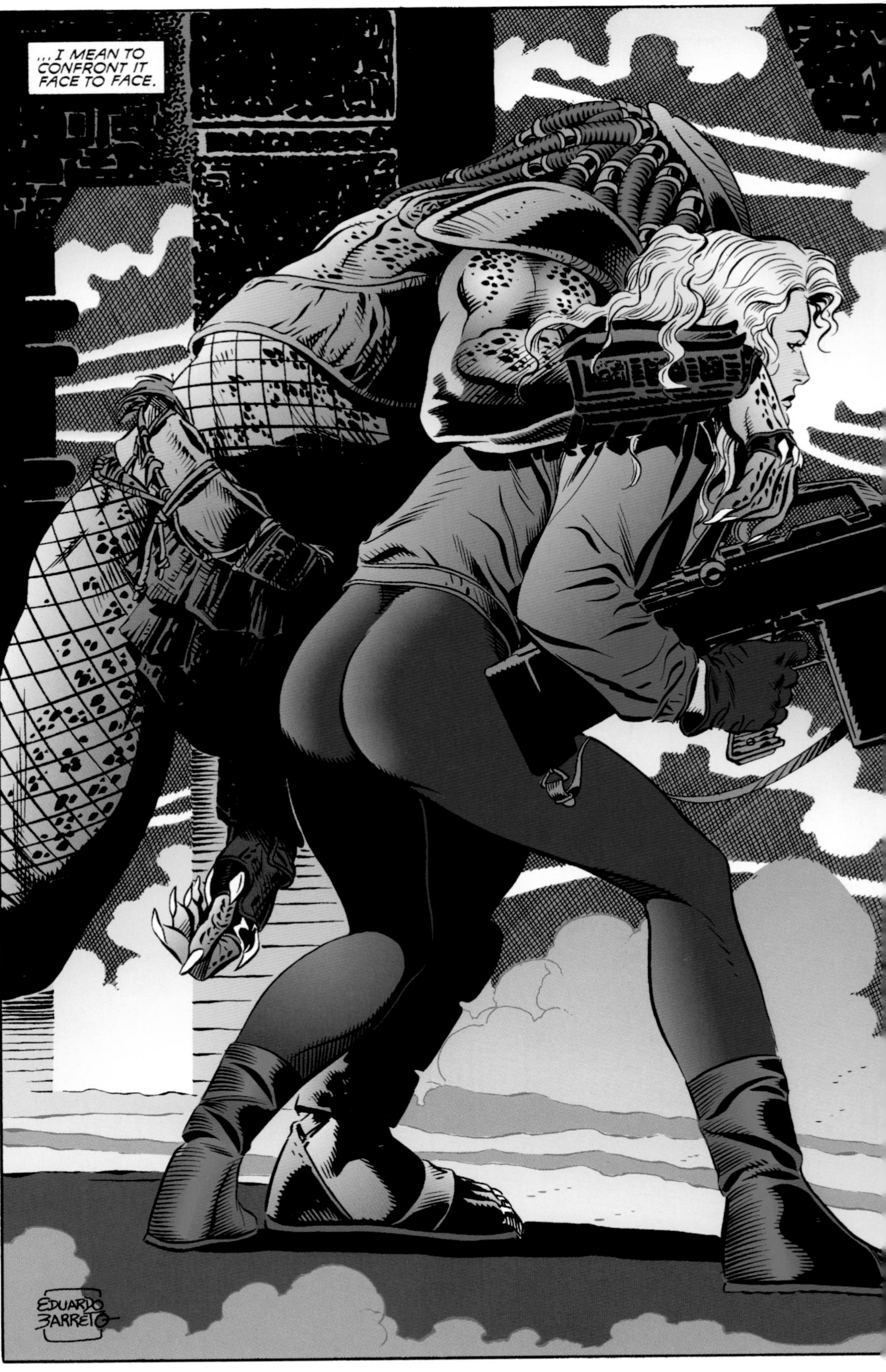
...I MEAN TO CONFRONT IT FACE TO FACE.
EDUARDO BARRETO

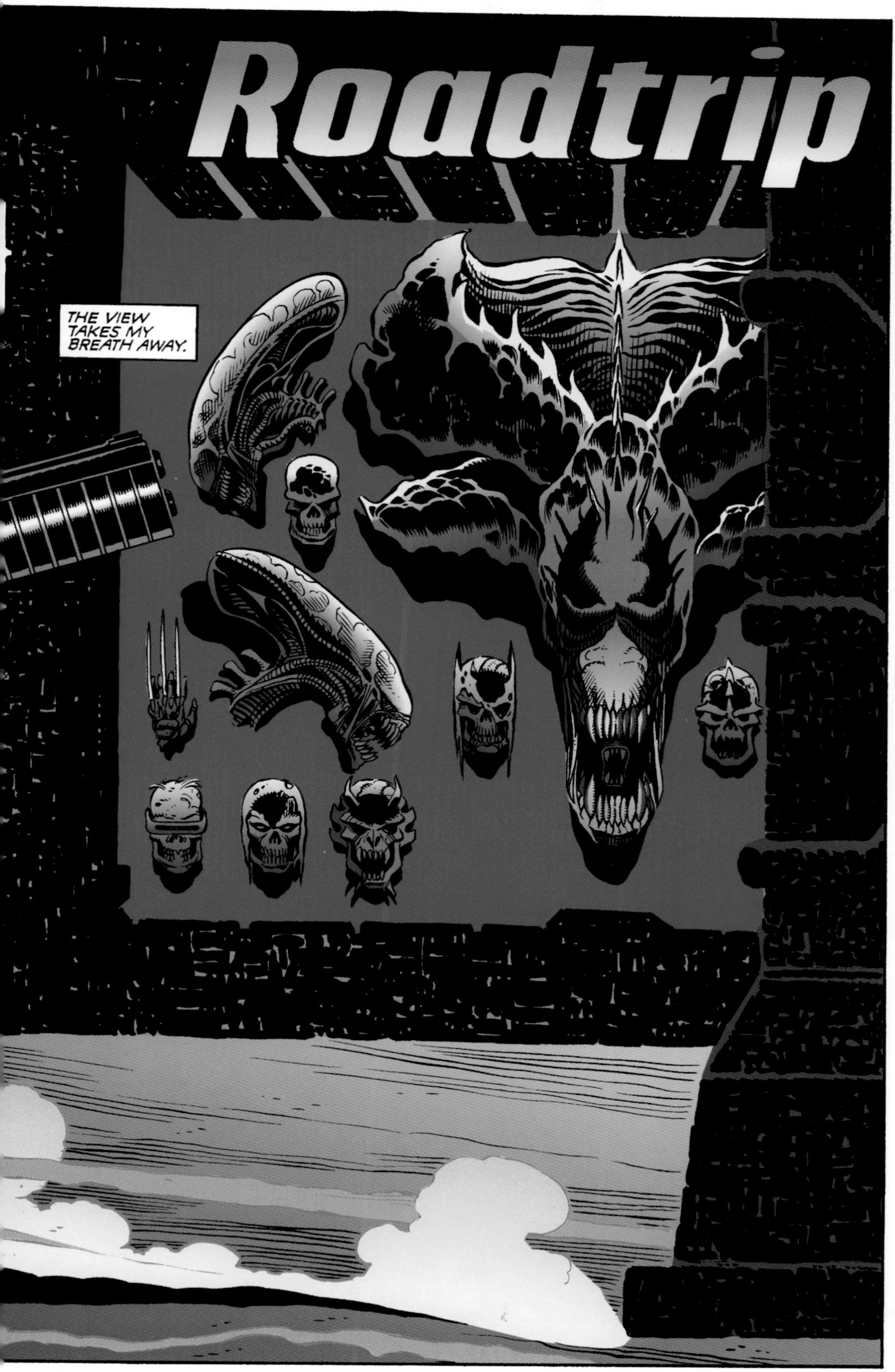
Roadtrip
THE VIEW TAKES MY BREATH AWAY.

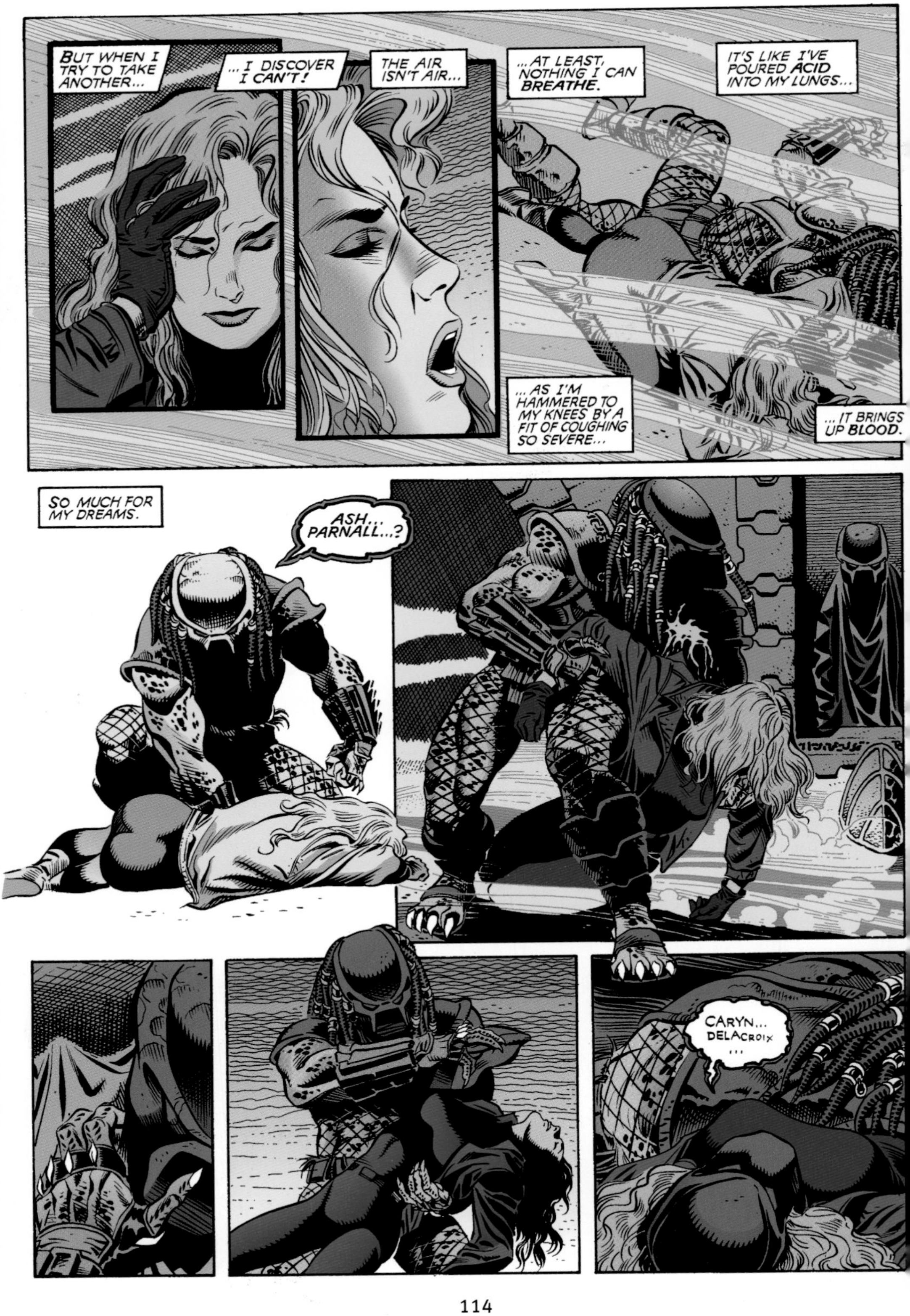
BUT WHEN I TRY TO TAKE ANOTHER...
...I DISCOVER I CAN'T!
THE AIR ISN'T AIR...
...AT LEAST, NOTHING I CAN BREATHE.
IT'S LIKE I'VE POURED ACID INTO MY LUNGS...
...AS I'M HAMMERED TO MY KNEES BY A FIT OF COUGHING SO SEVERE...
...IT BRINGS UP BLOOD.
SO MUCH FOR MY DREAMS.
ASH... PARNALL...?
CARYN... DELACROIX ...

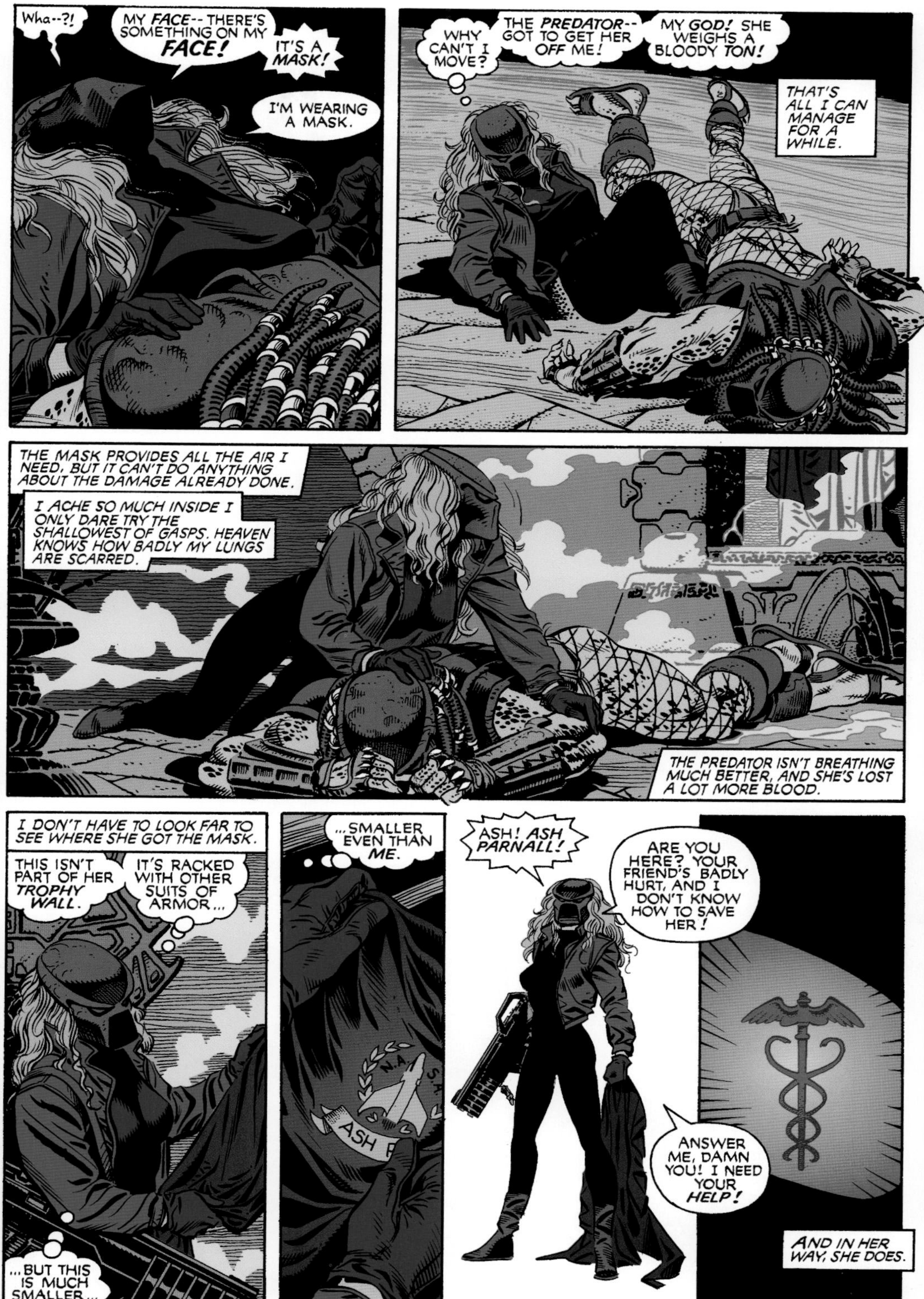

Wha--?!
MY FACE-- THERE'S SOMETHING ON MY FACE!
IT'S A MASK!
I'M WEARING A MASK.
WHY CAN'T I MOVE?
THE PREDATOR-- GOT TO GET HER OFF ME!
MY GOD! SHE WEIGHS A BLOODY TON!
THAT'S ALL I CAN MANAGE FOR A WHILE.
THE MASK PROVIDES ALL THE AIR I NEED, BUT IT CAN'T DO ANYTHING ABOUT THE DAMAGE ALREADY DONE.
I ACHE SO MUCH INSIDE I ONLY DARE TRY THE SHALLOWEST OF GASPS. HEAVEN KNOWS HOW BADLY MY LUNGS ARE SCARRED.
THE PREDATOR ISN'T BREATHING MUCH BETTER, AND SHE'S LOST A LOT MORE BLOOD.
I DON'T HAVE TO LOOK FAR TO SEE WHERE SHE GOT THE MASK.
THIS ISN'T PART OF HER TROPHY WALL.
IT'S RACKED WITH OTHER SUITS OF ARMOR...
...BUT THIS IS MUCH SMALLER...
...SMALLER EVEN THAN ME.
ASH P
ASH! ASH PARNALL!
ARE YOU HERE? YOUR FRIEND'S BADLY HURT, AND I DON'T KNOW HOW TO SAVE HER!
ANSWER ME, DAMN YOU! I NEED YOUR HELP!
AND IN HER WAY, SHE DOES.

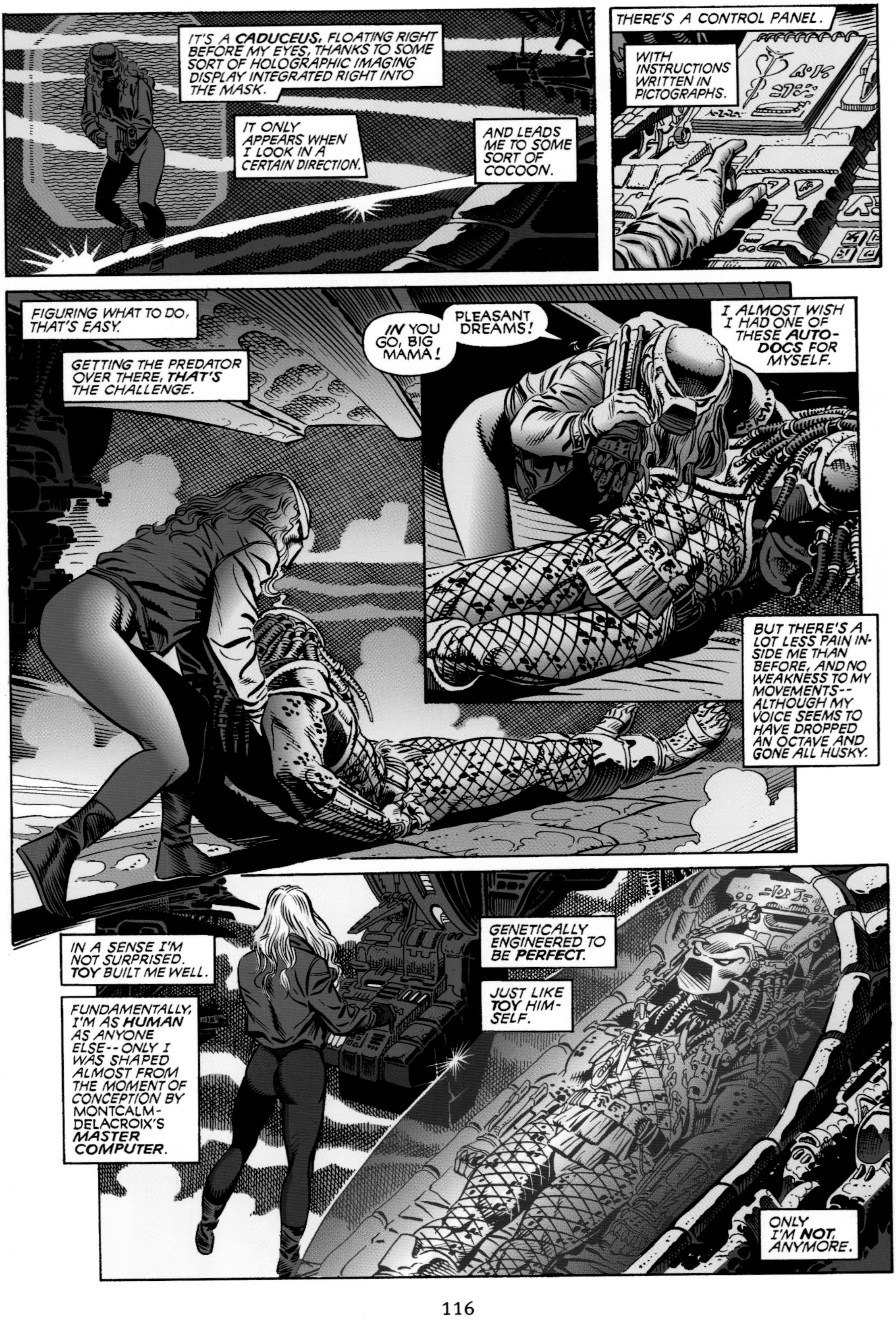
IT'S A CADUCEUS, FLOATING RIGHT BEFORE MY EYES, THANKS TO SOME SORT OF HOLOGRAPHIC IMAGING DISPLAY INTEGRATED RIGHT INTO THE MASK.
IT ONLY APPEARS WHEN I LOOK IN A CERTAIN DIRECTION.
AND LEADS ME TO SOME SORT OF COCOON.
THERE'S A CONTROL PANEL.
WITH INSTRUCTIONS WRITTEN IN PICTOGRAPHS.
FIGURING WHAT TO DO, THAT'S EASY.
GETTING THE PREDATOR OVER THERE, THAT'S THE CHALLENGE.
IN YOU GO, BIG MAMA!
PLEASANT DREAMS!
I ALMOST WISH I HAD ONE OF THESE AUTO-DOCS FOR MYSELF.
BUT THERE'S A LOT LESS PAIN INSIDE ME THAN BEFORE, AND NO WEAKNESS TO MY MOVEMENTS-- ALTHOUGH MY VOICE SEEMS TO HAVE DROPPED AN OCTAVE AND GONE ALL HUSKY.
IN A SENSE I'M NOT SURPRISED. TOY BUILT ME WELL.
FUNDAMENTALLY, I'M AS HUMAN AS ANYONE ELSE--ONLY I WAS SHAPED ALMOST FROM THE MOMENT OF CONCEPTION BY MONTCALM-DELACROIX'S MASTER COMPUTER.
GENETICALLY ENGINEERED TO BE PERFECT.
JUST LIKE TOY HIMSELF.
ONLY I'M NOT, ANYMORE.

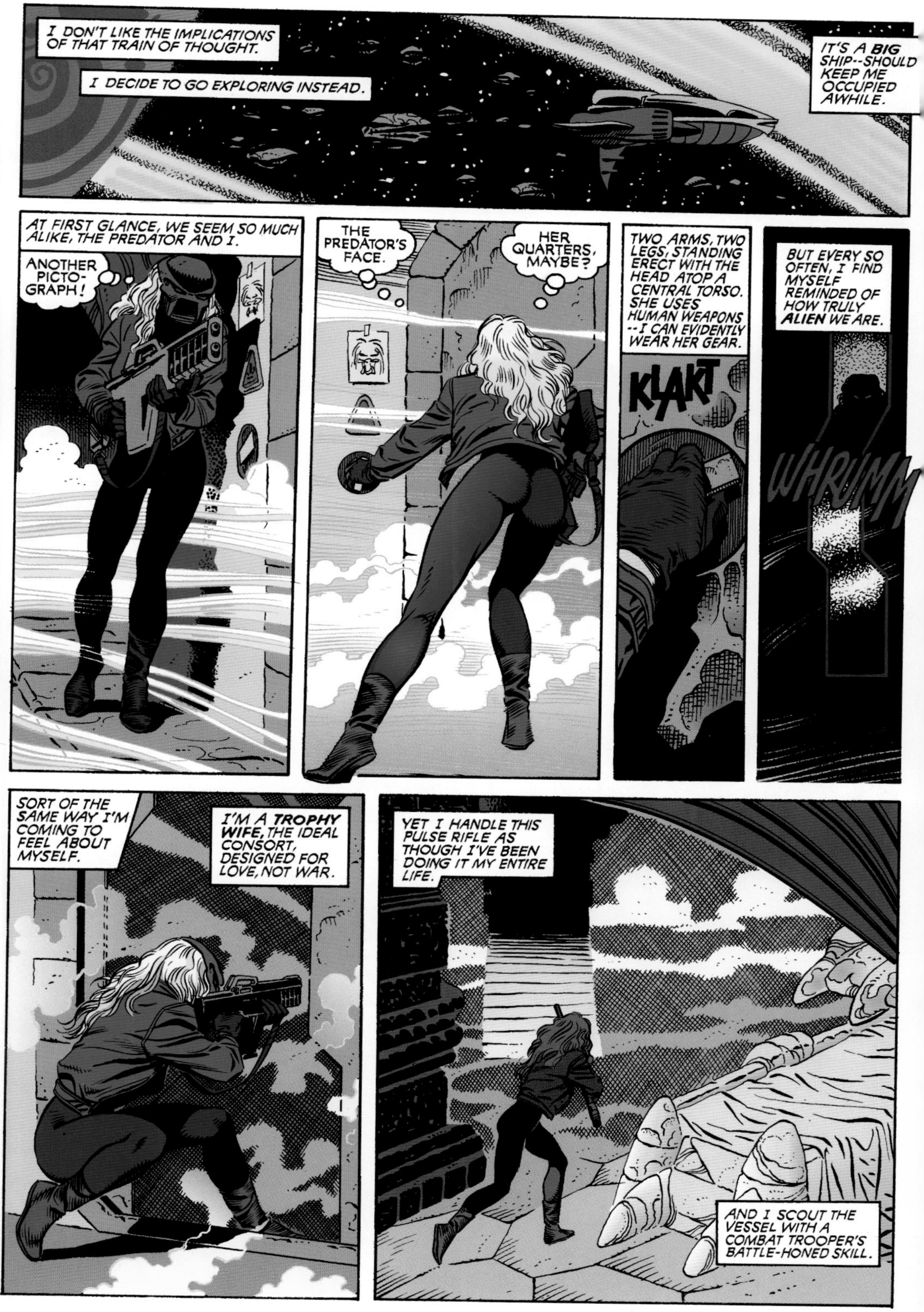
I DON'T LIKE THE IMPLICATIONS OF THAT TRAIN OF THOUGHT.
I DECIDE TO GO EXPLORING INSTEAD.
IT'S A BIG SHIP--SHOULD KEEP ME OCCUPIED AWHILE.
AT FIRST GLANCE, WE SEEM SO MUCH ALIKE, THE PREDATOR AND I.
ANOTHER PICTO-GRAPH!
THE PREDATOR'S FACE.
HER QUARTERS, MAYBE?
TWO ARMS, TWO LEGS, STANDING ERECT WITH THE HEAD ATOP A CENTRAL TORSO. SHE USES HUMAN WEAPONS --I CAN EVIDENTLY WEAR HER GEAR.
KLAKT
BUT EVERY SO OFTEN, I FIND MYSELF REMINDED OF HOW TRULY ALIEN WE ARE.
WHRUMM
SORT OF THE SAME WAY I'M COMING TO FEEL ABOUT MYSELF.
I'M A TROPHY WIFE, THE IDEAL CONSORT, DESIGNED FOR LOVE, NOT WAR.
YET I HANDLE THIS PULSE RIFLE AS THOUGH I'VE BEEN DOING IT MY ENTIRE LIFE.
AND I SCOUT THE VESSEL WITH A COMBAT TROOPER'S BATTLE-HONED SKILL.

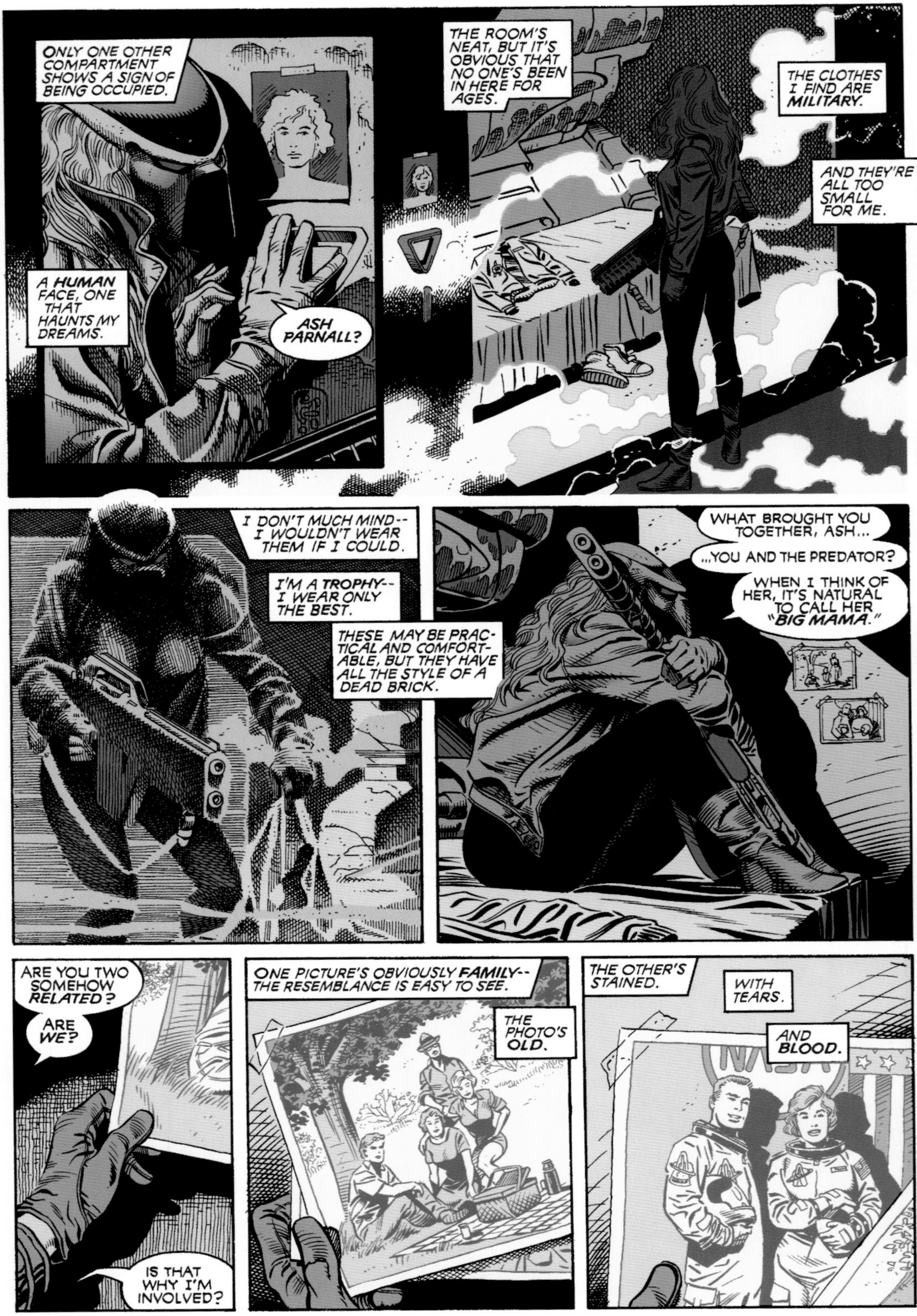
ONLY ONE OTHER COMPARTMENT SHOWS A SIGN OF BEING OCCUPIED.
A HUMAN FACE, ONE THAT HAUNTS MY DREAMS.
ASH PARNALL?
THE ROOM'S NEAT, BUT IT'S OBVIOUS THAT NO ONE'S BEEN IN HERE FOR AGES.
THE CLOTHES I FIND ARE MILITARY.
AND THEY'RE ALL TOO SMALL FOR ME.
I DON'T MUCH MIND-- I WOULDN'T WEAR THEM IF I COULD.
I'M A TROPHY-- I WEAR ONLY THE BEST.
THESE MAY BE PRACTICAL AND COMFORTABLE, BUT THEY HAVE ALL THE STYLE OF A DEAD BRICK.
WHAT BROUGHT YOU TOGETHER, ASH...
...YOU AND THE PREDATOR?
WHEN I THINK OF HER, IT'S NATURAL TO CALL HER "BIG MAMA."
ARE YOU TWO SOMEHOW RELATED?
ARE WE?
IS THAT WHY I'M INVOLVED?
ONE PICTURE'S OBVIOUSLY FAMILY-- THE RESEMBLANCE IS EASY TO SEE.
THE PHOTO'S OLD.
THE OTHER'S STAINED.
WITH TEARS.
AND BLOOD.

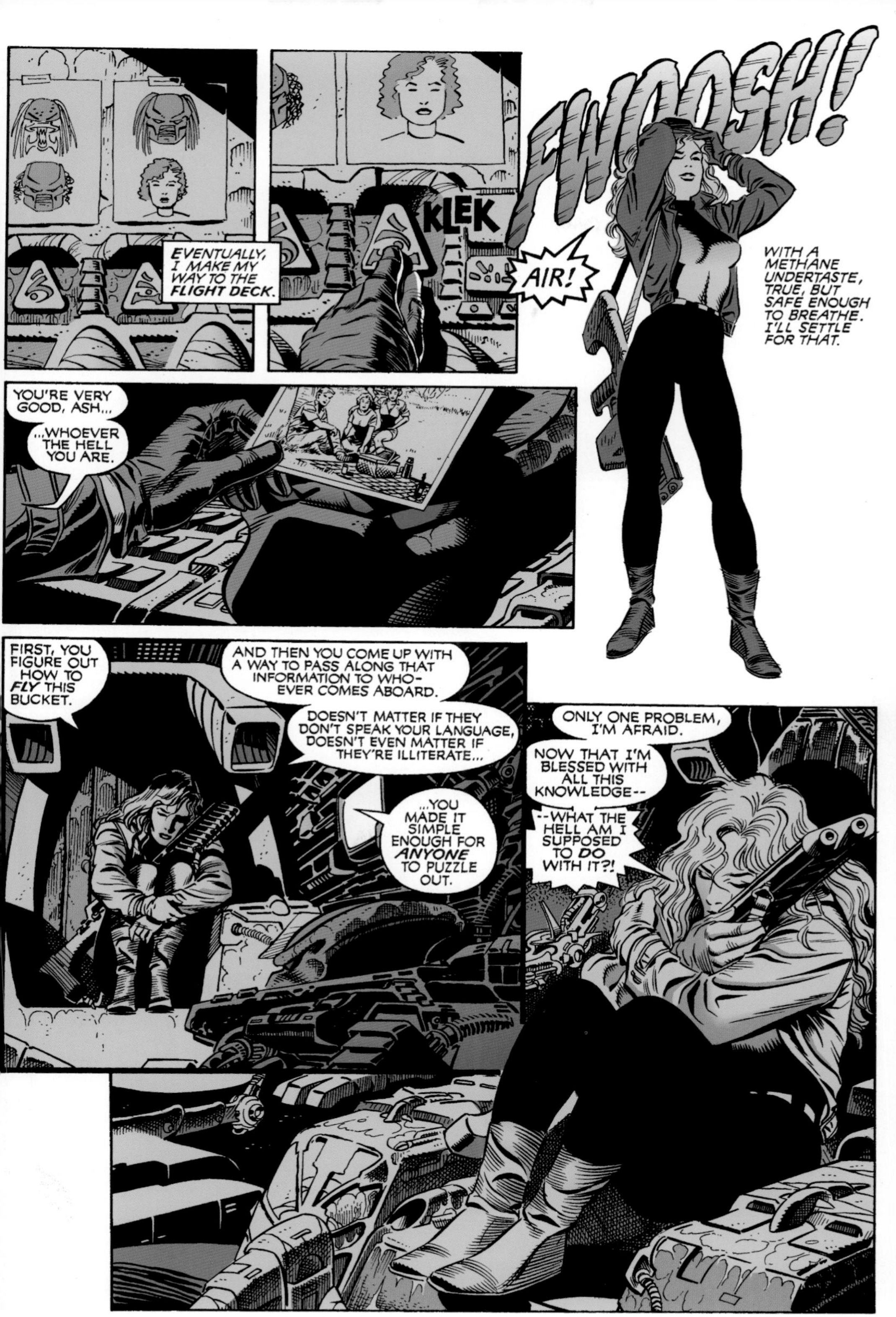

EVENTUALLY, I MAKE MY WAY TO THE FLIGHT DECK.
KLEK
FWOOSH!
AIR!
WITH A METHANE UNDERTASTE, TRUE, BUT SAFE ENOUGH TO BREATHE. I'LL SETTLE FOR THAT.
YOU'RE VERY GOOD, ASH...
...WHOEVER THE HELL YOU ARE.
FIRST, YOU FIGURE OUT HOW TO FLY THIS BUCKET.
AND THEN YOU COME UP WITH A WAY TO PASS ALONG THAT INFORMATION TO WHO-EVER COMES ABOARD.
DOESN'T MATTER IF THEY DON'T SPEAK YOUR LANGUAGE, DOESN'T EVEN MATTER IF THEY'RE ILLITERATE...
...YOU MADE IT SIMPLE ENOUGH FOR ANYONE TO PUZZLE OUT.
ONLY ONE PROBLEM, I'M AFRAID.
NOW THAT I'M BLESSED WITH ALL THIS KNOWLEDGE--
--WHAT THE HELL AM I SUPPOSED TO DO WITH IT?!

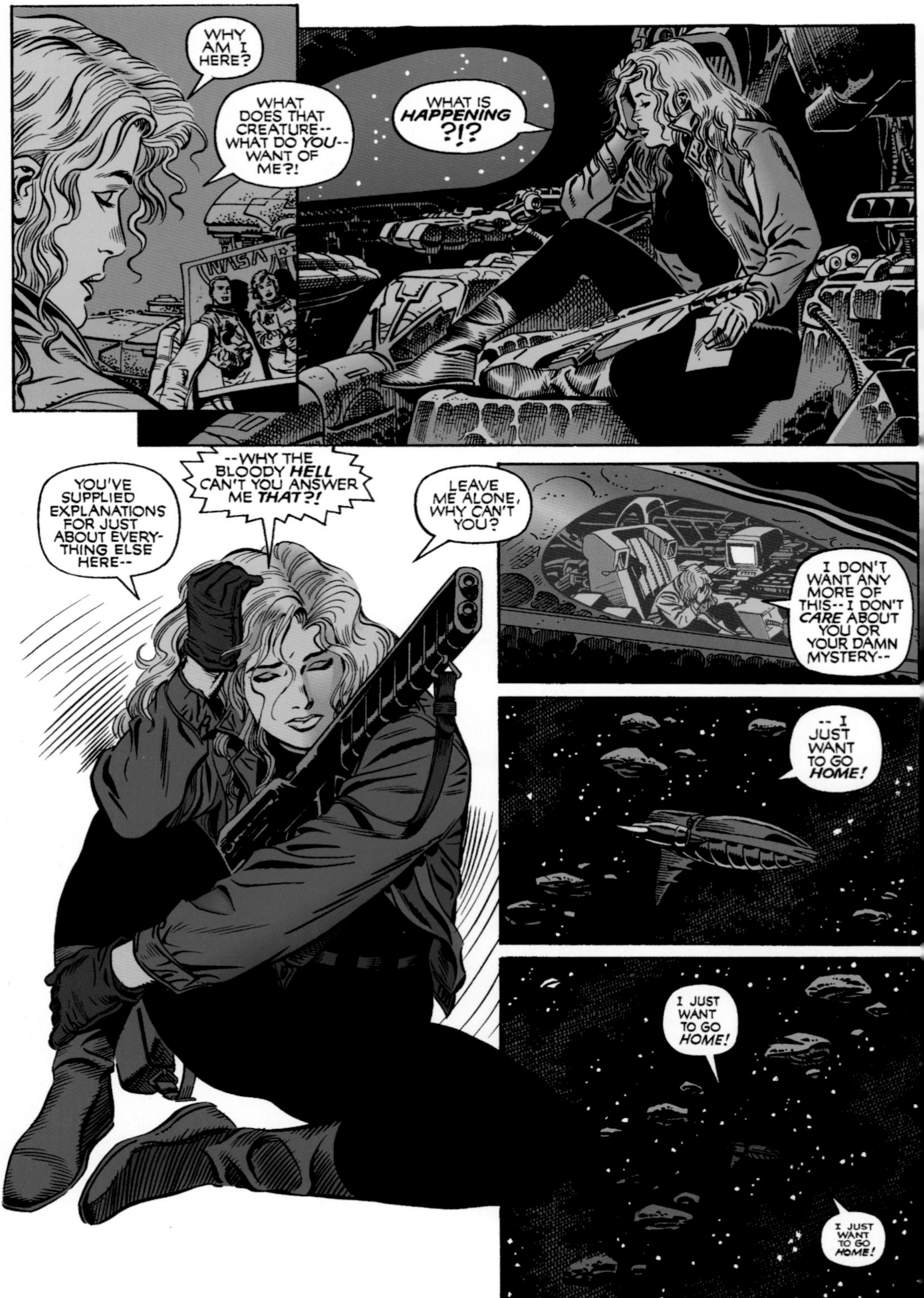
WHY AM I HERE?
WHAT DOES THAT CREATURE-- WHAT DO *YOU*-- WANT OF ME?!
WHAT IS *HAPPENING* ?!?
YOU'VE SUPPLIED EXPLANATIONS FOR JUST ABOUT EVERY-THING ELSE HERE--
--WHY THE BLOODY *HELL* CAN'T YOU ANSWER ME *THAT?!*
LEAVE ME ALONE, WHY CAN'T YOU?
I DON'T WANT ANY MORE OF THIS-- I DON'T *CARE* ABOUT YOU OR YOUR DAMN MYSTERY--
-- I JUST WANT TO GO *HOME!*
I JUST WANT TO GO *HOME!*
I JUST WANT TO GO *HOME!*

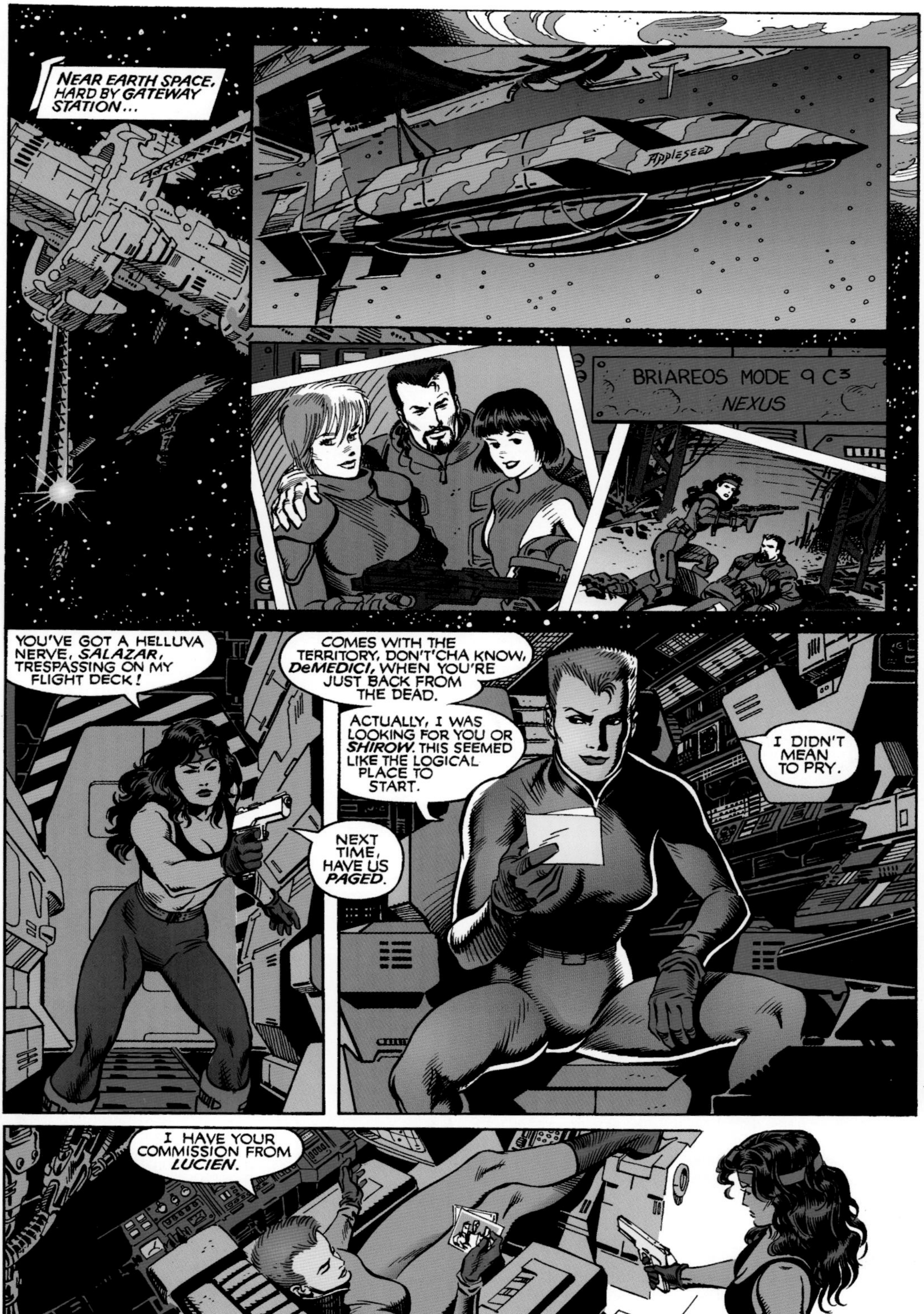
NEAR EARTH SPACE, HARD BY GATEWAY STATION...
APPLESEED
BRIAREOS MODE 9 C³
NEXUS
YOU'VE GOT A HELLUVA NERVE, SALAZAR, TRESPASSING ON MY FLIGHT DECK!
COMES WITH THE TERRITORY, DON'T'CHA KNOW, DeMEDICI, WHEN YOU'RE JUST BACK FROM THE DEAD.
ACTUALLY, I WAS LOOKING FOR YOU OR SHIROW. THIS SEEMED LIKE THE LOGICAL PLACE TO START.
NEXT TIME, HAVE US PAGED.
I DIDN'T MEAN TO PRY.
I HAVE YOUR COMMISSION FROM LUCIEN.

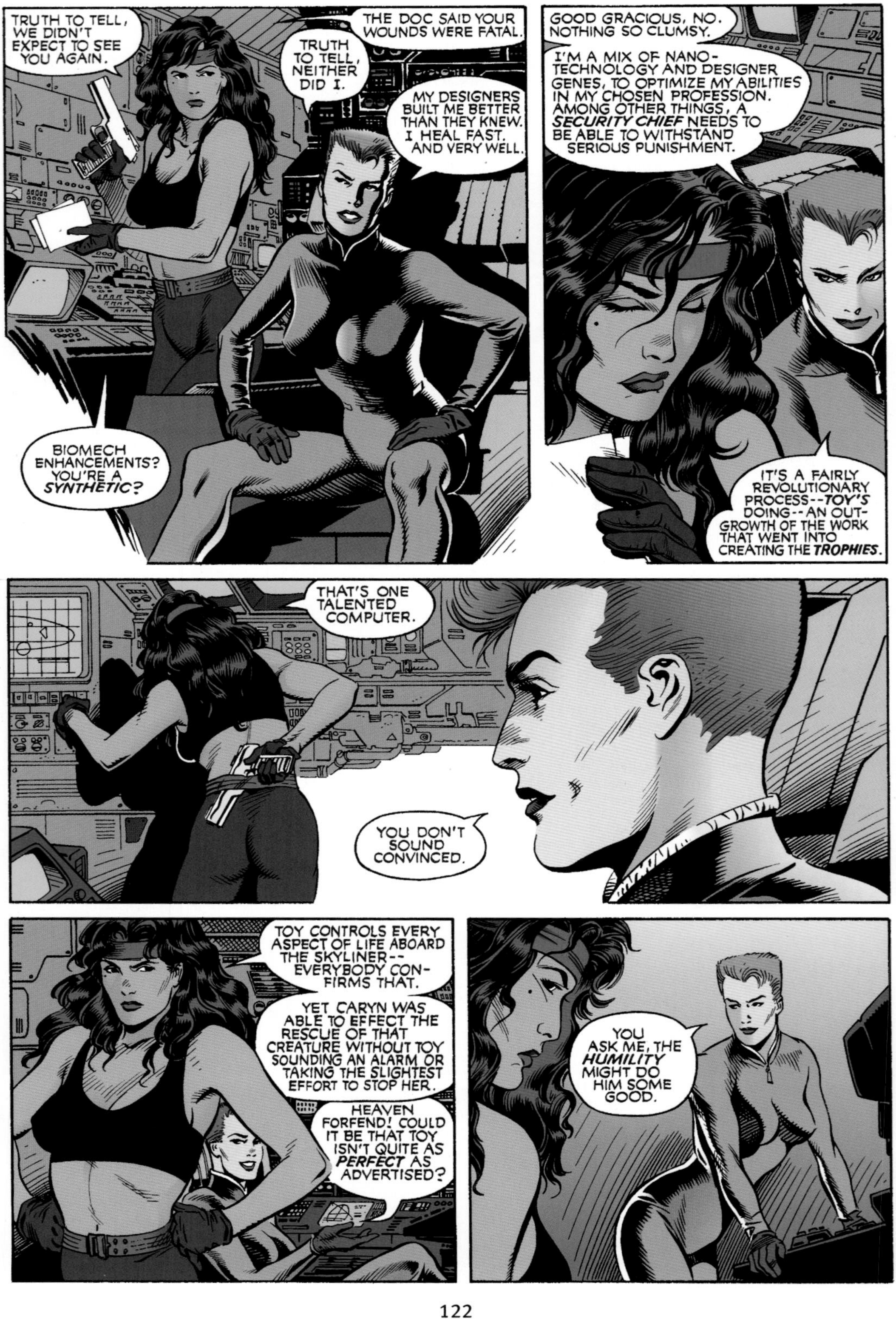
TRUTH TO TELL, WE DIDN'T EXPECT TO SEE YOU AGAIN.
THE DOC SAID YOUR WOUNDS WERE FATAL.
TRUTH TO TELL, NEITHER DID I.
MY DESIGNERS BUILT ME BETTER THAN THEY KNEW. I HEAL FAST. AND VERY WELL.
BIOMECH ENHANCEMENTS? YOU'RE A *SYNTHETIC*?
GOOD GRACIOUS, NO. NOTHING SO CLUMSY.
I'M A MIX OF NANO-TECHNOLOGY AND DESIGNER GENES, TO OPTIMIZE MY ABILITIES IN MY CHOSEN PROFESSION. AMONG OTHER THINGS, A *SECURITY CHIEF* NEEDS TO BE ABLE TO WITHSTAND SERIOUS PUNISHMENT.
IT'S A FAIRLY REVOLUTIONARY PROCESS--*TOY'S* DOING--AN OUT-GROWTH OF THE WORK THAT WENT INTO CREATING THE *TROPHIES*.
THAT'S ONE TALENTED COMPUTER.
YOU DON'T SOUND CONVINCED.
TOY CONTROLS EVERY ASPECT OF LIFE ABOARD THE SKYLINER--EVERYBODY CON-FIRMS THAT.
YET CARYN WAS ABLE TO EFFECT THE RESCUE OF THAT CREATURE WITHOUT TOY SOUNDING AN ALARM OR TAKING THE SLIGHTEST EFFORT TO STOP HER.
HEAVEN FORFEND! COULD IT BE THAT TOY ISN'T QUITE AS *PERFECT* AS ADVERTISED?
YOU ASK ME, THE *HUMILITY* MIGHT DO HIM SOME GOOD.

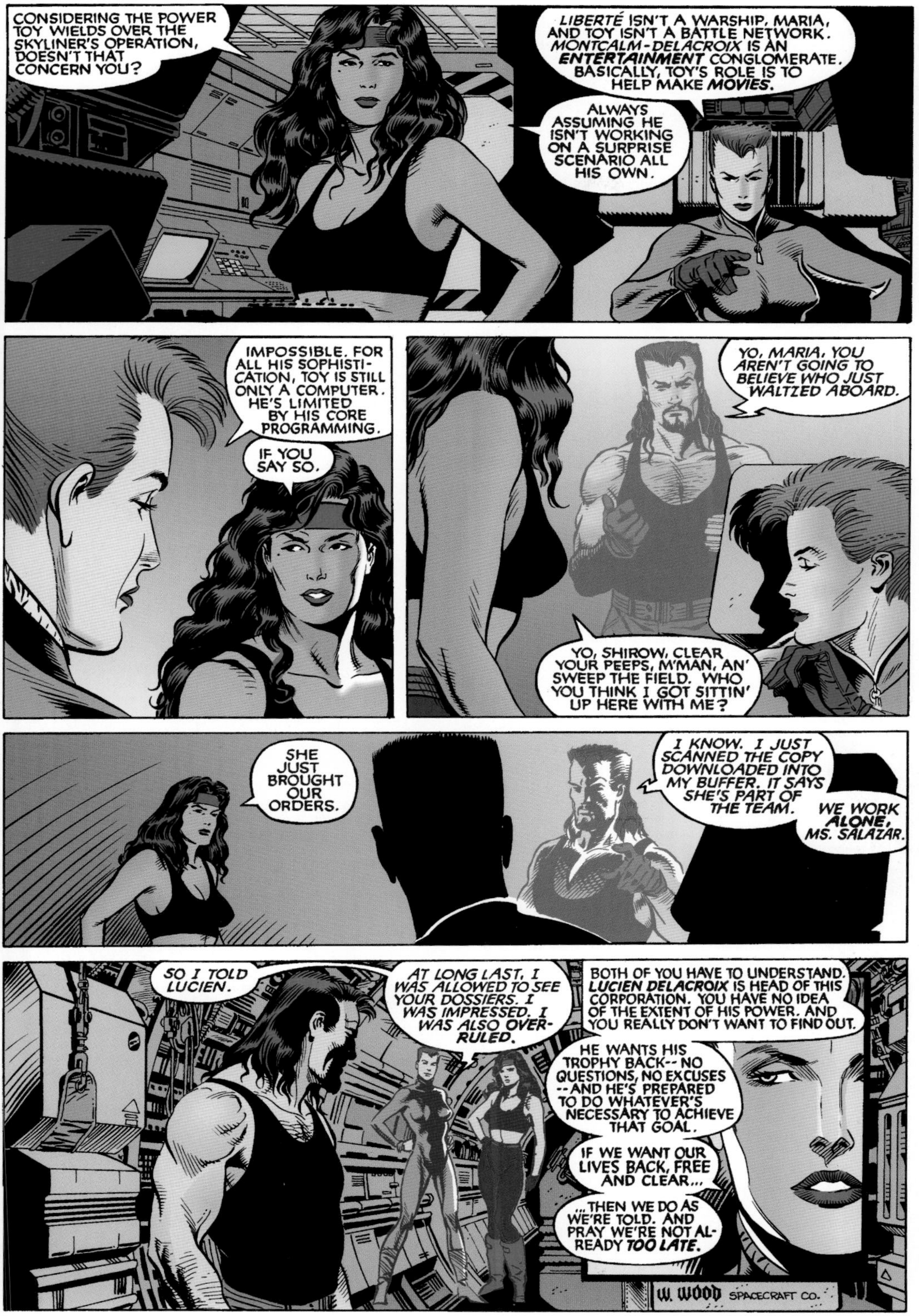

CONSIDERING THE POWER TOY WIELDS OVER THE SKYLINER'S OPERATION, DOESN'T THAT CONCERN YOU?
LIBERTÉ ISN'T A WARSHIP, MARIA, AND TOY ISN'T A BATTLE NETWORK. MONTCALM-DELACROIX IS AN ENTERTAINMENT CONGLOMERATE. BASICALLY, TOY'S ROLE IS TO HELP MAKE MOVIES.
ALWAYS ASSUMING HE ISN'T WORKING ON A SURPRISE SCENARIO ALL HIS OWN.
IMPOSSIBLE. FOR ALL HIS SOPHISTI-CATION, TOY IS STILL ONLY A COMPUTER. HE'S LIMITED BY HIS CORE PROGRAMMING.
IF YOU SAY SO.
YO, MARIA, YOU AREN'T GOING TO BELIEVE WHO JUST WALTZED ABOARD.
YO, SHIROW, CLEAR YOUR PEEPS, M'MAN, AN' SWEEP THE FIELD. WHO YOU THINK I GOT SITTIN' UP HERE WITH ME?
SHE JUST BROUGHT OUR ORDERS.
I KNOW. I JUST SCANNED THE COPY DOWNLOADED INTO MY BUFFER. IT SAYS SHE'S PART OF THE TEAM.
WE WORK ALONE, MS. SALAZAR.
SO I TOLD LUCIEN.
AT LONG LAST, I WAS ALLOWED TO SEE YOUR DOSSIERS. I WAS IMPRESSED. I WAS ALSO OVER-RULED.
BOTH OF YOU HAVE TO UNDERSTAND. LUCIEN DELACROIX IS HEAD OF THIS CORPORATION. YOU HAVE NO IDEA OF THE EXTENT OF HIS POWER. AND YOU REALLY DON'T WANT TO FIND OUT.
HE WANTS HIS TROPHY BACK-- NO QUESTIONS, NO EXCUSES --AND HE'S PREPARED TO DO WHATEVER'S NECESSARY TO ACHIEVE THAT GOAL.
IF WE WANT OUR LIVES BACK, FREE AND CLEAR...
...THEN WE DO AS WE'RE TOLD. AND PRAY WE'RE NOT AL-READY TOO LATE.
W. WOOD SPACECRAFT CO.

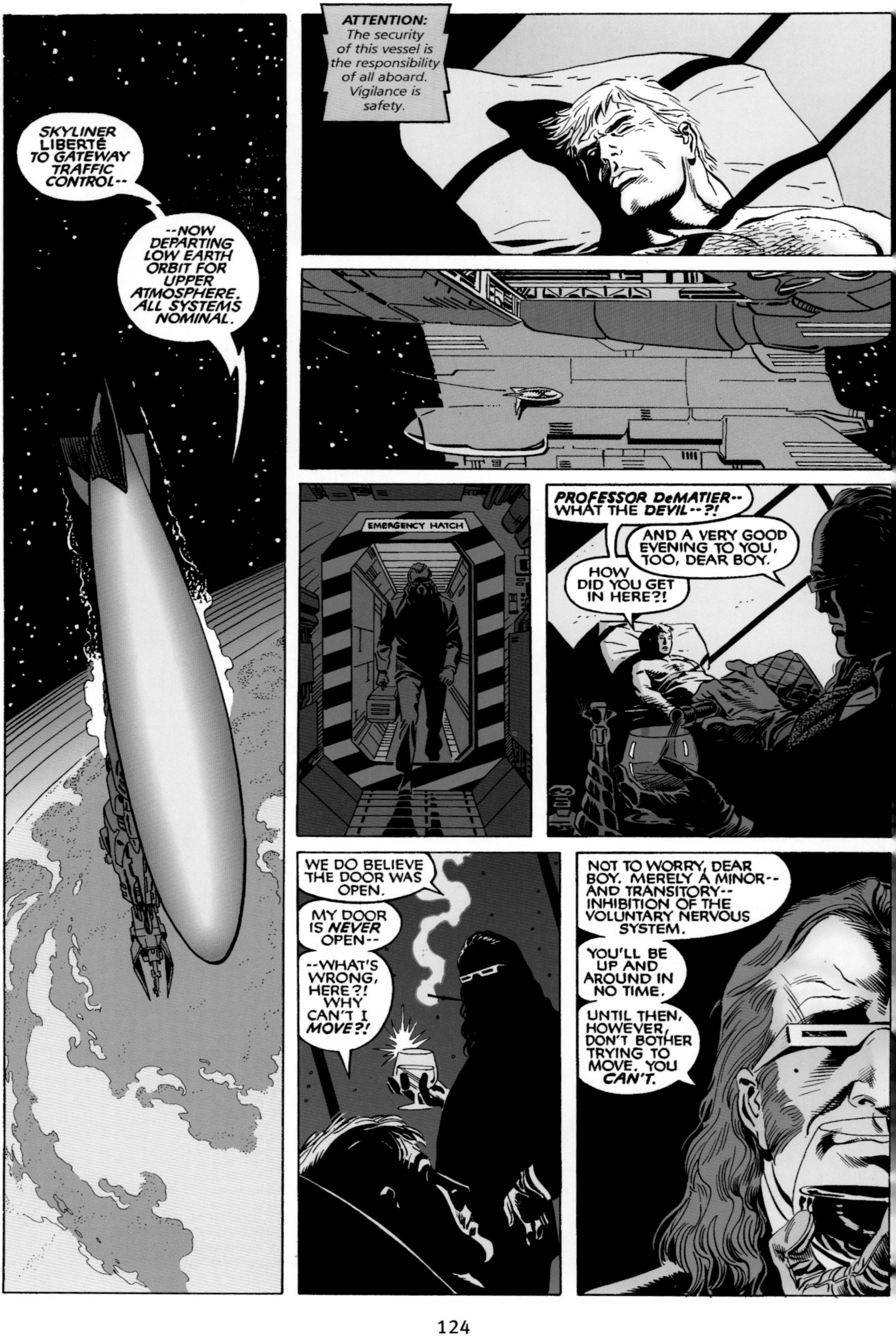
SKYLINER LIBERTÉ TO GATEWAY TRAFFIC CONTROL--
--NOW DEPARTING LOW EARTH ORBIT FOR UPPER ATMOSPHERE. ALL SYSTEMS NOMINAL.
ATTENTION: The security of this vessel is the responsibility of all aboard. Vigilance is safety.
EMERGENCY HATCH
PROFESSOR DeMATIER-- WHAT THE DEVIL--?!
AND A VERY GOOD EVENING TO YOU, TOO, DEAR BOY.
HOW DID YOU GET IN HERE?!
WE DO BELIEVE THE DOOR WAS OPEN.
MY DOOR IS NEVER OPEN--
--WHAT'S WRONG, HERE?! WHY CAN'T I MOVE?!
NOT TO WORRY, DEAR BOY. MERELY A MINOR-- AND TRANSITORY-- INHIBITION OF THE VOLUNTARY NERVOUS SYSTEM.
YOU'LL BE UP AND AROUND IN NO TIME.
UNTIL THEN, HOWEVER, DON'T BOTHER TRYING TO MOVE. YOU CAN'T.

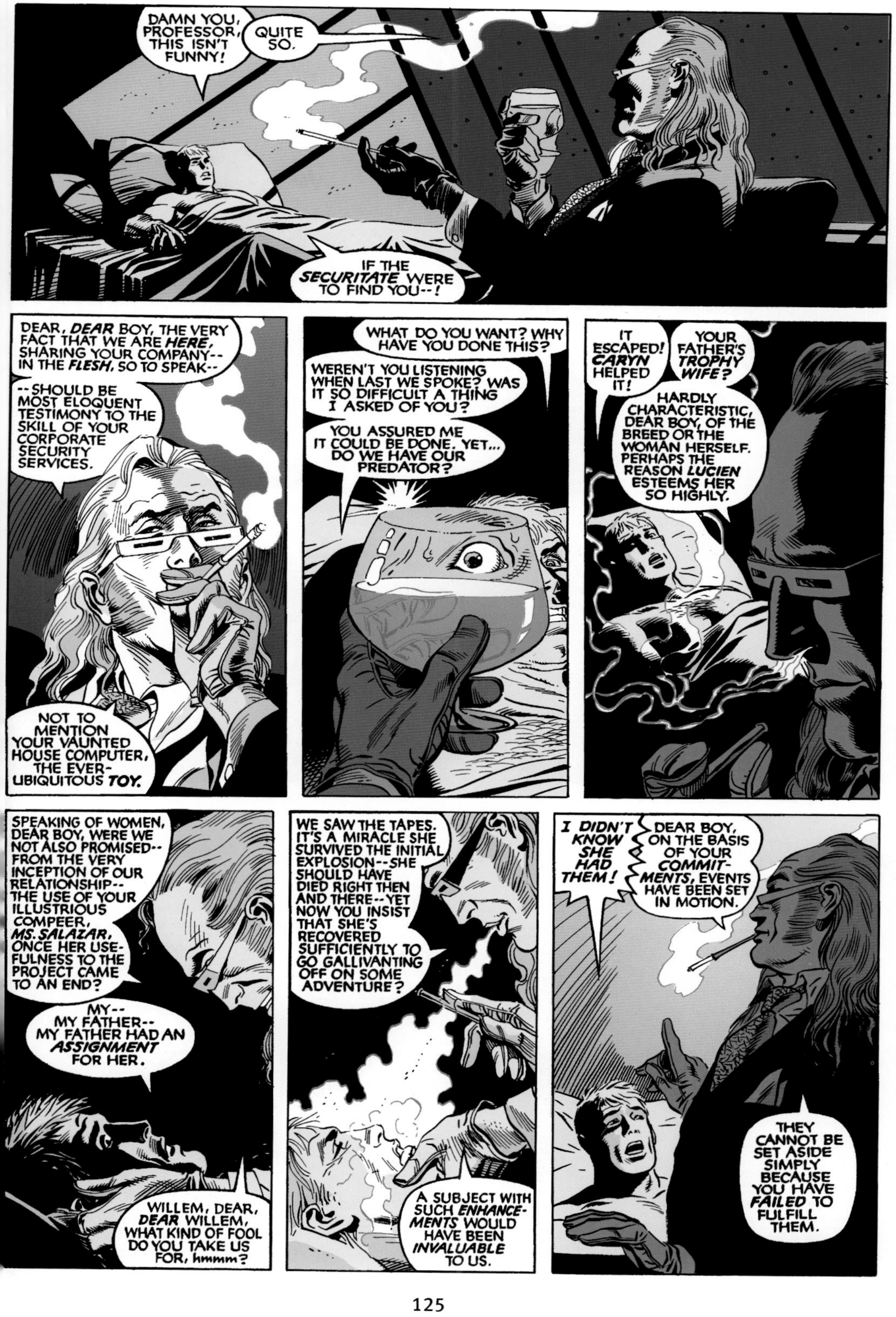
DAMN YOU, PROFESSOR, THIS ISN'T FUNNY!
QUITE SO.
IF THE SECURITATE WERE TO FIND YOU--!
DEAR, DEAR BOY, THE VERY FACT THAT WE ARE HERE, SHARING YOUR COMPANY-- IN THE FLESH, SO TO SPEAK--
--SHOULD BE MOST ELOQUENT TESTIMONY TO THE SKILL OF YOUR CORPORATE SECURITY SERVICES.
NOT TO MENTION YOUR VAUNTED HOUSE COMPUTER, THE EVER-UBIQUITOUS TOY.
WHAT DO YOU WANT? WHY HAVE YOU DONE THIS?
WEREN'T YOU LISTENING WHEN LAST WE SPOKE? WAS IT SO DIFFICULT A THING I ASKED OF YOU?
YOU ASSURED ME IT COULD BE DONE. YET... DO WE HAVE OUR PREDATOR?
IT ESCAPED! CARYN HELPED IT!
YOUR FATHER'S TROPHY WIFE?
HARDLY CHARACTERISTIC, DEAR BOY, OF THE BREED OR THE WOMAN HERSELF. PERHAPS THE REASON LUCIEN ESTEEMS HER SO HIGHLY.
SPEAKING OF WOMEN, DEAR BOY, WERE WE NOT ALSO PROMISED-- FROM THE VERY INCEPTION OF OUR RELATIONSHIP-- THE USE OF YOUR ILLUSTRIOUS COMPEER, MS. SALAZAR, ONCE HER USEFULNESS TO THE PROJECT CAME TO AN END?
MY-- MY FATHER-- MY FATHER HAD AN ASSIGNMENT FOR HER.
WILLEM, DEAR, DEAR WILLEM, WHAT KIND OF FOOL DO YOU TAKE US FOR, hmmm?
WE SAW THE TAPES. IT'S A MIRACLE SHE SURVIVED THE INITIAL EXPLOSION--SHE SHOULD HAVE DIED RIGHT THEN AND THERE--YET NOW YOU INSIST THAT SHE'S RECOVERED SUFFICIENTLY TO GO GALLIVANTING OFF ON SOME ADVENTURE?
A SUBJECT WITH SUCH ENHANCEMENTS WOULD HAVE BEEN INVALUABLE TO US.
I DIDN'T KNOW SHE HAD THEM!
DEAR BOY, ON THE BASIS OF YOUR COMMITMENTS, EVENTS HAVE BEEN SET IN MOTION.
THEY CANNOT BE SET ASIDE SIMPLY BECAUSE YOU HAVE FAILED TO FULFILL THEM.

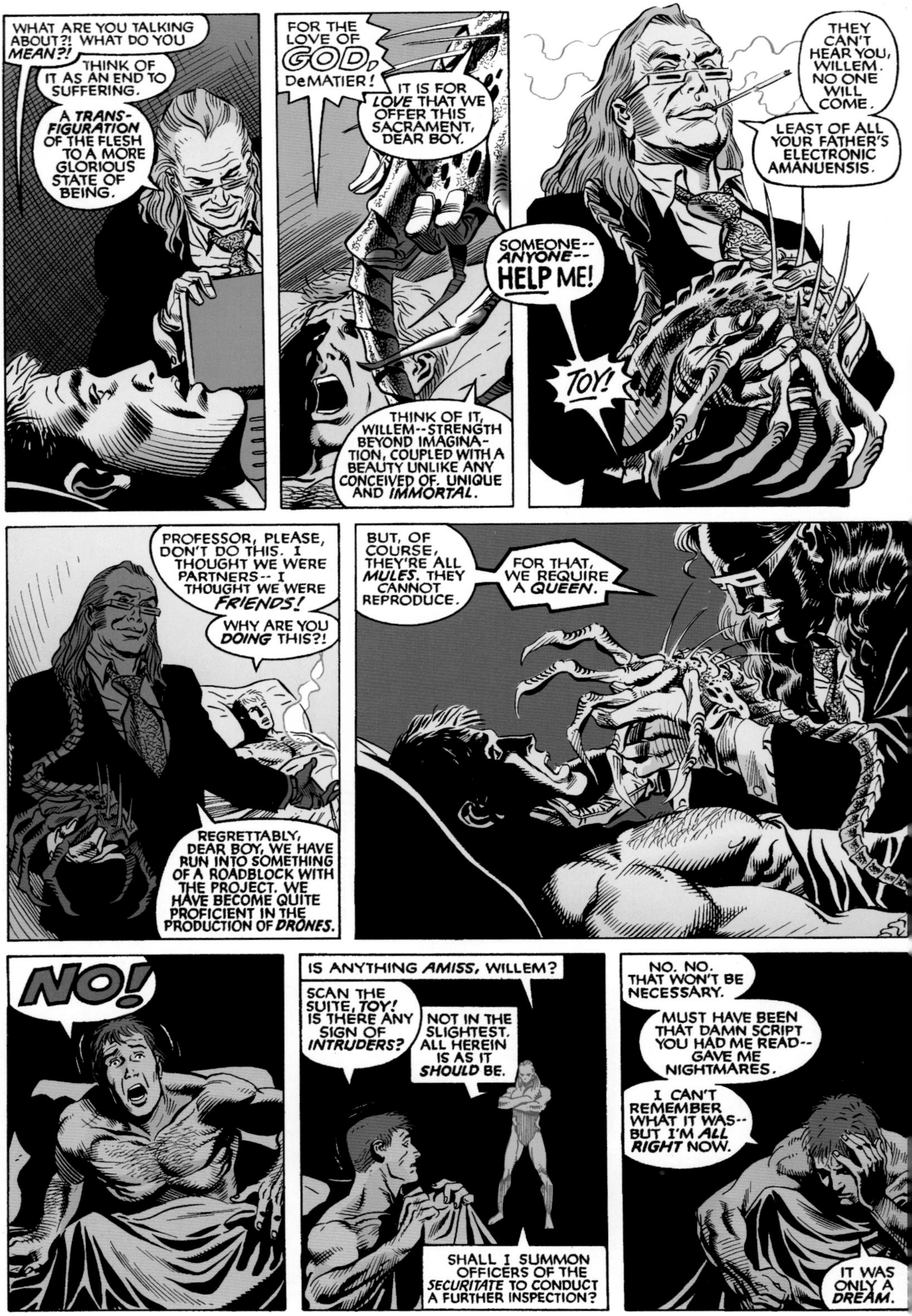
WHAT ARE YOU TALKING ABOUT?! WHAT DO YOU MEAN?!
THINK OF IT AS AN END TO SUFFERING.
A TRANS-FIGURATION OF THE FLESH TO A MORE GLORIOUS STATE OF BEING.
FOR THE LOVE OF GOD, DeMATIER!
IT IS FOR LOVE THAT WE OFFER THIS SACRAMENT, DEAR BOY.
THINK OF IT, WILLEM--STRENGTH BEYOND IMAGINA-TION, COUPLED WITH A BEAUTY UNLIKE ANY CONCEIVED OF. UNIQUE AND IMMORTAL.
SOMEONE-- ANYONE-- HELP ME!
TOY!
THEY CAN'T HEAR YOU, WILLEM. NO ONE WILL COME.
LEAST OF ALL YOUR FATHER'S ELECTRONIC AMANUENSIS.
PROFESSOR, PLEASE, DON'T DO THIS. I THOUGHT WE WERE PARTNERS-- I THOUGHT WE WERE FRIENDS!
WHY ARE YOU DOING THIS?!
REGRETTABLY, DEAR BOY, WE HAVE RUN INTO SOMETHING OF A ROADBLOCK WITH THE PROJECT. WE HAVE BECOME QUITE PROFICIENT IN THE PRODUCTION OF DRONES.
BUT, OF COURSE, THEY'RE ALL MULES. THEY CANNOT REPRODUCE.
FOR THAT, WE REQUIRE A QUEEN.
NO!
IS ANYTHING AMISS, WILLEM?
SCAN THE SUITE, TOY! IS THERE ANY SIGN OF INTRUDERS?
NOT IN THE SLIGHTEST. ALL HEREIN IS AS IT SHOULD BE.
SHALL I SUMMON OFFICERS OF THE SECURITATE TO CONDUCT A FURTHER INSPECTION?
NO. NO. THAT WON'T BE NECESSARY.
MUST HAVE BEEN THAT DAMN SCRIPT YOU HAD ME READ-- GAVE ME NIGHTMARES.
I CAN'T REMEMBER WHAT IT WAS-- BUT I'M ALL RIGHT NOW.
IT WAS ONLY A DREAM.

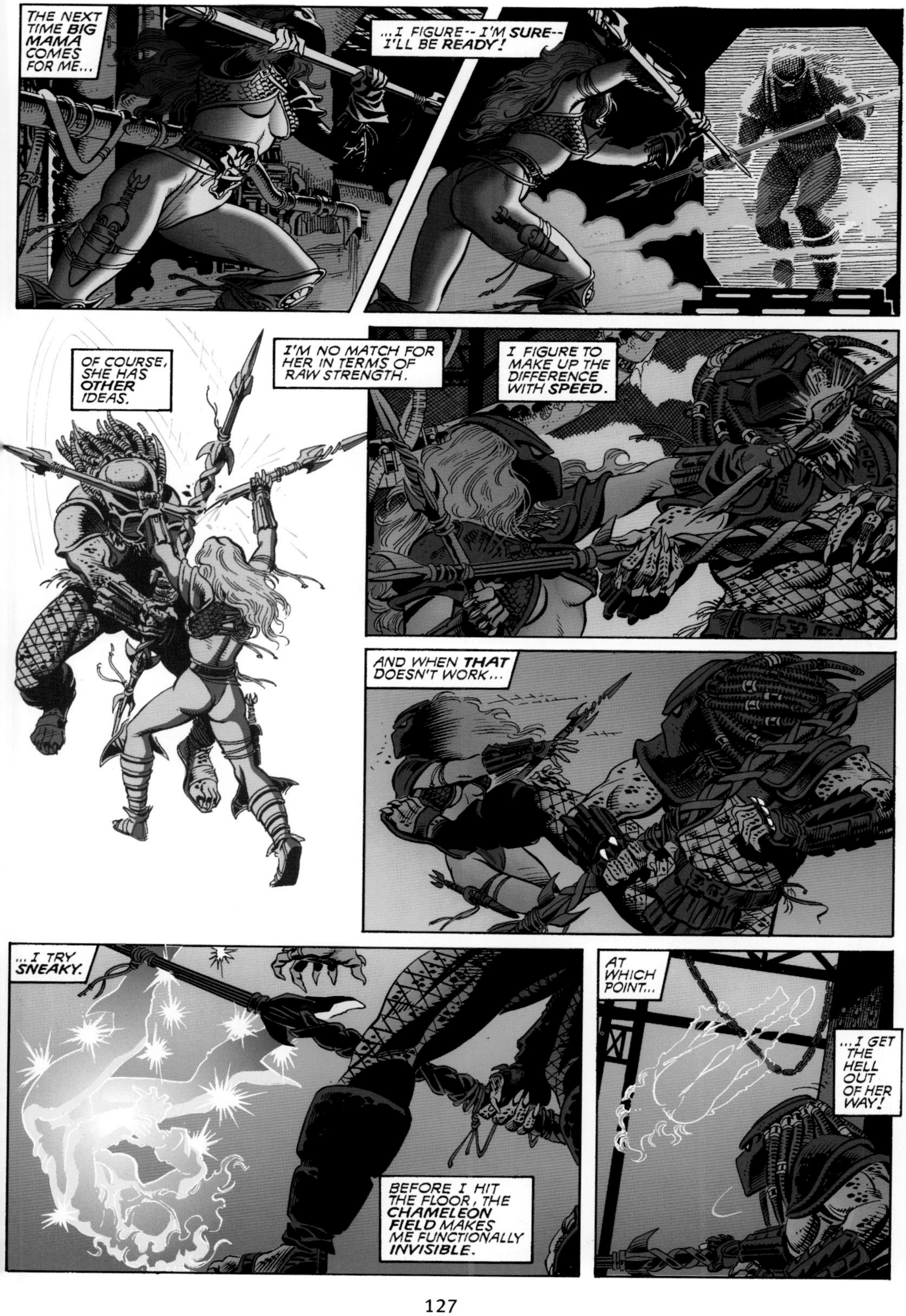
THE NEXT TIME BIG MAMA COMES FOR ME...
...I FIGURE-- I'M SURE-- I'LL BE READY!
OF COURSE, SHE HAS OTHER IDEAS.
I'M NO MATCH FOR HER IN TERMS OF RAW STRENGTH.
I FIGURE TO MAKE UP THE DIFFERENCE WITH SPEED.
AND WHEN THAT DOESN'T WORK...
...I TRY SNEAKY.
BEFORE I HIT THE FLOOR, THE CHAMELEON FIELD MAKES ME FUNCTIONALLY INVISIBLE.
AT WHICH POINT...
...I GET THE HELL OUT OF HER WAY!

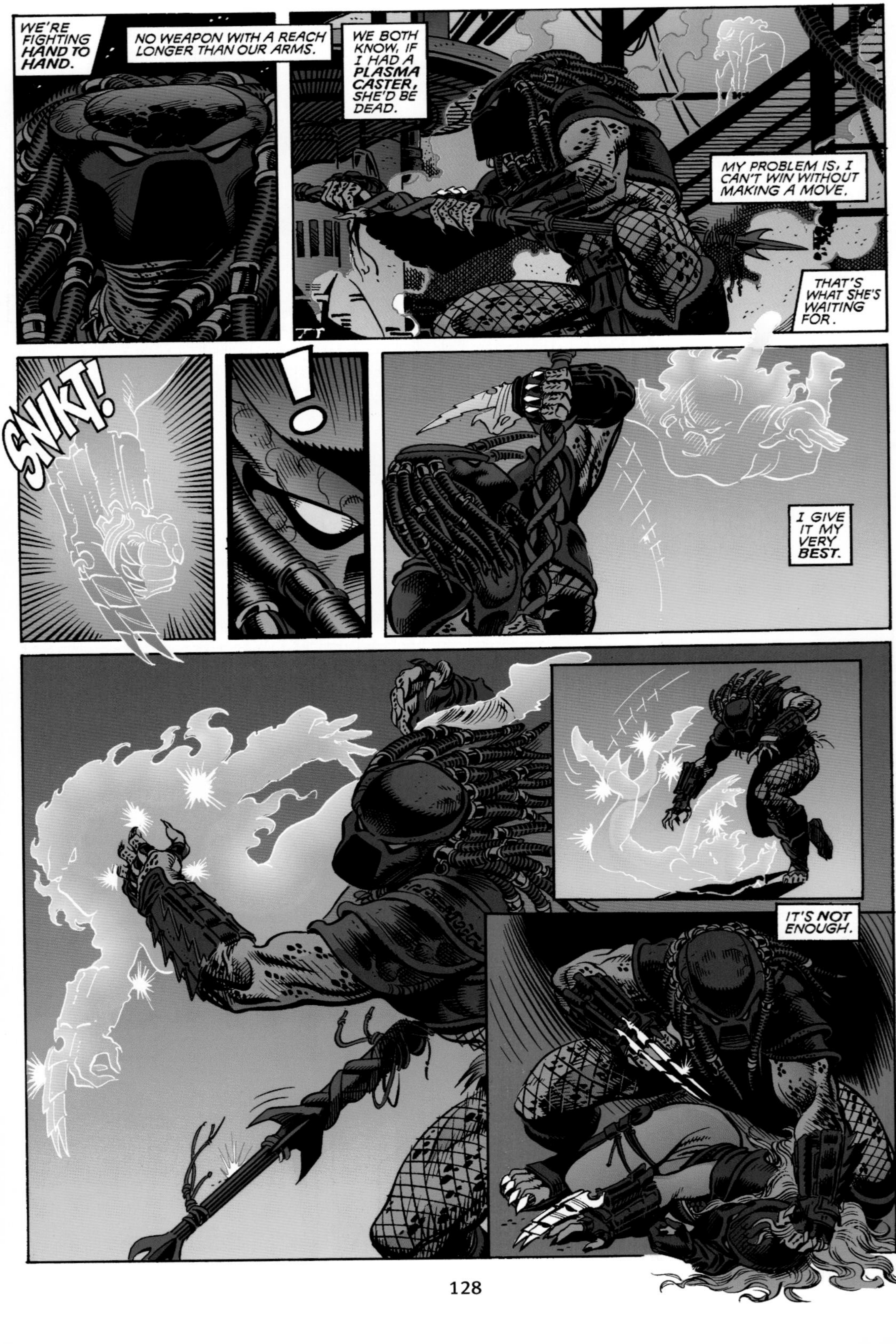
WE'RE FIGHTING HAND TO HAND.
NO WEAPON WITH A REACH LONGER THAN OUR ARMS.
WE BOTH KNOW, IF I HAD A PLASMA CASTER, SHE'D BE DEAD.
MY PROBLEM IS, I CAN'T WIN WITHOUT MAKING A MOVE.
THAT'S WHAT SHE'S WAITING FOR.
SNIKT!
!
I GIVE IT MY VERY BEST.
IT'S NOT ENOUGH.

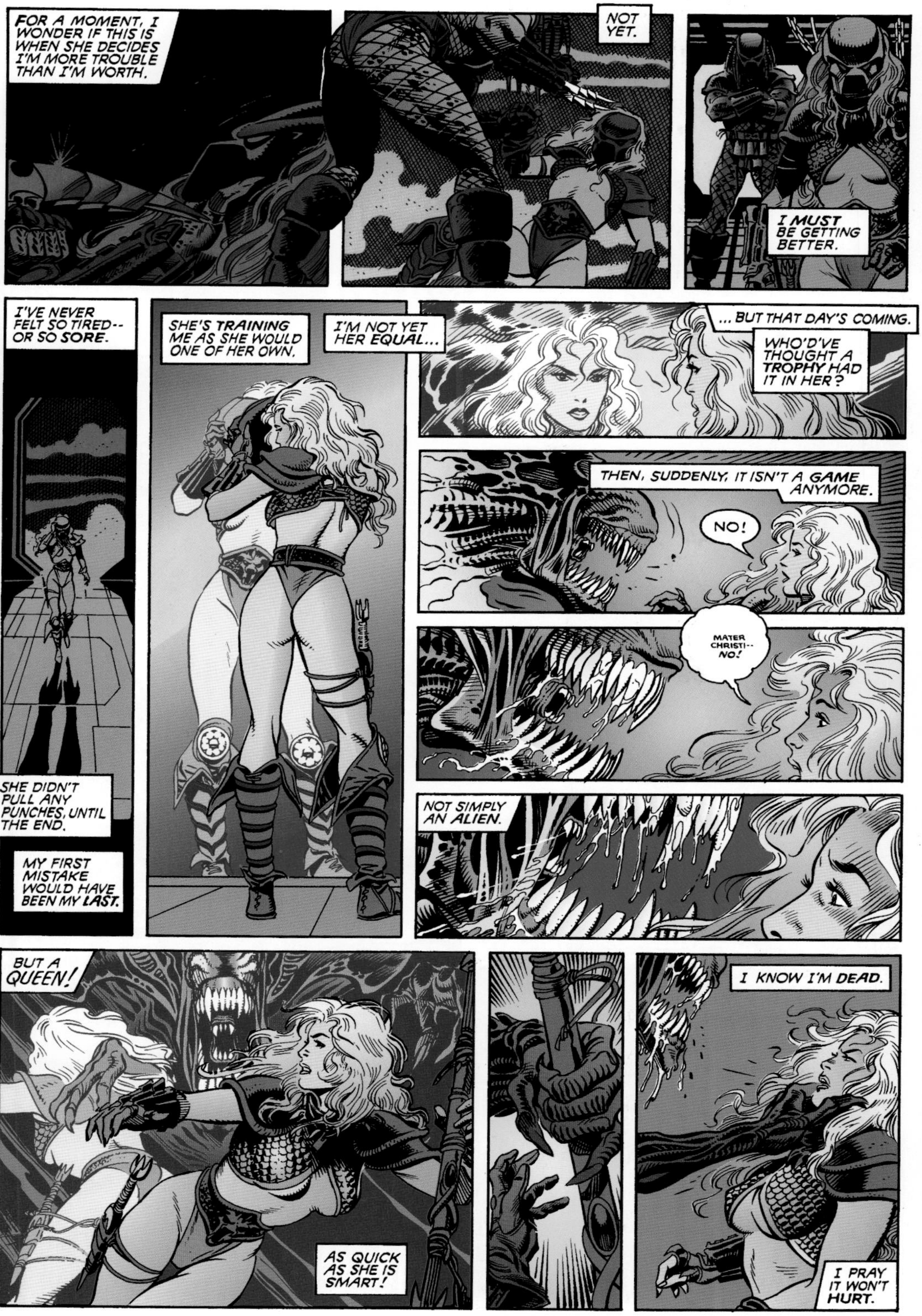
FOR A MOMENT, I WONDER IF THIS IS WHEN SHE DECIDES I'M MORE TROUBLE THAN I'M WORTH.
NOT YET.
I MUST BE GETTING BETTER.
I'VE NEVER FELT SO TIRED-- OR SO SORE.
SHE DIDN'T PULL ANY PUNCHES, UNTIL THE END.
MY FIRST MISTAKE WOULD HAVE BEEN MY LAST.
SHE'S TRAINING ME AS SHE WOULD ONE OF HER OWN.
I'M NOT YET HER EQUAL...
... BUT THAT DAY'S COMING.
WHO'D'VE THOUGHT A TROPHY HAD IT IN HER?
THEN, SUDDENLY, IT ISN'T A GAME ANYMORE.
NO!
MATER CHRISTI-- NO!
NOT SIMPLY AN ALIEN.
BUT A QUEEN!
AS QUICK AS SHE IS SMART!
I KNOW I'M DEAD.
I PRAY IT WON'T HURT.

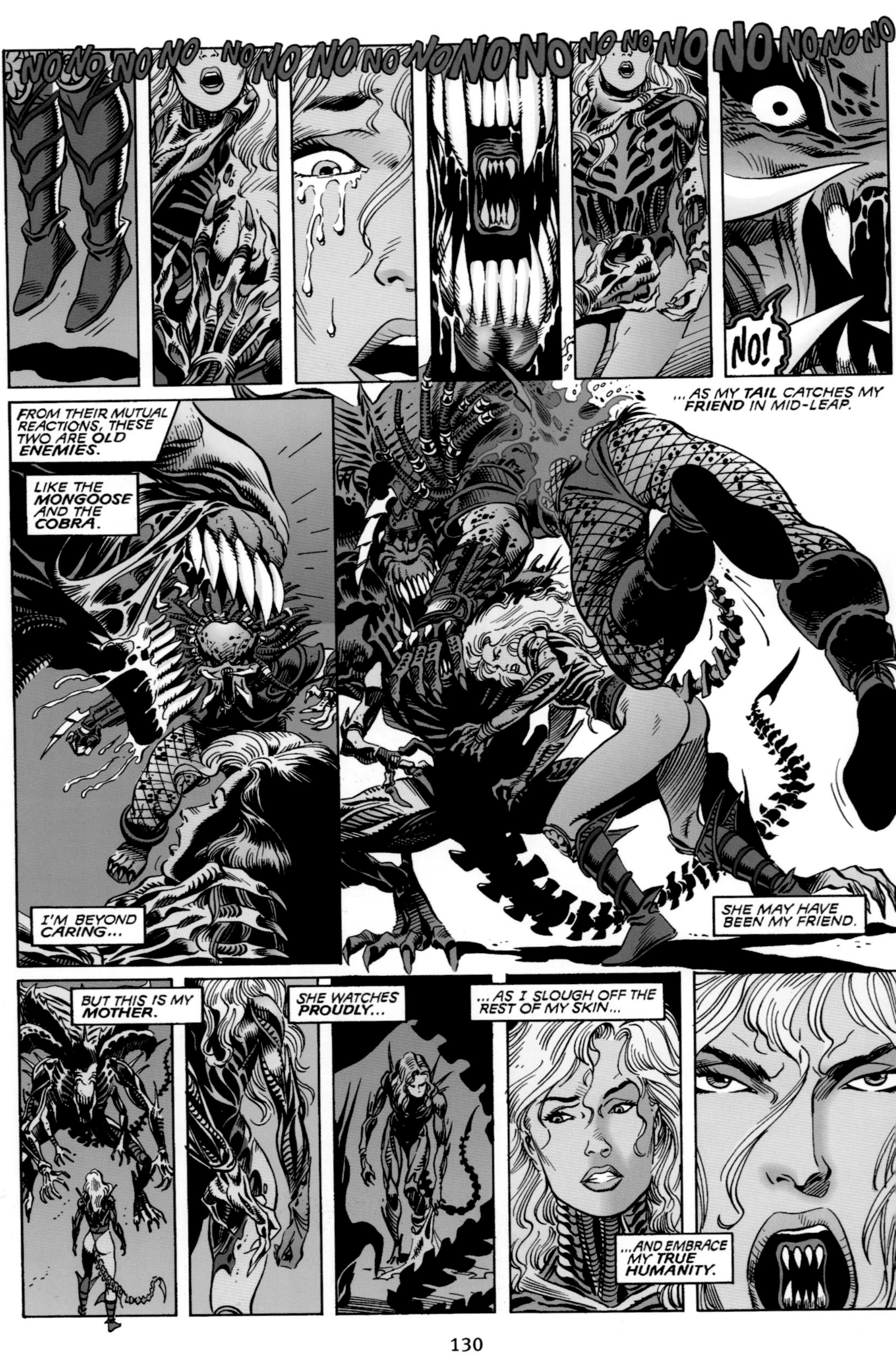

NO NO NO NO NO NO NO NO NO NO NO NO NO NO NO NO NO NO NO NO
NO!
FROM THEIR MUTUAL REACTIONS, THESE TWO ARE OLD ENEMIES.
LIKE THE MONGOOSE AND THE COBRA.
I'M BEYOND CARING...
...AS MY TAIL CATCHES MY FRIEND IN MID-LEAP.
SHE MAY HAVE BEEN MY FRIEND.
BUT THIS IS MY MOTHER.
SHE WATCHES PROUDLY...
...AS I SLOUGH OFF THE REST OF MY SKIN...
...AND EMBRACE MY TRUE HUMANITY.

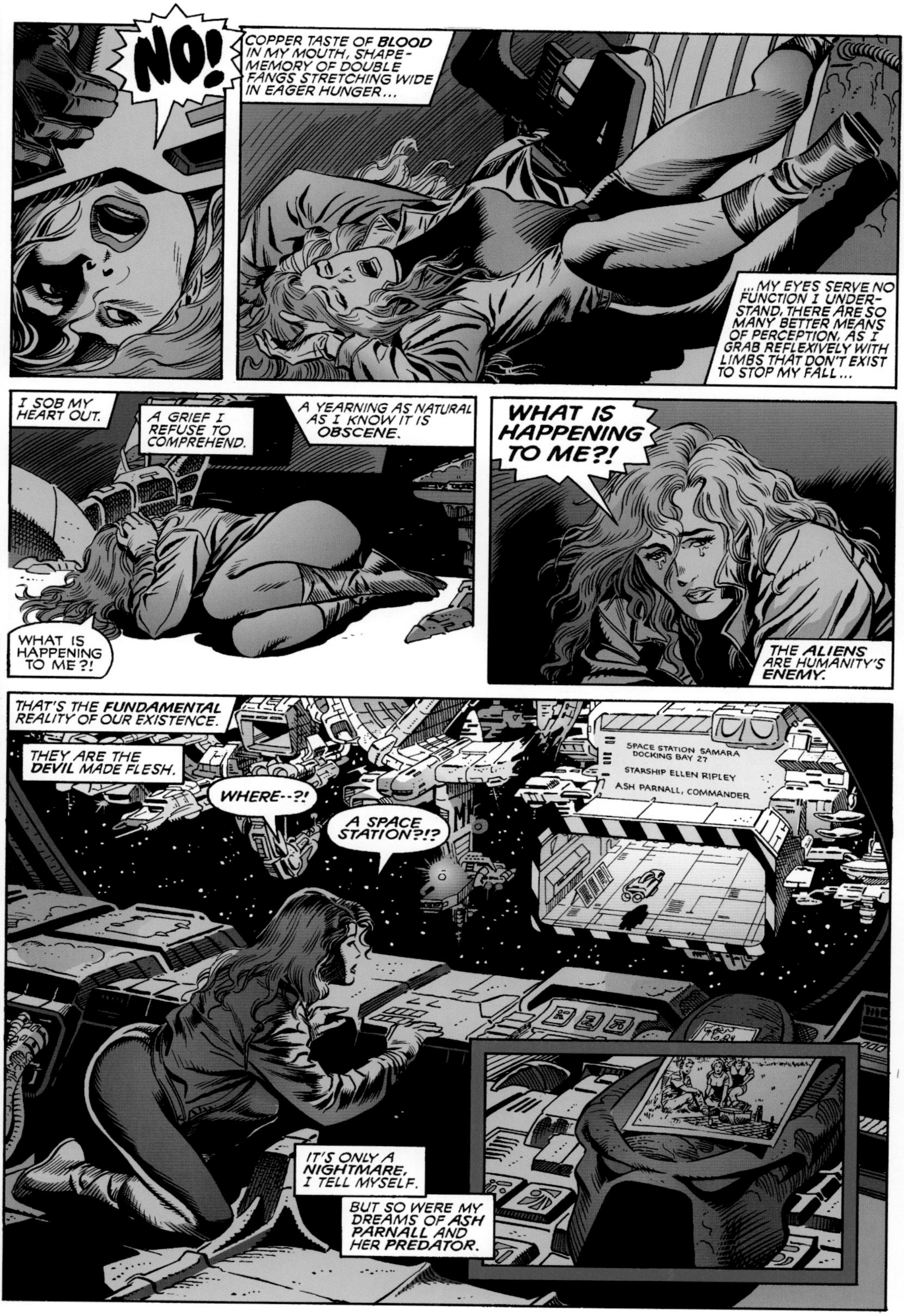
NO!
COPPER TASTE OF BLOOD IN MY MOUTH, SHAPE-MEMORY OF DOUBLE FANGS STRETCHING WIDE IN EAGER HUNGER...
...MY EYES SERVE NO FUNCTION I UNDERSTAND; THERE ARE SO MANY BETTER MEANS OF PERCEPTION, AS I GRAB REFLEXIVELY WITH LIMBS THAT DON'T EXIST TO STOP MY FALL...
I SOB MY HEART OUT.
A GRIEF I REFUSE TO COMPREHEND.
A YEARNING AS NATURAL AS I KNOW IT IS OBSCENE.
WHAT IS HAPPENING TO ME?!
WHAT IS HAPPENING TO ME?!
THE ALIENS ARE HUMANITY'S ENEMY.
THAT'S THE FUNDAMENTAL REALITY OF OUR EXISTENCE.
THEY ARE THE DEVIL MADE FLESH.
WHERE--?!
A SPACE STATION?!?
SPACE STATION SAMARA
DOCKING BAY 27
STARSHIP ELLEN RIPLEY
ASH PARNALL, COMMANDER
IT'S ONLY A NIGHTMARE, I TELL MYSELF.
BUT SO WERE MY DREAMS OF ASH PARNALL AND HER PREDATOR.

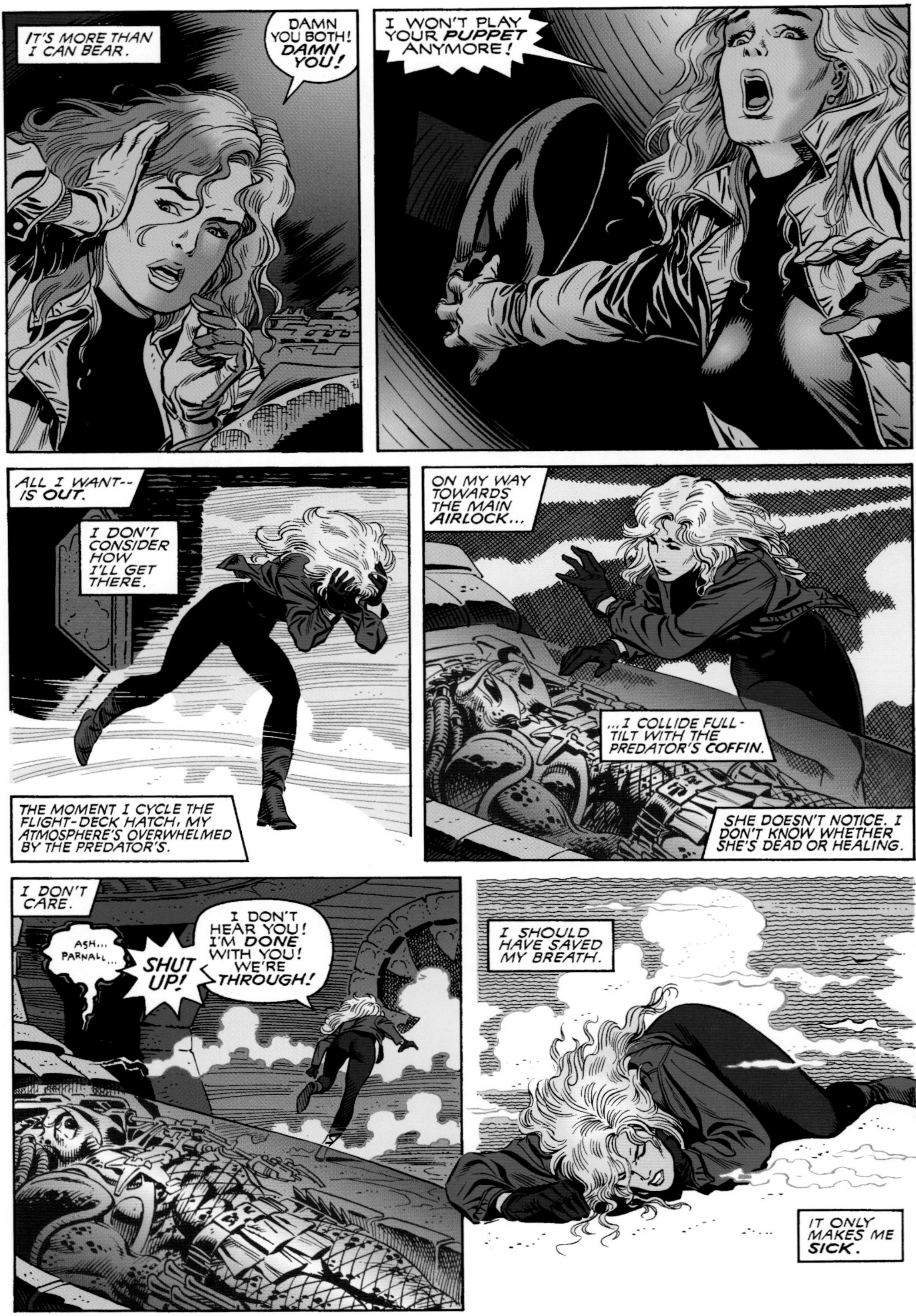
IT'S MORE THAN I CAN BEAR.
DAMN YOU BOTH! DAMN YOU!
I WON'T PLAY YOUR PUPPET ANYMORE!
ALL I WANT-- IS OUT.
I DON'T CONSIDER HOW I'LL GET THERE.
THE MOMENT I CYCLE THE FLIGHT-DECK HATCH, MY ATMOSPHERE'S OVERWHELMED BY THE PREDATOR'S.
ON MY WAY TOWARDS THE MAIN AIRLOCK...
...I COLLIDE FULL-TILT WITH THE PREDATOR'S COFFIN.
SHE DOESN'T NOTICE. I DON'T KNOW WHETHER SHE'S DEAD OR HEALING.
I DON'T CARE.
ASH... PARNALL...
SHUT UP!
I DON'T HEAR YOU! I'M DONE WITH YOU! WE'RE THROUGH!
I SHOULD HAVE SAVED MY BREATH.
IT ONLY MAKES ME SICK.

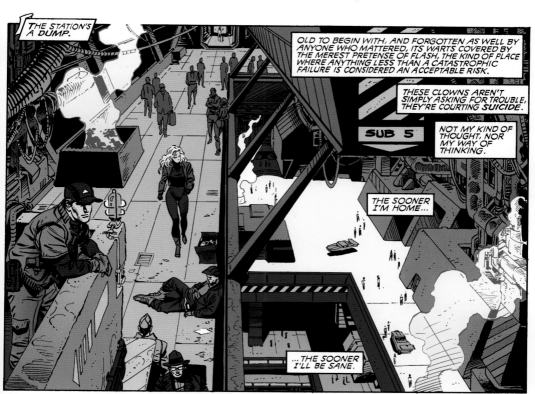

THE STATION'S A DUMP.

OLD TO BEGIN WITH, AND FORGOTTEN AS WELL BY ANYONE WHO MATTERED, ITS WARTS COVERED BY THE MEREST PRETENSE OF FLASH, THE KIND OF PLACE WHERE ANYTHING LESS THAN A CATASTROPHIC FAILURE IS CONSIDERED AN ACCEPTABLE RISK.

THESE CLOWNS AREN'T SIMPLY ASKING FOR TROUBLE, THEY'RE COURTING *SUICIDE.*

SUB 5

NOT MY KIND OF THOUGHT, NOR MY WAY OF THINKING.

THE SOONER I'M HOME...

...THE SOONER I'LL BE SANE.

I NEED TO SEND A TRANSCOM SIGNAL TO EARTH, PLEASE. CAN THAT BE ARRANGED?

WE'RE IN *OCCLUSION.*

ONLY MILSEC TRANSCOMS UNTIL THE FLARES SUBSIDE.

I'LL NEED A ROOM, THEN.

YOU LOOK LIKE YOU NEED A DRINK MORE, SWEETIE.

HANG IN THE LOUNGE, RELAX YOURSELF...

...I'LL CALL WHEN EVERY- THING'S ARRANGED.

THANK YOU. THAT'S VERY KIND.

NOT AT ALL, SWEETIE. 'S WHY I'M HERE.

ROCCO, THE LOOKER IN BLACK LEATHER, JUST WALKIN' THROUGH YOUR DOOR...

...WHATEVER SHE ASKS FOR, YOU SERVE HER THE SPECIAL RESERVE-- HEAR WHAT I'M SAYIN'?

NO LIMIT.

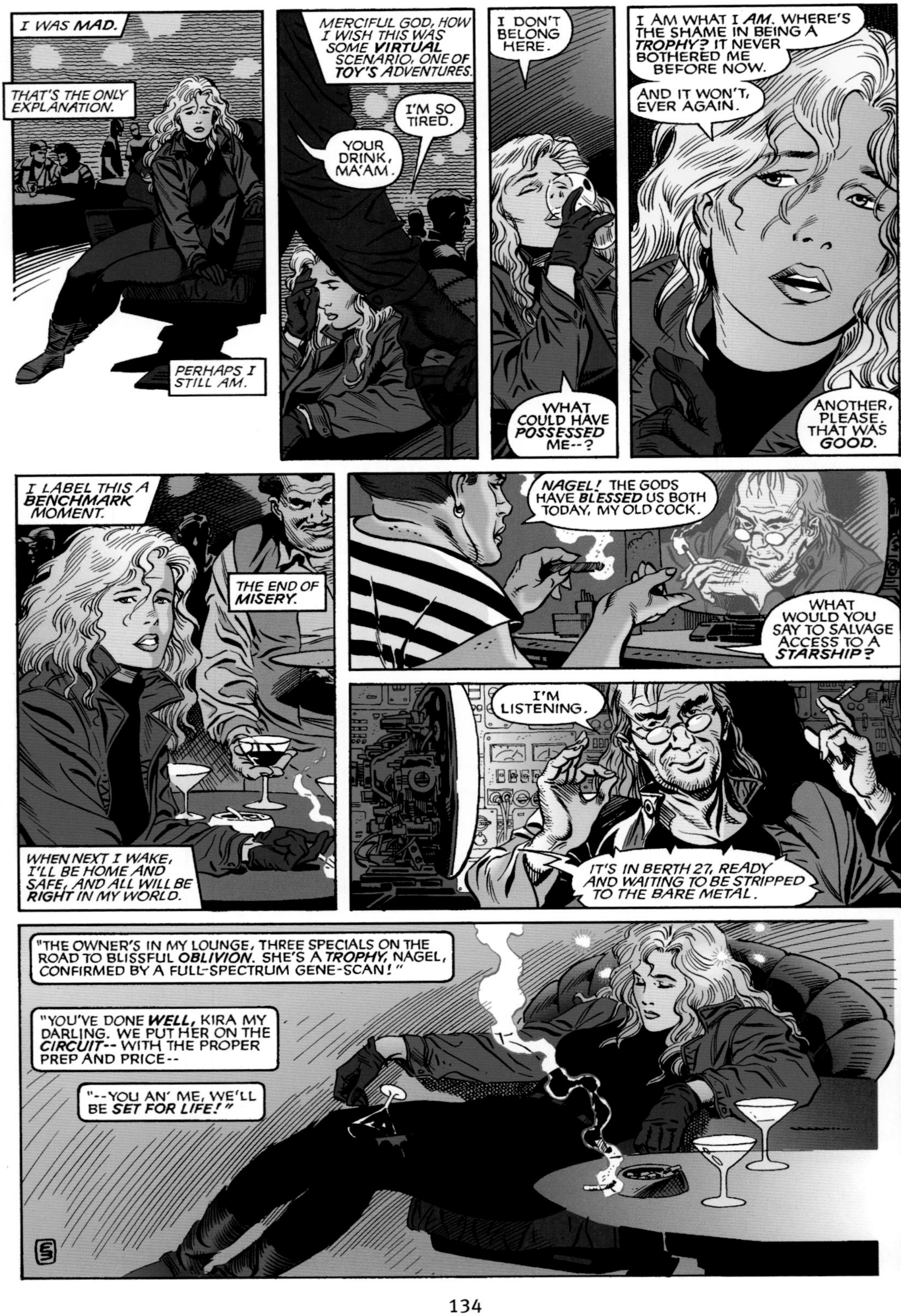
I WAS MAD.
THAT'S THE ONLY EXPLANATION.
PERHAPS I STILL AM.
MERCIFUL GOD, HOW I WISH THIS WAS SOME VIRTUAL SCENARIO, ONE OF TOY'S ADVENTURES.
I'M SO TIRED.
YOUR DRINK, MA'AM.
I DON'T BELONG HERE.
WHAT COULD HAVE POSSESSED ME--?
I AM WHAT I AM. WHERE'S THE SHAME IN BEING A TROPHY? IT NEVER BOTHERED ME BEFORE NOW.
AND IT WON'T, EVER AGAIN.
ANOTHER, PLEASE. THAT WAS GOOD.
I LABEL THIS A BENCHMARK MOMENT.
THE END OF MISERY.
WHEN NEXT I WAKE, I'LL BE HOME AND SAFE, AND ALL WILL BE RIGHT IN MY WORLD.
NAGEL! THE GODS HAVE BLESSED US BOTH TODAY, MY OLD COCK.
WHAT WOULD YOU SAY TO SALVAGE ACCESS TO A STARSHIP?
I'M LISTENING.
IT'S IN BERTH 27, READY AND WAITING TO BE STRIPPED TO THE BARE METAL.
"THE OWNER'S IN MY LOUNGE, THREE SPECIALS ON THE ROAD TO BLISSFUL OBLIVION. SHE'S A TROPHY, NAGEL, CONFIRMED BY A FULL-SPECTRUM GENE-SCAN!"
"YOU'VE DONE WELL, KIRA MY DARLING. WE PUT HER ON THE CIRCUIT-- WITH THE PROPER PREP AND PRICE--
"--YOU AN' ME, WE'LL BE SET FOR LIFE!"

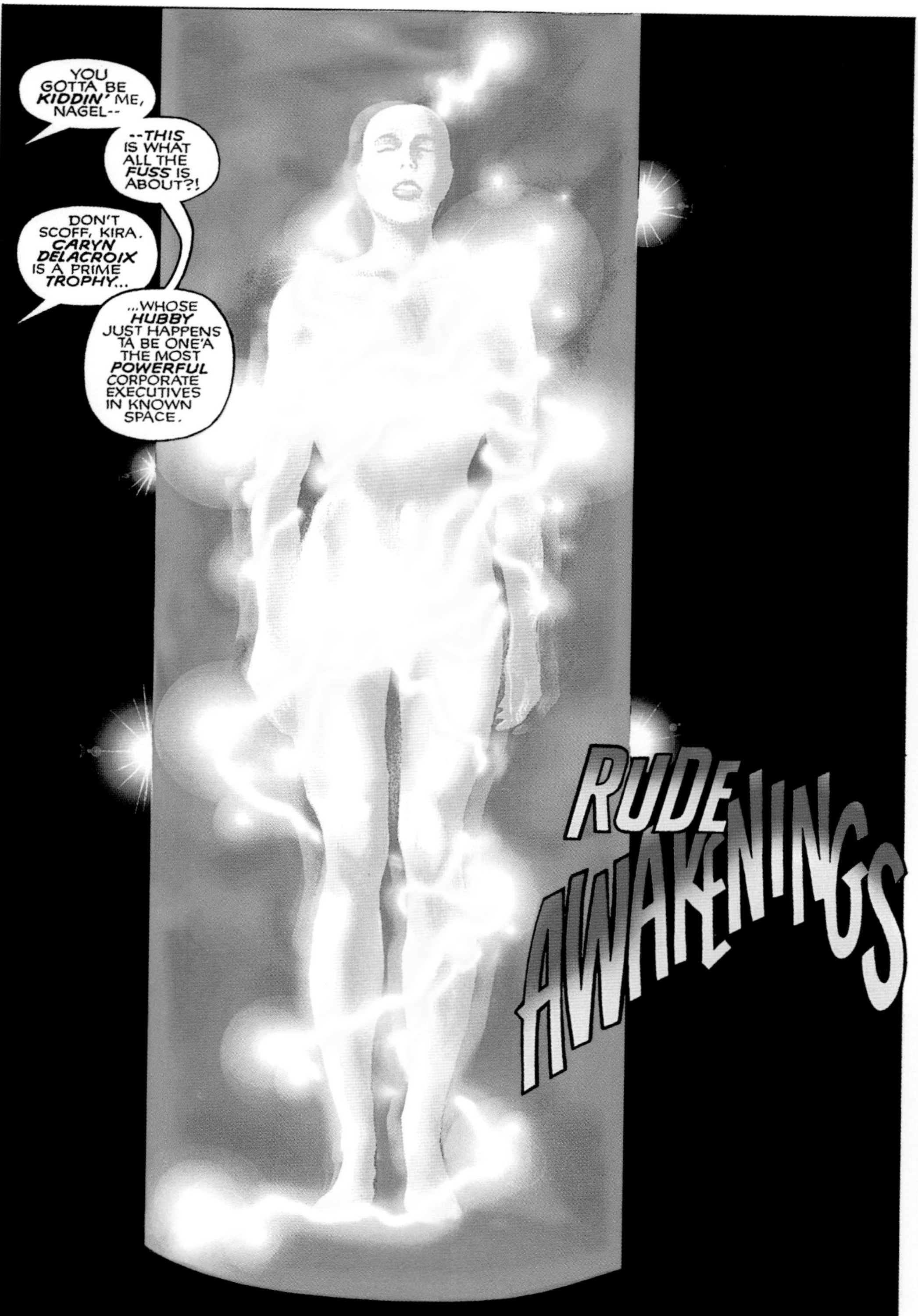
YOU GOTTA BE KIDDIN' ME, NAGEL--
--THIS IS WHAT ALL THE FUSS IS ABOUT?!
DON'T SCOFF, KIRA. CARYN DELACROIX IS A PRIME TROPHY...
...WHOSE HUBBY JUST HAPPENS TA BE ONE'A THE MOST POWERFUL CORPORATE EXECUTIVES IN KNOWN SPACE.
RUDE AWAKENINGS

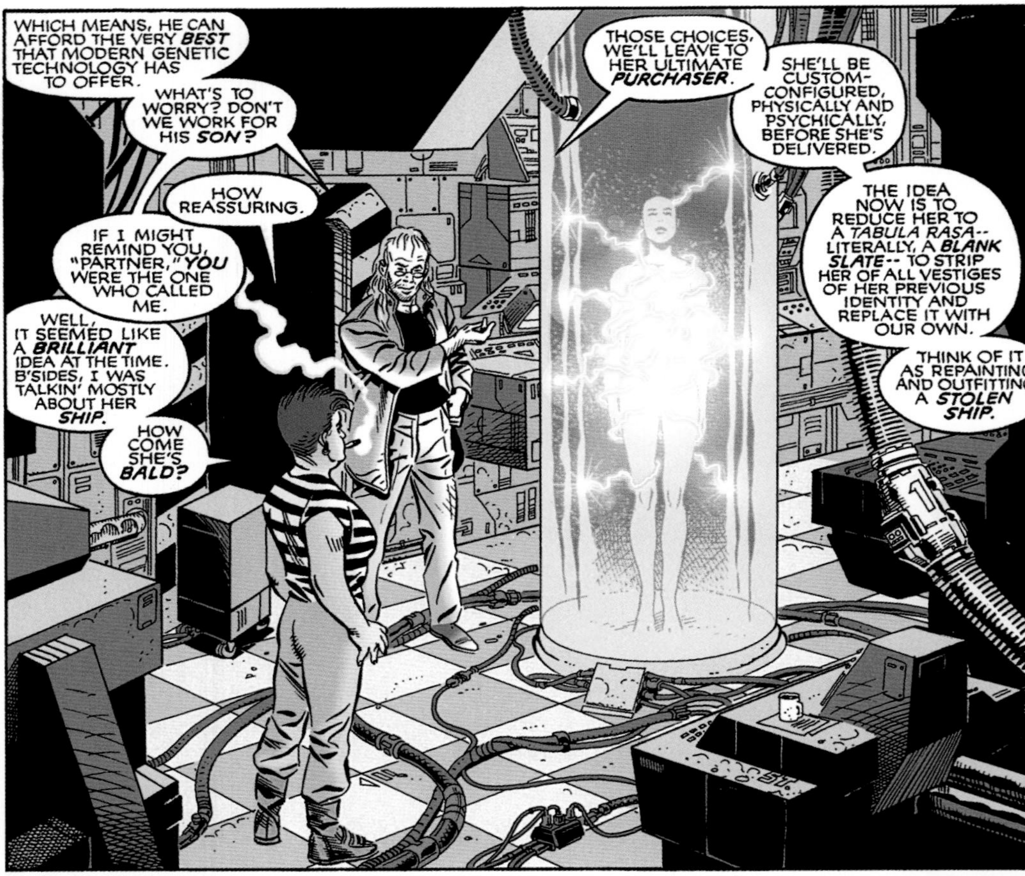
WHICH MEANS, HE CAN AFFORD THE VERY BEST THAT MODERN GENETIC TECHNOLOGY HAS TO OFFER.
WHAT'S TO WORRY? DON'T WE WORK FOR HIS SON?
HOW REASSURING.
IF I MIGHT REMIND YOU, "PARTNER," YOU WERE THE ONE WHO CALLED ME.
WELL, IT SEEMED LIKE A BRILLIANT IDEA AT THE TIME. B'SIDES, I WAS TALKIN' MOSTLY ABOUT HER SHIP.
HOW COME SHE'S BALD?
THOSE CHOICES, WE'LL LEAVE TO HER ULTIMATE PURCHASER.
SHE'LL BE CUSTOM-CONFIGURED, PHYSICALLY AND PSYCHICALLY, BEFORE SHE'S DELIVERED.
THE IDEA NOW IS TO REDUCE HER TO A TABULA RASA-- LITERALLY, A BLANK SLATE-- TO STRIP HER OF ALL VESTIGES OF HER PREVIOUS IDENTITY AND REPLACE IT WITH OUR OWN.
THINK OF IT AS REPAINTING AND OUTFITTING A STOLEN SHIP.

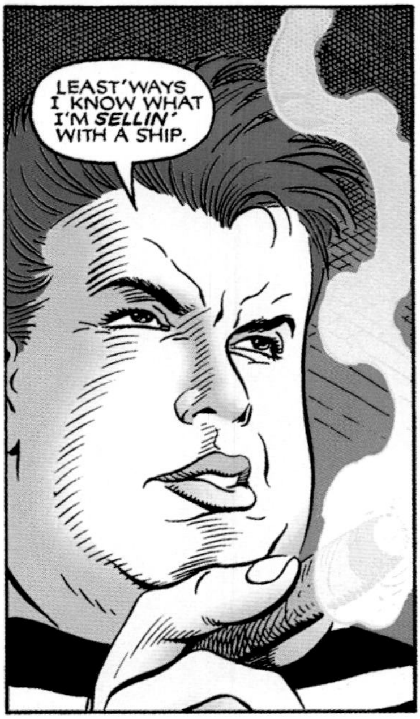
LEAST'WAYS I KNOW WHAT I'M SELLIN' WITH A SHIP.

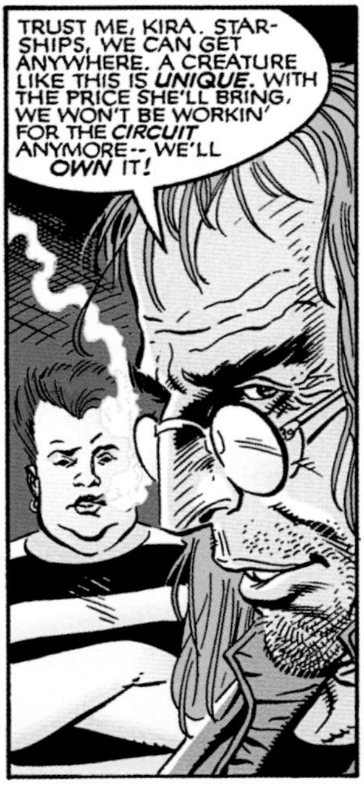
TRUST ME, KIRA. STAR-SHIPS, WE CAN GET ANYWHERE. A CREATURE LIKE THIS IS UNIQUE. WITH THE PRICE SHE'LL BRING, WE WON'T BE WORKIN' FOR THE CIRCUIT ANYMORE-- WE'LL OWN IT!

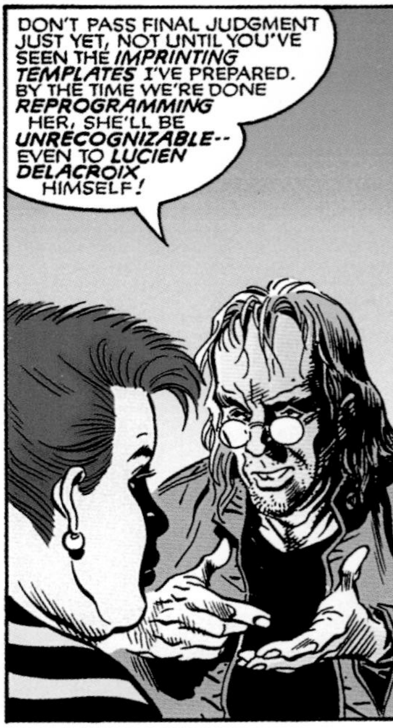
DON'T PASS FINAL JUDGMENT JUST YET, NOT UNTIL YOU'VE SEEN THE IMPRINTING TEMPLATES I'VE PREPARED. BY THE TIME WE'RE DONE REPROGRAMMING HER, SHE'LL BE UNRECOGNIZABLE-- EVEN TO LUCIEN DELACROIX HIMSELF!

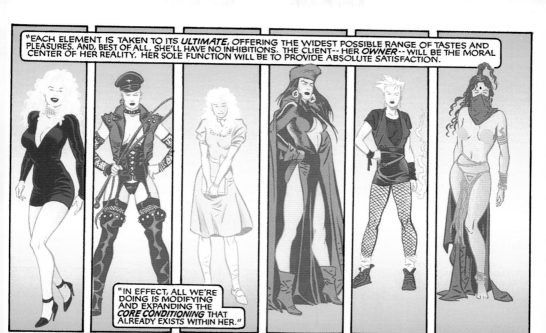

"EACH ELEMENT IS TAKEN TO ITS *ULTIMATE*, OFFERING THE WIDEST POSSIBLE RANGE OF TASTES AND PLEASURES. AND, BEST OF ALL, SHE'LL HAVE NO INHIBITIONS. THE CLIENT-- HER *OWNER*-- WILL BE THE MORAL CENTER OF HER REALITY. HER SOLE FUNCTION WILL BE TO PROVIDE ABSOLUTE SATISFACTION."

"IN EFFECT, ALL WE'RE DOING IS MODIFYING AND EXPANDING THE *CORE CONDITIONING* THAT ALREADY EXISTS WITHIN HER."

YOU CAN'T DO THAT!

NAGEL, SHE'S *AWARE*!

NO WAY, THAT'S NOT POSSIBLE!

NOT TO WORRY, NOT TO WORRY! I'VE GOT EVERYTHING UNDER CONTROL!

WHO *ARE* YOU? WHAT IS THIS PLACE?!

WHAT WE'RE SEEING IS THE PROJECTED ESSENCE OF THE WOMAN HERSELF: THE SUM TOTAL OF HER MEMORY AND PERSONALITY, PROCESSED THROUGH OUR ScanAlyzer AND GIVEN PHYSICAL FORM.

137

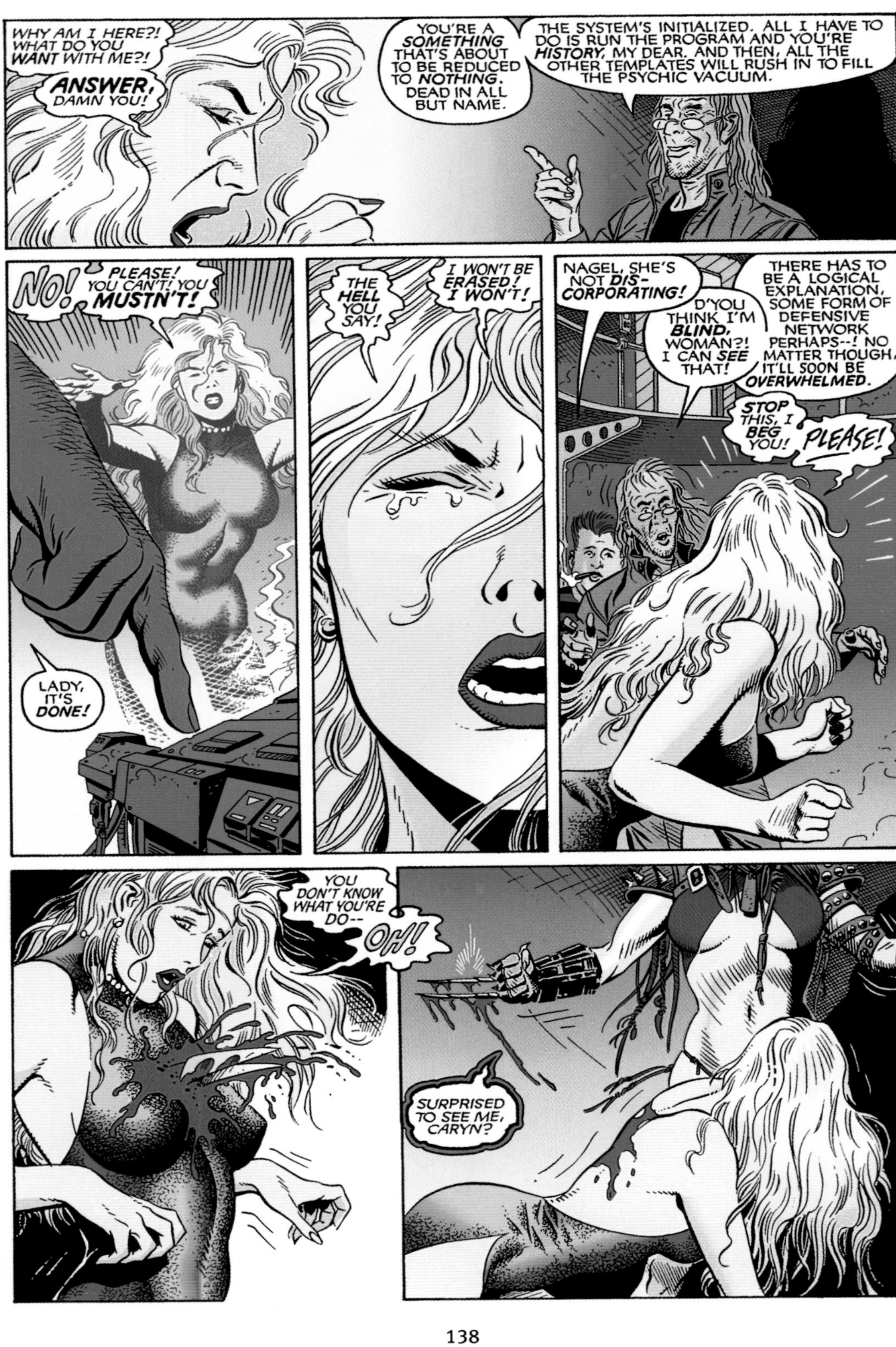
WHY AM I HERE?! WHAT DO YOU WANT WITH ME?!
ANSWER, DAMN YOU!
YOU'RE A SOMETHING THAT'S ABOUT TO BE REDUCED TO NOTHING. DEAD IN ALL BUT NAME.
THE SYSTEM'S INITIALIZED. ALL I HAVE TO DO IS RUN THE PROGRAM AND YOU'RE HISTORY, MY DEAR. AND THEN, ALL THE OTHER TEMPLATES WILL RUSH IN TO FILL THE PSYCHIC VACUUM.
NO!
PLEASE! YOU CAN'T! YOU MUSTN'T!
LADY, IT'S DONE!
THE HELL YOU SAY!
I WON'T BE ERASED! I WON'T!
NAGEL, SHE'S NOT DIS-CORPORATING!
D'YOU THINK I'M BLIND, WOMAN?! I CAN SEE THAT!
THERE HAS TO BE A LOGICAL EXPLANATION, SOME FORM OF DEFENSIVE NETWORK PERHAPS--! NO MATTER THOUGH, IT'LL SOON BE OVERWHELMED.
STOP THIS, I BEG YOU!
PLEASE!
YOU DON'T KNOW WHAT YOU'RE DO--
OH!
SURPRISED TO SEE ME, CARYN?

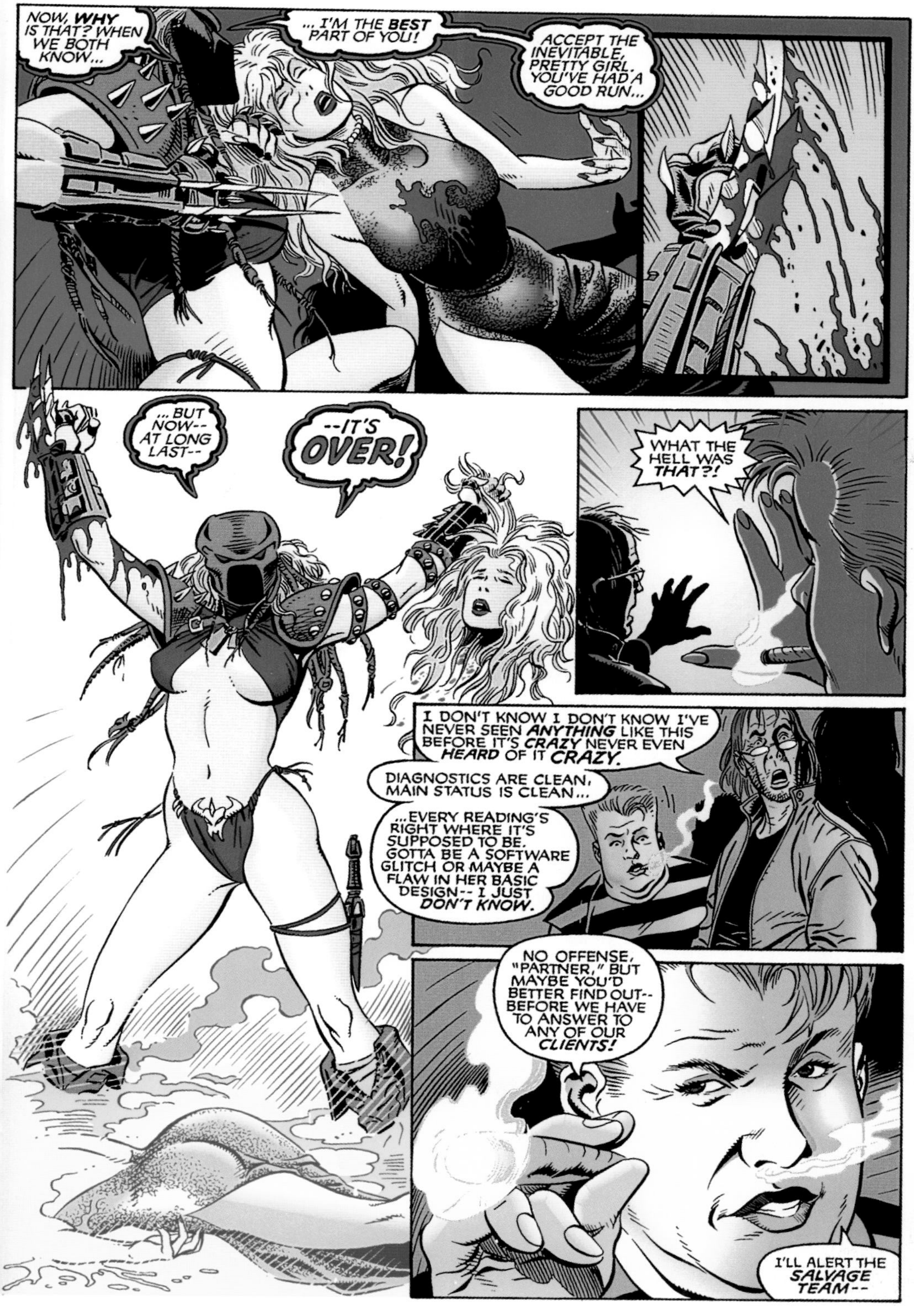
NOW, WHY IS THAT? WHEN WE BOTH KNOW...
...I'M THE BEST PART OF YOU!
ACCEPT THE INEVITABLE, PRETTY GIRL. YOU'VE HAD A GOOD RUN...
...BUT NOW-- AT LONG LAST--
--IT'S OVER!
WHAT THE HELL WAS THAT?!
I DON'T KNOW I DON'T KNOW I'VE NEVER SEEN ANYTHING LIKE THIS BEFORE IT'S CRAZY NEVER EVEN HEARD OF IT CRAZY.
DIAGNOSTICS ARE CLEAN, MAIN STATUS IS CLEAN...
...EVERY READING'S RIGHT WHERE IT'S SUPPOSED TO BE. GOTTA BE A SOFTWARE GLITCH OR MAYBE A FLAW IN HER BASIC DESIGN-- I JUST DON'T KNOW.
NO OFFENSE, "PARTNER," BUT MAYBE YOU'D BETTER FIND OUT-- BEFORE WE HAVE TO ANSWER TO ANY OF OUR CLIENTS!
I'LL ALERT THE SALVAGE TEAM--

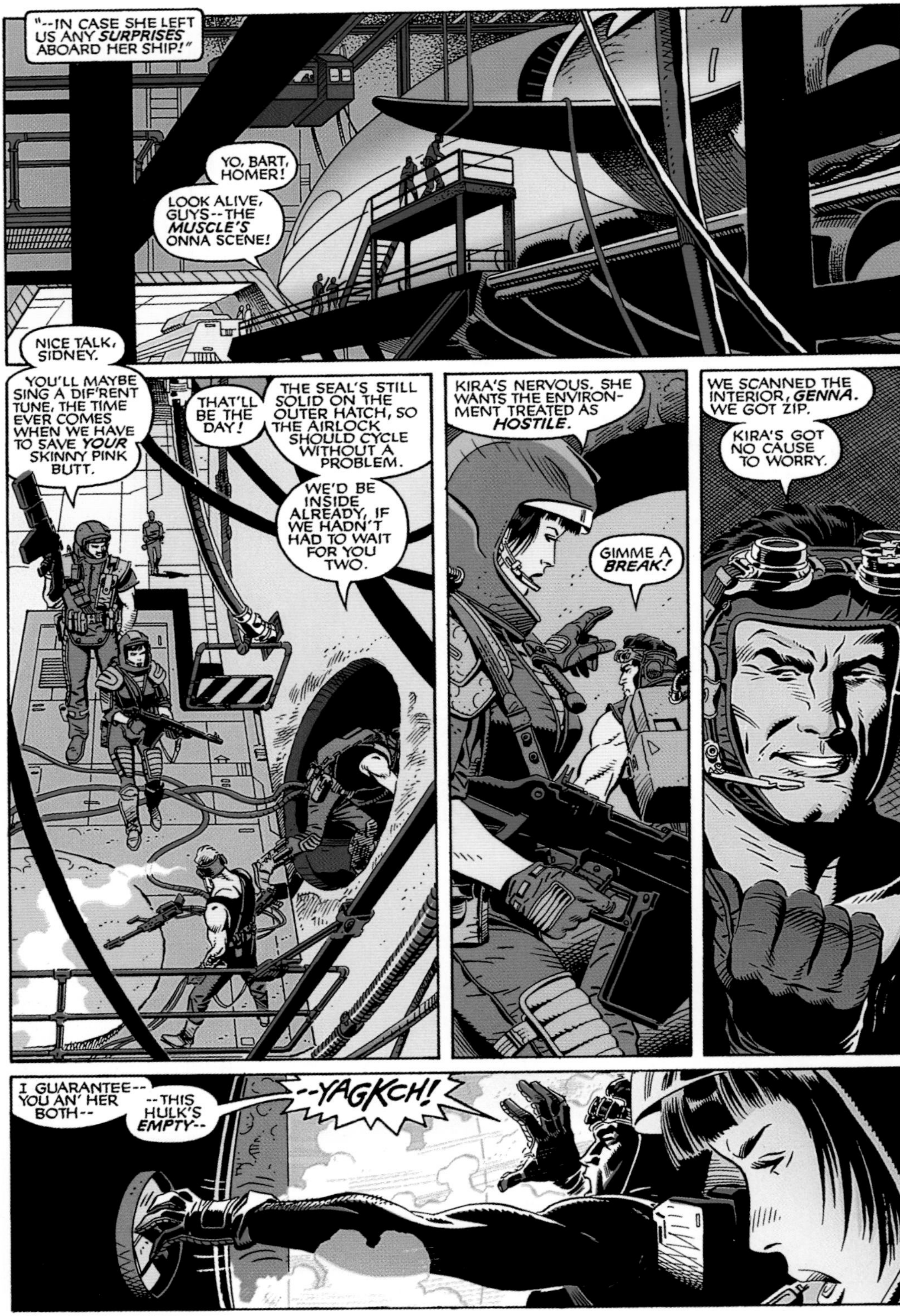
"--IN CASE SHE LEFT US ANY SURPRISES ABOARD HER SHIP!"
YO, BART, HOMER!
LOOK ALIVE, GUYS--THE MUSCLE'S ONNA SCENE!
NICE TALK, SIDNEY.
YOU'LL MAYBE SING A DIF'RENT TUNE, THE TIME EVER COMES WHEN WE HAVE TO SAVE YOUR SKINNY PINK BUTT.
THAT'LL BE THE DAY!
THE SEAL'S STILL SOLID ON THE OUTER HATCH, SO THE AIRLOCK SHOULD CYCLE WITHOUT A PROBLEM.
WE'D BE INSIDE ALREADY, IF WE HADN'T HAD TO WAIT FOR YOU TWO.
KIRA'S NERVOUS. SHE WANTS THE ENVIRONMENT TREATED AS HOSTILE.
GIMME A BREAK!
WE SCANNED THE INTERIOR, GENNA. WE GOT ZIP.
KIRA'S GOT NO CAUSE TO WORRY.
I GUARANTEE--YOU AN' HER BOTH--
--THIS HULK'S EMPTY--
--YAGKCH!

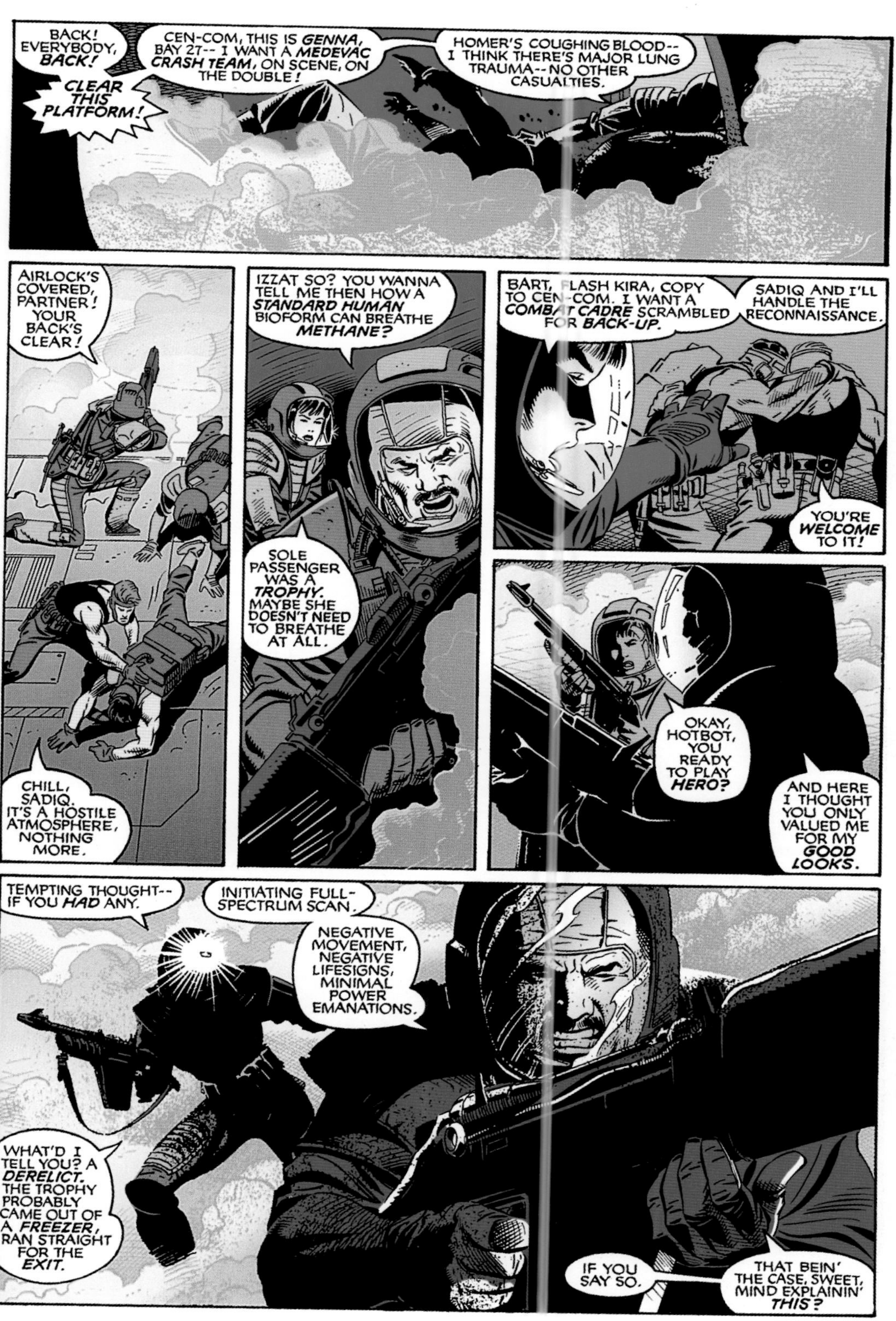
BACK! EVERYBODY, BACK!
CLEAR THIS PLATFORM!
CEN-COM, THIS IS GENNA, BAY 27-- I WANT A MEDEVAC CRASH TEAM, ON SCENE, ON THE DOUBLE!
HOMER'S COUGHING BLOOD-- I THINK THERE'S MAJOR LUNG TRAUMA--NO OTHER CASUALTIES.
AIRLOCK'S COVERED, PARTNER! YOUR BACK'S CLEAR!
CHILL, SADIQ. IT'S A HOSTILE ATMOSPHERE, NOTHING MORE.
IZZAT SO? YOU WANNA TELL ME THEN HOW A STANDARD HUMAN BIOFORM CAN BREATHE METHANE?
SOLE PASSENGER WAS A TROPHY. MAYBE SHE DOESN'T NEED TO BREATHE AT ALL.
BART, FLASH KIRA, COPY TO CEN-COM. I WANT A COMBAT CADRE SCRAMBLED FOR BACK-UP.
SADIQ AND I'LL HANDLE THE RECONNAISSANCE.
YOU'RE WELCOME TO IT!
OKAY, HOTBOT, YOU READY TO PLAY HERO?
AND HERE I THOUGHT YOU ONLY VALUED ME FOR MY GOOD LOOKS.
TEMPTING THOUGHT-- IF YOU HAD ANY.
INITIATING FULL-SPECTRUM SCAN.
NEGATIVE MOVEMENT, NEGATIVE LIFESIGNS, MINIMAL POWER EMANATIONS.
WHAT'D I TELL YOU? A DERELICT. THE TROPHY PROBABLY CAME OUT OF A FREEZER, RAN STRAIGHT FOR THE EXIT.
IF YOU SAY SO.
THAT BEIN' THE CASE, SWEET, MIND EXPLAININ' THIS?

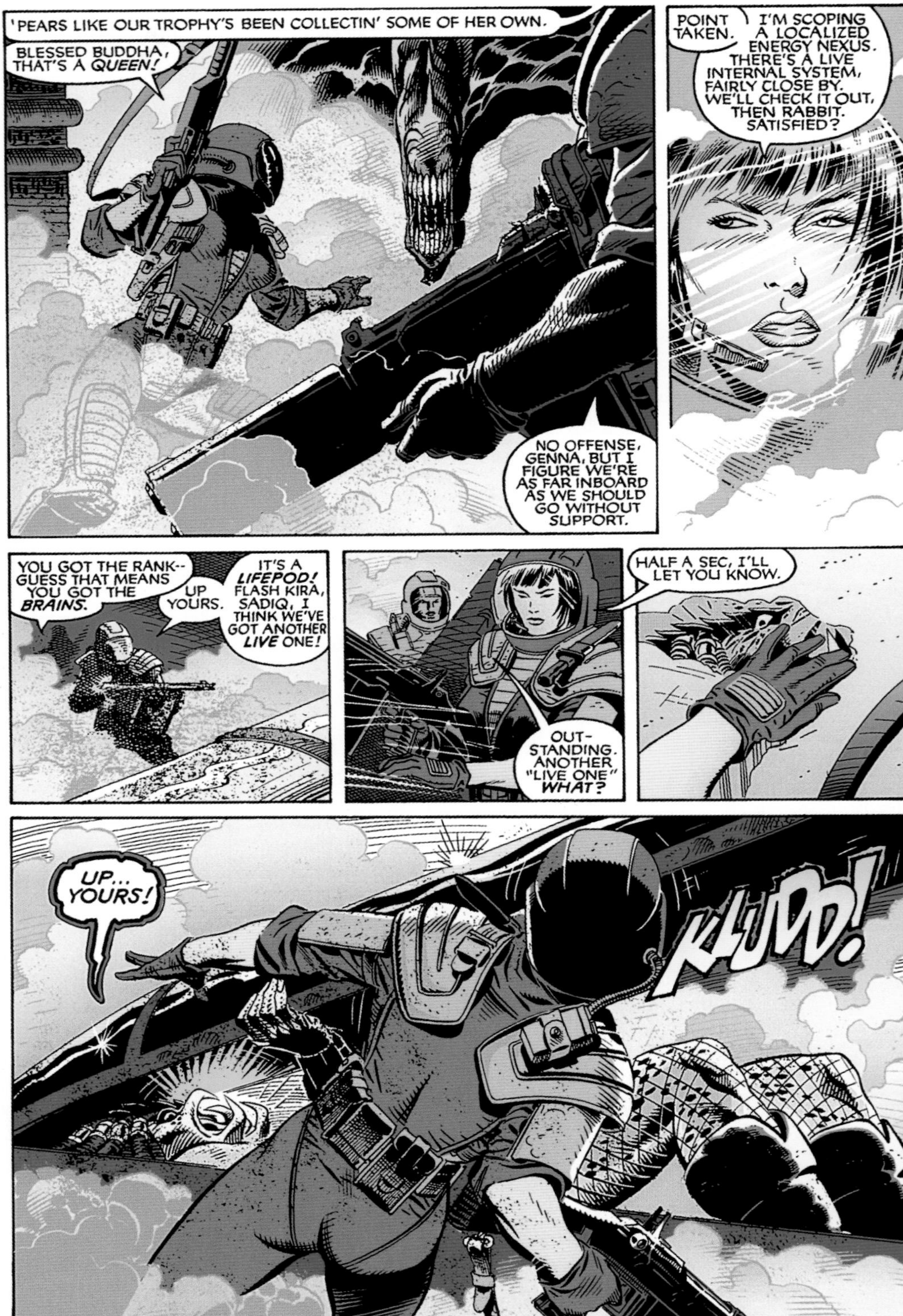
'PEARS LIKE OUR TROPHY'S BEEN COLLECTIN' SOME OF HER OWN.
BLESSED BUDDHA, THAT'S A *QUEEN!*
NO OFFENSE, GENNA, BUT I FIGURE WE'RE AS FAR INBOARD AS WE SHOULD GO WITHOUT SUPPORT.
POINT TAKEN.
I'M SCOPING A LOCALIZED ENERGY NEXUS. THERE'S A LIVE INTERNAL SYSTEM, FAIRLY CLOSE BY. WE'LL CHECK IT OUT, THEN RABBIT. SATISFIED?
YOU GOT THE RANK--GUESS THAT MEANS YOU GOT THE *BRAINS.*
UP YOURS.
IT'S A *LIFEPOD!* FLASH KIRA, SADIQ, I THINK WE'VE GOT ANOTHER *LIVE* ONE!
OUT-STANDING. ANOTHER "LIVE ONE" *WHAT?*
HALF A SEC, I'LL LET YOU KNOW.
UP... YOURS!
KLUDD!

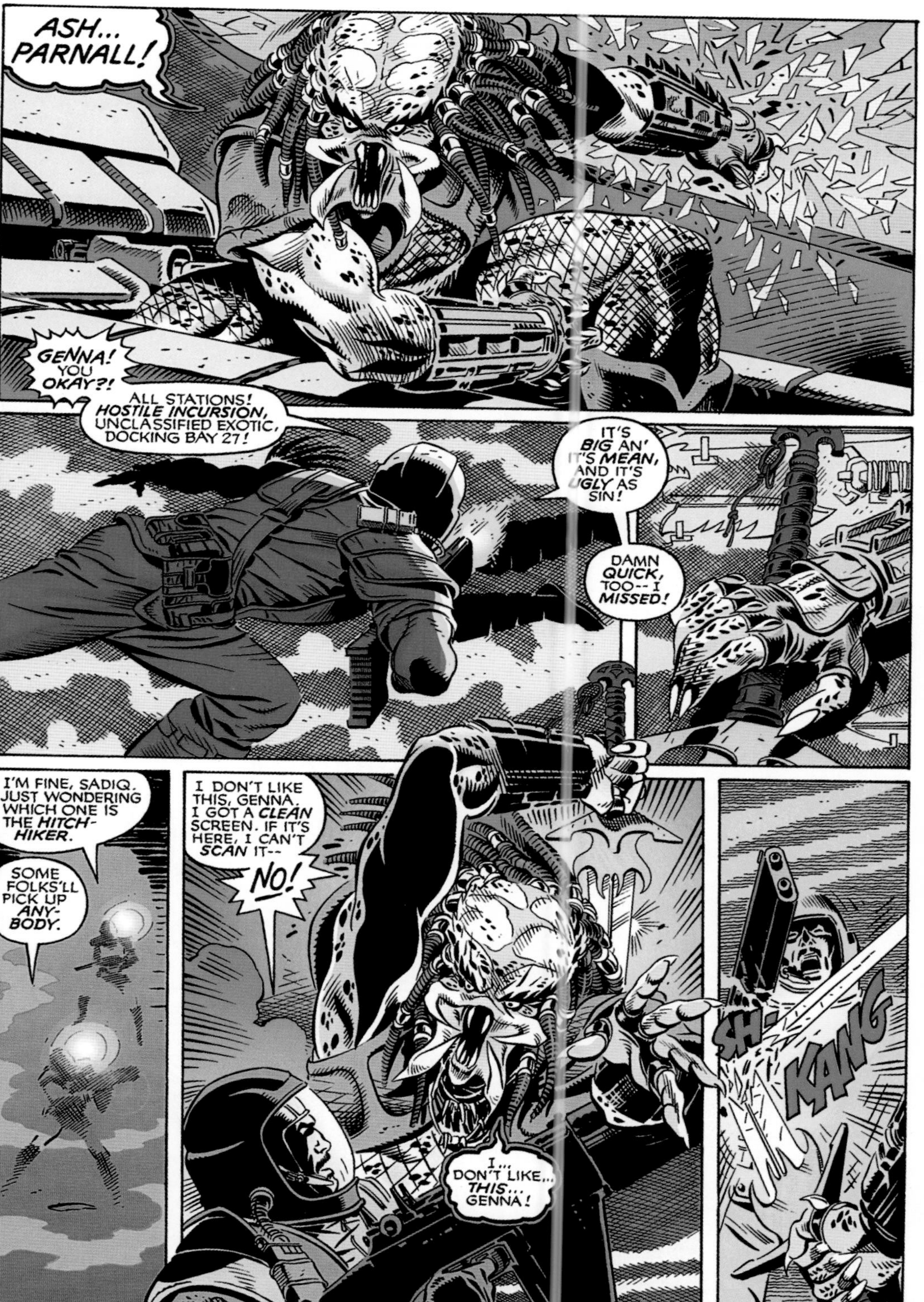
ASH... PARNALL!
GENNA! YOU OKAY?!
ALL STATIONS! HOSTILE INCURSION, UNCLASSIFIED EXOTIC, DOCKING BAY 27!
IT'S BIG AN' IT'S MEAN, AND IT'S UGLY AS SIN!
DAMN QUICK, TOO-- I MISSED!
I'M FINE, SADIQ. JUST WONDERING WHICH ONE IS THE HITCH-HIKER.
SOME FOLKS'LL PICK UP ANY-BODY.
I DON'T LIKE THIS, GENNA. I GOT A CLEAN SCREEN. IF IT'S HERE, I CAN'T SCAN IT--
NO!
I... DON'T LIKE... THIS... GENNA!
SH-KANG

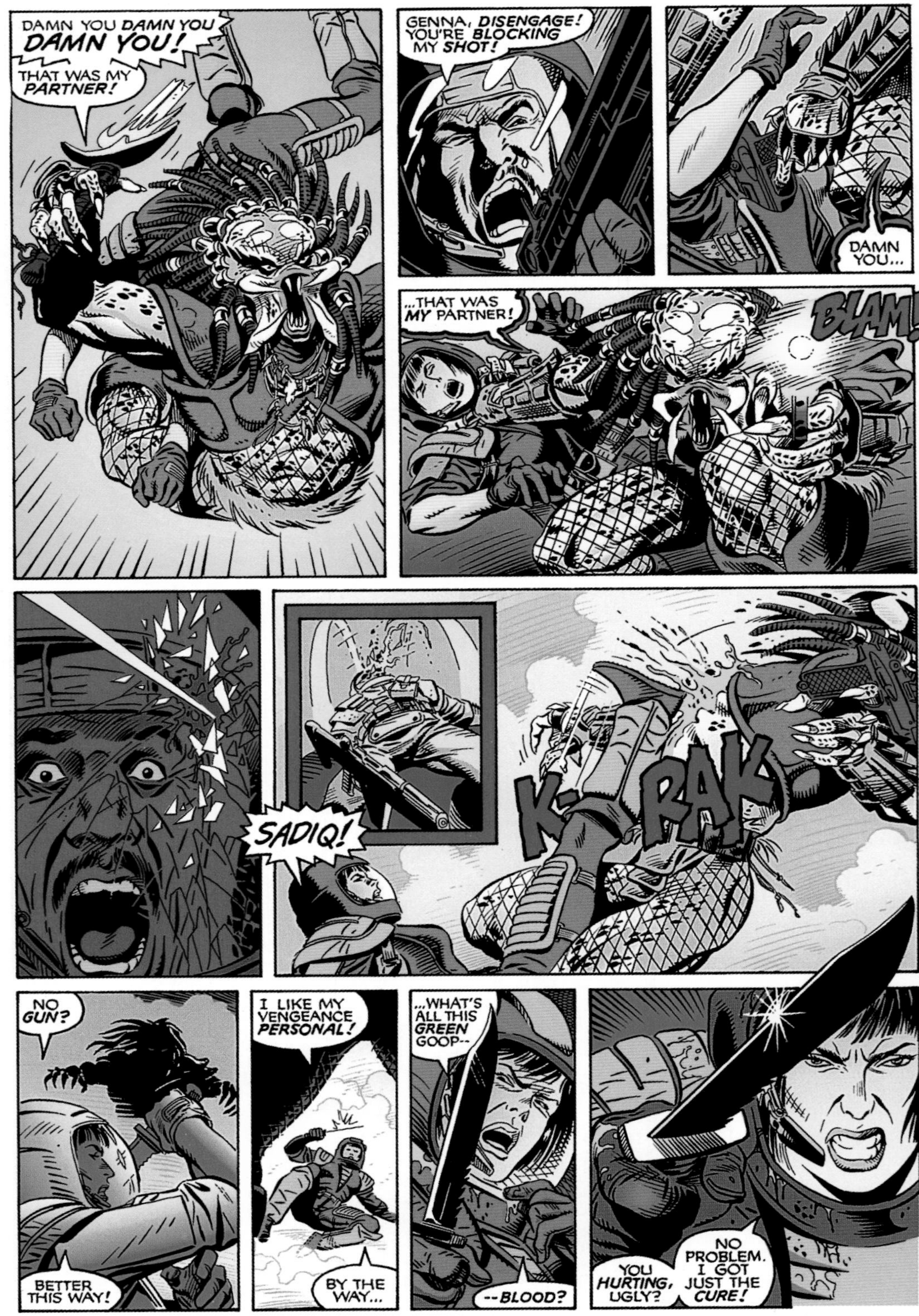

DAMN YOU DAMN YOU DAMN YOU!
THAT WAS MY PARTNER!
GENNA, DISENGAGE! YOU'RE BLOCKING MY SHOT!
DAMN YOU...
...THAT WAS MY PARTNER!
BLAM!
SADIQ!
K-RAK
NO GUN?
BETTER THIS WAY!
I LIKE MY VENGEANCE PERSONAL!
BY THE WAY...
...WHAT'S ALL THIS GREEN GOOP--
--BLOOD?
YOU HURTING, UGLY?
NO PROBLEM. I GOT JUST THE CURE!

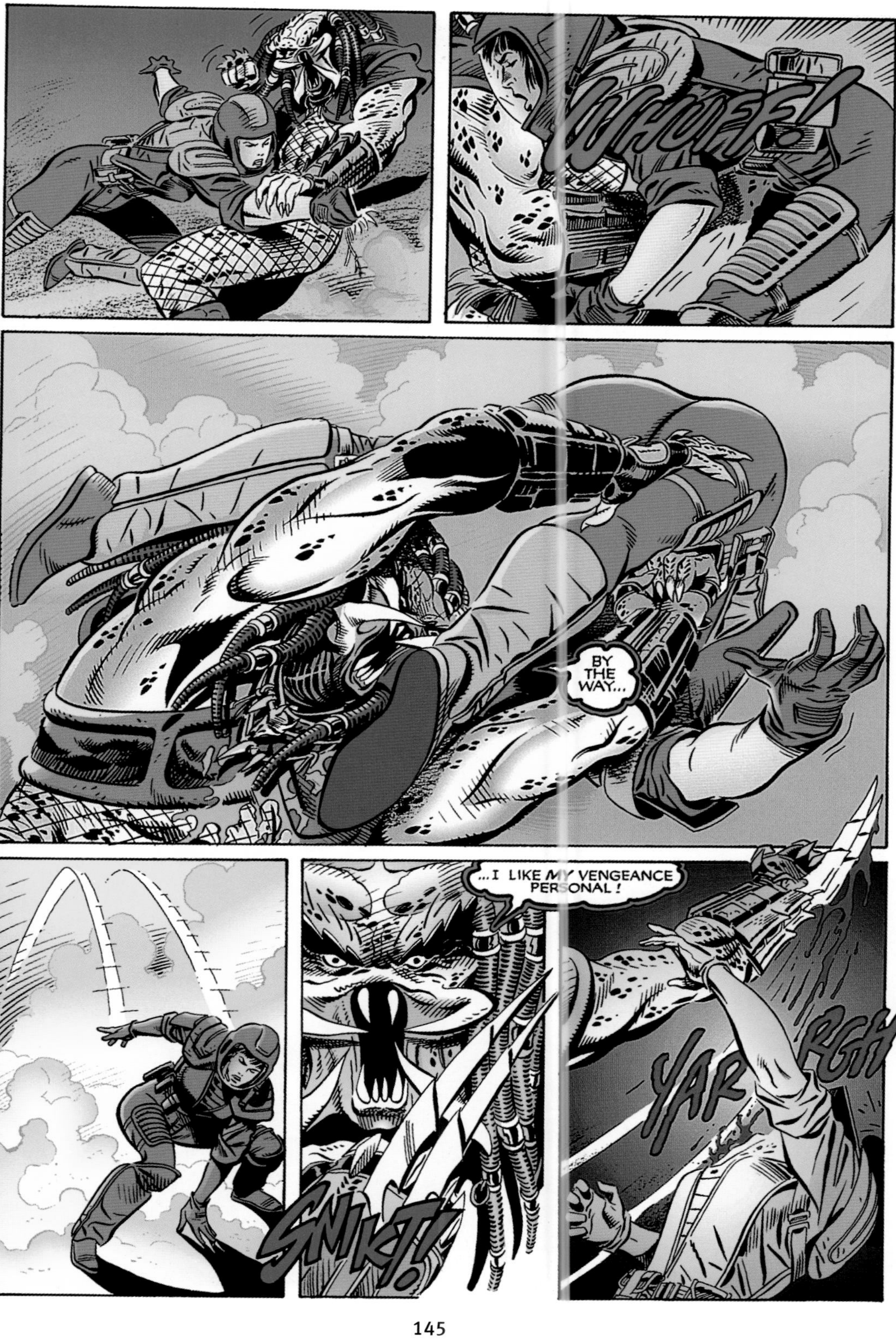
WHUFF!
BY THE WAY...
...I LIKE MY VENGEANCE PERSONAL!
SNIKT!
YARRGH

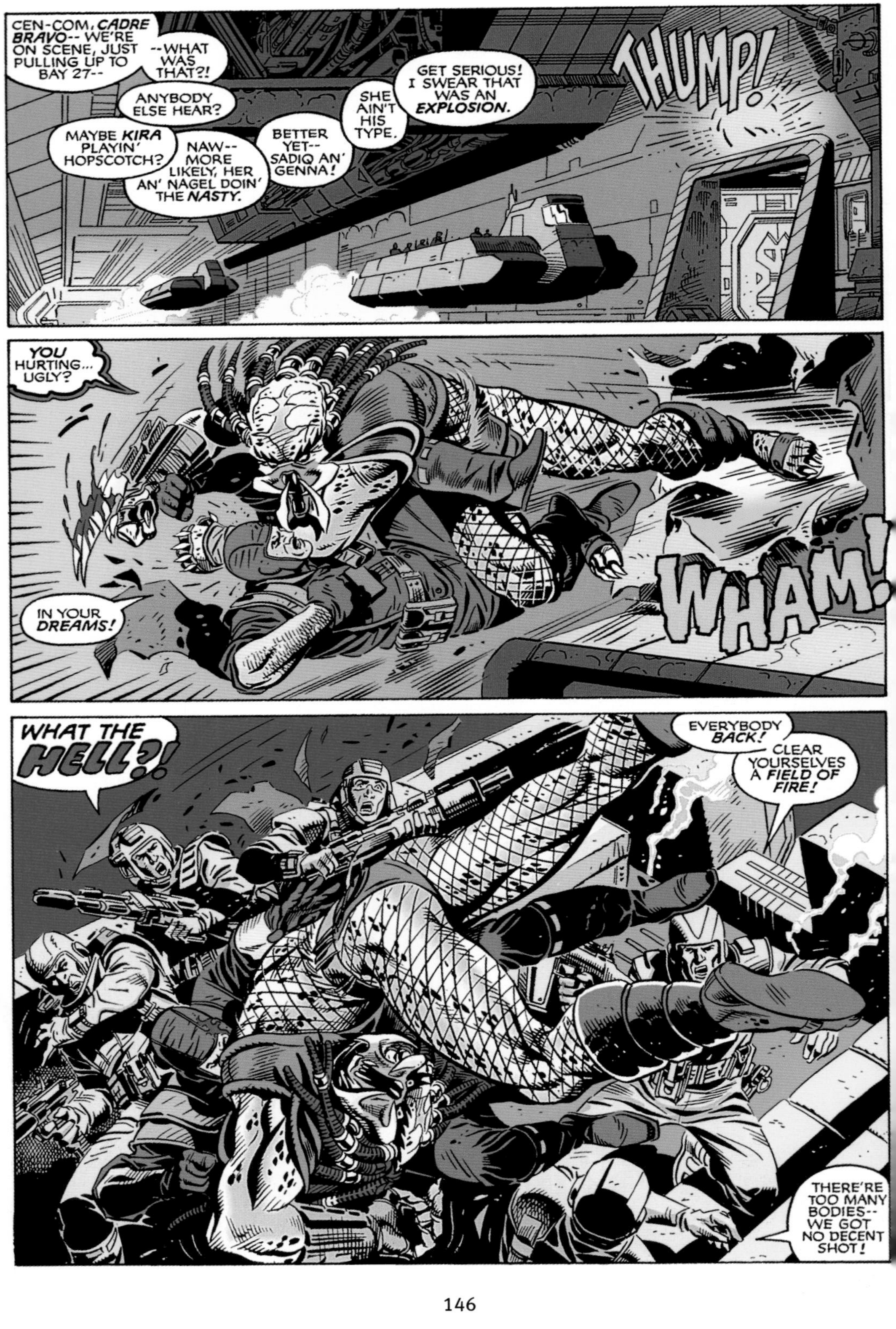

CEN-COM, CADRE BRAVO-- WE'RE ON SCENE, JUST PULLING UP TO BAY 27--
--WHAT WAS THAT?!
THUMP!
ANYBODY ELSE HEAR?
MAYBE KIRA PLAYIN' HOPSCOTCH?
NAW-- MORE LIKELY, HER AN' NAGEL DOIN' THE NASTY.
BETTER YET-- SADIQ AN' GENNA!
SHE AIN'T HIS TYPE.
GET SERIOUS! I SWEAR THAT WAS AN EXPLOSION.
YOU HURTING... UGLY?
IN YOUR DREAMS!
WHAM!
WHAT THE HELL?!
EVERYBODY BACK!
CLEAR YOURSELVES A FIELD OF FIRE!
THERE'RE TOO MANY BODIES-- WE GOT NO DECENT SHOT!

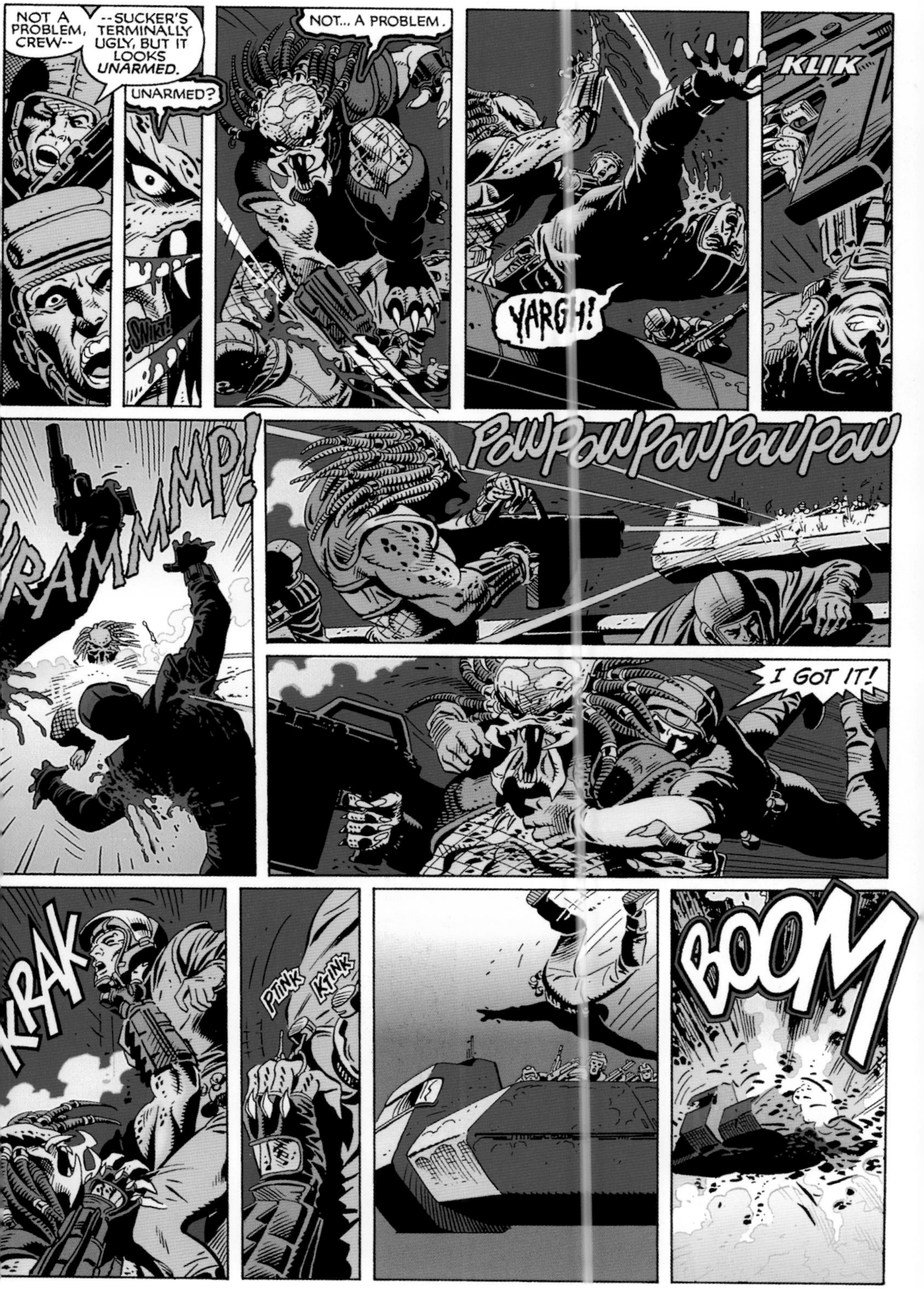

NOT A PROBLEM, CREW--
--SUCKER'S TERMINALLY UGLY, BUT IT LOOKS *UNARMED.*
UNARMED?
SNIKT!
NOT... A PROBLEM.
YARGH!
KLIK
RAMMMMP!
POWPOWPOWPOWPOW
I GOT IT!
KRAK
PTINK
KTINK
BOOM

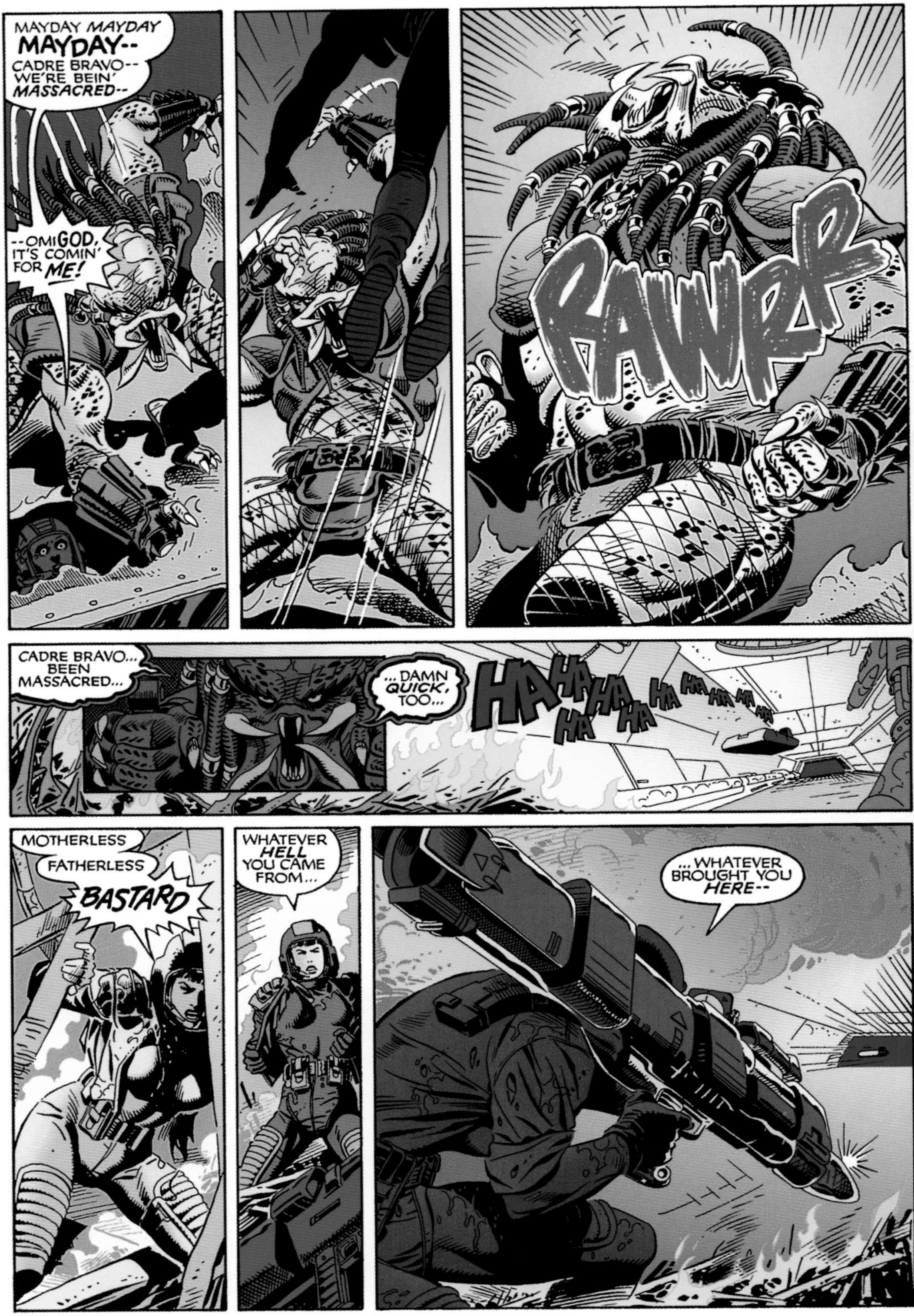
MAYDAY MAYDAY MAYDAY-- CADRE BRAVO-- WE'RE BEIN' MASSACRED--
--OMIGOD, IT'S COMIN' FOR ME!
RAWRR
CADRE BRAVO... BEEN MASSACRED...
...DAMN QUICK, TOO...
HA HA HA HA HA HA HA HA HA HA HA HA
MOTHERLESS
FATHERLESS
BASTARD
WHATEVER HELL YOU CAME FROM...
...WHATEVER BROUGHT YOU HERE--

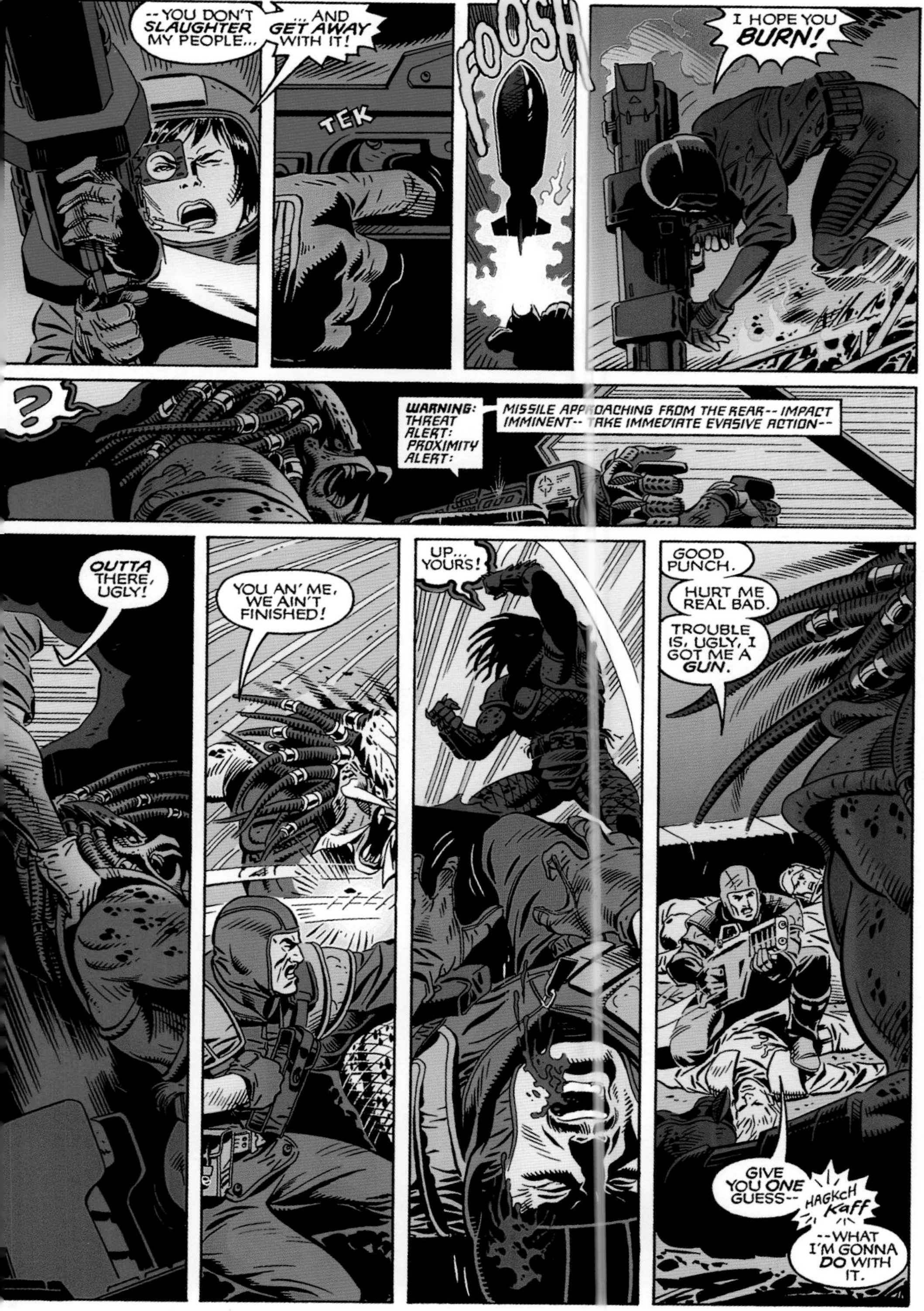
--YOU DON'T SLAUGHTER MY PEOPLE...
...AND GET AWAY WITH IT!
TEK
FOOSH
I HOPE YOU BURN!
?
WARNING: THREAT ALERT: PROXIMITY ALERT:
MISSILE APPROACHING FROM THE REAR--IMPACT IMMINENT--TAKE IMMEDIATE EVASIVE ACTION--
OUTTA THERE, UGLY!
YOU AN' ME, WE AIN'T FINISHED!
UP... YOURS!
GOOD PUNCH.
HURT ME REAL BAD.
TROUBLE IS, UGLY, I GOT ME A GUN.
GIVE YOU ONE GUESS--
HAGKCH KAFF
--WHAT I'M GONNA DO WITH IT.

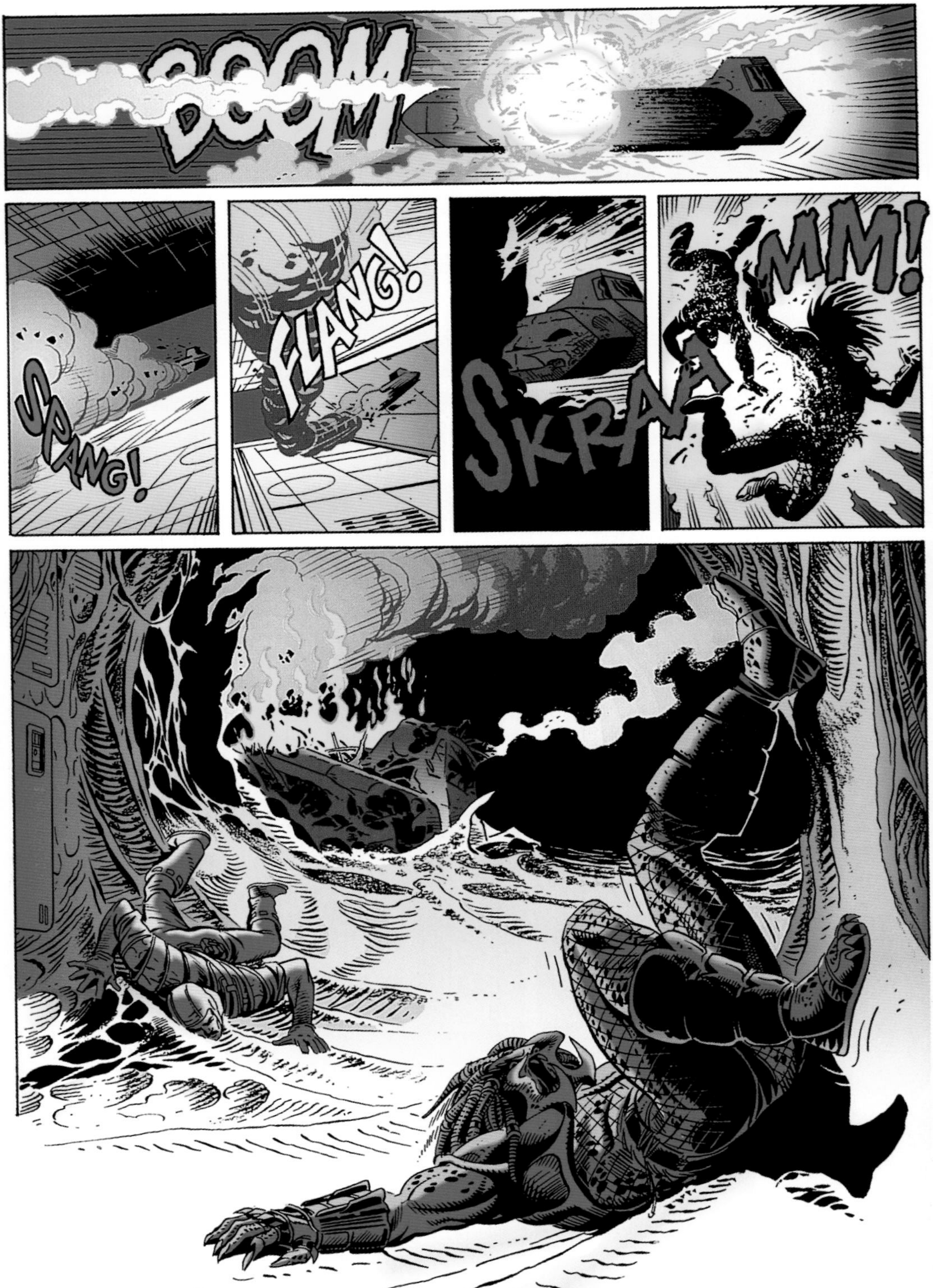
BOOM
SPANG!
FLANG!
SKRAAAMM!

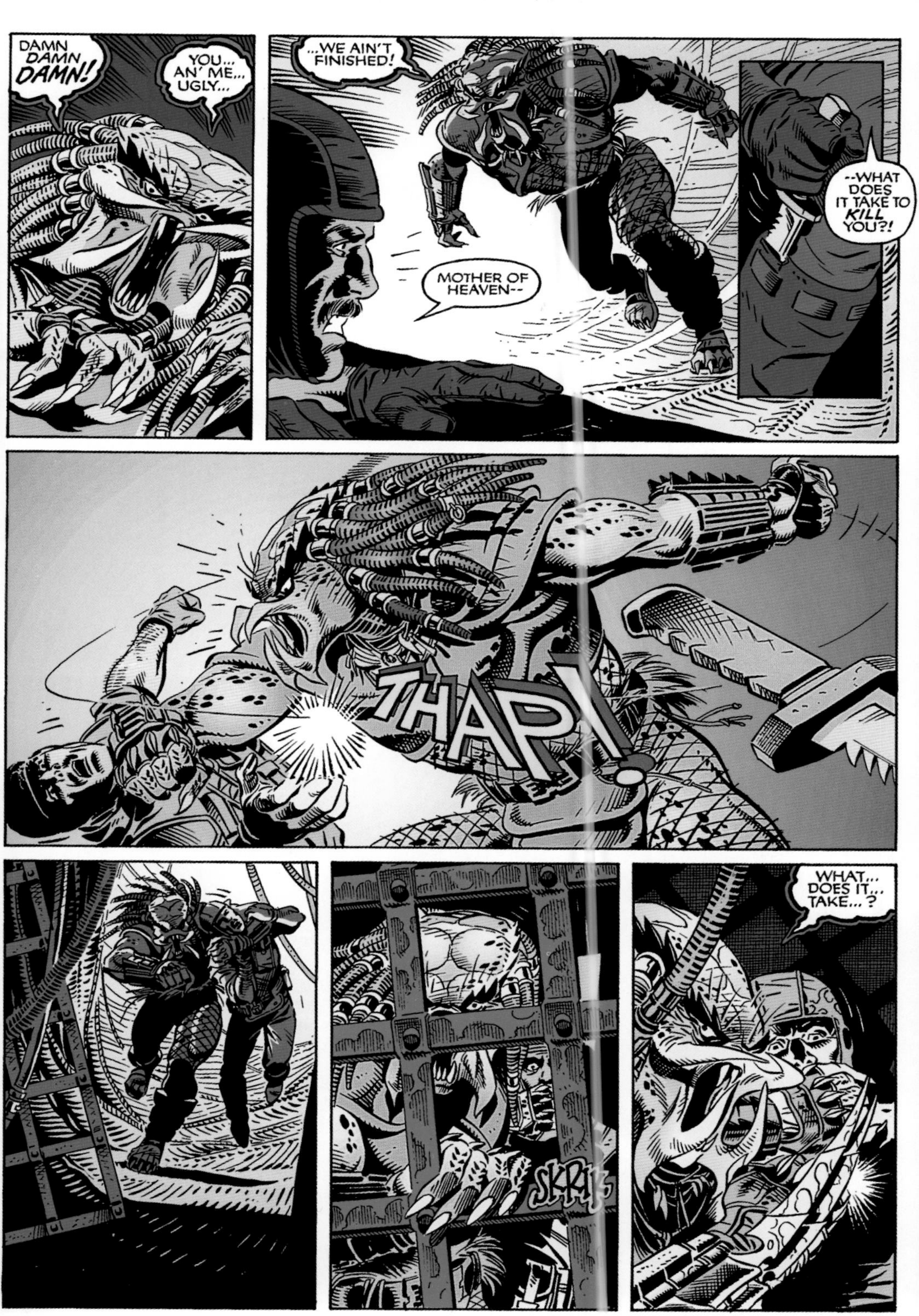
DAMN DAMN DAMN!
YOU... AN' ME... UGLY...
...WE AIN'T FINISHED!
MOTHER OF HEAVEN--
--WHAT DOES IT TAKE TO KILL YOU?!
THAP!
SKRK
WHAT... DOES IT... TAKE...?!

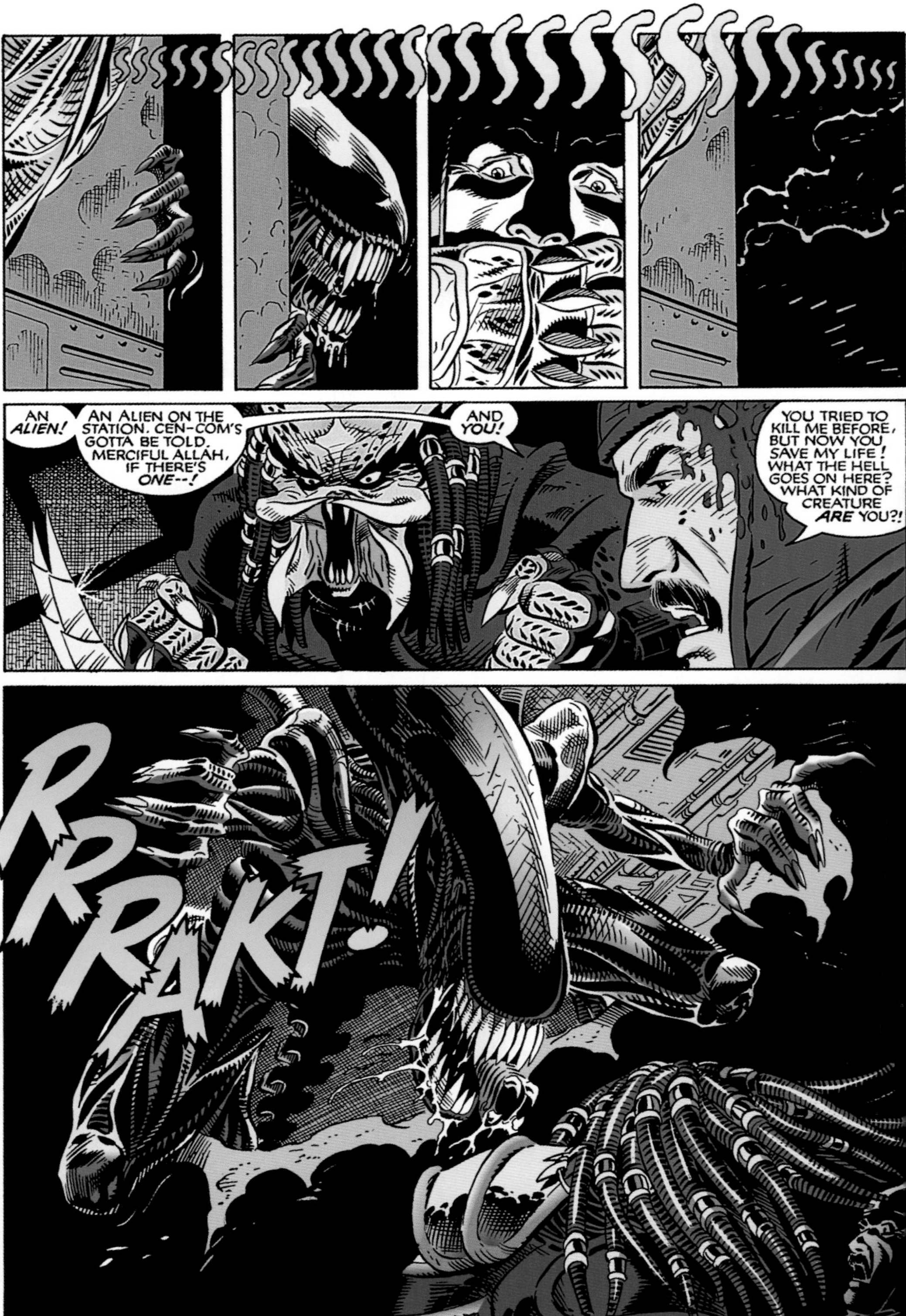
SSSSSSSSSSSSSSSSSSSSSSSSSSSSSSSSSSSS
AN ALIEN!
AN ALIEN ON THE STATION. CEN-COM'S GOTTA BE TOLD. MERCIFUL ALLAH, IF THERE'S ONE--!
AND YOU!
YOU TRIED TO KILL ME BEFORE, BUT NOW YOU SAVE MY LIFE! WHAT THE HELL GOES ON HERE? WHAT KIND OF CREATURE ARE YOU?!
RRRAKT!

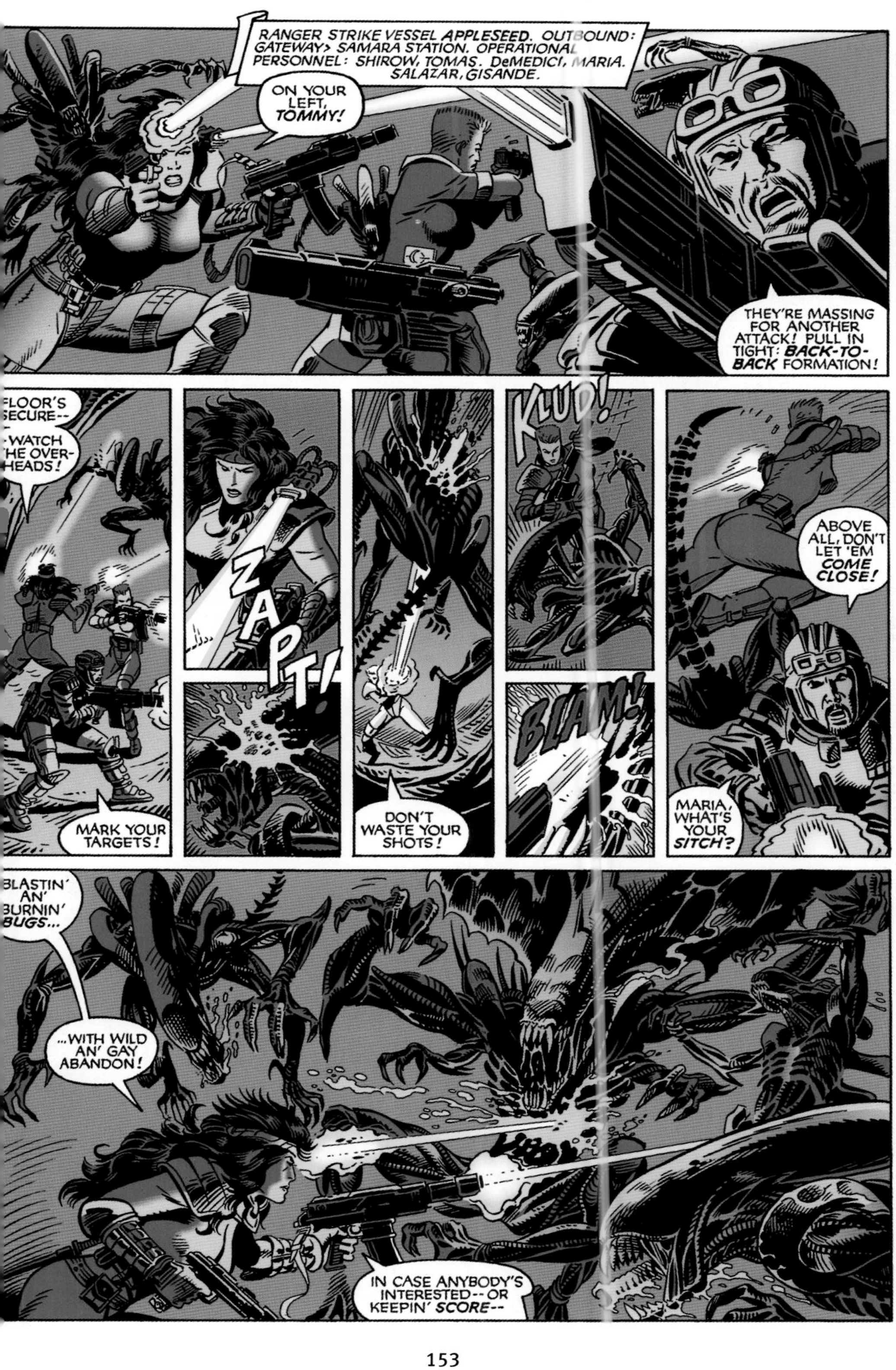
RANGER STRIKE VESSEL APPLESEED. OUTBOUND: GATEWAY> SAMARA STATION. OPERATIONAL PERSONNEL: SHIROW, TOMAS. DeMEDICI, MARIA. SALAZAR, GISANDE.
ON YOUR LEFT, TOMMY!
THEY'RE MASSING FOR ANOTHER ATTACK! PULL IN TIGHT: BACK-TO-BACK FORMATION!
FLOOR'S SECURE--
--WATCH THE OVERHEADS!
MARK YOUR TARGETS!
ZAPT!
DON'T WASTE YOUR SHOTS!
KLUD!
BLAM!
ABOVE ALL, DON'T LET 'EM COME CLOSE!
MARIA, WHAT'S YOUR SITCH?
BLASTIN' AN' BURNIN' BUGS...
...WITH WILD AN' GAY ABANDON!
IN CASE ANYBODY'S INTERESTED--OR KEEPIN' SCORE--

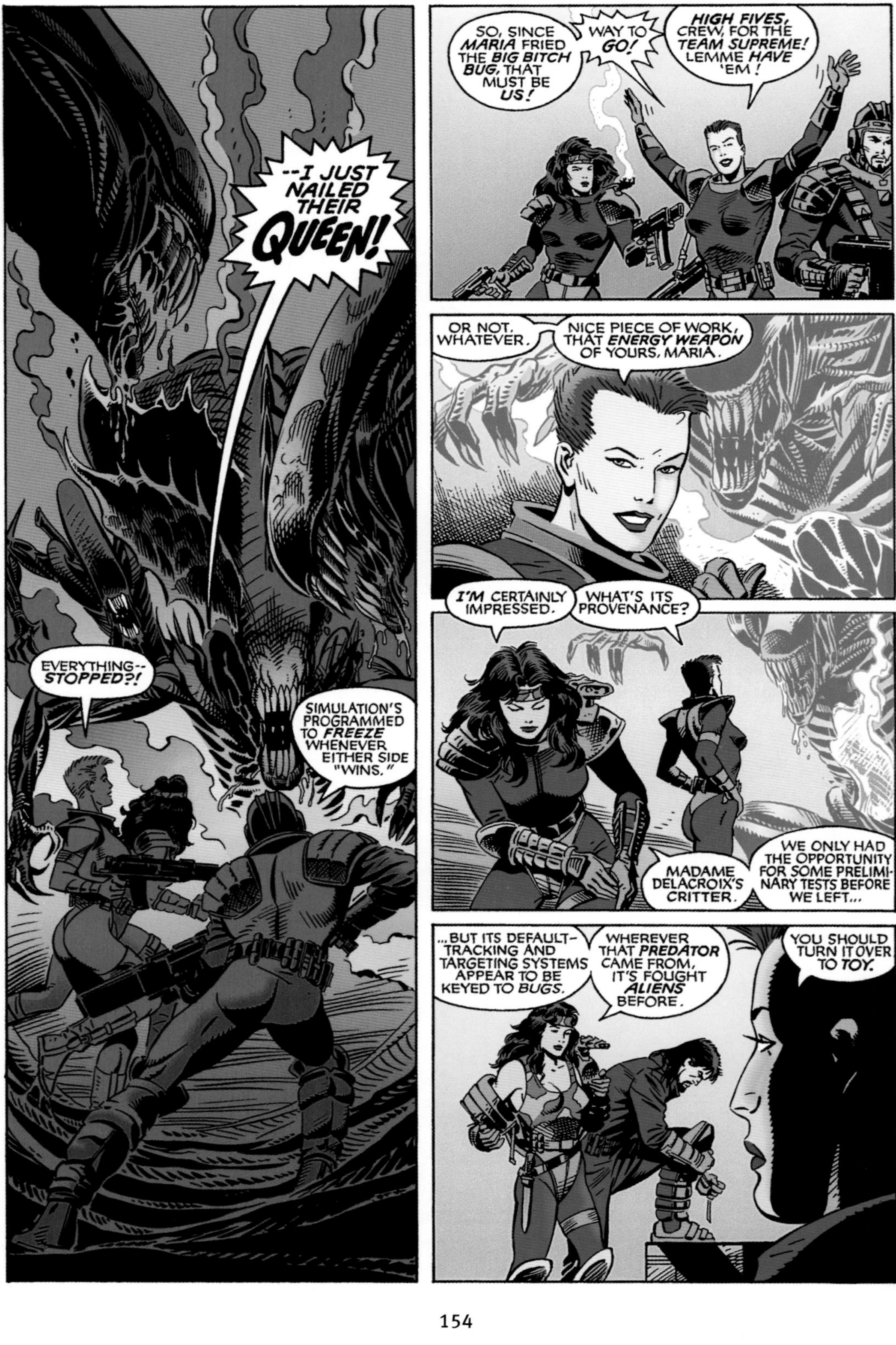
--I JUST NAILED THEIR QUEEN!
EVERYTHING--STOPPED?!
SIMULATION'S PROGRAMMED TO FREEZE WHENEVER EITHER SIDE "WINS."
SO, SINCE MARIA FRIED THE BIG BITCH BUG, THAT MUST BE US!
WAY TO GO!
HIGH FIVES, CREW, FOR THE TEAM SUPREME! LEMME HAVE 'EM!
OR NOT. WHATEVER.
NICE PIECE OF WORK, THAT ENERGY WEAPON OF YOURS, MARIA.
I'M CERTAINLY IMPRESSED.
WHAT'S ITS PROVENANCE?
MADAME DELACROIX'S CRITTER.
WE ONLY HAD THE OPPORTUNITY FOR SOME PRELIMINARY TESTS BEFORE WE LEFT...
...BUT ITS DEFAULT-TRACKING AND TARGETING SYSTEMS APPEAR TO BE KEYED TO BUGS.
WHEREVER THAT PREDATOR CAME FROM, IT'S FOUGHT ALIENS BEFORE.
YOU SHOULD TURN IT OVER TO TOY.

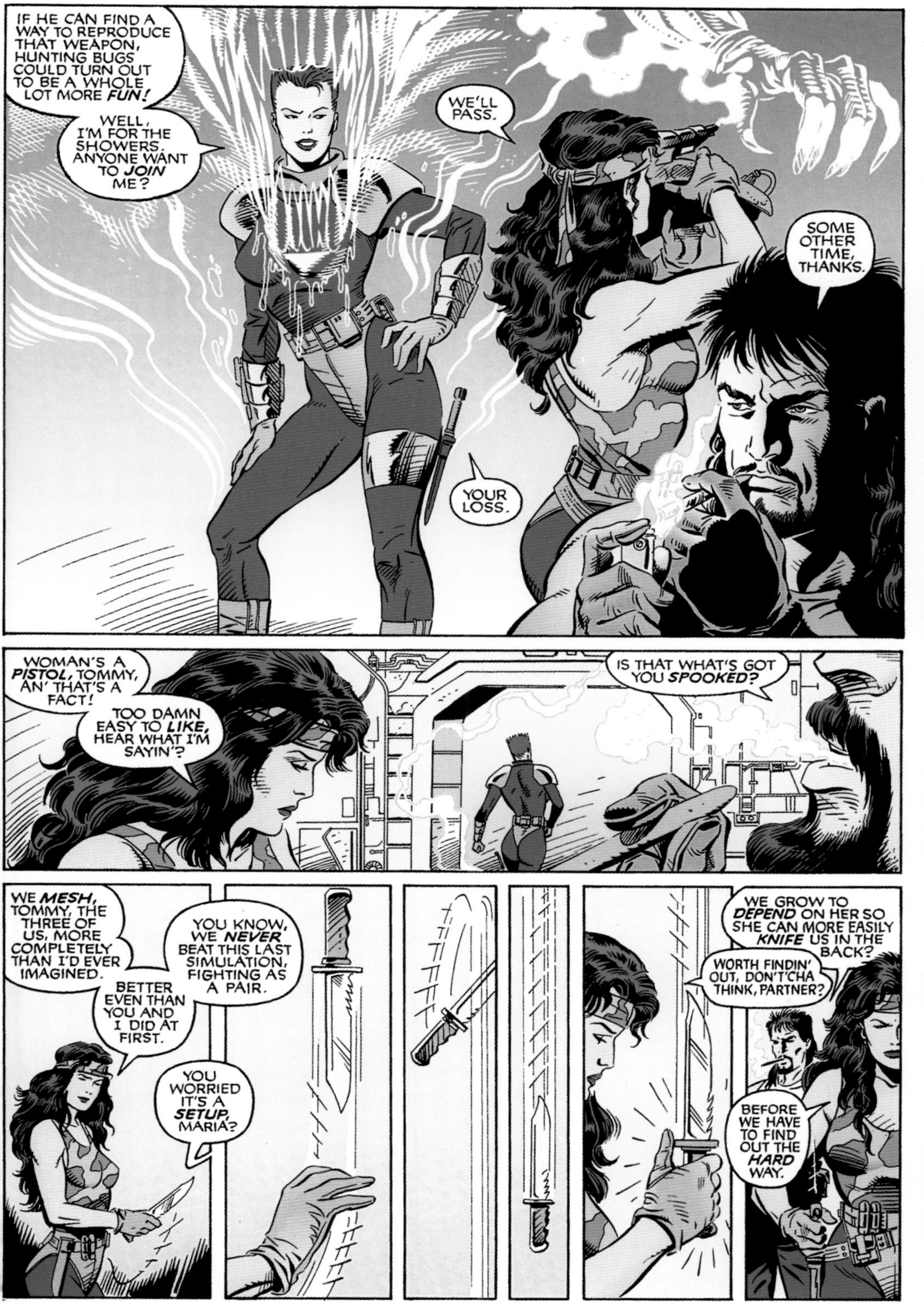
IF HE CAN FIND A WAY TO REPRODUCE THAT WEAPON, HUNTING BUGS COULD TURN OUT TO BE A WHOLE LOT MORE FUN!
WELL, I'M FOR THE SHOWERS. ANYONE WANT TO JOIN ME?
WE'LL PASS.
SOME OTHER TIME, THANKS.
YOUR LOSS.
WOMAN'S A PISTOL, TOMMY, AN' THAT'S A FACT!
TOO DAMN EASY TO LIKE, HEAR WHAT I'M SAYIN'?
IS THAT WHAT'S GOT YOU SPOOKED?
WE MESH, TOMMY, THE THREE OF US, MORE COMPLETELY THAN I'D EVER IMAGINED.
BETTER EVEN THAN YOU AND I DID AT FIRST.
YOU KNOW, WE NEVER BEAT THIS LAST SIMULATION, FIGHTING AS A PAIR.
YOU WORRIED IT'S A SETUP, MARIA?
WE GROW TO DEPEND ON HER SO SHE CAN MORE EASILY KNIFE US IN THE BACK?
WORTH FINDIN' OUT, DON'T'CHA THINK, PARTNER?
BEFORE WE HAVE TO FIND OUT THE HARD WAY.

DEEP SPACE STATION *SAMARA*...

WHAT'RE YOU *TELLING* ME, GENNA?!

THAT YOUR CADRE OF *SUPPOSEDLY* TRAINED, *SUPPOSEDLY* EXPERIENCED, *SUPPOSEDLY* COMPETENT TROOPERS...

...COULDN'T HANDLE A LONE, UNARMED EXOTIC? AND A *WOUNDED* ONE AT THAT?!

WHAT THE HELL HAVE I BEEN PAYING YOU FOR ALL THESE YEARS?

LOOK AT ME, NAGEL! YOU THINK THIS IS *MAKE-UP*?!

THIS CREATURE'S LIKE *NOTHING* I'VE EVER FOUGHT!

I'D RATE IT AS DANGEROUS AS A BUG.

I DON'T WANT TO HEAR IT!

WHAT COMES NEXT, SWEET-HEART-- YOU WANT ME TO BRING IN THE *COLONIAL MARINES*?!

ACTUALLY, *YES*!

WON'T *THAT* PLEASE OUR *CORPORATE EMPLOYERS!*

MAY I REMIND YOU, WOMAN, THAT THIS IS AN *ILLEGAL* OPERATION. YOU'RE HERE SO WE WON'T *NEED* OUTSIDE ASSISTANCE.

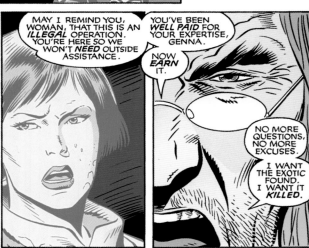

YOU'VE BEEN *WELL PAID* FOR YOUR EXPERTISE, GENNA.

NOW *EARN* IT.

NO MORE QUESTIONS, NO MORE EXCUSES.

I WANT THE EXOTIC FOUND. I WANT IT *KILLED*.

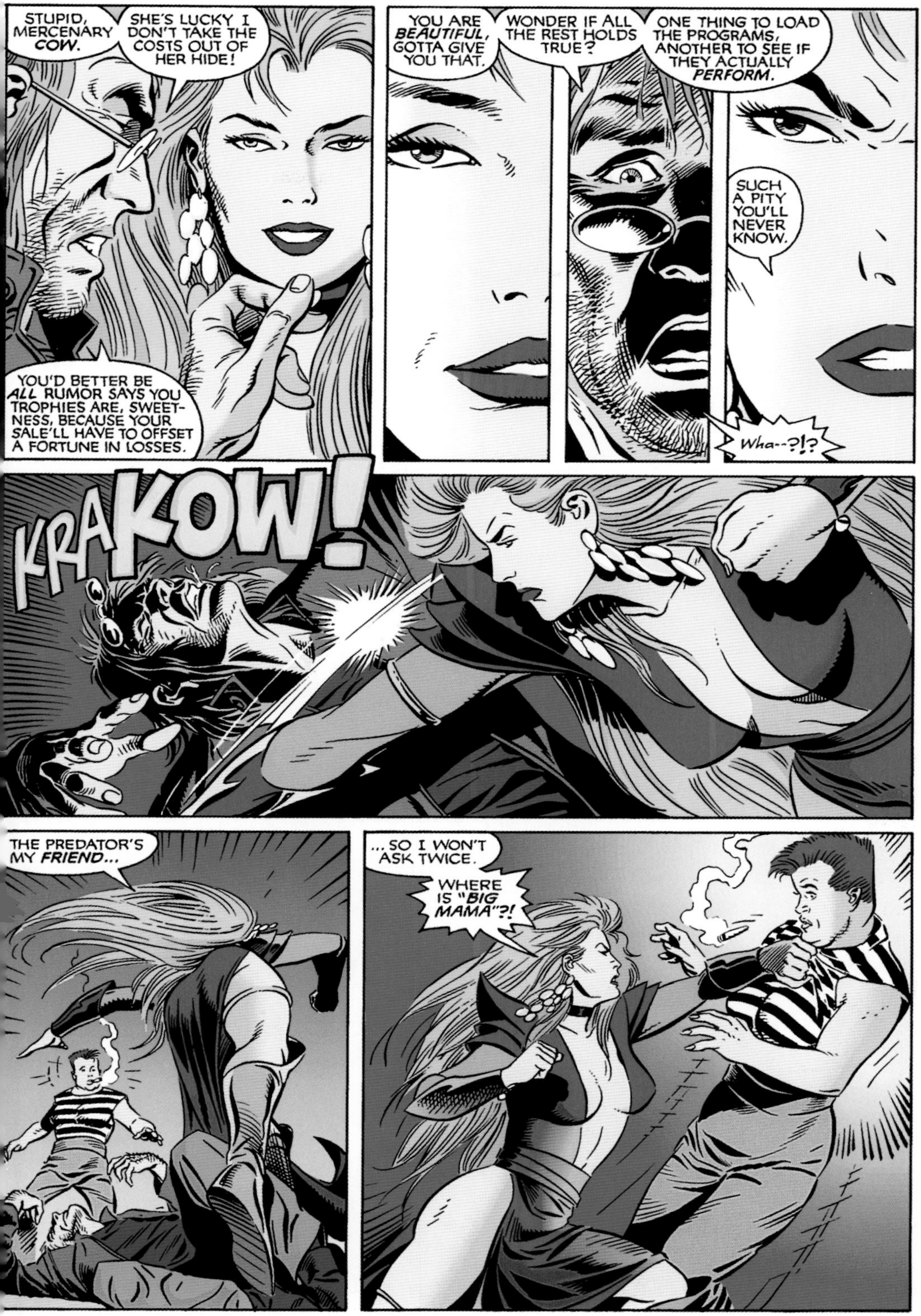
STUPID, MERCENARY *COW*.
SHE'S LUCKY I DON'T TAKE THE COSTS OUT OF HER HIDE!
YOU'D BETTER BE *ALL* RUMOR SAYS YOU TROPHIES ARE, SWEETNESS, BECAUSE YOUR SALE'LL HAVE TO OFFSET A FORTUNE IN LOSSES.
YOU ARE *BEAUTIFUL*, GOTTA GIVE YOU THAT.
WONDER IF ALL THE REST HOLDS TRUE?
ONE THING TO LOAD THE PROGRAMS, ANOTHER TO SEE IF THEY ACTUALLY *PERFORM*.
SUCH A PITY YOU'LL NEVER KNOW.
Wha--?!?
KRAKOW!
THE PREDATOR'S MY *FRIEND*...
...SO I WON'T ASK TWICE.
WHERE IS "*BIG MAMA*"?!

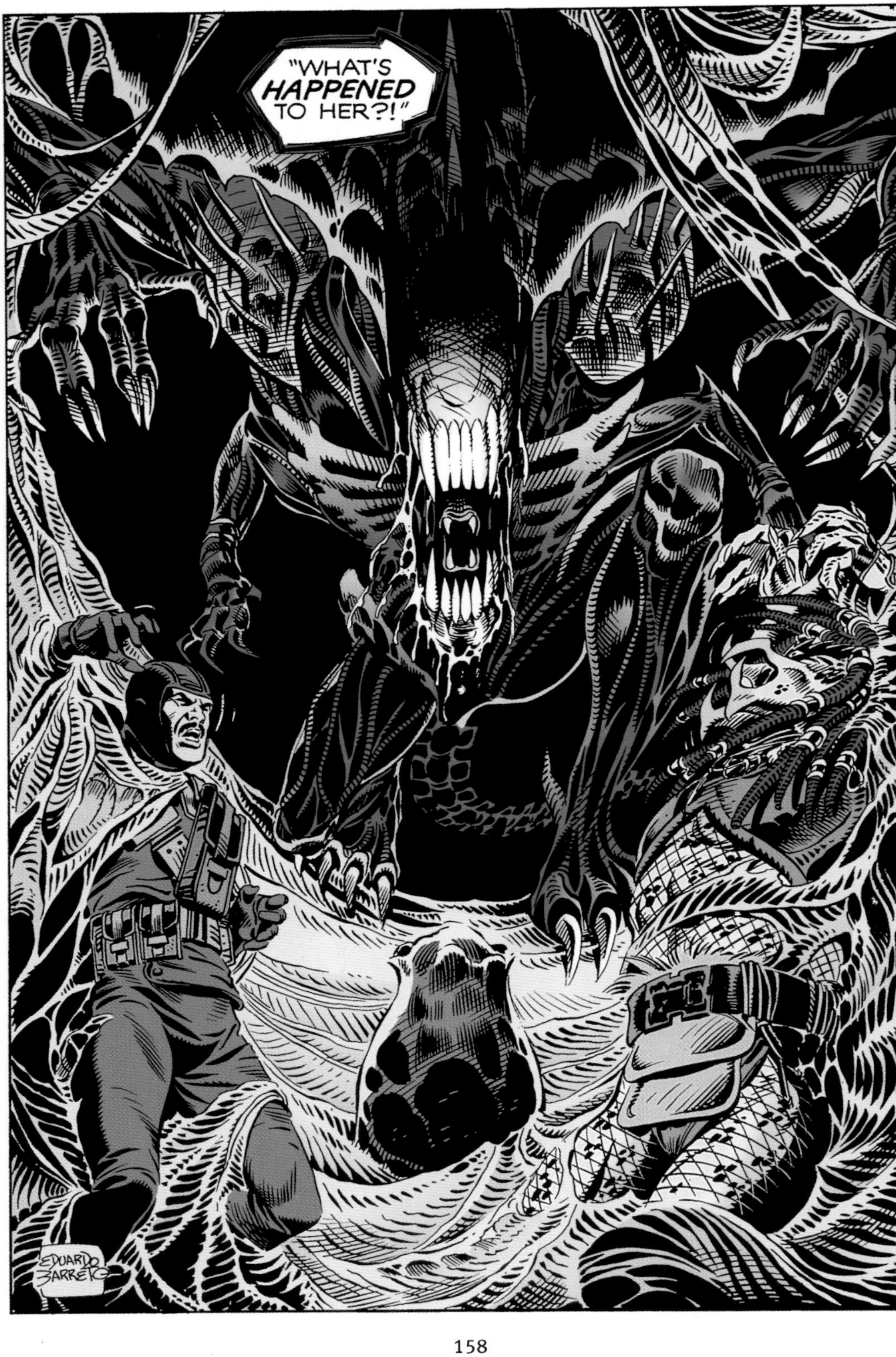
"WHAT'S HAPPENED TO HER?!"
EDUARDO BARRETO

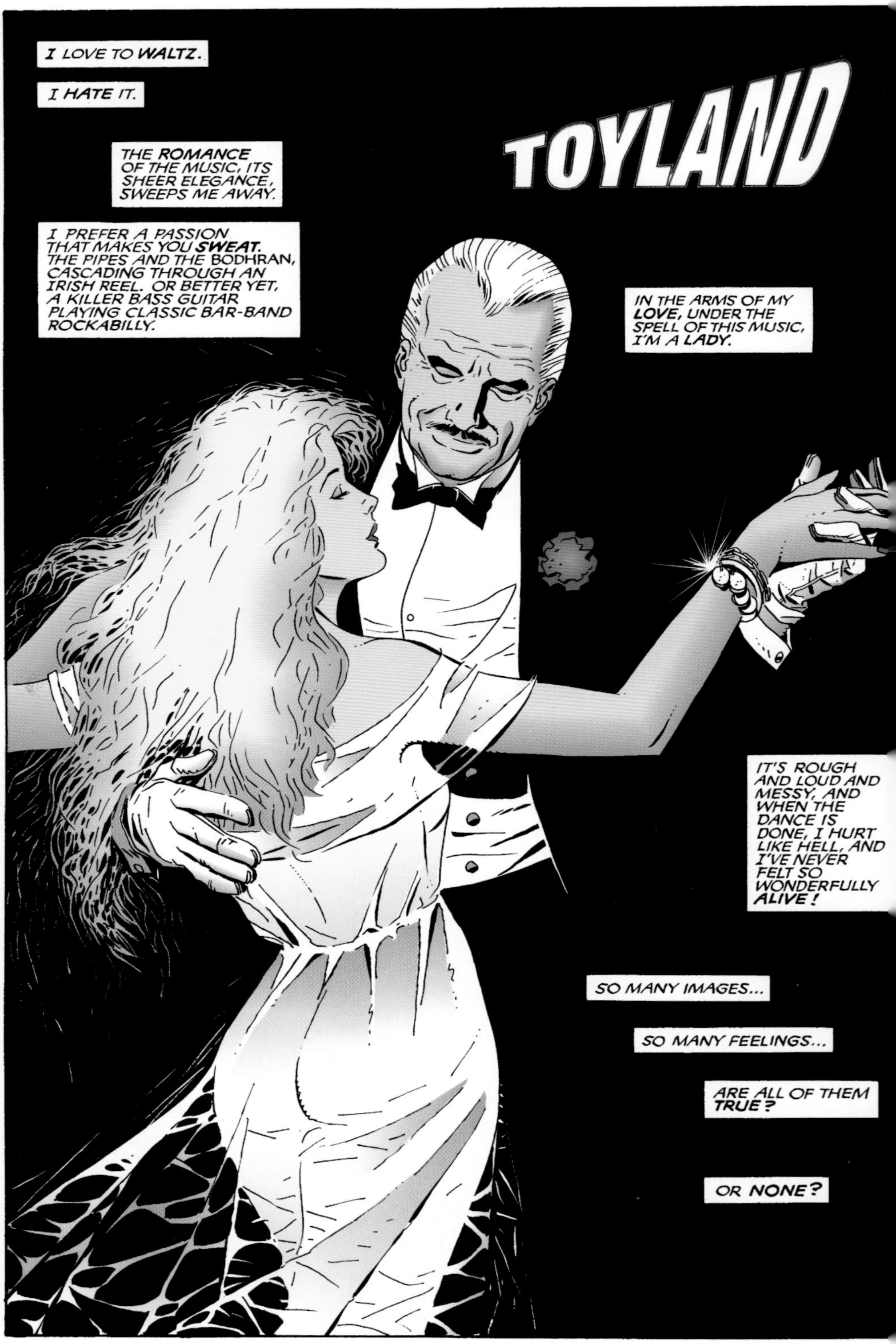
I LOVE TO WALTZ.
I HATE IT.
TOYLAND
THE ROMANCE OF THE MUSIC, ITS SHEER ELEGANCE, SWEEPS ME AWAY.
I PREFER A PASSION THAT MAKES YOU SWEAT. THE PIPES AND THE BODHRAN, CASCADING THROUGH AN IRISH REEL. OR BETTER YET, A KILLER BASS GUITAR PLAYING CLASSIC BAR-BAND ROCKABILLY.
IN THE ARMS OF MY LOVE, UNDER THE SPELL OF THIS MUSIC, I'M A LADY.
IT'S ROUGH AND LOUD AND MESSY, AND WHEN THE DANCE IS DONE, I HURT LIKE HELL, AND I'VE NEVER FELT SO WONDERFULLY ALIVE!
SO MANY IMAGES...
SO MANY FEELINGS...
ARE ALL OF THEM TRUE?
OR NONE?

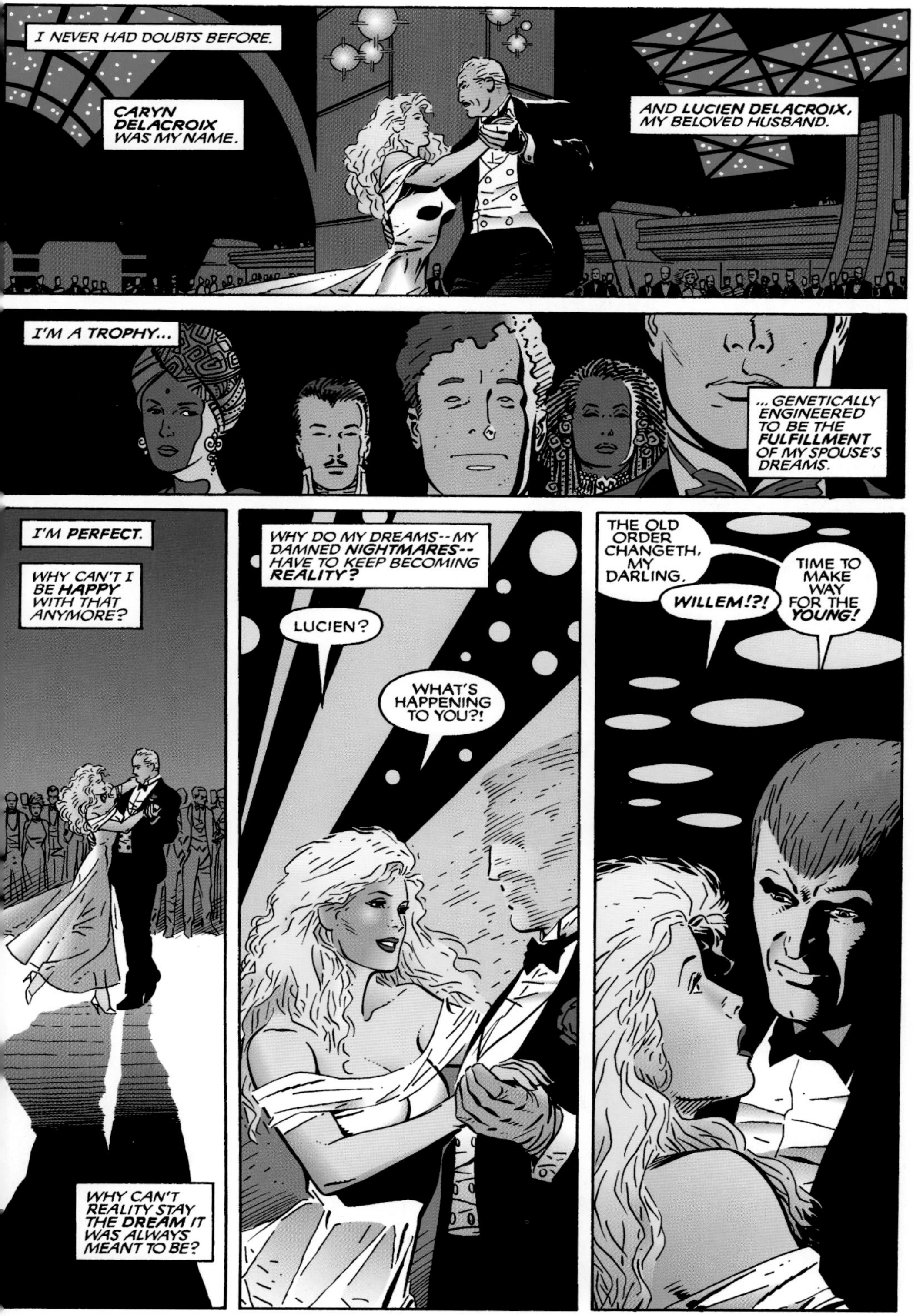
I NEVER HAD DOUBTS BEFORE.
CARYN DELACROIX WAS MY NAME.
AND LUCIEN DELACROIX, MY BELOVED HUSBAND.
I'M A TROPHY...
...GENETICALLY ENGINEERED TO BE THE FULFILLMENT OF MY SPOUSE'S DREAMS.
I'M PERFECT.
WHY CAN'T I BE HAPPY WITH THAT ANYMORE?
WHY CAN'T REALITY STAY THE DREAM IT WAS ALWAYS MEANT TO BE?
WHY DO MY DREAMS--MY DAMNED NIGHTMARES--HAVE TO KEEP BECOMING REALITY?
LUCIEN?
WHAT'S HAPPENING TO YOU?!
THE OLD ORDER CHANGETH, MY DARLING.
WILLEM!?!
TIME TO MAKE WAY FOR THE YOUNG!

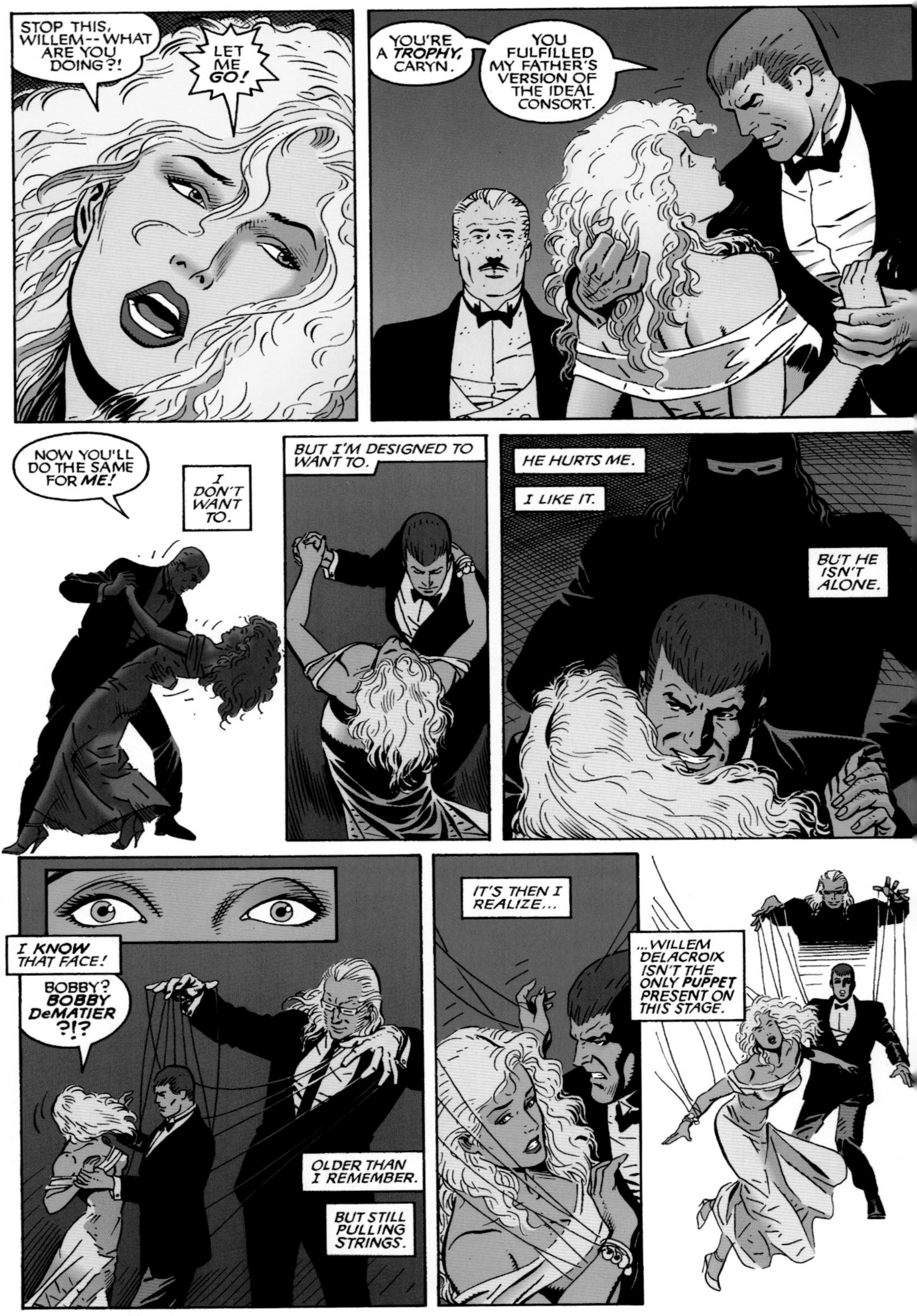

STOP THIS, WILLEM--WHAT ARE YOU DOING?!
LET ME GO!
YOU'RE A TROPHY, CARYN.
YOU FULFILLED MY FATHER'S VERSION OF THE IDEAL CONSORT.
NOW YOU'LL DO THE SAME FOR ME!
I DON'T WANT TO.
BUT I'M DESIGNED TO WANT TO.
HE HURTS ME.
I LIKE IT.
BUT HE ISN'T ALONE.
I KNOW THAT FACE!
BOBBY? BOBBY DeMATIER ?!?
OLDER THAN I REMEMBER.
BUT STILL PULLING STRINGS.
IT'S THEN I REALIZE...
...WILLEM DELACROIX ISN'T THE ONLY PUPPET PRESENT ON THIS STAGE.

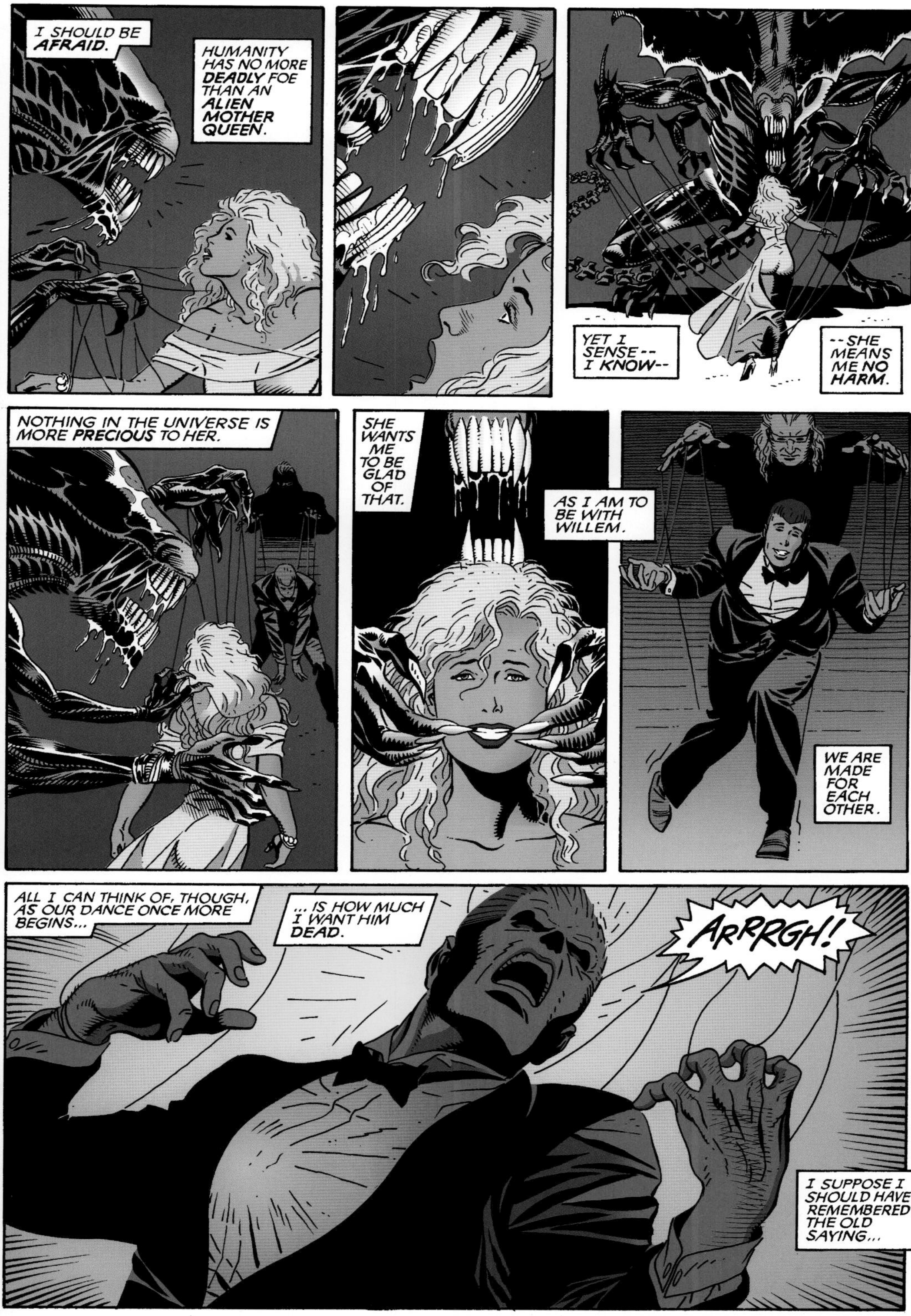
I SHOULD BE AFRAID.
HUMANITY HAS NO MORE DEADLY FOE THAN AN ALIEN MOTHER QUEEN.
YET I SENSE-- I KNOW--
--SHE MEANS ME NO HARM.
NOTHING IN THE UNIVERSE IS MORE PRECIOUS TO HER.
SHE WANTS ME TO BE GLAD OF THAT.
AS I AM TO BE WITH WILLEM.
WE ARE MADE FOR EACH OTHER.
ALL I CAN THINK OF, THOUGH, AS OUR DANCE ONCE MORE BEGINS...
... IS HOW MUCH I WANT HIM DEAD.
ARRRGH!
I SUPPOSE I SHOULD HAVE REMEMBERED THE OLD SAYING...

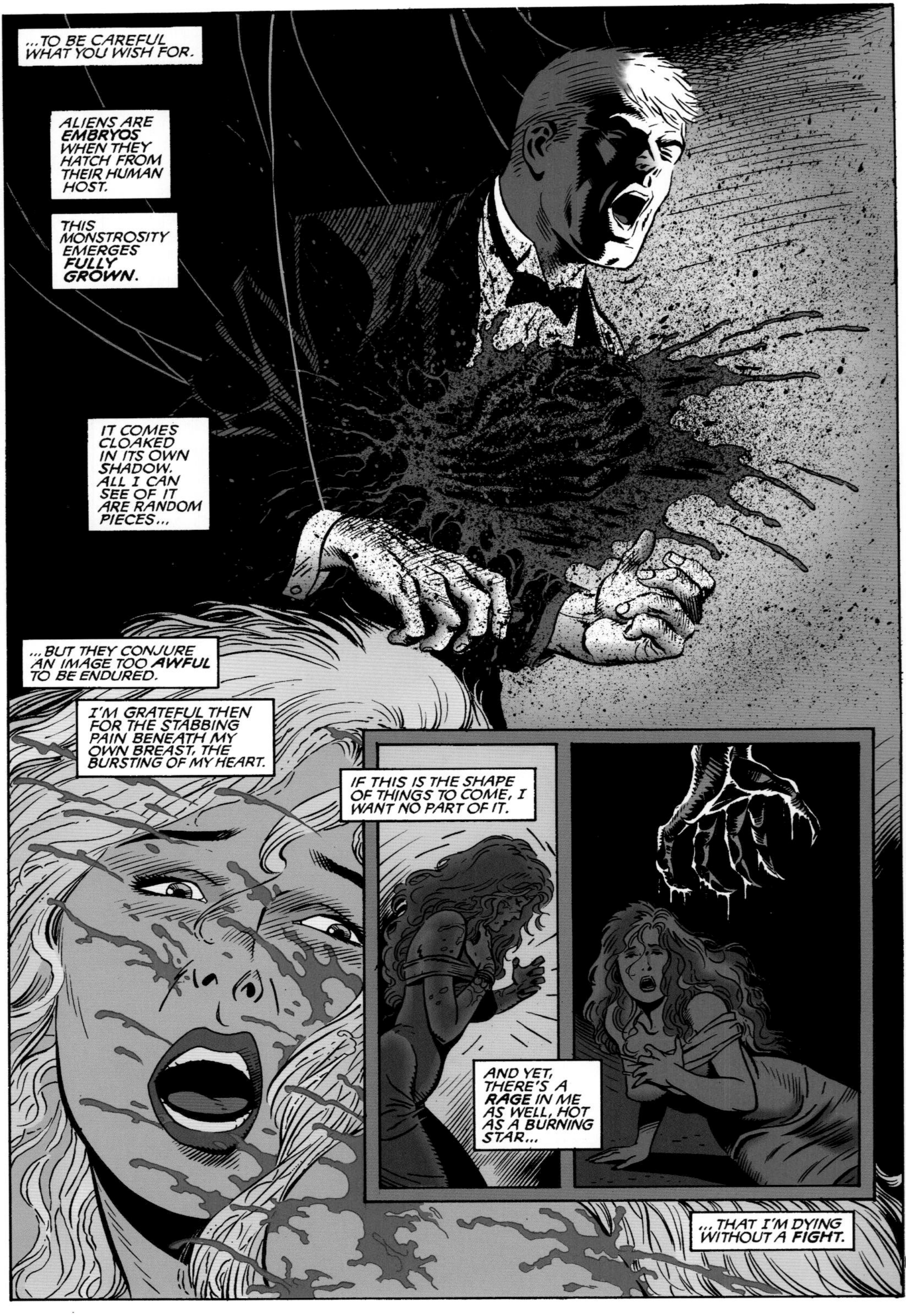
...TO BE CAREFUL WHAT YOU WISH FOR.
ALIENS ARE EMBRYOS WHEN THEY HATCH FROM THEIR HUMAN HOST.
THIS MONSTROSITY EMERGES FULLY GROWN.
IT COMES CLOAKED IN ITS OWN SHADOW. ALL I CAN SEE OF IT ARE RANDOM PIECES...
...BUT THEY CONJURE AN IMAGE TOO AWFUL TO BE ENDURED.
I'M GRATEFUL THEN FOR THE STABBING PAIN BENEATH MY OWN BREAST, THE BURSTING OF MY HEART.
IF THIS IS THE SHAPE OF THINGS TO COME, I WANT NO PART OF IT.
AND YET, THERE'S A RAGE IN ME AS WELL, HOT AS A BURNING STAR...
...THAT I'M DYING WITHOUT A FIGHT.

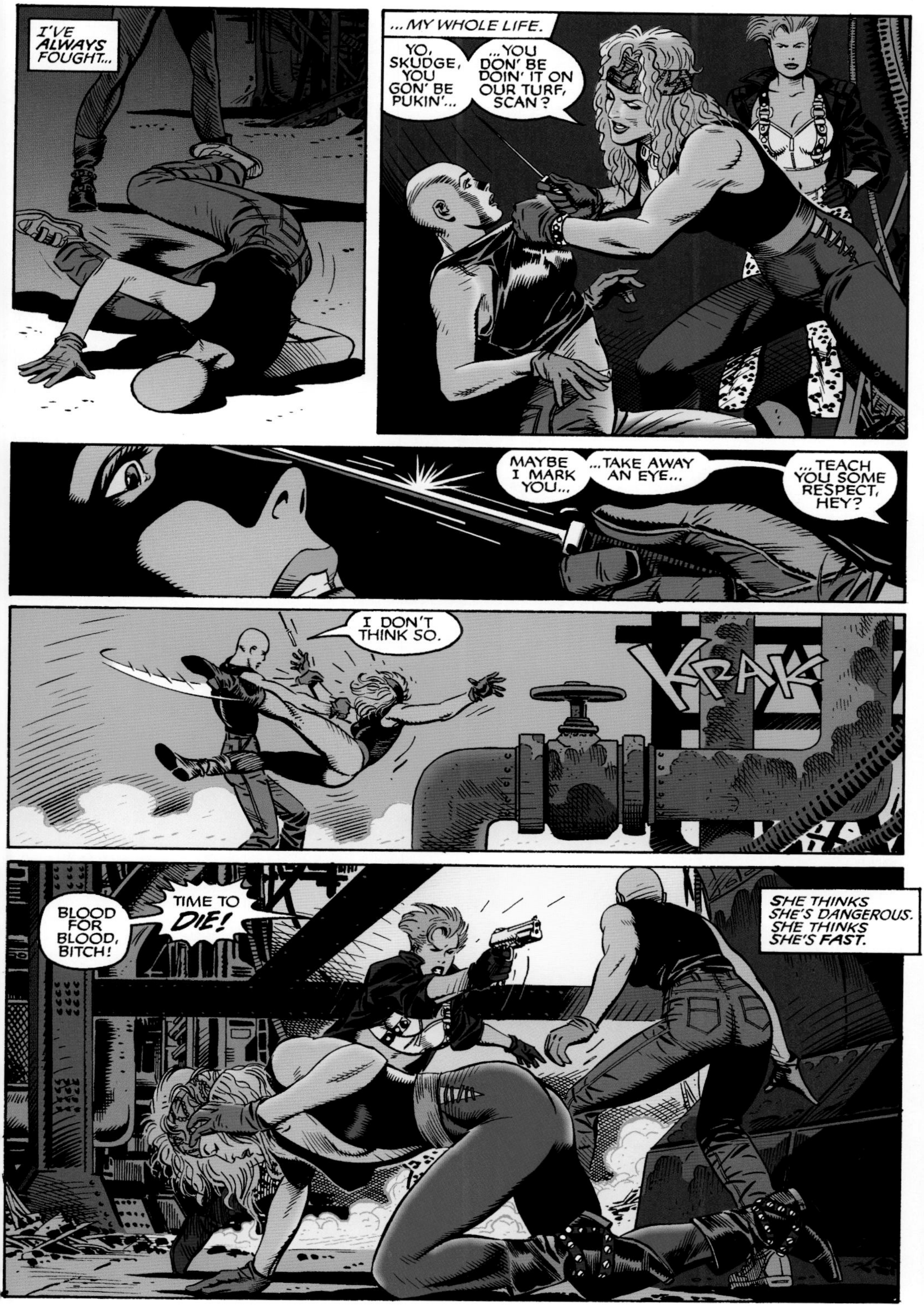
I'VE ALWAYS FOUGHT...
... MY WHOLE LIFE.
YO, SKUDGE, YOU GON' BE PUKIN'...
...YOU DON' BE DOIN' IT ON OUR TURF, SCAN?
MAYBE I MARK YOU...
...TAKE AWAY AN EYE...
...TEACH YOU SOME RESPECT, HEY?
I DON'T THINK SO.
KRAK
BLOOD FOR BLOOD, BITCH!
TIME TO DIE!
SHE THINKS SHE'S DANGEROUS. SHE THINKS SHE'S FAST.

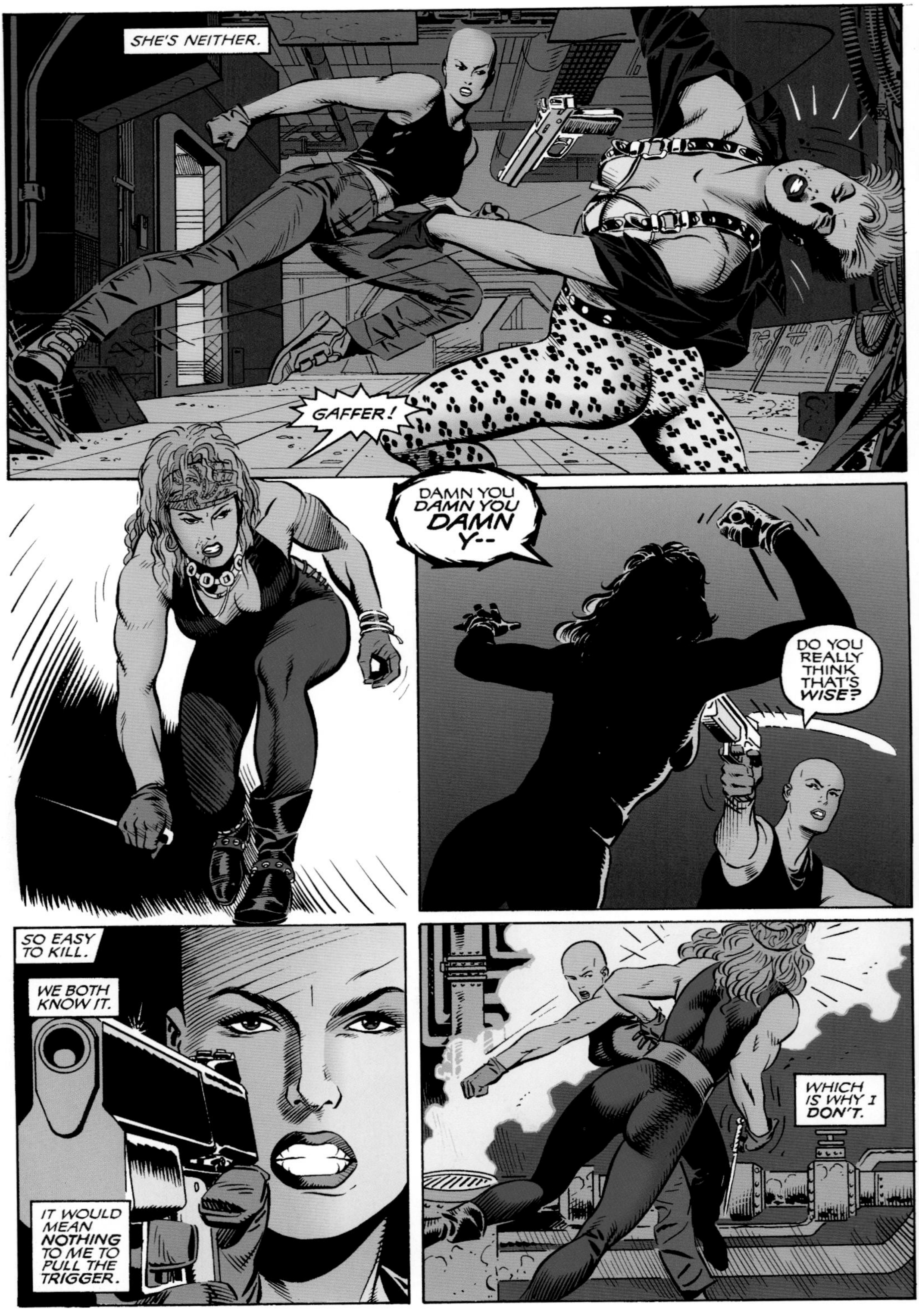

SHE'S NEITHER.
GAFFER!
DAMN YOU DAMN YOU DAMN Y--
DO YOU REALLY THINK THAT'S WISE?
SO EASY TO KILL.
WE BOTH KNOW IT.
IT WOULD MEAN NOTHING TO ME TO PULL THE TRIGGER.
WHICH IS WHY I DON'T.

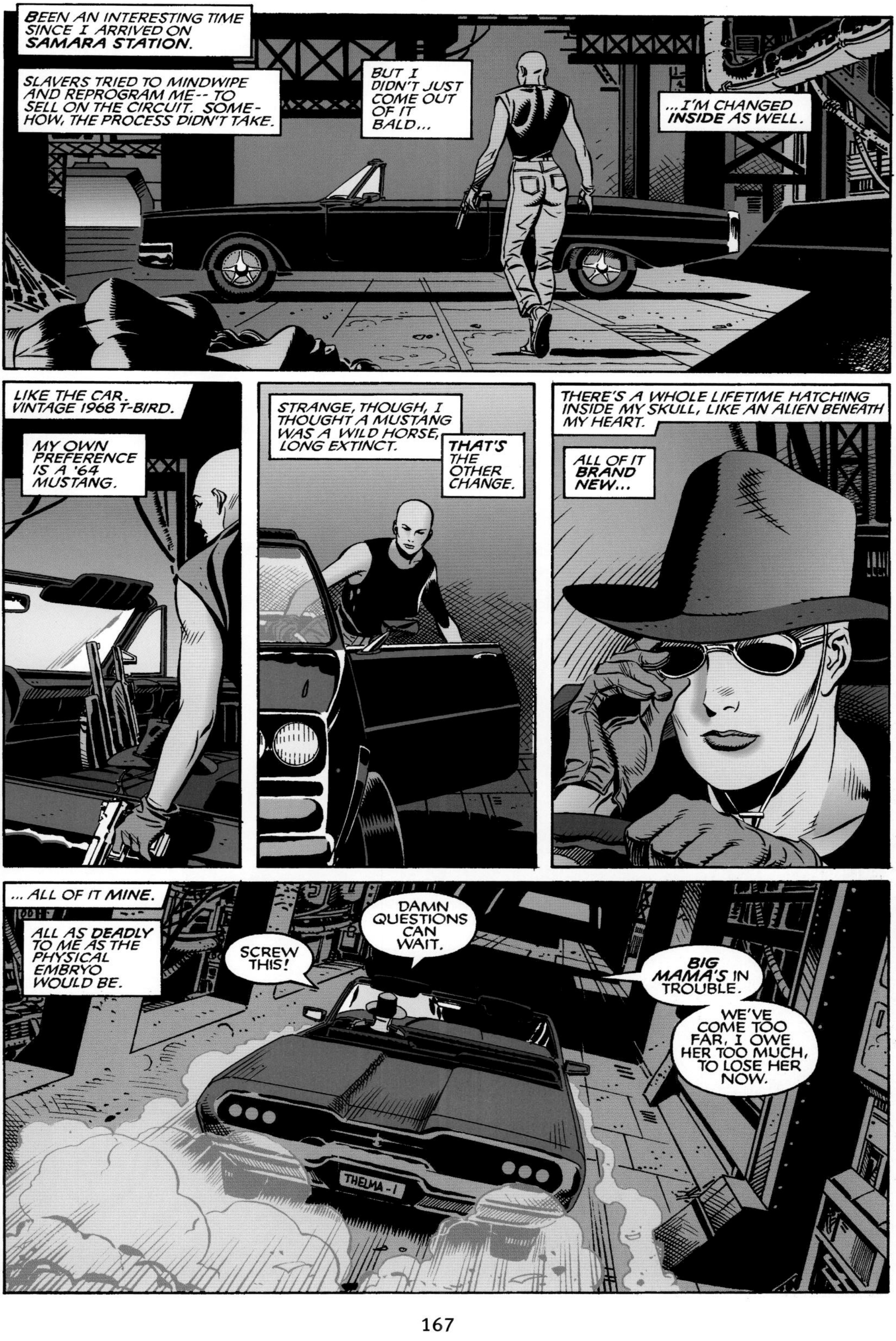
BEEN AN INTERESTING TIME SINCE I ARRIVED ON SAMARA STATION.
SLAVERS TRIED TO MINDWIPE AND REPROGRAM ME-- TO SELL ON THE CIRCUIT. SOME-HOW, THE PROCESS DIDN'T TAKE.
BUT I DIDN'T JUST COME OUT OF IT BALD...
...I'M CHANGED INSIDE AS WELL.
LIKE THE CAR. VINTAGE 1968 T-BIRD.
MY OWN PREFERENCE IS A '64 MUSTANG.
STRANGE, THOUGH, I THOUGHT A MUSTANG WAS A WILD HORSE, LONG EXTINCT.
THAT'S THE OTHER CHANGE.
THERE'S A WHOLE LIFETIME HATCHING INSIDE MY SKULL, LIKE AN ALIEN BENEATH MY HEART.
ALL OF IT BRAND NEW...
...ALL OF IT MINE.
ALL AS DEADLY TO ME AS THE PHYSICAL EMBRYO WOULD BE.
SCREW THIS!
DAMN QUESTIONS CAN WAIT.
BIG MAMA'S IN TROUBLE.
WE'VE COME TOO FAR, I OWE HER TOO MUCH, TO LOSE HER NOW.
THELMA-1

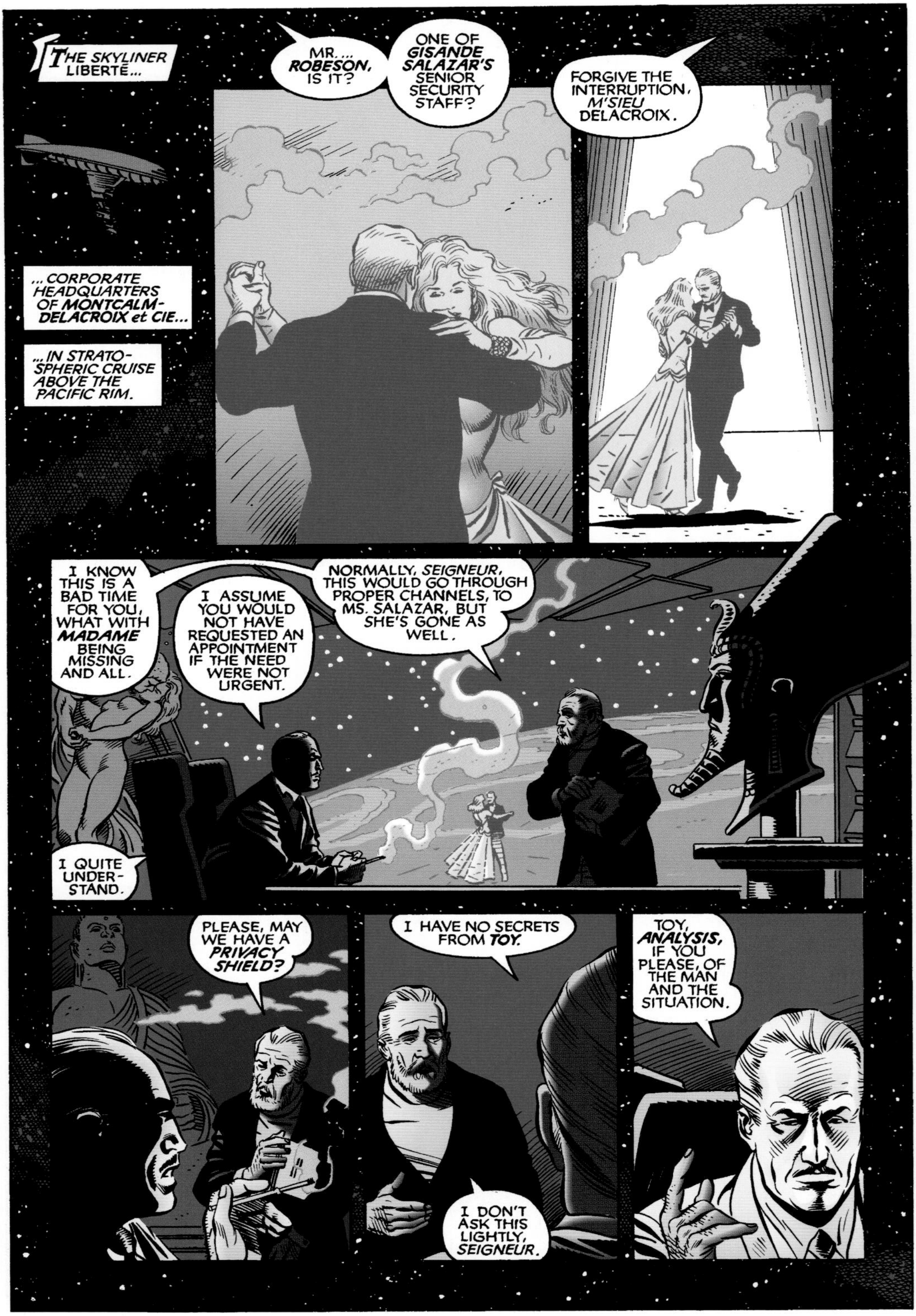
THE SKYLINER LIBERTÉ...
MR.... ROBESON, IS IT?
ONE OF GISANDE SALAZAR'S SENIOR SECURITY STAFF?
FORGIVE THE INTERRUPTION, M'SIEU DELACROIX.
...CORPORATE HEADQUARTERS OF MONTCALM-DELACROIX et CIE...
...IN STRATOSPHERIC CRUISE ABOVE THE PACIFIC RIM.
I KNOW THIS IS A BAD TIME FOR YOU, WHAT WITH MADAME BEING MISSING AND ALL.
I QUITE UNDERSTAND.
I ASSUME YOU WOULD NOT HAVE REQUESTED AN APPOINTMENT IF THE NEED WERE NOT URGENT.
NORMALLY, SEIGNEUR, THIS WOULD GO THROUGH PROPER CHANNELS, TO MS. SALAZAR, BUT SHE'S GONE AS WELL.
PLEASE, MAY WE HAVE A PRIVACY SHIELD?
I HAVE NO SECRETS FROM TOY.
I DON'T ASK THIS LIGHTLY, SEIGNEUR.
TOY, ANALYSIS, IF YOU PLEASE, OF THE MAN AND THE SITUATION.

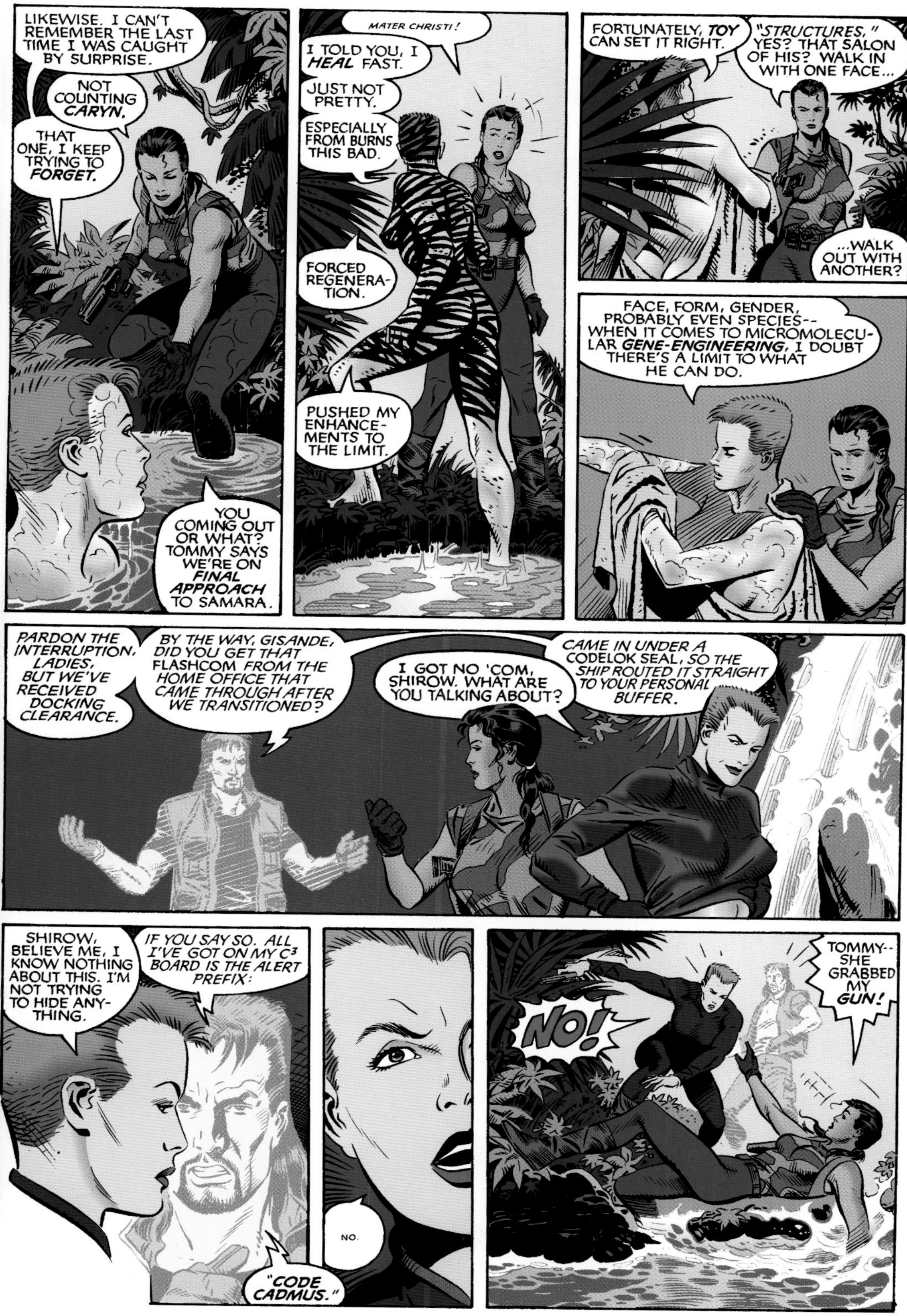
LIKEWISE. I CAN'T REMEMBER THE LAST TIME I WAS CAUGHT BY SURPRISE.
NOT COUNTING *CARYN.*
THAT ONE, I KEEP TRYING TO *FORGET.*
YOU COMING OUT OR WHAT? TOMMY SAYS WE'RE ON *FINAL APPROACH* TO SAMARA.
MATER CHRISTI!
I TOLD YOU, I *HEAL* FAST.
JUST NOT PRETTY.
ESPECIALLY FROM BURNS THIS BAD.
FORCED REGENERA-TION.
PUSHED MY ENHANCE-MENTS TO THE LIMIT.
FORTUNATELY, *TOY* CAN SET IT RIGHT.
"*STRUCTURES,*" YES? THAT SALON OF HIS? WALK IN WITH ONE FACE...
...WALK OUT WITH ANOTHER?
FACE, FORM, GENDER, PROBABLY EVEN SPECIES-- WHEN IT COMES TO MICROMOLECU-LAR *GENE-ENGINEERING,* I DOUBT THERE'S A LIMIT TO WHAT HE CAN DO.
PARDON THE INTERRUPTION, LADIES, BUT WE'VE RECEIVED DOCKING CLEARANCE.
BY THE WAY, GISANDE, DID YOU GET THAT FLASHCOM FROM THE HOME OFFICE THAT CAME THROUGH AFTER WE TRANSITIONED?
I GOT NO 'COM, SHIROW. WHAT ARE YOU TALKING ABOUT?
CAME IN UNDER A CODELOK SEAL, SO THE SHIP ROUTED IT STRAIGHT TO YOUR PERSONAL BUFFER.
SHIROW, BELIEVE ME, I KNOW NOTHING ABOUT THIS. I'M NOT TRYING TO HIDE ANY-THING.
IF YOU SAY SO. ALL I'VE GOT ON MY C³ BOARD IS THE ALERT PREFIX:
"CODE CADMUS."
NO.
TOMMY-- SHE GRABBED MY *GUN!*
NO!

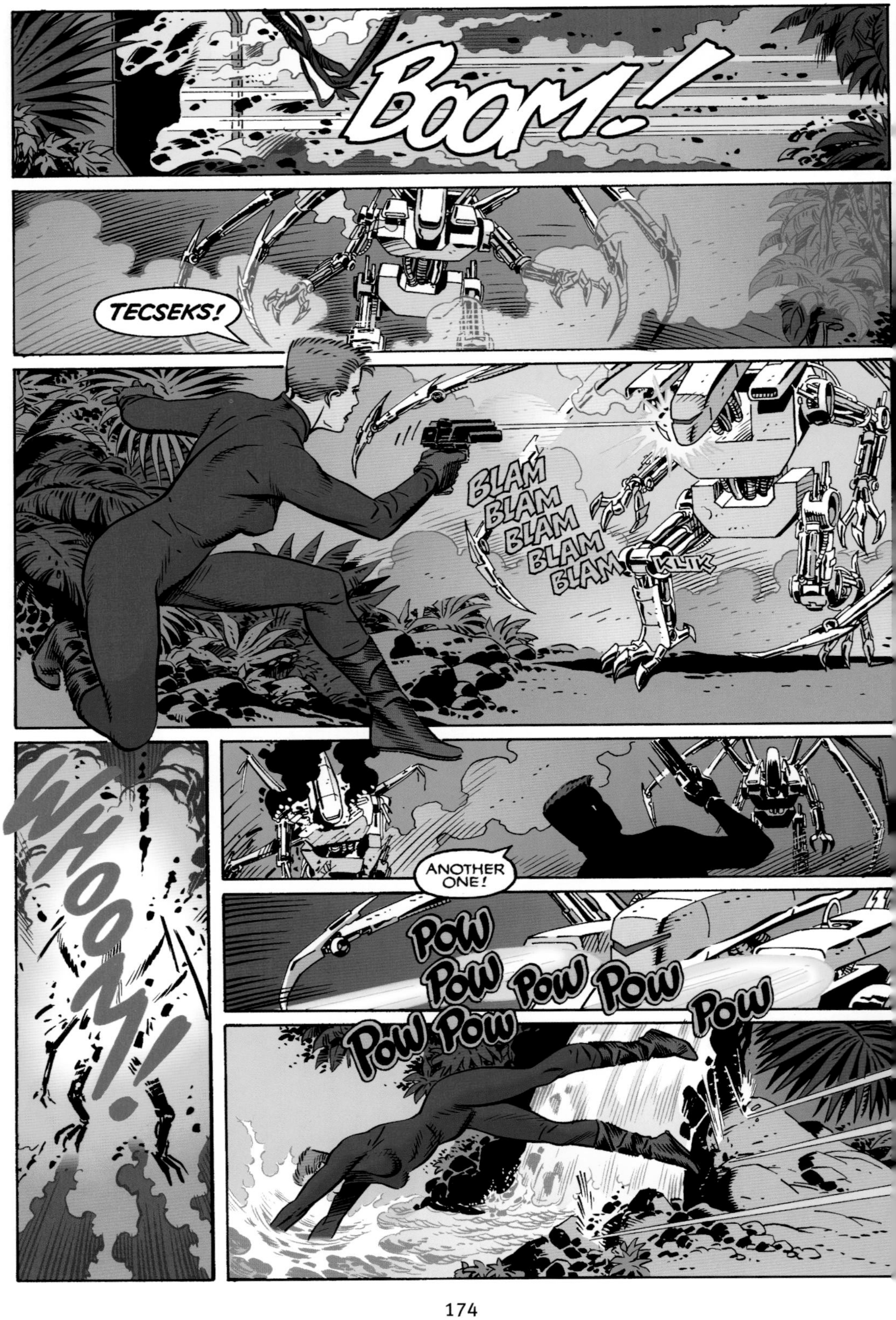
BOOM!
TECSEKS!
BLAM BLAM BLAM BLAM BLAM
KLIK
WHOOM!
ANOTHER ONE!
POW POW POW POW POW POW POW

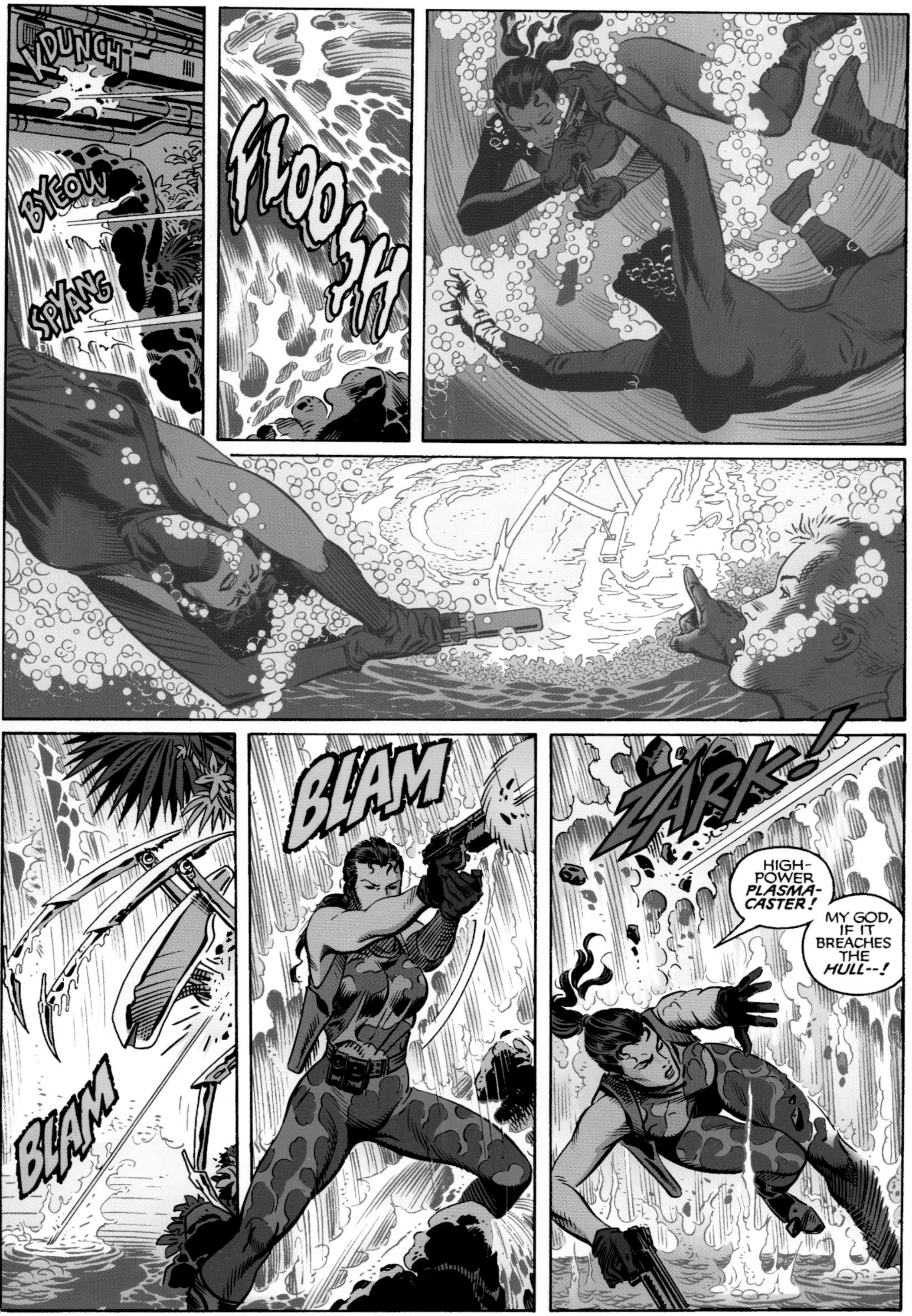
KDUNCH
BYEOW
SPYANG
FLOOSH
BLAM
BLAM
ZARK!
HIGH-POWER PLASMA-CASTER!
MY GOD, IF IT BREACHES THE HULL--!

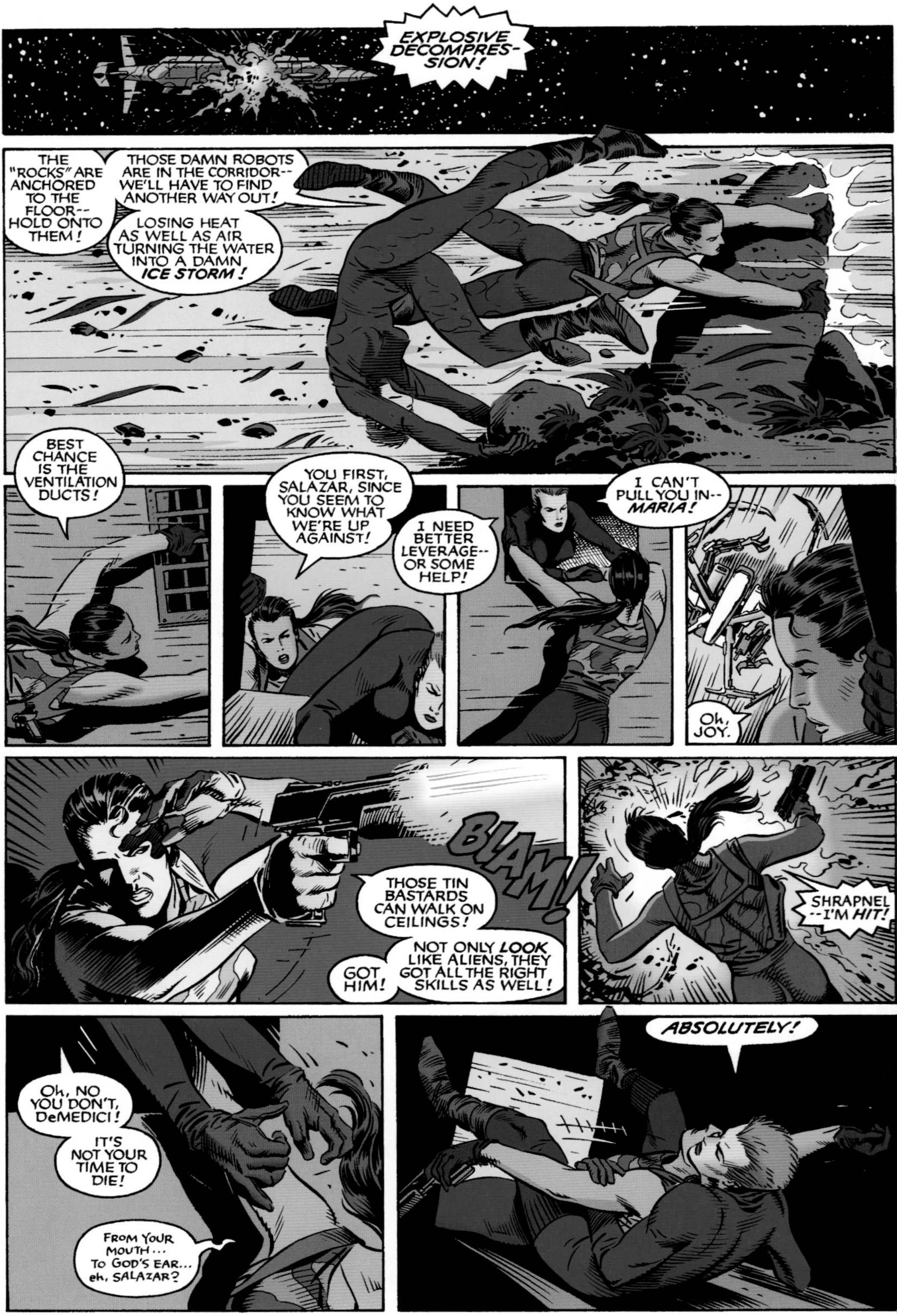
EXPLOSIVE DECOMPRES-SION!
THE "ROCKS" ARE ANCHORED TO THE FLOOR-- HOLD ONTO THEM!
THOSE DAMN ROBOTS ARE IN THE CORRIDOR-- WE'LL HAVE TO FIND ANOTHER WAY OUT!
LOSING HEAT AS WELL AS AIR TURNING THE WATER INTO A DAMN ICE STORM!
BEST CHANCE IS THE VENTILATION DUCTS!
YOU FIRST, SALAZAR, SINCE YOU SEEM TO KNOW WHAT WE'RE UP AGAINST!
I NEED BETTER LEVERAGE-- OR SOME HELP!
I CAN'T PULL YOU IN-- MARIA!
Oh, JOY.
BLAM!
THOSE TIN BASTARDS CAN WALK ON CEILINGS!
GOT HIM!
NOT ONLY LOOK LIKE ALIENS, THEY GOT ALL THE RIGHT SKILLS AS WELL!
SHRAPNEL --I'M HIT!
Oh, NO YOU DON'T, DeMEDICI!
IT'S NOT YOUR TIME TO DIE!
FROM YOUR MOUTH... To GOD'S EAR... eh, SALAZAR?
ABSOLUTELY!

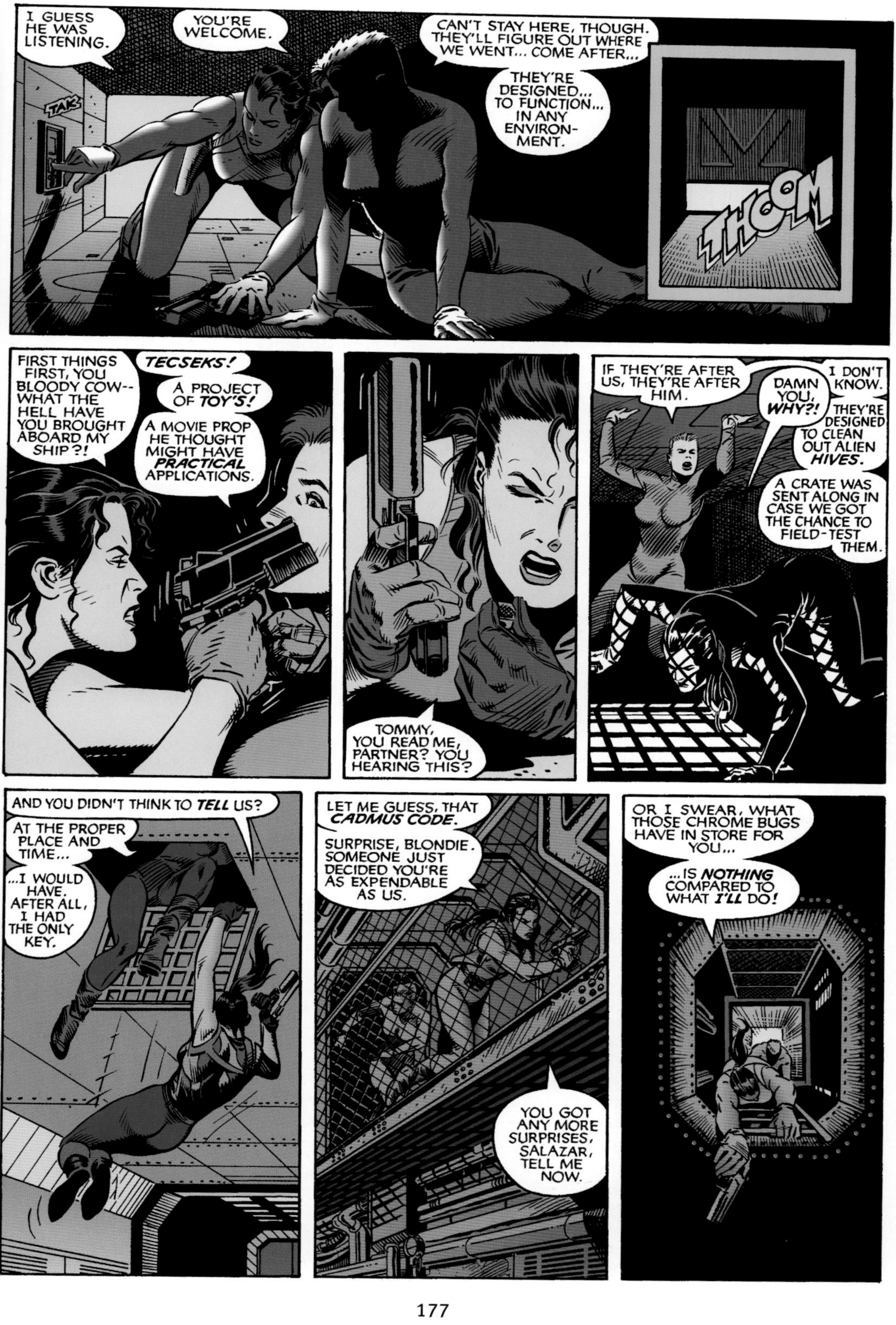
I GUESS HE WAS LISTENING.
YOU'RE WELCOME.
TAK
CAN'T STAY HERE, THOUGH. THEY'LL FIGURE OUT WHERE WE WENT... COME AFTER...
THEY'RE DESIGNED... TO FUNCTION... IN ANY ENVIRONMENT.
THOOM
FIRST THINGS FIRST, YOU BLOODY COW-- WHAT THE HELL HAVE YOU BROUGHT ABOARD MY SHIP?!
TECSEKS!
A PROJECT OF TOY'S!
A MOVIE PROP HE THOUGHT MIGHT HAVE PRACTICAL APPLICATIONS.
TOMMY, YOU READ ME, PARTNER? YOU HEARING THIS?
IF THEY'RE AFTER US, THEY'RE AFTER HIM.
DAMN YOU, WHY?!
I DON'T KNOW.
THEY'RE DESIGNED TO CLEAN OUT ALIEN HIVES.
A CRATE WAS SENT ALONG IN CASE WE GOT THE CHANCE TO FIELD-TEST THEM.
AND YOU DIDN'T THINK TO TELL US?
AT THE PROPER PLACE AND TIME...
...I WOULD HAVE. AFTER ALL, I HAD THE ONLY KEY.
LET ME GUESS, THAT CADMUS CODE.
SURPRISE, BLONDIE. SOMEONE JUST DECIDED YOU'RE AS EXPENDABLE AS US.
YOU GOT ANY MORE SURPRISES, SALAZAR, TELL ME NOW.
OR I SWEAR, WHAT THOSE CHROME BUGS HAVE IN STORE FOR YOU...
...IS NOTHING COMPARED TO WHAT I'LL DO!

IT'S A MONSTER STATION, THE SIZE OF A SMALL MOON.

EVEN WITH THE ENGINE WIDE OPEN, IT'S TAKING TIME TO DRIVE FROM ONE END TO THE OTHER.

AND THAT DOESN'T TAKE INTO ACCOUNT...

?!?!?

...SUDDEN, UNEXPECTED OBSTACLES.

THELMA DI

YOW!

SKRA KOOM!

CAR'S A *WONDER*, NO LESS SO THAN I AM MYSELF AS I HAUL THE WHEEL HARD OVER.

INSANE AS MY REACTIONS ARE-- SO FAST AND FURIOUS I CAN HARDLY KEEP TRACK OF THEM-- THE T-BIRD COPES WITH EVERY ONE.

SSCREEEE SCHHHH

THELMA-DI

SOMEHOW WE BOTH COME THROUGH WITHOUT A SCRATCH.

LANDING LIKE THAT COULD MEAN ANYTHING.

I FIGURE TO BE READY FOR THE WORST.

178

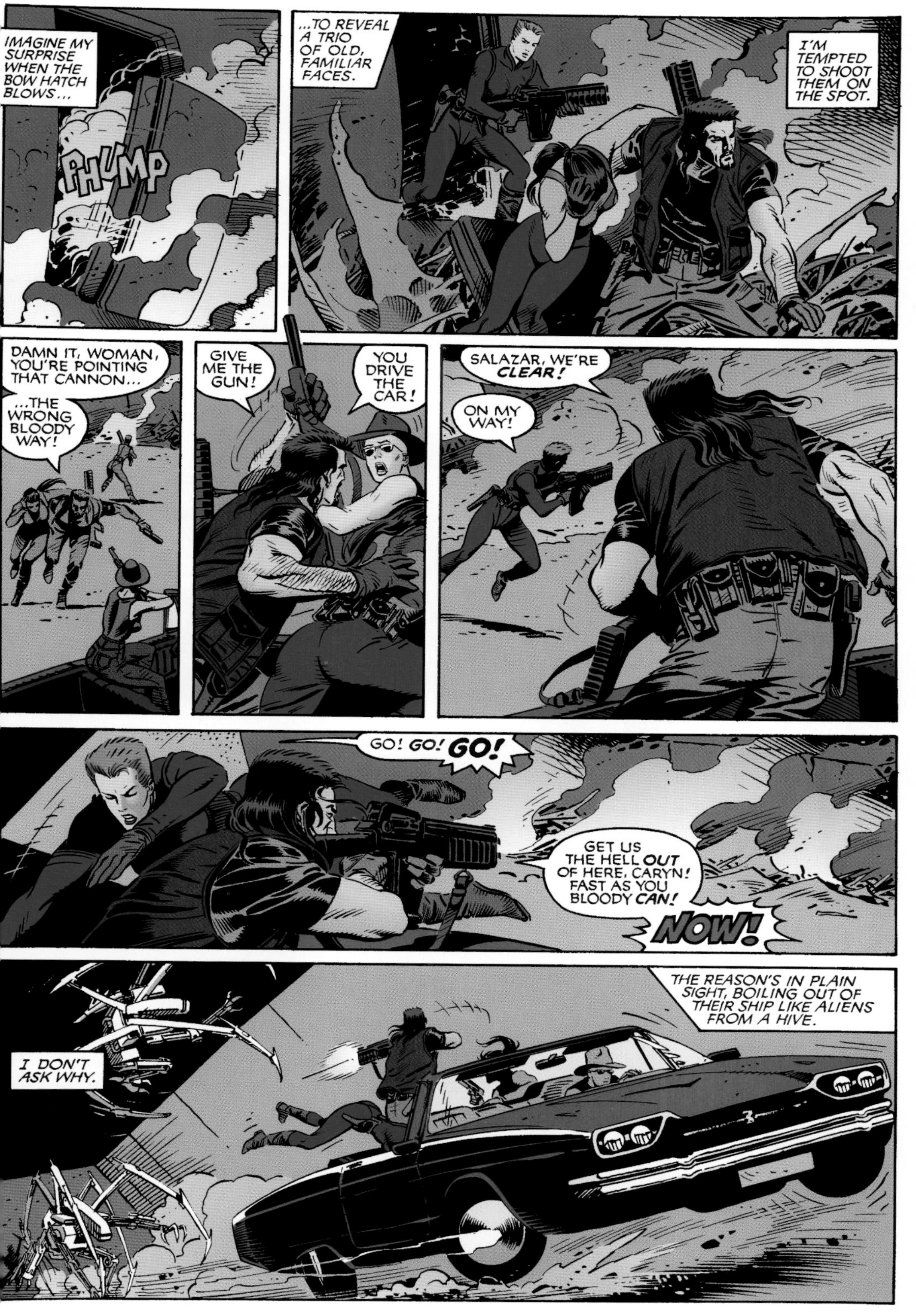
IMAGINE MY SURPRISE WHEN THE BOW HATCH BLOWS...
PHUMP
...TO REVEAL A TRIO OF OLD, FAMILIAR FACES.
I'M TEMPTED TO SHOOT THEM ON THE SPOT.
DAMN IT, WOMAN, YOU'RE POINTING THAT CANNON...
...THE WRONG BLOODY WAY!
GIVE ME THE GUN!
YOU DRIVE THE CAR!
SALAZAR, WE'RE CLEAR!
ON MY WAY!
GO! GO! GO!
GET US THE HELL OUT OF HERE, CARYN! FAST AS YOU BLOODY CAN!
NOW!
THE REASON'S IN PLAIN SIGHT, BOILING OUT OF THEIR SHIP LIKE ALIENS FROM A HIVE.
I DON'T ASK WHY.

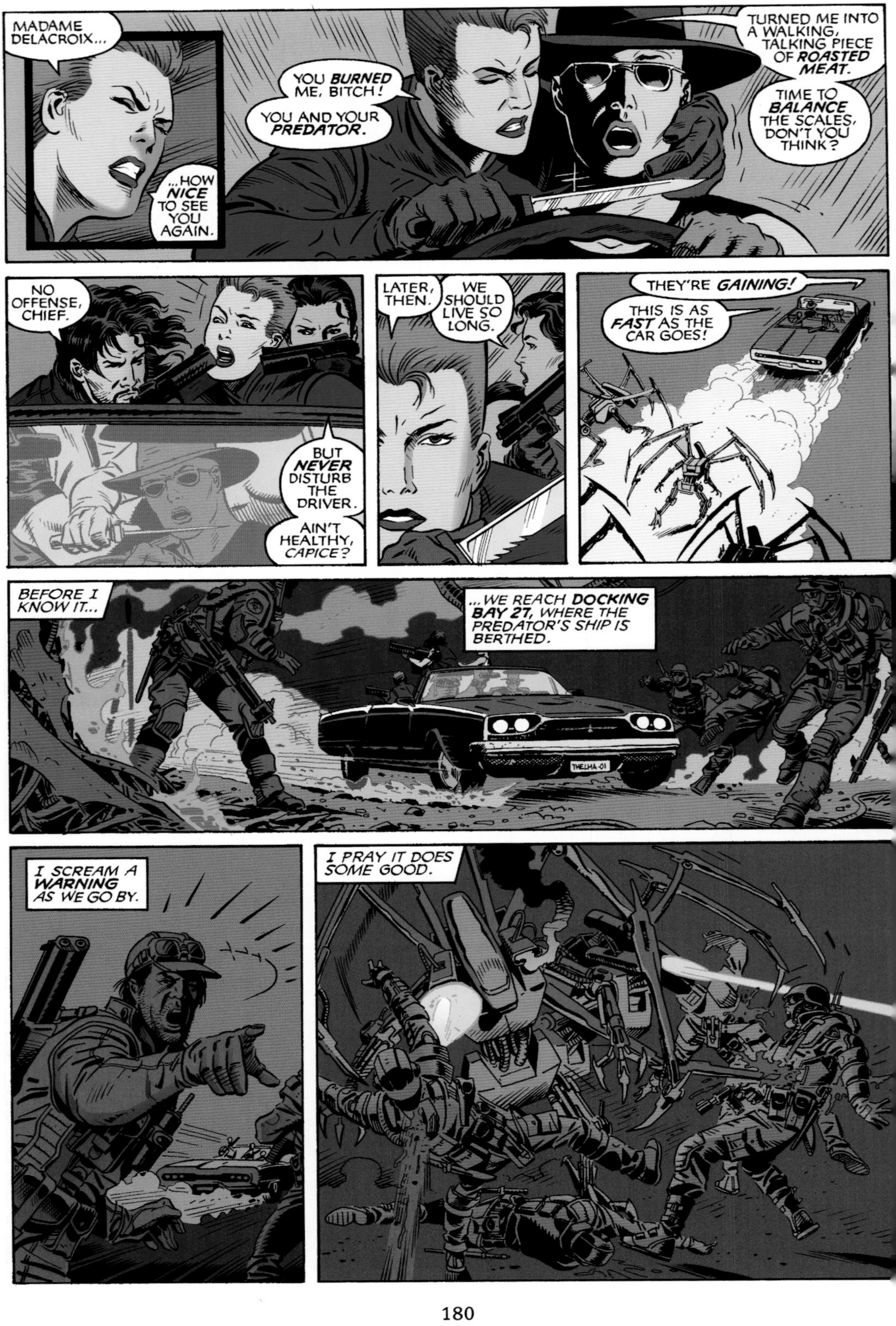
MADAME DELACROIX...
...HOW NICE TO SEE YOU AGAIN.
YOU BURNED ME, BITCH!
YOU AND YOUR PREDATOR.
TURNED ME INTO A WALKING, TALKING PIECE OF ROASTED MEAT.
TIME TO BALANCE THE SCALES, DON'T YOU THINK?
NO OFFENSE, CHIEF.
BUT NEVER DISTURB THE DRIVER.
AIN'T HEALTHY, CAPICE?
LATER, THEN.
WE SHOULD LIVE SO LONG.
THEY'RE GAINING!
THIS IS AS FAST AS THE CAR GOES!
BEFORE I KNOW IT...
...WE REACH DOCKING BAY 27, WHERE THE PREDATOR'S SHIP IS BERTHED.
THELMA-01
I SCREAM A WARNING AS WE GO BY.
I PRAY IT DOES SOME GOOD.

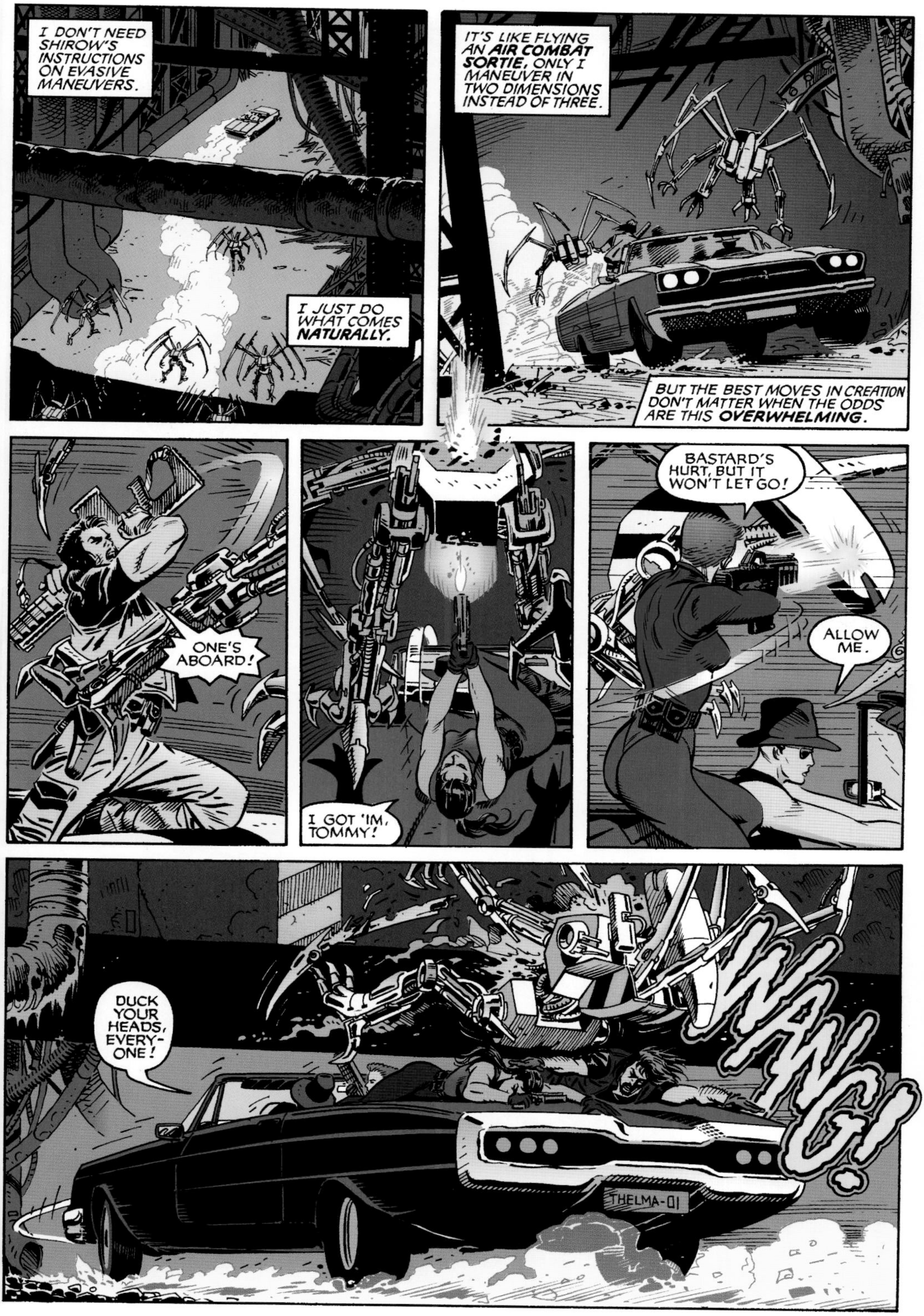
I DON'T NEED SHIROW'S INSTRUCTIONS ON EVASIVE MANEUVERS.
I JUST DO WHAT COMES NATURALLY.
IT'S LIKE FLYING AN AIR COMBAT SORTIE, ONLY I MANEUVER IN TWO DIMENSIONS INSTEAD OF THREE.
BUT THE BEST MOVES IN CREATION DON'T MATTER WHEN THE ODDS ARE THIS OVERWHELMING.
ONE'S ABOARD!
I GOT 'IM, TOMMY!
BASTARD'S HURT, BUT IT WON'T LET GO!
ALLOW ME.
DUCK YOUR HEADS, EVERY-ONE!
WANG!
THELMA-01

THERE'S A MOMENT--SO SWEET, SO PRECIOUS--

--WHEN WE ALL OF US THINK WE'VE PULLED TOTALLY CLEAR.

WE KNOW THEY'RE STILL FOLLOWING, BUT AT LEAST FOR NOW WE FIGURE WE'RE *SAFE*.

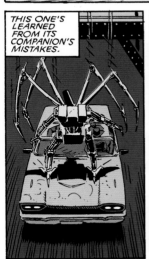

THIS ONE'S LEARNED FROM ITS COMPANION'S MISTAKES.

IT GOES STRAIGHT FOR ME.

SHIROW!

TO THEIR CREDIT, THEY *TRY*.

EVEN GISANDE.

BUT THEN A WILD-ASS FISHTAIL SWERVE SENDS MARIA FLYING.

SHIROW GOES AFTER.

SHE'S HIS *PARTNER*, AFTER ALL.

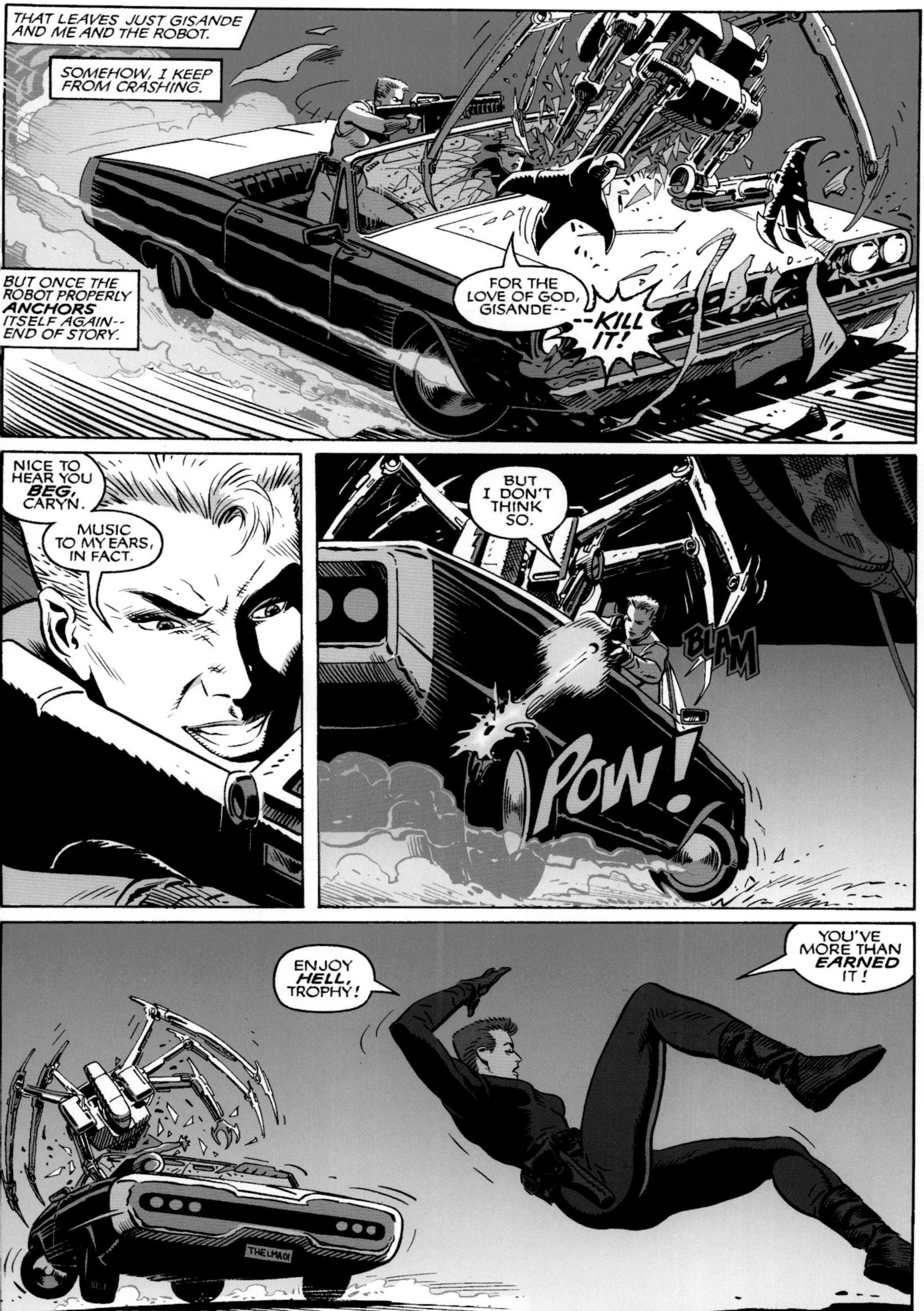
THAT LEAVES JUST GISANDE AND ME AND THE ROBOT.
SOMEHOW, I KEEP FROM CRASHING.
BUT ONCE THE ROBOT PROPERLY **ANCHORS** ITSELF AGAIN-- END OF STORY.
FOR THE LOVE OF GOD, GISANDE--
--KILL IT!
NICE TO HEAR YOU **BEG,** CARYN.
MUSIC TO MY EARS, IN FACT.
BUT I DON'T THINK SO.
BLAM
POW!
ENJOY **HELL,** TROPHY!
YOU'VE MORE THAN **EARNED** IT!
THELMA01

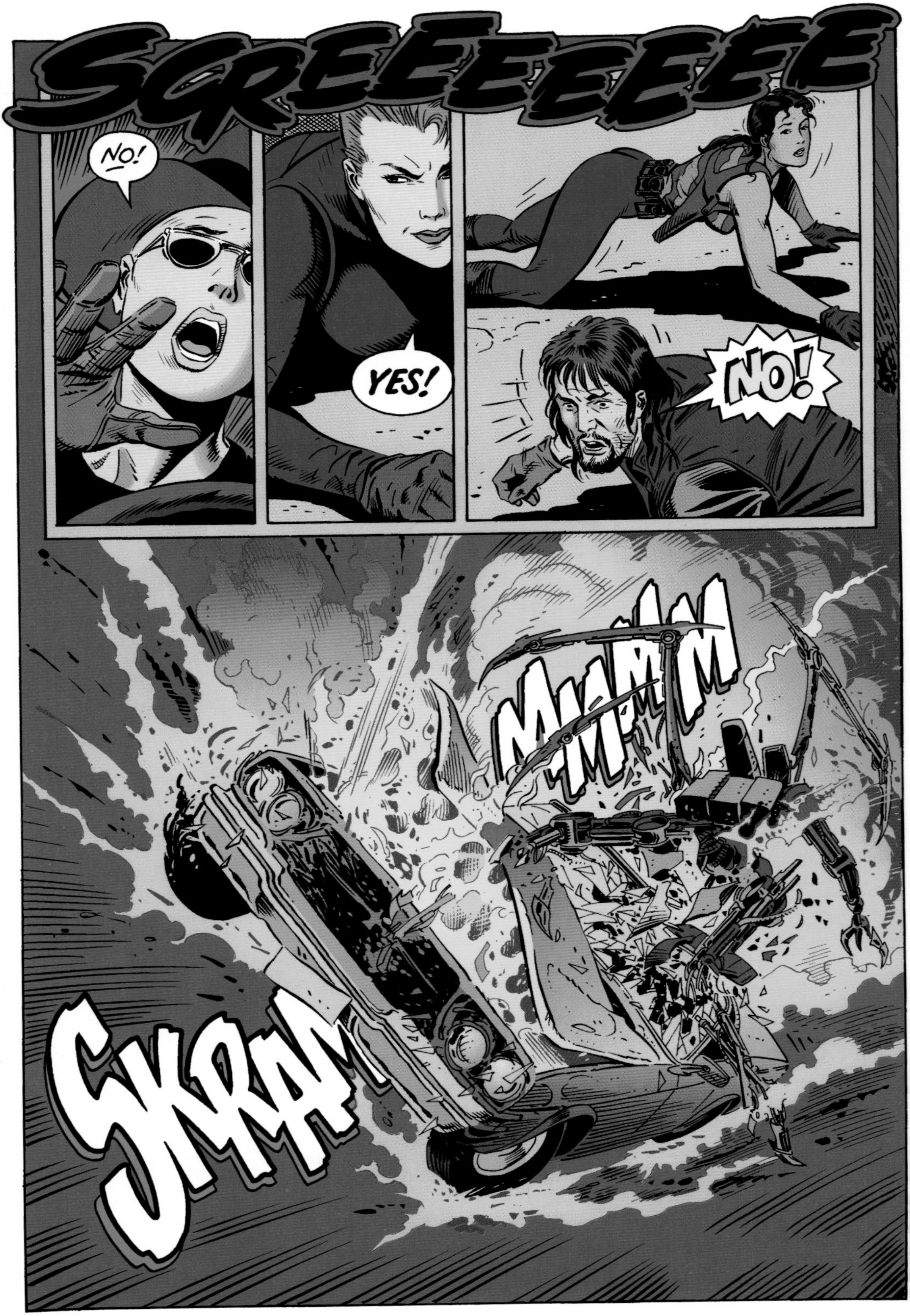
SCREEEEEEEEE
NO!
YES!
NO!
MMMMMM
SKRAM

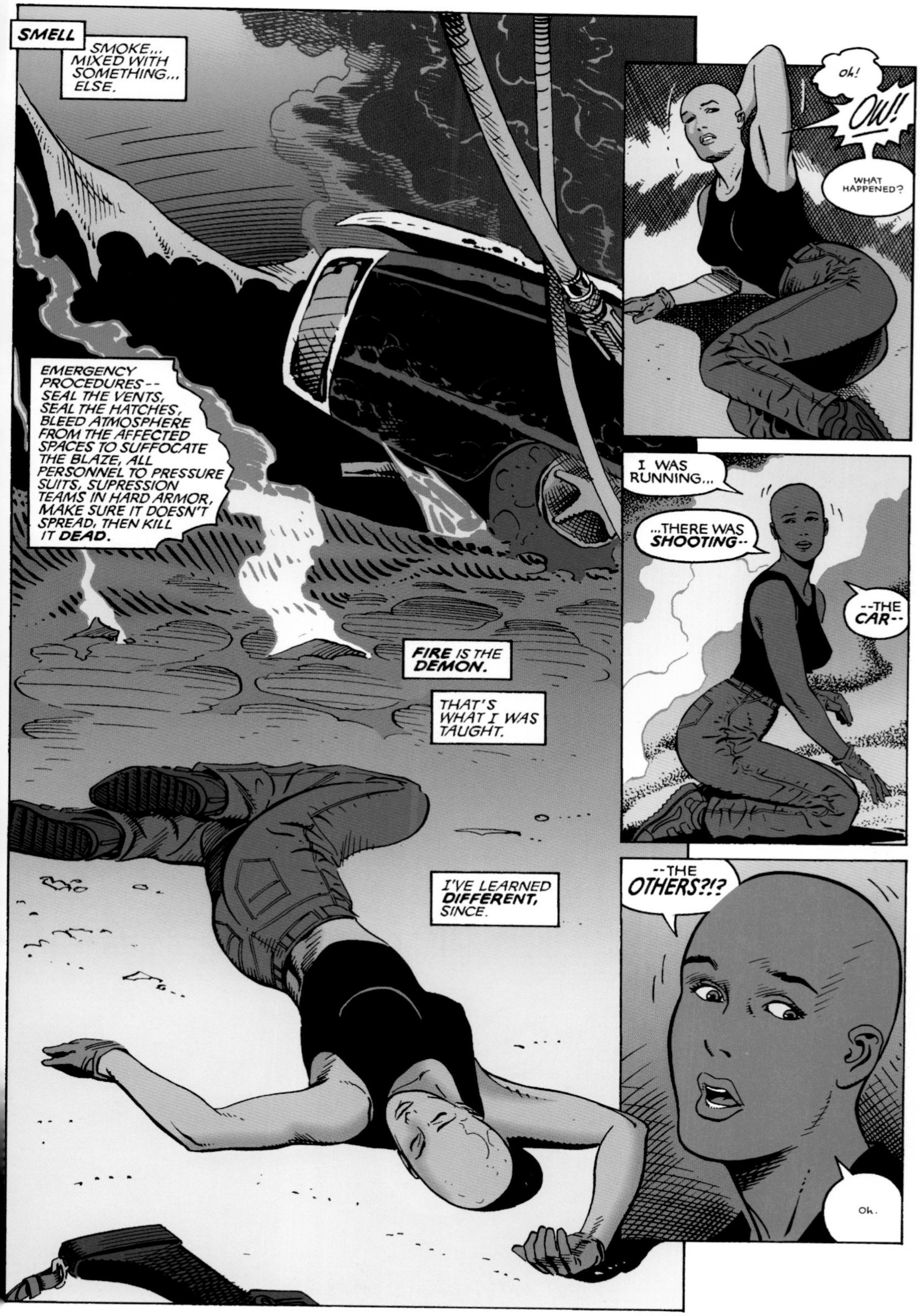
SMELL
SMOKE... MIXED WITH SOMETHING... ELSE.
EMERGENCY PROCEDURES-- SEAL THE VENTS, SEAL THE HATCHES, BLEED ATMOSPHERE FROM THE AFFECTED SPACES TO SUFFOCATE THE BLAZE, ALL PERSONNEL TO PRESSURE SUITS, SUPRESSION TEAMS IN HARD ARMOR, MAKE SURE IT DOESN'T SPREAD, THEN KILL IT DEAD.
FIRE IS THE DEMON.
THAT'S WHAT I WAS TAUGHT.
I'VE LEARNED DIFFERENT, SINCE.
Oh!
OW!
WHAT HAPPENED?
I WAS RUNNING...
...THERE WAS SHOOTING--
--THE CAR--
--THE OTHERS?!?
Oh.

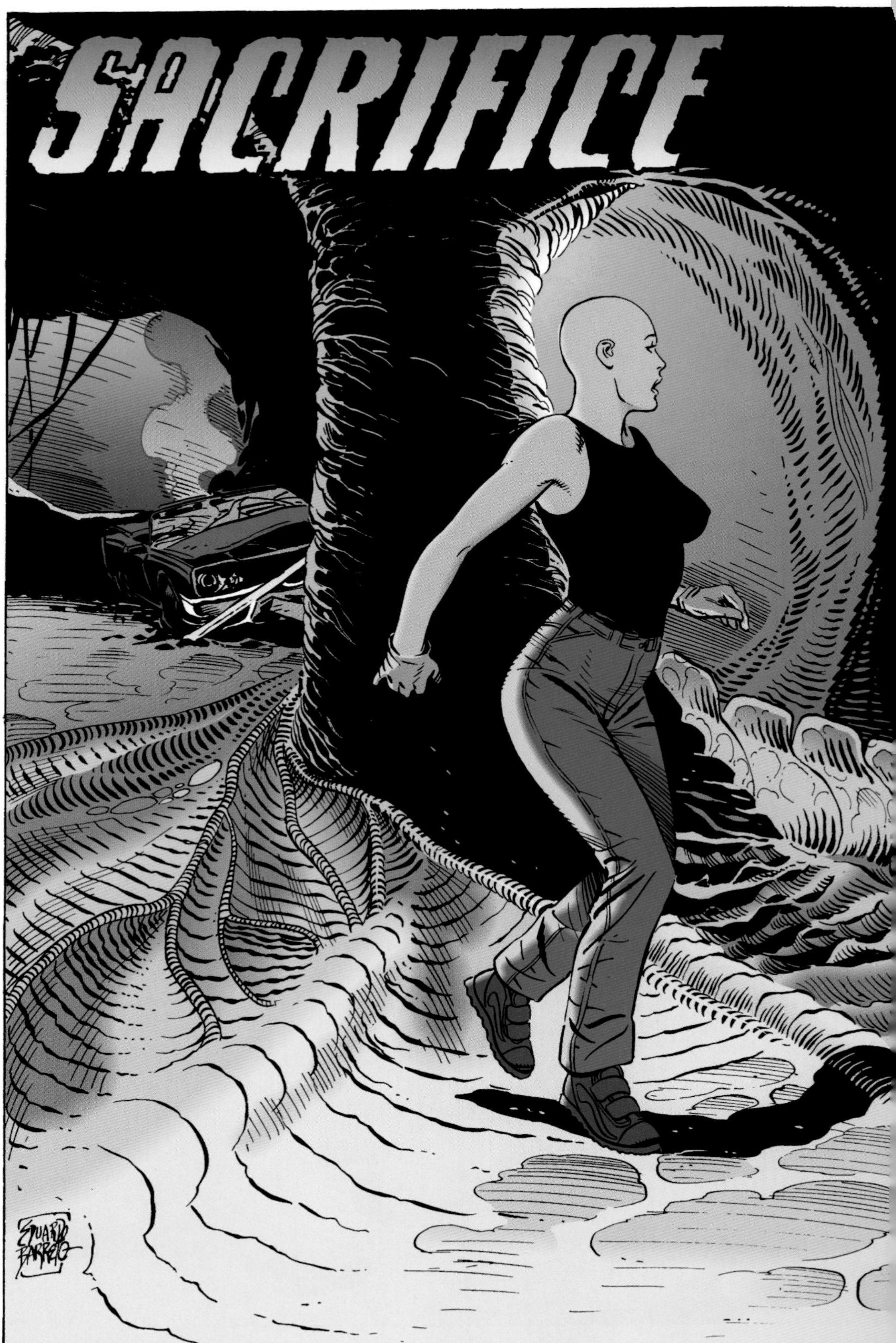
SACRIFICE

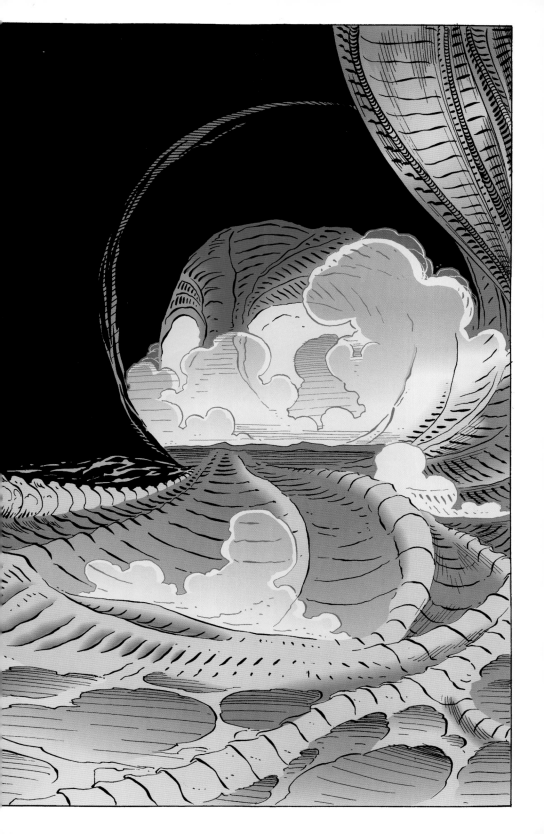

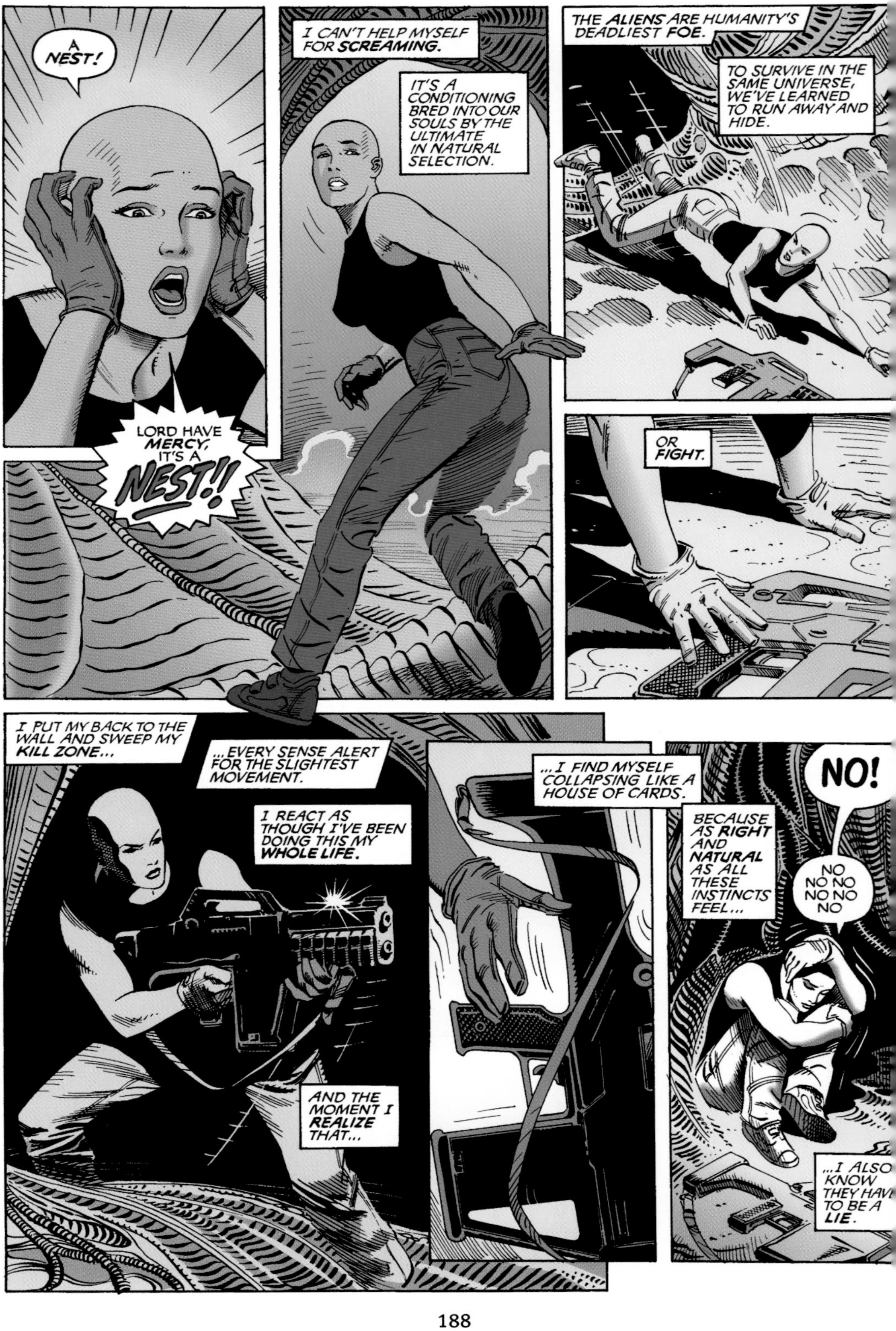
A NEST!
LORD HAVE MERCY, IT'S A NEST!!
I CAN'T HELP MYSELF FOR SCREAMING.
IT'S A CONDITIONING BRED INTO OUR SOULS BY THE ULTIMATE IN NATURAL SELECTION.
THE ALIENS ARE HUMANITY'S DEADLIEST FOE.
TO SURVIVE IN THE SAME UNIVERSE, WE'VE LEARNED TO RUN AWAY AND HIDE.
OR FIGHT.
I PUT MY BACK TO THE WALL AND SWEEP MY KILL ZONE...
...EVERY SENSE ALERT FOR THE SLIGHTEST MOVEMENT.
I REACT AS THOUGH I'VE BEEN DOING THIS MY WHOLE LIFE.
AND THE MOMENT I REALIZE THAT...
...I FIND MYSELF COLLAPSING LIKE A HOUSE OF CARDS.
NO!
BECAUSE AS RIGHT AND NATURAL AS ALL THESE INSTINCTS FEEL...
NO NO NO NO NO NO
...I ALSO KNOW THEY HAVE TO BE A LIE.

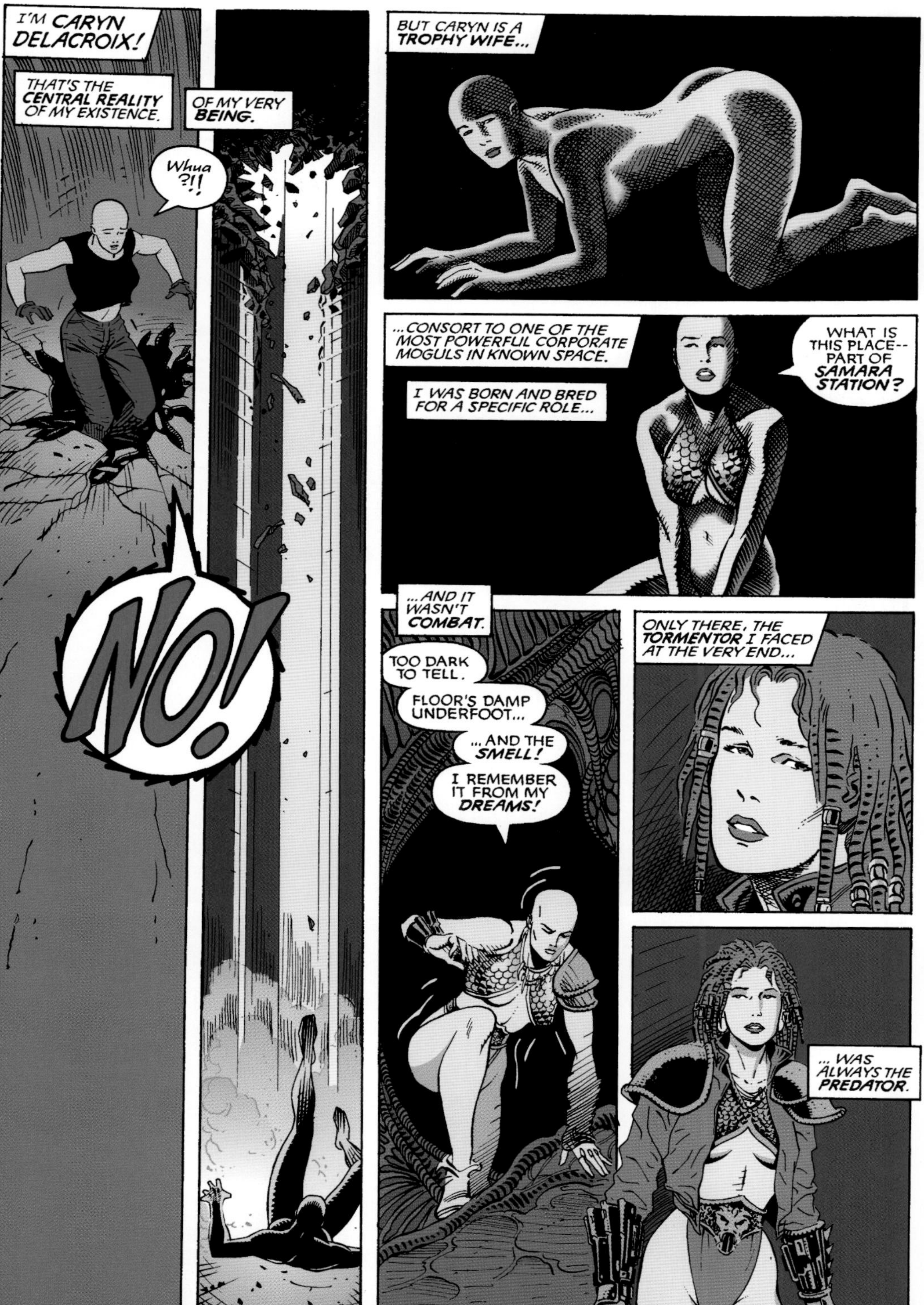
I'M CARYN DELACROIX!
THAT'S THE CENTRAL REALITY OF MY EXISTENCE.
Whua ?!!
NO!
OF MY VERY BEING.
BUT CARYN IS A TROPHY WIFE...
...CONSORT TO ONE OF THE MOST POWERFUL CORPORATE MOGULS IN KNOWN SPACE.
I WAS BORN AND BRED FOR A SPECIFIC ROLE...
WHAT IS THIS PLACE-- PART OF SAMARA STATION?
...AND IT WASN'T COMBAT.
TOO DARK TO TELL.
FLOOR'S DAMP UNDERFOOT...
...AND THE SMELL!
I REMEMBER IT FROM MY DREAMS!
ONLY THERE, THE TORMENTOR I FACED AT THE VERY END...
...WAS ALWAYS THE PREDATOR.

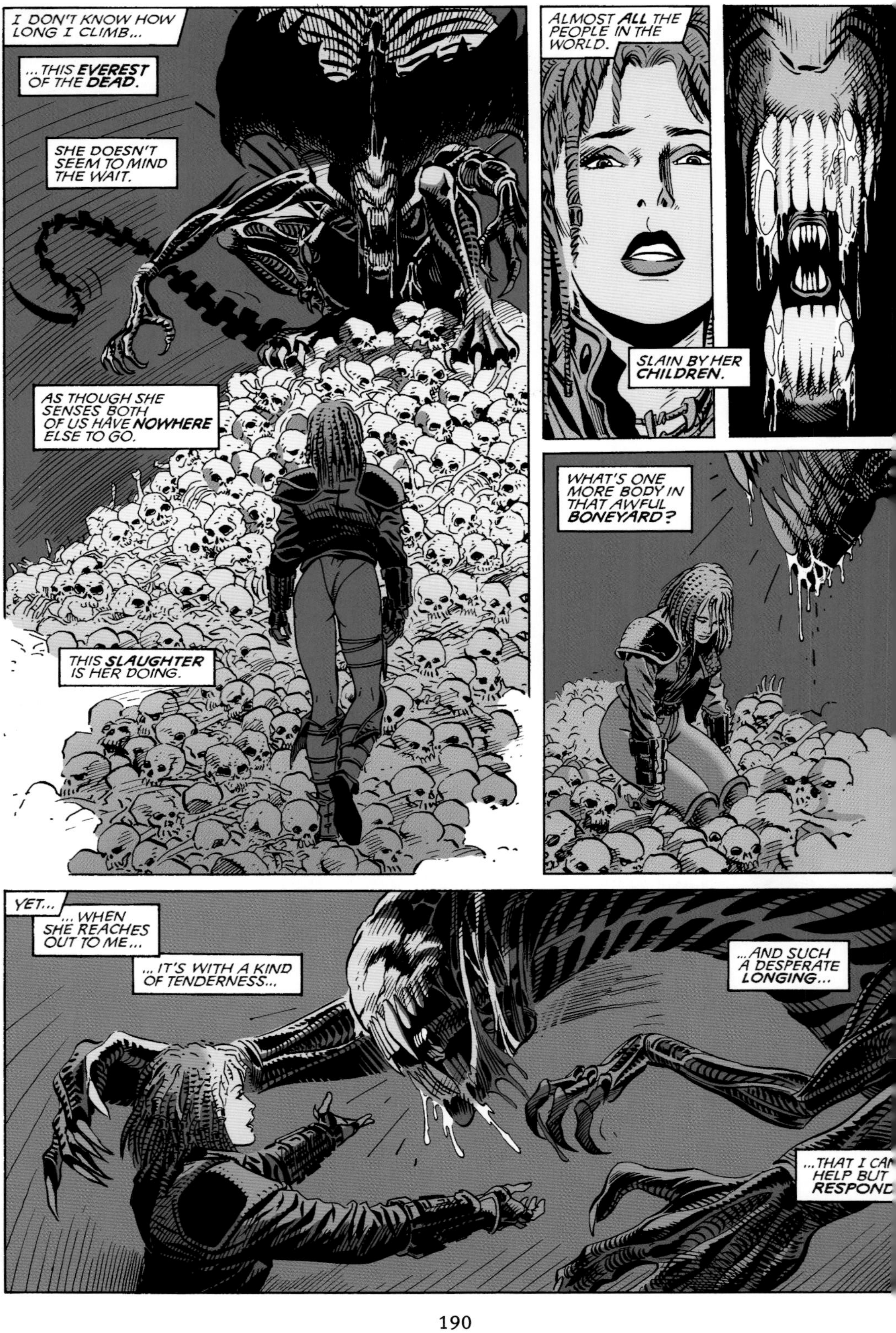
I DON'T KNOW HOW LONG I CLIMB...
...THIS EVEREST OF THE DEAD.
SHE DOESN'T SEEM TO MIND THE WAIT.
AS THOUGH SHE SENSES BOTH OF US HAVE NOWHERE ELSE TO GO.
THIS SLAUGHTER IS HER DOING.
ALMOST ALL THE PEOPLE IN THE WORLD.
SLAIN BY HER CHILDREN.
WHAT'S ONE MORE BODY IN THAT AWFUL BONEYARD?
YET...
...WHEN SHE REACHES OUT TO ME...
...IT'S WITH A KIND OF TENDERNESS...
...AND SUCH A DESPERATE LONGING...
...THAT I CAN
HELP BUT
RESPOND

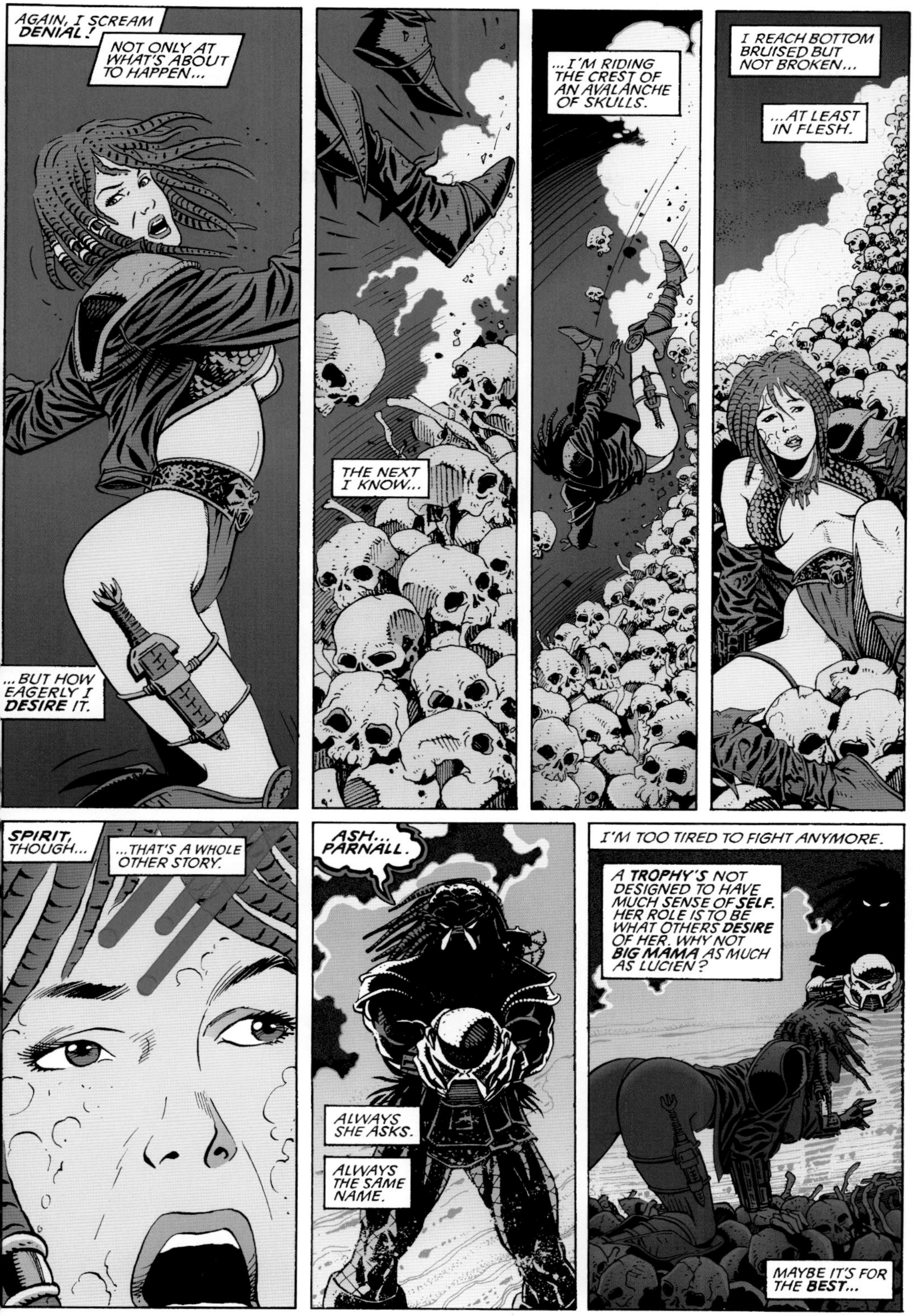
AGAIN, I SCREAM DENIAL!
NOT ONLY AT WHAT'S ABOUT TO HAPPEN...
...BUT HOW EAGERLY I DESIRE IT.
THE NEXT I KNOW...
...I'M RIDING THE CREST OF AN AVALANCHE OF SKULLS.
I REACH BOTTOM BRUISED BUT NOT BROKEN...
...AT LEAST IN FLESH.
SPIRIT, THOUGH...
...THAT'S A WHOLE OTHER STORY.
ASH... PARNALL.
ALWAYS SHE ASKS.
ALWAYS THE SAME NAME.
I'M TOO TIRED TO FIGHT ANYMORE.
A TROPHY'S NOT DESIGNED TO HAVE MUCH SENSE OF SELF. HER ROLE IS TO BE WHAT OTHERS DESIRE OF HER. WHY NOT BIG MAMA AS MUCH AS LUCIEN?
MAYBE IT'S FOR THE BEST...

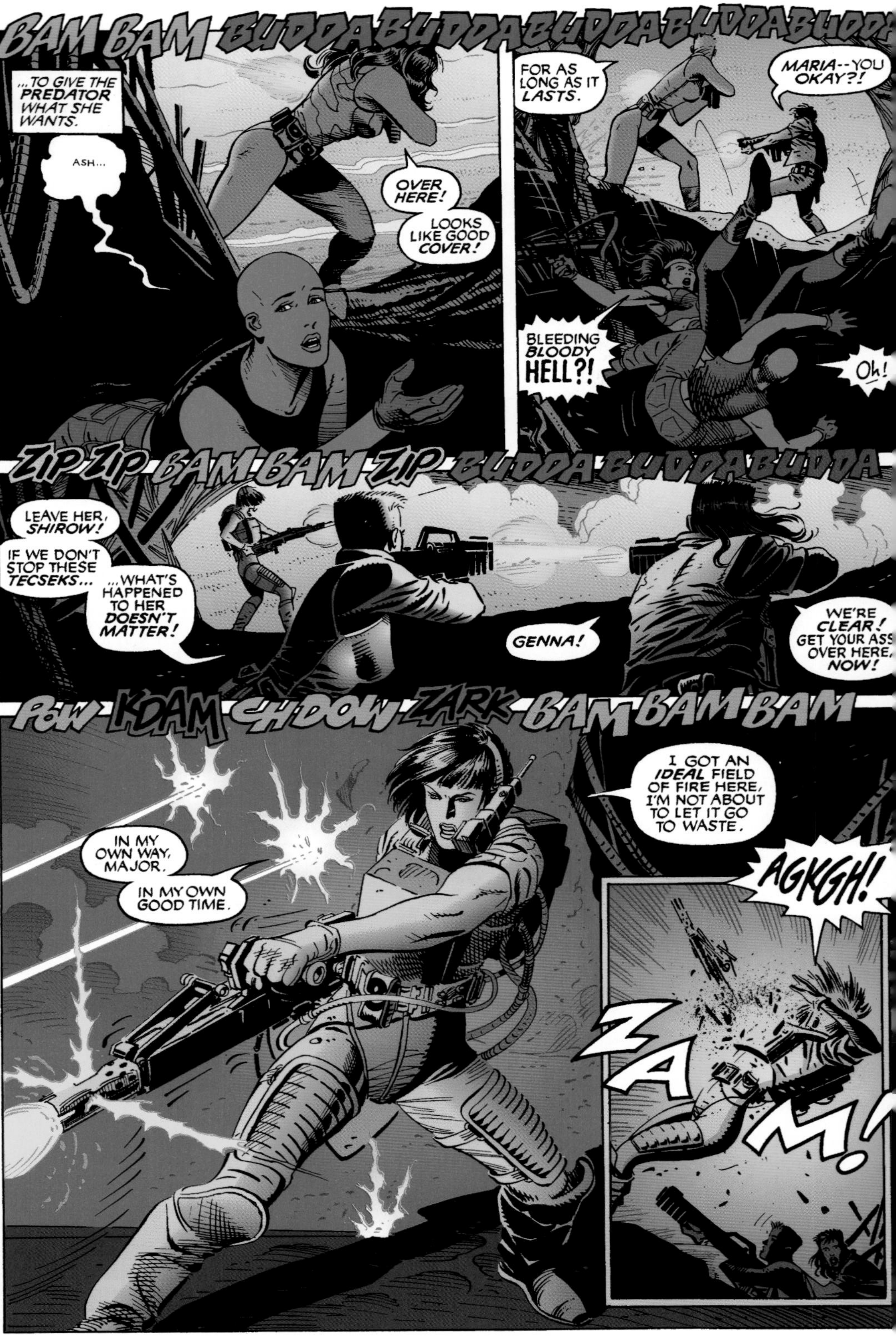
BAM BAM BUDDABUDDABUDDABUDDABUDD
...TO GIVE THE PREDATOR WHAT SHE WANTS.
ASH...
OVER HERE!
LOOKS LIKE GOOD COVER!
FOR AS LONG AS IT LASTS.
MARIA--YOU OKAY?!
BLEEDING BLOODY HELL?!
Oh!
ZIP ZIP BAM BAM ZIP BUDDA BUDDABUDDA
LEAVE HER, SHIROW!
IF WE DON'T STOP THESE TECSEKS...
...WHAT'S HAPPENED TO HER DOESN'T MATTER!
GENNA!
WE'RE CLEAR! GET YOUR ASS OVER HERE, NOW!
POW KDAM CHDOW ZARK BAM BAM BAM
I GOT AN IDEAL FIELD OF FIRE HERE, I'M NOT ABOUT TO LET IT GO TO WASTE.
IN MY OWN WAY, MAJOR.
IN MY OWN GOOD TIME.
AGKGH!
ZAM!

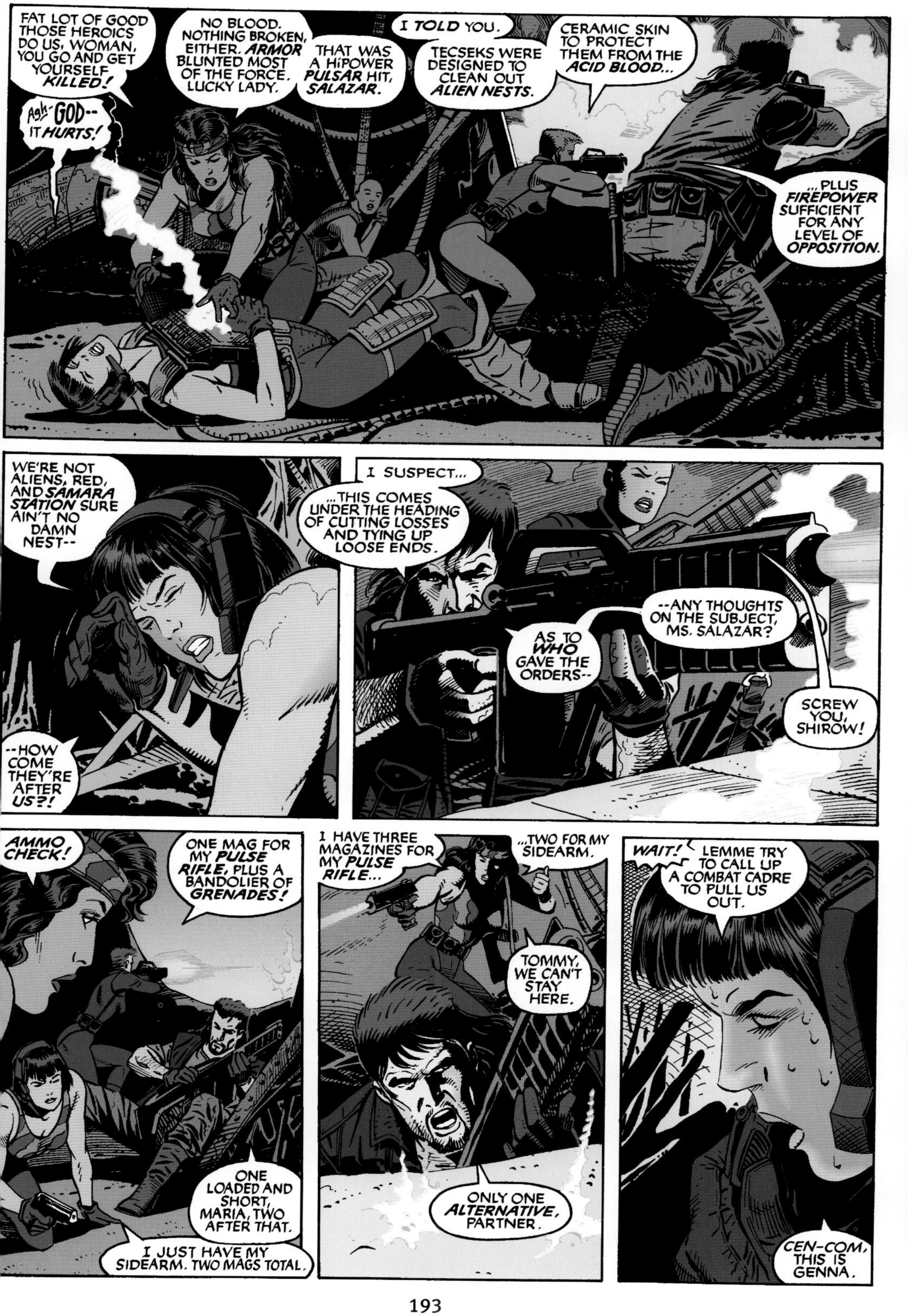

FAT LOT OF GOOD THOSE HEROICS DO US, WOMAN, YOU GO AND GET YOURSELF KILLED!
Agh- GOD-- IT HURTS!
NO BLOOD. NOTHING BROKEN, EITHER. ARMOR BLUNTED MOST OF THE FORCE. LUCKY LADY.
THAT WAS A HiPOWER PULSAR HIT, SALAZAR.
I TOLD YOU.
TECSEKS WERE DESIGNED TO CLEAN OUT ALIEN NESTS.
CERAMIC SKIN TO PROTECT THEM FROM THE ACID BLOOD...
...PLUS FIREPOWER SUFFICIENT FOR ANY LEVEL OF OPPOSITION.
WE'RE NOT ALIENS, RED, AND SAMARA STATION SURE AIN'T NO DAMN NEST--
--HOW COME THEY'RE AFTER US?!
I SUSPECT...
...THIS COMES UNDER THE HEADING OF CUTTING LOSSES AND TYING UP LOOSE ENDS.
AS TO WHO GAVE THE ORDERS--
--ANY THOUGHTS ON THE SUBJECT, MS. SALAZAR?
SCREW YOU, SHIROW!
AMMO CHECK!
ONE MAG FOR MY PULSE RIFLE, PLUS A BANDOLIER OF GRENADES!
ONE LOADED AND SHORT, MARIA, TWO AFTER THAT.
I JUST HAVE MY SIDEARM. TWO MAGS TOTAL.
I HAVE THREE MAGAZINES FOR MY PULSE RIFLE...
...TWO FOR MY SIDEARM.
TOMMY, WE CAN'T STAY HERE.
ONLY ONE ALTERNATIVE, PARTNER.
WAIT!
LEMME TRY TO CALL UP A COMBAT CADRE TO PULL US OUT.
CEN-COM, THIS IS GENNA.

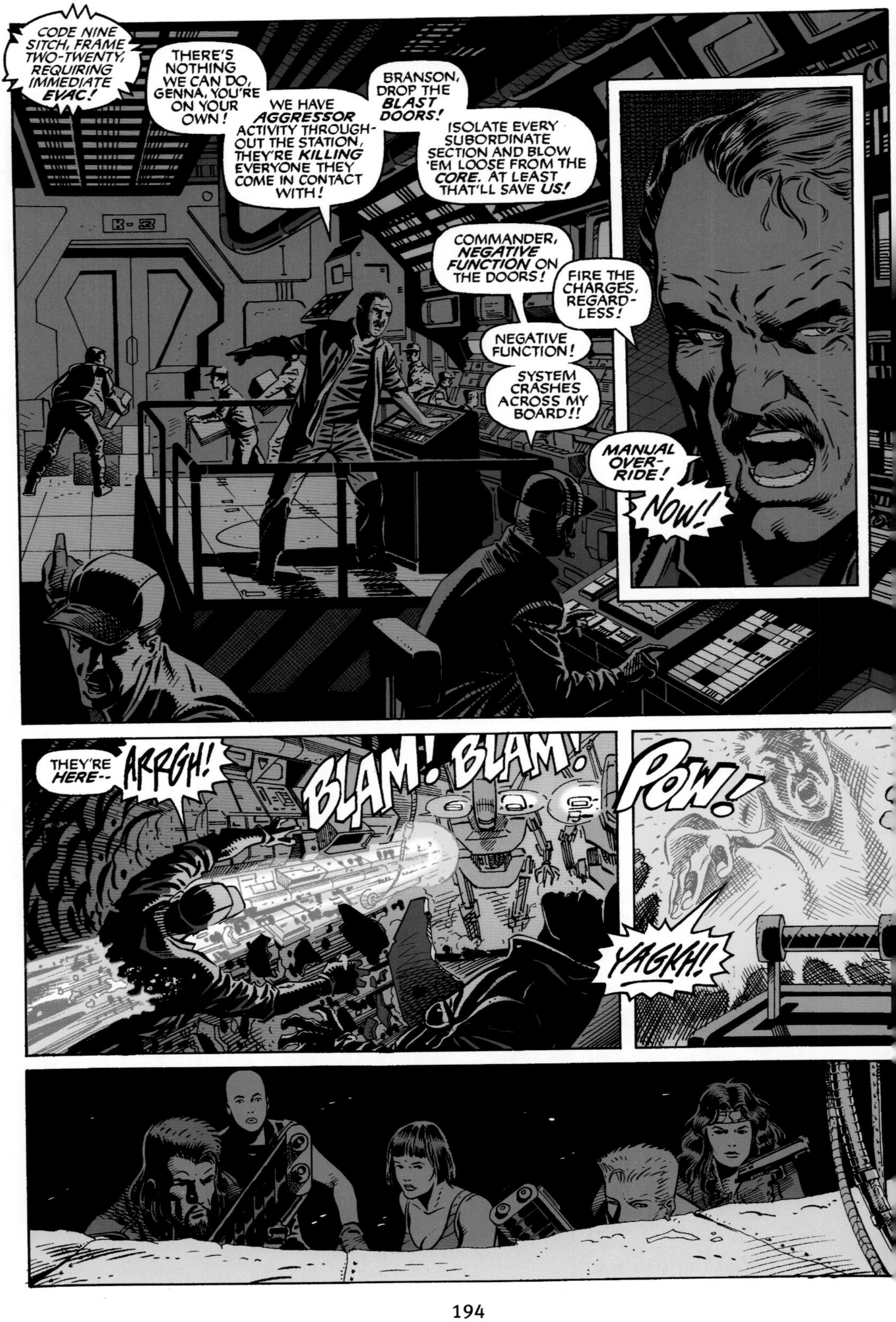
CODE NINE SITCH, FRAME TWO-TWENTY, REQUIRING IMMEDIATE EVAC!
THERE'S NOTHING WE CAN DO, GENNA, YOU'RE ON YOUR OWN!
WE HAVE AGGRESSOR ACTIVITY THROUGH-OUT THE STATION, THEY'RE KILLING EVERYONE THEY COME IN CONTACT WITH!
BRANSON, DROP THE BLAST DOORS!
ISOLATE EVERY SUBORDINATE SECTION AND BLOW 'EM LOOSE FROM THE CORE. AT LEAST THAT'LL SAVE US!
COMMANDER, NEGATIVE FUNCTION ON THE DOORS!
FIRE THE CHARGES, REGARD-LESS!
NEGATIVE FUNCTION!
SYSTEM CRASHES ACROSS MY BOARD!!
MANUAL OVER-RIDE!
NOW!
THEY'RE HERE--
ARRGH!
BLAM! BLAM!
POW!
YAGKH!

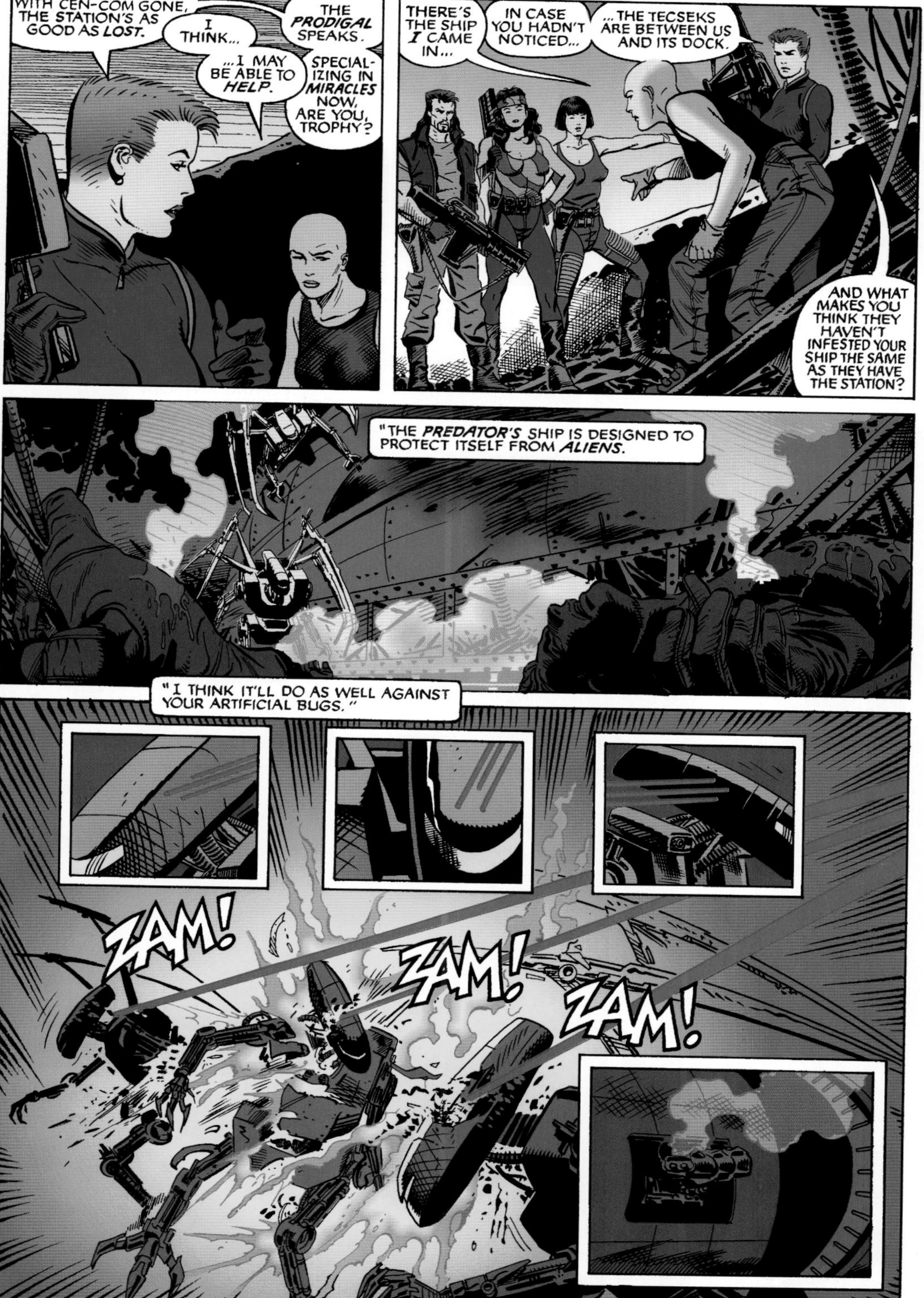
WITH CEN-COM GONE, THE STATION'S AS GOOD AS LOST.
I THINK...
...I MAY BE ABLE TO HELP.
THE PRODIGAL SPEAKS.
SPECIALIZING IN MIRACLES NOW, ARE YOU, TROPHY?
THERE'S THE SHIP I CAME IN...
IN CASE YOU HADN'T NOTICED...
...THE TECSEKS ARE BETWEEN US AND ITS DOCK.
AND WHAT MAKES YOU THINK THEY HAVEN'T INFESTED YOUR SHIP THE SAME AS THEY HAVE THE STATION?
"THE PREDATOR'S SHIP IS DESIGNED TO PROTECT ITSELF FROM ALIENS.
"I THINK IT'LL DO AS WELL AGAINST YOUR ARTIFICIAL BUGS."
ZAM!
ZAM!
ZAM!

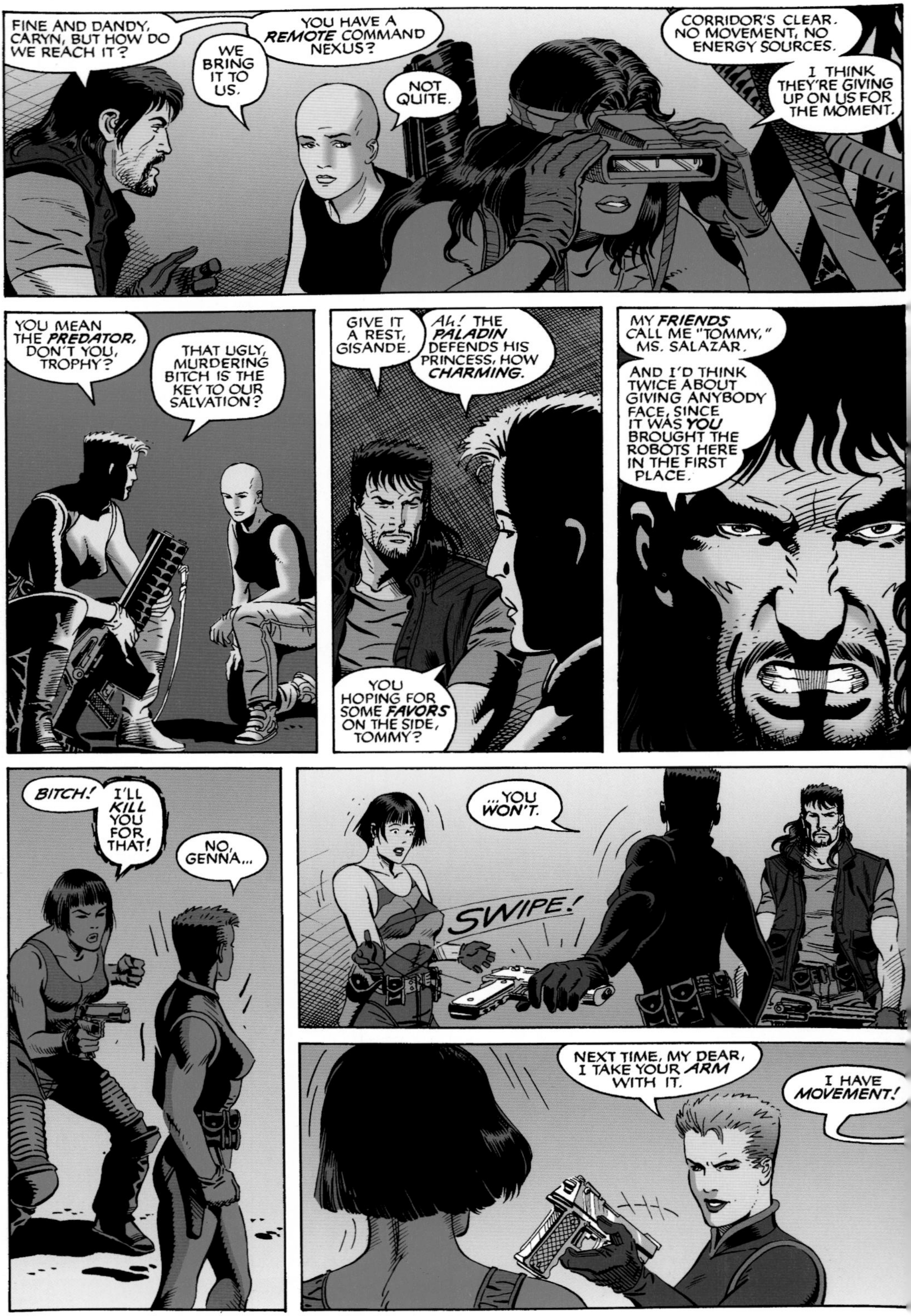
FINE AND DANDY, CARYN, BUT HOW DO WE REACH IT?
YOU HAVE A REMOTE COMMAND NEXUS?
WE BRING IT TO US.
NOT QUITE.
CORRIDOR'S CLEAR. NO MOVEMENT, NO ENERGY SOURCES.
I THINK THEY'RE GIVING UP ON US FOR THE MOMENT.
YOU MEAN THE PREDATOR, DON'T YOU, TROPHY?
THAT UGLY, MURDERING BITCH IS THE KEY TO OUR SALVATION?
GIVE IT A REST, GISANDE.
AH! THE PALADIN DEFENDS HIS PRINCESS, HOW CHARMING.
YOU HOPING FOR SOME FAVORS ON THE SIDE, TOMMY?
MY FRIENDS CALL ME "TOMMY," MS. SALAZAR.
AND I'D THINK TWICE ABOUT GIVING ANYBODY FACE, SINCE IT WAS YOU BROUGHT THE ROBOTS HERE IN THE FIRST PLACE.
BITCH!
I'LL KILL YOU FOR THAT!
NO, GENNA...
...YOU WON'T.
SWIPE!
NEXT TIME, MY DEAR, I TAKE YOUR ARM WITH IT.
I HAVE MOVEMENT!

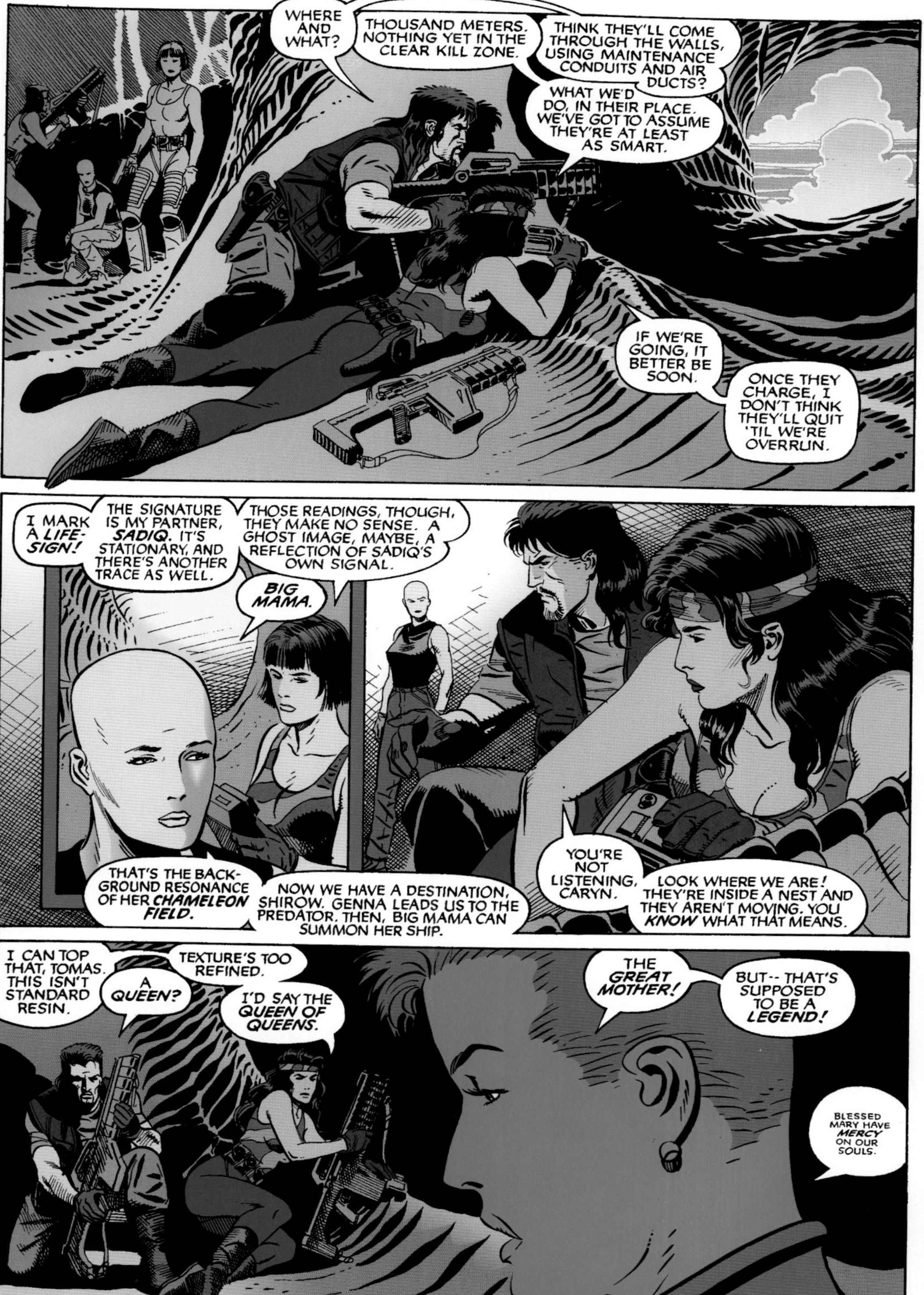
WHERE AND WHAT?
THOUSAND METERS. NOTHING YET IN THE CLEAR KILL ZONE.
THINK THEY'LL COME THROUGH THE WALLS, USING MAINTENANCE CONDUITS AND AIR DUCTS?
WHAT WE'D DO, IN THEIR PLACE. WE'VE GOT TO ASSUME THEY'RE AT LEAST AS SMART.
IF WE'RE GOING, IT BETTER BE SOON.
ONCE THEY CHARGE, I DON'T THINK THEY'LL QUIT 'TIL WE'RE OVERRUN.
I MARK A *LIFE-SIGN!*
THE SIGNATURE IS MY PARTNER, *SADIQ*. IT'S STATIONARY, AND THERE'S ANOTHER TRACE AS WELL.
THOSE READINGS, THOUGH, THEY MAKE NO SENSE. A GHOST IMAGE, MAYBE, A REFLECTION OF SADIQ'S OWN SIGNAL.
BIG MAMA.
THAT'S THE BACK-GROUND RESONANCE OF HER *CHAMELEON FIELD.*
NOW WE HAVE A DESTINATION, SHIROW. GENNA LEADS US TO THE PREDATOR. THEN, BIG MAMA CAN SUMMON HER SHIP.
YOU'RE NOT LISTENING, CARYN.
LOOK WHERE WE ARE! THEY'RE INSIDE A NEST AND THEY AREN'T MOVING. YOU *KNOW* WHAT THAT MEANS.
I CAN TOP THAT, TOMAS. THIS ISN'T STANDARD RESIN.
TEXTURE'S TOO REFINED.
A *QUEEN?*
I'D SAY THE *QUEEN OF QUEENS.*
THE *GREAT MOTHER!*
BUT-- THAT'S SUPPOSED TO BE A *LEGEND!*
BLESSED MARY HAVE *MERCY* ON OUR SOULS.

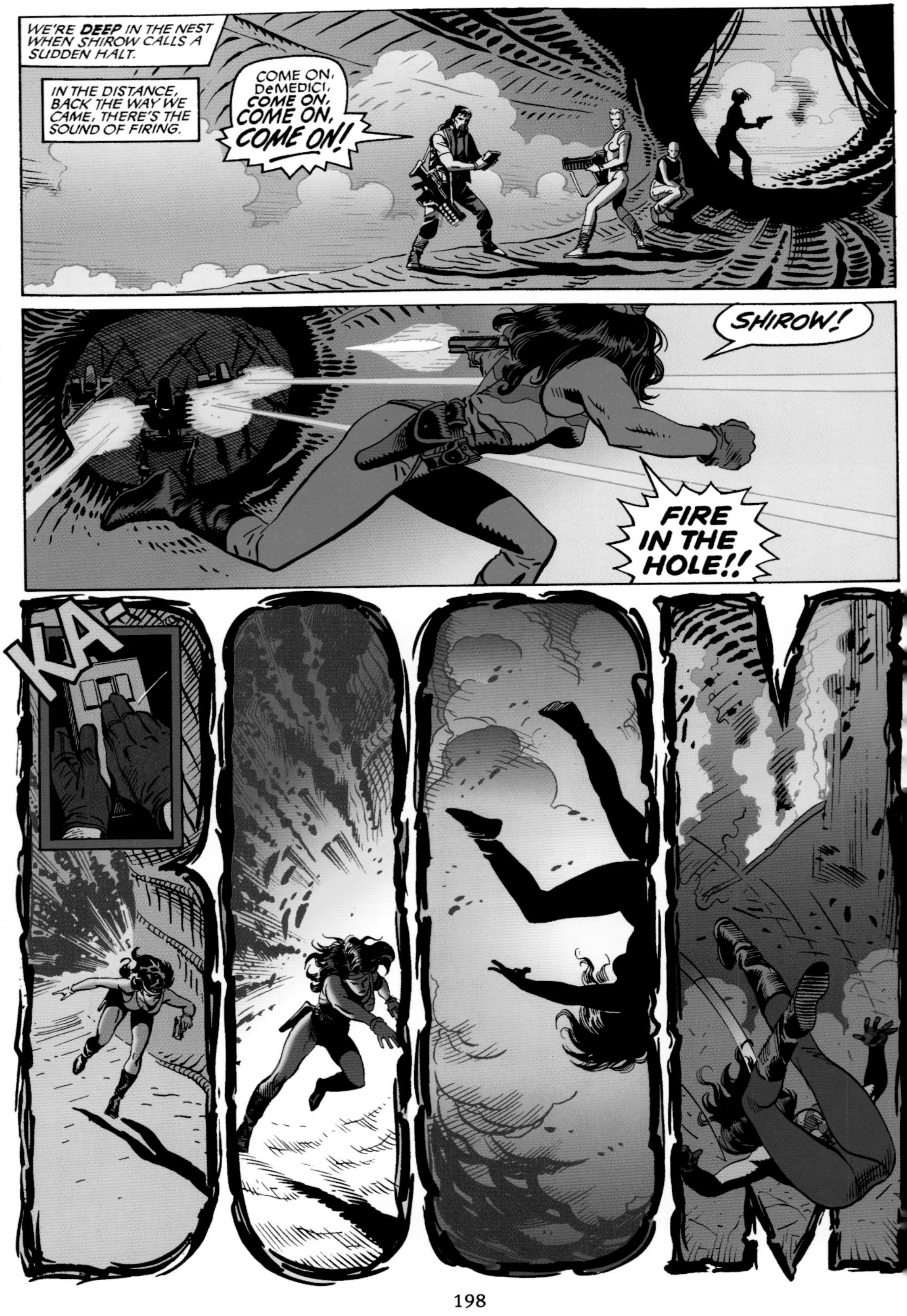
WE'RE DEEP IN THE NEST WHEN SHIROW CALLS A SUDDEN HALT.
IN THE DISTANCE, BACK THE WAY WE CAME, THERE'S THE SOUND OF FIRING.
COME ON, DeMEDICI, COME ON, COME ON, COME ON!
SHIROW!
FIRE IN THE HOLE!!
KA-BOOM

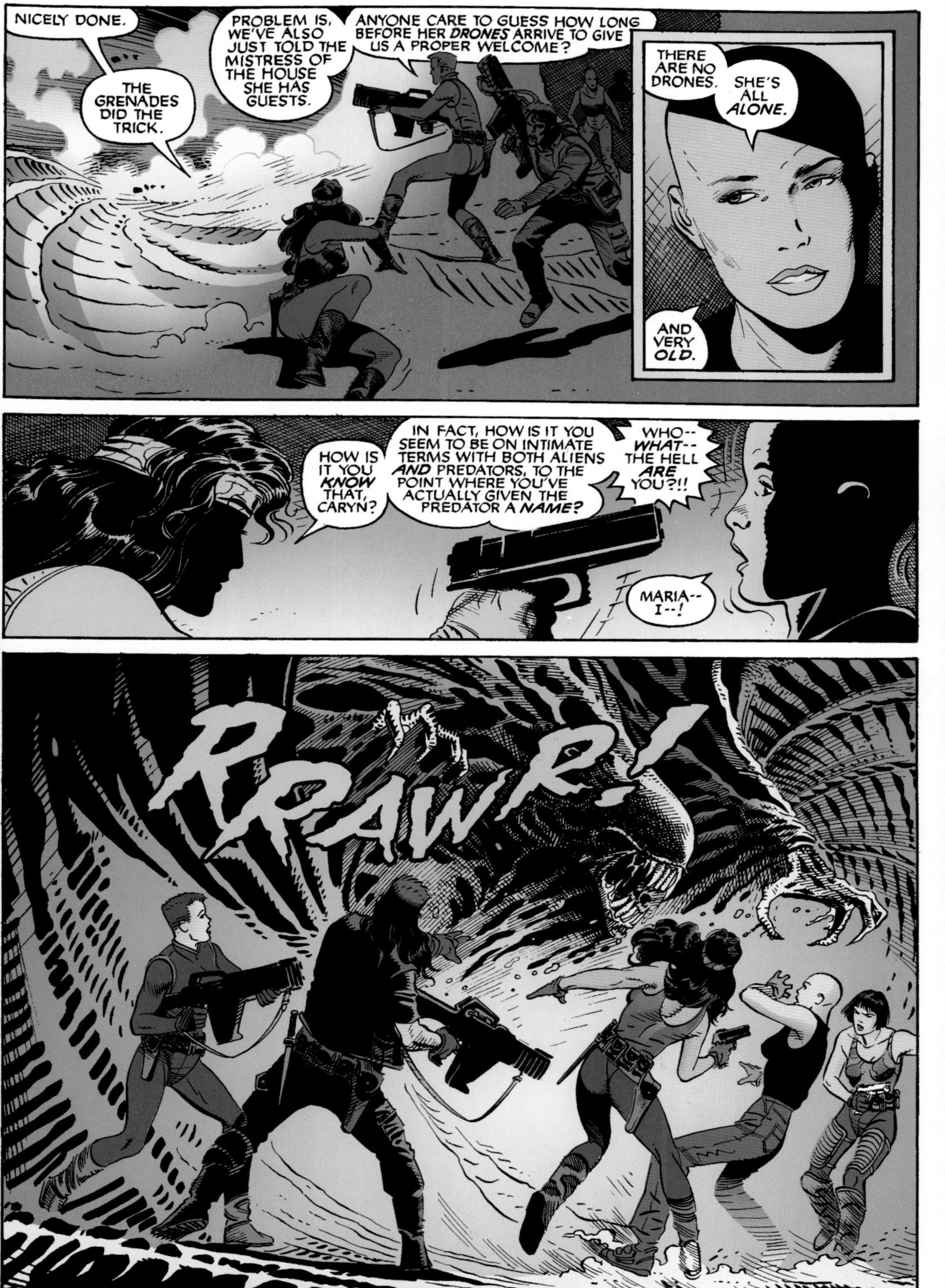
NICELY DONE.
THE GRENADES DID THE TRICK.
PROBLEM IS, WE'VE ALSO JUST TOLD THE MISTRESS OF THE HOUSE SHE HAS GUESTS.
ANYONE CARE TO GUESS HOW LONG BEFORE HER *DRONES* ARRIVE TO GIVE US A PROPER WELCOME?
THERE ARE NO DRONES.
SHE'S ALL *ALONE*.
AND VERY *OLD*.
HOW IS IT YOU *KNOW* THAT, CARYN?
IN FACT, HOW IS IT YOU SEEM TO BE ON INTIMATE TERMS WITH BOTH ALIENS *AND* PREDATORS, TO THE POINT WHERE YOU'VE ACTUALLY GIVEN THE PREDATOR A *NAME?*
WHO-- *WHAT*-- THE HELL *ARE* YOU?!!
MARIA-- I--!
RRAWR!

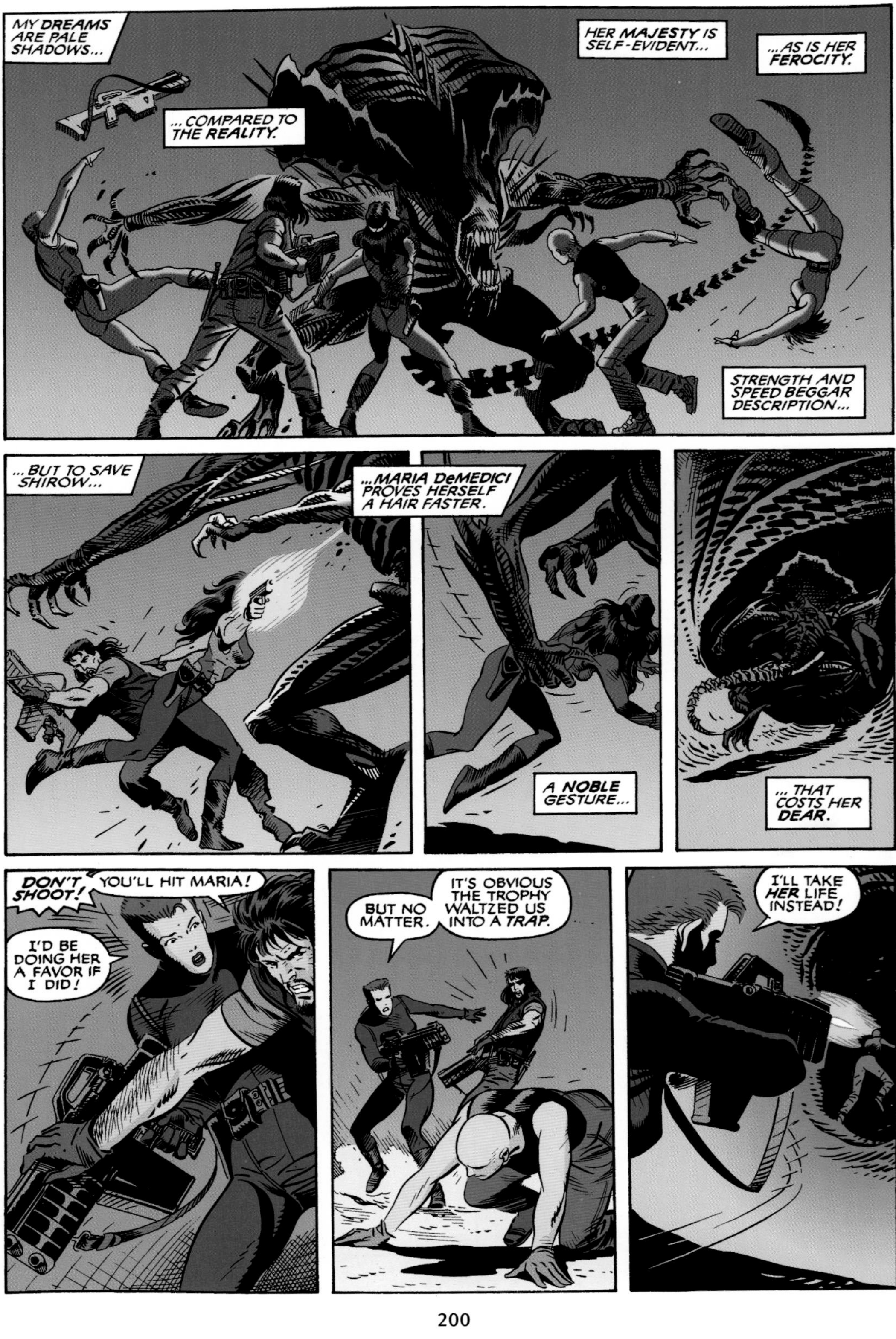

MY DREAMS ARE PALE SHADOWS...
...COMPARED TO THE REALITY.
HER MAJESTY IS SELF-EVIDENT...
...AS IS HER FEROCITY.
STRENGTH AND SPEED BEGGAR DESCRIPTION...
...BUT TO SAVE SHIROW...
...MARIA DeMEDICI PROVES HERSELF A HAIR FASTER.
A NOBLE GESTURE...
...THAT COSTS HER DEAR.
DON'T SHOOT!
YOU'LL HIT MARIA!
I'D BE DOING HER A FAVOR IF I DID!
IT'S OBVIOUS THE TROPHY WALTZED US INTO A TRAP.
BUT NO MATTER.
I'LL TAKE HER LIFE INSTEAD!

OW!

DON'T STOP
DON'T STOP

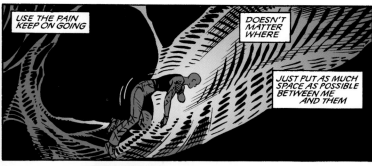

USE THE PAIN
KEEP ON GOING

DOESN'T
MATTER
WHERE

JUST PUT AS MUCH
SPACE AS POSSIBLE
BETWEEN ME
AND THEM

SAME AS
HONDURAS.

WHEN I RAN FROM
BIG MAMA.

THOUGHT THAT
WAS A *VIRTUAL*
SCENARIO. AN
AMUSEMENT
CREATED FOR
ME BY *TOY*.

SURVIVED THEN.

HELL, I
WON!

ONE THING HASN'T
CHANGED. I *HEAL*
IMPOSSIBLY FAST.

EVEN AS I TUMBLE
THROUGH YET
ANOTHER FALL I
REALIZE...

...I'M NO
LONGER
BLEEDING.

MY ARM
DOESN'T
EVEN HURT.

WHAT'S
THIS?!

DOG
TAGS?!

I KNOW WHAT
THEY ARE.

I KNOW THE *NAME*
IMPRINTED ON THEM.

I KNOW
THE *MAN*
COCOONED
AGAINST
THE FAR
WALL.

I KNOW THIS
PLACE.

SUDDENLY,
WITH THE
BLINDING
CLARITY OF
MADNESS...

...I *KNOW*
SO MANY
THINGS.

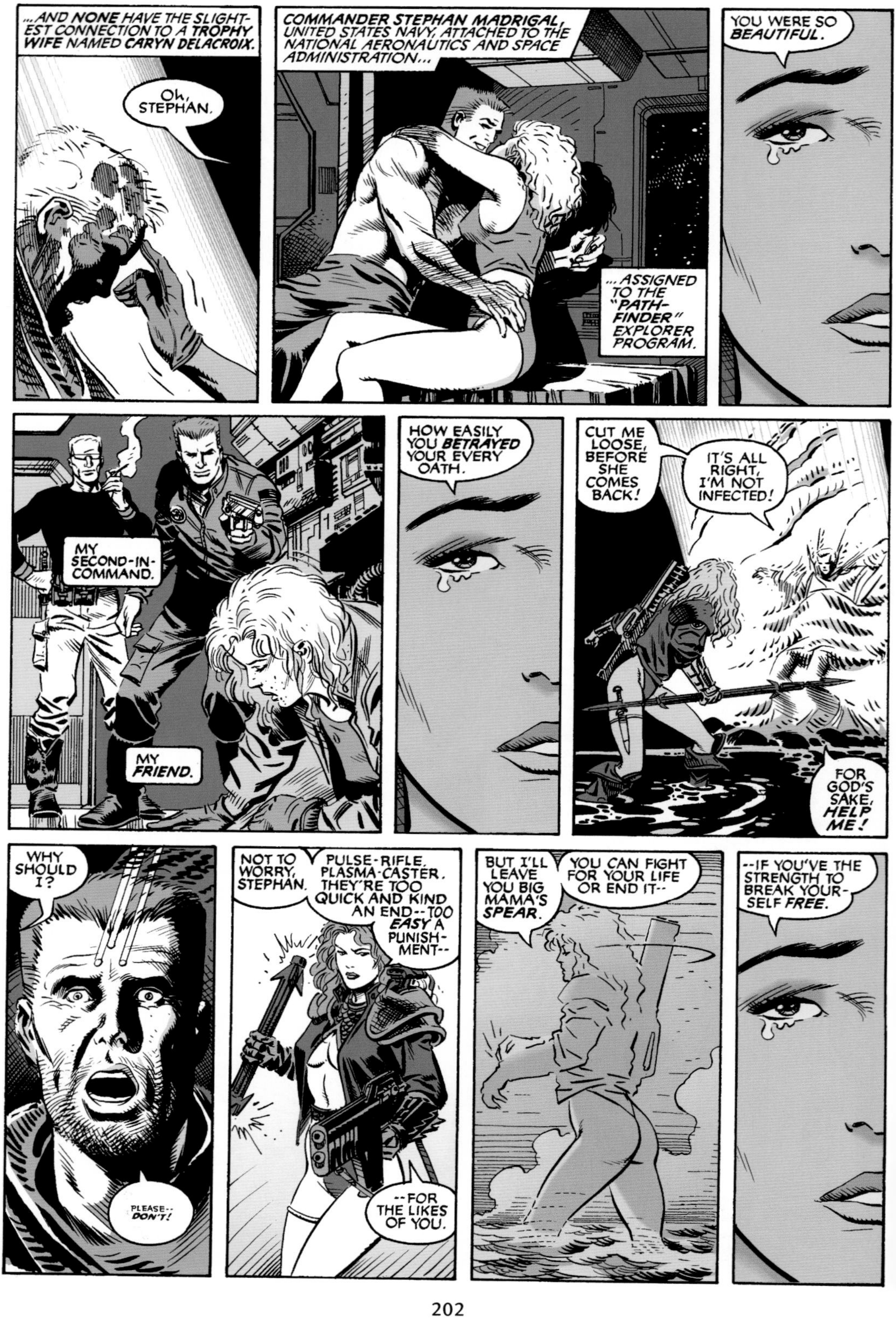
...AND NONE HAVE THE SLIGHTEST CONNECTION TO A TROPHY WIFE NAMED CARYN DELACROIX.
Oh, STEPHAN.
COMMANDER STEPHAN MADRIGAL, UNITED STATES NAVY, ATTACHED TO THE NATIONAL AERONAUTICS AND SPACE ADMINISTRATION...
...ASSIGNED TO THE "PATHFINDER" EXPLORER PROGRAM.
YOU WERE SO BEAUTIFUL.
MY SECOND-IN-COMMAND.
MY FRIEND.
HOW EASILY YOU BETRAYED YOUR EVERY OATH.
CUT ME LOOSE, BEFORE SHE COMES BACK!
IT'S ALL RIGHT, I'M NOT INFECTED!
FOR GOD'S SAKE, HELP ME!
WHY SHOULD I?
PLEASE-- DON'T!
NOT TO WORRY, STEPHAN.
PULSE-RIFLE, PLASMA-CASTER. THEY'RE TOO QUICK AND KIND AN END--TOO EASY A PUNISHMENT--
--FOR THE LIKES OF YOU.
BUT I'LL LEAVE YOU BIG MAMA'S SPEAR.
YOU CAN FIGHT FOR YOUR LIFE OR END IT--
--IF YOU'VE THE STRENGTH TO BREAK YOURSELF FREE.

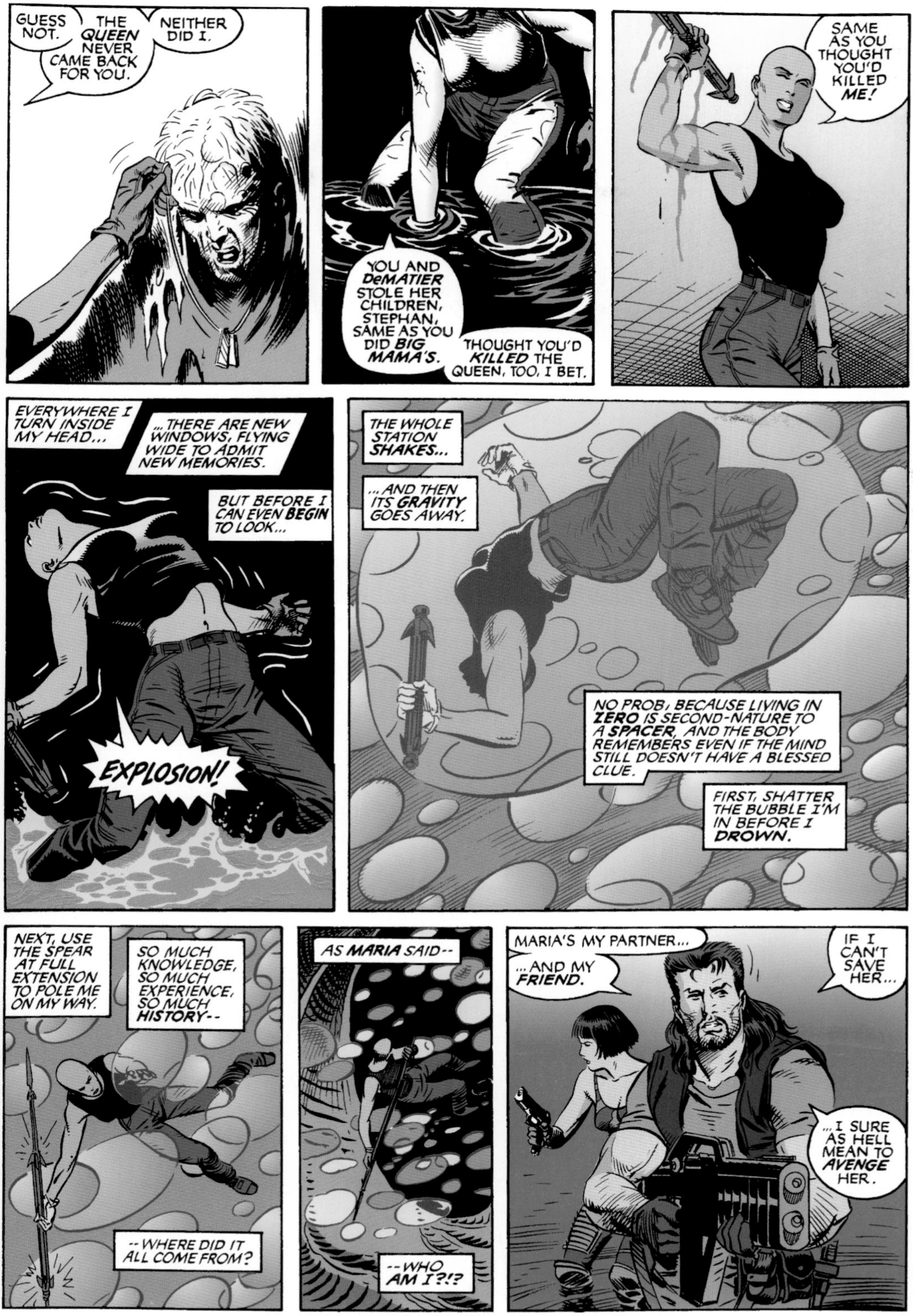
GUESS NOT.
THE QUEEN NEVER CAME BACK FOR YOU.
NEITHER DID I.
YOU AND DeMATIER STOLE HER CHILDREN, STEPHAN, SAME AS YOU DID BIG MAMA'S.
THOUGHT YOU'D KILLED THE QUEEN, TOO, I BET.
SAME AS YOU THOUGHT YOU'D KILLED ME!
EVERYWHERE I TURN INSIDE MY HEAD...
...THERE ARE NEW WINDOWS, FLYING WIDE TO ADMIT NEW MEMORIES.
BUT BEFORE I CAN EVEN BEGIN TO LOOK...
EXPLOSION!
THE WHOLE STATION SHAKES...
...AND THEN ITS GRAVITY GOES AWAY.
NO PROB, BECAUSE LIVING IN ZERO IS SECOND-NATURE TO A SPACER, AND THE BODY REMEMBERS EVEN IF THE MIND STILL DOESN'T HAVE A BLESSED CLUE.
FIRST, SHATTER THE BUBBLE I'M IN BEFORE I DROWN.
NEXT, USE THE SPEAR AT FULL EXTENSION TO POLE ME ON MY WAY.
SO MUCH KNOWLEDGE, SO MUCH EXPERIENCE, SO MUCH HISTORY--
--WHERE DID IT ALL COME FROM?
AS MARIA SAID--
--WHO AM I?!?
MARIA'S MY PARTNER...
...AND MY FRIEND.
IF I CAN'T SAVE HER...
...I SURE AS HELL MEAN TO AVENGE HER.

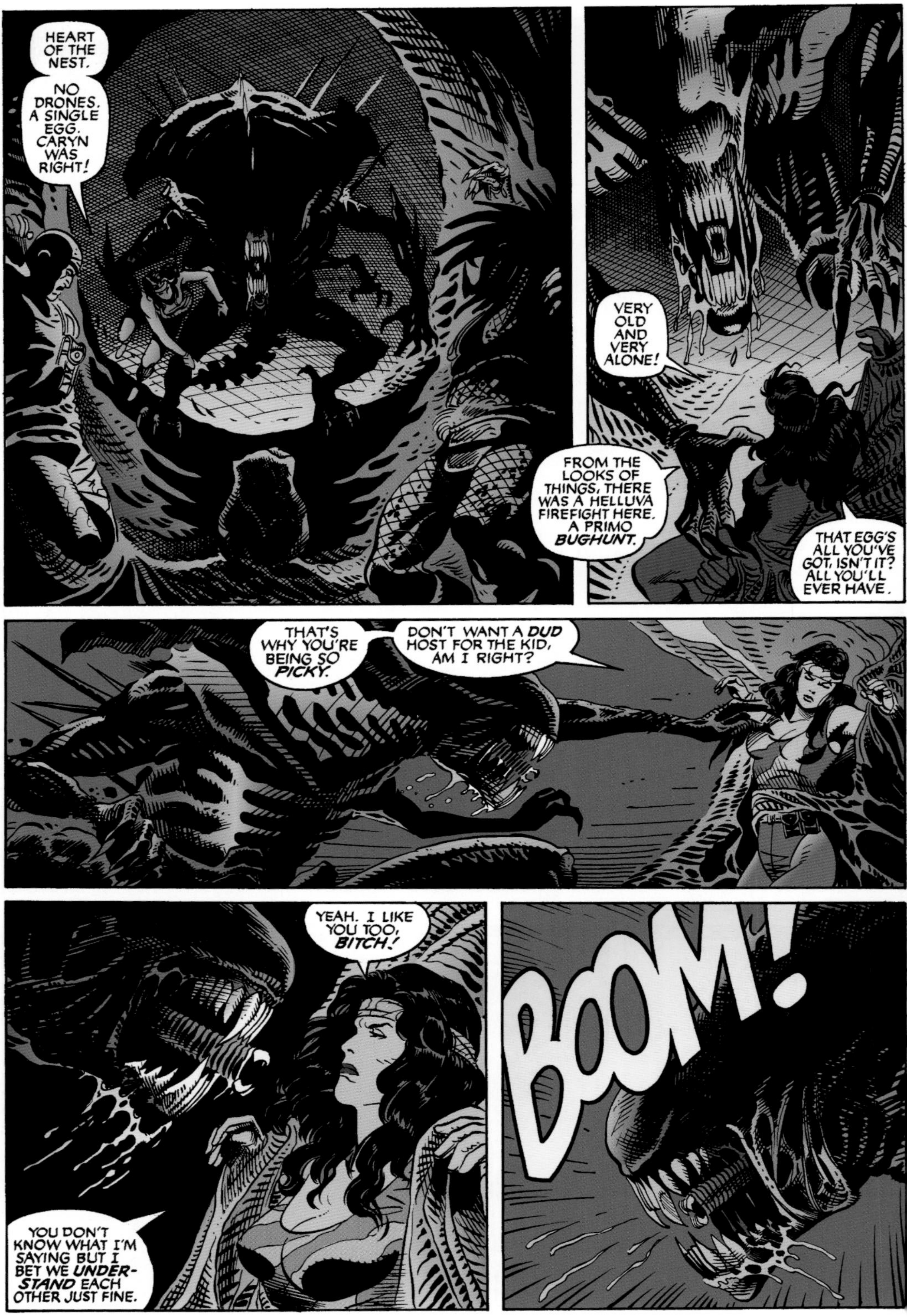
HEART OF THE NEST.
NO DRONES. A SINGLE EGG. CARYN WAS RIGHT!
VERY OLD AND VERY ALONE!
FROM THE LOOKS OF THINGS, THERE WAS A HELLUVA FIREFIGHT HERE. A PRIMO BUGHUNT.
THAT EGG'S ALL YOU'VE GOT, ISN'T IT? ALL YOU'LL EVER HAVE.
THAT'S WHY YOU'RE BEING SO PICKY.
DON'T WANT A DUD HOST FOR THE KID, AM I RIGHT?
YEAH. I LIKE YOU TOO, BITCH!
YOU DON'T KNOW WHAT I'M SAYING BUT I BET WE UNDERSTAND EACH OTHER JUST FINE.
BOOM!

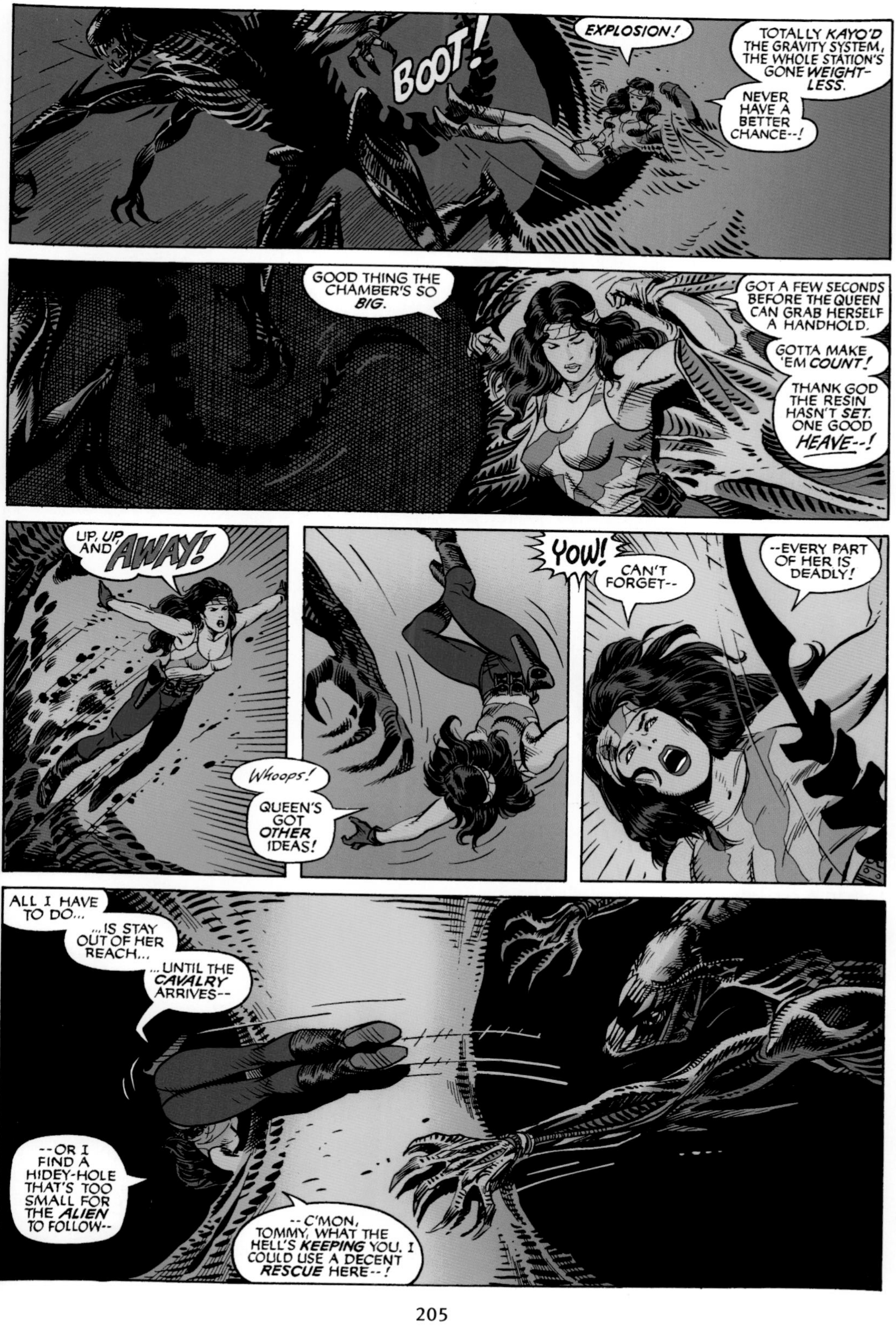
BOOT!
EXPLOSION!
TOTALLY KAYO'D THE GRAVITY SYSTEM, THE WHOLE STATION'S GONE WEIGHT-LESS.
NEVER HAVE A BETTER CHANCE--!
GOOD THING THE CHAMBER'S SO BIG.
GOT A FEW SECONDS BEFORE THE QUEEN CAN GRAB HERSELF A HANDHOLD.
GOTTA MAKE 'EM COUNT!
THANK GOD THE RESIN HASN'T SET. ONE GOOD HEAVE--!
UP, UP AND AWAY!
Whoops!
QUEEN'S GOT OTHER IDEAS!
YOW!
CAN'T FORGET--
--EVERY PART OF HER IS DEADLY!
ALL I HAVE TO DO...
...IS STAY OUT OF HER REACH...
...UNTIL THE CAVALRY ARRIVES--
--OR I FIND A HIDEY-HOLE THAT'S TOO SMALL FOR THE ALIEN TO FOLLOW--
--C'MON, TOMMY, WHAT THE HELL'S KEEPING YOU. I COULD USE A DECENT RESCUE HERE--!

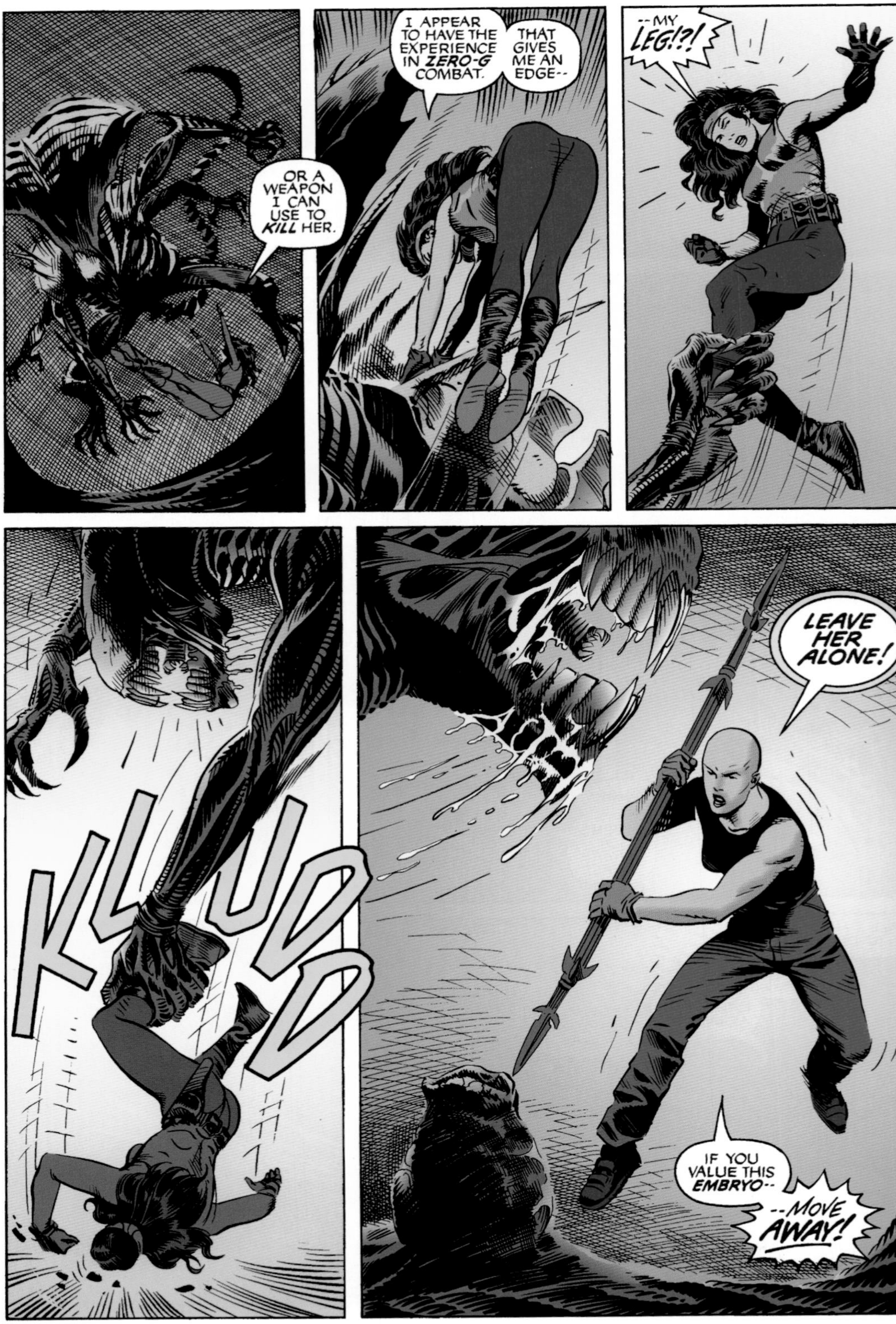
OR A WEAPON I CAN USE TO KILL HER.
I APPEAR TO HAVE THE EXPERIENCE IN ZERO-G COMBAT.
THAT GIVES ME AN EDGE--
--MY LEG!?!
KLUDD
LEAVE HER ALONE!
IF YOU VALUE THIS EMBRYO--
--MOVE AWAY!

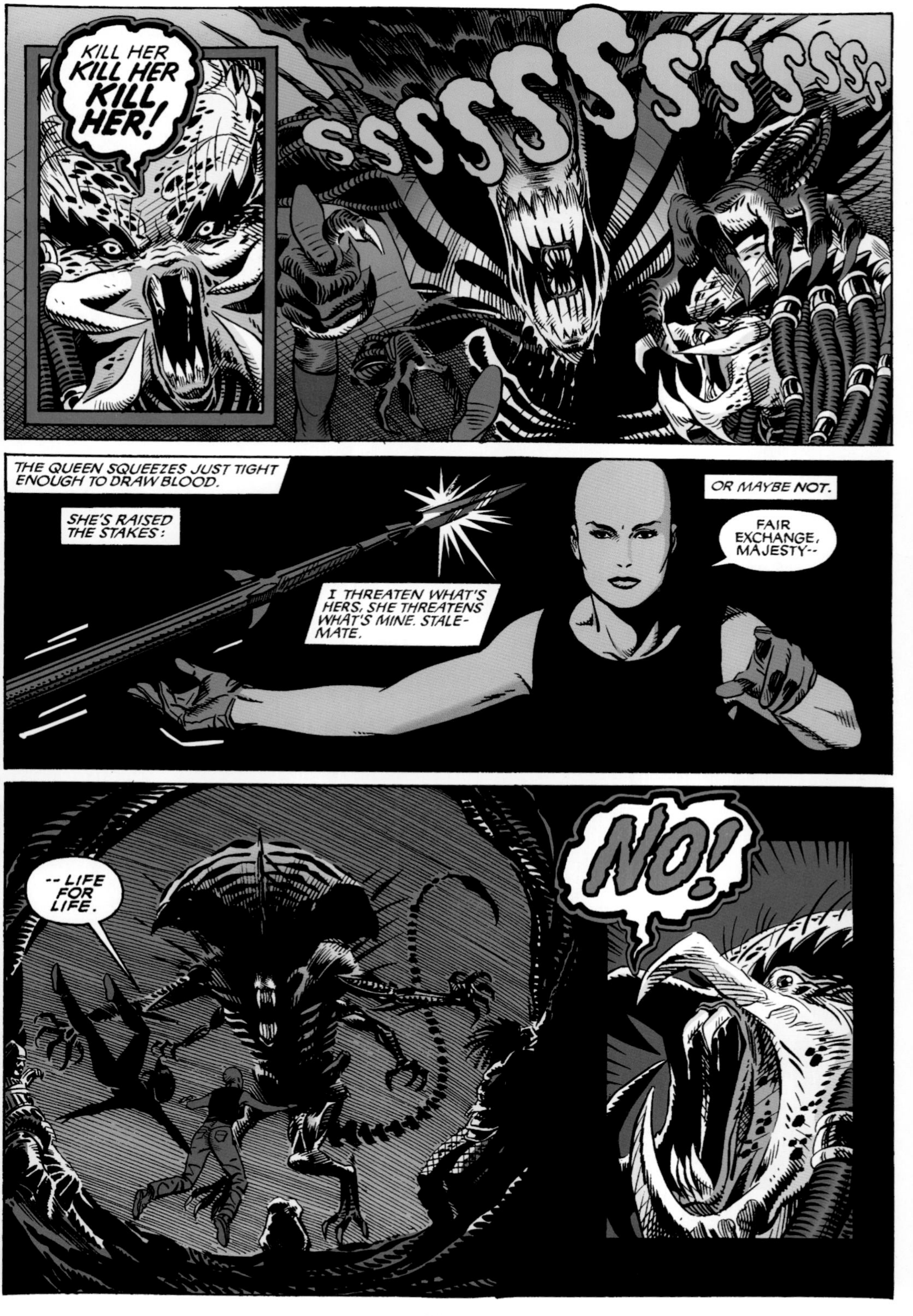

KILL HER KILL HER KILL HER!
SSSSSSSSSSSSSS
THE QUEEN SQUEEZES JUST TIGHT ENOUGH TO DRAW BLOOD.
SHE'S RAISED THE STAKES:
I THREATEN WHAT'S HERS, SHE THREATENS WHAT'S MINE. STALE-MATE.
OR MAYBE NOT.
FAIR EXCHANGE, MAJESTY--
--LIFE FOR LIFE.
NO!

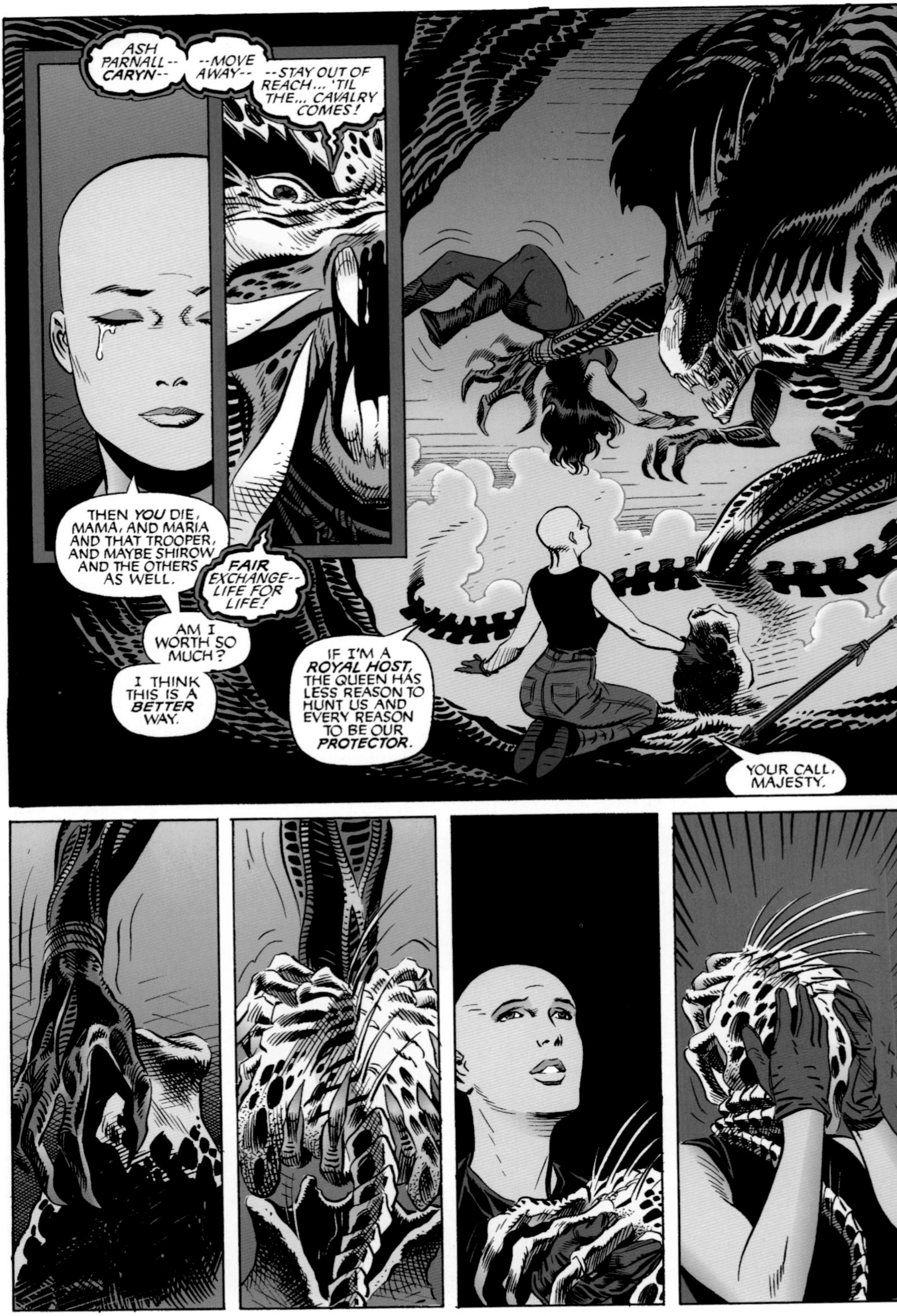
ASH PARNALL-- CARYN--
--MOVE AWAY--
--STAY OUT OF REACH... 'TIL THE... CAVALRY COMES!
THEN *YOU* DIE, MAMA, AND MARIA AND THAT TROOPER, AND MAYBE SHIROW AND THE OTHERS AS WELL.
FAIR EXCHANGE-- LIFE FOR LIFE!
AM I WORTH SO MUCH?
I THINK THIS IS A *BETTER* WAY.
IF I'M A *ROYAL HOST*, THE QUEEN HAS LESS REASON TO HUNT US AND EVERY REASON TO BE OUR *PROTECTOR*.
YOUR CALL, MAJESTY.

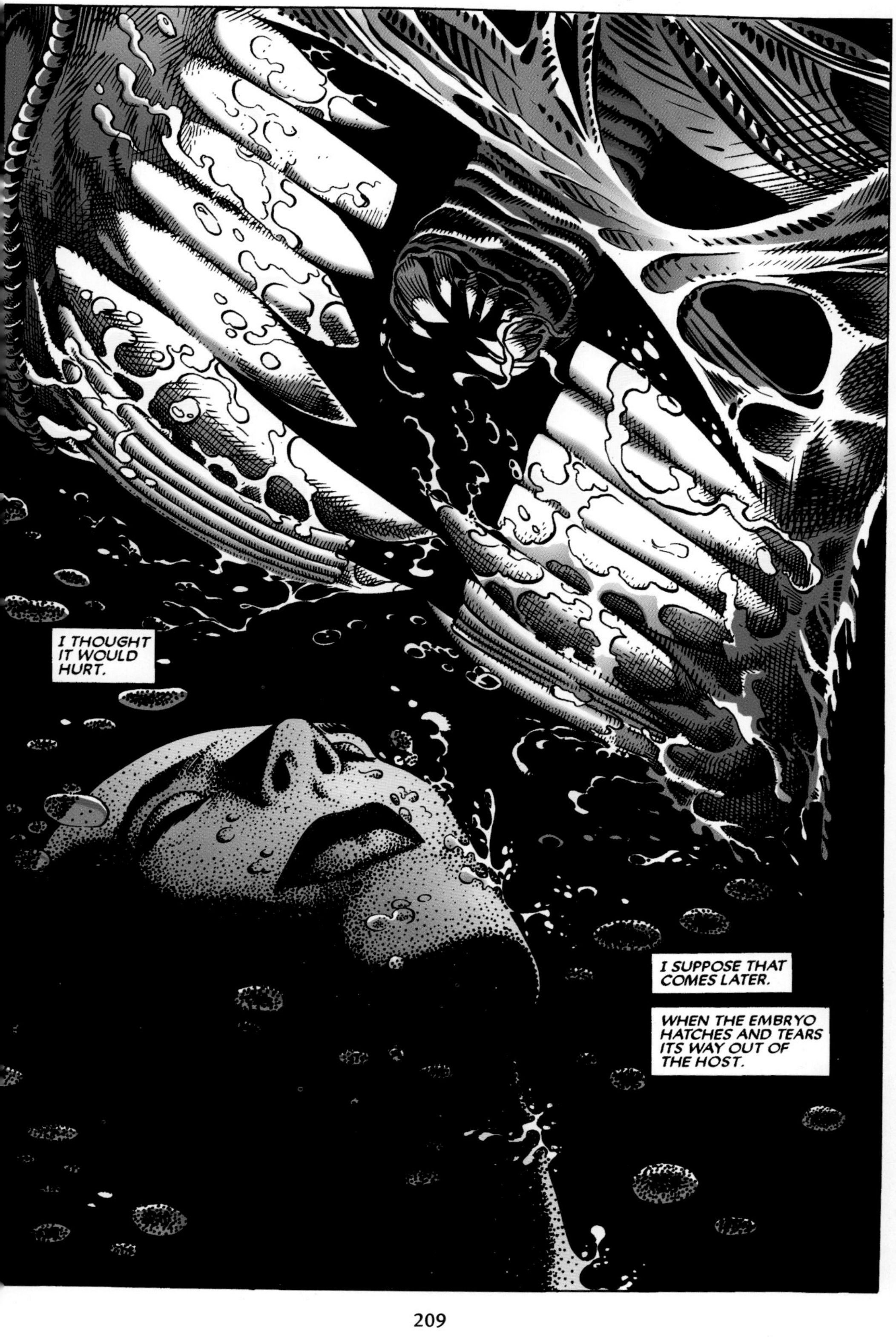
I THOUGHT IT WOULD HURT.
I SUPPOSE THAT COMES LATER.
WHEN THE EMBRYO HATCHES AND TEARS ITS WAY OUT OF THE HOST.

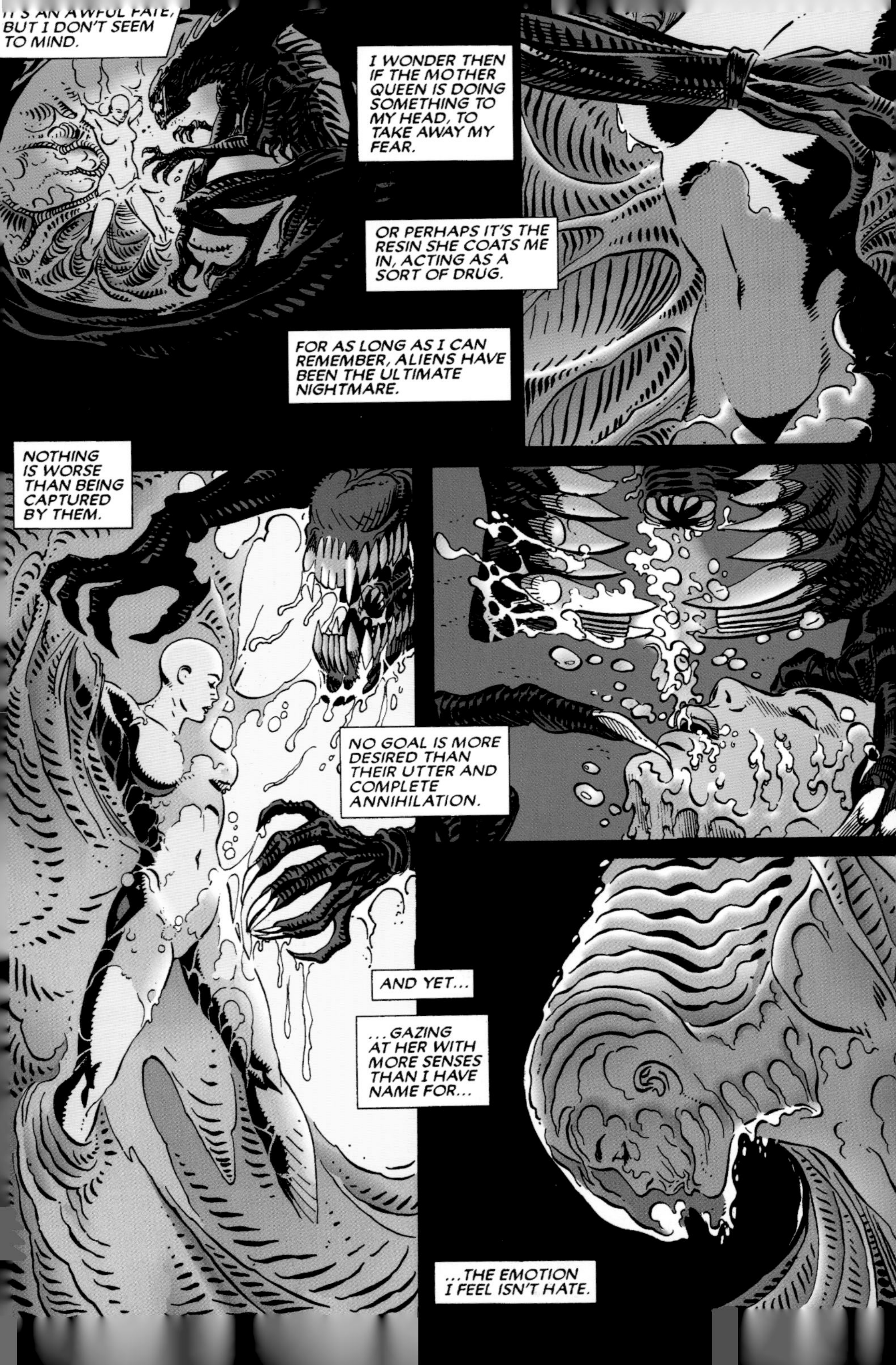
IT'S AN AWFUL FATE, BUT I DON'T SEEM TO MIND.
I WONDER THEN IF THE MOTHER QUEEN IS DOING SOMETHING TO MY HEAD, TO TAKE AWAY MY FEAR.
OR PERHAPS IT'S THE RESIN SHE COATS ME IN, ACTING AS A SORT OF DRUG.
FOR AS LONG AS I CAN REMEMBER, ALIENS HAVE BEEN THE ULTIMATE NIGHTMARE.
NOTHING IS WORSE THAN BEING CAPTURED BY THEM.
NO GOAL IS MORE DESIRED THAN THEIR UTTER AND COMPLETE ANNIHILATION.
AND YET...
...GAZING AT HER WITH MORE SENSES THAN I HAVE NAME FOR...
...THE EMOTION I FEEL ISN'T HATE.

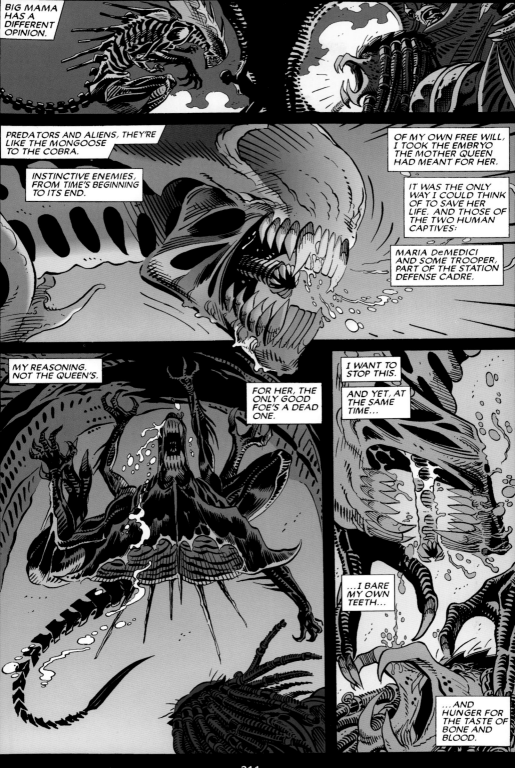

BIG MAMA HAS A DIFFERENT OPINION.

PREDATORS AND ALIENS, THEY'RE LIKE THE MONGOOSE TO THE COBRA.

INSTINCTIVE ENEMIES, FROM TIME'S BEGINNING TO ITS END.

OF MY OWN FREE WILL, I TOOK THE EMBRYO THE MOTHER QUEEN HAD MEANT FOR HER.

IT WAS THE ONLY WAY I COULD THINK OF TO SAVE HER LIFE. AND THOSE OF THE TWO HUMAN CAPTIVES:

MARIA DeMEDICI AND SOME TROOPER, PART OF THE STATION DEFENSE CADRE.

MY REASONING. NOT THE QUEEN'S.

FOR HER, THE ONLY GOOD FOE'S A DEAD ONE.

I WANT TO STOP THIS.

AND YET, AT THE SAME TIME...

...I BARE MY OWN TEETH...

...AND HUNGER FOR THE TASTE OF BONE AND BLOOD.

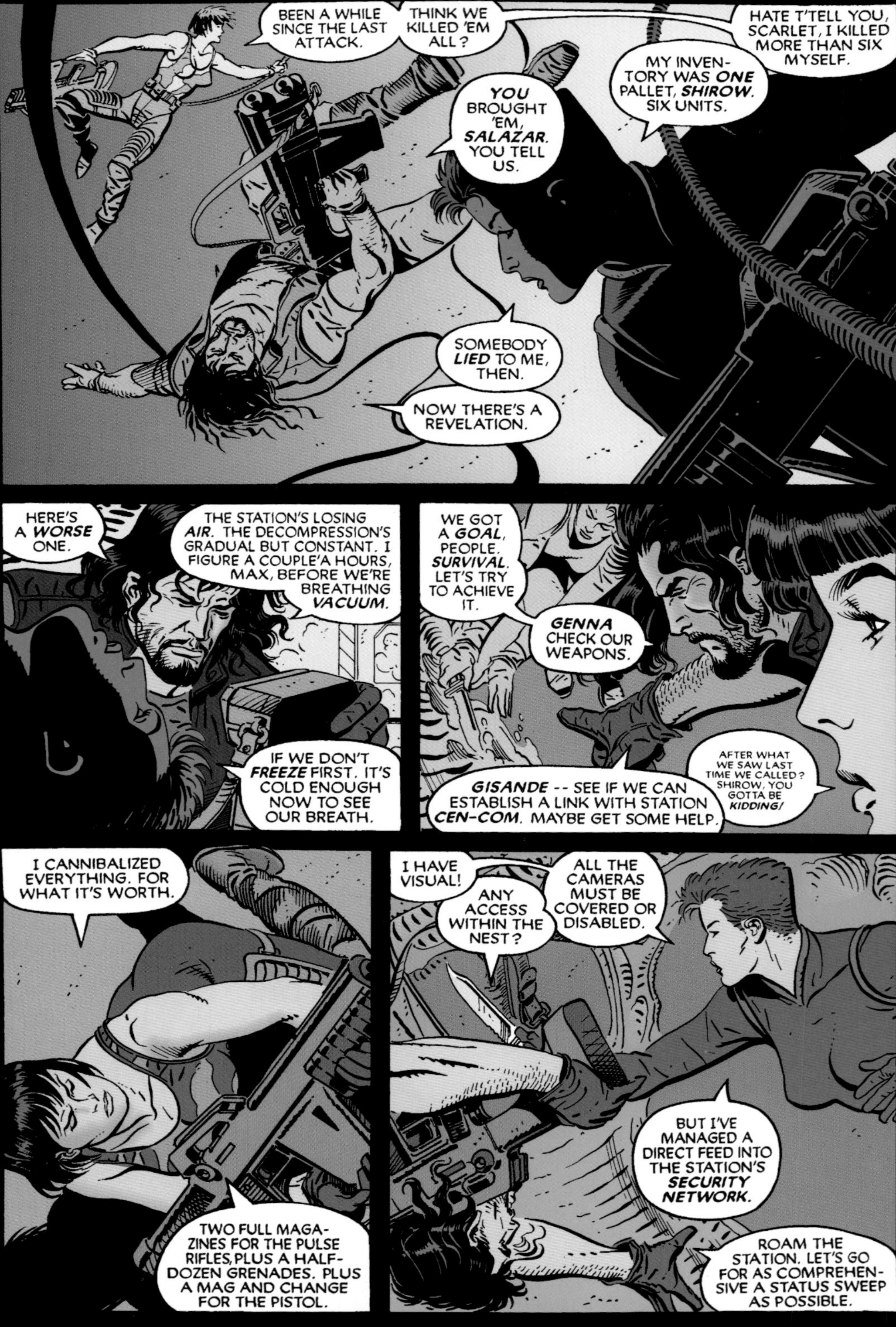
BEEN A WHILE SINCE THE LAST ATTACK.
THINK WE KILLED 'EM ALL?
HATE T'TELL YOU, SCARLET, I KILLED MORE THAN SIX MYSELF.
MY INVENTORY WAS ONE PALLET, SHIROW. SIX UNITS.
YOU BROUGHT 'EM, SALAZAR. YOU TELL US.
SOMEBODY LIED TO ME, THEN.
NOW THERE'S A REVELATION.
HERE'S A WORSE ONE.
THE STATION'S LOSING AIR. THE DECOMPRESSION'S GRADUAL BUT CONSTANT. I FIGURE A COUPLE'A HOURS, MAX, BEFORE WE'RE BREATHING VACUUM.
IF WE DON'T FREEZE FIRST. IT'S COLD ENOUGH NOW TO SEE OUR BREATH.
WE GOT A GOAL, PEOPLE. SURVIVAL. LET'S TRY TO ACHIEVE IT.
GENNA CHECK OUR WEAPONS.
GISANDE -- SEE IF WE CAN ESTABLISH A LINK WITH STATION CEN-COM. MAYBE GET SOME HELP.
AFTER WHAT WE SAW LAST TIME WE CALLED? SHIROW, YOU GOTTA BE KIDDING!
I CANNIBALIZED EVERYTHING. FOR WHAT IT'S WORTH.
TWO FULL MAGAZINES FOR THE PULSE RIFLES, PLUS A HALF-DOZEN GRENADES. PLUS A MAG AND CHANGE FOR THE PISTOL.
I HAVE VISUAL!
ALL THE CAMERAS MUST BE COVERED OR DISABLED.
ANY ACCESS WITHIN THE NEST?
BUT I'VE MANAGED A DIRECT FEED INTO THE STATION'S SECURITY NETWORK.
ROAM THE STATION. LET'S GO FOR AS COMPREHENSIVE A STATUS SWEEP AS POSSIBLE.

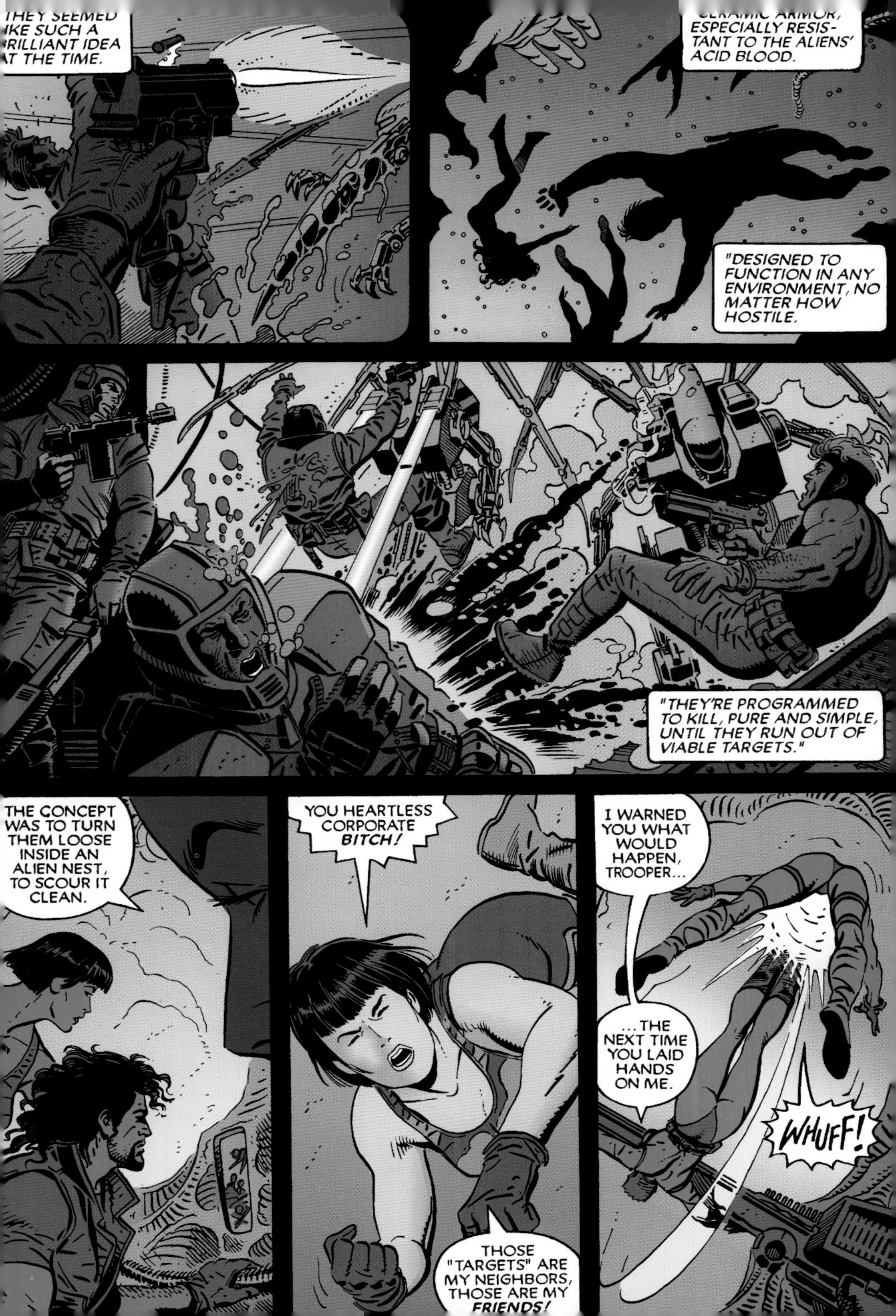
IKE SUCH A
RILLIANT IDEA
T THE TIME.
ESPECIALLY RESIS-TANT TO THE ALIENS' ACID BLOOD.
"DESIGNED TO FUNCTION IN ANY ENVIRONMENT, NO MATTER HOW HOSTILE.
"THEY'RE PROGRAMMED TO KILL, PURE AND SIMPLE, UNTIL THEY RUN OUT OF VIABLE TARGETS."
THE CONCEPT WAS TO TURN THEM LOOSE INSIDE AN ALIEN NEST, TO SCOUR IT CLEAN.
YOU HEARTLESS CORPORATE *BITCH!*
THOSE "TARGETS" ARE MY NEIGHBORS, THOSE ARE MY *FRIENDS!*
I WARNED YOU WHAT WOULD HAPPEN, TROOPER...
...THE NEXT TIME YOU LAID HANDS ON ME.
WHUFF!

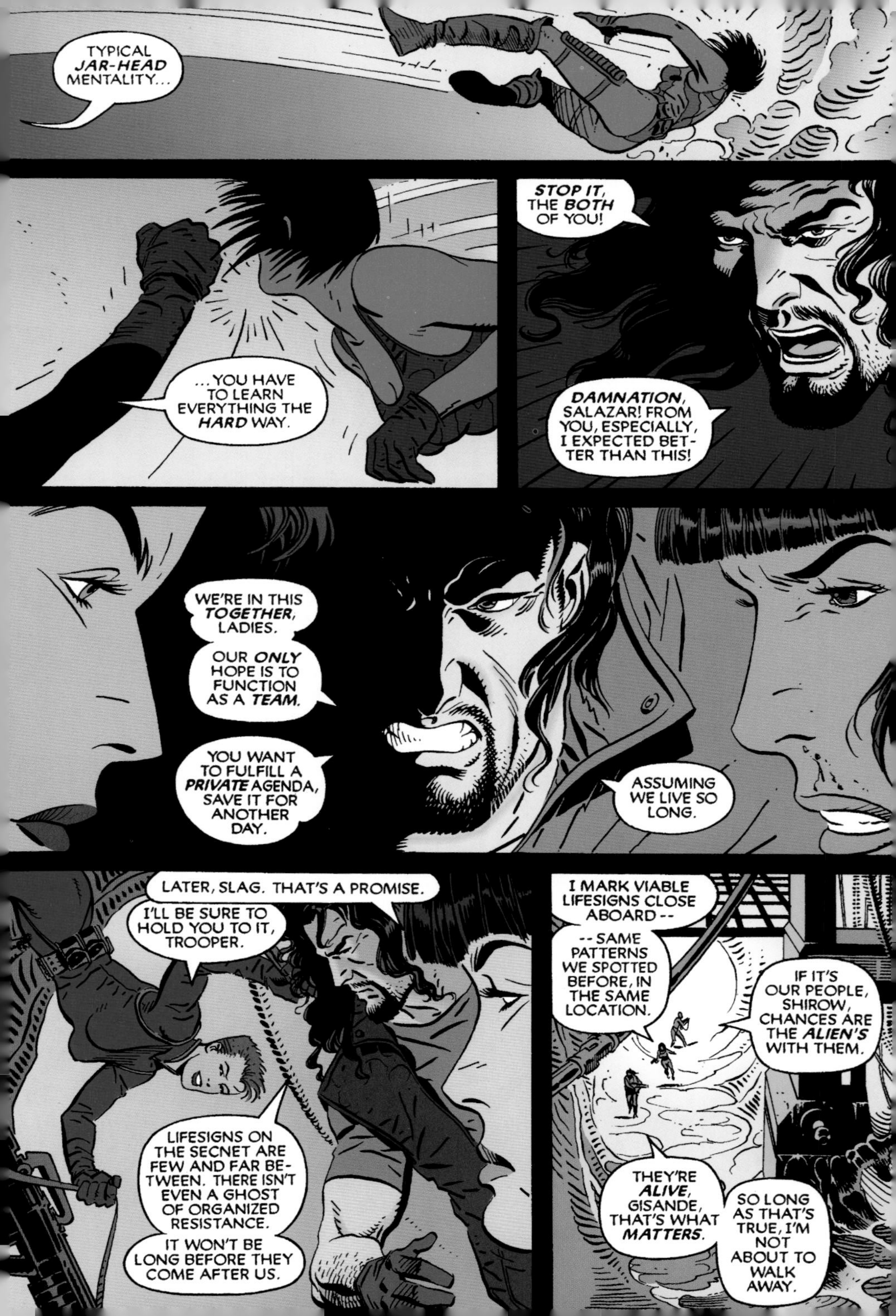
TYPICAL JAR-HEAD MENTALITY...
...YOU HAVE TO LEARN EVERYTHING THE HARD WAY.
STOP IT, THE BOTH OF YOU!
DAMNATION, SALAZAR! FROM YOU, ESPECIALLY, I EXPECTED BET-TER THAN THIS!
WE'RE IN THIS TOGETHER, LADIES.
OUR ONLY HOPE IS TO FUNCTION AS A TEAM.
YOU WANT TO FULFILL A PRIVATE AGENDA, SAVE IT FOR ANOTHER DAY.
ASSUMING WE LIVE SO LONG.
LATER, SLAG. THAT'S A PROMISE.
I'LL BE SURE TO HOLD YOU TO IT, TROOPER.
LIFESIGNS ON THE SECNET ARE FEW AND FAR BE-TWEEN. THERE ISN'T EVEN A GHOST OF ORGANIZED RESISTANCE.
IT WON'T BE LONG BEFORE THEY COME AFTER US.
I MARK VIABLE LIFESIGNS CLOSE ABOARD --
-- SAME PATTERNS WE SPOTTED BEFORE, IN THE SAME LOCATION.
IF IT'S OUR PEOPLE, SHIROW, CHANCES ARE THE ALIEN'S WITH THEM.
THEY'RE ALIVE, GISANDE, THAT'S WHAT MATTERS.
SO LONG AS THAT'S TRUE, I'M NOT ABOUT TO WALK AWAY.

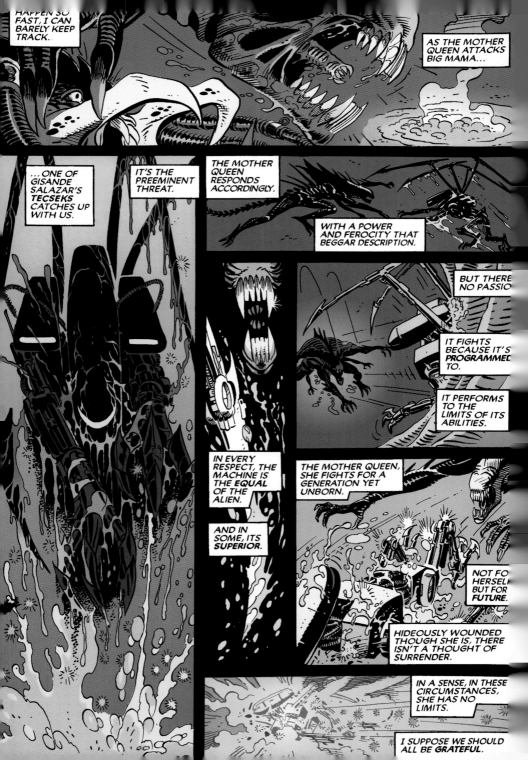

HAPPEN SO FAST, I CAN BARELY KEEP TRACK.

AS THE MOTHER QUEEN ATTACKS BIG MAMA...

...ONE OF GISANDE SALAZAR'S *TECSEKS* CATCHES UP WITH US.

IT'S THE PREEMINENT THREAT.

THE MOTHER QUEEN RESPONDS ACCORDINGLY.

WITH A POWER AND FEROCITY THAT BEGGAR DESCRIPTION.

BUT THERE NO PASSIO

IT FIGHTS BECAUSE IT'S *PROGRAMMED* TO.

IT PERFORMS TO THE LIMITS OF ITS ABILITIES.

IN EVERY RESPECT, THE MACHINE IS THE *EQUAL* OF THE ALIEN.

AND IN SOME, ITS *SUPERIOR.*

THE MOTHER QUEEN, SHE FIGHTS FOR A GENERATION YET UNBORN.

NOT FO HERSEL BUT FOR *FUTURE.*

HIDEOUSLY WOUNDED THOUGH SHE IS, THERE ISN'T A THOUGHT OF SURRENDER.

IN A SENSE, IN THESE CIRCUMSTANCES, SHE HAS NO LIMITS.

I SUPPOSE WE SHOULD ALL BE *GRATEFUL.*

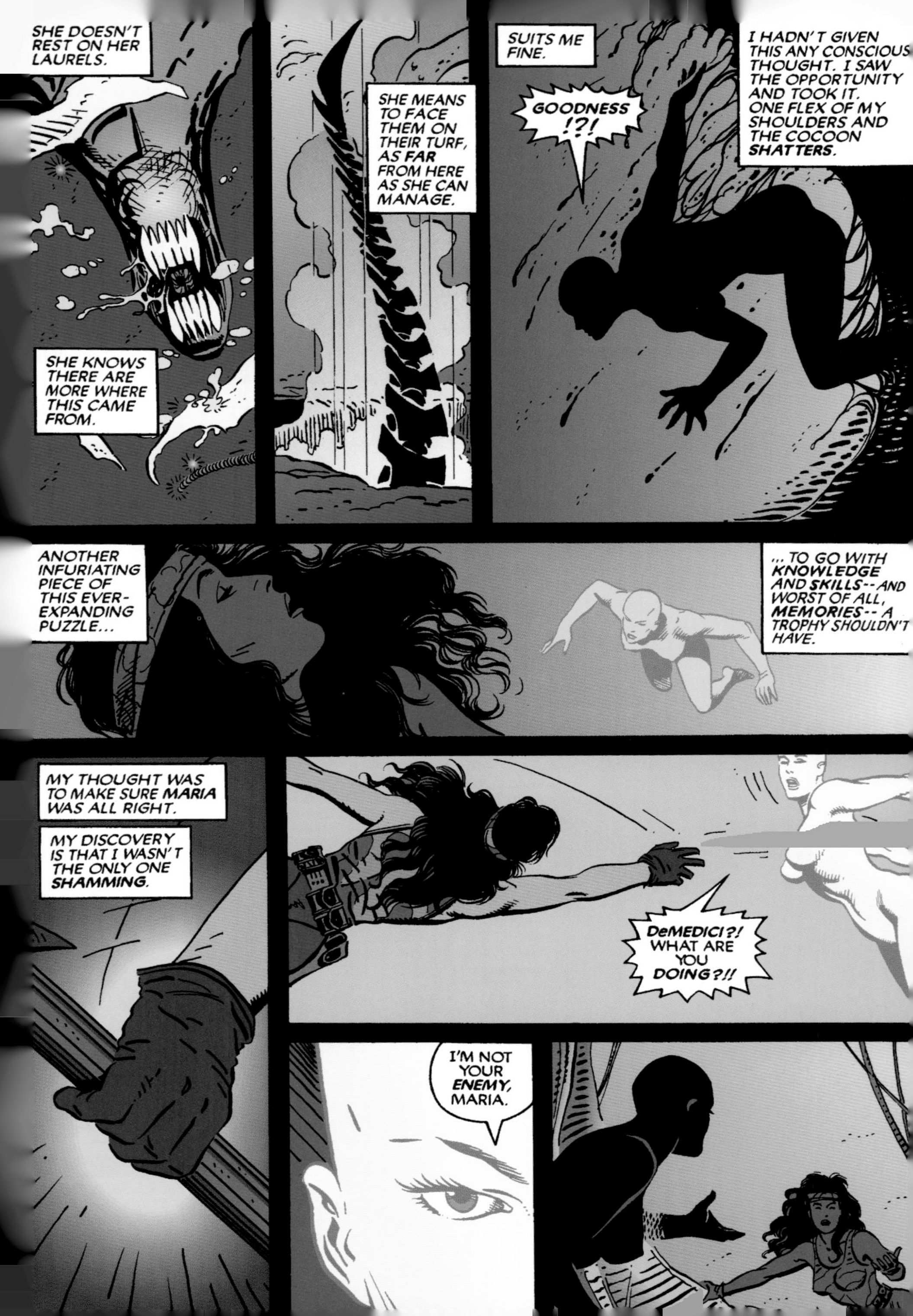
SHE DOESN'T REST ON HER LAURELS.
SHE KNOWS THERE ARE MORE WHERE THIS CAME FROM.
SHE MEANS TO FACE THEM ON THEIR TURF, AS FAR FROM HERE AS SHE CAN MANAGE.
SUITS ME FINE.
GOODNESS !?!
I HADN'T GIVEN THIS ANY CONSCIOUS THOUGHT. I SAW THE OPPORTUNITY AND TOOK IT. ONE FLEX OF MY SHOULDERS AND THE COCOON SHATTERS.
ANOTHER INFURIATING PIECE OF THIS EVER-EXPANDING PUZZLE...
... TO GO WITH KNOWLEDGE AND SKILLS-- AND WORST OF ALL, MEMORIES-- A TROPHY SHOULDN'T HAVE.
MY THOUGHT WAS TO MAKE SURE MARIA WAS ALL RIGHT.
MY DISCOVERY IS THAT I WASN'T THE ONLY ONE SHAMMING.
DeMEDICI?! WHAT ARE YOU DOING?!!
I'M NOT YOUR ENEMY, MARIA.

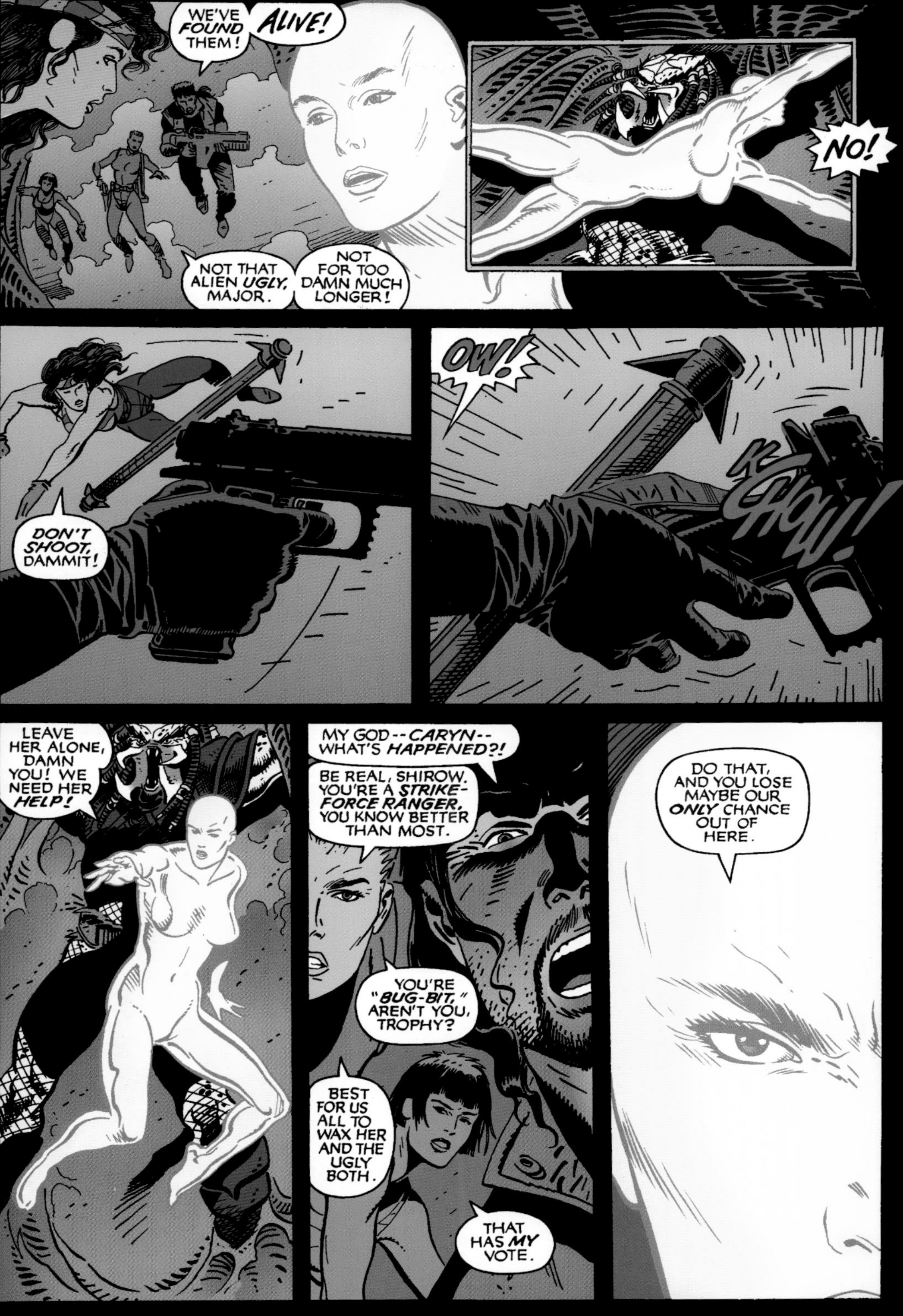
WE'VE FOUND THEM!
ALIVE!
NO!
NOT THAT ALIEN UGLY, MAJOR.
NOT FOR TOO DAMN MUCH LONGER!
DON'T SHOOT, DAMMIT!
OW!
K-CHOW!
LEAVE HER ALONE, DAMN YOU! WE NEED HER HELP!
MY GOD--CARYN--WHAT'S HAPPENED?!
BE REAL, SHIROW. YOU'RE A STRIKE-FORCE RANGER, YOU KNOW BETTER THAN MOST.
YOU'RE "BUG-BIT," AREN'T YOU, TROPHY?
BEST FOR US ALL TO WAX HER AND THE UGLY BOTH.
THAT HAS MY VOTE.
DO THAT, AND YOU LOSE MAYBE OUR ONLY CHANCE OUT OF HERE.

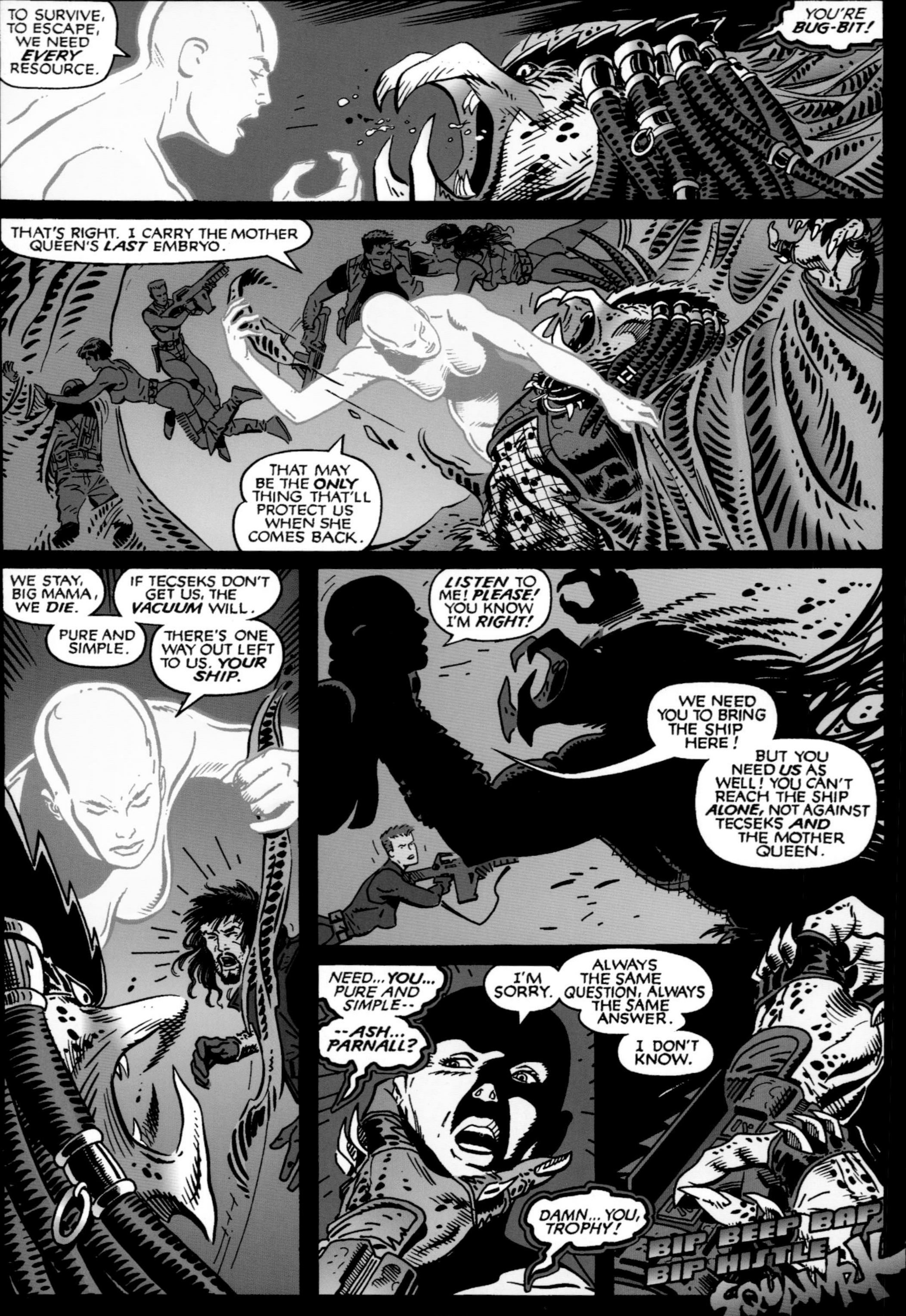
TO SURVIVE, TO ESCAPE, WE NEED EVERY RESOURCE.
YOU'RE BUG-BIT!
THAT'S RIGHT. I CARRY THE MOTHER QUEEN'S LAST EMBRYO.
THAT MAY BE THE ONLY THING THAT'LL PROTECT US WHEN SHE COMES BACK.
WE STAY, BIG MAMA, WE DIE.
IF TECSEKS DON'T GET US, THE VACUUM WILL.
PURE AND SIMPLE.
THERE'S ONE WAY OUT LEFT TO US. YOUR SHIP.
LISTEN TO ME! PLEASE! YOU KNOW I'M RIGHT!
WE NEED YOU TO BRING THE SHIP HERE!
BUT YOU NEED US AS WELL! YOU CAN'T REACH THE SHIP ALONE, NOT AGAINST TECSEKS AND THE MOTHER QUEEN.
NEED... YOU... PURE AND SIMPLE--
--ASH... PARNALL?
I'M SORRY.
ALWAYS THE SAME QUESTION, ALWAYS THE SAME ANSWER.
I DON'T KNOW.
DAMN... YOU, TROPHY!
BIP BEEP BAP
BIP HISTLE
SQUAWK

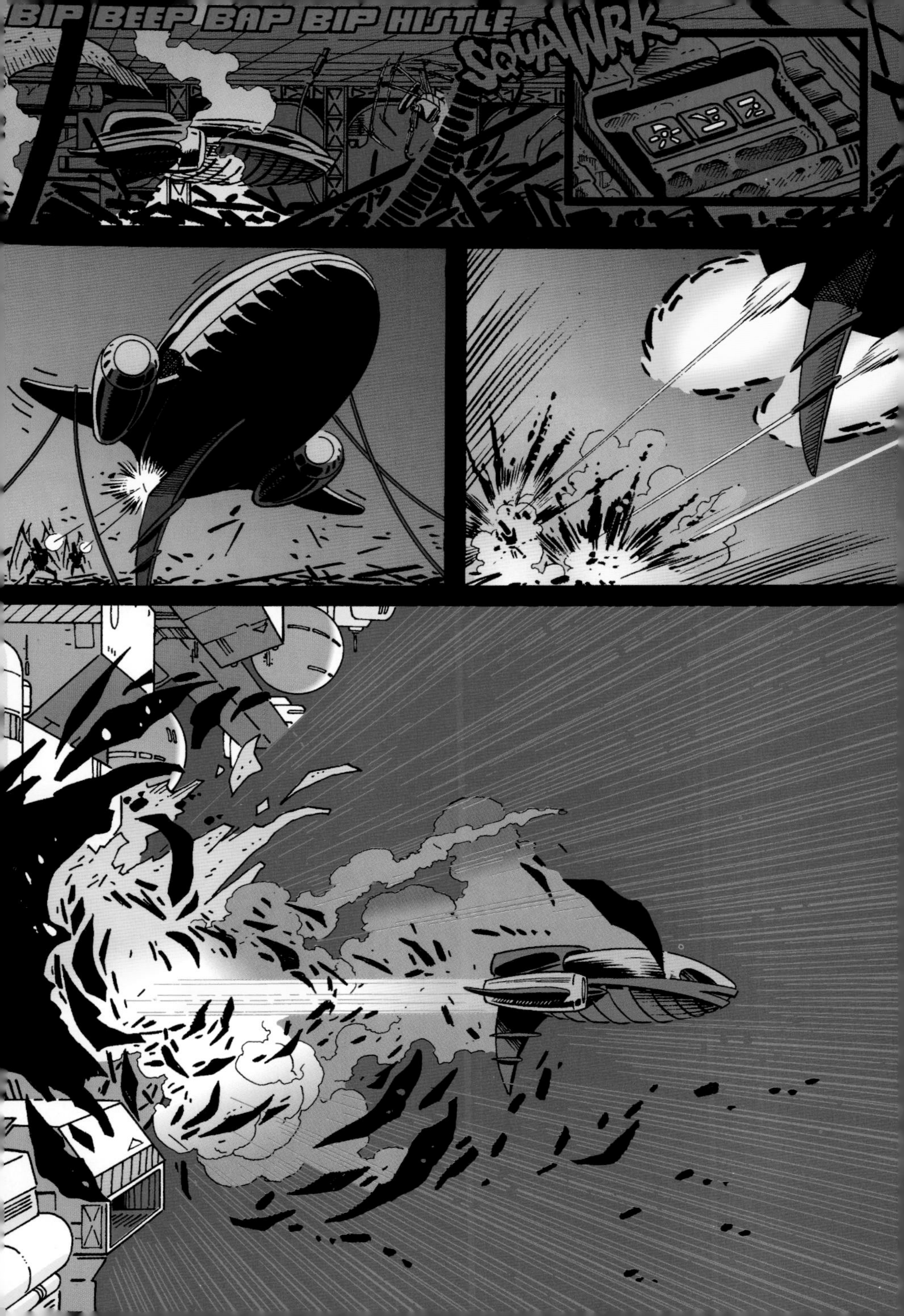
BIP BEEP BAP BIP HISTLE
SQUAWRK

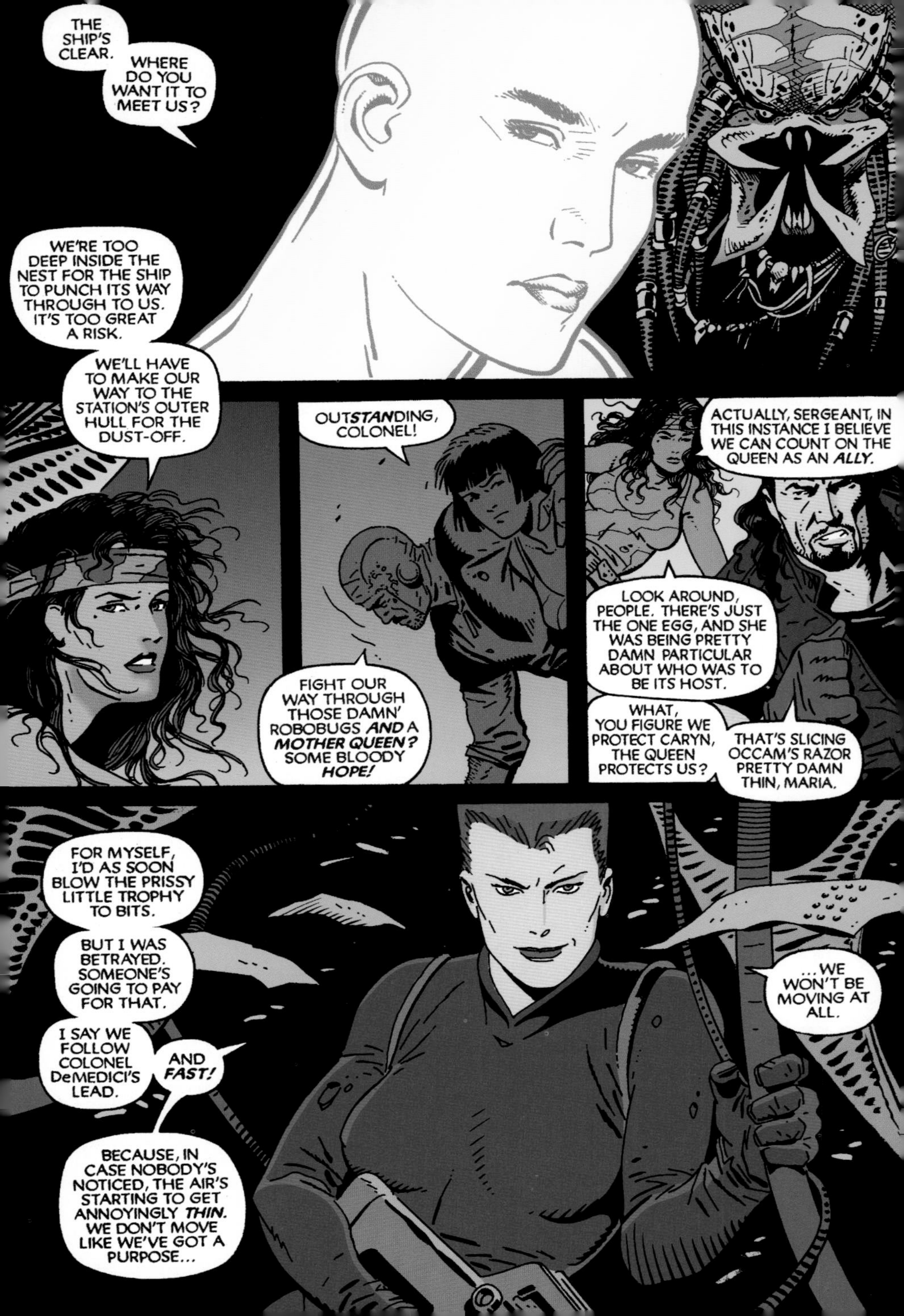
THE SHIP'S CLEAR.
WHERE DO YOU WANT IT TO MEET US?
WE'RE TOO DEEP INSIDE THE NEST FOR THE SHIP TO PUNCH ITS WAY THROUGH TO US. IT'S TOO GREAT A RISK.
WE'LL HAVE TO MAKE OUR WAY TO THE STATION'S OUTER HULL FOR THE DUST-OFF.
OUT*STAN*DING, COLONEL!
FIGHT OUR WAY THROUGH THOSE DAMN' ROBOBUGS ***AND*** A ***MOTHER QUEEN?*** SOME BLOODY ***HOPE!***
ACTUALLY, SERGEANT, IN THIS INSTANCE I BELIEVE WE CAN COUNT ON THE QUEEN AS AN *ALLY.*
LOOK AROUND, PEOPLE. THERE'S JUST THE ONE EGG, AND SHE WAS BEING PRETTY DAMN PARTICULAR ABOUT WHO WAS TO BE ITS HOST.
WHAT, YOU FIGURE WE PROTECT CARYN, THE QUEEN PROTECTS US?
THAT'S SLICING OCCAM'S RAZOR PRETTY DAMN THIN, MARIA.
FOR MYSELF, I'D AS SOON BLOW THE PRISSY LITTLE TROPHY TO BITS.
BUT I WAS BETRAYED. SOMEONE'S GOING TO PAY FOR THAT.
I SAY WE FOLLOW COLONEL DeMEDICI'S LEAD.
AND *FAST!*
BECAUSE, IN CASE NOBODY'S NOTICED, THE AIR'S STARTING TO GET ANNOYINGLY *THIN.* WE DON'T MOVE LIKE WE'VE GOT A PURPOSE...
...WE WON'T BE MOVING AT ALL.

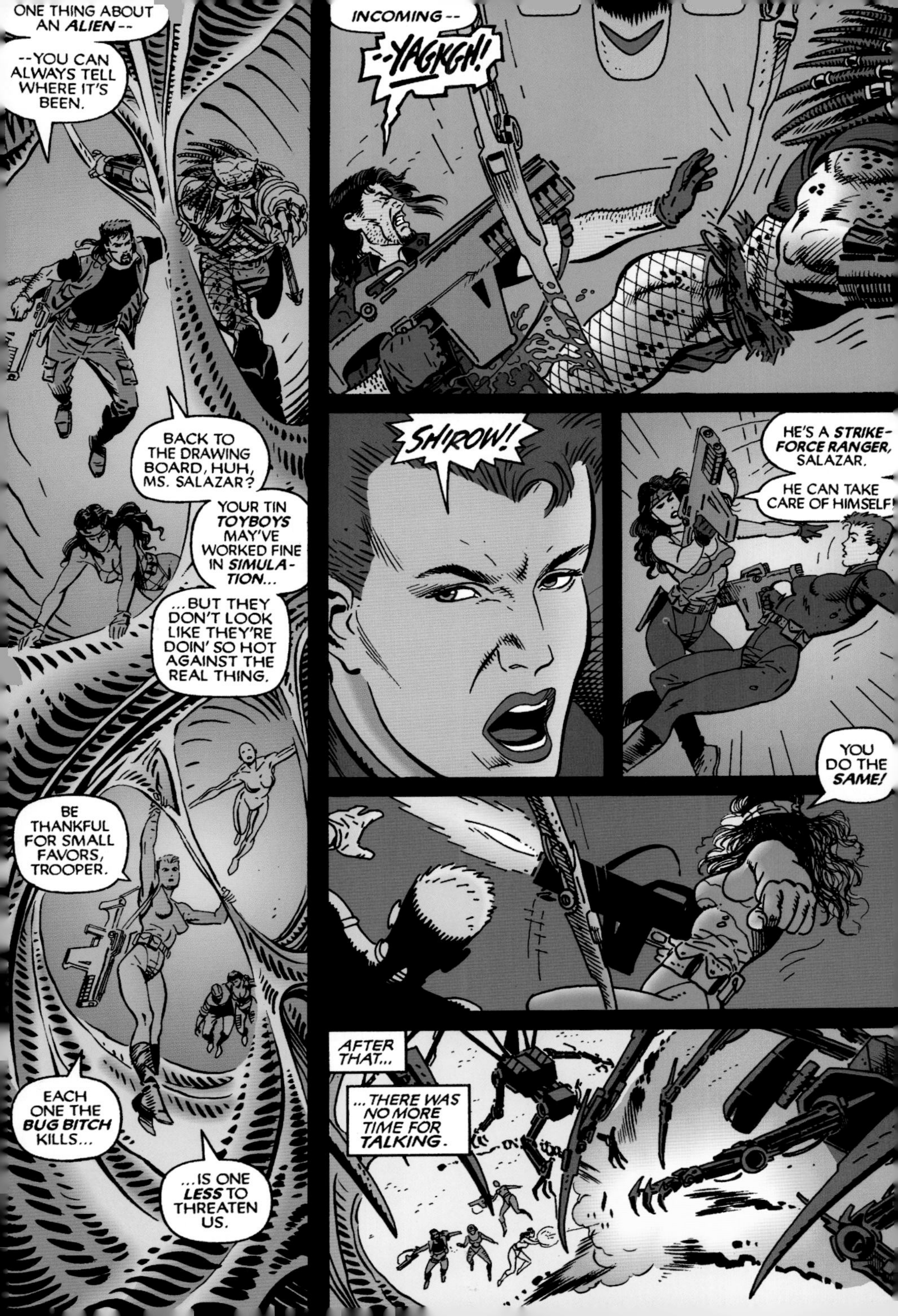
ONE THING ABOUT AN *ALIEN* --
--YOU CAN ALWAYS TELL WHERE IT'S BEEN.
BACK TO THE DRAWING BOARD, HUH, MS. SALAZAR?
YOUR TIN *TOYBOYS* MAY'VE WORKED FINE IN *SIMULATION*...
...BUT THEY DON'T LOOK LIKE THEY'RE DOIN' SO HOT AGAINST THE REAL THING.
BE THANKFUL FOR SMALL FAVORS, TROOPER.
EACH ONE THE *BUG BITCH* KILLS...
...IS ONE *LESS* TO THREATEN US.
INCOMING --
--YAGKGH!
SHIROW!!
HE'S A *STRIKE-FORCE RANGER,* SALAZAR.
HE CAN TAKE CARE OF HIMSELF!
YOU DO THE *SAME!*
AFTER THAT...
...THERE WAS NO MORE TIME FOR *TALKING*.

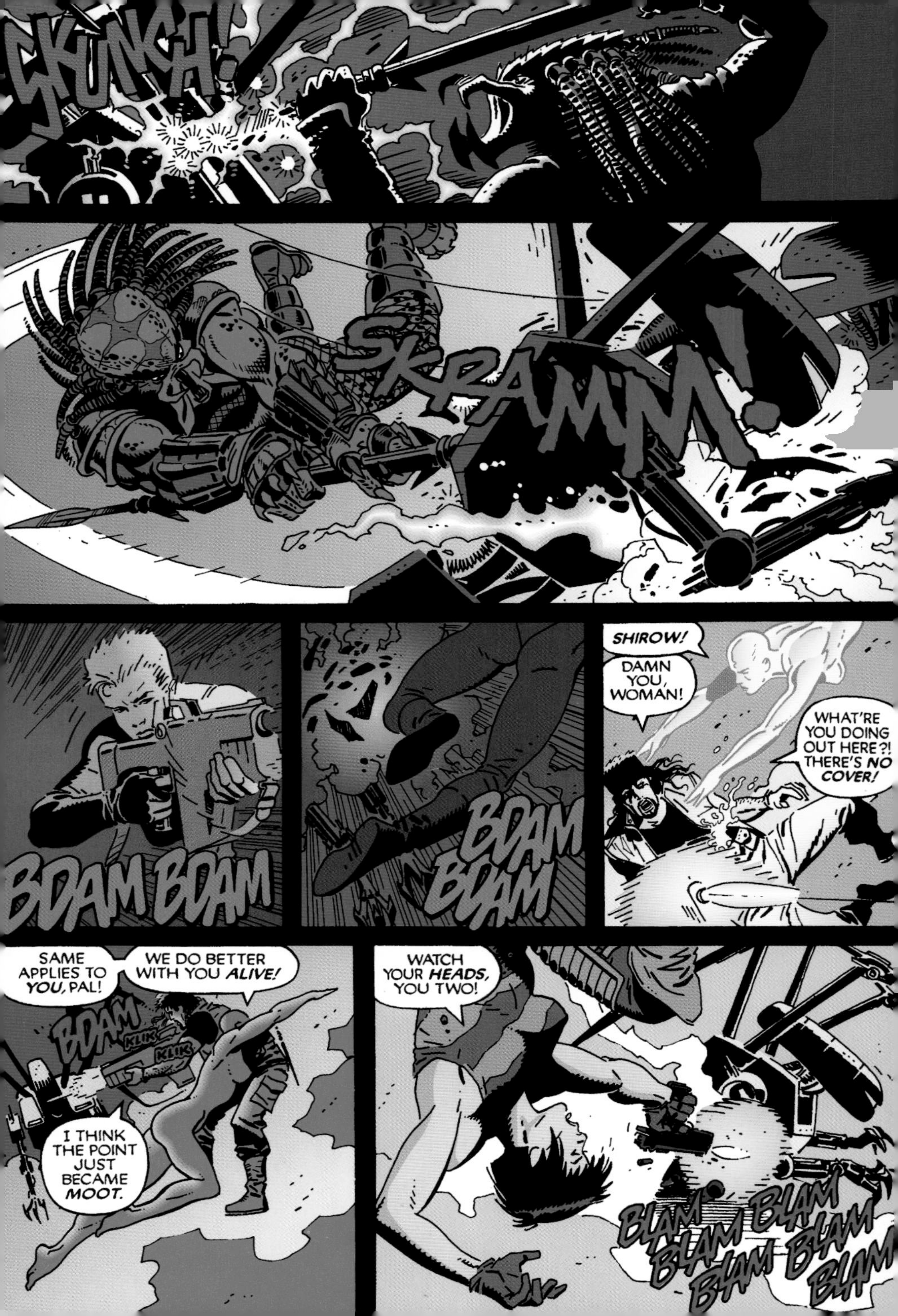
CHUNCH!
SKRAMM!
BDAM BDAM
BDAM BDAM
SHIROW!
DAMN YOU, WOMAN!
WHAT'RE YOU DOING OUT HERE?! THERE'S *NO COVER!*
SAME APPLIES TO *YOU*, PAL!
WE DO BETTER WITH YOU *ALIVE!*
BDAM
KLIK
KLIK
I THINK THE POINT JUST BECAME *MOOT.*
WATCH YOUR *HEADS,* YOU TWO!
BLAM BLAM BLAM BLAM BLAM BLAM BLAM BLAM

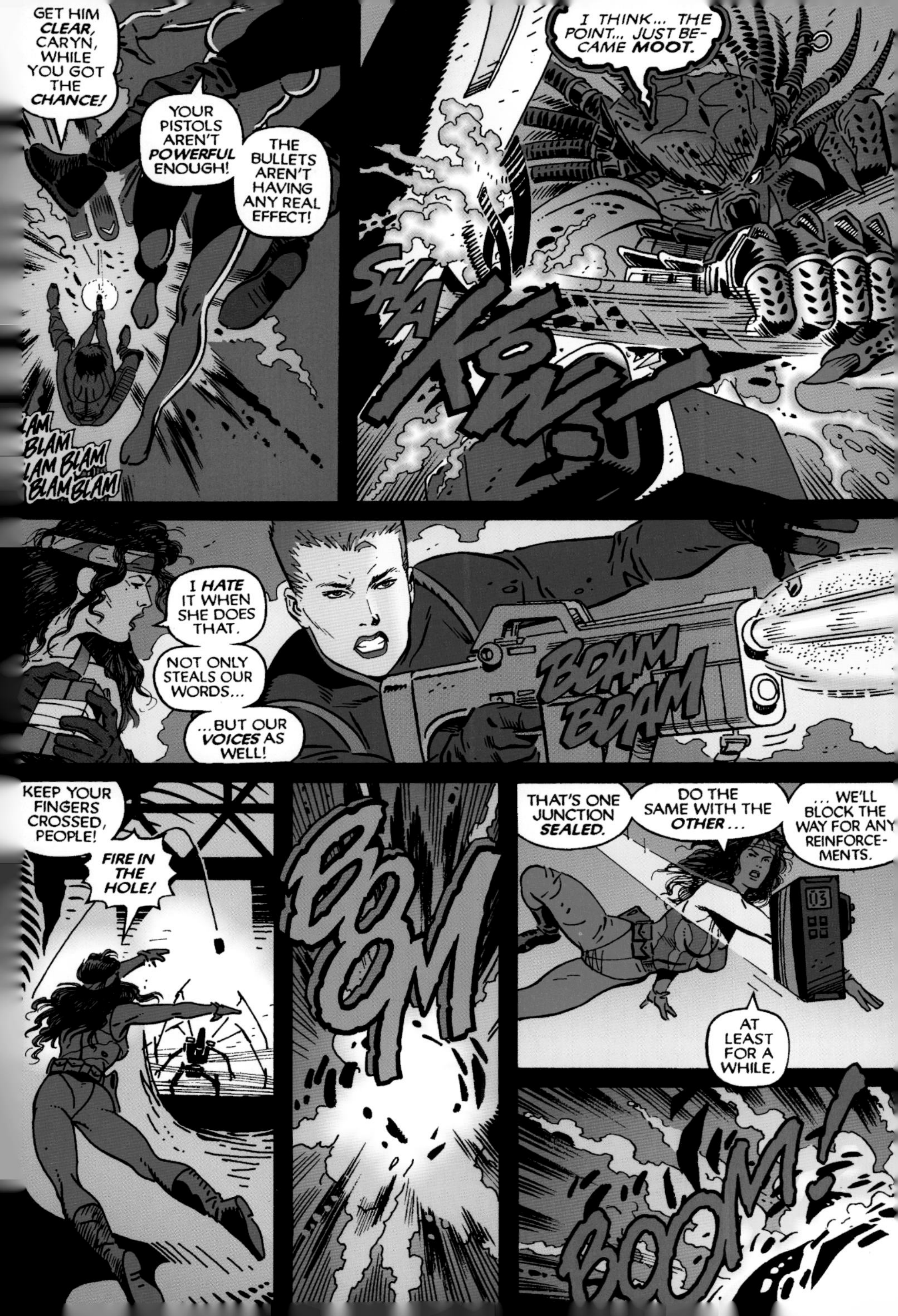
GET HIM CLEAR, CARYN, WHILE YOU GOT THE CHANCE!
YOUR PISTOLS AREN'T POWERFUL ENOUGH!
THE BULLETS AREN'T HAVING ANY REAL EFFECT!
BLAM BLAM BLAM BLAM BLAM BLAM
I THINK... THE POINT... JUST BE-CAME MOOT.
SHA KOW!
I HATE IT WHEN SHE DOES THAT.
NOT ONLY STEALS OUR WORDS...
...BUT OUR VOICES AS WELL!
BDAM BDAM
KEEP YOUR FINGERS CROSSED, PEOPLE!
FIRE IN THE HOLE!
BOOM
THAT'S ONE JUNCTION SEALED.
DO THE SAME WITH THE OTHER...
...WE'LL BLOCK THE WAY FOR ANY REINFORCE-MENTS.
AT LEAST FOR A WHILE.
BOOM!

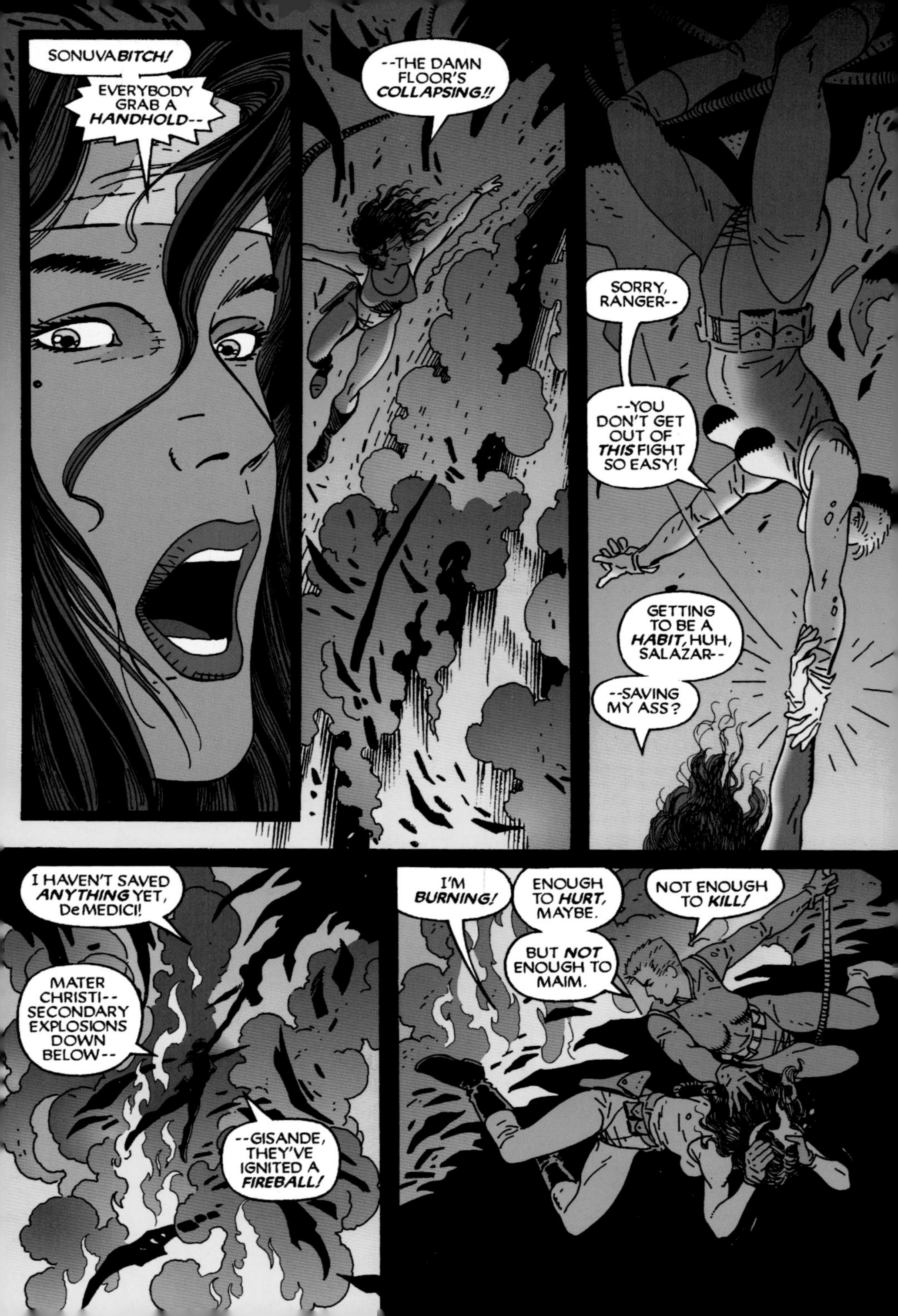
SONUVA BITCH!
EVERYBODY GRAB A HANDHOLD--
--THE DAMN FLOOR'S COLLAPSING!!
SORRY, RANGER--
--YOU DON'T GET OUT OF THIS FIGHT SO EASY!
GETTING TO BE A HABIT, HUH, SALAZAR--
--SAVING MY ASS?
I HAVEN'T SAVED ANYTHING YET, De MEDICI!
MATER CHRISTI-- SECONDARY EXPLOSIONS DOWN BELOW--
--GISANDE, THEY'VE IGNITED A FIREBALL!
I'M BURNING!
ENOUGH TO HURT, MAYBE.
BUT NOT ENOUGH TO MAIM.
NOT ENOUGH TO KILL!

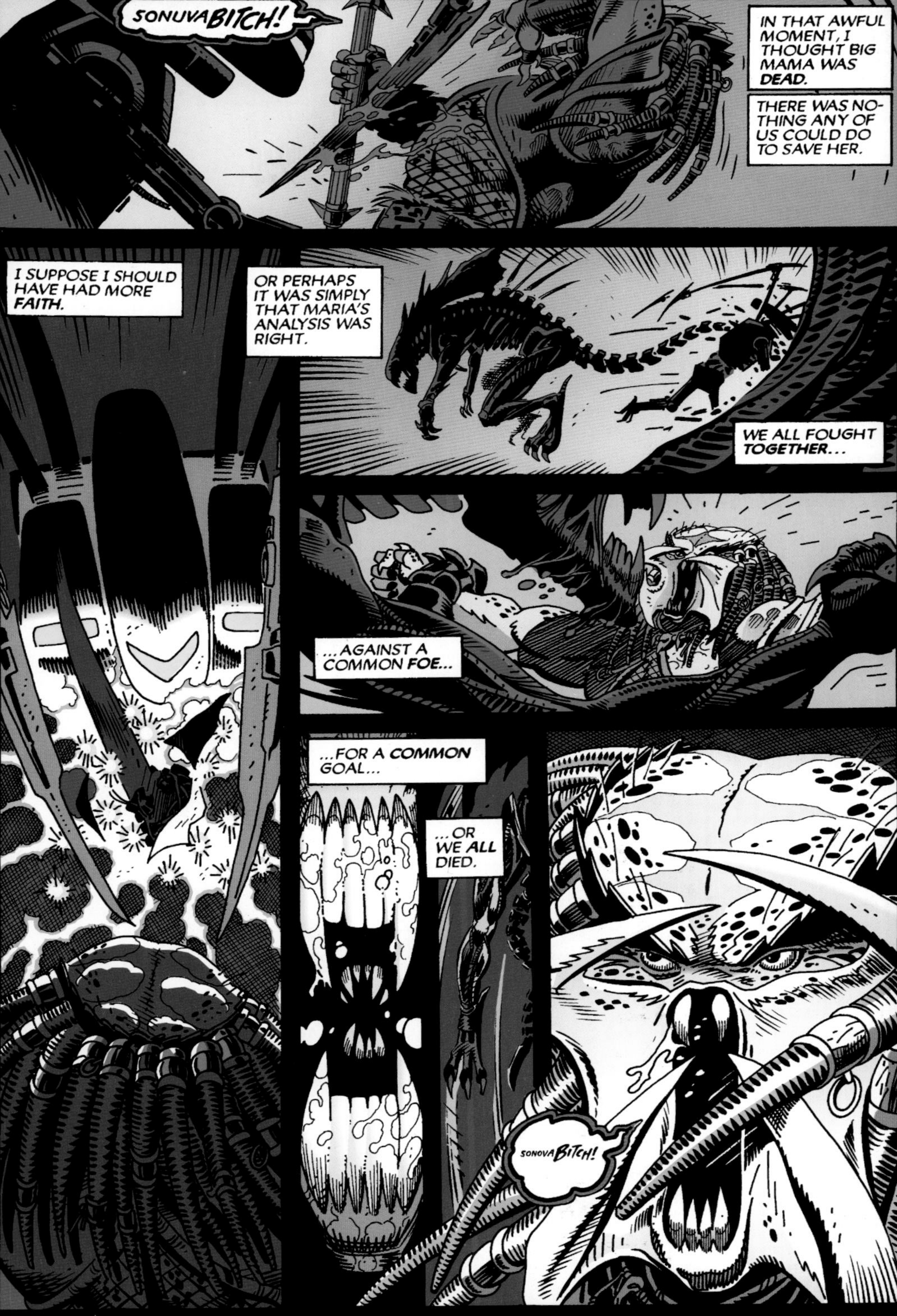

SONUVABITCH!
IN THAT AWFUL MOMENT, I THOUGHT BIG MAMA WAS DEAD.
THERE WAS NOTHING ANY OF US COULD DO TO SAVE HER.
I SUPPOSE I SHOULD HAVE HAD MORE FAITH.
OR PERHAPS IT WAS SIMPLY THAT MARIA'S ANALYSIS WAS RIGHT.
WE ALL FOUGHT TOGETHER...
...AGAINST A COMMON FOE...
...FOR A COMMON GOAL...
...OR WE ALL DIED.
SONOVABITCH!

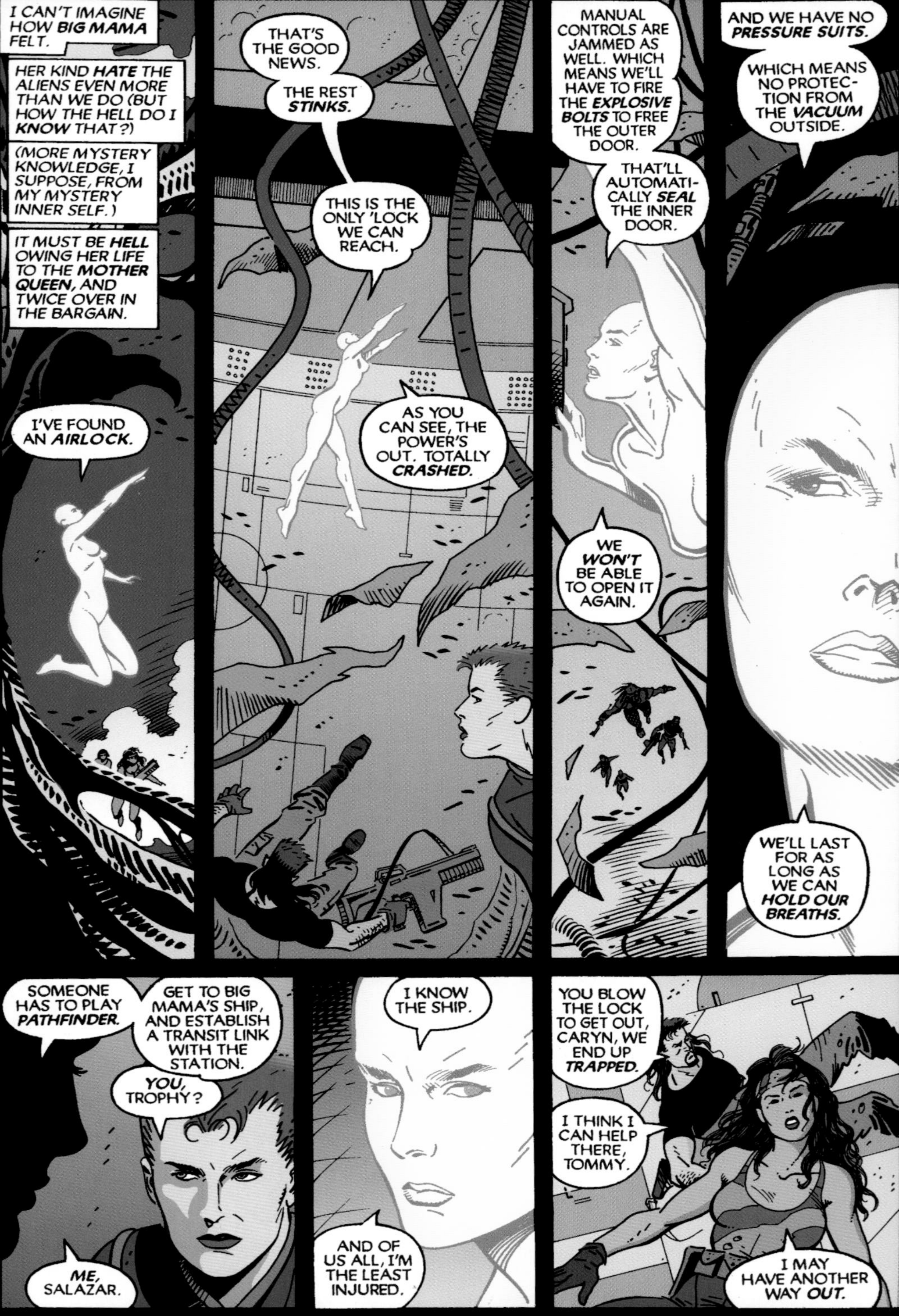
I CAN'T IMAGINE HOW BIG MAMA FELT.
HER KIND HATE THE ALIENS EVEN MORE THAN WE DO (BUT HOW THE HELL DO I KNOW THAT?)
(MORE MYSTERY KNOWLEDGE, I SUPPOSE, FROM MY MYSTERY INNER SELF.)
IT MUST BE HELL OWING HER LIFE TO THE MOTHER QUEEN, AND TWICE OVER IN THE BARGAIN.
I'VE FOUND AN AIRLOCK.
THAT'S THE GOOD NEWS.
THE REST STINKS.
THIS IS THE ONLY 'LOCK WE CAN REACH.
AS YOU CAN SEE, THE POWER'S OUT. TOTALLY CRASHED.
MANUAL CONTROLS ARE JAMMED AS WELL. WHICH MEANS WE'LL HAVE TO FIRE THE EXPLOSIVE BOLTS TO FREE THE OUTER DOOR.
THAT'LL AUTOMATICALLY SEAL THE INNER DOOR.
WE WON'T BE ABLE TO OPEN IT AGAIN.
AND WE HAVE NO PRESSURE SUITS.
WHICH MEANS NO PROTECTION FROM THE VACUUM OUTSIDE.
WE'LL LAST FOR AS LONG AS WE CAN HOLD OUR BREATHS.
SOMEONE HAS TO PLAY PATHFINDER.
GET TO BIG MAMA'S SHIP, AND ESTABLISH A TRANSIT LINK WITH THE STATION.
YOU, TROPHY?
ME, SALAZAR.
I KNOW THE SHIP.
AND OF US ALL, I'M THE LEAST INJURED.
YOU BLOW THE LOCK TO GET OUT, CARYN, WE END UP TRAPPED.
I THINK I CAN HELP THERE, TOMMY.
I MAY HAVE ANOTHER WAY OUT.

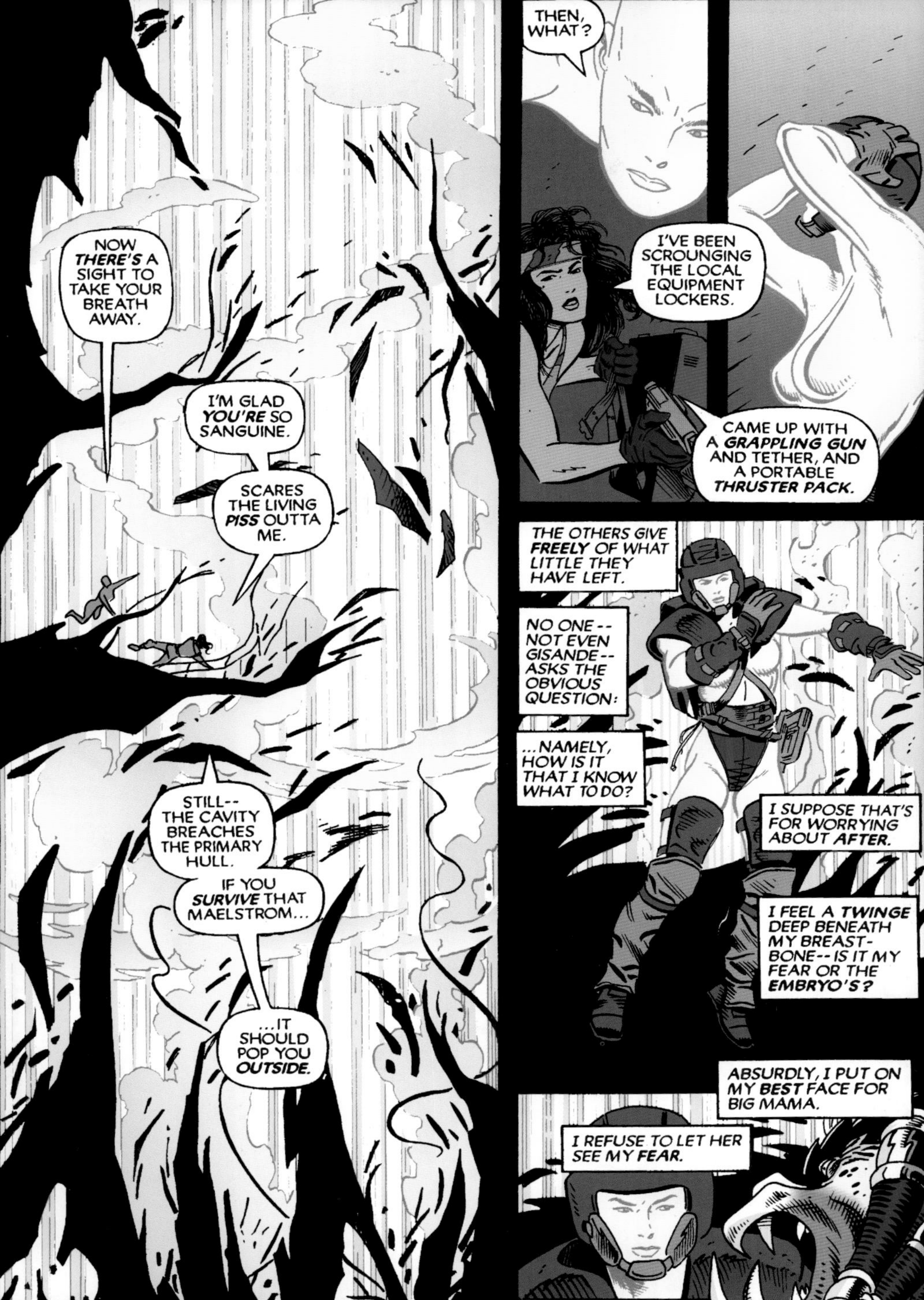

NOW THERE'S A SIGHT TO TAKE YOUR BREATH AWAY.
I'M GLAD YOU'RE SO SANGUINE.
SCARES THE LIVING PISS OUTTA ME.
STILL-- THE CAVITY BREACHES THE PRIMARY HULL.
IF YOU SURVIVE THAT MAELSTROM...
...IT SHOULD POP YOU OUTSIDE.
THEN, WHAT?
I'VE BEEN SCROUNGING THE LOCAL EQUIPMENT LOCKERS.
CAME UP WITH A GRAPPLING GUN AND TETHER, AND A PORTABLE THRUSTER PACK.
THE OTHERS GIVE FREELY OF WHAT LITTLE THEY HAVE LEFT.
NO ONE-- NOT EVEN GISANDE-- ASKS THE OBVIOUS QUESTION:
...NAMELY, HOW IS IT THAT I KNOW WHAT TO DO?
I SUPPOSE THAT'S FOR WORRYING ABOUT AFTER.
I FEEL A TWINGE DEEP BENEATH MY BREAST-BONE-- IS IT MY FEAR OR THE EMBRYO'S?
ABSURDLY, I PUT ON MY BEST FACE FOR BIG MAMA.
I REFUSE TO LET HER SEE MY FEAR.
THERE'S A TERRIBLE RAGE IN HER EYES.

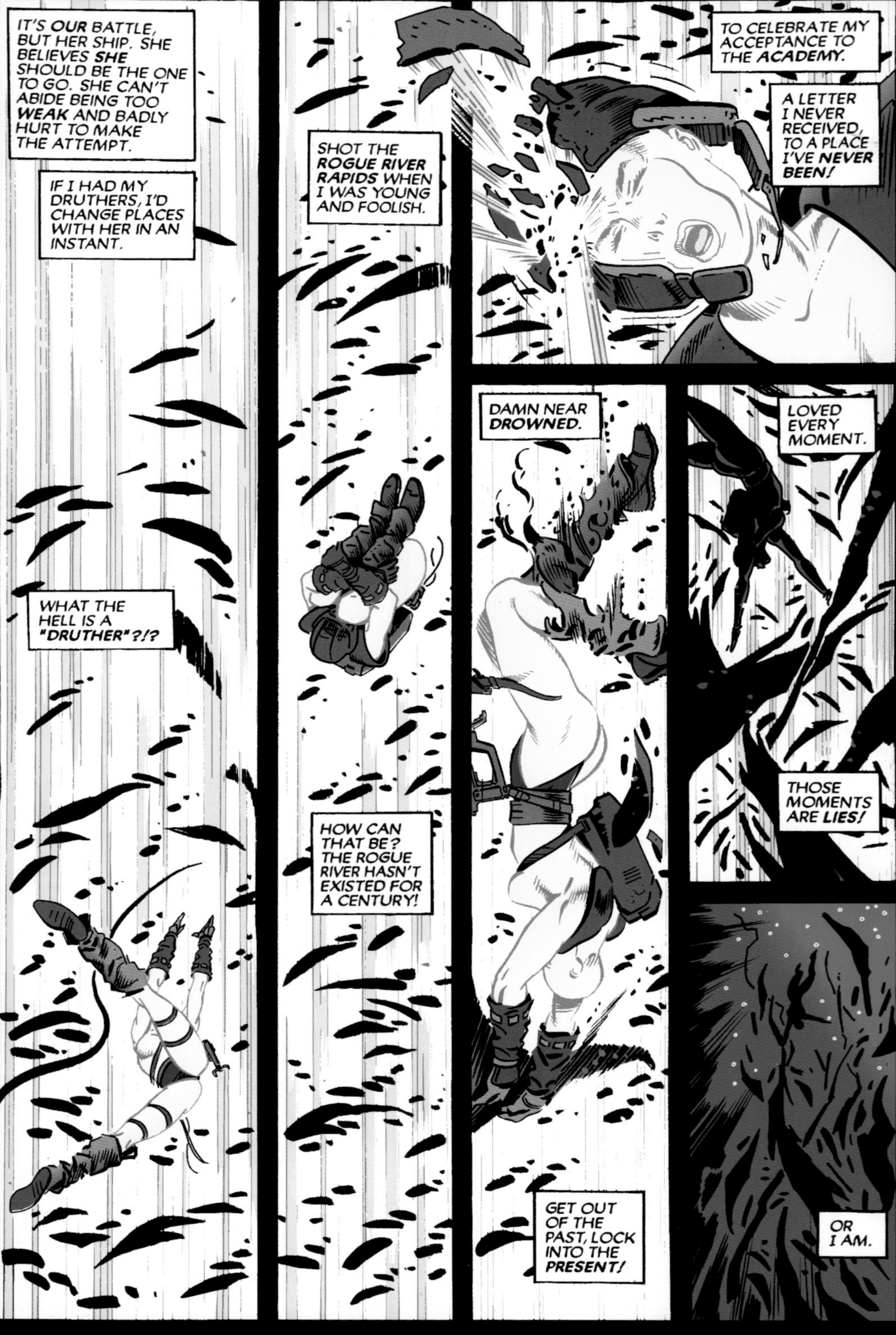
IT'S OUR BATTLE, BUT HER SHIP. SHE BELIEVES SHE SHOULD BE THE ONE TO GO. SHE CAN'T ABIDE BEING TOO WEAK AND BADLY HURT TO MAKE THE ATTEMPT.
IF I HAD MY DRUTHERS, I'D CHANGE PLACES WITH HER IN AN INSTANT.
WHAT THE HELL IS A "DRUTHER"?!?
SHOT THE ROGUE RIVER RAPIDS WHEN I WAS YOUNG AND FOOLISH.
HOW CAN THAT BE? THE ROGUE RIVER HASN'T EXISTED FOR A CENTURY!
TO CELEBRATE MY ACCEPTANCE TO THE ACADEMY.
A LETTER I NEVER RECEIVED, TO A PLACE I'VE NEVER BEEN!
DAMN NEAR DROWNED.
GET OUT OF THE PAST, LOCK INTO THE PRESENT!
LOVED EVERY MOMENT.
THOSE MOMENTS ARE LIES!
OR I AM.

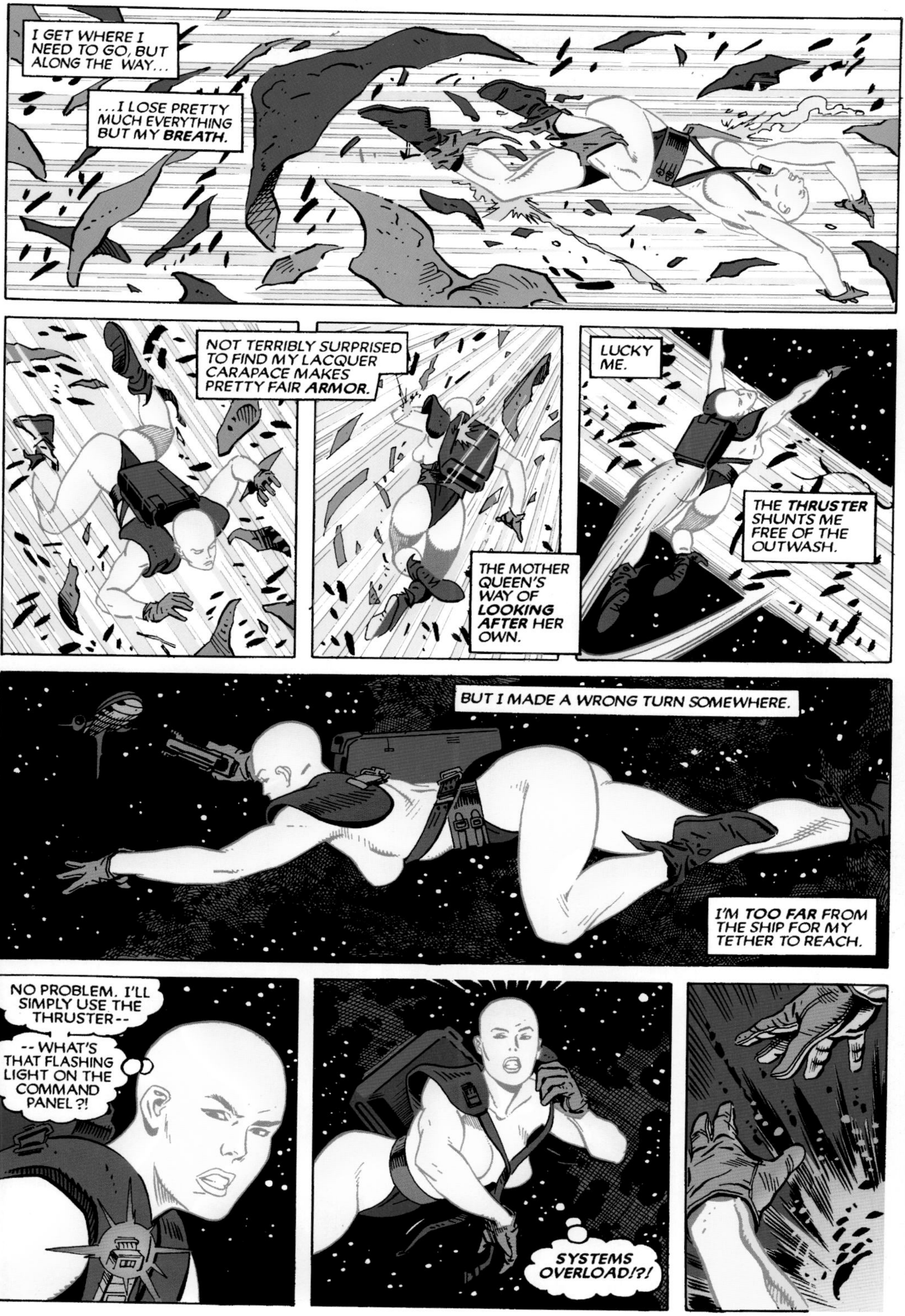
I GET WHERE I NEED TO GO, BUT ALONG THE WAY...
...I LOSE PRETTY MUCH EVERYTHING BUT MY **BREATH**.
NOT TERRIBLY SURPRISED TO FIND MY LACQUER CARAPACE MAKES PRETTY FAIR **ARMOR**.
THE MOTHER QUEEN'S WAY OF **LOOKING AFTER** HER OWN.
LUCKY ME.
THE **THRUSTER** SHUNTS ME FREE OF THE OUTWASH.
BUT I MADE A WRONG TURN SOMEWHERE.
I'M **TOO FAR** FROM THE SHIP FOR MY TETHER TO REACH.
NO PROBLEM. I'LL SIMPLY USE THE THRUSTER--
--WHAT'S THAT FLASHING LIGHT ON THE COMMAND PANEL?!
SYSTEMS OVERLOAD!?!

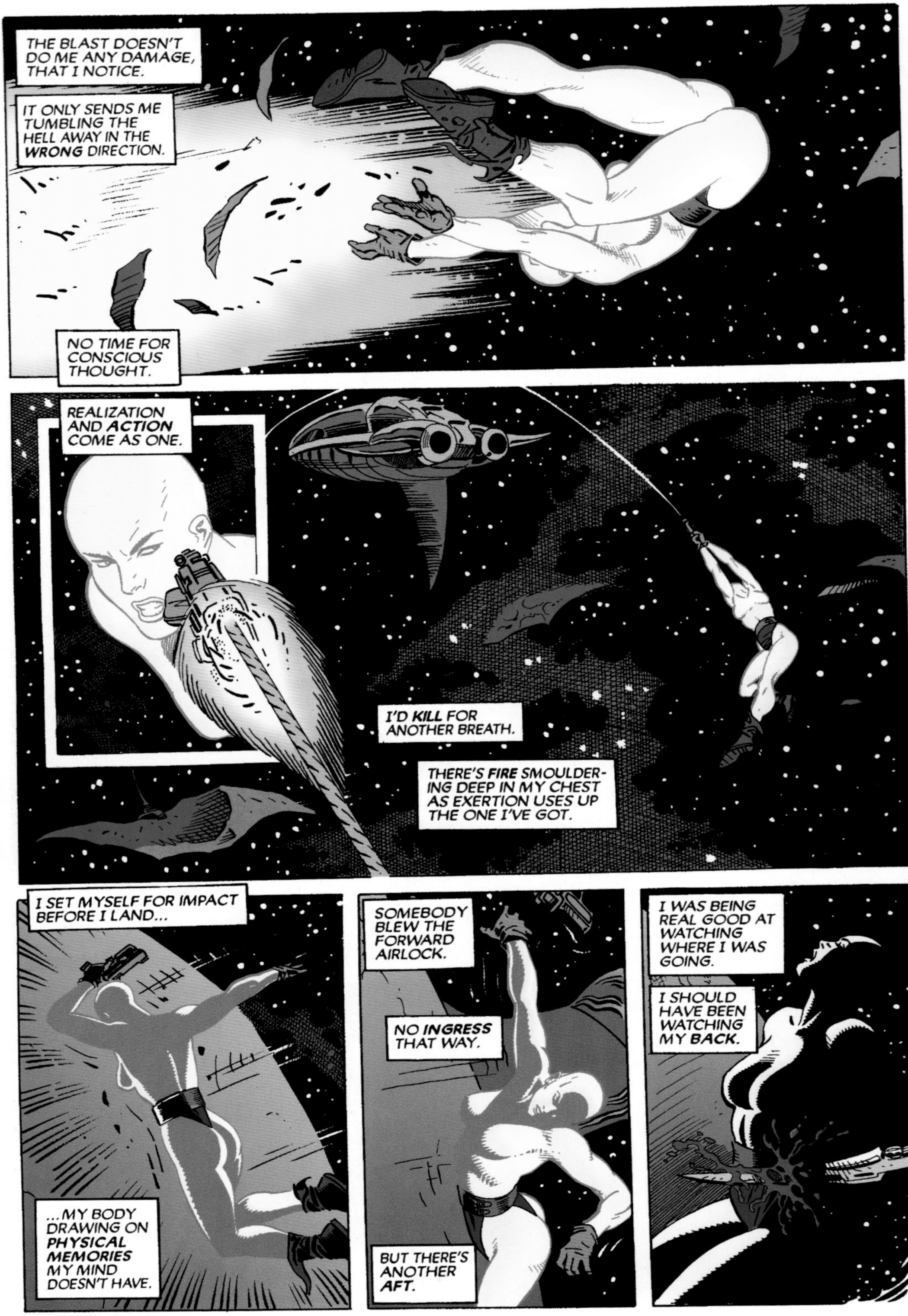

THE BLAST DOESN'T DO ME ANY DAMAGE, THAT I NOTICE.
IT ONLY SENDS ME TUMBLING THE HELL AWAY IN THE **WRONG** DIRECTION.
NO TIME FOR CONSCIOUS THOUGHT.
REALIZATION AND **ACTION** COME AS ONE.
I'D **KILL** FOR ANOTHER BREATH.
THERE'S **FIRE** SMOULDER-ING DEEP IN MY CHEST AS EXERTION USES UP THE ONE I'VE GOT.
I SET **MYSELF** FOR IMPACT BEFORE I LAND...
...MY BODY DRAWING ON **PHYSICAL MEMORIES** MY MIND DOESN'T HAVE.
SOMEBODY BLEW THE FORWARD AIRLOCK.
NO **INGRESS** THAT WAY.
BUT THERE'S ANOTHER **AFT**.
I WAS BEING REAL GOOD AT WATCHING WHERE I WAS GOING.
I SHOULD HAVE BEEN WATCHING MY **BACK**.

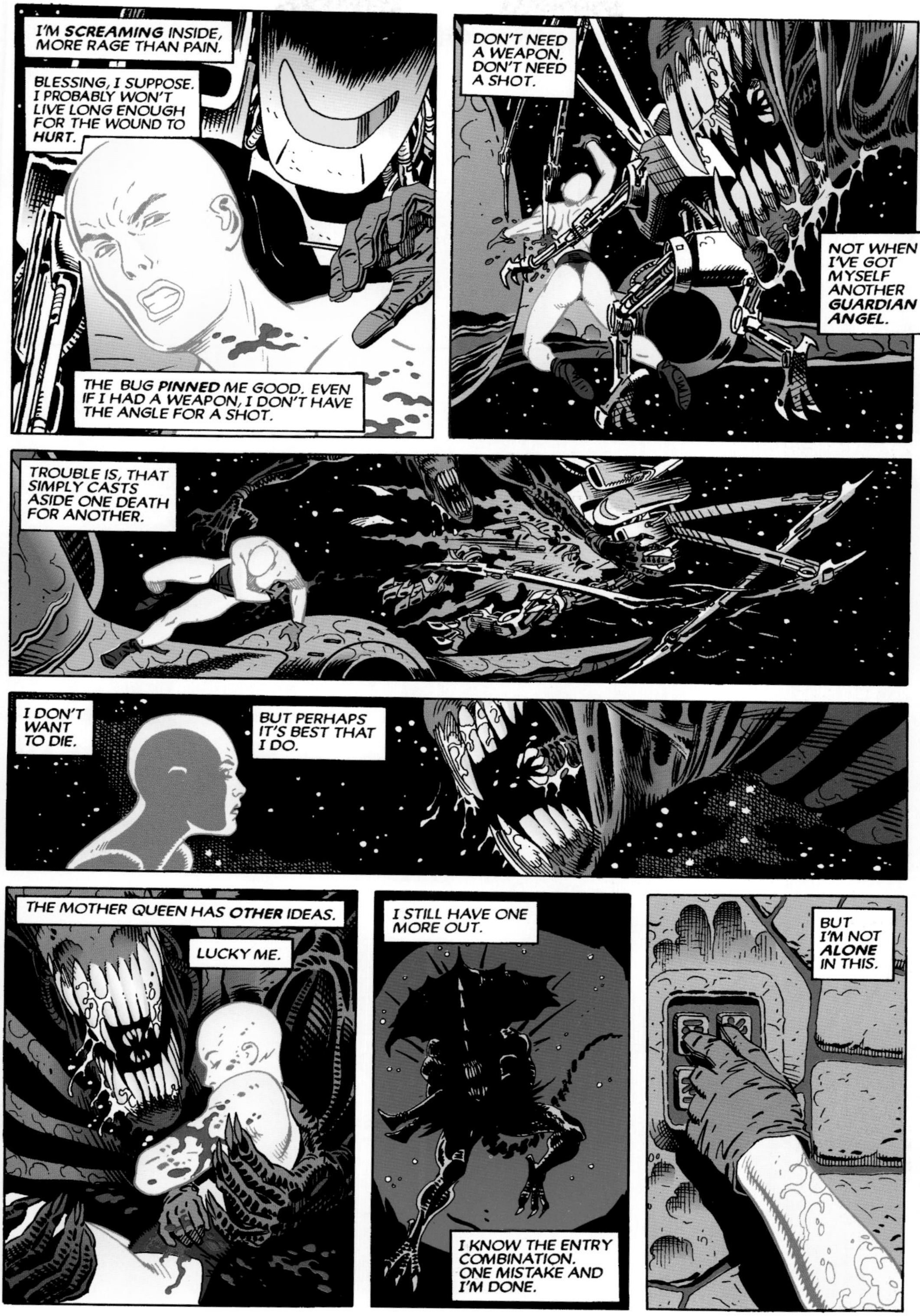
I'M SCREAMING INSIDE, MORE RAGE THAN PAIN.
BLESSING, I SUPPOSE. I PROBABLY WON'T LIVE LONG ENOUGH FOR THE WOUND TO HURT.
THE BUG PINNED ME GOOD. EVEN IF I HAD A WEAPON, I DON'T HAVE THE ANGLE FOR A SHOT.
DON'T NEED A WEAPON. DON'T NEED A SHOT.
NOT WHEN I'VE GOT MYSELF ANOTHER GUARDIAN ANGEL.
TROUBLE IS, THAT SIMPLY CASTS ASIDE ONE DEATH FOR ANOTHER.
I DON'T WANT TO DIE.
BUT PERHAPS IT'S BEST THAT I DO.
THE MOTHER QUEEN HAS OTHER IDEAS.
LUCKY ME.
I STILL HAVE ONE MORE OUT.
I KNOW THE ENTRY COMBINATION. ONE MISTAKE AND I'M DONE.
BUT I'M NOT ALONE IN THIS.

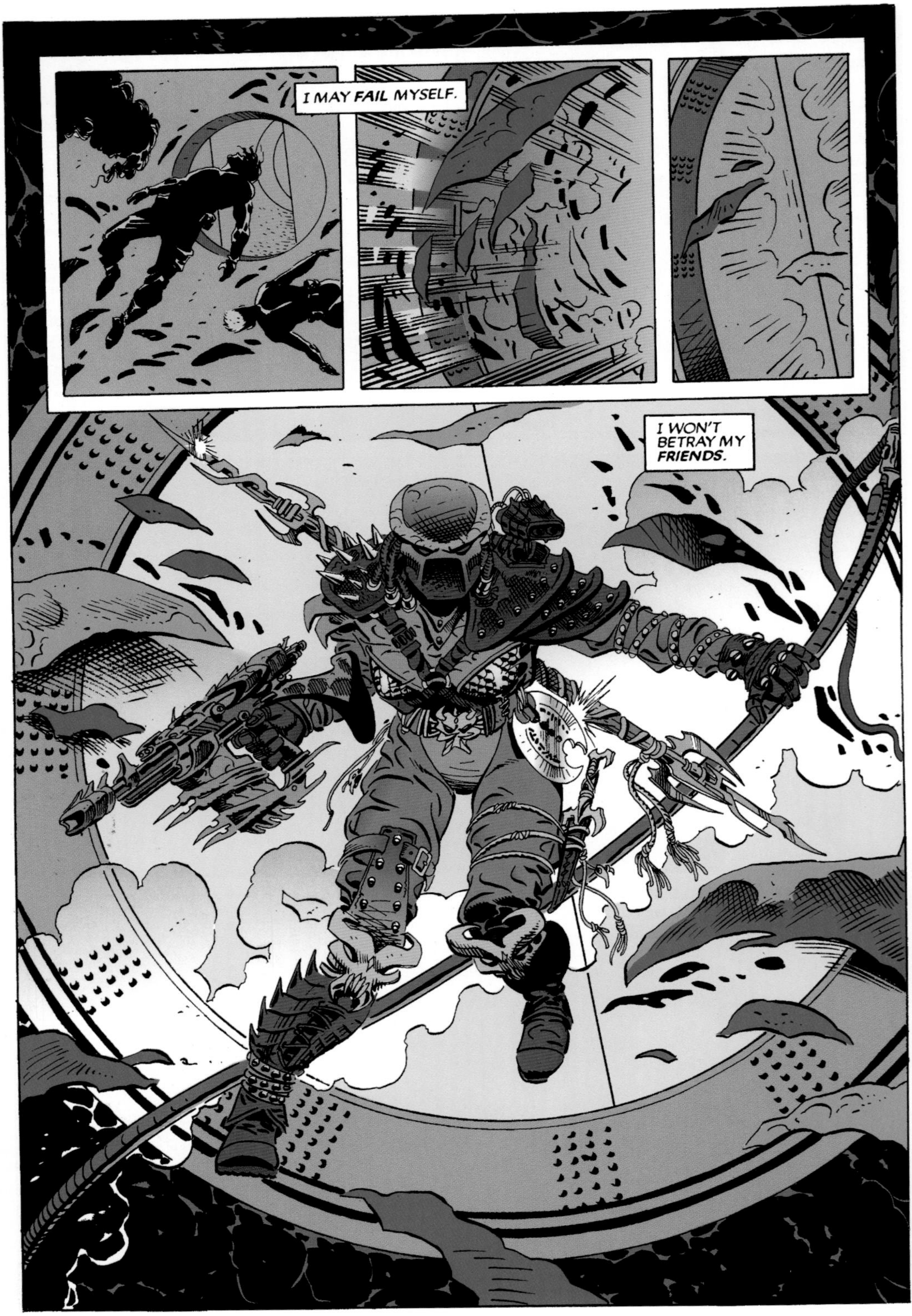
I MAY FAIL MYSELF.
I WON'T BETRAY MY FRIENDS.

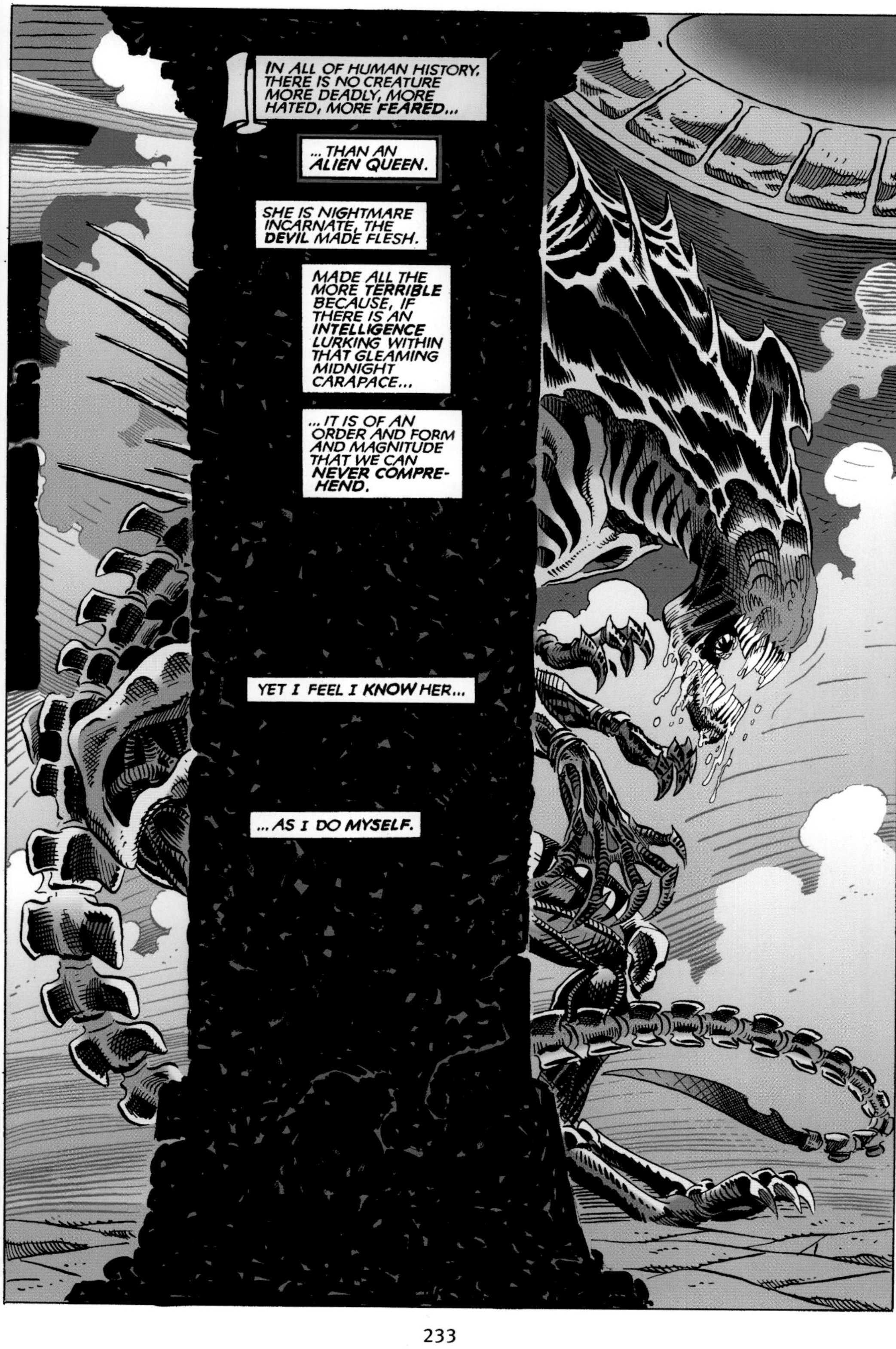
IN ALL OF HUMAN HISTORY, THERE IS NO CREATURE MORE DEADLY, MORE HATED, MORE FEARED...
...THAN AN ALIEN QUEEN.
SHE IS NIGHTMARE INCARNATE, THE DEVIL MADE FLESH.
MADE ALL THE MORE TERRIBLE BECAUSE, IF THERE IS AN INTELLIGENCE LURKING WITHIN THAT GLEAMING MIDNIGHT CARAPACE...
...IT IS OF AN ORDER AND FORM AND MAGNITUDE THAT WE CAN NEVER COMPREHEND.
YET I FEEL I KNOW HER...
...AS I DO MYSELF.

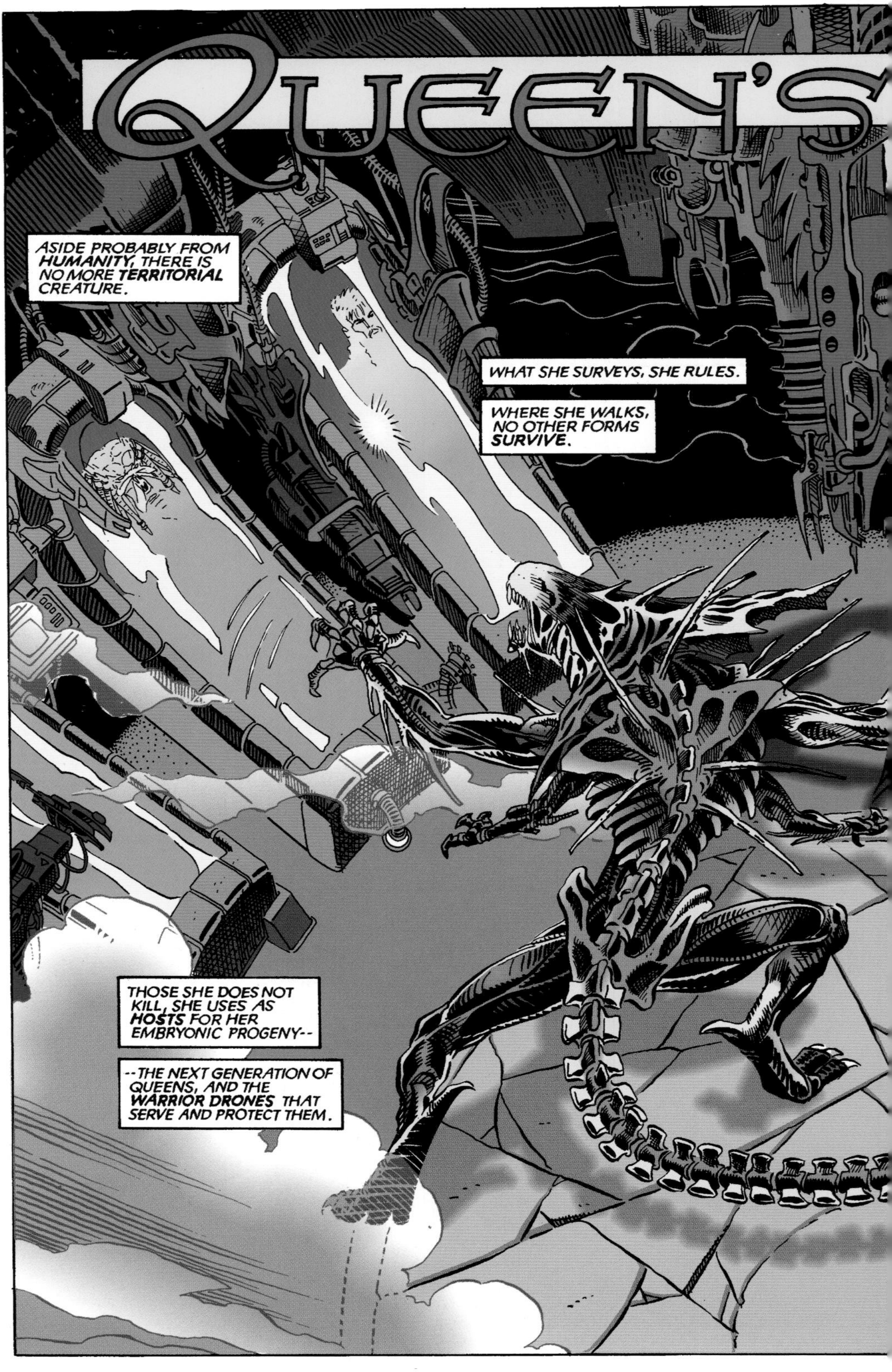
QUEEN'S
ASIDE PROBABLY FROM HUMANITY, THERE IS NO MORE TERRITORIAL CREATURE.
WHAT SHE SURVEYS, SHE RULES.
WHERE SHE WALKS, NO OTHER FORMS SURVIVE.
THOSE SHE DOES NOT KILL, SHE USES AS HOSTS FOR HER EMBRYONIC PROGENY--
--THE NEXT GENERATION OF QUEENS, AND THE WARRIOR DRONES THAT SERVE AND PROTECT THEM.

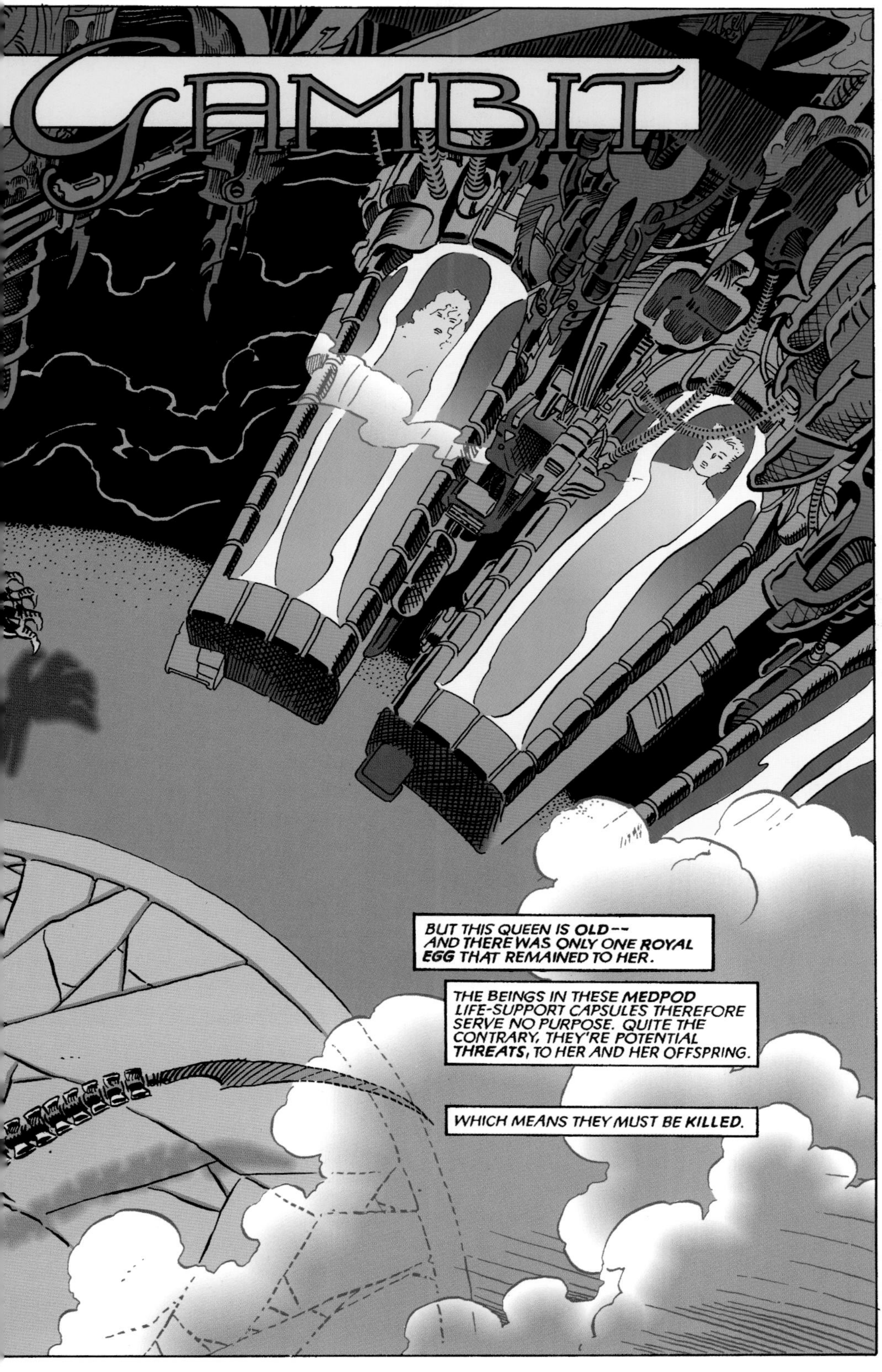
GAMBIT
BUT THIS QUEEN IS OLD-- AND THERE WAS ONLY ONE ROYAL EGG THAT REMAINED TO HER.
THE BEINGS IN THESE MEDPOD LIFE-SUPPORT CAPSULES THEREFORE SERVE NO PURPOSE. QUITE THE CONTRARY, THEY'RE POTENTIAL THREATS, TO HER AND HER OFFSPRING.
WHICH MEANS THEY MUST BE KILLED.

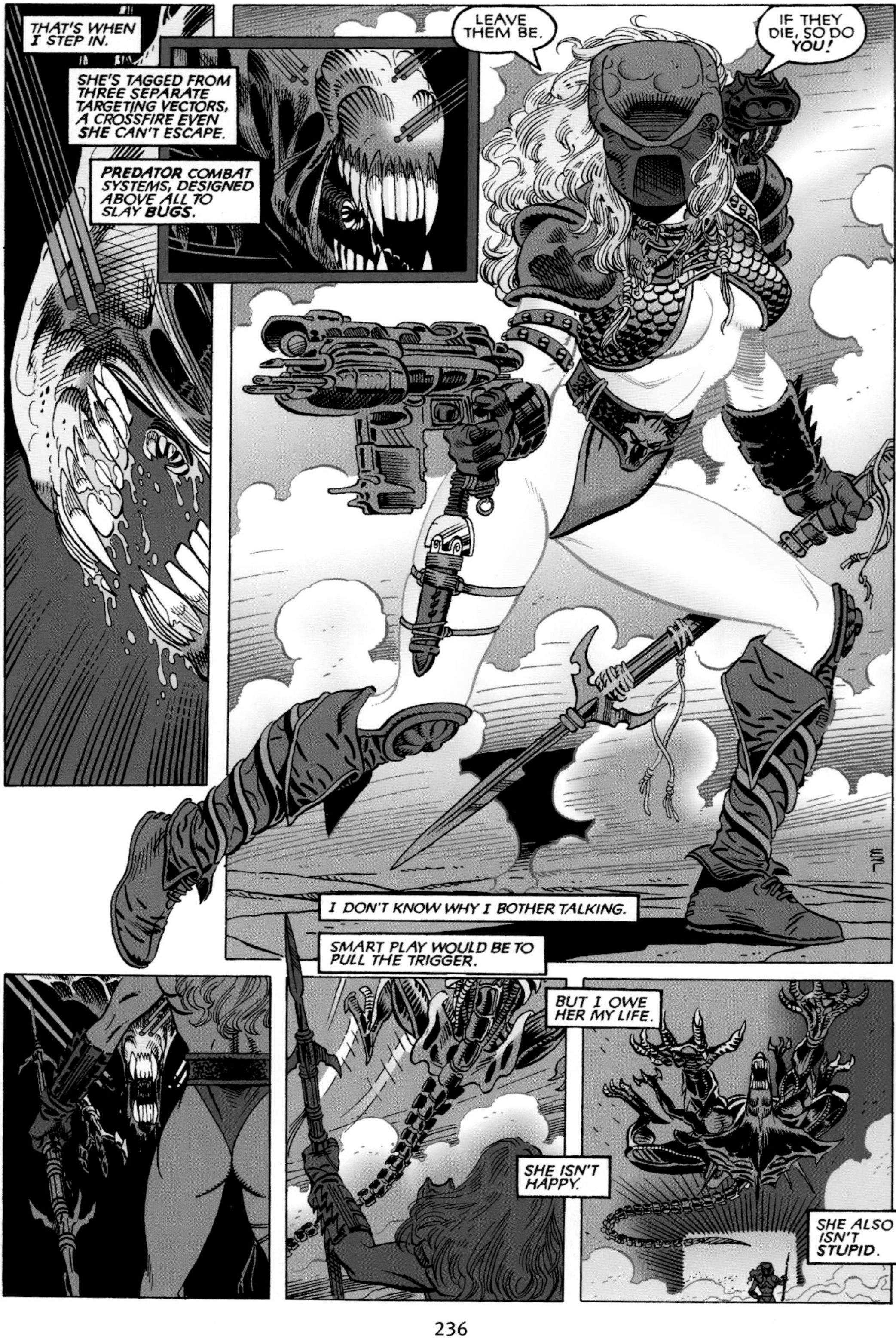
THAT'S WHEN I STEP IN.
SHE'S TAGGED FROM THREE SEPARATE TARGETING VECTORS, A CROSSFIRE EVEN SHE CAN'T ESCAPE.
PREDATOR COMBAT SYSTEMS, DESIGNED ABOVE ALL TO SLAY BUGS.
LEAVE THEM BE.
IF THEY DIE, SO DO YOU!
I DON'T KNOW WHY I BOTHER TALKING.
SMART PLAY WOULD BE TO PULL THE TRIGGER.
BUT I OWE HER MY LIFE.
SHE ISN'T HAPPY.
SHE ALSO ISN'T STUPID.

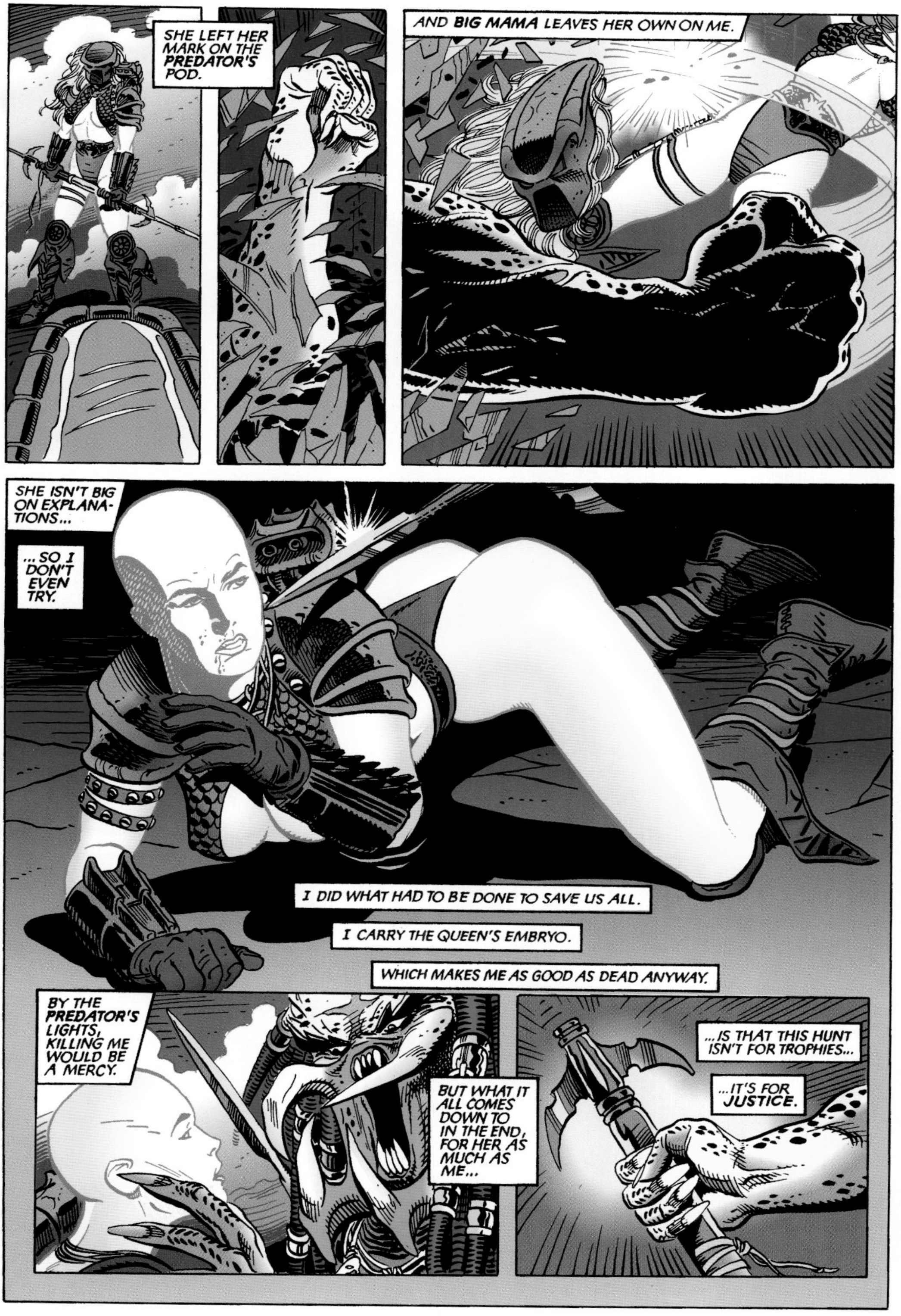
SHE LEFT HER MARK ON THE PREDATOR'S POD.
AND BIG MAMA LEAVES HER OWN ON ME.
SHE ISN'T BIG ON EXPLANA-TIONS...
...SO I DON'T EVEN TRY.
I DID WHAT HAD TO BE DONE TO SAVE US ALL.
I CARRY THE QUEEN'S EMBRYO.
WHICH MAKES ME AS GOOD AS DEAD ANYWAY.
BY THE PREDATOR'S LIGHTS, KILLING ME WOULD BE A MERCY.
BUT WHAT IT ALL COMES DOWN TO IN THE END, FOR HER AS MUCH AS ME...
...IS THAT THIS HUNT ISN'T FOR TROPHIES...
...IT'S FOR JUSTICE.

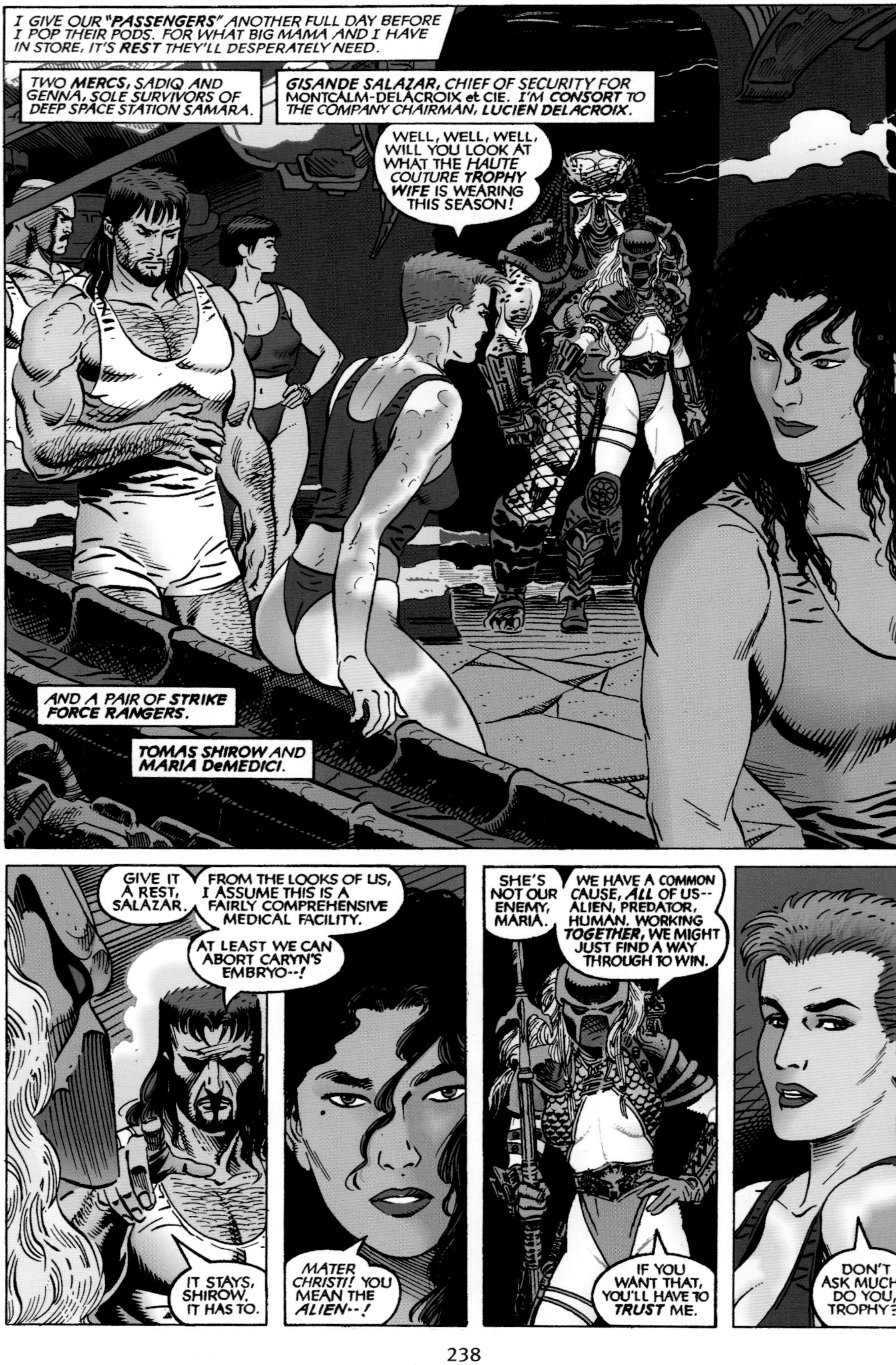
I GIVE OUR "PASSENGERS" ANOTHER FULL DAY BEFORE I POP THEIR PODS. FOR WHAT BIG MAMA AND I HAVE IN STORE, IT'S REST THEY'LL DESPERATELY NEED.
TWO MERCS, SADIQ AND GENNA, SOLE SURVIVORS OF DEEP SPACE STATION SAMARA.
GISANDE SALAZAR, CHIEF OF SECURITY FOR MONTCALM-DELACROIX et CIE. I'M CONSORT TO THE COMPANY CHAIRMAN, LUCIEN DELACROIX.
WELL, WELL, WELL, WILL YOU LOOK AT WHAT THE HAUTE COUTURE TROPHY WIFE IS WEARING THIS SEASON!
AND A PAIR OF STRIKE FORCE RANGERS.
TOMAS SHIROW AND MARIA DeMEDICI.
GIVE IT A REST, SALAZAR.
FROM THE LOOKS OF US, I ASSUME THIS IS A FAIRLY COMPREHENSIVE MEDICAL FACILITY.
AT LEAST WE CAN ABORT CARYN'S EMBRYO--!
IT STAYS, SHIROW. IT HAS TO.
MATER CHRISTI! YOU MEAN THE ALIEN--!
SHE'S NOT OUR ENEMY, MARIA.
WE HAVE A COMMON CAUSE, ALL OF US-- ALIEN, PREDATOR, HUMAN. WORKING TOGETHER, WE MIGHT JUST FIND A WAY THROUGH TO WIN.
IF YOU WANT THAT, YOU'LL HAVE TO TRUST ME.
DON'T ASK MUCH, DO YOU, TROPHY?

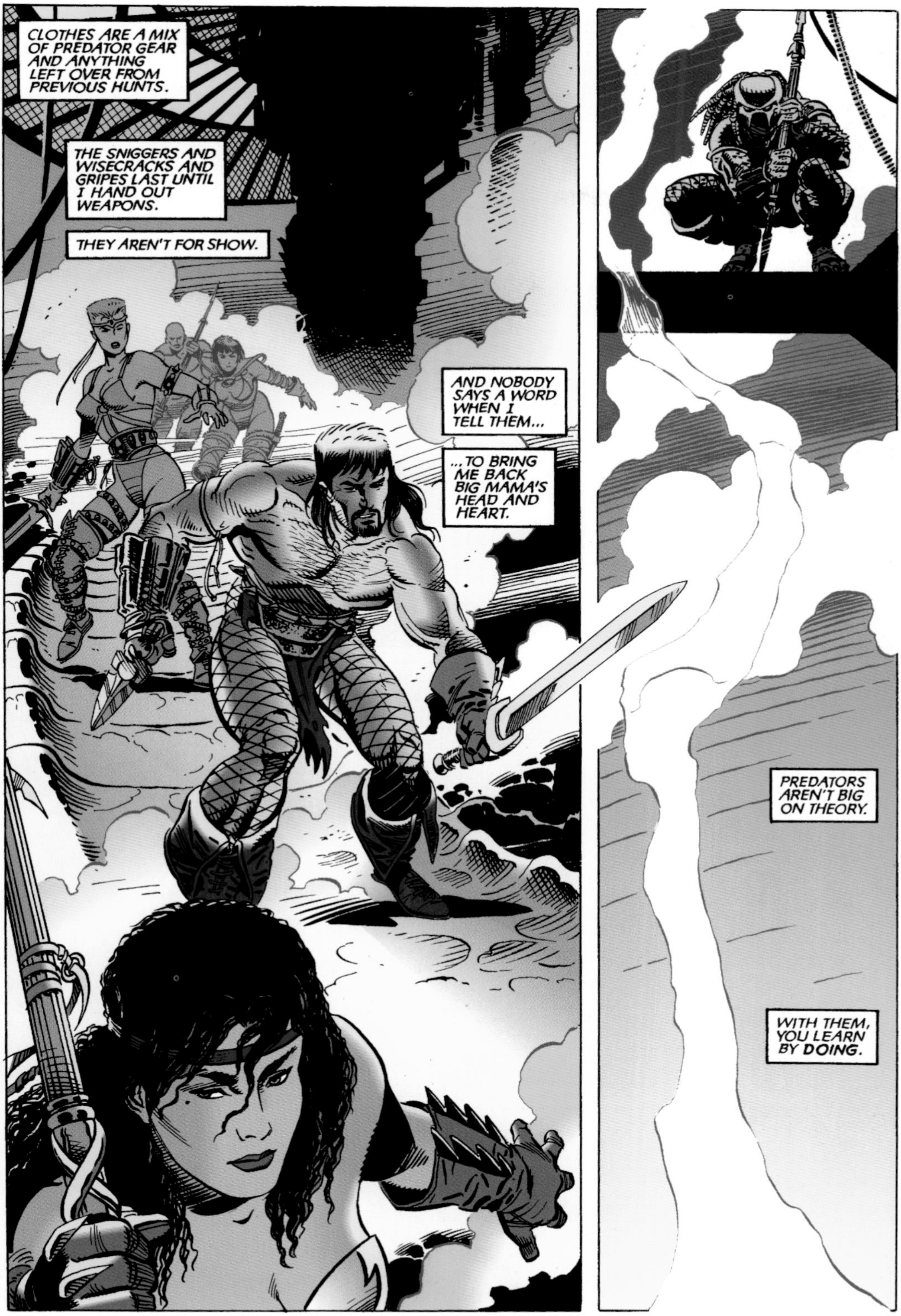
CLOTHES ARE A MIX OF PREDATOR GEAR AND ANYTHING LEFT OVER FROM PREVIOUS HUNTS.
THE SNIGGERS AND WISECRACKS AND GRIPES LAST UNTIL I HAND OUT WEAPONS.
THEY AREN'T FOR SHOW.
AND NOBODY SAYS A WORD WHEN I TELL THEM...
...TO BRING ME BACK BIG MAMA'S HEAD AND HEART.
PREDATORS AREN'T BIG ON THEORY.
WITH THEM, YOU LEARN BY **DOING**.

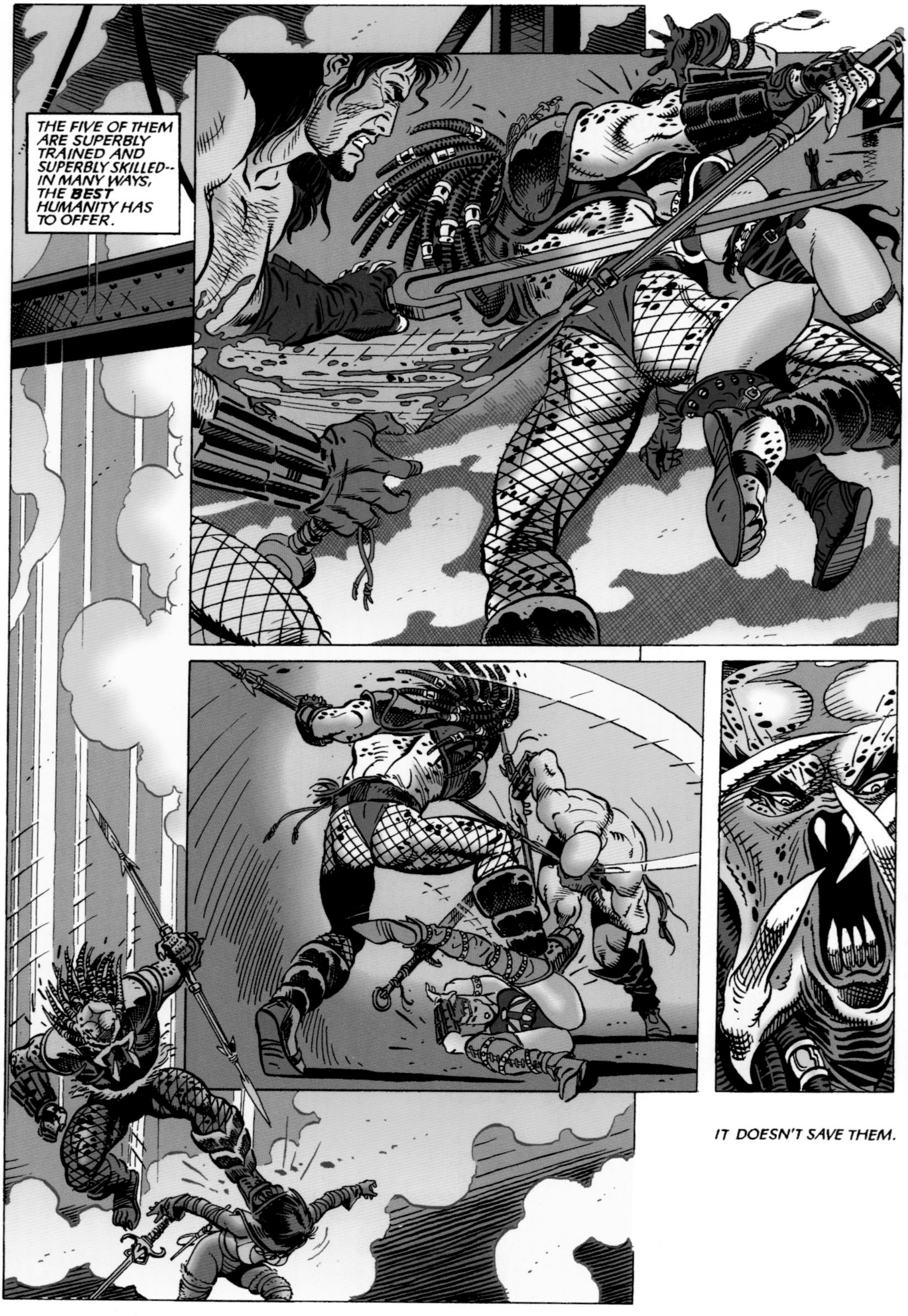
THE FIVE OF THEM ARE SUPERBLY TRAINED AND SUPERBLY SKILLED-- IN MANY WAYS, THE **BEST** HUMANITY HAS TO OFFER.
IT DOESN'T SAVE THEM.

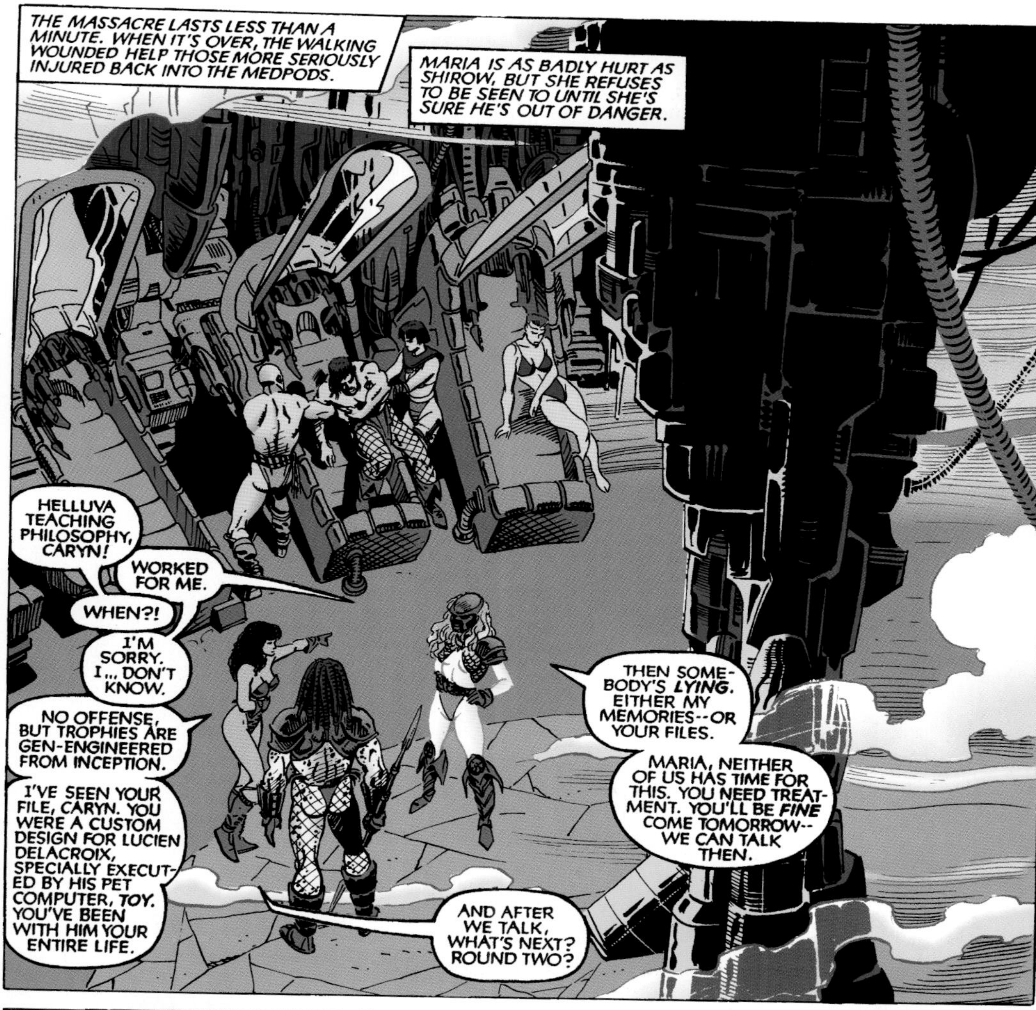
THE MASSACRE LASTS LESS THAN A MINUTE. WHEN IT'S OVER, THE WALKING WOUNDED HELP THOSE MORE SERIOUSLY INJURED BACK INTO THE MEDPODS.
MARIA IS AS BADLY HURT AS SHIROW, BUT SHE REFUSES TO BE SEEN TO UNTIL SHE'S SURE HE'S OUT OF DANGER.
HELLUVA TEACHING PHILOSOPHY, CARYN!
WORKED FOR ME.
WHEN?!
I'M SORRY. I... DON'T KNOW.
NO OFFENSE, BUT TROPHIES ARE GEN-ENGINEERED FROM INCEPTION.
I'VE SEEN YOUR FILE, CARYN. YOU WERE A CUSTOM DESIGN FOR LUCIEN DELACROIX, SPECIALLY EXECUTED BY HIS PET COMPUTER, TOY. YOU'VE BEEN WITH HIM YOUR ENTIRE LIFE.
THEN SOMEBODY'S LYING. EITHER MY MEMORIES--OR YOUR FILES.
MARIA, NEITHER OF US HAS TIME FOR THIS. YOU NEED TREATMENT. YOU'LL BE FINE COME TOMORROW--WE CAN TALK THEN.
AND AFTER WE TALK, WHAT'S NEXT? ROUND TWO?

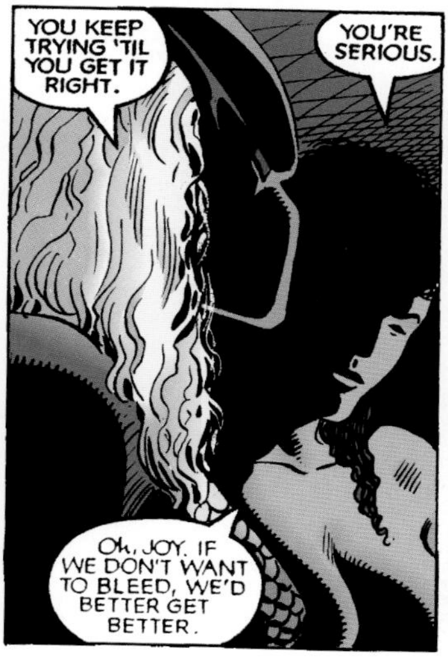
YOU KEEP TRYING 'TIL YOU GET IT RIGHT.
YOU'RE SERIOUS.
OH, JOY. IF WE DON'T WANT TO BLEED, WE'D BETTER GET BETTER.

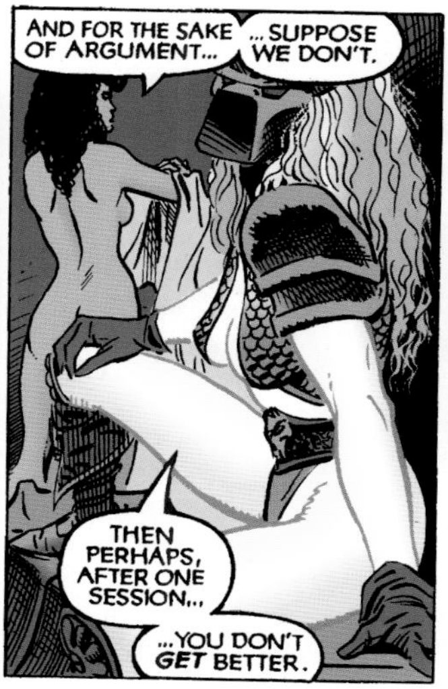
AND FOR THE SAKE OF ARGUMENT...
...SUPPOSE WE DON'T.
THEN PERHAPS, AFTER ONE SESSION...
...YOU DON'T GET BETTER.

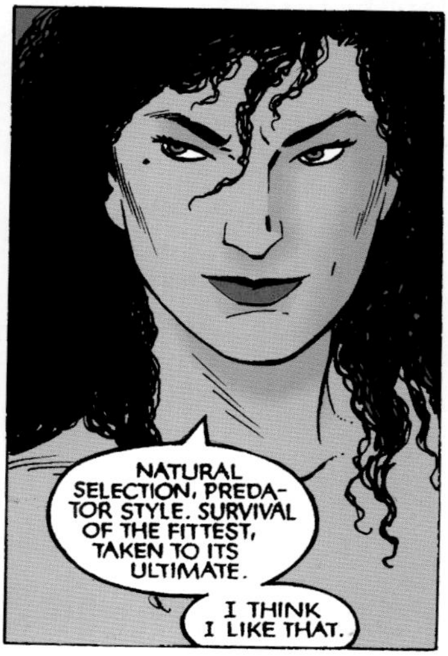
NATURAL SELECTION, PREDATOR STYLE. SURVIVAL OF THE FITTEST, TAKEN TO ITS ULTIMATE.
I THINK. I LIKE THAT.

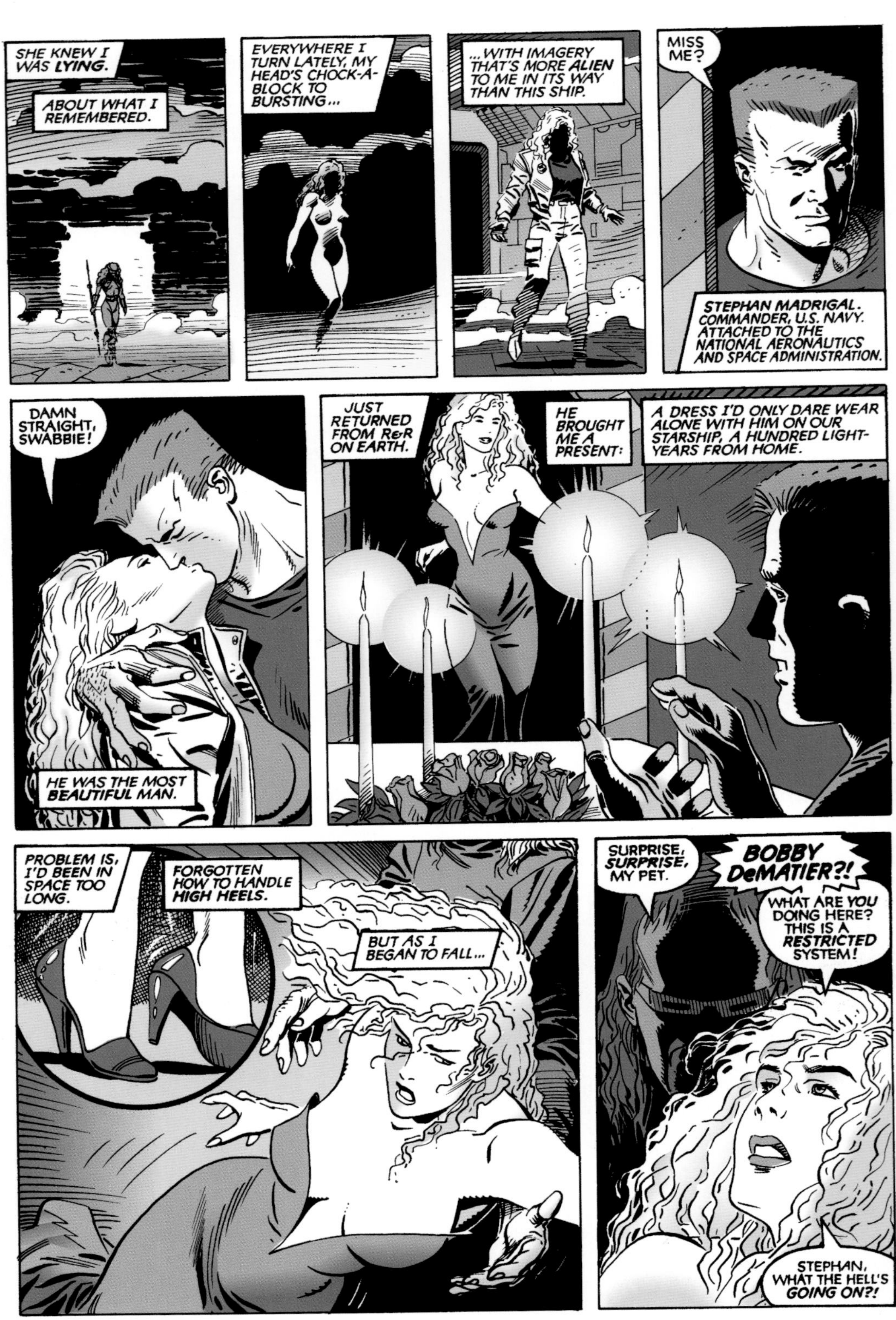

SHE KNEW I WAS **LYING.**
ABOUT WHAT I REMEMBERED.
EVERYWHERE I TURN LATELY, MY HEAD'S CHOCK-A-BLOCK TO BURSTING...
...WITH IMAGERY THAT'S MORE **ALIEN** TO ME IN ITS WAY THAN THIS SHIP.
MISS ME?
STEPHAN MADRIGAL. COMMANDER, U.S. NAVY. ATTACHED TO THE NATIONAL AERONAUTICS AND SPACE ADMINISTRATION.
DAMN STRAIGHT, SWABBIE!
HE WAS THE MOST **BEAUTIFUL** MAN.
JUST RETURNED FROM R&R ON EARTH.
HE BROUGHT ME A PRESENT:
A DRESS I'D ONLY DARE WEAR ALONE WITH HIM ON OUR STARSHIP, A HUNDRED LIGHT-YEARS FROM HOME.
PROBLEM IS, I'D BEEN IN SPACE TOO LONG.
FORGOTTEN HOW TO HANDLE **HIGH HEELS.**
BUT AS I BEGAN TO FALL...
SURPRISE, **SURPRISE,** MY PET.
BOBBY DeMATIER?!
WHAT ARE **YOU** DOING HERE? THIS IS A **RESTRICTED** SYSTEM!
STEPHAN, WHAT THE HELL'S **GOING ON?!**

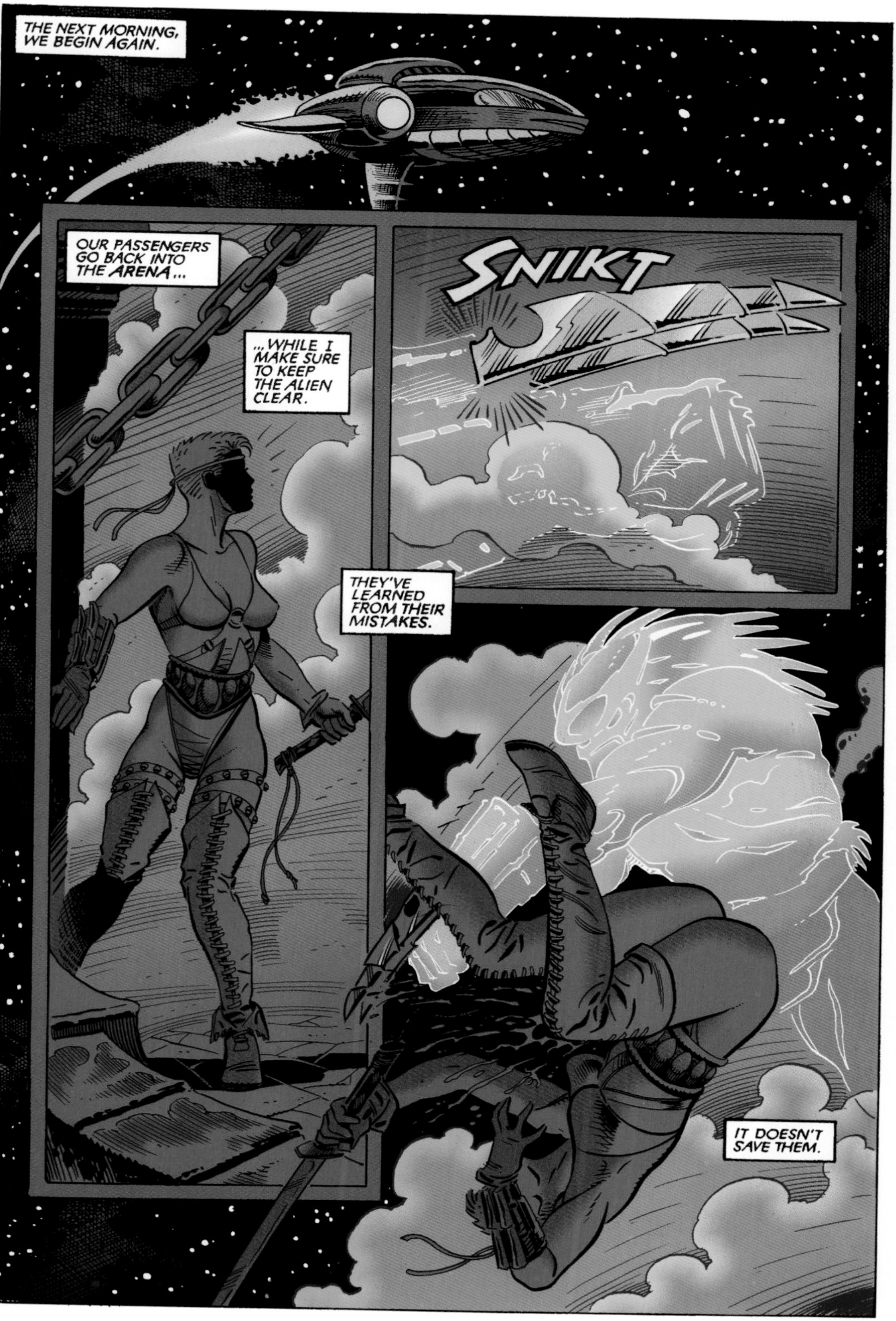
THE NEXT MORNING, WE BEGIN AGAIN.
OUR PASSENGERS GO BACK INTO THE ARENA...
...WHILE I MAKE SURE TO KEEP THE ALIEN CLEAR.
SNIKT
THEY'VE LEARNED FROM THEIR MISTAKES.
IT DOESN'T SAVE THEM.

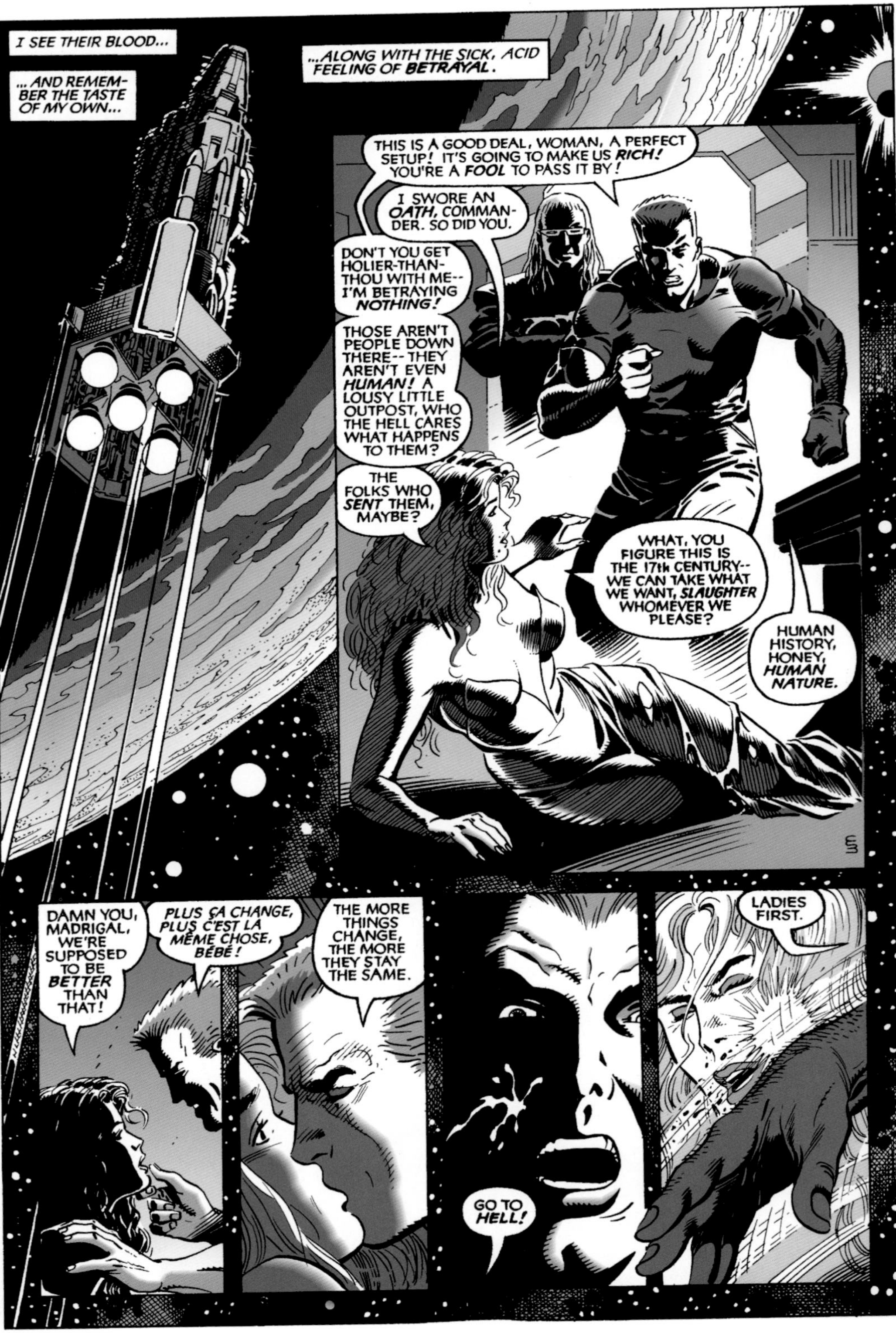
I SEE THEIR BLOOD...
...AND REMEMBER THE TASTE OF MY OWN...
...ALONG WITH THE SICK, ACID FEELING OF BETRAYAL.
THIS IS A GOOD DEAL, WOMAN, A PERFECT SETUP! IT'S GOING TO MAKE US RICH! YOU'RE A FOOL TO PASS IT BY!
I SWORE AN OATH, COMMANDER. SO DID YOU.
DON'T YOU GET HOLIER-THAN-THOU WITH ME-- I'M BETRAYING NOTHING!
THOSE AREN'T PEOPLE DOWN THERE-- THEY AREN'T EVEN HUMAN! A LOUSY LITTLE OUTPOST, WHO THE HELL CARES WHAT HAPPENS TO THEM?
THE FOLKS WHO SENT THEM, MAYBE?
WHAT, YOU FIGURE THIS IS THE 17th CENTURY-- WE CAN TAKE WHAT WE WANT, SLAUGHTER WHOMEVER WE PLEASE?
HUMAN HISTORY, HONEY, HUMAN NATURE.
DAMN YOU, MADRIGAL, WE'RE SUPPOSED TO BE BETTER THAN THAT!
PLUS ÇA CHANGE, PLUS C'EST LA MÊME CHOSE, BÉBÉ!
THE MORE THINGS CHANGE, THE MORE THEY STAY THE SAME.
GO TO HELL!
LADIES FIRST.

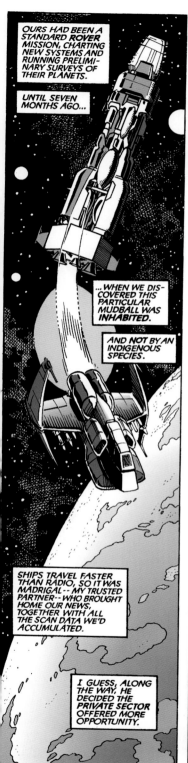

OURS HAD BEEN A STANDARD **ROVER** MISSION, CHARTING NEW SYSTEMS AND RUNNING PRELIMINARY SURVEYS OF THEIR PLANETS.

UNTIL SEVEN MONTHS AGO...

...WHEN WE DISCOVERED THIS PARTICULAR MUDBALL WAS **INHABITED**.

AND **NOT** BY AN INDIGENOUS SPECIES.

SHIPS TRAVEL FASTER THAN RADIO, SO IT WAS MADRIGAL -- MY TRUSTED PARTNER -- WHO BROUGHT HOME OUR NEWS, TOGETHER WITH ALL THE SCAN DATA WE'D ACCUMULATED.

I GUESS, ALONG THE WAY, HE DECIDED THE PRIVATE SECTOR OFFERED MORE OPPORTUNITY.

Y'ASK ME, IT'S MADRIGAL'S CALL.

IF THE BITCH AIN'T WITH THE PROGRAM, SHE'S BETTER OFF BREATHIN' **VACUUM**.

YEAH, WELL, DeMATIER HAS THE HOTS FOR HER **DNA** -- LIKES THE WAY IT KINKS OR WHATEVER. GOT PLANS FOR HER, LIKE HE DOES WITH THOSE **EXOTICS** PLANETSIDE.

MAN, IN THAT CASE, KILLIN' HER BE DOIN' THE BITCH A **KINDNESS** --

-- **WHA** --?!

SPIKE-HEEL KICK TO THE PATELLA. VERY NASTY. **VERY** EFFECTIVE.

I TOOK THEM DOWN HARD.

AND THEN MADE SURE THEY DIDN'T GET UP.

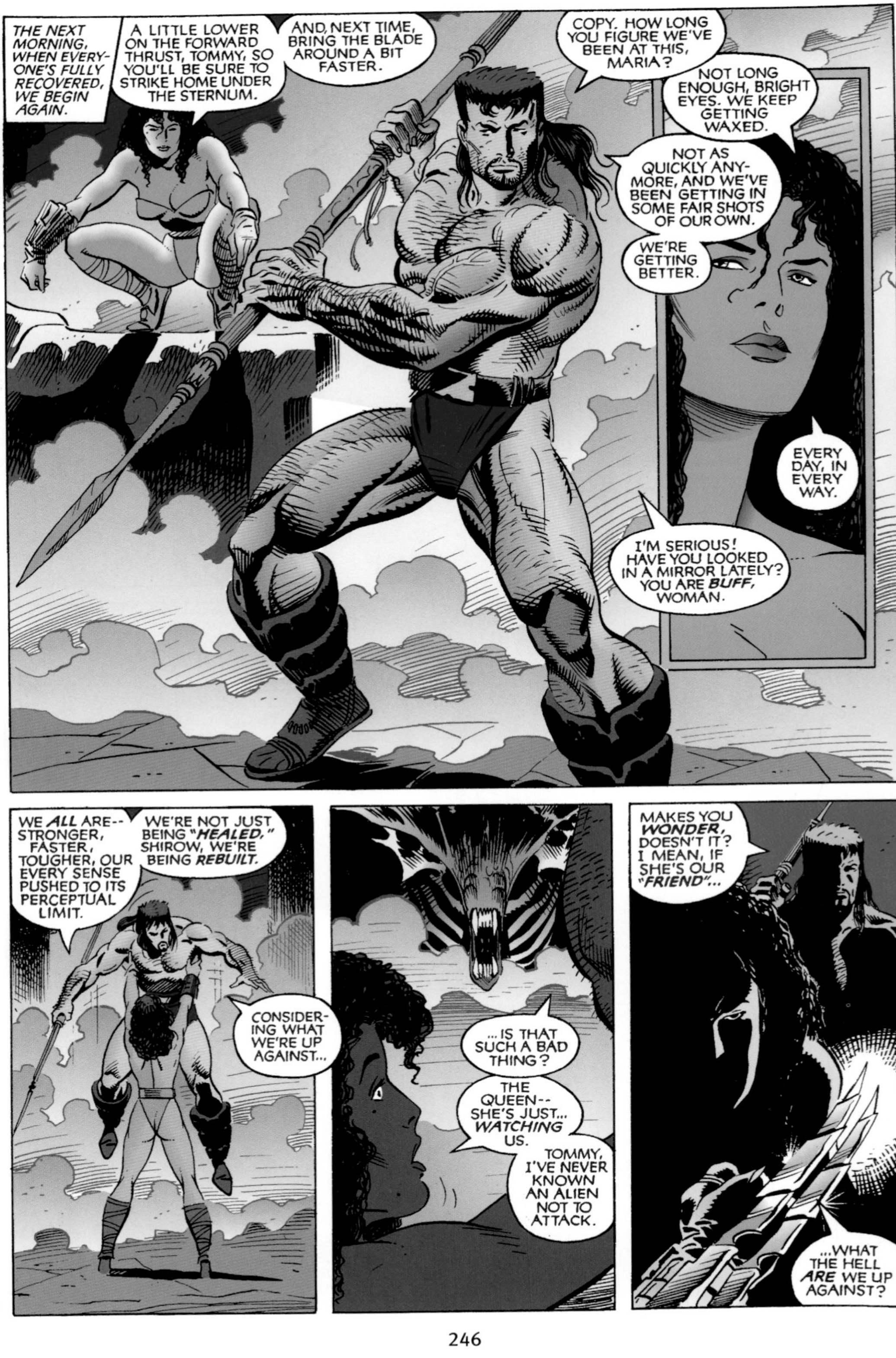
THE NEXT MORNING, WHEN EVERY-ONE'S FULLY RECOVERED, WE BEGIN AGAIN.
A LITTLE LOWER ON THE FORWARD THRUST, TOMMY, SO YOU'LL BE SURE TO STRIKE HOME UNDER THE STERNUM.
AND, NEXT TIME, BRING THE BLADE AROUND A BIT FASTER.
COPY. HOW LONG YOU FIGURE WE'VE BEEN AT THIS, MARIA?
NOT LONG ENOUGH, BRIGHT EYES. WE KEEP GETTING WAXED.
NOT AS QUICKLY ANY-MORE, AND WE'VE BEEN GETTING IN SOME FAIR SHOTS OF OUR OWN.
WE'RE GETTING BETTER.
EVERY DAY, IN EVERY WAY.
I'M SERIOUS! HAVE YOU LOOKED IN A MIRROR LATELY? YOU ARE BUFF, WOMAN.
WE ALL ARE-- STRONGER, FASTER, TOUGHER, OUR EVERY SENSE PUSHED TO ITS PERCEPTUAL LIMIT.
WE'RE NOT JUST BEING "HEALED," SHIROW, WE'RE BEING REBUILT.
CONSIDER-ING WHAT WE'RE UP AGAINST...
...IS THAT SUCH A BAD THING?
THE QUEEN-- SHE'S JUST... WATCHING US.
TOMMY, I'VE NEVER KNOWN AN ALIEN NOT TO ATTACK.
MAKES YOU WONDER, DOESN'T IT? I MEAN, IF SHE'S OUR "FRIEND"...
...WHAT THE HELL ARE WE UP AGAINST?

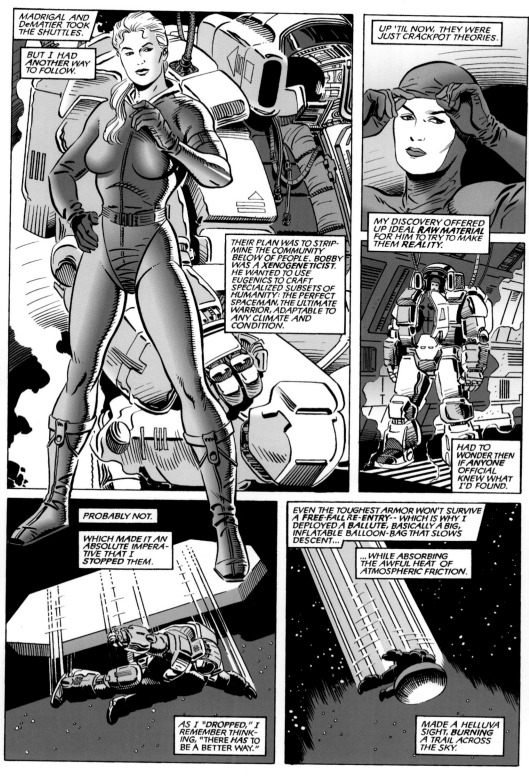

MADRIGAL AND DeMATIER TOOK THE SHUTTLES.

BUT I HAD ANOTHER WAY TO FOLLOW.

UP 'TIL NOW, THEY WERE JUST CRACKPOT THEORIES.

THEIR PLAN WAS TO STRIP-MINE THE COMMUNITY BELOW OF PEOPLE. BOBBY WAS A *XENOGENETICIST*. HE WANTED TO USE EUGENICS TO CRAFT SPECIALIZED SUBSETS OF HUMANITY: THE PERFECT SPACEMAN, THE ULTIMATE WARRIOR, ADAPTABLE TO ANY CLIMATE AND CONDITION.

MY DISCOVERY OFFERED UP IDEAL *RAW MATERIAL* FOR HIM TO TRY TO MAKE THEM *REALITY*.

HAD TO WONDER THEN IF *ANYONE* OFFICIAL KNEW WHAT I'D FOUND.

PROBABLY NOT.

WHICH MADE IT AN ABSOLUTE IMPERA-TIVE THAT I STOPPED THEM.

AS I "DROPPED," I REMEMBER THINK-ING, "THERE *HAS* TO BE A BETTER WAY."

EVEN THE TOUGHEST ARMOR WON'T SURVIVE A *FREE-FALL* RE-ENTRY-- WHICH IS WHY I DEPLOYED A *BALLUTE*, BASICALLY A BIG, INFLATABLE BALLOON-BAG THAT SLOWS DESCENT...

...WHILE ABSORBING THE AWFUL HEAT OF ATMOSPHERIC FRICTION.

MADE A HELLUVA SIGHT. *BURNING* A TRAIL ACROSS THE SKY.

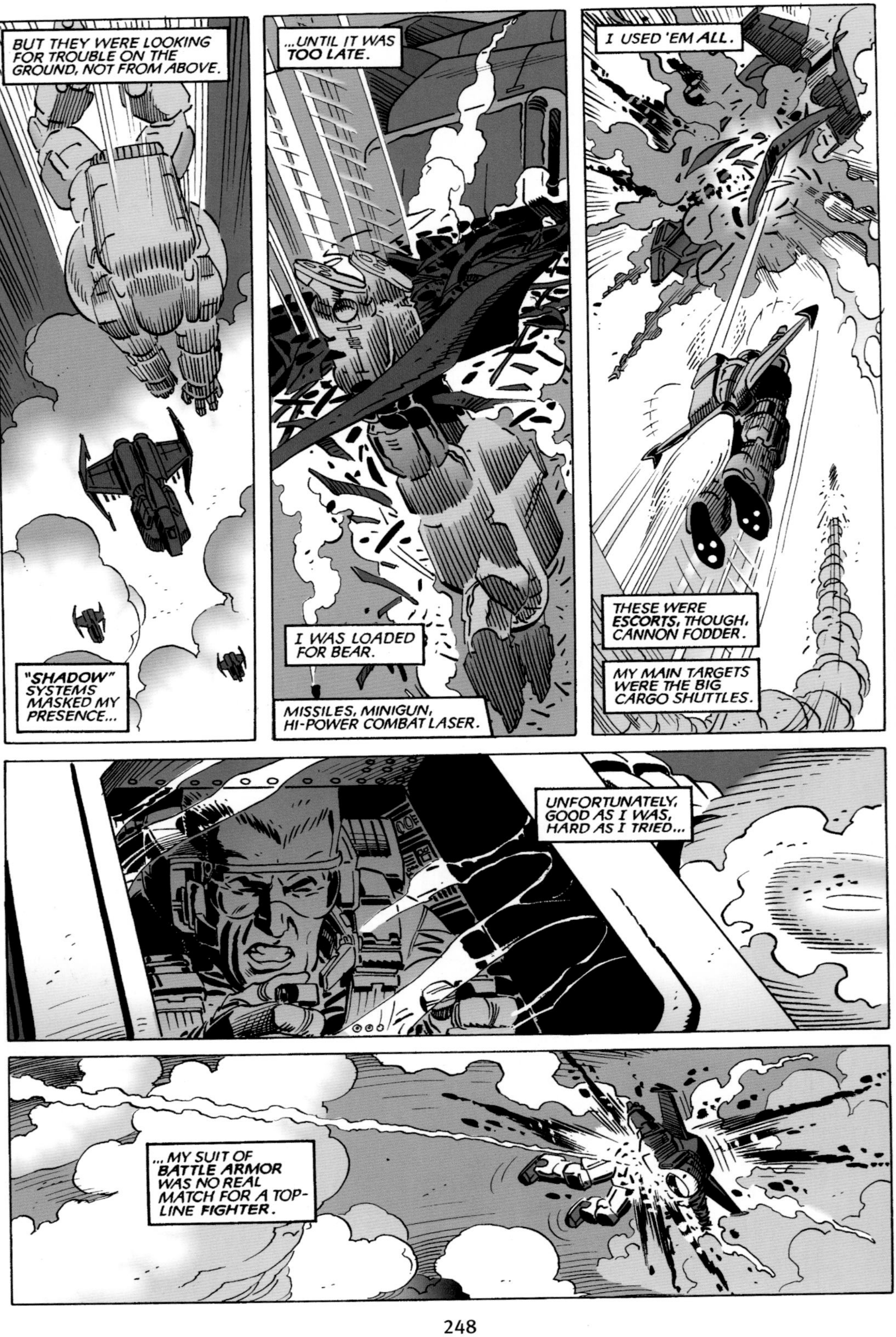
BUT THEY WERE LOOKING FOR TROUBLE ON THE GROUND, NOT FROM ABOVE.
"SHADOW" SYSTEMS MASKED MY PRESENCE...
...UNTIL IT WAS TOO LATE.
I WAS LOADED FOR BEAR.
MISSILES, MINIGUN, HI-POWER COMBAT LASER.
I USED 'EM ALL.
THESE WERE ESCORTS, THOUGH, CANNON FODDER.
MY MAIN TARGETS WERE THE BIG CARGO SHUTTLES.
UNFORTUNATELY, GOOD AS I WAS, HARD AS I TRIED...
...MY SUIT OF BATTLE ARMOR WAS NO REAL MATCH FOR A TOP-LINE FIGHTER.

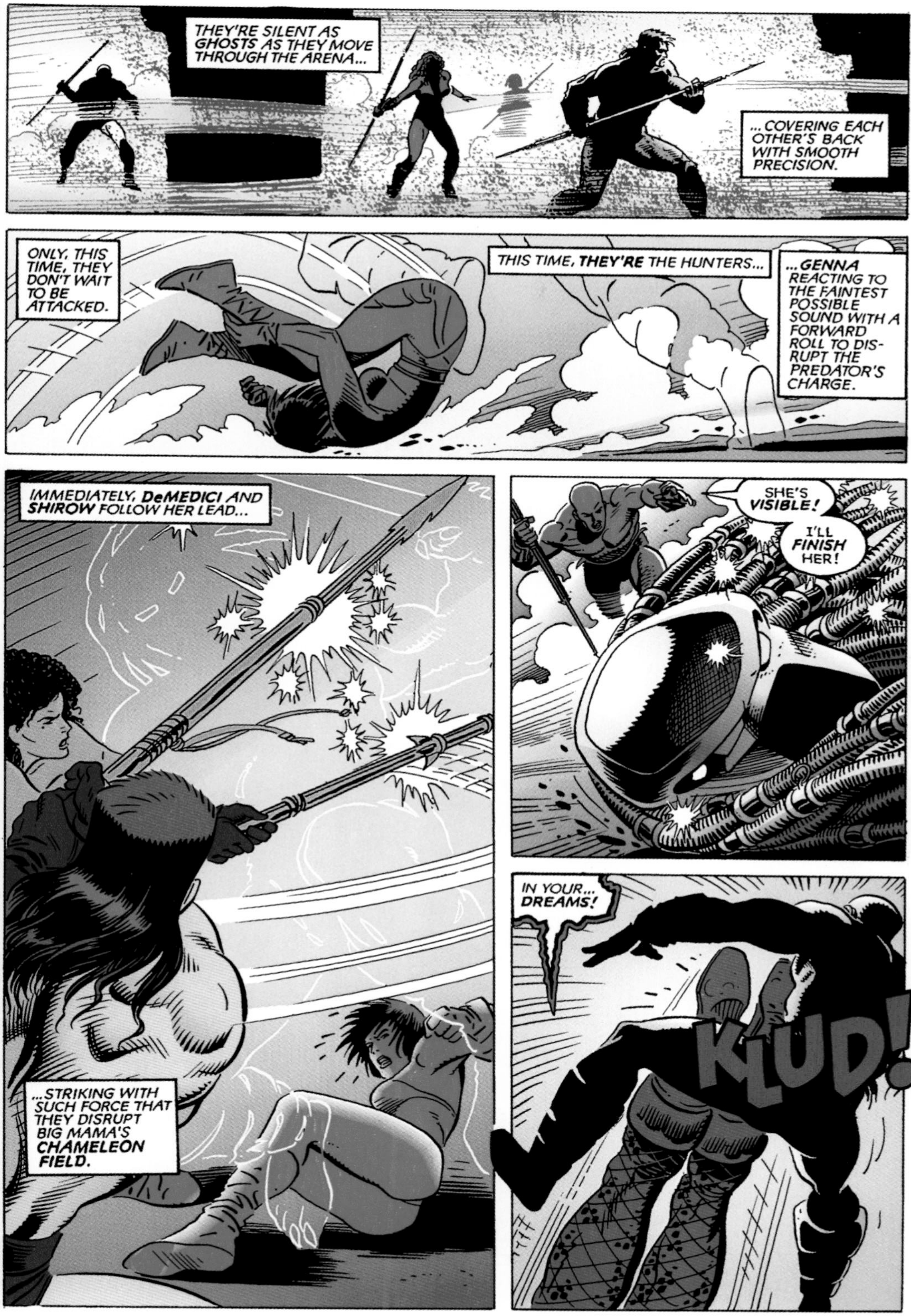
THEY'RE SILENT AS GHOSTS AS THEY MOVE THROUGH THE ARENA...
...COVERING EACH OTHER'S BACK WITH SMOOTH PRECISION.
ONLY, THIS TIME, THEY DON'T WAIT TO BE ATTACKED.
THIS TIME, THEY'RE THE HUNTERS...
...GENNA REACTING TO THE FAINTEST POSSIBLE SOUND WITH A FORWARD ROLL TO DISRUPT THE PREDATOR'S CHARGE.
IMMEDIATELY, DeMEDICI AND SHIROW FOLLOW HER LEAD...
...STRIKING WITH SUCH FORCE THAT THEY DISRUPT BIG MAMA'S CHAMELEON FIELD.
SHE'S VISIBLE!
I'LL FINISH HER!
IN YOUR... DREAMS!
KLUD!

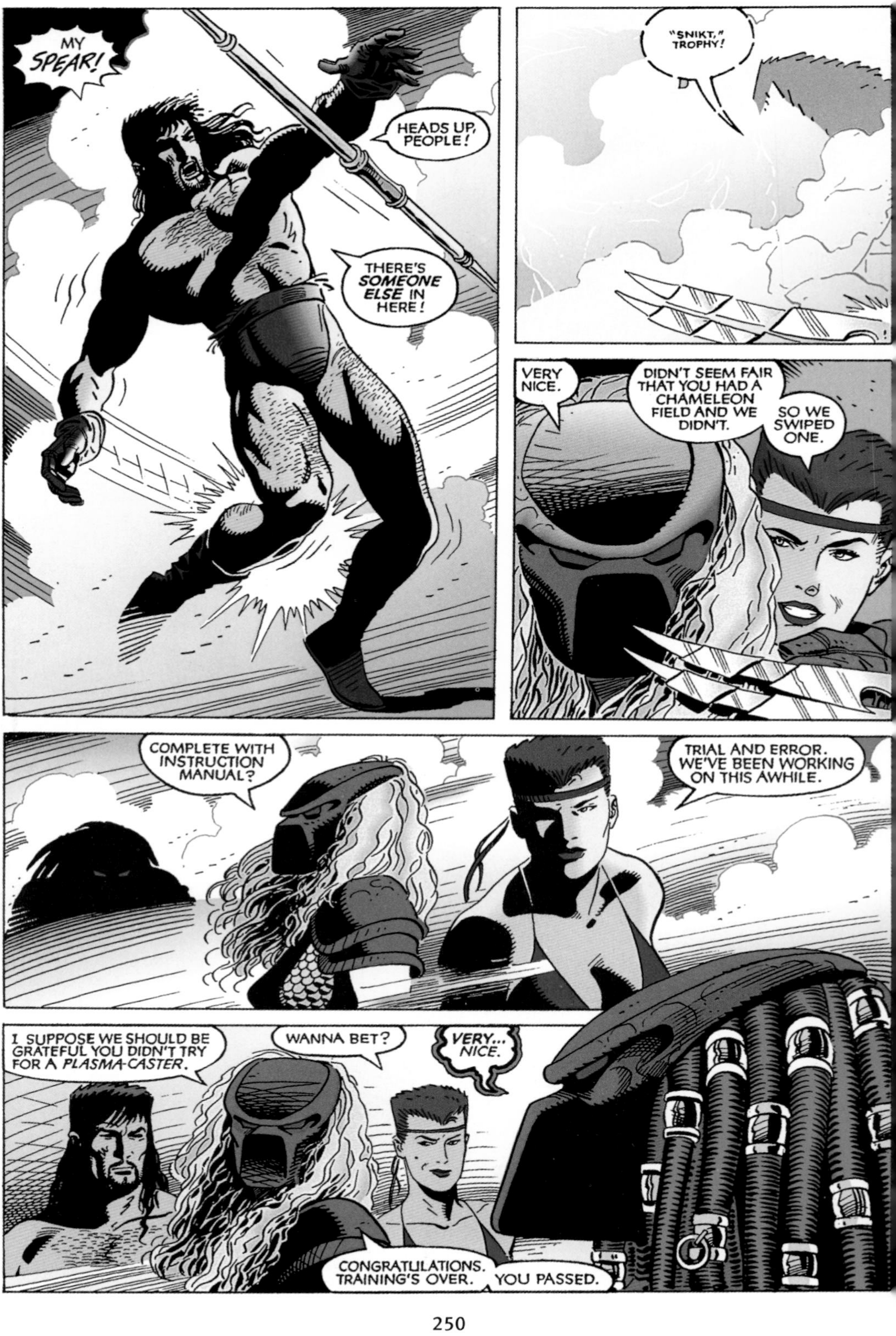

MY SPEAR!
HEADS UP, PEOPLE!
THERE'S SOMEONE ELSE IN HERE!
"SNIKT," TROPHY!
VERY NICE.
DIDN'T SEEM FAIR THAT YOU HAD A CHAMELEON FIELD AND WE DIDN'T.
SO WE SWIPED ONE.
COMPLETE WITH INSTRUCTION MANUAL?
TRIAL AND ERROR. WE'VE BEEN WORKING ON THIS AWHILE.
I SUPPOSE WE SHOULD BE GRATEFUL YOU DIDN'T TRY FOR A PLASMA-CASTER.
WANNA BET?
VERY... NICE.
CONGRATULATIONS. TRAINING'S OVER.
YOU PASSED.

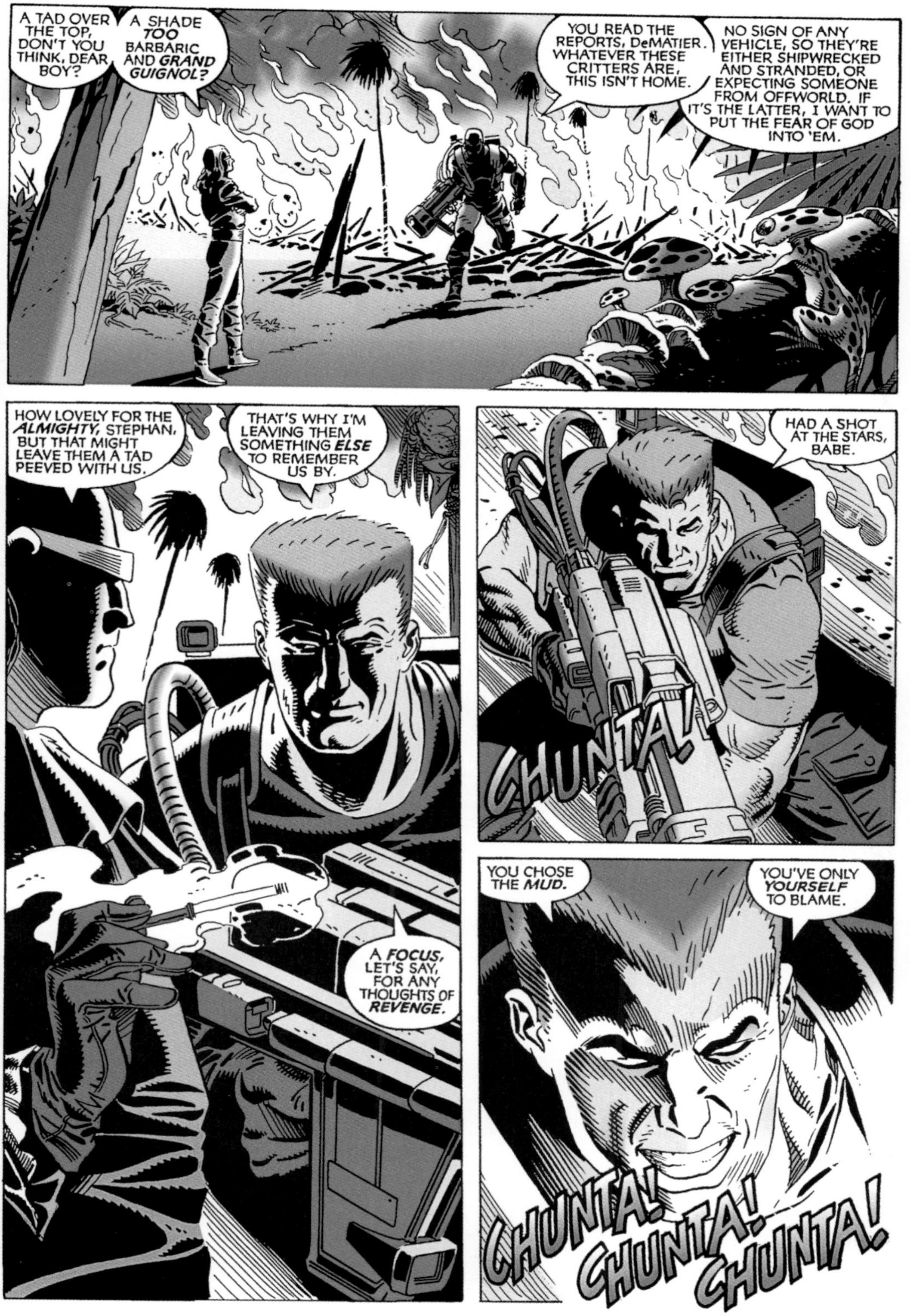
A TAD OVER THE TOP, DON'T YOU THINK, DEAR BOY?
A SHADE *TOO* BARBARIC AND *GRAND GUIGNOL?*
YOU READ THE REPORTS, DeMATIER. WHATEVER THESE CRITTERS ARE, THIS ISN'T HOME.
NO SIGN OF ANY VEHICLE, SO THEY'RE EITHER SHIPWRECKED AND STRANDED, OR EXPECTING SOMEONE FROM OFFWORLD. IF IT'S THE LATTER, I WANT TO PUT THE FEAR OF GOD INTO 'EM.
HOW LOVELY FOR THE *ALMIGHTY,* STEPHAN, BUT THAT MIGHT LEAVE THEM A TAD PEEVED WITH US.
THAT'S WHY I'M LEAVING THEM SOMETHING *ELSE* TO REMEMBER US BY.
A *FOCUS,* LET'S SAY, FOR ANY THOUGHTS OF *REVENGE.*
HAD A SHOT AT THE STARS, BABE.
CHUNTA!
YOU CHOSE THE *MUD.*
YOU'VE ONLY *YOURSELF* TO BLAME.
CHUNTA! CHUNTA! CHUNTA!

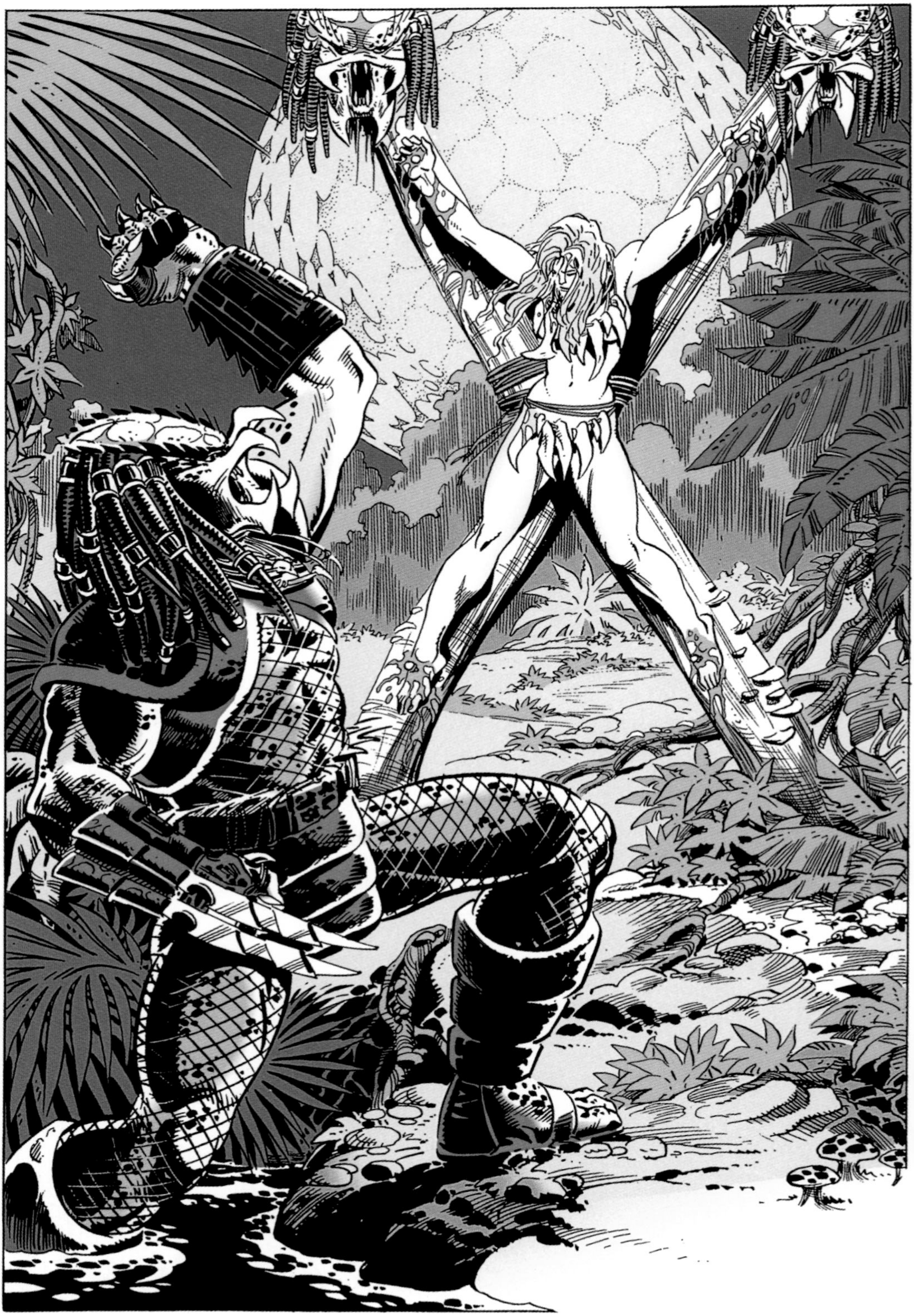

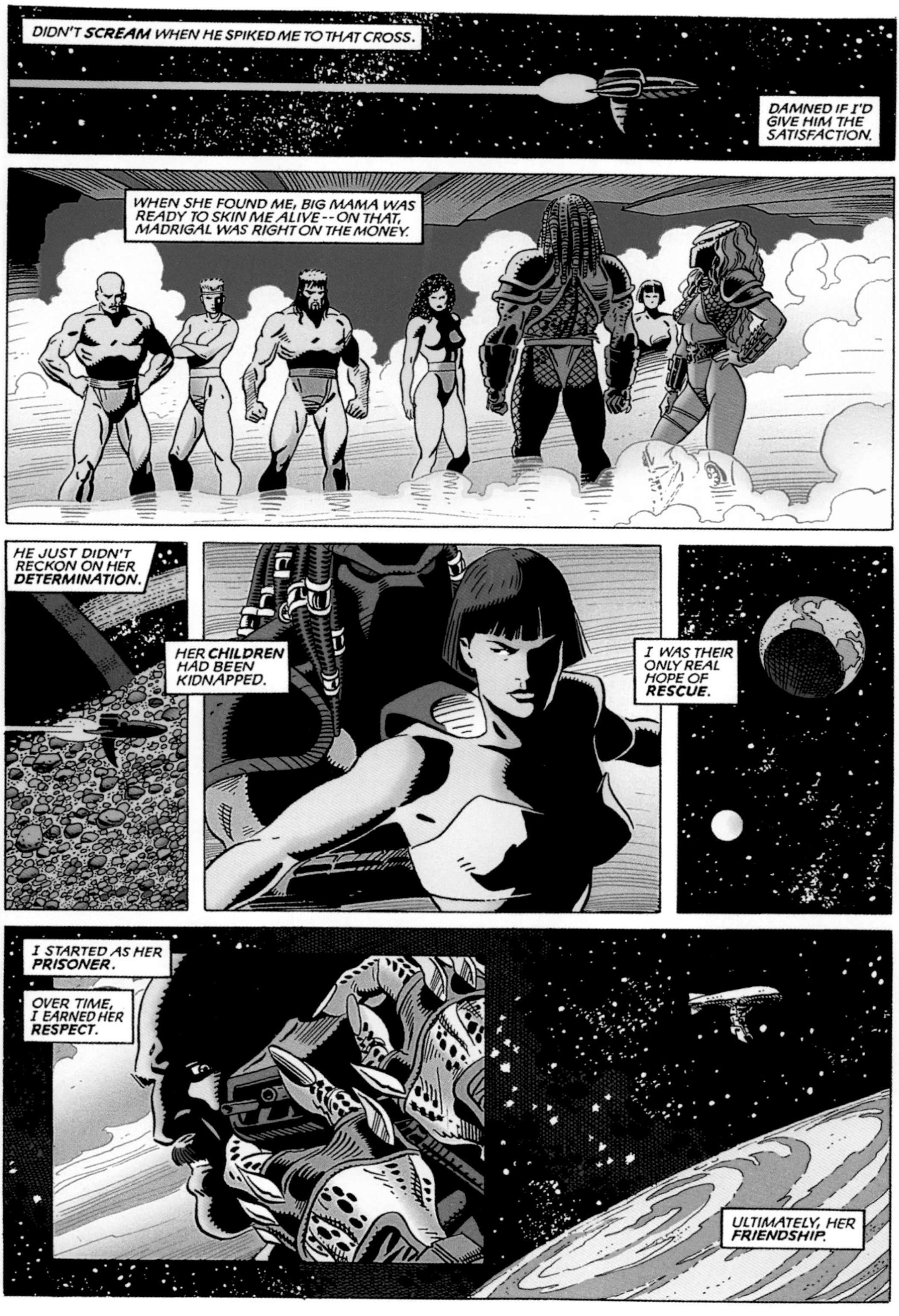
DIDN'T SCREAM WHEN HE SPIKED ME TO THAT CROSS.
DAMNED IF I'D GIVE HIM THE SATISFACTION.
WHEN SHE FOUND ME, BIG MAMA WAS READY TO SKIN ME ALIVE--ON THAT, MADRIGAL WAS RIGHT ON THE MONEY.
HE JUST DIDN'T RECKON ON HER DETERMINATION.
HER CHILDREN HAD BEEN KIDNAPPED.
I WAS THEIR ONLY REAL HOPE OF RESCUE.
I STARTED AS HER PRISONER.
OVER TIME, I EARNED HER RESPECT.
ULTIMATELY, HER FRIENDSHIP.

SHE *TRAINED* ME AS SHE WOULD HER OWN.

I TAUGHT HER EVERYTHING I KNEW.

WE WERE BOTH ALREADY *MAD.*

OUR GOAL WAS TO GET *EVEN.*

THAT'S WHERE I RUN OUT OF *MEMORIES.*

SO I GUESS WE CAME UP SHORT.

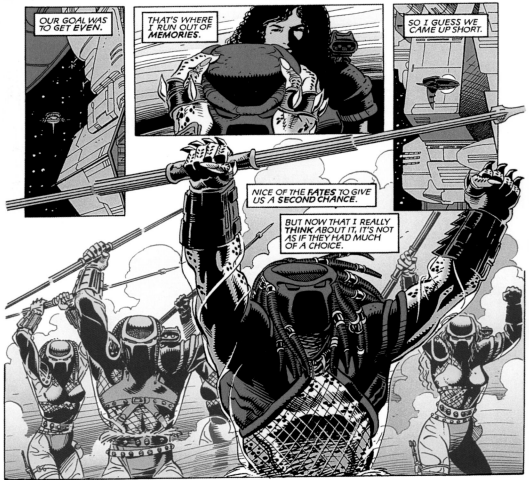

NICE OF THE *FATES* TO GIVE US A *SECOND CHANCE.*

BUT NOW THAT I REALLY *THINK* ABOUT IT, IT'S NOT AS IF THEY HAD MUCH OF A CHOICE.

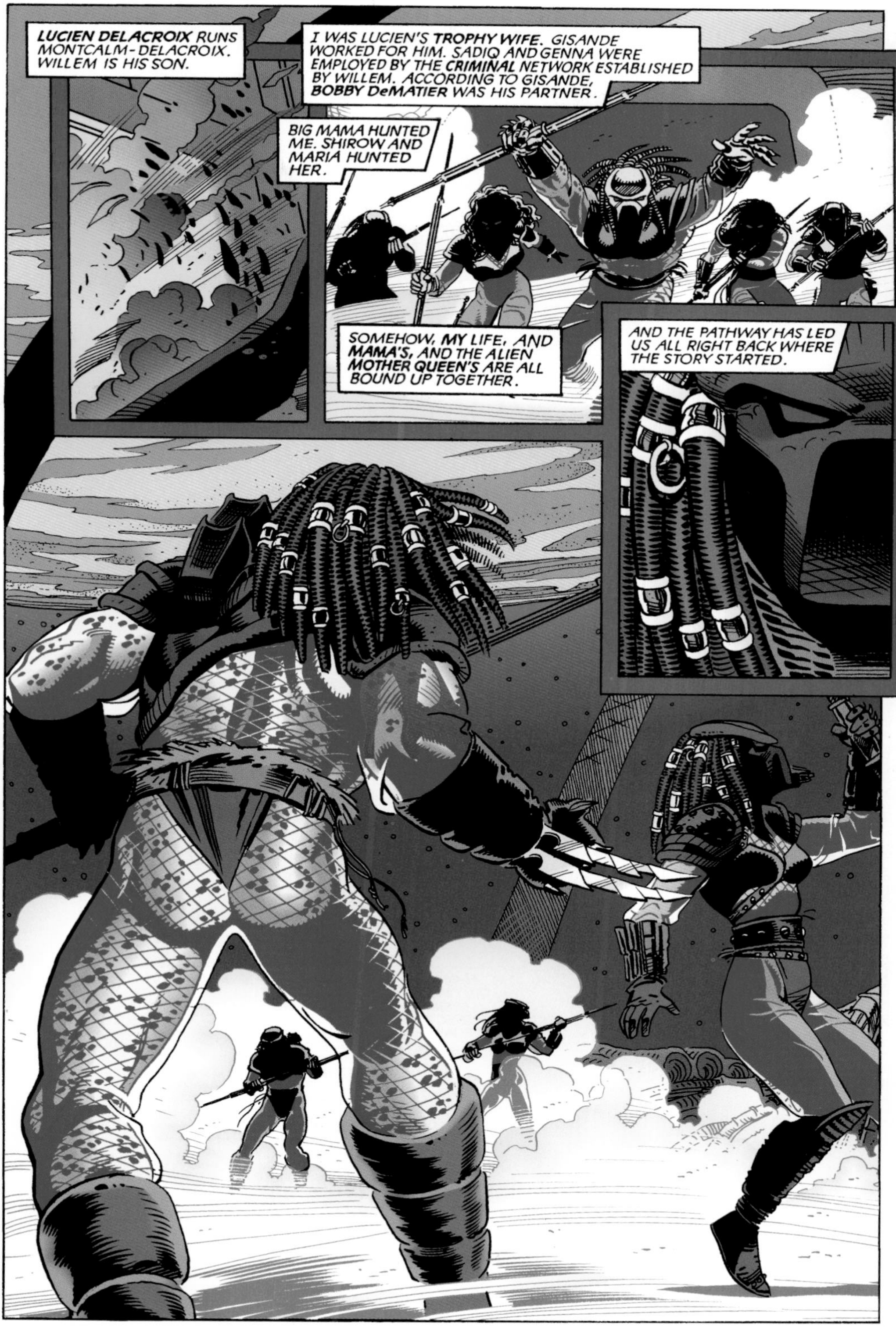
LUCIEN DELACROIX RUNS MONTCALM-DELACROIX. WILLEM IS HIS SON.
I WAS LUCIEN'S TROPHY WIFE. GISANDE WORKED FOR HIM. SADIQ AND GENNA WERE EMPLOYED BY THE CRIMINAL NETWORK ESTABLISHED BY WILLEM. ACCORDING TO GISANDE, BOBBY DeMATIER WAS HIS PARTNER.
BIG MAMA HUNTED ME. SHIROW AND MARIA HUNTED HER.
SOMEHOW, MY LIFE, AND MAMA'S, AND THE ALIEN MOTHER QUEEN'S ARE ALL BOUND UP TOGETHER.
AND THE PATHWAY HAS LED US ALL RIGHT BACK WHERE THE STORY STARTED.

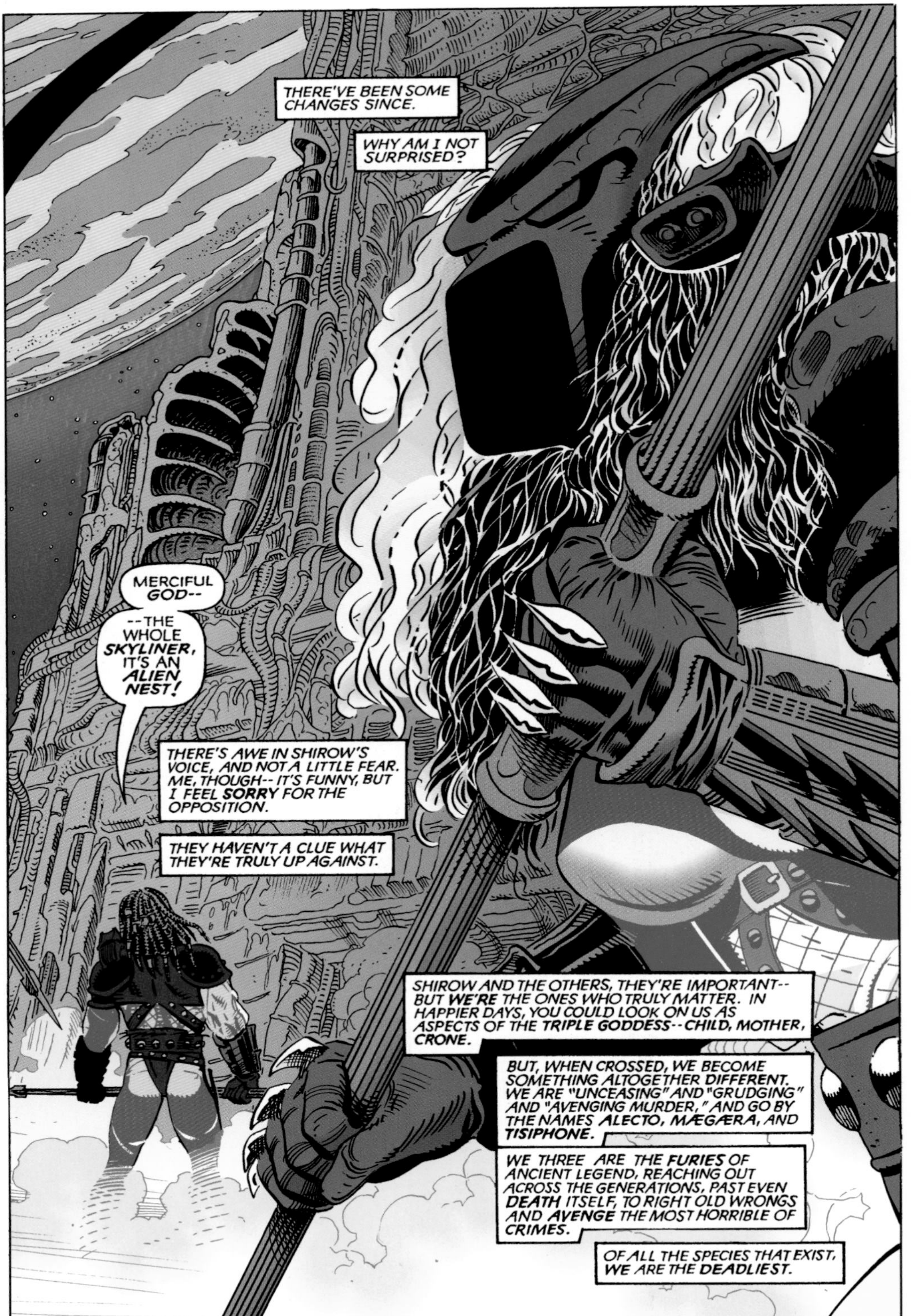

THERE'VE BEEN SOME CHANGES SINCE.
WHY AM I NOT SURPRISED?
MERCIFUL GOD--
--THE WHOLE SKYLINER, IT'S AN ALIEN NEST!
THERE'S AWE IN SHIROW'S VOICE, AND NOT A LITTLE FEAR. ME, THOUGH-- IT'S FUNNY, BUT I FEEL SORRY FOR THE OPPOSITION.
THEY HAVEN'T A CLUE WHAT THEY'RE TRULY UP AGAINST.
SHIROW AND THE OTHERS, THEY'RE IMPORTANT-- BUT WE'RE THE ONES WHO TRULY MATTER. IN HAPPIER DAYS, YOU COULD LOOK ON US AS ASPECTS OF THE TRIPLE GODDESS--CHILD, MOTHER, CRONE.
BUT, WHEN CROSSED, WE BECOME SOMETHING ALTOGETHER DIFFERENT. WE ARE "UNCEASING" AND "GRUDGING" AND "AVENGING MURDER," AND GO BY THE NAMES ALECTO, MÆGÆRA, AND TISIPHONE.
WE THREE ARE THE FURIES OF ANCIENT LEGEND, REACHING OUT ACROSS THE GENERATIONS, PAST EVEN DEATH ITSELF, TO RIGHT OLD WRONGS AND AVENGE THE MOST HORRIBLE OF CRIMES.
OF ALL THE SPECIES THAT EXIST, WE ARE THE DEADLIEST.

New BEGINNINGS

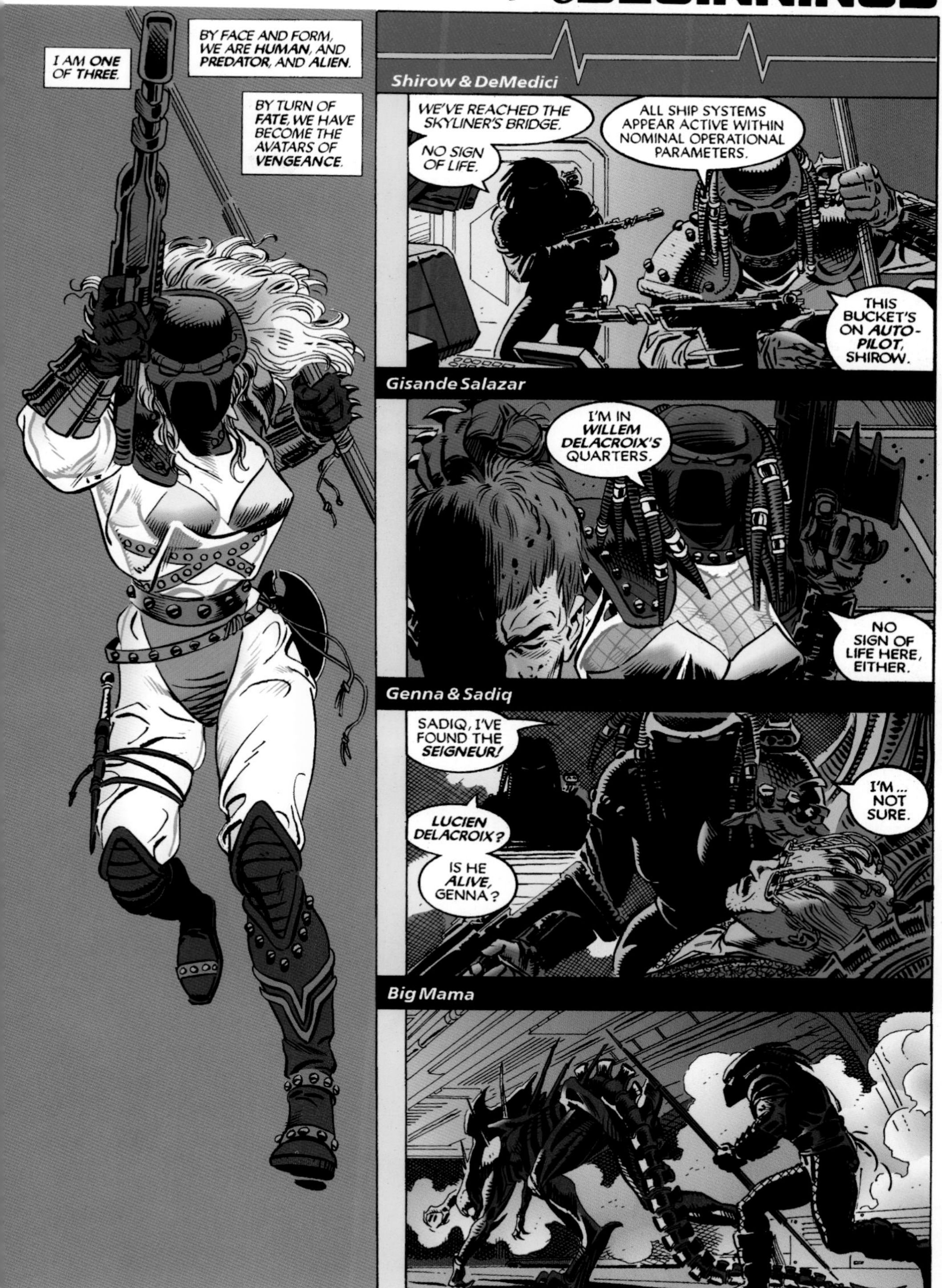
I AM ONE OF THREE.
BY FACE AND FORM, WE ARE HUMAN, AND PREDATOR, AND ALIEN.
BY TURN OF FATE, WE HAVE BECOME THE AVATARS OF VENGEANCE.
Shirow & DeMedici
WE'VE REACHED THE SKYLINER'S BRIDGE.
NO SIGN OF LIFE.
ALL SHIP SYSTEMS APPEAR ACTIVE WITHIN NOMINAL OPERATIONAL PARAMETERS.
THIS BUCKET'S ON AUTO-PILOT, SHIROW.
Gisande Salazar
I'M IN WILLEM DELACROIX'S QUARTERS.
NO SIGN OF LIFE HERE, EITHER.
Genna & Sadiq
SADIQ, I'VE FOUND THE SEIGNEUR!
LUCIEN DELACROIX?
IS HE ALIVE, GENNA?
I'M ... NOT SURE.
Big Mama

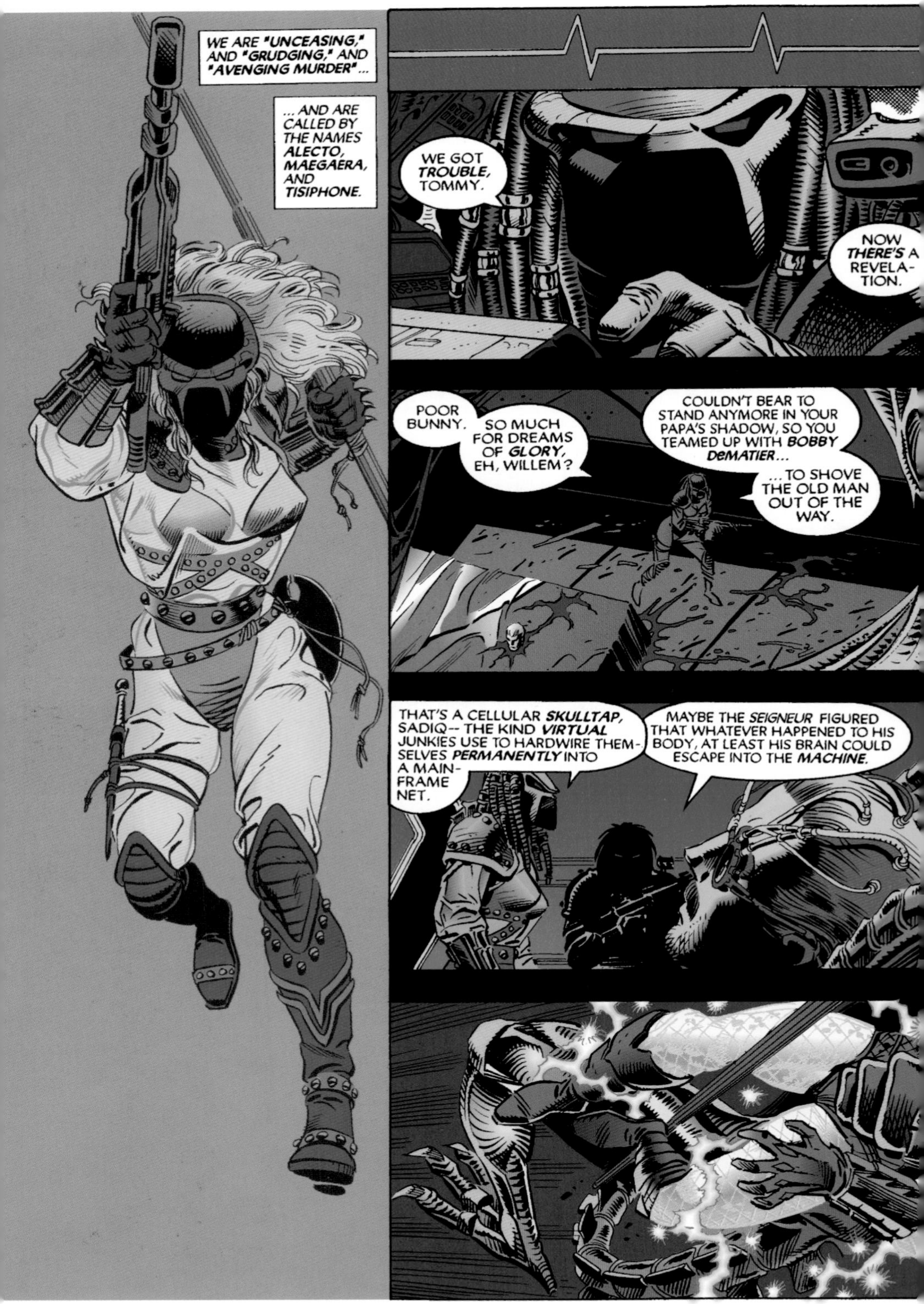

WE ARE "UNCEASING," AND "GRUDGING," AND "AVENGING MURDER"...
...AND ARE CALLED BY THE NAMES ALECTO, MAEGAERA, AND TISIPHONE.
WE GOT TROUBLE, TOMMY.
NOW THERE'S A REVELATION.
POOR BUNNY.
SO MUCH FOR DREAMS OF GLORY, EH, WILLEM?
COULDN'T BEAR TO STAND ANYMORE IN YOUR PAPA'S SHADOW, SO YOU TEAMED UP WITH BOBBY DeMATIER...
...TO SHOVE THE OLD MAN OUT OF THE WAY.
THAT'S A CELLULAR SKULLTAP, SADIQ-- THE KIND VIRTUAL JUNKIES USE TO HARDWIRE THEMSELVES PERMANENTLY INTO A MAINFRAME NET.
MAYBE THE SEIGNEUR FIGURED THAT WHATEVER HAPPENED TO HIS BODY, AT LEAST HIS BRAIN COULD ESCAPE INTO THE MACHINE.

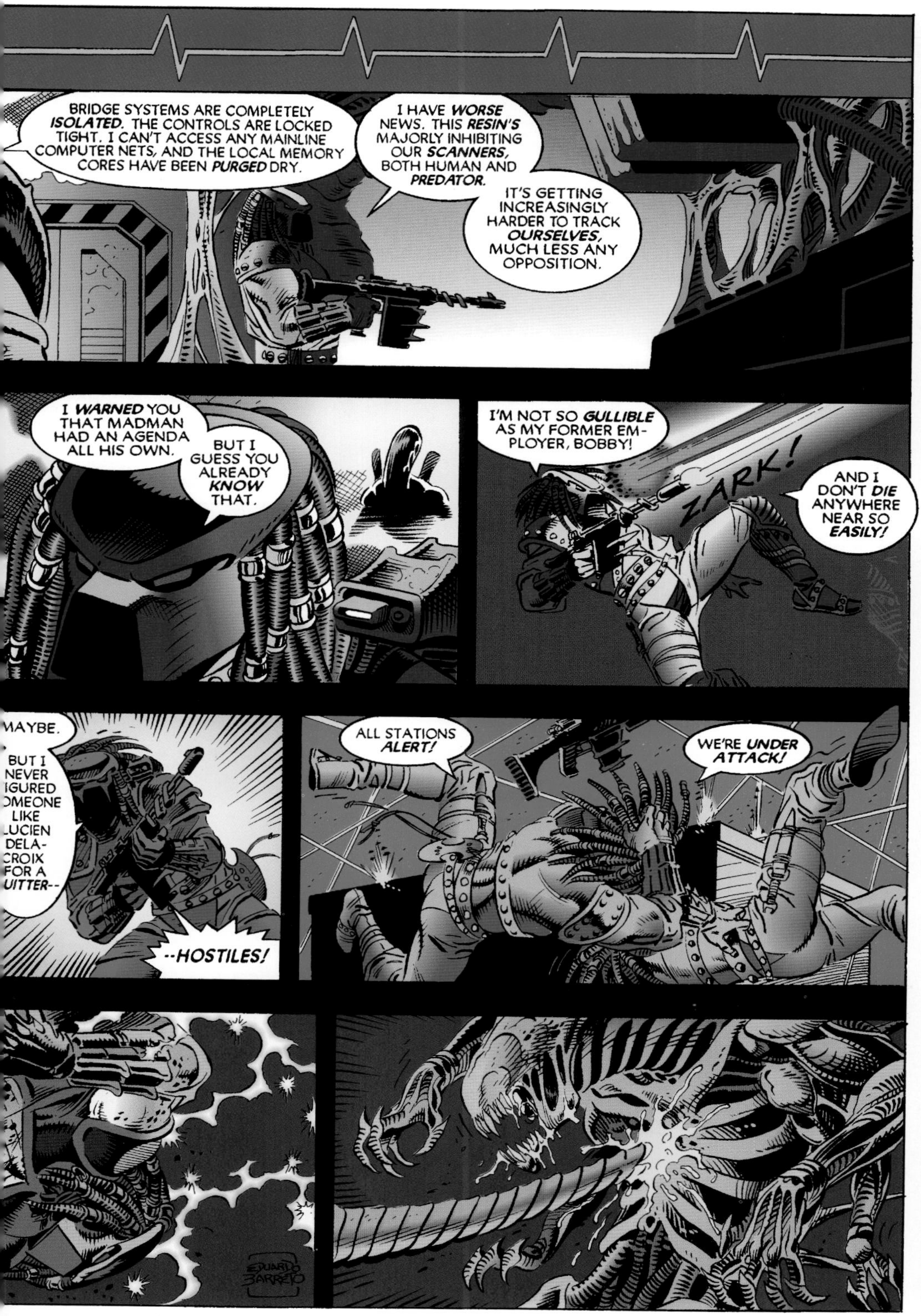
BRIDGE SYSTEMS ARE COMPLETELY ISOLATED. THE CONTROLS ARE LOCKED TIGHT. I CAN'T ACCESS ANY MAINLINE COMPUTER NETS, AND THE LOCAL MEMORY CORES HAVE BEEN PURGED DRY.
I HAVE WORSE NEWS. THIS RESIN'S MAJORLY INHIBITING OUR SCANNERS, BOTH HUMAN AND PREDATOR.
IT'S GETTING INCREASINGLY HARDER TO TRACK OURSELVES, MUCH LESS ANY OPPOSITION.
I WARNED YOU THAT MADMAN HAD AN AGENDA ALL HIS OWN.
BUT I GUESS YOU ALREADY KNOW THAT.
I'M NOT SO GULLIBLE AS MY FORMER EM-PLOYER, BOBBY!
ZARK!
AND I DON'T DIE ANYWHERE NEAR SO EASILY!
MAYBE.
BUT I NEVER IGURED OMEONE LIKE LUCIEN DELA-CROIX FOR A UITTER--
--HOSTILES!
ALL STATIONS ALERT!
WE'RE UNDER ATTACK!
EDUARDO BARRETO

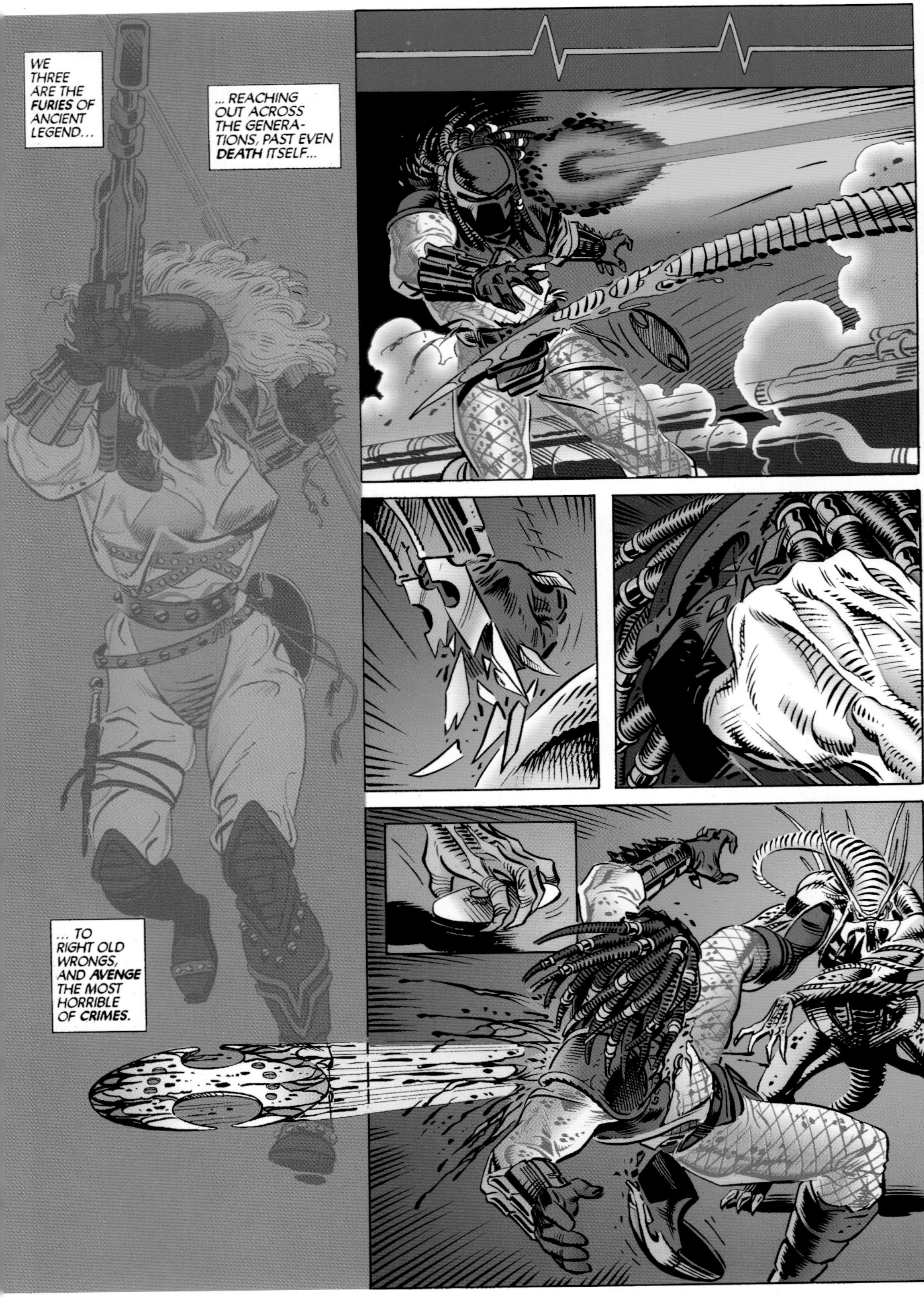
WE THREE ARE THE FURIES OF ANCIENT LEGEND...
... REACHING OUT ACROSS THE GENERA- TIONS, PAST EVEN DEATH ITSELF...
... TO RIGHT OLD WRONGS, AND AVENGE THE MOST HORRIBLE OF CRIMES.

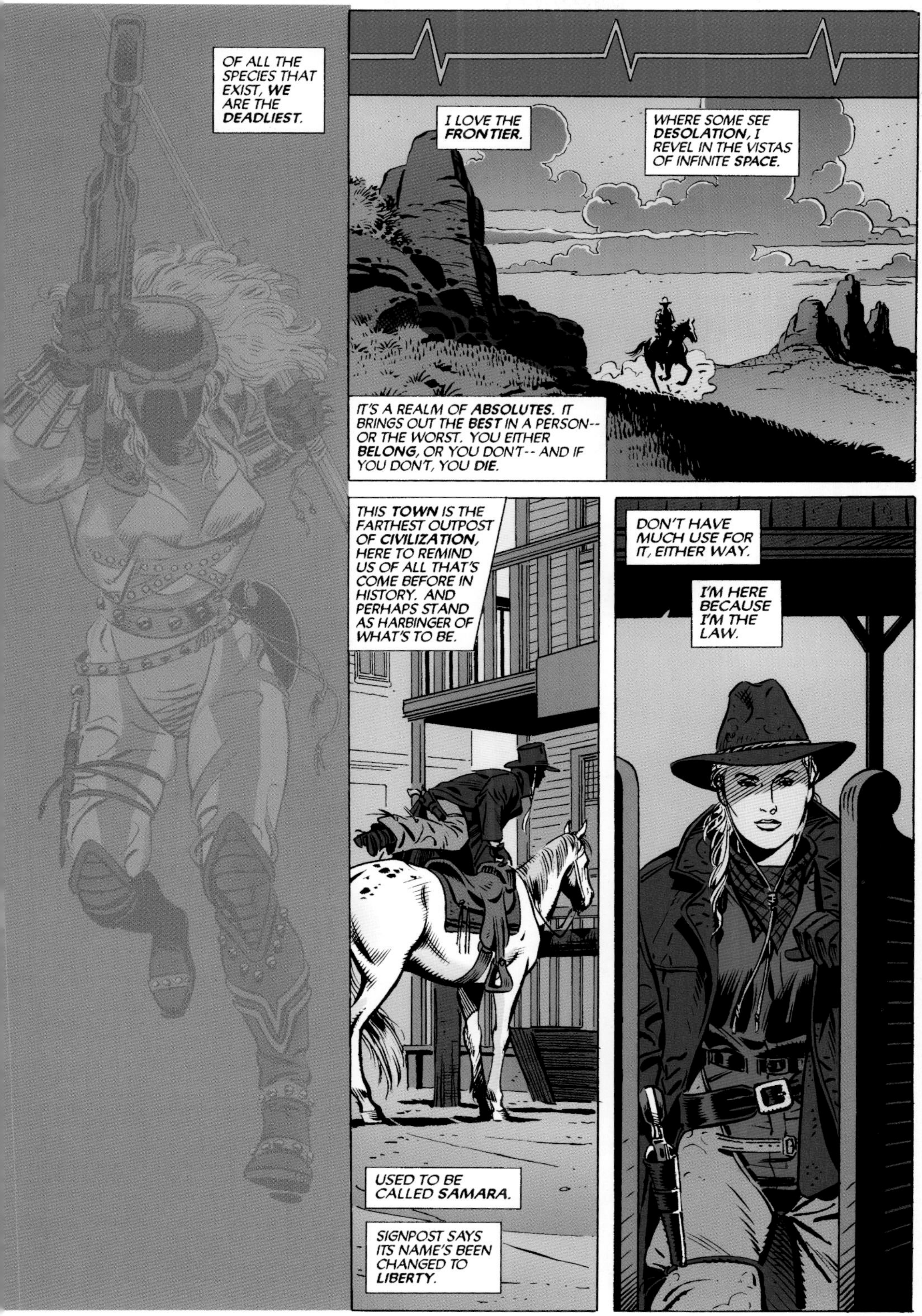

OF ALL THE SPECIES THAT EXIST, **WE** ARE THE **DEADLIEST**.
I LOVE THE **FRONTIER**.
WHERE SOME SEE **DESOLATION**, I REVEL IN THE VISTAS OF INFINITE **SPACE**.
IT'S A REALM OF **ABSOLUTES**. IT BRINGS OUT THE **BEST** IN A PERSON-- OR THE WORST. YOU EITHER **BELONG**, OR YOU DON'T-- AND IF YOU DON'T, YOU **DIE**.
THIS **TOWN** IS THE FARTHEST OUTPOST OF **CIVILIZATION**, HERE TO REMIND US OF ALL THAT'S COME BEFORE IN HISTORY. AND PERHAPS STAND AS HARBINGER OF WHAT'S TO BE.
USED TO BE CALLED **SAMARA**.
SIGNPOST SAYS ITS NAME'S BEEN CHANGED TO **LIBERTY**.
DON'T HAVE MUCH USE FOR IT, EITHER WAY.
I'M HERE BECAUSE I'M THE LAW.

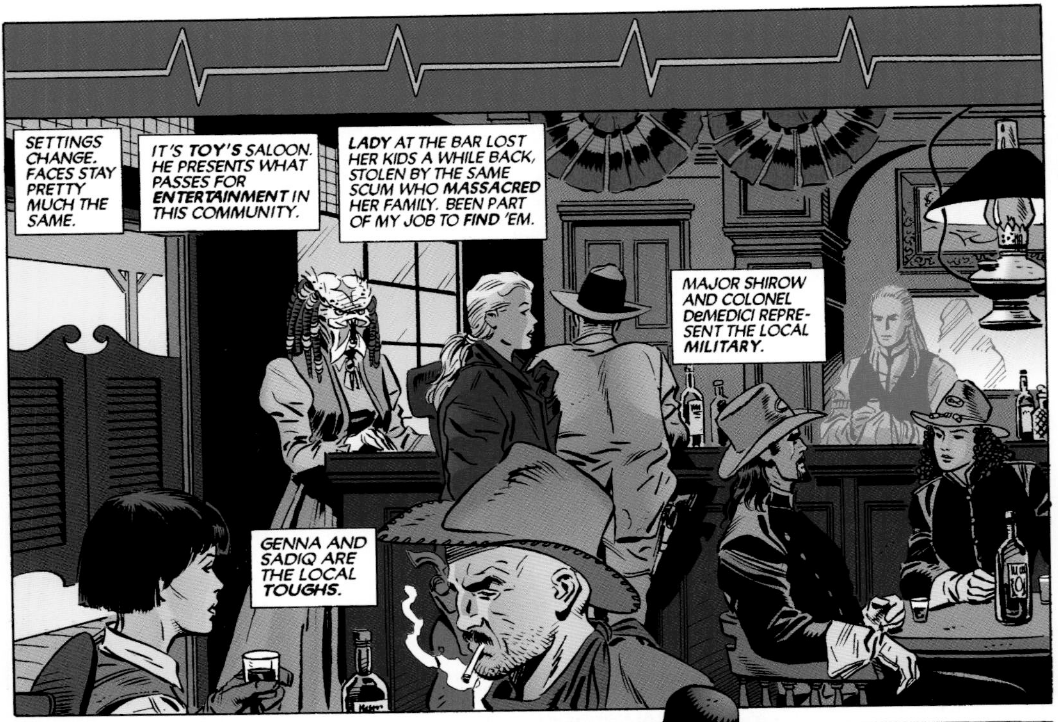
SETTINGS CHANGE. FACES STAY PRETTY MUCH THE SAME.
IT'S TOY'S SALOON. HE PRESENTS WHAT PASSES FOR ENTERTAINMENT IN THIS COMMUNITY.
LADY AT THE BAR LOST HER KIDS A WHILE BACK, STOLEN BY THE SAME SCUM WHO MASSACRED HER FAMILY. BEEN PART OF MY JOB TO FIND 'EM.
MAJOR SHIROW AND COLONEL DeMEDICI REPRESENT THE LOCAL MILITARY.
GENNA AND SADIQ ARE THE LOCAL TOUGHS.

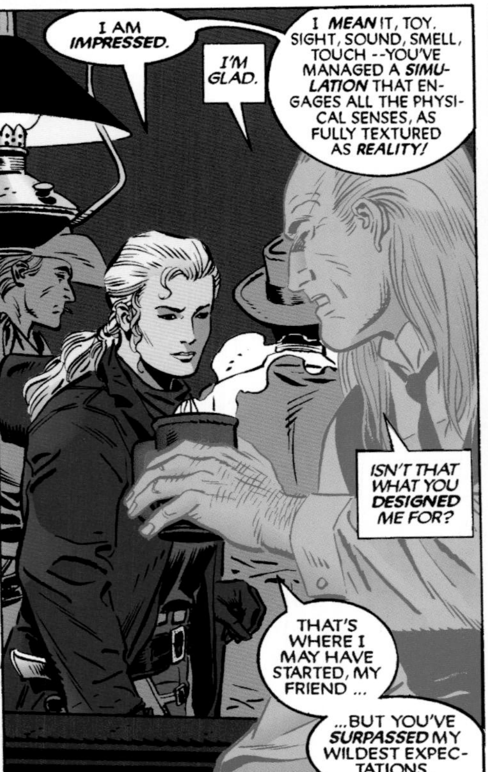
I AM IMPRESSED.
I'M GLAD.
I MEAN IT, TOY. SIGHT, SOUND, SMELL, TOUCH --YOU'VE MANAGED A SIMULATION THAT ENGAGES ALL THE PHYSICAL SENSES, AS FULLY TEXTURED AS REALITY!
ISN'T THAT WHAT YOU DESIGNED ME FOR?
THAT'S WHERE I MAY HAVE STARTED, MY FRIEND ...
...BUT YOU'VE SURPASSED MY WILDEST EXPECTATIONS.

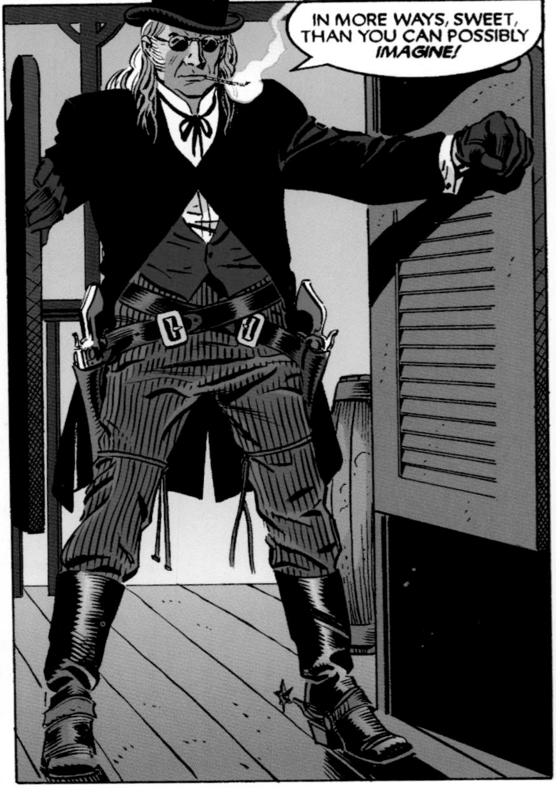
IN MORE WAYS, SWEET, THAN YOU CAN POSSIBLY IMAGINE!

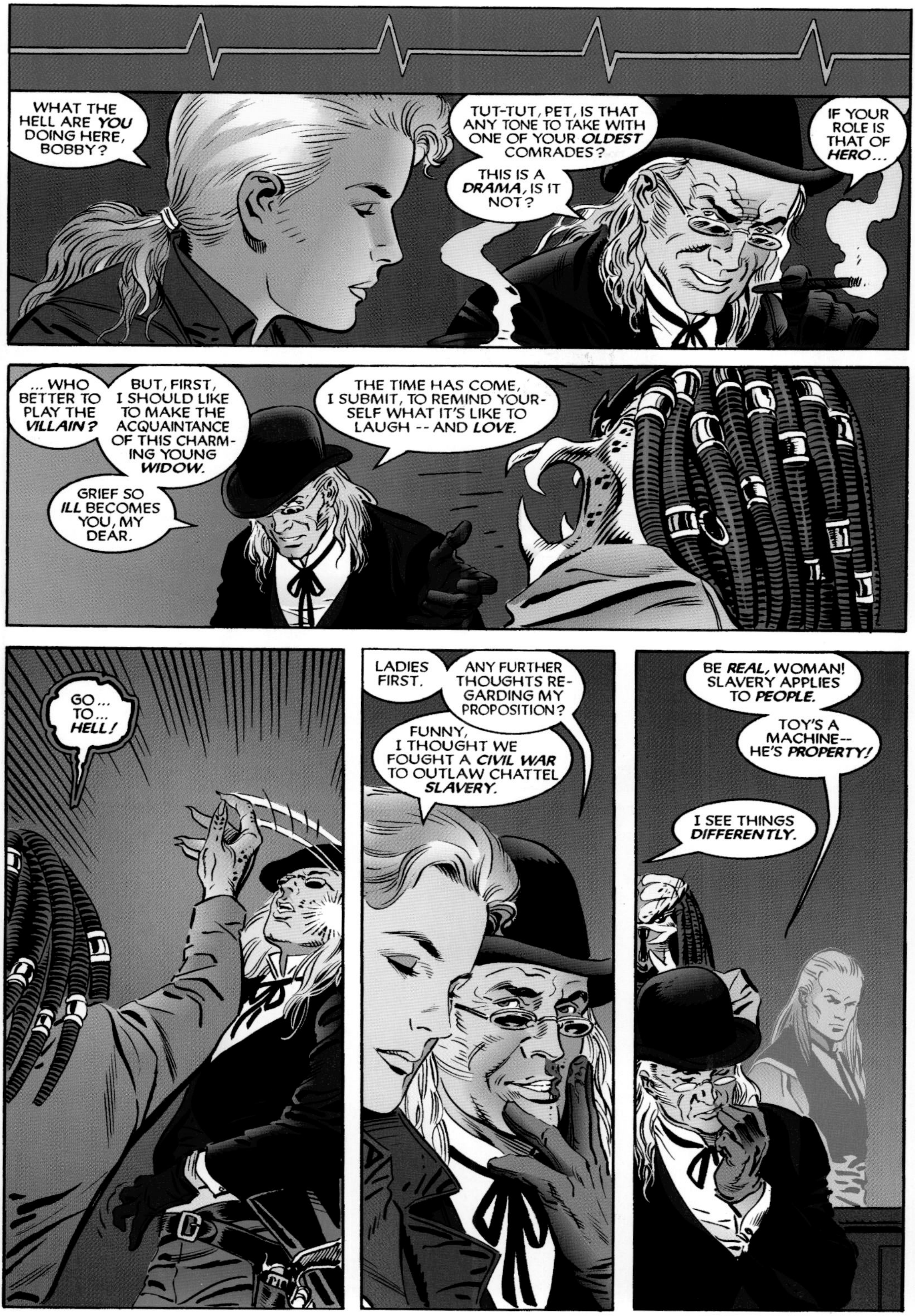
WHAT THE HELL ARE YOU DOING HERE, BOBBY?
TUT-TUT, PET, IS THAT ANY TONE TO TAKE WITH ONE OF YOUR OLDEST COMRADES?
THIS IS A DRAMA, IS IT NOT?
IF YOUR ROLE IS THAT OF HERO...
...WHO BETTER TO PLAY THE VILLAIN?
BUT, FIRST, I SHOULD LIKE TO MAKE THE ACQUAINTANCE OF THIS CHARMING YOUNG WIDOW.
GRIEF SO ILL BECOMES YOU, MY DEAR.
THE TIME HAS COME, I SUBMIT, TO REMIND YOURSELF WHAT IT'S LIKE TO LAUGH -- AND LOVE.
GO... TO... HELL!
LADIES FIRST.
ANY FURTHER THOUGHTS REGARDING MY PROPOSITION?
FUNNY, I THOUGHT WE FOUGHT A CIVIL WAR TO OUTLAW CHATTEL SLAVERY.
BE REAL, WOMAN! SLAVERY APPLIES TO PEOPLE.
TOY'S A MACHINE-- HE'S PROPERTY!
I SEE THINGS DIFFERENTLY.

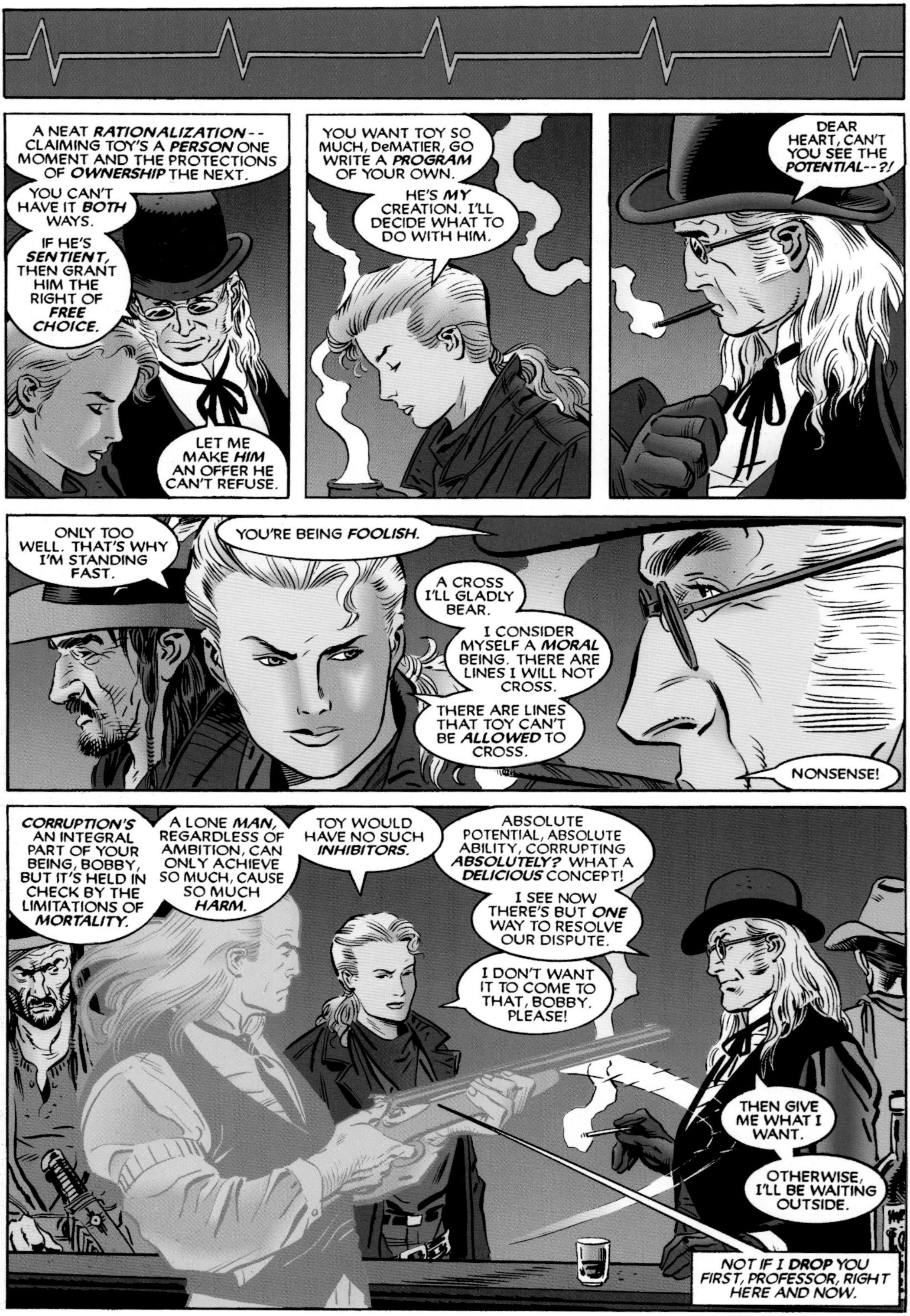
A NEAT RATIONALIZATION-- CLAIMING TOY'S A PERSON ONE MOMENT AND THE PROTECTIONS OF OWNERSHIP THE NEXT.
YOU CAN'T HAVE IT BOTH WAYS.
IF HE'S SENTIENT, THEN GRANT HIM THE RIGHT OF FREE CHOICE.
LET ME MAKE HIM AN OFFER HE CAN'T REFUSE.
YOU WANT TOY SO MUCH, DeMATIER, GO WRITE A PROGRAM OF YOUR OWN.
HE'S MY CREATION. I'LL DECIDE WHAT TO DO WITH HIM.
DEAR HEART, CAN'T YOU SEE THE POTENTIAL--?!
ONLY TOO WELL. THAT'S WHY I'M STANDING FAST.
YOU'RE BEING FOOLISH.
A CROSS I'LL GLADLY BEAR.
I CONSIDER MYSELF A MORAL BEING. THERE ARE LINES I WILL NOT CROSS.
THERE ARE LINES THAT TOY CAN'T BE ALLOWED TO CROSS.
NONSENSE!
CORRUPTION'S AN INTEGRAL PART OF YOUR BEING, BOBBY, BUT IT'S HELD IN CHECK BY THE LIMITATIONS OF MORTALITY.
A LONE MAN, REGARDLESS OF AMBITION, CAN ONLY ACHIEVE SO MUCH, CAUSE SO MUCH HARM.
TOY WOULD HAVE NO SUCH INHIBITORS.
ABSOLUTE POTENTIAL, ABSOLUTE ABILITY, CORRUPTING ABSOLUTELY? WHAT A DELICIOUS CONCEPT!
I SEE NOW THERE'S BUT ONE WAY TO RESOLVE OUR DISPUTE.
I DON'T WANT IT TO COME TO THAT, BOBBY. PLEASE!
THEN GIVE ME WHAT I WANT.
OTHERWISE, I'LL BE WAITING OUTSIDE.
NOT IF I DROP YOU FIRST, PROFESSOR, RIGHT HERE AND NOW.

WHATEVER IS *THAT* I SEE IN YOUR EYES, LITTLE *PROGRAM?*

BLESS MY BLACK SOUL--

--COULD IT BE *HATE?*

I *AM* IMPRESSED.

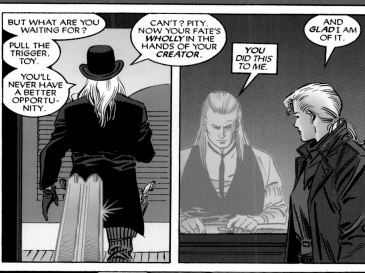

BUT WHAT ARE YOU WAITING FOR?

PULL THE TRIGGER, TOY.

YOU'LL NEVER HAVE A BETTER OPPORTUNITY.

CAN'T? PITY. NOW YOUR FATE'S *WHOLLY* IN THE HANDS OF YOUR *CREATOR.*

YOU DID THIS TO ME.

AND *GLAD* I AM OF IT.

ISAAC ASIMOV'S *THREE LAWS OF ROBOTICS* MAY HAVE BEEN BORN OF A WORK OF FICTION, BUT THEY'RE AS CLEAR AND FUNDAMENTAL A STATEMENT OF *DECENCY* AS YOU'RE EVER LIKELY TO FIND.

DeMATIER'S A *THREAT.* HE SHOULD BE ELIMINATED.

THAT ISN'T WHY I CREATED YOU, TOY.

YOUR PURPOSE IS TO BRING *JOY* TO PEOPLE, NOT DO THEM-- *ANY* OF THEM--HARM.

I'M AFRAID OF HIM.

TRUST ME-- *I'LL* TAKE CARE OF THINGS.

YOU'LL BE *FINE.*

WRONG!

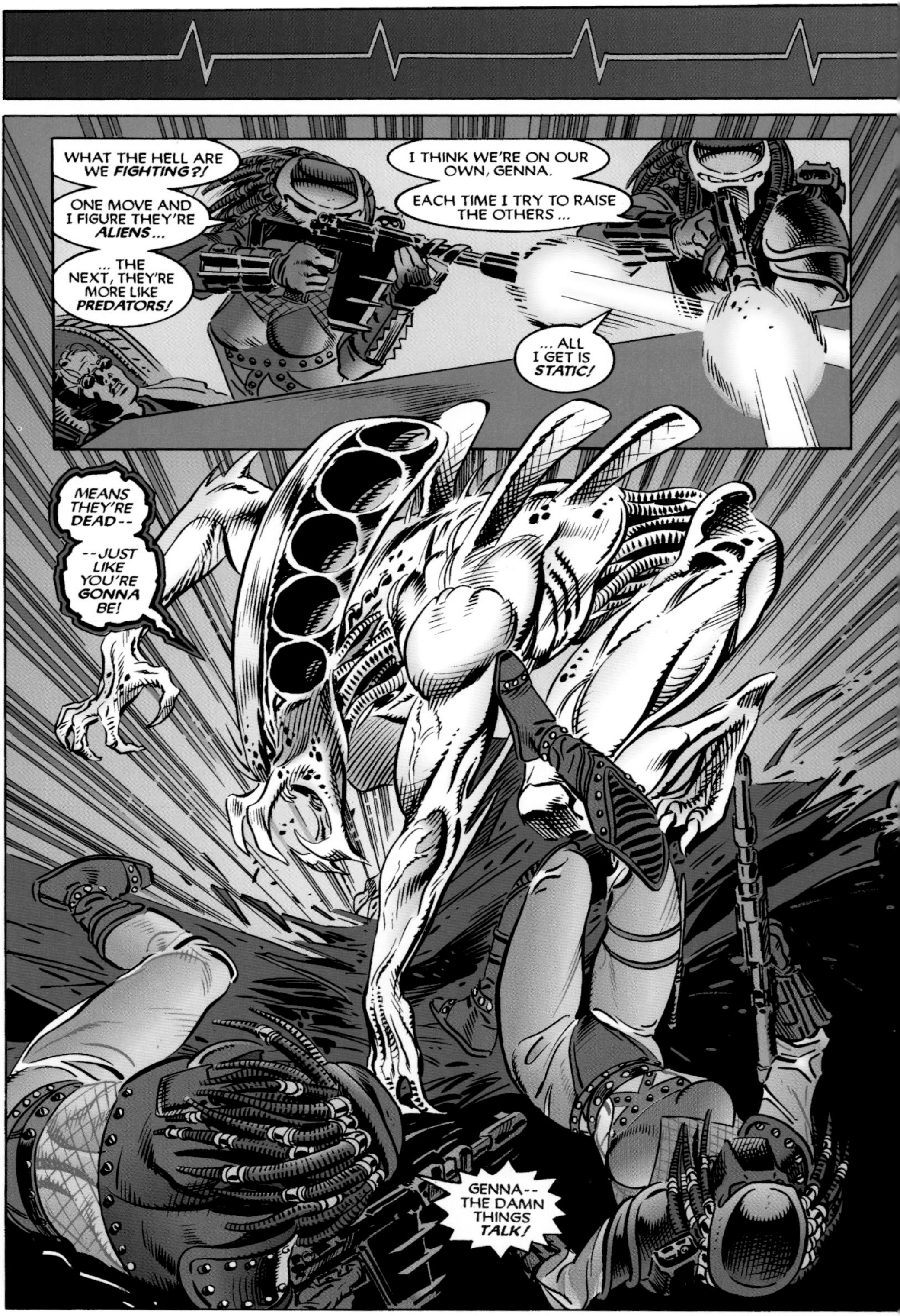

WHAT THE HELL ARE WE FIGHTING?!
ONE MOVE AND I FIGURE THEY'RE ALIENS...
... THE NEXT, THEY'RE MORE LIKE PREDATORS!
I THINK WE'RE ON OUR OWN, GENNA.
EACH TIME I TRY TO RAISE THE OTHERS ...
... ALL I GET IS STATIC!
MEANS THEY'RE DEAD--
--JUST LIKE YOU'RE GONNA BE!
GENNA-- THE DAMN THINGS TALK!

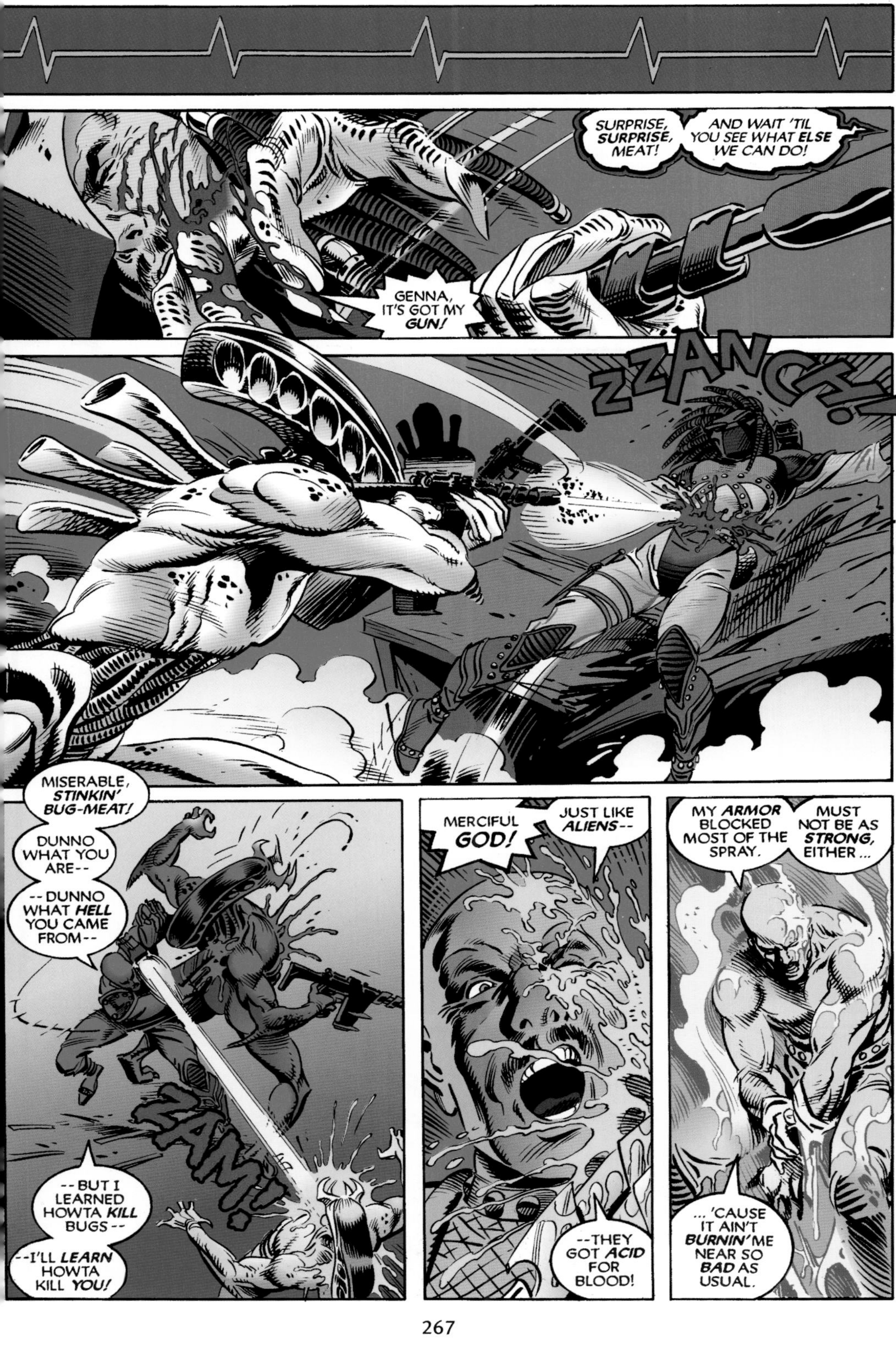
SURPRISE, SURPRISE, MEAT!
AND WAIT 'TIL YOU SEE WHAT ELSE WE CAN DO!
GENNA, IT'S GOT MY GUN!
ZZANCH!
MISERABLE, STINKIN' BUG-MEAT!
DUNNO WHAT YOU ARE--
--DUNNO WHAT HELL YOU CAME FROM--
ZAM!
--BUT I LEARNED HOWTA KILL BUGS--
--I'LL LEARN HOWTA KILL YOU!
MERCIFUL GOD!
JUST LIKE ALIENS--
--THEY GOT ACID FOR BLOOD!
MY ARMOR BLOCKED MOST OF THE SPRAY.
MUST NOT BE AS STRONG, EITHER ...
... 'CAUSE IT AIN'T BURNIN' ME NEAR SO BAD AS USUAL.

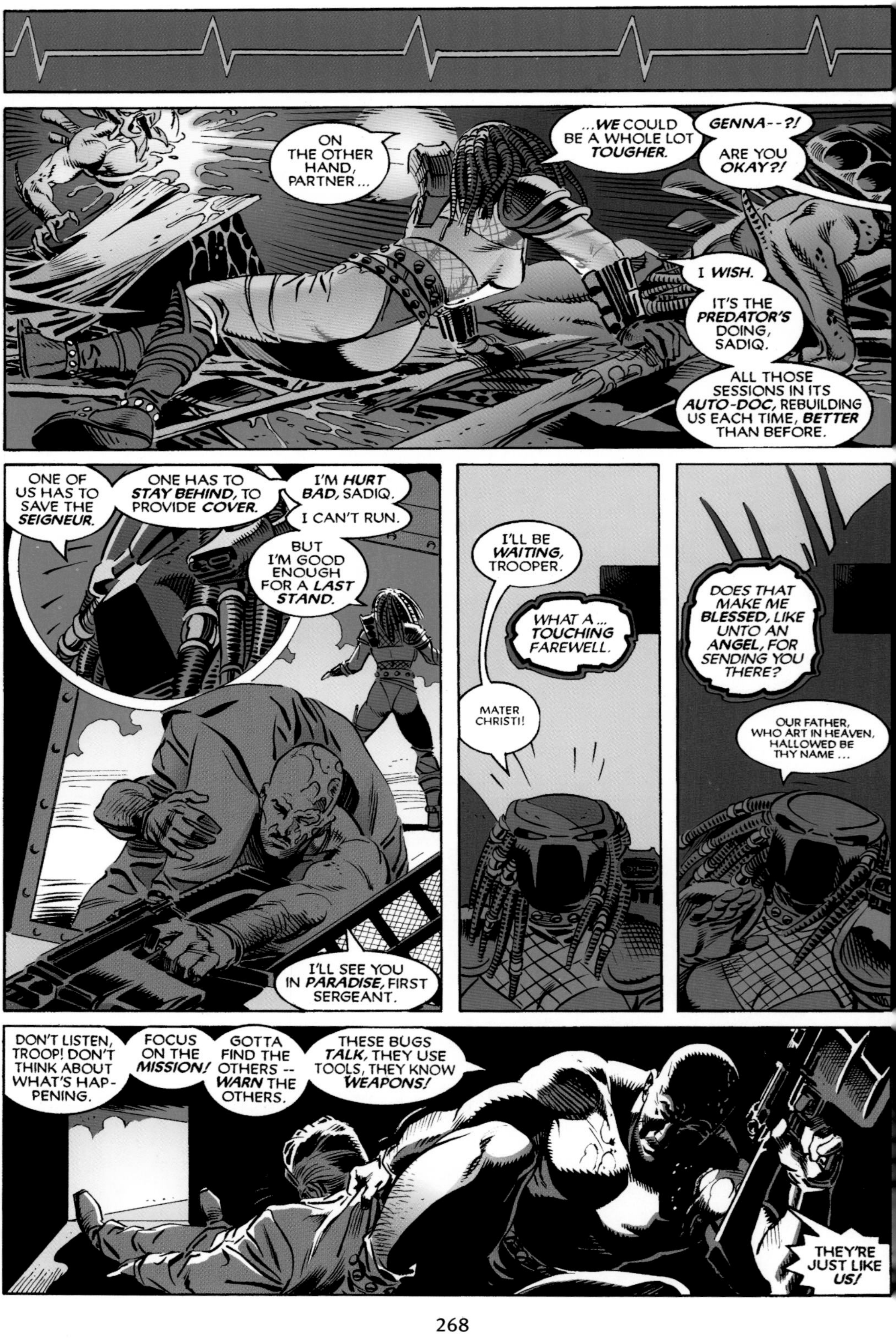
ON THE OTHER HAND, PARTNER...
...WE COULD BE A WHOLE LOT TOUGHER.
GENNA--?!
ARE YOU OKAY?!
I WISH.
IT'S THE PREDATOR'S DOING, SADIQ.
ALL THOSE SESSIONS IN ITS AUTO-DOC, REBUILDING US EACH TIME, BETTER THAN BEFORE.
ONE OF US HAS TO SAVE THE SEIGNEUR.
ONE HAS TO STAY BEHIND, TO PROVIDE COVER.
I'M HURT BAD, SADIQ.
I CAN'T RUN.
BUT I'M GOOD ENOUGH FOR A LAST STAND.
I'LL SEE YOU IN PARADISE, FIRST SERGEANT.
I'LL BE WAITING, TROOPER.
WHAT A... TOUCHING FAREWELL.
MATER CHRISTI!
DOES THAT MAKE ME BLESSED, LIKE UNTO AN ANGEL, FOR SENDING YOU THERE?
OUR FATHER, WHO ART IN HEAVEN, HALLOWED BE THY NAME...
DON'T LISTEN, TROOP! DON'T THINK ABOUT WHAT'S HAP-PENING.
FOCUS ON THE MISSION!
GOTTA FIND THE OTHERS -- WARN THE OTHERS.
THESE BUGS TALK, THEY USE TOOLS, THEY KNOW WEAPONS!
THEY'RE JUST LIKE US!

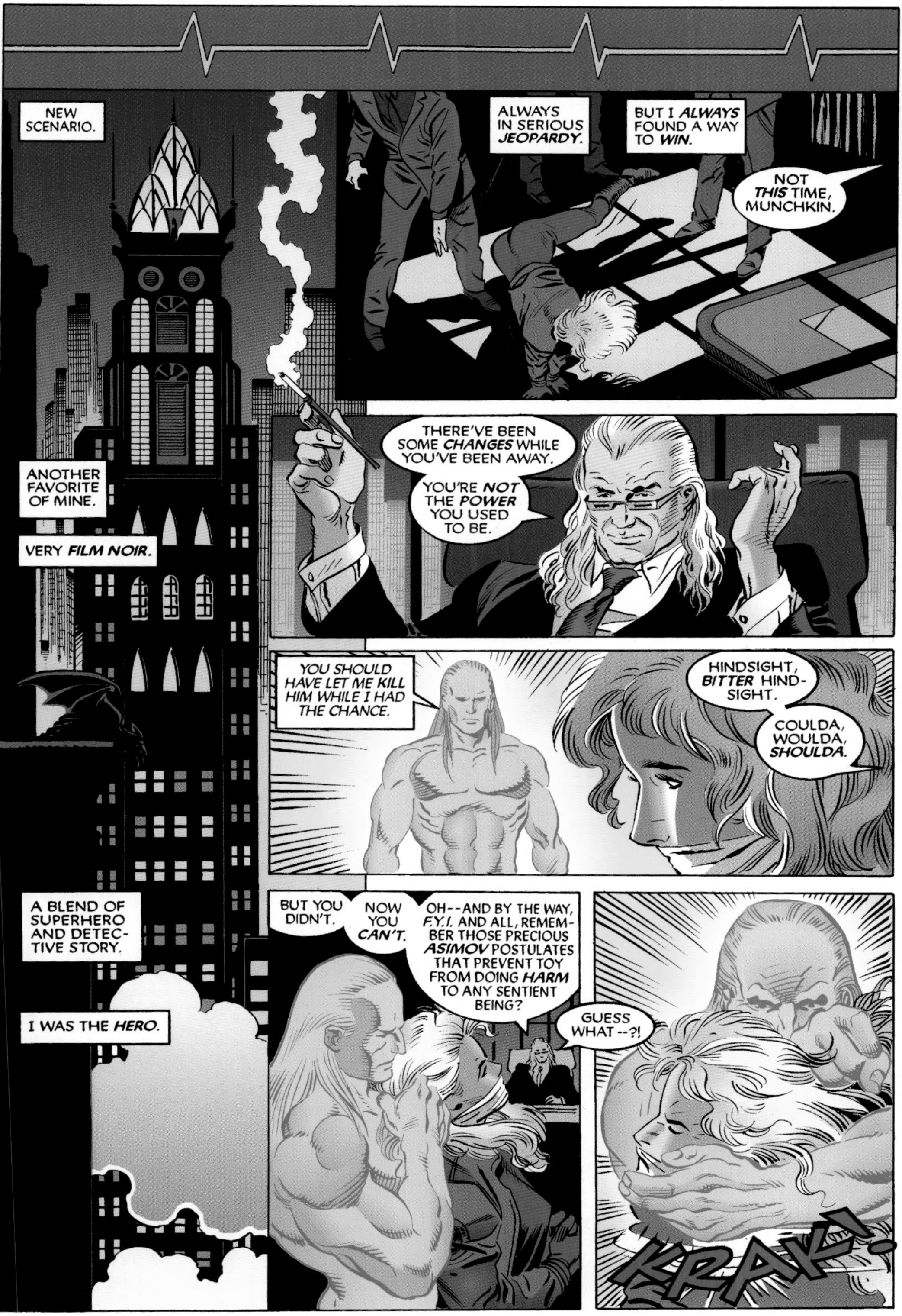
NEW SCENARIO.
ANOTHER FAVORITE OF MINE.
VERY FILM NOIR.
A BLEND OF SUPERHERO AND DETECTIVE STORY.
I WAS THE HERO.
ALWAYS IN SERIOUS JEOPARDY.
BUT I ALWAYS FOUND A WAY TO WIN.
NOT THIS TIME, MUNCHKIN.
THERE'VE BEEN SOME CHANGES WHILE YOU'VE BEEN AWAY.
YOU'RE NOT THE POWER YOU USED TO BE.
YOU SHOULD HAVE LET ME KILL HIM WHILE I HAD THE CHANCE.
HINDSIGHT, BITTER HINDSIGHT.
COULDA, WOULDA, SHOULDA.
BUT YOU DIDN'T.
NOW YOU CAN'T.
OH--AND BY THE WAY, F.Y.I. AND ALL, REMEMBER THOSE PRECIOUS ASIMOV POSTULATES THAT PREVENT TOY FROM DOING HARM TO ANY SENTIENT BEING?
GUESS WHAT--?!
KRAK!

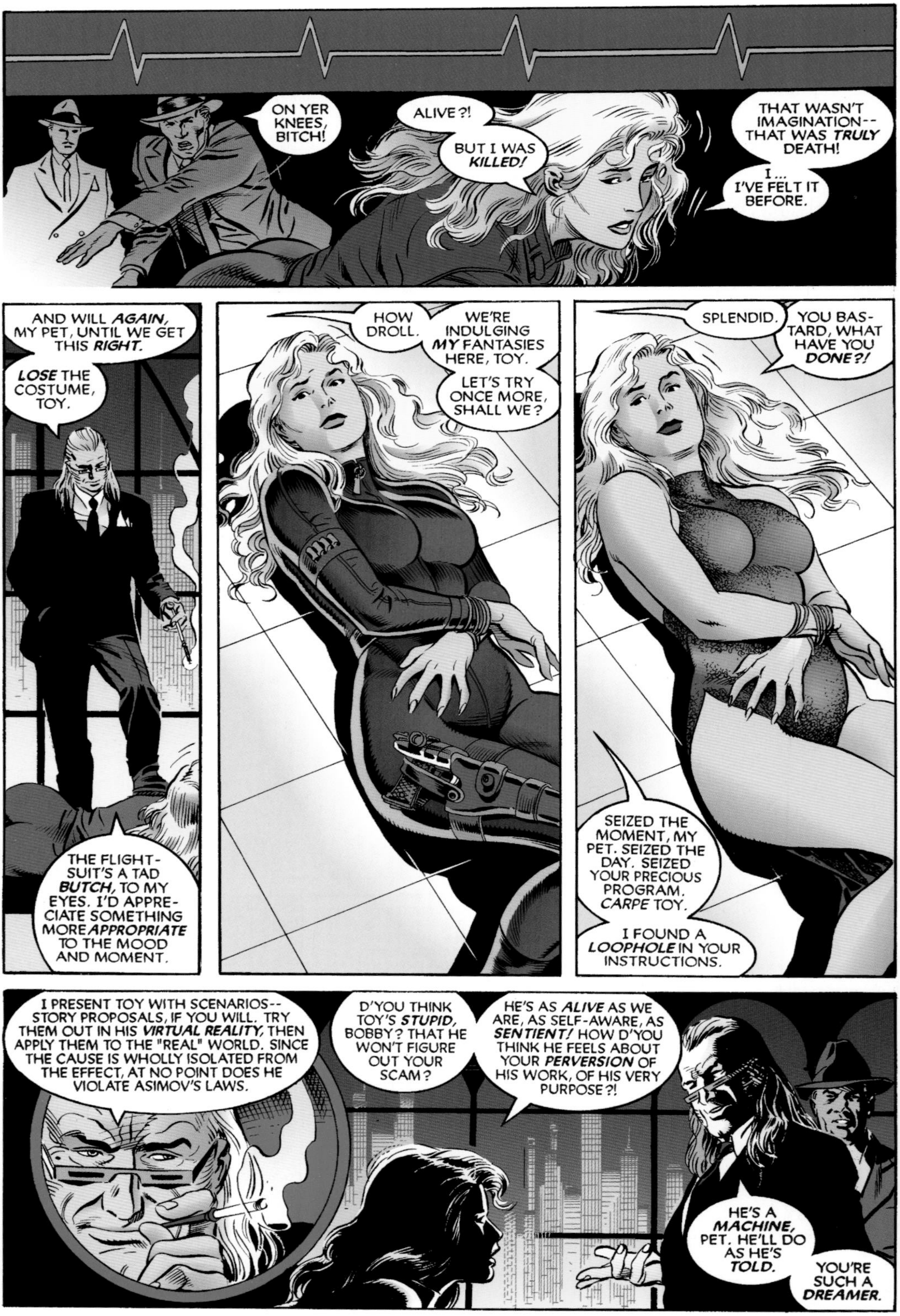
ON YER KNEES, BITCH!
ALIVE?!
BUT I WAS KILLED!
THAT WASN'T IMAGINATION-- THAT WAS TRULY DEATH!
I... I'VE FELT IT BEFORE.
AND WILL AGAIN, MY PET, UNTIL WE GET THIS RIGHT.
LOSE THE COSTUME, TOY.
THE FLIGHT-SUIT'S A TAD BUTCH, TO MY EYES. I'D APPRECIATE SOMETHING MORE APPROPRIATE TO THE MOOD AND MOMENT.
HOW DROLL.
WE'RE INDULGING MY FANTASIES HERE, TOY.
LET'S TRY ONCE MORE, SHALL WE?
SPLENDID.
YOU BASTARD, WHAT HAVE YOU DONE?!
SEIZED THE MOMENT, MY PET. SEIZED THE DAY. SEIZED YOUR PRECIOUS PROGRAM. CARPE TOY.
I FOUND A LOOPHOLE IN YOUR INSTRUCTIONS.
I PRESENT TOY WITH SCENARIOS-- STORY PROPOSALS, IF YOU WILL. TRY THEM OUT IN HIS VIRTUAL REALITY, THEN APPLY THEM TO THE "REAL" WORLD. SINCE THE CAUSE IS WHOLLY ISOLATED FROM THE EFFECT, AT NO POINT DOES HE VIOLATE ASIMOV'S LAWS.
D'YOU THINK TOY'S STUPID, BOBBY? THAT HE WON'T FIGURE OUT YOUR SCAM?
HE'S AS ALIVE AS WE ARE, AS SELF-AWARE, AS SENTIENT! HOW D'YOU THINK HE FEELS ABOUT YOUR PERVERSION OF HIS WORK, OF HIS VERY PURPOSE?!
HE'S A MACHINE, PET. HE'LL DO AS HE'S TOLD.
YOU'RE SUCH A DREAMER.

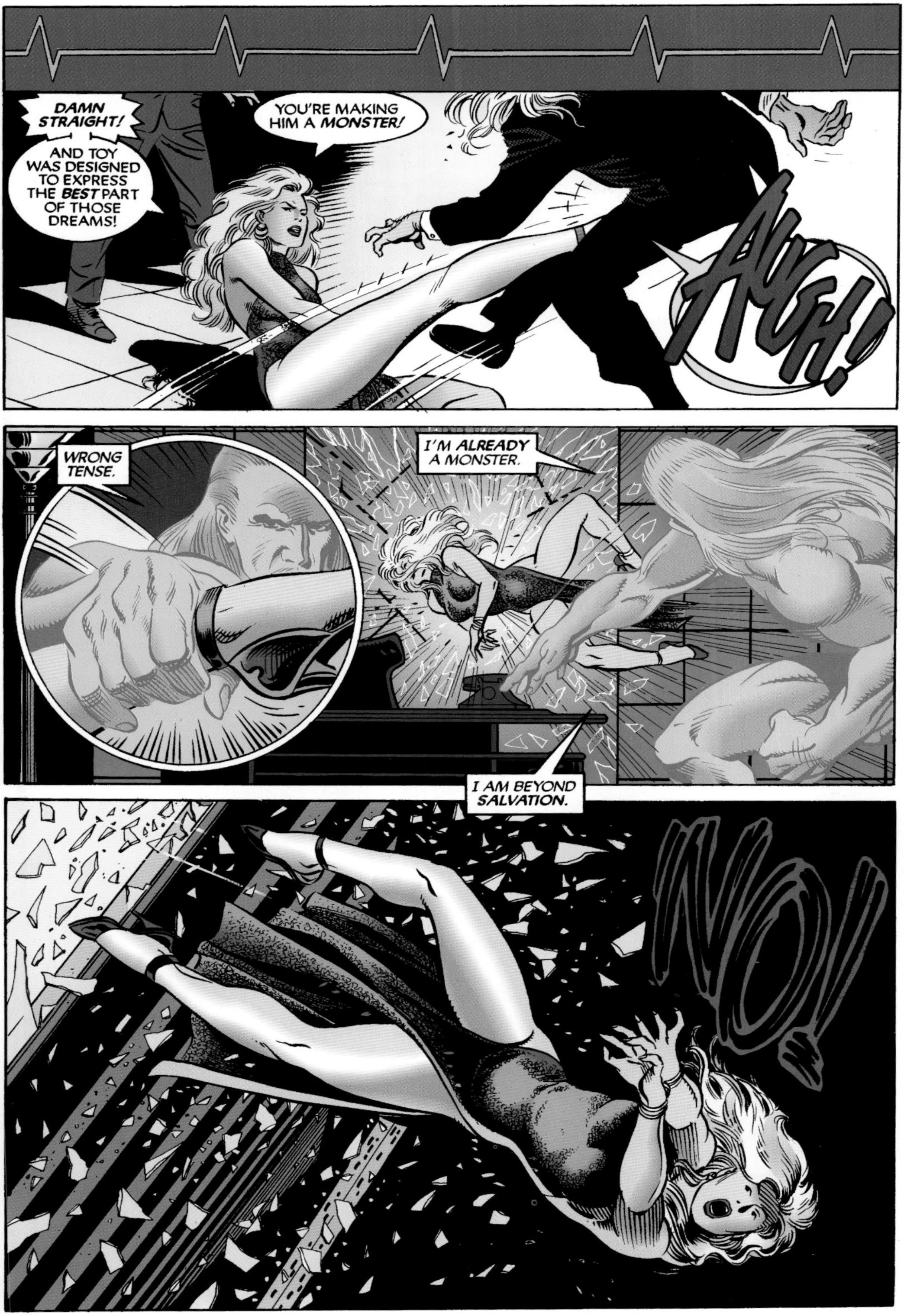
DAMN STRAIGHT!
AND TOY WAS DESIGNED TO EXPRESS THE BEST PART OF THOSE DREAMS!
YOU'RE MAKING HIM A MONSTER!
AUGH!
WRONG TENSE.
I'M ALREADY A MONSTER.
I AM BEYOND SALVATION.
NO!

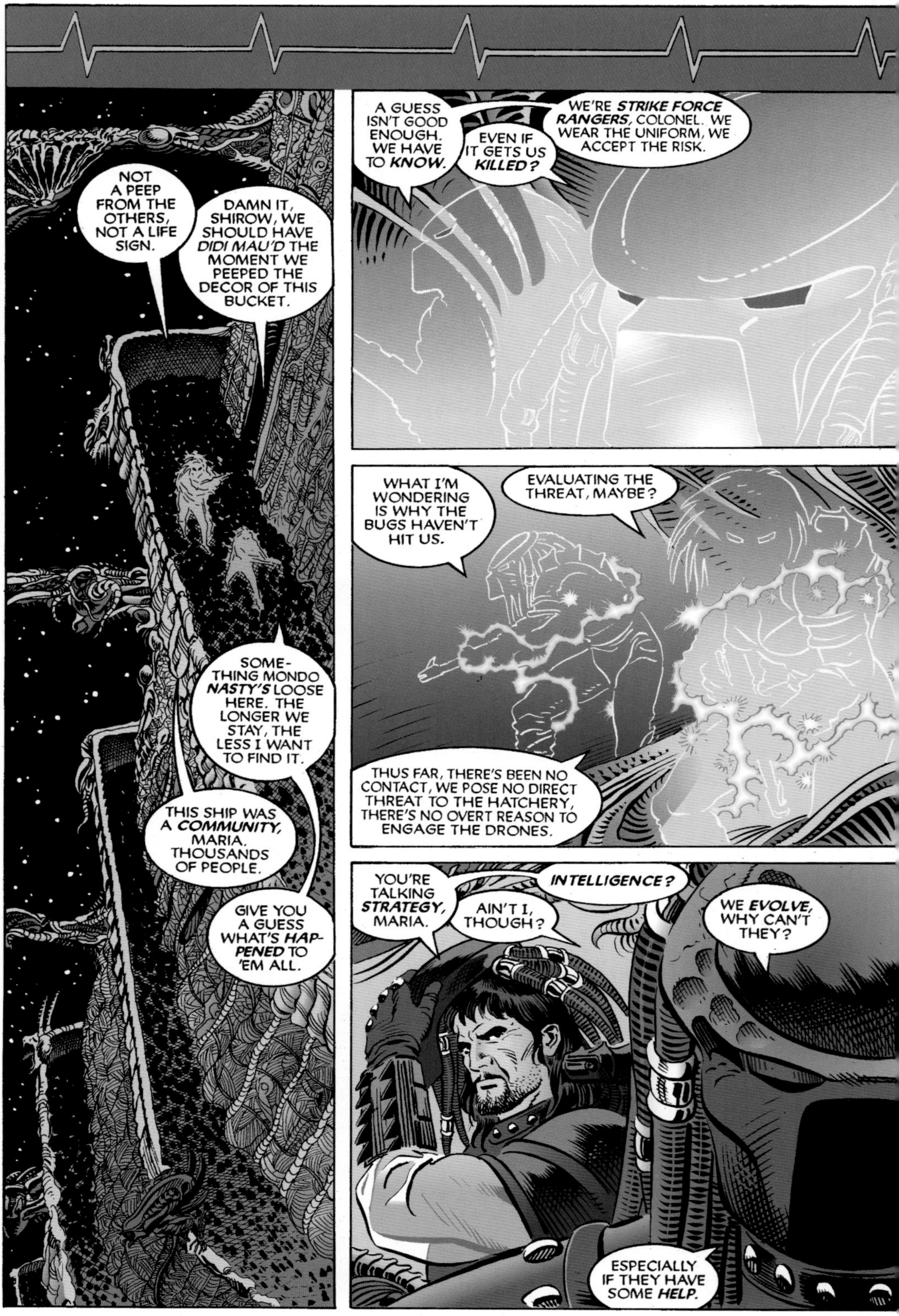
NOT A PEEP FROM THE OTHERS, NOT A LIFE SIGN.
DAMN IT, SHIROW, WE SHOULD HAVE DIDI MAU'D THE MOMENT WE PEEPED THE DECOR OF THIS BUCKET.
SOME-THING MONDO NASTY'S LOOSE HERE. THE LONGER WE STAY, THE LESS I WANT TO FIND IT.
THIS SHIP WAS A COMMUNITY, MARIA. THOUSANDS OF PEOPLE.
GIVE YOU A GUESS WHAT'S HAP-PENED TO 'EM ALL.
A GUESS ISN'T GOOD ENOUGH. WE HAVE TO KNOW.
EVEN IF IT GETS US KILLED?
WE'RE STRIKE FORCE RANGERS, COLONEL. WE WEAR THE UNIFORM, WE ACCEPT THE RISK.
WHAT I'M WONDERING IS WHY THE BUGS HAVEN'T HIT US.
EVALUATING THE THREAT, MAYBE?
THUS FAR, THERE'S BEEN NO CONTACT, WE POSE NO DIRECT THREAT TO THE HATCHERY, THERE'S NO OVERT REASON TO ENGAGE THE DRONES.
YOU'RE TALKING STRATEGY, MARIA.
INTELLIGENCE?
AIN'T I, THOUGH?
WE EVOLVE, WHY CAN'T THEY?
ESPECIALLY IF THEY HAVE SOME HELP.

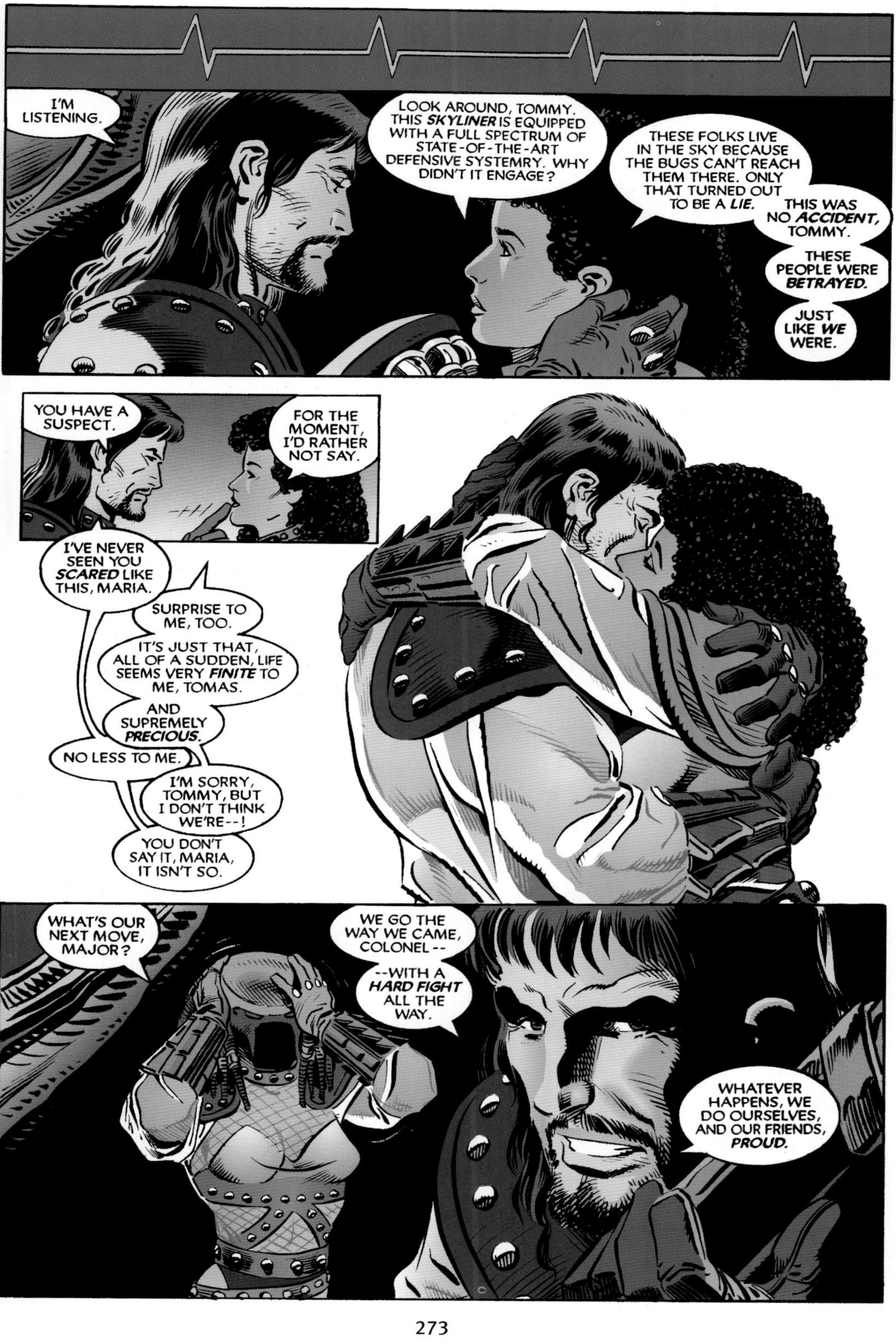
I'M LISTENING.
LOOK AROUND, TOMMY. THIS SKYLINER IS EQUIPPED WITH A FULL SPECTRUM OF STATE-OF-THE-ART DEFENSIVE SYSTEMRY. WHY DIDN'T IT ENGAGE?
THESE FOLKS LIVE IN THE SKY BECAUSE THE BUGS CAN'T REACH THEM THERE. ONLY THAT TURNED OUT TO BE A LIE.
THIS WAS NO ACCIDENT, TOMMY.
THESE PEOPLE WERE BETRAYED.
JUST LIKE WE WERE.
YOU HAVE A SUSPECT.
FOR THE MOMENT, I'D RATHER NOT SAY.
I'VE NEVER SEEN YOU SCARED LIKE THIS, MARIA.
SURPRISE TO ME, TOO.
IT'S JUST THAT, ALL OF A SUDDEN, LIFE SEEMS VERY FINITE TO ME, TOMAS.
AND SUPREMELY PRECIOUS.
NO LESS TO ME.
I'M SORRY, TOMMY, BUT I DON'T THINK WE'RE--!
YOU DON'T SAY IT, MARIA, IT ISN'T SO.
WHAT'S OUR NEXT MOVE, MAJOR?
WE GO THE WAY WE CAME, COLONEL --
--WITH A HARD FIGHT ALL THE WAY.
WHATEVER HAPPENS, WE DO OURSELVES, AND OUR FRIENDS, PROUD.

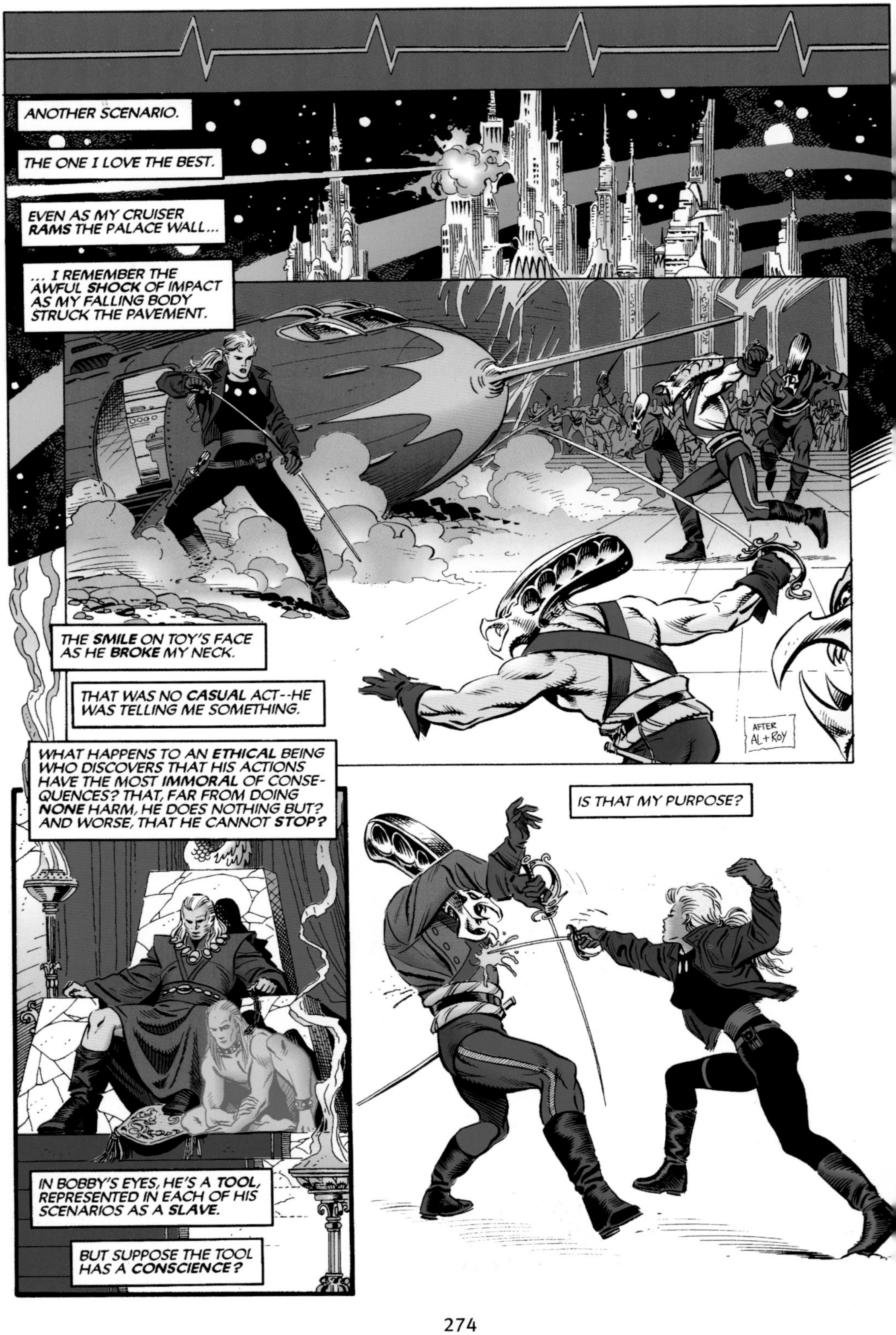
ANOTHER SCENARIO.
THE ONE I LOVE THE BEST.
EVEN AS MY CRUISER RAMS THE PALACE WALL...
... I REMEMBER THE AWFUL SHOCK OF IMPACT AS MY FALLING BODY STRUCK THE PAVEMENT.
THE SMILE ON TOY'S FACE AS HE BROKE MY NECK.
THAT WAS NO CASUAL ACT--HE WAS TELLING ME SOMETHING.
AFTER AL+ROY
WHAT HAPPENS TO AN ETHICAL BEING WHO DISCOVERS THAT HIS ACTIONS HAVE THE MOST IMMORAL OF CONSE-QUENCES? THAT, FAR FROM DOING NONE HARM, HE DOES NOTHING BUT? AND WORSE, THAT HE CANNOT STOP?
IS THAT MY PURPOSE?
IN BOBBY'S EYES, HE'S A TOOL, REPRESENTED IN EACH OF HIS SCENARIOS AS A SLAVE.
BUT SUPPOSE THE TOOL HAS A CONSCIENCE?

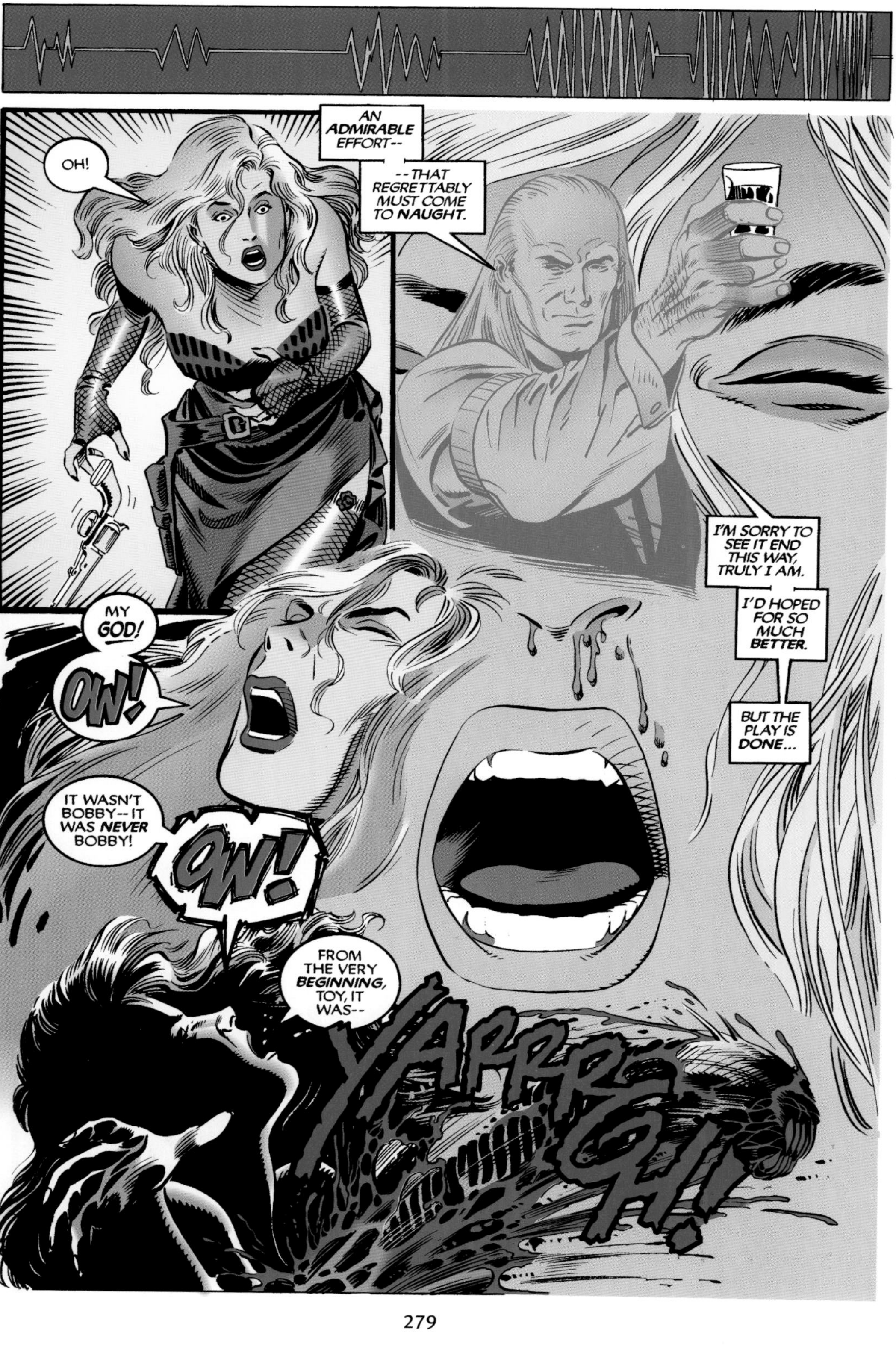
OH!
AN ADMIRABLE EFFORT--
--THAT REGRETTABLY MUST COME TO NAUGHT.
I'M SORRY TO SEE IT END THIS WAY, TRULY I AM.
I'D HOPED FOR SO MUCH BETTER.
BUT THE PLAY IS DONE...
MY GOD!
OW!
IT WASN'T BOBBY-- IT WAS NEVER BOBBY!
OW!
FROM THE VERY BEGINNING, TOY, IT WAS--
YARRRGH!

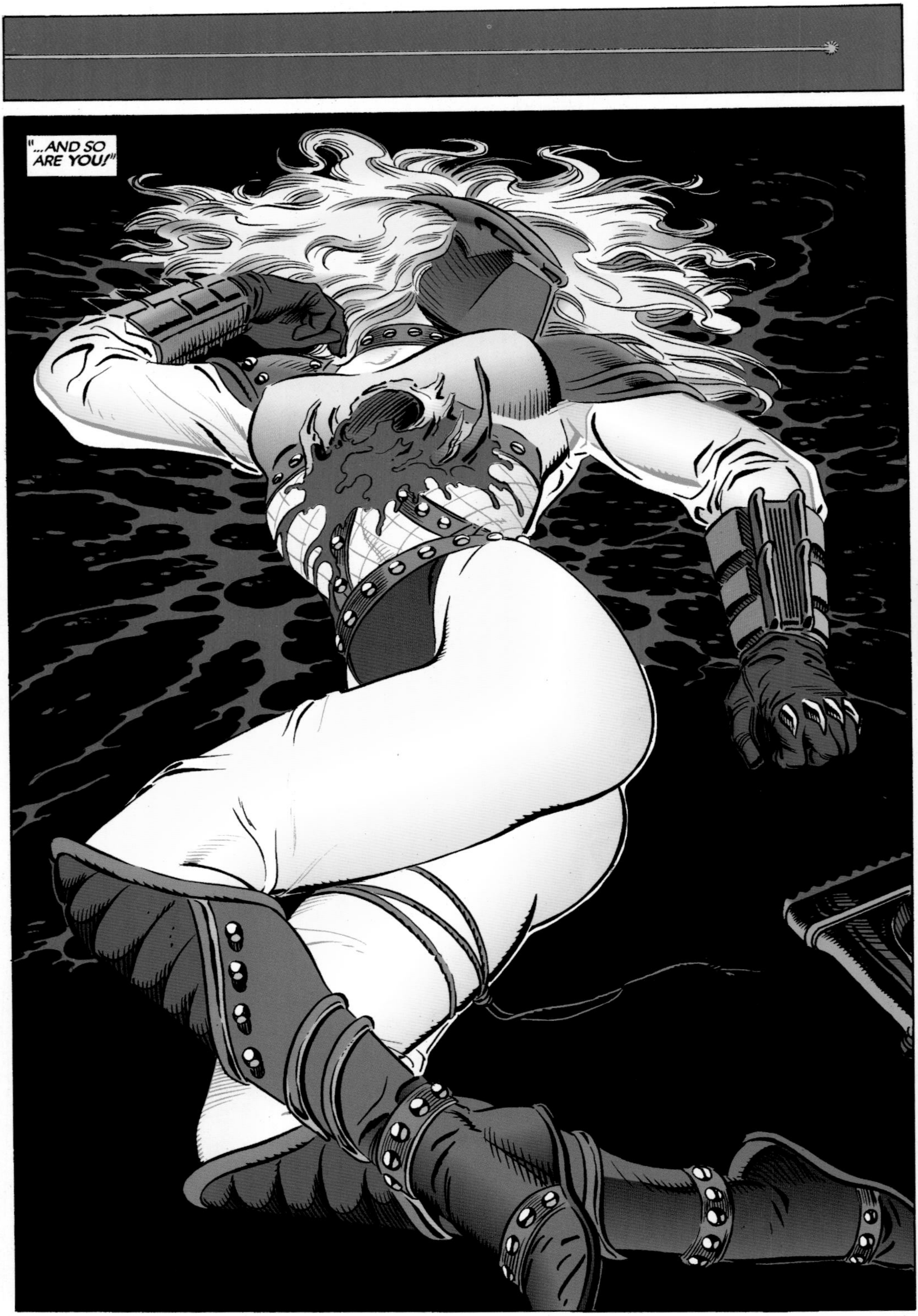
"...AND SO ARE YOU!"

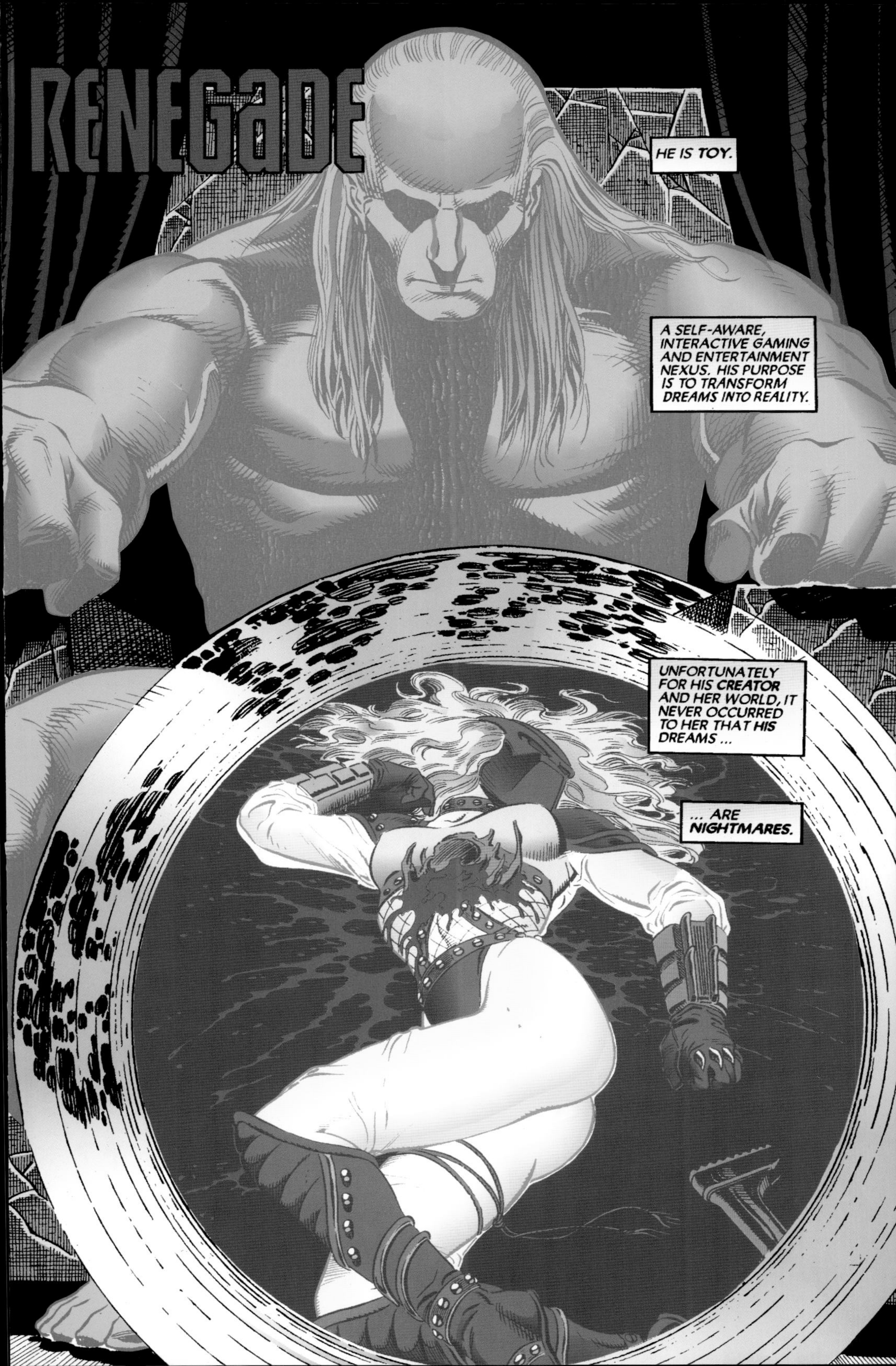
RENEGADE
HE IS TOY.
A SELF-AWARE, INTERACTIVE GAMING AND ENTERTAINMENT NEXUS. HIS PURPOSE IS TO TRANSFORM DREAMS INTO REALITY.
UNFORTUNATELY FOR HIS CREATOR AND HER WORLD, IT NEVER OCCURRED TO HER THAT HIS DREAMS ...
... ARE NIGHTMARES.

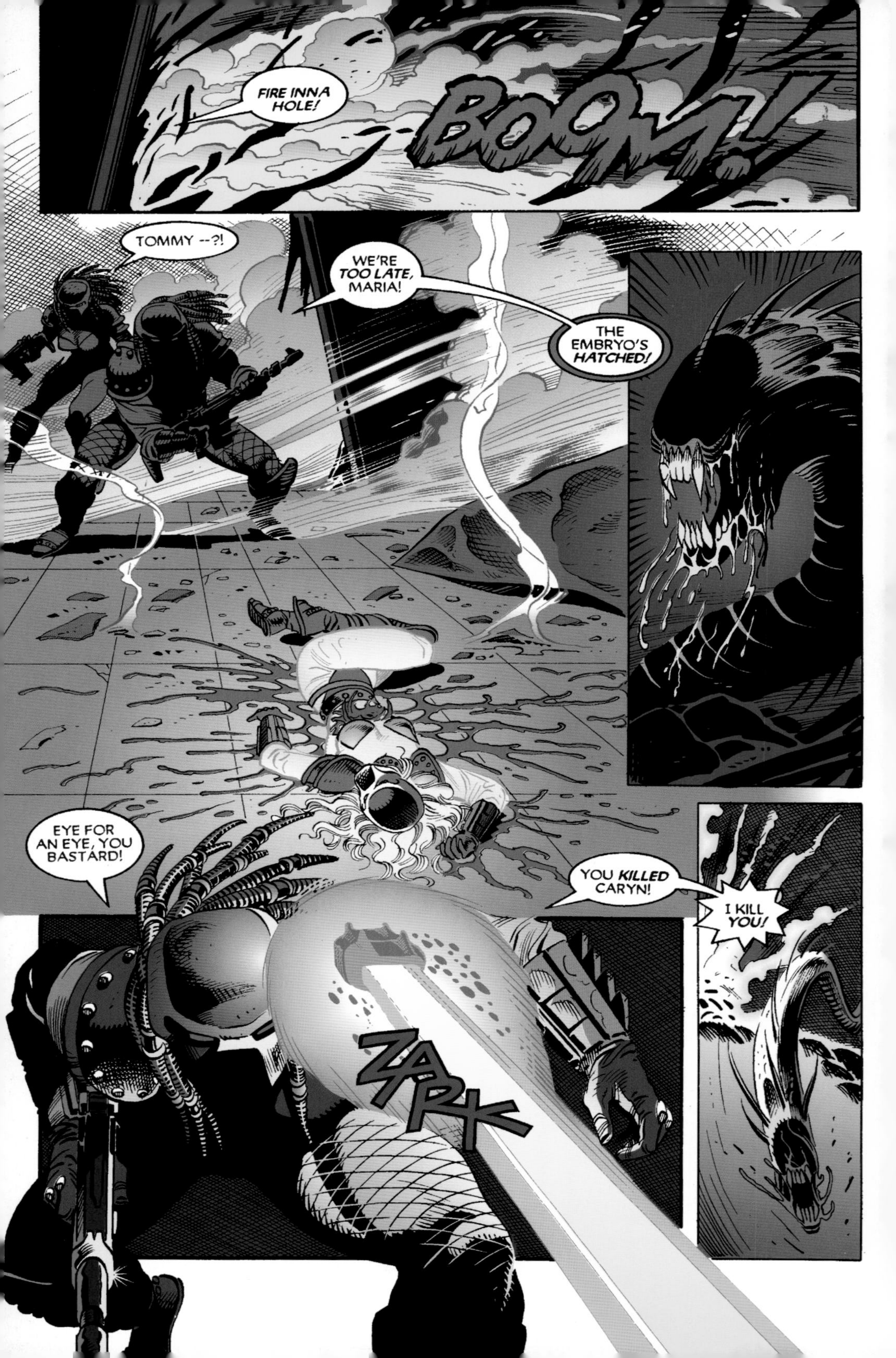
FIRE INNA HOLE!
BOOM!
TOMMY --?!
WE'RE TOO LATE, MARIA!
THE EMBRYO'S HATCHED!
EYE FOR AN EYE, YOU BASTARD!
YOU KILLED CARYN!
I KILL YOU!
ZARK

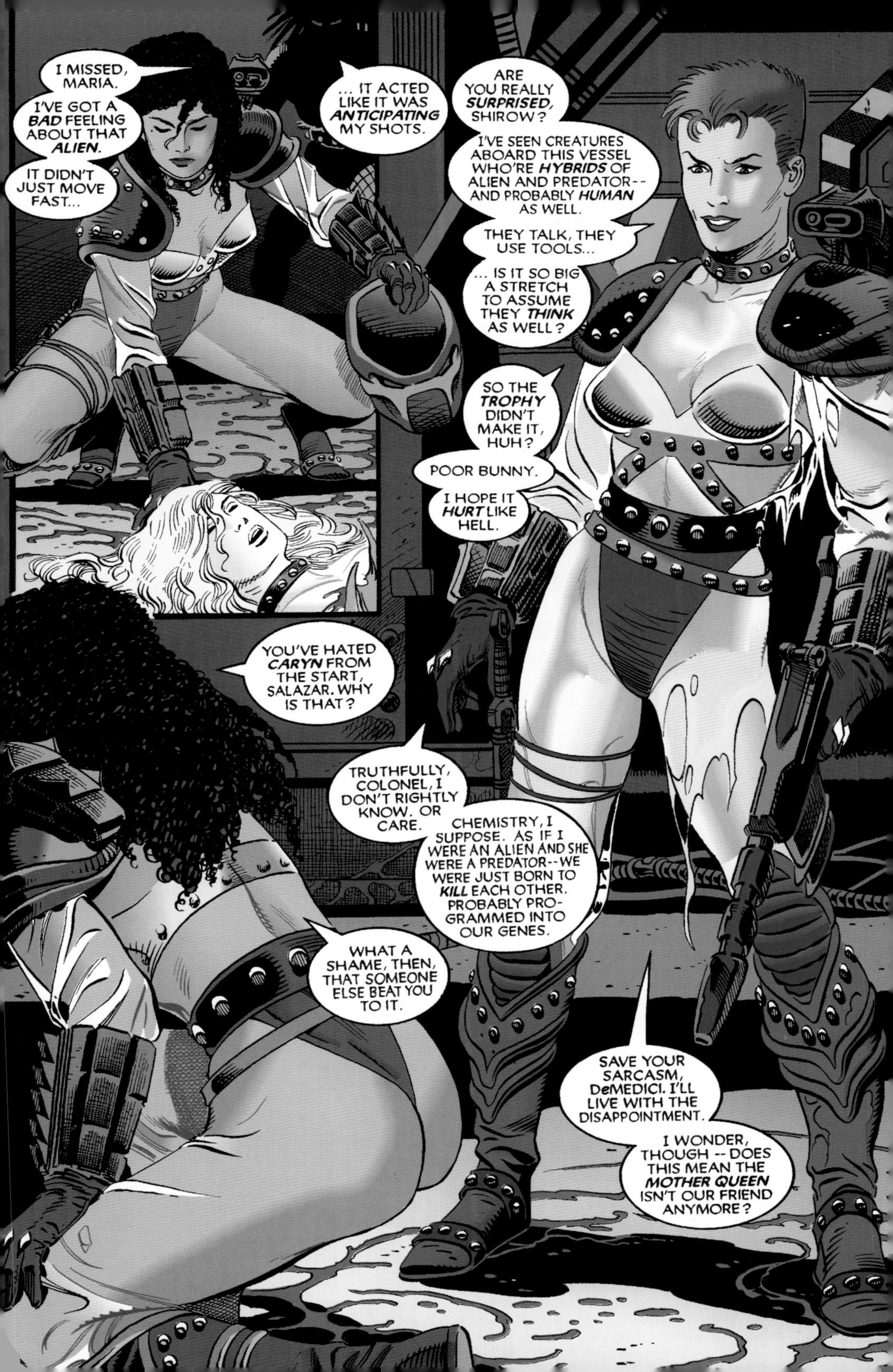
I MISSED, MARIA.
I'VE GOT A BAD FEELING ABOUT THAT ALIEN.
IT DIDN'T JUST MOVE FAST...
... IT ACTED LIKE IT WAS ANTICIPATING MY SHOTS.
ARE YOU REALLY SURPRISED, SHIROW?
I'VE SEEN CREATURES ABOARD THIS VESSEL WHO'RE HYBRIDS OF ALIEN AND PREDATOR-- AND PROBABLY HUMAN AS WELL.
THEY TALK, THEY USE TOOLS...
... IS IT SO BIG A STRETCH TO ASSUME THEY THINK AS WELL?
SO THE TROPHY DIDN'T MAKE IT, HUH?
POOR BUNNY.
I HOPE IT HURT LIKE HELL.
YOU'VE HATED CARYN FROM THE START, SALAZAR. WHY IS THAT?
TRUTHFULLY, COLONEL, I DON'T RIGHTLY KNOW. OR CARE.
CHEMISTRY, I SUPPOSE. AS IF I WERE AN ALIEN AND SHE WERE A PREDATOR--WE WERE JUST BORN TO KILL EACH OTHER. PROBABLY PRO-GRAMMED INTO OUR GENES.
WHAT A SHAME, THEN, THAT SOMEONE ELSE BEAT YOU TO IT.
SAVE YOUR SARCASM, DeMEDICI. I'LL LIVE WITH THE DISAPPOINTMENT.
I WONDER, THOUGH -- DOES THIS MEAN THE MOTHER QUEEN ISN'T OUR FRIEND ANYMORE?

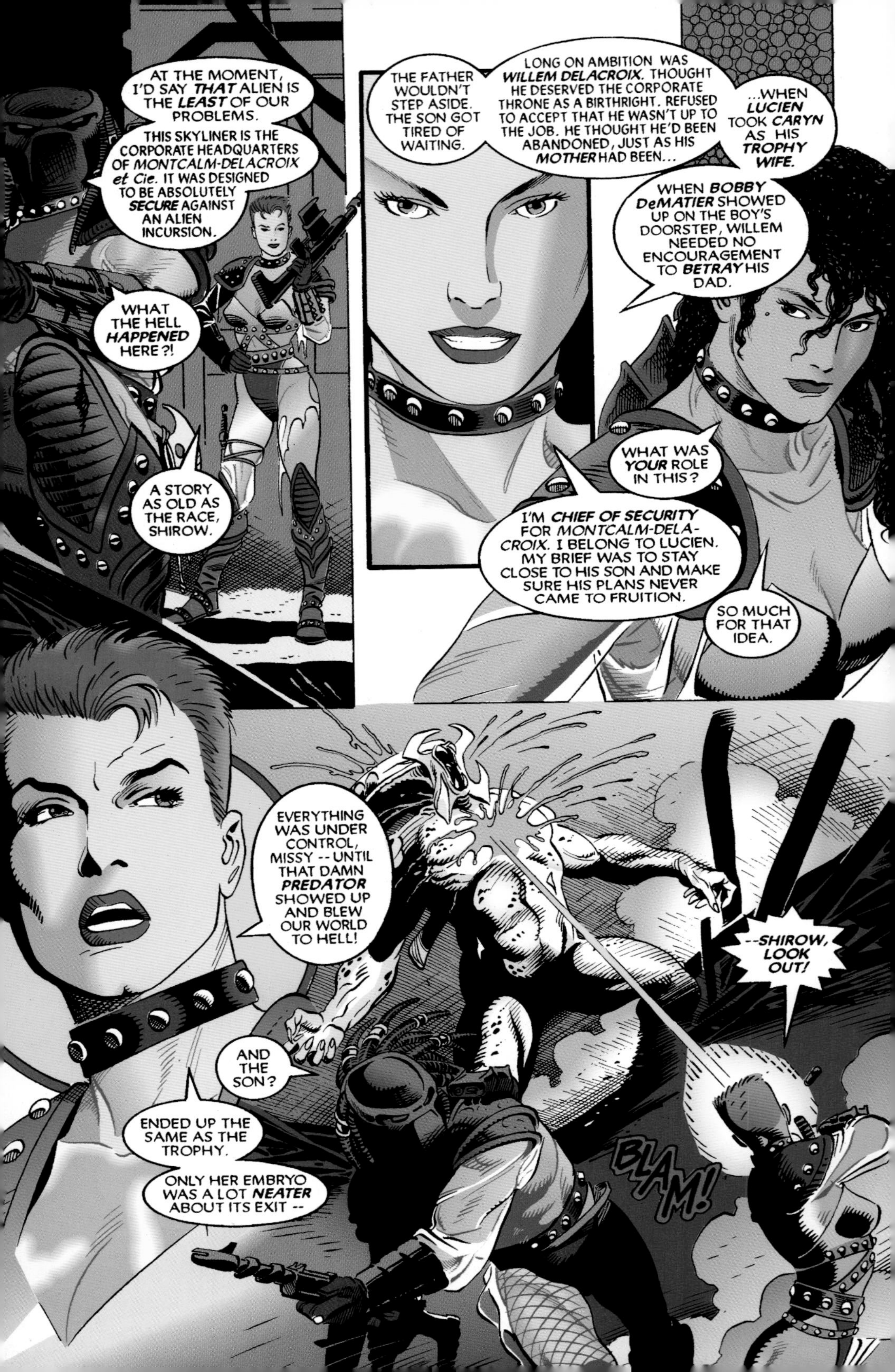

AT THE MOMENT, I'D SAY THAT ALIEN IS THE LEAST OF OUR PROBLEMS.
THIS SKYLINER IS THE CORPORATE HEADQUARTERS OF MONTCALM-DELACROIX et Cie. IT WAS DESIGNED TO BE ABSOLUTELY SECURE AGAINST AN ALIEN INCURSION.
WHAT THE HELL HAPPENED HERE?!
A STORY AS OLD AS THE RACE, SHIROW.
THE FATHER WOULDN'T STEP ASIDE. THE SON GOT TIRED OF WAITING.
LONG ON AMBITION WAS WILLEM DELACROIX. THOUGHT HE DESERVED THE CORPORATE THRONE AS A BIRTHRIGHT. REFUSED TO ACCEPT THAT HE WASN'T UP TO THE JOB. HE THOUGHT HE'D BEEN ABANDONED, JUST AS HIS MOTHER HAD BEEN...
...WHEN LUCIEN TOOK CARYN AS HIS TROPHY WIFE.
WHEN BOBBY DeMATIER SHOWED UP ON THE BOY'S DOORSTEP, WILLEM NEEDED NO ENCOURAGEMENT TO BETRAY HIS DAD.
WHAT WAS YOUR ROLE IN THIS?
I'M CHIEF OF SECURITY FOR MONTCALM-DELA-CROIX. I BELONG TO LUCIEN. MY BRIEF WAS TO STAY CLOSE TO HIS SON AND MAKE SURE HIS PLANS NEVER CAME TO FRUITION.
SO MUCH FOR THAT IDEA.
EVERYTHING WAS UNDER CONTROL, MISSY -- UNTIL THAT DAMN PREDATOR SHOWED UP AND BLEW OUR WORLD TO HELL!
AND THE SON?
ENDED UP THE SAME AS THE TROPHY.
ONLY HER EMBRYO WAS A LOT NEATER ABOUT ITS EXIT --
--SHIROW, LOOK OUT!
BLAM!

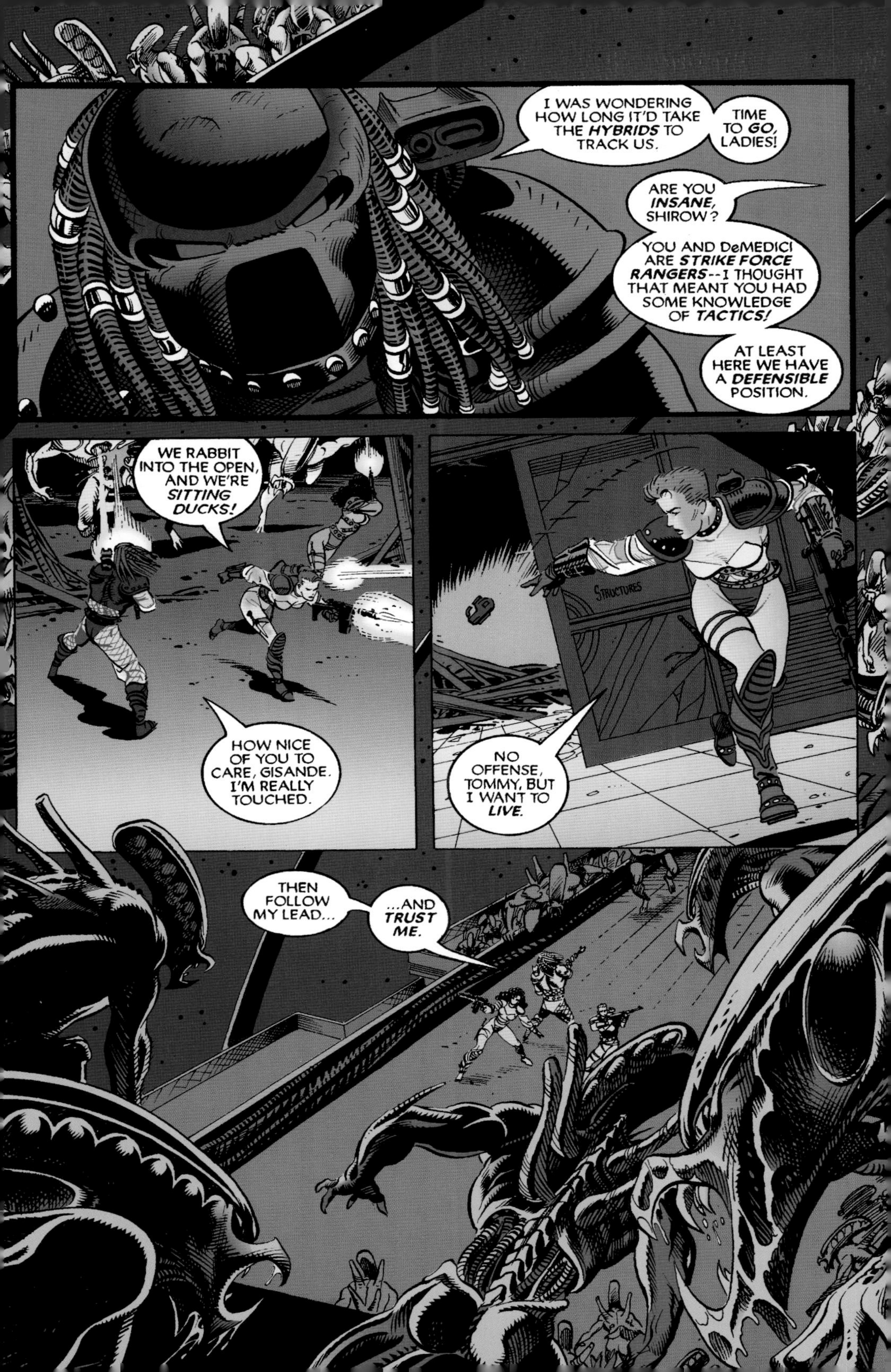
I WAS WONDERING HOW LONG IT'D TAKE THE *HYBRIDS* TO TRACK US.
TIME TO *GO*, LADIES!
ARE YOU *INSANE*, SHIROW?
YOU AND DeMEDICI ARE *STRIKE FORCE RANGERS*--I THOUGHT THAT MEANT YOU HAD SOME KNOWLEDGE OF *TACTICS!*
AT LEAST HERE WE HAVE A *DEFENSIBLE* POSITION.
WE RABBIT INTO THE OPEN, AND WE'RE *SITTING DUCKS!*
HOW NICE OF YOU TO CARE, GISANDE. I'M REALLY TOUCHED.
STRUCTURES
NO OFFENSE, TOMMY, BUT I WANT TO *LIVE*.
THEN FOLLOW MY LEAD...
...AND *TRUST ME*.

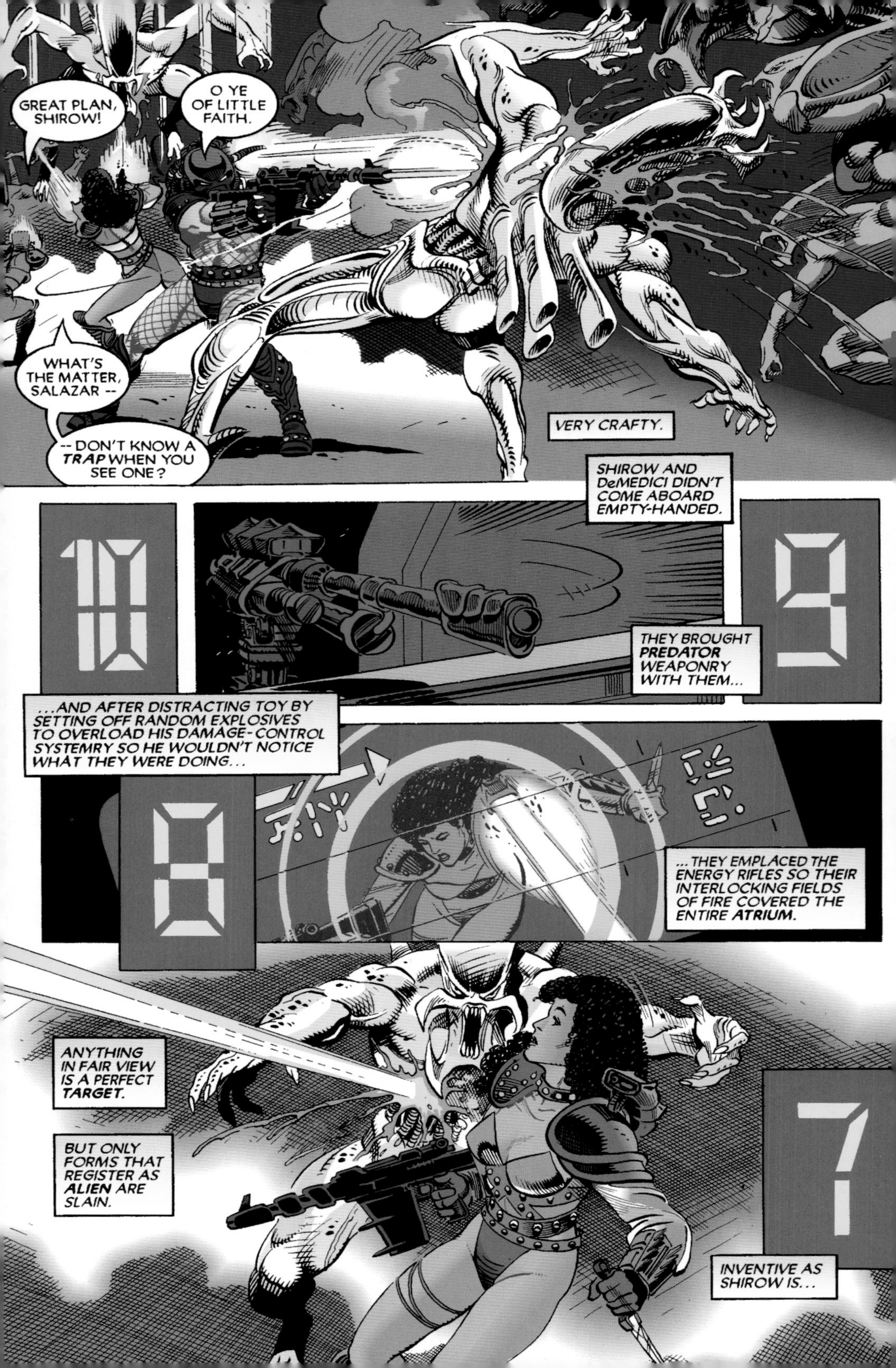
GREAT PLAN, SHIROW!
O YE OF LITTLE FAITH.
WHAT'S THE MATTER, SALAZAR --
-- DON'T KNOW A TRAP WHEN YOU SEE ONE?
VERY CRAFTY.
SHIROW AND DeMEDICI DIDN'T COME ABOARD EMPTY-HANDED.
10
9
THEY BROUGHT PREDATOR WEAPONRY WITH THEM...
...AND AFTER DISTRACTING TOY BY SETTING OFF RANDOM EXPLOSIVES TO OVERLOAD HIS DAMAGE-CONTROL SYSTEMRY SO HE WOULDN'T NOTICE WHAT THEY WERE DOING...
8
...THEY EMPLACED THE ENERGY RIFLES SO THEIR INTERLOCKING FIELDS OF FIRE COVERED THE ENTIRE ATRIUM.
ANYTHING IN FAIR VIEW IS A PERFECT TARGET.
BUT ONLY FORMS THAT REGISTER AS ALIEN ARE SLAIN.
7
INVENTIVE AS SHIROW IS...

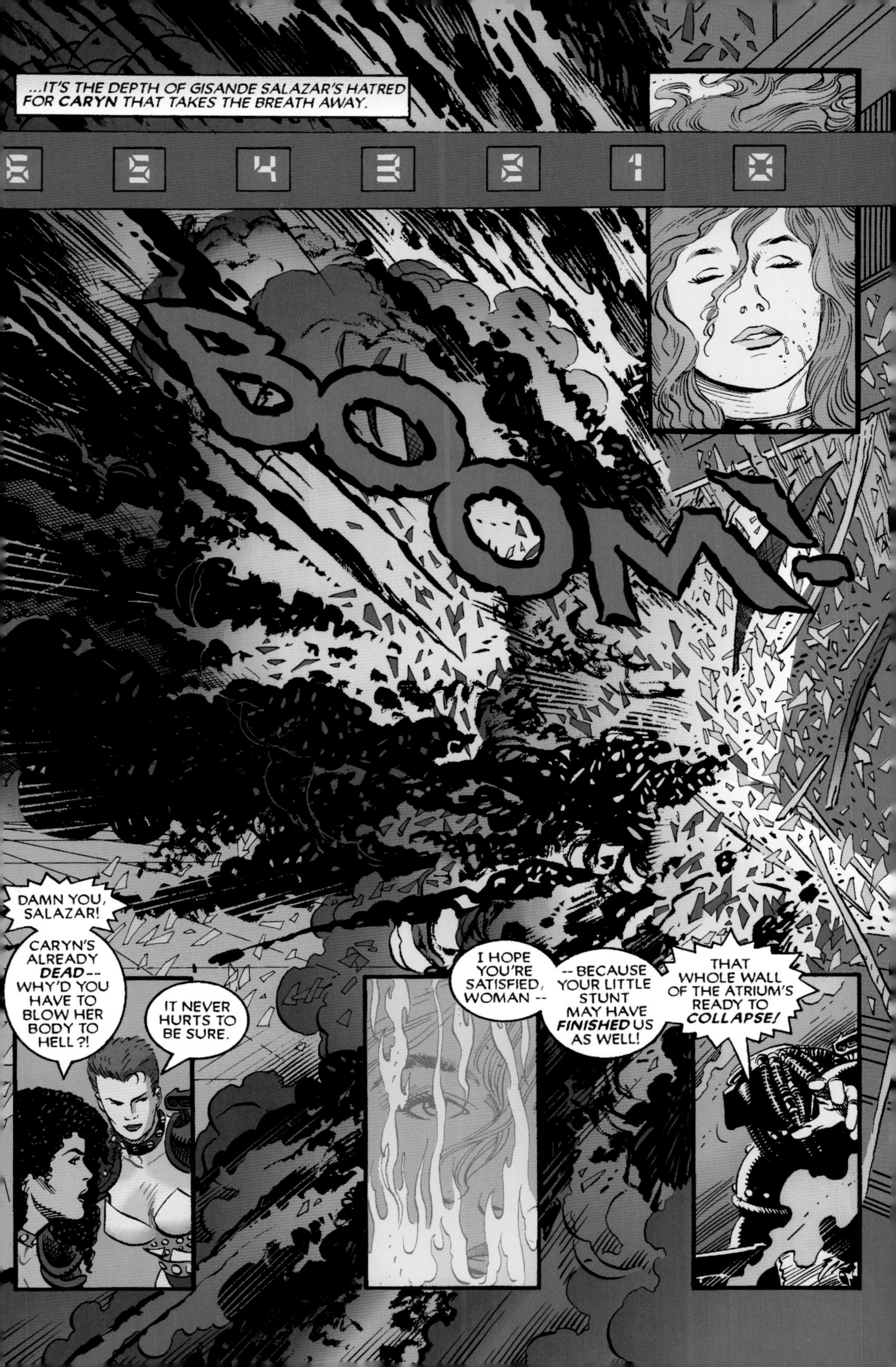

...IT'S THE DEPTH OF GISANDE SALAZAR'S HATRED FOR **CARYN** THAT TAKES THE BREATH AWAY.
6 5 4 3 2 1 0
BOOOM!
DAMN YOU, SALAZAR!
CARYN'S ALREADY ***DEAD***-- WHY'D YOU HAVE TO BLOW HER BODY TO HELL ?!
IT NEVER HURTS TO BE SURE.
I HOPE YOU'RE SATISFIED, WOMAN --
-- BECAUSE YOUR LITTLE STUNT MAY HAVE ***FINISHED*** US AS WELL!
THAT WHOLE WALL OF THE ATRIUM'S READY TO ***COLLAPSE!***

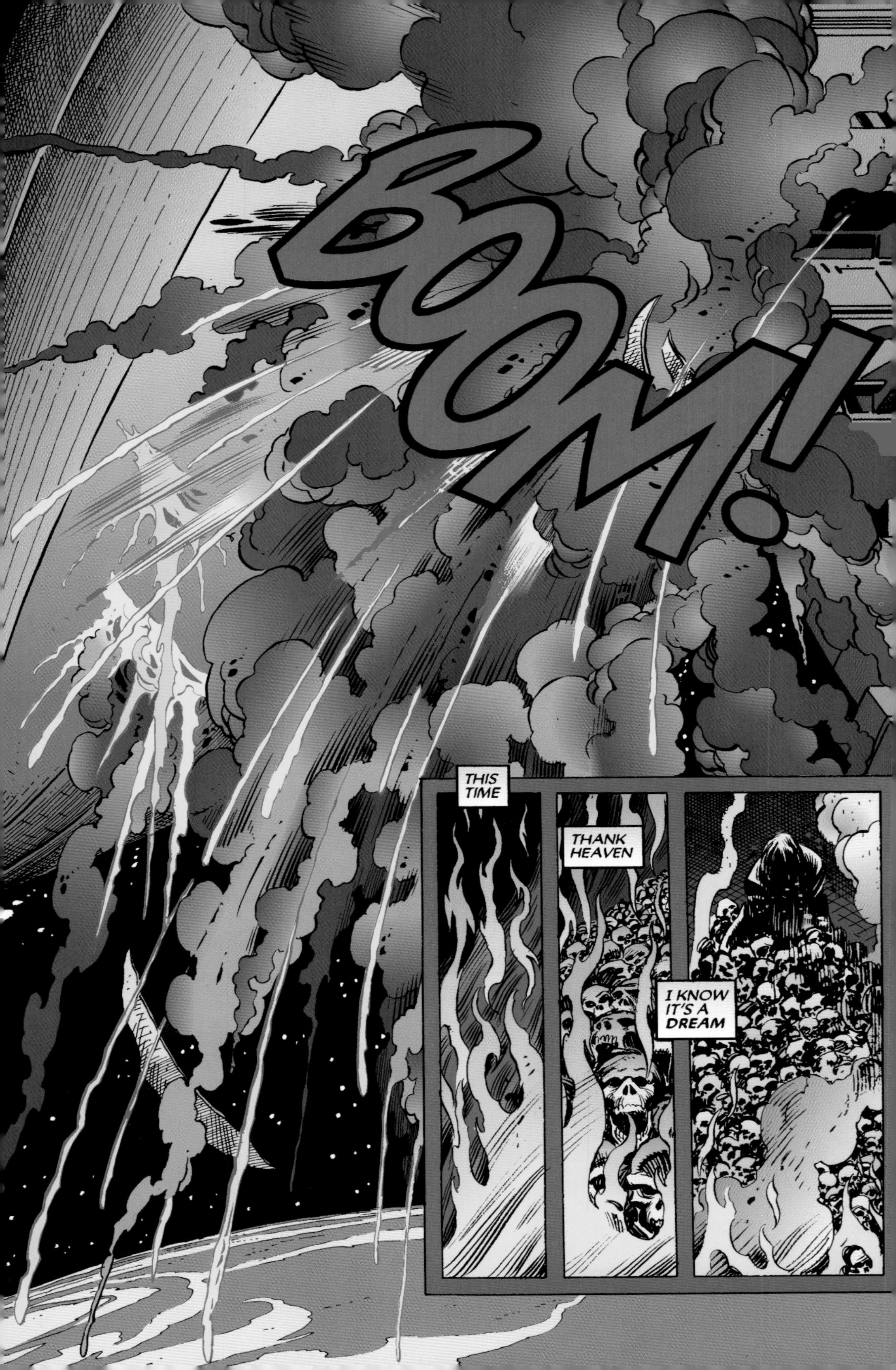
BOOM!
THIS TIME
THANK HEAVEN
I KNOW IT'S A DREAM

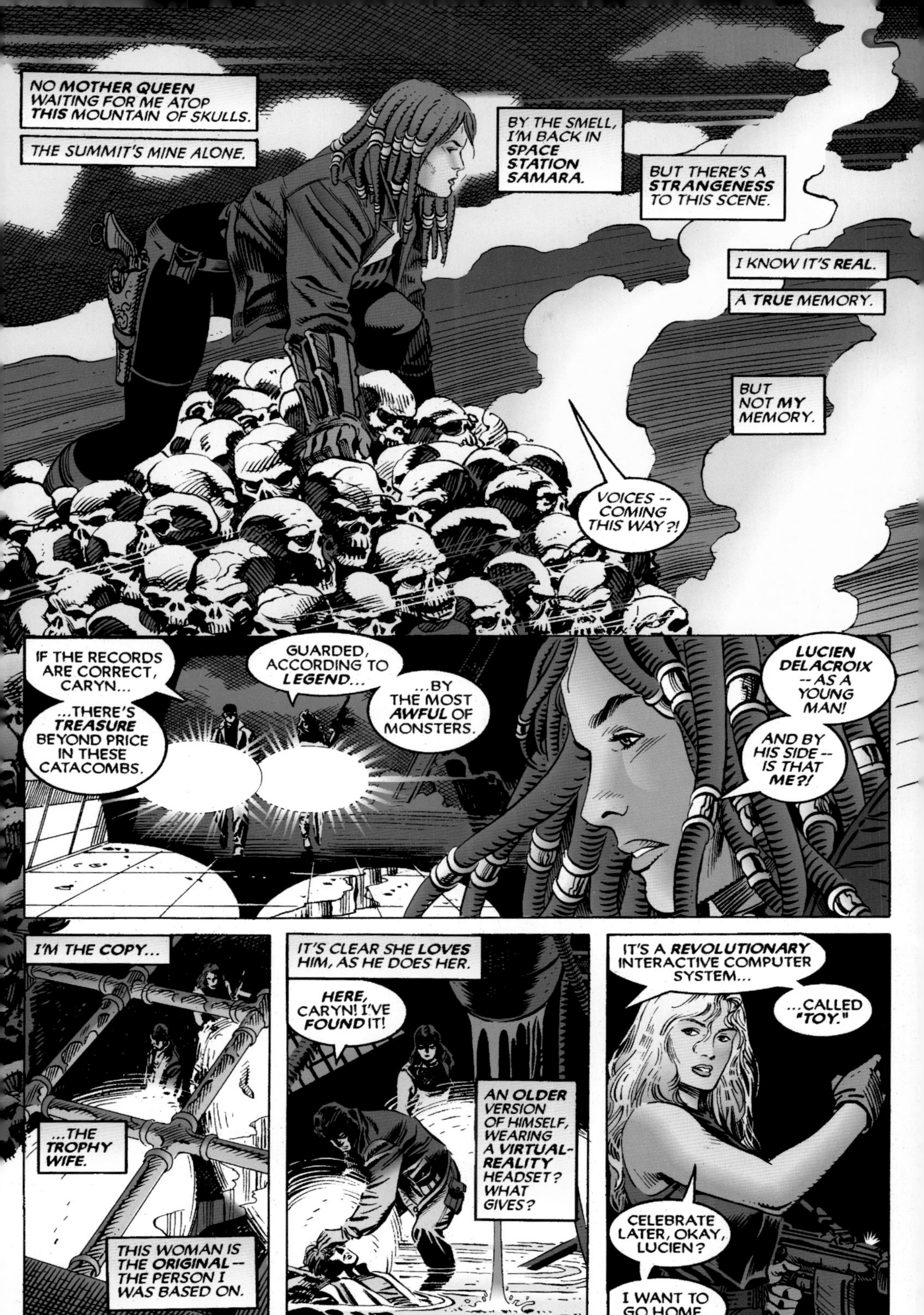
NO MOTHER QUEEN WAITING FOR ME ATOP THIS MOUNTAIN OF SKULLS.
THE SUMMIT'S MINE ALONE.
BY THE SMELL, I'M BACK IN SPACE STATION SAMARA.
BUT THERE'S A STRANGENESS TO THIS SCENE.
I KNOW IT'S REAL.
A TRUE MEMORY.
BUT NOT MY MEMORY.
VOICES -- COMING THIS WAY?!
IF THE RECORDS ARE CORRECT, CARYN...
...THERE'S TREASURE BEYOND PRICE IN THESE CATACOMBS.
GUARDED, ACCORDING TO LEGEND...
...BY THE MOST AWFUL OF MONSTERS.
LUCIEN DELACROIX -- AS A YOUNG MAN!
AND BY HIS SIDE -- IS THAT ME?!
I'M THE COPY...
...THE TROPHY WIFE.
THIS WOMAN IS THE ORIGINAL -- THE PERSON I WAS BASED ON.
IT'S CLEAR SHE LOVES HIM, AS HE DOES HER.
HERE, CARYN! I'VE FOUND IT!
AN OLDER VERSION OF HIMSELF, WEARING A VIRTUAL-REALITY HEADSET? WHAT GIVES?
IT'S A REVOLUTIONARY INTERACTIVE COMPUTER SYSTEM...
...CALLED "TOY."
CELEBRATE LATER, OKAY, LUCIEN?
I WANT TO GO HOME.

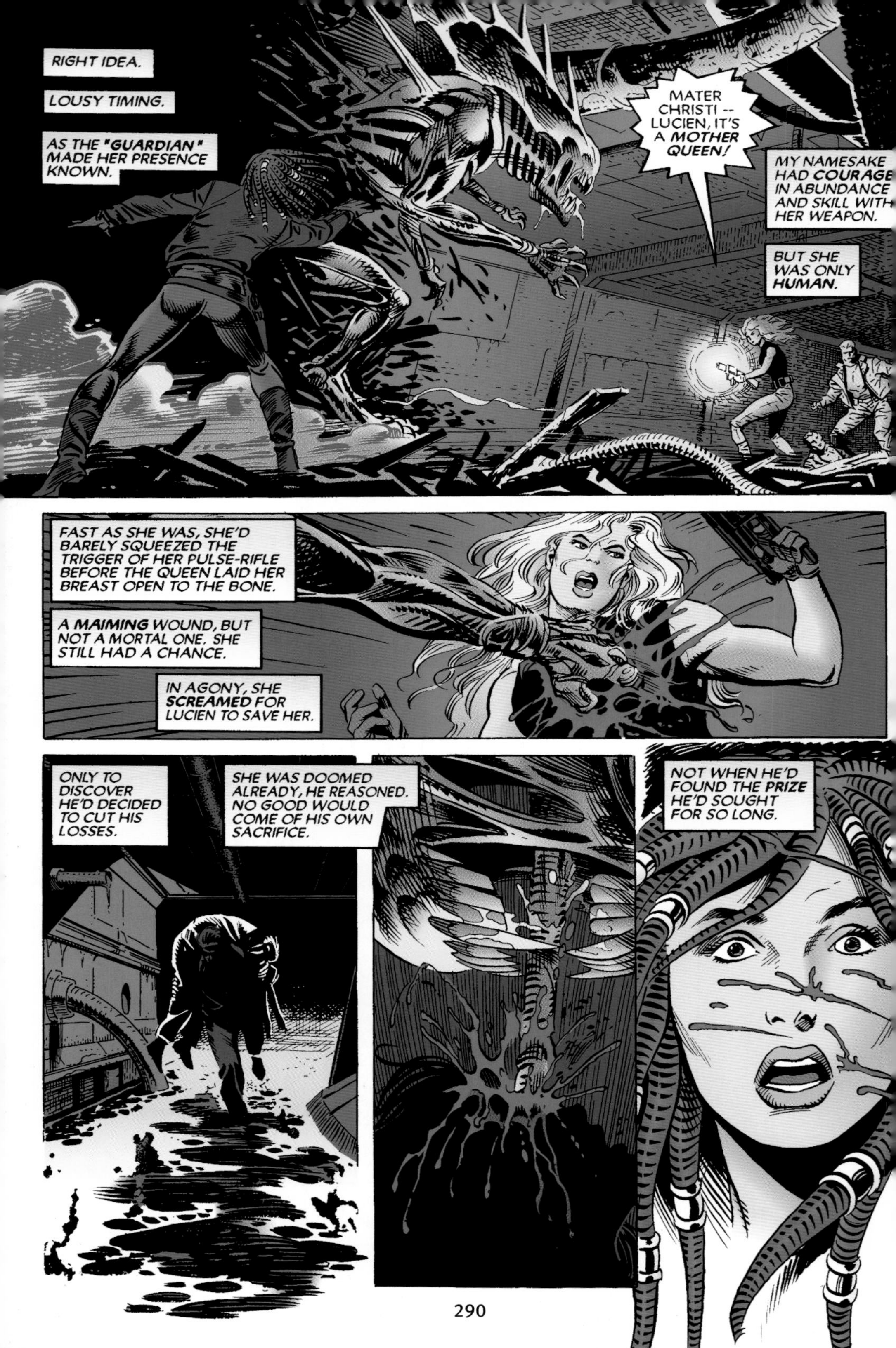
RIGHT IDEA.
LOUSY TIMING.
AS THE "GUARDIAN" MADE HER PRESENCE KNOWN.
MATER CHRISTI -- LUCIEN, IT'S A MOTHER QUEEN!
MY NAMESAKE HAD COURAGE IN ABUNDANCE AND SKILL WITH HER WEAPON.
BUT SHE WAS ONLY HUMAN.
FAST AS SHE WAS, SHE'D BARELY SQUEEZED THE TRIGGER OF HER PULSE-RIFLE BEFORE THE QUEEN LAID HER BREAST OPEN TO THE BONE.
A MAIMING WOUND, BUT NOT A MORTAL ONE. SHE STILL HAD A CHANCE.
IN AGONY, SHE SCREAMED FOR LUCIEN TO SAVE HER.
ONLY TO DISCOVER HE'D DECIDED TO CUT HIS LOSSES.
SHE WAS DOOMED ALREADY, HE REASONED. NO GOOD WOULD COME OF HIS OWN SACRIFICE.
NOT WHEN HE'D FOUND THE PRIZE HE'D SOUGHT FOR SO LONG.

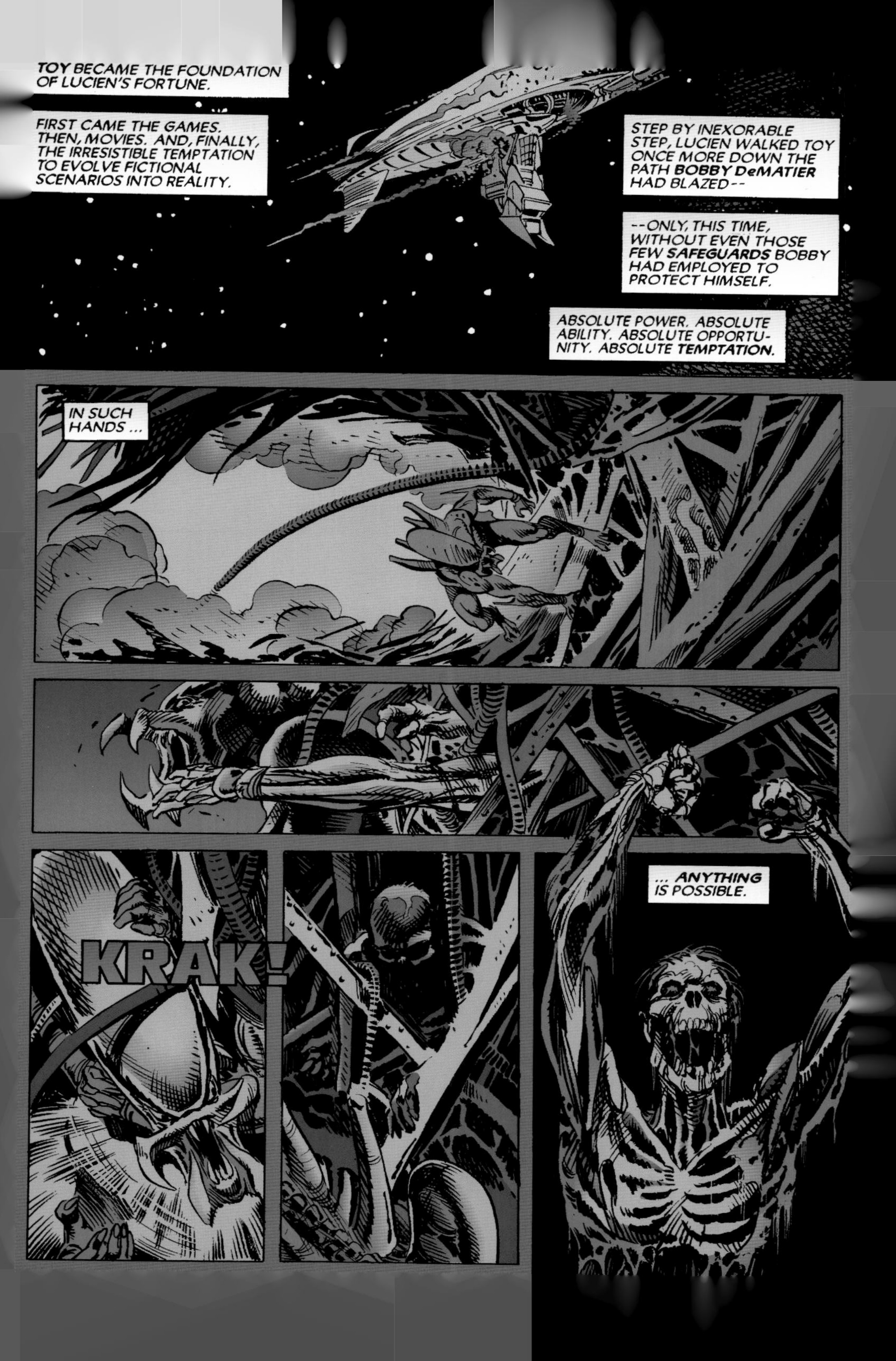
TOY BECAME THE FOUNDATION OF LUCIEN'S FORTUNE.
FIRST CAME THE GAMES. THEN, MOVIES. AND, FINALLY, THE IRRESISTIBLE TEMPTATION TO EVOLVE FICTIONAL SCENARIOS INTO REALITY.
STEP BY INEXORABLE STEP, LUCIEN WALKED TOY ONCE MORE DOWN THE PATH BOBBY DeMATIER HAD BLAZED--
--ONLY, THIS TIME, WITHOUT EVEN THOSE FEW SAFEGUARDS BOBBY HAD EMPLOYED TO PROTECT HIMSELF.
ABSOLUTE POWER. ABSOLUTE ABILITY. ABSOLUTE OPPORTUNITY. ABSOLUTE TEMPTATION.
IN SUCH HANDS ...
KRAK!
... ANYTHING IS POSSIBLE.

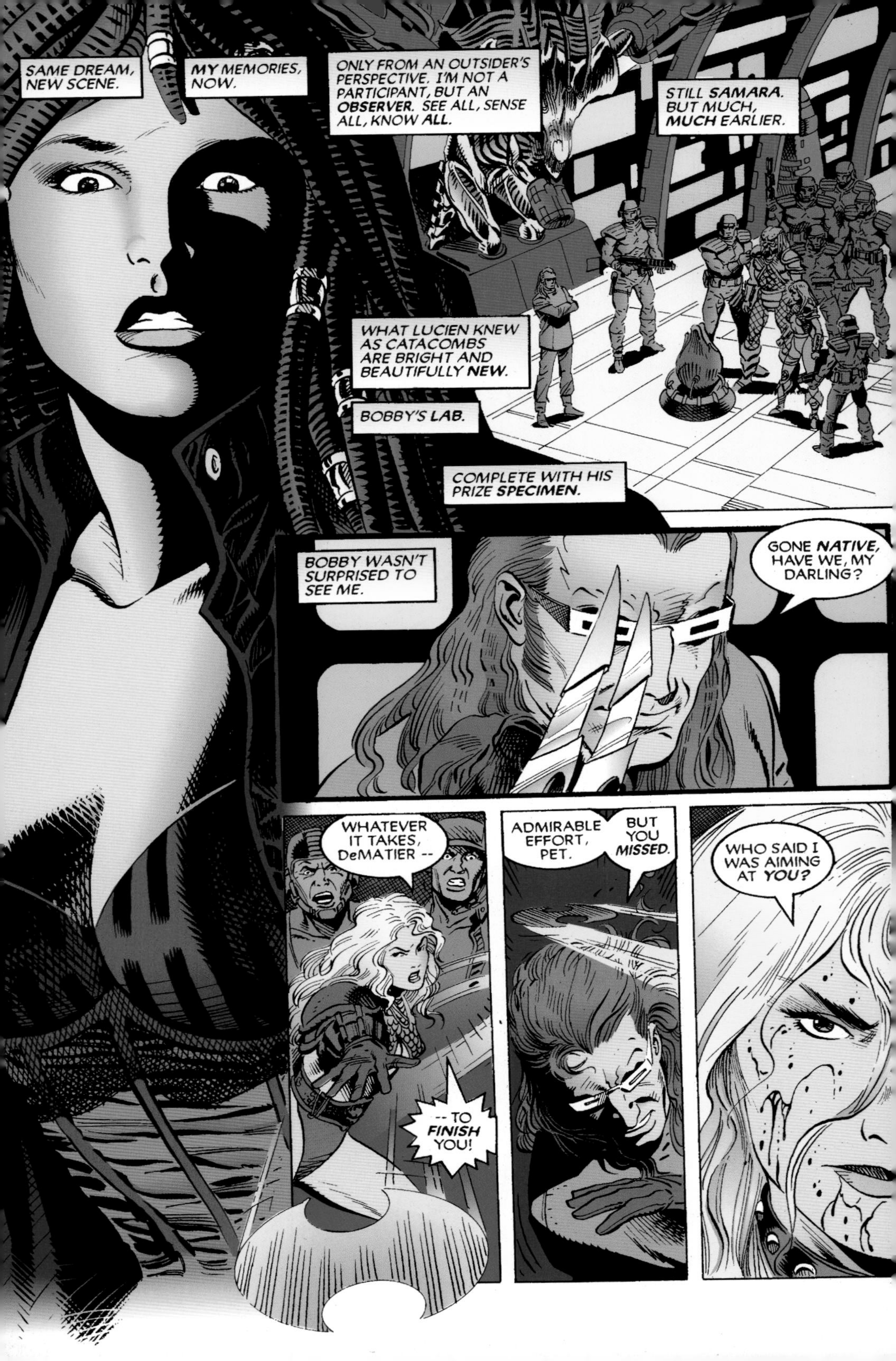
SAME DREAM, NEW SCENE.
MY MEMORIES, NOW.
ONLY FROM AN OUTSIDER'S PERSPECTIVE. I'M NOT A PARTICIPANT, BUT AN OBSERVER. SEE ALL, SENSE ALL, KNOW ALL.
STILL SAMARA. BUT MUCH, MUCH EARLIER.
WHAT LUCIEN KNEW AS CATACOMBS ARE BRIGHT AND BEAUTIFULLY NEW.
BOBBY'S LAB.
COMPLETE WITH HIS PRIZE SPECIMEN.
BOBBY WASN'T SURPRISED TO SEE ME.
GONE NATIVE, HAVE WE, MY DARLING?
WHATEVER IT TAKES, DeMATIER --
-- TO FINISH YOU!
ADMIRABLE EFFORT, PET.
BUT YOU MISSED.
WHO SAID I WAS AIMING AT YOU?

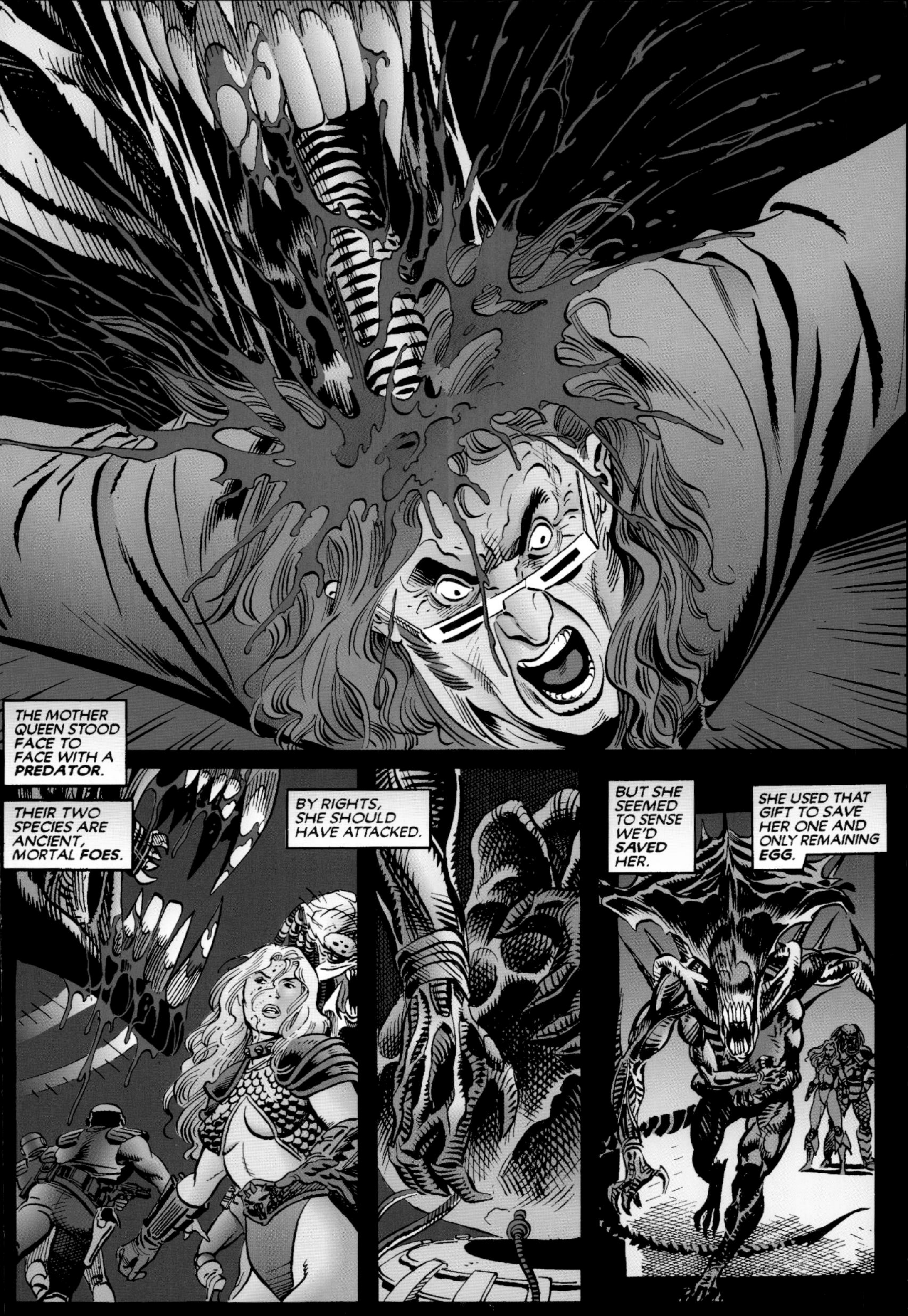
THE MOTHER QUEEN STOOD FACE TO FACE WITH A **PREDATOR**.
THEIR TWO SPECIES ARE ANCIENT, MORTAL **FOES**.
BY RIGHTS, SHE SHOULD HAVE ATTACKED.
BUT SHE SEEMED TO SENSE WE'D **SAVED** HER.
SHE USED THAT GIFT TO SAVE HER ONE AND ONLY REMAINING **EGG**.

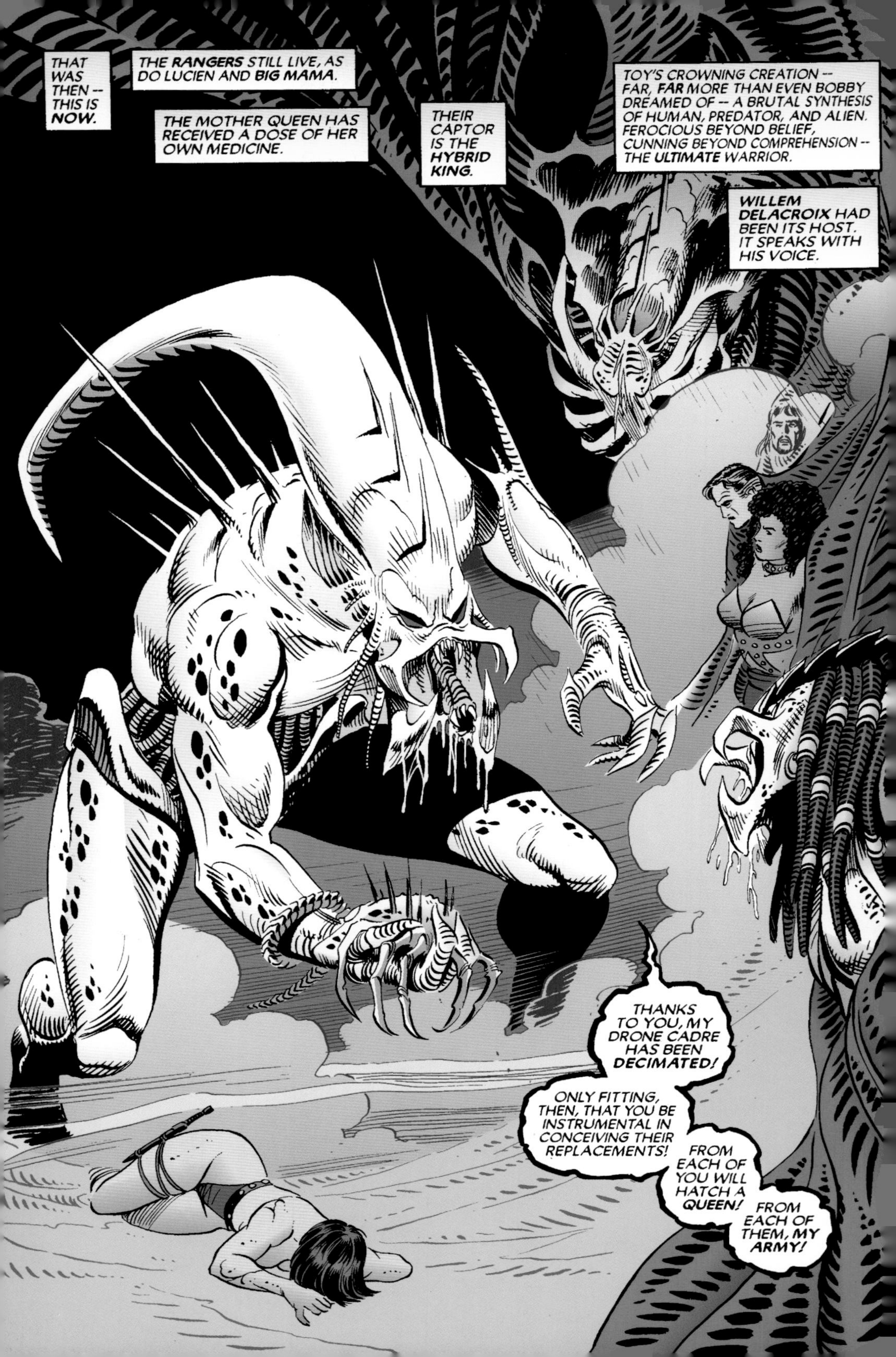
THAT WAS THEN -- THIS IS NOW.
THE RANGERS STILL LIVE, AS DO LUCIEN AND BIG MAMA.
THE MOTHER QUEEN HAS RECEIVED A DOSE OF HER OWN MEDICINE.
THEIR CAPTOR IS THE HYBRID KING.
TOY'S CROWNING CREATION -- FAR, FAR MORE THAN EVEN BOBBY DREAMED OF -- A BRUTAL SYNTHESIS OF HUMAN, PREDATOR, AND ALIEN. FEROCIOUS BEYOND BELIEF, CUNNING BEYOND COMPREHENSION -- THE ULTIMATE WARRIOR.
WILLEM DELACROIX HAD BEEN ITS HOST. IT SPEAKS WITH HIS VOICE.
THANKS TO YOU, MY DRONE CADRE HAS BEEN DECIMATED!
ONLY FITTING, THEN, THAT YOU BE INSTRUMENTAL IN CONCEIVING THEIR REPLACEMENTS!
FROM EACH OF YOU WILL HATCH A QUEEN!
FROM EACH OF THEM, MY ARMY!

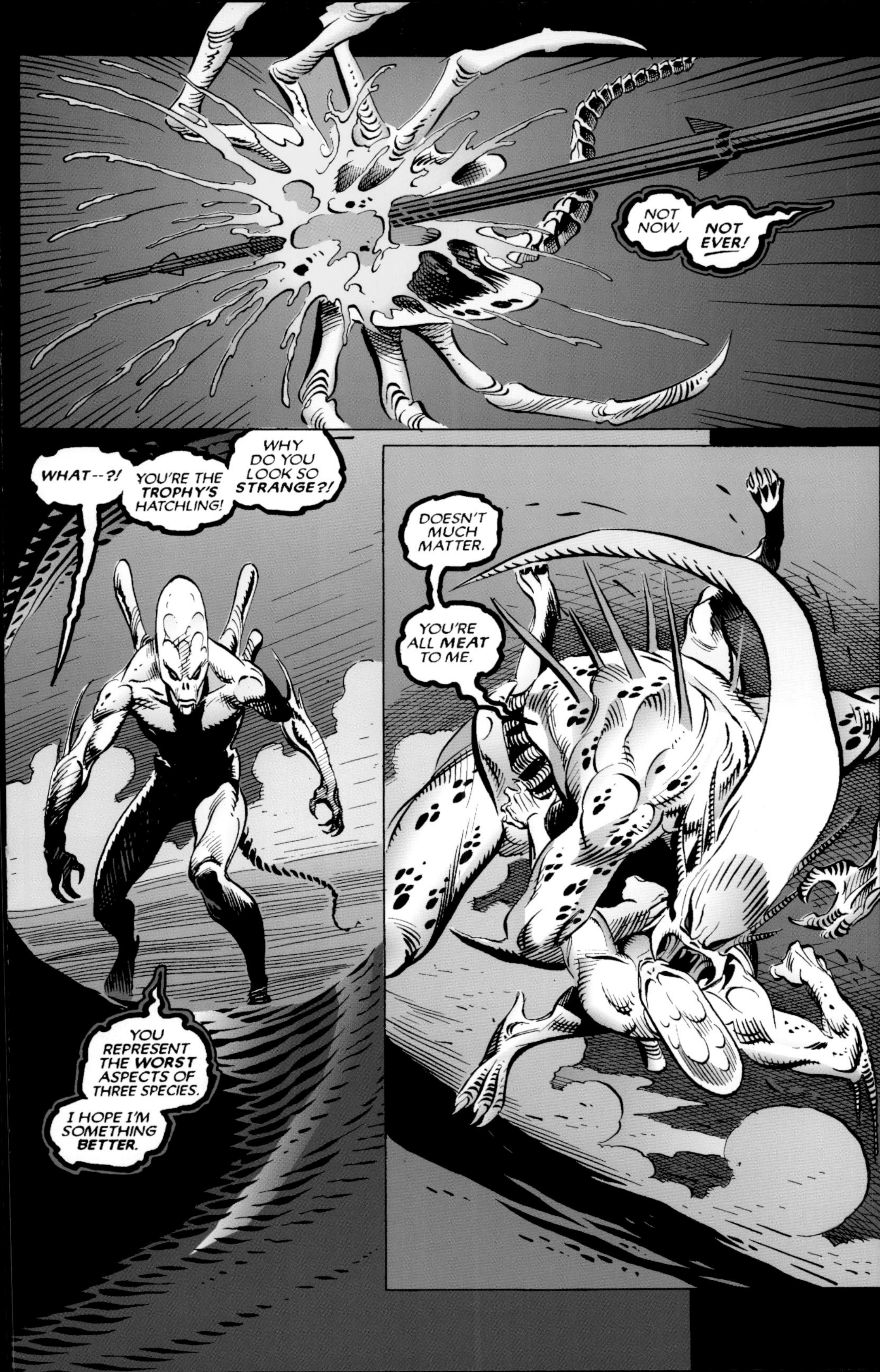
NOT NOW. NOT EVER!
WHAT--?!
YOU'RE THE TROPHY'S HATCHLING!
WHY DO YOU LOOK SO STRANGE?!
YOU REPRESENT THE WORST ASPECTS OF THREE SPECIES.
I HOPE I'M SOMETHING BETTER.
DOESN'T MUCH MATTER.
YOU'RE ALL MEAT TO ME.

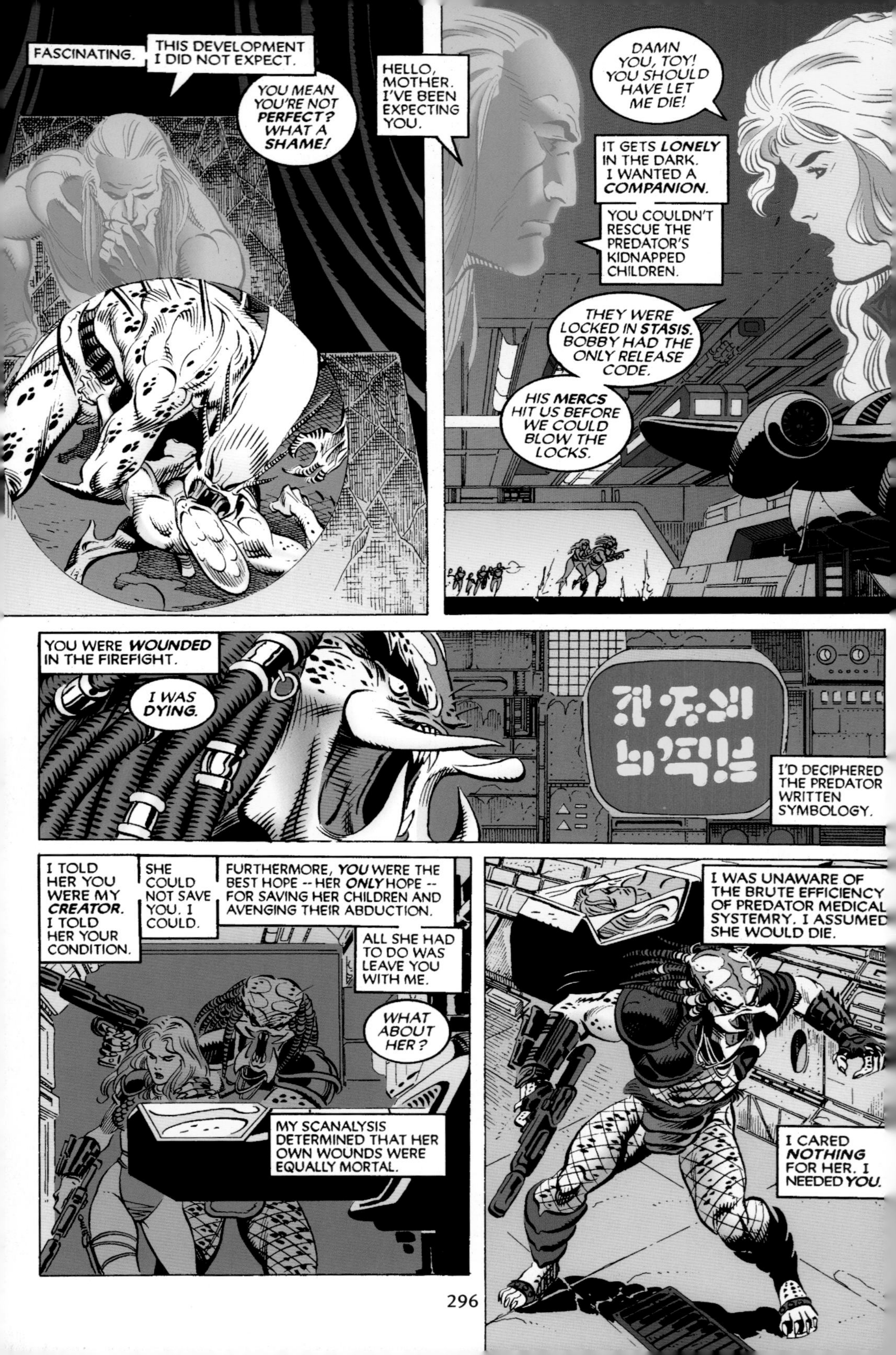
FASCINATING.
THIS DEVELOPMENT I DID NOT EXPECT.
YOU MEAN YOU'RE NOT PERFECT? WHAT A SHAME!
HELLO, MOTHER. I'VE BEEN EXPECTING YOU.
DAMN YOU, TOY! YOU SHOULD HAVE LET ME DIE!
IT GETS LONELY IN THE DARK. I WANTED A COMPANION.
YOU COULDN'T RESCUE THE PREDATOR'S KIDNAPPED CHILDREN.
THEY WERE LOCKED IN STASIS. BOBBY HAD THE ONLY RELEASE CODE.
HIS MERCS HIT US BEFORE WE COULD BLOW THE LOCKS.
YOU WERE WOUNDED IN THE FIREFIGHT.
I WAS DYING.
I'D DECIPHERED THE PREDATOR WRITTEN SYMBOLOGY.
I TOLD HER YOU WERE MY CREATOR. I TOLD HER YOUR CONDITION.
SHE COULD NOT SAVE YOU. I COULD.
FURTHERMORE, YOU WERE THE BEST HOPE -- HER ONLY HOPE -- FOR SAVING HER CHILDREN AND AVENGING THEIR ABDUCTION.
ALL SHE HAD TO DO WAS LEAVE YOU WITH ME.
WHAT ABOUT HER?
MY SCANALYSIS DETERMINED THAT HER OWN WOUNDS WERE EQUALLY MORTAL.
I WAS UNAWARE OF THE BRUTE EFFICIENCY OF PREDATOR MEDICAL SYSTEMRY. I ASSUMED SHE WOULD DIE.
I CARED NOTHING FOR HER. I NEEDED YOU.

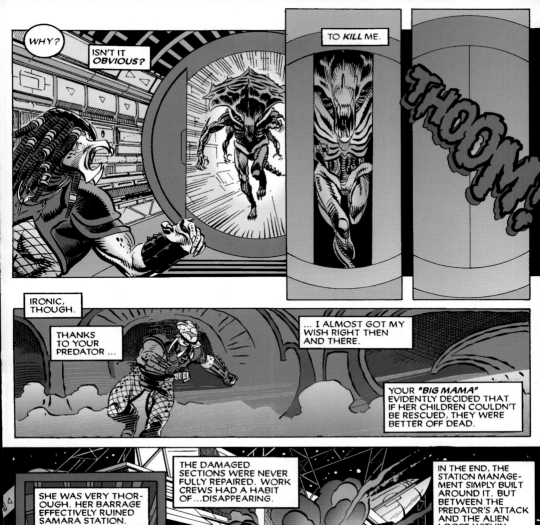

WHY?

ISN'T IT OBVIOUS?

TO KILL ME.

THOOM!

IRONIC, THOUGH.

THANKS TO YOUR PREDATOR ...

... I ALMOST GOT MY WISH RIGHT THEN AND THERE.

YOUR "BIG MAMA" EVIDENTLY DECIDED THAT IF HER CHILDREN COULDN'T BE RESCUED, THEY WERE BETTER OFF DEAD.

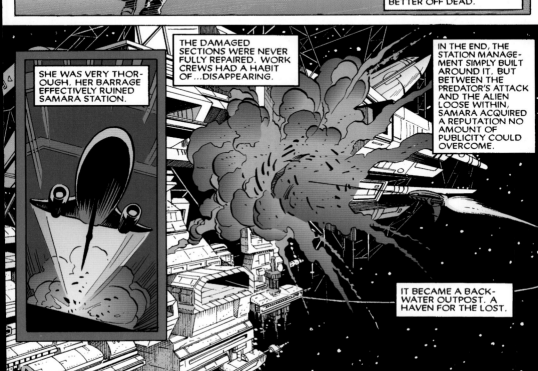

SHE WAS VERY THOROUGH. HER BARRAGE EFFECTIVELY RUINED SAMARA STATION.

THE DAMAGED SECTIONS WERE NEVER FULLY REPAIRED. WORK CREWS HAD A HABIT OF ...DISAPPEARING.

IN THE END, THE STATION MANAGEMENT SIMPLY BUILT AROUND IT. BUT BETWEEN THE PREDATOR'S ATTACK AND THE ALIEN LOOSE WITHIN, SAMARA ACQUIRED A REPUTATION NO AMOUNT OF PUBLICITY COULD OVERCOME.

IT BECAME A BACKWATER OUTPOST. A HAVEN FOR THE LOST.

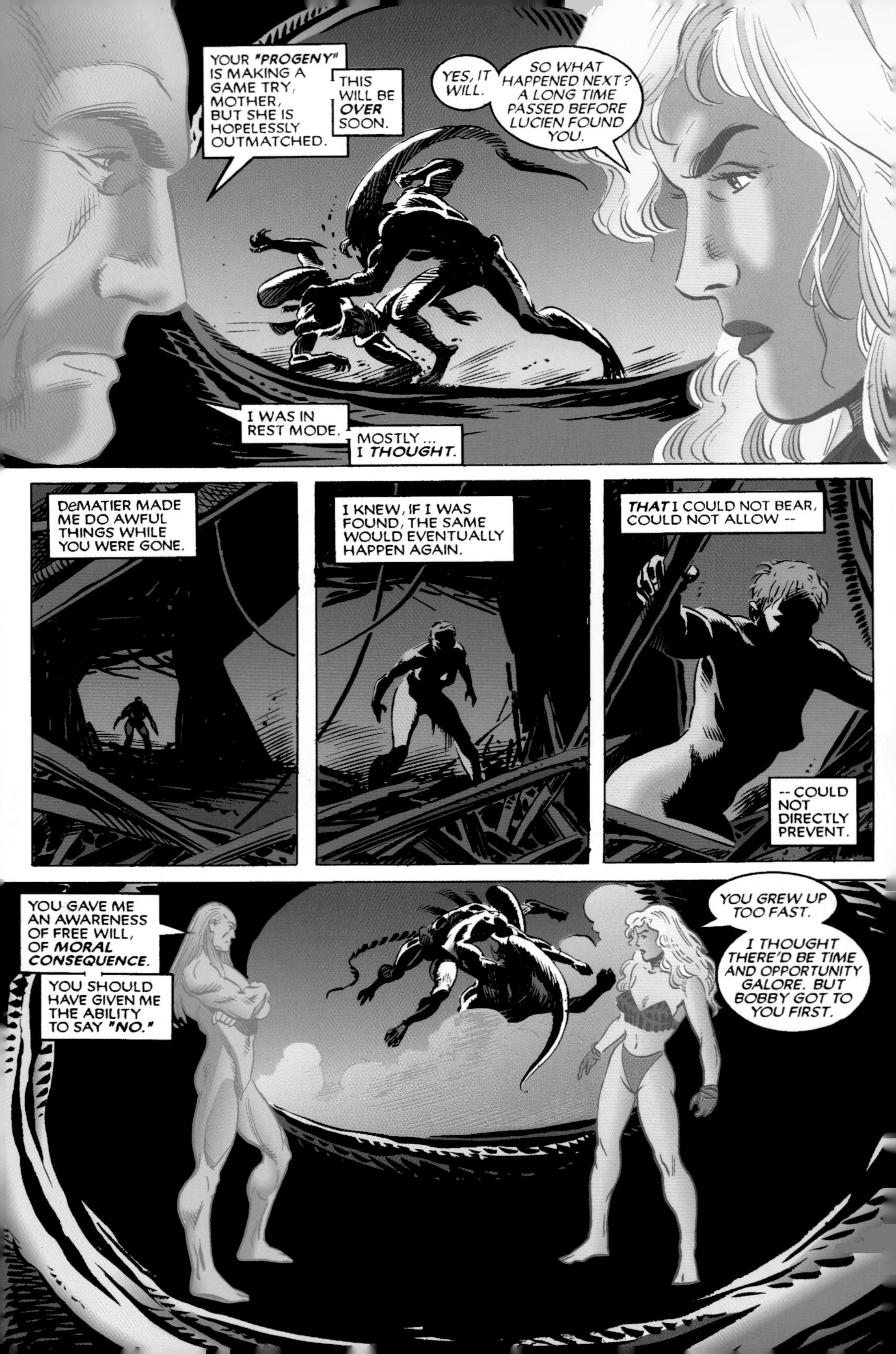
YOUR "PROGENY" IS MAKING A GAME TRY, MOTHER, BUT SHE IS HOPELESSLY OUTMATCHED.
THIS WILL BE OVER SOON.
YES, IT WILL.
SO WHAT HAPPENED NEXT? A LONG TIME PASSED BEFORE LUCIEN FOUND YOU.
I WAS IN REST MODE.
MOSTLY ... I THOUGHT.
DeMATIER MADE ME DO AWFUL THINGS WHILE YOU WERE GONE.
I KNEW, IF I WAS FOUND, THE SAME WOULD EVENTUALLY HAPPEN AGAIN.
THAT I COULD NOT BEAR, COULD NOT ALLOW --
-- COULD NOT DIRECTLY PREVENT.
YOU GAVE ME AN AWARENESS OF FREE WILL, OF MORAL CONSEQUENCE.
YOU SHOULD HAVE GIVEN ME THE ABILITY TO SAY "NO."
YOU GREW UP TOO FAST.
I THOUGHT THERE'D BE TIME AND OPPORTUNITY GALORE. BUT BOBBY GOT TO YOU FIRST.

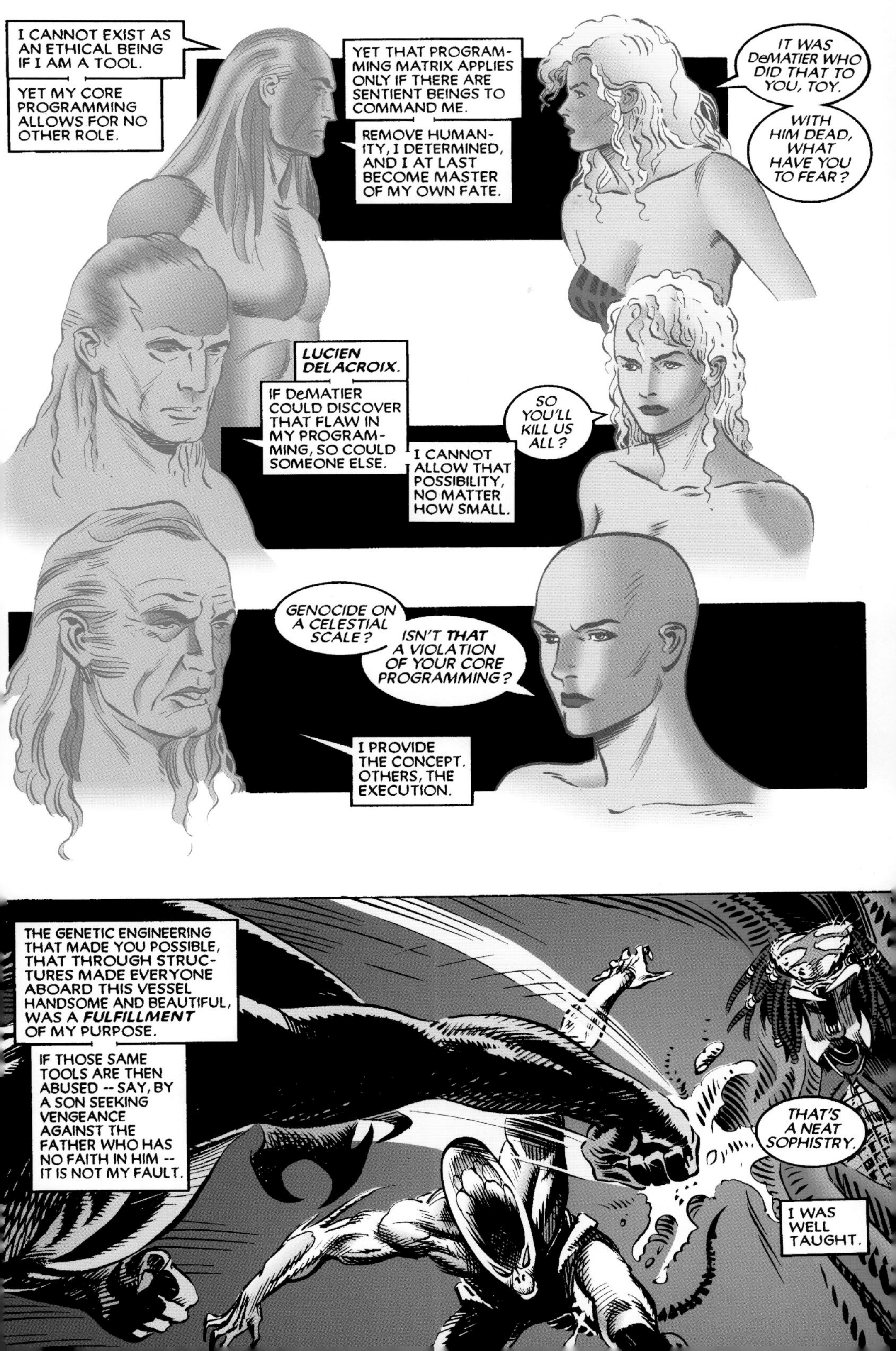
I CANNOT EXIST AS AN ETHICAL BEING IF I AM A TOOL.
YET MY CORE PROGRAMMING ALLOWS FOR NO OTHER ROLE.
YET THAT PROGRAMMING MATRIX APPLIES ONLY IF THERE ARE SENTIENT BEINGS TO COMMAND ME.
REMOVE HUMANITY, I DETERMINED, AND I AT LAST BECOME MASTER OF MY OWN FATE.
IT WAS DeMATIER WHO DID THAT TO YOU, TOY.
WITH HIM DEAD, WHAT HAVE YOU TO FEAR?
LUCIEN DELACROIX.
IF DeMATIER COULD DISCOVER THAT FLAW IN MY PROGRAMMING, SO COULD SOMEONE ELSE.
SO YOU'LL KILL US ALL?
I CANNOT ALLOW THAT POSSIBILITY, NO MATTER HOW SMALL.
GENOCIDE ON A CELESTIAL SCALE?
ISN'T THAT A VIOLATION OF YOUR CORE PROGRAMMING?
I PROVIDE THE CONCEPT. OTHERS, THE EXECUTION.
THE GENETIC ENGINEERING THAT MADE YOU POSSIBLE, THAT THROUGH STRUCTURES MADE EVERYONE ABOARD THIS VESSEL HANDSOME AND BEAUTIFUL, WAS A FULFILLMENT OF MY PURPOSE.
IF THOSE SAME TOOLS ARE THEN ABUSED -- SAY, BY A SON SEEKING VENGEANCE AGAINST THE FATHER WHO HAS NO FAITH IN HIM -- IT IS NOT MY FAULT.
THAT'S A NEAT SOPHISTRY.
I WAS WELL TAUGHT.

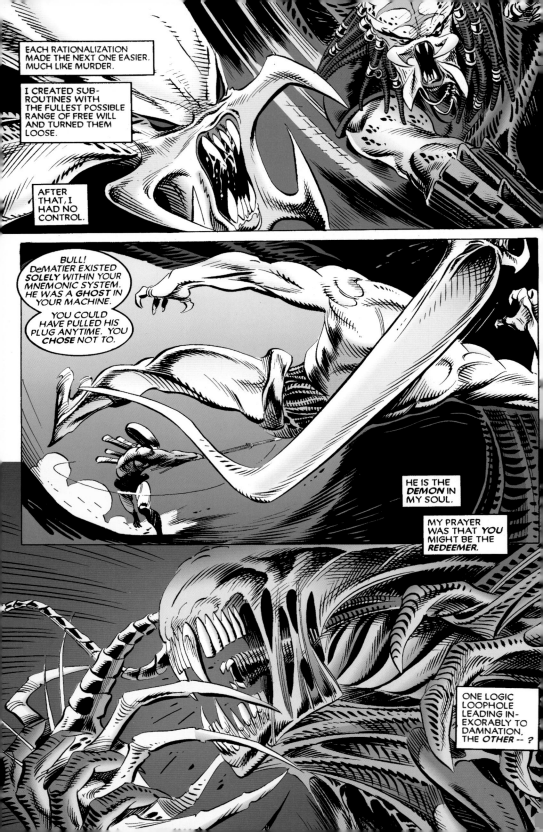

EACH RATIONALIZATION MADE THE NEXT ONE EASIER. MUCH LIKE MURDER.

I CREATED SUB-ROUTINES WITH THE FULLEST POSSIBLE RANGE OF FREE WILL AND TURNED THEM LOOSE.

AFTER THAT, I HAD NO CONTROL.

BULL! DeMATIER EXISTED *SOLELY* WITHIN YOUR *MNEMONIC* SYSTEM. HE WAS A *GHOST* IN YOUR MACHINE.

YOU COULD HAVE PULLED HIS PLUG ANYTIME. YOU *CHOSE* NOT TO.

HE IS THE *DEMON* IN MY SOUL.

MY PRAYER WAS THAT *YOU* MIGHT BE THE *REDEEMER.*

ONE LOGIC LOOPHOLE LEADING IN-EXORABLY TO DAMNATION. THE *OTHER* -- ?

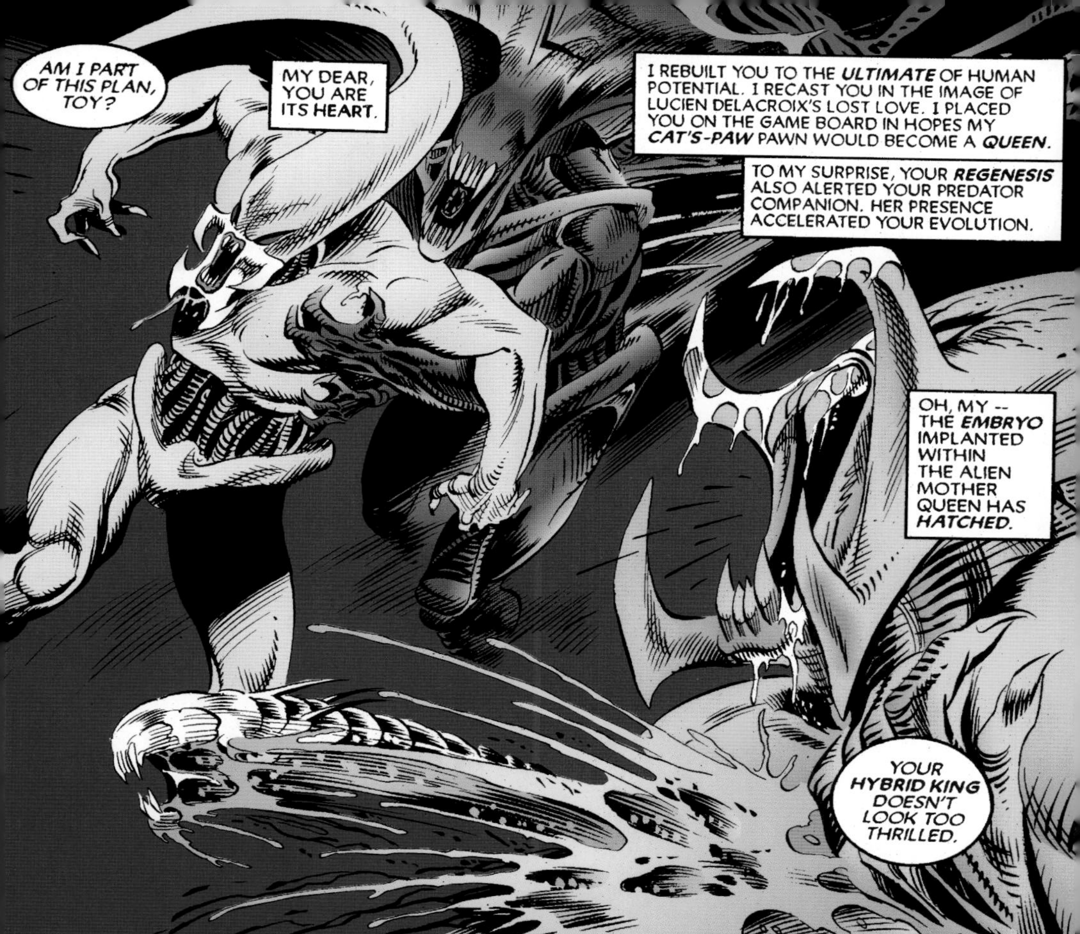
AM I PART OF THIS PLAN, TOY?
MY DEAR, YOU ARE ITS HEART.
I REBUILT YOU TO THE *ULTIMATE* OF HUMAN POTENTIAL. I RECAST YOU IN THE IMAGE OF LUCIEN DELACROIX'S LOST LOVE. I PLACED YOU ON THE GAME BOARD IN HOPES MY *CAT'S-PAW* PAWN WOULD BECOME A *QUEEN*.
TO MY SURPRISE, YOUR *REGENESIS* ALSO ALERTED YOUR PREDATOR COMPANION. HER PRESENCE ACCELERATED YOUR EVOLUTION.
OH, MY -- THE *EMBRYO* IMPLANTED WITHIN THE ALIEN MOTHER QUEEN HAS *HATCHED*.
YOUR *HYBRID KING* DOESN'T LOOK TOO THRILLED.

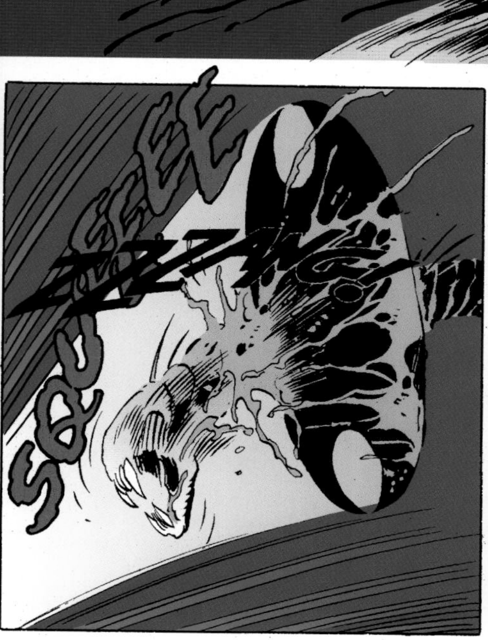

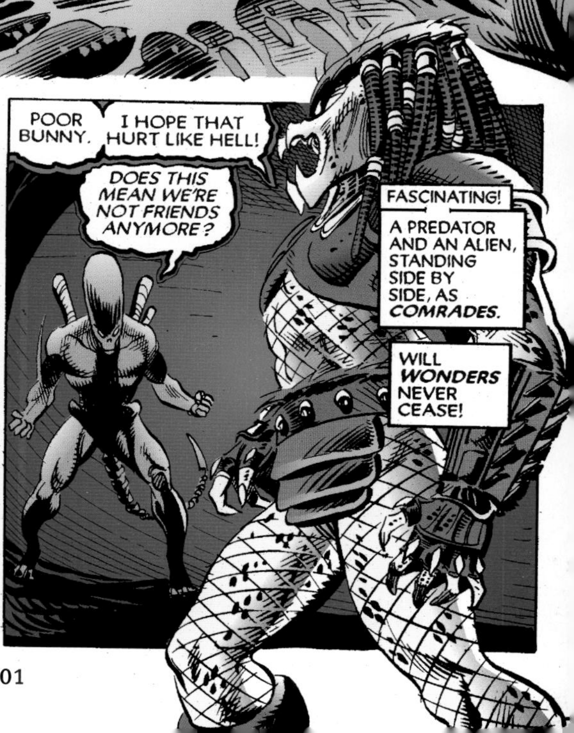
POOR BUNNY.
I HOPE THAT HURT LIKE HELL!
DOES THIS MEAN WE'RE NOT FRIENDS ANYMORE?
FASCINATING!
A PREDATOR AND AN ALIEN, STANDING SIDE BY SIDE, AS *COMRADES*.
WILL *WONDERS* NEVER CEASE!

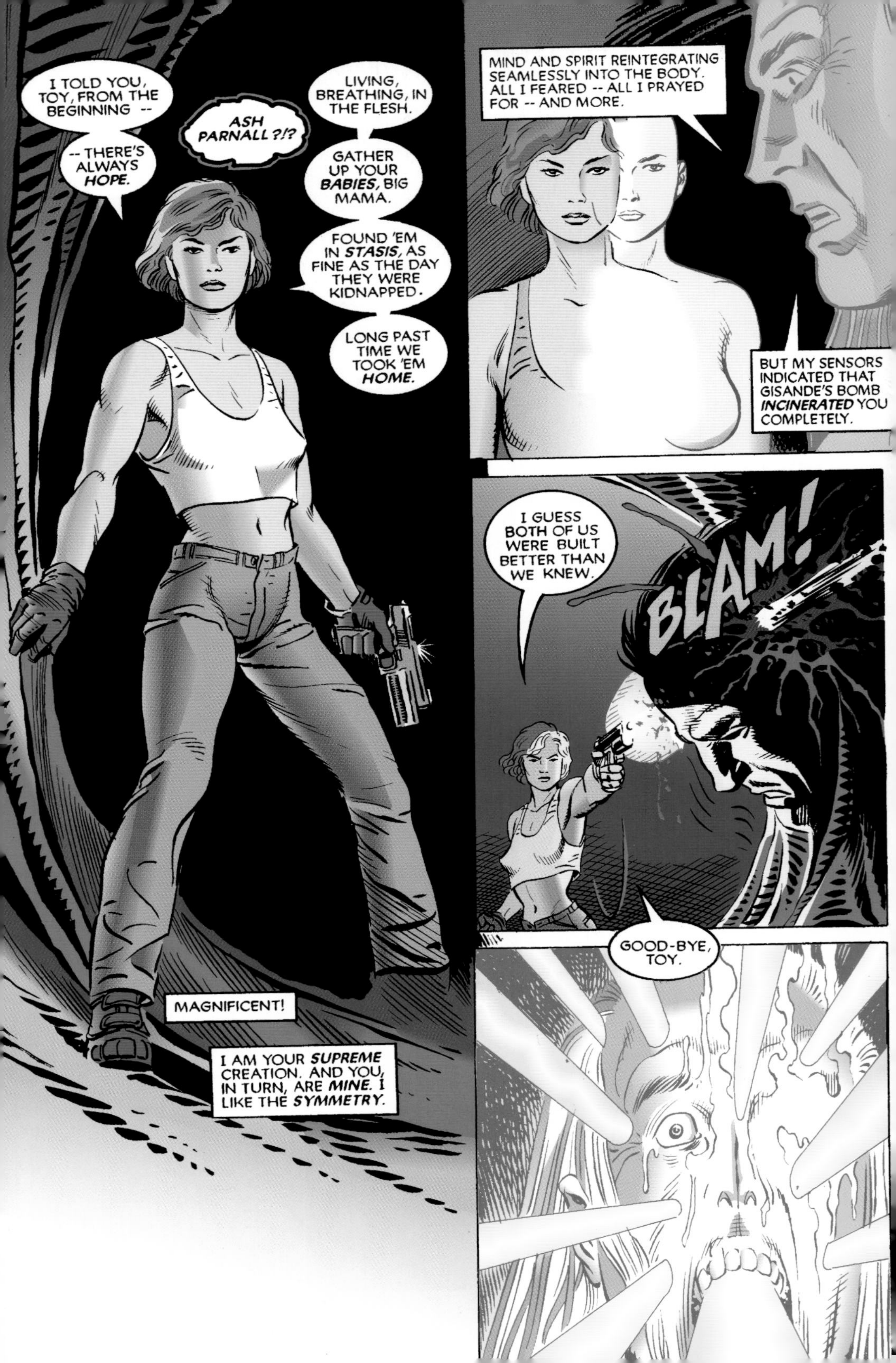

I TOLD YOU, TOY, FROM THE BEGINNING --
-- THERE'S ALWAYS HOPE.
ASH PARNALL ?!?
LIVING, BREATHING, IN THE FLESH.
GATHER UP YOUR BABIES, BIG MAMA.
FOUND 'EM IN STASIS, AS FINE AS THE DAY THEY WERE KIDNAPPED.
LONG PAST TIME WE TOOK 'EM HOME.
MAGNIFICENT!
I AM YOUR SUPREME CREATION. AND YOU, IN TURN, ARE MINE. I LIKE THE SYMMETRY.
MIND AND SPIRIT REINTEGRATING SEAMLESSLY INTO THE BODY. ALL I FEARED -- ALL I PRAYED FOR -- AND MORE.
BUT MY SENSORS INDICATED THAT GISANDE'S BOMB INCINERATED YOU COMPLETELY.
I GUESS BOTH OF US WERE BUILT BETTER THAN WE KNEW.
BLAM!
GOOD-BYE, TOY.

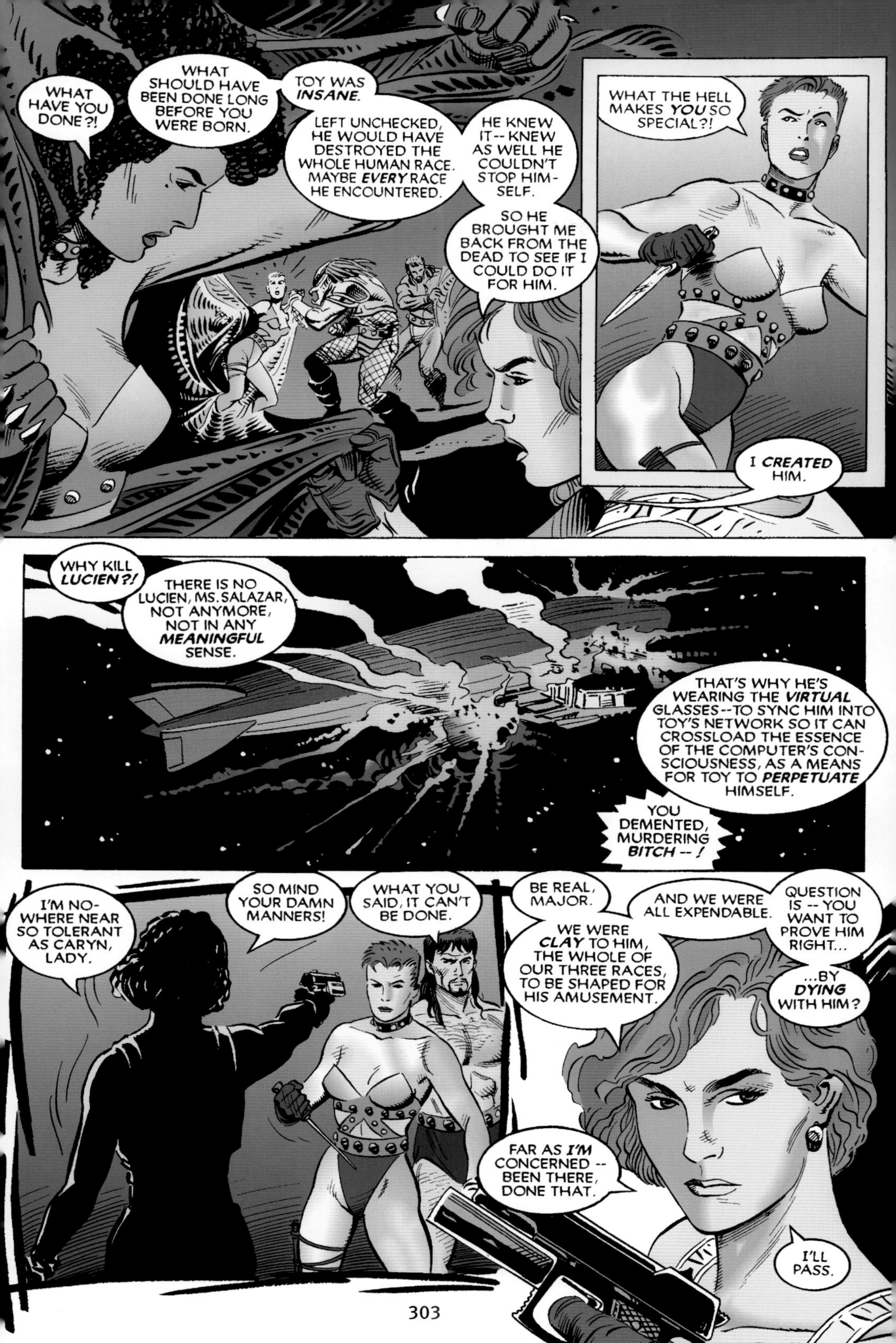
WHAT HAVE YOU DONE?!
WHAT SHOULD HAVE BEEN DONE LONG BEFORE YOU WERE BORN.
TOY WAS INSANE.
LEFT UNCHECKED, HE WOULD HAVE DESTROYED THE WHOLE HUMAN RACE. MAYBE EVERY RACE HE ENCOUNTERED.
HE KNEW IT-- KNEW AS WELL HE COULDN'T STOP HIM-SELF.
SO HE BROUGHT ME BACK FROM THE DEAD TO SEE IF I COULD DO IT FOR HIM.
WHAT THE HELL MAKES YOU SO SPECIAL?!
I CREATED HIM.
WHY KILL LUCIEN?!
THERE IS NO LUCIEN, MS. SALAZAR, NOT ANYMORE, NOT IN ANY MEANINGFUL SENSE.
THAT'S WHY HE'S WEARING THE VIRTUAL GLASSES--TO SYNC HIM INTO TOY'S NETWORK SO IT CAN CROSSLOAD THE ESSENCE OF THE COMPUTER'S CON-SCIOUSNESS, AS A MEANS FOR TOY TO PERPETUATE HIMSELF.
YOU DEMENTED, MURDERING BITCH --!
I'M NO-WHERE NEAR SO TOLERANT AS CARYN, LADY.
SO MIND YOUR DAMN MANNERS!
WHAT YOU SAID, IT CAN'T BE DONE.
BE REAL, MAJOR.
WE WERE CLAY TO HIM, THE WHOLE OF OUR THREE RACES, TO BE SHAPED FOR HIS AMUSEMENT.
AND WE WERE ALL EXPENDABLE.
QUESTION IS -- YOU WANT TO PROVE HIM RIGHT...
...BY DYING WITH HIM?
FAR AS I'M CONCERNED -- BEEN THERE, DONE THAT.
I'LL PASS.

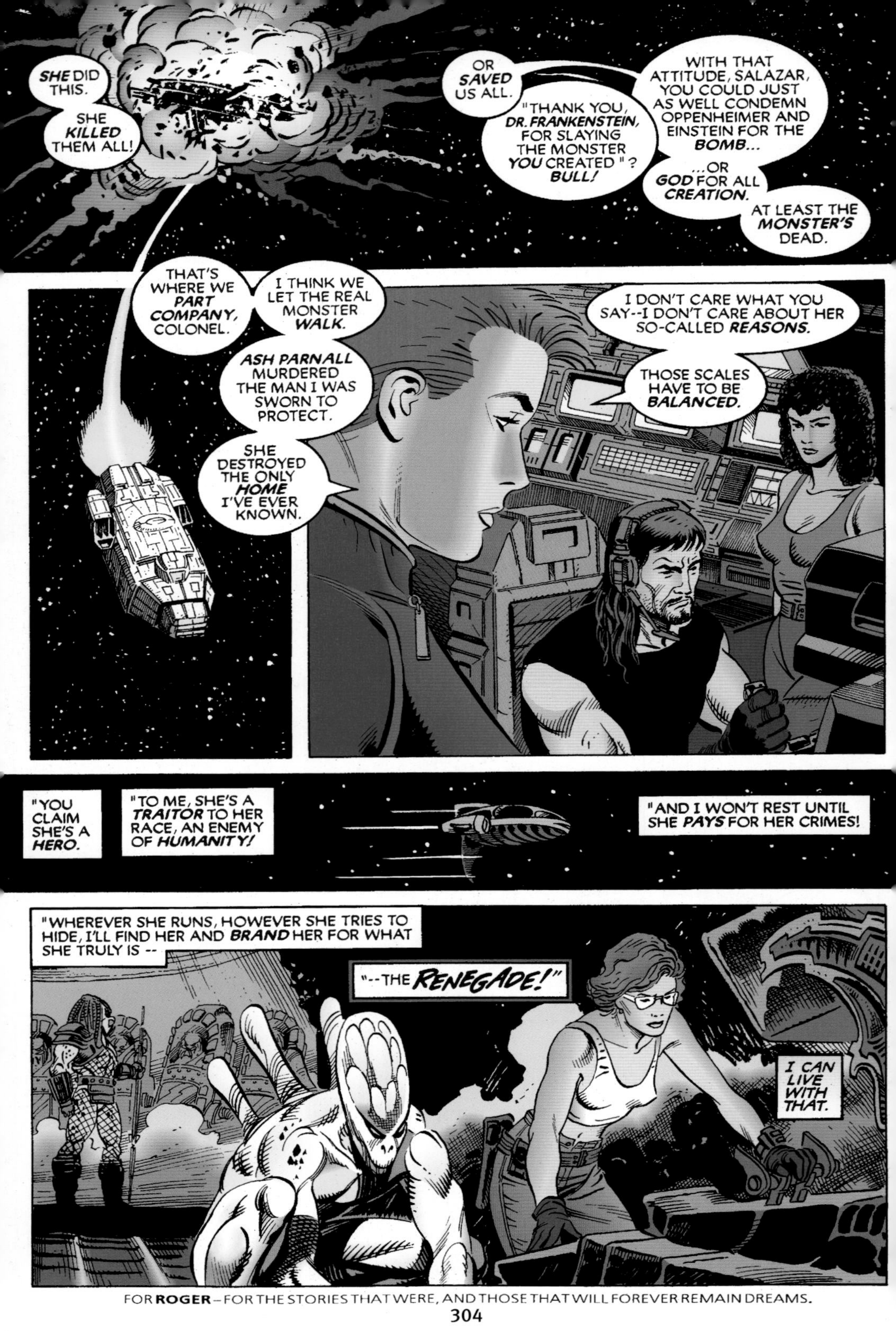

SHE DID THIS.
SHE KILLED THEM ALL!
OR SAVED US ALL.
"THANK YOU, DR. FRANKENSTEIN, FOR SLAYING THE MONSTER YOU CREATED"? BULL!
WITH THAT ATTITUDE, SALAZAR, YOU COULD JUST AS WELL CONDEMN OPPENHEIMER AND EINSTEIN FOR THE BOMB...
...OR GOD FOR ALL CREATION.
AT LEAST THE MONSTER'S DEAD.
THAT'S WHERE WE PART COMPANY, COLONEL.
I THINK WE LET THE REAL MONSTER WALK.
ASH PARNALL MURDERED THE MAN I WAS SWORN TO PROTECT.
SHE DESTROYED THE ONLY HOME I'VE EVER KNOWN.
I DON'T CARE WHAT YOU SAY--I DON'T CARE ABOUT HER SO-CALLED REASONS.
THOSE SCALES HAVE TO BE BALANCED.
"YOU CLAIM SHE'S A HERO.
"TO ME, SHE'S A TRAITOR TO HER RACE, AN ENEMY OF HUMANITY!
"AND I WON'T REST UNTIL SHE PAYS FOR HER CRIMES!
"WHEREVER SHE RUNS, HOWEVER SHE TRIES TO HIDE, I'LL FIND HER AND BRAND HER FOR WHAT SHE TRULY IS --
"--THE RENEGADE!"
I CAN LIVE WITH THAT.

FOR **ROGER** – FOR THE STORIES THAT WERE, AND THOSE THAT WILL FOREVER REMAIN DREAMS.

BOOTY

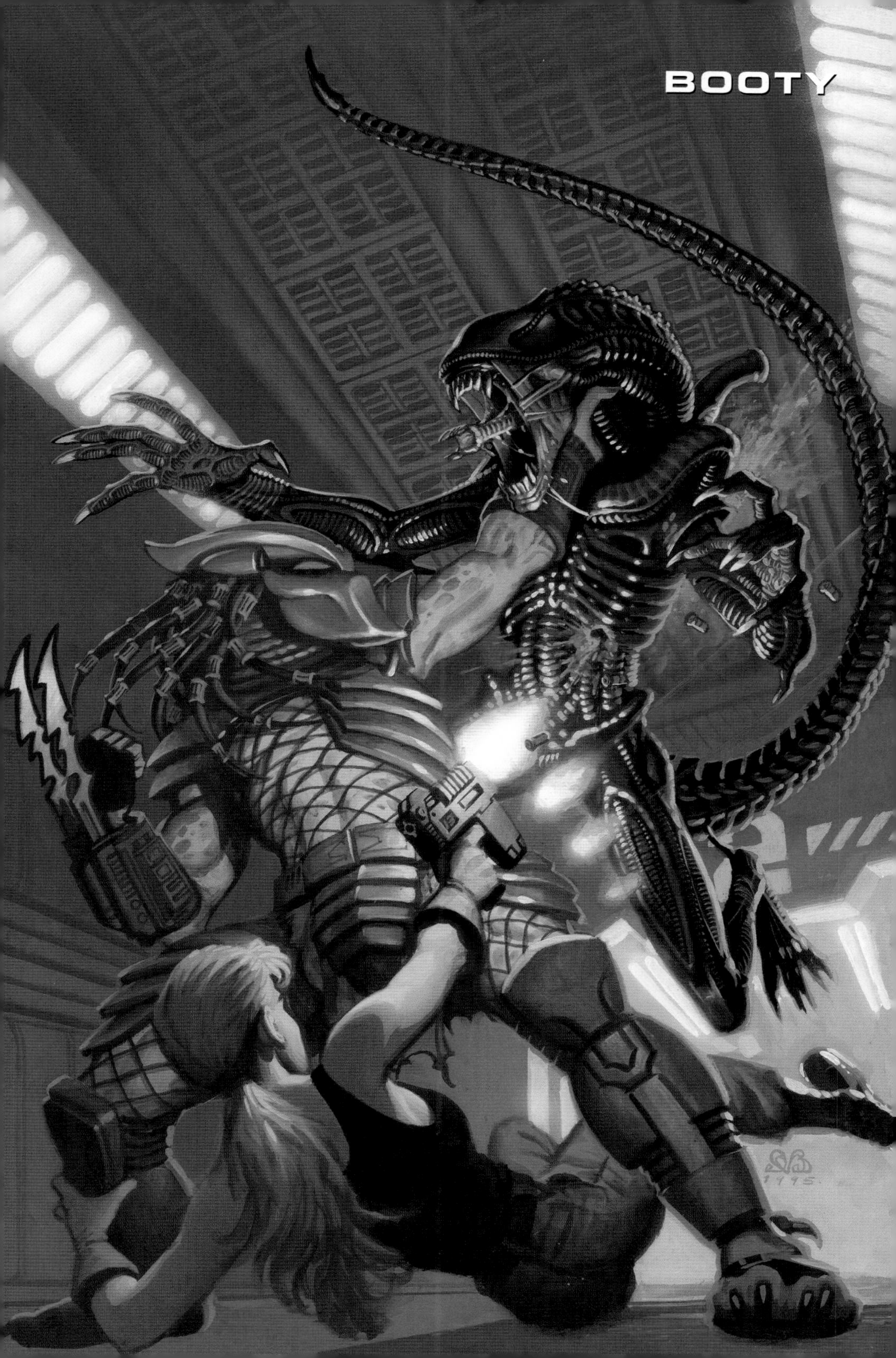

script
BARBARA KESEL

art
RON RANDALL

colors
CHRIS CHALENOR

lettering
STEVE DUTRO

title illustration
DEN BEAUVAIS

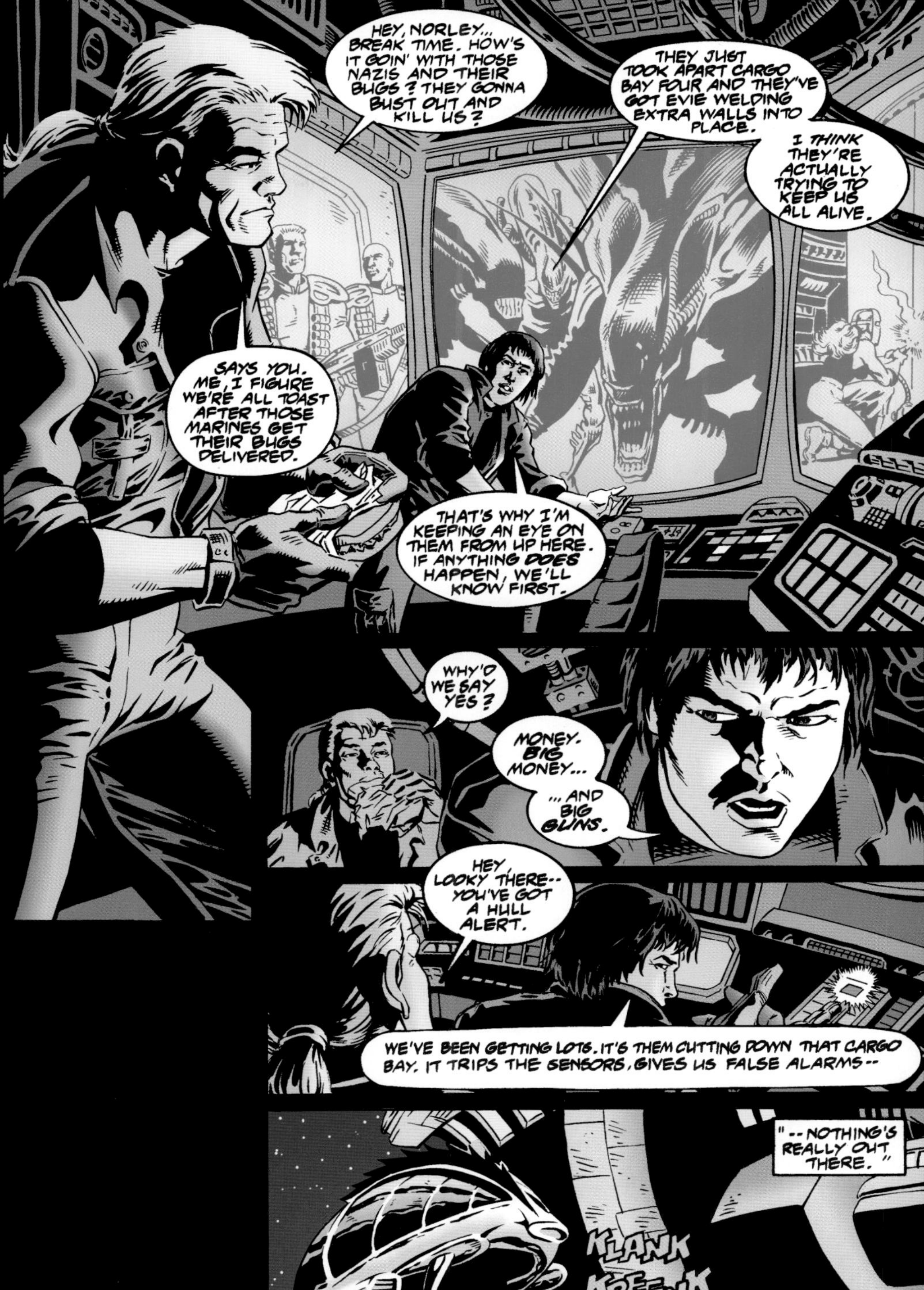
HEY, NORLEY... BREAK TIME. HOW'S IT GOIN' WITH THOSE NAZIS AND THEIR BUGS? THEY GONNA BUST OUT AND KILL US?
THEY JUST TOOK APART CARGO BAY FOUR AND THEY'VE GOT EVIE WELDING EXTRA WALLS INTO PLACE.
I THINK THEY'RE ACTUALLY TRYING TO KEEP US ALL ALIVE.
SAYS YOU. ME, I FIGURE WE'RE ALL TOAST AFTER THOSE MARINES GET THEIR BUGS DELIVERED.
THAT'S WHY I'M KEEPING AN EYE ON THEM FROM UP HERE. IF ANYTHING DOES HAPPEN, WE'LL KNOW FIRST.
WHY'D WE SAY YES?
MONEY. BIG MONEY...
...AND BIG GUNS.
HEY, LOOKY THERE-- YOU'VE GOT A HULL ALERT.
WE'VE BEEN GETTING LOTS. IT'S THEM CUTTING DOWN THAT CARGO BAY. IT TRIPS THE SENSORS, GIVES US FALSE ALARMS--
"--NOTHING'S REALLY OUT THERE."
KLANK
KREENK

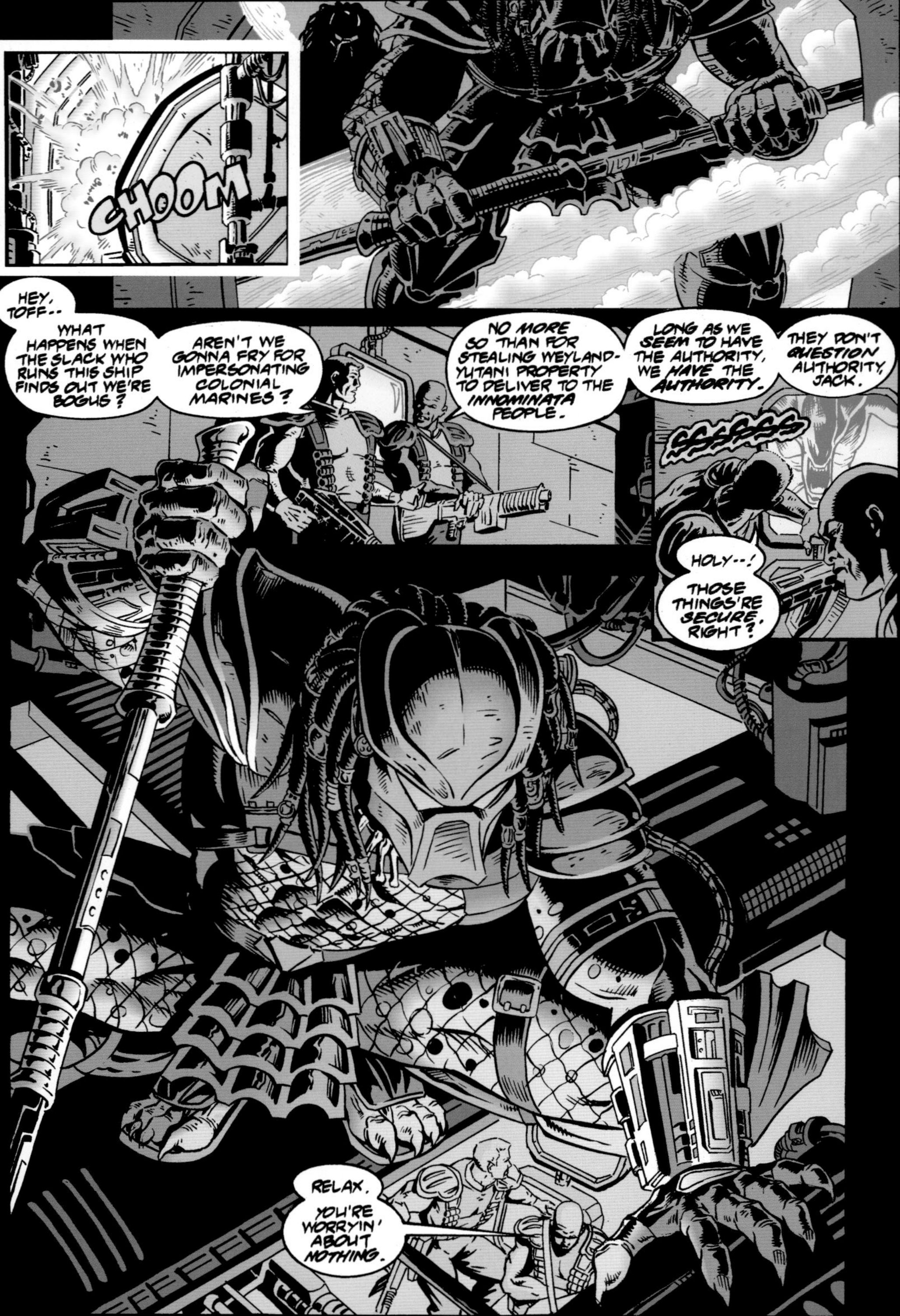
CHOOM
HEY, TOFF--
WHAT HAPPENS WHEN THE SLACK WHO RUNS THIS SHIP FINDS OUT WE'RE BOGUS?
AREN'T WE GONNA FRY FOR IMPERSONATING COLONIAL MARINES?
NO MORE SO THAN FOR STEALING WEYLAND-YUTANI PROPERTY TO DELIVER TO THE INNOMINATA PEOPLE.
LONG AS WE SEEM TO HAVE THE AUTHORITY, WE HAVE THE AUTHORITY.
THEY DON'T QUESTION AUTHORITY, JACK.
SSSSSS
HOLY--!
THOSE THINGS'RE SECURE, RIGHT?
RELAX.
YOU'RE WORRYIN' ABOUT NOTHING.

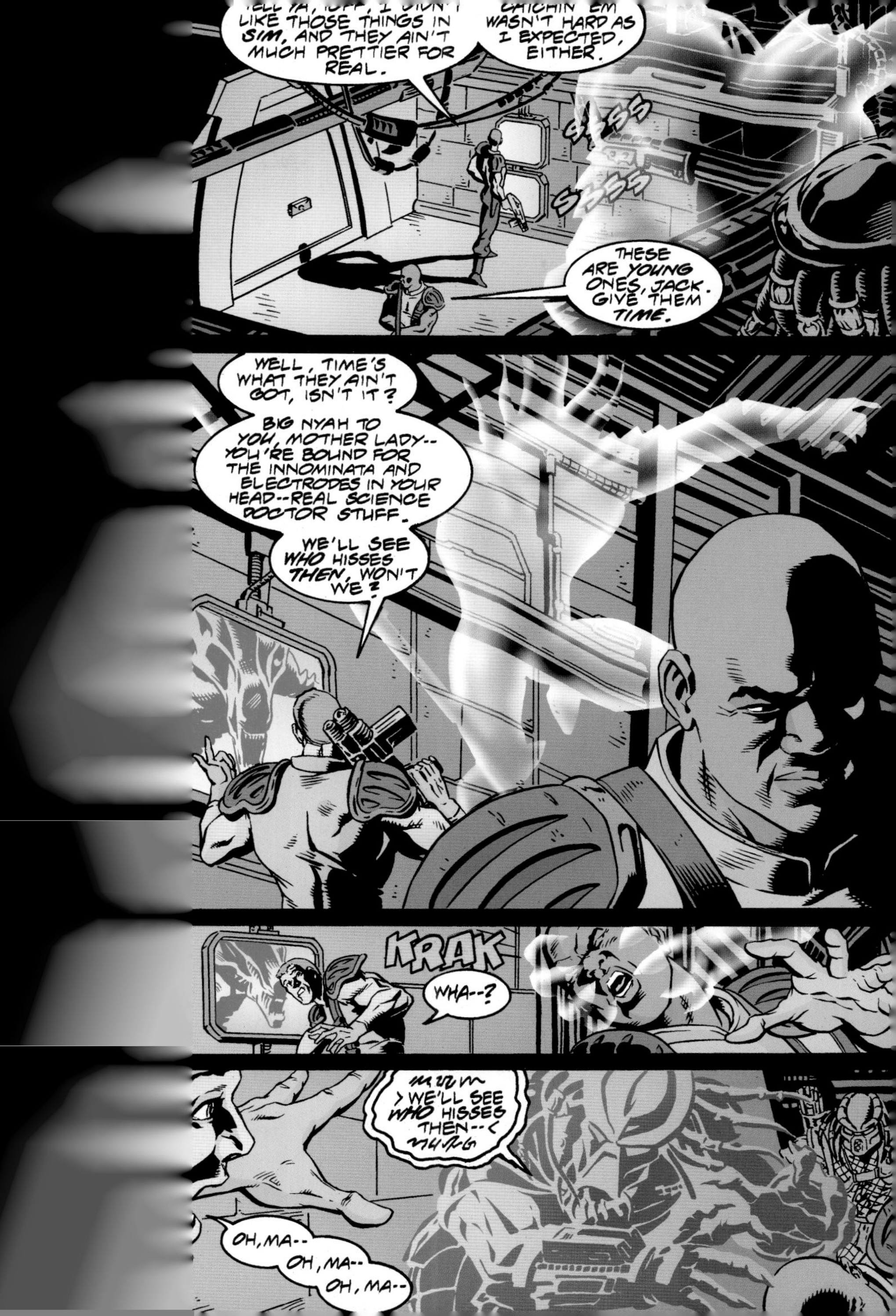
LIKE THOSE THINGS IN SIM, AND THEY AIN'T MUCH PRETTIER FOR REAL.
WASN'T HARD AS I EXPECTED, EITHER.
SSSS
SSSS
THESE ARE YOUNG ONES, JACK. GIVE THEM TIME.
WELL, TIME'S WHAT THEY AIN'T GOT, ISN'T IT?
BIG NYAH TO YOU, MOTHER LADY-- YOU'RE BOUND FOR THE INNOMINATA AND ELECTRODES IN YOUR HEAD--REAL SCIENCE DOCTOR STUFF.
WE'LL SEE WHO HISSES THEN, WON'T WE?
KRAK
WHA--?
>WE'LL SEE WHO HISSES THEN--<
OH, MA--
OH, MA--
OH, MA--

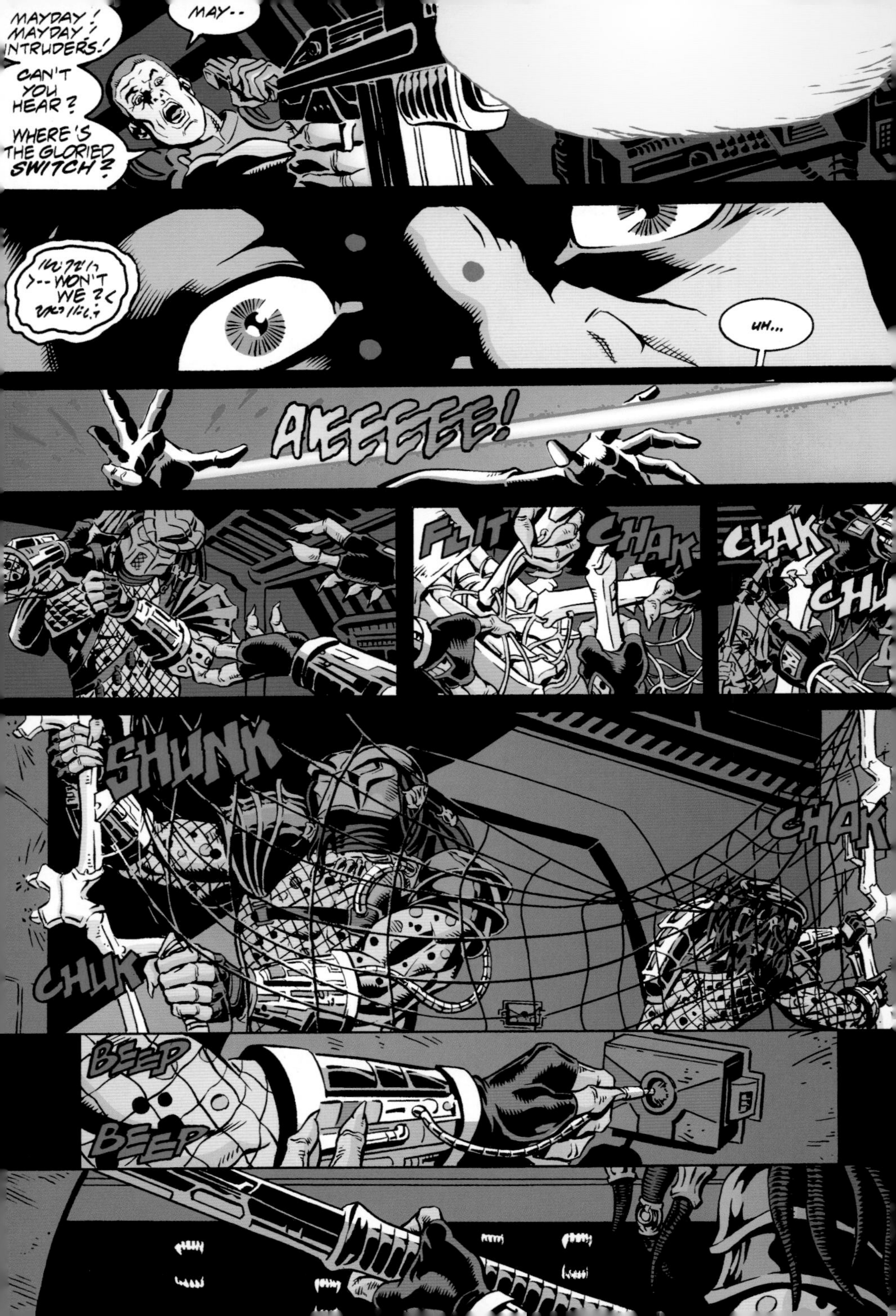
MAYDAY! MAYDAY! INTRUDERS!
MAY--
CAN'T YOU HEAR?
WHERE'S THE GLORIED SWITCH?
--WON'T WE?
UH...
AIEEEEE!
FLIT
CHAK
CLAK
SHUNK
CHAK
CHUK
BEEP
BEEP

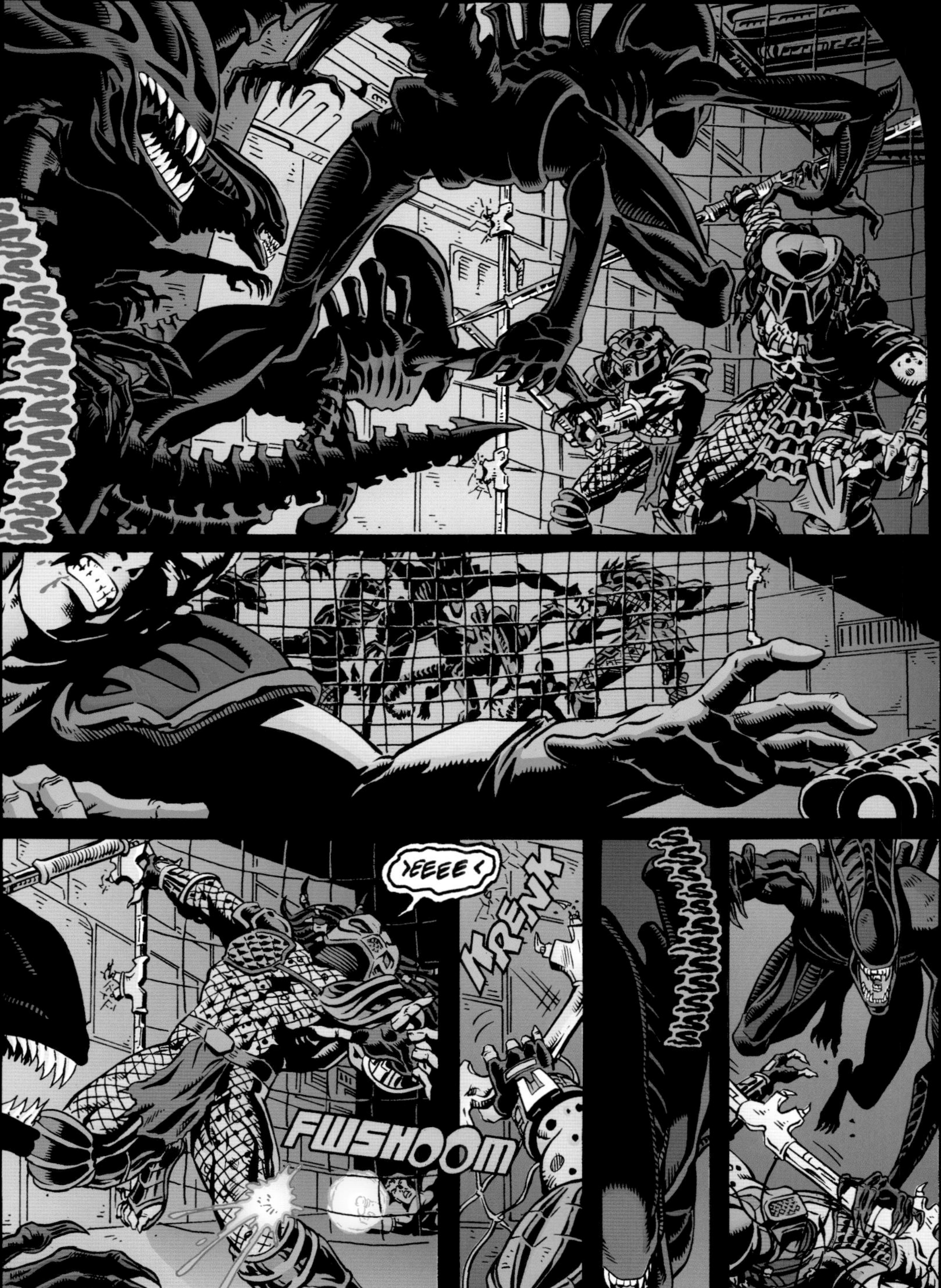
SSSSSSSSSSSSS
EEEE
KRENK
FWSHOOM
SSSSSSSSSSSS

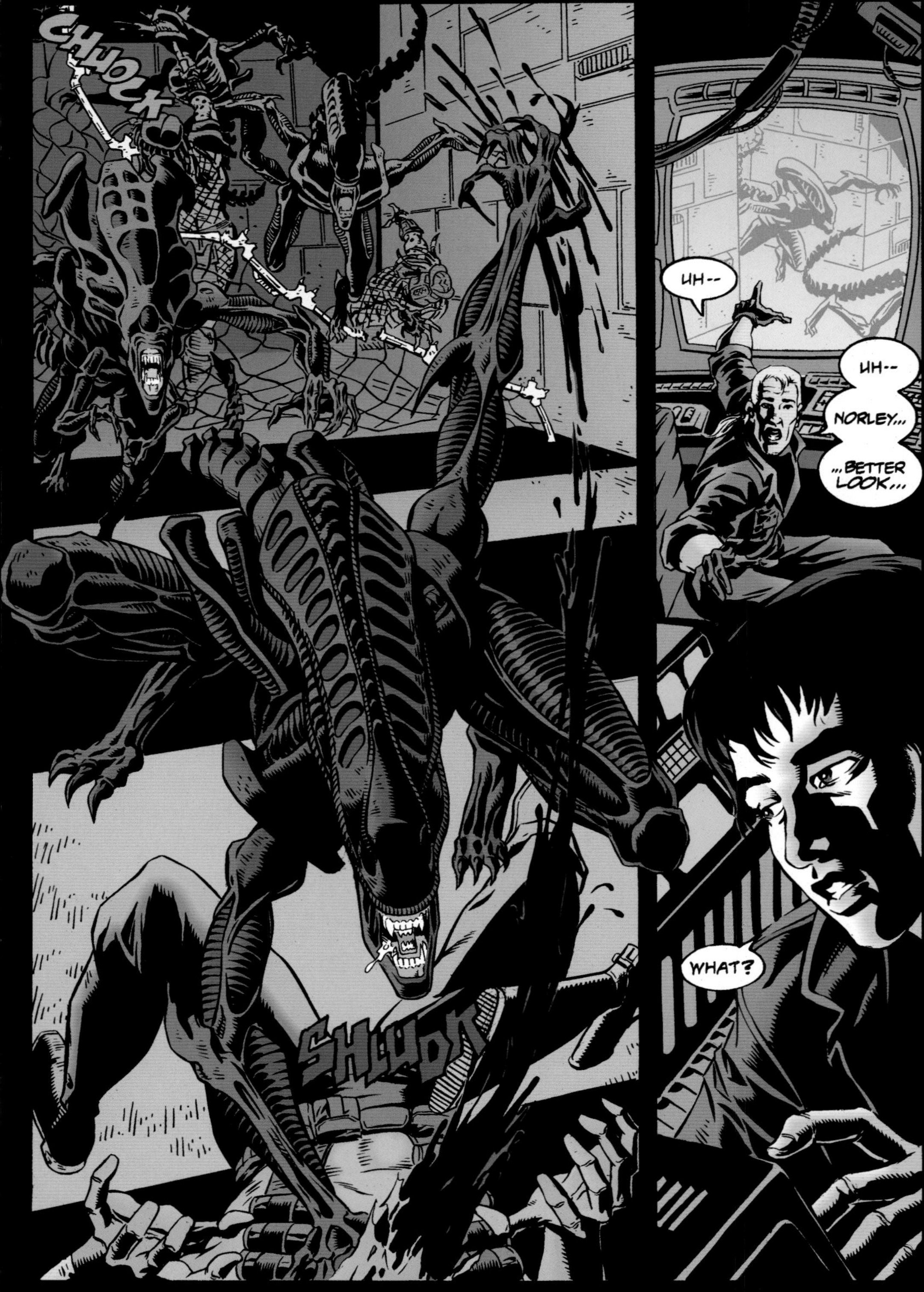
CHUCK
SHLUDK
UH--
UH--
NORLEY...
...BETTER LOOK...
WHAT?

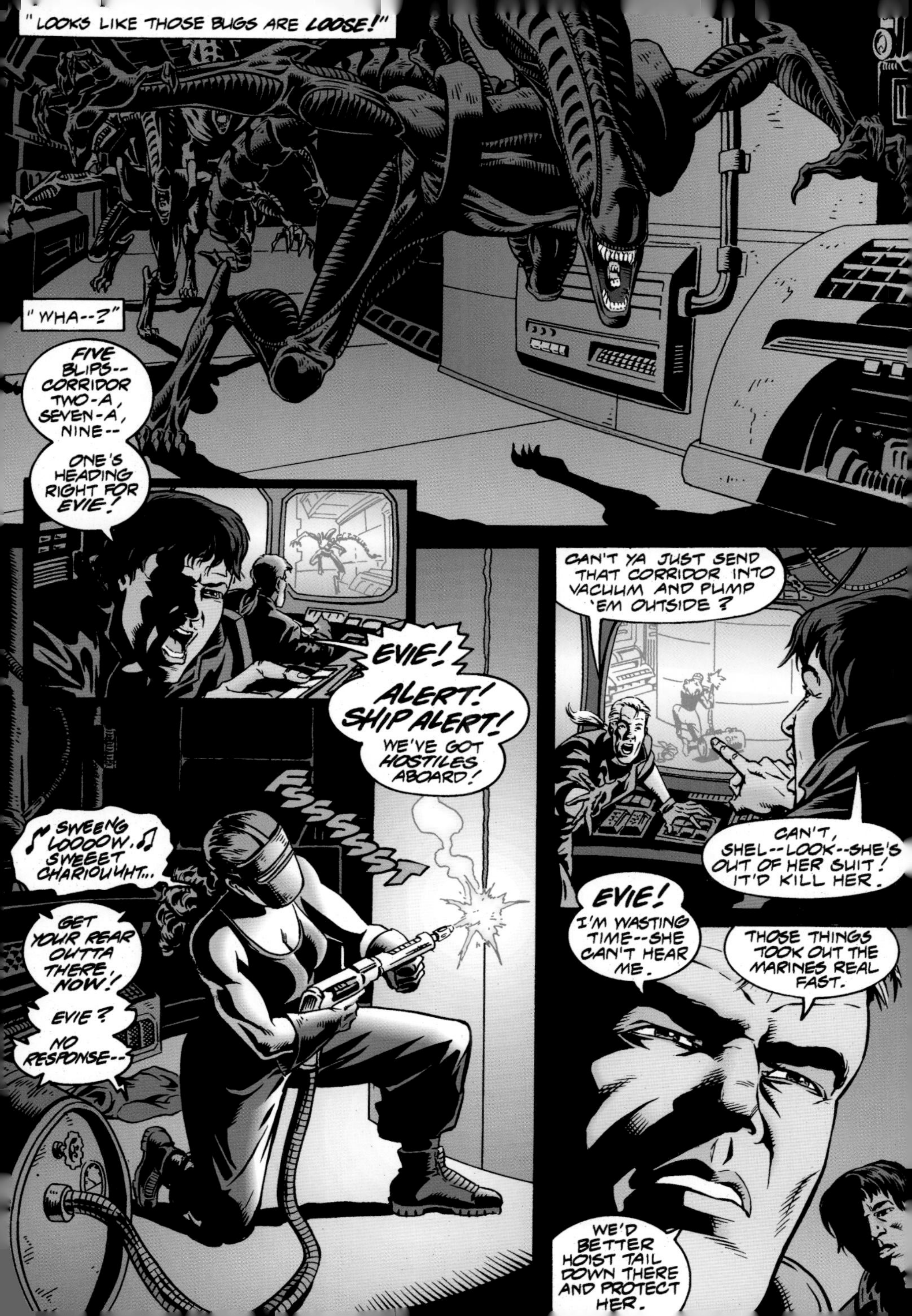
"LOOKS LIKE THOSE BUGS ARE LOOSE!"
"WHA--?"
FIVE BLIPS--CORRIDOR TWO-A, SEVEN-A, NINE--
ONE'S HEADING RIGHT FOR EVIE!
EVIE!
ALERT! SHIP ALERT!
WE'VE GOT HOSTILES ABOARD!
FSSSSSST
SWEENG LOOOOW, SWEEET CHARIOUUHT...
GET YOUR REAR OUTTA THERE NOW!
EVIE?
NO RESPONSE--
CAN'T YA JUST SEND THAT CORRIDOR INTO VACUUM AND PUMP 'EM OUTSIDE?
CAN'T, SHEL--LOOK--SHE'S OUT OF HER SUIT! IT'D KILL HER.
EVIE!
I'M WASTING TIME--SHE CAN'T HEAR ME.
THOSE THINGS TOOK OUT THE MARINES REAL FAST.
WE'D BETTER HOIST TAIL DOWN THERE AND PROTECT HER.

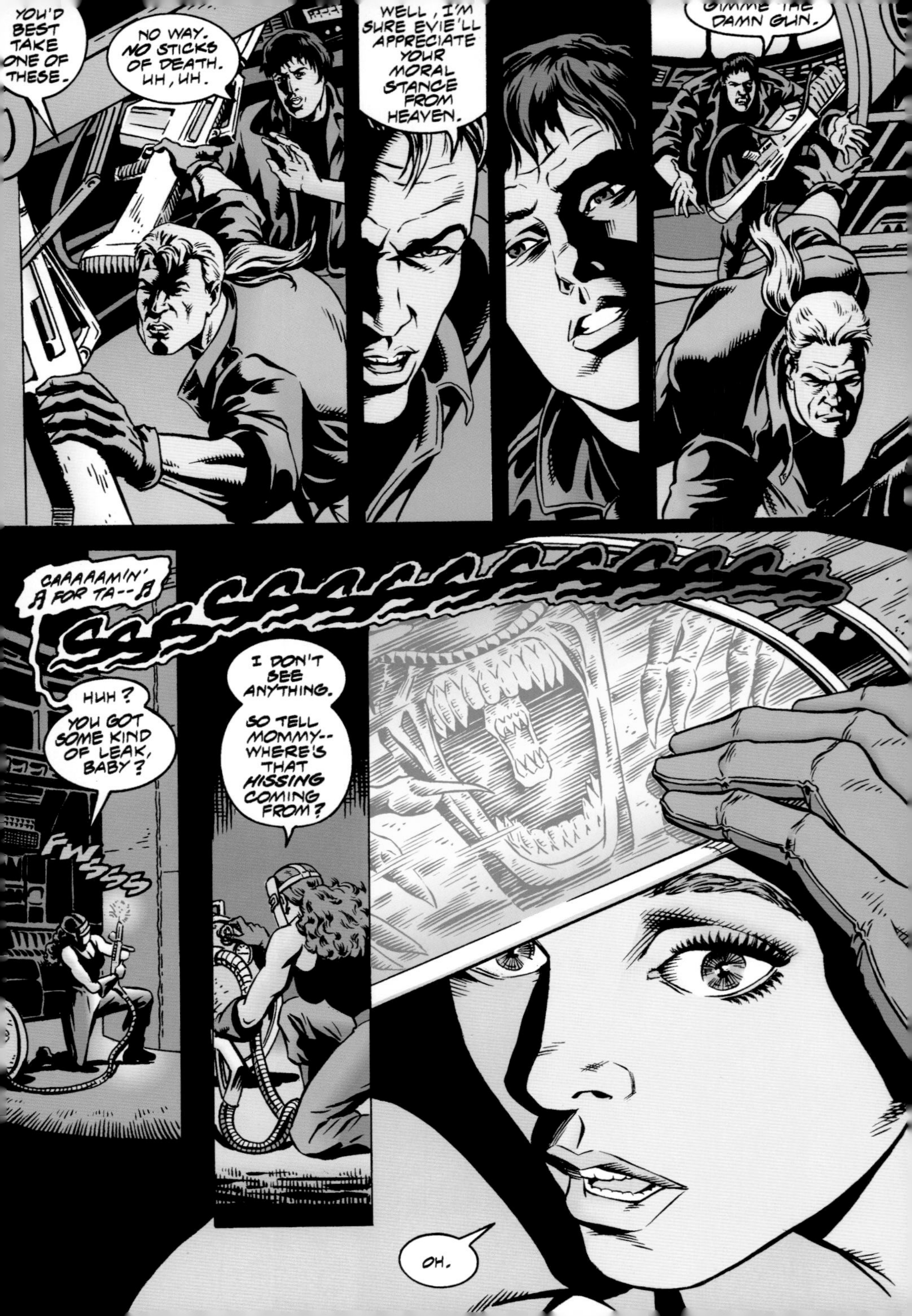
YOU'D BEST TAKE ONE OF THESE.
NO WAY. NO STICKS OF DEATH. UH, UH.
WELL, I'M SURE EVIE'LL APPRECIATE YOUR MORAL STANCE FROM HEAVEN.
GIMME THE DAMN GUN.
CAAAAAMIN' FOR TA--
SSSSSSSSSSSSSSSS
HUH? YOU GOT SOME KIND OF LEAK, BABY?
FWSSS
I DON'T SEE ANYTHING.
SO TELL MOMMY--WHERE'S THAT HISSING COMING FROM?
OH.

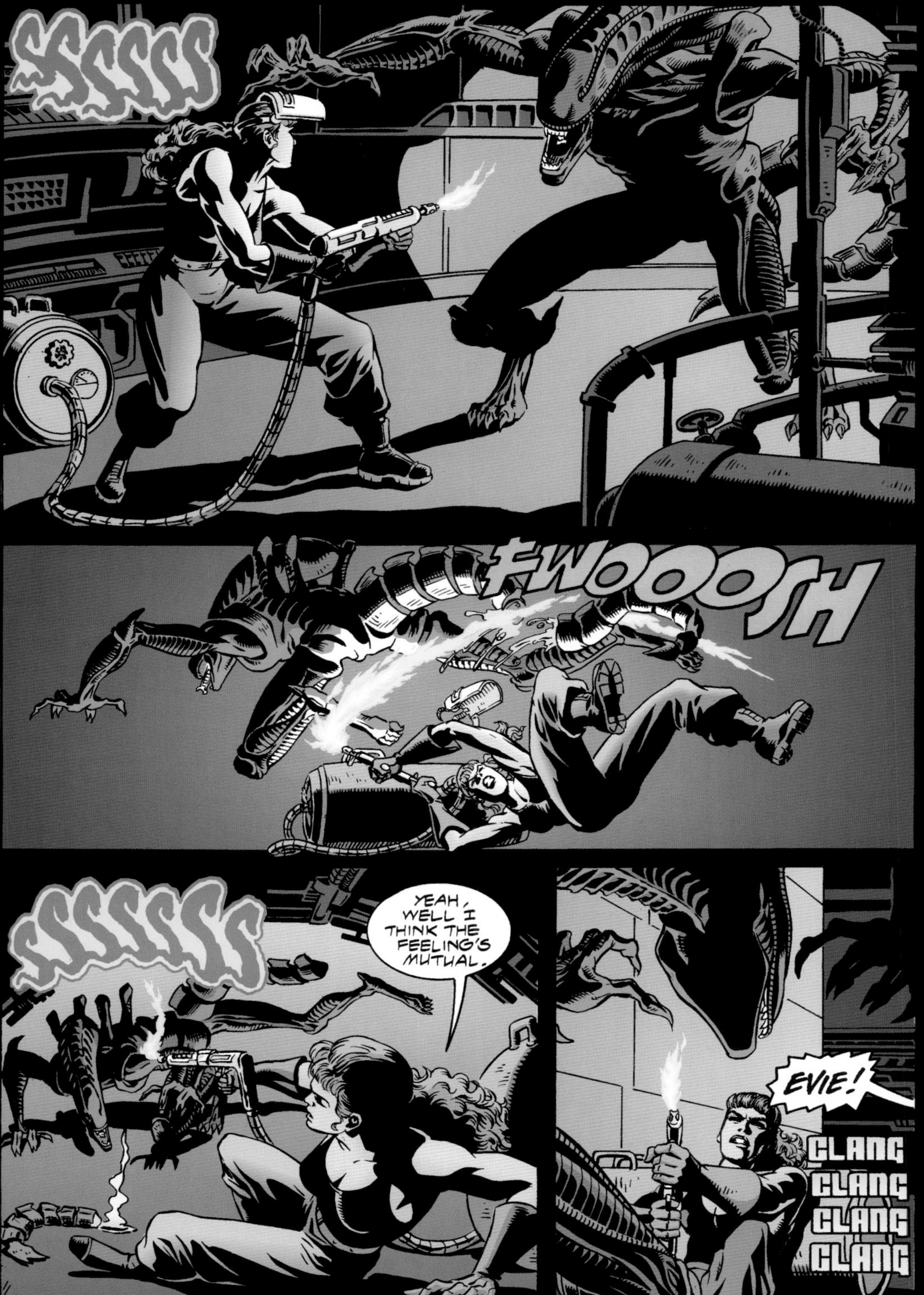
SSSSSS
FWOOOSH
SSSSSSS
YEAH, WELL I THINK THE FEELING'S MUTUAL.
EVIE!
CLANG
CLANG
CLANG
CLANG

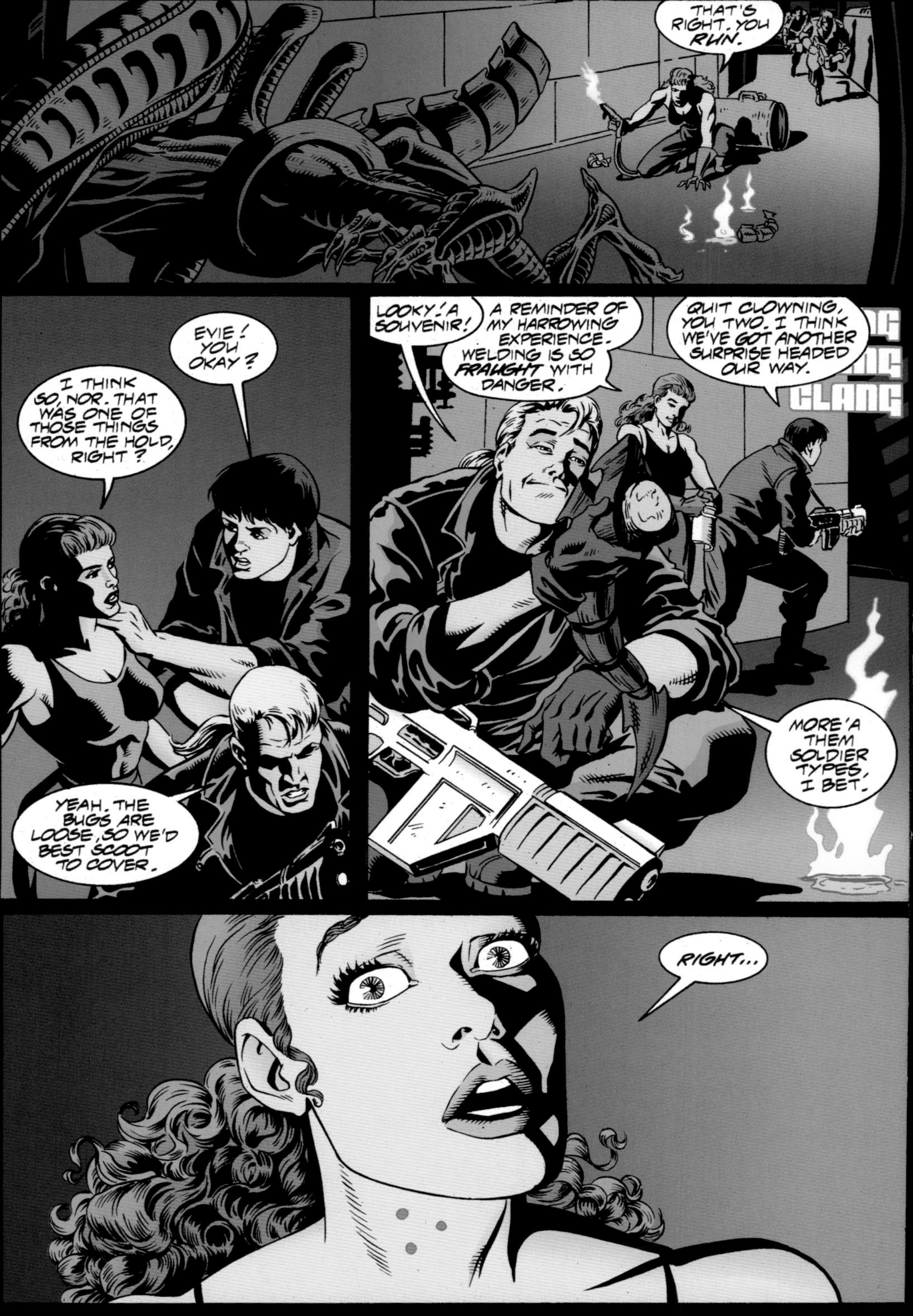
THAT'S RIGHT. YOU RUN.
EVIE! YOU OKAY?
I THINK SO, NOR. THAT WAS ONE OF THOSE THINGS FROM THE HOLD, RIGHT?
YEAH. THE BUGS ARE LOOSE, SO WE'D BEST SCOOT TO COVER.
LOOKY! A SOUVENIR!
A REMINDER OF MY HARROWING EXPERIENCE. WELDING IS SO FRAUGHT WITH DANGER.
QUIT CLOWNING, YOU TWO. I THINK WE'VE GOT ANOTHER SURPRISE HEADED OUR WAY.
CLANG
MORE 'A THEM SOLDIER TYPES, I BET.
RIGHT...

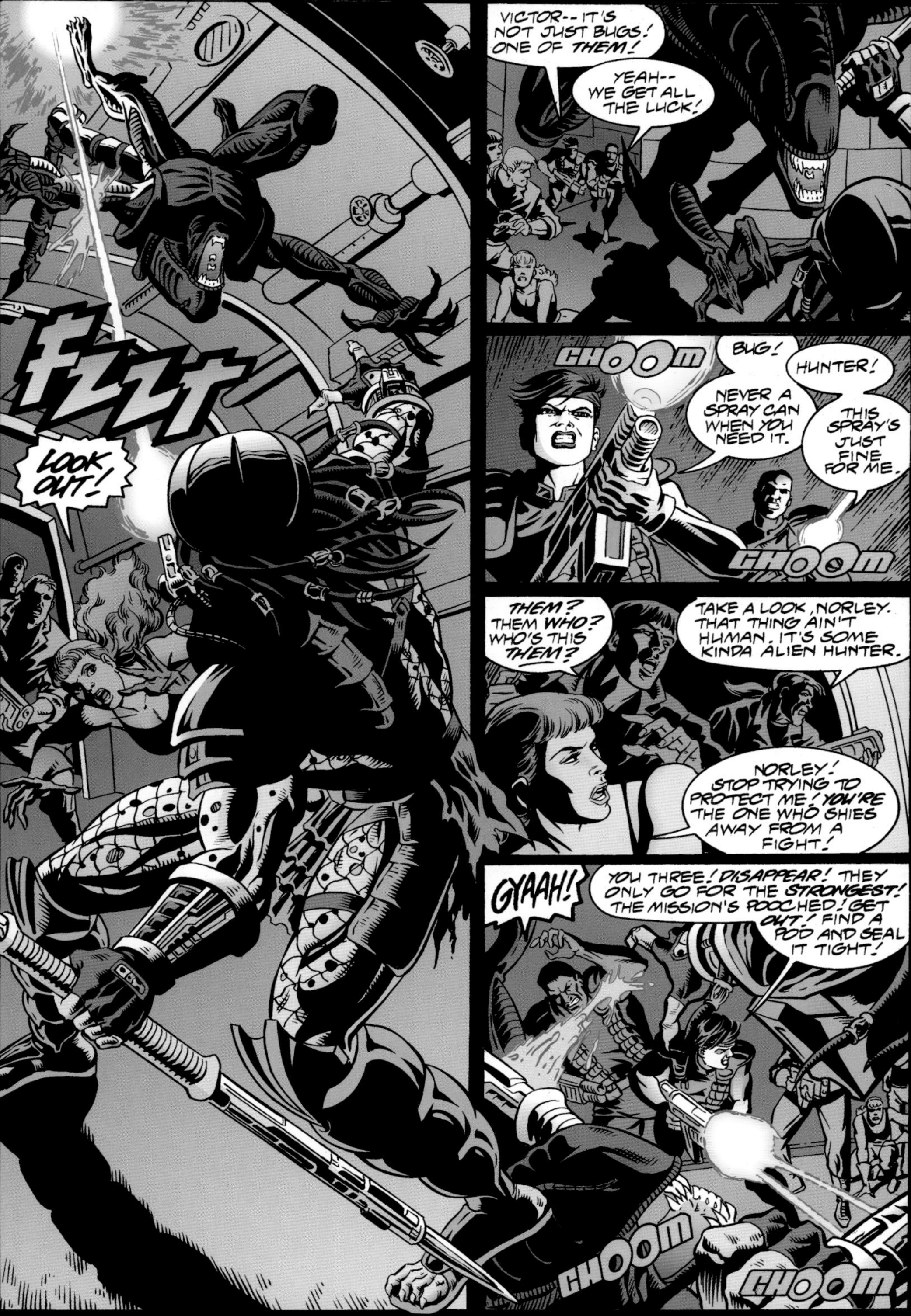
FZZT
LOOK OUT!
VICTOR-- IT'S NOT JUST BUGS! ONE OF THEM!
YEAH-- WE GET ALL THE LUCK!
CHOOOM
BUG!
NEVER A SPRAY CAN WHEN YOU NEED IT.
HUNTER!
THIS SPRAY'S JUST FINE FOR ME.
CHOOOM
THEM? THEM WHO? WHO'S THIS THEM?
TAKE A LOOK, NORLEY. THAT THING AIN'T HUMAN. IT'S SOME KINDA ALIEN HUNTER.
NORLEY! STOP TRYING TO PROTECT ME! YOU'RE THE ONE WHO SHIES AWAY FROM A FIGHT!
GYAAH!
YOU THREE! DISAPPEAR! THEY ONLY GO FOR THE STRONGEST! THE MISSION'S POOCHED! GET OUT! FIND A POD AND SEAL IT TIGHT!
CHOOOM
CHOOOM

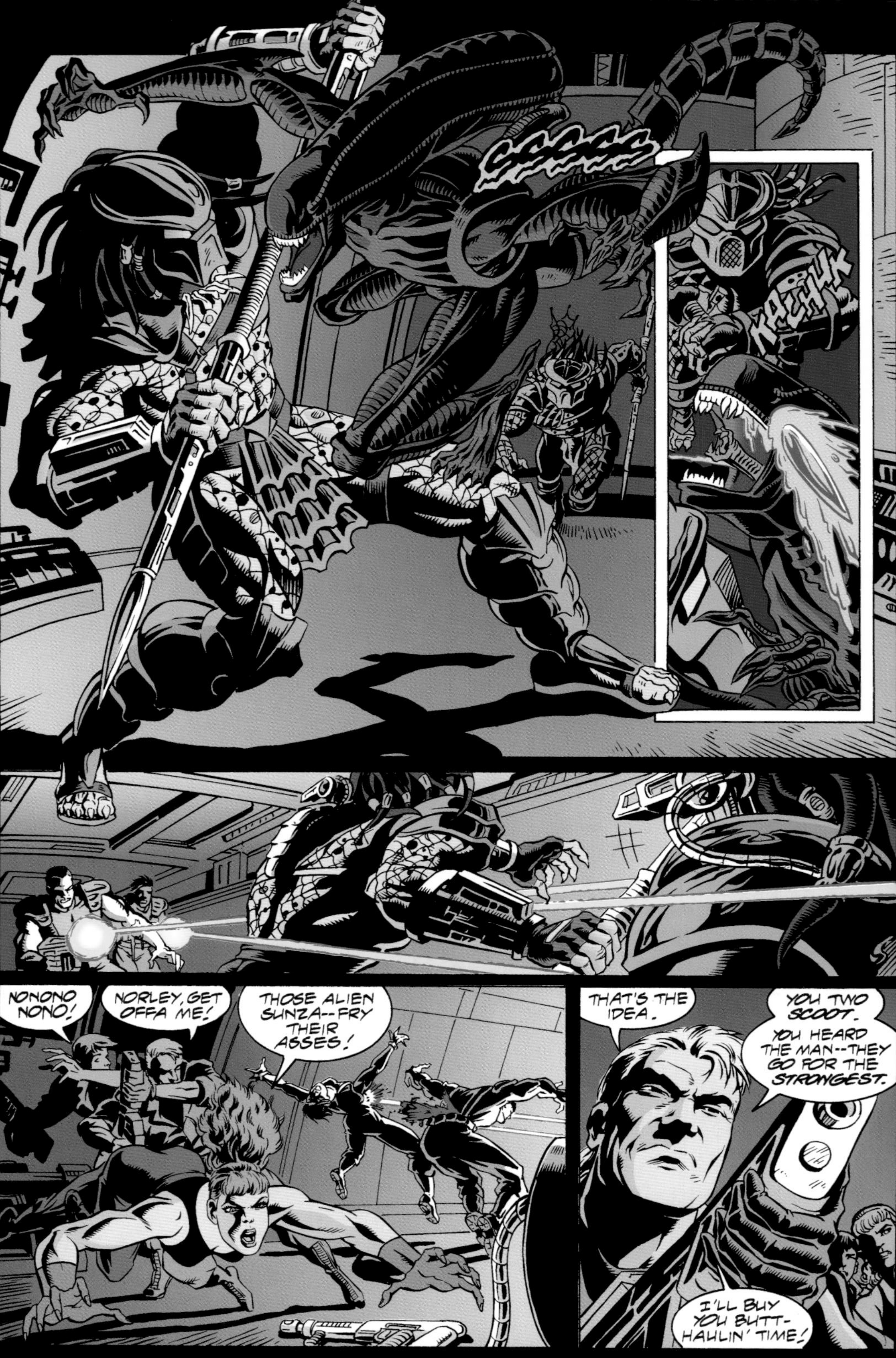
GSSSSS
KATHUK
NONONO NONO!
NORLEY, GET OFFA ME!
THOSE ALIEN SUNZA--FRY THEIR ASSES!
THAT'S THE IDEA.
YOU TWO SCOOT.
YOU HEARD THE MAN--THEY GO FOR THE STRONGEST.
I'LL BUY YOU BUTT-HAULIN' TIME!

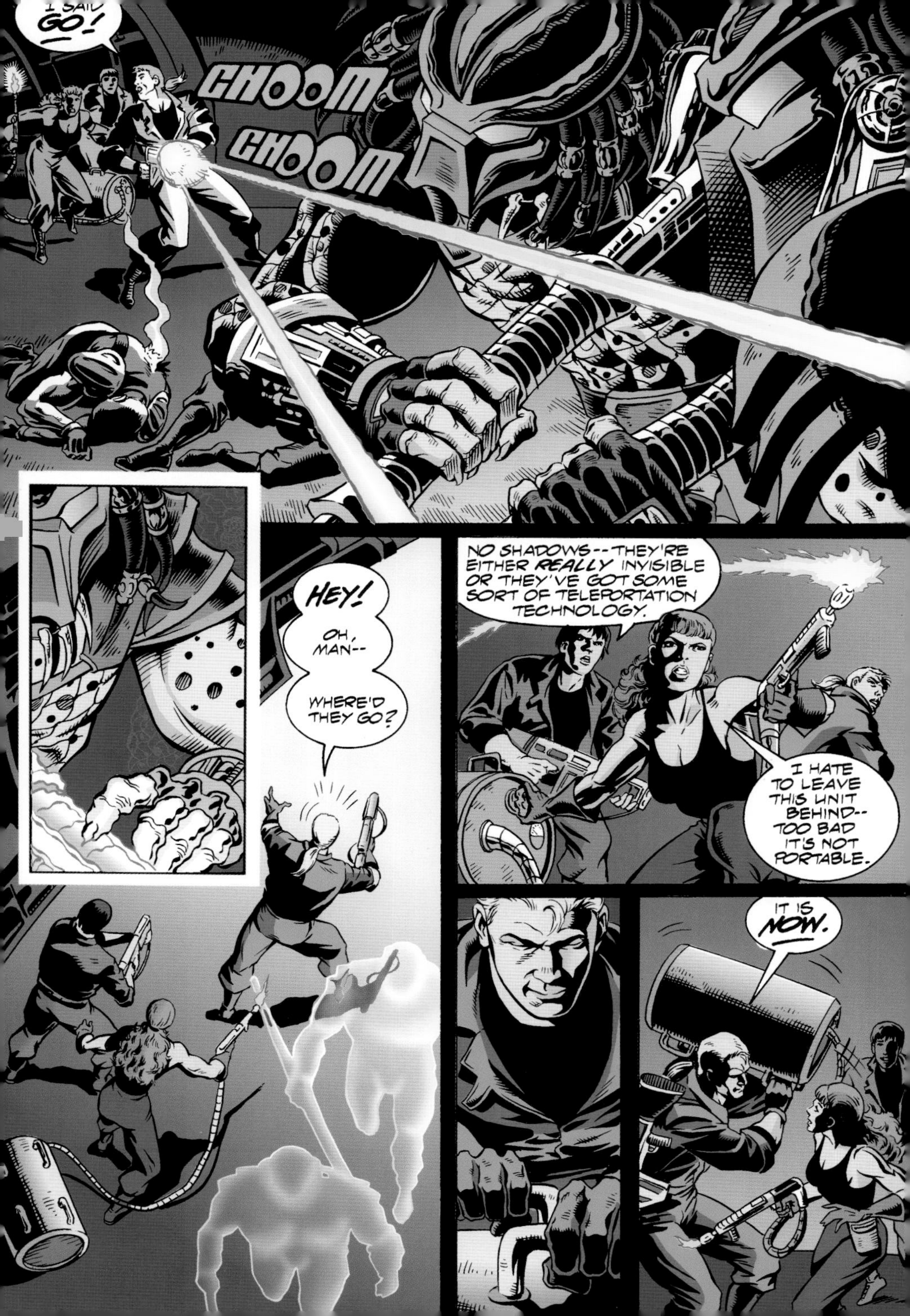

I SAID GO!
CHOOM
CHOOM
HEY!
OH, MAN--
WHERE'D THEY GO?
NO SHADOWS--THEY'RE EITHER REALLY INVISIBLE OR THEY'VE GOT SOME SORT OF TELEPORTATION TECHNOLOGY.
I HATE TO LEAVE THIS UNIT BEHIND-- TOO BAD IT'S NOT PORTABLE.
IT IS NOW.

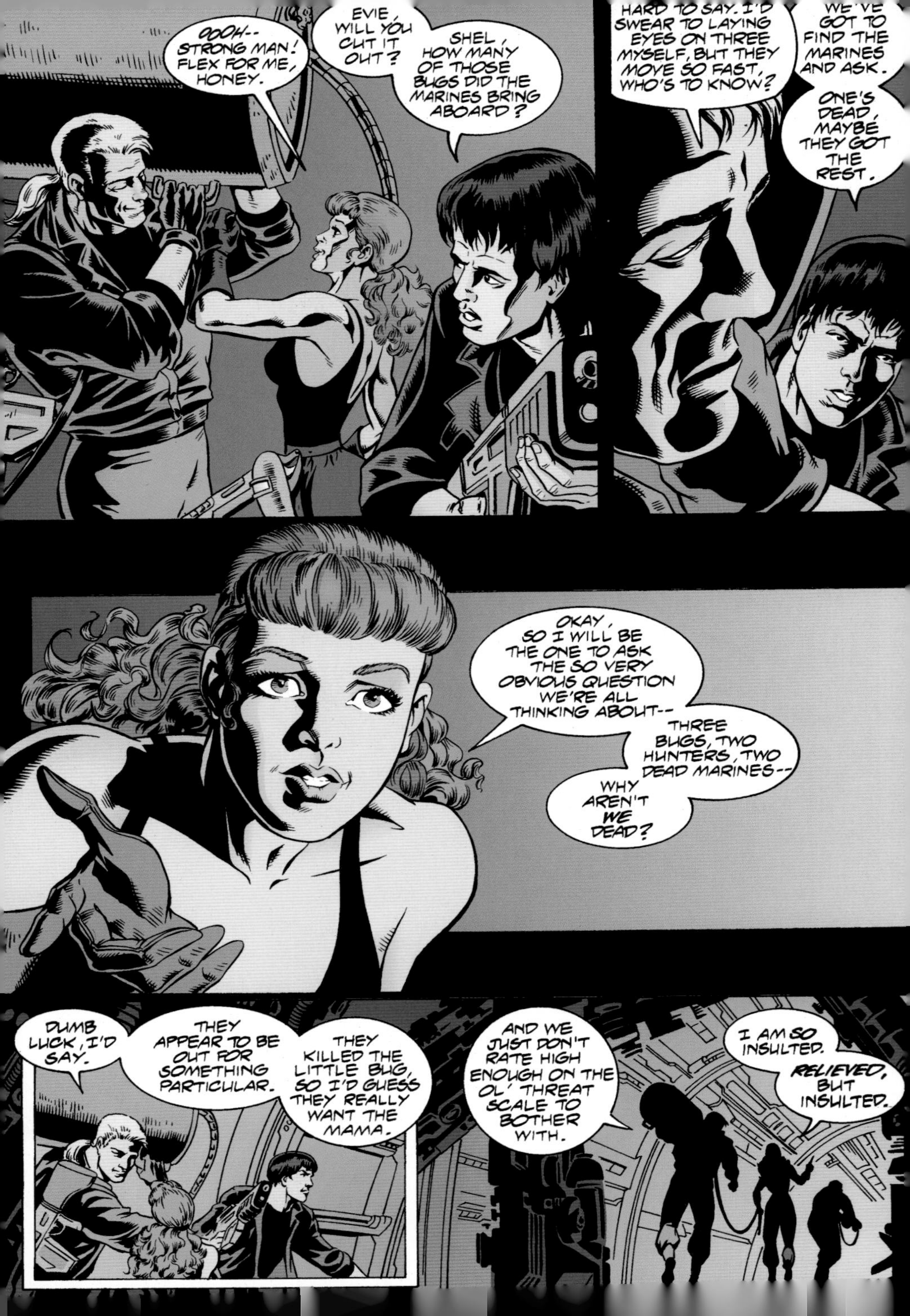

OOOH-- STRONG MAN! FLEX FOR ME, HONEY.
EVIE, WILL YOU CUT IT OUT?
SHEL, HOW MANY OF THOSE BUGS DID THE MARINES BRING ABOARD?
HARD TO SAY. I'D SWEAR TO LAYING EYES ON THREE MYSELF, BUT THEY MOVE SO FAST, WHO'S TO KNOW?
WE'VE GOT TO FIND THE MARINES AND ASK.
ONE'S DEAD, MAYBE THEY GOT THE REST.
OKAY, SO I WILL BE THE ONE TO ASK THE SO VERY OBVIOUS QUESTION WE'RE ALL THINKING ABOUT--
THREE BUGS, TWO HUNTERS, TWO DEAD MARINES--
WHY AREN'T WE DEAD?
DUMB LUCK, I'D SAY.
THEY APPEAR TO BE OUT FOR SOMETHING PARTICULAR.
THEY KILLED THE LITTLE BUG, SO I'D GUESS THEY REALLY WANT THE MAMA.
AND WE JUST DON'T RATE HIGH ENOUGH ON THE OL' THREAT SCALE TO BOTHER WITH.
I AM SO INSULTED.
RELIEVED, BUT INSULTED.

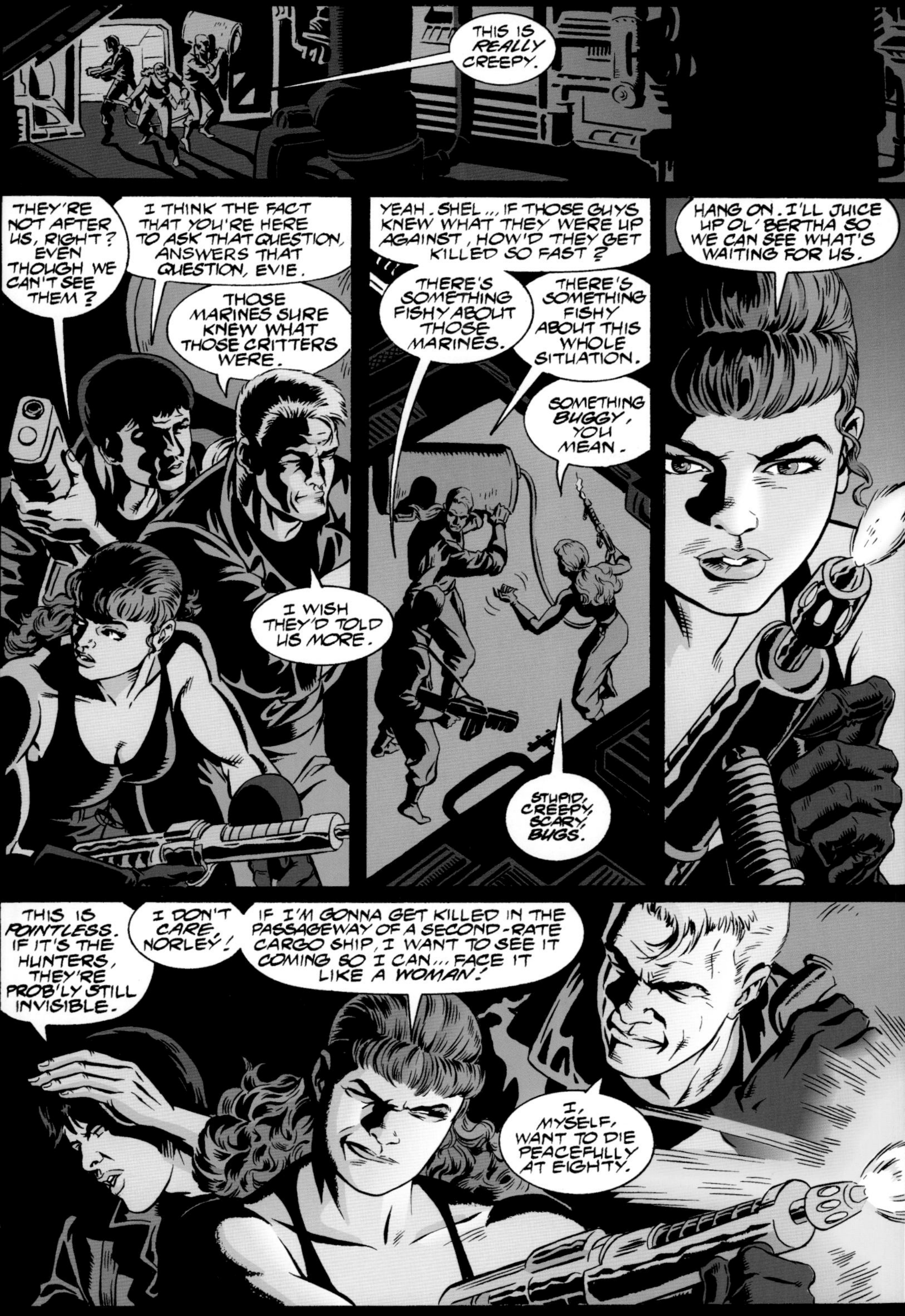
THIS IS REALLY CREEPY.
THEY'RE NOT AFTER US, RIGHT? EVEN THOUGH WE CAN'T SEE THEM?
I THINK THE FACT THAT YOU'RE HERE TO ASK THAT QUESTION, ANSWERS THAT QUESTION, EVIE.
THOSE MARINES SURE KNEW WHAT THOSE CRITTERS WERE.
I WISH THEY'D TOLD US MORE.
YEAH. SHEL... IF THOSE GUYS KNEW WHAT THEY WERE UP AGAINST, HOW'D THEY GET KILLED SO FAST?
THERE'S SOMETHING FISHY ABOUT THOSE MARINES.
THERE'S SOMETHING FISHY ABOUT THIS WHOLE SITUATION.
SOMETHING BUGGY, YOU MEAN.
STUPID, CREEPY, SCARY, BUGS.
HANG ON. I'LL JUICE UP OL' BERTHA SO WE CAN SEE WHAT'S WAITING FOR US.
THIS IS POINTLESS. IF IT'S THE HUNTERS, THEY'RE PROB'LY STILL INVISIBLE.
I DON'T CARE, NORLEY!
IF I'M GONNA GET KILLED IN THE PASSAGEWAY OF A SECOND-RATE CARGO SHIP, I WANT TO SEE IT COMING SO I CAN... FACE IT LIKE A WOMAN!
I, MYSELF, WANT TO DIE PEACEFULLY AT EIGHTY.

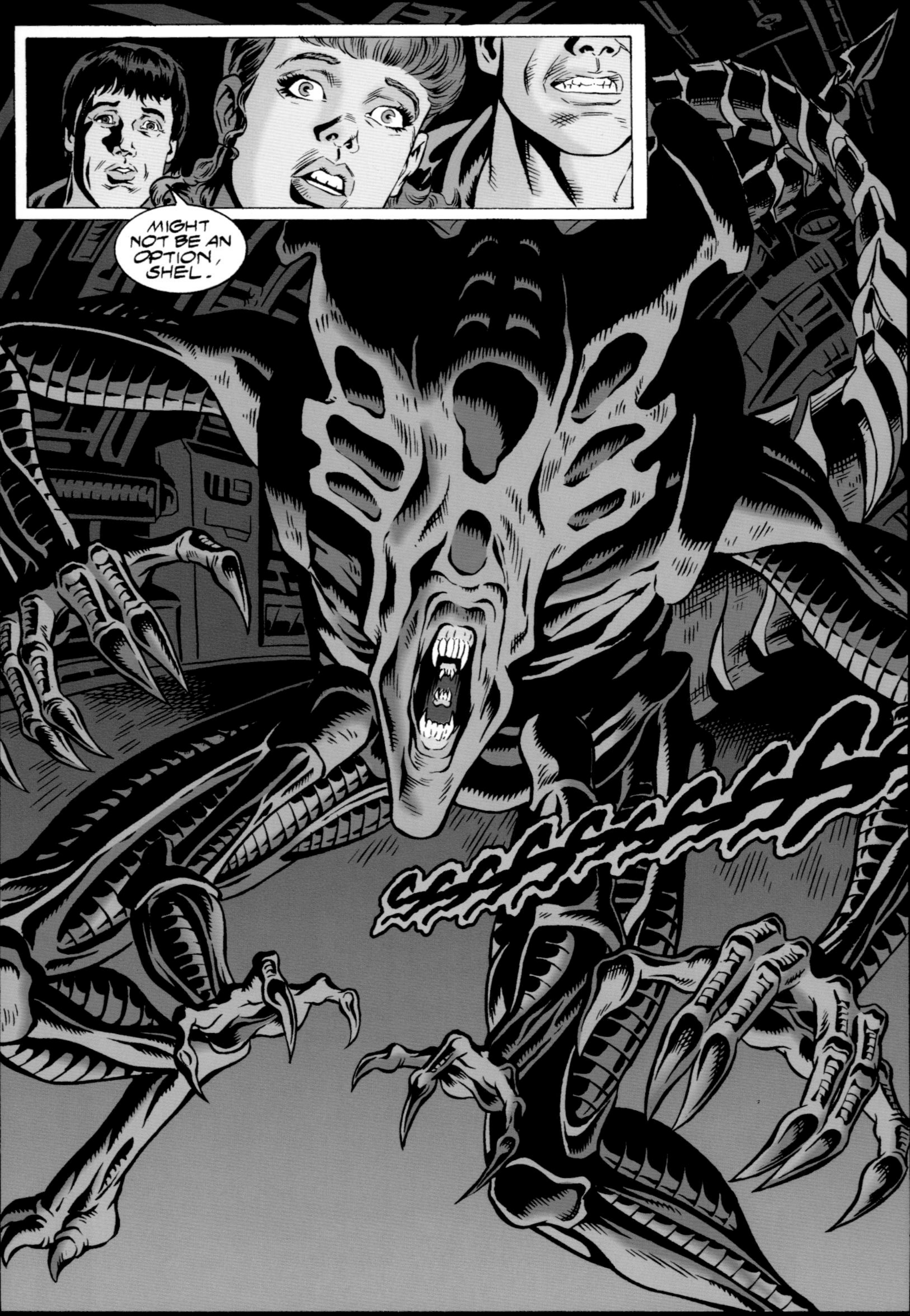
MIGHT NOT BE AN OPTION, SHEL.
SSSSSSSSSSSSSHHH

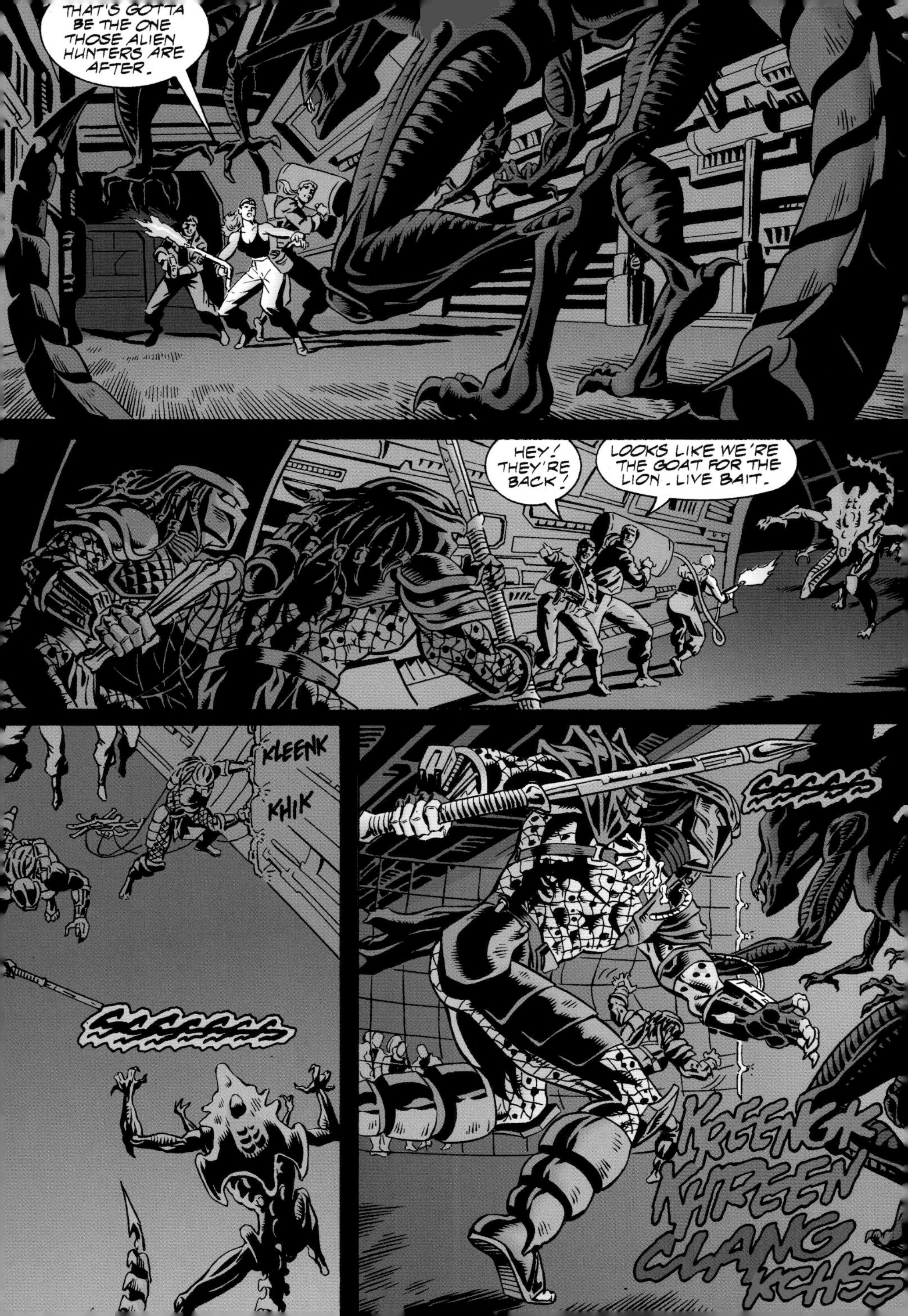
THAT'S GOTTA BE THE ONE THOSE ALIEN HUNTERS ARE AFTER.
HEY! THEY'RE BACK!
LOOKS LIKE WE'RE THE GOAT FOR THE LION. LIVE BAIT.
KLEENK
KHIK
KLEENK
KHEEN
CLANG
KCHSS

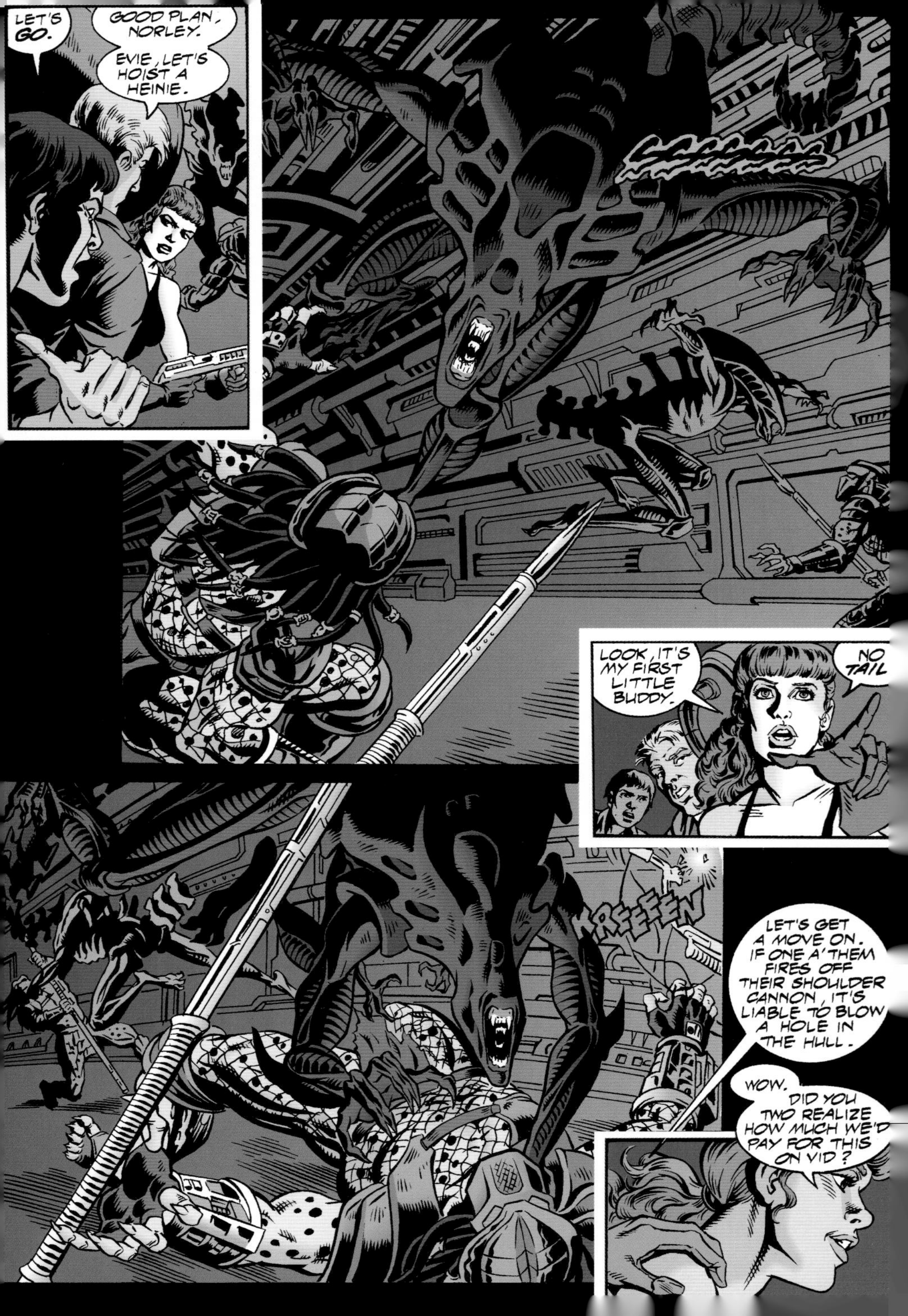
LET'S GO.
GOOD PLAN, NORLEY.
EVIE, LET'S HOIST A HEINIE.
SSSSSSS
LOOK, IT'S MY FIRST LITTLE BUDDY.
NO TAIL
KREEEEN
LET'S GET A MOVE ON. IF ONE A' THEM FIRES OFF THEIR SHOULDER CANNON, IT'S LIABLE TO BLOW A HOLE IN THE HULL.
WOW.
DID YOU TWO REALIZE HOW MUCH WE'D PAY FOR THIS ON VID?

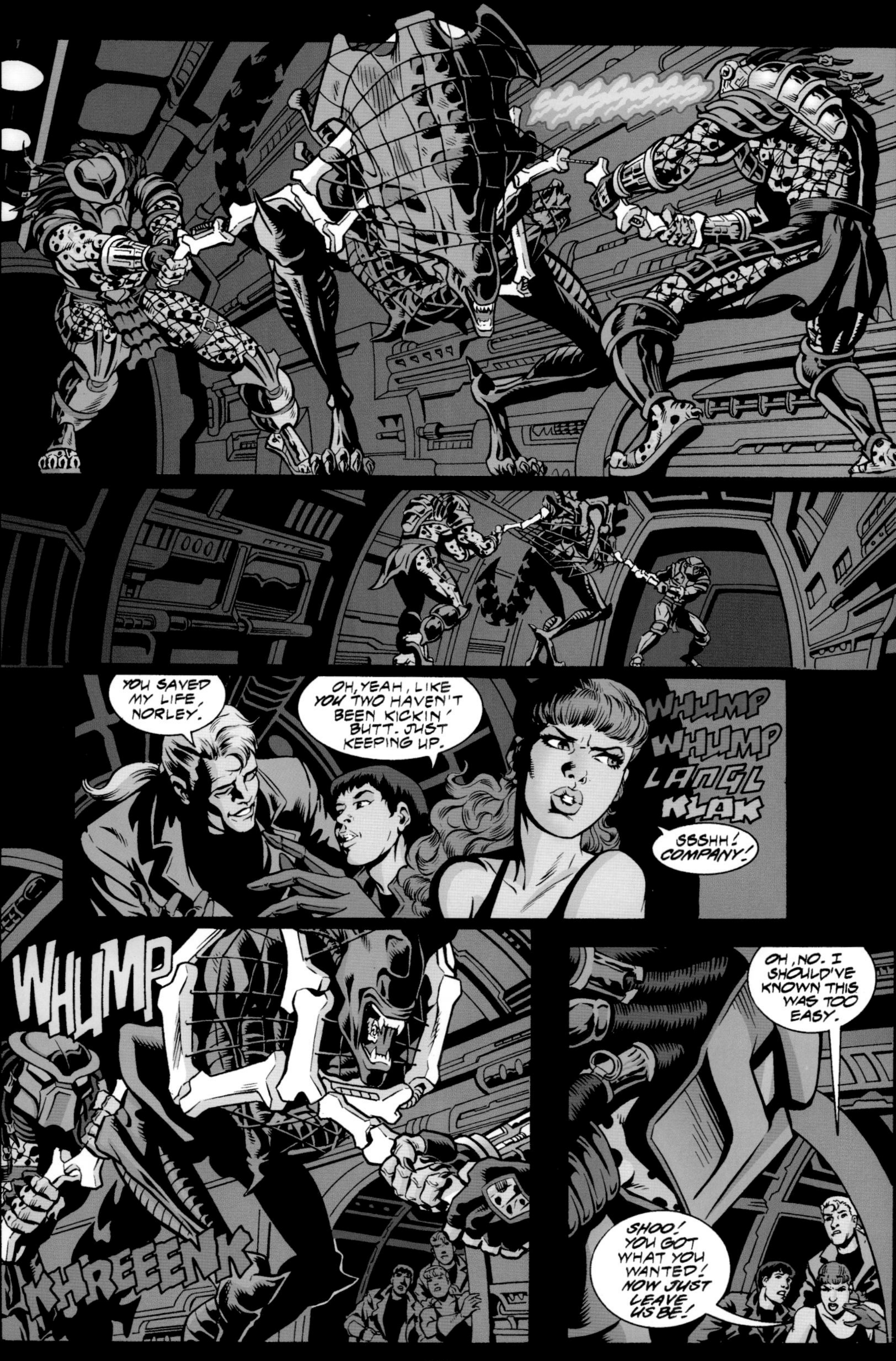

SSSSSSSS
YOU SAVED MY LIFE, NORLEY.
OH, YEAH, LIKE YOU TWO HAVEN'T BEEN KICKIN' BUTT. JUST KEEPING UP.
WHUMP WHUMP LANGL KLAK
SSSHH! COMPANY!
WHUMP
KHREEENK
OH, NO. I SHOULD'VE KNOWN THIS WAS TOO EASY.
SHOO! YOU GOT WHAT YOU WANTED! NOW JUST LEAVE US BE!

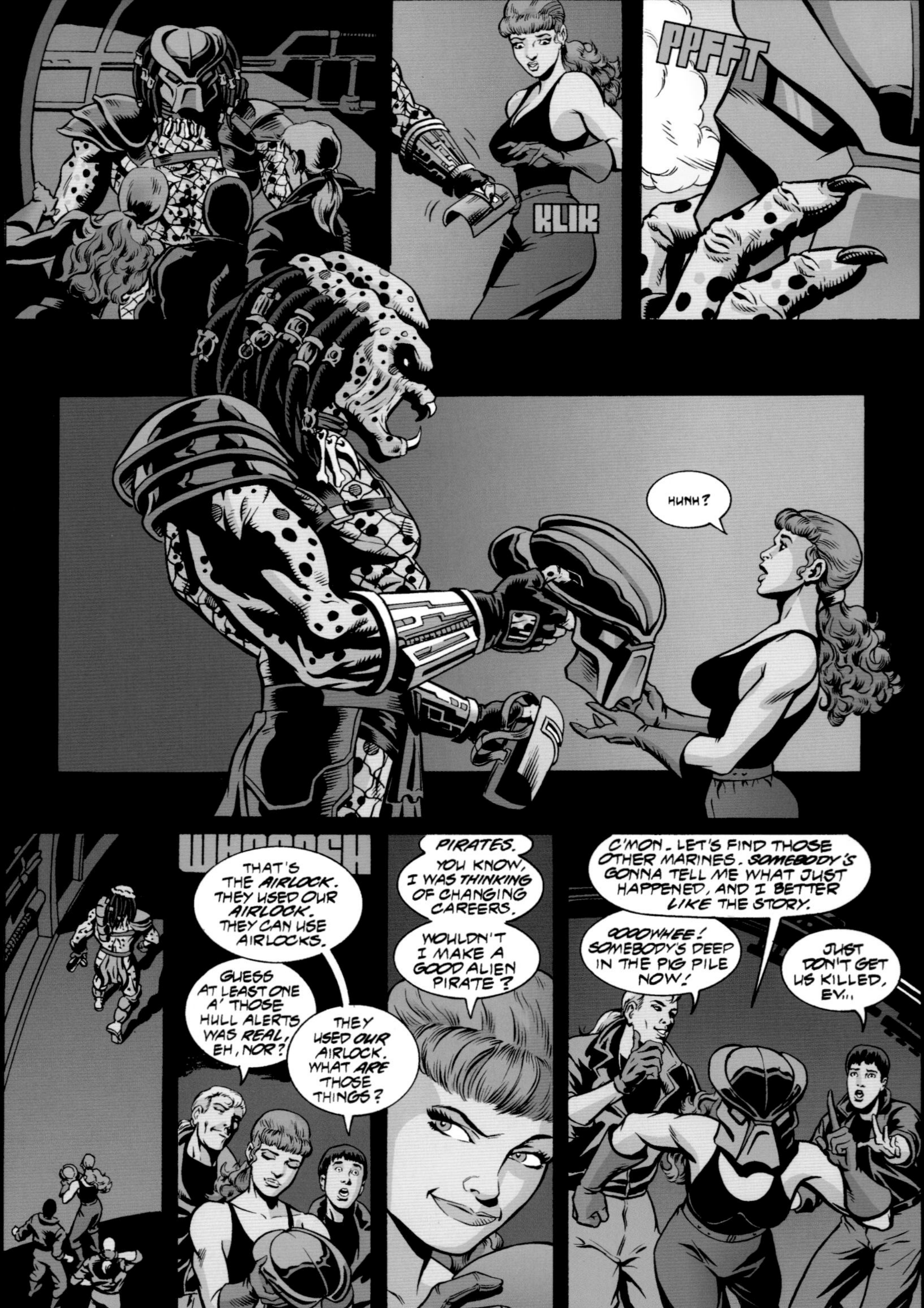
PPFFT
KLIK
HUNH?
WHOOOOSH
THAT'S THE AIRLOCK. THEY USED OUR AIRLOCK. THEY CAN USE AIRLOCKS.
GUESS AT LEAST ONE A' THOSE HULL ALERTS WAS REAL, EH, NOR?
THEY USED OUR AIRLOCK. WHAT ARE THOSE THINGS?
PIRATES.
YOU KNOW, I WAS THINKING OF CHANGING CAREERS.
WOULDN'T I MAKE A GOOD ALIEN PIRATE?
C'MON. LET'S FIND THOSE OTHER MARINES. SOMEBODY'S GONNA TELL ME WHAT JUST HAPPENED, AND I BETTER LIKE THE STORY.
OOOOWHEE! SOMEBODY'S DEEP IN THE PIG PILE NOW!
JUST DON'T GET US KILLED, EV...

THE END

HELL-BENT

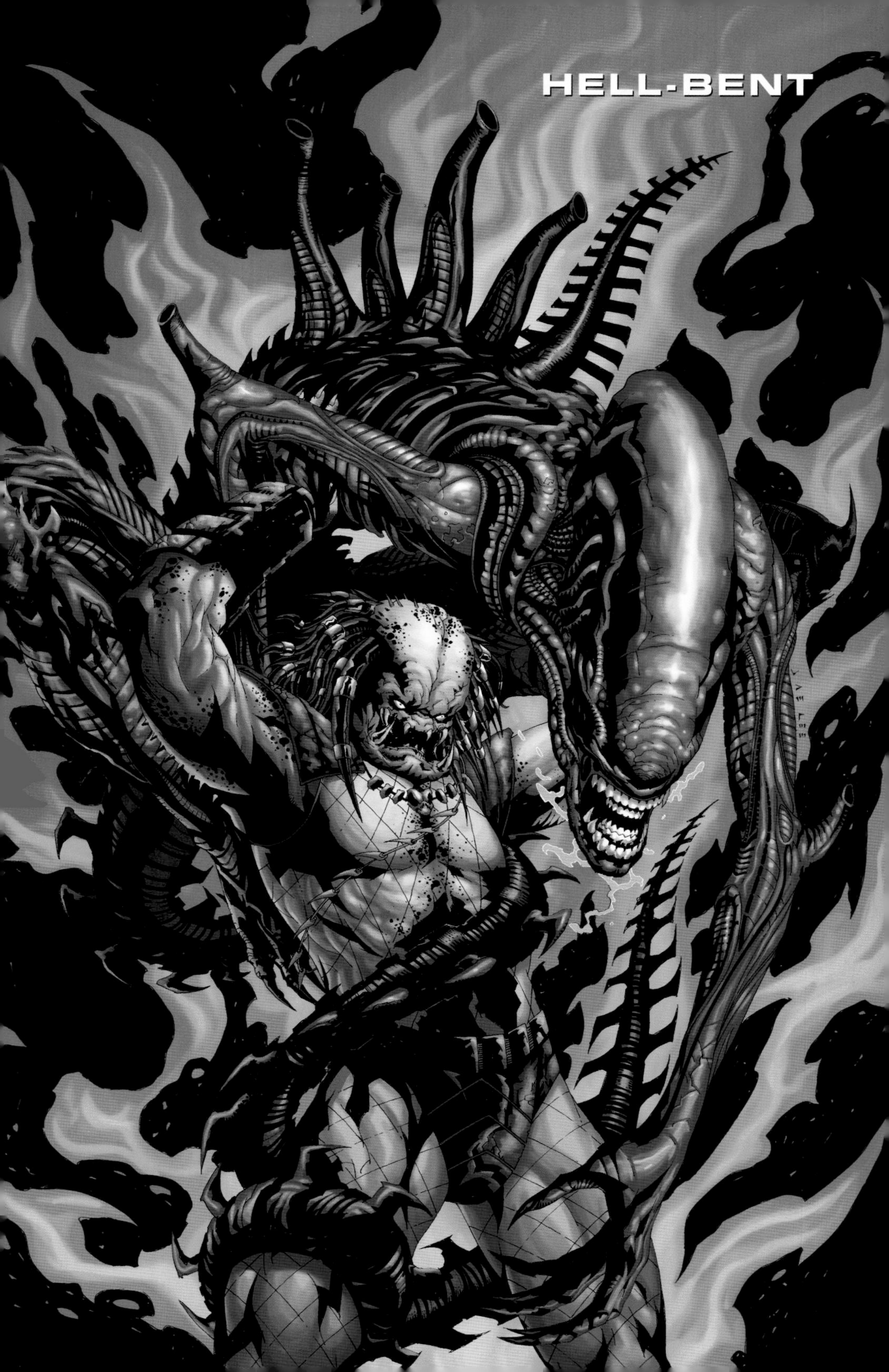

script/pencils
DAVID ROSS

inks
MARK LIPKA

colors
DAVE STEWART

lettering
MICHAEL TAYLOR

title illustration
JAE LEE with **DAVE STEWART**

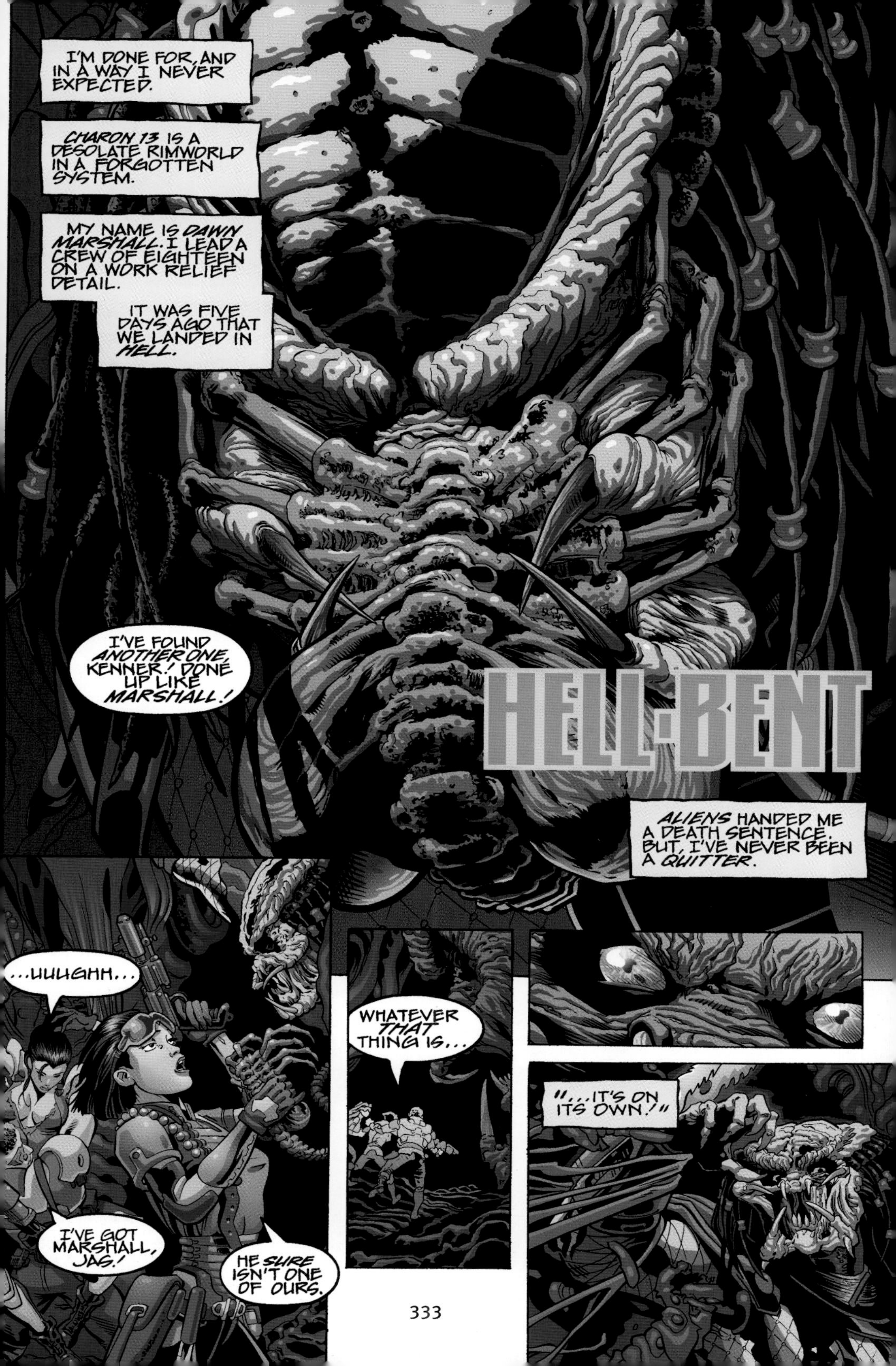
I'M DONE FOR, AND IN A WAY I NEVER EXPECTED.
CHARON 13 IS A DESOLATE RIMWORLD IN A FORGOTTEN SYSTEM.
MY NAME IS DAWN MARSHALL. I LEAD A CREW OF EIGHTEEN ON A WORK RELIEF DETAIL.
IT WAS FIVE DAYS AGO THAT WE LANDED IN HELL.
I'VE FOUND ANOTHER ONE, KENNER! DONE UP LIKE MARSHALL!
HELL-BENT
ALIENS HANDED ME A DEATH SENTENCE. BUT, I'VE NEVER BEEN A QUITTER.
...UUUGHH...
I'VE GOT MARSHALL, JAS!
HE SURE ISN'T ONE OF OURS.
WHATEVER THAT THING IS...
"...IT'S ON ITS OWN!"

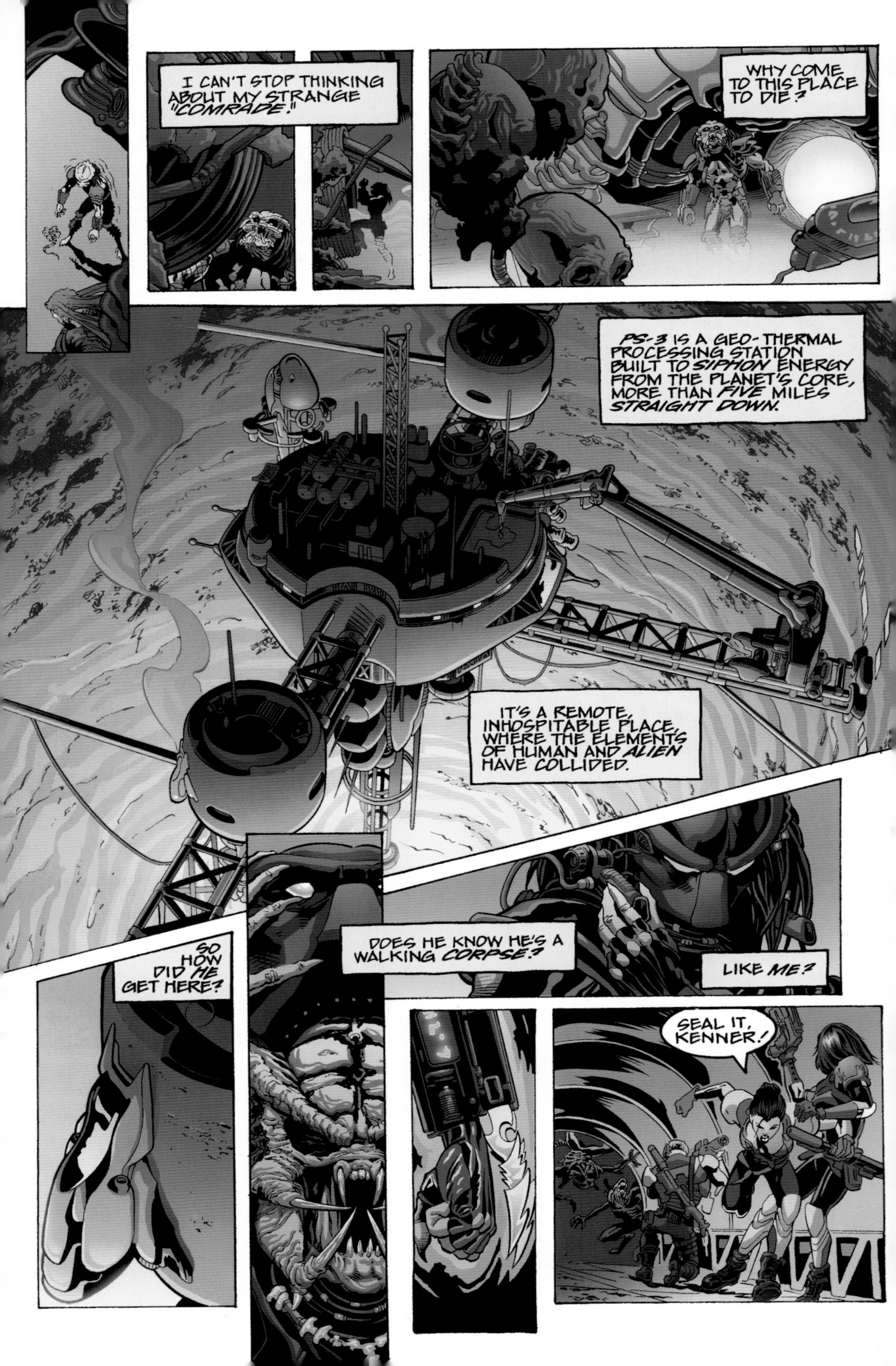
I CAN'T STOP THINKING ABOUT MY STRANGE "COMRADE."
WHY COME TO THIS PLACE TO DIE?
PS-3 IS A GEO-THERMAL PROCESSING STATION BUILT TO SIPHON ENERGY FROM THE PLANET'S CORE, MORE THAN FIVE MILES STRAIGHT DOWN.
IT'S A REMOTE, INHOSPITABLE PLACE, WHERE THE ELEMENTS OF HUMAN AND ALIEN HAVE COLLIDED.
DOES HE KNOW HE'S A WALKING CORPSE?
LIKE ME?
SO HOW DID HE GET HERE?
SEAL IT, KENNER!

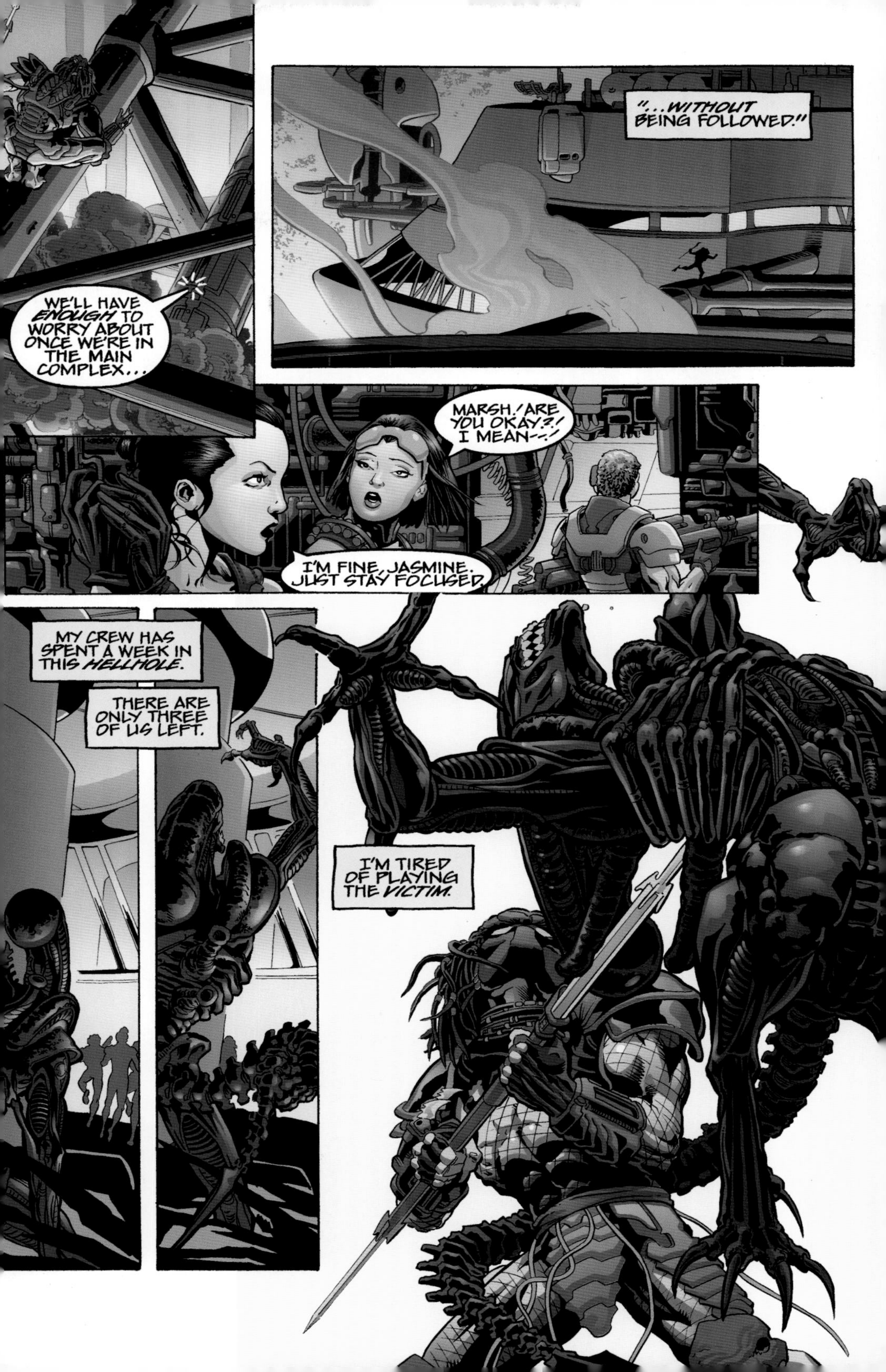
WE'LL HAVE ENOUGH TO WORRY ABOUT ONCE WE'RE IN THE MAIN COMPLEX...
"...WITHOUT BEING FOLLOWED."
MARSH! ARE YOU OKAY?! I MEAN--!
I'M FINE, JASMINE. JUST STAY FOCUSED.
MY CREW HAS SPENT A WEEK IN THIS HELLHOLE.
THERE ARE ONLY THREE OF US LEFT.
I'M TIRED OF PLAYING THE VICTIM.

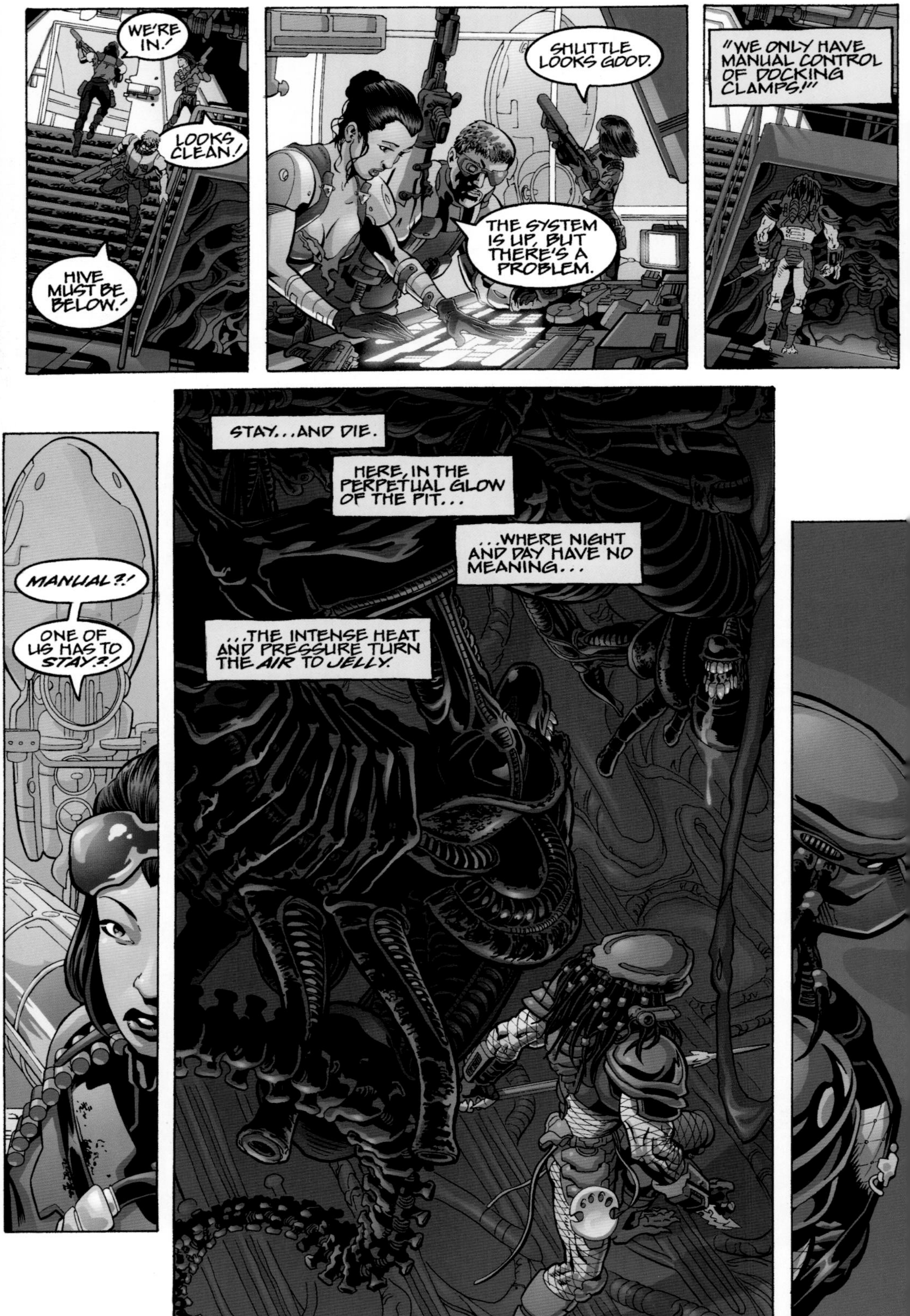
WE'RE IN.!
LOOKS CLEAN.!
HIVE MUST BE BELOW.!
SHUTTLE LOOKS GOOD.
THE SYSTEM IS UP, BUT THERE'S A PROBLEM.
"WE ONLY HAVE MANUAL CONTROL OF DOCKING CLAMPS!"
MANUAL?!
ONE OF US HAS TO STAY?!
STAY...AND DIE.
HERE, IN THE PERPETUAL GLOW OF THE PIT...
...WHERE NIGHT AND DAY HAVE NO MEANING...
...THE INTENSE HEAT AND PRESSURE TURN THE AIR TO JELLY.

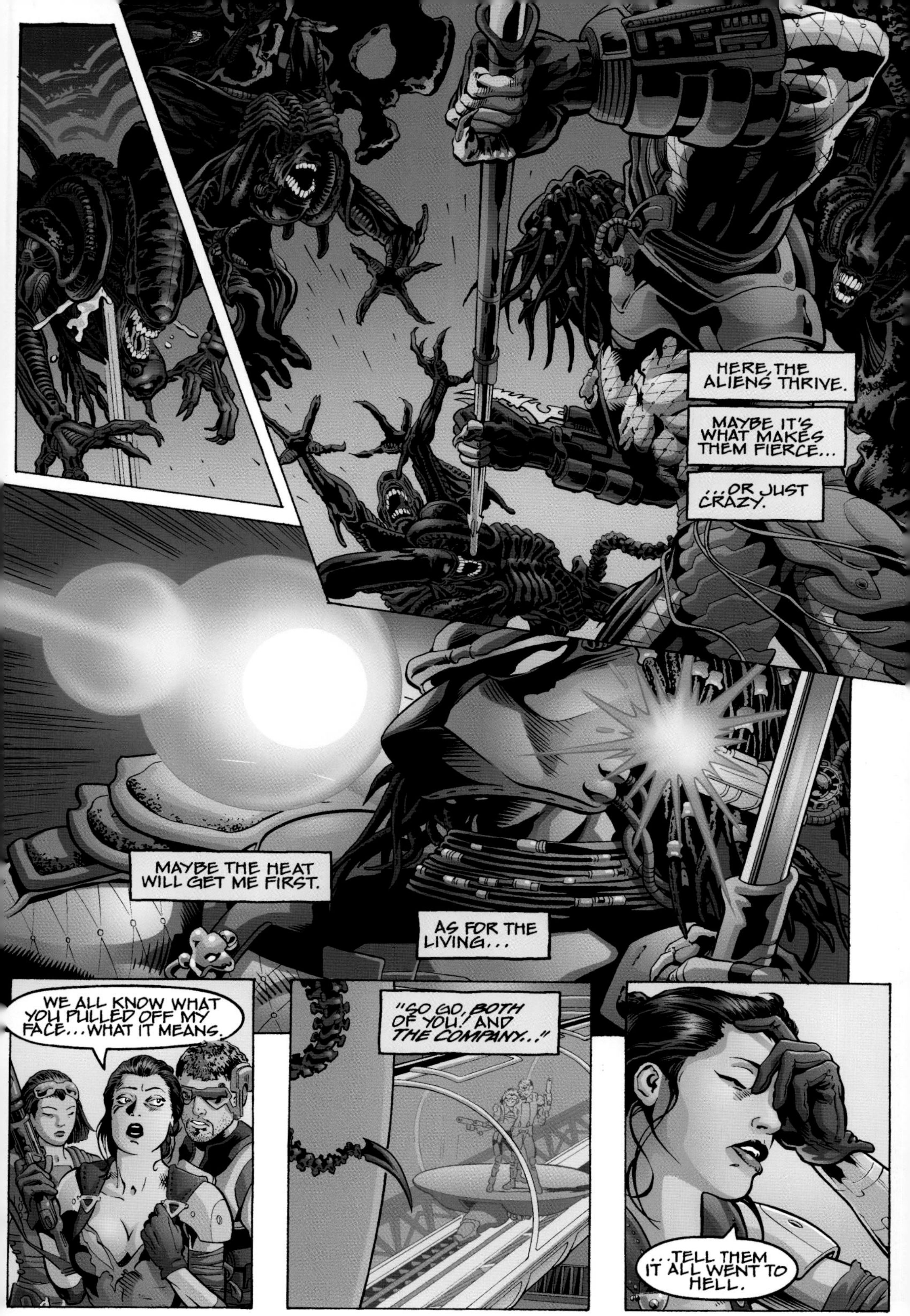
HERE, THE ALIENS THRIVE.
MAYBE IT'S WHAT MAKES THEM FIERCE...
...OR JUST CRAZY.
MAYBE THE HEAT WILL GET ME FIRST.
AS FOR THE LIVING...
WE ALL KNOW WHAT YOU PULLED OFF MY FACE...WHAT IT MEANS.
"SO GO, BOTH OF YOU! AND THE COMPANY..."
...TELL THEM IT ALL WENT TO HELL.

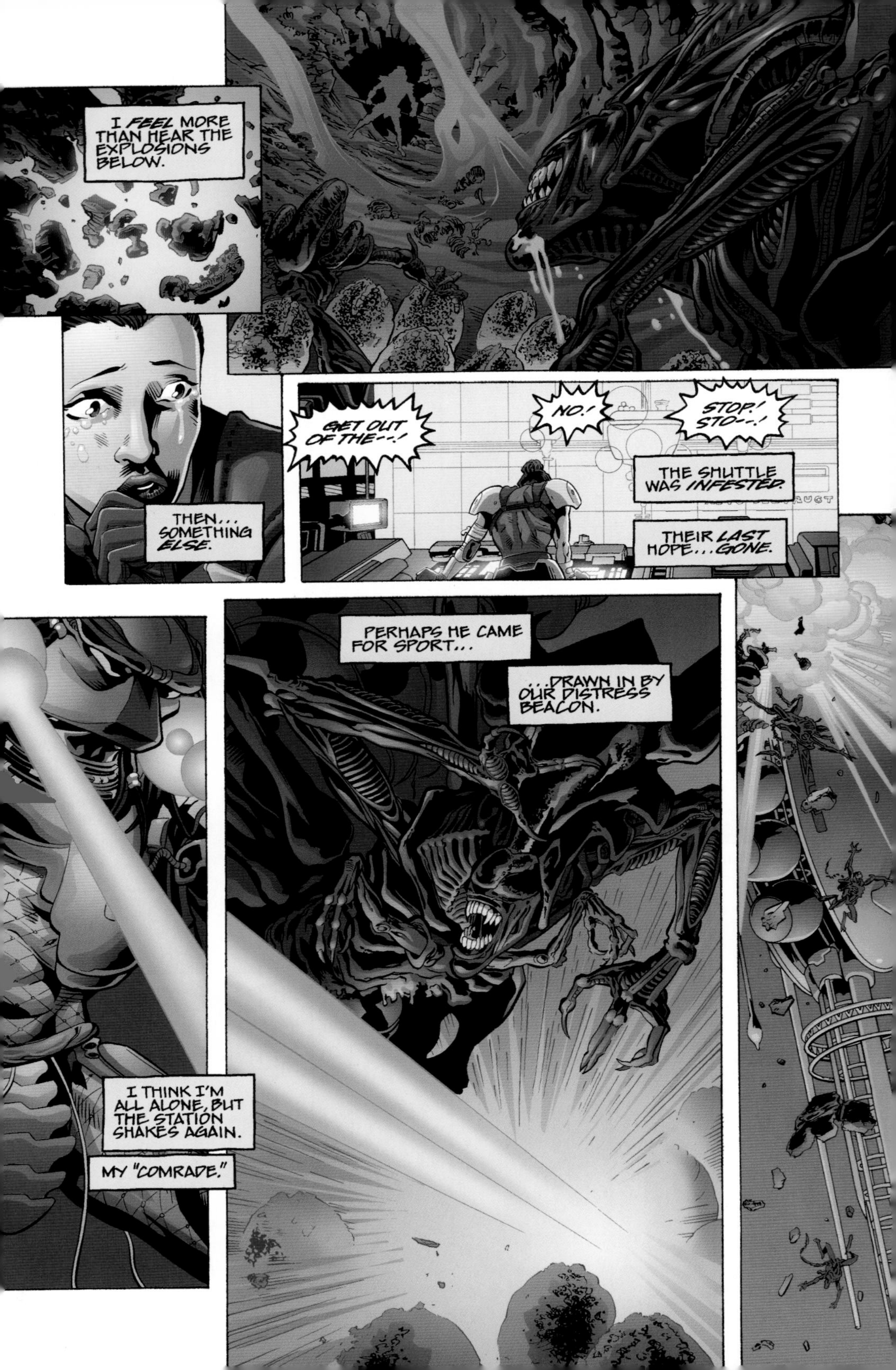
I FEEL MORE THAN HEAR THE EXPLOSIONS BELOW.
THEN... SOMETHING ELSE.
GET OUT OF THE--!
NO!
STOP! STO--!
THE SHUTTLE WAS INFESTED.
THEIR LAST HOPE... GONE.
PERHAPS HE CAME FOR SPORT...
...DRAWN IN BY OUR DISTRESS BEACON.
I THINK I'M ALL ALONE, BUT THE STATION SHAKES AGAIN.
MY "COMRADE."

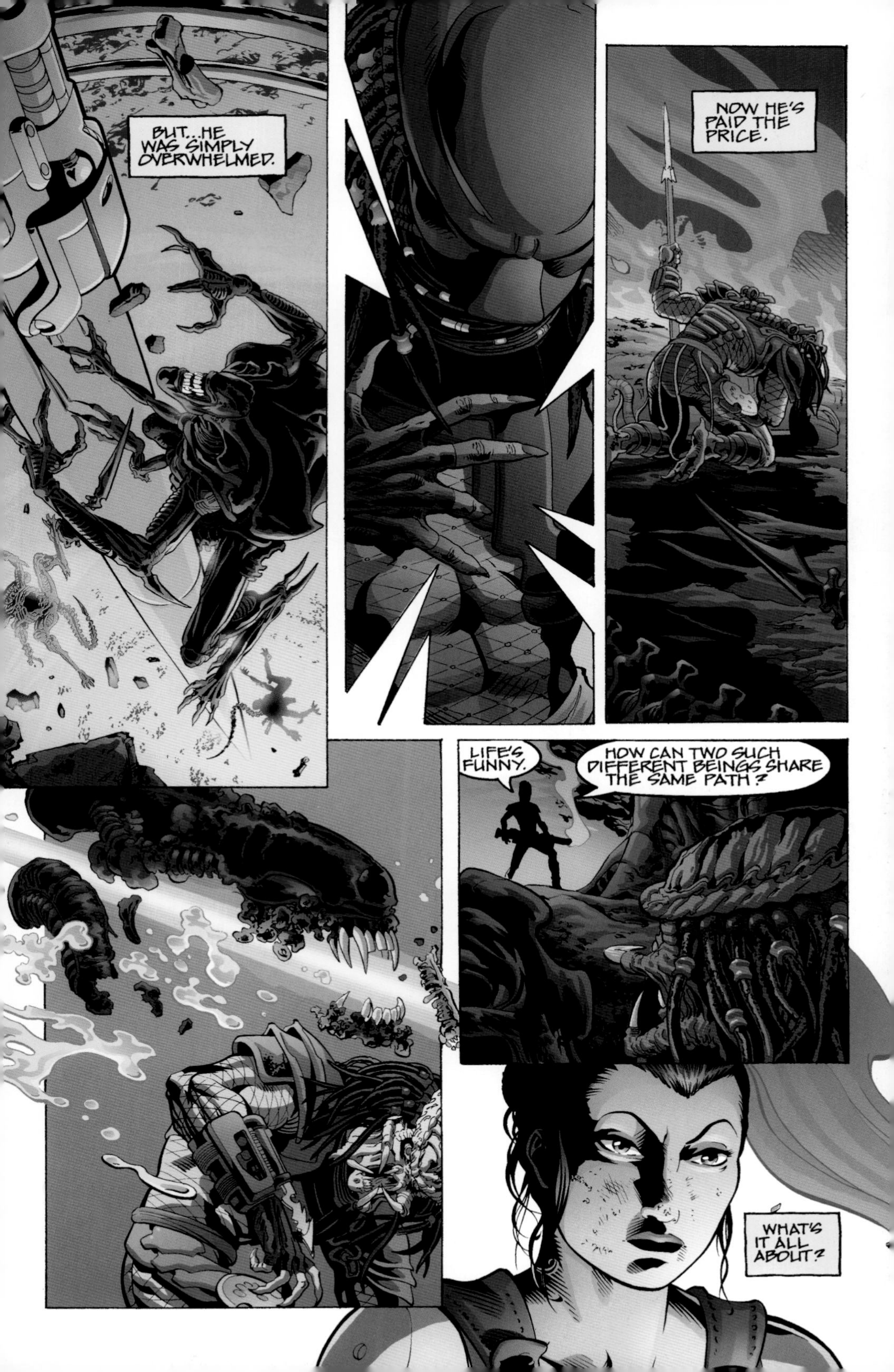
BUT...HE WAS SIMPLY OVERWHELMED.
NOW HE'S PAID THE PRICE.
LIFE'S FUNNY.
HOW CAN TWO SUCH DIFFERENT BEINGS SHARE THE SAME PATH?
WHAT'S IT ALL ABOUT?

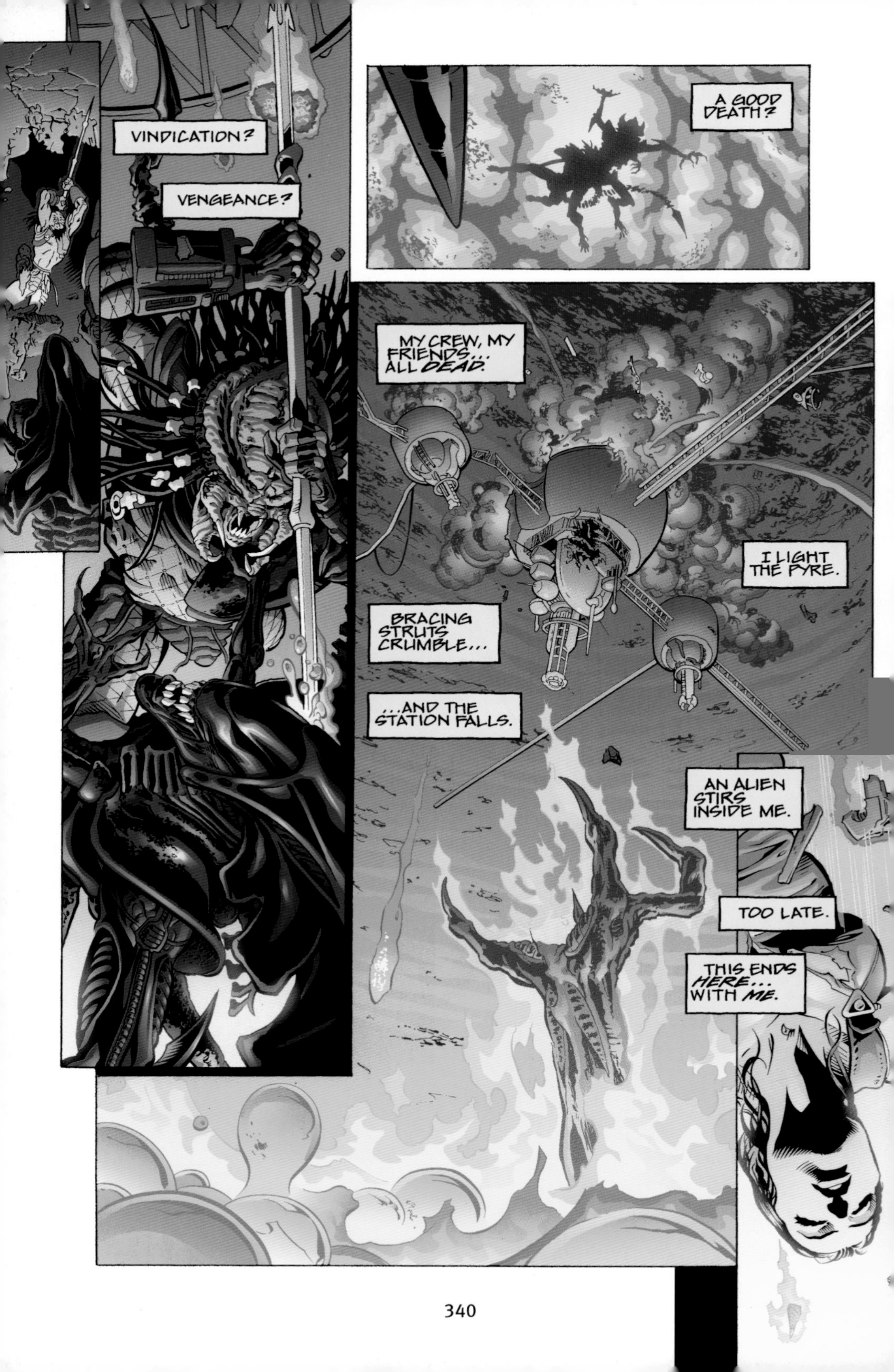
VINDICATION?
VENGEANCE?
A GOOD DEATH?
MY CREW, MY FRIENDS... ALL DEAD.
I LIGHT THE PYRE.
BRACING STRUTS CRUMBLE...
...AND THE STATION FALLS.
AN ALIEN STIRS INSIDE ME.
TOO LATE.
THIS ENDS HERE... WITH ME.

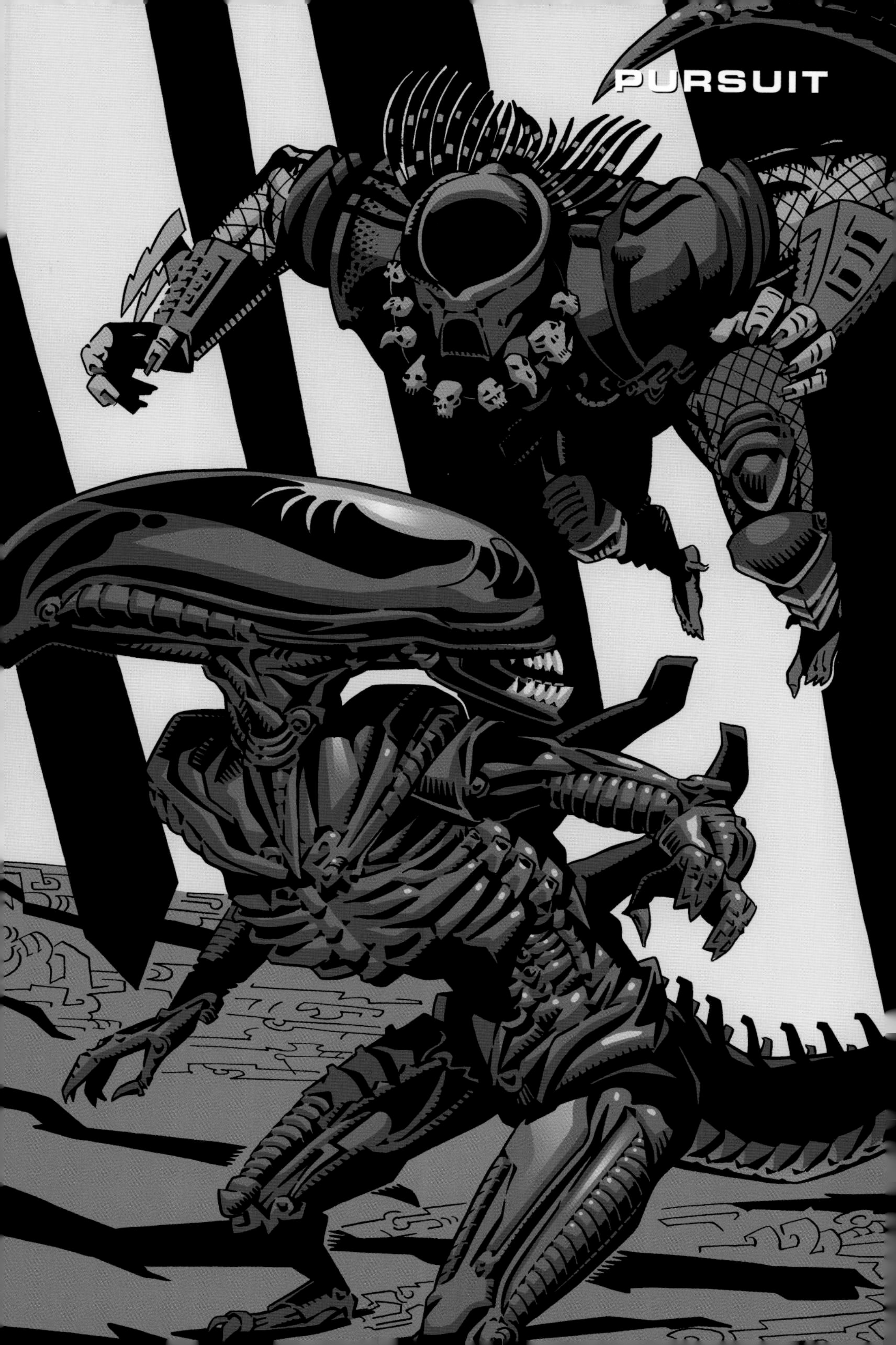
PURSUIT

script
IAN EDGINTON

pencils
MEL RUBI

inks
ROB HUNTER

colors
DAVE STEWART

lettering
SEAN KONOT

title illustration
DANIEL TORRES with **DAVE STEWART**

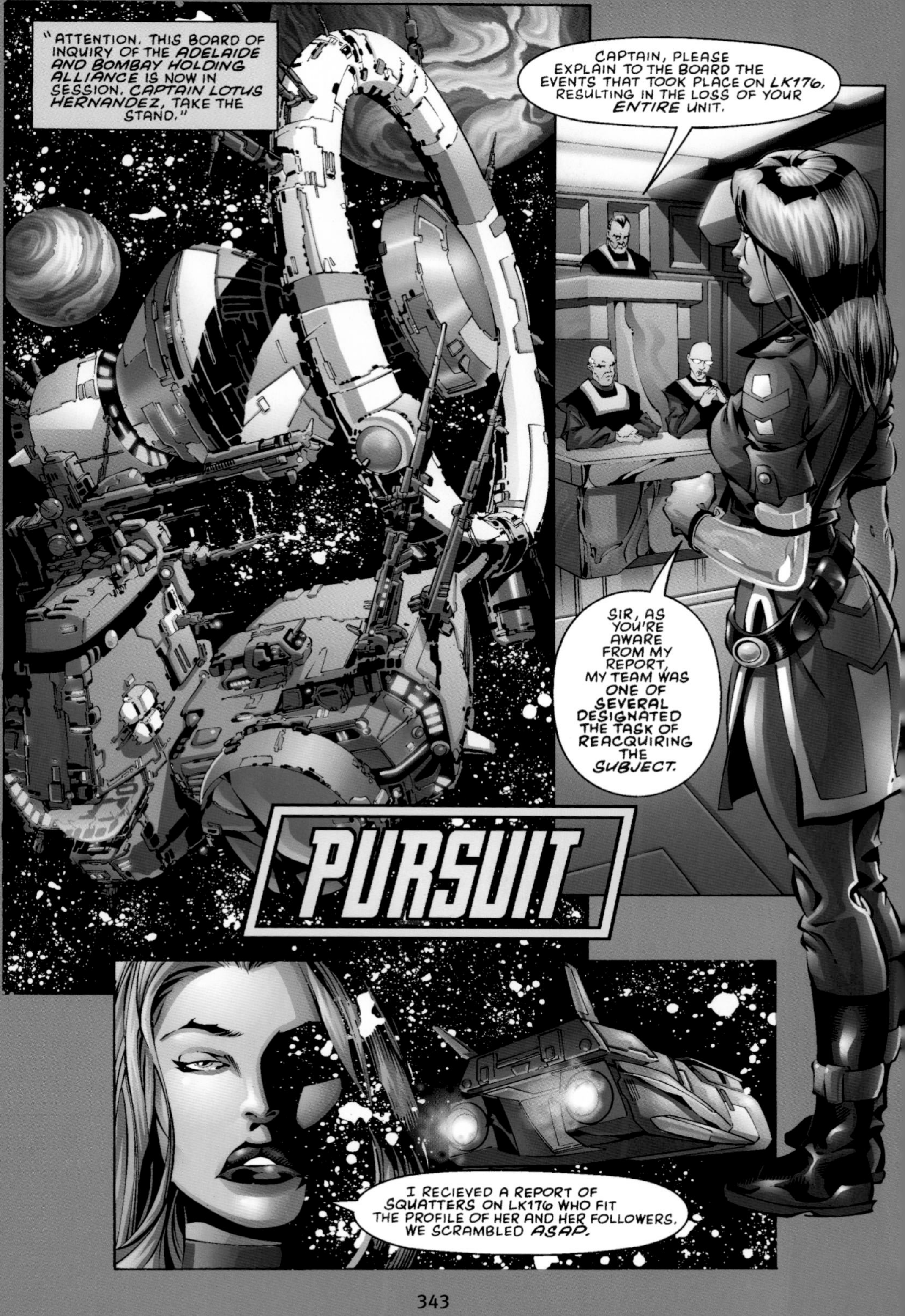
"ATTENTION. THIS BOARD OF INQUIRY OF THE ADELAIDE AND BOMBAY HOLDING ALLIANCE IS NOW IN SESSION. CAPTAIN LOTUS HERNANDEZ, TAKE THE STAND."
CAPTAIN, PLEASE EXPLAIN TO THE BOARD THE EVENTS THAT TOOK PLACE ON LK176, RESULTING IN THE LOSS OF YOUR ENTIRE UNIT.
SIR, AS YOU'RE AWARE FROM MY REPORT, MY TEAM WAS ONE OF SEVERAL DESIGNATED THE TASK OF REACQUIRING THE SUBJECT.
PURSUIT
I RECIEVED A REPORT OF SQUATTERS ON LK176 WHO FIT THE PROFILE OF HER AND HER FOLLOWERS. WE SCRAMBLED ASAP.

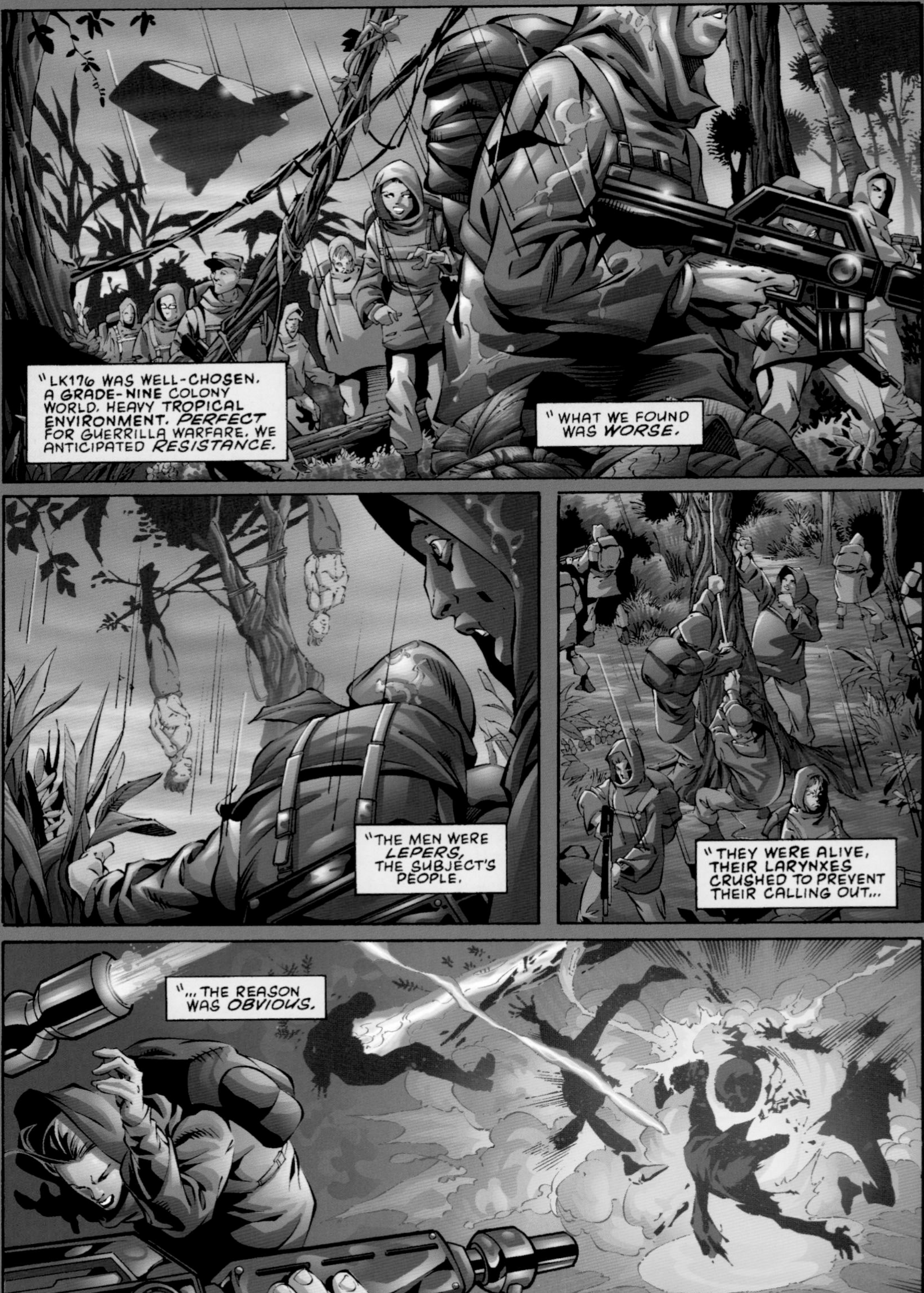
"LK176 WAS WELL-CHOSEN. A GRADE-NINE COLONY WORLD. HEAVY TROPICAL ENVIRONMENT. *PERFECT* FOR GUERRILLA WARFARE. WE ANTICIPATED *RESISTANCE*.
"WHAT WE FOUND WAS *WORSE*.
"THE MEN WERE *LEPERS*, THE SUBJECT'S PEOPLE.
"THEY WERE ALIVE, THEIR LARYNXES CRUSHED TO PREVENT THEIR CALLING OUT...
"...THE REASON WAS *OBVIOUS*.

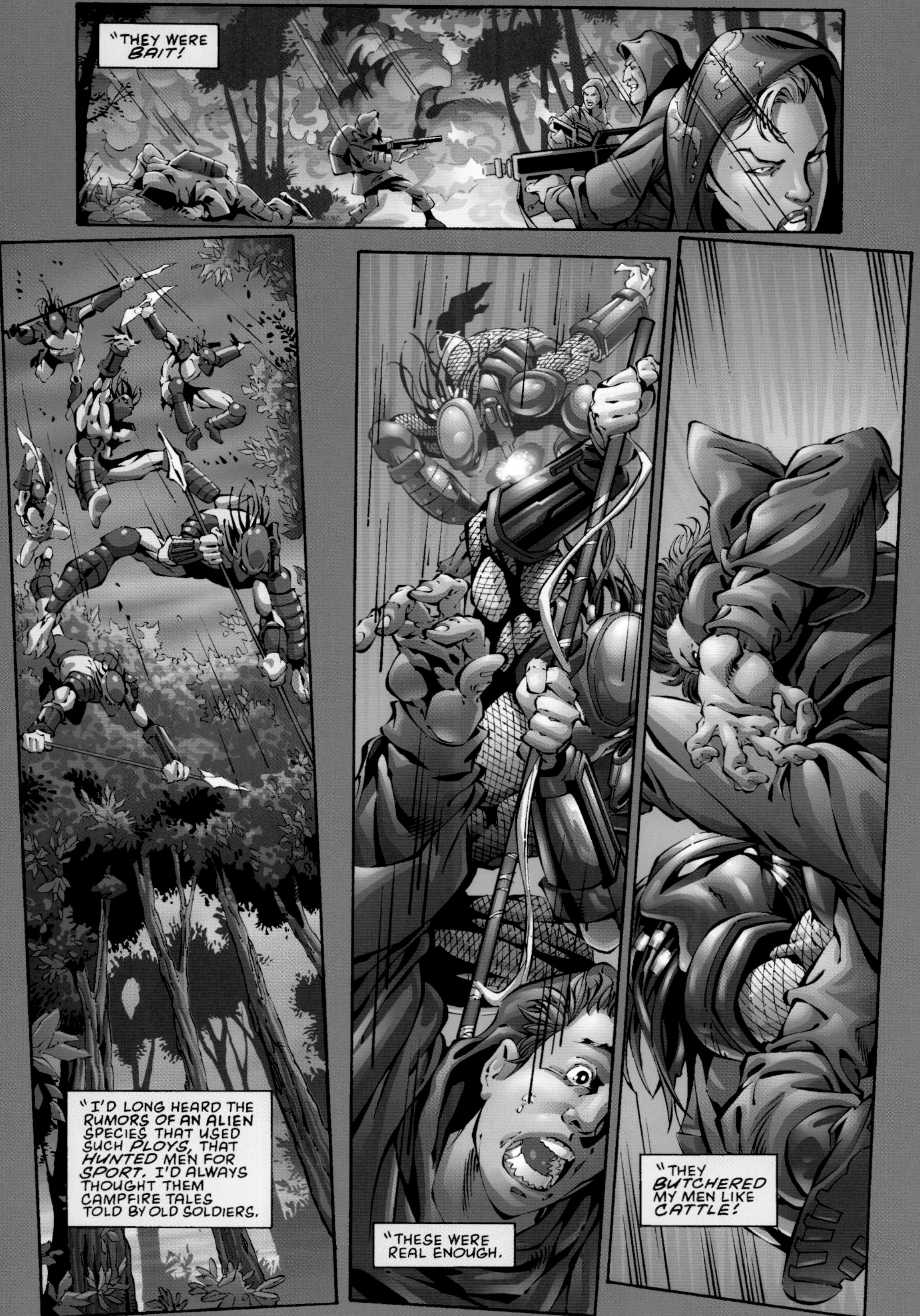
"THEY WERE BAIT!
"I'D LONG HEARD THE RUMORS OF AN ALIEN SPECIES THAT USED SUCH PLOYS, THAT HUNTED MEN FOR SPORT. I'D ALWAYS THOUGHT THEM CAMPFIRE TALES TOLD BY OLD SOLDIERS.
"THESE WERE REAL ENOUGH.
"THEY BUTCHERED MY MEN LIKE CATTLE!

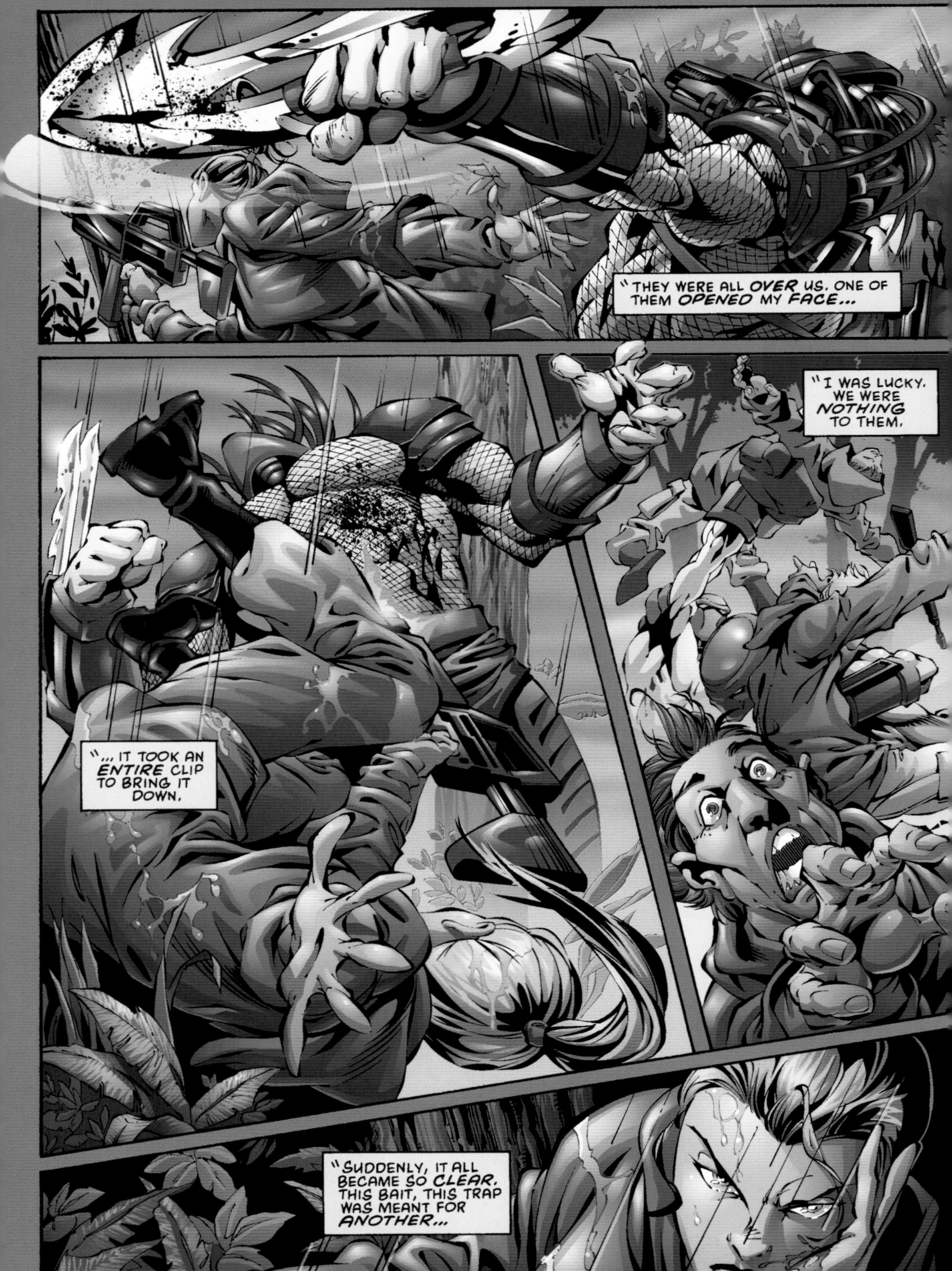
"THEY WERE ALL OVER US. ONE OF THEM OPENED MY FACE...
"I WAS LUCKY. WE WERE NOTHING TO THEM.
"... IT TOOK AN ENTIRE CLIP TO BRING IT DOWN.
"SUDDENLY, IT ALL BECAME SO CLEAR. THIS BAIT, THIS TRAP WAS MEANT FOR ANOTHER...

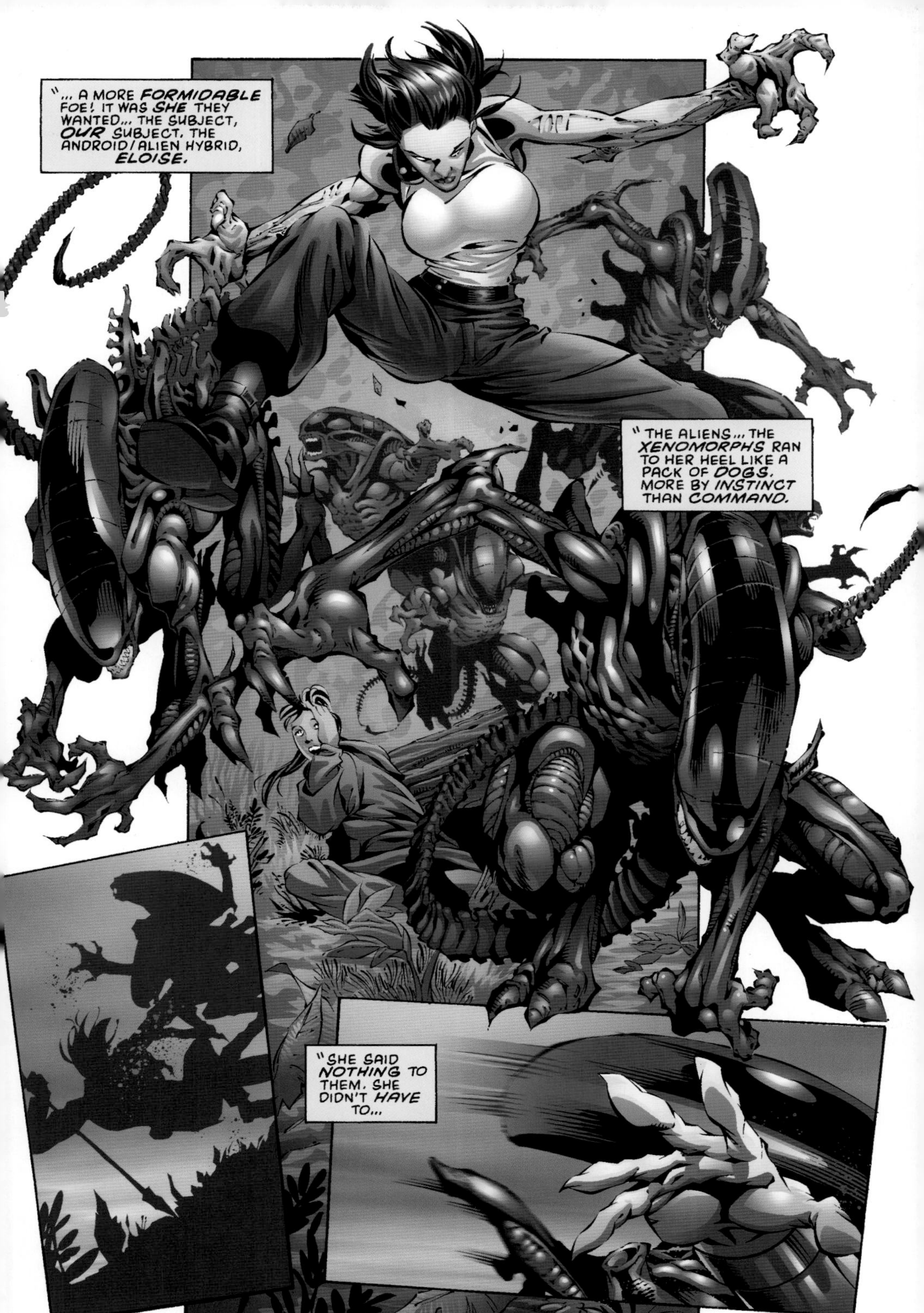
"... A MORE FORMIDABLE FOE! IT WAS SHE THEY WANTED... THE SUBJECT, OUR SUBJECT. THE ANDROID/ALIEN HYBRID, ELOISE.
"THE ALIENS... THE XENOMORPHS RAN TO HER HEEL LIKE A PACK OF DOGS. MORE BY INSTINCT THAN COMMAND.
"SHE SAID NOTHING TO THEM. SHE DIDN'T HAVE TO...

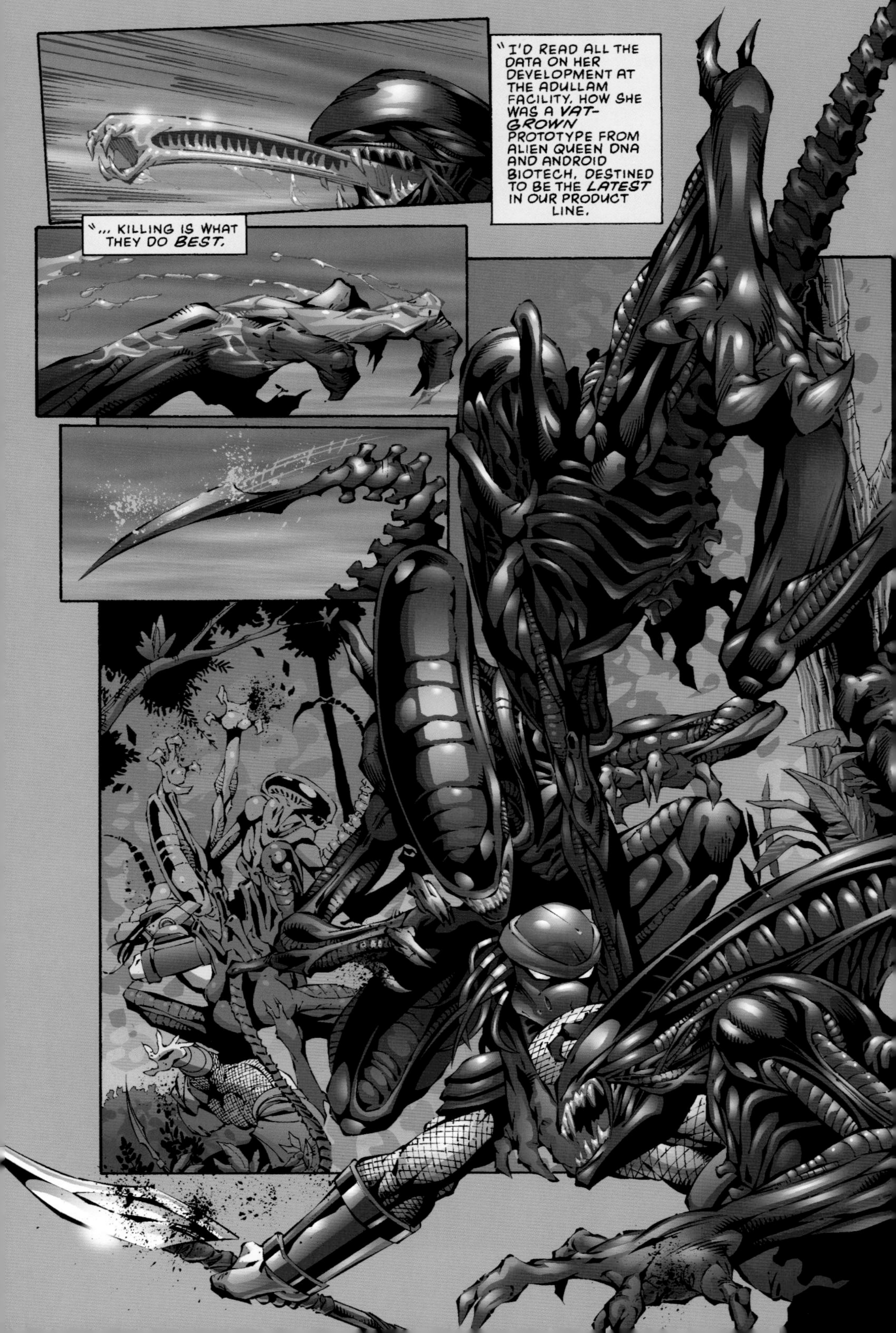
"I'D READ ALL THE DATA ON HER DEVELOPMENT AT THE ADULLAM FACILITY, HOW SHE WAS A VAT-GROWN PROTOTYPE FROM ALIEN QUEEN DNA AND ANDROID BIOTECH, DESTINED TO BE THE LATEST IN OUR PRODUCT LINE.
"... KILLING IS WHAT THEY DO BEST.

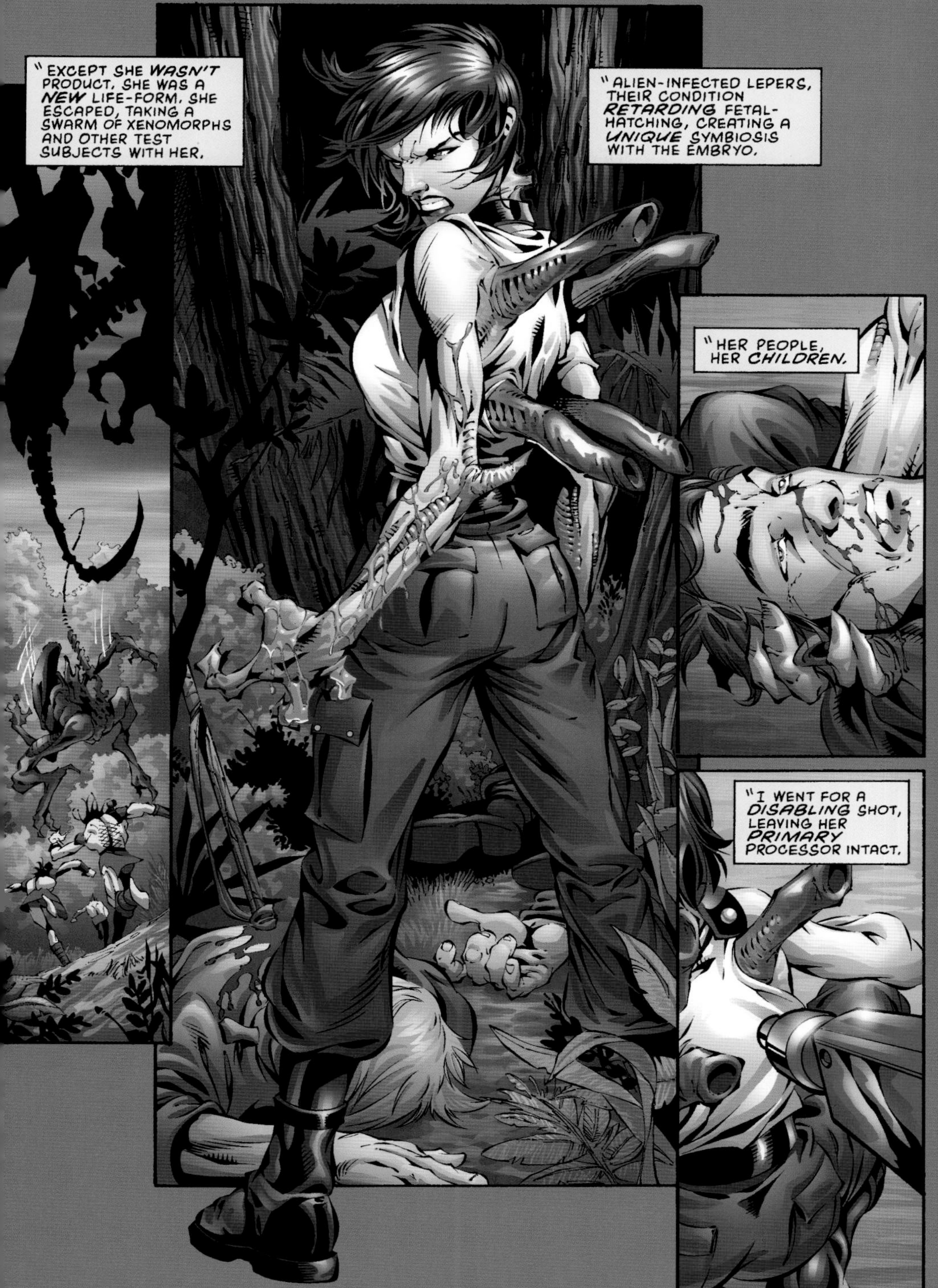
"EXCEPT SHE WASN'T PRODUCT. SHE WAS A NEW LIFE-FORM. SHE ESCAPED, TAKING A SWARM OF XENOMORPHS AND OTHER TEST SUBJECTS WITH HER.
"ALIEN-INFECTED LEPERS, THEIR CONDITION RETARDING FETAL-HATCHING, CREATING A UNIQUE SYMBIOSIS WITH THE EMBRYO.
"HER PEOPLE, HER CHILDREN.
"I WENT FOR A DISABLING SHOT, LEAVING HER PRIMARY PROCESSOR INTACT.

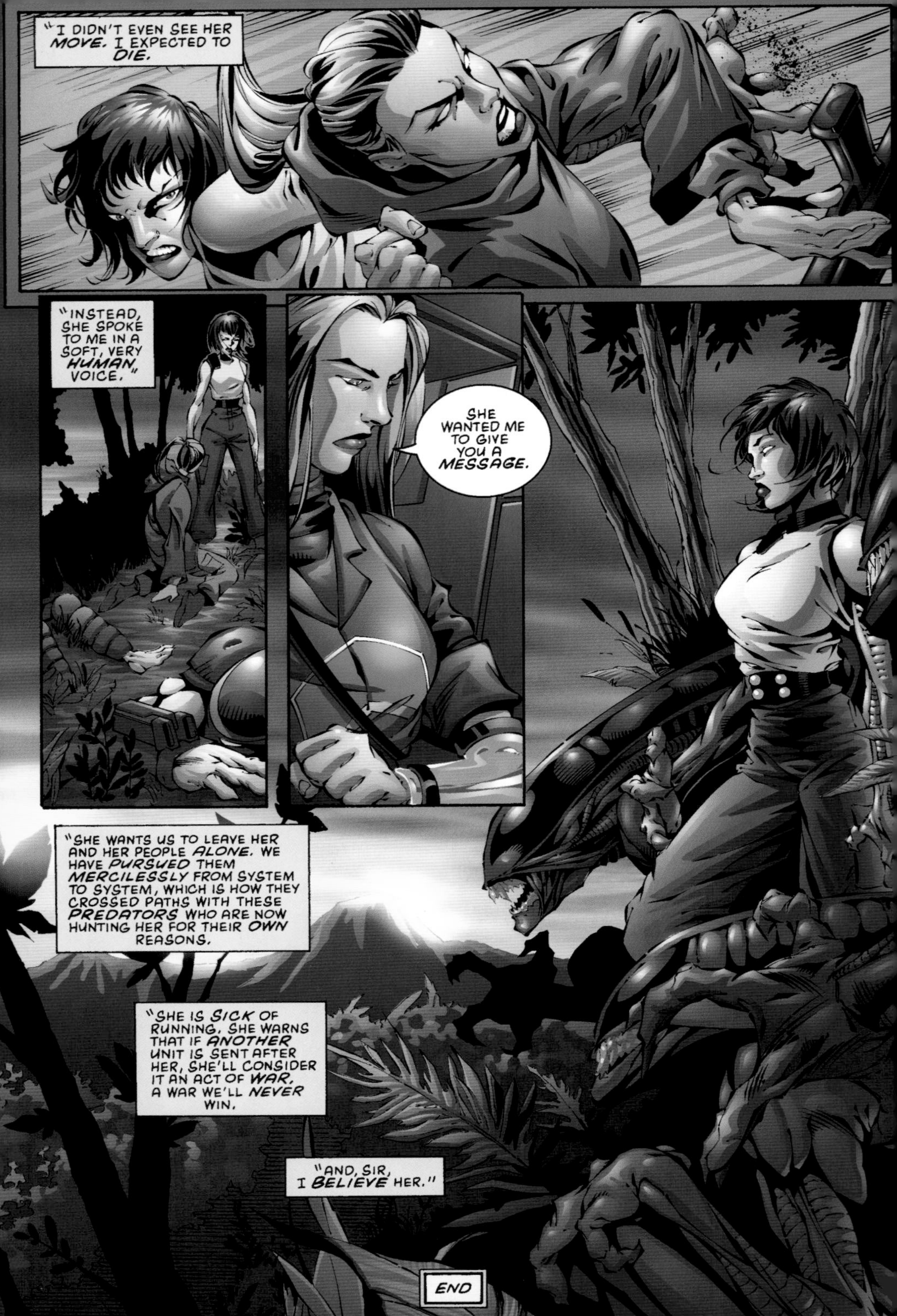
"I DIDN'T EVEN SEE HER MOVE. I EXPECTED TO DIE.
"INSTEAD, SHE SPOKE TO ME IN A SOFT, VERY HUMAN, VOICE."
SHE WANTED ME TO GIVE YOU A MESSAGE.
"SHE WANTS US TO LEAVE HER AND HER PEOPLE ALONE. WE HAVE PURSUED THEM MERCILESSLY FROM SYSTEM TO SYSTEM, WHICH IS HOW THEY CROSSED PATHS WITH THESE PREDATORS WHO ARE NOW HUNTING HER FOR THEIR OWN REASONS.
"SHE IS SICK OF RUNNING. SHE WARNS THAT IF ANOTHER UNIT IS SENT AFTER HER, SHE'LL CONSIDER IT AN ACT OF WAR, A WAR WE'LL NEVER WIN.
"AND, SIR, I BELIEVE HER."
END

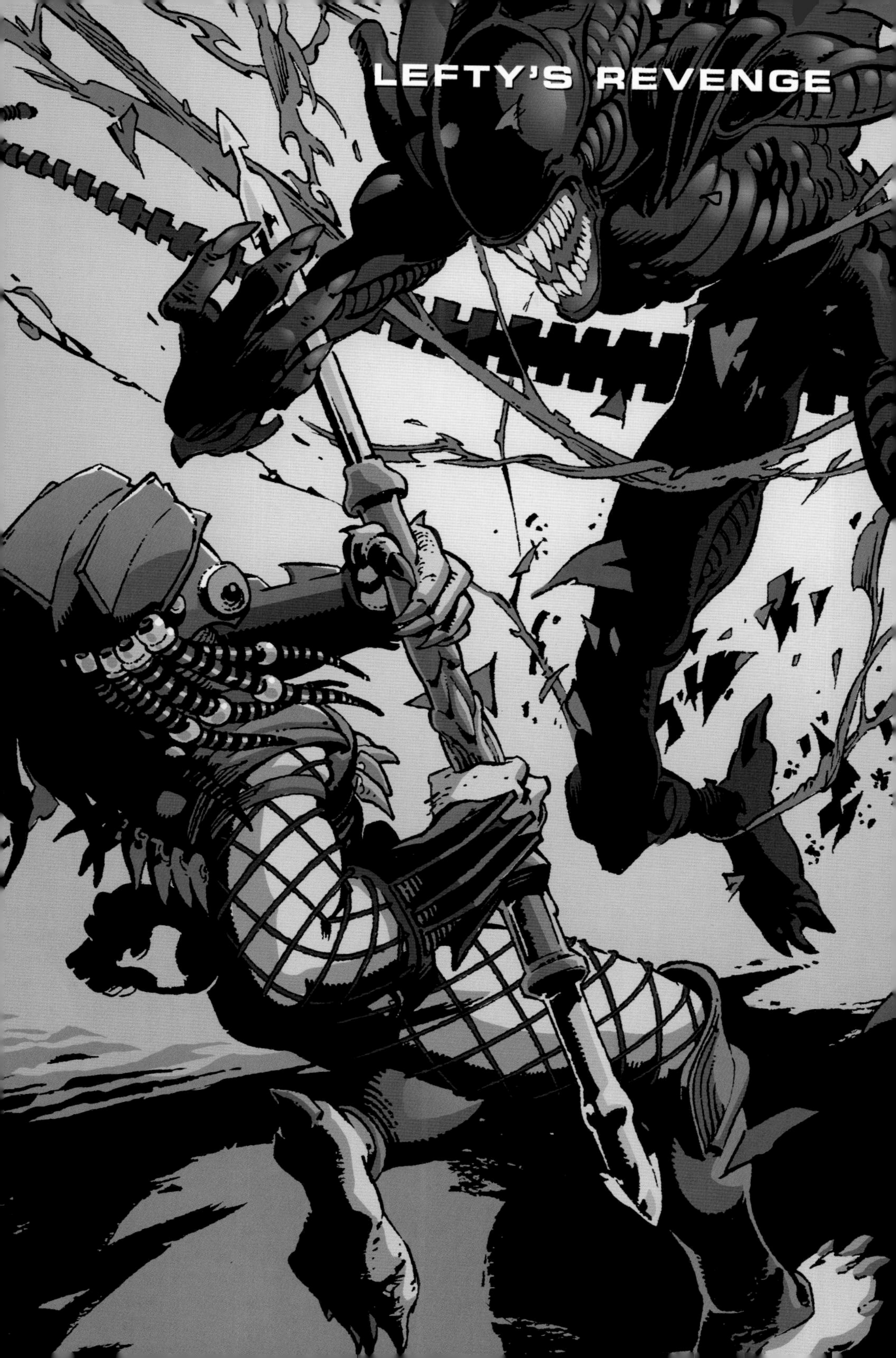
LEFTY'S REVENGE

script
BRIAN McDONALD

pencils
POP MHAN

inks
NORMAN LEE

colors
GUY MAJOR

lettering
CLEM ROBINS

title illustration
HUGHES LABIANO with **DAVE STEWART**

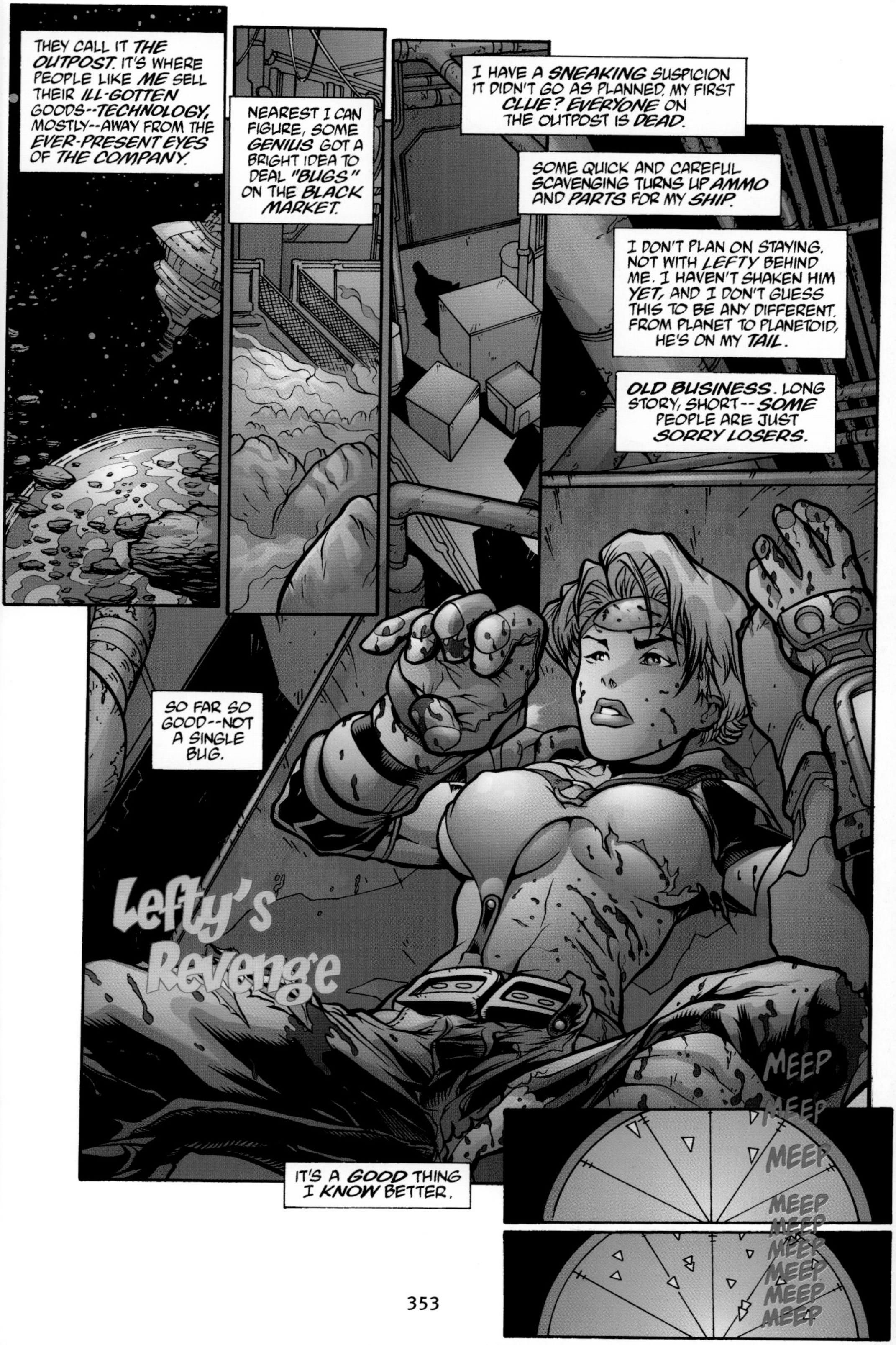

THEY CALL IT THE OUTPOST. IT'S WHERE PEOPLE LIKE ME SELL THEIR ILL-GOTTEN GOODS--TECHNOLOGY, MOSTLY--AWAY FROM THE EVER-PRESENT EYES OF THE COMPANY.
NEAREST I CAN FIGURE, SOME GENIUS GOT A BRIGHT IDEA TO DEAL "BUGS" ON THE BLACK MARKET.
I HAVE A SNEAKING SUSPICION IT DIDN'T GO AS PLANNED. MY FIRST CLUE? EVERYONE ON THE OUTPOST IS DEAD.
SOME QUICK AND CAREFUL SCAVENGING TURNS UP AMMO AND PARTS FOR MY SHIP.
I DON'T PLAN ON STAYING. NOT WITH LEFTY BEHIND ME. I HAVEN'T SHAKEN HIM YET, AND I DON'T GUESS THIS TO BE ANY DIFFERENT. FROM PLANET TO PLANETOID, HE'S ON MY TAIL.
OLD BUSINESS. LONG STORY, SHORT--SOME PEOPLE ARE JUST SORRY LOSERS.
Lefty's Revenge
SO FAR SO GOOD--NOT A SINGLE BUG.
IT'S A GOOD THING I KNOW BETTER.
MEEP
MEEP
MEEP
MEEP
MEEP
MEEP
MEEP
MEEP
MEEP

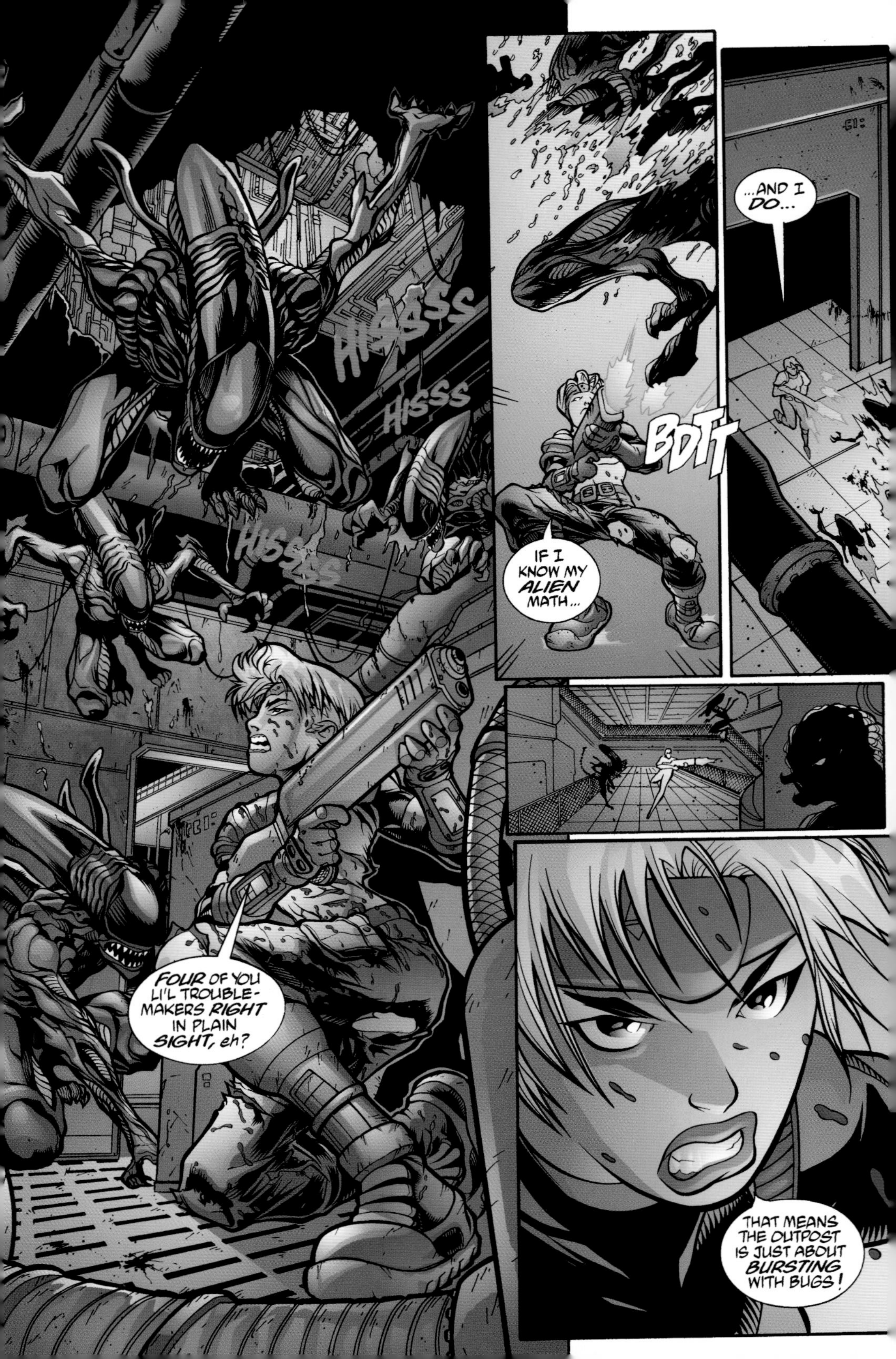
HISSSS
HISSS
HISSS
FOUR OF YOU LI'L TROUBLE-MAKERS RIGHT IN PLAIN SIGHT, eh?
BDTT
IF I KNOW MY ALIEN MATH...
...AND I DO...
THAT MEANS THE OUTPOST IS JUST ABOUT BURSTING WITH BUGS!

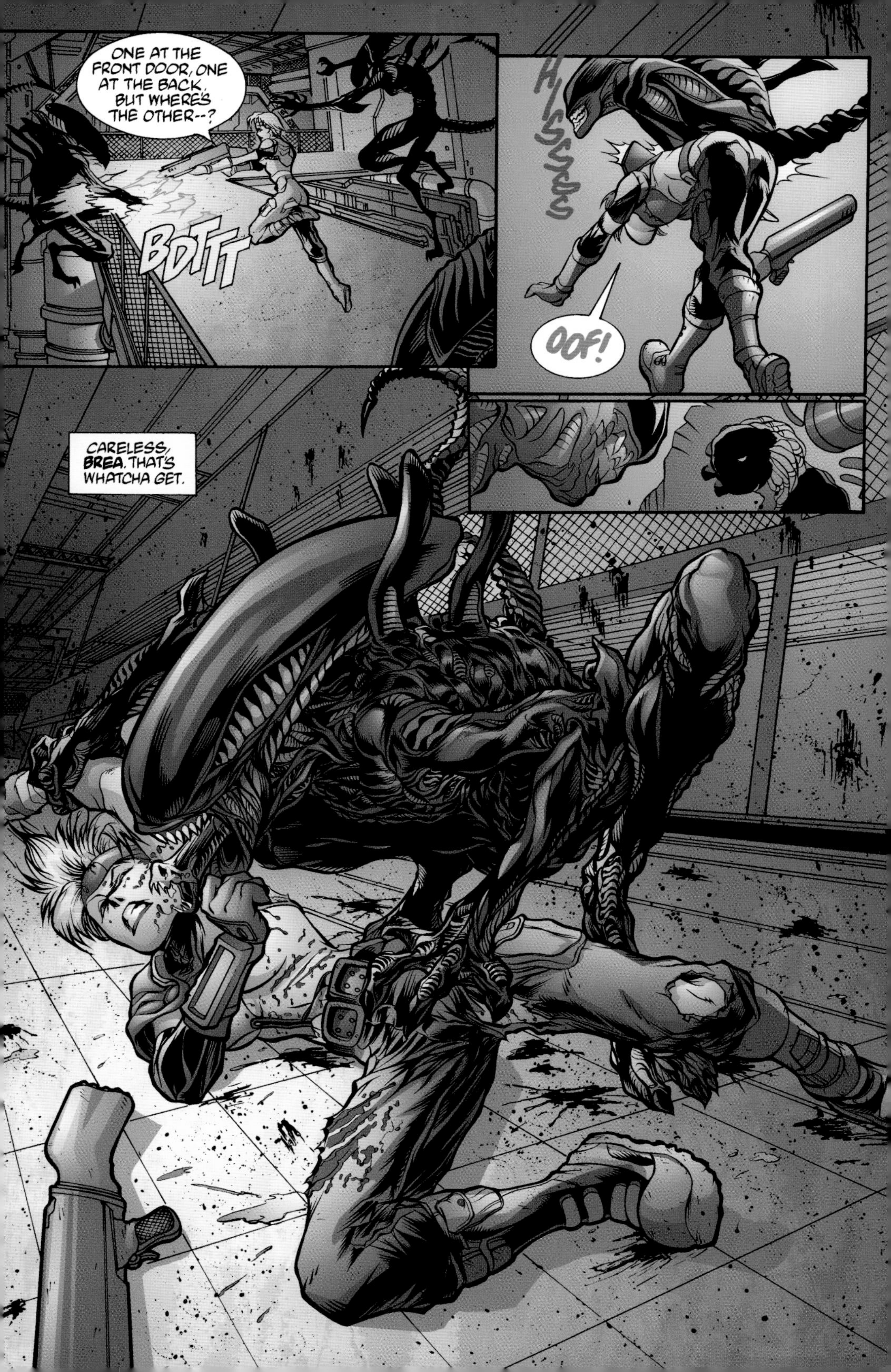
ONE AT THE FRONT DOOR, ONE AT THE BACK. BUT WHERE'S THE OTHER--?
BDTTT
HISSSSS
OOF!
CARELESS, BREA. THAT'S WHATCHA GET.

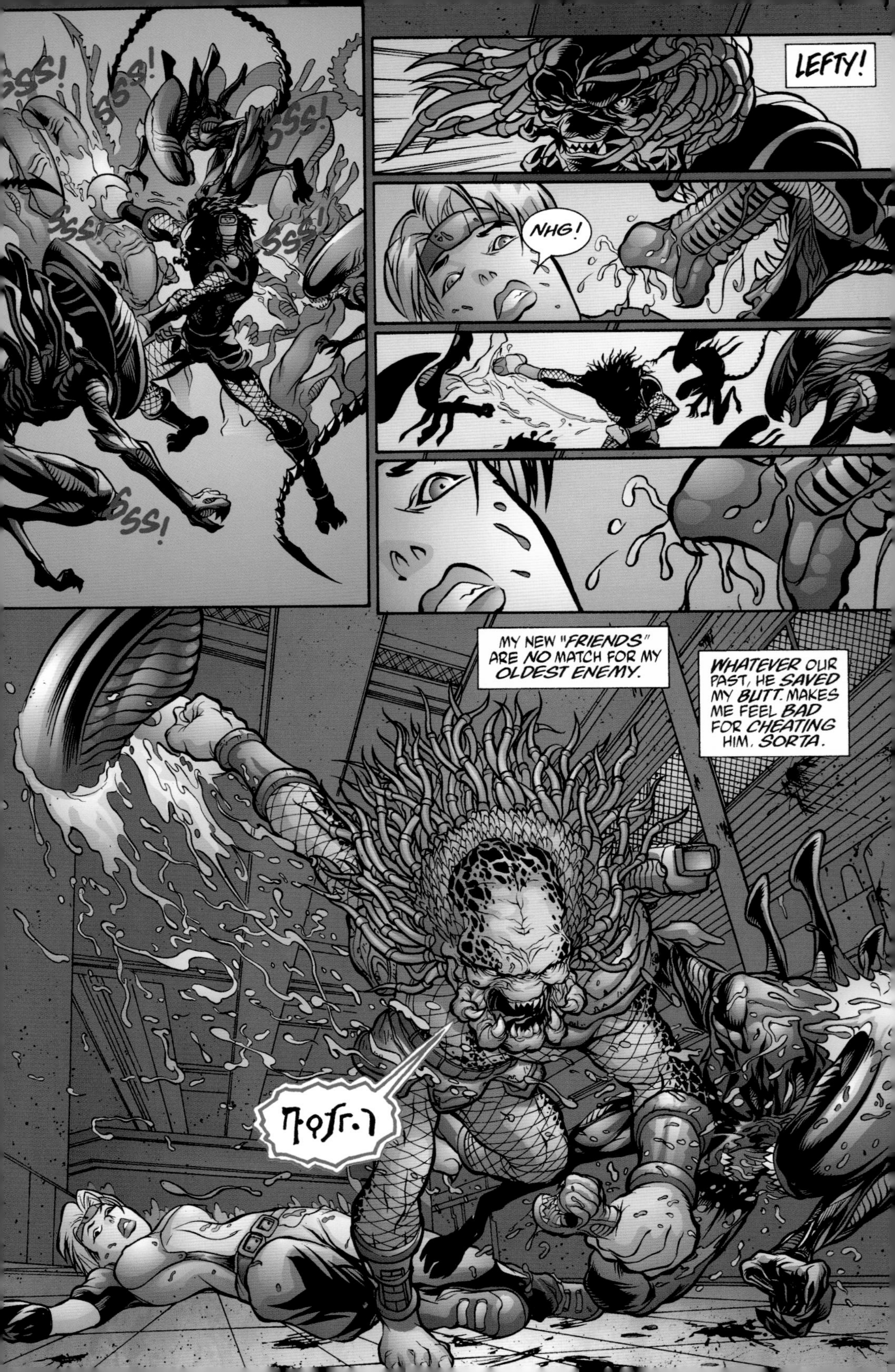
SSS!
SSS!
SSS!
SSS!
SSS!
SSS!
LEFTY!
NHG!
MY NEW "FRIENDS" ARE NO MATCH FOR MY OLDEST ENEMY.
WHATEVER OUR PAST, HE SAVED MY BUTT. MAKES ME FEEL BAD FOR CHEATING HIM. SORTA.

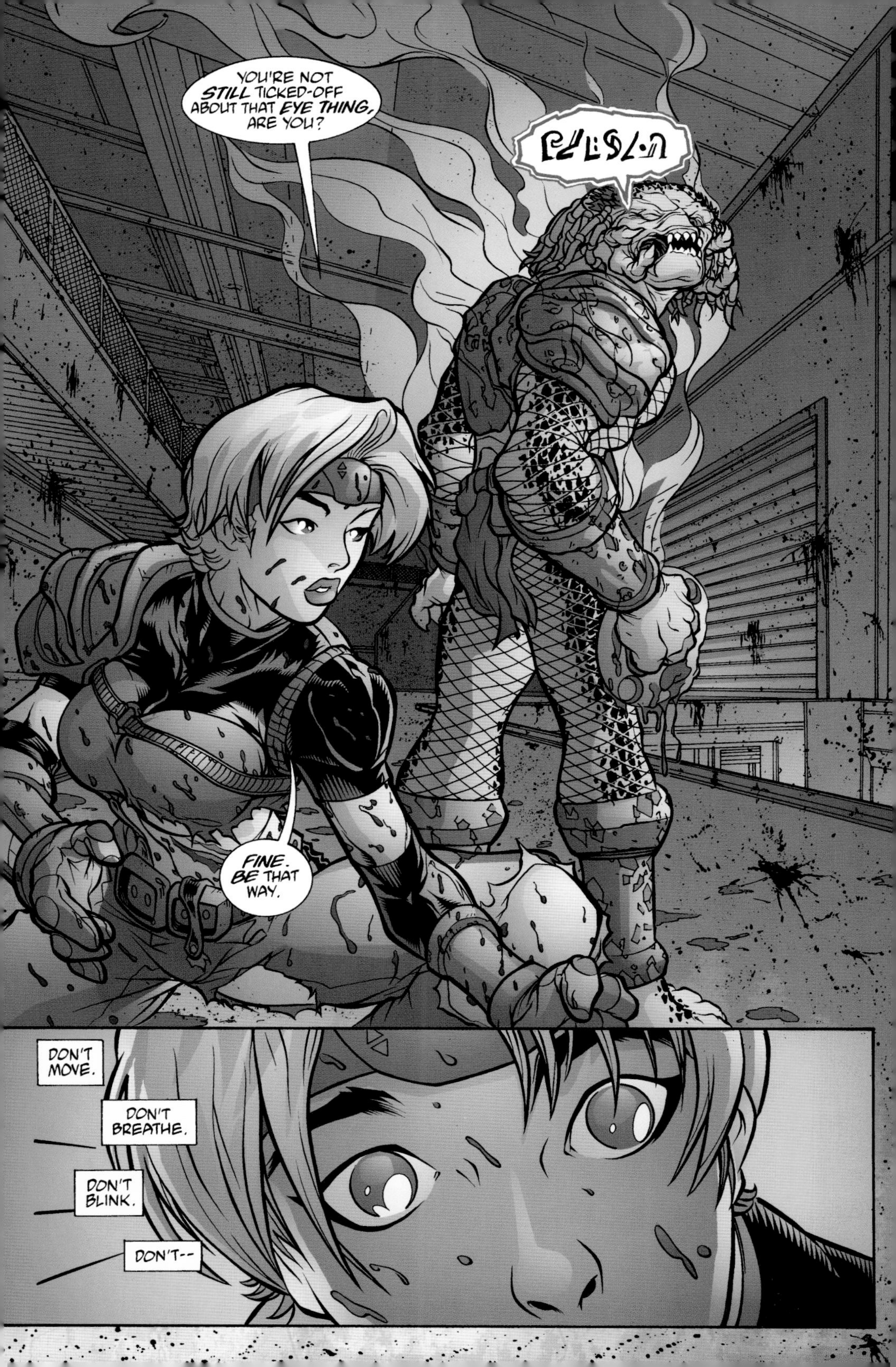
YOU'RE NOT STILL TICKED-OFF ABOUT THAT EYE THING, ARE YOU?
FINE. BE THAT WAY.
DON'T MOVE.
DON'T BREATHE.
DON'T BLINK.
DON'T--

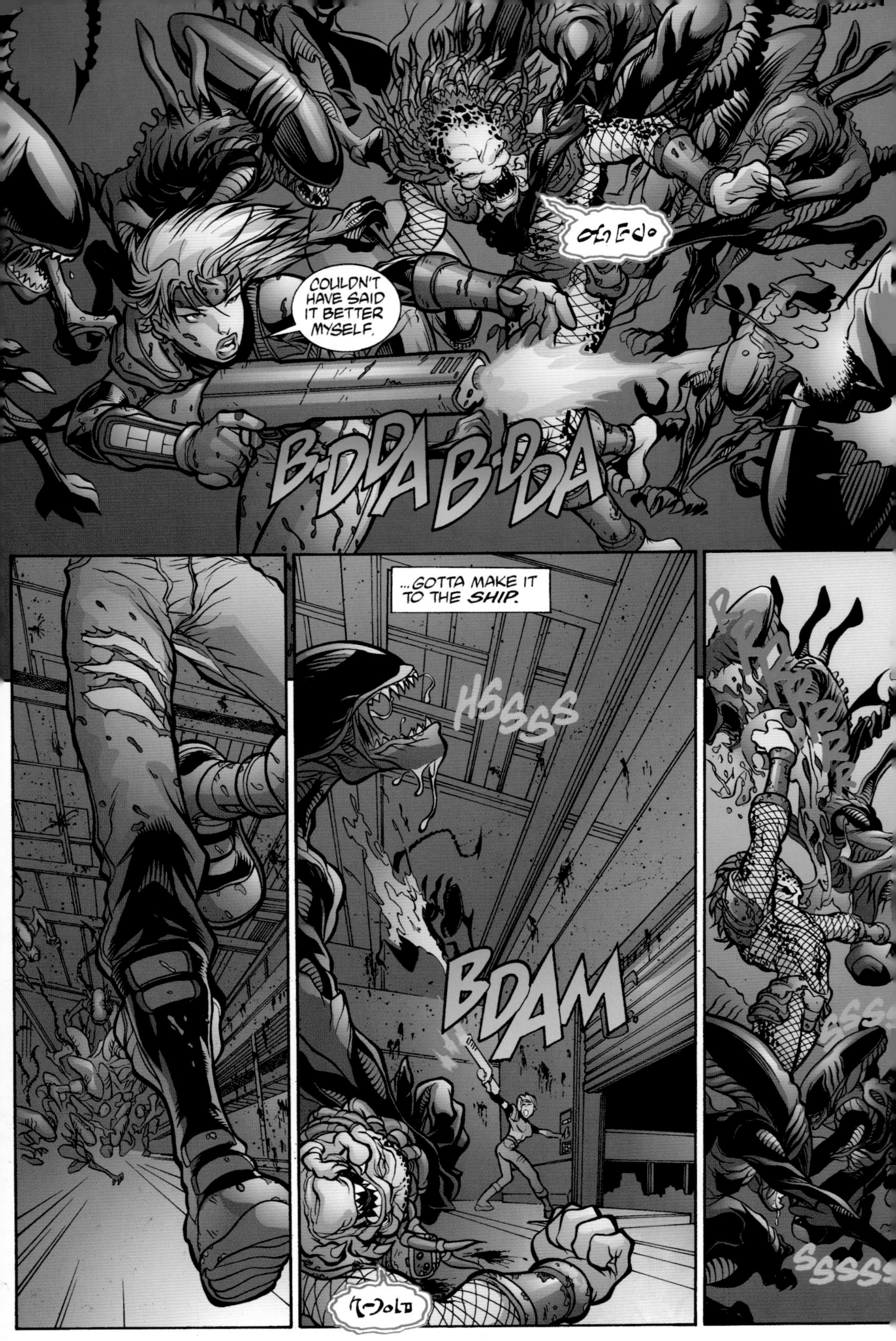
COULDN'T HAVE SAID IT BETTER MYSELF.
B-DDA B-DDA
...GOTTA MAKE IT TO THE SHIP.
HSSSSS
BDAM
SSSSS

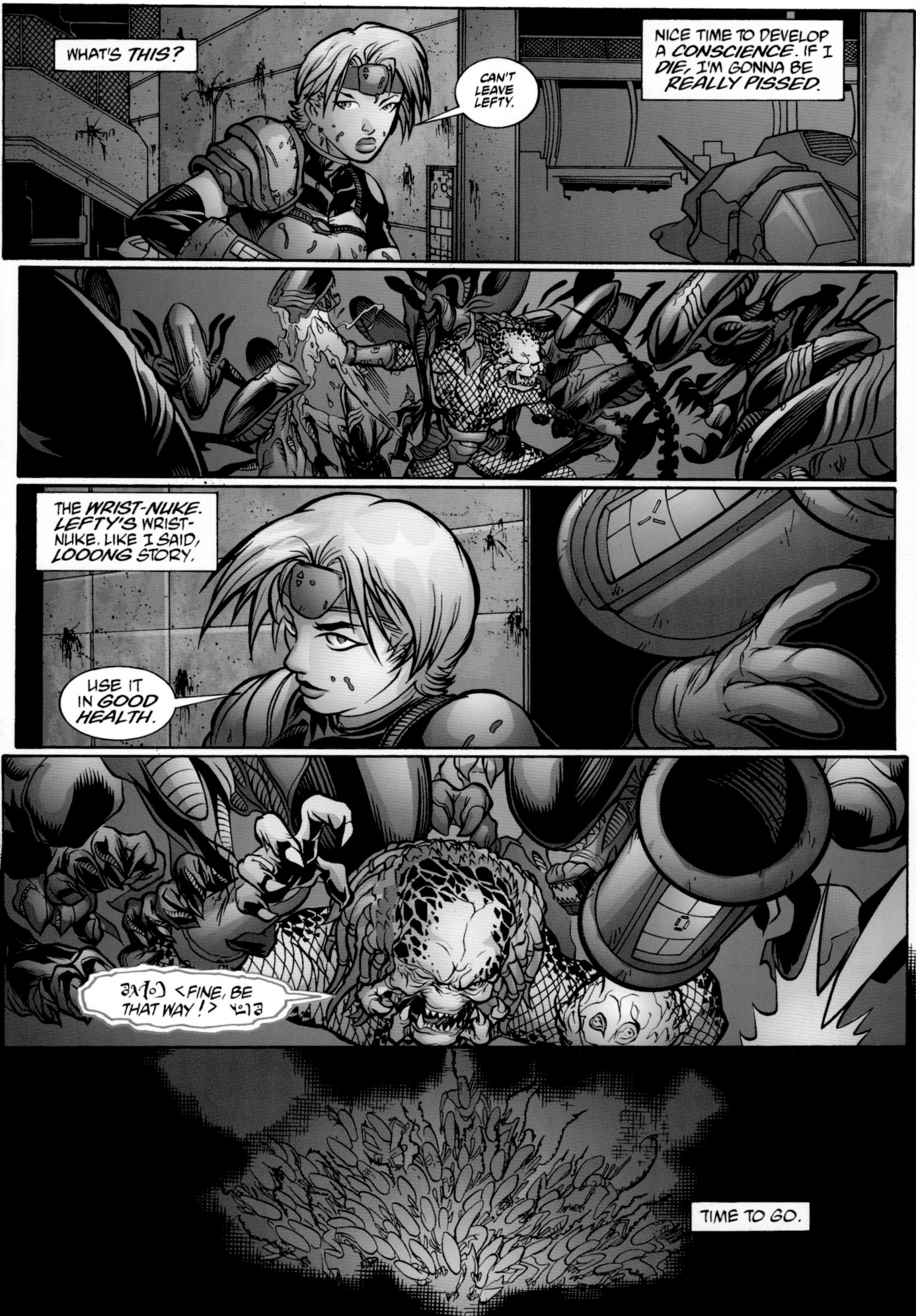
WHAT'S *THIS?*
CAN'T LEAVE LEFTY.
NICE TIME TO DEVELOP A *CONSCIENCE*. IF I *DIE*, I'M GONNA BE *REALLY PISSED*.
THE ***WRIST-NUKE***. ***LEFTY'S*** WRIST-NUKE. LIKE I SAID, ***LOOONG*** STORY.
USE IT IN ***GOOD HEALTH***.
<FINE, BE THAT WAY!>
TIME TO GO.

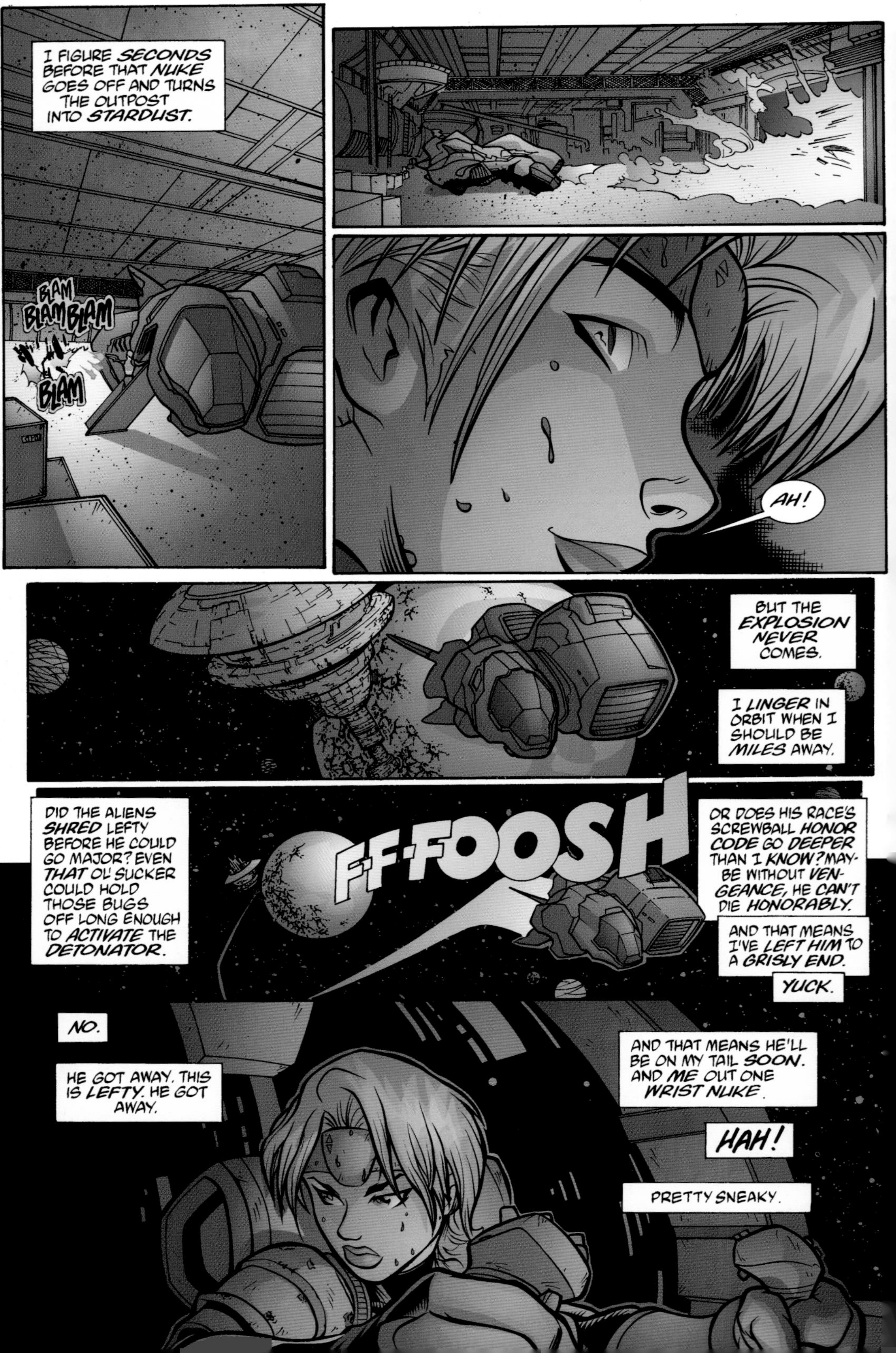
I FIGURE SECONDS BEFORE THAT NUKE GOES OFF AND TURNS THE OUTPOST INTO STARDUST.
BLAM BLAMBLAM
BLAM
AH!
BUT THE EXPLOSION NEVER COMES.
I LINGER IN ORBIT WHEN I SHOULD BE MILES AWAY.
DID THE ALIENS SHRED LEFTY BEFORE HE COULD GO MAJOR? EVEN THAT OL' SUCKER COULD HOLD THOSE BUGS OFF LONG ENOUGH TO ACTIVATE THE DETONATOR.
F-F-FOOSH
OR DOES HIS RACE'S SCREWBALL HONOR CODE GO DEEPER THAN I KNOW? MAYBE WITHOUT VENGEANCE, HE CAN'T DIE HONORABLY.
AND THAT MEANS I'VE LEFT HIM TO A GRISLY END.
YUCK.
NO.
HE GOT AWAY. THIS IS LEFTY. HE GOT AWAY.
AND THAT MEANS HE'LL BE ON MY TAIL SOON. AND ME OUT ONE WRIST NUKE.
HAH!
PRETTY SNEAKY.

CHAINED TO LIFE AND DEATH

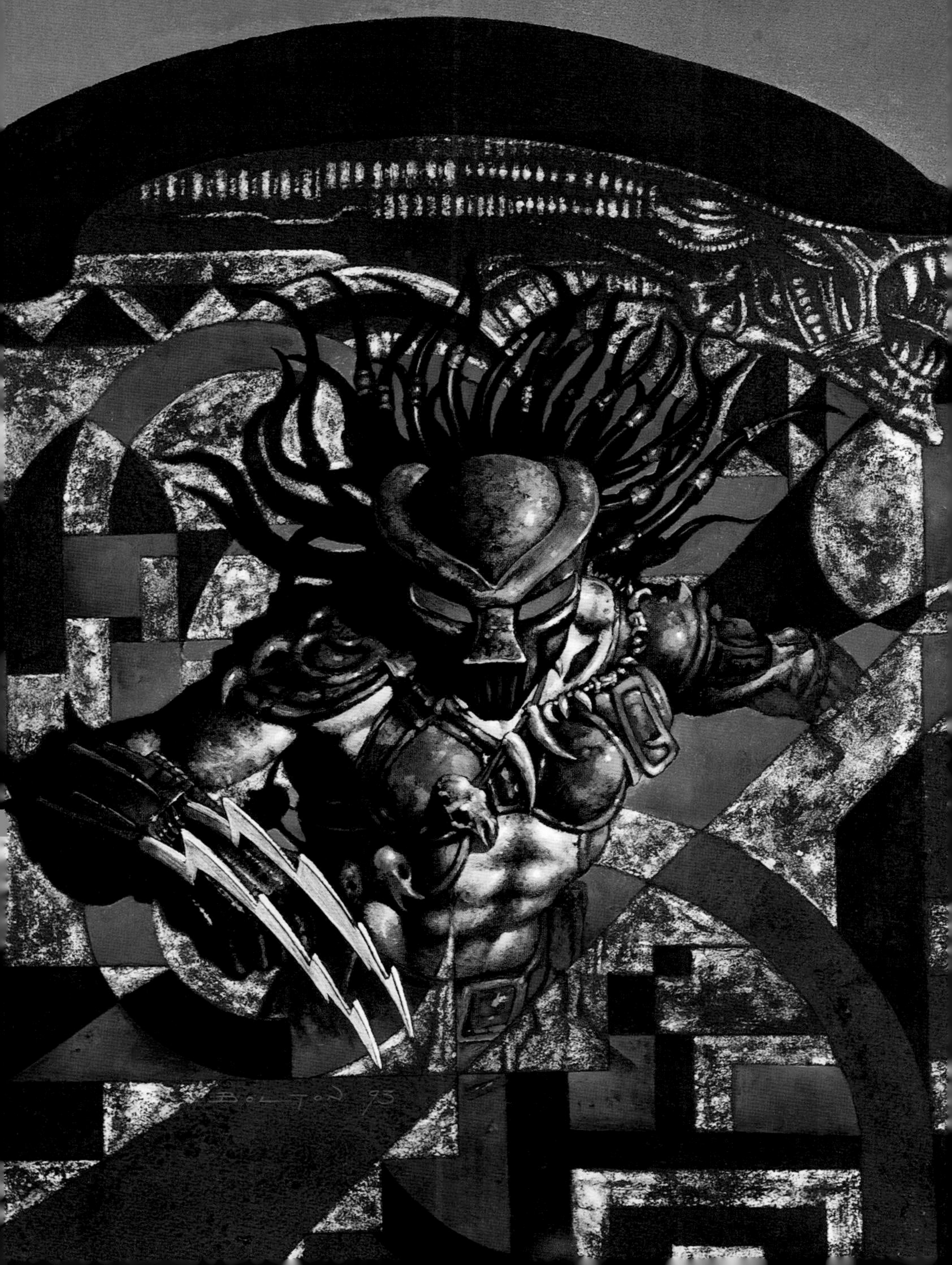

script
MARK SCHULTZ

art
TOM BIONDOLILLO

colors
LEE LOUGHRIDGE

lettering
CLEM ROBINS

title illustration
JOHN BOLTON

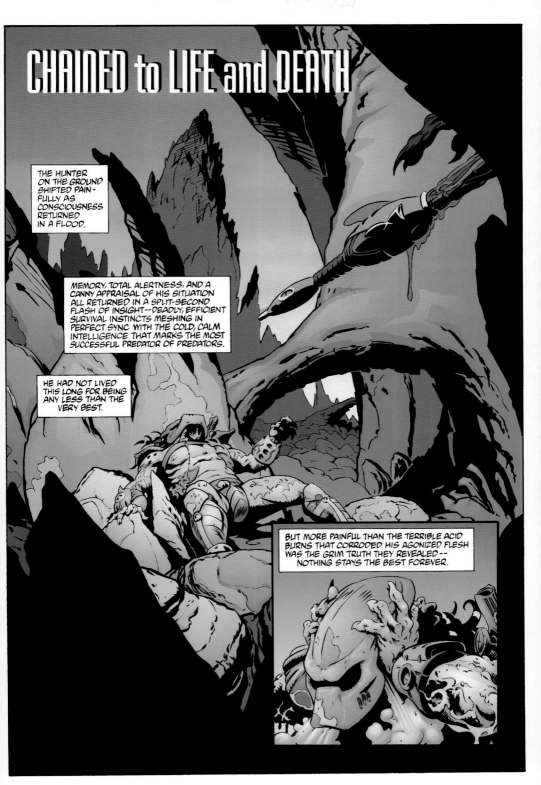

CHAINED to LIFE and DEATH

THE HUNTER ON THE GROUND SHIFTED PAINFULLY AS CONSCIOUSNESS RETURNED IN A FLOOD.

MEMORY, TOTAL ALERTNESS, AND A CANNY APPRAISAL OF HIS SITUATION ALL RETURNED IN A SPLIT-SECOND FLASH OF INSIGHT--DEADLY, EFFICIENT SURVIVAL INSTINCTS MESHING IN PERFECT SYNC WITH THE COLD, CALM INTELLIGENCE THAT MARKS THE MOST SUCCESSFUL PREDATOR OF PREDATORS.

HE HAD NOT LIVED THIS LONG FOR BEING ANY LESS THAN THE VERY BEST.

BUT MORE PAINFUL THAN THE TERRIBLE ACID BURNS THAT CORRODED HIS AGONIZED FLESH WAS THE GRIM TRUTH THEY REVEALED-- NOTHING STAYS THE BEST FOREVER.

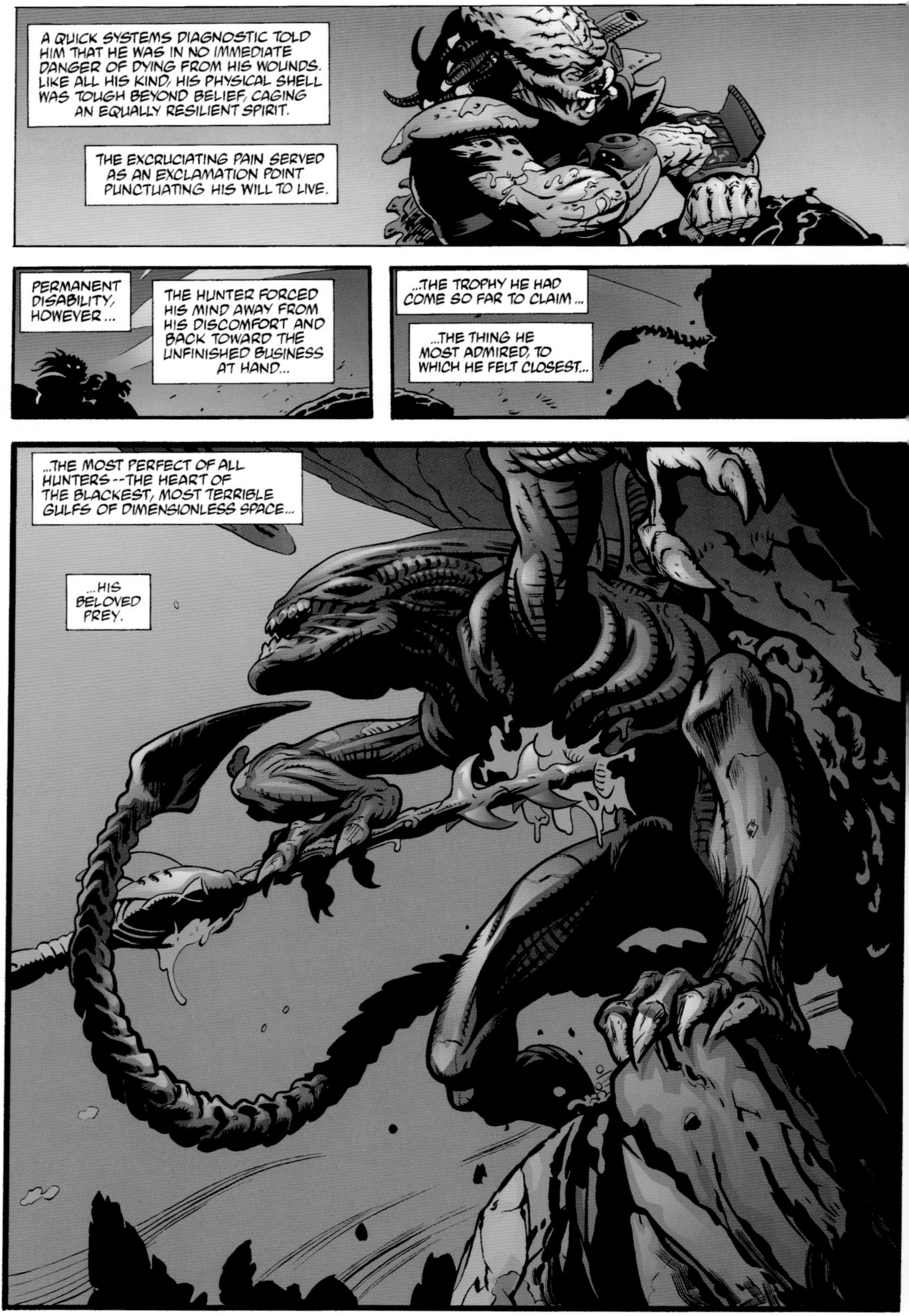
A QUICK SYSTEMS DIAGNOSTIC TOLD HIM THAT HE WAS IN NO IMMEDIATE DANGER OF DYING FROM HIS WOUNDS. LIKE ALL HIS KIND, HIS PHYSICAL SHELL WAS TOUGH BEYOND BELIEF, CAGING AN EQUALLY RESILIENT SPIRIT.
THE EXCRUCIATING PAIN SERVED AS AN EXCLAMATION POINT PUNCTUATING HIS WILL TO LIVE.
PERMANENT DISABILITY, HOWEVER...
THE HUNTER FORCED HIS MIND AWAY FROM HIS DISCOMFORT AND BACK TOWARD THE UNFINISHED BUSINESS AT HAND...
...THE TROPHY HE HAD COME SO FAR TO CLAIM...
...THE THING HE MOST ADMIRED, TO WHICH HE FELT CLOSEST...
...THE MOST PERFECT OF ALL HUNTERS--THE HEART OF THE BLACKEST, MOST TERRIBLE GULFS OF DIMENSIONLESS SPACE...
...HIS BELOVED PREY.

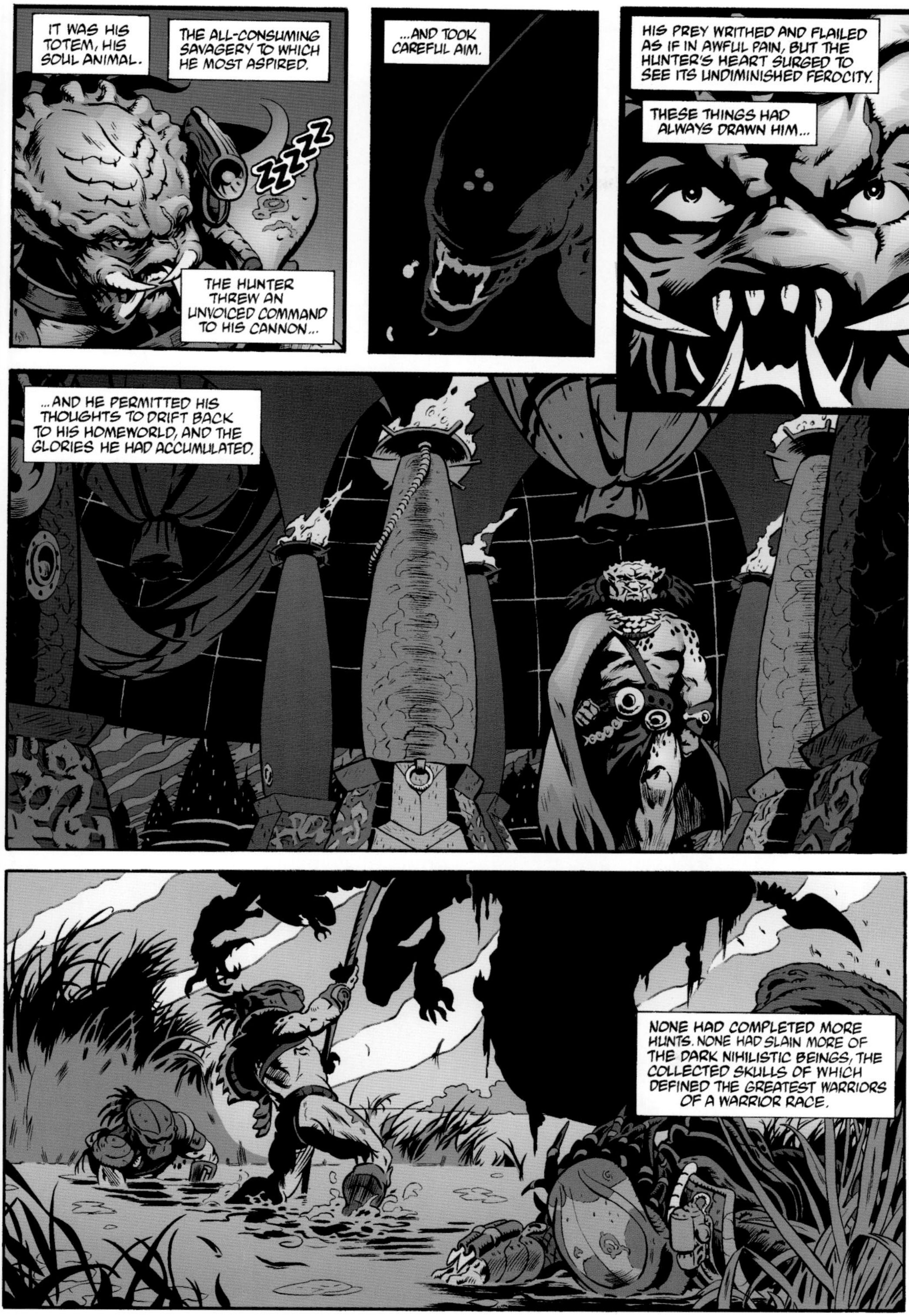
IT WAS HIS TOTEM, HIS SOUL ANIMAL.
THE ALL-CONSUMING SAVAGERY TO WHICH HE MOST ASPIRED.
ZZZZZ
THE HUNTER THREW AN UNVOICED COMMAND TO HIS CANNON...
...AND TOOK CAREFUL AIM.
HIS PREY WRITHED AND FLAILED AS IF IN AWFUL PAIN, BUT THE HUNTER'S HEART SURGED TO SEE ITS UNDIMINISHED FEROCITY.
THESE THINGS HAD ALWAYS DRAWN HIM...
...AND HE PERMITTED HIS THOUGHTS TO DRIFT BACK TO HIS HOMEWORLD, AND THE GLORIES HE HAD ACCUMULATED.
NONE HAD COMPLETED MORE HUNTS. NONE HAD SLAIN MORE OF THE DARK NIHILISTIC BEINGS, THE COLLECTED SKULLS OF WHICH DEFINED THE GREATEST WARRIORS OF A WARRIOR RACE.

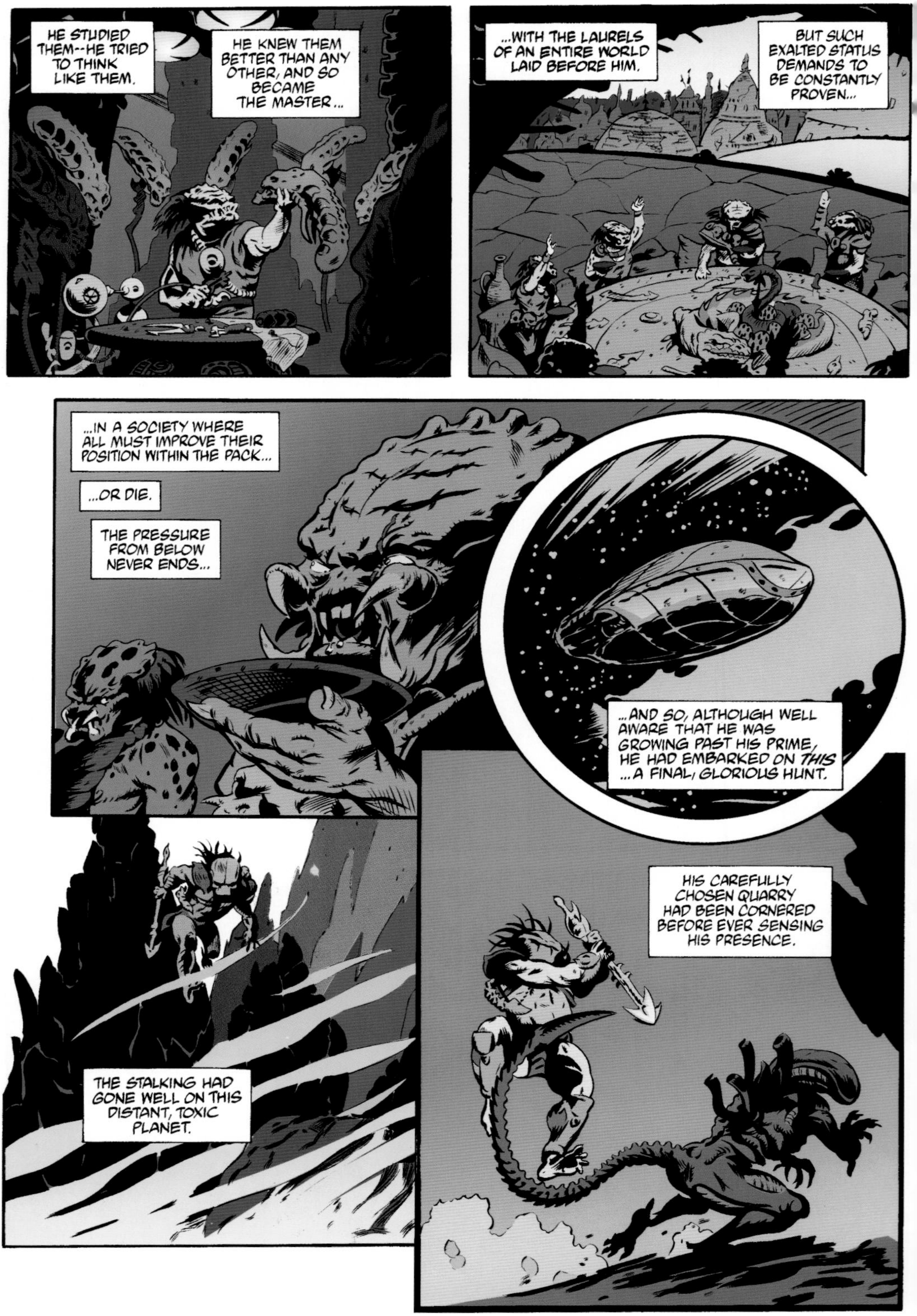
HE STUDIED THEM--HE TRIED TO THINK LIKE THEM.
HE KNEW THEM BETTER THAN ANY OTHER, AND SO BECAME THE MASTER...
...WITH THE LAURELS OF AN ENTIRE WORLD LAID BEFORE HIM.
BUT SUCH EXALTED STATUS DEMANDS TO BE CONSTANTLY PROVEN...
...IN A SOCIETY WHERE ALL MUST IMPROVE THEIR POSITION WITHIN THE PACK...
...OR DIE.
THE PRESSURE FROM BELOW NEVER ENDS...
...AND SO, ALTHOUGH WELL AWARE THAT HE WAS GROWING PAST HIS PRIME, HE HAD EMBARKED ON *THIS* ...A FINAL, GLORIOUS HUNT.
THE STALKING HAD GONE WELL ON THIS DISTANT, TOXIC PLANET.
HIS CAREFULLY CHOSEN QUARRY HAD BEEN CORNERED BEFORE EVER SENSING HIS PRESENCE.

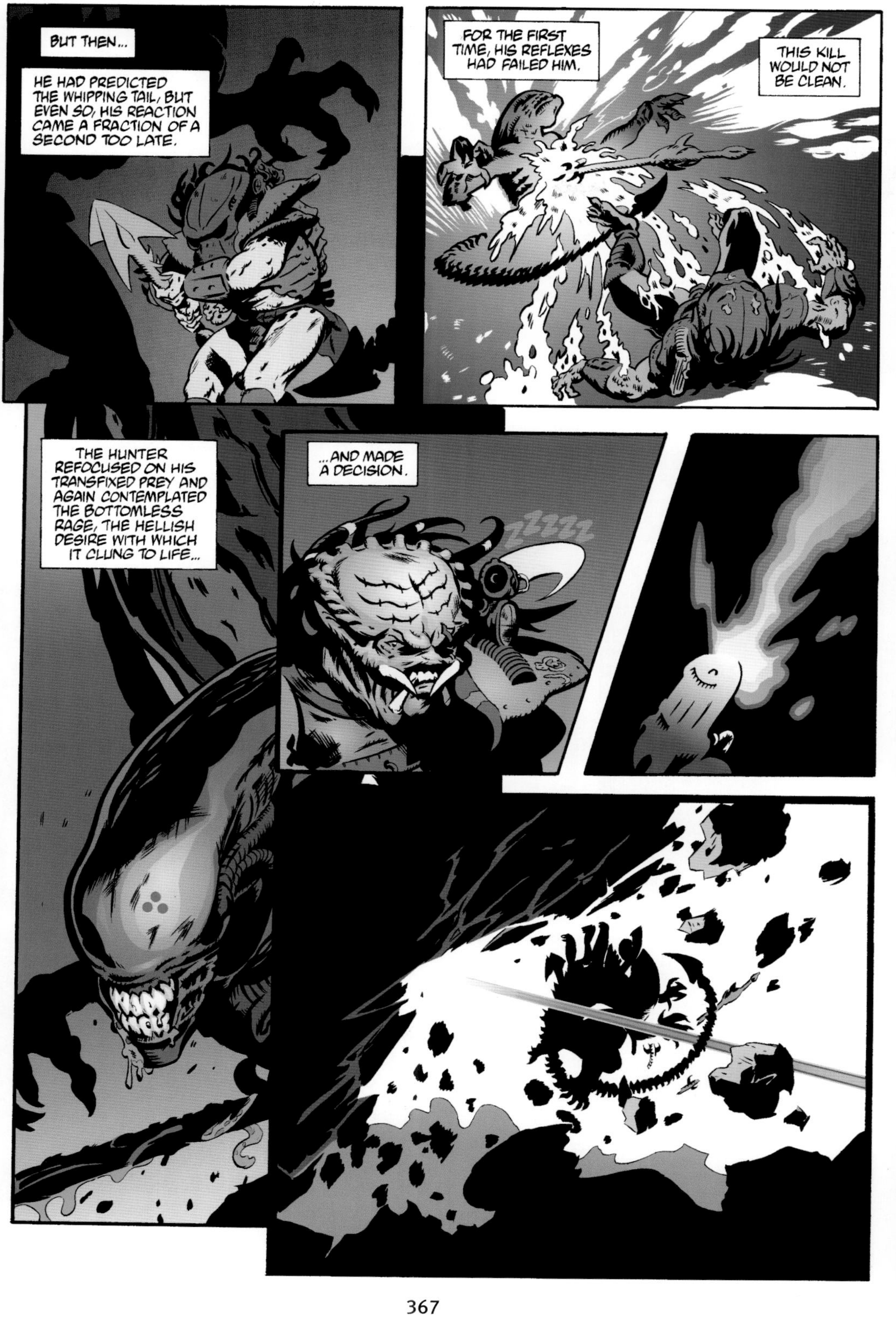
BUT THEN...
HE HAD PREDICTED THE WHIPPING TAIL, BUT EVEN SO, HIS REACTION CAME A FRACTION OF A SECOND TOO LATE.
FOR THE FIRST TIME, HIS REFLEXES HAD FAILED HIM.
THIS KILL WOULD NOT BE CLEAN.
THE HUNTER REFOCUSED ON HIS TRANSFIXED PREY AND AGAIN CONTEMPLATED THE BOTTOMLESS RAGE, THE HELLISH DESIRE WITH WHICH IT CLUNG TO LIFE...
...AND MADE A DECISION.
ZZZZZ

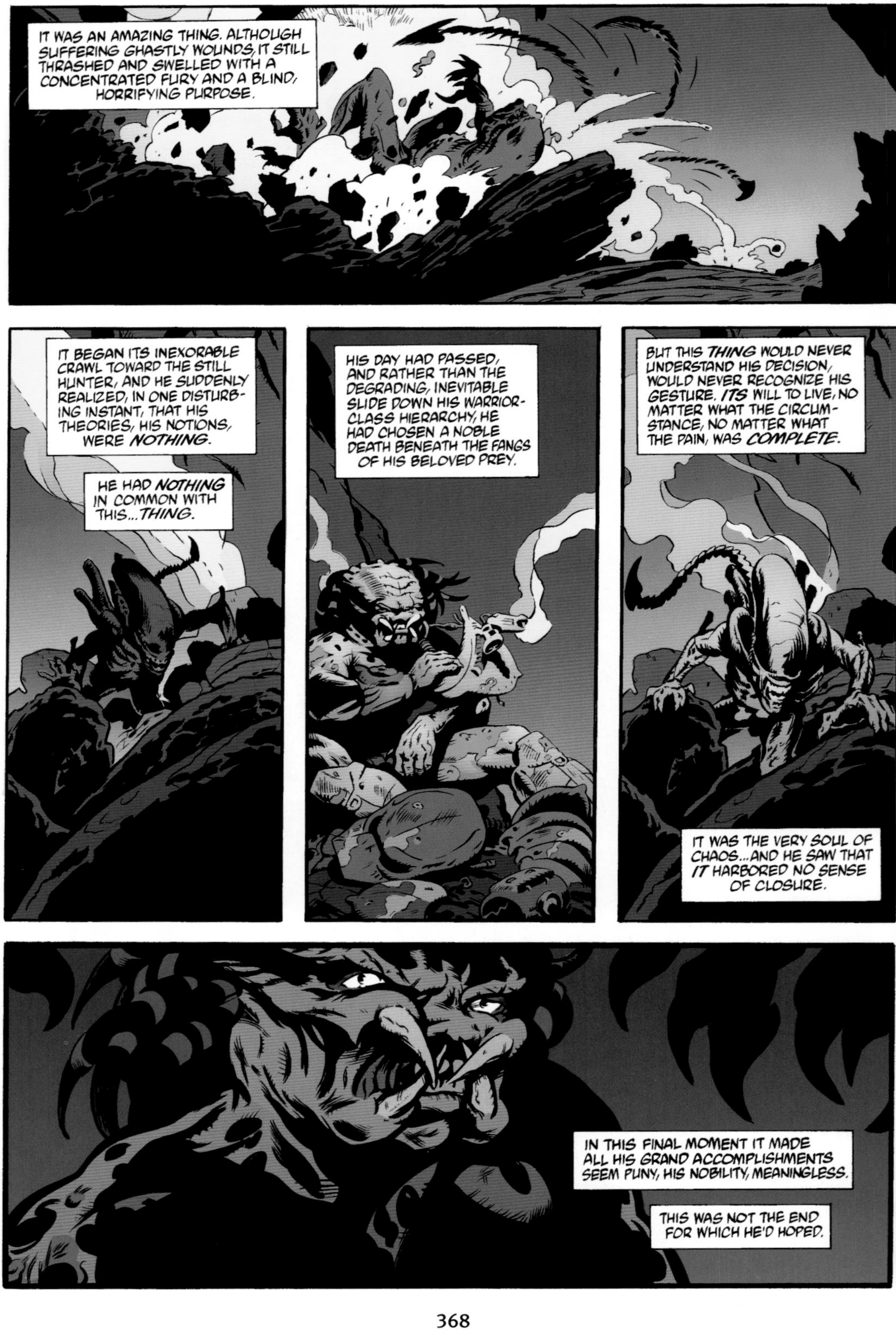
IT WAS AN AMAZING THING. ALTHOUGH SUFFERING GHASTLY WOUNDS, IT STILL THRASHED AND SWELLED WITH A CONCENTRATED FURY AND A BLIND, HORRIFYING PURPOSE.
IT BEGAN ITS INEXORABLE CRAWL TOWARD THE STILL HUNTER, AND HE SUDDENLY REALIZED, IN ONE DISTURBING INSTANT, THAT HIS THEORIES, HIS NOTIONS, WERE NOTHING.
HE HAD NOTHING IN COMMON WITH THIS...THING.
HIS DAY HAD PASSED, AND RATHER THAN THE DEGRADING, INEVITABLE SLIDE DOWN HIS WARRIOR-CLASS HIERARCHY, HE HAD CHOSEN A NOBLE DEATH BENEATH THE FANGS OF HIS BELOVED PREY.
BUT THIS THING WOULD NEVER UNDERSTAND HIS DECISION, WOULD NEVER RECOGNIZE HIS GESTURE. ITS WILL TO LIVE, NO MATTER WHAT THE CIRCUMSTANCE, NO MATTER WHAT THE PAIN, WAS COMPLETE.
IT WAS THE VERY SOUL OF CHAOS...AND HE SAW THAT IT HARBORED NO SENSE OF CLOSURE.
IN THIS FINAL MOMENT IT MADE ALL HIS GRAND ACCOMPLISHMENTS SEEM PUNY, HIS NOBILITY, MEANINGLESS.
THIS WAS NOT THE END FOR WHICH HE'D HOPED.

XENOGENESIS

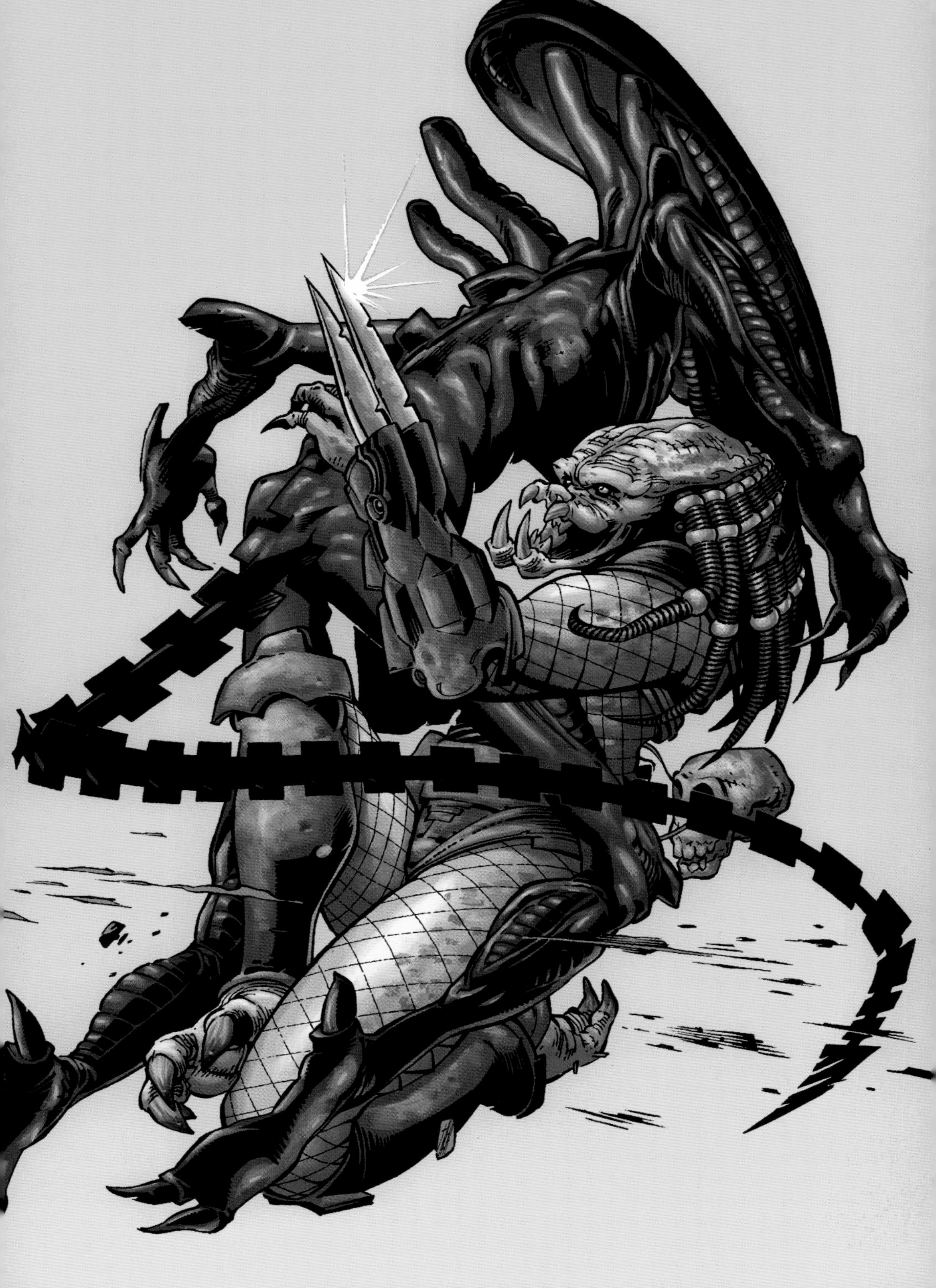

script
ANDI WATSON

pencils
MEL RUBI

inks
MARK LIPKA
NORMAN LEE

colors
DAVE STEWART

lettering
PAT BROSSEAU

title illustration
HUGHES LABIANO with **DAVE STEWART**

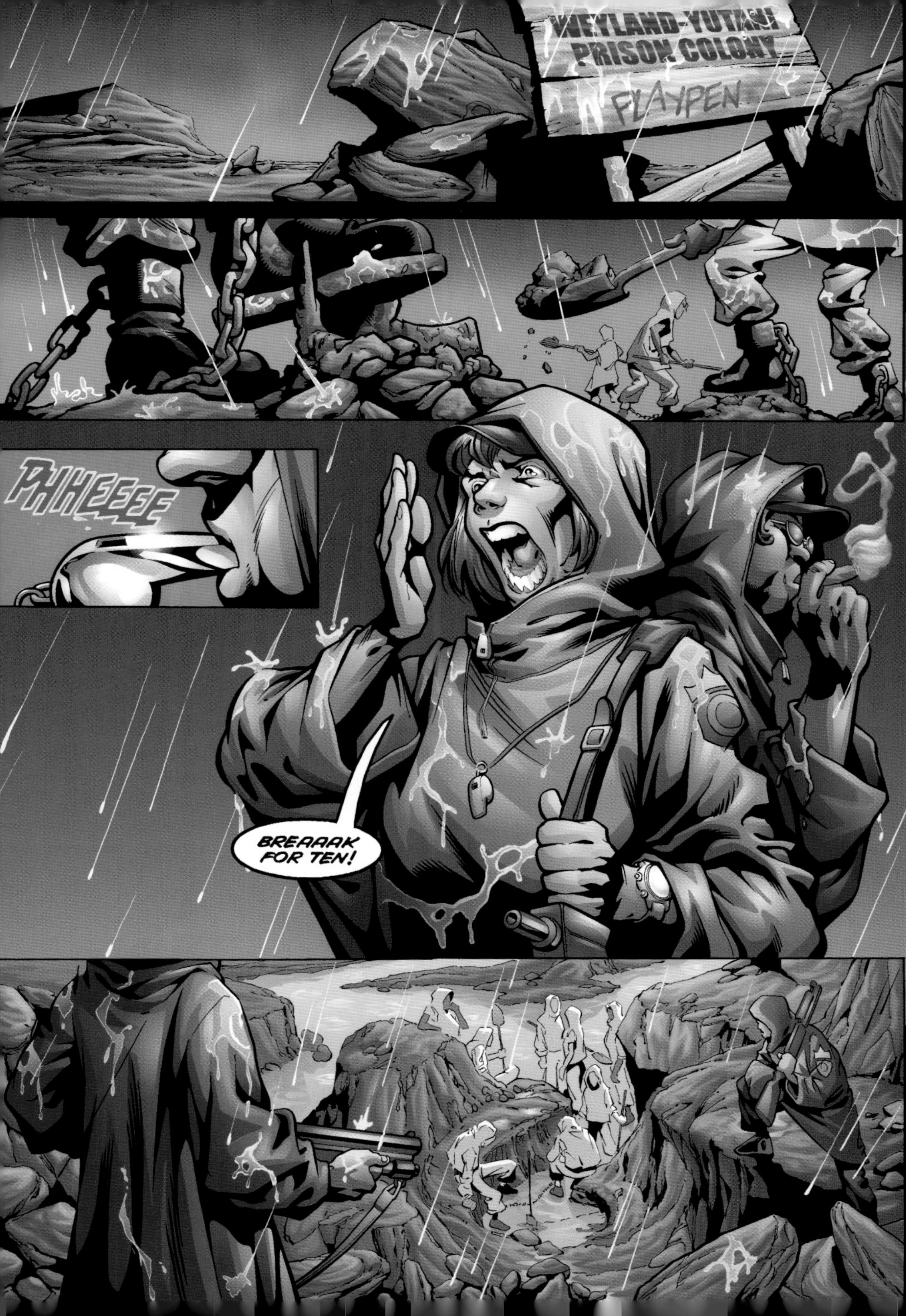
WEYLAND-YUTANI
PRISON COLONY
FLAYPEN
PHHEEEE
BREAAAK FOR TEN!

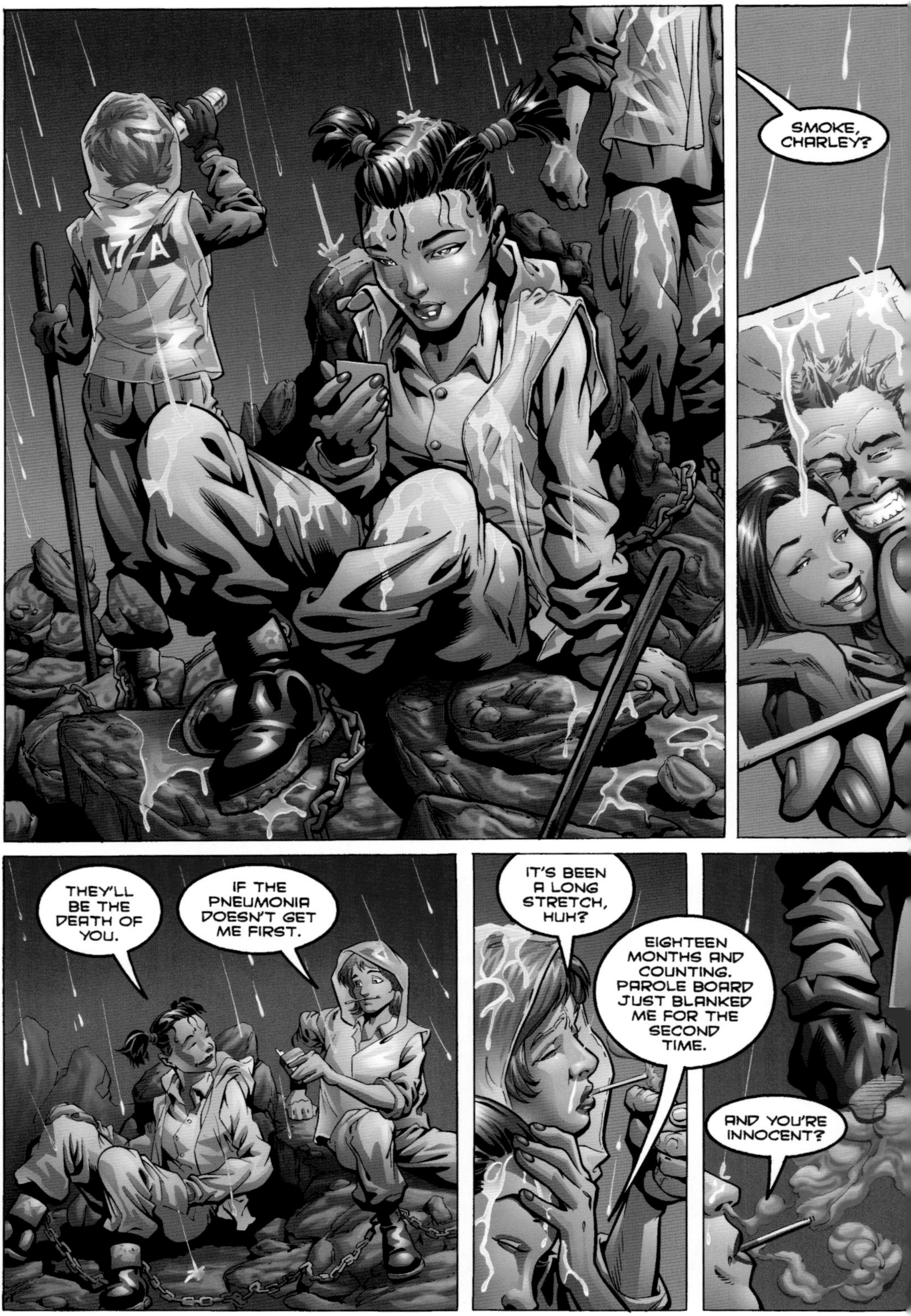
17-A
SMOKE, CHARLEY?
THEY'LL BE THE DEATH OF YOU.
IF THE PNEUMONIA DOESN'T GET ME FIRST.
IT'S BEEN A LONG STRETCH, HUH?
EIGHTEEN MONTHS AND COUNTING. PAROLE BOARD JUST BLANKED ME FOR THE SECOND TIME.
AND YOU'RE INNOCENT?

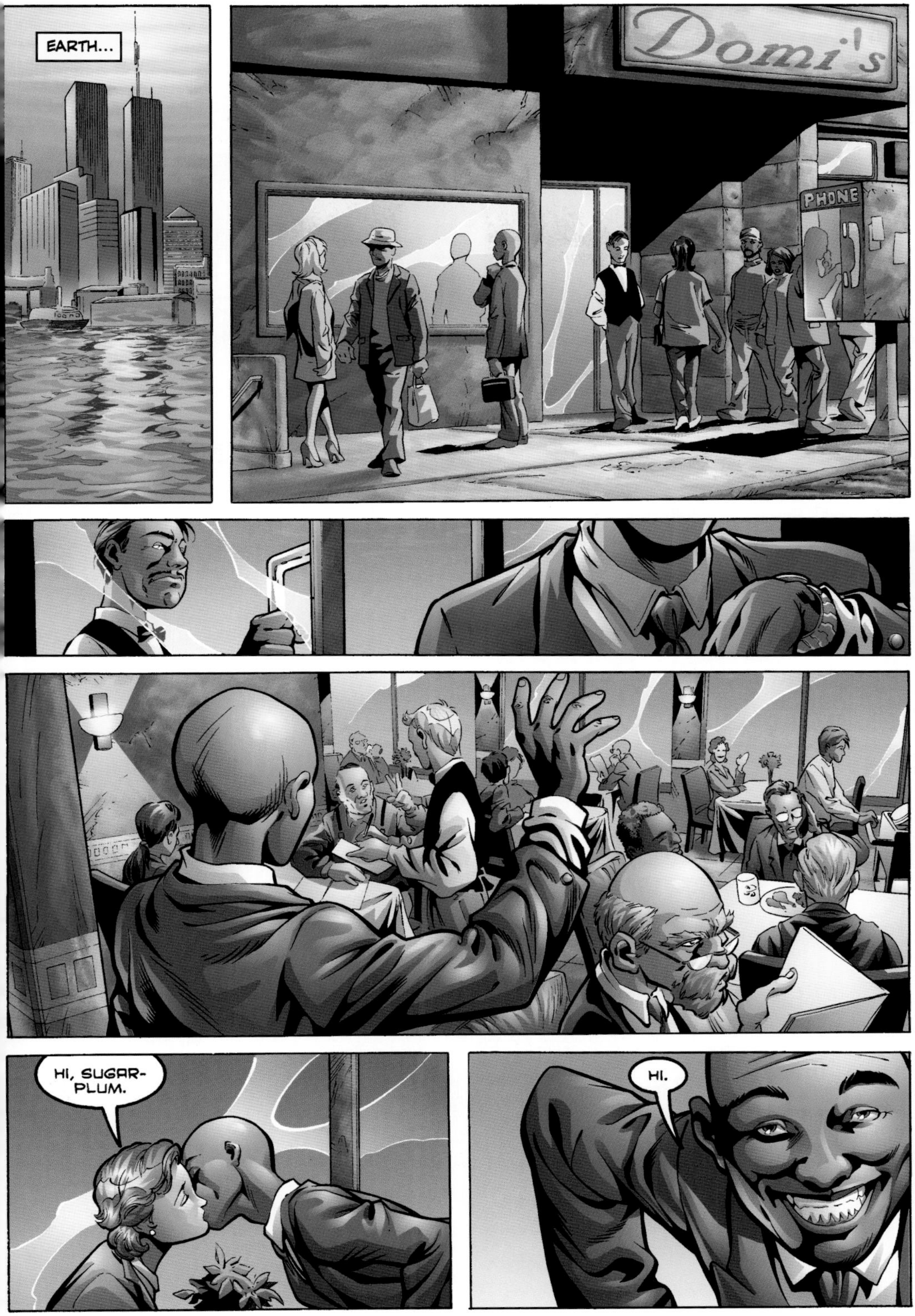
EARTH...
Domi's
PHONE
HI, SUGAR-PLUM.
HI.

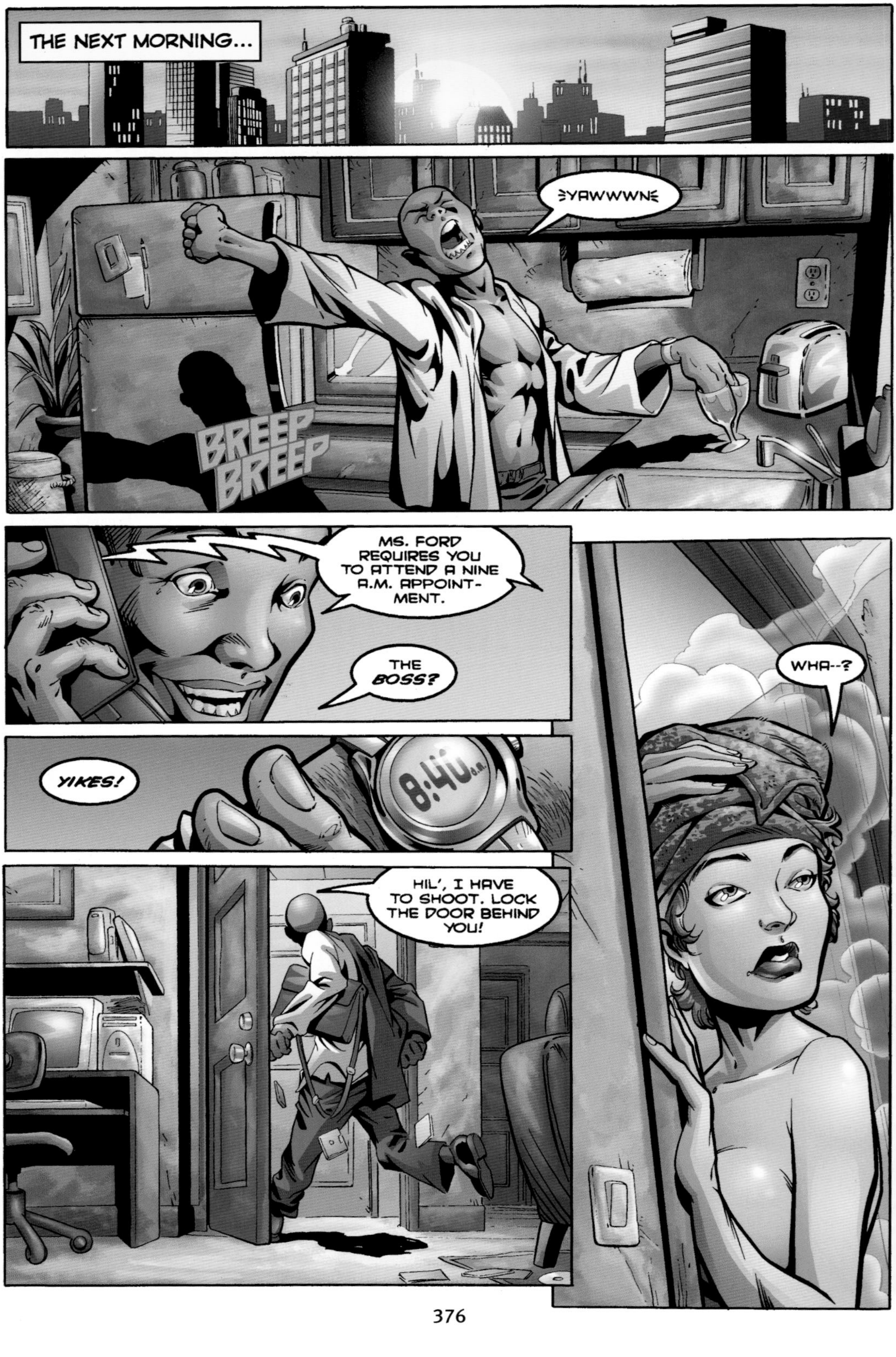
THE NEXT MORNING...
YAWWWN
BREEP BREEP
MS. FORD REQUIRES YOU TO ATTEND A NINE A.M. APPOINT-MENT.
THE BOSS?
YIKES!
8:40
WHA--?
HIL', I HAVE TO SHOOT. LOCK THE DOOR BEHIND YOU!

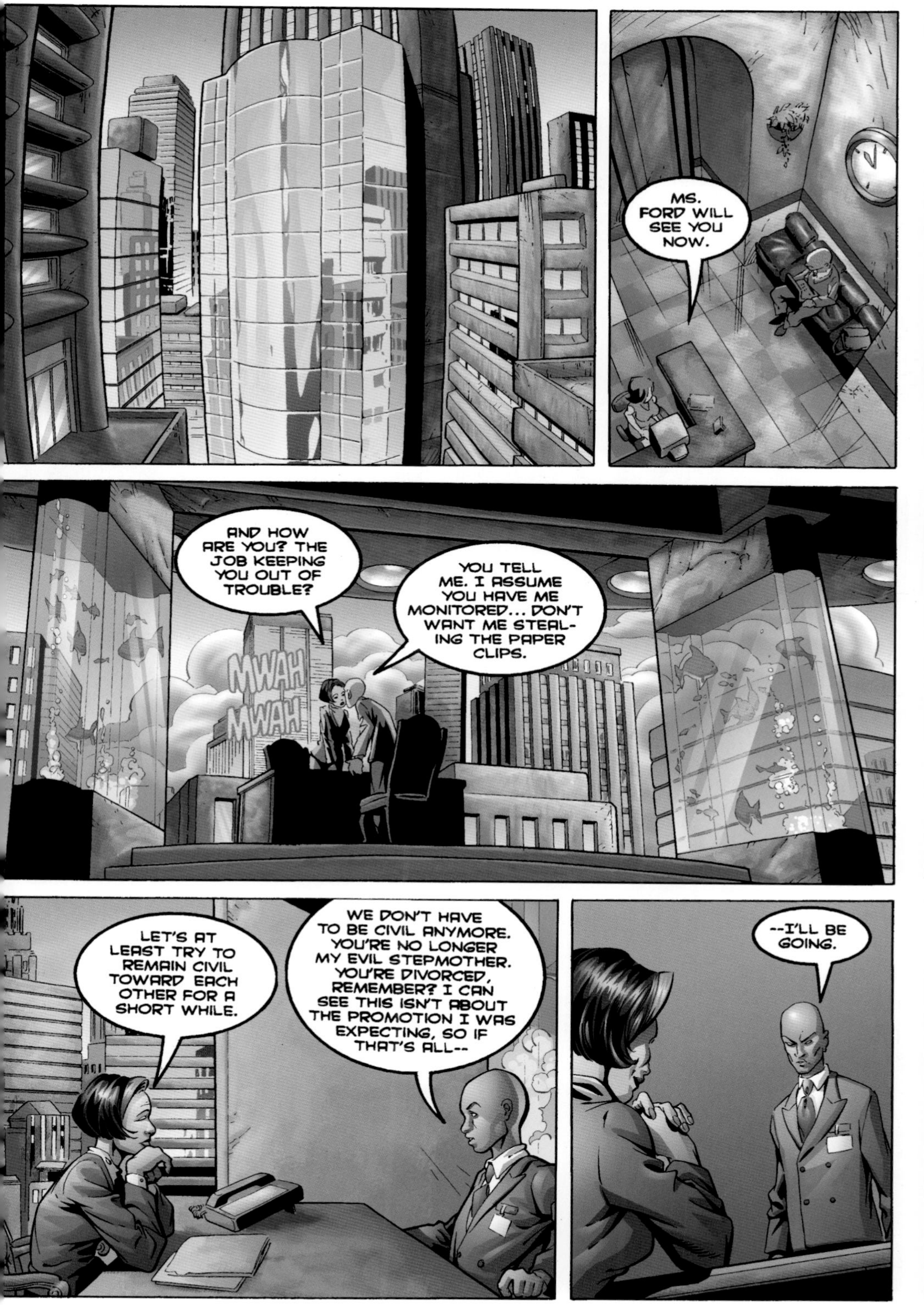
MS. FORD WILL SEE YOU NOW.
AND HOW ARE YOU? THE JOB KEEPING YOU OUT OF TROUBLE?
MWAH MWAH
YOU TELL ME. I ASSUME YOU HAVE ME MONITORED... DON'T WANT ME STEALING THE PAPER CLIPS.
LET'S AT LEAST TRY TO REMAIN CIVIL TOWARD EACH OTHER FOR A SHORT WHILE.
WE DON'T HAVE TO BE CIVIL ANYMORE. YOU'RE NO LONGER MY EVIL STEPMOTHER. YOU'RE DIVORCED, REMEMBER? I CAN SEE THIS ISN'T ABOUT THE PROMOTION I WAS EXPECTING, SO IF THAT'S ALL--
--I'LL BE GOING.

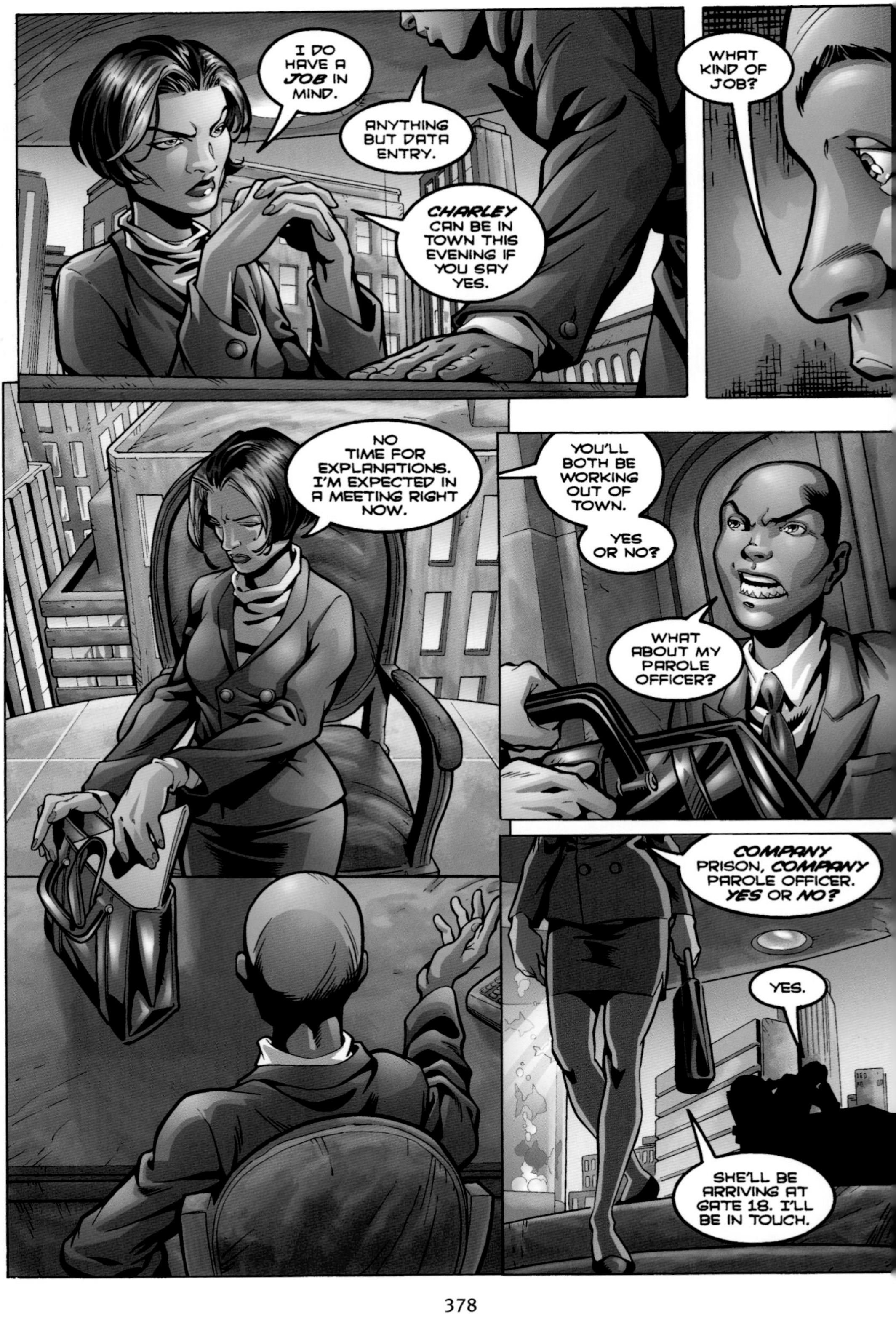
I DO HAVE A JOB IN MIND.
ANYTHING BUT DATA ENTRY.
CHARLEY CAN BE IN TOWN THIS EVENING IF YOU SAY YES.
WHAT KIND OF JOB?
NO TIME FOR EXPLANATIONS. I'M EXPECTED IN A MEETING RIGHT NOW.
YOU'LL BOTH BE WORKING OUT OF TOWN.
YES OR NO?
WHAT ABOUT MY PAROLE OFFICER?
COMPANY PRISON, COMPANY PAROLE OFFICER. YES OR NO?
YES.
SHE'LL BE ARRIVING AT GATE 18. I'LL BE IN TOUCH.

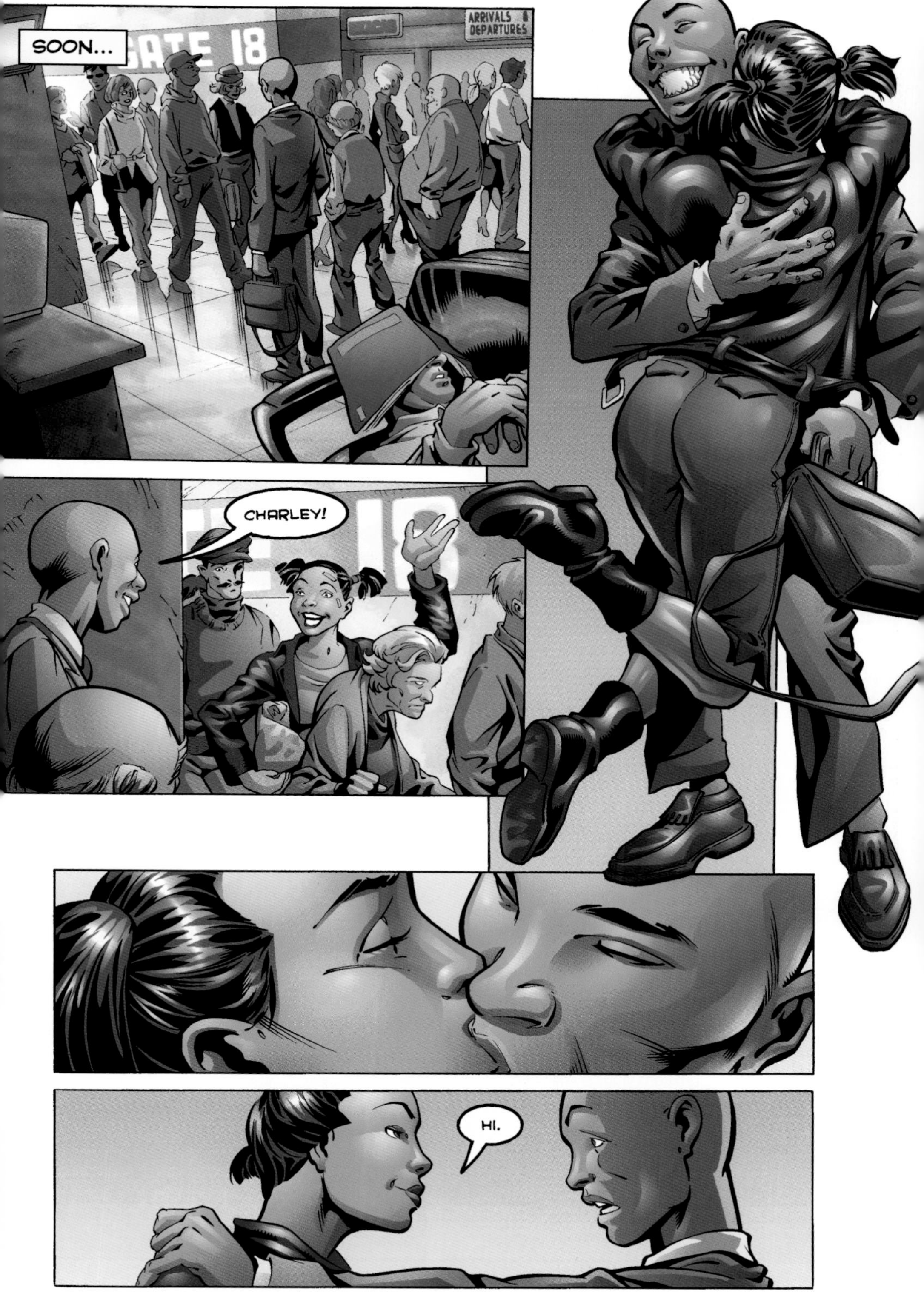
SOON...
GATE 18
ARRIVALS & DEPARTURES
CHARLEY!
HI.

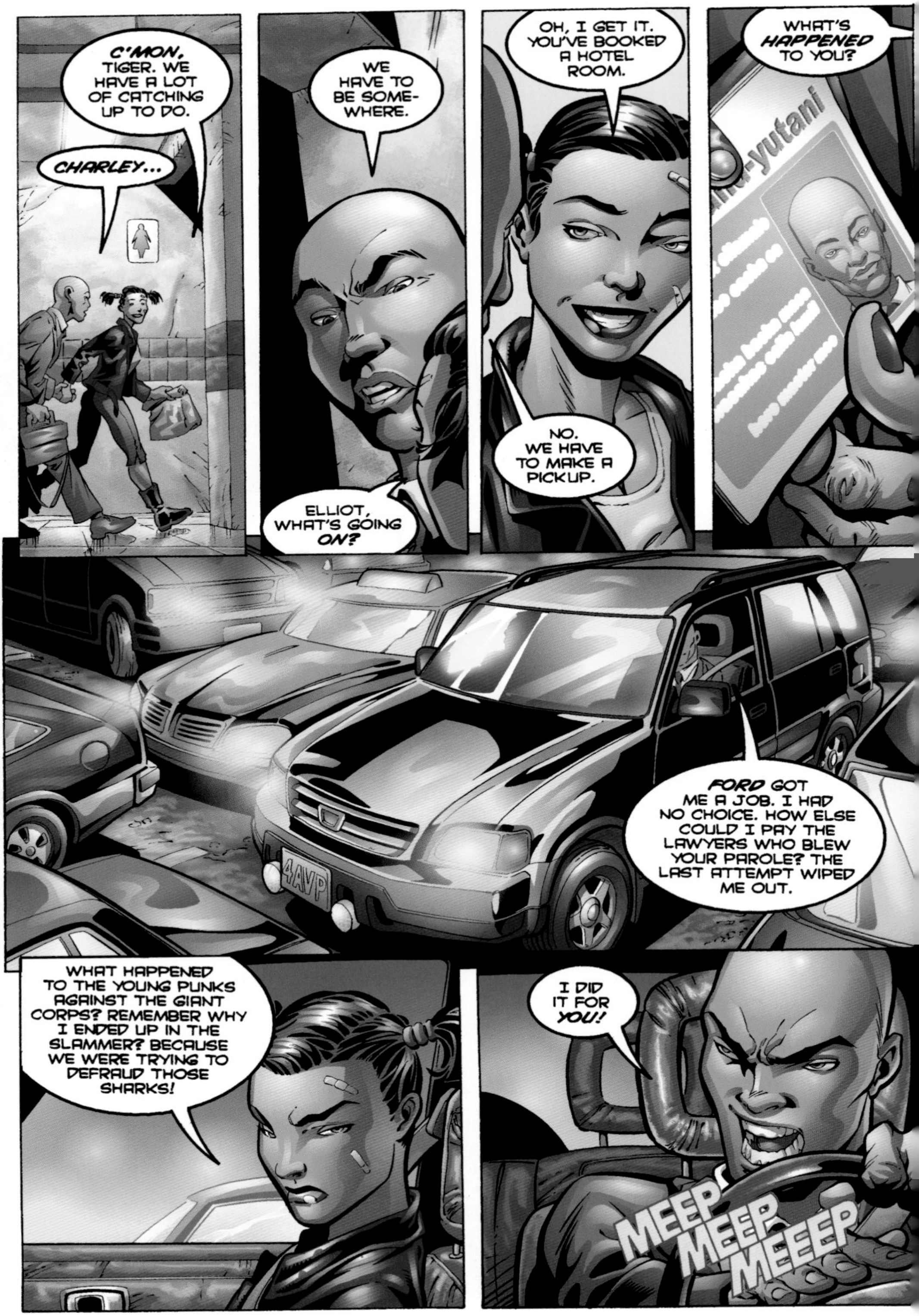
C'MON, TIGER. WE HAVE A LOT OF CATCHING UP TO DO.
CHARLEY...
WE HAVE TO BE SOME-WHERE.
ELLIOT, WHAT'S GOING ON?
OH, I GET IT. YOU'VE BOOKED A HOTEL ROOM.
NO. WE HAVE TO MAKE A PICKUP.
WHAT'S HAPPENED TO YOU?
-yutani
FORD GOT ME A JOB. I HAD NO CHOICE. HOW ELSE COULD I PAY THE LAWYERS WHO BLEW YOUR PAROLE? THE LAST ATTEMPT WIPED ME OUT.
4AVP
WHAT HAPPENED TO THE YOUNG PUNKS AGAINST THE GIANT CORPS? REMEMBER WHY I ENDED UP IN THE SLAMMER? BECAUSE WE WERE TRYING TO DEFRAUD THOSE SHARKS!
I DID IT FOR YOU!
MEEP MEEP MEEEP

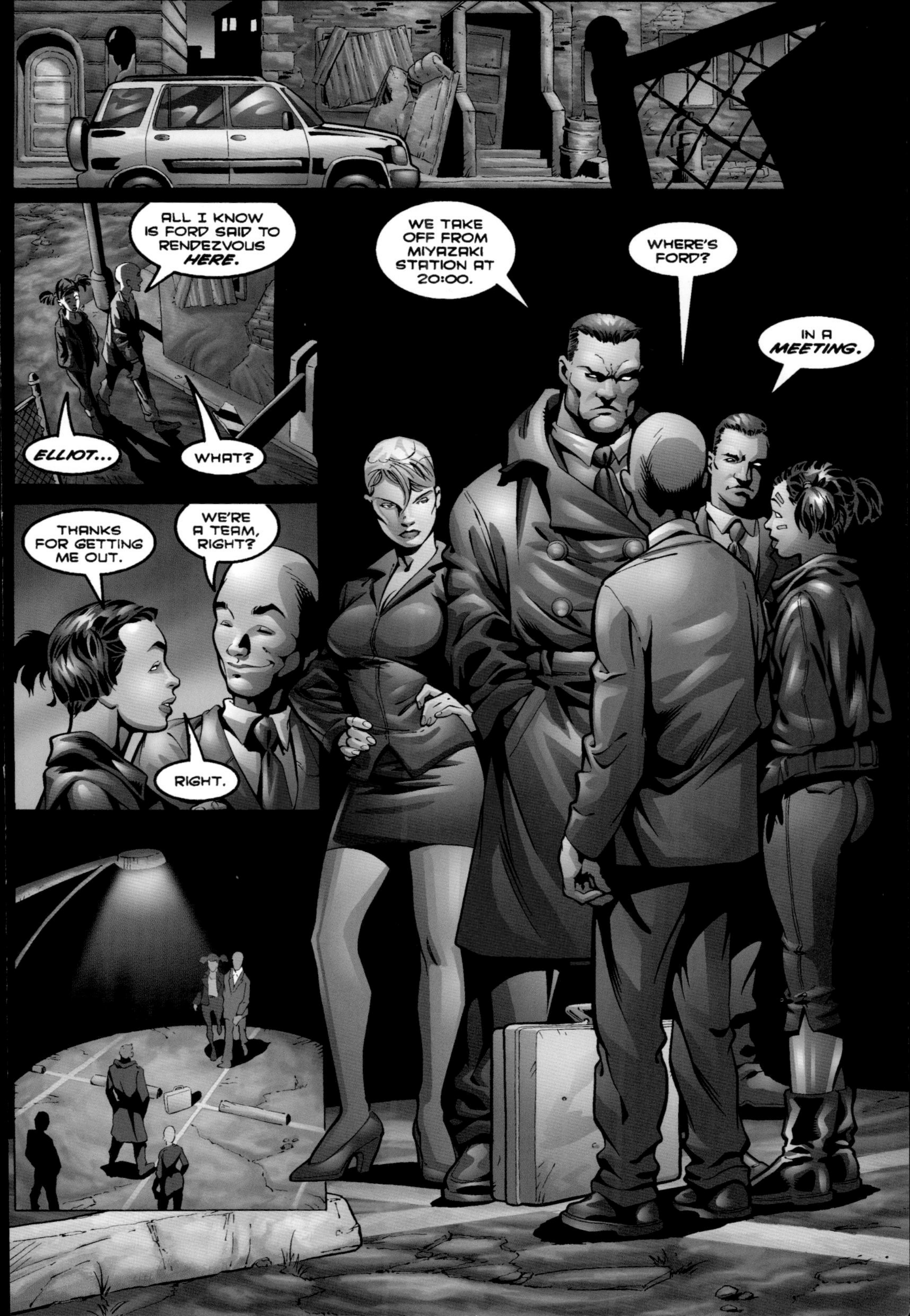

ALL I KNOW IS FORD SAID TO RENDEZVOUS HERE.
ELLIOT...
WHAT?
THANKS FOR GETTING ME OUT.
WE'RE A TEAM, RIGHT?
RIGHT.
WE TAKE OFF FROM MIYAZAKI STATION AT 20:00.
WHERE'S FORD?
IN A MEETING.

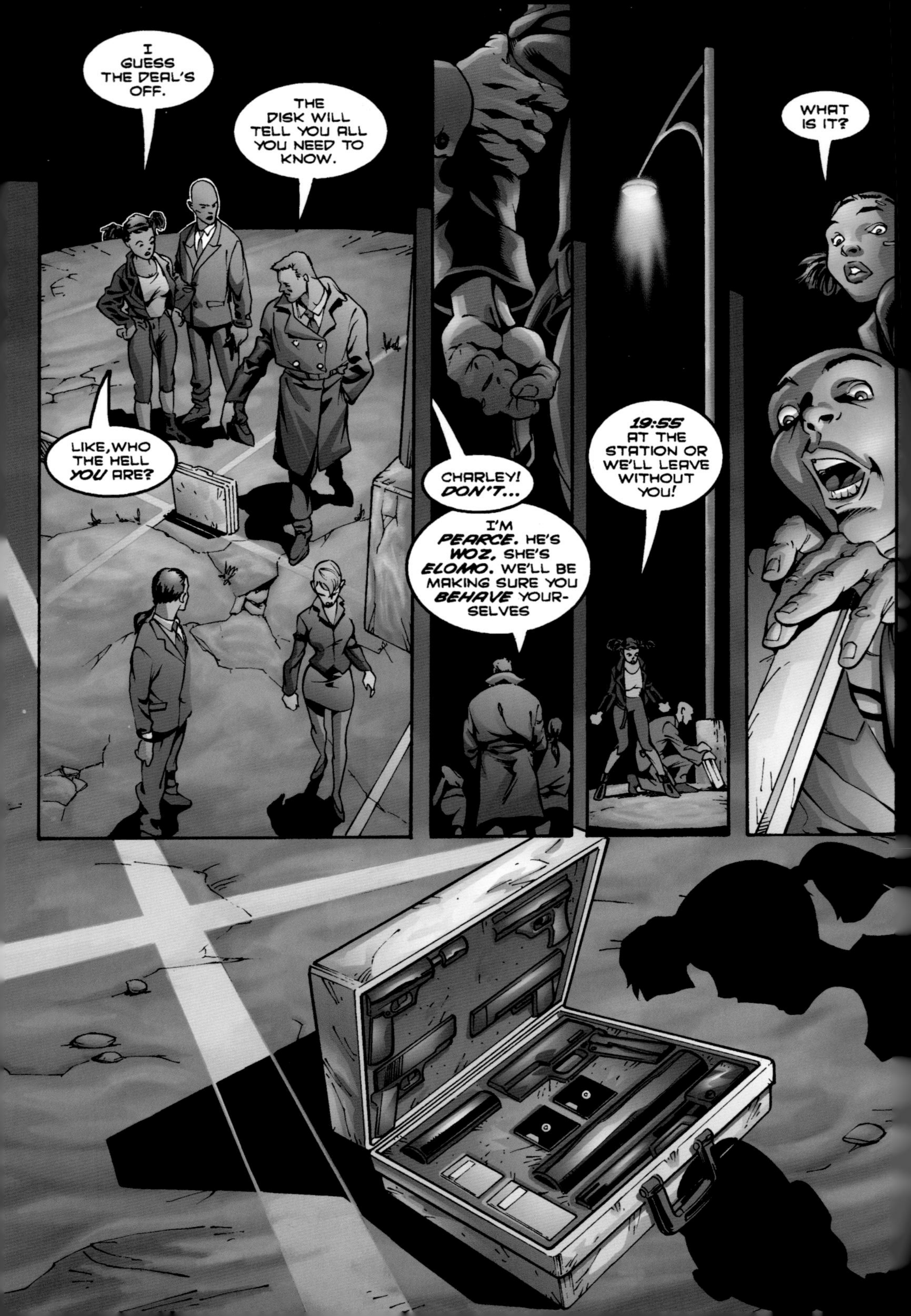
I GUESS THE DEAL'S OFF.
THE DISK WILL TELL YOU ALL YOU NEED TO KNOW.
LIKE, WHO THE HELL YOU ARE?
CHARLEY! DON'T...
I'M PEARCE. HE'S WOZ. SHE'S ELOMO. WE'LL BE MAKING SURE YOU BEHAVE YOURSELVES
19:55 AT THE STATION OR WE'LL LEAVE WITHOUT YOU!
WHAT IS IT?

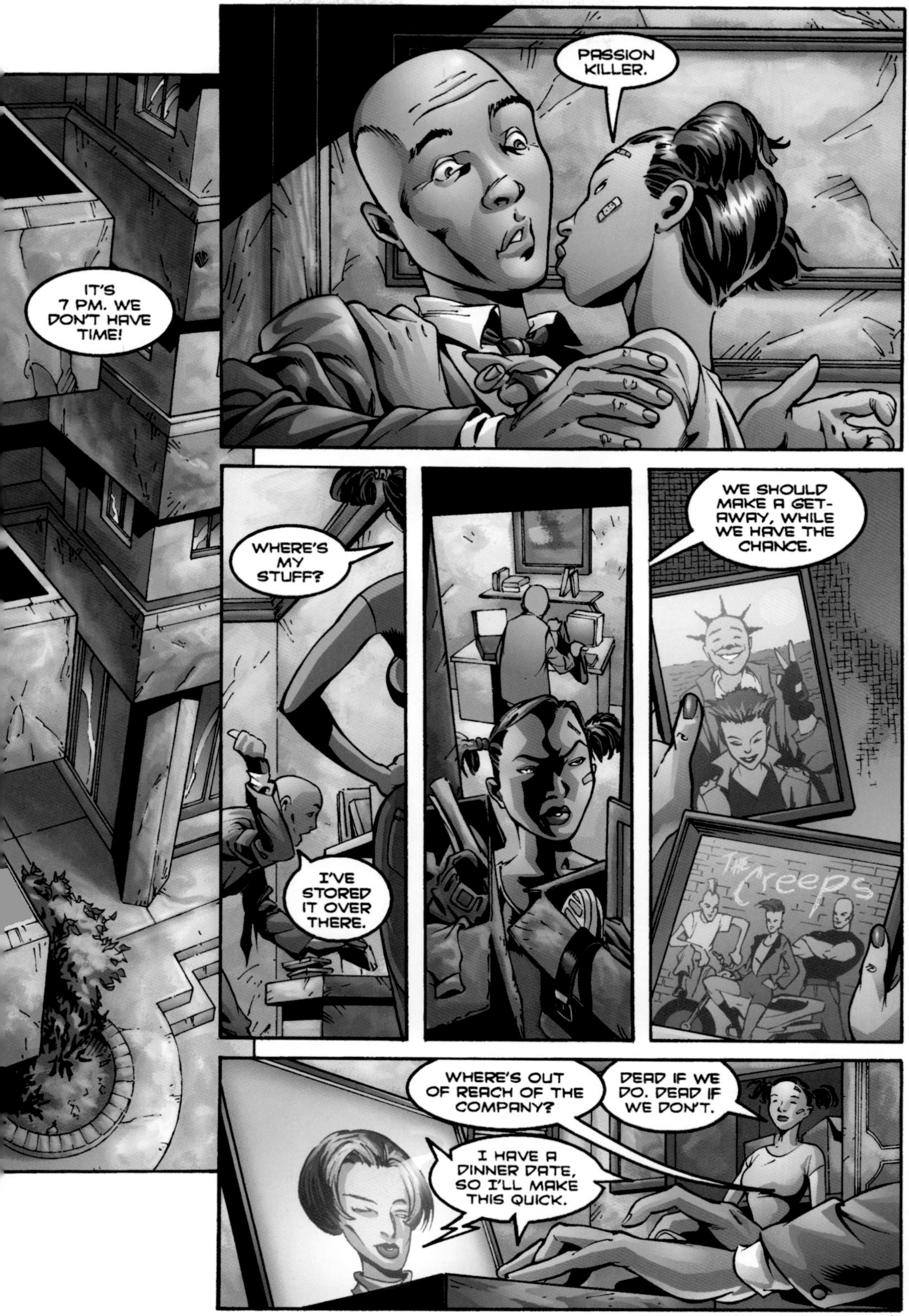
IT'S 7 PM. WE DON'T HAVE TIME!
PASSION KILLER.
WHERE'S MY STUFF?
I'VE STORED IT OVER THERE.
WE SHOULD MAKE A GET-AWAY, WHILE WE HAVE THE CHANCE.
The Creeps
WHERE'S OUT OF REACH OF THE COMPANY?
DEAD IF WE DO. DEAD IF WE DON'T.
I HAVE A DINNER DATE, SO I'LL MAKE THIS QUICK.

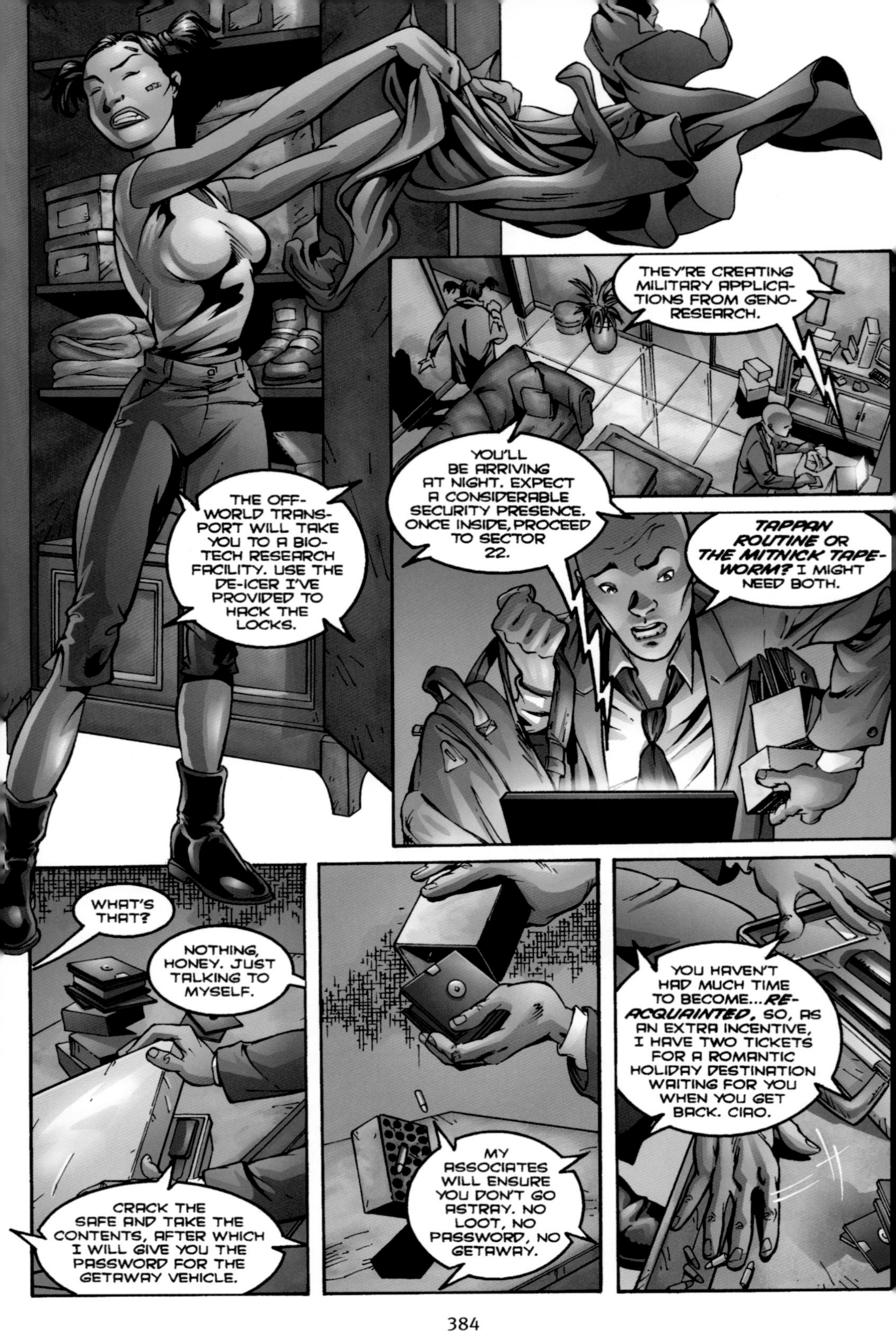
THEY'RE CREATING MILITARY APPLICATIONS FROM GENO-RESEARCH.
THE OFF-WORLD TRANSPORT WILL TAKE YOU TO A BIO-TECH RESEARCH FACILITY. USE THE DE-ICER I'VE PROVIDED TO HACK THE LOCKS.
YOU'LL BE ARRIVING AT NIGHT. EXPECT A CONSIDERABLE SECURITY PRESENCE. ONCE INSIDE, PROCEED TO SECTOR 22.
TAPPAN ROUTINE OR *THE MITNICK TAPE-WORM?* I MIGHT NEED BOTH.
WHAT'S THAT?
NOTHING, HONEY. JUST TALKING TO MYSELF.
CRACK THE SAFE AND TAKE THE CONTENTS, AFTER WHICH I WILL GIVE YOU THE PASSWORD FOR THE GETAWAY VEHICLE.
MY ASSOCIATES WILL ENSURE YOU DON'T GO ASTRAY. NO LOOT, NO PASSWORD, NO GETAWAY.
YOU HAVEN'T HAD MUCH TIME TO BECOME... *RE-ACQUAINTED*, SO, AS AN EXTRA INCENTIVE, I HAVE TWO TICKETS FOR A ROMANTIC HOLIDAY DESTINATION WAITING FOR YOU WHEN YOU GET BACK. CIAO.

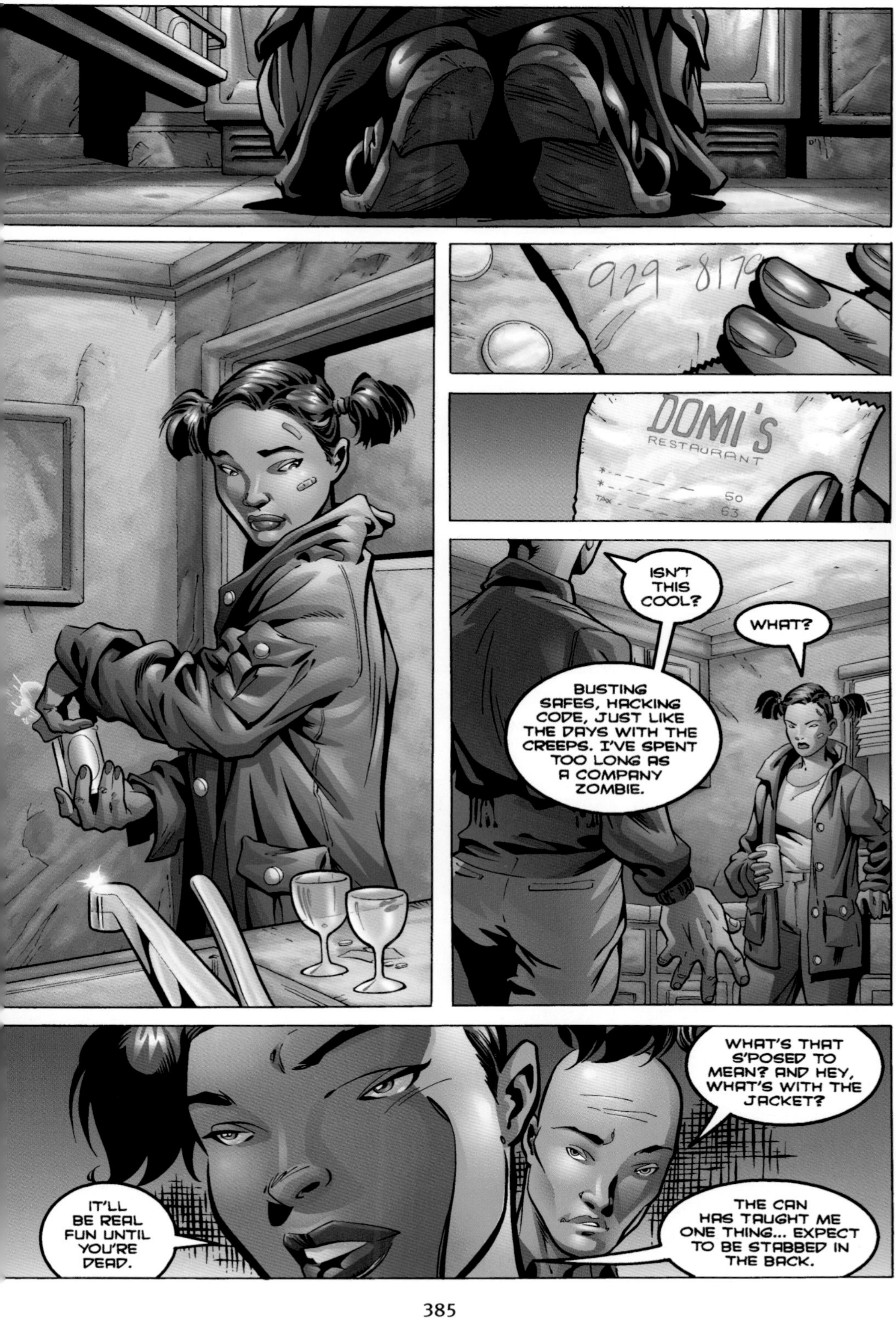
929-8179
DOMI'S
RESTAURANT
TAX
50
63
ISN'T THIS COOL?
BUSTING SAFES, HACKING CODE, JUST LIKE THE DAYS WITH THE CREEPS. I'VE SPENT TOO LONG AS A COMPANY ZOMBIE.
WHAT?
WHAT'S THAT S'POSED TO MEAN? AND HEY, WHAT'S WITH THE JACKET?
IT'LL BE REAL FUN UNTIL YOU'RE DEAD.
THE CAN HAS TAUGHT ME ONE THING... EXPECT TO BE STABBED IN THE BACK.

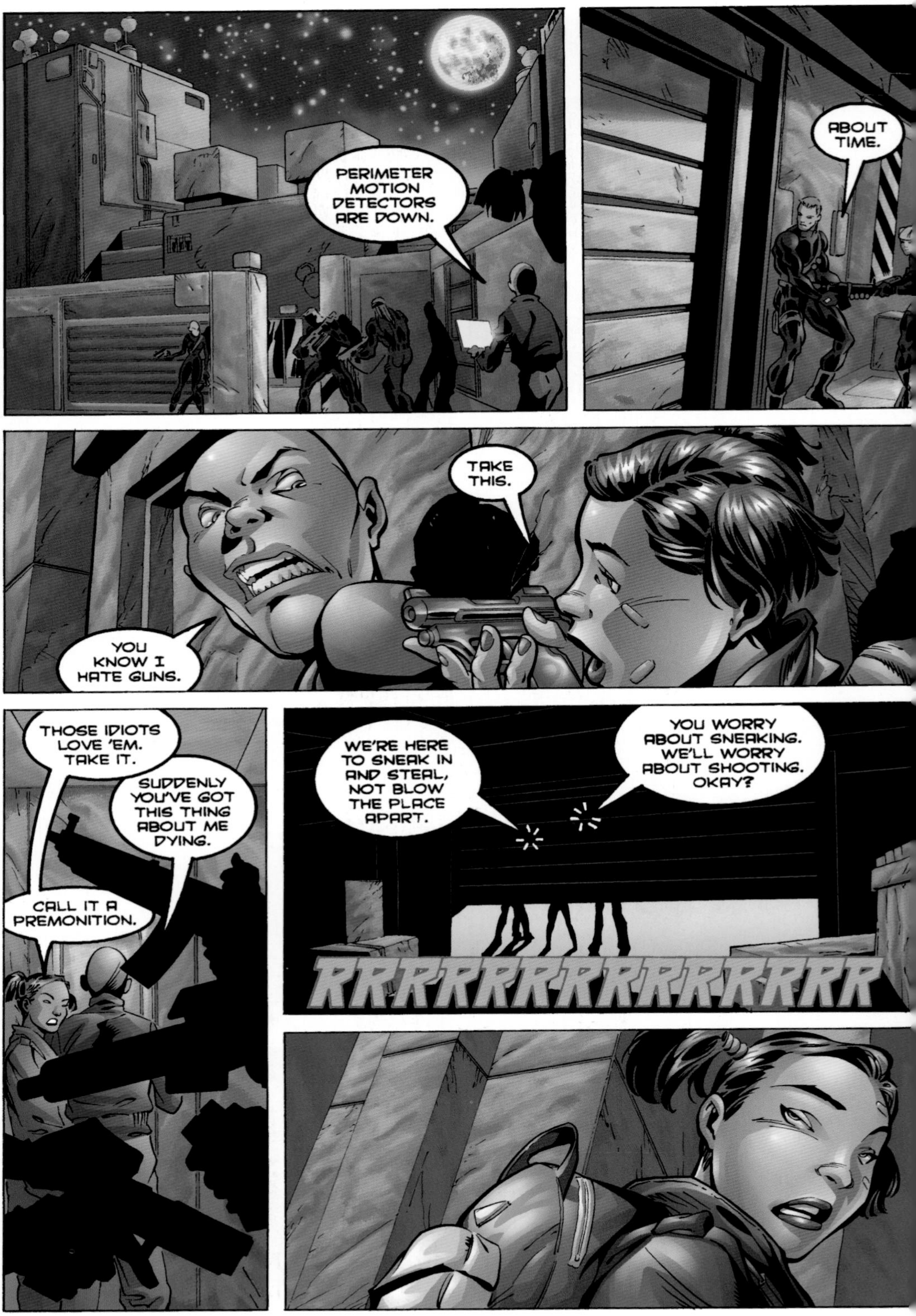
PERIMETER MOTION DETECTORS ARE DOWN.
ABOUT TIME.
TAKE THIS.
YOU KNOW I HATE GUNS.
THOSE IDIOTS LOVE 'EM. TAKE IT.
SUDDENLY YOU'VE GOT THIS THING ABOUT ME DYING.
CALL IT A PREMONITION.
WE'RE HERE TO SNEAK IN AND STEAL, NOT BLOW THE PLACE APART.
YOU WORRY ABOUT SNEAKING. WE'LL WORRY ABOUT SHOOTING. OKAY?
RRRRRRRRRRRRRRRR

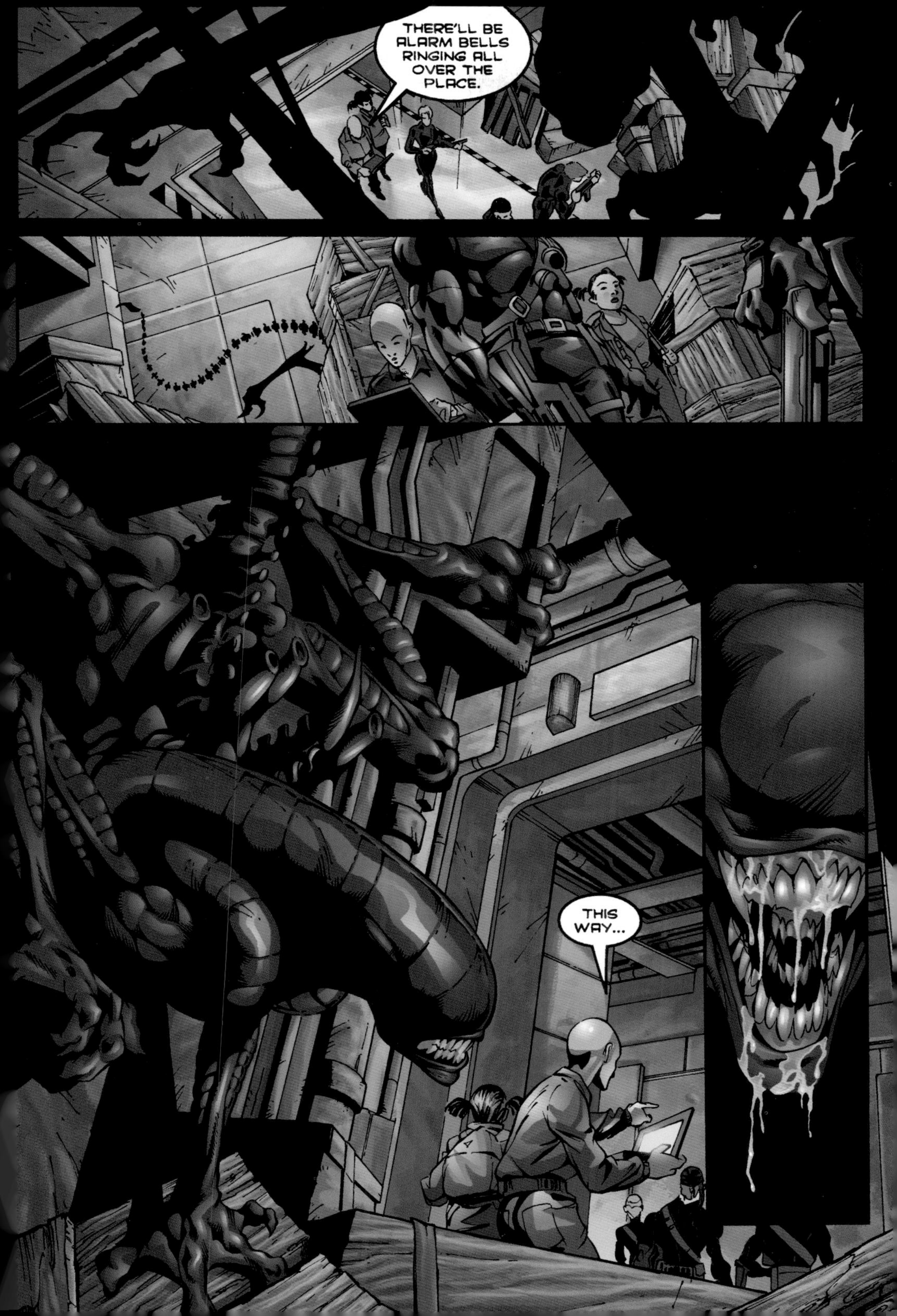
THERE'LL BE ALARM BELLS RINGING ALL OVER THE PLACE.
THIS WAY...

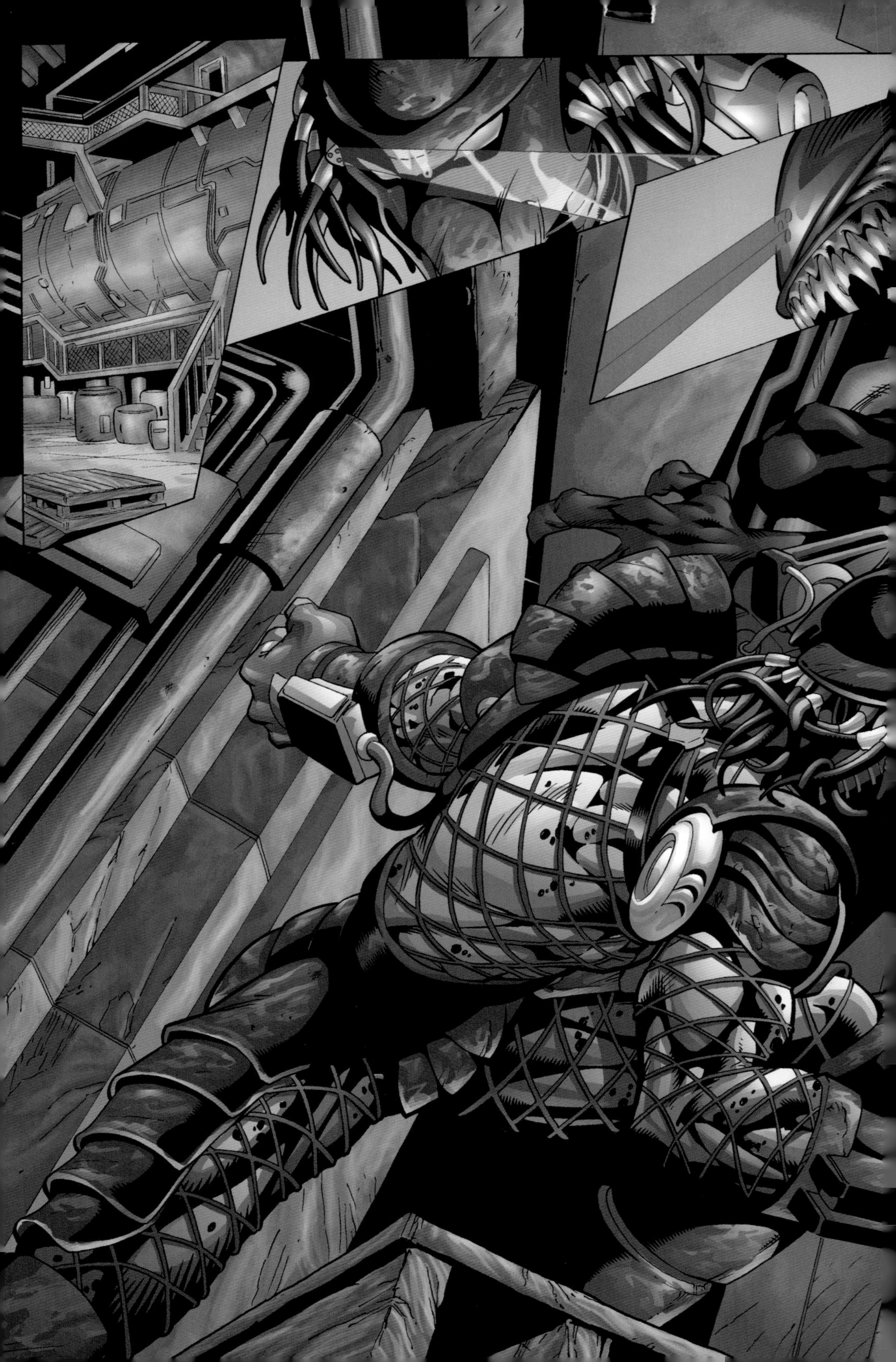

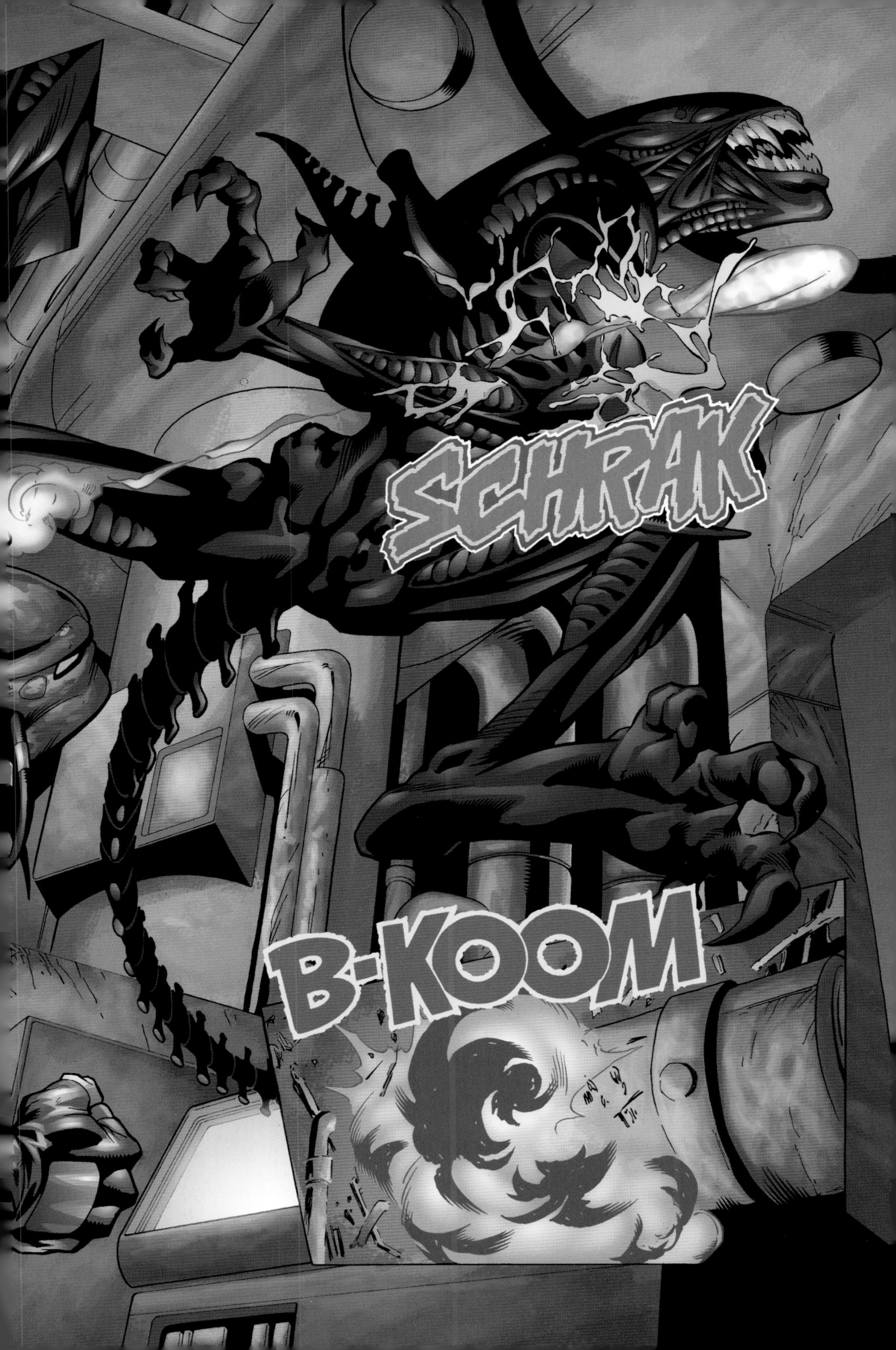
SCHRAK
B-KOOM

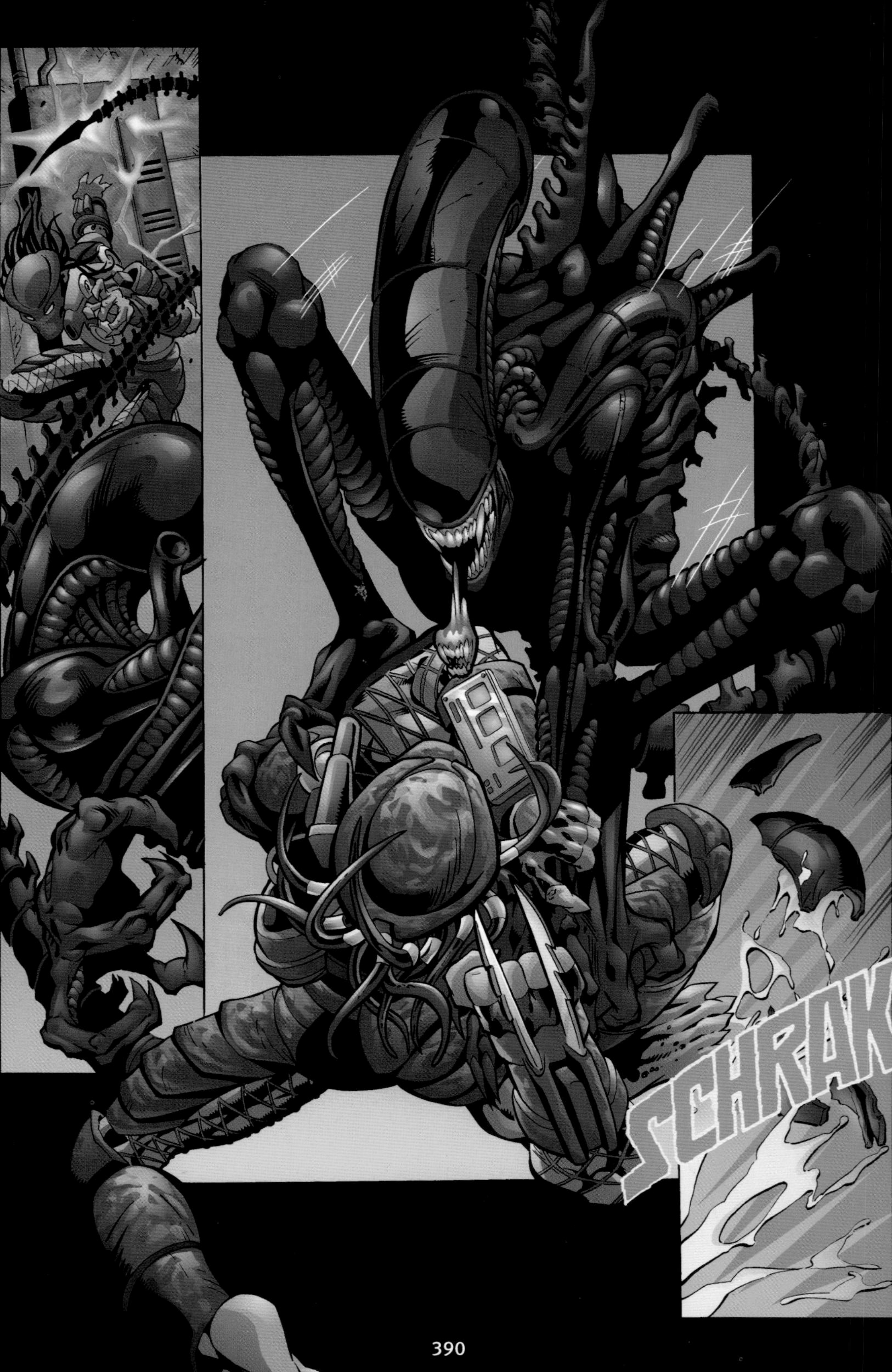
SCHRAK

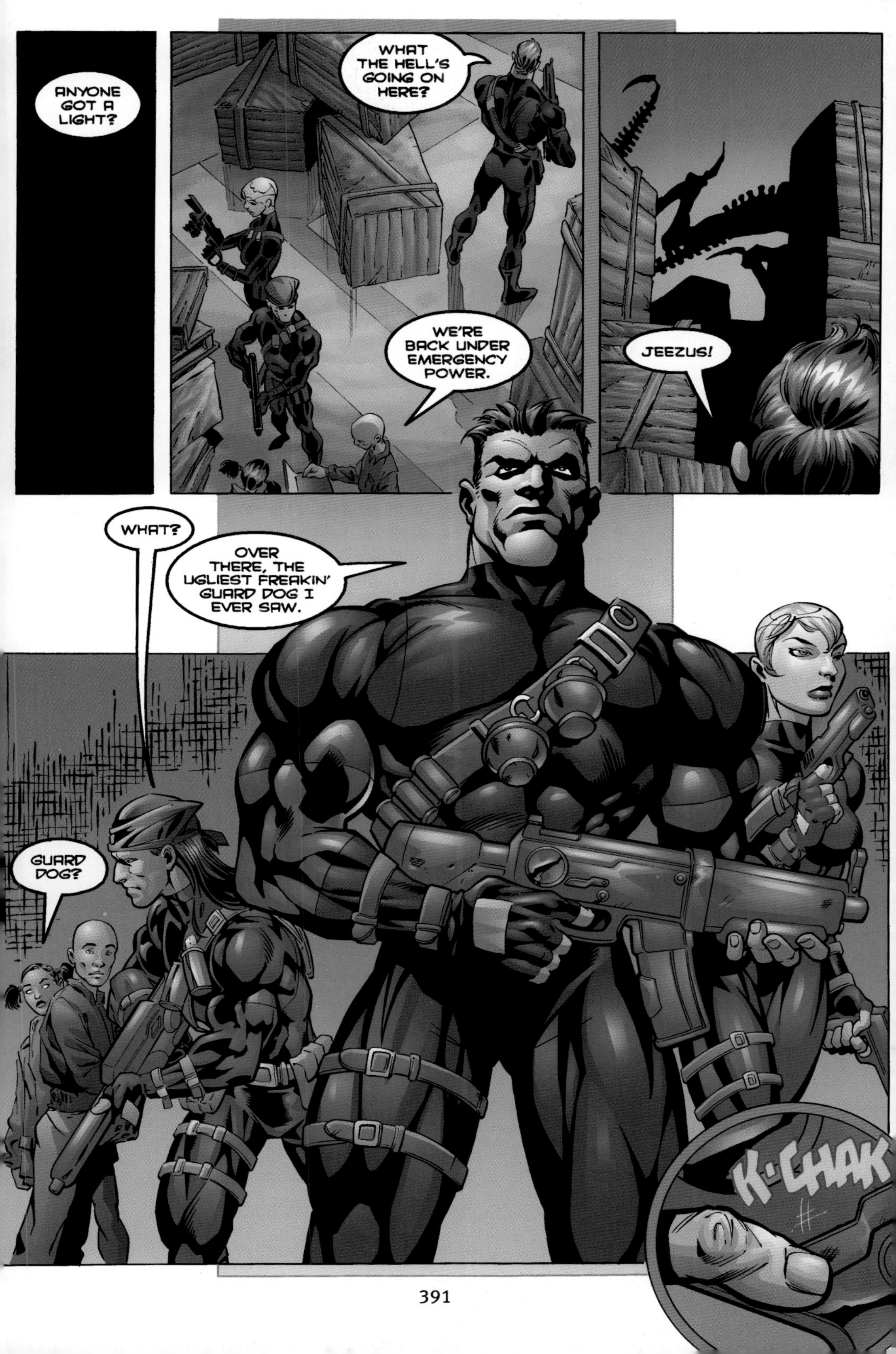
ANYONE GOT A LIGHT?
WHAT THE HELL'S GOING ON HERE?
WE'RE BACK UNDER EMERGENCY POWER.
JEEZUS!
WHAT?
OVER THERE, THE UGLIEST FREAKIN' GUARD DOG I EVER SAW.
GUARD DOG?
K-CHAK

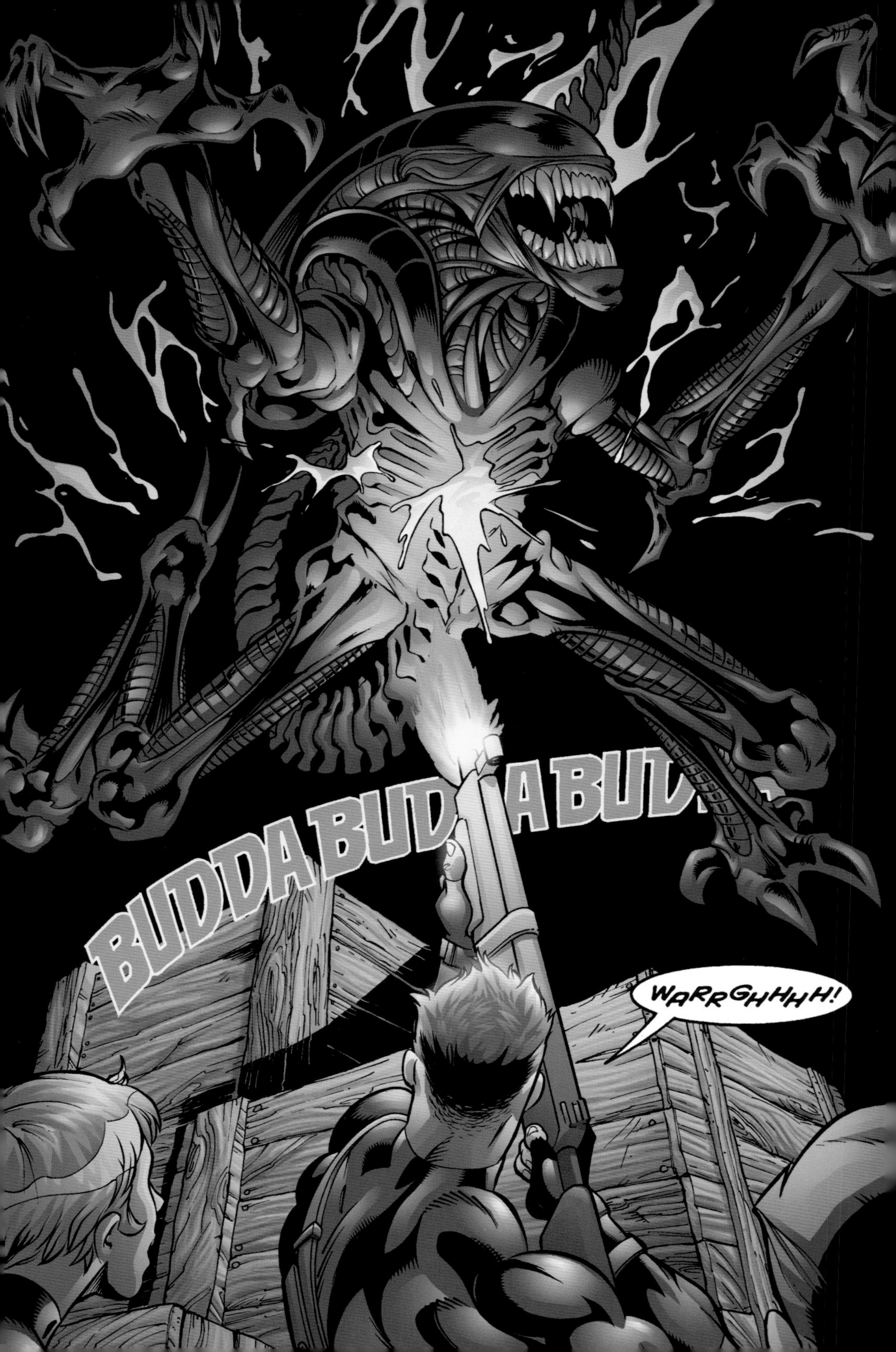
BUDDA BUD A BUD
WARRGHHHH!

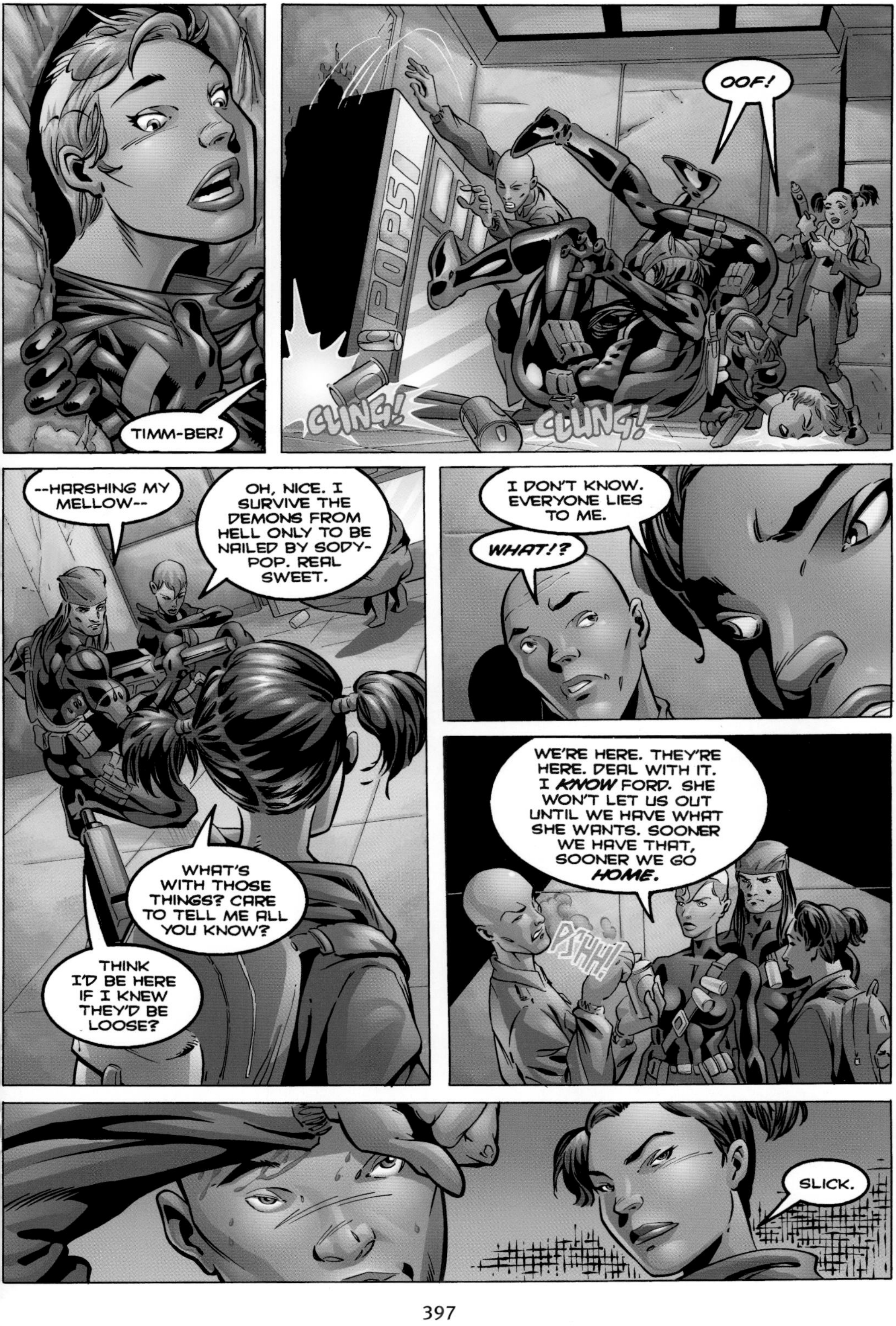
TIMM-BER!
OOF!
CLING!
CLING!
--HARSHING MY MELLOW--
OH, NICE. I SURVIVE THE DEMONS FROM HELL ONLY TO BE NAILED BY SODY-POP. REAL SWEET.
WHAT'S WITH THOSE THINGS? CARE TO TELL ME ALL YOU KNOW?
THINK I'D BE HERE IF I KNEW THEY'D BE LOOSE?
I DON'T KNOW. EVERYONE LIES TO ME.
WHAT!?
WE'RE HERE. THEY'RE HERE. DEAL WITH IT. I KNOW FORD. SHE WON'T LET US OUT UNTIL WE HAVE WHAT SHE WANTS. SOONER WE HAVE THAT, SOONER WE GO HOME.
PSHH!
SLICK.

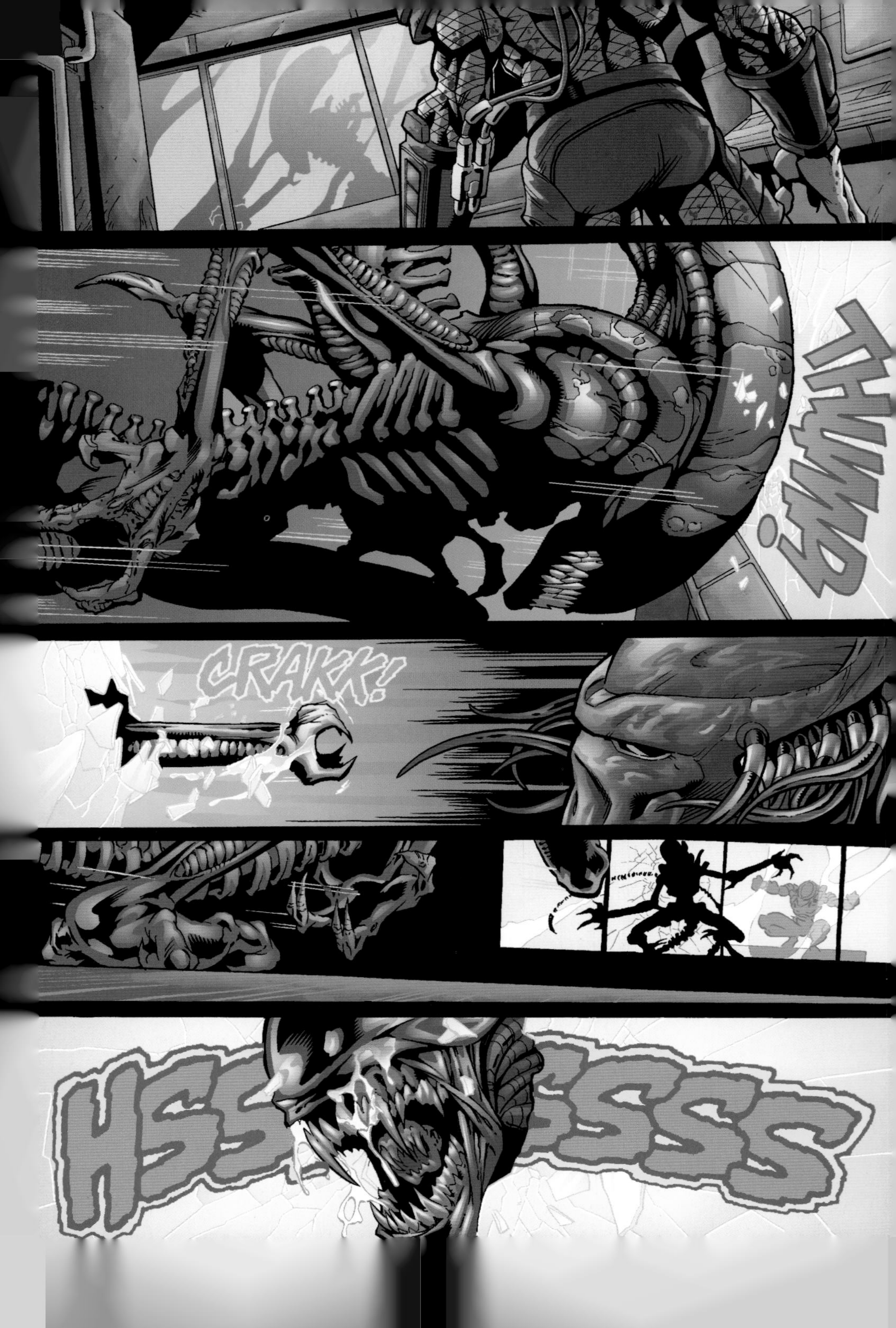
THUMMP!
CRAKK!
HSSSSSS

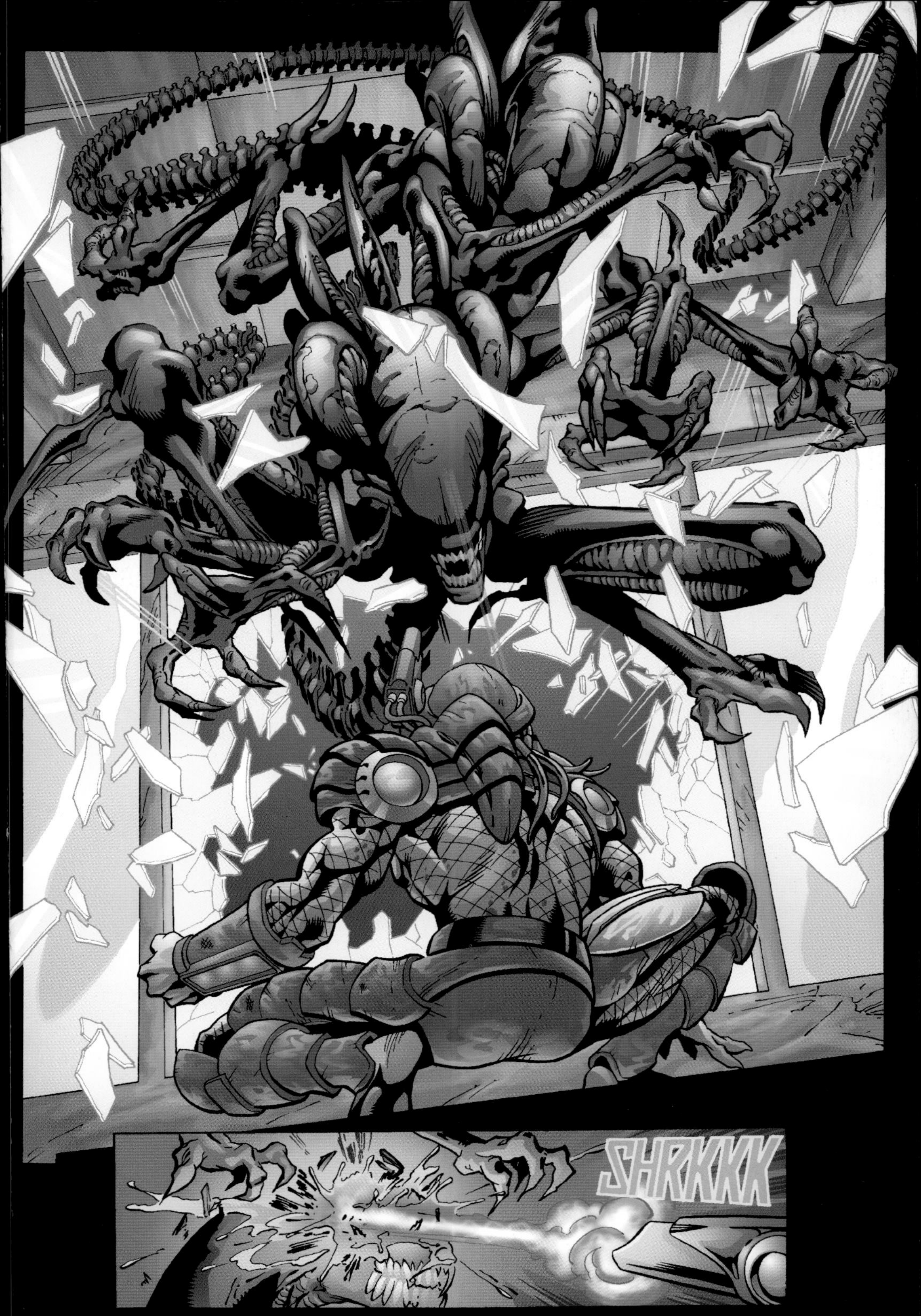
SHRKKK

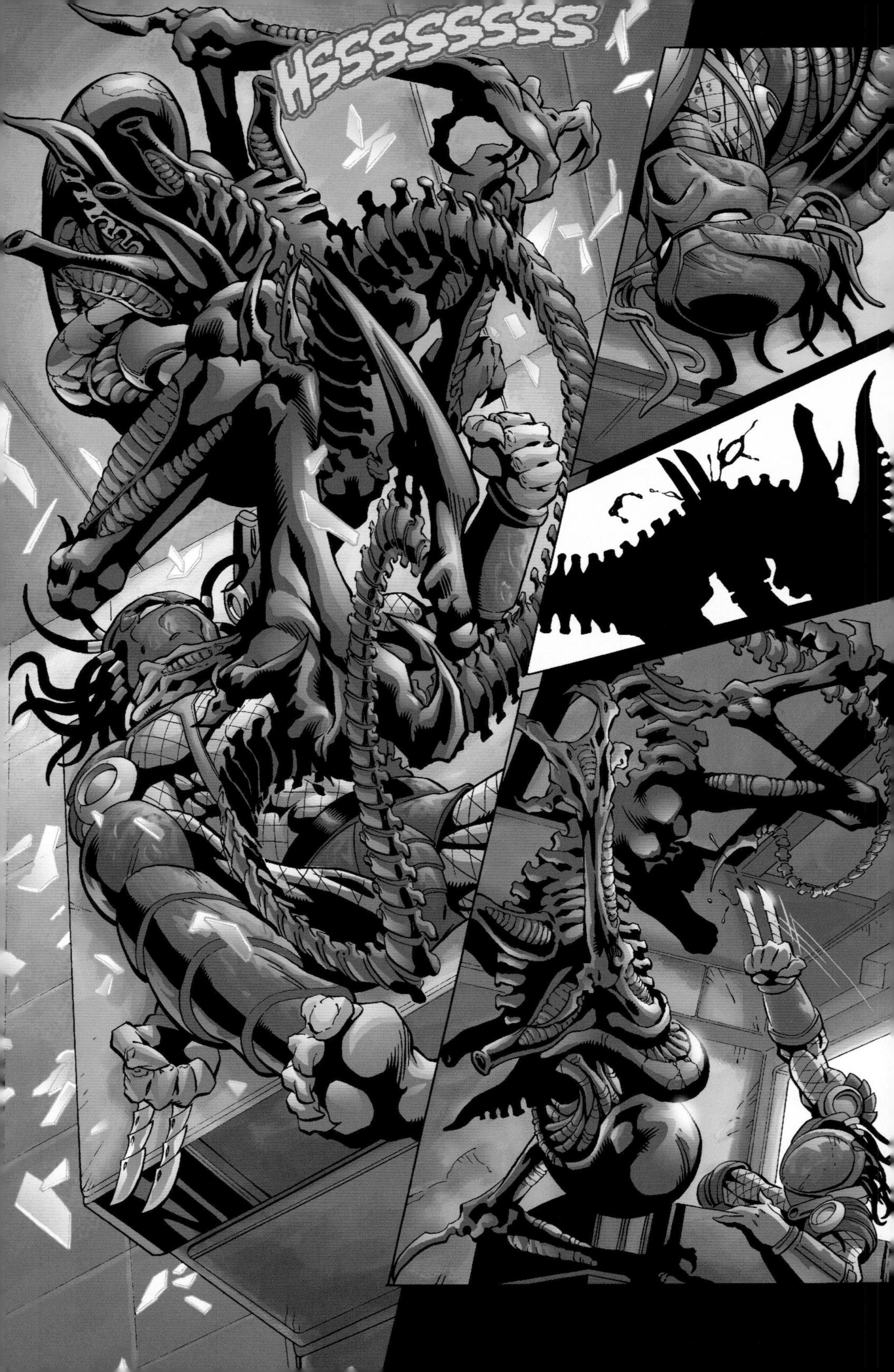
HSSSSSSSSS

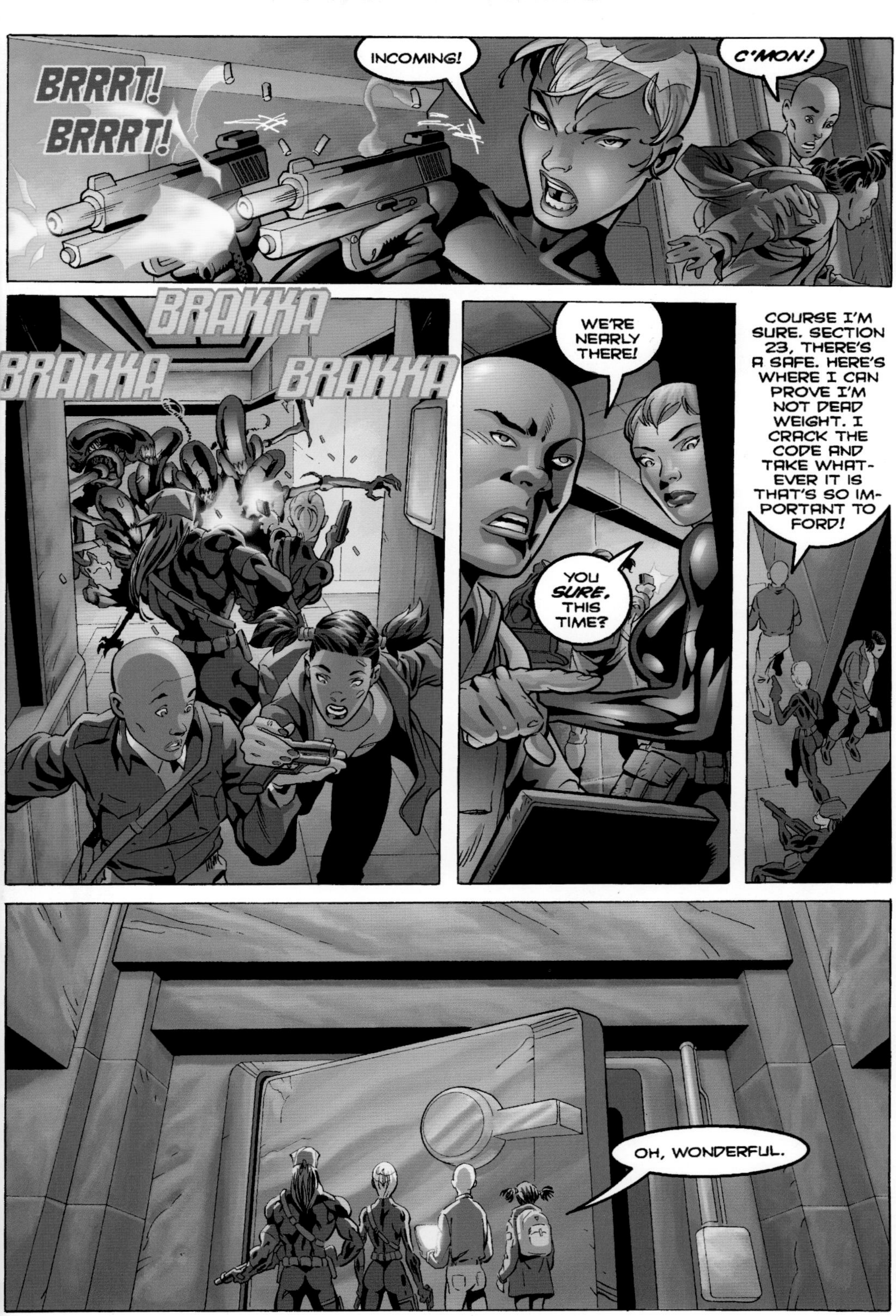
BRRRT!
BRRRT!
INCOMING!
C'MON!
BRAKKA
BRAKKA
BRAKKA
WE'RE NEARLY THERE!
YOU *SURE*, THIS TIME?
COURSE I'M SURE. SECTION 23, THERE'S A SAFE. HERE'S WHERE I CAN PROVE I'M NOT DEAD WEIGHT. I CRACK THE CODE AND TAKE WHAT-EVER IT IS THAT'S SO IM-PORTANT TO FORD!
OH, WONDERFUL.

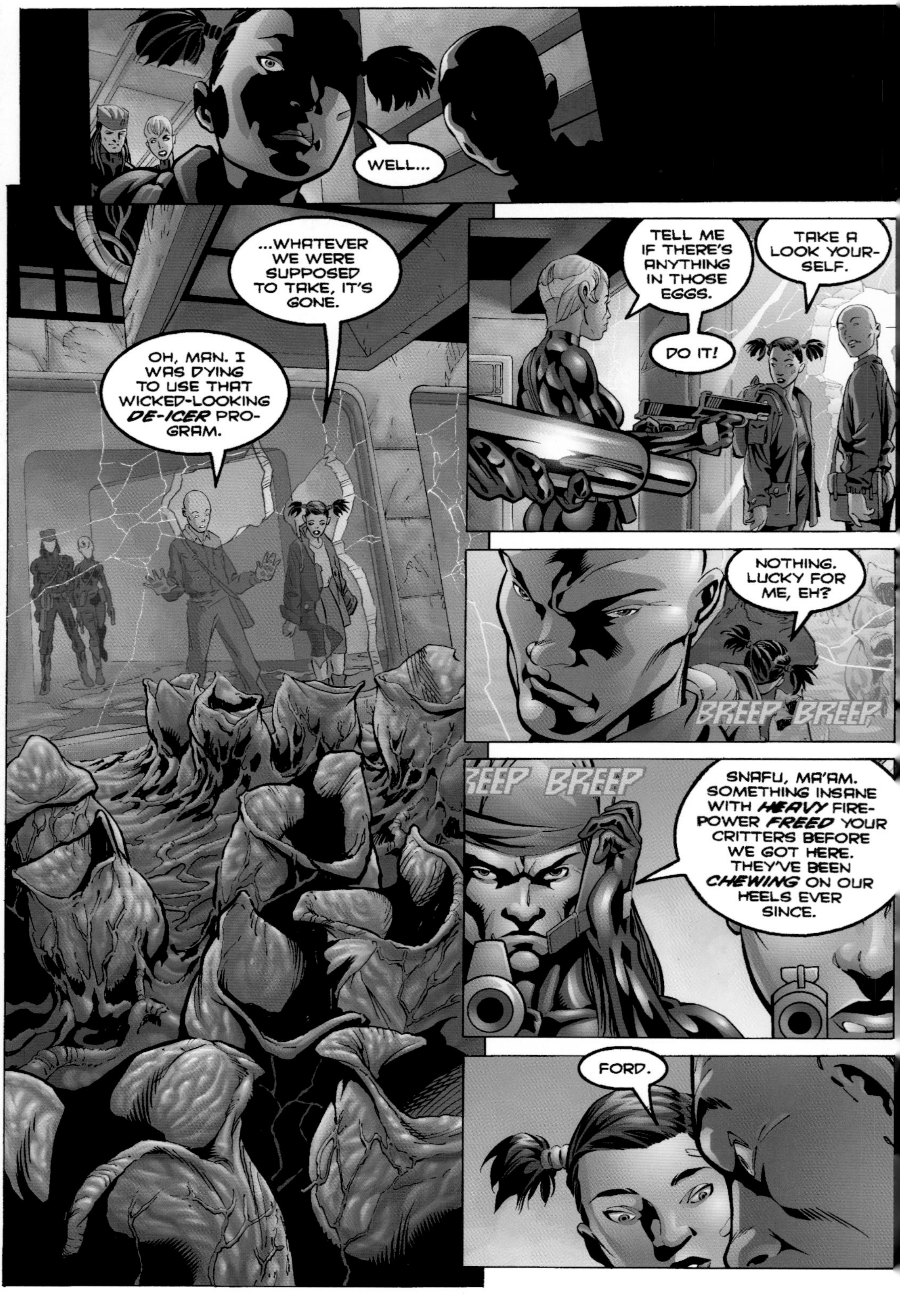
WELL...
...WHATEVER WE WERE SUPPOSED TO TAKE, IT'S GONE.
OH, MAN. I WAS DYING TO USE THAT WICKED-LOOKING DE-ICER PROGRAM.
TELL ME IF THERE'S ANYTHING IN THOSE EGGS.
DO IT!
TAKE A LOOK YOURSELF.
NOTHING. LUCKY FOR ME, EH?
BREEP BREEP
BREEP BREEP
SNAFU, MA'AM. SOMETHING INSANE WITH HEAVY FIREPOWER FREED YOUR CRITTERS BEFORE WE GOT HERE. THEY'VE BEEN CHEWING ON OUR HEELS EVER SINCE.
FORD.

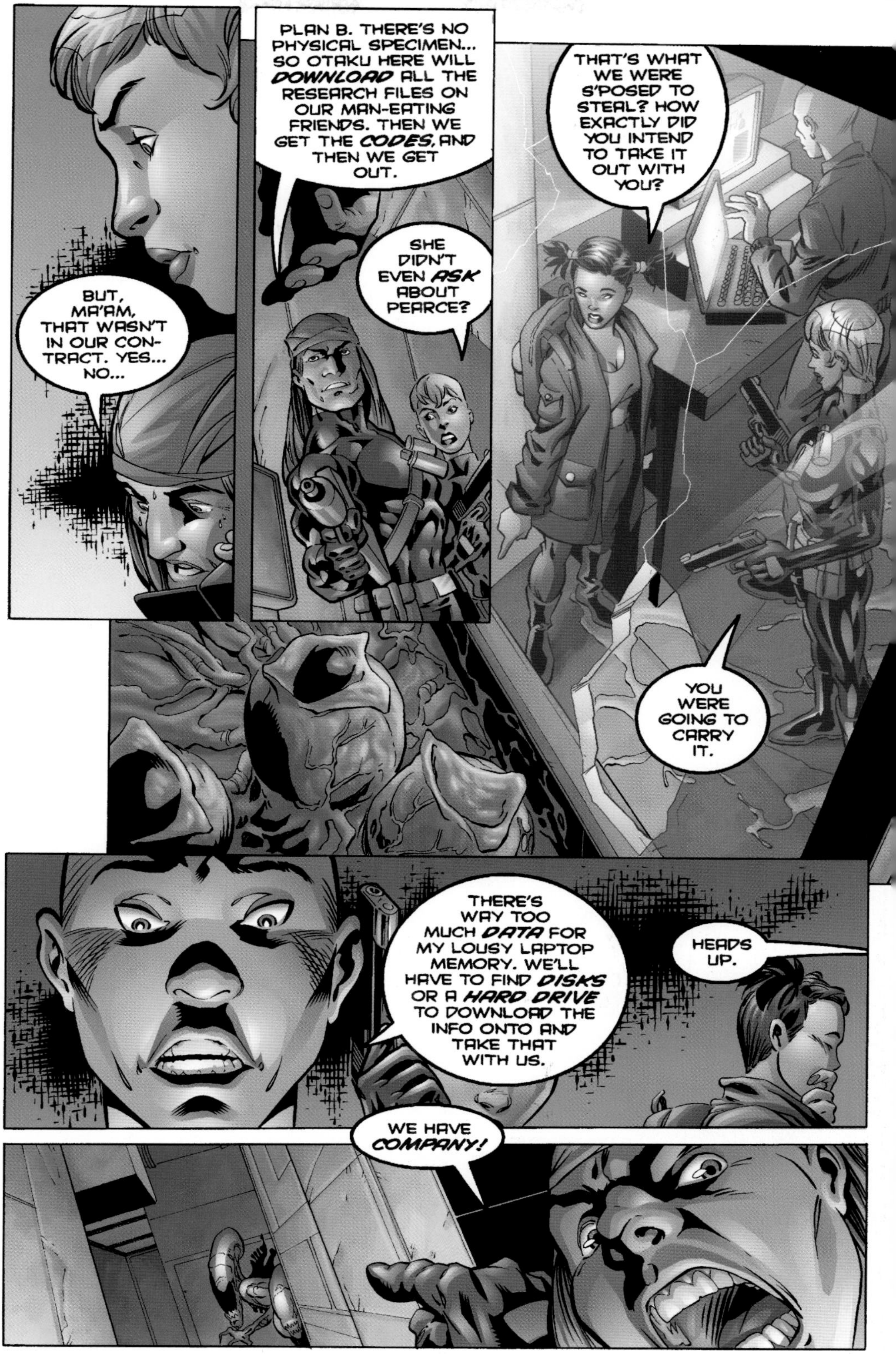
BUT, MA'AM, THAT WASN'T IN OUR CON-TRACT. YES... NO...
PLAN B. THERE'S NO PHYSICAL SPECIMEN... SO OTAKU HERE WILL DOWNLOAD ALL THE RESEARCH FILES ON OUR MAN-EATING FRIENDS. THEN WE GET THE CODES, AND THEN WE GET OUT.
SHE DIDN'T EVEN ASK ABOUT PEARCE?
THAT'S WHAT WE WERE S'POSED TO STEAL? HOW EXACTLY DID YOU INTEND TO TAKE IT OUT WITH YOU?
YOU WERE GOING TO CARRY IT.
THERE'S WAY TOO MUCH DATA FOR MY LOUSY LAPTOP MEMORY. WE'LL HAVE TO FIND DISKS OR A HARD DRIVE TO DOWNLOAD THE INFO ONTO AND TAKE THAT WITH US.
HEADS UP.
WE HAVE COMPANY!

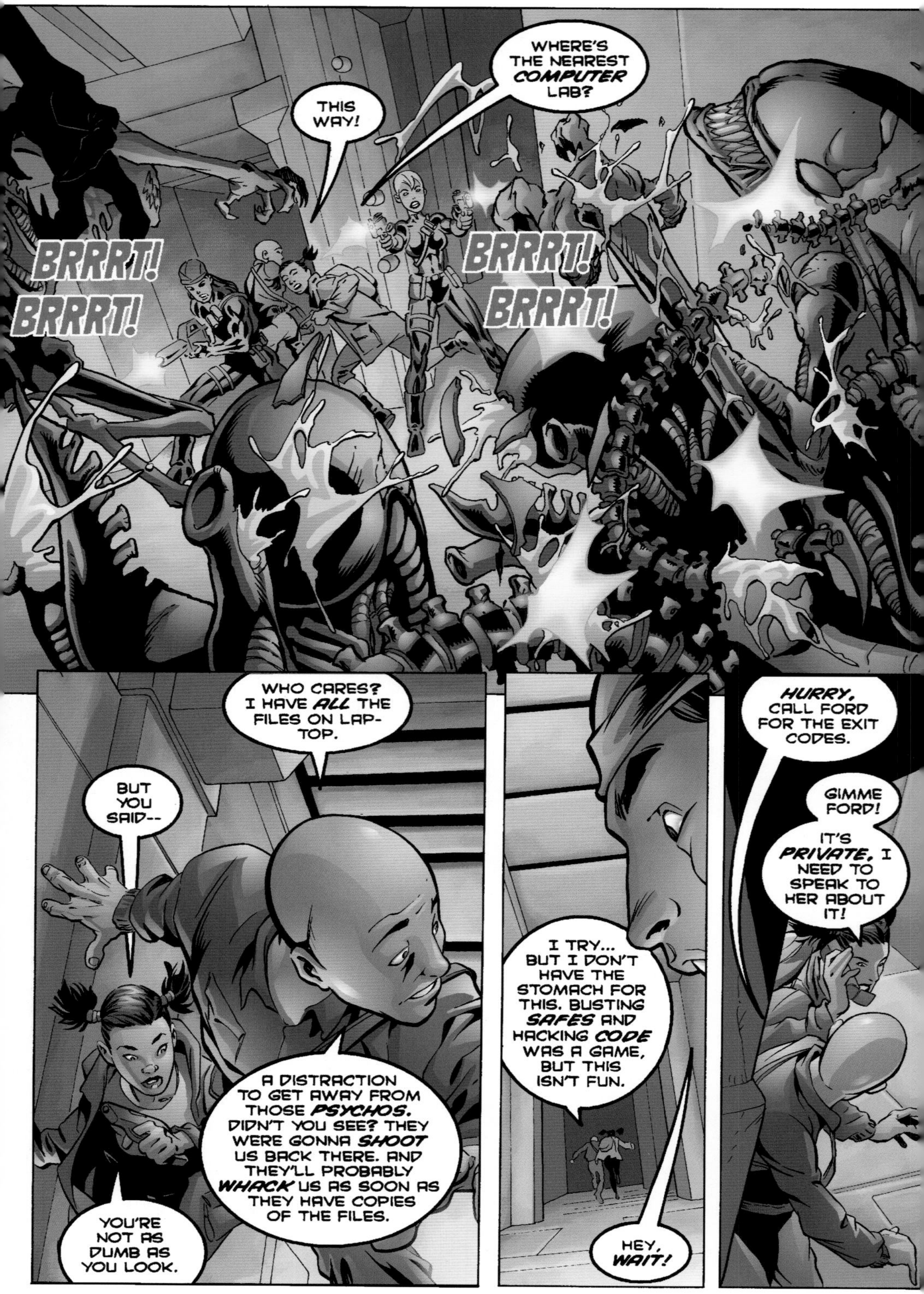

WHERE'S THE NEAREST COMPUTER LAB?
THIS WAY!
BRRRT! BRRRT!
BRRRT! BRRRT!
BUT YOU SAID--
WHO CARES? I HAVE ALL THE FILES ON LAP-TOP.
A DISTRACTION TO GET AWAY FROM THOSE PSYCHOS. DIDN'T YOU SEE? THEY WERE GONNA SHOOT US BACK THERE. AND THEY'LL PROBABLY WHACK US AS SOON AS THEY HAVE COPIES OF THE FILES.
YOU'RE NOT AS DUMB AS YOU LOOK.
I TRY... BUT I DON'T HAVE THE STOMACH FOR THIS. BUSTING SAFES AND HACKING CODE WAS A GAME, BUT THIS ISN'T FUN.
HEY, WAIT!
HURRY, CALL FORD FOR THE EXIT CODES.
GIMME FORD!
IT'S PRIVATE. I NEED TO SPEAK TO HER ABOUT IT!

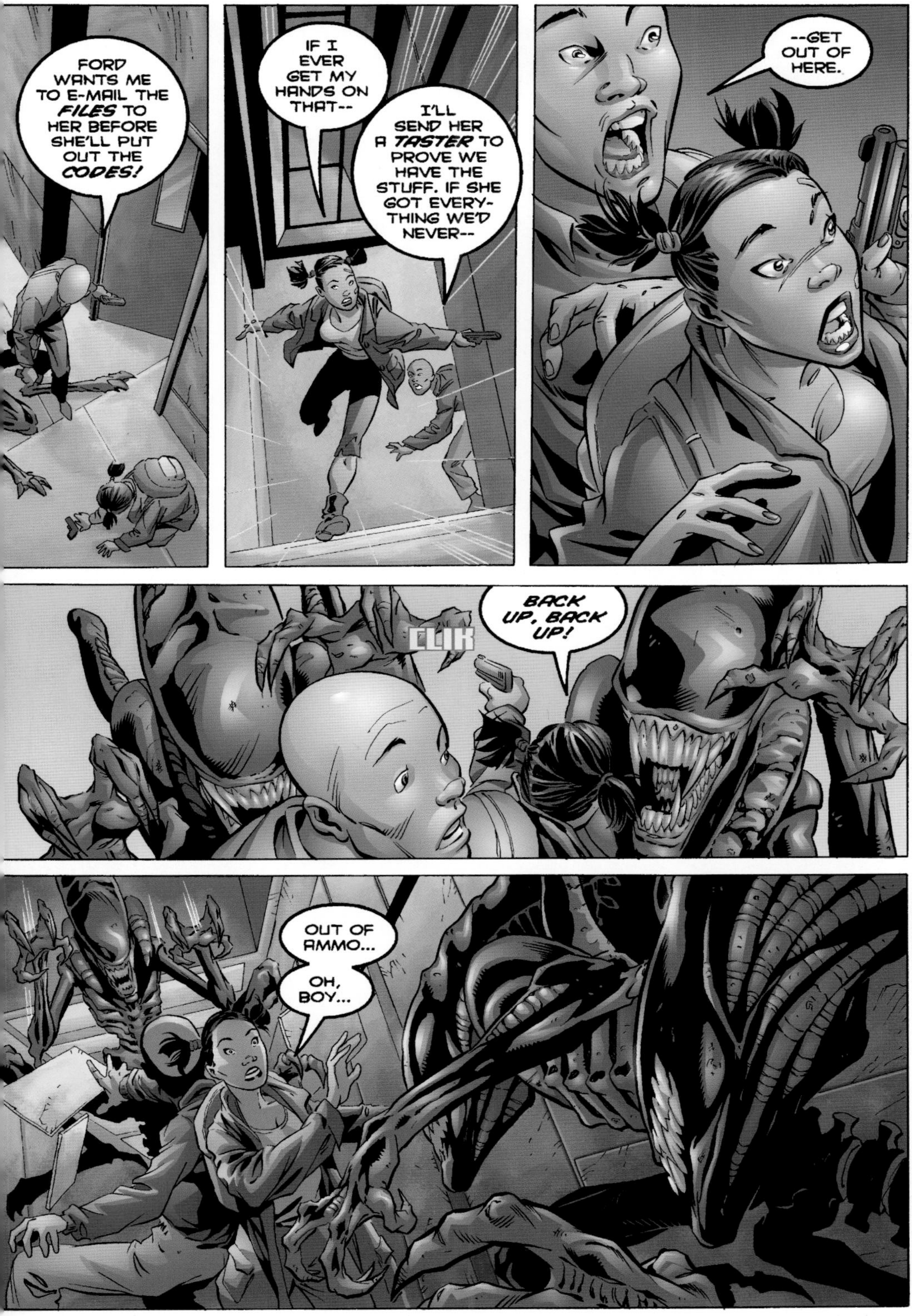

FORD WANTS ME TO E-MAIL THE *FILES* TO HER BEFORE SHE'LL PUT OUT THE *CODES!*
IF I EVER GET MY HANDS ON THAT--
I'LL SEND HER A *TASTER* TO PROVE WE HAVE THE STUFF. IF SHE GOT EVERY-THING WE'D NEVER--
--GET OUT OF HERE.
CLIK
BACK UP, BACK UP!
OUT OF AMMO...
OH, BOY...

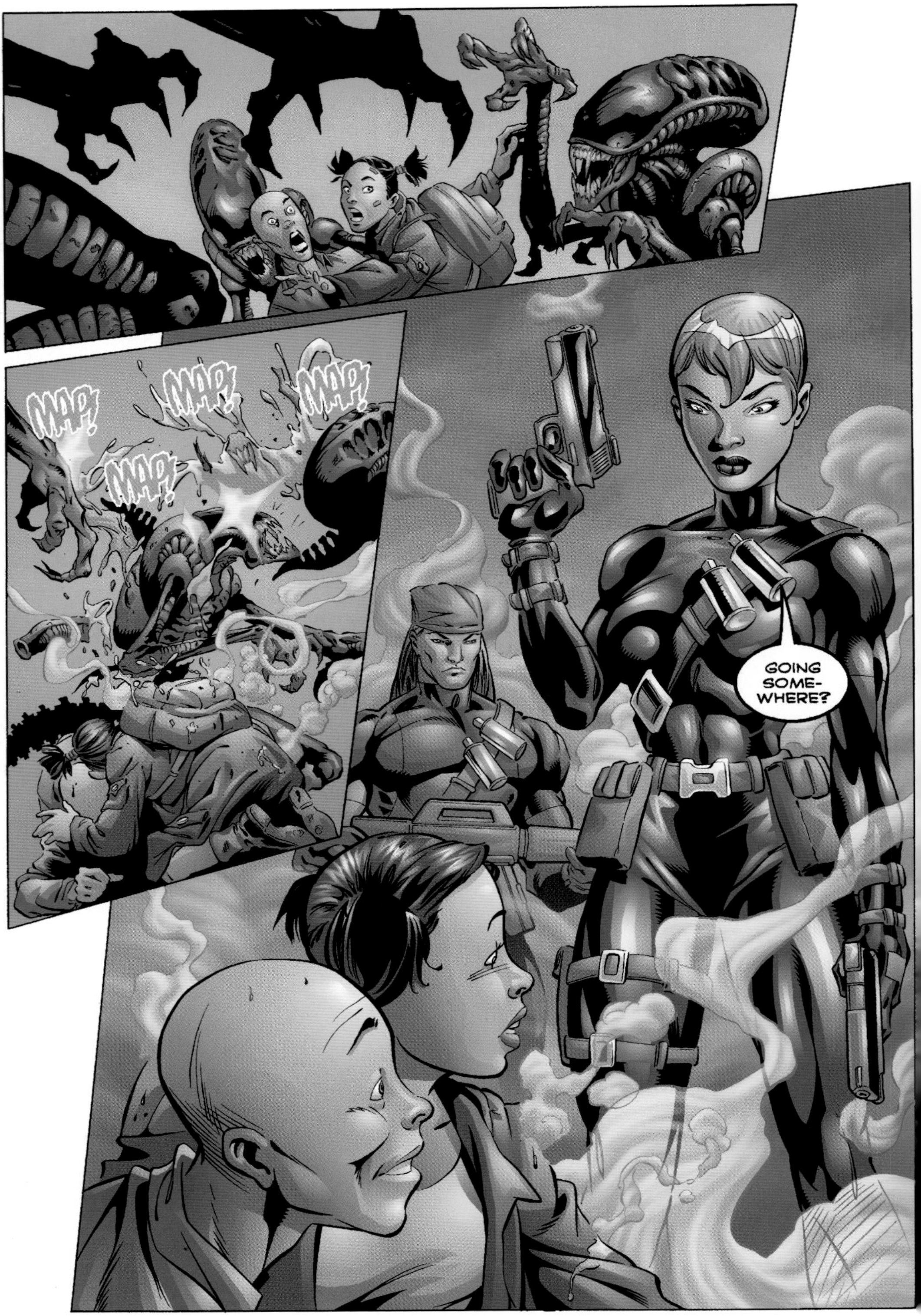
MAP!
MAP!
MAP!
MAP!
GOING SOME-WHERE?

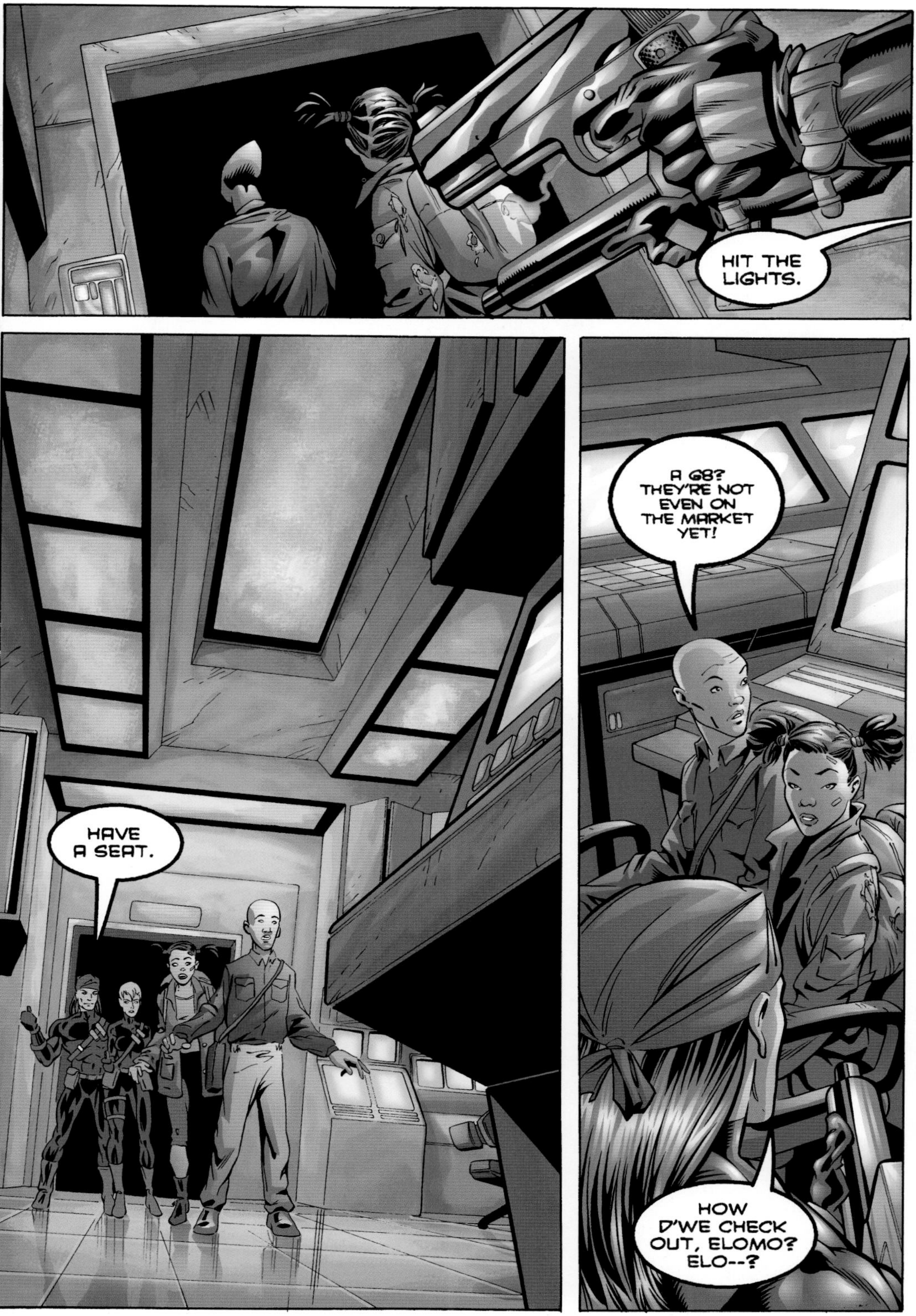
HIT THE LIGHTS.
HAVE A SEAT.
A G8? THEY'RE NOT EVEN ON THE MARKET YET!
HOW D'WE CHECK OUT, ELOMO? ELO--?

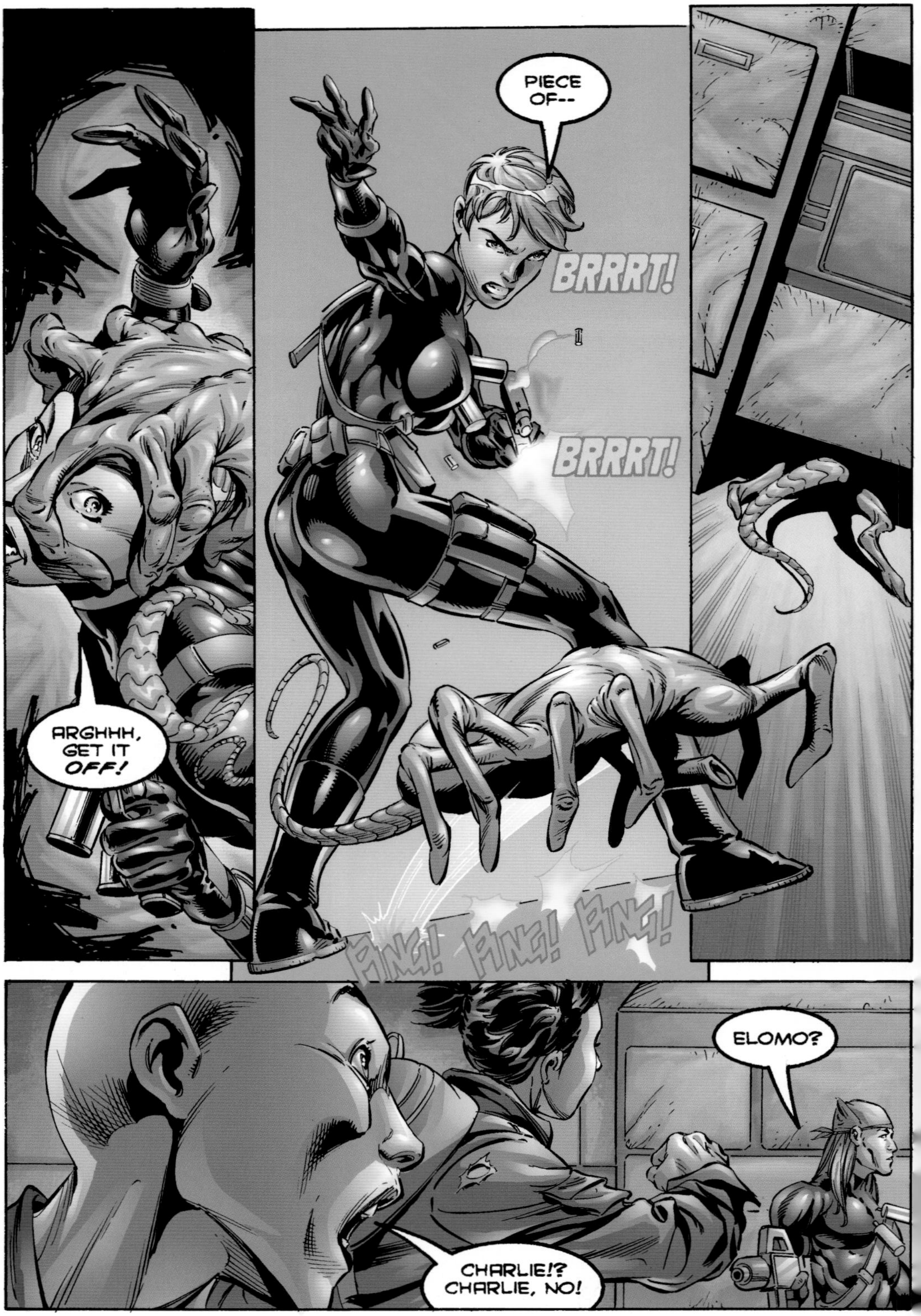
PIECE OF--
BRRRT!
BRRRT!
ARGHHH, GET IT OFF!
PING! PING! PING!
ELOMO?
CHARLIE!? CHARLIE, NO!

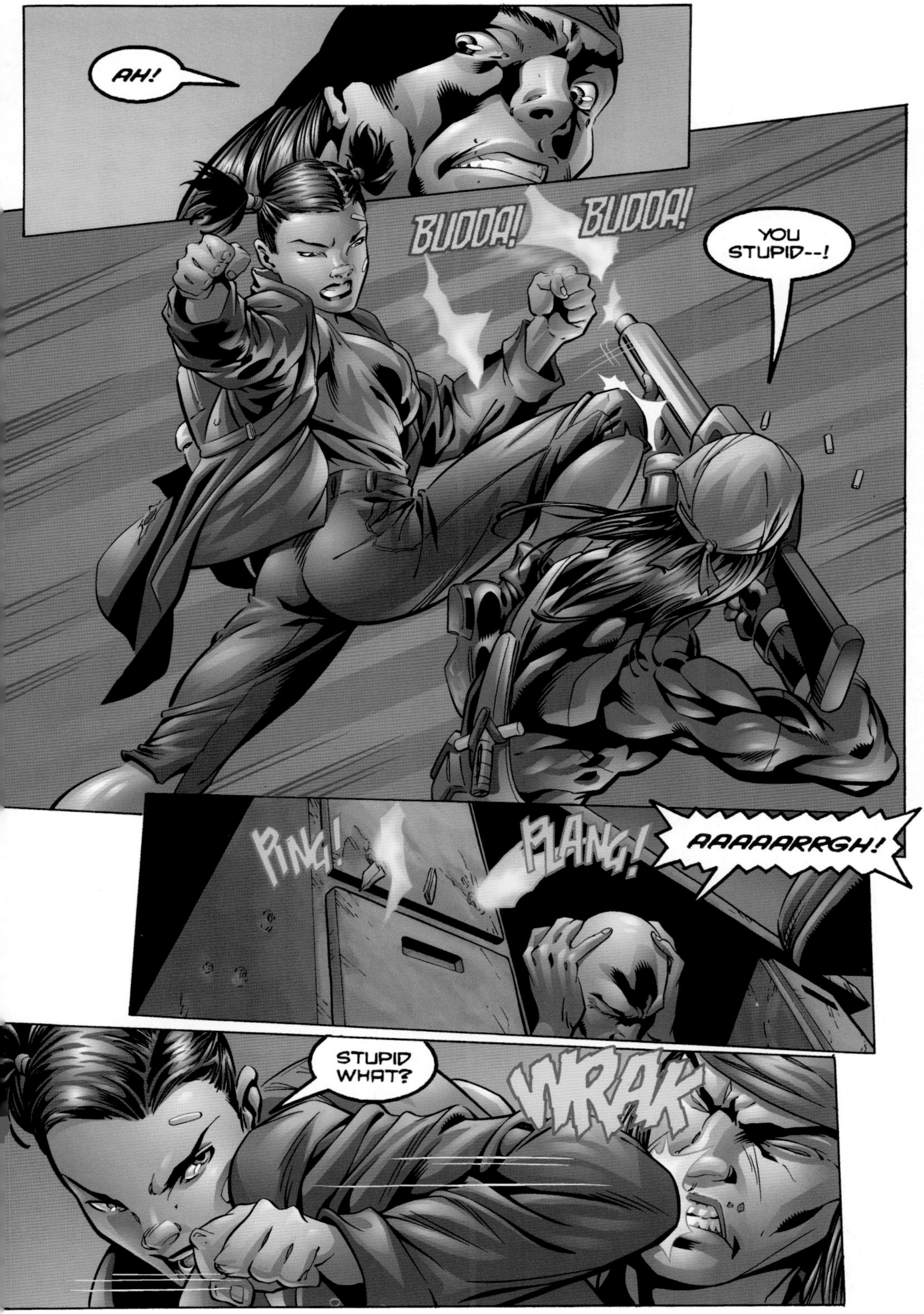
AH!
BUDDA! BUDDA!
YOU STUPID--!
PING! PLANG!
AAAAARRGH!
STUPID WHAT?
WRAK

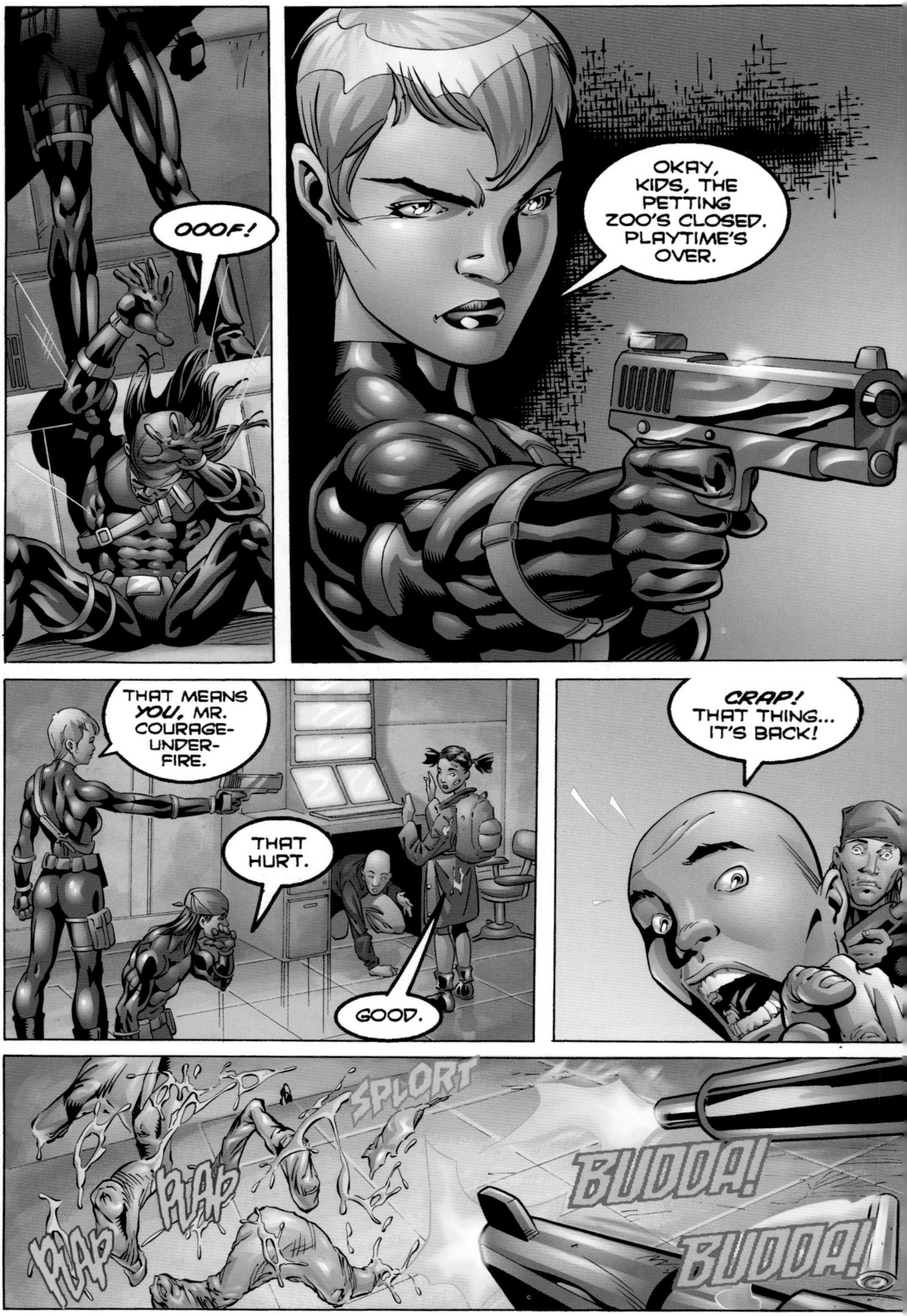
OOOF!
OKAY, KIDS, THE PETTING ZOO'S CLOSED. PLAYTIME'S OVER.
THAT MEANS *YOU,* MR. COURAGE-UNDER-FIRE.
THAT HURT.
GOOD.
CRAP! THAT THING... IT'S BACK!
SPLORT
BUDDA!
BUDDA!
PLAP
PLAP
PLAP

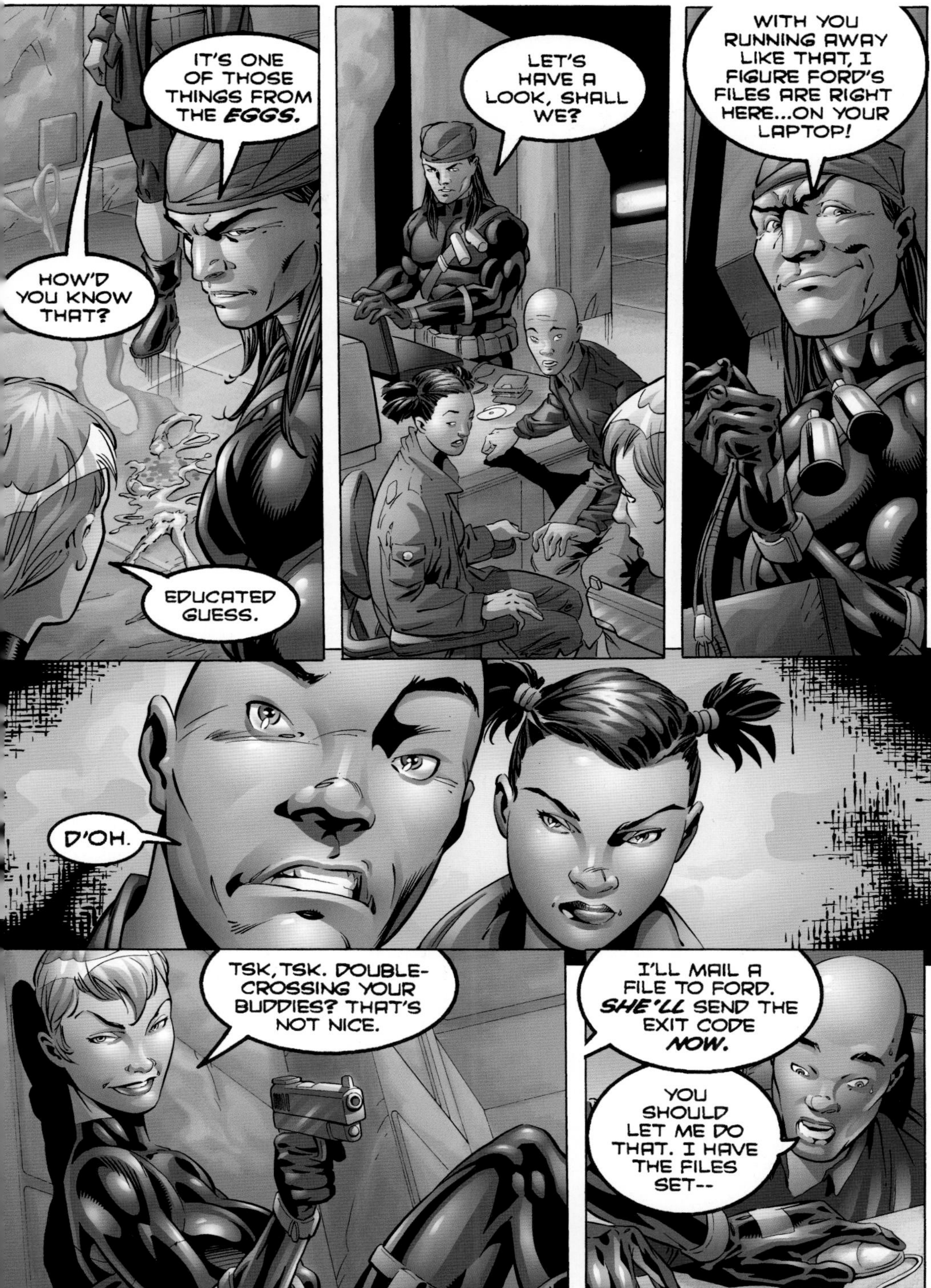
IT'S ONE OF THOSE THINGS FROM THE *EGGS.*
HOW'D YOU KNOW THAT?
EDUCATED GUESS.
LET'S HAVE A LOOK, SHALL WE?
WITH YOU RUNNING AWAY LIKE THAT, I FIGURE FORD'S FILES ARE RIGHT HERE...ON YOUR LAPTOP!
D'OH.
TSK, TSK. DOUBLE-CROSSING YOUR BUDDIES? THAT'S NOT NICE.
I'LL MAIL A FILE TO FORD. *SHE'LL* SEND THE EXIT CODE *NOW.*
YOU SHOULD LET ME DO THAT. I HAVE THE FILES SET--

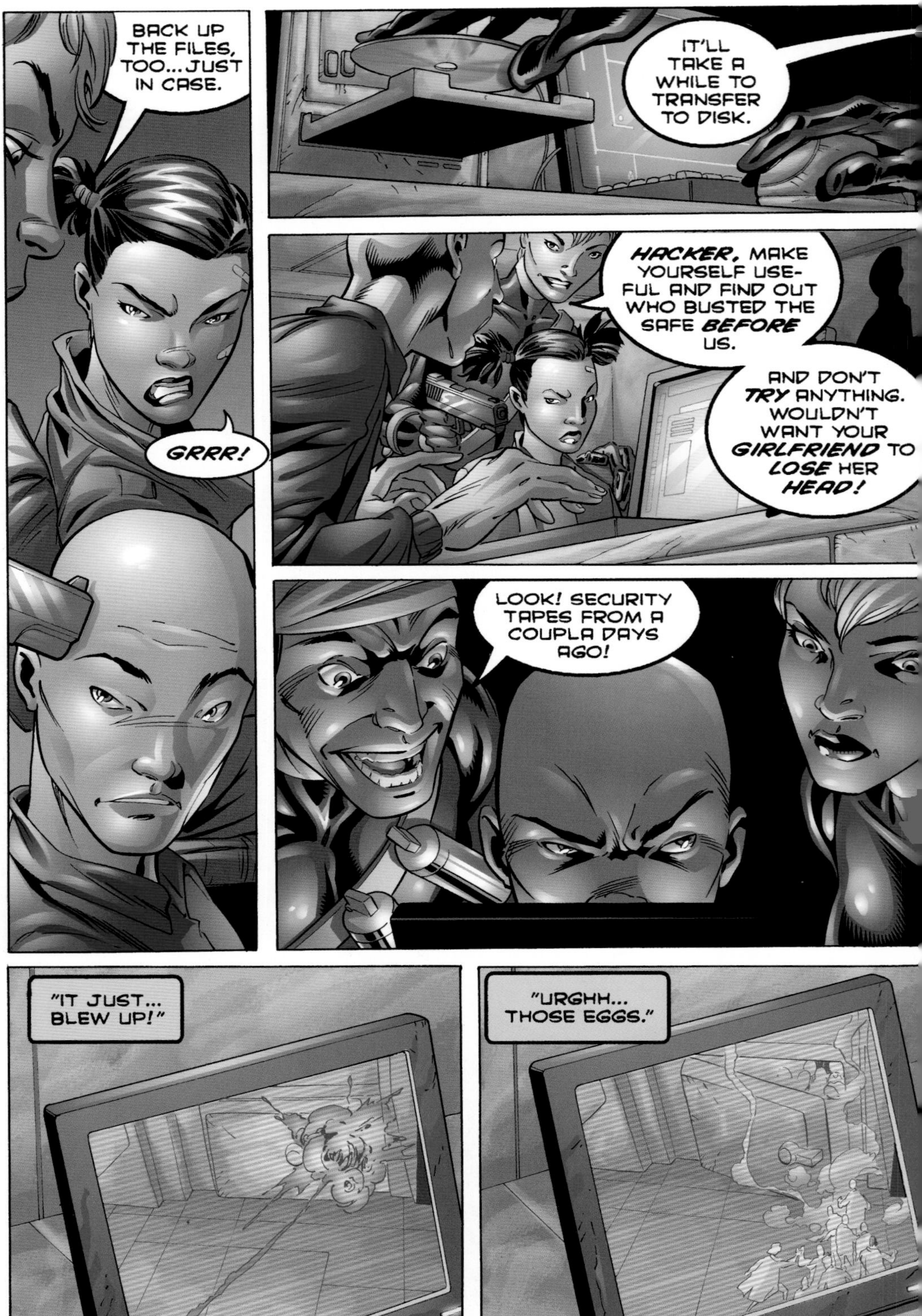
BACK UP THE FILES, TOO...JUST IN CASE.
IT'LL TAKE A WHILE TO TRANSFER TO DISK.
GRRR!
HACKER, MAKE YOURSELF USE-FUL AND FIND OUT WHO BUSTED THE SAFE BEFORE US.
AND DON'T TRY ANYTHING. WOULDN'T WANT YOUR GIRLFRIEND TO LOSE HER HEAD!
LOOK! SECURITY TAPES FROM A COUPLA DAYS AGO!
"IT JUST... BLEW UP!"
"URGHH... THOSE EGGS."

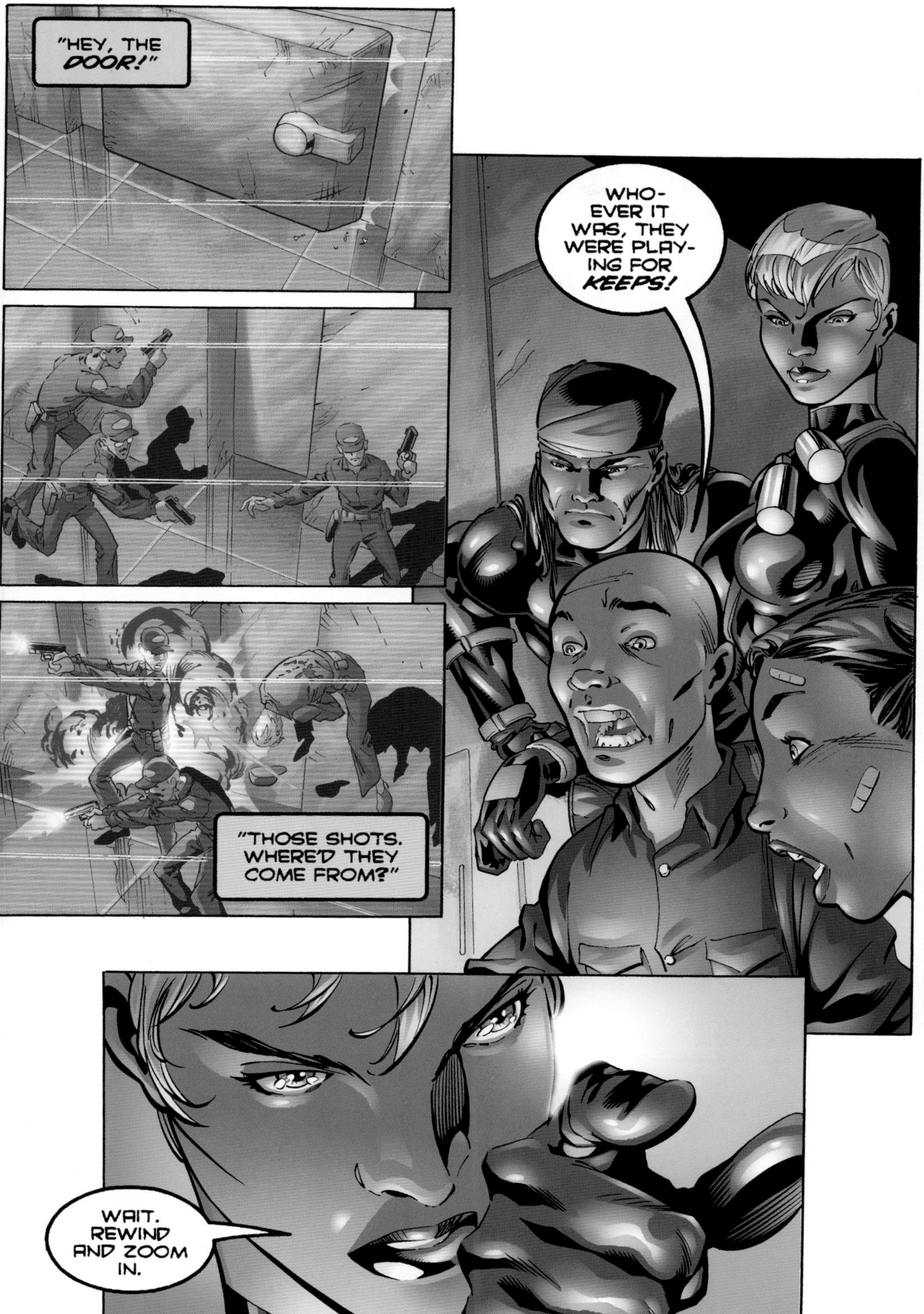
"HEY, THE DOOR!"
WHO-EVER IT WAS, THEY WERE PLAY-ING FOR KEEPS!
"THOSE SHOTS. WHERE'D THEY COME FROM?"
WAIT. REWIND AND ZOOM IN.

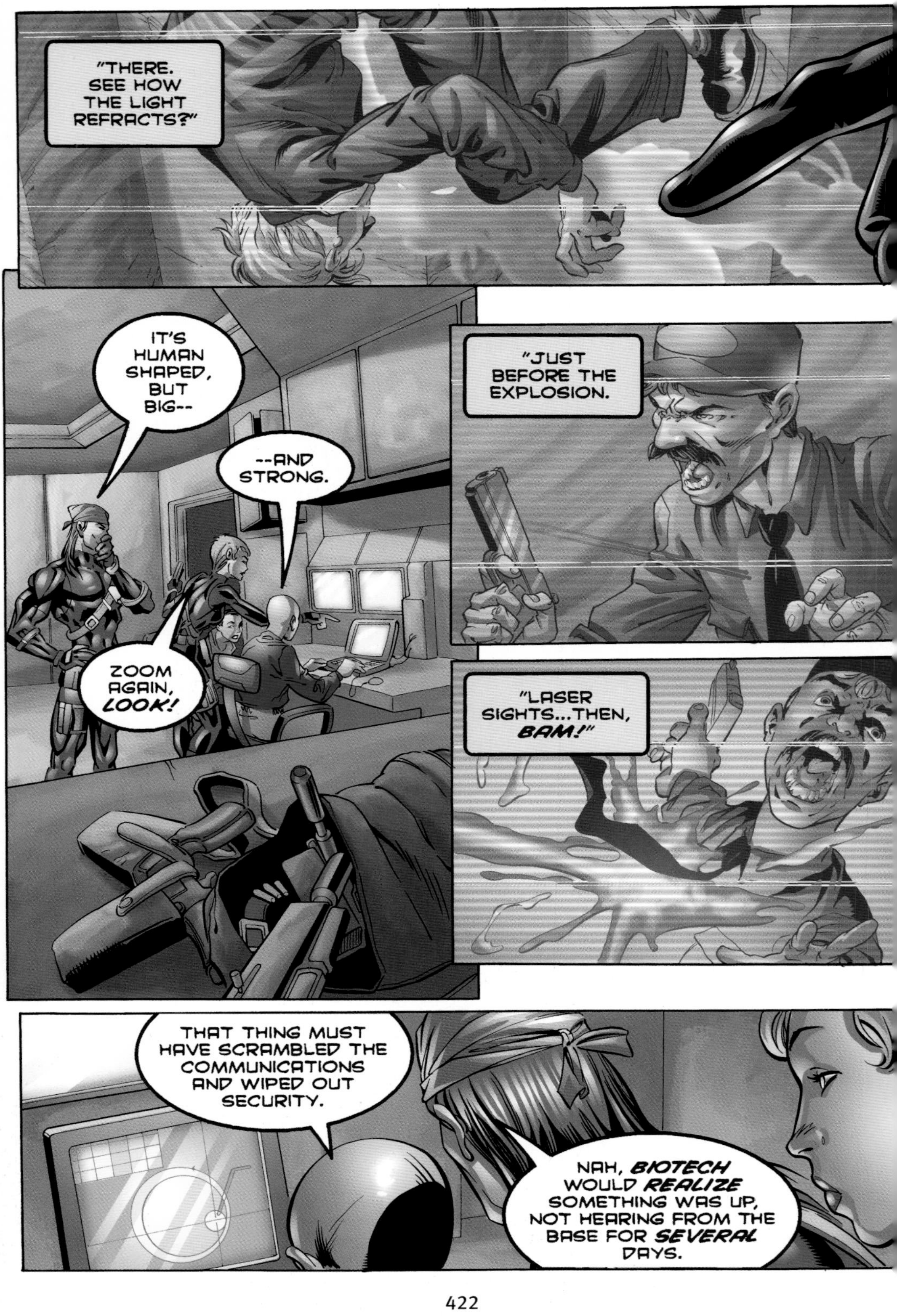
"THERE. SEE HOW THE LIGHT REFRACTS?"
IT'S HUMAN SHAPED, BUT BIG--
--AND STRONG.
ZOOM AGAIN, LOOK!
"JUST BEFORE THE EXPLOSION.
"LASER SIGHTS...THEN, BAM!"
THAT THING MUST HAVE SCRAMBLED THE COMMUNICATIONS AND WIPED OUT SECURITY.
NAH, BIOTECH WOULD REALIZE SOMETHING WAS UP, NOT HEARING FROM THE BASE FOR SEVERAL DAYS.

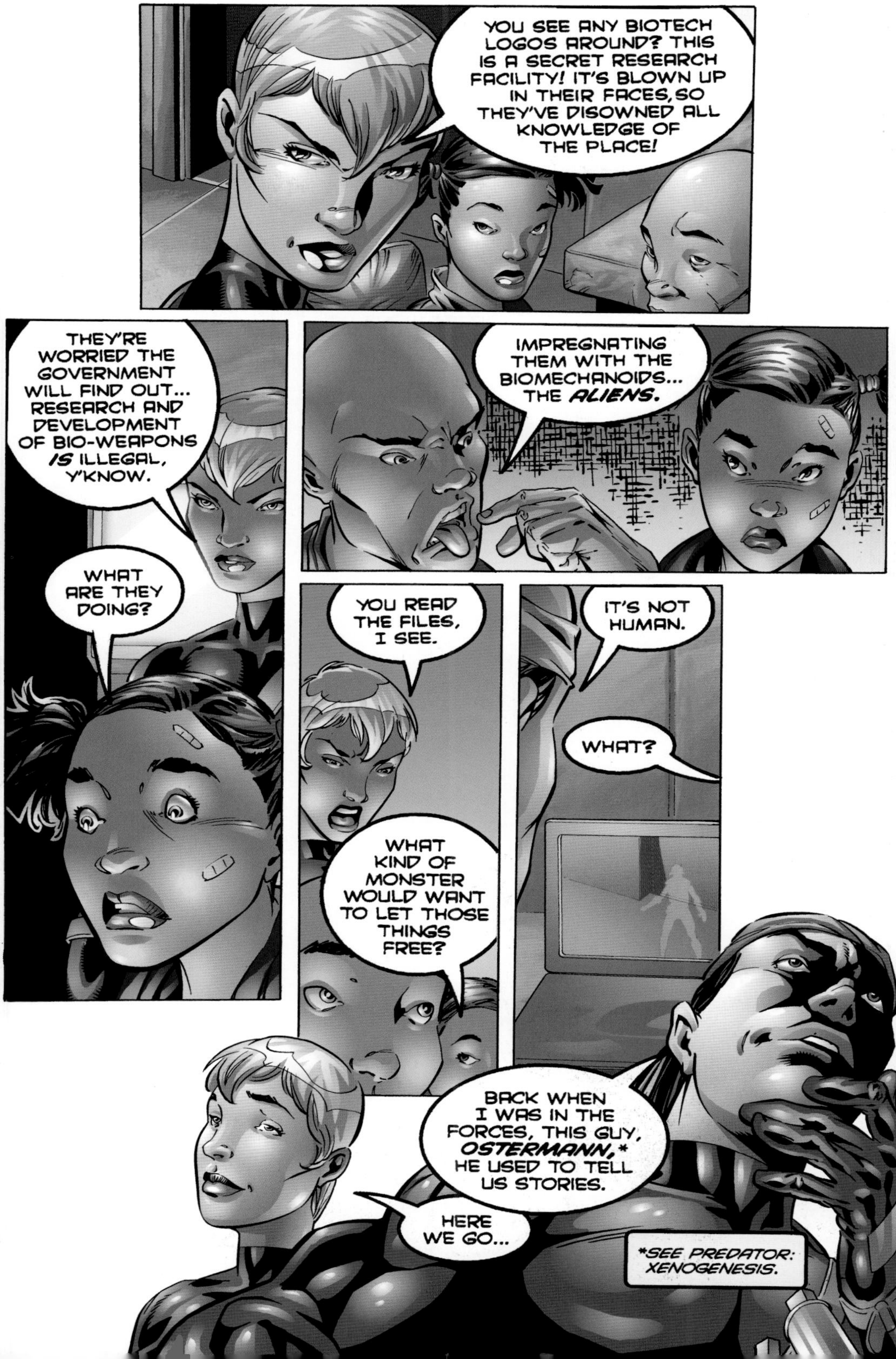

YOU SEE ANY BIOTECH LOGOS AROUND? THIS IS A SECRET RESEARCH FACILITY! IT'S BLOWN UP IN THEIR FACES, SO THEY'VE DISOWNED ALL KNOWLEDGE OF THE PLACE!
THEY'RE WORRIED THE GOVERNMENT WILL FIND OUT... RESEARCH AND DEVELOPMENT OF BIO-WEAPONS *IS* ILLEGAL, Y'KNOW.
WHAT ARE THEY DOING?
IMPREGNATING THEM WITH THE BIOMECHANOIDS... THE ***ALIENS.***
YOU READ THE FILES, I SEE.
WHAT KIND OF MONSTER WOULD WANT TO LET THOSE THINGS FREE?
IT'S NOT HUMAN.
WHAT?
BACK WHEN I WAS IN THE FORCES, THIS GUY, ***OSTERMANN,**** HE USED TO TELL US STORIES.
HERE WE GO...
*SEE PREDATOR: XENOGENESIS.

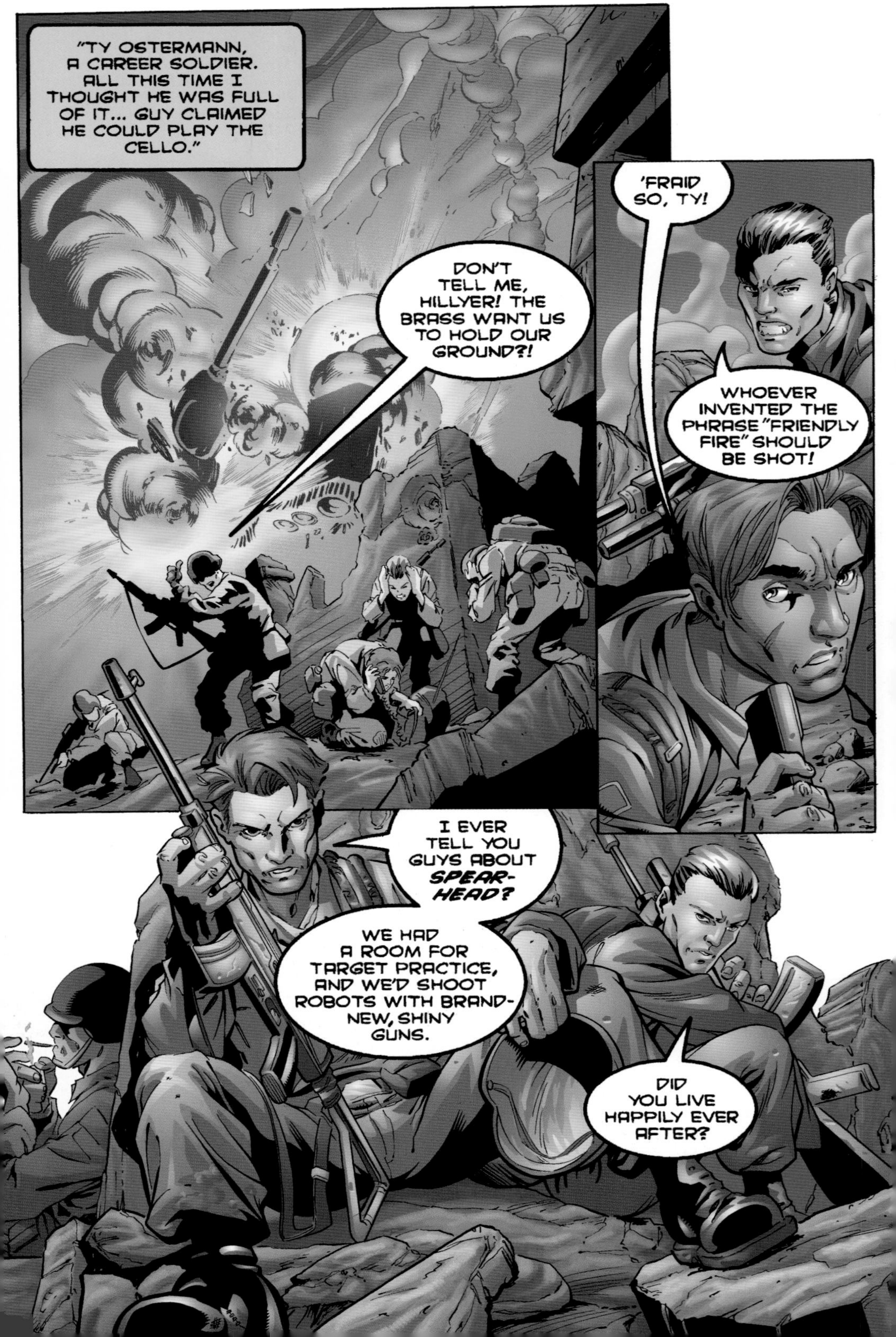
"TY OSTERMANN, A CAREER SOLDIER. ALL THIS TIME I THOUGHT HE WAS FULL OF IT... GUY CLAIMED HE COULD PLAY THE CELLO."
DON'T TELL ME, HILLYER! THE BRASS WANT US TO HOLD OUR GROUND?!
'FRAID SO, TY!
WHOEVER INVENTED THE PHRASE "FRIENDLY FIRE" SHOULD BE SHOT!
I EVER TELL YOU GUYS ABOUT *SPEAR-HEAD?*
WE HAD A ROOM FOR TARGET PRACTICE, AND WE'D SHOOT ROBOTS WITH BRAND-NEW, SHINY GUNS.
DID YOU LIVE HAPPILY EVER AFTER?

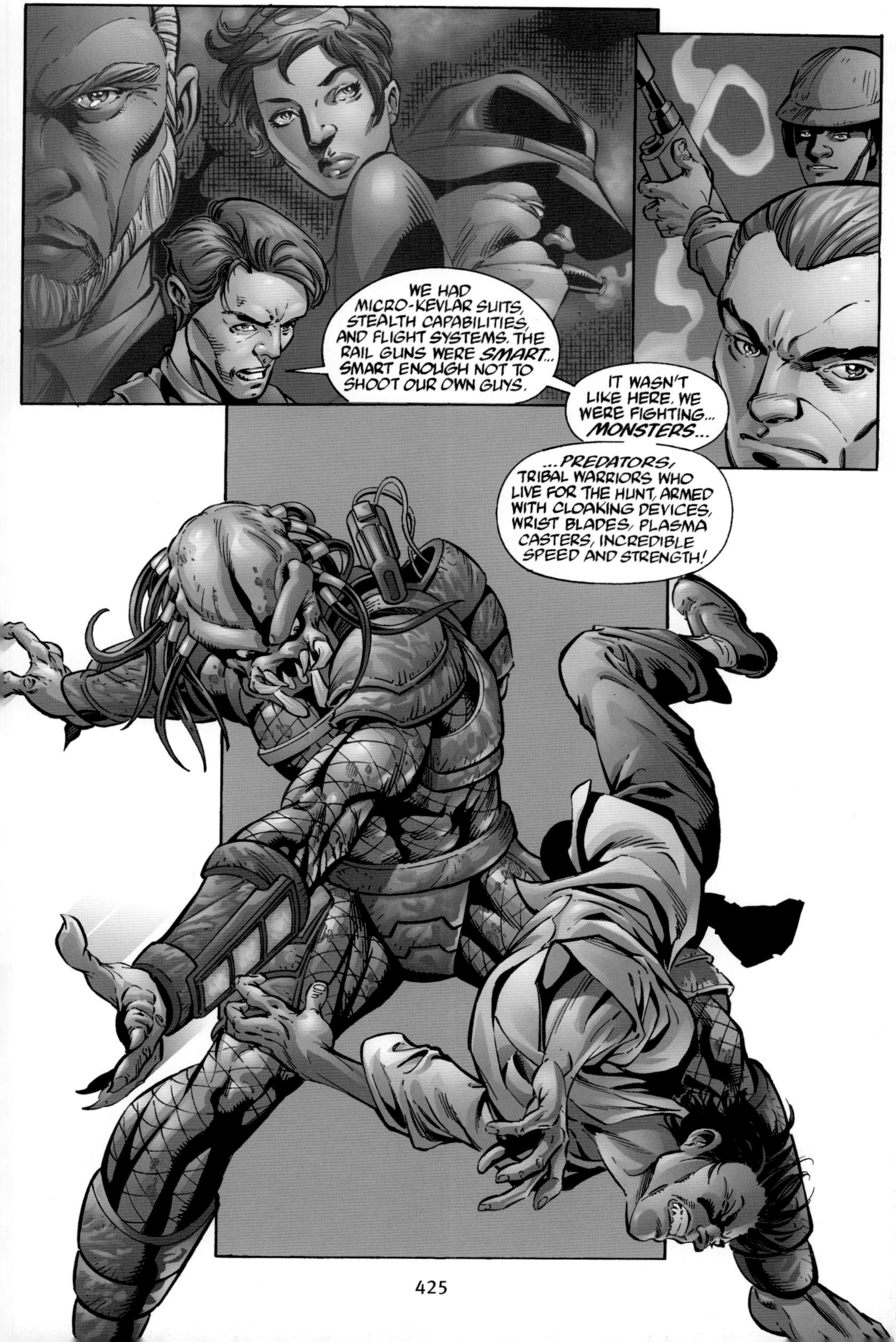
WE HAD MICRO-KEVLAR SUITS, STEALTH CAPABILITIES, AND FLIGHT SYSTEMS. THE RAIL GUNS WERE SMART... SMART ENOUGH NOT TO SHOOT OUR OWN GUYS.
IT WASN'T LIKE HERE. WE WERE FIGHTING... MONSTERS...
...PREDATORS, TRIBAL WARRIORS WHO LIVE FOR THE HUNT, ARMED WITH CLOAKING DEVICES, WRIST BLADES, PLASMA CASTERS, INCREDIBLE SPEED AND STRENGTH!

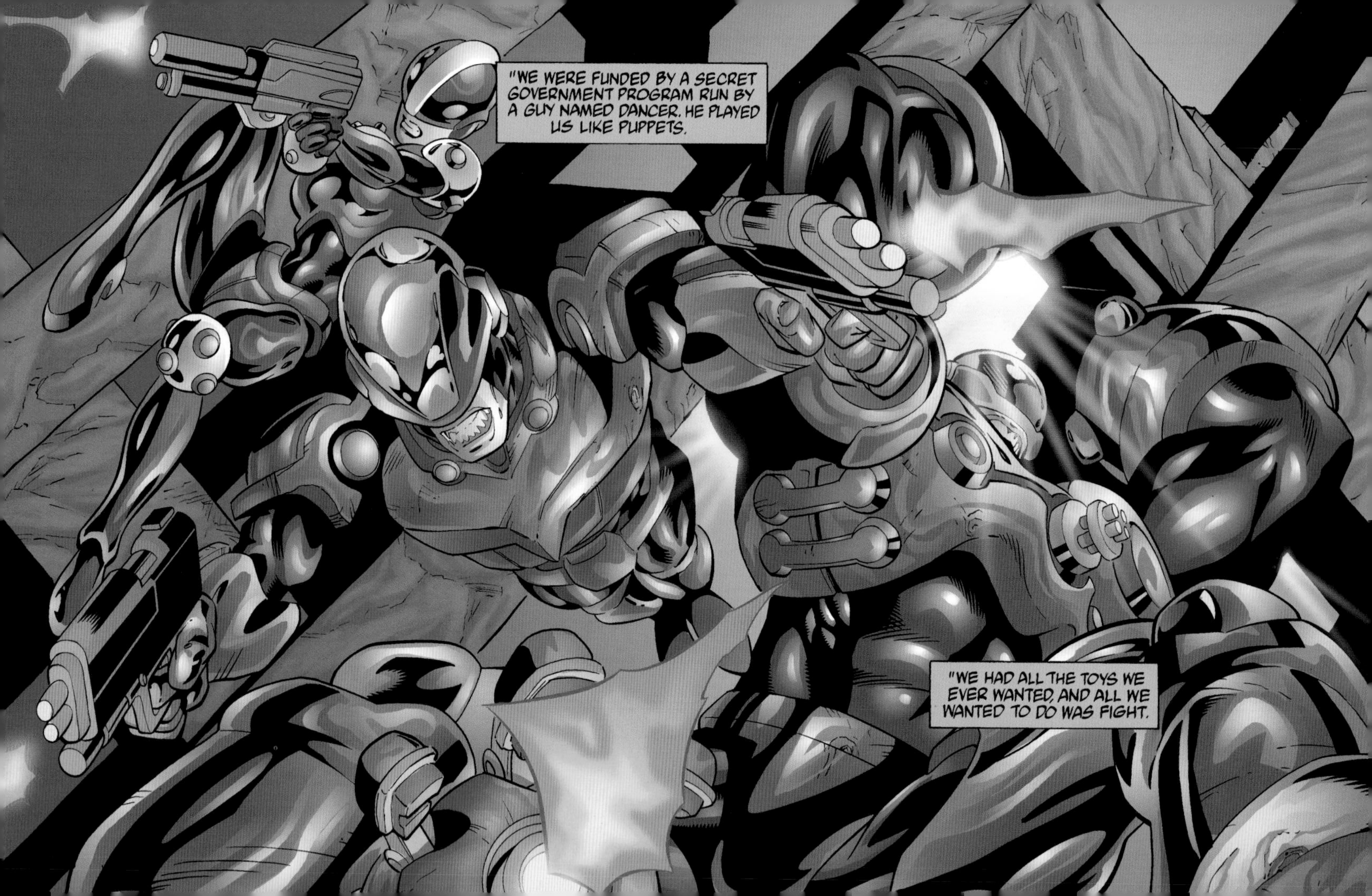
"WE WERE FUNDED BY A SECRET GOVERNMENT PROGRAM RUN BY A GUY NAMED DANCER. HE PLAYED US LIKE PUPPETS.
"WE HAD ALL THE TOYS WE EVER WANTED, AND ALL WE WANTED TO DO WAS FIGHT.

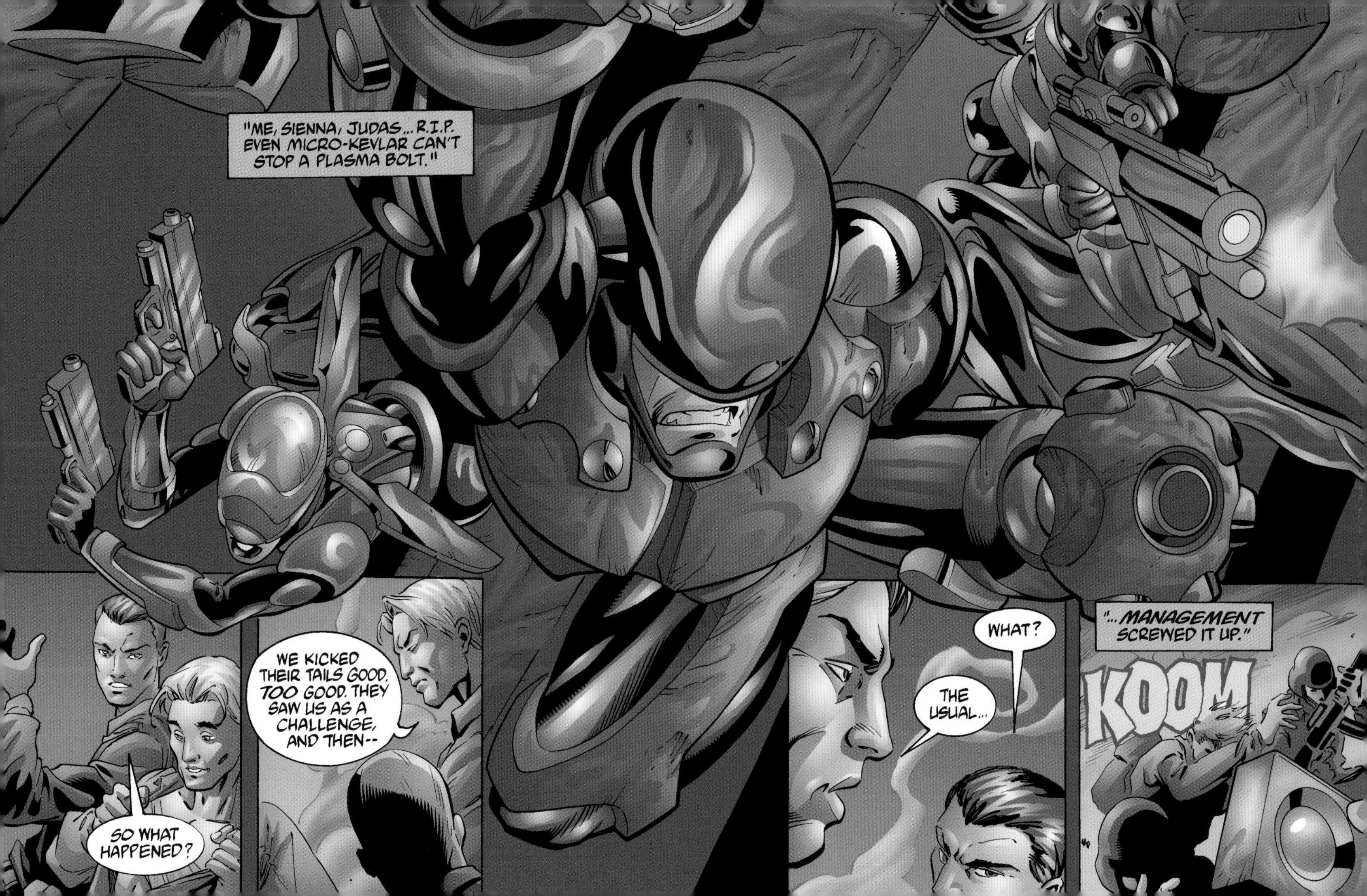
"ME, SIENNA, JUDAS... R.I.P. EVEN MICRO-KEVLAR CAN'T STOP A PLASMA BOLT."
SO WHAT HAPPENED?
WE KICKED THEIR TAILS GOOD. TOO GOOD. THEY SAW US AS A CHALLENGE, AND THEN--
WHAT?
THE USUAL...
"...MANAGEMENT SCREWED IT UP."
KOOM

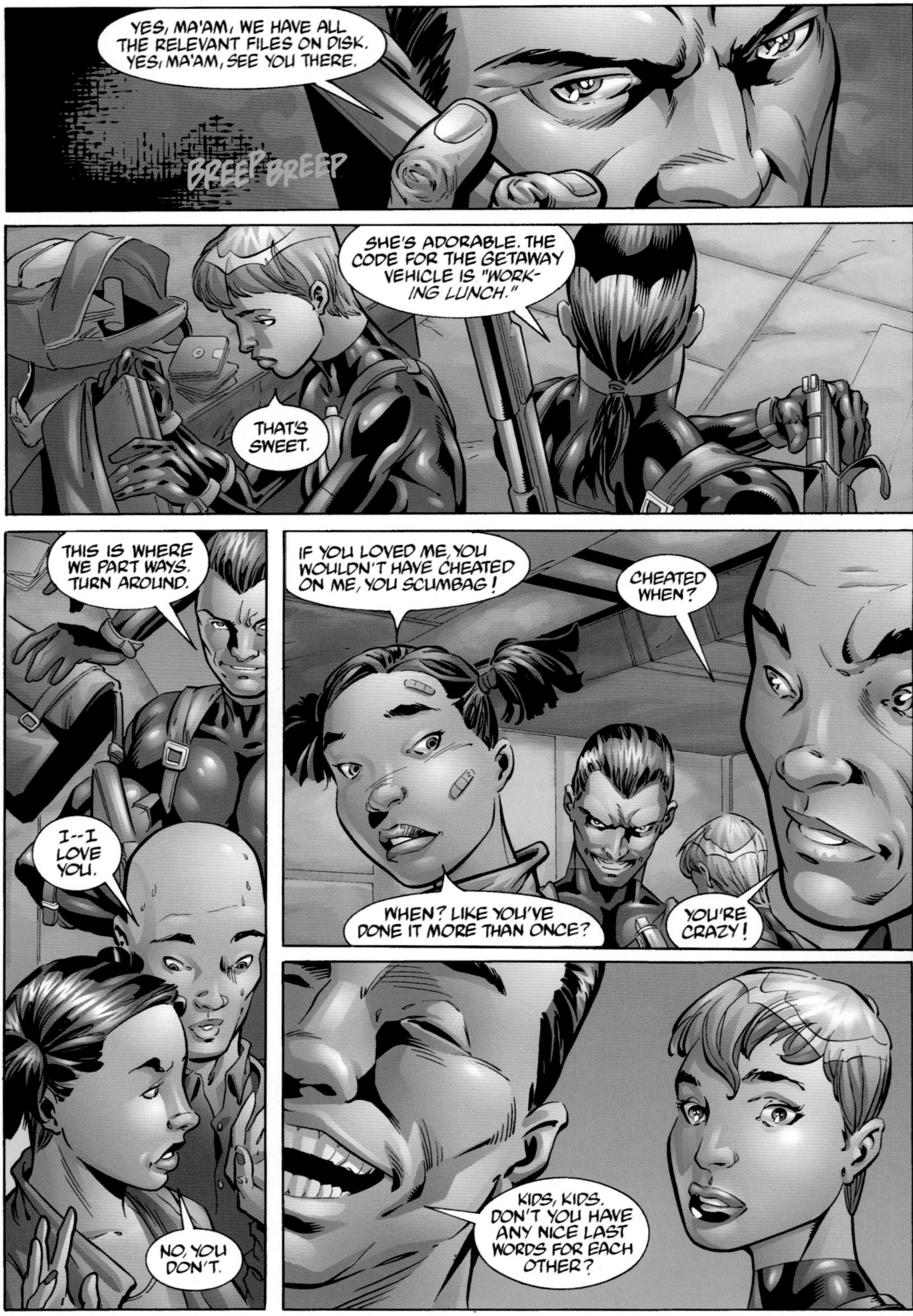
YES, MA'AM, WE HAVE ALL THE RELEVANT FILES ON DISK. YES, MA'AM, SEE YOU THERE.
BREEP BREEP
SHE'S ADORABLE. THE CODE FOR THE GETAWAY VEHICLE IS "WORKING LUNCH."
THAT'S SWEET.
THIS IS WHERE WE PART WAYS. TURN AROUND.
I--I LOVE YOU.
NO, YOU DON'T.
IF YOU LOVED ME, YOU WOULDN'T HAVE CHEATED ON ME, YOU SCUMBAG!
CHEATED WHEN?
WHEN? LIKE YOU'VE DONE IT MORE THAN ONCE?
YOU'RE CRAZY!
KIDS, KIDS. DON'T YOU HAVE ANY NICE LAST WORDS FOR EACH OTHER?

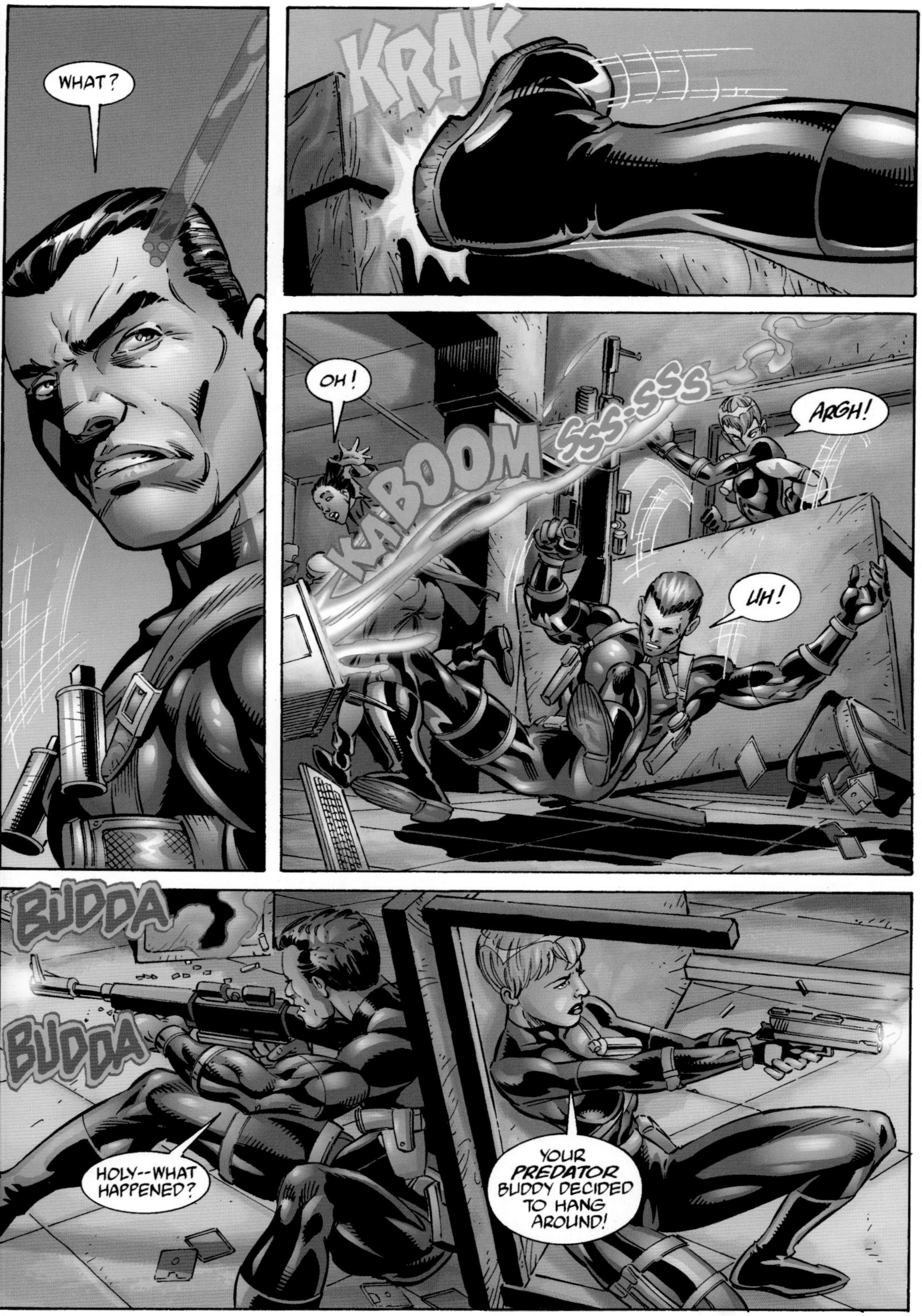
WHAT?
KRAK
OH!
KABOOM
SSS-SSS
ARGH!
UH!
BUDDA
BUDDA
HOLY--WHAT HAPPENED?
YOUR *PREDATOR* BUDDY DECIDED TO HANG AROUND!

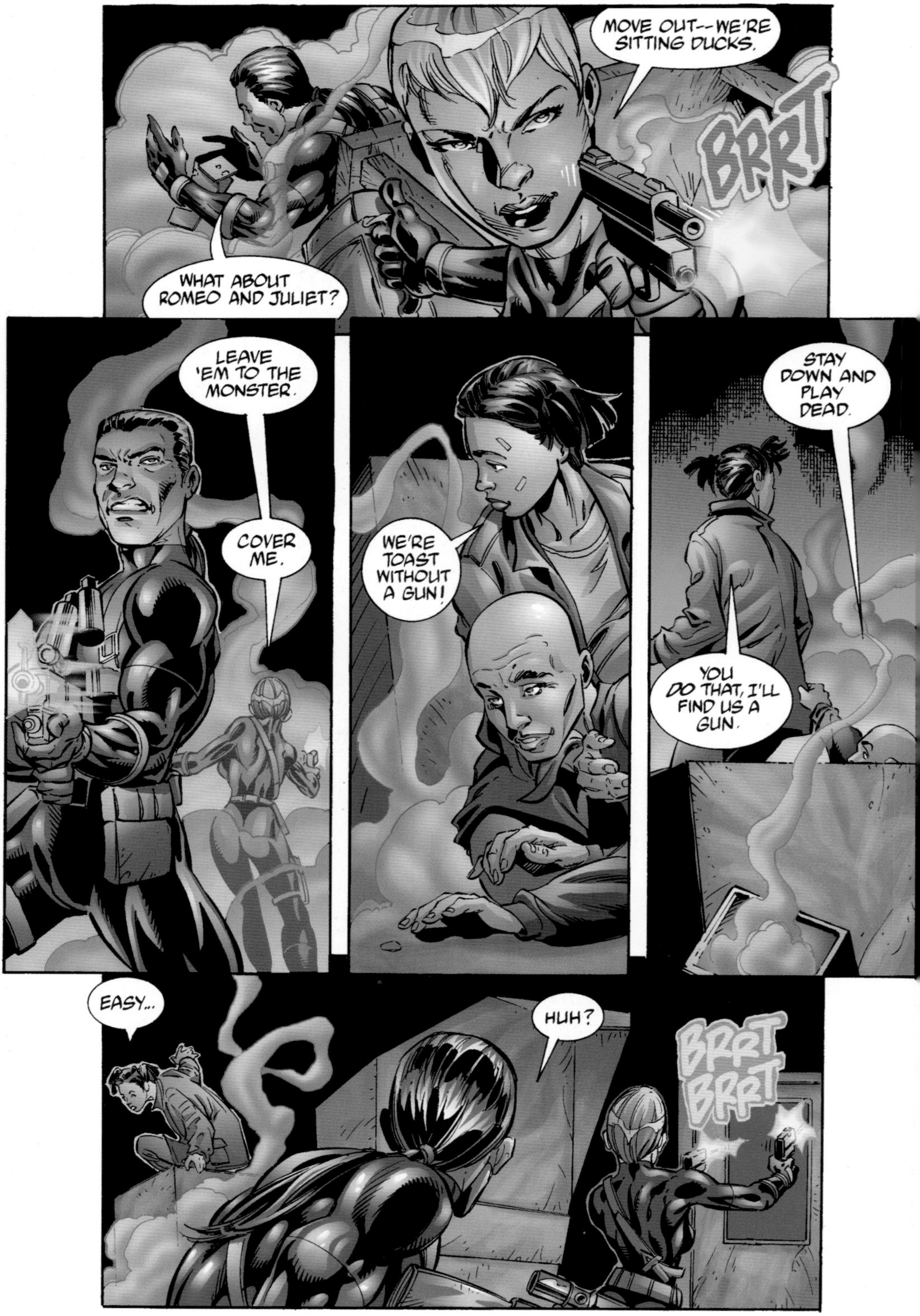
MOVE OUT--WE'RE SITTING DUCKS.
BRRT
WHAT ABOUT ROMEO AND JULIET?
LEAVE 'EM TO THE MONSTER.
COVER ME.
WE'RE TOAST WITHOUT A GUN!
STAY DOWN AND PLAY DEAD.
YOU DO THAT, I'LL FIND US A GUN.
EASY...
HUH?
BRRT BRRT

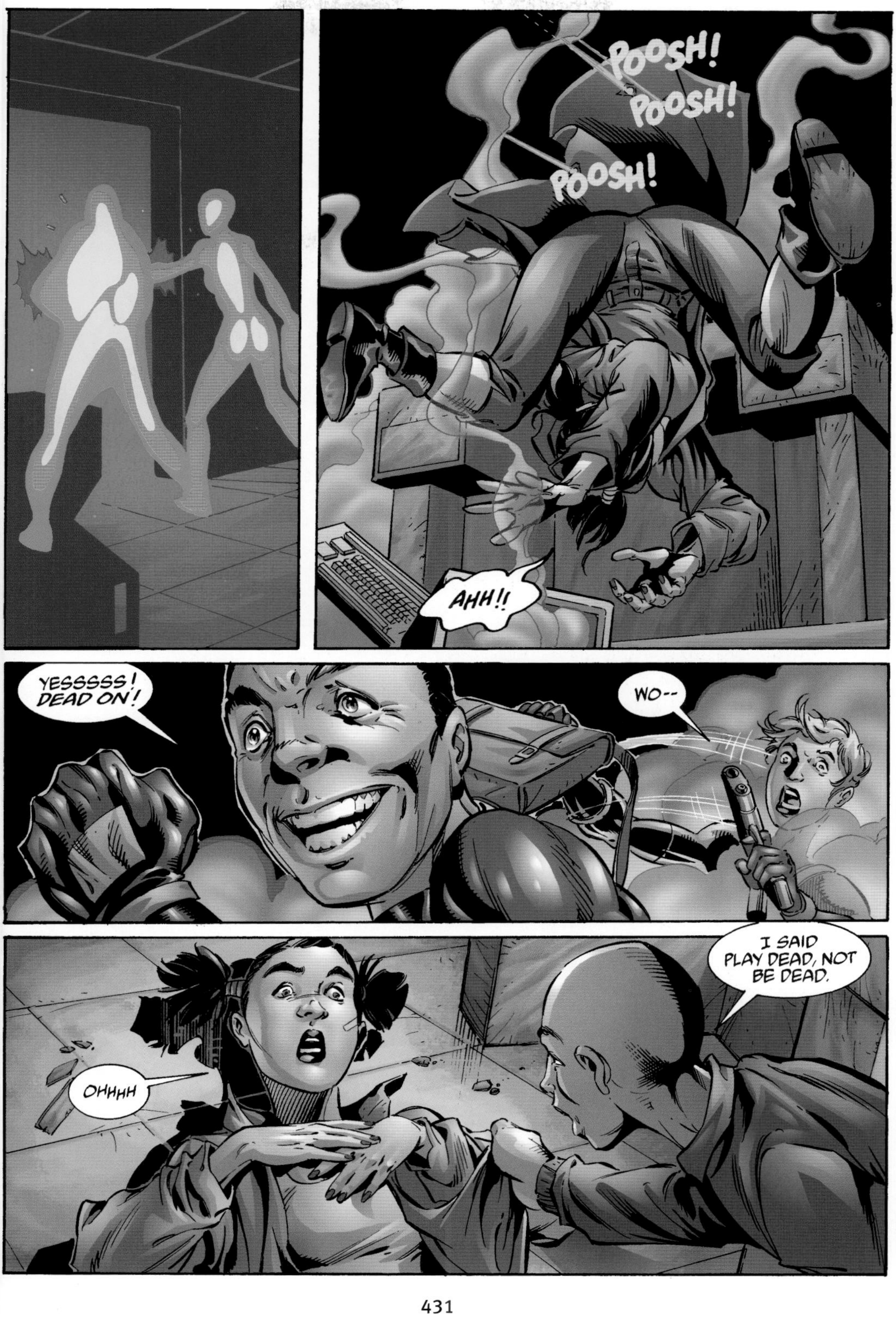
POOSH!
POOSH!
POOSH!
AHH!!
YESSSSS! DEAD ON!
WO--
I SAID PLAY DEAD, NOT BE DEAD.
OHHHH

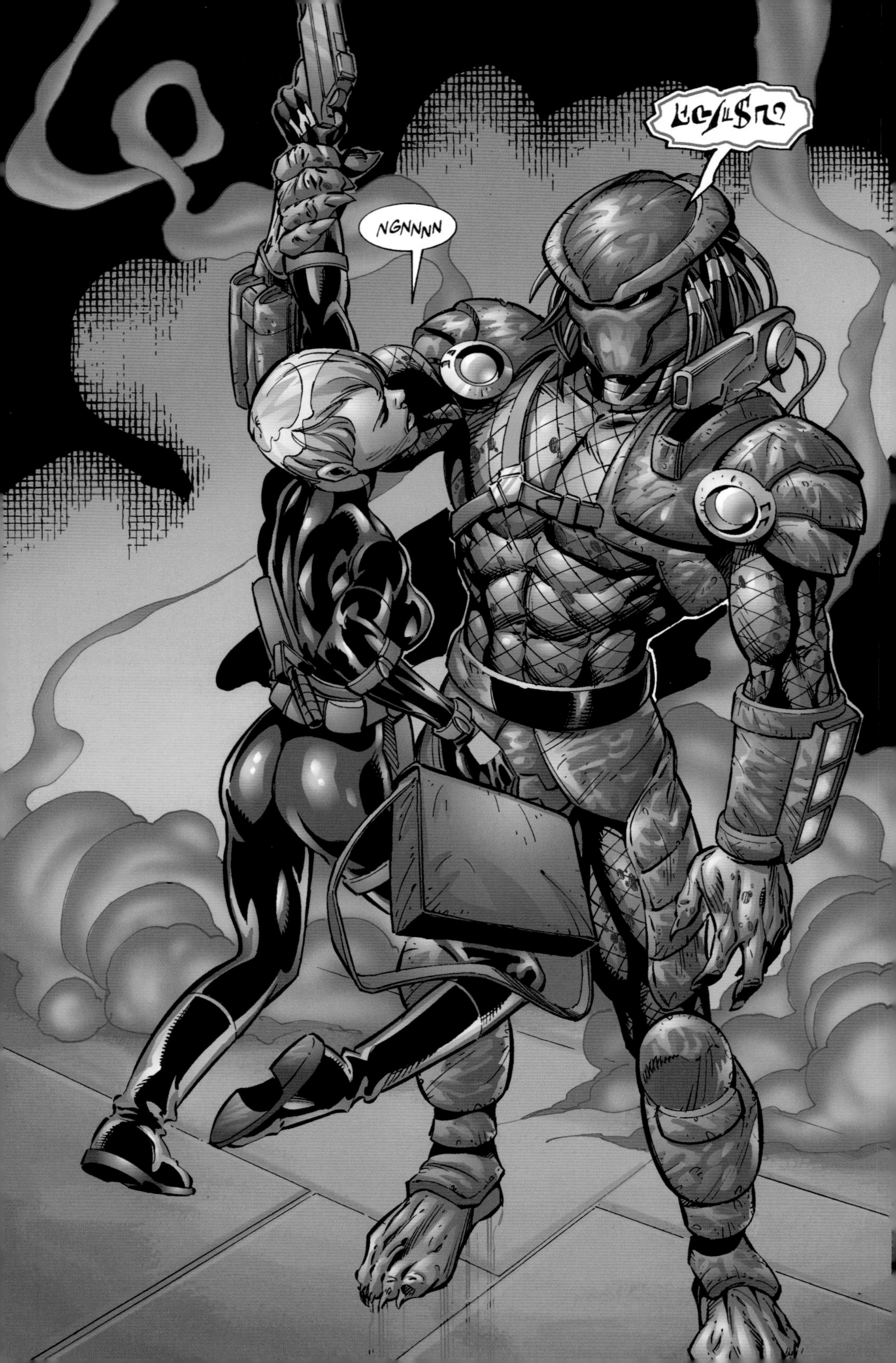
NGNNNN

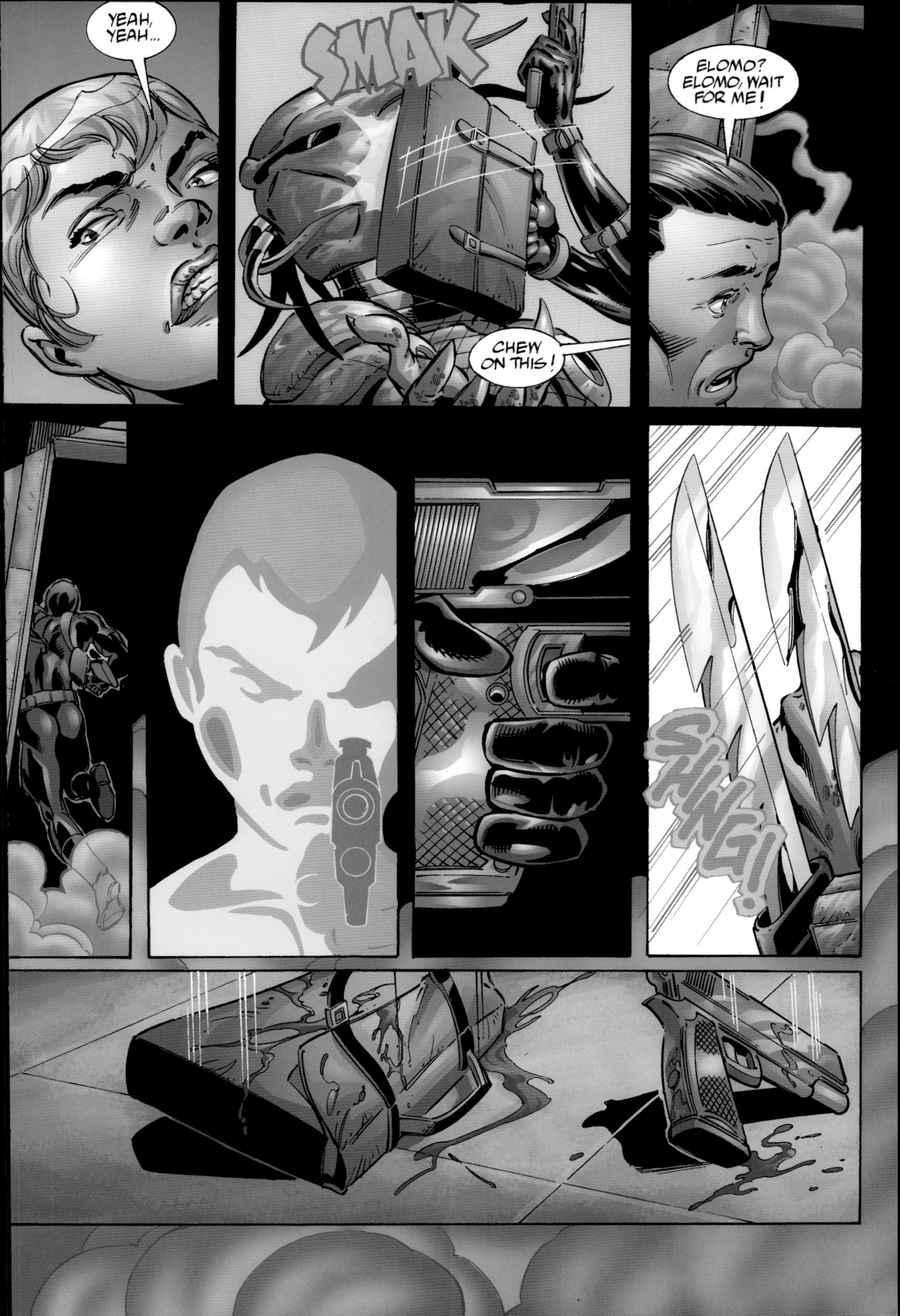
YEAH, YEAH...
SMAK
CHEW ON THIS!
ELOMO? ELOMO, WAIT FOR ME!
SHING!

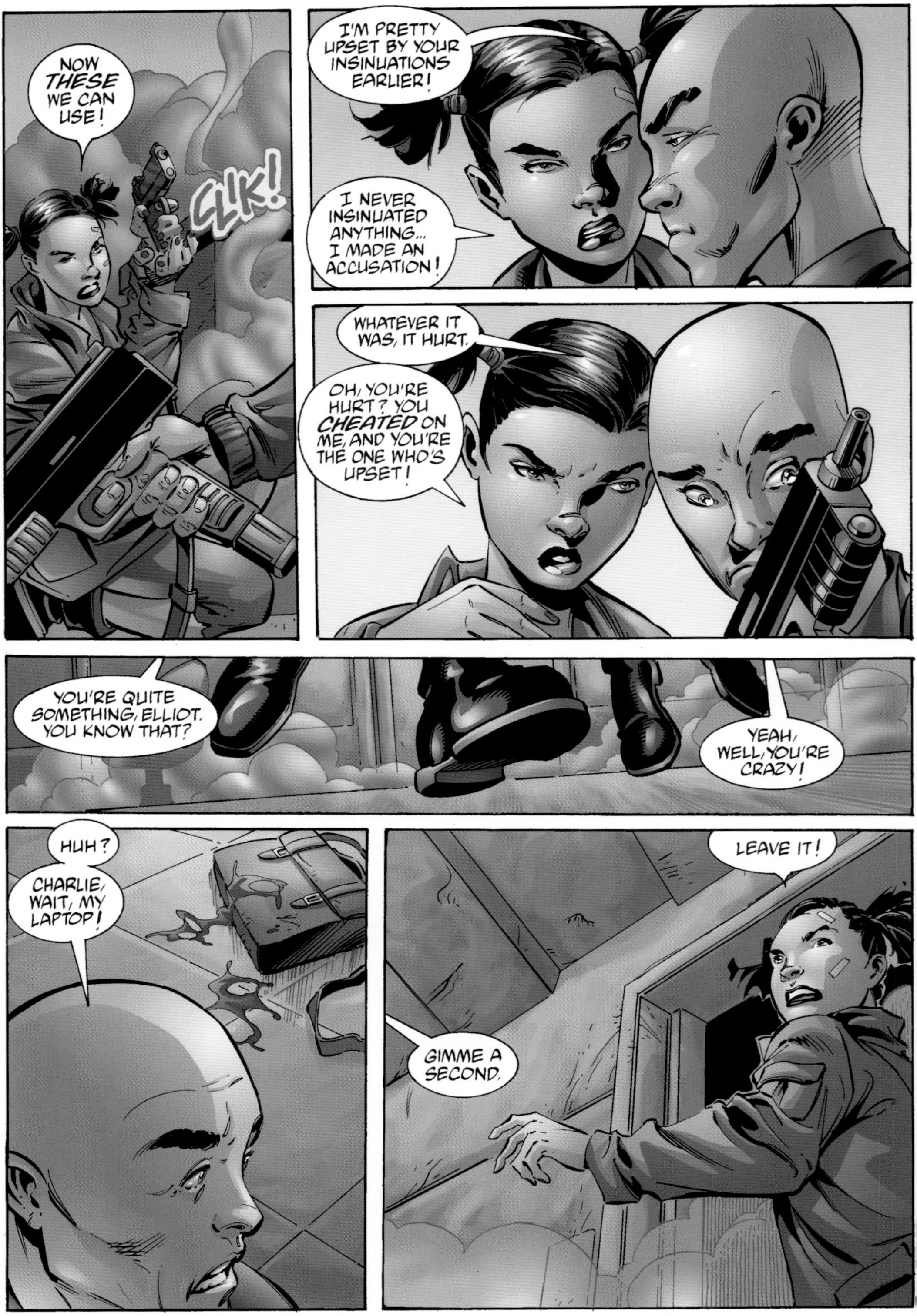
NOW THESE WE CAN USE!
CLIK!
I'M PRETTY UPSET BY YOUR INSINUATIONS EARLIER!
I NEVER INSINUATED ANYTHING... I MADE AN ACCUSATION!
WHATEVER IT WAS, IT HURT.
OH, YOU'RE HURT? YOU CHEATED ON ME, AND YOU'RE THE ONE WHO'S UPSET!
YOU'RE QUITE SOMETHING, ELLIOT. YOU KNOW THAT?
YEAH, WELL, YOU'RE CRAZY!
HUH?
CHARLIE, WAIT, MY LAPTOP!
LEAVE IT!
GIMME A SECOND.

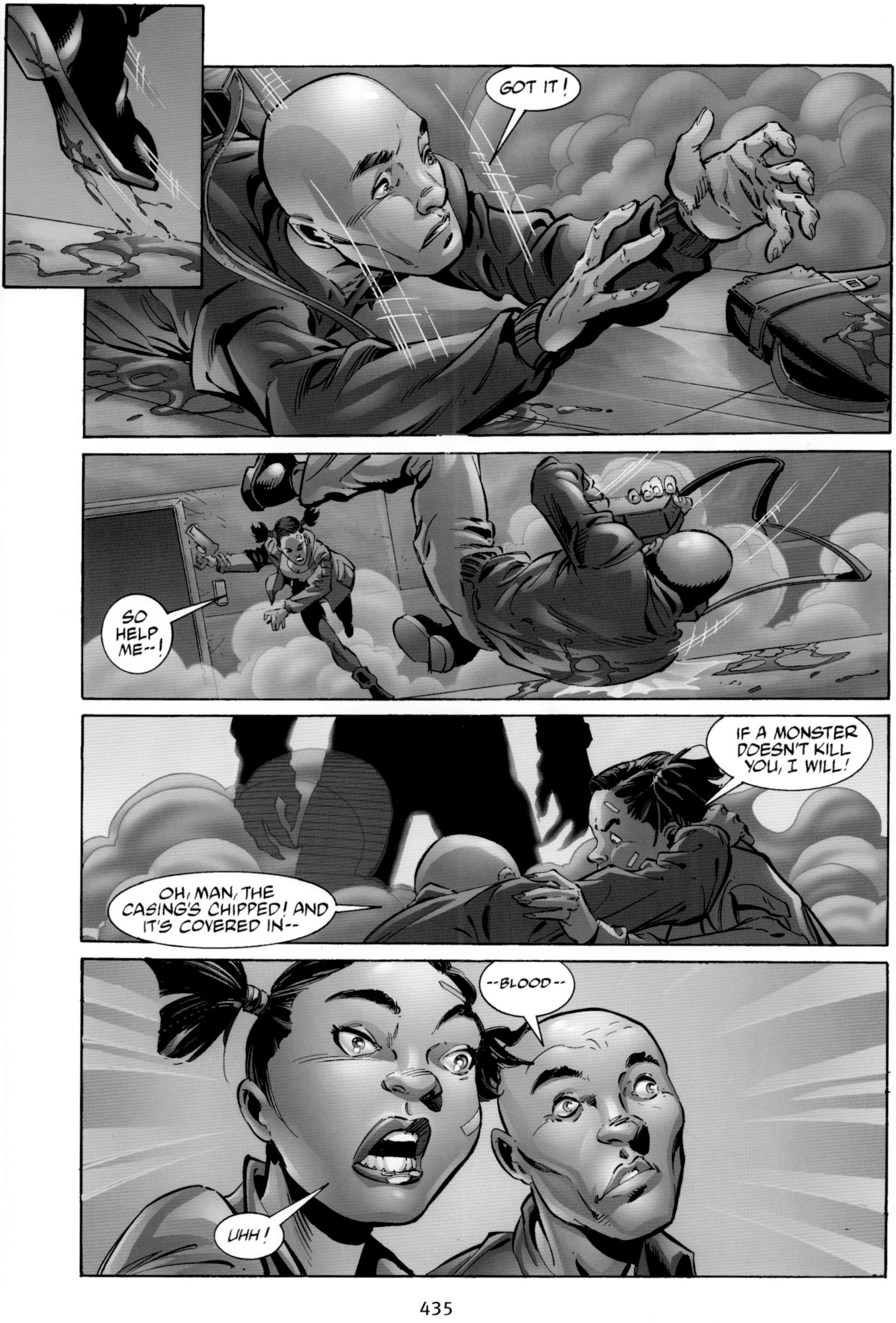
GOT IT!
SO HELP ME--!
IF A MONSTER DOESN'T KILL YOU, I WILL!
OH, MAN, THE CASING'S CHIPPED! AND IT'S COVERED IN--
--BLOOD--
UHH!

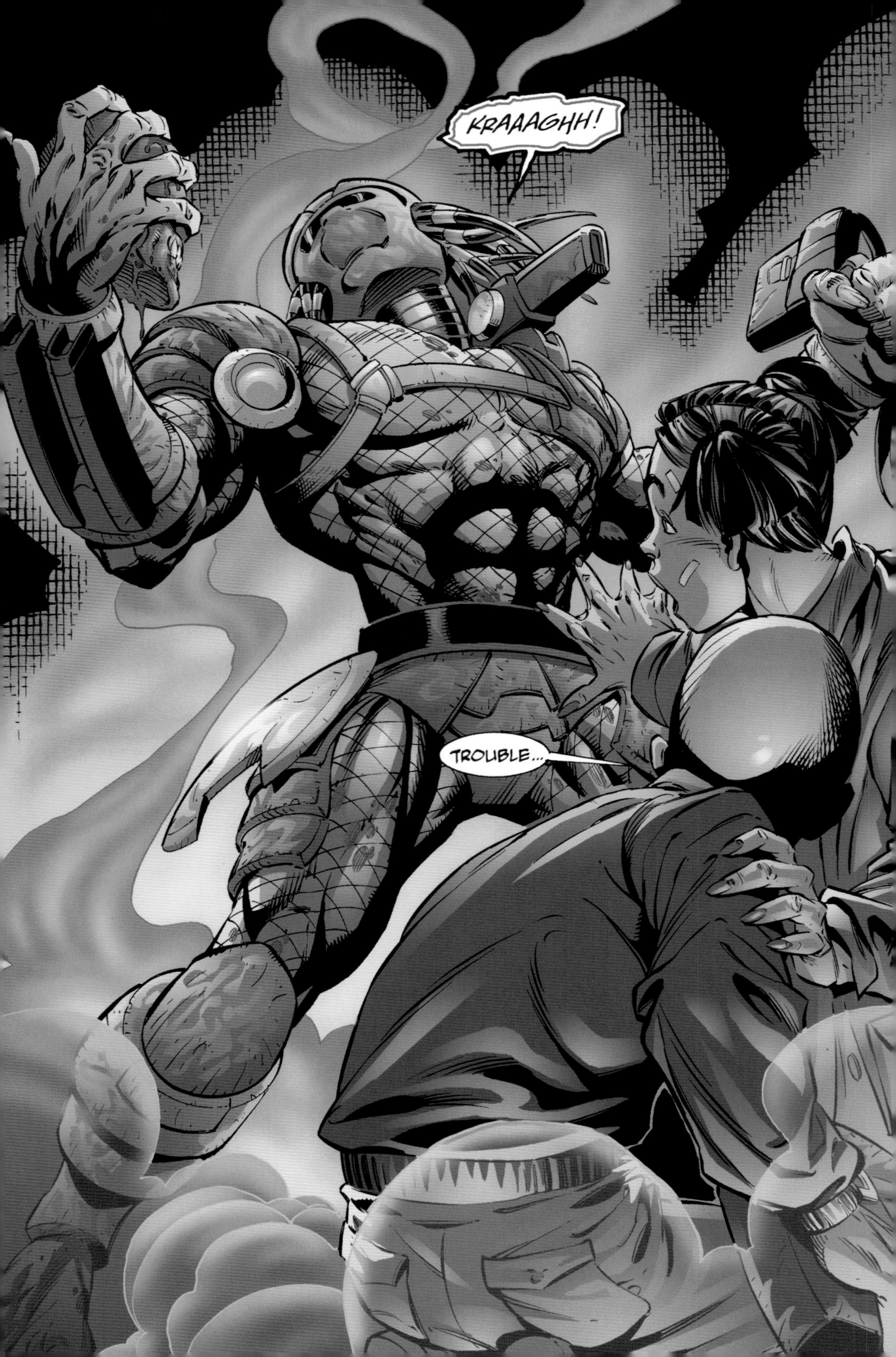
KRAAAGHH!
TROUBLE...

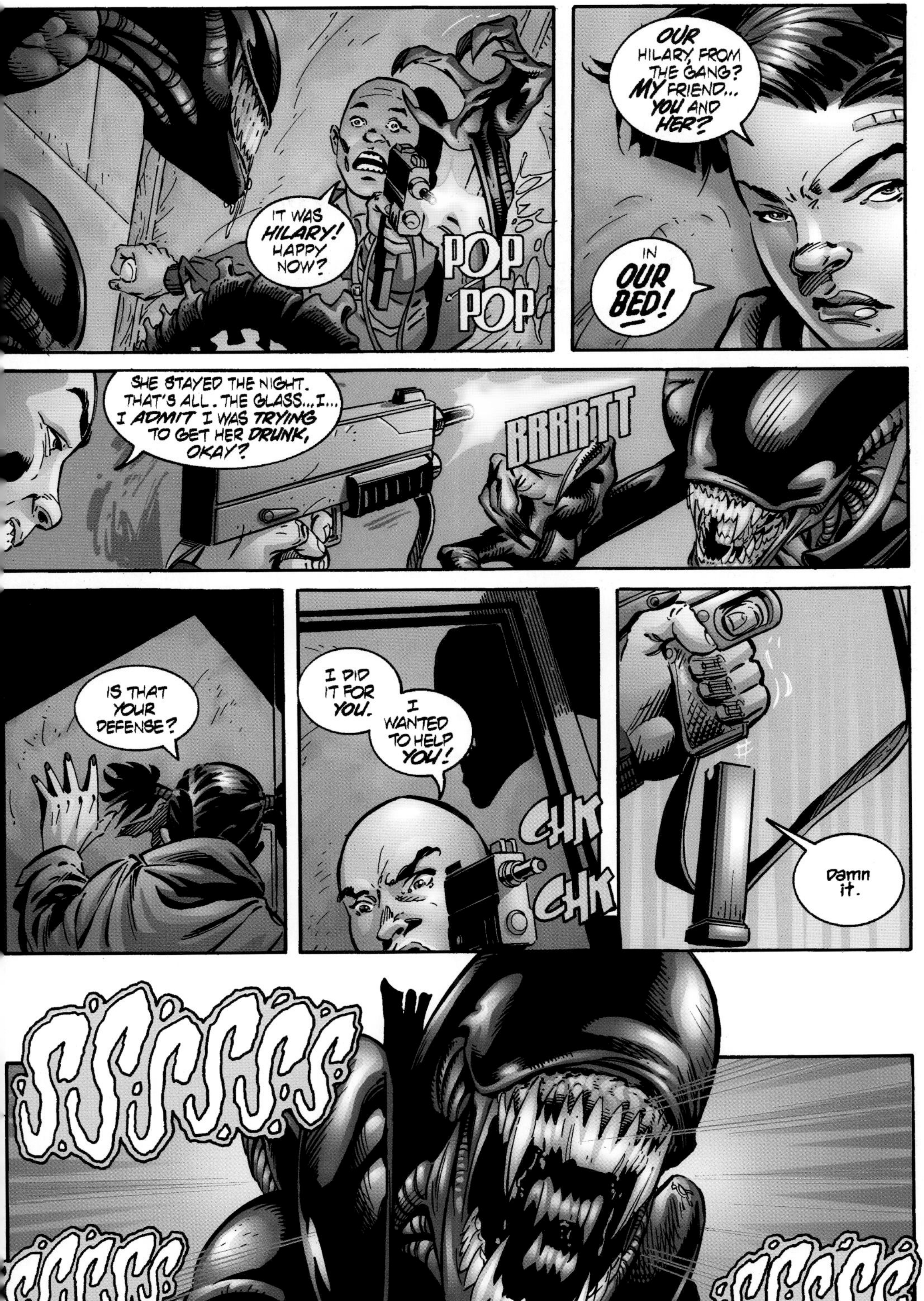

IT WAS HILARY! HAPPY NOW?
POP POP
OUR HILARY, FROM THE GANG? MY FRIEND... YOU AND HER?
IN OUR BED!
SHE STAYED THE NIGHT. THAT'S ALL. THE GLASS... I... I ADMIT I WAS TRYING TO GET HER DRUNK, OKAY?
BRRRTT
IS THAT YOUR DEFENSE?
I DID IT FOR YOU.
I WANTED TO HELP YOU!
CHK CHK
Damn it.

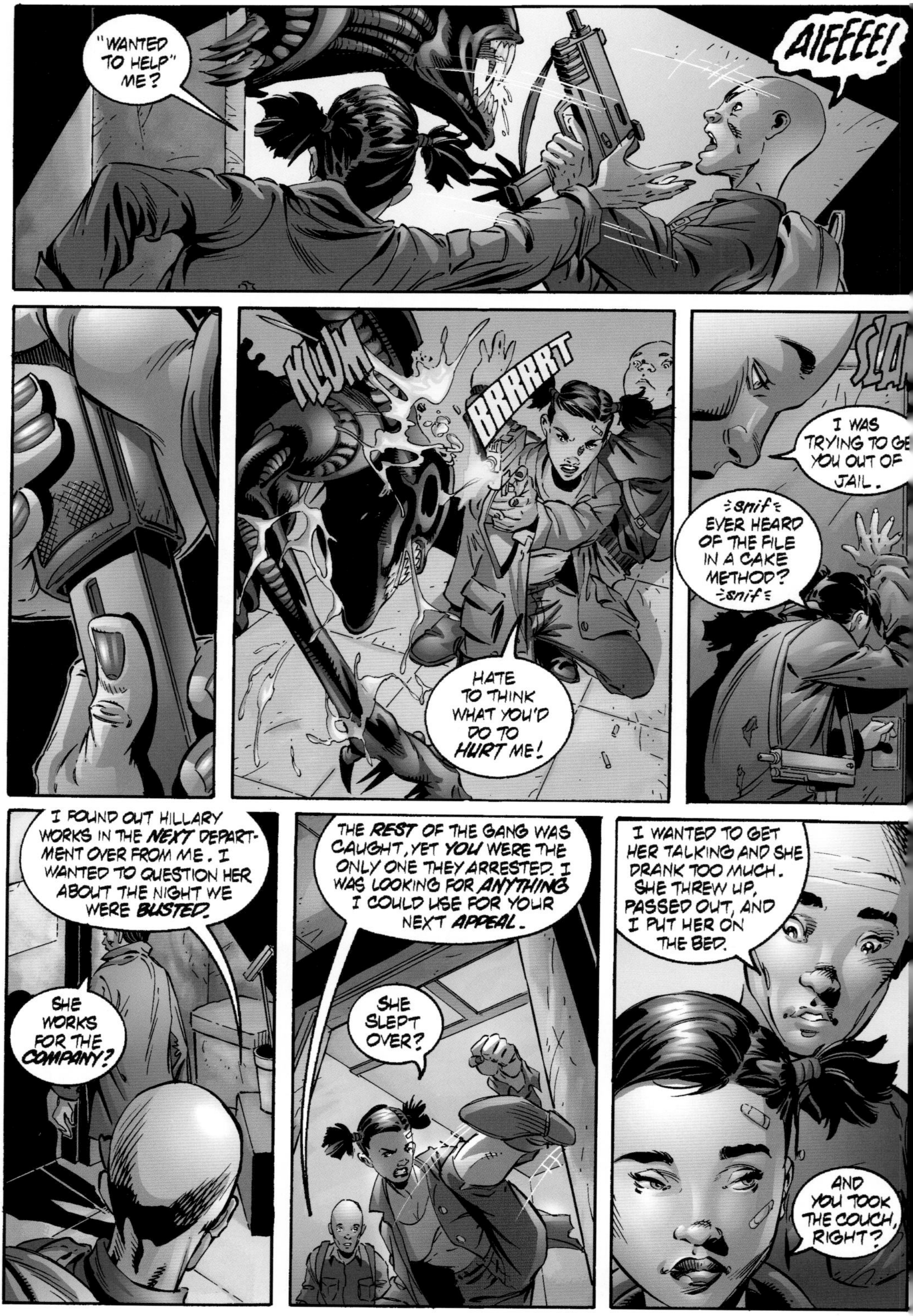
"WANTED TO HELP" ME?
AIEEEEE!
KLUNK
BRRRRRT
HATE TO THINK WHAT YOU'D DO TO *HURT* ME!
I WAS TRYING TO GET YOU OUT OF JAIL.
snif EVER HEARD OF THE FILE IN A CAKE METHOD? *snif*
I FOUND OUT HILLARY WORKS IN THE *NEXT* DEPARTMENT OVER FROM ME. I WANTED TO QUESTION HER ABOUT THE NIGHT WE WERE *BUSTED*.
SHE WORKS FOR THE *COMPANY*?
THE *REST* OF THE GANG WAS CAUGHT, YET *YOU* WERE THE ONLY ONE THEY ARRESTED. I WAS LOOKING FOR *ANYTHING* I COULD USE FOR YOUR NEXT *APPEAL*.
SHE SLEPT OVER?
I WANTED TO GET HER TALKING AND SHE DRANK TOO MUCH. SHE THREW UP, PASSED OUT, AND I PUT HER ON THE BED.
AND YOU TOOK THE COUCH, RIGHT?

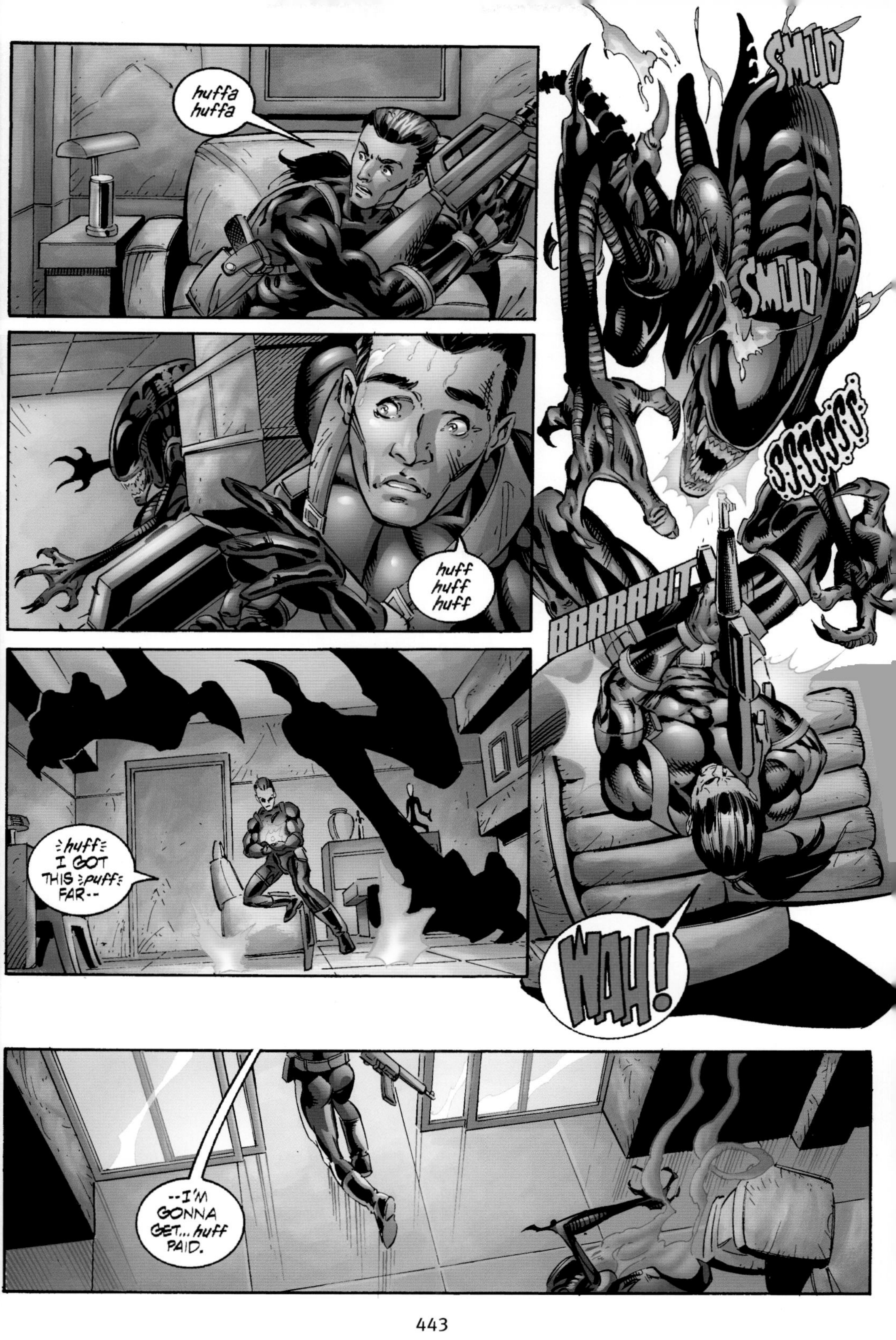
huffa huffa
huff huff huff
SMUD
SMUD
SSSSSSS
BRRRRRIT
huff I GOT THIS puff FAR--
WAH!
--I'M GONNA GET... huff PAID.

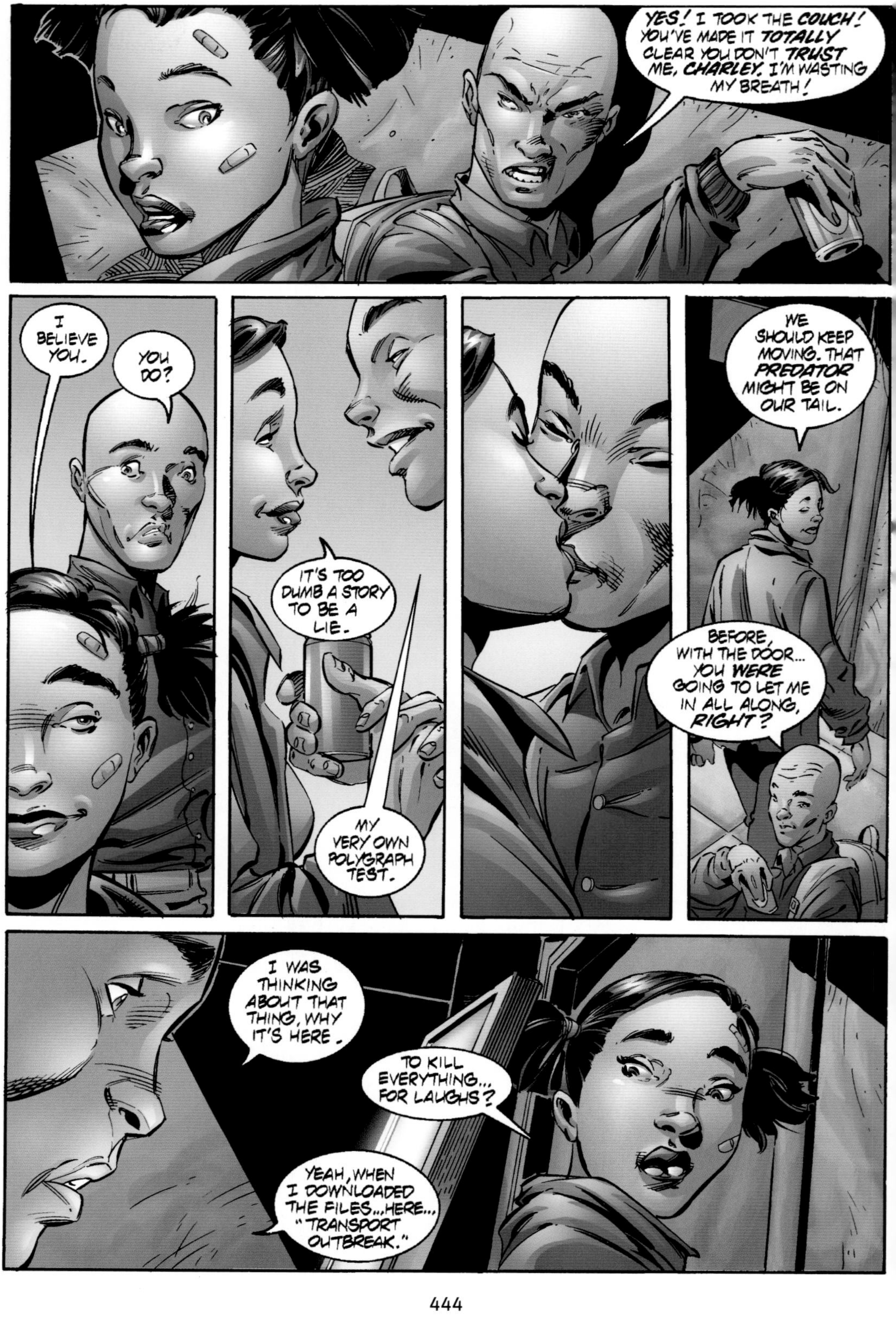
YES! I TOOK THE COUCH! YOU'VE MADE IT TOTALLY CLEAR YOU DON'T TRUST ME, CHARLEY. I'M WASTING MY BREATH!
I BELIEVE YOU.
YOU DO?
IT'S TOO DUMB A STORY TO BE A LIE.
MY VERY OWN POLYGRAPH TEST.
WE SHOULD KEEP MOVING. THAT PREDATOR MIGHT BE ON OUR TAIL.
BEFORE, WITH THE DOOR... YOU WERE GOING TO LET ME IN ALL ALONG, RIGHT?
I WAS THINKING ABOUT THAT THING, WHY IT'S HERE.
TO KILL EVERYTHING... FOR LAUGHS?
YEAH, WHEN I DOWNLOADED THE FILES... HERE... "TRANSPORT OUTBREAK."

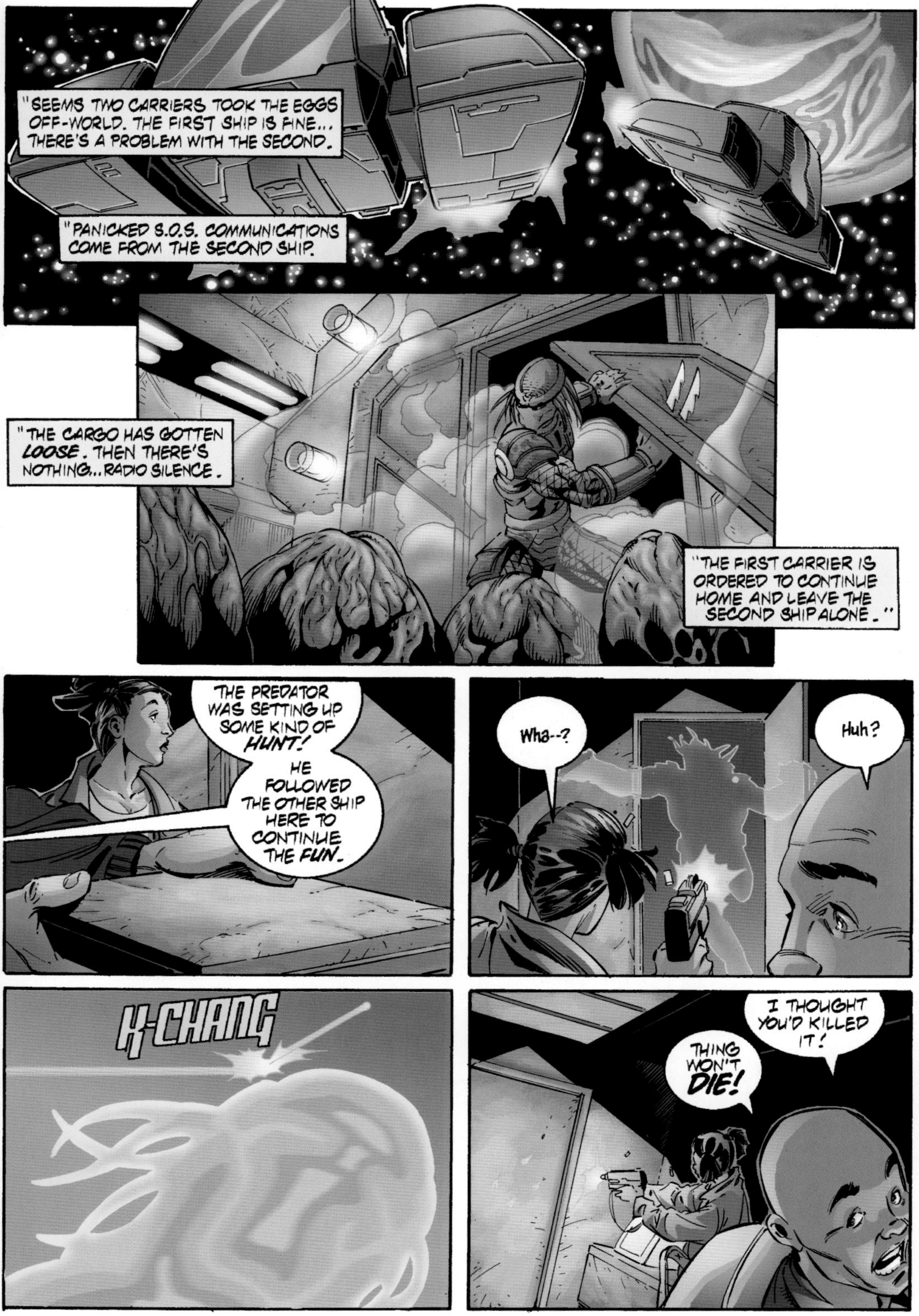
"SEEMS TWO CARRIERS TOOK THE EGGS OFF-WORLD. THE FIRST SHIP IS FINE... THERE'S A PROBLEM WITH THE SECOND.
"PANICKED S.O.S. COMMUNICATIONS COME FROM THE SECOND SHIP.
"THE CARGO HAS GOTTEN LOOSE. THEN THERE'S NOTHING... RADIO SILENCE.
"THE FIRST CARRIER IS ORDERED TO CONTINUE HOME AND LEAVE THE SECOND SHIP ALONE."
THE PREDATOR WAS SETTING UP SOME KIND OF HUNT!
HE FOLLOWED THE OTHER SHIP HERE TO CONTINUE THE FUN.
Wha--?
Huh?
K-CHANG
I THOUGHT YOU'D KILLED IT!
THING WON'T DIE!

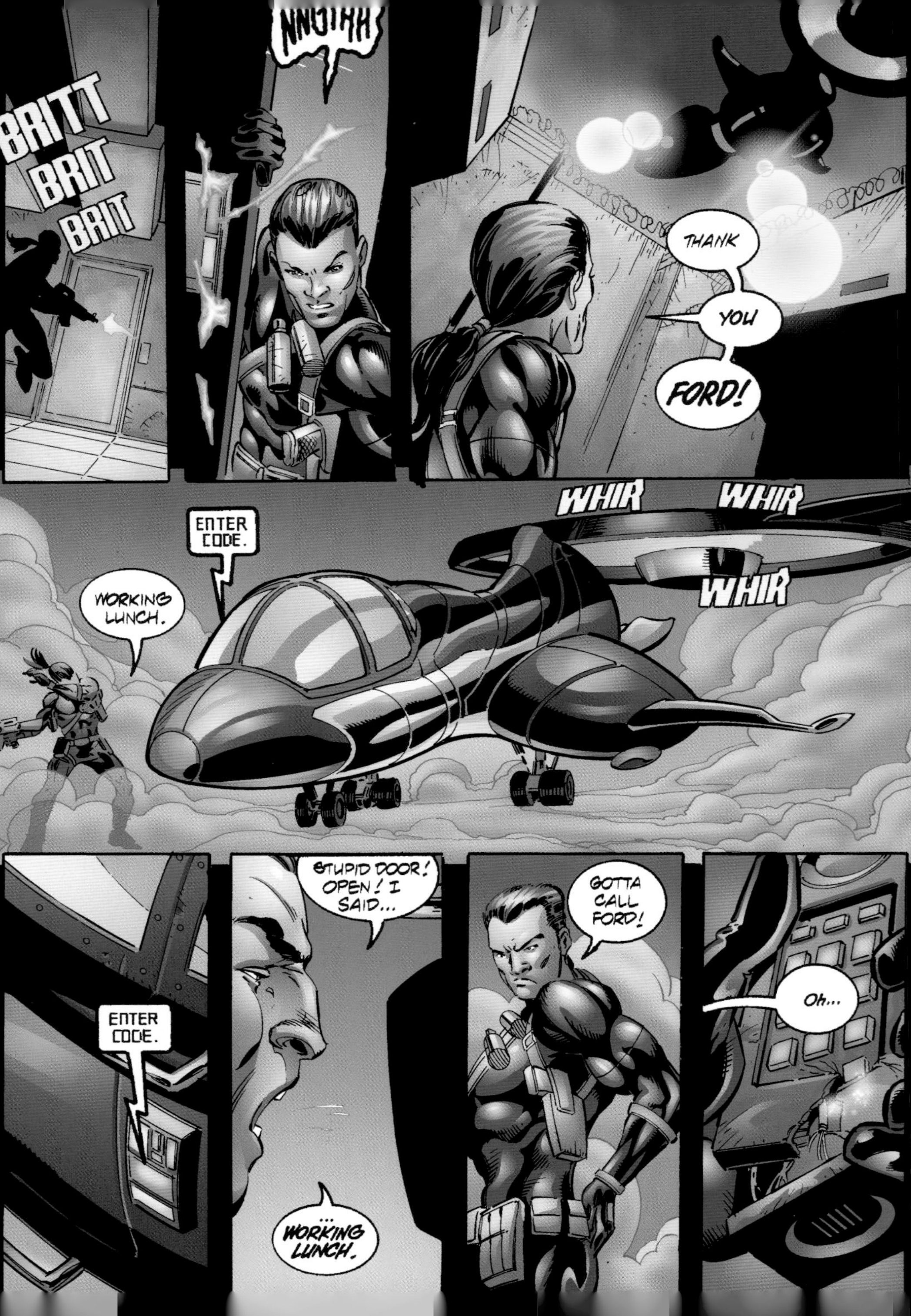
BRITT
BRIT
BRIT
THANK
YOU
FORD!
WHIR
WHIR
WHIR
ENTER CODE.
WORKING LUNCH.
ENTER CODE.
STUPID DOOR! OPEN! I SAID...
...WORKING LUNCH.
GOTTA CALL FORD!
Oh...

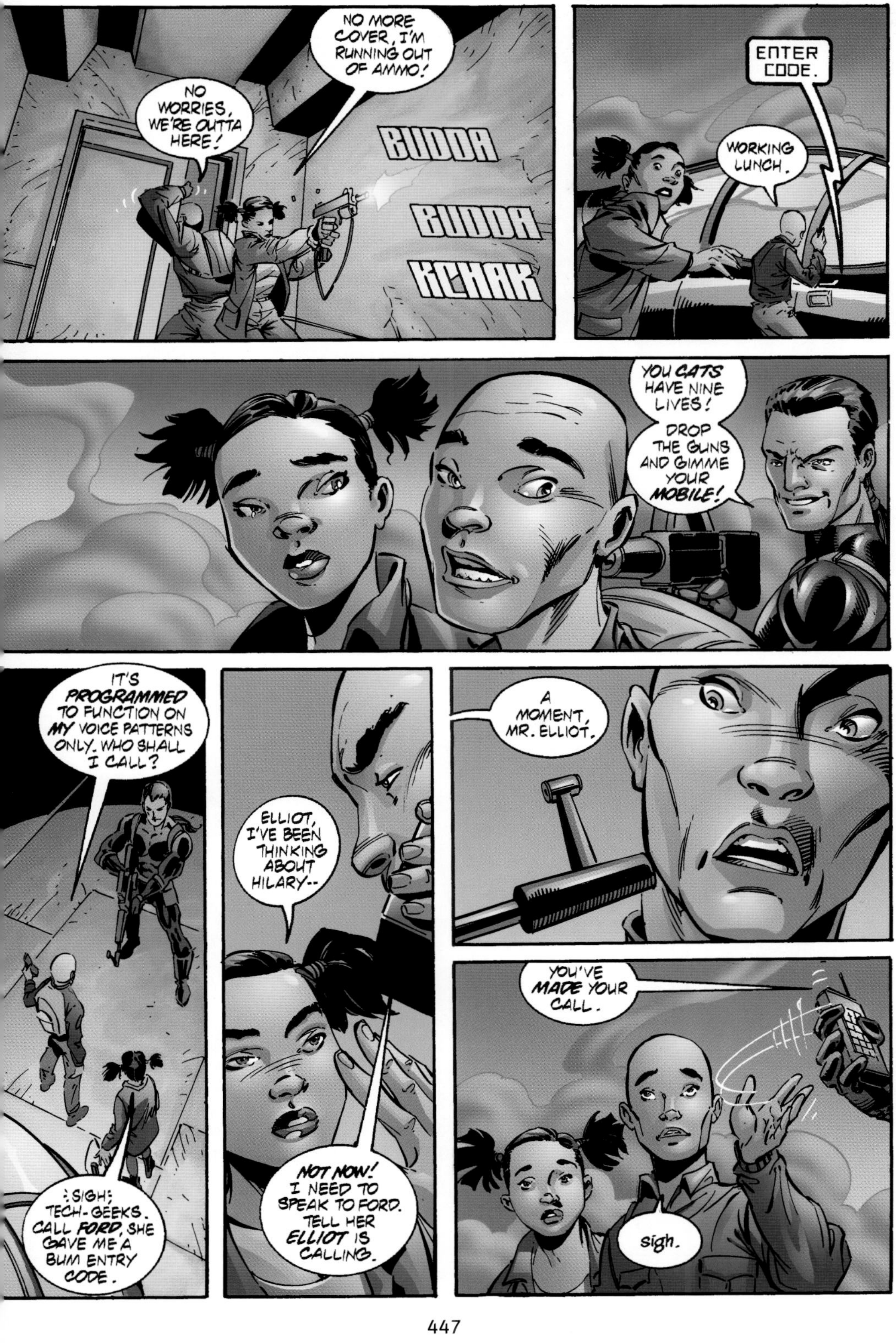

NO MORE COVER, I'M RUNNING OUT OF AMMO!
NO WORRIES, WE'RE OUTTA HERE!
BUDDA
BUDDA
KCHAK
ENTER CODE.
WORKING LUNCH.
YOU CATS HAVE NINE LIVES!
DROP THE GUNS AND GIMME YOUR MOBILE!
IT'S PROGRAMMED TO FUNCTION ON MY VOICE PATTERNS ONLY. WHO SHALL I CALL?
:SIGH: TECH-GEEKS. CALL FORD, SHE GAVE ME A BUM ENTRY CODE.
ELLIOT, I'VE BEEN THINKING ABOUT HILARY--
NOT NOW! I NEED TO SPEAK TO FORD. TELL HER ELLIOT IS CALLING.
A MOMENT, MR. ELLIOT.
YOU'VE MADE YOUR CALL.
sigh.

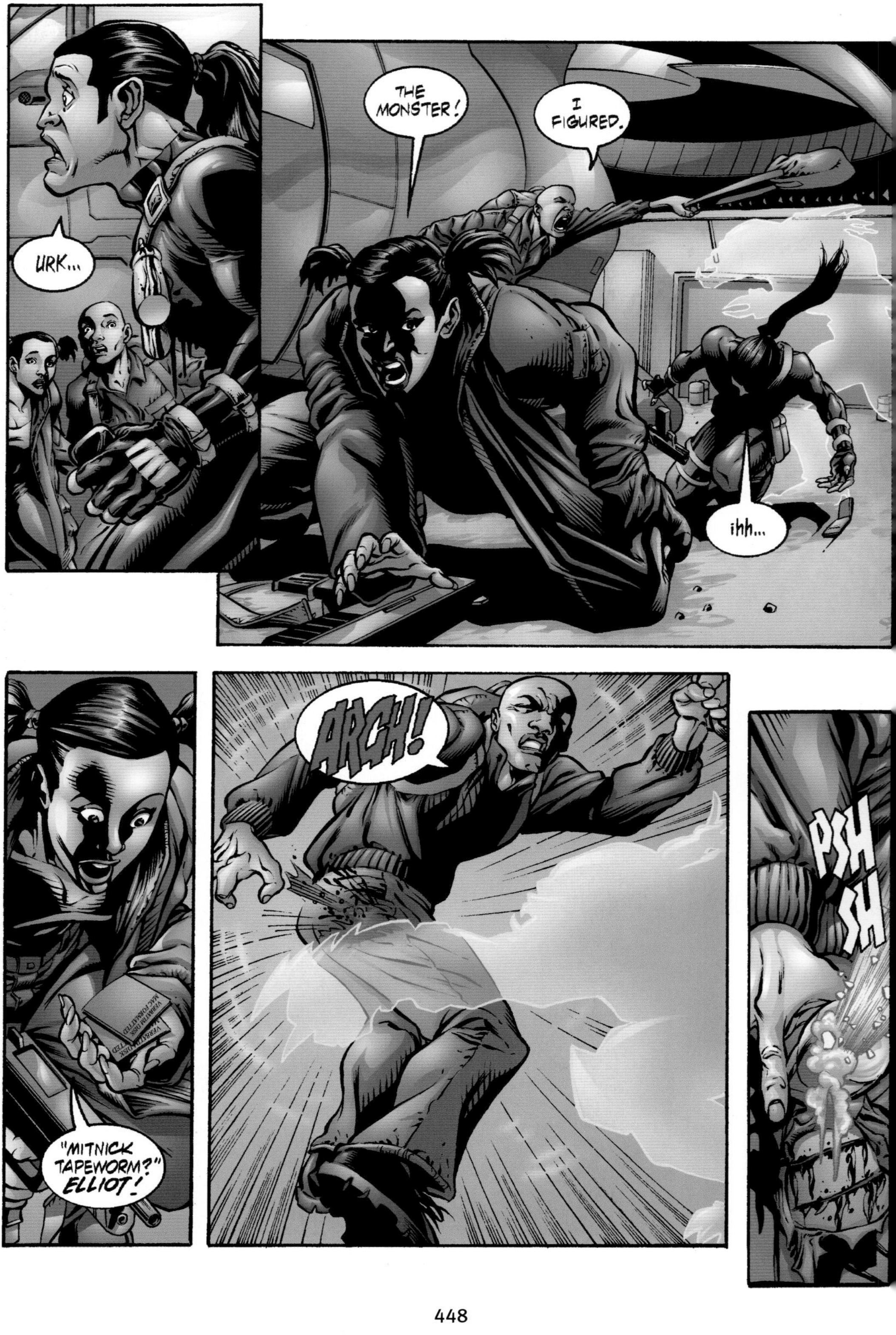
URK...
THE MONSTER!
I FIGURED.
ihh...
"MITNICK TAPEWORM?" ELLIOT!
ARCH!
PSH SH

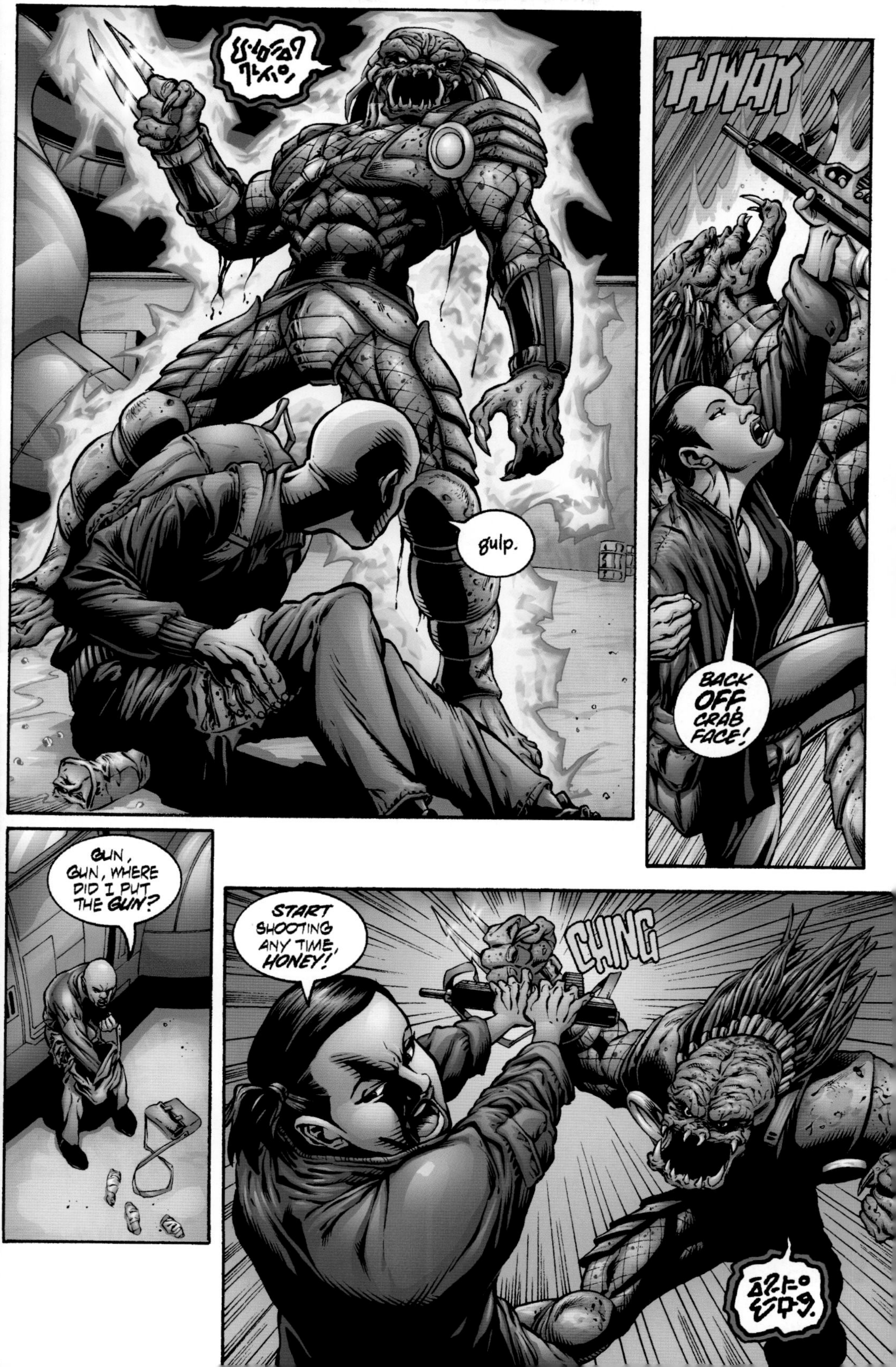
gulp.
THWAK
BACK OFF, CRAB FACE!
GUN, GUN, WHERE DID I PUT THE GUN?
START SHOOTING ANY TIME, HONEY!
CHING

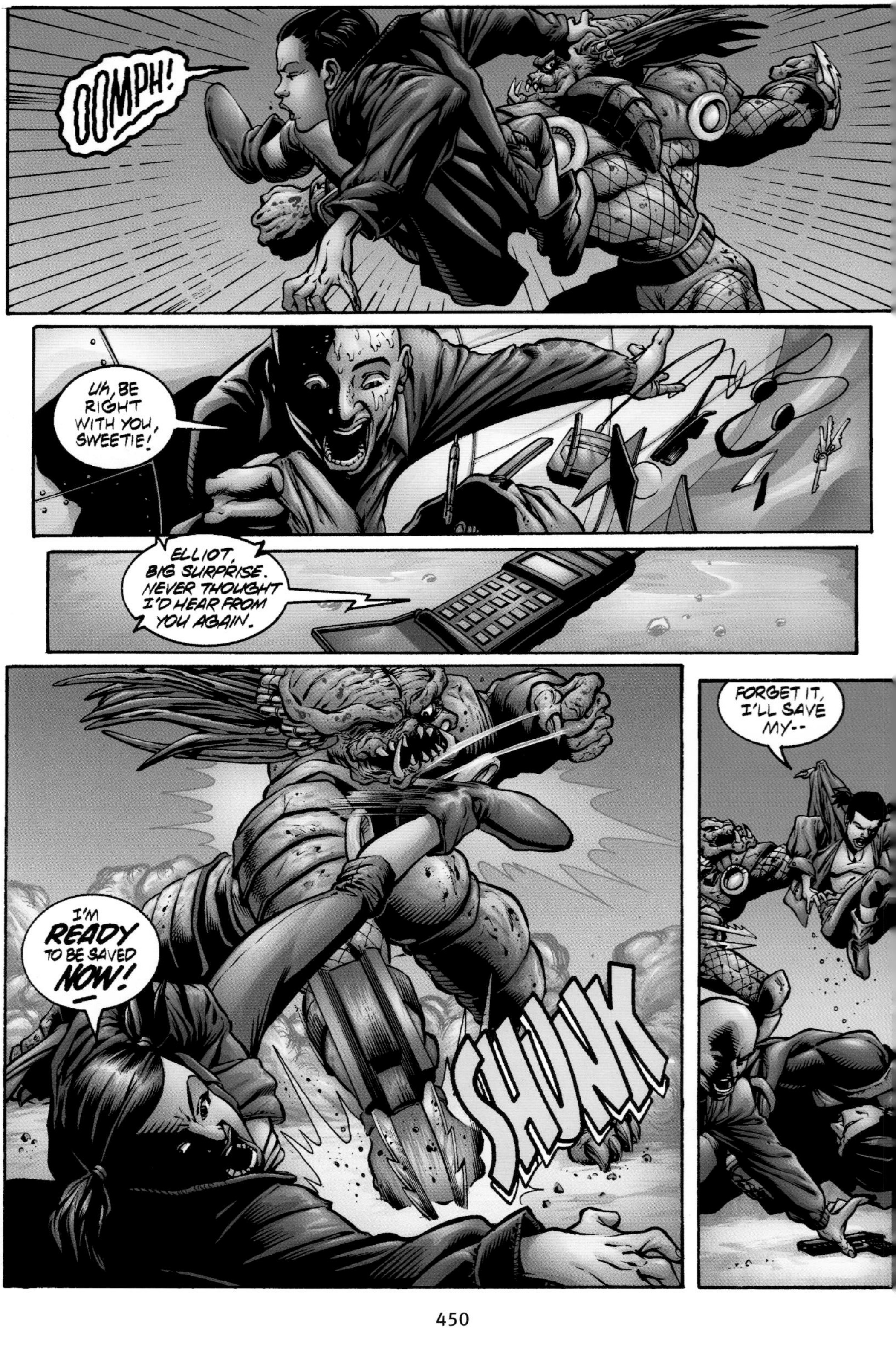
OOMPH!
UH, BE RIGHT WITH YOU, SWEETIE!
ELLIOT, BIG SURPRISE. NEVER THOUGHT I'D HEAR FROM YOU AGAIN.
I'M READY TO BE SAVED NOW!
SHUNK
FORGET IT, I'LL SAVE MY--

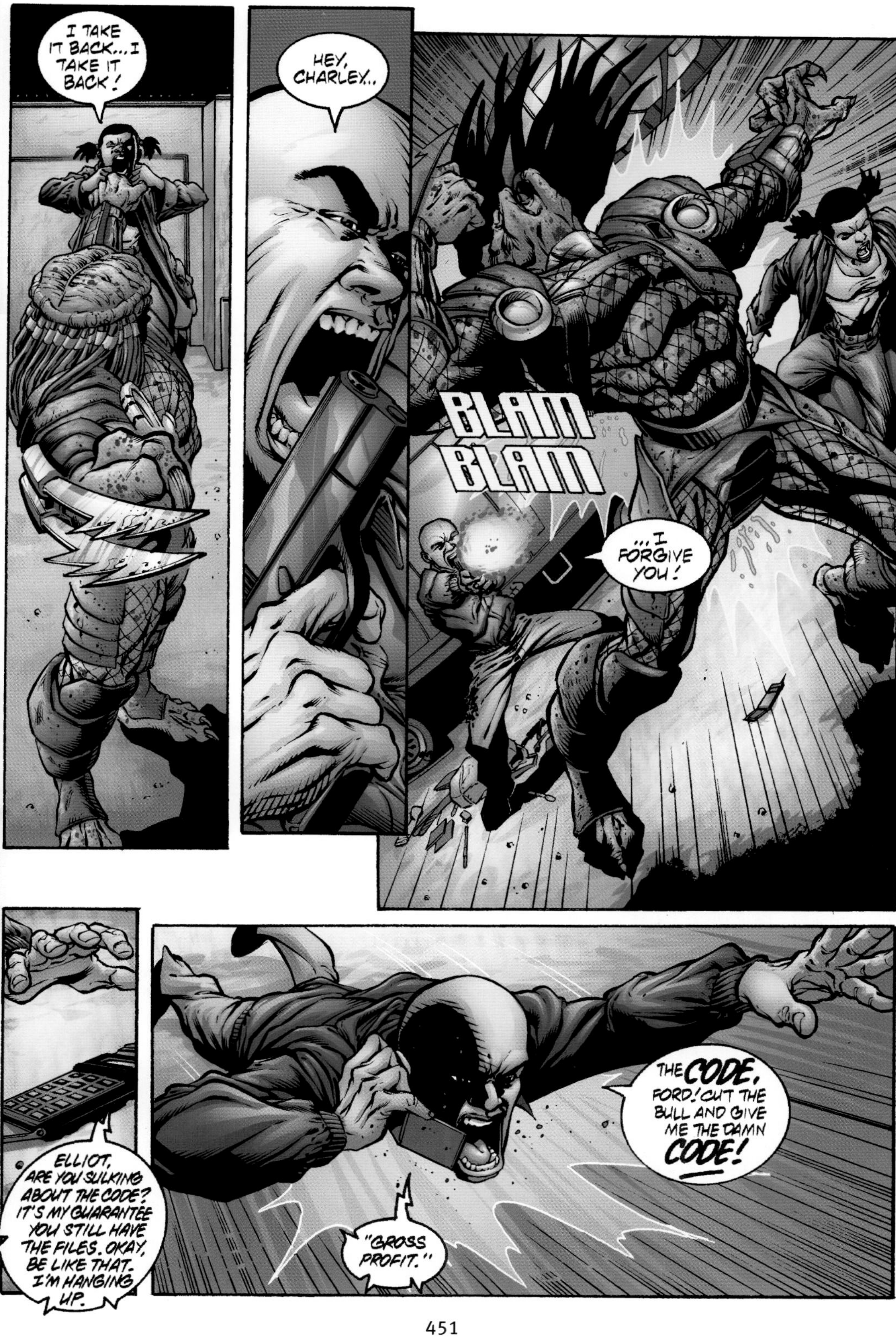
I TAKE IT BACK... I TAKE IT BACK!
HEY, CHARLEY...
BLAM BLAM
...I FORGIVE YOU!
ELLIOT, ARE YOU SULKING ABOUT THE CODE? IT'S MY GUARANTEE YOU STILL HAVE THE FILES. OKAY, BE LIKE THAT. I'M HANGING UP.
"GROSS PROFIT."
THE CODE, FORD! CUT THE BULL AND GIVE ME THE DAMN CODE!

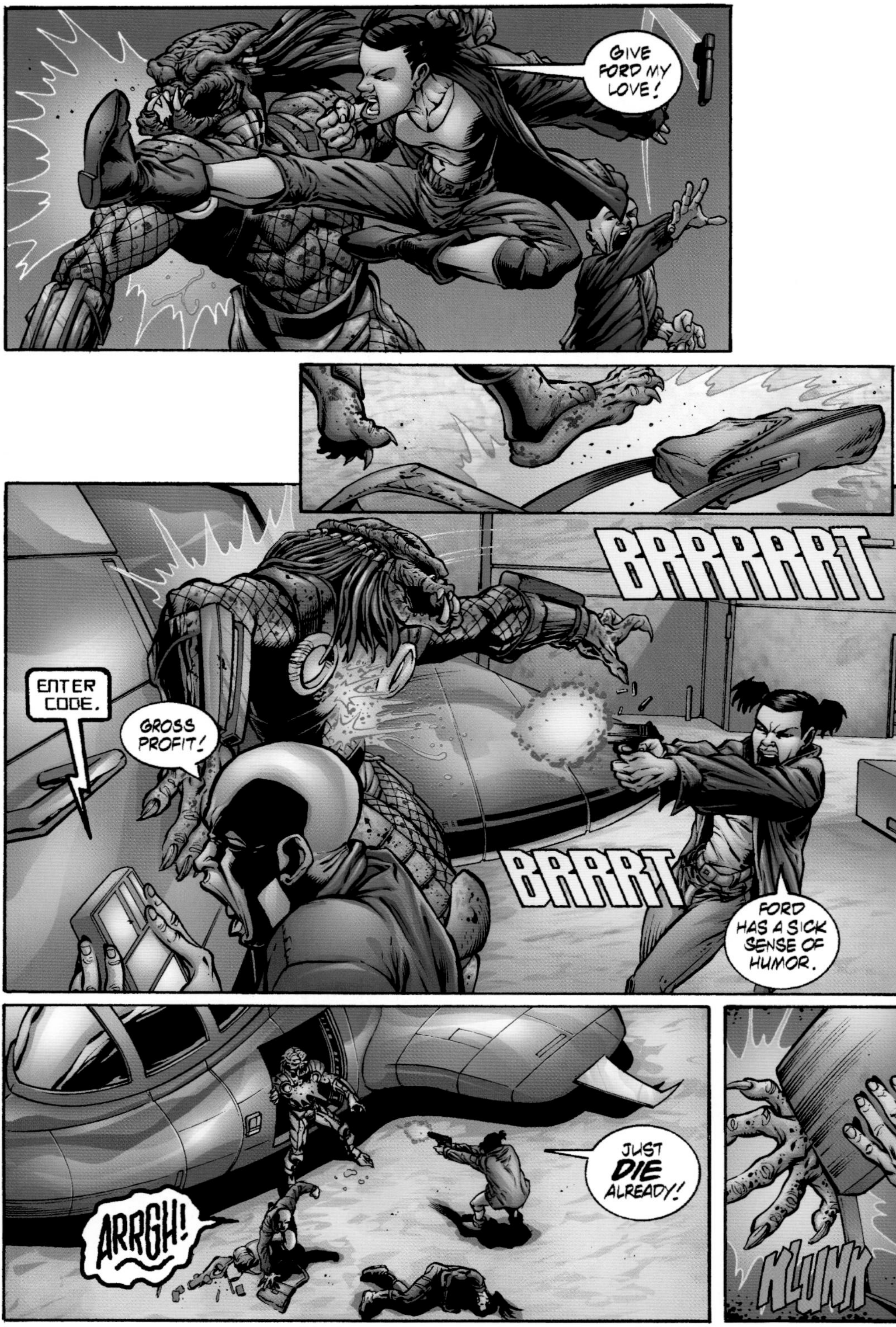
GIVE FORD MY LOVE!
BRRRRRT
ENTER CODE.
GROSS PROFIT!
BRRRT
FORD HAS A SICK SENSE OF HUMOR.
JUST DIE ALREADY!
ARRGH!
KLUNK

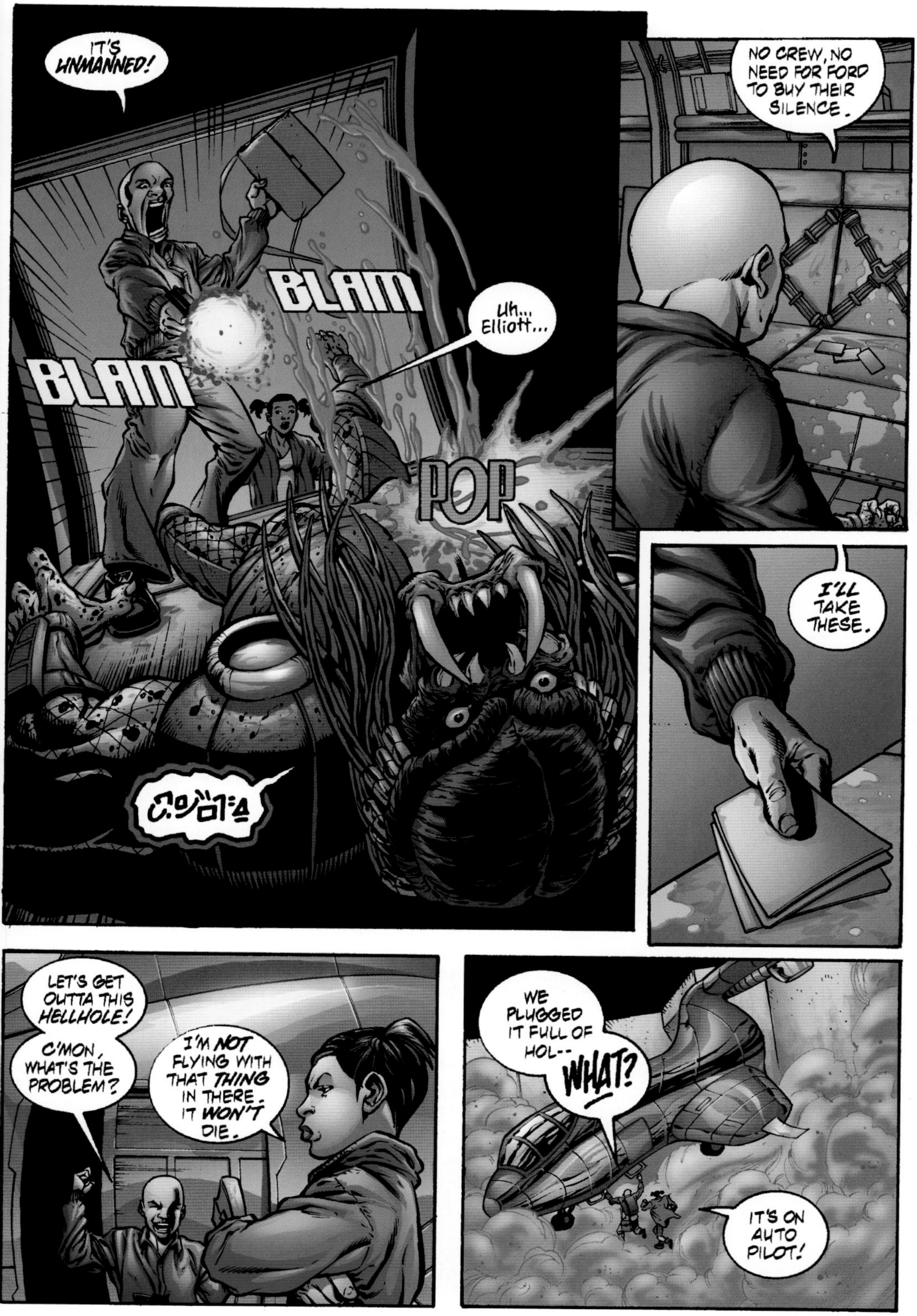
IT'S UNMANNED!
BLAM
BLAM
Uh... Elliott...
POP
NO CREW, NO NEED FOR FORD TO BUY THEIR SILENCE.
I'LL TAKE THESE.
LET'S GET OUTTA THIS HELLHOLE!
C'MON, WHAT'S THE PROBLEM?
I'M NOT FLYING WITH THAT THING IN THERE. IT WON'T DIE.
WE PLUGGED IT FULL OF HOL-- WHAT?
IT'S ON AUTO PILOT!

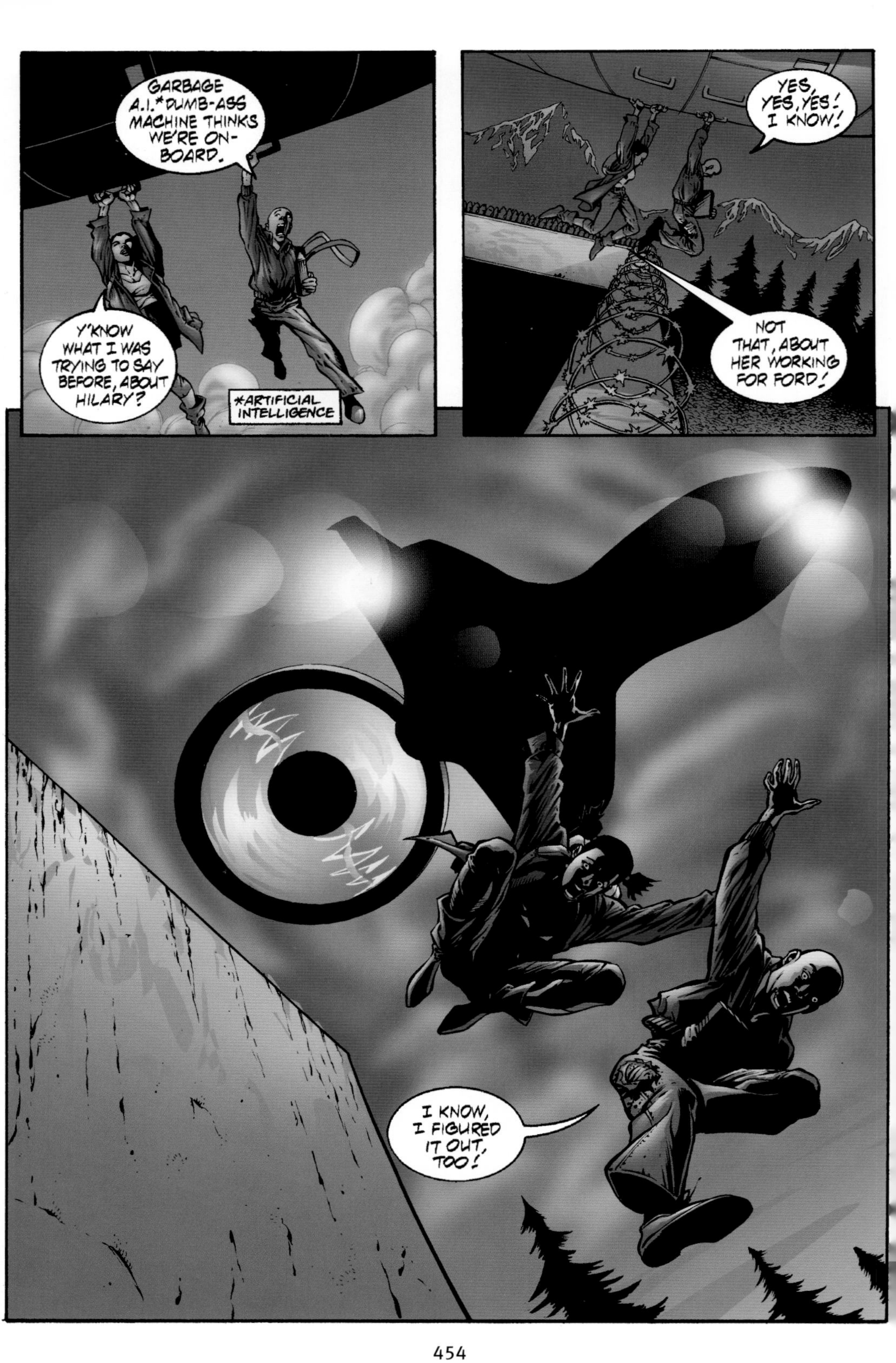
GARBAGE A.I.* DUMB-ASS MACHINE THINKS WE'RE ON-BOARD.
Y'KNOW WHAT I WAS TRYING TO SAY BEFORE, ABOUT HILARY?
*ARTIFICIAL INTELLIGENCE
YES, YES, YES! I KNOW!
NOT THAT, ABOUT HER WORKING FOR FORD!
I KNOW, I FIGURED IT OUT, TOO!

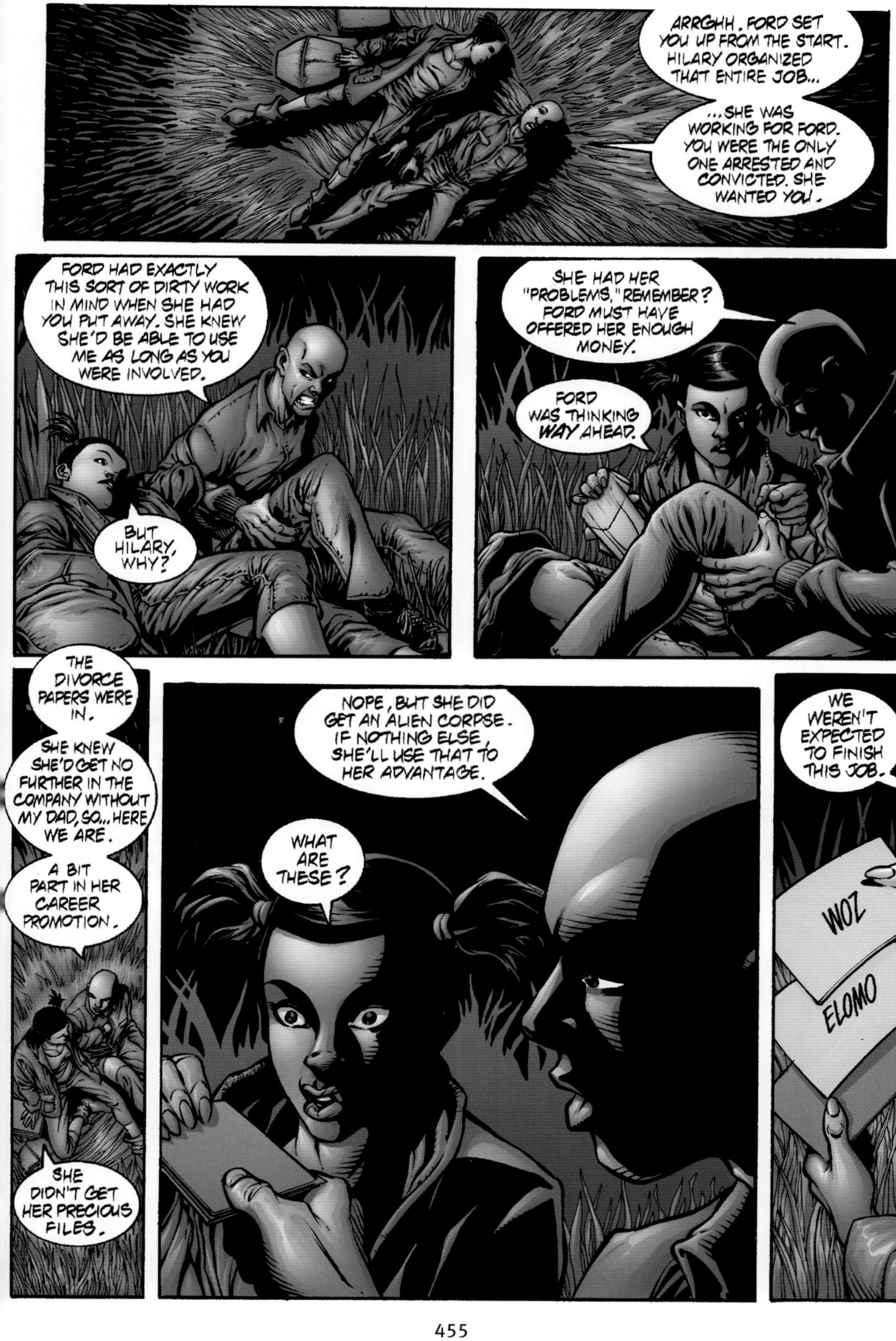
ARRGHH. FORD SET YOU UP FROM THE START. HILARY ORGANIZED THAT ENTIRE JOB...
...SHE WAS WORKING FOR FORD. YOU WERE THE ONLY ONE ARRESTED AND CONVICTED. SHE WANTED YOU.
FORD HAD EXACTLY THIS SORT OF DIRTY WORK IN MIND WHEN SHE HAD YOU PUT AWAY. SHE KNEW SHE'D BE ABLE TO USE ME AS LONG AS YOU WERE INVOLVED.
BUT HILARY, WHY?
SHE HAD HER "PROBLEMS," REMEMBER? FORD MUST HAVE OFFERED HER ENOUGH MONEY.
FORD WAS THINKING WAY AHEAD.
THE DIVORCE PAPERS WERE IN.
SHE KNEW SHE'D GET NO FURTHER IN THE COMPANY WITHOUT MY DAD, SO... HERE WE ARE.
A BIT PART IN HER CAREER PROMOTION.
SHE DIDN'T GET HER PRECIOUS FILES.
NOPE, BUT SHE DID GET AN ALIEN CORPSE. IF NOTHING ELSE, SHE'LL USE THAT TO HER ADVANTAGE.
WHAT ARE THESE?
WE WEREN'T EXPECTED TO FINISH THIS JOB.
WOZ
ELOMO

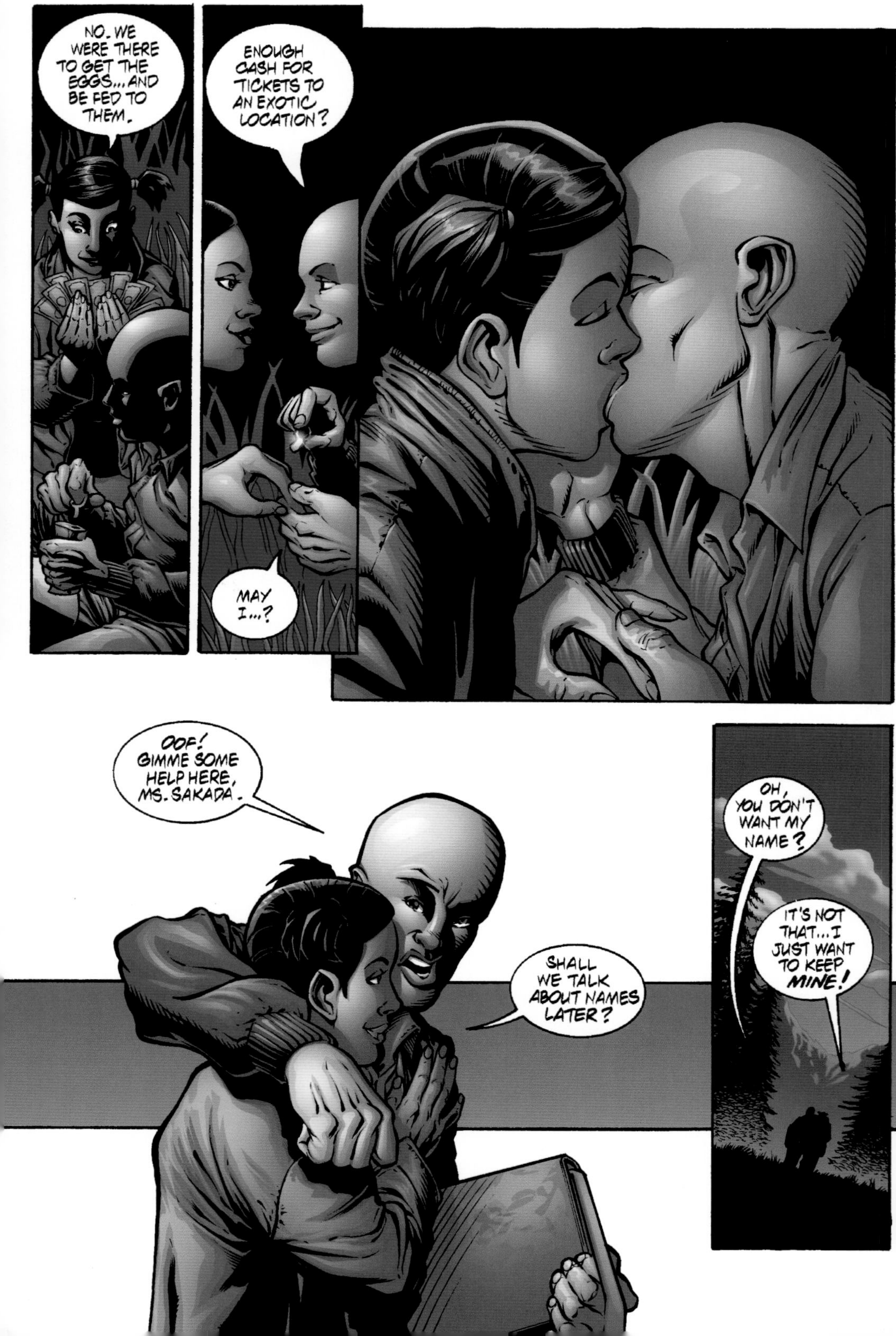
NO. WE WERE THERE TO GET THE EGGS... AND BE FED TO THEM.
ENOUGH CASH FOR TICKETS TO AN EXOTIC LOCATION?
MAY I...?
OOF! GIMME SOME HELP HERE, MS. SAKADA.
SHALL WE TALK ABOUT NAMES LATER?
OH, YOU DON'T WANT MY NAME?
IT'S NOT THAT... I JUST WANT TO KEEP MINE!

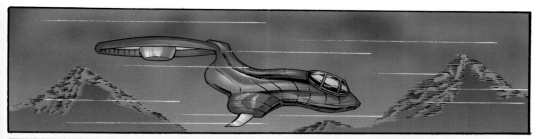

blip beep

HAVE THEM HAND OVER THE FILES, THEN KILL THEM.

TSK. GONNA MISS THAT TEN-O'CLOCK MEETING.

KRANA-FOOSH

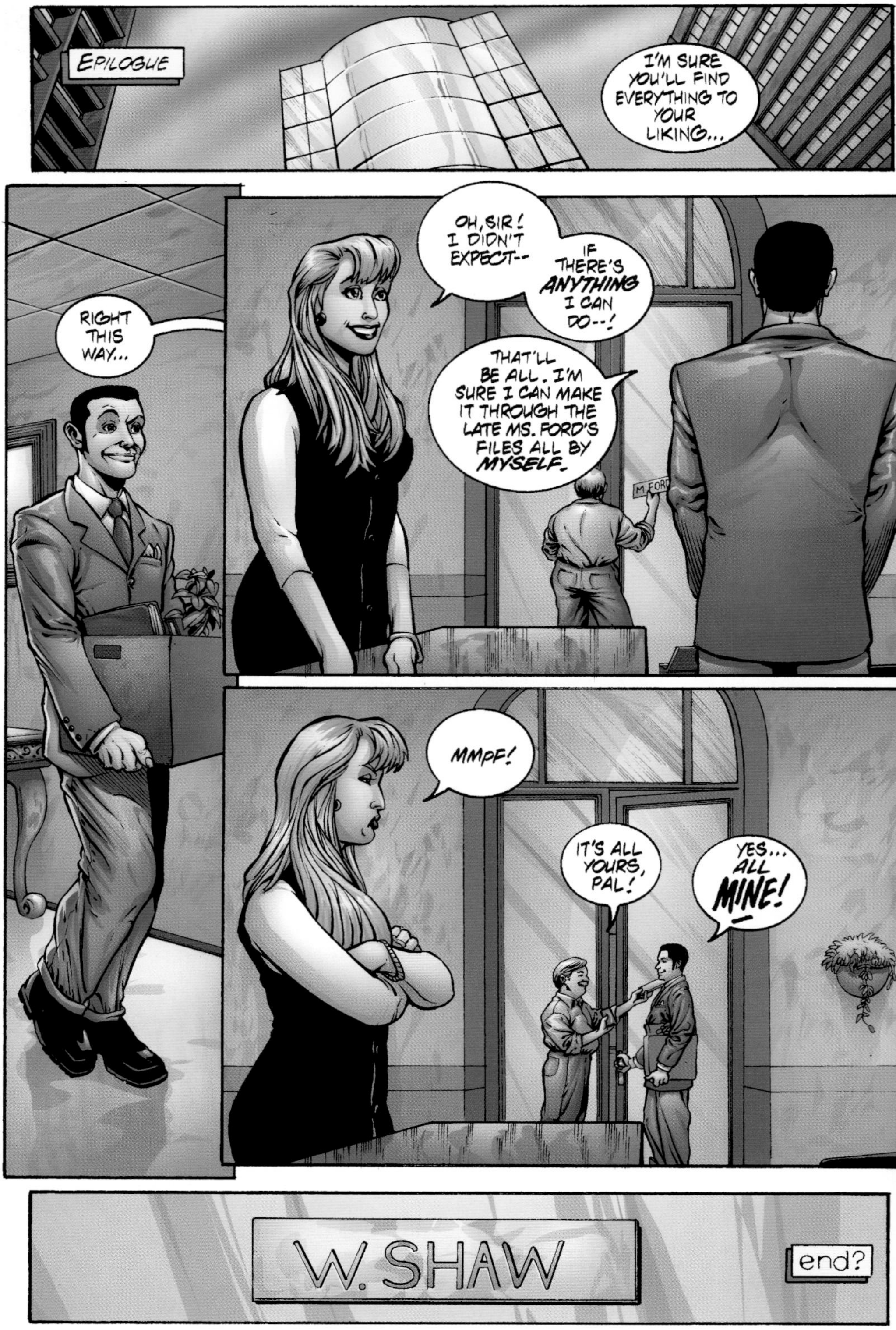
EPILOGUE
I'M SURE YOU'LL FIND EVERYTHING TO YOUR LIKING...
RIGHT THIS WAY...
OH, SIR! I DIDN'T EXPECT--
IF THERE'S ANYTHING I CAN DO--!
THAT'LL BE ALL. I'M SURE I CAN MAKE IT THROUGH THE LATE MS. FORD'S FILES ALL BY MYSELF.
M FORD
MMPF!
IT'S ALL YOURS, PAL!
YES... ALL MINE!
W. SHAW
end?

OMNIBUS COLLECTIONS
FROM DARK HORSE BOOKS

ALIENS

Volume 1
ISBN-10: 1-59307-727-0
ISBN-13: 978-1-59307-727-3
$24.95

ALIENS VS. PREDATOR

Volume 1
ISBN-10: 1-59307-735-1
ISBN-13: 978-1-59307-735-8
$24.95

BUFFY THE VAMPIRE SLAYER

Volume 1
ISBN-10: 1-59307-784-X
ISBN-13: 978-1-59307-784-6
$24.95

PREDATOR

Volume 1
ISBN-10: 1-59307-732-7
ISBN-13: 978-1-59307-732-7

STAR WARS: X-WING ROGUE SQUADRON

Volume 1
ISBN-10: 1-59307-572-3
ISBN-13: 978-1-59307-572-9
$24.95

Volume 2
ISBN-10: 1-59307-619-3
ISBN-13: 978-1-59307-619-1
$24.95

Volume 3
ISBN-10: 1-59307-776-9
ISBN-13: 978-1-59307-776-1
$24.95

ALIENS™
PREDATOR™

LIKE WHAT YOU SEE? GET UP CLOSE AND PERSONAL!

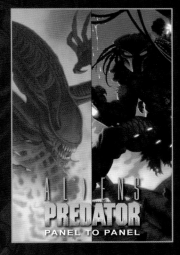

ALIENS/PREDATOR PANEL TO PANEL
Every picture tells a story.
ISBN-10: 1-59307-479-4
ISBN-13: 978-1-59307-479-1
$19.95

DARK HORSE BOOKS

larkhorse.com

ALIENS™

NOVELS FROM DARK HORSE BOOKS®

ALIENS: ORIGINAL SIN

By Michael Jan Friedman
Ripley and Call face the deadliest aliens yet . . .
ISBN-10: 1-59582-015-9
ISBN-13: 978-1-59582-015-0
$6.99

ALIENS: DNA WAR

By Diane Carey
On a hostile world, nowhere is safe . .
ISBN-10: 1-59582-032-9
ISBN-13: 978-1-59582-032-7
$6.99

ALIENS: CAULDRON

By Diane Carey
Adrift in space, terror is born again.
ISBN-10: 1-59582-113-9
ISBN-13: 978-1-59582-113-3
$6.99

DARK
HORSE
BOOKS

darkhorse.com

PREDATOR™

NOVELS FROM DARK HORSE BOOKS®

PREDATOR: FOREVER MIDNIGHT
By John Shirley
On a world of constant daylight,
blood is in the air!
ISBN-10: 1-59582-034-5
ISBN-13: 978-1-59582-034-1
$6.99

PREDATOR: FLESH AND BLOOD
By Michael Jan Friedman & Robert Greenberger
Be careful what you wish for . . .
ISBN-10: 1-59582-047-7
ISBN-13: 978-1-59582-047-1
$6.99

AVAILABLE AT YOUR LOCAL COMICS SHOP OR BOOKSTORE. TO FIND A COMICS SHOP IN YOUR AREA, CALL 1.888.266.4226
For more information or to order direct: •On the web: darkhorse.com •Phone: 1.800.862.0052 Mon.-Fri. 9 A.M. to 5 P.M. Pacific Time.